Costa Rica

Rob Rachowiecki

John Thompson

LONELY PLANET PUBLICATIONS
Melbourne · Oakland · London · Paris

COSTA RICA

Parque Nacional Santa Rosa

The largest remaining tropical dry forest in Central America offers good camping and wildlife watching.

Volcán Arenal

The most active volcano in Central America has spectacular lava flows and erupts every few hours.

Playa Tamarindo

Relax at this beach resort with turtle-watching, surfing, sea kayaking, and good hotels.

Monteverde

Escape to cooler temperatures amid the cloud forests and search for the elusive quetzal.

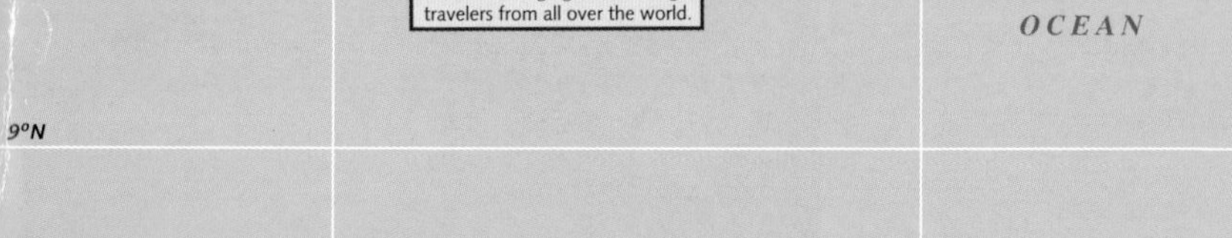

Montezuma

Beaches, wildlife reserves, and affordable lodging attract budget travelers from all over the world.

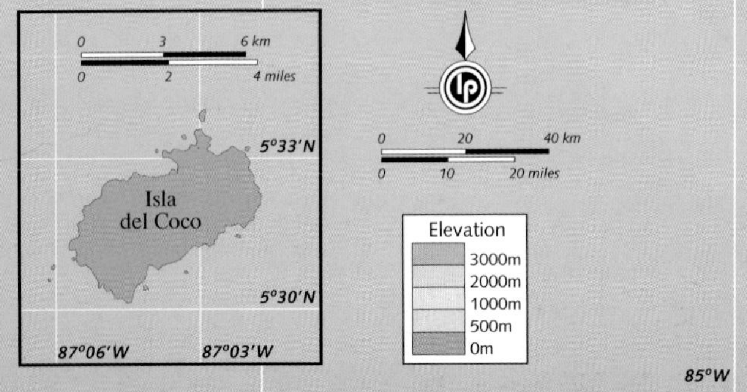

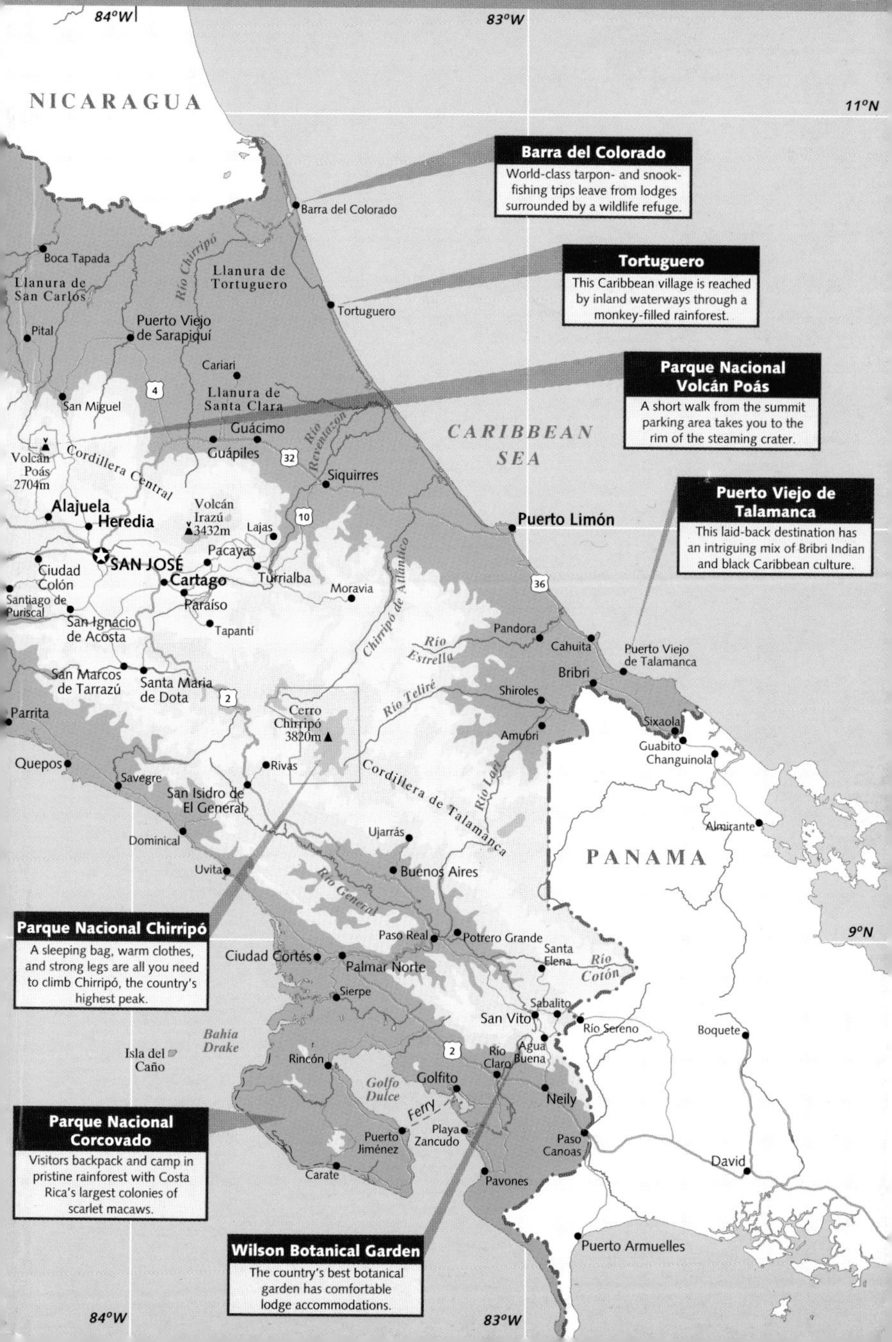

84°W 83°W 11°N 9°N

NICARAGUA

CARIBBEAN SEA

PANAMA

Barra del Colorado

World-class tarpon- and snook-fishing trips leave from lodges surrounded by a wildlife refuge.

Tortuguero

This Caribbean village is reached by inland waterways through a monkey-filled rainforest.

Parque Nacional Volcán Poás

A short walk from the summit parking area takes you to the rim of the steaming crater.

Puerto Viejo de Talamanca

This laid-back destination has an intriguing mix of Bribri Indian and black Caribbean culture.

Parque Nacional Chirripó

A sleeping bag, warm clothes, and strong legs are all you need to climb Chirripó, the country's highest peak.

Parque Nacional Corcovado

Visitors backpack and camp in pristine rainforest with Costa Rica's largest colonies of scarlet macaws.

Wilson Botanical Garden

The country's best botanical garden has comfortable lodge accommodations.

Barra del Colorado, Boca Tapada, Llanura de San Carlos, Río Chirripó, Llanura de Tortuguero, Tortuguero, Pital, Puerto Viejo de Sarapiquí, Cariari, Llanura de Santa Clara, San Miguel, Guácimo, Guápiles, Río Reventazón, Volcán Poás 2704m, Cordillera Central, Siquirres, Alajuela, Heredia, Volcán Irazú 3432m, Lajas, Puerto Limón, SAN JOSÉ, Pacayas, Ciudad Colón, Cartago, Turrialba, Moravia, Chirripó de Atlántico, Santiago de Puriscal, Paraíso, San Ignacio de Acosta, Tapantí, Pandora, Cahuita, Puerto Viejo de Talamanca, Río Estrella, Bribri, San Marcos de Tarrazú, Santa María de Dota, Río Teliré, Shiroles, Parrita, Cerro Chirripó 3820m, Sixaola, Amubri, Guabito, Changuinola, Quepos, Rivas, Savegre, Cordillera de Talamanca, Río Lari, San Isidro de El General, Almirante, Dominical, Ujarrás, Uvita, Buenos Aires, Río General, Paso Real, Potrero Grande, Santa Elena, Río Cotón, Ciudad Cortés, Palmar Norte, Sierpe, Sabalito, San Vito, Río Sereno, Boquete, Bahía Drake, Isla del Caño, Agua Buena, Río Claro, Rincón, Golfito, Golfo Dulce, Neily, Ferry, Puerto Jiménez, Playa Zancudo, Paso Canoas, David, Carate, Pavones, Puerto Armuelles

Route numbers: 4, 32, 10, 36, 2

Costa Rica
4th edition – May 2000
First published – September 1991

Published by
Lonely Planet Publications Pty Ltd ABN 36 005 607 983
90 Maribyrnong St, Footscray, Victoria 3011, Australia

Lonely Planet Offices
Australia Locked Bag 1, Footscray, Victoria 3011
USA 150 Linden St, Oakland, CA 94607
UK 10a Spring Place, London NW5 3BH
France 1 rue du Dahomey, 75011 Paris

Photographs
Frank Balthis, Erwin & Peggy Bauer, Janis Burger, Jan Butchofsky-Houser, Bruce Coleman, Nicholas DeVore, Michael Fogden, Lee Foster, Dave G Houser, Carol Hughes, Richard Laval, David Madison, Lindsey P Martin, Buddy Mays, Rob Rachowiecki, Chris Salcedo, Kevin Schafer, Errol D Sehnke, Norman Owen Tomalin, Eric L Wheater, Nik Wheeler, Robert Winslow

Many of the images in this guide are available for licensing from Lonely Planet Images.
email: lpi@lonelyplanet.com.au

Illustrations
Hugh D'Andrade, Jim Fadeff, Hayden Foell, Beth Grundvidg, Justin Marler, Hannah Reineck, Jim Swanson, Wendy Yanagihara

Front cover photograph
Buddy Mays, Travel Stock

ISBN 0 86442 760 3

Printed by The Bookmaker International Ltd
Printed in China

Although the authors and Lonely Planet try to make the information as accurate as possible, we accept no responsibility for any loss, injury or inconvenience sustained by anyone using this book.

Contents

CENTRAL VALLEY & SURROUNDING HIGHLANDS 166

NORTHWESTERN COSTA RICA 209

PENÍNSULA DE NICOYA 279

CENTRAL PACIFIC COAST 480

LANGUAGE 532

COSTA RICA WILDLIFE GUIDE 537

GLOSSARY 573

ACKNOWLEDGMENTS 575

INDEX 581

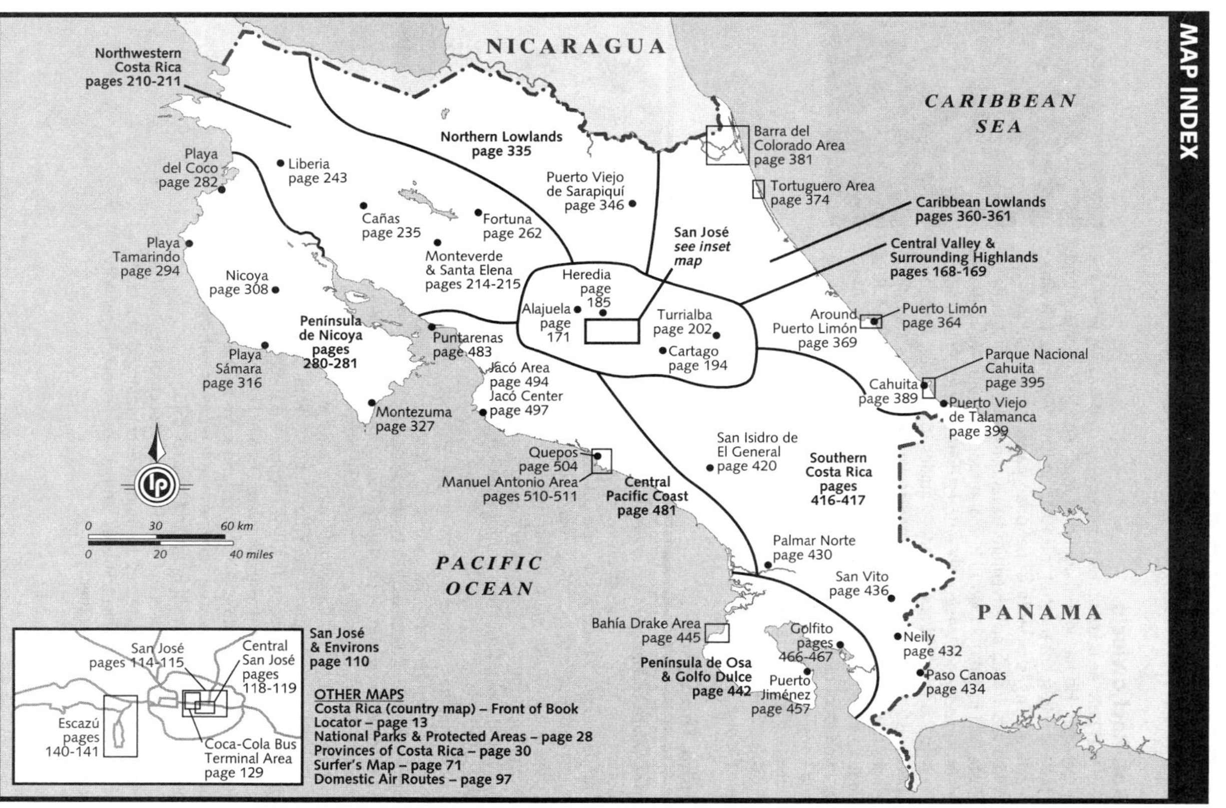
MAP INDEX
NICARAGUA
CARIBBEAN SEA
PANAMA
PACIFIC OCEAN
Northwestern Costa Rica pages 210-211
Playa del Coco page 282
Playa Tamarindo page 294
Liberia page 243
Nicoya page 308
Playa Sámara page 316
Península de Nicoya pages 280-281
Montezuma page 327
Cañas page 235
Northern Lowlands page 335
Monteverde & Santa Elena pages 214-215
Fortuna page 262
Puntarenas page 483
Jacó Area page 494
Jacó Center page 497
Puerto Viejo de Sarapiquí page 346
Alajuela page 171
Heredia page 185
San José see inset map
Turrialba page 202
Cartago page 194
Quepos page 504
Manuel Antonio Area pages 510-511
Central Pacific Coast page 481
Barra del Colorado Area page 381
Tortuguero Area page 374
Caribbean Lowlands pages 360-361
Central Valley & Surrounding Highlands pages 168-169
Puerto Limón page 364
Around Puerto Limón page 369
Cahuita page 389
Parque Nacional Cahuita page 395
Puerto Viejo de Talamanca page 399
San Isidro de El General page 420
Southern Costa Rica pages 416-417
Palmar Norte page 430
San Vito page 436
Neily page 432
Paso Canoas page 434
Golfito pages 466-467
Puerto Jiménez page 457
Bahía Drake Area page 445
Península de Osa & Golfo Dulce page 442
0 30 60 km
0 20 40 miles
San José pages 114-115
Central San José pages 118-119
Coca-Cola Bus Terminal Area page 129
Escazú pages 140-141
San José & Environs page 110
OTHER MAPS
Costa Rica (country map) – Front of Book
Locator – page 13
National Parks & Protected Areas – page 28
Provinces of Costa Rica – page 30
Surfer's Map – page 71
Domestic Air Routes – page 97

The Authors

Rob Rachowiecki

Rob was born near London and became an avid traveler while still a teenager. He has visited countries as diverse as Greenland and Thailand. He spent most of the 1980s in Latin America, traveling, teaching English, visiting national parks, and working for Wilderness Travel, an adventure travel company. His first visits to Costa Rica in 1980-81 led to his co-authorship, with Hilary Bradt, of *Backpacking in Mexico & Central America*, Bradt Publications. He is the author of Lonely Planet's guides to *Ecuador*, *Peru*, and *Southwest*, and he has contributed to Lonely Planet's shoestring guides to *South America* and *Central America*, as well as *USA*. Rob finds Costa Rica to be an ideal country for combining his particular interests of birding and natural history, visiting wilderness areas, and conservation. Rob has a master's degree in biology from the University of Arizona. When not traveling, he lives in Arizona with his wife, Cathy, and their three school-aged children, Julia, Alison, and David.

John Thompson

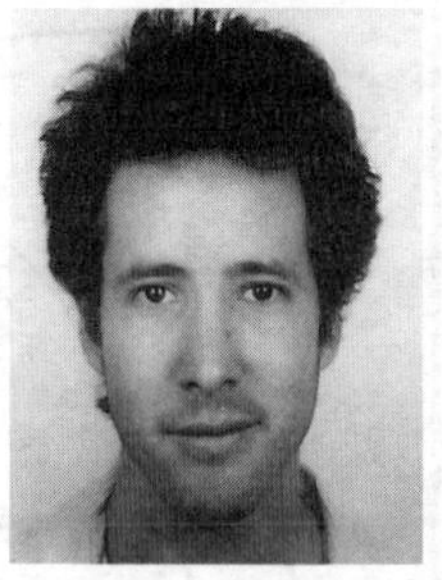

John was conceived in New York City, born in Zambia, and crossed the equator by air, land, and sea by the time he was two. He's still looking for a place to call home. So far, he has lived in Ethiopia (during the reign of Emperor Haile Selassie), Texas (during experiments with public school integration), Hawaii (when *Jaws* and *Star Wars* opened), northern Idaho (when Mt St Helens blew), Wisconsin (summer lakes and winter ice), Scotland (rural Fife, in sight of the sea), Costa Rica (during the Gulf War), and Somerville, Massachusetts.

John has had around 40 jobs. In the '80s, during his college years, he wrote Let's Go guides to Wisconsin, Iowa, Wales, Northern Ireland, Scotland, Finland, and Norway. In the '90s, he wrote obsessively and incompletely about Bruce Chatwin and co-founded, with Gordon Strause, the City Quest treasure hunt series. In the '00s, John will be writing *Driveaway: An Improvisational Pilgrimage* – a web-based USA travelogue – with Matt Hutton, lyricist for the Boston band The Red Telephone. Currently, John has deferred his enrollment at the Harvard Divinity School to help create the Washington Street Arts Center and serve on the Somerville city arts council. For living expenses, he interviews witnesses for private investigator David Prum and teaches ESL.

Each time John returns to Costa Rica, his respect for the low-key friendliness of ticos increases. He finds it encouraging that a landscape of beautiful microclimates and a cosmopolitan geniality seem to sustain each other.

FROM THE AUTHORS

From Rob

My biggest thanks go to the good people who lent me the boats that got me to remote parts of the Osa Peninsula and the north Caribbean coast – among my favorite areas in Costa Rica. Herb and Marleny of Drake Bay got me to all the lodges on that coast and to Corcovado National Park, as well as introducing me to their new airstrip; Nicole Dupont of La Paloma was my patient buddy on a great dive off Isla del Caño; and Ray and Shawn of Barra del Colorado kindly enabled me to voyage to the lodges in that area. In Tortuguero, Michael Kaye of Costa Rica Expeditions insisted on being my boatman and took me everywhere I wanted to go, plus a few places I didn't know about.

Michael and his lovely wife, Yolanda, also provided me with a place to crash at their home on the outskirts of San José – it felt like coming home when I was there. I also thank Jeff and Bill of Nuevo Arenal for making sure I visited all the best places to eat in that area.

As always, I thank the travelers who took the time to write to me and those whom I met on the road and gave me up-to-the-minute information. I also thank the excellent journalists of *The Tico Times* for their insightful comments and for answering my questions. Finally, a big hug and thanks to my wife for holding down the fort while I'm gone, and hugs and love to my children, who understand why I'm gone.

Dedication For my dear Alison, because she loves all the animals in this book.

From John

Special thanks go to the ever-questing Caroline Somerville and the ever-loquacious Lucy Gorman for a home away from home, to Shannon Gilliam and Shay Wotring for the shirt on my back, and to Sarah Goodman. Special thanks also to Lisa McCarrell and the Hano Crew for good pool, invaluable help with research, and reminding me why travel is worth the travail; the enlightened Darren Mora of Mora Books for his tico kindness and worldly wisdom; Fernando Muñoz of the CyberCafe for his untiring good humor and intelligence; Guillermo Escofet of *The Tico Times* for introducing me to the newspaper's Thursday night drinking club and for help with environmental facts; Dan Stasiuk for showing me Guanacaste by horseback; and Kevin Yardley of Diamond Tropical Hardwoods for his unblinking generosity and Tasmanian devil-like energy. For help and hospitality along the way, thanks to Haymo Heyder of Arco Iris in Monteverde, Fernando Gutiérrez Coto of Santa Rosa National Park, Katie Duncan of Land Sea Tours in

Golfito, Alex Martinez of Posada Andrea Cristina B&B and Beatriz Gomez of La Quinta Inn near Puerto Viejo de Sarapiquí, Wanda and Wolf of the Playa Chiquita Inn and Lisa and Steve Brooks of Earth Connect near Puerto Viejo de Talamanca, Toine and Sara of the Montaña Linda Hostel in Orosi, Gonzalo at Mohila Inn in Montezuma, and Raymond and Reymar of Dolphin Quest near Golfito. For generous last-minute help with research, thanks to webmasters Joel Jones of extranjero.net – an excellent general site on traveling and living in Costa Rica – and Robert J Gordon of southerncostarica.com. I met many inspiring travelers along the way, and would like to thank particularly Gary Negbaur, Chris Van Arsdale, Judith Thompson, Lina Lindblom, Kelly from WV, Joshua Stinson, Cari McIntyre, Sue Lavalle, Tania Rodriguez, Susa Oñate, Rob from BC, the Traveling Smartaleck's Club (Marcia, Dick, Diane, Tracy, and, of course, Ron), and Lene Ladekjaer. Back in the USA at the LP office, thanks to Carolyn Hubbard for cheerfully launching the project, to David Zingarelli for gracefully weathering the turbulence of seeing it through, and to Laura Harger for blessing it with clarity and perspective.

Dedication I would like to dedicate my work on this book to Cliff Thompson, James Thompson, and Les Pennington – all good fathers.

This Book

The early editions of Costa Rica were researched and written by Rob Rachowiecki. This 4th edition was revised and updated by Rob and contributing author John Thompson. Rob was the coordinating author, and he updated the book's introductory chapters as well as sections of the Northwestern Costa Rica, Caribbean Lowlands, and Península de Osa & Golfo Dulce chapters, as well as the Wildlife Guide. John updated all of the regional chapters of this edition. Some general information was drawn from Scott Doggett's *Panama* (1st edition).

FROM THE PUBLISHER

This 4th edition of Costa Rica was produced in Lonely Planet's Oakland office. David Zingarelli was the lead editor. Ample support was lent by senior editor Laura Harger and the rest of the editorial team: Christine Lee, Erin Corrigan, and Roxane Buck-Ezcurra. Erin, Christine, Laura, David, and Vivian Numaguchi diligently proofed the maps and text.

Maps for this book were produced by Colin Bishop and Dion Good, with oversight from senior cartographer Tracey Croom and cartography manager Alex Guilbert. Colin worked the maps into their final form and saw them through layout. Cartographic contributions were also made by Matthew DeMartini, Chris Gillis, Guphy, Mary Hagemann, Monica Lepe, Connie Lock, Kimberly Moses, Annette Olson, Patrick Phelan, and John Spelman. Ruth Askevold designed the book's color pages and guided pre-production. Ruth and Joshua Schefers skillfully laid out the book's pages with direction from design manager Susan Rimerman. Ken DellaPenta indexed the book, Hayden Foell created the chapter end, and Rini Keagy designed the cover.

THANKS
Many thanks to the travelers who used the last edition and wrote to us with helpful hints, advice and interesting anecdotes. Your names appear in the back of this book.

Foreword

ABOUT LONELY PLANET GUIDEBOOKS

The story begins with a classic travel adventure: Tony and Maureen Wheeler's 1972 journey across Europe and Asia to Australia. Useful information about the overland trail did not exist at that time, so Tony and Maureen published the first Lonely Planet guidebook to meet a growing need.

From a kitchen table, then from a tiny office in Melbourne (Australia), Lonely Planet has become the largest independent travel publisher in the world, an international company with offices in Melbourne, Oakland (USA), London (UK) and Paris (France).

Today Lonely Planet guidebooks cover the globe. There is an ever-growing list of books, and there's information in a variety of forms and media. Some things haven't changed. The main aim is still to help make it possible for adventurous travelers to get out there – to explore and better understand the world.

At Lonely Planet we believe travelers can make a positive contribution to the countries they visit – if they respect their host communities and spend their money wisely. Since 1986 a percentage of the income from each book has been donated to aid projects and human-rights campaigns.

Updates Lonely Planet thoroughly updates each guidebook as often as possible. This usually means there are around two years between editions, although for more unusual or more stable destinations the gap can be longer. Check the imprint page (following the color map at the beginning of the book) for publication dates.

Between editions, up-to-date information is available in two free newsletters – the paper *Planet Talk* and email *Comet* (to subscribe, contact any Lonely Planet office) – and on our website at www.lonelyplanet.com. The *Upgrades* section of the website covers a number of important and volatile destinations and is regularly updated by Lonely Planet authors. *Scoop* covers news and current affairs relevant to travelers. And, lastly, the *Thorn Tree* bulletin board and *Postcards* section of the site carry unverified, but fascinating, reports from travelers.

Correspondence The process of creating new editions begins with the letters, postcards and emails received from travelers. This correspondence often includes suggestions, criticisms and comments about the current editions. Interesting excerpts are immediately passed on via newsletters and the website, and everything goes to our authors to be verified when they're researching on the road. We're keen to get more feedback from organizations or individuals who represent communities visited by travelers.

Lonely Planet gathers information for everyone who's curious about the planet – and especially for those who explore it firsthand. Through guidebooks, phrasebooks, activity guides, maps, literature, newsletters, image library, TV series and website, we act as an information exchange for a worldwide community of travelers.

Research Authors aim to gather sufficient practical information to enable travelers to make informed choices and to make the mechanics of a journey run smoothly. They also research historical and cultural background to help enrich the travel experience and allow travelers to understand and respond appropriately to cultural and environmental issues.

Authors don't stay in every hotel because that would mean spending a couple of months in each medium-size city and, no, they don't eat at every restaurant because that would mean stretching belts beyond capacity. They do visit hotels and restaurants to check standards and prices, but feedback based on readers' direct experiences can be very helpful.

Many of our authors work undercover; others aren't so secretive. None of them accept freebies in exchange for positive write-ups. And none of our guidebooks contain any advertising.

Production Authors submit their raw manuscripts and maps to offices in Australia, the USA, the UK or France. Editors and cartographers – all experienced travelers themselves – then begin the process of assembling the pieces. When the book finally hits the shops, some things are already out of date, we start getting feedback from readers and the process begins again....

WARNING & REQUEST

Things change – prices go up, schedules change, good places go bad and bad places go bankrupt – nothing stays the same. So, if you find things better or worse, recently opened or long since closed, please tell us and help make the next edition even more accurate and useful. We genuinely value all the feedback we receive. Julie Young coordinates a well-traveled team that reads and acknowledges every letter, postcard and email and ensures that every morsel of information finds its way to the appropriate authors, editors and cartographers for verification.

Everyone who writes to us will find their name in the next edition of the appropriate guidebook. They will also receive the latest issue of *Planet Talk*, our quarterly printed newsletter, or *Comet*, our monthly email newsletter. Subscriptions to both newsletters are free. The very best contributions will be rewarded with a free guidebook.

Excerpts from your correspondence may appear in new editions of Lonely Planet guidebooks, the Lonely Planet website, *Planet Talk* or *Comet*, so please let us know if you *don't* want your letter published or your name acknowledged.

Send all correspondence to the Lonely Planet office closest to you:

Australia: Locked Bag 1, Footscray, Victoria 3011
USA: 150 Linden St, Oakland, CA 94607
UK: 10A Spring Place, London NW5 3BH
France: 1 rue du Dahomey, 75011 Paris

Or email us at: talk2us@lonelyplanet.com.au

For news, views and updates, see our website: www.lonelyplanet.com

HOW TO USE A LONELY PLANET GUIDEBOOK

The best way to use a Lonely Planet guidebook is any way you choose. At Lonely Planet, we believe the most memorable travel experiences are often those that are unexpected, and the finest discoveries are those you make yourself. Guidebooks are not intended to be used as if they provided a detailed set of infallible instructions!

Contents All Lonely Planet guidebooks follow the same format. The Facts about the Country chapters or sections give background information ranging from history to weather. Facts for the Visitor gives practical information on issues like visas and health. Getting There & Away gives a brief starting point for researching travel to and from the destination. Getting Around gives an overview of the transport options available when you arrive.

The peculiar demands of each destination determine how subsequent chapters are broken up, but some things remain constant. We always start with background, then proceed to sights, places to stay, places to eat, entertainment, getting there and away, and getting around information – in that order.

Heading Hierarchy Lonely Planet headings are used in a strict hierarchical structure that can be visualized as a set of Russian dolls. Each heading (and its following text) is encompassed by any preceding heading that is higher on the hierarchical ladder.

Entry Points We do not assume guidebooks will be read from beginning to end, but that people will dip into them. The traditional entry points are the list of contents and the index. In addition, however, some books have a complete list of maps and an index map illustrating map coverage.

There may also be a color map that shows highlights. These highlights are dealt with in greater detail later in the book, along with planning questions. Each chapter covering a geographical region usually begins with a locator map and another list of highlights. Once you find something of interest in a list of highlights, turn to the index.

Maps Maps play a crucial role in Lonely Planet guidebooks and include a huge amount of information. A legend is printed on the back page. We seek to have complete consistency between maps and text, and to have every important place in the text captured on a map. Map key numbers usually start in the top left corner.

Although inclusion in a guidebook usually implies a recommendation, we cannot list every good place. Exclusion does not necessarily imply criticism. In fact, there are a number of reasons why we might exclude a place – sometimes it is simply inappropriate to encourage an influx of travelers.

Introduction

Travelers today are turning increasingly toward the tropics as an exciting, adventurous, and exotic destination. Of the many attractive tropical countries to choose from, Costa Rica stands out as one of the most delightful in the world. There are not only tropical rainforests and beautiful beaches, but also some surprises – active volcanoes and windswept mountaintops. So although Costa Rica is a small country, a large variety of tropical habitats is found within it – and they are protected by the best-developed conservation program in Latin America.

Costa Rica is famous for its enlightened approach to conservation. About 27% of the country is protected in one form or another, and over 13% is within the national park system. This means that the traveler who wishes to do so can experience the tropics in a natural way. The variety and density of wildlife in the preserved areas attract people whose dream is to see monkeys, sloths, caimans, sea turtles, and exotic birds in their natural habitats. And see them they will! Many other animals can be seen, and, with a lot of luck, such rare and elusive animals as jaguars, tapirs, and harpy eagles may be glimpsed.

With both Pacific and Caribbean coasts, there is no shortage of beaches in Costa Rica. Some have been developed for tourism, while others are remote and rarely visited. For a relaxing seaside vacation, you can stay in a luxurious hotel or you can camp – the choice is yours. And wherever you stay, you are likely to find a preserved area within driving distance where you will find monkeys in the trees by the ocean's edge.

Active volcanoes are surely one of the most dramatic natural sights, and few visitors to Costa Rica can resist the opportunity to peer into the crater of a smoking giant. Whether you want to take a guided bus tour to a volcanic summit or hike up through the rainforest and camp out amid a landscape of boiling mud pools and steaming vents, you will find the information you need within the pages of this book.

Apart from hiking and camping in rainforests and mountains and on beaches, the

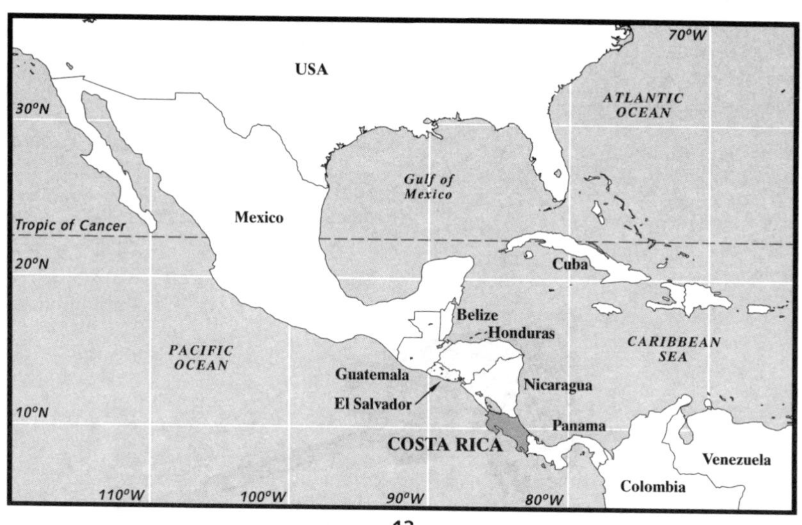

adventurous traveler will find the opportunity to snorkel on tropical reefs, surf the best waves in Central America, and raft some of the most thrilling white water in the tropics. Pristine rivers tumble down the lower slopes of the mountains, and the riverbanks are clothed with curtains of rainforest – a truly unique white-water experience. Those who like to fish will find that the rivers and lakes offer a beautiful setting for their sport, and the ocean fishing is definitely world-class.

In addition to this natural beauty and outdoor excitement, there is the added attraction of a country that has long had the most stable political climate in Latin America. Costa Rica has had democratic elections since the 19th century and is one of the most peaceful nations in the world. The armed forces were abolished after the 1948 civil war, and Costa Rica has avoided the despotic dictatorships, frequent military coups, terrorism, and internal strife that have torn apart other countries in the region. Costa Rica is the safest country to visit in Latin America.

But it is not only safe – it is friendly. Costa Ricans delight in showing off their lovely country to visitors, and wherever you go, you will find the locals to be a constant source of help, smiles, and information. The transportation system is inexpensive and covers the whole country, so Costa Rica is not only one of the most beautiful tropical countries, but also one of the easiest in which to travel.

Facts about Costa Rica

HISTORY

Pre-Conquest

Of all the Central American countries, Costa Rica is the one that has been most influenced by the Spanish conquest, and there are relatively few signs of pre-Columbian cultures. The well-known Mexican and northern Central American civilizations, such as the Aztecs, Olmecs, and Mayas, did not reach as far south as Costa Rica. Those peoples who did exist in Costa Rica were few in number and relatively poorly organized. They offered slight resistance to the Spanish, left us little in the way of ancient archaeological monuments, and had no written language.

This is not to say that Costa Rica's pre-Columbian peoples were uncivilized. A visit to San José's Museo de Jade (Jade Museum) or Museo de Oro Precolombino (Pre-Columbian Gold Museum) will awe the visitor. The Museo de Jade has the world's largest collection of pre-Columbian jade – and most of it comes from the Costa Rican area. The Museo de Oro has approximately 2000 pieces on display. Unfortunately, not a great deal is known about the cultures that produced these treasures.

The Greater Nicoya area (consisting of Costa Rica's Península de Nicoya and reaching north along the Pacific coast into Nicaragua) has recently been the focus of archaeological study. In this area, still noteworthy for its pottery, workers have found a wealth of ceramics, stonework, and jade, which has provided excellent insight into the pre-Columbian peoples who lived here. Although it is almost certain that people were living in Central America prior to 20,000 BC, the first definite evidence (in the form of ceramics) is dated to about 2000 BC, which corresponds to what is called Period III by archaeologists.

Period IV, from 1000 BC to 500 AD, was characterized by the establishment of villages and of social hierarchies, and the development of jade production. Ceramics and jade from Mayan areas indicate the influence of other peoples through trade. Skill in making pottery improved during Period V (500-1000 AD), and by Period VI (1000-1520 AD) society had developed into a number of settlements, some with populations of about 20,000 and ruled over by a chief. Most of these were quickly destroyed by the Spanish conquest and its aftermath. Today, the few remaining Indian groups are often known by the name of their last chief, as noted by the Spanish chroniclers. Particularly important in the Greater Nicoya area are the Chorotegas.

The Nicoya area had a dry season and a wet season; this led to a greater development in ceramics than on the Caribbean side, where water was easier to obtain and rarely had to be stored or transported long distances. In addition, the many bays and safe anchorages of the Península de Nicoya area fostered trading there, so it is not surprising that the Greater Nicoya area has left archaeologists with more artifacts than has the Caribbean coast.

The major archaeological site in Costa Rica is the Monumento Nacional Guayabo, which is about 85km east of the capital, San José. Guayabo is currently under investigation and is thought to have been inhabited from about 1000 BC to 1400 AD. Streets, aqueducts, and causeways can be seen, though most of the buildings have collapsed and have not yet been restored. Gold and stone artifacts have been discovered there. Archaeologists believe Guayabo was an important religious and cultural center, although minor compared to Aztec, Inca, or Maya sites.

Of all the existing remnants of pre-Columbian culture, none are more mysterious than the stone spheres of the Diquis region. This region covers the southern half of Costa Rica. Dotted throughout the area are perfectly shaped spheres of granite, some as tall as a person, and others as small as a grapefruit. They can be seen in the Museo Nacional and various parks and gardens in San José, as well as throughout the Diquis region. Some, undisturbed for centuries, have been found on Isla del Caño, 20km west of the southern Pacific coast. Who carved these enigmatic orbs? What was their purpose? How did they get to Isla del Caño? No one has the answers to these questions. The puzzling granite spheres of southern Costa Rica serve to underscore how little we know and understand of the pre-Columbian cultures of the region.

Spanish Conquest

Because of the lack of a large and rich Indian empire at the time of the arrival of the Spaniards, the conquest of Costa Rica is euphemistically called a 'settlement' by some writers. In reality, the Spanish arrival was accompanied by diseases to which the Indians had no resistance, and they died of sickness as much as by the sword. Although the Indians did try to fight the Spanish, the small numbers of natives were unable to stop the ever larger groups of Spaniards that arrived every few years attempting to colonize the land.

The first arrival was Christopher Columbus himself, who landed near present-day Puerto Limón on September 18, 1502, during his fourth and last voyage to the Americas. He was treated well by the coastal Indians during his stay of 17 days, and he noted that some of the natives wore gold decorations. Because of this, the area was dubbed 'costa rica' (rich coast) by the Spaniards, who imagined that there must be a rich empire lying farther inland.

Spanish King Ferdinand appointed Diego de Nicuesa as governor of the region and sent him to colonize it in 1506. This time the Indians did not provide a friendly welcome – perhaps they had become aware of the deadly diseases that accompanied the Europeans. The colonizers were hampered by the jungle, tropical diseases, and the small bands of Indians who used guerrilla tactics to fight off the invaders. About half the colonizers died and the rest returned home, unsuccessful.

Further expeditions followed. The most successful, from the Spaniards' point of view, was a 1522 expedition to the Golfo de Nicoya area led by Gil González Dávila. Although the expedition returned home with a hoard of gold and other treasures and claimed to have converted tens of thousands of Indians to Catholicism, it was unable to form a permanent colony and many expedition members died of hunger and disease.

By the 1560s, the Spanish had unsuccessfully attempted colonization several more times. By this time, the Indian resistance, such as it was, had been worn down; many Indians had died or were dying of disease and others had simply moved on to more inhospitable terrain.

In 1562, Juan Vásquez de Coronado arrived as governor and decided that the best place to found a colony was in the central highlands. This was an unusual move because the Spanish were a seafaring people and had naturally tried to colonize the coastal areas where they could build ports and maintain contact with Spain. This proved problematic because the coastal areas harbored disease. When Coronado founded Cartago in 1563, his followers encountered a healthy climate and fertile volcanic soil and the colony survived.

Cartago was quite different from Spanish colonies in other parts of the New World. There were few Indians, so the Spanish did not have a huge workforce available, nor were they able to intermarry with the Indians to form the *mestizo* culture prevalent in many other parts of Latin America. The imagined riches of Costa Rica turned out to be very little and were soon plundered. The small highland colony soon became removed from the mainstream of Spanish influence.

For the next century and a half, the colony remained a forgotten backwater, isolated from the coast and major trading routes. It survived only by dint of hard work and the generosity and friendliness that have become the hallmarks of the contemporary Costa Rican character.

In the 1700s, the colony began to spread and change. Settlements became established throughout the fertile plains of the central highlands (now known as the *meseta central*). Heredia was founded in 1717, San José in 1737, and Alajuela in 1782, although at the time of their founding the cities had different names. Much of Cartago was destroyed in an eruption of Volcán Irazú in 1723, but the survivors rebuilt the town. This expansion reflected slow growth from within Costa Rica, but the colony remained one of the poorest and most isolated in the Spanish empire.

Independence

Central America became independent from Spain on September 15, 1821, although Costa Rica was not aware of this situation until at least a month later. It briefly became part of the Mexican empire, then a state within the Central American United Provinces. The first elected head of state was Juan Mora Fernández, who governed from 1824 to 1833. During his time in office, export of coffee, introduced in 1808 from Cuba, began in modest amounts.

The rest of the 19th century saw a steady increase in coffee exports, and this turned Costa Rica from an extremely poor and struggling country into a more successful and worldly one. Inevitably, some of the coffee growers became relatively rich, and a class structure began to emerge. In 1849, a successful coffee grower, Juan Rafael Mora, became president and governed for 10 years.

Mora's presidency is remembered both for economic and cultural growth, and for a somewhat bizarre military incident that has earned a place in every Costa Rican child's history books. In June 1855, the US filibuster William Walker arrived in Nicaragua with the aim of conquering Central America and converting it into slaving territory, then using the slaves to build a Nicaraguan canal to join the Atlantic and Pacific. Walker defeated the Nicaraguans and marched for Costa Rica, which he entered more or less unopposed, reaching a hacienda at Santa Rosa (now a national park in northwestern Costa Rica).

Costa Rica had no army, so Mora organized 9000 civilians to gather what arms they could and march north in February 1856. In a short but determined battle, the Costa Ricans defeated Walker, who retreated to Rivas, Nicaragua, followed by the victorious Costa Ricans. Walker and his soldiers made a stand in a wooden fort, and Juan Santamaría, a drummer boy from Alajuela, volunteered to torch the building, thus forcing Walker to flee. Santamaría was killed in this action and is now remembered as one of Costa Rica's favorite national heroes.

Despite his defeat, Walker returned unsuccessfully to Central America several more times before finally being shot in Honduras in 1860. Meanwhile, Mora lost favor in his country – he and his army were thought to have brought back the cholera that caused a massive epidemic in Costa Rica. He was deposed in 1859, led a coup in 1860, failed, and was executed in the same year that Walker died.

Democracy

The next three decades were characterized by power struggles among members of the coffee-growing elite. In 1869, a free and compulsory elementary education system was established – though, inevitably, families in more remote areas were not able to send children to schools. In 1889, the first democratic elections were held, with the poor *campesinos* (peasants) as well as the rich coffee growers able to vote, although women and blacks had not yet received that right.

Democracy has been a hallmark of Costa Rican politics since then, and there have been few lapses. One occurred between 1917 and 1919, when the Minister of War, Federico Tinoco, overthrew the democratically elected president and formed a dictatorship. This ended in Tinoco's exile after opposition from the rest of Costa Rica and from the US government.

In 1940, Rafael Angel Calderón Guardia became president. His presidency was marked by reforms that were supported by the poor but criticized by the rich. These reforms included workers' rights to organize, minimum wages, and social security. To further widen his power base, Calderón allied himself, strangely, with both the Catholic church and the Communist party to form a Christian Socialist group. This further alienated him from the conservatives, the intellectuals, and the upper classes.

Calderón was succeeded in 1944 by the Christian Socialist Teodoro Picado, who was a supporter of Calderón's policies, but the conservative opposition claimed the elections were a fraud. In 1948, Calderón again ran for the presidency, against Otilio Ulate. Ulate won the election but Calderón claimed fraud because some of the ballots had been destroyed. Picado's government did not recognize Ulate's victory, and the tense situation escalated into civil war.

Calderón and Picado were opposed by José (Don Pepe) Figueres Ferrer. After several weeks of civil warfare, in which over 2000 people were killed, Figueres emerged victorious. He took over an interim government and in 1949 handed the presidency to Otilio Ulate.

That year marked the formation of the Costa Rican constitution, which is still in effect. Women and blacks finally received the vote, presidents were not allowed to run for successive terms, and a neutral electoral tribunal was established to guarantee free and fair elections. Voting in elections, held every four years, was made mandatory for all citizens over the age of 18. But the constitutional dissolution of the armed forces is the act that has had the most long-lasting impact on the nation. Today, half a century later, Costa Rica is known as 'the country that doesn't have an army.'

Although there are well over a dozen political parties, since 1949 the Partido de Liberación Nacional (PLN; National Liberation Party), formed by Don Pepe Figueres, has dominated, usually being elected every other four years. Figueres continued to be popular and was returned to two more terms of office, in 1953 and 1970. He died in 1990. Another famous PLN president was Oscar Arias, who governed from 1986 to 1990. For his work in attempting to spread peace from Costa Rica to all of Central America, Arias received the Nobel Peace Prize in 1987.

In recent years, the Christian Socialists have continued to be the favored party of the poor and working classes, and Calderón's son, Rafael Angel Calderón Fournier, has played a large role in that party, running for president three times. After two losses, he was finally elected president in 1990, succeeding Oscar Arias.

During 1993, six PLN politicians vied for their party's candidacy for the 1994 presidential elections. These included Margarita Penon, who was the first woman to reach such an advanced position in a presidential race in Costa Rica. Penon is the wife of ex-president Oscar Arias. The winner of the PLN candidacy, however, was José María Figueres, Don Pepe's son.

PLN's Figueres was opposed by the Partido Unidad Social Cristiana (PUSC; Social Christian Unity Party). The PUSC pre-candidates for the 1994 presidential elections included Juan José Trejos, the son of ex-president José Juaquin Trejos (1966-70), and economist Miguel Angel Rodríguez, who became the PUSC candidate. There were also some presidential candidates from other minor parties.

Clearly, the history of politics in Costa Rica is strongly influenced by a handful of families, as shown by the father-son, husband-wife associations mentioned above. In fact, 75% of the 44 presidents of Costa Rica prior to 1970 were descended from just three original colonizers.

The winner of the 1994 election was Figueres, who received 49.6% of the vote, closely followed by Rodríguez with 47.6%. Figueres had campaigned on a populist platform, promising improved health care and education, but his presidency was unpopular, marked by price hikes, tax increases, bank closures, and strikes by teachers and other groups.

In 1998, Miguel Angel Rodríguez again represented the PUSC party in the election on February 1. He was opposed by PLN candidate José Miguel Corrales (incumbents are not allowed to run) and 11 others, including the country's first black candidate, and the first all-female ticket. Also for the first time, the two front-runners had women running in both vice-presidential positions. The campaign was marked by voter apathy, partly because Rodríguez's consistent 10% lead over Corrales in pre-election polls made the race unexciting, partly because neither candidate was considered charismatic, and partly because the public was disillusioned with the two-party dominance in Costa Rican politics.

Rodríguez is a conservative economist and led the polls because the public perceived that he could improve the economic woes of the previous administration. Election results favored Rodríguez with 46.6% of the vote, barely 2% more than Corrales and much closer than expected. However, a 30% abstention level was notably higher than in most Costa Rican elections. Rodríguez took office on May 8, 1998, and will lead the country until the next elections, in 2002. However, only 27 of the 57 congresspeople elected belonged to the PUSC. This was two short of a majority, forcing Rodríguez to search for a consensus with opposition groups. He cut the number of cabinet ministers from 18 to 12, promising a leaner government dedicated to improving the economy.

The new president tried to push a tough austerity plan but came under severe criticism after almost quadrupling the presidential annual salary, from US$70,000 to over US$250,000. In comparison, the average Costa Rican professional earns about US$12,000. After widespread public outcry, Rodríguez apologized for his 'error' and returned the salary to close to its previous level.

Other noteworthy events of recent years include several natural disasters that caused widespread flooding, road damage, and destruction of homes. In July 1996, Hurricane César resulted in several dozen deaths and cut off much of southern Costa Rica from the rest of the country. The Carretera Interamericana (Interamerican Hwy) was closed for about two months and the overall damage was estimated at about US$100 million. The ill-famed Hurricane Mitch of November 1998 caused substantial damage to Costa Rica, but the most catastrophic events occurred in the countries to the north, especially Honduras, Nicaragua, and El Salvador.

GEOGRAPHY

Costa Rica is bordered to the north by Nicaragua, to the northeast by the Caribbean Sea, to the southeast by Panama, and to the west and southwest by the Pacific Ocean. This tropical country lies between latitudes 11°13'N and 8°N and longitudes 82°33'W and 85°58'W. In addition, Costa Rica claims Isla del Coco (25 sq km), at about 5°30'N and 87°05'W.

Costa Rica is an extremely varied country despite its tiny size, which, at 51,100 sq km, is almost half the size of the state of Kentucky in the USA, two-thirds the size of Scotland, or three-quarters the size of Tasmania in Australia.

A series of volcanic mountain chains runs from the Nicaraguan border in the northwest to the Panamanian border in the southeast, splitting the country in two. The northwesternmost range is the Cordillera de Guanacaste, consisting of a spectacular chain of volcanoes that can be appreciated by the traveler heading south from the Nicaraguan border along the Carretera Interamericana. These include Volcán Orosí (1487m) in Parque Nacional Guanacaste, the gently steaming Volcán Rincón de la Vieja (1895m) and Volcán Santa María (1916m), both in Parque Nacional Rincón de la Vieja, as well as Volcán Miravalles (2026m) and Volcán Tenorio (1916m).

Farther to the southeast is the Cordillera de Tilarán, which includes the renowned Monteverde cloud forest reserve and, just north of the main massif, the continually exploding Volcán Arenal (1633m), the most active volcano in Costa Rica.

The Cordillera de Tilarán runs into the Cordillera Central, which includes the famous Volcán Poás (2704m) and Volcán Irazú (3432m), both of which are active volcanoes lying at the center of national parks that are named after them, and Volcán Barva (2906m), which is in Parque Nacional Braulio Carrillo.

The southeasternmost mountains are associated with the Cordillera de Talamanca, which is higher, geologically older, more remote, and more rugged than the other ranges. About 16 separate peaks reach in excess of 3000m, the highest being Cerro Chirripó (3820m). Changing altitudes play an important part in determining geographical, climatic, and ecological variation. Many

BUDDY MAYS

Costa Rica's most active volcanic giant, Volcán Arenal

different ecological habitats are found, corresponding with altitudinal changes up the mountains.

In the center of the highlands lies the meseta central, which is surrounded by mountains (the Cordillera Central to the north and east, the Cordillera de Talamanca to the south). It is this central plain, between about 1000 and 1500m above sea level, that contains four of Costa Rica's five largest cities, including San José, the capital. Over half of the population lives on this plain, which contains fertile volcanic soil.

On either side of the volcanic central highlands lie coastal lowlands, which differ greatly in form. The smooth Caribbean coastline is 212km long and is characterized by year-round rain, mangroves, swamps, an intracoastal waterway, sandy beaches, and small tides. The Pacific coast is much more rugged and rocky. The tortuous coastline is 1016km long, with various gulfs and peninsulas. It is bordered by tropical dry forests, which receive almost no rain for several months each year, as well as by mangroves, swamps, and beaches. Tidal variation is quite large and there are many offshore islands.

The two most important peninsulas are the Nicoya, separated from the mainland by a gulf of the same name, and the Osa, separated from the mainland by the Golfo Dulce. The Península de Nicoya is hilly, dry, and dusty. It is known for its cattle farming and its beach resorts. The Península de Osa contains Parque Nacional Corcovado, which is one of Costa Rica's protected rainforests.

GEOLOGY

Geologists believe that the surface of the earth is covered with a number of huge tectonic plates that move slowly over millions of years, causing the earth's surface to change constantly. Like most of Central America, Costa Rica's geological history can be traced back to the impact of the Cocos Plate moving northeast and crashing into the Caribbean Plate at a rate of about 10cm every year – quite fast by geological standards. The point of impact is called a subduction zone, in which the Cocos Plate forces the edge of the Caribbean Plate to break up and become uplifted. This is not a smooth process, and hence Central America is an area prone to earthquakes and volcanic activity (see Dangers & Annoyances in the Facts for the Visitor chapter).

This process began underwater and has been going on for about 5 million years. Most of Costa Rica itself is about 3 million years old, with the exception of the Península de Nicoya which is many millions of years older. Most of the mountain ranges in Costa Rica are volcanic; the exception is the massive Cordillera de Talamanca in the south, which is the largest range in Costa Rica. This is a granite batholith, or intruded igneous rock that formed under great pressure below the surface of the earth and was uplifted.

CLIMATE

Like many tropical countries, Costa Rica experiences two seasons, the wet and the dry, rather than the four seasons of temperate regions. The dry season lasts from about late

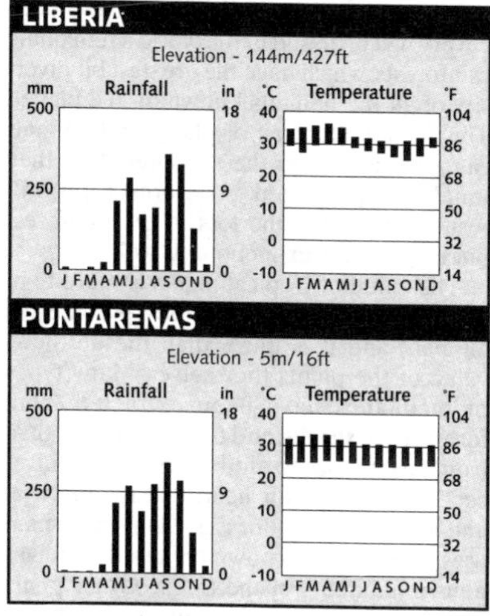

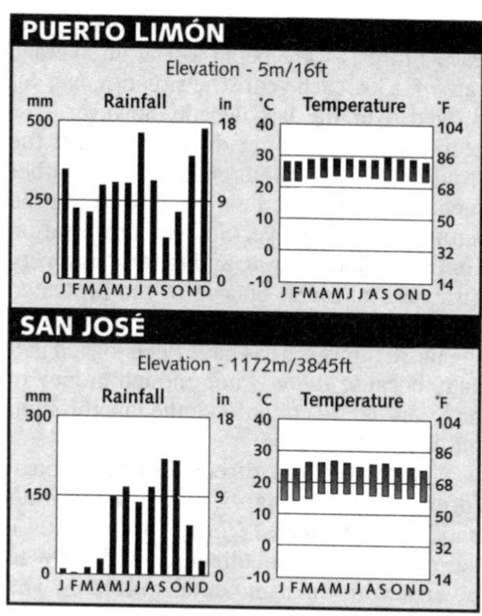

December to April and is called *verano* (summer) by Costa Ricans. The rest of the year tends to be wet, and is called *invierno* (winter).

The Caribbean coastal region is rainy year-round. The dry season is characterized by fewer rainy days and spells of fine weather sometimes lasting a week or more. In the highlands, the dry season really is dry, with only one or two rainy days per month. It can, however, rain up to 20 days per month in the wet season. The north and central Pacific coastal regions have rain patterns similar to the highlands, while the southern Pacific coast can experience rain year-round, though less so in the dry season.

Temperatures vary little from season to season, and the main influencing factor is altitude. San José, at 1150m, has a climate the locals refer to as 'eternal spring.' Lows average a mild 15°C year-round, while highs are a pleasant 26°C. The coasts are much hotter – the Caribbean averages 21°C at night and over 30°C during the day; the Pacific is 2°C or 3°C warmer. Visitors used to a more temperate climate may find the high heat and humidity of the coastal areas oppressive, but most adjust to the conditions after a few days.

ECOLOGY & ENVIRONMENT

Life Zones

Ecologists define 12 tropical life zones in Costa Rica, which are named according to forest type and altitude. Thus, there are dry, moist, wet, and rain forests in tropical, premontane, lower montane, montane, and subalpine areas.

Within a life zone, several types of habitat may occur. Much of Parque Nacional Santa Rosa, for example, is tropical dry forest, but types of vegetation within this zone include deciduous forest, evergreen forest, mangrove swamp, and littoral woodland. Thus Costa Rica has a huge variety of habitats, each with particular associations of plants and animals. The country's extensive and ambitious national park system is an attempt to protect them all.

Major Environmental Problems

Despite Costa Rica's national park system (see National Parks & Protected Areas, later in this chapter), the major problem facing the nation's environment is deforestation. Costa Rica's natural vegetation was originally almost all forest, but most of this has been cleared, mainly for pasture or agriculture. The UN Food and Agriculture Organization estimates that between 1973 and 1989, Costa Rica's forests were being lost at an average rate of 2.3% each year. The situation has improved over the last decade, however: tree plantations are being developed, and the availability of commercially grown timber means that there is less pressure to log the natural forests. Nevertheless, deforestation continues at a high rate and there is now very little natural forest outside of the protected areas. Even within national parks, some of the more remote areas have been logged illegally because there is not enough money to hire park guards to enforce the law throughout the parks.

Apart from the direct loss of tropical forests and the plants and animals that depend on them (see Conservation, below), deforestation has led directly or indirectly to other severe environmental problems. The first and greatest issue is that of soil erosion. Forests protect the soil beneath them from the ravages of tropical rainstorms, and after deforestation much of the topsoil is washed away, lowering the productivity of the land and silting up watersheds. Some deforested lands are planted with Costa Rica's main agricultural product, bananas, the production of which entails the use of pesticides and blue plastic bags to protect the fruit. Both the pesticides and the plastic bags end up polluting the environment.

Conservation

The loss of key habitats, particularly tropical forests, is a pressing problem. Deforestation is happening at such a rate that most of Costa Rica's (and the world's) tropical forests will have disappeared by the first decades of the 21st century; loss of other habitats is a less publicized but equally pressing concern. With this in mind, two important questions arise: Why are habitats such as the tropical rainforests so important, and what can be done to prevent their loss?

Much of Costa Rica's remaining natural vegetation is tropical forest, and there are many reasons why this particular habitat is important. Almost a million of the known species on earth live in tropical rainforests; scientists predict that most of the millions more plant and animal species that await discovery will be found in the world's remaining rainforests, which have the greatest biodiversity of all the habitats known on the planet. This incredible array of plants and animals cannot exist unless the rainforest that they inhabit is protected – deforestation will result not only in the loss of the rainforest but in countless extinctions as well.

The value of tropical plants is more than just the habitat and food they provide for animals, and it is more than the aesthetic value of the plants themselves. Many types of medicines have been extracted from forest trees, shrubs, and flowers. These range from anesthetics to antibiotics, from contraceptives to cures for heart disease, malaria, and various other illnesses. Many medicinal uses of plants are known only to the indigenous inhabitants of the forest. Other pharmaceutical treasures remain locked up in tropical forests, unknown to anybody. They may never be discovered if the forests are destroyed.

Costa Rica's Instituto Nacional de Biodiversidad (INBio) has signed contracts with pharmaceutical companies such as Merck & Company of the USA, the world's largest pharmaceutical company. Funding from the companies is used to support INBio's efforts to protect the rainforests by training local campesinos to make plant and animal collections in the field and to make detailed inventories. Simple preliminary studies are carried out to identify those species that may have medical significance. Thus, local people are involved at a grass-roots level, and pharmaceutical companies receive selections of species that may lead to vital medical breakthroughs. The deal doesn't stop there, however. The contracts earmark a percentage of the potential profits for conservation and preservation efforts.

Deforestation leads not only to species extinction, but also to loss of the genetic diversity that could help species adapt to a changing world. Many crops are monocultures that suffer from a lack of genetic diversity. In other words, all the plants are almost identical because agriculturists have bred strains that are high yielding, easy to harvest, good tasting, etc. If these monocultures are attacked by a new disease or pest epidemic, they could be wiped out because the resistant strains may have been bred out of the population. Plants such as bananas, an important part of Costa Rica's economy, are found in the wild in tropical forests, so in the event of an epidemic scientists could look for disease-resistant wild strains to breed into the commercially raised crops.

While biodiversity for aesthetic, medicinal, and genetic reasons may be important to us, it is even more important to the local indigenous peoples who still survive in tropical rainforests. In Costa Rica, Bribri Indian groups still live in the rainforest in a more or less traditional manner. A few remaining Cabecar Indians still practice shifting agriculture, hunting, and gathering. Over 60% of Costa Rica's remaining Indian people are protected in the Reserva de La Biosfera La Amistad, which comprises two national parks and a host of indigenous and biological reserves in the Talamanca region on the Costa Rica-Panama border. Various international agencies are working with the Costa Rican authorities to protect this area and the cultural and anthropological treasures within it.

Rainforests are important on a global scale because they moderate global climatic patterns. Scientists have determined that the destruction of the rainforests is a major contributing factor to global warming, which would lead to disastrous changes to our world. These changes include the melting of ice caps, causing rising ocean levels and flooding of major coastal cities, many of which are only a scant few meters above the present sea level. Global warming would also make many of the world's 'breadbasket' regions unsuitable for crop production.

All these are good reasons why the rainforest and other habitats should be preserved and protected, but the reality of the economic importance of forest exploitation by the developing nations that own tropical forests must also be considered. It is undeniably true that the clearing of the rainforest provides resources in the way of timber, pasture, and possible mineral wealth, but this is a short-sighted view.

The long-term importance of the rainforest, both from a global view and as a resource of biodiversity, genetic variation, and pharmaceutical wealth, is becoming recognized by the countries that contain forest as well as other nations of the world that will be affected by the destruction of these rainforests. Efforts are now underway to show that the economic value of the standing rainforest is greater than the wealth realized by deforestation.

One important way of making the tropical forest an economically productive resource without cutting it down is to protect it in national parks and preserves and make it accessible to visitors. This type of ecotourism has become extremely important to the economy of Costa Rica and other nations with similar natural resources. More people are likely to visit Costa Rica to see monkeys in the forest than to see cows in a pasture. The visitors spend money on hotels, transport, tours, food, and souvenirs. In addition, many people who spend time in the tropics gain a better understanding of the natural beauty within forests, and the importance of preserving them. The result is that when the visitors return home, they become goodwill ambassadors for tropical forests.

The fundamental concept of ecotourism is excellent, and it has been very successful – so successful that there have been inevitable problems and abuses (see the boxed text 'Ecotourism'). Apart from ecotourism, other innovative projects for sustainable development of tropical forests are being developed. Many of these developments are on private reserves such as Monteverde and Rara Avis. Here, individuals not connected with the government are showing how forests can be preserved and yield a higher economic return than if they were cut down for a one-time sale of lumber and the land then turned into low-yield pasture.

FLORA & FAUNA

Costa Rica is a small country, but its range of habitats gives it an incredibly rich diversity of flora and fauna. The World Resources Institute, in a chart published in 1995, shows

Ecotourism

Costa Rica has so much to offer the wildlife enthusiast that it is small wonder that ecotourism is growing in the country. Over 70% of foreign travelers visit one or more nature destinations; half of these visitors come specifically to see Costa Rica's wildlife.

During the past few years, the natural wonders of Costa Rica have been discovered. From the late 1980s to the mid-1990s, the annual number of visitors doubled, and now over 700,000 foreign tourists visit every year. The tourism industry recently surpassed bananas and coffee as the nation's biggest industry (though 1998 figures placed it second, behind electronics, another newcomer). Prices for the traveler have risen substantially.

The financial bonanza generated by the tourism boom means that new operations are starting up all the time – many are good, some are not. The big word in Costa Rica is 'ecotourism' – everyone wants to jump on the green bandwagon. There are 'ecological' car rental agencies and 'ecological' menus in restaurants! Taking advantage of Costa Rica's 'green' image, some developers are promoting mass tourism and are building large hotels with accompanying environmental problems. Apart from the immediate impacts, such as cutting down vegetation, diverting or damming rivers, and driving away wildlife, there are secondary impacts like erosion, lack of adequate waste treatment facilities for a huge hotel in an area away from sewerage lines, and the building of socially, environmentally, and economically inadequate 'shanty towns' to house the maids, waiters, cooks, cleaners, and many other employees needed. I recommend staying in smaller hotels that have a positive attitude about the environment rather than the large, mass-tourism destinations.

At first, the growth in tourism took the nation by surprise – there was no overall development plan, and the growth was poorly controlled. Some people wanted to cash in on the short term, with little thought for the future. Many developers are foreigners – they say that they are giving the local people jobs, but locals don't want to spend their lives being waiters and maids while watching the big money go out of the country.

Traditionally, tourism in Costa Rica has been on a small and intimate scale. About 90% of the country's hotels are small (fewer than 50 rooms), and the friendly local people have worked closely with tourists, to the benefit of both. This intimacy and friendliness was a hallmark of a visit to Costa Rica, but this is changing.

The developers of a recent project to build a 402-room hotel (the first of a chain) on a remote Pacific beach were sued for causing environmental damage and treating employees unfairly. Although the government agreed that laws were broken, the Spanish-owned hotel opened in 1992 and sparked off a spirited controversy within Costa Rica.

The big question is whether future tourism developments should continue to focus on the traditional small-hotel, ecotourism approach, or turn to mass tourism, with planeloads of visitors accommodated in 'mega-resorts' like the ones in Cancún, Mexico. From the top levels of government on down, the debate has been fierce. Local and international tour operators and travel agents, journalists, developers, airline operators, hotel owners, writers, environmentalists, and politicians have all been vocal in their support of either ecotourism or mass tourism. Many believe that the country is too small to handle both forms of tourism properly.

– **Rob Rachowiecki**

that Costa Rica has the most varied fauna of any country on the planet. A huge tropical country like Brazil will have more species than tiny Costa Rica, so the biodiversity (variety of species) is measured in terms of different species per unit area rather than per country. Counting all birds and mammals per every 10,000 sq km, Costa Rica comes out on top with 615 species (and neighboring Panama has a noteworthy 581 species). In comparison, the highest-ranked African countries are Rwanda and Gambia, with 596 and 574 species. The USA has just 104 species of birds and mammals per 10,000 sq km. Costa Rica's leading level of biodiversity attracts nature lovers from all over the world.

Flora

The floral biodiversity is also high; some 10,000 species of vascular plants have been described, and more are being added to the list every year. Orchids alone account for over 1200 species, the most famous of which is the March-blooming *Cattleya skinneri* (or *guaria morada* in Spanish), Costa Rica's national flower.

The tropical forest is very different from the temperate forests that many North Americans or Europeans may be used to. Temperate forests, such as the coniferous forests of the far north or the deciduous woodlands of milder regions, tend to have little variety. They are pines, pines, and more pines, or endless tracts of oaks, beech, and birch.

Tropical forests, on the other hand, have great variety; over 1400 tree species have been recorded in Costa Rica. If you stand in one spot and look around, you'll see scores of different species of trees, but often you'll have to walk several hundred meters to find another example of any particular species.

This incredible variety generates biodiversity in the animals that live within the forests. There are several dozen species of fig trees in Costa Rica, for example, and the fruit of each species is the home of one particular wasp species. The wasp benefits by obtaining food and protection; when it flies to another fig tree, the fig benefits because the wasp carries pollen on its body. Many trees and plants of the forest provide fruit, seeds, or nectar for insects, birds, and bats. They rely upon these visitors to carry pollen across several hundred meters of forest to fertilize another member of the appropriate plant species.

These complex interrelationships and the high biodiversity are among the reasons why biologists and conservationists are calling for a halt to the destruction of tropical forests. It is a sobering thought that three-quarters of Costa Rica was forested in the late 1940s; by the early 1990s, less than a quarter of the country remained covered by forest. To try to control this deforestation and protect its wildlife, Costa Rica has instigated the most progressive national park system in Latin America.

Fauna

The primary attractions for many naturalists are the birds, of which some 850 species have been recorded in the country. This is far more than what is found in any one of the continents of North America, Australia, or Europe. Also, there are well over 200 mammal species, at least 35,000 classified insect species (with many thousands more

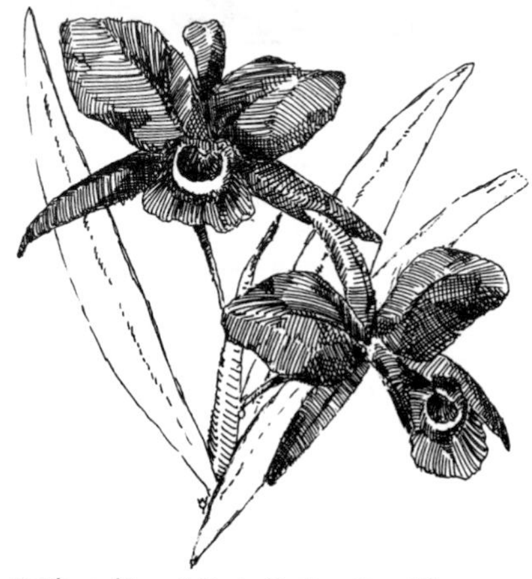

***Cattleya skinneri*, Costa Rica's national flower**

remaining to be described), about 160 species of amphibians, 220 species of reptiles (of which over half are snakes), and about 130 species of freshwater fish. (See the Wildlife Guide at the end of the book and related boxed text for more information.)

Endangered Species

According to the World Resources Institute, Costa Rica is home to many threatened species, including 10 bird species, eight mammal species, seven reptile species, one amphibian, and 456 plants. These are the most extremely endangered cases. In addition, Costa Rican laws passed in 1992 protect many more species against hunting, capturing, or trafficking. Locally, 87 birds, 27 mammals, 36 amphibians, 16 reptiles, all species of orchids, cacti, and tree ferns, and some palms are listed as endangered under Costa Rican law.

Watching Wildlife

The best places to see wildlife are in the many national parks and private preserves in the country. While the forest in these protected areas supports a great deal of wildlife, it is often not very easy to observe it. The main reason for this is the forest itself – you could be 30m away from a jaguar and never even know it is there because of the dense vegetation. Wildlife observation in the rainforest is much more difficult than in the open plains of East Africa, for example.

Various strategies can be used to increase your chances of seeing wildlife. The best ideas are to hire a guide or go on a guided tour. Local guides often know where the animals in their area are hanging out and also have a great eye for the tiny movement that can give away an animal's presence. Animals tend to be the most active and visible in the hours after dawn and just before dusk; it is more difficult to see an animal asleep in the middle of the day. Turn your thoughts away from the exotic but rarely seen large mammals, such as jaguars and tapirs, and concentrate instead on smaller things that are relatively easy to observe, such as the marching columns of leaf-cutter ants found in most rainforests or bright red poison-arrow frogs seen hopping around many parts of the Caribbean coast.

Look for wildlife using more than just your eyes. Some guides can smell a herd of peccaries before they see them. Everyone should use their ears, especially for birding. A walk through the cloud forest is often made eerie by the penetrating whistles and ventriloqual

Bird Extinction

Some Costa Rican birds are recent arrivals from other areas but have now become increasingly common here. This has occurred because of dramatic changes in Costa Rica's countryside in recent decades. As forests are replaced with pastures and agricultural land, the original fauna is put under pressure, and new species, better adapted at living in disturbed and more open land, move in and take over. Examples of recent arrivals are the cattle egret and black-shouldered kite, both of which were first recorded in Costa Rica in the 1950s and are now common (see the Wildlife Guide). Meanwhile, a famous species that has become almost extinct because of deforestation is the spectacular harpy eagle.

– Rob Rachowiecki

'bonk!' calls of the three-wattled bellbird, a member of the cotinga family. The haunting notes sound so loud that they can easily be heard half a kilometer away. Spotting this large, chestnut-brown bird, with its pure white head and neck decorated with three black wormlike wattles, is another matter. They call from display perches at the tops of the highest trees and are heard more often than seen. The male howler monkeys are heard as often as they are seen; their eerie vocalizations carry long distances and have been likened to a baby crying or the wind moaning through the trees. Many visitors are unable to believe they are hearing a monkey when they first hear the mournful sound.

NATIONAL PARKS & PROTECTED AREAS

The national park system began in the 1960s, and now there are about three dozen national parks, wildlife refuges, biological reserves, monuments, and recreation areas in Costa Rica. These comprise about 13% of the total land area. In addition, there are various buffer zones, such as forest reserves and Indian reservations, that boost the total area of 'protected' land to about 27%. These buffer zones still allow farming, logging, and other exploitation, however, so the environment is not totally protected within them.

As well as the national park system, there are dozens of small, privately owned lodges, reserves, and haciendas that have been set up to protect the land, and these are well worth visiting.

A project is slowly developing to link geographically close groups of national parks and reserves, private preserves, and national forests into a national system of conservation areas (Sistema Nacional de Areas de Conservación – SINAC), of which there are now 11. Carefully managed agricultural land will help create buffer zones to protect the more critical areas, called core zones. Wildlife corridors will be used to enable wildlife to range over larger areas. These areas have been dubbed 'megaparks' by local conservationists, and it has been suggested that they will eventually cover about a quarter of Costa Rica's land area.

The system will have two major effects. First, larger areas of wildlife habitats will be protected in blocks, allowing greater numbers of species and individuals to exist. Second, the administration of the national parks will be delegated to regional offices, allowing a more individualized management approach for each particular area. This is already happening to a certain extent, although many regional offices play what appear to be obscure bureaucratic roles rather than providing necessary management and guidance.

Most of the national park system has been created in order to protect the different habitats and wildlife of Costa Rica. A few parks are designed to preserve other valued areas, such as the country's best pre-Columbian ruins, at Monumento Nacional Guayabo; an important cave system at Parque Nacional Barra Honda; a site of national historic importance as well as the tropical dry forest in Parque Nacional Santa Rosa; and a series of geologically active and inactive volcanoes in several parks and reserves.

SINAC has a toll-free number (☎ 192 in Costa Rica) that can provide up-to-date admission and other information from 7 am to 5 pm weekdays. For specific parks, call the numbers given in the regional chapters of the book.

Most national parks can be entered without permits, but a few of the biological reserves do require a permit that can be obtained by applying to the public information office. The entrance fee to most parks is US$6 for foreigners, plus an additional US$2 for overnight camping.

Many national parks are in remote areas and are rarely visited – they suffer from a lack of rangers and protection. Others are extremely – and deservedly – popular for their world-class scenic and natural beauty, as well as their wildlife. In the idyllic Parque Nacional Manuel Antonio, a tiny park on the Pacific coast, the number of visitors has reached 1000 per day in the high season. Annual visitation rocketed from about 36,000 visitors in 1982 to over 150,000 by 1991. This number of visitors threatened to ruin the diminutive area by driving away the

NATIONAL PARKS & PROTECTED AREAS
NICARAGUA
CARIBBEAN SEA
PACIFIC OCEAN
PANAMA
Bahía de Coronado
11°N
10°N
9°N
85°W
84°W
83°W
La Cruz
Liberia
Santa Cruz
Nicoya
Puntarenas
Alajuela
Heredia
SAN JOSÉ
Ciudad Colón
Cartago
Jacó
Quepos
San Isidro de El General
Palmar Norte
Golfito
Puerto Jiménez
Barra del Colorado
Tortuguero
Guácimo
Puerto Limón
87°06'W
87°03'W
5°33'N
5°30'N
Isla del Coco
0 3 6 km
0 2 4 miles
0 40 80 km
0 25 50 miles
1 Refugio Nacional de Fauna Silvestre Isla Bolaños
2 Refugio Nacional de Vida Silvestre Bahía Junquillal
3 Parque Nacional Guanacaste
4 Parque Nacional Santa Rosa
5 Estación Experimental Horizontes
6 Parque Nacional Rincón de la Vieja
7 Refugio Nacional de Vida Silvestre Caño Negro
8 Parque Nacional Marino Las Baulas de Guanacaste
9 Reserva Biológica Lomas Barbudal
10 Parque Nacional Volcán Tenorio
11 Reserva Indígena Guatuso
12 Parque Nacional Volcán Arenal
13 Refugio Nacional de Fauna Silvestre Barra del Colorado
14 Parque Nacional Tortuguero
15 Refugio Nacional de Fauna Silvestre Ostional
16 Reserva Indígena Matambú
17 Parque Nacional Barra Honda
18 Parque Nacional Palo Verde
19 Reserva Biológica Bosque Nuboso Monteverde
20 Refugio Silvestre de Peñas Blancas
21 Parque Nacional Juan Castro Blanco
22 Parque Nacional Volcán Poás
23 Estación Biológica La Selva
24 Parque Nacional Braulio Carrillo
25 Reserva Biológica Isla de Los Pájaros
26 Reserva Biológica de Isla Guayabo
27 Refugio Nacional de Vida Silvestre Curú
28 Reserva Natural Absoluta Cabo Blanco
29 Reserva Biológica Islas Negritos
30 Reserva Biológica Carara
31 Reserva Indígena Quitirrisí
32 Reserva Indígena Zapatón
33 Parque Nacional Volcán Irazú
34 Monumento Nacional Guayabo
35 Parque Nacional Tapantí
36 Reserva Indígena Barbilla
37 Reserva Biológica Barbilla
38 Reserva Indígena Alto y Bajo Chirripó
39 Parque Nacional Manuel Antonio
40 Parque Nacional Chirripó
41 Reserva Indígena Tayní
42 Reserva Biológica Hitoy Cerere
43 Reserva Indígena Telire
44 Reserva Indígena Talamanca Cabécar
45 Parque Internacional La Amistad
46 Reserva Indígena Talamanca Bribri
47 Parque Nacional Cahuita
48 Reserva Indígena Cocles/KéköLdi
49 Refugio Nacional de Vida Silvestre Gandoca-Manzanillo
50 Parque Nacional Marino Ballena
51 Reserva Indígena Ujarrás
52 Reserva Indígena Salitre
53 Reserva Indígena Cabagra
54 Reserva Indígena Térraba
55 Reserva Indígena Boruca
56 Reserva Indígena Curré
57 Zona Protectora Las Tablas
58 Reserva Biológica Isla del Caño
59 Humedal Nacional Térraba-Sierpe
60 Reserva Indígena Osa
61 Parque Nacional Corcovado
62 Parque Nacional Corcovado (Piedras Blancas Sector)
63 Refugio Nacional de Fauna Silvestre Golfito
64 Reserva Indígena Coto Brus
65 Reserva Indígena Abrojo-Montezuma
66 Reserva Indígena Conte Burica
67 Parque Nacional Isla del Coco

wildlife, polluting the beaches, and replacing wilderness with hotel development. Park visitation has been limited to 600 people a day and the park is closed on Mondays to allow it a brief respite from the onslaught.

Costa Rica has a world-famous reputation for the excellence and far-sightedness of its national park system – but lack of funds, concentrated visitor use, and sometimes fuzzy leadership have shown that there are problems in paradise.

GOVERNMENT & POLITICS

The government is based on the Constitution of November 9, 1949 (see History, earlier in this chapter). The president, who is both the head of government and head of state, wields executive power, assisted by two vice-presidents and a cabinet of 12 ministers. (Previous governments had 18 ministers; in 1998, the president downsized the cabinet and added a team of eight advisors.) The presidential elections are held every four years, and an incumbent cannot be reelected.

The country is divided into the seven provinces of San José, Alajuela, Cartago, Heredia, Guanacaste, Puntarenas, and Limón. Each province has a governor who is appointed by the president. The provinces are divided into 81 *cantones* (counties) and subdivided into 429 districts. For about every 30,000 people in each province, a *diputado/a* (congressman/woman) is elected every four years to the Legislative Assembly, or Congress, which totals 57 diputados in all. This is where much of the power of government lies. Incumbents cannot serve successive terms, which creates a lack of continuity: whatever one congressperson does politically is liable to be reversed by his or her successor.

The Legislative Assembly appoints 22 Supreme Court magistrates for minimum terms of eight years, and these judges select judges for the lower courts. The idea behind these three power structures is to prevent any one person or group from having too much control, thus ensuring a real democracy. There is also an Electoral Tribunal that is responsible for supervising elections and ensuring that the electoral process is fair and democratic. Known as the 'fourth power,' the Electoral Tribunal consists of three magistrates and six substitutes who are independent of the government.

There is no army in Costa Rica. Instead, there's a Fuerza Publica, a form of an armed police force.

Although there are about 30 political parties, only two groups have been in power since 1949: the National Liberation Party (PLN) and the Christian Socialist Party (PUSC). Since 1998, the PUSC has been in power, under the presidency of Miguel Angel Rodríguez.

The vote is officially mandatory for all citizens aged over 18 years. An up-to-date and validated electoral card must be carried by all Costa Ricans as identification and is needed for anything from opening a bank account to getting a job. Election day is very upbeat in Costa Rica – everyone treats it like a patriotic holiday, with flag waving, car-horn honking, and general euphoria. Still, voter apathy has been increasing in recent years, and almost 30% of eligible voters declined to vote in the 1998 elections.

ECONOMY

Until the middle of the 19th century, Costa Rica was a very poor country with an economy based on subsistence agriculture. Then the introduction of coffee began to provide a product suitable for export. This was followed by bananas, and today these two crops continue to be the most important in the country. Other important traditional exports include meat and sugar.

In the early 1990s, nontraditional export items such as ornamental plants and flowers, seafood, pineapples, pharmaceutical products, textiles and clothing, tires, furniture, and many other products began to rival the traditional exports. Also during the early 1990s, tourism experienced an unprecedented boom in Costa Rica. Numbers of foreign tourists visiting the country rose from 376,000 in 1989 to about 940,000 at present. The annual value of revenues from tourism soon rose to over US$500 million, making tourism the single most important earner of foreign currency over traditional banana and coffee exports from 1993 to 1997.

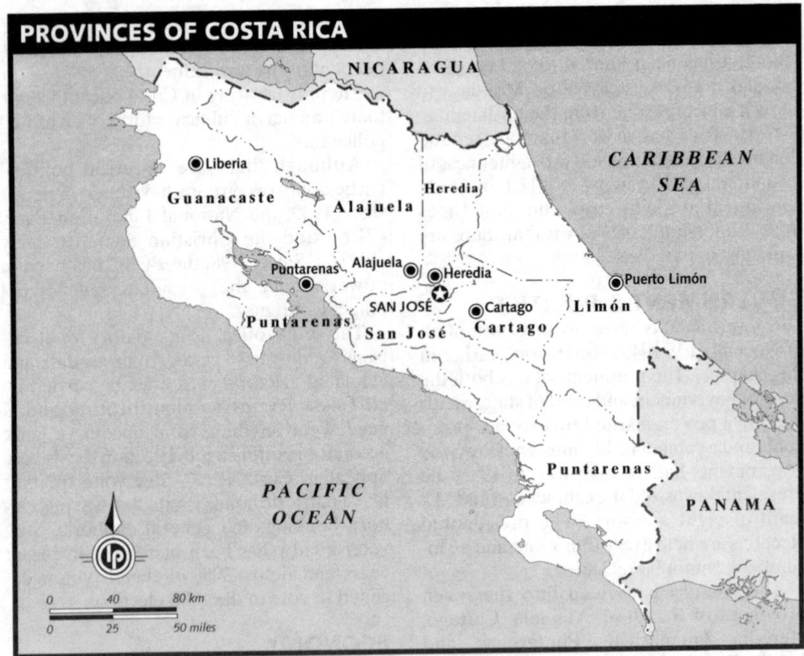

Changes since then have been in the electronics sector. Intel, the multinational manufacturer of computer chips, opened factories in Costa Rica. Their influence fueled the electronics industry to become Costa Rica's top dollar earner in 1998, bringing the country US$1.2 billion, of which about 78% was attributed to Intel. Also in 1998, tourism brought US$829 million to the country, followed by the textile industry (US$758 million), bananas (US$630 million), and coffee (US$409 million).

The USA is by far the most important export destination, followed by Europe, especially Germany. The USA is also the main supplier of imports, distantly followed by Japan (7.6%).

POPULATION & PEOPLE

The last census was in 1984, when 2,416,809 inhabitants were counted. The next census has been postponed because the government can't yet afford to do it. The estimated population in 1998 was 3,605,000, of which just over half was male. About 60% of the people live in the highlands. The annual population growth rate is about 2%, and infant mortality was 13 per 1000 live births in 1998. About 34% of the population is under 15. About 95% of those over 15 are literate – this is among the best literacy rates in Latin America.

The population density is over 70 people per square kilometer, the third highest in Central America, after El Salvador and Guatemala. This is about a quarter of the population density of the UK, but almost 2½ times higher than that of the USA.

The vast majority of the people are white, mainly of Spanish descent. About 2% of the population is black, except in the thinly populated Caribbean province of Limón. Here, about 35% of the inhabitants trace their ancestry mainly to the immigrant laborers from Jamaica who built the railways and worked the banana plantations in the late

1800s. As with other Caribbean blacks, many of them speak a lively dialect of English. They were actively discriminated against in the early 1900s, not even being allowed to spend a night in the highlands, but since the 1949 constitution they have legally had equal rights. Almost 1% of the population is of Asian (mainly Chinese) descent.

A small number of Indians remain, making up about 1% of the population. (Note that the literal translation of Indian is *indio*, which is an insulting term to Costa Rica's indigenous inhabitants. They prefer the term *indígena*, which means 'native inhabitant.') Estimates of the Indian population vary from 5000 to 40,000 – the higher figure is the most likely if one includes those that are not pureblooded. Many of these have integrated to the extent that they are more or less indistinguishable from other Costa Ricans. Small populations of culturally distinct tribes include the Bribri from the Talamanca area near the southeastern coast and Panamanian border, the Borucas in the southern Pacific coastal areas, and the Guayami, who straddle the Panamanian border. Other groups – the Chorotegas, Cabecares, Terrabas, and others – either have been assimilated into the mainstream Costa Rican way of life or were wiped out soon after the conquest.

There are 22 Indian reserves in Costa Rica, but, for the most part, these are of little interest to travelers, who often may not even know they are within a reserve. A few reserves discourage visitation, and a few have perhaps a store selling some local crafts, along with the usual country-store items like cans of sardines and bottles of soft drinks.

The Costa Rican people call themselves *ticos* and *ticas* (male and female). This supposedly stems from their love of the use of diminutives; *chico* (small) becomes *chiquito* and *chiquitito* or *chiquitico*. You don't hear the *tico* ending as much as before, though a waiter at the airport café once told me he'd be with me in a *momentico*.

I find most ticos to be consistently friendly, polite, and helpful. Visitors are constantly surprised at the warmth of the Costa Rican people. This is still a very family-oriented society, however, and the friendliness and politeness tend to form somewhat of a shell over their true personalities. It is easy to make friends with a tico, but it is much more difficult to form deeper relationships.

Living, Living & Living...

Costa Rican life expectancy in 1998 was estimated at an average of 76 years. In 1995, local newspapers reported that in a World Health Organization study ranking the life spans of the world, Costa Ricans were rated third! Only the Japanese, averaging an 80-year life span, and the French, with a 78-year average, ranked higher. Although the World Health Organization didn't give reasons for these countries' longevity records, I guess that if you want to live a long time, you should eat raw fish, rice, and beans, and drink plenty of wine.

– Rob Rachowiecki

EDUCATION

About 20% of the national budget goes toward education. With the highest literacy rate in Latin America and compulsory education through ninth grade (age 14), the education system appears to be in good shape. Appearances can be deceptive, however, and there are certainly problems that don't show up in the official picture. A Ministry of Public Education study, reported in the Costa Rican press in mid-1996, indicates that there are six times more dropouts from secondary school than there are students in the ninth grade – the final year of legally mandated study. This is blamed on various factors, including the need for conveniently located secondary schools, lack of student interest, lack of encouragement from parents, and a desire to enter the work force.

ARTS

Costa Rica is famous for its natural beauty and friendly people rather than for its culture. Because of the overwhelmingly European population, there is very little indigenous cultural influence. And because the country was a poor subsistence-agriculture nation until the middle of the 19th century, cultural and artistic activities have only really developed since the late 19th century. Ticos consider San José to be the cultural center of the country, and it is here that the most important museums are found.

Performing Arts

Theater is one of the favorite cultural activities in Costa Rica, and San José is the center of a thriving acting community. Plays are produced mainly in Spanish, but the Little Theater Group is well known for its English-language performances. (See the San José chapter for details.)

The most famous theater in the country is the Teatro Nacional, built between 1890 and 1897. The story goes that a noted European opera company, featuring the talented singer Adelina Patti, was on a Latin American tour but declined to perform in Costa Rica for lack of a suitable hall. Immediately, the coffee elite put a special cultural tax on coffee exports for the construction of a world-class theater.

The Teatro Nacional, in the heart of San José, is now the venue for plays, opera, performances by the National Symphony Orchestra, ballet, poetry readings, and other cultural events. It also is an architectural work in its own right and a landmark in any city tour of San José.

The National Symphony Orchestra is perhaps the most cosmopolitan of Costa Rica's performing arts groups. It has toured the USA, Eastern Europe, Spain, Asia, and other countries in recent years and has a high standard. International guest artists often perform with the orchestra, and tickets are inexpensive.

Blowing, Blowing & Blowing...

The world record for a musician holding a single note is held by Costa Rican saxophonist Geovanny Escalante of the famed local band Marfil, which has played in Costa Rica for many years. In 1998, the then 24-year-old artist held a steady 'A' for 90 minutes, 45 seconds, almost twice as long as the previous record held by the US saxophonist Kenny G.

– Rob Rachowiecki

International Arts Festival

Costa Rica's biggest cultural event is the International Arts Festival, held annually in San José for about two weeks in March. The festival features theater, music, dance, film, and a variety of art shows with participants from many countries. Also important is the annual Monteverde Music Festival, held in January and February.

Literature

Carmen Naranjo (born 1930) is the one Costa Rican writer who has risen to international acclaim. She is a novelist, poet, and short-story writer who also served her country in the 1970s as ambassador to India and as the Minister of Culture. In 1996, she was awarded the prestigious Gabriela Mistral medal from the Chilean government (Gabriela Mistral, a Chilean, won the 1945 Nobel Prize for Literature). Naranjo's works have been translated into several languages, including English. Two of her short stories are found in *Costa Rica – A Traveler's Literary Companion*, which is the best introduction to Costa Rican literature (see Books in the Facts for the Visitor chapter).

Crafts

Many crafts are available in Costa Rica, ranging from balsa birds to jungle-seed jewelry. Most of these are similar to crafts available in other tropical Latin American countries, but a few of them have a special Costa Rican niche.

A few decades ago, the *carretas*, gaily painted wooden carts drawn by oxen, were the common form of transportation in the countryside. Although carretas are rarely seen in use today (you'll occasionally see one in the most rural areas or during a fiesta), they have become something of a traditional craft form, both a symbol of agricultural Costa Rica and a souvenir peculiar to Costa Rica. They come in all sizes, from table-top models to nearly life-size replicas that double as liquor cabinets. They all fold down for transport. Sarchí is the main center for carreta construction.

Wooden bowls sound like a humble art form, yet they have been elevated to international art status by Barry Biesanz, working in Escazú, San José. Biesanz's handcrafted wooden bowls are light and luminous, almost defying the definition of wooden. His best pieces sell for close to US$1000, and some of his bowls have been presented to US presidents.

The village of Guaitil on the Península de Nicoya is famed for its pottery. The attractive pots are made from local clays and use natural colors in the pre-Columbian Chorotega Indian style. They come in a variety of shapes and sizes – many of the huge pots seen decorating houses and hotels in Guanacaste come from here. Other distinctive, boldly painted ceramics are made by Cecilia Facio Pecas Figueres, the sister-in-law of President Figueres (1994-98). Her work is often identifiable by the painted initials PF.

SOCIETY & CONDUCT

Costa Rican society is the least diverse of any Central American nation. As indicated under Population & People, above, most of the population is white. The majority are of Latin descent and practice Roman Catholicism. Traditionally, Costa Ricans have prided themselves on being a classless society.

Despite the apparent homogeneity, societal differences clearly exist. Historically, a small noble class *(hidalgos)* led the colony's

Carmen Naranjo

affairs, and since Costa Rica became independent the descendants of three hidalgo families have provided the country with most of its presidents and congressional representatives. Nevertheless, politicians from the president down take pride in mingling with the public and maintaining some semblance of a classless society. The distribution of land and wealth is clearly uneven, but much less so than in other Central American countries.

Until 1949, the small black minority (many of whom are descendants of Jamaican workers hired to build the railway in the 1870s and 1880s) was actively discriminated against. Blacks did not have Costa Rican citizenship and were not allowed to vote or to travel into the highlands away from their Caribbean coastal homes. This was changed by the new (and current) constitution of 1949. Now, racism is officially a thing of the past and black travelers are unlikely to encounter problems in the main cities and on the Caribbean coast, although some racist attitudes might still be encountered off the beaten path. One reader reported indifferent unfriendliness in San Vito, but most black foreign travelers with whom I have talked have not reported problems. I welcome any feedback travelers may have.

Other minority groups are even smaller in number than the black population. The few remaining Indian groups are but a tiny fraction of the population present when the Europeans arrived. There are far fewer Indians here than in any other Central American country, and their lot is a poor one. Although Indians do have reserves designed to enable them to live in a traditional manner, enforcing the boundaries and integrity of the reserves against loggers, plantations, colonists, mineral prospectors, and others has not been entirely successful. Indians, with very few exceptions, remain a marginal element of Costa Rican society, and little is being done to change this.

Other ethnic groups include small but reasonably successful Chinese and Jewish communities. Although Costa Ricans claim that these are well integrated into the culture, I have, unfortunately, heard occasional anti-Semitic statements made by a few ticos. In 1999, a false report that Chinese restaurants served rats led to a surprisingly strong wave of anti-Chinese sentiment that motivated the president to make a publicized visit to a Chinese restaurant in an attempt to improve their unfairly tarnished image. (I recommend Chinese restaurants.)

The San Vito area in southern Costa Rica is known for its Italian community, and the Monteverde area has a Quaker community that dates back to the arrival of a Quaker group from the USA about half a century ago. A new influx of US citizens has occurred in

Prostitution

Prostitution is legal in Costa Rica for women over 18. Professional prostitutes carry a health card showing how recently they had a medical check-up. Be aware, however, that some women don't bother with these cards. Also, some sexually transmitted diseases can take several days or weeks before they can be detected, so even an up-to-date health card doesn't guarantee that a prostitute is disease-free. AIDS is a growing problem in Costa Rica (see the Health and Gay & Lesbian Travelers sections in the Facts for the Visitor chapter).

A study reported in the Costa Rican newspaper *Al Día* says that there are 2000 children working as prostitutes in San José, hired both by foreign tourists and Costa Ricans. This is definitely not legal. There are publications that promote Costa Rica as a 'sex destination' partly because of legal prostitution and partly for pedophiles. This is discouraged by government officials, who do not consider legal sex for money to be a tourist attraction. Many of the children working as prostitutes have drug problems and no family to turn to. One of the few resources available to them is the Fundación Oratorio Don Bosco de Sor María Romero, a shelter for homeless street kids in San José. The Oratorio also provides food and counseling for addicted and abused kids. The shelter is funded by UNICEF and private donations. You can help by depositing money in their account at the Banco Nacional de Costa Rica No 174282-4 (in *colones*) or No 608592-2 (in US dollars) or calling the shelter (☎ 257-4470) for information about how to donate.

In 1999, the Costa Rican tourist board, encouraged by the Catholic church, attempted to link sex tourism with gay tourism. This is a clearly unfounded claim, as gay tourists usually come with partners or friends looking for a tropical vacation, and aren't interested in underage prostitutes. After protests from both straight and gay travelers and travel agencies, the official position was that sex tourism was discouraged, activity with underage prostitutes was illegal, and gay tourism was in the usual limbo in between – it's legal but folks don't want to talk about it.

– Rob Rachowiecki

recent decades – tens of thousands of retirees have decided that the year-round warmth and easygoing nature of Costa Rica are preferable to life in the USA. Both the capital and many of the coastal villages in the Península de Nicoya have large enclaves of US *pensionados*, as the retirees are called. Also in recent decades, there has been a surge of people from other Central American countries, who were trying to avoid the conflicts there.

Appearances are important to Costa Ricans. As they say, they want to *quedar bien*, which translates more or less into leaving a good impression. They do this by dressing both conservatively and as well as they can (and sometimes can't) afford, and by acting in an agreeable and friendly manner, which has become a hallmark of tico culture. Despite their conservatism, they can certainly loosen up in certain settings. Flirtation and public displays of affection, such as kissing, are unremarkable sights in the streets (but also see the section on Women Travelers in Facts for the Visitor). Conservative dress is appropriate in the cities, and few Costa Ricans wear shorts in the highlands (except in athletic or exercise settings) – though once you get down to the coast, shorts are fine in the beach resorts and beachwear may be quite skimpy. Nudity or toplessness is definitely considered inappropriate, however.

Costa Ricans, like most Latin Americans, consider greetings important. In all situations, politeness is a valued habit. A certain degree of formality and floweriness is often used in conversation – friends may say, *'Buenos días, cómo amaneció?'* (Good morning, how did you awake?). An appropriate response is *'Muy bien, por dicha, y usted?'* (Very well, fortunately, and you?). Strangers conducting business will, at the minimum, exchange a cordial *'Buenos días, cómo está?'* before launching into whatever they are doing. Male friends and casual acquaintances meeting one another in the street shake hands at the beginning and end of even a short meeting; women kiss one another on the cheek in greeting and farewell. Men often kiss women decorously on the cheek, except in a business setting, where a handshake is more appropriate.

Family life is a central part of Costa Rican life, and any conversation will often include inquiries about your family. Strangers will ask if you are married and how many children you have, which is a fairly normal conversational gambit that's not meant to seem overly inquisitive. Conversations are frequently laced with local colloquialisms (see the Language section at the back of the book). References to a person's appearance are practical endearments and are not meant to give offense, though non-tico recipients may find them tiresome. These include *chino* (person with a Chinese appearance), *flaco* (a skinny person), *gordo* (a plump person), and *negro* (a black person). They may be made more affectionate by adding a diminutive, eg, *la gordita*.

The concept of smoking being a hazard to one's health is not very big in Costa Rica compared to the USA. Nonsmoking areas are infrequent and some restaurants allow diners to smoke wherever they please.

RELIGION

This can be summed up in one word: Catholicism. Depending on which statistics you read, about 80% or 90% of the population is Roman Catholic, at least in principle. In practice, many people tend to go to church only at the time of birth, marriage, and death, but they consider themselves Catholic nevertheless. Religious processions on holy days are generally less fervent or colorful than those found in other Latin American countries. Holy Week (the week before Easter) is a national holiday; everything, including buses, stops operating at lunchtime on Maundy Thursday and doesn't start up again till Holy Saturday.

The blacks on the Caribbean coast tend to be Protestant, though some traditional African and Caribbean beliefs persist. Most other denominations have a church in or around San José. Various fundamentalist and evangelist groups, as well as Mormons, are slowly gaining some adherents. There is a small Jewish community with a B'Nai Israel temple and a synagogue, and a sprinkling of people hold Middle Eastern and Asian religious beliefs.

LANGUAGE

Spanish is the official language and is the main language for the traveler. English is understood in the better hotels, airline offices, and tourist agencies, as well as along much of the Caribbean coast.

Indian languages, primarily Bribri, are spoken in isolated areas. Bribri is understood by an estimated 10,000 people living on both sides of the Cordillera de Talamanca.

If you don't speak Spanish, take heart. It is an easy language to learn. Courses are available in San José as well as in other towns (see under the town descriptions), or you can study books, records, and tapes before your trip. These study aids are often available free from many public libraries, or you might want to consider taking an evening or college course. Once you have learned the basics, you'll find it possible to travel all over Latin America because, apart from Brazil, which is Portuguese-speaking, most of the countries use Spanish.

Spanish is easy to learn for several reasons. It uses Roman script and, with few exceptions, the language is written phonetically. Imagine trying to explain to someone learning English that there are seven different ways of pronouncing 'ough.' This isn't a problem in Spanish. Also, many words in Spanish are similar enough to English that you can figure them out by guesswork. Instituto Geográfico Nacional means the National Geographical Institute, for example.

Even if you don't have time to take a course, at least bring a phrasebook (Lonely Planet's *Latin American Spanish phrasebook* is a good choice) and dictionary. Don't dispense with the dictionary, because the phrasebook limits you to asking where the bus station is and won't help you translate the local newspaper. For a quick reference to vocabulary and pronunciation, see the Language section near the back of this guidebook.

Facts for the Visitor

HIGHLIGHTS

The greatest attractions are natural. Rainforests, active volcanoes, and prolific birdlife are certainly at the top of the list because they are more accessible in Costa Rica than in most other countries with similar attractions. The national park system is the best in Central America and provides visitors with memorable experiences: you can safely peer into a smoking volcanic crater one day and photograph a flock of scarlet macaws flying over a coastal rainforest the next day.

The most accessible volcanoes are Poás and Irazú, both of which have roads reaching overlooks of their active craters, and Arenal, which is one of the most active volcanoes in the world and best viewed from afar (head to the town of Fortuna for a good look). For rainforest, the national park at Corcovado is the wildest (though comfortable lodges are nearby), and Manuel Antonio is the prettiest. Tortuguero is excellent for wildlife, and Caño Negro is the least well known but is superb for birding.

Birders find Costa Rica offers exceptional opportunities almost anywhere they go. Vacations specifically designed to yield numerous excellent sightings every day are offered by tour companies that specialize in birding.

Outdoor enthusiasts also find top-notch surfing, white-water rafting, windsurfing, and fishing. Beaches at Puerto Viejo de Talamanca on the Caribbean coast and at Pavones, Dominical, Jacó, and Tamarindo on the Pacific coast are all favorite surfers' hangouts. River running through the rainforests on the Pacuare or Reventazón rivers is offered daily by outfitters in San José and Turrialba, and overnight trips with riverside camping are also available. Windsurfers consider Laguna de Arenal to be among the best windsurfing spots in the world. Anglers routinely hook (and release) world-class tarpon and sailfish on both coasts, and first-class fishing resorts and experienced boat skippers provide all the necessary expertise. On the Caribbean, Barra del Colorado is excellent; on the Pacific, there are several other choices.

Combining outdoor adventure with the rainforest has resulted in places where you can climb into the canopy and spend time on platforms gazing out over the tropical treetops. Some of these places are good for looking at birds or monkeys; others are

What Visitors Do

The Costa Rican Tourist Institute reports that travelers from the USA average nine to 10 days per visit, while Europeans average about two weeks per visit. With cheap airfares available from Miami, it is quite feasible for US travelers to come down on a one-week visit, though many who do this end up returning because they like the country so much.

One poll asking visitors why they come to Costa Rica indicated that 58% of visitors came to see Costa Rica's natural beauty, followed by 17% who said they were attracted by the people and 9.5% who came for the beaches. Over 70% of visitors said that they visited national parks, and 75% went to the beach. Birding was an important activity for 40% of visitors. About 22% of visitors went snorkeling or scuba diving, 15% went river running, 12% went fishing, and 9% were surfers.

Clearly, then, outdoor activities, especially wildlife watching in national parks and visiting the beach, are the main purposes of trips. Many people get around by public transport (bus or plane) and others prefer to rent a car, although the poor condition of the country's roads (especially potholes) is the single factor that visitors complain about the most. Guided tours are another popular option, taking care of all travel arrangements.

– Rob Rachowiecki

geared more to fun rappelling and zip-lining through the forest; and yet others are a combination of the two. For wildlife, Corcovado Lodge Tent Camp, on the Península de Osa, and Hacienda Barú, on the central Pacific coast, are good choices; for zip-lining, the Canopy Tour in Monteverde is the most experienced; and for a combo, the Rainforest Aerial Tram, in the Central Valley, provides a ski-lift-style gondola through the rainforest.

Many other interests are catered to, but aren't as noteworthy as the above because, well, you can find equally good or better options in other places. But you can certainly laze on beaches, go scuba diving or snorkeling, try to pay for your vacation at a casino, go mountain biking or hiking, or visit museums and art galleries.

Your itinerary will depend on your interests. Many visitors go specifically to practice a hobby such as surfing, fishing, or birding. Others rent a car and strike out on their own, or join a tour and visit the highlights. Budget travelers can use the public bus system to get around. Those wishing to relax can spend a week in one of the many wilderness lodges or in a charming B&B or comfortable hotel by the beach. The choice is yours.

PLANNING

If this is your first trip to Central America, you might want to check out Lonely Planet's *Read This First: Central & South America*. It's full of useful predeparture information on planning, buying tickets, visa applications, health issues, and what to expect from this region of the world. It also includes a country profile section with full-color maps and stories from Lonely Planet authors about their adventures (and misadventures) on their first trip to the region. See Books, later in this chapter, for other useful titles.

When to Go

In general, visitors are told that the late December to mid-April dry season is the best time to visit Costa Rica. During this time, beach resorts tend to be busy and often full on weekends and holidays; Easter week is booked months ahead. Schoolchildren have their main vacations from December to February.

Starting in late April, when the rains begin, many of the dirt roads in the backcountry require 4WD vehicles (which can be rented). However, travel in the wet season also means smaller crowds and lower hotel prices. Bring your umbrella and take advantage of it! I have traveled in Costa Rica in both seasons, and have thoroughly enjoyed myself at both times.

To travel in the least crowded months, try late April and May and from mid-October to mid-December.

Maps

If you want a good map of Costa Rica before you go, the best choice is the very detailed 1:500,000 sheet with a 1:250,000 *Environs of San José* inset, published by and available from International Travel Map Productions (ITM), 530 West Broadway, Vancouver, British Columbia, V5Z 1E9, Canada. ITM also publishes an excellent regional map, *Traveller's Reference Map of Central America*. These provide road, rail, topography, national park, and private reserve information.

Once you arrive in Costa Rica, there are several choices. The Instituto Costarricense de Turismo (ICT) has published several useful maps, all of which are free, subject to availability. Maps include the 1:10,000 *Center of San José Map*, 1:200,000 *San José Area Map*, and 1:1,000,000 *Costa Rica Road Map*.

The Instituto Geográfico Nacional de Costa Rica (IGN) publishes four kinds of maps that can be bought at the IGN in San José (☎ 257-7798), Avenida 20, Calles 9 & 11, or in major bookstores in the capital. There is a single-sheet 1:500,000 map of Costa Rica, which is very good but not as detailed as the ITM map, and there is a nine-sheet 1:200,000 map covering the country in detail. Unfortunately, several sheets were recently out of print. However, the same maps were used in Wilberth's *Mapa-Guía de la Naturaleza – Costa Rica* (see Books, later in this chapter). Most of the country is covered by 1:50,000 scale topographical maps, useful for hiking and backpacking, and some of the cities and urban areas are covered by a variety of 1:10,000 and 1:5000 maps. All these maps provide physical as well as political detail and are well produced.

Many private publishers in Costa Rica have produced country maps, available in bookstores in the country. Most are 1:500,000. One of the best of these is by Jimenez & Tanzi (often abbreviated to Jitan), which, in addition to the country map, has a 1:15,000 map of San José, as well as smaller route maps of the main cities and much background information. This map is updated most years. Another good map is the simpler 1:670,000 map by the Asociación de Carreteras y Caminos de Costa Rica (ACCCR), which also has a detailed 1:15,000 San José map on the reverse. The Fundación Neotropica has published a 1:500,000 map of the country showing all the national parks and other protected areas. These maps are available by mail order from Treaty Oak (☎ 512-326-4141, fax 512-443-0973, www.treatyoak.com), PO Box 50295, Austin, TX 78763-0295, USA. This company specializes in Latin American maps.

In Europe, the best source for maps is Stanfords (☎ 020-7836-1321, fax 020-7836-0189), 12-14 Long Acre, London WC2E 9LP, UK. A 1:650,000 map with a 1:20,000 map of San José on the reverse is also published by Berndtson & Berndtson, Germany.

What to Bring

The best advice is usually to travel as lightly as possible, but also to bring anything that is important to you. Binoculars are very important for wildlife observation, and you really should bring them if you plan on trying to see monkeys and birds. If you're interested in photography, you'll only curse every time you see a good shot if you haven't brought your telephoto lens, and if you're a musician, you won't enjoy the trip if you constantly worry about how out of practice your fingers are getting.

There's no denying, however, that traveling light is much less of a hassle, so don't bring things you can do without. Traveling on buses and trains is bound to make you slightly grubby, so bring one or two changes of dark clothes that don't show the dirt, rather than seven changes of smart clothes for a six-week trip. On the other hand, if you are going to spend a lot of time in the lowlands, dark clothes definitely feel hotter than light-colored ones. Of course, bring more than two or three changes of socks, underwear, and T- or sports-shirts. Bring clothes that wash and dry easily. (Jeans take forever to dry.)

The highlands can be cool, so bring a windproof jacket and a warm layer to wear underneath. A hat is indispensable; it'll keep you warm when it's cold, shade your eyes when it's sunny, and keep your head dry when it rains (a great deal!). A collapsible umbrella is great protection against sun and rain as well, particularly during the rainy season. Rainwear in tropical rainforests often makes you sweat, so an umbrella is preferred by many travelers.

You can buy clothes of almost any size if you need them, but shoes in large sizes are difficult to find. I have size 12 feet (don't laugh, they're not that big!) and I can't buy footwear in Costa Rica unless I have it specially made. This is true of most Latin American countries, so bring a spare pair of shoes if you're planning a long trip. Also, if you're planning a trip to the rainforest, remember that it will often be muddy even during the dry season, and very wet at other times, so bring a pair of shoes that you are prepared to get repeatedly wet and muddy. Rubber boots are popular with the locals and are readily available in small and medium sizes in Costa Rica. Some people swear by Teva-type sandals; others love reef-walking shoes or aqua socks – it's a matter of what you are most comfortable with. Long sleeves and pants are recommended for sun and insect protection in the tropics. Shorts and skirts are fine on the beaches but less useful in the rainforests. See also Society & Conduct in the Facts about Costa Rica chapter for dress-code etiquette.

The following is a checklist of small items you will find useful and will probably need:

- pocket torch (flashlight) with spare bulb and batteries
- travel alarm clock (or watch)
- Swiss Army-style pocket knife

- sewing and repairs kit (dental floss makes excellent, strong, and colorless emergency thread)
- a few meters of cord (also useful for clothesline and spare shoelaces)
- sunglasses
- plastic bags
- soap and dish, shampoo, toothbrush and paste, shaving gear, and towel (soap and towel are supplied in all but the cheapest hotels)
- toilet paper (rarely found in cheaper hotels and restaurants)
- earplugs to aid sleeping in noisy hotels
- sunblock (strong blocking lotions: SPF 20 and above)
- insect repellent (containing a high percentage of Deet – use with care)
- address book, notebook, pens, and pencils
- paperback book (easily exchanged with other travelers when you've finished)
- water bottle
- first-aid kit (see the Health section, later in this chapter)
- prescription medicines

Optional items include the following:

- camera and film
- binoculars and field guides (binoculars are essential if you want do a lot of nature observation; 7x35 are recommended)
- Spanish-English dictionary and phrasebook
- small padlock
- large folding nylon bag to leave things in storage
- snorkeling gear (only if you are really dedicated)
- folding umbrella (rainy season – they are reasonably priced in San José)
- light sleeping bag and camping mattress
- cup (supplied in many hotels, but not the cheaper ones)
- tampons (available but heavily taxed, so you may want to bring your own supply if you like a particular brand or size)
- contraceptives (available in the major cities, but if you use a preferred brand or method, bring it from home)

You need something to carry everything around in. A backpack is recommended because carrying your baggage on your back is less exhausting than carrying it in your hands. On the other hand, it's often more difficult to get at things inside a pack, so some travelers prefer a duffel bag with a full-length zip. Also, in crowded places (eg, buses, busy street corners), backpacks occasionally get slit by thieves who run off with whatever falls out.

Whichever you choose, ensure that it is a good, strong piece of luggage, or you'll find that you spend much of your trip replacing zips, straps, and buckles. Hard traveling is notoriously wearing on your luggage, and if you bring a backpack, I suggest one with an internal frame. External frames snag on bus doors, luggage racks, and airline baggage belts, and are prone to getting twisted, cracked, or broken.

A good idea once you're in San José is to divide your gear into two piles. One is what you need for the next section of your trip; the rest you can stash in the storage room at your hotel (most hotels have one). Costa Rica is a small country, so you can use San José as a base and divide your traveling into, say, coastal, highland, and jungle portions, easily returning to the capital between sections and picking up the gear you need for the next. If you are just on a short trip and don't plan on returning to San José until your last night, you can at least leave a clean set of clothes waiting for your last night and flight home.

TOURIST OFFICES

Also see Useful Organizations, later in this chapter.

Local Tourist Offices

In San José, the Instituto Costarricense de Turismo (ICT) answers questions (in English!) and sometimes provides maps at its public information office (☎ 222-1090, 222-1733 ext 277, fax 223-1090, www.tourism-costarica.com). The street address is on the Plaza de la Cultura at Calle 5 and Avenida Central, next to the Museo de Oro, open 9 am to 5 pm weekdays (Monday to Friday), with a flexible lunch hour. It also has an information center at the airport.

In other towns, there is sometimes a locally run information center. These are mentioned in the text where appropriate.

Tourist Offices Abroad

Roughly 30% of all foreign visitors to Costa Rica come from the USA, where you can call ☎ 800-343-6332 for ICT brochures or information. The ICT's US public relations office is JGR and Associates (☎ 305-858-7277, fax 305-857-0071), 3361 SW 3rd Ave, suite 102, Miami, FL 33145.

The ICT's public relations office in Germany is Tourismusbuero Costa Rica (☎ 0049-221-9 62 47 00, fax 0049-221-9 62 47 01, amik@mail.k.magicvillage.de), Regenstrasse 17, 51063 Cologne.

Citizens of other countries can ask the local Costa Rican consulate for tourist information, or write to the Instituto Costarricense de Turismo in San José.

VISAS & DOCUMENTS

Passport

Citizens of all nations are required to have at least a passport to enter Costa Rica. Passports should be valid for at least six months beyond the dates of your trip.

Passport-carrying nationals of the following countries are allowed 90 days' stay with

Guidelines for Responsible Tourism

The term 'ecotourism' has been used and abused more than any other word during the huge growth of the tourism industry that Costa Rica has experienced since the late 1980s. Some developers, hotel owners, and tour operators have jumped on the ecotourism bandwagon, offering a packaged glimpse of nature without making any positive impact on the country. Other operators and hoteliers have arrived at a series of guidelines designed to minimize negative impacts of tourism and to emphasize sustainable development of the industry at all levels. These guidelines enable the traveler to make enlightened choices when visiting Costa Rica, and can generally be applied to countries worldwide. There are two main themes in the guidelines: conservation and cultural sensitivity.

1. Waste Disposal Don't litter. Patronize hotels with recycling programs. Some hotels will provide towel or sheet changes on request, rather than daily, to minimize unnecessary use of soap and water. Travel with tour operators who provide and use waste receptacles aboard buses and boats and who dispose of trash properly.

2. Wildlife Don't disturb animals or damage plants. Stay on trails. Observe wildlife from a distance with binoculars. Follow the instructions of trained naturalist guides. Never feed wild animals. Do not collect or buy endangered animals or plants.

3. Local Communities Allow the small communities at your destination to benefit from tourism. Use local guides. Patronize locally owned and operated restaurants and hotels. Buy locally made crafts and souvenirs (though never those made from endangered species such as turtles or black coral).

4. Cultural Sensitivity Interact with local people. Speak as much Spanish as you can. Appreciate and learn from the different cultural traditions of the areas you visit.

5. Education Learn about wildlife and local conservation, environmental, and cultural issues both before your trip and during your visit. Ask questions.

6. Sustainability Avoid overcrowded areas unless you really want to see them. Support tourism companies with conservation initiatives and long-term management plans.

– Rob Rachowiecki

no visa: most western European countries, Argentina, Brazil, Canada, Israel, Japan, Panama, Romania, South Korea, the UK, Uruguay, and the USA.

Passport-carrying nationals of the following countries are allowed 30 days' stay with no visa: most eastern European countries, Australia, Bolivia, Chile, Colombia, Ecuador, El Salvador, France, Guatemala, Honduras, Iceland, India, Ireland, Mexico, New Zealand, Russia, South Africa, Vatican City, Venezuela, and some others. Note that these lists are subject to change.

Officially, adult Canadians, Panamanians, and US citizens can enter the country for up to 30 days with a birth certificate or driver's license, upon payment of a US$2 fee. However, if they want to stay longer than 30 days, a passport is required. I advise bringing a passport because it makes life easier when changing money and also allows you to stay for more than 30 days if your travel plans change. Costa Rican entry requirements change frequently, so it is worth checking at a consulate before your trip, especially if you want to stay more than 30 days.

When you arrive, your passport will be stamped. During your stay, the law requires that you carry your passport or tourist card at all times. A photocopy of the pages bearing your photo, passport number, and entry stamp will suffice when walking around town, but the passport should at least be in the hotel where you are staying, not locked up in San José.

Visas

Most other nationalities are required to have a visa, which can be obtained from a Costa Rican consulate for US$20. A few nationalities are restricted by political problems and may have difficulty in obtaining a visa for tourism.

Visa Extensions If you overstay your allotted 30 or 90 days, you will need a bureaucratically time-consuming exit visa, and the rules change often. Don't overstay your allotted time without checking locally about the current situation. Many travel agents will be able to get an exit visa for you for a small fee. The cost varies, depending on how long you overstay, but usually starts at about US$45. A better alternative is to leave the country for 72 hours (by visiting Panama or Nicaragua) and then return. Requirements change regularly; check with Migración (☎ 223-7555 ext 240/276, 223-9465, fax 221-2066, 256-1650) before you decide whether to stay, leave, or visit another country for 72 hours.

The Migración office for visa extensions or exit visas is in San José opposite the Hospital Mexico, about 4km north of Parque La Sabana. Any Alajuela bus will drop you nearby. Hours are 8 am to 4 pm weekdays, and lines can be long. Some travel agencies will do the paperwork for you and charge a small processing fee; Tikal Tours is recommended.

Onward Tickets

Travelers officially need an exit ticket out of the country before they are allowed to enter, although this is often not asked for at the airport in San José because most airlines will not let you board their planes unless you have a return or onward ticket, or an MCO (miscellaneous charge order). Those travelers arriving without a passport (see the Passport section, above) do need onward tickets.

Travelers arriving by land may need an exit ticket, but the rules change and are enforced erratically. The easiest way for overland travelers to solve this requirement is to buy a ticket from the TICA Bus company, which has offices in both Managua (Nicaragua) and Panama City. (Ask other travelers – they can beat any guidebook for up-to-the-minute information.) Sometimes a show of cash is required to cross land borders – US$400 per month should be sufficient.

Travel Insurance

No matter how you're traveling, make sure you take out travel insurance. This should cover you not only for medical expenses and luggage theft or loss, but also for unavoidable cancellation or delays in your travel arrangements. It should also cover the worst possible case, such as an accident that requires hospital treatment and a flight home. Coverage depends on your insurance and type of ticket, so ask both your insurer and your ticket-issuing agency to explain the finer points. Council Travel and STA Travel (see the Getting There & Away chapter) offer a variety of travel insurance options at reasonable prices. Ticket loss is also covered by travel insurance. Make sure you have a separate record of all your ticket details – or, better still, a photocopy of it. Also make a copy of your policy in case the original is lost.

Buy travel insurance as early as possible. If you buy it the week before you fly, you may find, for instance, that you're not covered for delays to your flight caused by strikes or other industrial action that may have been in force before you took out the insurance.

Driver's License & Permits

If you plan to rent a car, your driver's license from your home country is normally accepted. If you plan to drive down to Costa Rica from North America, you will need all the usual insurance and ownership papers. In addition, you have to buy additional Costa Rican insurance at the border (about US$20 a month) and pay a US$10 road tax. You can stay in the country for up to 90 days. If you want to stay longer, you will need to get a Costa Rican driver's license. You are not allowed to sell the car in Costa Rica. If you need to leave the country without the car, you must leave the car in a customs warehouse in San José.

Other Documents

International health cards are not needed to enter Costa Rica.

There is a small network of youth hostels in Costa Rica that will give you a discount if you have a youth hostel card from your home country. Student cards are of limited use in Costa Rica and are accepted only if they have a photograph.

Photocopies

The cheapest insurance policy is keeping copies of your most important documents. I routinely photocopy the pages of my passport with my photograph and passport number. On the back of this I write the numbers of my traveler's checks, airline tickets, credit card contact telephone numbers (in case of loss), health insurance contact telephone numbers, and anything else that may be important. This can range from dates of birthdays to your mum's address. Then I photocopy this again and leave a copy at home, and carry my own copy (or two) separate from all my other documents.

CUSTOMS

When it comes to importing duty-free items like alcohol and tobacco, Costa Rica is less restrictive than many countries. You are allowed 500 cigarettes or 500g of tobacco, and 3 liters of wine or spirits.

Camera gear, binoculars, and camping, snorkeling, and other sporting equipment are readily allowed into the country. Officially, you are limited to six rolls of film, but this is rarely checked or enforced – I routinely carry 20 or 30 rolls of film into Costa Rica. Generally, if you are bringing in items for personal use, there's no problem. If you are trying to bring in new items that you want to sell, you may be asked to pay duty. Don't ask me how they know the difference.

MONEY

Currency

The Costa Rican currency is the *colón*, plural *colones*, named after Cristóbal Colón (Christopher Columbus). Colones are normally written ¢.

Bills come in 50, 100, 500, 1000, 2000, 5000, and 10,000 colones, though the 50 and 100 colones bills are being phased out. Coins come in one (rarely), five, 10, 20, 50, and 100 colones.

Exchange Rates

During the past years, the colón has fallen slowly against the US dollar at a rate of about two colones a month.

Prices in this book are quoted in US dollars, and the exchange rate is expected to reach 300 colones to US$1 by early 2000. Other currencies are rarely accepted; therefore I don't give exchange rates for them.

Exchanging Money

A few banks in the capital will change a handful of non-US currencies, but rates are generally very poor. Outside of San José, US dollars are the only way to go. Non-US travelers should buy US dollars before they arrive in Costa Rica. There is occasional talk of linking the colón to the US dollar, and you can change cash US dollars almost anywhere.

Embassies & Consulates

Some of the most important embassies are listed below; also see www.rree.go.cr.

Costa Rican Embassies & Consulates

Australia
(☎ 02-9261-1177, fax 02-9261-2953) 30 Clarence St, 11th floor, Sydney, NSW 2000

Canada
(☎ 613-562-2855, fax 613-562-2582) 135 York St, No 208, Ottawa, ONT K1N 5TA

France
(☎ 01 45 78 96 96, fax 01 45 78 99 66) 78 avenue Emile Zola, 75015 Paris

Germany
(☎ 02-28-54-00-40, fax 02-28-54-90-53) Langenbachstrasse 19, 53113 Bonn

Israel
(☎ 02-256-6197, fax 02-256-3259) 13 Diskin St, No 1, Jerusalem 91012

Italy
(☎ 06-4425-1046, fax 06-4425-1048) Via Bartolomeo, Eustacho 22, Interno 6, Rome

Japan
(☎ 03-3486-1812, fax 3486-1813) Kowa Building No 38 Floor 12-24 Nishi-Azabu 4, Chome Minato-Ku, Tokyo

Netherlands
(☎ 070-354-0780, 358-4754, fax 070-358-4754) Laan Copes Van Cattenburg 46, 2585 GM Den Haag

Nicaragua
(☎ 02-66-2404, 66-3986, fax 02-66-3955) De la Estatua de Montoya, dos cuadras al lado y media cuadra arriba (Callejón Zelaya), Managua

Panama
(☎ 264-2980, 264-2937, fax 264-4057) Calle Samuel Lewis, Edificio Plaza Omega 3 piso, contiguo Santuario Nacional, Panama City

Spain
(☎ 91-345-9622, fax 91-353-3709) Paseo de la Castellana 164, No 17A, 28046 Madrid

UK
(☎ 020-7706-8844, fax 020-7706-8655) Flat 1, 14 Lancaster Gate, London W2 3LH

USA
(☎ 202-234-2945, 234-2946, fax 202-265-4795) 2112 S St NW, Washington, DC 20008

Your Own Embassy

As a tourist, it's important to realize what your own embassy – the embassy of the country of which you are a citizen – can and can't do.

Generally speaking, it won't be much help in emergencies if the trouble you're in is remotely your own fault. Remember that you are bound by the laws of the country you are in. Your embassy will not be sympathetic if you end up in jail after committing a crime locally, even if such actions are legal in your own country.

In genuine emergencies, you might get some assistance, but only if other channels have been exhausted. For example, if you need to get home urgently, a free ticket home

Banks tend to be slow in changing money, especially the state-run institutions (like Banco Nacional, Banco Central, or Banco de Costa Rica), where it can sometimes take almost an hour. Private banks (Banco Popular, Banex, and many others) tend to be faster.

Banking hours are 9 am to 3 pm weekdays, though in San José the banks often open by 8:30 am and may remain open till

Embassies & Consulates

is exceedingly unlikely – the embassy would expect you to have insurance. If you have all your money and documents stolen, it should assist in getting a new passport, but a loan for onward travel is out of the question.

Embassies used to keep letters for travelers or have a small reading room with home newspapers, but these days the mail-holding service has been stopped, and newspapers tend to be out of date.

Embassies & Consulates in Costa Rica

The following countries have embassies or consulates in the San José area. Call ahead to confirm locations and get directions. Embassies tend to be open in the mornings more often than in the afternoons. Australia and New Zealand do not have consular representation but do have embassies in Mexico City.

Canada
(☎ 296-4149, fax 296-4270) Oficentro Ejecutivo La Sabana, Edificio 5, 3rd floor, detrás La Contraloría, Sabana Sur

France
(☎ 225-0733, 225-0933, 225-0058, fax 253-7027) 200m south, 25m west of the Indoor Club, Carretera a Curridabat

Germany
(☎ 232-5533, 232-5450, fax 231-6403) 200m north, 75m east of the Casa de Dr Oscar Arias, Rohrmoser

Israel
(☎ 221-6011, 221-6444, fax 257-0867) Edificio Centro Colón, 11th floor, Paseo Colón, Calles 38 & 40

Italy
(☎ 224-6574, 234-2326, fax 225-8200) Calle 33, Avenidas 8 & 10, quinta entrada de Los Yoses

Netherlands
(☎ 296-1490, fax 296-2933) Oficentro Ejecutivo La Sabana, Edificio 3, 3rd floor, detrás La Contraloría, Sabana Sur

Nicaragua
(☎ 222-2373, 233-3479, 233-8747, fax 221-5481) Avenida Central, Calles 25 & 27, in front of Pizza Hut

Panama
(☎ 257-3241, 256-5169, fax 257-4864) Calle 38, Avenidas 5 & 7

Spain
(☎ 222-1933, 221-7005, 222-5745, fax 222-4180) Calle 32, Paseo Colón & Avenida 2

Switzerland
(☎ 221-4829, 222-3229, fax 525-2831) Edificio Centro Colón, Paseo Colón, Calles 38 & 40

UK
(☎ 258-2025, fax 233-9938) Edificio Centro Colón, 11th floor, Paseo Colón, Calles 38 & 40

USA
(☎ 220-3939, fax 220-2305) Carretera Pavas, in front of the Centro Commercial

4 pm. Carry your passport when changing money.

Hotels and travel agencies sometimes give the same rate as the banks, and are much faster and more convenient. Most only allow guests and customers to use their services, although some places will serve outsiders – it's worth trying. Another drawback is that they have limited cash resources and sometimes don't have enough colones. Some hotels charge a 'commission.'

Changing money on the streets is not recommended, except possibly at land borders. Street changers don't give better rates, and scammers abound. A favorite scam is for the changer to say that the police are coming, and give you back your dollars – except that the dollars are counterfeit. Always count your colones carefully before handing over your dollars.

Try not to leave the country with many excess colones; it's difficult to buy back more than US$50 at the border or airport.

Cash US cash dollars with tears or in worn condition are not accepted by banks or anyone else. Make sure your bills are undamaged – Costa Rican banks are very picky about this.

You can use small-denomination bills (US$20 and less) to pay for anything from groceries in a corner store to cab fare. Larger bills can be used for more expensive purchases like tours, car rentals, and air tickets. Change some money into colones, as you'll need them for small expenses like a snack, budget hotel, or bus fare.

Traveler's Checks Major brands of traveler's checks in US dollars are readily exchanged into colones, but the rate is usually 1% or 2% lower than cash. Some banks will accept one kind of check but not another. Because they can be replaced in the event of loss, traveler's checks are safe. It's worth having some US cash for use when banks are closed.

ATMs Banco Popular, ATH (A Todo Hora), and Credomatic have the biggest ATM networks, though there are others. Visa cards are the most useful, though MasterCard works in some machines as well. You can find ATMs in cities and in some smaller towns, especially those that have a developed tourism industry. If you use a credit card in an ATM, you will begin paying very high interest from the moment you make a cash withdrawal, so either overpay your bill before you travel to have a positive balance or use a debit card that is connected with your checking account (again, with a positive balance) back home.

Credit & Debit Cards Holders of credit and debit cards can buy cash colones (and sometimes US dollars) in some banks. See ATMs, above, about avoiding high interest payments.

Cards can also be used at the more expensive hotels, restaurants, travel and car rental agencies, and stores. Visa and MasterCard are both widely accepted (especially Visa), you are charged at close to the normal bank rates, and commissions are low. American Express cards are less readily accepted. Although this is now illegal, some places still charge a 7% commission for card use (be sure to ask).

I suggest that card holders call the customer service of their credit card company at home before leaving for Costa Rica to find out the most current numbers to dial in the case of loss or other problems with credit cards in Costa Rica. Often, you are told to dial your home country collect to report a lost card rather than calling a number in Costa Rica.

Users of credit cards linked to a currency other than the US dollar get poor rates for cash withdrawal.

International Transfers The main branches of several banks in San José will accept cash transfers but charge a commission. Shop around for the best deal. Allow several days and plenty of bureaucracy for a bank transfer. Western Union arranges international cash transfers more quickly than a bank, but its commission is much higher. Transferring money internationally should be used only as a last resort.

Security

Pickpockets prey on easy targets, and unsuspecting tourists are a prime choice. Avoid losing your money by following a few basic precautions: Carry money in inside pockets, money belts, or pouches beneath your clothes. Don't carry a wallet in a trousers or jacket pocket, as this is the first thing pickpockets look for. Divide your money among several places so that if someone pickpockets you, you won't lose all your cash.

Costs

Costa Rica is pricier than many Central or South American countries, although usually cheaper than the USA or Europe. Generally speaking, San José and the most popular tourist areas (Monteverde, Jacó, Manuel Antonio, Guanacaste beaches) are more expensive than the rest of the country. The dry season (from December to April) is the high season and more expensive. Imported goods are also expensive.

Travelers on a tight budget will find the cheapest basic hotels start at about US$3 or US$4 per person for four walls and a bed. Fairly decent but still quite basic rooms with private bathroom, hot water, and maybe air-conditioning start at around US$10 per person, depending on the area. First-class hotels charge well over US$100 for a single room, but there are plenty of good ones for less than that.

Meals cost from about US$2 to US$30, depending on the quality of the restaurant. Budget travelers should stick to the cheaper set lunches offered in many restaurants, which usually cost about US$2. Cafés or lunch counters, called *sodas*, are cheap places for meals. Beer costs from US70¢ to US$3, depending on how fancy the restaurant or bar is. National parks have a standard fee of US$6 per person per day.

Public transportation is quite cheap: the longest bus journeys, from San José to the Panamanian or Nicaraguan borders, cost under US$7. Domestic airfares are also relatively cheap, ranging from US$70 to US$110 roundtrip with SANSA or US$93 to US$165 with Travelair. (Chartered flights are more expensive.) A taxi, particularly when you're in a group, isn't expensive and usually costs US$1 to US$2 for short rides. Car rental is expensive, however – figure on US$300 per week for the cheapest cars, including the mandatory insurance.

A budget traveler economizing hard can get by on US$12 to US$20 per day, especially if you are traveling with someone, because single rooms are more expensive. (Some readers have written to say that it's impossible to get by on US$12 a day – their definition of budget travel must be higher than rock-bottom.) If you want some basic comforts, such as rooms with private baths, meals other than set meals, and occasional flights, expect to pay about US$25 to US$50 per day. Travelers wanting to be very comfortable can spend from US$50 to over US$150 per day, depending on their definition of comfort. The best tours cost over US$200 per day, but these include flights and first-class accommodations and services. Cheaper tours are available.

Taxes & Tipping

Better hotels add a 16.39% tax to room prices; I include this tax in the prices in the book, but always ask. Most restaurants automatically add a 13% tax and 10% tip to the bill, which is legally correct. Cheaper restaurants might not do this. Tipping above the included amount is not necessary (*ticos* rarely do), but adding a few percent for excellent service is OK.

Tip bellhops in the better hotels about US50¢ to US$1 per bag. The person who cleans your hotel room deserves US50¢ to US$1 a day, except in the cheapest hotels, where they don't expect a tip.

Taxi drivers are not normally tipped, unless some special service is provided. Drivers tip boys and adults about US$1 (less for a short period) to watch their cars when parked on the street. The guardians take no responsibility for problems, but do keep thieves away.

On guided tours, tip the guide about US$1 to US$5 per person per day, depending on how good the guide is. (Tip more if the group is very small, less or nothing if the guide doesn't meet your expectations.) Tip the tour driver about half of what you tip the guide, unless, of course, the driver is great and the guide is poor!

POST & COMMUNICATIONS

Sending Mail

The better hotels provide stamps for your letters and postcards and will mail them for you; otherwise, go to the main post office in each town. There are no mailboxes. The postal system has been privatized since the last edition, and postal service is expected to improve, though costs will rise. Sending parcels is expensive.

In addresses, Apartado means PO Box; it is not a street or apartment address.

Receiving Mail

Unless you have a contact in Costa Rica, you can receive mail at the Correo Central (Main Post Office) of major towns. San José is the most efficient, and letters usually arrive within a week from North America, a little longer from more distant places. Post offices charge about US25¢ per letter received, and you need to show your passport to receive your mail – you can't pick up other people's.

Mail is filed alphabetically, but if it's addressed to John Gillis Payson, it could well

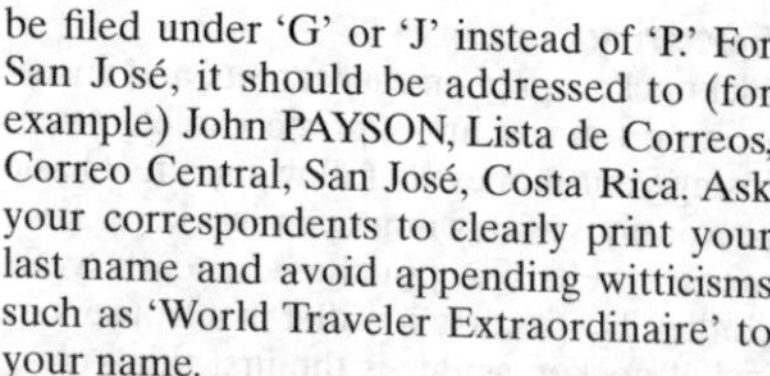

be filed under 'G' or 'J' instead of 'P.' For San José, it should be addressed to (for example) John PAYSON, Lista de Correos, Correo Central, San José, Costa Rica. Ask your correspondents to clearly print your last name and avoid appending witticisms such as 'World Traveler Extraordinaire' to your name.

Avoid having parcels sent to you, as they are held in customs and cannot be retrieved until you have paid a usually exorbitant customs fee and gone through a time-consuming bureaucratic process. This is true of even small packages.

Communicating with Costa Rica

Readers and travelers have commented that phone messages, faxes, and emails sent to Costa Rica can remain unanswered for a week or more. The reason is simply that the remote location of many of the hotels and lodges there means that someone must go into the nearest town to recover their messages (which might happen only once or twice a week) and then answer later. Some places rely on public Internet cabins and don't have a computer on their desk. So don't get discouraged if your communication doesn't get answered right away, and allow extra time for this when possible.

– Rob Rachowiecki

Telephone

Generally, the telephone system is quite good, although systems sometimes get congested and some areas can be cut off temporarily due to weather conditions.

Public telephones are found all over Costa Rica and accept either coins – of five, 10, and 20 colones – or the far more convenient CHIP telephone cards. The digital CHIP phones can now be found even in small villages. Telephone cards that work on any touch-tone phone by dialing a toll-free number and punching in the card's account number are also available. Both kinds of telephone cards can be purchased in many grocery stores, pharmacies, and other places, and can be bought for 500, 1000, 2000, 3000, and 10,000 colones. Recently, telephone cards for US$10 and US$20 were available for international calls, and they work for local calls as well.

Local Calls There are no area codes; just dial the seven-digit number. Calls are inexpensive, except for operator-assisted calls from hotels – the fancier the hotel, the more they seem to charge.

In remote areas of the country, look for the telephone symbol in even the most unlikely places. General stores in tiny villages often have a phone for public use.

For directory information, call ☎ 113.

Pagers Hotel owners and other businesses in remote areas sometimes receive messages on pagers, which are called 'beepers' in Costa Rica.

International Calls Calling internationally is quite straightforward, though not cheap. The cheapest calls are direct-dialed using a phone card. For collect (reverse charge) calls, dial ☎ 116 on any public phone to get an English-speaking international operator. The party you call can ring you back at many public telephones. Countries with reciprocal agreements with Costa Rica will accept collect calls, including the USA and many others.

Dial the following numbers from any phone to reach operators in these foreign countries:

Canada	☎ 0800-015-0161 or 0800-015-2000
France	☎ 0800-033-1033
Germany	☎ 00800-0049-0049
Israel	☎ 0800-972-1972
Italy	☎ 0800-039-1039
Netherlands	☎ 0800-031-1111
New Zealand	☎ 0800-064-1064
Spain	☎ 0800-034-1034
Switzerland	☎ 00800-2341-2341
UK	☎ 0800-044-1044
USA (AT&T)	☎ 0800-011-4114
USA (MCI)	☎ 0800-012-2222
USA (Sprint)	☎ 0800-013-0123
USA (Worldcom)	☎ 0800-014-4444

Many other countries are introducing similar systems, so check locally. After reaching the foreign operator, you can either call collect or charge the call to your calling-card number – you can get through in less than a minute. These methods are convenient but expensive; ask the operator for costs or find out from your home country before you travel.

To call Costa Rica from abroad, use the international code (506) before the seven-digit Costa Rican telephone number.

Fax

Radiográfica and ICE in San José have fax machines (see the San José chapter for office locations). They will also accept and hold telex and fax messages. Outside San José, the ICE office in many towns will send faxes. If you are faxing Costa Rica, make sure that you put your return fax number on the document; some machines in Costa Rica won't do this automatically.

Email & Internet Access

It's not difficult to stay connected to your email account in Costa Rica. Cybercafés in San José and several other towns are listed in the regional chapters of this book. In other towns, ask around; you can often find a place that offers access to the Internet so that you can read your email. Internet access enables you to reach Web-based email accounts such as Hotmail, Yahoo!, or other services with POP mail. Check with your provider before you leave and become familiar with the process in advance.

Travelers with a laptop and modem will find that hotels and some other locales (friends' houses and offices) have RJ-11 phone jacks similar to those used in the USA. Some online services, like AOL, allow members to access their email and the Internet from their laptop computer by dialing a number in San José. This normally costs an additional fee, so check with your online service for costs and the appropriate local number. Other providers may require an international call.

If you are traveling in Costa Rica frequently or for a long time, you can set up a local account. See the San José chapter for suggestions.

INTERNET RESOURCES

The World Wide Web is a rich resource for travelers. You can research your trip, hunt down bargain airfares, book hotels, check on weather conditions, or chat with locals and other travelers about the best places to visit (or avoid!).

Try the Lonely Planet website (www.lonelyplanet.com) for summaries on traveling to most places on earth, postcards from other travelers, and the Thorn Tree bulletin board, where you can ask questions before you go or dispense advice when you return. You can also find travel news and updates to some of our guidebooks, and the site's subWWWay section links you to useful travel resources elsewhere on the Web.

Many hotels, tour operators, etc, have websites – I rarely list them in this book unless they are especially interesting. However, I do list email addresses whenever I can; you can email to ask if the company has a Web page.

A useful background site on many aspects of Costa Rica (not much on travel, though) is http://lanic.utexas.edu/la/ca/cr. The official country site is the memorably named www.cr, but it is mainly in Spanish. For many useful links for anything from car rental to cosmetic surgery to the Costa Rica Chess Federation, try www.yellowweb.co.cr.

Numerous travel-oriented sites specialize mainly in the higher end of the market, including the better hotels, domestic air service, car rentals, etc. I think the best of these is www.centralamerica.com/cr/index.htm, although www.crica.com and www.ticonet.co.cr/tourism also offer travel information. Other websites are mentioned in appropriate parts of the text.

BOOKS

Some books are published in different editions by different publishers in different countries. As a result, a book might be rare in one country while it's readily available in another. Bookstores and libraries can search by title or author, so your local bookstore or library is the best place to find out about the availability of the following.

Many of the books listed below are available outside Costa Rica in good bookstores or catalogs specializing in travel and wildlife. A few bookstores in San José carry some titles, especially those published in Costa Rica. These bookstores are listed in the San José chapter. Books published outside Costa Rica are more expensive in San José, and few bookstores outside San José carry books of interest to the traveler.

Lonely Planet

Lonely Planet's *Central America on a shoestring* is useful for travelers visiting several Central American countries on a tight budget. There are many useful maps.

In *Green Dreams: Travels in Central America*, author Stephen Benz questions the impact that visitors are having on the region and its people.

Lonely Planet's *Latin American Spanish phrasebook* will come in handy for travelers who want to try out the local lingo.

If you are a first-time visitor to Central America, see the Planning section, earlier in this chapter, for another useful Lonely Planet title.

Guidebooks

Costa Rica has changed greatly over the past few years, and the tourism boom is one of the greatest changes of all. When choosing travel guidebooks, get a recent edition – older editions may be selling cheaply, but their travel information is way out of date.

Regional For those driving their own vehicle down to Costa Rica from the USA, there's *Driving the Pan-American Highway to Mexico and Central America*, by Raymond F and Aubrey Pritchard. See Lonely Planet, above, for further options.

Costa Rica *Mapa-Guía de la Naturaleza – Costa Rica*, by author Herrera S Wilberth (Incafo, Costa Rica), is a book of maps based upon the Costa Rican IGN 1:200,000 topographical series. All natural areas are highlighted and described in Spanish and English, accompanied by good color photographs. This guide is a cross between Boza's park book (described below) and the IGN maps.

The Essential Road Guide for Costa Rica, by Bill Baker (Baker, Apartado 1185-1011, San José, 1992), is a useful kilometer-by-kilometer guide for driving along the major roads of the country; it also has good maps and background information on bus terminals, getting around, and driving in Costa Rica.

Choose Costa Rica for Retirement, by John Howells, is the perhaps the best of the 'how to retire in Costa Rica' books, although some folks prefer *The New Golden Door to Retirement and Living in Costa Rica*, by Christopher Howard. In either case, get the most recent edition as the retirement laws have changed recently. Also useful is *The Rules of the Game – Buying Real Estate in Costa Rica*, by Bill Baker.

Vern Bell's Walking Tour of Downtown San José, subtitled 'with some glimpses of history, anecdotes, and a chuckle or two,' is a fun-to-read, 48-page booklet available from long-time resident Vernon Bell. Call ☎ 225-4752, fax 224-5884 in San José, or send US$6.50 to Vernon Bell, Dept 1432, PO Box 025216, Miami, FL 33102, USA. It's recommended if you have a day to walk around San José.

Adventure Travel

Backpacking in Central America, by Tim Burford, has plenty to keep the hiker busy. *Adventuring in Central America*, by David Rains Wallace, has lots of conservation-related background.

The Rivers of Costa Rica: A Canoeing, Kayaking, and Rafting Guide, by Michael W Mayfield et al, is just the ticket for river runners. *Costa Rica's National Parks and Preserves – A Visitor's Guide*, by Joseph Franke, provides useful maps and background.

Nature & Wildlife

Parques Nacionales Costa Rica (Incafo, Madrid) is written by Mario Boza, the former Costa Rican Vice-Minister of Natural Resources. The hardbound version is a coffee-table book with beautiful photographs and bilingual (Spanish-English) text describing the national parks; the softbound version is half the size but also has good photos and interesting text. Both books are readily available in San José.

Costa Rican Natural History, by Daniel H Janzen with 174 contributors, is an excellent, if weighty (almost 2kg and over 800 large pages), introduction for the biologist.

I recommend the entertaining and readable *Tropical Nature*, by Adrian Forsyth and Ken Miyata, for the layperson interested in biology, particularly of the rainforest. *A Neotropical Companion*, by John C Kricher and Mark Plotkin, is a readable book, subtitled 'An Introduction to the Animals, Plants, and Ecosystems of the New World Tropics' – which tells you all you need to know. *In the Rainforest*, by Catherine Caulfield, is another good choice. It emphasizes the problems of the loss of the rainforest.

Sarapiquí Chronicle, by Allen M Young, is subtitled 'A Naturalist in Costa Rica.' The book tells the story of the invertebrate zoologist's quarter century of expeditions to the rainforests near the Río Sarapiquí. A good read.

Field Guides

Costa Rica: The Ecotravellers' Wildlife Guide, by Les Beletsky, is the best wildlife guide if you want just one book for everything.

A Guide to the Birds of Costa Rica, by F Gary Stiles and Alexander F Skutch, is an excellent and thorough book and the only one recommended for birding. *Site Guides: Costa Rica & Panama – A Guide to the Best Birding Locations*, by Dennis W Rogers, is useful for finding out where to bird.

Neotropical Rainforest Mammals – A Field Guide, by Louise H Emmons, is also recommended. It's a detailed and portable book, with almost 300 mammal species described and illustrated. Although some of the mammals included are found only in other Neotropical countries, most of Costa Rica's mammals, and certainly all the rainforest ones, are found within the book's pages.

The Butterflies of Costa Rica and Their Natural History, by Philip J DeVries, is a detailed two-volume guide for lepidopterists.

A Field Guide to the Orchids of Costa Rica and Panama, by Robert Dressler, has 240 photos and almost as many drawings of orchids within its 274 pages.

People & Politics

The Costa Ricans, by Richard Biesanz et al, is a recommended book with a historical perspective (pre-1998) on politics and social change in Costa Rica and many insights into the tico character. *The Ticos: Culture and Social Change in Costa Rica*, by Mavis Biesanz, is a more recent (1998) resource. Both are available in Costa Rica at Biesanz Woodworks (see Shopping in the San José chapter).

What Happen: A Folk History of Costa Rica's Talamanca Coast and *Wa'apin Man* are both written by former Peace Corps volunteer and sociologist Paula Palmer, and are about the people of the south Caribbean coast of Costa Rica. Although out of print, they still show up in San José bookstores.

Taking Care of Sibö's Gifts, by Paula Palmer, Juanita Sánchez, and Gloria Mayorga, is also out of print, but found in Costa Rica. Subtitled 'An Environmental Treatise from Costa Rica's KéköLdi Indigenous Reserve,' this excellent booklet discusses the traditional Bribri lifestyle, focusing on their natural surroundings.

Fiction

Costa Rica – A Traveler's Literary Companion, edited by Barbara Ras, is an excellent compendium of 26 short stories by 20th-century Costa Rican writers. The selections offer a satisfying variety of Costa Rican writing that reveals special glimpses of tico life. The stories are grouped by geographical location, hence the title of the anthology.

When New Flowers Bloomed: Short Stories by Women Writers from Costa Rica and Panama, edited by Enrique Jaramillo Levi (Latin American Literary Review Press, 1991), is a little harder to get ahold of than the previous book, and a few of the stories are found in both. If you like the first one, look for the second.

La Loca de Gandoca, by Anacristina Rossi (EDUCA, San José), is written by a prize-winning *tica* novelist. It describes the struggle of a local conservationist trying to halt the development of a hotel in a protected area of the Caribbean coast, and the problems with corruption at various levels of government. Although the author claims that all the characters in her novel are imaginary and that any similarity to reality is coincidental, local cognoscenti will tell you that remarkably similar events happened here. It's a deplorable story, and will give you a different view of Costa Rica as a 'perfect environmental destination.' The book is available locally and only in Spanish, but is short and simply written. Thus, it makes a good choice for those interested in local conservation issues, even if their Spanish is limited. The book has been a hot seller and has sold out in several editions, so grab it if you see it.

Jurassic Park, by Michael Crichton – unless your interest in Hollywood blockbusters is zero, you've heard of the movie – is the novel that gave rise to the movie, and the dino-action is based in Costa Rica. Locals don't appreciate the references to the Costa Rican Air Force (there is no military force here) and 'ticans' (should be 'ticos'), but it beats *War and Peace* for those lazy moments of your trip (apologies to dedicated Tolstoy readers).

NEWSPAPERS & MAGAZINES

The best-established San José daily newspaper is *La Nación* (www.nacion.co.cr), which was founded in 1936. It has thorough but fairly right-wing coverage of tico news and the most important international news, and is the most widely distributed paper in Costa Rica. You can read the main headlines on the Internet. Its main competitor is *La República,* founded in 1950 and also quite conservative. For a more left-wing slant on the day's events, read *La Prensa Libre*, San José's only afternoon daily and also the oldest, having been published for over a century. There are several other tabloids. *Esta Semana* is the best local weekly news magazine.

An English-language newspaper appearing every Friday is *The Tico Times* (www.ticotimes.co.cr), published since the 1950s. It costs about US$1 and is a well-recommended source of information about things going on in Costa Rica. It publishes an annual tourism edition that is available in local bookstores or directly from the newspaper. Foreign subscriptions are available for one year for US$61 (USA), US$96 (Canada and other Western Hemisphere countries, Europe and the Middle East), and US$139 (Africa, Asia, and the Far East). Write to Apartado 4632-1000, San José, Costa Rica (fax 233-6378, ttcirc@sol.racsa.co.cr). US residents can write to SJO 717, PO Box 025216, Miami, FL 33102-5216.

A second English-language weekly, *Costa Rica Today*, was launched in 1992; publication day is Thursday. It doesn't give the news coverage of *The Tico Times* but caters to tourists and is relentlessly upbeat, though useful.

Costa Rica Outdoors is a newsletter on sportfishing, adventure sports, golf, and tico culture, with an emphasis on fishing. Written in English, it is available in Costa Rica every two months for about US$2 a copy, or by subscription in the Americas for US$20 a year and in other countries for US$30 a year. To subscribe, write or call Costa Rica Outdoors (☎ 800-308-3394, jruhlow@sol.racsa.co.cr), Dept SJO 2316, PO Box 025216, Miami, FL 33102-5216, USA.

Major bookstores in San José carry some North American and other newspapers as well as magazines such as *Time* and *Newsweek*. The international edition of the *Miami Herald* is usually the most up-to-date of the foreign newspapers.

RADIO & TV

There are several local TV stations (programming is poor), but many of the better hotels also receive cable TV from the USA.

There are over 100 local radio stations, some of which broadcast in English. Radio 2 (99.5 FM) has news, pop-rock favorites, and a US-style morning show from 6 to 9 am with trivia contests and telephone calls. For classical music, there's Radio Universidad (96.7 FM). Rock (107.5 FM) is one of the newest, with rock of the past decades. Superradio (102.3 FM) also plays US and British rock classics. Azul Stereo (99.9 FM) has a good variety of Latin music.

If you have a portable shortwave radio, you can listen to the BBC World Service and Voice of America, among many others.

PHOTOGRAPHY & VIDEO

Film & Equipment

Camera gear is expensive in Costa Rica, and film choice is limited. Film sold in Costa Rica might be outdated, so check the expiration date.

Film is easily developed in Costa Rica, but professionals prefer to bring their film home to their favorite processing lab. Don't carry around exposed rolls for months – that's asking for washed-out results. If you are on an extended trip, try to send film home as soon after it's exposed as possible. You'll often meet people heading back to whichever continent you're from, and they can usually be persuaded to do you the favor of carrying film home, particularly if you offer to take them out to dinner. I always buy either process-paid film or prepaid film mailers so I can place the exposed film in the mailer and not worry about the cost. The last thing you want to do on your return from a trip is worry about how you're going to find the money to develop a few dozen rolls of film.

Technical Tips

Tropical shadows are very strong and come out almost black on photographs. Often a bright but hazy day makes for better photographs than a very sunny one. Photography in open shade or using fill-in flash will help. The best time for shooting is when the sun is low – the first and last two hours of the day. If you are heading into the rainforest, you will need high-speed film, flash, a tripod, or a combination of these if you want to take photographs within the jungle. The amount of light penetrating the layers of vegetation is, surprisingly, very low.

Video Systems

Videos can be purchased in Costa Rica as souvenirs, but keep in mind that videos available in Costa Rica are compatible with the US video system NTSC, and don't work on European and Australian systems.

Photographing People

The Costa Rican people make wonderful subjects for photos. However, most people resent having a camera thrust in their faces. Ask for permission with a smile or a joke, and if this is refused (rarely), don't become offended. Be aware and sensitive of people's feelings – it is not worth upsetting someone to get a photograph.

Airport Security

The international airport in San José has a vicious X-ray machine. On one trip in the mid-1990s, my film came home with a grayish cast to it, and two friends who were there later reported the same thing. Carry all your film separately. I have received a report that the X-ray machine can also damage computer disks, although I can't figure out how.

TIME

Costa Rica is six hours behind Greenwich Mean Time (GMT), which means that Costa Rican time is equivalent to Central Time in North America. There is no daylight saving time.

ELECTRICITY

Costa Rica's electricity supply is 110 V AC at 60 Hz (same as the USA). You will need a voltage converter if you want to use 240/250 V AC-powered items. Most outlets accept two-pronged plugs with flat prongs of the kind used in the USA. Three-pronged outlets are occasionally found (but accept two-pronged plugs).

WEIGHTS & MEASURES

Costa Rica uses the metric system. There is a conversion table at the back of this book.

LAUNDRY

There are almost no self-service laundries in Costa Rica, although I did find a few in San José. This means you have to find someone to wash your clothes for you or wash them yourself.

Many hotels will have someone to do your laundry; this can cost very little in the cheaper hotels (about a dollar for a change of clothes). The problem is that you might not see your clothes again for two or three days, particularly if it is raining and they can't be dried. Better hotels have dryers but charge more. A few upscale coastal fishing lodges are now offering free laundry service because the charter flight to reach the lodges only permits a 25lb baggage allowance.

You can hand-wash your clothes; some cheaper hotels have sinks in which to do this.

TOILETS

Costa Rican plumbing is often poor and has very low pressure in all but the best hotels and buildings. Often, putting toilet paper into the bowl seems to clog up the system, so a waste receptacle is provided for the used paper. This may not seem particularly sanitary, but it is much better than clogged bowls and toilet water overflowing onto the floor. A well-run hotel, even if it is cheap, will ensure that the receptacle is emptied and the toilet cleaned every day. The same applies to restaurants and other public toilets. The better hotels have adequate flushing capabilities. In places where toilet paper baskets are provided, travelers are urged to use them.

Public toilets are limited mainly to bus terminals, airports, and restaurants. Lavatories are called *servicios higiénicos* and may be marked 'SS.HH' – a little confusing until you learn the abbreviation. People needing to use the lavatory can go into a restaurant and ask to use the *baño*; toilet paper is not always available, so the experienced traveler learns to carry a personal supply.

HEALTH

It's true that most people traveling for any length of time in Latin America are likely to have an occasional mild stomach upset. It's also true that if you take the appropriate precautions before, during, and after your trip, it's unlikely that you will become seriously ill. I've lived and traveled all over Latin America every year since 1980, and I'm happy to report I've picked up no major illnesses.

Dengue fever, a mosquito-spread disease, is on the rise. There have been several hundred recent cases of malaria in low-lying regions. Both diseases are most common on the Caribbean coast, although malaria has been reported on the Península de Osa. Despite this, Costa Rica has one of the highest standards of health care and hygiene in Latin America.

Predeparture Preparations

Vaccinations The Costa Rican authorities do not, at present, require anyone to have an up-to-date international vaccination card to enter the country, though you should make sure that all your normal vaccinations are up to date. Pregnant women should consult their doctors before taking any vaccinations. Rarely, if a widespread cholera or malaria outbreak is occurring, travelers (especially those arriving overland) may be subject to cholera jabs or asked to show they have anti-malarials.

Travel Insurance However fit and healthy you are, *do* take out travel insurance, preferably with provisions for flying you home in the event of a medical emergency. Even if you don't get sick, you might be involved in an accident.

First-Aid Kit How large or small your first-aid kit should be depends on your knowledge of first-aid procedures, where and how far off the beaten track you are going, how long you will need the kit for, and how many people will share it. The following is a suggested checklist, which you should amend as needed.

- your own prescription medications
- antiseptic cream
- antihistamine or other anti-itch cream for insect bites
- aspirin or similar painkiller
- Lomotil/Imodium and/or a nonprescription preparation such as Pepto-Bismol for diarrhea
- antibiotics such as ampicillin and tetracycline (only if you plan on going far off the beaten track. These are available by prescription only; carry the prescription and know what you are doing. Some people have severe allergic reactions to antibiotics.)
- throat lozenges
- ear and eye drops
- antacid tablets
- motion-sickness medication
- alcohol swabs
- water purification tablets
- powdered rehydration mixture for severe diarrhea – particularly useful if traveling with children
- lip salve
- sunburn salve (aloe vera gel works well)
- antifungal powder (for feet and groin)
- thermometer in a case
- surgical tape, assorted adhesive strips, gauze, bandages, butterfly closures
- moleskin
- scissors
- first-aid booklet

A convenient way of carrying your first-aid kit so that it doesn't get crushed is in a small plastic container with a sealing lid, such as Tupperware.

Don't use medications indiscriminately, and be aware of their side effects. Some people may be allergic to things as simple as aspirin. Antibiotics such as tetracycline can make you extra sensitive to the sun, thus increasing the chance of severe sunburn. Antibiotics are not recommended for prophylactic use – they destroy the body's natural resistance to bacteria that cause diarrhea and other diseases. Lomotil or Imodium will temporarily stop the symptoms of diarrhea, but will not cure the problem. Motion sickness or antihistamine medications can make you very drowsy.

Basic Rules

Water & Food Water is usually safe in San José and the major towns, though it is a good idea to boil, filter, or purify it in out-of-the-way places. The lowlands are the most likely places to find unsafe drinking water. When in doubt, ask: some better hotels may be able to show you a certificate of water purity. Bottled mineral water, soft drinks, and beer are readily available alternatives.

Some places have had problems with contaminated ice. Try to avoid ice if you're unsure of its safety. Uncooked foods (such as salads and fruits) are best avoided unless they can be peeled.

Health Precautions Check these details before leaving home. If you wear prescription glasses, make sure you have a spare pair and a copy of the prescription. The tropical sun is strong, so you may want to have a pair of prescription sunglasses made.

Ensure that you have an adequate supply of any prescription medicines you use regularly. If you haven't had a dental examination for a long time, you should have one rather than risk a dental problem on your trip.

Medical Problems & Treatment

Diarrhea The drastic change in diet experienced by travelers means that they are often susceptible to minor stomach ailments, such as diarrhea. After you've been traveling in Latin America for a while, you seem to build up some sort of immunity. If this is your first trip to the area, take heart. Costa Rica has one of the better health care systems in Latin America. Many people get minor stomach problems, but a simple nonprescription medicine such as Pepto-Bismol usually takes care of the discomfort quickly.

Dysentery If your diarrhea continues for days and is accompanied by nausea, severe abdominal pain, and fever, and you find blood in your stools, you may have contracted dysentery, which is uncommon in Costa Rica. If you contract dysentery, you should seek medical advice.

Hepatitis Hepatitis A is caused by ingesting contaminated food or water. Salads, uncooked or unpeeled fruit, and unboiled drinks are the worst offenders. Infection risks are minimized by using bottled drinks, except in major towns or places where you know the water has been purified, washing your own fruits and vegetables with purified water, and paying scrupulous attention to your toilet habits.

Hepatitis sufferers' skin and especially the whites of their eyes turn yellow, and they feel so tired that it literally takes all their effort to go to the toilet. There is no cure except rest for a few weeks. Protection can be provided with the antibody gamma globulin or with a newer vaccine called Havrix, also known as hepatitis A vaccine.

The incidence of hepatitis A is low in Costa Rica, so many travelers opt not to bother with these shots.

Cholera Very few cholera cases are reported from Costa Rica, and the chance of a tourist contracting this illness is almost nil.

Malaria Malarial mosquitoes aren't a problem in the highlands, but some cases of malaria are reported in the lowlands. Be particularly careful in the south Caribbean coastal area near the Panamanian border and the Península de Osa, although there is a risk in any lowland area. If you plan on visiting the lowlands, purchase anti-malarial pills in advance, because they should be taken from two weeks before until six weeks after your visit. Dosage and frequency of administration vary from brand to brand, so check this carefully.

Chloroquine (known as Aralen in Costa Rica) is recommended for short-term protection. The usual dose is 500mg once a week. Long-term use of chloroquine *may* cause side effects, and travelers planning a long trip into the lowlands should discuss this risk against the value of protection with their doctor. Pregnant women are at a higher risk when taking anti-malarials. Fansidar is now known to cause dangerous side effects, so this drug should be used only under medical supervision.

People who are going to spend a great deal of time in tropical lowlands and prefer not to take anti-malarial pills on a semipermanent basis should remember that malarial mosquitoes bite mostly at night. Wear long-sleeved shirts and long trousers from dusk till dawn, use frequent applications of insect repellent, and sleep under a mosquito net. Sleeping with a fan on is also effective; mosquitoes don't like wind.

A woman traveler suggests that getting changed or dressed for dinner is not a good idea in mosquito-prone areas, because dusk is a particularly bad time for mosquitoes and that dressy skirt does nothing to keep the insects away. Keep the long pants and bug repellent on.

Note that only some *Anopheles* species carry the disease and they generally bite standing on their heads with their back legs up – mosquitoes that bite in a position horizontal to the skin are not malarial mosquitoes.

Dengue Fever No prophylactic is available for this mosquito-spread disease; the main preventative measure is to avoid mosquito bites (see Malaria, above). The carrier is *Aedes aegypti* – a different species from that which carries the malarial parasite, but it is avoided in the same way.

A sudden onset of fever, headaches, and severe joint and muscle pains is the first sign, before a pink rash starts on the trunk of the body and spreads to the limbs and face. After about three or four days, the fever will subside and recovery will begin. A shorter, less severe second bout may occur about a day later. There is no treatment except for bed rest and painkillers. Aspirin should not be taken. Drink plenty of liquids to stay hydrated.

Serious complications are uncommon, but full recovery can take several weeks. Quite common in some Latin American countries, dengue fever is less common in Costa Rica, though a few hundred cases are reported every year. Less than 3% of cases in the Americas are of the more dangerous hemorrhagic dengue fever, which may be lethal. It's not easy to tell the difference, so medical help should be sought.

Insect Problems Insect repellents go a long way in preventing bites, but if you do get bitten, avoid scratching. Unfortunately, this is easier said than done.

To alleviate itching, try applying hydrocortisone cream, calamine lotion, or some other kind of anti-itch cream, or soaking in baking soda. Scratching will quickly open bites and cause them to become infected. Skin infections are slow to heal in the heat of the tropics, and all infected bites as well as cuts and grazes should be kept scrupulously clean, treated with antiseptic creams, and covered with dressings on a daily basis. A reader writes that rubbing lime or lemon juice on mosquito bites makes them itch like crazy for a short while, but then they stop itching entirely and heal more quickly – I haven't tried this!

Another insect problem is infestation with lice (including crabs) and scabies. Lice or crabs crawl around in your body hair and make you itch. To get rid of them, wash with

Insect Repellent

The most effective ingredient in insect repellent is diethyl-metatoluamide, also known as Deet. You can buy repellent with 90% or more of this ingredient; many brands (including those available in Costa Rica) contain less than 15%, so buy it ahead of time. I find that the rub-on lotions are the most effective, and pump sprays are good for spraying clothes, especially at the neck, wrist, waist, and ankle openings.

Some people find that Deet is irritating to the skin – they should use lower strengths. Everyone should avoid getting Deet in the eyes, on the lips, and on other sensitive regions. This stuff can dissolve plastic, so keep it off plastic lenses, etc. I know of someone who put plenty of Deet onto his face and forehead, then began sweating and got Deet-laden sweat in his eyes, resulting not only in eye irritation but clouding his plastic contact lenses!

Deet is toxic to children and shouldn't be used on their skin. Instead, try Avon's 'Skin So Soft,' which has insect-repellent properties and is not toxic – get the oil, not the lotion. Camping stores sometimes sell insect repellents with names such as 'Green Ban' – these are made with natural products and are not toxic, but I find them less effective than repellents with Deet.

Mosquito spirals (coils) can sometimes be bought in Costa Rica. They work like incense sticks and are fairly effective at keeping mosquitoes away.

– Rob Rachowiecki

a shampoo containing benzene hexachloride or shave the affected area. To avoid being reinfected, wash all your clothes and bedding in hot water and the shampoo; it's probably best to just throw away your underwear. Lice thrive on body warmth; those beasties lurking in clothes will die in about 72 hours if the clothing isn't worn.

Chiggers are mites that burrow into your skin and cause it to become red and itchy. The irritation lasts for weeks, but you don't feel the bites until it's too late. The recommended prevention is to sprinkle sulfur powder on socks, shoes, and lower legs when walking through grass. Liberal application of insect repellent works reasonably well.

Scorpions and spiders can give severely painful – but rarely fatal – stings or bites. A common way to get bitten is to put on your clothes and shoes in the morning without checking them first. Develop the habit of shaking out your clothing before putting it on, especially in the lowlands. Check your bedding before going to sleep. Don't walk barefoot, and look where you place your hands when reaching to a shelf or branch. It's unlikely that you will get stung, so don't worry too much about it, but take the precautions outlined above.

Snakebite This is also extremely unlikely. Should you be bitten, the snake may be a nonvenomous one (try to identify the offending creature). Do not try the slash-and-suck routine on the bite.

The venom of most dangerous snakes does its nasty work via the lymph system, not the bloodstream, so treatment aimed at reducing the flow of blood or removing venom from the bloodstream is likely to be futile. Aim to immobilize the bitten limb and bandage it tightly and completely (but don't make a tourniquet – now considered too dangerous and not particularly effective). Then, with a minimum of disturbance, particularly of the bound limb, get the victim to medical attention as soon as possible. Keep calm and reassure the victim.

One of the world's deadliest snakes is the fer-de-lance, and it has an anticoagulating agent in its venom. If you're bitten by a fer-de-lance, your blood coagulates twice as slowly as the average hemophiliac's, so slashing at the wound with a razor is a good way to help yourself bleed to death. The slash-and-suck routine does work in some cases, but this should be done only by people who know what they are doing. Even the deadly fer-de-lance succeeds in killing only a small percentage of its victims.

Sexually Transmitted Diseases Prostitution is legal in Costa Rica, and female prostitutes are required to be registered and receive regular medical checkups (see the boxed text 'Prostitution' in the Facts about Costa Rica chapter). Nevertheless, incidence of sexually transmitted diseases, including HIV/AIDS, is increasing among Costa Rican prostitutes. In addition, male prostitutes, including transvestites, are unlikely to receive the required medical checkups. There are two effective ways of avoiding contracting an STD: have a monogamous relationship with a healthy partner or abstain from sexual encounters.

Abstinence is easy to recommend but tough to practice. Travelers who have no sexual partner and are unwilling to abstain are strongly advised against using prostitutes. Having sex with a person other than a prostitute may be somewhat safer, but it's still far from risk-free. The use of condoms minimizes, but does not eliminate, the chances of contracting an STD. Condoms *(preservativos)*, including some imported brands, are available in Costa Rican pharmacies.

Diseases such as syphilis and gonorrhea are marked by rashes or sores in the genital area and burning pain during urination. Women's symptoms may be less obvious than men's. These diseases can be cured relatively easily by antibiotics. If untreated, they can become dormant, only to emerge in much more difficult-to-treat forms a few months or years later. Costa Rican doctors know how to treat most STDs – if you have a rash, discharge, or pain, see a doctor. Herpes and AIDS are incurable as of this writing. Herpes is not fatal.

HIV/AIDS HIV, the human immunodeficiency virus, may develop into AIDS, acquired immune deficiency syndrome (SIDA in Spanish). HIV is a significant problem in all Latin American countries, particularly among prostitutes of both sexes. Any exposure to blood, blood products, or bodily fluids may put the individual at risk. Transmission in Costa Rica is predominantly through homosexual sexual activity, with about 70% of cases reported in gay men. However, many of these men are bisexual, and the disease is spreading among women, too.

HIV/AIDS can also be spread through infected blood transfusions; if you need a transfusion, go to the best clinic available and make sure they screen blood used for transfusions. It can also be spread by dirty needles – vaccinations, acupuncture, tattooing, and body piercing can be as dangerous as intravenous drug use if the equipment is not clean. If you do need an injection, ask to see the syringe unwrapped in front of you, or buy a needle and syringe pack from a pharmacy if you have any doubt about the sterility of the needle.

Apart from abstinence, the most effective way to prevent sexual transmission of HIV is to always practice safe sex using latex barriers, such as condoms and dams. Condoms are available in Costa Rican pharmacies. It is impossible to detect the HIV+ status of a healthy-looking person without a blood test.

A psychologist working with HIV+ men in San José in the mid-1990s reported that between 10,000 and 15,000 Costa Ricans were affected by the disease, and the number has undoubtedly grown since that report. Unfortunately, many of them don't know they are infected and continue to be sexually active, so the virus is spreading rapidly. Equally unfortunately, information about safe sex and condoms – indeed, any kind of sex education – is sadly lacking in Costa Rica because sex education is opposed by the powerful Roman Catholic church. Other problems are cultural and have to do with *machismo* – a 'real' man doesn't need to use a condom. Also, it is widely thought that HIV+ people look sick, when the reality is that HIV+ people are likely to look and act completely healthy for several years after infection, all the time carrying and perhaps spreading the disease.

Fear of HIV infection should never preclude treatment for serious medical conditions. Although there may be a risk of infection, it is very small indeed.

Altitude Sickness This may occur when you ascend to high altitude quickly, for example, when you fly into the highlands. This is not a problem in San José (1150m), which is not high enough to cause altitude problems.

If you are planning on driving up one of the volcanoes such as Poás (2704m) or Irazú (3432m), you may experience some shortness of breath and headache. Overnight stays are not allowed on these volcanoes, so you will be able to descend quickly if you feel unwell. Heading south from San José on the Interamericana, the road crosses the continental divide at 3335m, 95km south of the capital. Again, you will probably be going down again before you get sick.

If you climb Chirripó (3819m, the highest mountain in Costa Rica and south Central America), you may experience much more severe symptoms, including vomiting, fatigue, insomnia, loss of appetite, a rapid pulse, and irregular (or Cheyne-Stokes) breathing during sleep.

The best thing you can do to avoid altitude sickness is to climb gradually. Consider

A Terrific Tumor

Costa Rican surgeons were amazed recently when they discovered a huge abdominal tumor in a 52-year-old patient. After extraction, they found that the tumor weighed a record-breaking 46lb, over three times heavier than the previously recorded largest tumor of this type. Five days after surgery, the much lighter patient was able to return to work.

– Rob Rachowiecki

taking two days for the Chirripó ascent rather than one. If you feel sick, the best treatment is rest, deep breathing, an adequate fluid intake, and a mild painkiller such as Tylenol to alleviate headaches. If symptoms are very severe, the only effective cure is to descend to a lower elevation.

Heat & Sun The heat and humidity of the coastal tropics make you sweat profusely and can also make you feel apathetic. It is important to maintain a high fluid intake and ensure that your food is well salted. If fluids lost through perspiration are not replaced, heat exhaustion and cramps may result. The feeling of apathy that some people experience usually fades after a week or two.

If you're arriving in the tropics with a great desire to improve your tan, you've certainly come to the right place. The tropical sun will not only improve your tan, it will burn you to a crisp. I know several travelers who have enjoyed themselves in the sun for an afternoon, and then spent the next couple of days with severe sunburn. An effective way of immobilizing yourself is to cover yourself with sunblock, walk down to the beach, remove your shoes, and badly burn your feet, which you forgot to put lotion on and which are especially untanned.

The power of the tropical sun cannot be overemphasized. Don't spoil your trip by trying to tan too quickly; use strong sunblock lotion frequently and put it on all exposed skin. Wearing a wide-brimmed sun hat is also a good idea.

Rabies Rabid dogs are more common in Latin America than in more developed nations. If you are bitten by a dog, try to have it captured for tests. If you are unable to test the dog, you must assume that you have rabies, which is invariably fatal if untreated, so you cannot take the risk of hoping that the dog was not infected. Treatment consists of a series of injections. Rabies takes from five days (exceptionally) to several months to develop, so if you are bitten, don't panic. You've got plenty of time to get treated. Ensure that any bite or scratch is cleaned immediately and thoroughly with soap and running water or swabbed with alcohol to prevent potential infections or tetanus.

Rabies is also carried by vampire bats, which actually prefer to bite the toes of their sleeping human victims, rather than necks, as popular folklore suggests. Don't stick your toes out from your mosquito net or blanket if you're sleeping in an area where there are bats. Other carriers are monkeys, cats…in fact, many mammals. A rabies vaccine is available and should be considered if you are in a high-risk category (for example, if you intend to explore caves with bats or work with animals).

Medical Attention

If you've taken the precautions mentioned in the previous sections, you can look forward to a generally healthy trip. Should something go wrong, however, you can get good medical advice and treatment in San José.

The social security hospitals provide free emergency services to everyone, including foreigners. The main one in San José is the Hospital San Juan de Dios (☎ 257-6282) on Paseo Colón, Calle 14. Private clinics are also available and are listed under San José and other main towns in this book. Their services are normally of a higher standard than the social security hospitals.

An emergency phone number worth knowing is the Red Cross (Cruz Roja; ☎ 128, no coin needed) for ambulances in the San José area. Outside San José, the Cruz Roja has a different number in each province:

Alajuela	☎ 441-3939
Cartago	☎ 551-0421
Heredia	☎ 237-1115
Guanacaste	☎ 666-0994
Puerto Limón	☎ 758-0125
Puntarenas	☎ 661-0184

Most prescription drugs are available in Costa Rica; some are sold over the counter. For minor ailments and illnesses, pharmacists will often advise and prescribe for you.

Healthcare Tourism

Medical care in Costa Rica is generally less expensive than it is in most Western countries, although the standards in San José are high. Costa Rica is experiencing a boom in dental, cosmetic, and plastic surgery. Foreigners come here specifically to have these nonessential medical procedures done at lower cost than at home. One couple wrote that they had what would have been US$10,000 worth of dental work (in the USA) done in Costa Rica for a third of the cost – the savings more than paid for their trip!

Many surgeons have received medical training in the USA, speak English, and are well qualified. You can get lists of plastic surgeons from the College of Physicians and Surgeons of Costa Rica (☎ 232-3433). Health Holidays of Costa Rica (☎ 240-6645, fax 236-8527, www.health.co.cr) arranges everything from medical procedures to hotels and tours. Holistic health retreats and resorts are also springing up in Costa Rica; several are listed in appropriate parts of the text.

– Rob Rachowiecki

If you have insurance to cover medical emergencies, note that many doctors expect to be paid up front; then you have to claim from the insurance company in order to get reimbursed.

WOMEN TRAVELERS

Attitudes toward Women

Generally, women travelers find Costa Rica safe and pleasant to visit. Women are traditionally respected in Costa Rica (Mother's Day is a national holiday), and women have made gains in the workplace. A woman vice-president, Victoria Garrón, was elected in 1986, and another woman, Margarita Penon, ran as a presidential candidate in 1993. Both vice-presidents (Costa Rica has two) elected in 1998 were women, Astrid Fischel and Elizabeth Odio. Women routinely occupy roles in the political, legal, scientific, and medical fields – professions that used to be overpoweringly dominated by men.

This is not to say that machismo is a thing of the past. On the contrary, it is very much alive and practiced. Costa Rican men generally consider *gringas* to have looser morals and to be easier 'conquests' than ticas. They often make flirtatious comments to or stare at unaccompanied women, both local and foreign. Women traveling together are not exempt from this attention; women traveling with men are less likely to receive attention.

Comments are rarely blatantly rude; the usual thing is a smiling *'Mi amor'* or an appreciative hiss. The best way to deal with this is to do what the ticas do – ignore the comments completely and do not look at the man making them.

Women travelers will meet pleasant and friendly Costa Rican men. It is worth remembering, though, that gentle seduction is a sport, a challenge, even a way of life for many Costa Rican men, particularly in San José. Men may conveniently forget to mention that they are married, and declarations of undying love might mean little in this Catholic society where divorce is frowned upon.

Women who firmly resist unwanted verbal advances from men are normally treated with respect. But there are always a small number of men who insist on trying to hold hands or give a 'friendly' hug or kiss – if the feeling is not mutual, turn them down firmly and explicitly. Some women find that wearing a cheap 'wedding' ring helps – though, of course, you have to be ready to answer the inevitable 'Where is your husband?'

There have been reports of some cab drivers making inappropriate advances to women – women alone may want to use cabs from a hotel rather than a cab on the street. Pirate cabs (without the insignia of a cab company) are more likely to present a problem. Lone women might avoid those, especially after dark if going for a long ride. (Nevertheless, I get the impression that cab drivers are generally OK – use your best judgment.)

What to Wear

Costa Ricans are generally quite conservative, and that applies to dress. Women travelers are advised to follow suit to avoid calling unnecessary attention to themselves. On the beach, skimpy bathing costumes are quite acceptable, although topless bathing and nudity are not. Some women travelers, especially Europeans, tend to think that what they do on the Mediterranean they can do in Costa Rican beach areas. Going topless may be fine in other places, but it is seen in Costa Rica as insensitive, rude, and generally unacceptable.

Organizations

CEFEMINA, the Centro Feminista de Información y Acción (☎ 224-3986), in San Pedro, is the main Costa Rican feminist organization. It publishes a newsletter and can provide information and assistance to women travelers.

Magazines & Newsletters

Newsletters aimed specifically at advising women travelers are of a general nature and not specifically about Costa Rica. *Journeywoman* is an online magazine, at www.journeywoman.com, with many useful links. Also check out *Maiden Voyages* (www.maiden-voyages.com), which has both text and online versions and many links to travel books for and about women.

GAY & LESBIAN TRAVELERS

Although Costa Rica is known for its good human rights record, the situation for gays and lesbians is still poor, though better than in most Central American countries. Legally, homosexuality is not singled out as a criminal offense (except with minors under 18), and most Costa Ricans are tolerant of gay and lesbian people as long as they don't show affection for one another in public, which means that homosexual life is pretty low-key in Costa Rica. The tolerance of gay people only goes as far as a 'Don't ask; don't tell' philosophy. Despite the legal protection and theoretical equal rights of all Costa Ricans, gay or straight, police harassment in gay clubs and other locales has resulted in a string of human rights violations. People who come out publicly are often discriminated against by their employers and even their own families. This results in a high level of depression, drug and alcohol abuse, and other psychological problems within the gay community.

In 1992, Triángulo Rosa (Pink Triangle), the first legally recognized gay group in Central America, was founded to support human rights for all members of the gay and bisexual community, despite opposition from the political and religious establishment. Triángulo Rosa works in various fields, including AIDS and safe sex education, struggling against discrimination, supporting HIV+ people and those with AIDS, operating a community center, forging positive relationships within the gay community and with the straight community, and providing information. Travelers will find that Triángulo Rosa can recommend gay-friendly hotels, bars, and meeting places in Costa Rica (especially in San José).

Leaders of Triángulo Rosa write that the situation with the gay rights movement in San José is about where it was in the USA in the 1960s. In addition, the culture of machismo makes life 'a veritable hell for gays and lesbians,' according to a local psychologist who treats HIV+ patients. The Triángulo Rosa is staffed by about 20 volunteers and is supported mainly by local donations with some international funding. The volunteers say that their main aim is to save lives through education. For more on the AIDS situation in Costa Rica, see the Health section, earlier in this chapter.

In 1998, a gay and lesbian festival that had been planned in San José was canceled following comments from the Roman Catholic clergy that promoted heavy opposition to gay rights. The church has continued to lead homophobic sentiment in Costa Rica, forcing the cancellation of a gay and lesbian tour to Manuel Antonio and encouraging the blockade of a coastal hotel hosting a group of North American gays. The situation took an embarrassing turn in 1999, when the president of the ICT said that Costa Rica should not be a destination for sex tourism or homosexuals or lesbians. The gay community made it clear that they were against sex tourism, and that the linking of gay tourism with sex tourism was both untrue and defamatory. The official position in Costa Rica shifted toward stating that gay tourism was neither discriminated against nor encouraged.

However, the bottom line remains that discreet gay couples generally enjoy their vacations, and harassment is not a problem if they don't call attention to their sexual orientation.

Organizations

You can contact Triángulo Rosa (☎ 234-2411 English, 258-0214 Spanish, atrirosa@sol.racsa.co.cr) for information or to make donations. They also run regular meetings of the Gay & Lesbian Club (☎ 222-1047, 222-1185).

Instituto Latinoamericano de Prevención y Educación en Salud (ILPES; ☎ 256-0082, 222-3921, ilpes@sol.racsa.co.cr) gives support to people living with or at risk for HIV/AIDS.

The International Gay & Lesbian Travel Association (IGLTA) has a list of hundreds of travel agents, tour operators, and tourism industry professionals all over the world. Browse its home page at www.iglta.org.

The local gay magazine, *Gente 10*, is available at some of the hotels listed below and in some of the bars listed under Gay & Lesbian Venues in the Entertainment section of the San José chapter.

Meeting Places

Some gay-friendly hotels, described later in this book, are the Hotel Kekoldi, Joluva Guesthouse, Colors, and Apartamentos Scotland in San José, and the Hotel Casa Blanca and the Hotel Mariposa in Manuel Antonio. Manuel Antonio also has a nude beach for gay people – one of the few places in the country where a blind eye is turned to nudity.

There is a good number of gay and lesbian nightclubs, especially in San José. These range from slightly dangerous meat markets to raving dance clubs to quiet places for a drink and talk. The main street action is in the blocks south of the Parque Central, but some blocks (though not all) are somewhat dangerous at night, so don't go around alone unless you know how to look after yourself or have good local information. There are also clubs in other areas. See the San José chapter for details.

DISABLED TRAVELERS

Although there is an Equal Opportunities for Disabled Persons Law, its provisions are much less strict than those of similar laws in first world countries. Still, it is a small move in the right direction for disabled people.

Unfortunately, the law only applies to new or newly remodeled businesses (including hotels and restaurants), so older businesses (built prior to the mid-1990s) are exempt. New businesses are required to have a barrier-free entrance for disabled people.

Realistically, independent travel is difficult for disabled people. Very few hotels and restaurants, except for the newest, have features specifically suited to wheelchair use, for example. Many don't even have the basic minimum of a wheelchair ramp and room or bathroom doors wide enough to accommodate a wheelchair. Special phones for hearing-impaired people or signs in Braille for blind people are very rare.

Outside of the buildings, streets and sidewalks are potholed and poorly paved, making wheelchair use frustrating everywhere. Public buses don't have provisions that allow wheelchairs to be carried.

Organizations

In Costa Rica, Vaya con Silla de Ruedas (☎ 391-5045 cellular, fax 454-2810, vayacon@sol.racsa.co.cr) translates into 'Go with Wheelchairs.' This company has a van especially designed to transport travelers in wheelchairs; equipment meets international accessibility standards and up to three wheelchairs can be transported. It can help with other arrangements such as bilingual guides, hotel reservations, and tours lasting from a few hours to a few days.

La Fundacion Kosta Roda (☎/fax 771-7482, chabote@sol.racsa.co.cr) in San Isidro is a nonprofit organization working with the ICT to list accessible sites of interest to disabled travelers.

SENIOR TRAVELERS

Though many seniors travel in Costa Rica, I am aware of no special discounts available to them. Seniors normally pay the same fares, hotel costs, museum entrances, etc. However, international airlines flying into Costa Rica may offer discounted tickets.

Elderhostel (☎ 877-426-8056, 978-323-4141, www.elderhostel.org), 75 Federal St, Boston, MA 02110, USA, is one of the best agencies for learning vacations for those 55 and older. See also the earlier Books section for titles about retiring in Costa Rica.

TRAVEL WITH CHILDREN

Children pay full fare on buses if they occupy a seat, but often ride for free if they sit on a parent's knee. Children under 12 pay a discounted fare (variable) on domestic airline flights and get a seat, while infants under two pay 10% of the fare but don't get a seat. Children's car seats are not always available in Costa Rican car rental agencies, so bring one if you plan on driving.

In hotels, the general rule is simply to bargain, except in top-end hotels, where discounts are normally posted. Children should never have to pay as much as an adult, but whether they stay for half price or free is open to discussion. A few hotels don't allow children under a certain age in order to maintain a quiet atmosphere.

While 'kids' meals' (small portions at small prices) are not normally offered in restaurants, it is perfectly acceptable to order a meal to split between two children or an adult and a child.

Foreigners traveling with children will meet with extra, generally friendly, attention and interest. For more suggestions, see Lonely Planet's *Travel with Children* by Maureen Wheeler.

USEFUL ORGANIZATIONS

In addition to the specific groups listed above, others of a more general nature are given here.

The South American Explorers Club

The SAEC (☎ 607-277-0488, fax 607-277-6122, www.samexplo.org) is at 126 Indian Creek Rd, Ithaca, NY 14850, USA. The club is an information center for travelers, has clubhouses in Peru and Ecuador, and provides information for travelers to Central America as well.

The club has books, maps, and trip reports left by other travelers. Maps and books are sold through a print and online catalog. This is a membership-supported nonprofit organization. Membership costs US$40 and lasts for four quarterly issues of the informative *South American Explorer* magazine. Members can make use of the clubhouses (if heading on to Peru or Ecuador) as well as the extensive information facilities and books available by mail before they go.

Latin American Travel Advisor

You can get up-to-date information on safety, political and economic situations, health risks, costs, etc, for all the Latin American countries (including Costa Rica) from *The Latin American Travel Advisor*. This impartial, 16-page quarterly newsletter is published in Ecuador. Four issues are US$39, the most recent issue is US$15, and back issues are US$7.50, sent by airmail. The Latin American Travel Advisor (☎ 888-215-9511 in the USA, fax 562-566 in Ecuador, www.amerispan.com/lata) is reachable at PO Box 17-17-908, Quito, Ecuador.

DANGERS & ANNOYANCES

Thefts & Muggings

Locals and frequent visitors have noted an increase in tourist-oriented crime in recent years – likely precipitated by the increase in tourism. Although rip-offs are a fact of life when traveling anywhere, you'll find Costa Rica is still less prone to theft than many countries. You should, nevertheless, take some simple precautions to avoid being robbed.

Armed robbery is rare, but sneak theft is more common, and you should remember that crowded places are the haunts of pickpockets – places such as badly lit bus stations or bustling streets. Crowded streets around the market and east of the Coca-Cola bus terminal in San José, as well as along Avenida 2 west of the Parque Central, are areas noted for thefts. Muggings have been reported after dark – so keep alert. This is also the heart of the tourist area, with many budget hotels nearby and high-quality hotels on the edges. I spend many a night walking these streets and rarely have a problem.

Occasionally, a couple of women may try to physically harass a man – one tries lasciviously to gain your attention while the other tries to pull your wallet. Other scams include being squirted with mustard or some other noxious substance; 'Samaritans' offering to help wipe you off are lifting your wallet at the same time. Alertness helps – don't allow yourself to be distracted. If you are used to dealing with big-city hassles, you should have no great problem.

Thieves look for easy targets. Tourists carrying a wallet or passport in a hip pocket are asking for trouble. Leave your wallet at home; it's an easy mark for a pickpocket. Carrying a small roll of bills loosely wadded under a handkerchief in your front pocket is as safe a way as any of carrying your daily spending money. The rest should be hidden. Always use at least an inside pocket or preferably a body pouch, money belt, or leg pouch to protect your money and passport. Separate your money into different places.

Carry some of your money as traveler's checks or credit cards. The former can be refunded if lost or stolen; the latter can be canceled and reissued. Carry an emergency packet somewhere separate from all your other valuables. This should contain a photocopy of the identifying pages of your passport; on the back of the photocopy list important numbers such as traveler's checks serial numbers, airline ticket numbers, and credit card or bank account numbers. Also, keep one high-denomination bill in with this emergency stash. You will probably never have to use it, but it's a good idea not to put all your eggs into one basket.

Take out travelers' luggage insurance if you're carrying valuable gear such as a good camera. But don't get paranoid: Costa Rica is still a reasonably safe country.

If you are robbed, get a police report as soon as possible. This is a requirement for any insurance claims, although it is unlikely that the police will be able to recover the property. Police reports should be filed with the Organismo de Investigación Judicial (OIJ) in the Corte Suprema de Justicia (Supreme Court) complex at Avenida 6, Calles 17 & 19, in San José. If you don't speak Spanish, bring a translator. In addition, travelers who have suffered crimes or price-gouging can write to the Costa Rican Tourist Board, Apartado 777-1000, San José. By Costa Rican law, the tourist board is obliged to represent foreign tourists who are victims of tourist-related crimes in court cases if necessary, thus allowing the tourist to go elsewhere (like home).

Costa Rica has a long history of business-related crimes – real estate and investment scams have occurred frequently over the years. If you want to sink money into any kind of Costa Rican business, make sure you both know what you are doing and check it out thoroughly.

Swimming Safety

The tourist brochures, with their enticing photographs of tropical paradises, do not mention that approximately 200 drownings a year occur in Costa Rican waters. Of these, an estimated 80% are caused by riptides.

A riptide is a strong current that pulls the swimmer out to sea. It can occur in waist-deep water. It is most important to remember that riptides will pull you *out but not under*. Many deaths are caused by panicked swimmers struggling to the point of exhaustion.

If you are caught in a riptide, float, do not struggle. Let the riptide carry you out beyond the breakers. If you swim, do so parallel to the beach, not directly back in. You are very unlikely to be able to swim against a riptide and will only exhaust yourself. When you are carried out beyond the breakers, you will find that the riptide will dissipate – it won't carry you out for miles. Then you can swim back to shore. Swim at a 45° angle to the shore to avoid being caught by the current again.

If you feel a riptide while you are wading, try to come back in sideways, thus offering less body surface to the current. Also remember to walk parallel to the beach if you cannot make headway, so that you can get out of the riptide. Some riptides are permanent; others come and go or move along a beach. Beaches with a reputation for rips are Playa Bonita near Limón; the area at the entrance of Parque Nacional Cahuita; Playa Doña Ana and Playa Barranca near Puntarenas; and Playa Espadilla at Parque Nacional Manuel Antonio.

Other swimming problems are occasional huge waves that can knock waders over – stay within your limits and remember that few beaches have lifeguards.

Some beaches are polluted by litter or, worse, sewage and other contamination, which can pose a health hazard. Beaches are now checked by the local authorities, and the cleanest are marked with a blue flag.

Hiking Safety

Many visitors like to hike in the national parks and wilderness areas. Hikers should be adequately prepared for their trips. Always carry plenty of water, even on short trips. In 1993, two German hikers going for a short 90-minute hike in Parque Nacional Barra Honda got lost and died of heat prostration and thirst. Hikers have been known to get lost in rainforests. Carry maps and extra food, and let someone know where you are going to narrow the search area in the event of an emergency (for more information on hiking, see Hiking & Backpacking under Activities, later in this chapter).

Earthquakes

It comes as no surprise that Costa Rica, with its mountain chains of active volcanoes, should be earthquake prone. Recent major quakes occurred on March 25, 1990 (7.1 on the Richter scale), and on April 22, 1991 (7.4 on the Richter scale, killing over 50 people in Costa Rica and about 30 more in Panama). Smaller quakes and tremors happen quite often.

If you are caught in a quake, make sure you are not standing under heavy objects that could fall and injure you. The best places to take shelter if you are in a building are in a door frame or under a sturdy table. If you are in the open, don't stand near walls, telegraph poles, etc, that could collapse on you.

Racial Discrimination

Despite Costa Rica's apparent friendly, democratic image, racism does exist, though many ticos will deny it. The predominantly white (or *mestizo*) population of the highlands tends to act as if they are the only ones living there. Racism is rarely overt (it is illegal), but racist attitudes are encountered. One black traveler told me he felt reasonably comfortable most of the time, but occasionally encountered cold stares in some smaller highland towns. Anti-Semitic statements and 'jokes' are also encountered; however, most Jewish travelers in Western clothing are treated like other Americans or Europeans. In 1999, a false report that a Chinese restaurant was serving rat meat disguised as shrimp made newspaper headlines, and the Asian population noted a drastic decline of patronage in their restaurants and unkind 'jokes' about *'latoncitos flitos'* (flied lats). Asian ticos noted that they have constantly been the subject of immature jokes. Matters came to a head when the president ate a well-publicized meal in a Chinese restaurant in an attempt to improve the tico image.

EMERGENCY

The general emergency number (☎ 911) is available in the central provinces and is slowly expanding, although it does not yet cover the whole country. Police (☎ 117) and fire (☎ 118) are, theoretically, reachable throughout the country.

LEGAL MATTERS

If you get into legal trouble and are jailed, your embassy can offer only limited assistance. This may include an occasional visit from an embassy staff member to make sure that your human rights have not been violated, letting your family know where you are, and putting you in contact with a

Costa Rican lawyer, whom you must pay yourself. Embassy officials will not bail you out, and you are subject to the laws of Costa Rica, not to the laws of your home country.

Penalties in Costa Rica for possession of even small amounts of illegal drugs are much stricter than in the USA or Europe. Defendants often spend many months in jail before they are brought to trial and, if convicted (as is usually the case), can expect sentences of several years in jail.

Drivers should carry their passport as well as driver's license. In the event of an accident, leave the vehicles where they are until the police arrive and make a report. This is essential for all insurance claims. While waiting for the police, keep your eye on the vehicle to protect it from theft or vandalism. After the police have made the report, you can move the car. Call the rental company to find out where they want the car taken for repairs or whom they want to tow it if it isn't driveable. If the accident results in injury or death, you may be prevented from leaving the country until all legalities are handled. Drive as defensively as you can.

BUSINESS HOURS

Banks are open 9 am to 3 pm weekdays (Monday to Friday), with a few exceptions in San José. Government offices are supposedly open 8 am to 4 pm weekdays, but often close for lunch between about 11:30 am and 1 pm. Stores are open 8 am to 6 or 7 pm Monday to Saturday, but a two-hour lunch break is not uncommon.

PUBLIC HOLIDAYS & SPECIAL EVENTS

National holidays *(días feriados)* are taken seriously in Costa Rica, and banks, public offices, and many stores close. There are no buses at all on the Thursday afternoon and Friday before Easter, and many businesses are closed for the entire week before Easter. From Thursday to Easter Sunday, all bars are closed and locked and alcohol sales are prohibited. Beach hotels are usually booked weeks ahead for this week, though a limited choice of rooms is often available. Public transport tends to be tight on all holidays and the days immediately preceding or following them, so book tickets ahead.

National Holidays

Until 1996, there were 15 official national holidays, but in that year four holidays lost their official status in a governmental reform of the work code. Older books may, therefore, show more official holidays than the 11 indicated in this section.

Of these 11, all but two (August 2 and October 12) require that employees get paid if they take the day off, or receive double pay if they must work. Previously, only six holidays had obligatory pay, so although there are fewer total official holidays, employees who take them are entitled to more pay than previously.

– Rob Rachowiecki

The week between Christmas and New Year's Day is an unofficial holiday, especially in San José. In addition, various towns have celebrations for their own particular day. These other holidays and special events are not official public holidays, and banks, etc, remain open. All the official national holidays plus the most important other events are listed below. Those marked with an asterisk (*) are official national holidays when banks and businesses are closed throughout the country. See the regional chapters for details on events.

January

New Year's Day* – the 1st

Fiesta de Santa Cruz – mid-January; this town on the Península de Nicoya features a religious procession, rodeo, bullfight, music, and dancing.

February

Fiesta de los Diablitos – dates vary; one of the few indigenous festivals, it features masked dancing held on the Reserva Indígena Boruca near Curré.

March

Día del Boyero – second Sunday; in honor of ox-cart drivers, this festival held in Escazú features a colorful ox-cart parade and associated events.

Día de San José (St Joseph's Day) – the 19th; honors the patron saint of the capital; a former national holiday.

Semana Santa (Holy Week)* – March or April; moveable; the Thursday and Friday before Easter are both national public holidays when everything stops nationwide.

April

Día de Juan Santamaría* – the 11th; honors the national hero who fought at the Battle of Rivas against William Walker in 1856. Major events (dances, parades, etc) are held in Alajuela, his home town.

May

Labor Day* – the 1st; especially colorful around Puerto Limón, where there are dances and cricket matches.

June

Día de San Pedro & San Pablo (St Peter & St Paul Day) – the 29th; a former national holiday; some religious processions are held in villages of those names.

July

Fiesta de La Virgen del Mar (Fiesta of the Virgin of the Sea) – mid-July; held in Puntarenas and Playa del Coco, with a colorful regatta and boat parade as well as many land-based festivities.

Día de Guanacaste* – the 25th; annexation of Guanacaste Province, formerly part of Nicaragua, is celebrated with a nationwide holiday and many events in Guanacaste towns.

August

Virgen de Los Angeles* – the 2nd; the patron saint of Costa Rica is celebrated with a particularly important religious parade from San José to Cartago.

Día del Madre (Mother's Day)* – the 15th; coincides with the Catholic feast of the Assumption.

September

Independence Day* – the 15th; children march in evening lantern-lit parades.

October

Día de la Raza* – the 12th; the local name for Columbus Day (discovery of the Americas), celebrated especially near Puerto Limón with a carnival-like fiesta.

November

Día de los Muertos (All Souls' Day) – the 2nd; celebrated, as in most of Latin America, with family visits to graveyards and religious parades.

December

Immaculate Conception – the 8th; a former national holiday.

Christmas Day* – the 25th; the 24th is often an (unofficial) holiday as well.

Last week in December – The last week in December (the 25th to the 31st) is a nonstop holiday in San José, with bullfights, equestrian processions and events, and a dance on New Year's Eve.

ACTIVITIES

San José is the cultural center of Costa Rica, with good restaurants, the Teatro Nacional (which puts on theater, dance, symphony, and other musical performances), cinemas, art galleries, museums, and shopping centers. But many of Costa Rica's greatest attractions are found away from the capital.

Costa Rica's conservationist attitude and activities are the most developed in Latin America. The wonderful array of national parks and private preserves and their attendant wildlife and scenery draw travelers from all over the world. Visitors can enjoy an intimate look at habitats and environments ranging from tropical rainforest to highland *páramo*, from beautiful beaches to active volcanoes, and from white-water rivers to mountain ranges. The wildlife and vegetation are magnificent and accessible. No wonder most visitors travel to at least one park or preserve, and that the primary focus of many trips is natural history, especially birding, which is among the best in the world.

Outdoor enthusiasts will find much to their liking. From running some of the best white water in Central America to just relaxing on palm-fringed beaches, from backpacking through the rainforest to horseback riding, from camping on mountaintops to record-breaking deep-sea sportfishing, from snorkeling to world-class surfing, many adventures are possible.

The more sedentary visitor can enjoy leisurely drives through the pretty countryside, perhaps visiting a coffee *finca* (farm) or villages known for handicrafts. Luxurious lunch or dinner cruises on elegant boats in the Golfo de Nicoya on the Pacific coast are also popular activities, as are day trips to peer into the crater of one of Costa Rica's many volcanoes.

See the Getting There & Away and Getting Around chapters for some suggested international and local tour operators that can arrange the following activities.

Wildlife Watching

Scarlet macaws, marine turtles, hummingbirds, sloths, leaf-cutter ants, quetzals, marine toads, monkeys, blue morpho butterflies, tanagers, poison-arrow frogs, crocodiles, toucans, bats, iguanas, parrots – the list of Costa Rican wildlife seems endless, and there are many opportunities to see these animals. An overview of the most important, interesting, and frequently seen species is provided in the Wildlife Guide at the end of this book. Unless you spend your entire time in San José, you cannot fail to see some tropical wildlife in Costa Rica. Many people come specifically to spend their days watching wildlife or birds, and many companies arrange guided natural history tours.

Tours aren't cheap and will be beyond the pocketbooks of shoestring travelers. Here are some tips for budget travelers who want to view as much wildlife as possible (though travelers on an expensive tour should also follow these suggestions). The national parks and preserves are all good places for observation, but private areas such as gardens around rural hotels can also yield a good number of birds, insects, reptiles, and even monkeys. Always be alert for these possibilities. Early morning and late afternoon are the best times to watch for wildlife activity anywhere; the hot and bright middle of the day is when many animals rest. Carry binoculars. An inexpensive lightweight pair brought from home will improve wildlife observation tremendously; they don't have to be the most expensive.

Have realistic expectations. Wildlife is plentiful in the fantastic rainforest environment, but it is *hard* to see because the vegetation is so thick. You could be 15m from a jaguar and not even know it is there. Don't expect to see jaguars, ocelots, tapirs, and many other mammals, which are shy, well camouflaged, and often rare. Concentrate on things that are easier to observe and enjoy them – most of the animals listed at the beginning of this section can be seen fairly easily if you visit different parts of the country. Walk slowly and quietly; listen as well as look.

The single best area for wildlife watching is, in my opinion, the Península de Osa; this is also one of the most difficult areas to get to, which is perhaps why the animals have remained relatively undisturbed. Other excellent places are the national parks, especially Santa Rosa, Tortuguero, and Caño Negro, although all of them are good. Of these, Santa Rosa is the easiest to get to on a tight budget (a bus from San José passes the park entrance; then you can walk in) and Tortuguero the most difficult (you have to take a rather pricey boat ride). But they are all definitely worthwhile.

Fishing

Sportfishing of the 'catch and release' variety (though a small number of fish are kept to eat or mount as trophies) is a tremendously popular activity despite the very high costs involved. People on fishing vacations routinely spend several hundred dollars a day to fish, and the most exclusive all-inclusive fishing packages can cost over US$1000 a day. This doesn't stop 12% of foreign tourists from saying that one of the reasons they are here is to fish. They say it's worth it because the fishing is world-class and several of the fish caught in Costa Rican waters have broken world records. Local anglers say that a bad day of fishing in Costa Rica is often better than a good day of fishing in most other places!

To help protect this resource, local skippers, guides, and anglers adhere to the 'catch and release' philosophy – if they didn't, the excellent fishing would become endangered.

The most popular fishing areas are on the coast, rather than inland. People often stay at coastal fishing lodges and go out to sea on a daily basis in modern boats outfitted with state-of-the-art fishing and navigation equipment. Some people prefer to spend their entire time living aboard a boat, and this option is also available. Further information is given in the chapters on the Caribbean Lowlands, Southern Costa Rica, Central Pacific Coast, Península de Osa, and Península de Nicoya. The best places to look for fishing lodges and boats are in Parismina, Tortuguero, and (especially) Barra del Colorado on the Caribbean side and in the Golfito and Quepos areas and many parts of the Península de Nicoya on the Pacific side, though there certainly are other places.

Note that while most of the fishing lodges described in the book provide tackle, inveterate anglers may prefer to bring their own. Lures and other essentials are sold by the lodges but, because of import duties, are more expensive than at home. Lures are not included in the packages. The lodges will be happy to advise you about all aspects of fishing equipment if you make a reservation with them.

Inland, trout fishing in rivers and lake fishing are also popular, though not as much as the coastal fishing. Particularly recommended are the Río Savegre near San Gerardo de Dota for trout fishing and Laguna de Arenal for *guapote* or rainbow bass, although you can fish almost anywhere you have a mind to.

You can fish almost any time. Laguna de Arenal has a closed season from October to December and certain rivers may have closed seasons sometimes – check with local operators. The ocean is always open and, if you are prepared to fish on either coast and accept what species are biting, there is fishing year-round. Some books and brochures provide month-by-month breakdowns of what fish to catch where. Having looked at several of these, all I can say is that anglers love to tell stories – and each one is different! Certainly, fishing varies from season to season. As a general rule, the Pacific coast is slowest from September to November, though you'll get better fishing if you are on the south coast in those months, and the Caribbean can be fished year-round, though June and July are the slowest months.

The fish that are most sought after by anglers are tarpon and snook on the Caribbean side and sailfish and black marlin on the Pacific side.

Fishing licenses are required, but are cheap and included in outfitters' packages and tours. *Costa Rica Outdoors* (see Newspapers & Magazines, earlier in this chapter) has news about fishing in Costa Rica.

Surfing

Point and beach breaks, lefts and rights, reefs and river mouths, warm water and waves year-round make Costa Rica a favorite surfers' destination. Some beaches may be hard to get to but are totally uncrowded (sometimes you'll be the only one surfing there all day), and even the easily accessible ones tend to be much less crowded than the beaches of Hawaii, southern California, or Sydney.

The waves are often quite big, though not as huge as the almost mythical ones in Hawaii. But they make up for this in length, with fast kilometer-long waves at Pavones on the south Pacific coast giving rides of two or three minutes. It's an athletic challenge to stay upright on such a long wave.

Dedicated surfers bring their own boards from home. Most airlines accept a surfboard (properly packed in a padded bag designed for surfboards) as one of the two pieces of checked luggage. However, once in Costa Rica, the two domestic airlines either don't allow them or charge extra for them, and many surfers prefer to rent a jeep to give themselves mobility. At the end of your trip, you can easily sell the board in Costa Rica.

A few places rent equipment. These are mainly in the popular coastal towns and villages such as Jacó, Quepos, Tamarindo, and Puerto Viejo de Talamanca. In the San José area, there is the Mango Surf Shop (☎ 225-1067) near the Banco Popular in the San Pedro suburb, with branches at the San Pedro Mall (☎ 283-7697) and in Alajuela, Avenida 4, Calles 4 & 6 (☎ 442-5862), or Shaka Bra Surf Shop (☎ 250-3741) in La Pacífica suburb.

There are dozens of surfing areas, and some of the best are shown on the accompanying surfing map. Further details are given in

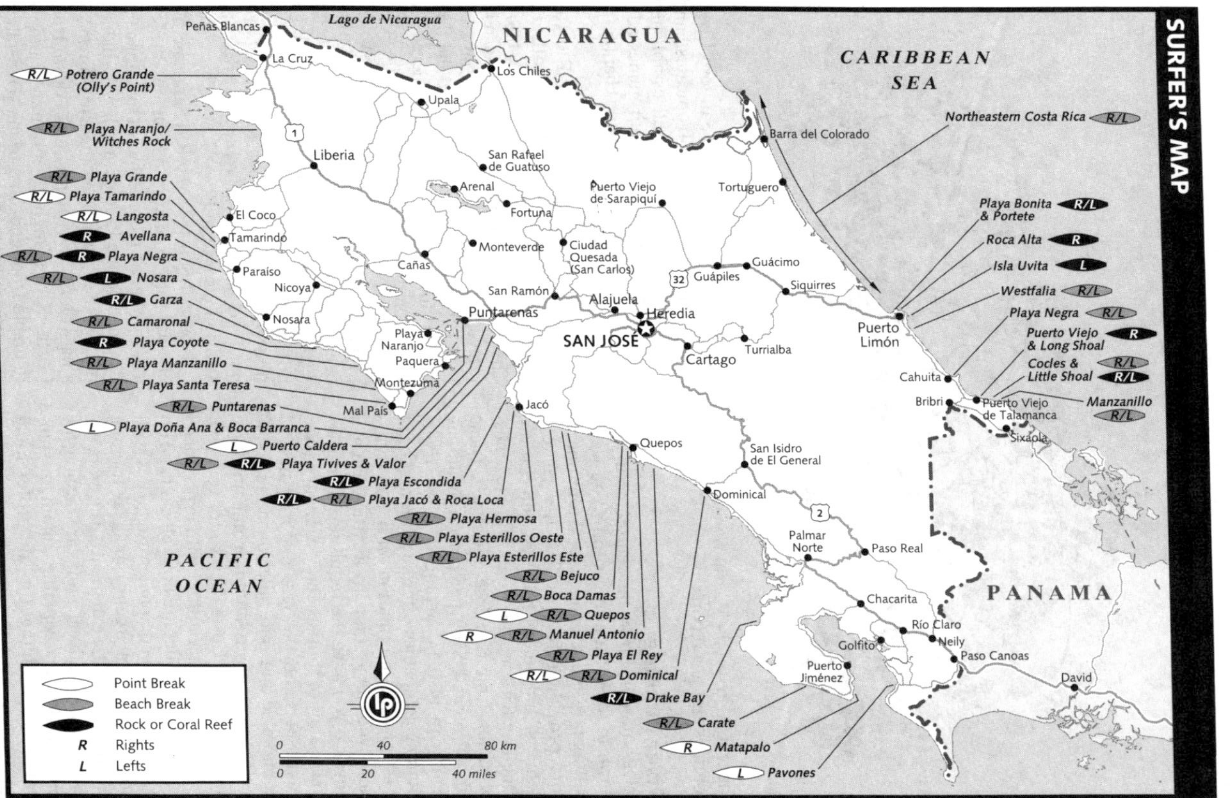
SURFER'S MAP
Lago de Nicaragua
NICARAGUA
CARIBBEAN SEA
PACIFIC OCEAN
PANAMA
R/L Potrero Grande (Olly's Point)
R/L Playa Naranjo/ Witches Rock
R/L Playa Grande
R/L Playa Tamarindo
R/L Langosta
R Avellana
R/L R Playa Negra
R/L L Nosara
R/L Garza
R/L Camaronal
R Playa Coyote
R/L Playa Manzanillo
R/L Playa Santa Teresa
R/L Puntarenas
L Playa Doña Ana & Boca Barranca
L Puerto Caldera
R/L R/L Playa Tivives & Valor
R/L Playa Escondida
R/L R/L Playa Jacó & Roca Loca
R/L Playa Hermosa
R/L Playa Esterillos Oeste
R/L Playa Esterillos Este
R/L Bejuco
R/L Boca Damas
L R/L Quepos
R R/L Manuel Antonio
R/L Playa El Rey
R/L R/L Dominical
R/L Drake Bay
R/L Carate
R Matapalo
L Pavones
Northeastern Costa Rica R/L
Playa Bonita & Portete R/L
Roca Alta R
Isla Uvita L
Westfalia R/L
Playa Negra R/L
Puerto Viejo & Long Shoal R
Cocles & Little Shoal R/L R/L
Manzanillo R/L
Peñas Blancas
La Cruz
Los Chiles
Upala
Liberia
San Rafael de Guatuso
Arenal
Fortuna
Puerto Viejo de Sarapiquí
Tortuguero
Barra del Colorado
El Coco
Tamarindo
Paraíso
Nicoya
Nosara
Cañas
Monteverde
Ciudad Quesada (San Carlos)
Guápiles
Guácimo
Siquirres
San Ramón
Alajuela
Heredia
Puntarenas
SAN JOSÉ
Cartago
Turrialba
Puerto Limón
Playa Naranjo
Paquera
Montezuma
Mal País
Jacó
Quepos
San Isidro de El General
Dominical
Cahuita
Bribri
Puerto Viejo de Talamanca
Sixaola
Palmar Norte
Paso Real
Chacarita
Río Claro
Neily
Golfito
Paso Canoas
Puerto Jiménez
David
1
32
2
Point Break
Beach Break
Rock or Coral Reef
R Rights
L Lefts
0 40 80 km
0 20 40 miles

the text. Also surf the Web at www.crsurf.com for tides and surf reports.

River Running

Rivers tumbling from the central mountains down to the coast afford good white-water rafting possibilities, and several tour operators provide rafts, paddles, life jackets, helmets, and guides for these adventures. One-day trips include roundtrip bus transportation from San José and lunch. These start around US$69 per person. Multiday trips can also be arranged. Most river-running companies offer kayak rental or at least provide information on it, and sometimes you can accompany a rafting trip in a kayak if you have the requisite experience. Thousands of tourists enjoy running a river each year, and the vast majority have a memorable and enjoyable adventure.

However, river-running companies are not regulated in Costa Rica, so, for your own safety, go with an outfitter with experienced guides. Most guides are not well paid and do it for fun. Some companies use guides with no rescue or emergency medical training and relatively little experience. The more experienced and ethical guides are pushing for internationally acceptable minimum standards and training for all professional guides, but this had yet to happen at this writing. Of the companies in San José, Costa Rica Expeditions, Ríos Tropicales, and Aventuras Naturales are well established and do the most to train their guides adequately (see the Getting Around chapter for contact information).

The best-known rivers are the Río Reventazón and the Río Pacuare, both described in more detail later in this book. These rivers on the Caribbean slopes can be run year-round and have rapids of Classes II to V, depending on the section and the time of year. June to October are considered the wildest and wettest months, but you'll get wet whatever time of year you go. Runs are available for all levels of experience. Rafters need to put on plenty of sunblock and bring a spare change of clothes. Going barefoot is not recommended because the rubber-floored boats sometimes hit rocks fairly hard, so sneakers or river sandals (like Tevas) are suggested.

North of San José, the Río Sarapiquí has one-day runs from May to November. This is a narrower and more technical river than the Reventazón and Pacuare, and less frequently run. On the Pacific slope, the Río Chirripó is a big-volume river that tumbles down from Costa Rica's highest mountain and is runnable from mid-June to mid-December. Trips here usually last three or four days.

The gentlest river is the Río Corobicí, near Cañas, which is basically a float trip, but with good chances of spotting many birds and, often, monkeys. This is a good trip for the whole family and can be done year-round.

Details on these river-running trips are given in the regional chapters of this book.

Scuba Diving & Snorkeling

This is a good news and bad news story. The good news is that there are huge numbers of large fish and other animals (eels, turtles, starfish, etc) to see. The bad news is that the visibility is poor to adequate, but never excellent. The good news is that the water is warm, and the diving is uncrowded. The bad news is...yeah, that mediocre visibility. If the water was crystalline, this would be world-class diving. Still, there are decent places to dive and enjoy the diversity of marine life, despite the visibility. As a general rule, the worst visibility is during the rainy months, when rivers swell and their outflow clouds the ocean. The solution is to go on a boat trip to offshore islands or undersea walls and get away from the rivers.

Some of the best areas for diving are off the northern part of the Península de Nicoya; at Playa del Coco, Playa Ocotal, and Playa Hermosa, dive shops provide gear, boats, and guides and can also teach and certify you if you're a beginner. The diving here is offshore, and inshore snorkeling is not too good. Better snorkeling is found near the popular beach areas at Montezuma and Manuel Antonio. Farther south along the Pacific coast, Isla del Caño has good diving and snorkeling and can be reached from the lodges on Bahía Drake (Drake Bay).

On the Caribbean side, the best diving and snorkeling is over the coral reefs near Cahuita, but these are quite close to the shore and have suffered from silting from the rivers (see the 'Coral Reefs' boxed text in the Caribbean Lowlands chapter). Here, because the reef is close to shore, you definitely have better visibility in the dry months.

The best diving by far is off Isla del Coco – but this island is about 500km southwest of the Costa Rican mainland. Diving tours do go there, but they are expensive and have to be planned ahead. (See Organized Tours in the Getting There & Away chapter.) The diving is excellent but challenging – not recommended for novices. (Also see the boxed text 'Parque Nacional Isla del Coco' in the Península de Osa & Golfo Dulce chapter.)

Hiking & Backpacking

There are many opportunities for short hikes of a few hours in most of the national parks and other reserves. There are always short nature trails where wildlife watching is more the point than hiking. Assaults and robberies have been reported in some national parks, in particular Carara and Braulio Carrillo, so if you plan on visiting these areas, go with a group or a guided tour and seek local information. Other parks don't seem to have this bad reputation. However short your hike, always remember to carry plenty of water (bring extra in case you get lost), insect repellent, and sun protection when hiking in the tropics.

For longer distance and overnight hiking, there are several good choices. If you've always wanted to try backpacking in the rainforest, then Parque Nacional Corcovado

Swimming, Swimming & Swimming...

Costa Rican swimmer Claudia Poll won a gold medal at the 1996 Atlanta Olympics in the women's 200m freestyle event. This was the first ever Olympic gold for the country. Poll continues to dominate the world swimming circuit with gold medals in many major meets and is considered the best female swimmer in the world.

– Rob Rachowiecki

offers some adventurous opportunities. If you prefer to get away from the heat and humidity, try a climb of Chirripó, Costa Rica's highest peak, located in the national park of the same name. Other good hiking trips include a visit to Parque Nacional Santa Rosa, where you hike through tropical dry forest down to the beach and camp. The hike from the Arenal area to Monteverde, which can be done in one long day, has recently become popular. More details are given in the text for the appropriate places. See the Dangers & Annoyances section, earlier, for advice on hiking safety.

Mountain Biking

Some cyclists claim that the steep, narrow, winding, and potholed roads and aggressive Costa Rican drivers add up to a generally poor cycling experience. This may be true of the main roads, but there are numerous less-trafficked roads that offer good adventures. Local outfitters and tour companies from the USA arrange guided bike trips, which lets you avoid the hassle of finding the best roads. Because of the poor condition of the roads, mountain bikes are a better option than road bikes.

Most airlines will fly your bike as one of your pieces of checked baggage if you box it. However, boxing the bike gives baggage handlers little clue to the contents and the box is liable to be roughly handled, possibly damaging the bike. An alternative is wrapping it in heavy-duty plastic or bubble wrap – baggage handlers are less likely to drop or throw the bike in this case. Airlines' bicycle-carrying policies do vary a lot, so shop around. It is also possible to cycle down from the USA through Central America, and a handful of people do that every year.

There are several tour operators and bicycle outfitters who can rent you a bike and give you a map or provide you with a complete tour package with bike, guide, and support vehicle. These packages cost about US$50 to US$75 a day. Unless you are really dedicated and insist on your own bike, there is no reason to bring your own, as you can rent a decent mountain bike with helmet and water bottle for about US$15 to US$30 a day.

Windsurfing

Laguna de Arenal, Costa Rica's largest lake, is the nation's undisputed windsurfing center and, from December to March, is considered one of the three best windsurfing spots in the world. Winds are often strong and steady, especially at the western end during the dry season. The lake has a year-round water temperature of 18°C to 21°C with 1m-high swells and winds averaging 20 knots in the dry season, a little less in the wet. May and June and September and October are the least windy months; December to February are the most windy. Maximum winds often go over 30 knots, and windless days are a rarity. These consistently high winds attract experienced windsurfers – beginners will require expert instruction.

Complete windsurfing equipment is available for rent in several hotels at the west end of the lake. Of these, the Hotel Tilawa has the best selection and location, is open year-round, and has top-notch instructors (see the Northwestern Costa Rica chapter for details).

Puerto Soley, on the far northern Pacific coast, is also developing windsurfing schools and resorts.

Horseback Riding

Riding horses has been part of rural Costa Rican life for as long as anyone can remember. Wherever you go, you are sure to find someone renting a horse. Most of the resort and tourist areas have horses available for rides along the beaches or up into the mountains. Guides are available to lead you to scenic waterfalls and views. Rates vary from about US$40 to US$100 a day, and shorter (two hours) or overnight trips can also be arranged.

Some areas have become very popular for horse treks, and the increased demand for rides has led to unscrupulous 'outfitters' cashing in on the popularity by providing undernourished and overworked horses for rides. The worst area at this time seems to be the popular Arenal to Monteverde (or vice versa) ride, where a number of outfitters cut costs by overworking their horses. Numerous readers have written to say that they have witnessed guides beating horses, emaciated animals with sores, and even horses dying on this trail, which is steep, often muddy, and difficult for horses. Taking the cheapest tour is not in the best interest of the horses. Riders weighing over 100kg cannot expect the small local horses to carry them very far. (See the 'To Ride or Not to Ride?' boxed text near the end of the Northwestern Costa Rica chapter.)

Horseback riding is a pleasure if it's done right. It's certainly part of the tico culture. I welcome further feedback from readers about caring (or otherwise) outfitters.

Rainforest Canopy Tours

Until recently, most visitors to the rainforest had to make do with either walking through it or traveling by boat. You could see what was around you, but seeing the top of the canopy was not easy. Over the past decade, several ways of exploring the rainforest canopy have been devised.

At the most simple level are tree platforms, where you are winched up on a rope and scramble out onto a platform some 20m or more above the ground. Sitting in a platform, you wait, hoping that a flock of birds or troop of monkeys will come close – which, often, they do. Good places for sitting on a platform are at Hacienda Barú (see the Central Pacific Coast chapter) and Corcovado Lodge Tent Camp (see the Península de Osa & Golfo Dulce chapter).

Another system consists of a series of platforms joined by cables. You climb or are winched up to the first platform, then slide (in a sling) along the cable to the next platform. This rather adventurous activity is offered in several places by Canopy Tour (see contact information under Organized Tours in the Getting Around chapter). These tours are exciting but don't offer many opportunities for observing wildlife.

The most technologically advanced is the Rainforest Aerial Tram (see the Central Valley chapter). This is like a ski lift stretching for almost 2km through various levels of the canopy just east of Parque Nacional Braulio Carrillo. Passengers ride in open gondolas carrying five visitors plus a guide. This is the easiest way of seeing the canopy.

Safety is the most important concern in these operations. The ones mentioned here have properly trained staff and use high-quality equipment. There are numerous spin-off rainforest canopy tours, not all of which maintain the most rigorous safety conditions.

Sea Kayaking

This is still a small but growing activity in Costa Rica. Sea kayaks range from inflatable toys to slim, elegant craft with foot rudders that can be paddled by one or two people and used on overnight kayaking/beach-camping trips. It's easy enough to learn at least the basics of getting around, so this could be a good activity for beginners as well as experienced people. Kayakers at Bahía Drake told me of expeditions up jungle rivers where they were able to glide noiselessly up to wildlife (in one case, a tapir) without disturbing the animals. Combining ease of learning with an enhanced chance of spotting wildlife, a coastal kayaking trip is a great experience – no wonder sea kayaking is such a growing sport. Many places along the coast rent sea kayaks.

Hot-Air Ballooning

This is a fledgling activity in Costa Rica. Contact Serendipity Adventures for more information (see Organized Tours in the Getting There & Away chapter).

Bungee Jumping

Yes, finally in Costa Rica...you can safely make a head-first, screaming plunge off a bridge to which you are safely attached with a 60m elastic rope. After safely bouncing around for a while, you are hauled back up to the bridge. Highly trained jump masters guarantee your safety. I prefer playing chess.

For further information, contact Tropical Bungee (☎ 232-3956). They do jumps off the Río Colorado bridge near the Grecia turnoff from the Interamericana. The first jump costs US$45, and you can do it again for US$25. If you just want to watch the jumpers from the safety of solid ground (or bridge), contact them anyway. They'll provide transportation for spectators as well as jumpers.

LANGUAGE COURSES

Spanish language courses are offered mainly in San José, but also in Alajuela, Manuel Antonio, and a few other places. These are popular ways for travelers to visit the country, learn the language, and become aware of tico lifestyle and culture. Language schools are listed under San José and other appropriate parts of the text.

WORK

It is difficult, but not impossible, to find work in Costa Rica. The most likely source of paid employment is as an English teacher in language institutes in San José, which advertise courses in the local newspapers. Word of mouth from other travelers is another way of finding out about this kind of work.

Writers can occasionally sell work to the English-language weekly, *The Tico Times*. Naturalists or river guides may be able to find work with the private lodges or adventure travel operators. Don't expect to make more than survival wages from these jobs, and don't arrive in Costa Rica expecting to get a job easily and immediately. Getting a bona fide job requires a work permit, which is a bureaucratic, time-consuming, and difficult process.

Volunteer Work

Volunteer work in nature preserves or national parks is sometimes possible. Volunteers usually provide their own transport to Costa Rica and pay about US$10 per day for living expenses. Volunteers live with park rangers in ranger stations and help with a variety of jobs ranging from providing visitor information to constructing trails or buildings to office work or surveys.

Some volunteers are needed in the San José headquarters as well as in remote areas – efforts are made to match volunteers' interests and skills with the projects available. A minimum commitment of 60 days is requested, and volunteers work six days a week. Several hundred volunteers are used each year; almost half of them are foreign and the rest are Costa Rican.

If you are interested in working in the national parks, contact the Asociación Voluntarias de Parques Nacionales (☎/fax 233-4989, asvo89@sol.racsa.co.cr) in San José for more information and an application. Many people apply, but few actually end up volunteering. Some travelers report that you can just show up at the park of your choice and ask to volunteer.

A few private lodges and organizations need English-speaking volunteers – see COTERC, Pacuare Nature Reserve, Caribbean Conservation Corporation, and ANAI in the Caribbean Lowlands chapter; Genesis II in Southern Costa Rica; the Reserva Biológica Bosque Nuboso Monteverde in Northwestern Costa Rica; and others mentioned in the text.

ACCOMMODATIONS

Youth Hostels & Camping

There is a small Hostelling International youth hostel system, and the charge for a night in a hostel varies from about US$8 to US$40, depending on the hostel. The more expensive hostels are usually good hotels or lodges giving a discount to youth hostel members. The San José hostel is the headquarters for the network of Costa Rican youth hostels, and information and reservations for the others can be made there. Budget travelers will find cheaper rooms in basic hotels.

There are rarely campsites in the towns; the constant availability of cheap hotels makes town campsites unnecessary.

Cheap camping facilities are available in many of the national parks. The handful of campgrounds suitable for caravans or for motorhomes are mentioned in the text.

B&Bs

Almost unknown in Costa Rica in the 1980s, the B&B phenomenon has swept San José and has begun to expand over the country in the last decade. B&B places vary from mid-range to top end in prices, and have been generally well received and recommended by travelers.

Hotels

There is great variety and no shortage of places to stay in Costa Rica. It is rare to arrive in a town and be unable to find somewhere to sleep, but during Easter week or weekends in the dry season, the beach hotels can be full. Indeed, most beach hotels are booked several weeks in advance for Easter week. Hotel accommodations can also be tight if a special event is going on in a particular town. Private lodges and expensive hotels in remote areas should always be reserved in advance if you want specific dates. However, the cheapest hotels are more likely to have a room available at any time. In the low season, you can often find rooms in most hotels on the day you arrive. Note that reservations made abroad will always be at the highest rates, and discounts can be obtained in-country.

Some travelers prefer to make advance reservations everywhere – this is possible even in the cheapest hotels and recommended in the better places. Faxes and emails are being used increasingly to make reservations as they are cheaper than phone calls and solve the problem of language difficulties – they can be translated readily enough. Mail is slow. Note that most hotels will give rainy season discounts (from about late April to mid-December). If you are already in Costa Rica, a telephone call a day or two ahead will often yield a reservation.

Sometimes it's a little difficult to find single rooms, and you may get a room with two beds. In most cases, though, you will be charged the single rate. The single rate is rarely half of the double rate, except in a few of the cheapest hotels. In a few hotels, single and double rates are the same. If you are economizing, travel with someone and share a room.

Before accepting a room, look around the hotel if possible. The same prices are often charged for rooms of widely differing quality. Even in the US$4-a-night cheapies, it's worth looking around. If you get shown into a horrible airless box with just a bed and a bare lightbulb, you can ask to see a better room without giving offense. You'll often be amazed at the results. At the other end of the scale, hotels may want to rent you their most expensive suites – ask if they have more economical rooms if you don't want the suite.

Hotel Categories Budget hotels are certainly the cheapest, but not necessarily the worst. Although they are sometimes very basic, with just a bed and four walls, they can nevertheless be well looked after, very clean, and amazing value for the money. They are often good places to meet other budget travelers, both Costa Rican and foreign.

Prices in the budget section begin at about US$3 per person and go up to US$20 for a double room. Almost every town (except exclusive tourist resorts) has hotels in this price range. Although you'll usually have to use communal bathrooms in the cheapest hotels, you can sometimes find rooms with a private bathroom for as low as US$10 a double.

Hotels in the mid-range category usually charge from about US$30 to US$80 for a double room, but the cheaper ones are not always better than the best hotels in the budget price range. On the whole, you can find some very decent hotels here. Even if you're traveling on a budget, there may be occasions when you feel like indulging in comparative luxury for a day or two.

'Top-end' hotels charge over US$100 a double and can ask over twice that in San José, the beach resorts, and some of the upscale lodges. The prices and services compare favorably with international standards in the best places.

Apartotels are like a cross between an apartment and a hotel and can be rented for extended stays. They are mostly found in San José, and occasionally elsewhere. See the San José chapter for a detailed description.

Hotel Tax A 16.39% tax is currently added to hotel prices. The hotel tax situation changes from government to government and year to year, but expect to pay a tax percentage somewhere in the teens. Some hotels give prices including tax, others give prices without tax, so always clarify this point when asking about room rates. I have tried to give full prices, including taxes, for the 2000 high season. Some hotel prices have risen dramatically with the tourism boom of the past few years, and you should not be surprised by further increases. However, some hotels may lower prices to attract guests.

Bathrooms Bathroom facilities in the cheaper hotels are rarely what you may be used to at home. The cheapest hotels don't always have hot water. Even if they do, it might not work or it may be turned on only at certain hours of the day.

An intriguing device to know about is the electric shower: a cold-water showerhead hooked up to an electric heating element that is switched on when you want a hot (more likely tepid) shower. Don't touch anything metal while you're in the shower or you may discover what a (mild) electric shock feels like. The power is never high enough to actually throw you across the room, but it's unpleasant nevertheless – kind of like holding a 9-volt battery across your tongue, if you're really interested! Electric showers vary from just taking the chill off the water to warm; they are rarely hot, and they sometimes simply don't work at all and you have to be content with a cold shower. They work best when heating a small amount of water, so if you turn the water on all the way, you'll get a fairly cold flow, but if you turn it on just enough to be able to wash with, the water will be warmer. These showers are found in some budget hotels; more expensive hotels rarely use them.

Flushing a toilet in the cheaper hotels creates another hazard – overflow. See the Toilets section for details on that problem.

Security Although hotels give you room keys, carrying your own padlock is a good idea if you plan on staying in the most basic hotels.

Once in a while, you'll find that a room doesn't look very secure – perhaps there's a window that doesn't close or the wall doesn't come to the ceiling and can be climbed over. It's worth finding another room. This is another reason why it's good to look at a room before you rent it.

You should never leave valuables lying around the room; it's just too tempting for someone who makes less than US$1 an hour for their work. Money and passport should be in a secure body pouch; other valuables can usually be kept in the hotel strongbox, although some cheaper hotels might not want to take this responsibility. In this case, keep your valuables locked in your bag and not in plain sight. Beware of local 'fishermen' – people who poke sticks with hooks on them through openable windows to fish out whatever they can get. If you do use a hotel strongbox, insist on a signed receipt; occasional pilfering is reported.

Homestays

The option of staying with a family is another relatively recent phenomenon in Costa Rica, mainly in San José. See the San José chapter for details.

FOOD

If you're on a tight budget, food is the most important part of your expenses. You can stay in rock-bottom hotels, travel by bus, and never consider buying a souvenir, but you've got to eat well. This doesn't mean expensively, but it does mean that you want to avoid spending half your trip sitting on the toilet.

The worst culprits for making you sick are salads and unpeeled fruit. With the fruit, stick to bananas, oranges, pineapples, and other fruit that you can peel yourself. With unpeeled fruit or salad vegetables, wash them yourself in water that you can trust (see the Health section). It can be a lot of fun getting a group together, heading out to the market to buy salad vegetables, and preparing a huge salad.

As long as you take heed of the salad warning, you'll find plenty of good things to eat at reasonable prices. You certainly don't have to eat at a fancy restaurant – their kitchen facilities may not be as clean as their white tablecloths. A good sign for any restaurant is that the locals eat there – restaurants aren't empty if the food is delicious and healthy.

If you're on a tight budget, eat the set meal offered in most restaurants at lunchtime – it's usually filling and cheap. Also try the cheap luncheon counters called sodas. The sodas in the central markets of most towns are locally popular and usually very cheap. Eat at one that is frequented by ticos and you'll probably find that the food is good and clean. There are reasonably priced Chinese and Italian restaurants in most towns.

Whatever your budget, I have given a good range of restaurants at all price levels throughout this book. Remember that a combined 25% in taxes and services is added to restaurant bills in all but the cheapest sodas. Further tipping is not necessary unless you want to. Where I give an idea of prices for the restaurant meals in this book, I include the tax for a main course. Drinks and desserts, for example, cost extra.

What to Order

Most restaurants serve *bistek* (beef), *pollo* (chicken), and *pescado* (fish) dishes. Vegetarians should note that *carne* literally means meat, but in Costa Rica it tends to refer to beef. Chicken, *puerco* (pork), and *chivo* (goat) aren't necessarily included, so be specific if you want something without any meat. Many visitors from North America, used to spicy Mexican food capable of burning out taste buds, mistakenly assume that Costa Rican food is very spicy too. Generally, it's tasty rather than spicy-hot.

Of course, internationally popular food is available: pizzas, spaghetti, hamburgers, sandwiches, Chinese rice dishes, steaks, etc. However, Costa Rican specialties include the following:

gallo pinto – literally 'spotted rooster,' a mixture of rice and black beans that is traditionally served for breakfast, sometimes with *natilla* (something like a cross between sour cream and custard) or *huevos fritos/revueltos* (fried/scrambled eggs). This dish is lightly seasoned with herbs and is filling and tasty.

tortillas – either Mexican-style corn pancakes or omelets, depending on what kind of meal you're having.

casado – a set meal that is often filling and always economical. It normally contains *arroz* (rice), *frijoles* (black beans), *platano* (fried plantain), beef, chopped *repollo* (cabbage), and maybe an egg or an avocado.

olla de carne – a soup containing beef and vegetables such as potatoes, corn, squash, a local tuber called *yuca*, and plantains.

palmitos – hearts of palm, usually served in a salad with vinegar dressing; *pejibaye* is a rather starchy-tasting palm fruit also eaten as a salad.

arroz con pollo – a basic dish of rice and chicken.

elote – corn on the cob served boiled *(elote cocinado)* or roasted *(elote asado)*.

Desserts *(postres)* include the following:

mazamorra – a pudding made from cornstarch.

queque seco – simply a pound cake.

dulce de leche – milk and sugar boiled to make a thick syrup that may be used in a layered cake called *torta chilena*.

cajeta – similar to dulce de leche, but thicker still, like a fudge.

flan – a cold caramel custard.

These snacks are often obtained in sodas:

arreglados – little puff pastries stuffed with beef, chicken, or cheese; this term might also be used for sandwiches.

enchiladas – heavier pastries stuffed with potatoes and cheese and maybe meat.

empanadas – Chilean-style turnovers stuffed with meat or cheese and raisins.

pupusas – El Salvadoran-style fried corn and cheese cakes.

gallos – tortilla sandwiches containing meat, beans, or cheese.

ceviche – seafood marinated with lemon, onion, garlic, sweet red peppers, and coriander. Also made with *corvina* (a white sea bass), or occasionally with *langostinos* (shrimps) or *conchas* (shellfish).

patacones – a coastal specialty, especially on the Caribbean side, consisting of slices of plantain deep-fried like French-fried potatoes – delicious.

tamales – boiled cornmeal pasties, usually wrapped in a banana leaf (you don't eat the leaf). At Christmas they traditionally come stuffed with chicken or pork; at other times of year they may come stuffed with corn and wrapped in a corn leaf. *Tamales asado* are sweet cornmeal cakes.

Many bars serve *bocas*, also known as *boquitas*. These are little savory side dishes such as black beans, ceviche, chicken stew, potato chips, and sausages, and are designed to make your drink more pleasurable – maybe you'll have another one! If you have several rounds, you could eat enough bocas to make a very light meal. Many of the cheaper bars have free bocas, some charge a small amount extra for them, and some don't have them at all.

Occasionally, a boca might be a turtle egg. These used to be common, but now that marine turtles are endangered, their eggs are less frequently offered as bar bocas. Although, technically, it is still possible to harvest marine turtle eggs legally, poaching goes on as well. It is very difficult to establish whether turtle eggs have been taken legally, and a large number have not. Until turtles recover, I urge travelers to refrain from eating turtle eggs.

DRINKS

Nonalcoholic Drinks

Coffee is traditionally served very strong and mixed with hot milk to taste, but increasingly fewer establishments serve it this way. As far as I am concerned, this is just as well, because the hot milk tends to form a skin, which I find quite unappetizing. I much prefer it strong, tasty, and black. Tea (including herb tea) is also available. Milk is pasteurized and safe to drink.

The usual brands of soft drinks are available, although many people prefer *refrescos* – fruit drinks made either *con agua* (with water) or *con leche* (with milk). Possible fruit drinks to sample are mango, papaya, *piña* (pineapple), *sandía* (watermelon), *melón* (cantaloupe), *mora* (blackberry), *zanahoria* (carrot), *cebada* (barley), or *tamarindo* (a slightly tart but refreshing drink made from the fruit of the tamarind tree). Be careful where you buy these to avoid getting sick.

Pipas are green coconuts that have a hole macheted into the top of them and a straw stuck in so you can drink the coconut 'milk' – a slightly bitter but refreshing and filling drink.

Agua dulce is simply boiled water mixed with brown sugar, and *horchata* is a cornmeal drink flavored with cinnamon.

Alcoholic Drinks

Costa Ricans like to drink, but they don't like drunks. Most restaurants serve a good variety of alcoholic drinks. Imported drinks are expensive; local ones are quite cheap.

There are some half-dozen brands of local beer. Pilsen and Imperial are both good, popular beers; I prefer Imperial. (It's also the largest-selling beer in the country and its nickname is *una águila* for the black eagle on the label.) Tropical is a low-calorie 'lite' beer, not available everywhere. Bavaria has a gold foil around the cap and is a little more expensive and supposedly more full-bodied than the first two, though I can't say it's much better. Also, a local version of Heineken is made, which costs about the same as Bavaria. Most of these are 4% or 4.5% alcohol. Rock Ice, with a 4.7% alcohol content, has a slightly more bitter taste. Other beers are imported and expensive.

Local beers cost about US60¢ in the very cheapest bars; they cost about US$1.25 in average bars and restaurants, and almost US$3 in some of the fancy tourist lodges, restaurants, hotels, and resorts.

Costa Rican wines are cheap, taste cheap, and provide a memorable hangover. Good imported wines are available but expensive. Chilean brands are your best bet for a palatable wine at an affordable price.

Sugarcane is grown in Costa Rica, so liquor made from this is cheap. The cheapest is *guaro*, which is the local firewater, drunk by the shot. Also inexpensive and good is local rum, usually drunk as a *cuba libre* (rum and cola). A 750ml bottle of local Gold Ron Rico is only US$5.

Local vodka and gin aren't bad, but whisky is not as good. Expensive imported liquors are available, as are imported liqueurs. One locally made liqueur is Café Rica, which, predictably, is based on coffee and tastes like the better-known Mexican Kahlua.

Drinkers Beware

No alcohol can be served or sold on election days and from the Thursday to Saturday before Easter. This applies to stores, bars, and restaurants, so plan ahead.

– Rob Rachowiecki

ENTERTAINMENT

San José has the best selection of entertainment, though it is modest compared to many other capital cities. Traditionally, family get-togethers are what ticos do to entertain themselves. There are plenty of cinemas, theaters, and nightclubs in San José (see details in that chapter), but relatively few elsewhere. Certainly, I would not recommend Costa Rica as a destination for travelers looking for entertainment of the nightlife variety.

SPECTATOR SPORTS

Soccer *(fútbol)* is by far the most important spectator sport. It is almost a national passion, especially for men (although girls and women do play and show some interest). Costa Rica's most memorable soccer appearance was at the 1990 Men's World Cup in Italy, when the national team made the quarterfinals. This was the only year in which Costa Rica qualified to play in the World Cup.

The regular season is from August to May, and the games are played at 11 am on Sunday mornings, and sometimes on Wednesday evenings. Competition is fierce and fan rivalry does not support the notion that ticos are friendly. They can get really wild during games!

There are 12 teams in the First Division. At the end of each season, the 12th team is relegated to the Second Division while the top team in the Second Division is promoted to the First Division. In addition, the 11th team in the First Division has to play against the runner-up in the Second Division to determine which of these plays in the First Division the next season. The top teams in the regular season then play another championship in June or July, so there are matches almost year-round.

At the end of the 1998-99 season, the champions were Saprissa, the main San José team, followed by La Liga, the team from Alajuela. These two teams have finished at the top of the league for most of the past years. You can watch Saprissa play at home in the suburb of Tibas (any cab driver knows it). Tickets cost about US$2 to US$10 and are usually available on the day of the game. The more expensive tickets give you seats in the shade *(sombra)* with a more sedate crowd; the cheapest tickets are in direct sun *(sol)* with a wilder crowd of fans.

Other popular spectator sports (though not even close rivals to soccer) are basketball and bullfighting. In Costa Rica, the bull is not killed, so international matadors don't bother to come here. Local bullfights are held at various times of year; in San José the main season is from Christmas to just after New Year's Day.

SHOPPING

Coffee

Coffee is excellent; many visitors bring a bag of freshly roasted coffee beans back home. Gift stores sell expensive, elegantly wrapped packages of coffee beans for export, but you can also shop ordinary grocery stores. The national coffee liqueur, Café Rica, is also a popular buy.

Handicrafts

The things to buy are wood and leather items, which are well made and inexpensive. Wood items include salad bowls, plates, carving boards and other useful kitchen utensils, jewelry boxes, and a variety of carvings and ornaments. Furniture is also made but is hard to bring home, and having it shipped is expensive. Leatherwork includes the usual wallets and purses, handbags, and briefcases, and is usually cheaper than at home.

Interesting wood/leather combinations are the rocking chairs seen in many tourist lodges and better hotels in the country. Because of their leather seats and backs, they can be folded for transport and are usually packed two to a carton. If you're not bringing too much else back, you could check a pair of them in your airline baggage.

There are plenty of excellent souvenir shops in San José. Many people, however, opt to visit a village such as Sarchí where many souvenirs are made, especially woodwork, and where you can watch artisans at work. Although it is undeniably touristy, Sarchí is the center for making the colorfully painted replicas of the ox carts *(carretas)* that were traditionally used for hauling produce and people in the countryside – and still are in some remote regions. These ox carts are, as much as anything else, a typical souvenir peculiar to Costa Rica. They come in all sizes, from table-top models to nearly life-size replicas that double as drink cabinets. They all fold down for transport.

Ceramics and jewelry are also popular souvenirs. Some ceramics are replicas of pre-Columbian artifacts. Colorful posters and T-shirts with wildlife, national park, and ecological themes are also very popular, attractive, and reasonably priced. Some of the profits from these go to conservation organizations in Costa Rica. Indian handicrafts from Guatemala and Panama are also available.

Getting There & Away

Costa Rica is reached by air, land, and sea. However, few people use the ocean route (unless stopping briefly on a cruise) because it is less convenient and usually more expensive than flying.

AIR

Airports & Airlines

Juan Santamaría international airport, 17km outside San José, is where almost all international flights to Costa Rica arrive. The airport in Liberia, 217km northwest of San José on the Carretera Interamericana (Interamerican Hwy), is the backup international airport but is little used. The facilities at the Liberia airport have been improved, and since 1996, this airport has seen a few direct flights from Miami and Canada, which cater to travelers wanting to go to the Península de Nicoya and other northwestern areas of the country without stopping unnecessarily in San José.

Usually, going through immigration, baggage pickup, and customs at the main airport is fairly straightforward and takes about 30 minutes to an hour, occasionally longer if several international charters and regular flights land at almost the same time.

Most airlines serving Costa Rica fly from the USA. These include American Airlines, Continental, Delta, and United, all based in the USA; Lacsa, the international Costa Rican carrier (part of the TACA Central American airline group, which includes Aviateca of Guatemala, Taca of El Salvador, and Nica of Nicaragua); and Mexicana.

From Europe, most airlines connect with flights from Miami; those airlines that do fly to Costa Rica may stop in the Caribbean instead. Carriers from Europe change every year. Recently, Martinair (a KLM subsidiary) from the Netherlands, Iberia from Spain, British Airways, and Condor charters from Germany offered service to Costa Rica. See the San José chapter for a list of airline offices in that city.

> **Warning**
>
> The information in this chapter is particularly vulnerable to change: prices for international travel are volatile, routes are introduced and canceled, schedules change, special deals come and go, and rules and visa requirements are amended. Airlines and governments often seem to make price structures and regulations as complicated as possible. You should check directly with the airline or a travel agent to make sure you understand how a fare (and any ticket you may buy) works. In addition, the travel industry is highly competitive and there are many hidden costs and benefits.
>
> The upshot of this is that you should get opinions, quotes, and advice from as many airlines and travel agents as possible before you part with your hard-earned cash. The details given in this chapter should be regarded as pointers and are not a substitute for your own careful, up-to-date research.

Buying Tickets

The ordinary tourist or full economy-class fare is not the most economical way to go. It is convenient, however, because it enables you to fly on the next plane out and your ticket is valid for 12 months. In my experience, contacting the airlines directly is a waste of time. A good travel agent is more likely to find the airline with the best deal for you. If you want to economize further, there are several options. (For information on travel seasons in Costa Rica, see When to Go in the Facts for the Visitor chapter.)

Youth & Student Fares Students with international student ID cards and anyone under 26 years of age can get discounts with most airlines. Although youth and student airfares can be arranged through most travel agents and airlines, it is a good idea to go through agents that specialize in student travel – several are listed in the regional sections later in this chapter. Note that student fares are not only cheap, but often include free stopovers, don't require advance purchase, and may be valid for up to a year – a great deal if you are a student.

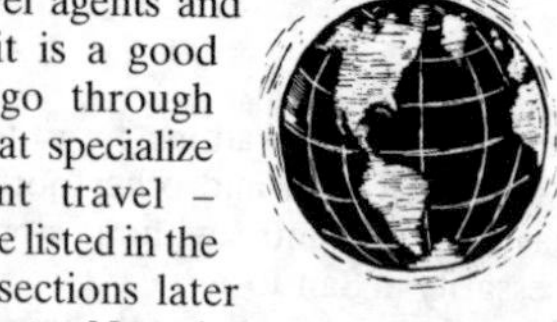

In Costa Rica, OTEC (☎ 256-0633, fax 233-8678), Calle 3, Avenida 3, in San José, specializes in student and youth fares and works closely with most of the student travel specialists listed in the following sections.

Airline Deals Whatever your age, if you purchase your ticket in advance, you can buy a ticket that costs about 30% or 40% less than the full economy fare. These are often called APEX, excursion, or promotional fares, depending on the country you are flying from and the rules and fare structures that apply there.

Often, the following restrictions apply: you must purchase your ticket at least 21 days (sometimes more or fewer days) in advance; you must stay a minimum period (about 14 days on average); and you must return within 180 days (sometimes fewer). Individual airlines have different requirements and these change from time to time. Most of these tickets do not allow stopovers, and there are extra charges if you change your itinerary or dates of travel. These tickets may sell out well in advance, so try to book early.

You can also use the Internet to hunt for low fares. Most airlines have their own websites with online ticket sales, often discounted for online customers. The airlines may sell seats by auction, offer last-minute specials, or simply cut prices to reflect the reduced cost of electronic selling. To buy a ticket via the Web, you'll need to use a credit card – this is straightforward and secure, as card details are encrypted. Commercial reservation networks offer airline ticketing as well as information and bookings for hotels, car rental, and other services.

Discounted Tickets Another cheap way to go is via consolidators (also called 'bucket shops,' though this term is less in vogue these days) that are allowed to sell discounted tickets to help airlines fill their flights. These tickets are often the cheapest of all, particularly in the low season, but they may sell out fast and you may be limited to only a few available dates.

While youth and student fares, economy fares, and discounted tickets are available direct from the airlines or from a travel agency (there is no extra charge for any of these tickets if you buy them from an agent rather than direct from the airline), consolidated discount tickets are available only from the discount ticket agencies themselves. Most of them are good, reputable, bonded companies, but once in a while a fly-by-night operator comes along, taking your money for a supercheap flight and giving you an invalid or unusable ticket. Carefully check what you are buying before handing over your money.

Discount ticket agencies often advertise in Sunday newspapers and travel-oriented magazines; there is much competition, and a variety of fares and schedules are available. Fares to Latin America are traditionally quite expensive, but discount ticket agencies have recently been able to offer increasingly economical fares.

Courier Flights If you are flexible with travel dates and can get by with minimal luggage, you can fly to Costa Rica as a courier. (This is most practical from the USA.) Couriers are hired by companies that need to have packages delivered to Costa Rica (and many other international destinations). The company will give the courier exceptionally cheap tickets in return for the use of his or her checked-baggage allowance. The traveler can bring carry-on luggage only. These are legitimate operations – all baggage that you are to deliver is completely legal. And it is amazing how much you can bring in your carry-on luggage! I have heard of couriers boarding an aircraft wearing two pairs of trousers and two shirts under a sweater and rain jacket and stuffing the pockets with travel essentials. Bring a folded plastic shopping bag and, once you have boarded the aircraft, you can remove the extra clothes and place them in the plastic bag! (Try not to have metal objects in inside pockets when you go through the metal detector at the airport! Also bear in mind that most courier companies want their agents to look reasonably neat, so don't overdo the baggy routine.) Remember, you can buy things like T-shirts, a towel, and soap after you arrive at your destination, so traveling with just carry-on luggage is certainly feasible.

Courier flights are more common from the USA than Europe. This is an especially good option for people flying from New York or Miami. For up-to-date information, contact *Travel Unlimited,* PO Box 1058, Allston, MA 02134, USA, which publishes monthly listings of courier and other cheap flights to Costa Rica and many other countries – this newsletter is recommended for bargain fare hunters. A year's subscription costs US$25, or US$35 for residents outside the US. You can get a single issue for US$5. Also contact the International Association of Air Travel Couriers (IAATC; ☎ 561-582-8320, fax 561-582-1581, www.courier.org), 220 South Dixie Hwy No 3, PO Box 1349, Lake Worth, FL 33460, USA.

Most courier flights to San José originate in Miami, though not many are offered. Another option is taking a courier flight to Mexico City, Guatemala City, or Panama City (flights are available from Los Angeles and New York as well as Miami) and continuing overland by bus.

Other Considerations Roundtrip fares are always much cheaper than two one-way tickets. They are also cheaper than 'open-jaw' tickets, which enable you to fly into one city (say San José) and leave via another (say Panama City). However, a few agencies can offer good fares on open-jaw tickets, which are suitable for someone who wants to do a little overland travel in Central America, so it pays to shop around.

If, because of a late flight (but not a rescheduled one), you miss a connection or are forced to stay overnight, the carrier is responsible for providing you with help in making the earliest possible connection and paying for a room in a hotel of its choice. The airline should also provide you with meal vouchers. If you are seriously delayed on an international flight, ask for these services.

Travelers are sometimes confused about the meaning of the term 'direct flight.' A direct flight goes from your departure point to San José and does not require that you get off the plane. However, unless it is specifically called a nonstop direct flight, the plane can stop in several cities en route to its final destination.

Baggage & Other Restrictions

These vary depending on the airline and the class of service you have chosen. The airline or your travel agent will be able to explain restrictions to you. At minimum, you will be allowed two pieces of luggage totaling 20kg, plus a carry-on bag that fits under the seat in front of you. On some airlines or in business and 1st class, you will be allowed more.

Restrictions on cheaper tickets usually mean that you cannot get a refund, and if you change your dates of travel, you must pay an additional charge.

Travelers with Special Needs

Most airlines can accommodate travelers with special needs, but only if such services are requested some days in advance. On flights with meals, a variety of special cuisines can be ordered in advance at no extra charge. These may include most of the following meals: vegetarian, low fat, low salt, children's, kosher, Muslim, and/or others. Ask.

Airlines can easily accommodate travelers requiring physical assistance. Wheelchairs designed to fit in aircraft aisles, plus an employee to push the chair if necessary, are available with advance notice. Passengers can check their own wheelchairs as luggage. Blind passengers can request that an employee take them through the check-in procedure and all the way to their seats. Again, ask if you have special needs – airlines usually work to oblige.

Departure Tax

A US$17 departure tax is payable at the international airport by all foreign passengers departing on international flights (*ticos* pay more). Payment can be in cash US dollars or *colones*.

The USA

The Sunday travel sections in the major newspapers advertise cheap fares to Central America, although these are sometimes no cheaper than the APEX fares offered by one of the several airlines serving Costa Rica.

Any reputable travel agent can help you find a reasonably priced ticket to Costa Rica. Students and people under 26 years of age should try one of the following experts in student travel – they also deal with regular fares and can help with things like international student ID cards, guidebooks, and youth hostel memberships.

A travel agent that can find you the best deal is Council Travel, a subsidiary of the Council on International Educational Exchange (CIEE). You can find its office locations and phone numbers in the telephone directories of many US cities, particularly those with universities. Alternatively, you can contact its national reservations center (☎ 800-226-8624, fax 617-528-2091, www.counciltravel.com), 6 Hamilton Place, 4th floor, Boston, MA 02108. Council Travel works with all age groups.

Also good for cheap airfares, mainly for students, is STA Travel (☎ 800-777-0112, 800-781-4040, www.statravel.com), with office locations worldwide. The toll-free numbers automatically connect you to the nearest office.

Another excellent contact is Tico Travel (☎ 800-493-8426, info@ticotravel.com), which offers discounted airfares from US gateway cities to anywhere in Central America and can provide connecting flights from all major US cities. Recent roundtrip fares to San José with Tico Travel varied from US$325 from Miami to US$600 from San Francisco, plus about US$50 in taxes. Another excellent source of cheap tickets is eXito Latin America Travel Specialists (☎ 800-655-4053, fax 510-655-4566, exito@wonderlink.com, www.exitotravel.com), 1212 Broadway, suite 910, Oakland, CA 94612. It specializes in Latin America exclusively and can arrange both short- and long-term tickets with multiple stopovers if desired.

APEX fares vary wildly depending on whether there's a price war going on, which airline you fly with, and when and how long you travel. At this writing, Iberia was offering a US$365 roundtrip fare from Miami to San José, while the Central and North American airlines were all quoting about US$570. Note that the lowest fares are usually available from consolidators, who may be able to give even lower quotes; fares under US$300 are sometimes reported from Miami. Other (more expensive) gateway cities include Los Angeles, New York, Houston, New Orleans, Dallas-Fort Worth, San Francisco, and Washington, DC, among others.

Because of the bewildering number of possibilities for air travel between the USA and Costa Rica, booking through a reputable travel agent is a good idea. The following airlines currently offer flights to Costa Rica from the USA:

American	☎ 800-433-7300
Continental	☎ 800-231-0856
Delta	☎ 800-221-1212
Iberia	☎ 800-772-4642
Lacsa	☎ 800-225-2272
Mexicana	☎ 800-531-7921
Taca	☎ 800-535-8780
United	☎ 800-241-6522

Courier travel is another possibility; see Courier Flights, earlier in this chapter, for details.

Also see the Organized Tours section at the end of this chapter. Note that 'tours' doesn't necessarily mean a tour group – there are companies that will customize a tour for just a couple of people.

Canada

Most travelers to Costa Rica must connect through one of the US gateway cities, though there may be direct charters. Canadian Airlines flies from Canada to San José, stopping in the USA. The airlines listed above under the USA all offer good connections from major Canadian cities.

Travel CUTS (☎ 416-614-2887, 800-667-2887, fax 416-614-9670, www.travelcuts.com), 200 Ronson Drive, suite 300, Toronto, ON M9W 5Z9, is a good choice for student, youth, and budget airfares. Travel CUTS has about 60 offices nationwide.

See the entry under the USA for eXito, which can arrange discounted fares from Canada.

Canadians will find that various companies arrange cheap winter getaway charters to Costa Rica. These normally include several days of hotel accommodations in San José and/or a beach resort, but represent a good value for the money if the hotels happen to be to your liking. It's easiest to go through a travel agent, as charter companies don't always sell directly to the public.

Latin America

Central American airlines Lacsa and Taca provide services between all the Central American capitals and San José. In addition, Copa (Panama) and Tan/SAHSA (Honduras) provide services to San José.

For South America, you'll find that Lacsa (or other members of the TACA group) flies to/from Venezuela, Colombia, Ecuador, Peru, Chile, and Argentina. American Airlines, Continental, Delta, and United all have connections to several Latin American countries. A few South American national airlines fly to Costa Rica, but routes change often.

Flights from Latin America are expensive because most Latin American countries tax airfares heavily (usually over 10%), and the number of APEX fares is limited. Consolidators aren't found easily. If you plan on traveling from outside the region to several Latin American countries by air, it is better to book tickets from home in advance rather than pay as you go. You can save hundreds of dollars this way, but the downside is that by booking in advance, you lose flexibility with your travel dates.

The UK & Ireland

Discount ticket agencies ('bucket shops') generally provide the cheapest fares from Europe to Latin America. Fares from London, where competition is fiercest, are often cheaper than from other European cities. Some Europeans find it cheaper to fly via London than direct from their home countries.

Agencies advertise in newspaper classifieds. I have heard consistently good reports about Journey Latin America (JLA; ☎ 020-8747-8315 for tours, 020-8747-3108 for flights, fax 020-8742-1312, sales@journeylatinamerica.co.uk, www.journeylatinamerica.co.uk), 12 & 13 Heathfield Terrace, Chiswick, London W4 4JE. There is also an office in Manchester. JLA specializes in cheap fares to most Latin American countries and arranges itineraries for both independent and escorted travel. Ask for its free magazine, *Papagaio,* which offers helpful information. JLA agents will make arrangements for you over the phone or by fax.

Another reputable budget travel agency in the UK is Trailfinders (☎ 020-7937-5400, www.trailfinder.co.uk), 215 Kensington High St, London W8 6BD. Trailfinders also has branches in several other British cities. Its useful travel publication, *Trailfinder Magazine*, is available free from the agency.

Flightbookers (☎ 020-7757-2611, www.flightbookers.net), 177 Tottenham Court Rd, London W1P OLX, also offers cheap flights from the UK.

Agencies specializing in student fares and youth discounts include STA Travel (☎ 020-7581-4132, fax 020-7368-0075), 86 Old Brompton Rd, London, SW7 3LQ, with several other addresses in London, as well as other offices in many university cities in the UK. Council Travel (☎ 020-7437-7767), 28A Poland St, Oxford Circus, London W1V 3DB, also offers student and youth fares but deals with nonstudents of all ages as well. See the USA section for Council's website.

Typical advance-purchase roundtrip fares from London to San José range from about UK£500 to UK£700. The variation in fares depends on how long you want to stay (longer stays are more expensive), which airline you choose, and when you travel. You need to go through a professional discount agent to get these fares, however. Note that the high season for air travel is the northern summer and December, which doesn't coincide with the Costa Rican high season of December to April.

Continental Europe

Some airlines from Europe will take you to Miami, where you connect with other flights to Costa Rica. Airlines that may fly direct to San José (with stops in either Miami or the Caribbean) are Martinair (a KLM subsidiary) from the Netherlands, Iberia from Spain, and British Airways; Condor has charter flights from Germany. Fares, routes, and low/high seasons change frequently; the best information to be had is from travel professionals.

On the Continent, try one of the following companies. Council Travel (see the USA section) has French offices in Aix-en-Provence and Lyon. Council Travel is also in Düsseldorf (☎ 0211-36-30-30) and Munich (☎ 089-39-50-22), Germany.

STA Travel (see the USA section) has offices in Denmark (☎ 45-97-42-50-00), Finland (☎ 358-9-818-34-91), and Sweden (☎ 46-46-13-72-05, 46-18-14-20-30). STA also has dozens of offices in major cities in Germany and Switzerland.

South Africa

STA has several offices in Cape Town (☎ 21-685-1808), Johannesburg (☎ 11-716-3045), and Pretoria (☎ 12-342-5292).

Australia & New Zealand

Travelers coming from Australia's east coast will usually fly to Costa Rica via the USA or Mexico. Most major airlines fly to Los Angeles, where you can get connecting flights to Costa Rica. Economy advance-purchase fares range from A$2200 to over A$3000 (though most should be under A$3000), so it pays to shop around. The low season in terms of fares is February and March (high season in Costa Rica) and mid-October to mid-November. The high season is mid-June to the end of July (mid- to low-season in Costa Rica) and mid-December to mid-January.

Qantas, Air New Zealand, and other trans-Pacific carriers fly to Los Angeles via Auckland, Nadi, or Honolulu, usually with one stopover allowed on the roundtrip, and connect with various carriers onward to San José. Also consider the overland route through Mexico as a cheaper alternative.

Fares from New Zealand via the Pacific will be somewhat lower than those from Australia's east coast. Routes via Asia are impractical.

Students and travelers under age 26 (though travelers of all ages can buy tickets) would do well to contact STA Travel in Australia or New Zealand. There are dozens of offices in the major cities, including the following:

Australia
(☎ 02-9361-4966) 79 Oxford St, Sydney, NSW 2010
(☎ 03-9349-2411) 222 Faraday St, Melbourne, VIC 3053

New Zealand
(☎ 09-309-0458) 10 High St, Auckland

Trailfinders also has several Australian offices including one (☎ 02-9247-7666, fax 02-9247-6566, www.trailfinders.com.au) at 8 Spring St, Sydney, NSW 2000.

Asia

There is also very little choice of direct flights between Asia and Latin America apart from Japan, and there certainly won't be any bargains there. The cheapest way is to travel to the US West Coast and connect with flights to Costa Rica from there.

In Japan, Council Travel (☎ 3-5467-5535, fax 3-5467-7031) is at Cosmos Aoyama, Gallery Floor, 5-53-67 Jingumae, Shibuya-ku, Tokyo 150.

STA has offices in the following Asian countries:

China
: (☎ 86-20-8667-1455) 179 Huan Shi Xi Rd, Guangzhou, China 510010

Japan
: (☎ 3-5391-2922, fax 3-5391-2923) 4F Nukariya Building, 1-16-20 Minami-Ikebukuro, Tokyo 171-0022; check telephone directories for other addresses in Tokyo and Osaka

Malaysia
: (☎ 3-248-9800, fax 3-243-3046) Lot 506, 5th floor, Plaza Magnum, Letter Box 506, 128 Jalan Pudu, 55100 Kuala Lumpur

Philippines
: (☎ 63-2-526-7919/20/21/22) 3rd floor, 511 Alonso St, Manila

Singapore
: (☎ 65-733-2218) 33A Cuppage Rd, Cuppage Terrace, Singapore 229458; also at the Singapore Polytechnic and the National University of Singapore

Thailand
: (☎ 2-233-2582, fax 2-237-6005) Wall Street Tower Building, Room 1406, 33 Surawong Rd (between Thaniya Rd and Patpong Rd), Bangkok 10500

LAND

If you live in North or Central America, it is possible to travel overland to Costa Rica. The nearest US town to San José is Brownsville, Texas, on the border with Mexico. From there it is about 4000km by road to San José, half of which traverses Mexico; the rest is through Guatemala, Honduras, Nicaragua, and Costa Rica. It is possible, though not necessary, to travel through El Salvador and Belize. Costa Rica has land borders with Nicaragua to the north and Panama to the south.

You can drive your own car, but the costs of insurance, fuel, border permits, food, and accommodations will be higher than that of an airline ticket. Many people fly down and rent a car in San José.

If you drive down, consider the following: driving even major Central American roads at night isn't recommended – they are narrow, unlit, rarely painted with a center stripe, often potholed, and subject to hazards such as cattle and pedestrians in rural areas. Traveling by day, allowing for time-consuming and bureaucratic border crossings, will take about a week from the US-Mexico border, or more to enjoy some of the sights (ruins, villages, markets, volcanoes, etc) en route. But it can certainly be done – get good insurance, be prepared for border bureaucracy, have your papers in impeccable order, and never leave your car unattended except in guarded parking areas. Don't leave anything of value in the car unless you are with it, and don't travel with fancy hubcaps, mirrors, etc, which are liable to be stolen. (US license plates are attractive to thieves, so display these inside the car.) Note that unleaded gas is not always available in Central America.

The American Automobile Association (AAA) publishes a map of Mexico and Central America (free to AAA members) that highlights the Carretera Interamericana and major side roads. The AAA sells insurance for driving in Mexico, but not in Central America. For insurance coverage in Mexico and Central America, call Sanborn's (☎ 210-686-0711) in McAllen, Texas. Sanborn's also has offices in several other cities near the US-Mexico border. For auto insurance details specific to travel within Costa Rica, see the Driver's License & Permits section in the Facts for the Visitor chapter.

A series of public buses will take you from the USA to San José. Bus travel is slow and cramped, but cheap and interesting. See Lonely Planet's *Mexico* and *Central America on a shoestring* for details on bus travel and accommodations en route. Direct buses from San José to the capitals of several Central American countries will cost you more than

Crossing Borders

When crossing borders, sometimes a show of cash is required – US$400 per month should be sufficient. Costa Ricans are sensitive to appearances; putting on your most presentable clothes and avoiding unusual fashions will make entrance procedures easier.

– Rob Rachowiecki

taking local buses to the borders and changing. Regardless of which buses you travel on, adding the cost of bus tickets to food and (budget) hotels, you'll pay as much as the airfare. You will, however, see and experience far more – it depends on your schedule.

The Carretera Interamericana continues as far south as Panama, then peters out in the Darién Gap, an area of roadless rainforest. It is not possible to drive on to South America; vehicles must be transported by ferry (or be airfreighted) from Panama to Colombia.

It is possible to ship a car from Miami to Costa Rica for about US$400 and up, depending on the car. Try contacting Latii Express International (☎ 800-590-3789, 305-593-8929, fax 305-593-8786, latiiexpress@prodigy.net) for specifics.

Nicaragua

The one major crossing point between Nicaragua and Costa Rica is at Peñas Blancas, on the Carretera Interamericana. Almost all international overland travelers enter Costa Rica through here, though there are other border posts.

Peñas Blancas This is the main border post, not a town, and so there is nowhere to stay.

The border is open from 8 am to noon and 1 to 8 pm daily on both the Costa Rican and Nicaraguan sides, though bus traffic stops in the afternoon. The earlier in the day that you get there, the better. The Costa Rican and Nicaraguan immigration offices are 4km apart – minibuses are available for about US$1 or there are taxis. On the Costa Rican side, the Migración office (☎ 677-0064) is in the immigration building next to the ***Restaurant La Frontera***, which serves adequate food.

A tiny Costa Rican tourist information office and a bus ticket office are also housed within the immigration building. Bus tickets are sold for departures to San José and Liberia; there are seven buses a day to San José, departing between 5 am and 3:30 pm, and four to Liberia, with departures between 6 am and 5 pm. Try to arrive early if you plan on taking a bus. Taxis are always an option.

If you are entering Costa Rica, sometimes an onward or exit ticket out of Costa Rica is requested – if you don't have one, you can buy a bus ticket back into Nicaragua from next to the tourist information office. This is acceptable to the Costa Rican authorities, who are generally helpful as long as your documents are in order. (Reports indicate that onward tickets, while legally required, are rarely asked for.)

If you are leaving Costa Rica, no special permit is required if you haven't overstayed the time allocated in your passport. If your time has expired, you need an exit visa, which you can pay for at the border (though you are less likely to encounter delays if you get your documents in order in San José).

International travelers between San José and Managua (or vice versa) on Sirca or TICA buses will find that the bus will wait for all passengers to be processed. This is time-consuming, and delays of up to eight hours have been occasionally reported (though two or three hours is more likely). To avoid the crowds, take local buses to the border post, a taxi or minibus to the other border post, and then continue on another bus – but cross as early in the day as possible. Several travelers have reported that luggage placed on the roofs of buses in Nicaragua has been pilfered, sometimes when only a bus employee has been allowed on the roof. Stolen objects are often mundane items such as deodorant or clothing. If you can't lock your luggage, try wrapping it in a large sack with a lock on that. Primitive – but it deters pilferers. Carry your luggage aboard the bus if possible. Note that poverty in Nicaragua is worse than in Costa Rica, and therefore thefts from buses are much more frequent; watch your gear very carefully.

The exit fees are reportedly no longer charged, though policies and fees change frequently. In the late 1990s, entry fees of US$7 into Nicaragua were (infrequently) charged for a tourist card, though the official price of the Nicaraguan tourist card was then US$2 – the extra US$5 appears to have gone into the officials' pockets!

Money changers at the Costa Rican post give better rates for US cash dollars than for traveler's checks. The border bank will cash traveler's checks at better rates; it is open from 8 am to 5 pm weekdays and 8 am to noon on Saturday. You can also change traveler's checks in the restaurant (see above); both Costa Rican colones and Nicaraguan *córdobas* are available. Excess córdobas or colones can also be sold, but usually at a small loss. Try to arrive at the border with as little local money as possible. The best place to sell córdobas is with the money changers on the street at the Nicaraguan border post.

The first (or last) Nicaraguan city of any size is Rivas, 37km north of the border, with several cheap hotels. There are frequent buses from the border to Rivas until 5 pm; get to the border by early afternoon to make sure you get on a bus. Alternatively, *colectivos* (buses, minivans, or cars operating as shared taxis) charge twice as much as a bus and leave more often. From Rivas, you can continue to the cities of Granada and Managua by bus, or across Lago de Nicaragua by boat.

Nicaraguan visa regulations change frequently, so check in with the Nicaraguan embassy in San José or in your home country. Recently, citizens of the USA, UK, and many European nations were allowed to enter Nicaragua for up to 90 days with a passport, which must be valid for at least six months after the date of entry. Citizens of Canada, Australia, New Zealand, and some European nations were only allowed 30 days with a valid passport. In most cases a tourist card is also required; the card costs US$5 and can be obtained at the border. Nationals of some African and Asian countries may require a visa.

Los Chiles Non-Nicaraguan and non-Costa Rican travelers rarely use this route, though it's possible for other nationals to cross here with the usual documents. Note that some nationals may require a visa; many don't.

Heading north from Costa Rica, a very rough road (a taxi with 4WD is essential; otherwise walk) traverses the 14km from Los Chiles to the Nicaraguan town of San Carlos, on the southeastern corner of Lago de Nicaragua at the beginning of the Río San Juan. Boats on the Río Frío go from Los Chiles to San Carlos every day.

San Carlos has a couple of extremely basic *pensiones* and regular boat service to Granada, a major Nicaraguan town on the northwestern corner of Lago de Nicaragua. This boat is usually full, so you should buy a ticket the day before if possible.

The Migración office (☎ 471-1223) is on the main road (ask anyone for directions) and is open from 8 am to 6 pm weekdays. The Nicaraguan consul is Sra Julieta Gómez (☎ 471-1053). The border crossing should be hassle-free if your papers are in order.

Panama

There are three road border crossings between Costa Rica and Panama. Note that Panama's time is one hour ahead of Costa Rica's.

Paso Canoas This border crossing on the Carretera Interamericana is by far the most frequently used entry and exit point with Panama.

Border hours are subject to change (and frequently do). Recently, the border was open from 6 am to 9 pm with two breaks (from 11 am to 1 pm, and 5 to 6 pm). There's not much point in arriving after dark, because buses leave during daylight hours only. If you are entering Panama from Costa Rica, you may need a visa or tourist card in addition to your passport. Visitors from the UK, some western European countries, and a few others need only a passport. Citizens of Australia, Canada, New Zealand, the USA, some western European countries, and others can buy a tourist card for US$5, which allows for a 30-day stay; longer stays require a visa. Visas typically cost up to about US$20, depending on your nationality. Visas are not obtainable at the border. Tourist cards are officially available, but the immigration office on the border has been known to run out, so get your visa or tourist card in advance if you need one. Panamanian officials often require that you have an onward ticket out of Panama before you are allowed to enter. If you don't have one, a roundtrip ticket to David can be purchased at the border and should suffice. Officials may also require that you have the equivalent of US$500 as proof of sufficient funds.

Regulations are subject to change, so you should check at the Panamanian consulate in San José about current requirements.

Once you are in Panama, there is a Panamanian bus terminal in front of the border post. The nearest town of any size and with decent hotels is David, about 1½ hours away by bus. There are buses to David every hour or two throughout the day, and the last one leaves the border at 7 pm. If you want to travel on to Panama City, you can either fly or catch a bus from David – the last bus leaves David at 5 pm and the trip takes about seven hours.

If you are entering Costa Rica, you may be required to show a ticket out of the country and US$400. If you don't have a ticket, buy a TRACOPA bus ticket in David for the roundtrip between David and Paso Canoas; this is acceptable to the Costa Rican authorities. Apparently, purchasing just the Paso Canoas-David section at the border isn't considered sufficient proof of intent to exit the country.

There are Costa Rican consulates in David and in Panama City.

People of most nationalities require only a passport and exit ticket to enter Costa Rica. See Visas & Documents in the Facts for the Visitor chapter for additional details. The border crossing in either direction is generally straightforward if your documents are in order.

Sixaola/Guabito This crossing is on the Caribbean coast, and the continuation of Sixaola on the Panamanian side is called Guabito. There are no banks, but stores in Guabito will accept colones, Panamanian *balboas*, or US dollars. The border is open from 7 to 11 am and 1 to 7 pm, but there are reports that the border guards are frequently late and may even take a day off on Friday, Saturday, or Sunday (though they claim that someone is there seven days a week). There are minibuses and taxis from near the border crossing to Changuinola, 16km into Panama.

In Changuinola, there is a bank and an airport with daily flights to David. There are several moderately priced hotels, including the ***Hotel Changuinola*** (☎ *758-8678*), near the airport.

From Changuinola, several buses travel the 30km to Almirante, where there are cheaper hotels. From Almirante, cheap public launches (US$3) or expensive water taxis (US$20) depart every day to Bocas del Toro, where there are pleasant beaches and reasonable hotels. (My friend Randy Galati suggests the ***Hotel Las Brisas*** as a reasonable budget choice for US$20 a double.) Many people begin their journey here from Puerto Viejo de Talamanca; be sure to take an early-morning bus to ensure getting to Bocas del Toro. There are no roads beyond Almirante, though some are planned. Also from Almirante, boats leave at 7 am daily to Chiriquí Grande, where there are hotels. From here, a road goes to David and the rest of Panama.

The Bocas del Toro area is becoming a popular destination, and people who have traveled this way say that it is attractive and worth seeing, but be prepared for delays. Almirante is the first (or last) place in Panama with a selection of reasonably priced accommodations, although the town is much less attractive than Bocas del Toro.

Río Sereno The road transiting this border crossing goes east from San Vito, through the border post by Río Sereno (a village on the Panamanian side), and on to the village of Volcán near the Parque Nacional Volcán Barú, the highest part of Panama. This is a remote and rarely used route, but it looks as if the scenery could be pretty amazing judging from the topographical maps. If I was in the area with plenty of time on my hands, I'd give it a go.

Reportedly, the Panamanian immigration officials here are sticklers on formalities: They require a return ticket to your country of origin, plus at least US$500 to show that you are solvent, as well as the usual passport with a visa or tourist card (if you need one). The immigration station is beside the police station. The Costa Rican officials, on the other hand, are not quite as fussy. The border crossing is open 8 am to 6 pm daily.

I'm told that there is a decent hotel on the Panamanian side, but that the banking facilities at the border do not deal with foreign exchange. However, you can pay for anything you need with small US bills.

Buses from Río Sereno travel to Concepción and David (in Panama); the last bus leaves the crossing at 5 pm daily.

SEA

Cruise lines stop in Costa Rican ports and enable passengers to make a quick foray into the country. Most cruises are, however, geared to shipboard life and ocean travel, so passengers can expect no more than a brief glimpse of Costa Rica – perhaps a day or so. Typically, cruise ships dock at either the Pacific port of Caldera (near Puntarenas) or the Caribbean port of Moín (near Puerto Limón). Passengers at Caldera get a chance to do a day trip to San José and the Central Valley or perhaps visit the Reserva Biológica Carara. Passengers at Moín may take a trip up the canals toward Parque Nacional Tortuguero or go on a river-rafting excursion. Other options are often possible – talk to your onboard excursion director.

Freighters also arrive in Costa Rica, but most are for cargo only. A few may accept a small number of passengers. Private yachts cruise down the Pacific coast from North America.

ORGANIZED TOURS

Scores of tour operators in North America and Europe run tours to Costa Rica. It is beyond the scope of this book to list them all (about three dozen tour operators in California alone run Costa Rica tours!). In contrast, there are few operators in other parts of the world.

Typical tours combine nature and adventure. Travelers visit one or more national parks and reserves, with overnight accommodations in comfortable lodges and hotels. Apart from birding and wildlife observation, and guided cloud or rainforest walks, other activities include river running, snorkeling, kayaking, deep-sea or freshwater fishing, horseback riding, touring the countryside, and just plain relaxing.

Many tours in Costa Rica tend to be first-class and expensive, and costs for the best trips can reach US$200 or more per person per day, plus airfare to San José. The best tours usually provide an experienced bilingual guide, the best accommodations available, all transport, and most meals. If you are shopping for a cheaper tour, ask about the guide. Is the guide fluent in English? What are the guide's particular interests and qualifications? Will they accompany you throughout the trip or will there be different guides for different portions? Other questions to consider are: How big will the tour group be? How many meals are included? What kind of lodging is used? Can you talk to past clients?

The advantage of a tour is that you have everything taken care of from the time you arrive till the time you leave. You don't have to worry about speaking Spanish, figuring out itineraries, finding bus stations, haggling with cab drivers, locating hotels with available rooms, or translating restaurant menus. Tours are often preferred by people who have a short vacation period and enough money to afford being taken care of. People on tours can have activities scheduled for every day of their trip and don't need to spend time figuring out what to do and how to do it once they get to San José.

Travelers who like these advantages but hate the idea of traveling with a tour group are served by several companies that arrange custom itineraries. These are never cheap but aren't necessarily super-expensive. Ask for moderate hotels and try to travel with a small group of friends and family to share the cost of a guide.

The following tour operators are reputable, but there are scores of others. Most are upscale, although some cheaper outfits are suggested as well. Most have a sliding price scale (a group of four on a two-week trip might pay about US$300 per person more than a group of 14, for example). Prices are based on double occupancy, and single travelers may pay several hundred dollars more. The ones listed here operate from outside of Costa Rica.

For information on Costa Rican companies (some of which also have a US address or contact phone number), see the Getting Around chapter.

The USA

General & Natural History These companies emphasize general sightseeing and natural history tours based in hotels, but may have other offerings.

Abercrombie & Kent
(☎ 708-954-2944, 800-323-7308, fax 708-954-3324, www.abercrombiekent.com) 1520 Kensington Rd, Oak Brook, IL 60521-2141. Among the most deluxe general tours.

Adventure Center
(☎ 510-654-1879, 800-227-8747, fax 510-654-4200, www.adventurecenter.com) 1311 63rd St, suite 200, Emeryville, CA 94608. Represents several different companies.

Ecotour Expeditions
(☎ 401-423-3377, 800-688-1822, fax 401-423-9630, www.naturetours.com) PO Box 128, Jamestown, RI 02835-0128. Offers five- to 10-day natural history and highlights tours.

Elderhostel
(☎ 978-323-4141, 877-426-8056, www.elderhostel.org) 75 Federal St, Boston, MA 02110. Excellent educational tours for travelers over 55 (younger companions permitted).

Geostar Tours
(☎ 707-579-2420, 800-624-6633, mansellw@sonic.net) 4754 Old Redwood Hwy, suite 650A, Santa Rosa, CA 95403. Mid-priced 10-day 'explorer' tours; also rainforest tours and an educational workshop.

International Expeditions
(☎ 205-428-1700, 800-633-4734, fax 205-428-1714, www.ietravel.com) 1 Environs Park, Helena, AL 35080. High-quality natural history tours include excellent guides and accommodations; eight- to 10-day tours from Miami from US$2300, including air; custom itineraries are also available.

Wilderness Travel
(☎ 510-558-2488, 800-368-2794, fax 510-558-2489, www.wildernesstravel.com) 1102 9th St, Berkeley, CA 94710. Ten- to 13-day comprehensive natural history adventures guided by bilingual local experts; comfortable lodge accommodations. The 13-day tours start at US$2200 plus airfare.

Wildland Adventures
(☎ 206-365-0686, 800-345-4453, fax 206-363-6615, www.wildland.com) 3546 NE 155th St, Seattle, WA 98155. Wide selection of seven- to 10-day tours, including some designed for families; costs range from US$1200 to US$2300 plus airfare.

Sportfishing For more information on fishing, see Activities in the Facts for the Visitor chapter.

JD's Watersports
(☎ 970-356-1028, 800-477-8971, fax 970-352-6324, www.jdwatersports.com) 1115 11th Ave, Greeley, CO 80631. Fishing from Hotel Punta Leona (near Jacó, but you don't have to stay there); also diving, kayaking, boogie boarding, river and sunset cruises. See the entry under Punta Leona Area in the Central Pacific Coast chapter for local contact information.

Rod & Reel Adventures
(☎ 209-785-0444, 800-356-6982, fax 209-785-0447, www.rodreeladventures.com) 566 Thomson Lane, Copperopolis, CA 95228. Well known, represents several of the best lodges and boats. Four-night/three-day ocean-fishing packages from US$1000 to US$2000, depending on accommodations and boats used; longer trips available. It also arranges freshwater trips on Laguna de Arenal.

Surfing For more information on surfing, see Activities in the Facts for the Visitor chapter.

Tico Travel
(☎ 800-493-8426) web: www.ticotravel.com Cheap fare specialist with plenty of surfing information.

Diving For more information on diving, see the Facts for the Visitor chapter.

JD's Watersports
(see Sportfishing, above) PADI-certified trips at the Hotel Punta Leona, resort courses (mini-courses for beginners to determine whether they like diving), and certification courses are offered.

Okeanos Aggressor
(☎ 504-385-2628, 800-348-2628, fax 504-384-0817, www.aggressor.com) PO Box 1470, Morgan City, LA 70381. Runs dive trips to Isla del Coco for experienced divers.

Tropical Adventures
(☎ 206-441-3483, 888-250-1799, fax 206-441-5431,

www.divetropical.com) 111 2nd North, Seattle, WA 98109. North America's biggest dive tour operator.

Other Activities These companies usually offer some specialized activities in addition to general and natural history tours.

Above the Clouds Trekking
(☎ 508-799-4499, 800-233-4499, fax 508-797-4779, info@aboveclouds.com) PO Box 398, Worcester, MA 01602. Eleven-day tours include five days of trekking and some river rafting; expert local guides. Cost from US$1625.

Backroads
(☎ 510-527-1555, 800-462-2848, fax 510-527-1444, www.backroads.com) 801 Cedar St, Berkeley, CA 94710-1800. Seven- or eight-day easy walking or mountain-biking adventures based in excellent hotels. Walk 4 to 10km a day, ride 16 to 70km a day, with river rafting and jungle hiking available. Tours only in dry season; expensive but reputable.

BattenKill Canoe Ltd
(☎ 802-362-2800, 800-421-5268, fax 802-362-0159, www.battenkill.com) PO Box 65, Historic Route 7a, Arlington, VT 05250. Eleven-day trips with an emphasis on canoeing in various areas of Costa Rica – no experience needed. Cost is about US$1950 plus airfare; custom itineraries or add-on days can be arranged.

Earthwatch
(☎ 617-926-8200, 800-776-0188, fax 617-926-8532, www.earthwatch.org) 680 Mt Auburn St, PO Box 403, Watertown, MA 02272. Ten-day turtle-tagging projects; 'volunteers' pay about US$1800 to assist scientists carrying out research; work at night and sleep by day. Longer and cheaper projects involving caterpillar studies, tropical forest research, and other trips are offered; all are tax deductible.

Mountain Travel/Sobek
(☎ 510-527-8100, 888-687-6235, fax 510-525-7710, www.mtsobek.com) 6420 Fairmount Ave, El Cerrito, CA 94530. Sea kayaking, river rafting, hiking, natural history. Costs are US$1500 to US$2500 on 10-day trips.

Serendipity Adventures
(☎ 734-995-0111, 800-635-2325, fax 734-426-5026; in Costa Rica ☎ 556-2592) web: www.serendipityadventures.com. PO Box 2325, Ann Arbor, MI 48106. All kinds of adventures, ranging from hot-air ballooning (US$900 for five people) to nine-day/eight-night cross-country biking trips (US$1900 per person in high season). Other activities include rafting, climbing, kayaking, snorkeling, tree-climbing, hiking, horseback riding, and camping, as well as the usual natural history; novices welcomed.

Customized Itineraries These companies will find a group tour or arrange a customized itinerary to suit your interests.

Costa Rica Connection
(☎ 805-543-8823, 800-345-7422, fax 805-543-3626, www.crconnect.com) 1124 Nipomo St, suite C, San Luis Obispo, CA 93401. Wide variety of itineraries at US$120 to US$300 per day, plus air.

Costa Rica Experts
(☎ 773-935-1009, 800-827-9046, fax 773-935-9252, www.crexpert.com) 3166 N Lincoln Ave, suite 424, Chicago, IL 60657. Specializes in Costa Rica and the best lodging options at upper-middle to top-end budgets. Many different activities.

Holbrook Travel
(☎ 352-377-7111, 800-451-7111, fax 352-371-3710, www.holbrooktravel.com) 3540 NW 13th St, Gainesville, FL 32609-2196. Holbrook owns and operates the Selva Verde Lodge and arranges various other trips from US$100 to over US$200 per day.

Lost World Adventures
(☎ 404-373-5820, 800-999-0558, fax 404-377-1902, www.gorp.com/lostworld.htm) 112 Church St, Decatur, GA 30030. Custom itineraries for US$125 to US$200 per day.

Preferred Adventures
(☎ 651-222-8131, 800-840-8687, fax 651-222-4221, www.preferredadventures.com) 1 W Water St, suite 300, St Paul, MN 55107. Well-recommended, experienced, environmentally sensitive adventure and nature travel with cheap airfares with any land package.

Tread Lightly
(☎ 860-868-1710, 800-643-0060, fax 860-868-1718, www.treadlightly.com) At 37 Juniper Meadow Rd, Washington Depot, CT 06794. Personal attention and an environmentally friendly approach.

Canada

Adventures Abroad
(☎ 604-303-1099, 800-665-3998, fax 604-303-1076, www.adventures-abroad.com) 20800 Westminster Hwy, suite 2148, Richmond, BC V6V 2W3. Moderately priced one- and two-week escorted bus tours; maximum of 20 participants.

GAP
(☎ 416-922-8899, 800-465-5600, fax 416-922-0822, www.gap.ca) 264 Dupont St, Toronto, ON M5R 1V7. Lower-priced escorted tours using public transport and inexpensive hotels.

Trek Holidays
(☎ 780-439-9118, 800-661-7265, www.trekholidays.com) 8412-109 St, Edmonton, AB T6G 1E2. Several other locations.

The UK

Journey Latin America
(JLA; ☎ 020-8747-8315, fax 020-8742-1312, www.journeylatinamerica.co.uk) At 12 & 13 Heathfield Terrace, Chiswick, London W4 4JE. Recommended flight, tour, and custom-itinerary specialists to Latin America, with many years of experience.

South American Experience
(☎ 020-7976-5511, fax 020-7976-6908, sax@mcmail.com) 47 Causton St, London SW1P 4AT. Custom itineraries and mid-priced three-week tours.

Sunvil Holidays
(☎ 020-8568-4499, fax 020-8568-8330, www.sunvil.co.uk) Sunvil House, 7-8 Upper Square, Old Isleworth, Middlesex TW7 7BJ. Arranges independent travel, including hotel reservations and car rentals, with some organized tours.

Australia & New Zealand

Adventure Associates
(☎ 02-9389-7466, fax 02-9369-1853, www.adventureassociates.com) 197 Oxford St, Bondi Junction, Sydney, NSW 2022. Standard one-week tours in addition to independent travel arrangements.

Adventure Specialists
(☎ 02-9261-2927, 800-643-465, fax 02-9261-2907) Level 1/69 Liverpool St, Sydney, NSW 2000. Tours of one to three weeks with river running and rainforest visits.

Adventure World
(☎ 02-9956-7766, 800-221-931) web: www.adventureworld.com.au. 73 Walker St, Sydney, NSW 2060. Also locations in other Australian cities. (☎ 09-524-5118,fax 09-520-6629) 101 Great South Rd, Remuera, Auckland. Specializes in San José and national park tours.

Contours
(☎ 03-9670-6900, fax 03-9670-7558, contours@compuserve.com) 1/84 William St, Melbourne, VIC 3000. Good variety of Latin American tours at mid-range to lower-top-end prices.

ERIC L WHEATER

Hanging out, Puerto Limón

BUDDY MAYS

San José fruit vendor selling mangoes, oranges, and papayas

JAN BUTCHOFSKY-HOUSER

Farm on the flanks of Volcán Arenal

ERIC L WHEATER

Street soccer, Puerto Limón

NIK WHEELER

Cowboy, Guanacaste province

BRUCE COLEMAN

NICHOLAS DEVORE

Potato fields and planting next year's potato crop, near Tortuguero

ERIC L WHEATER

Milkman, San José

BUDDY MAYS

CAROL HUGHES

Woman with bananas near Montezuma, Península de Nicoya, and banana plantation near Tortuguero

Getting Around

The population distribution of Costa Rica dictates how its public transport works. Roughly one quarter of the country's 3.6 million inhabitants live in the greater San José area, and roughly two-thirds live in the Central Valley, one of the most densely populated regions in Central America. This means that there are a lot of roads and buses in the center of the country. As you go farther afield, there are generally fewer roads and less public transport.

To get to most regions, you have to start from San José, which is the main center for public transport. It is often easier to go to one region and then return to San José to find transport to another area.

The majority of Costa Ricans do not own cars. Therefore, public transport is quite well developed and you can get buses to almost any part of the country. Remote or small towns may be served by only one bus a day, but you can get there.

AIR

Costa Rica's two domestic airlines are SANSA (Servicios Aéreos Nacionales SA; ☎ 221-9414) and Travelair (☎ 220-3054, www.travelair-costarica.com).

SANSA is now linked with Grupo TACA, and you can buy tickets through any travel agent. It has upgraded its fleet, services, and reservation system, though flights are still subject to delays and occasional cancellations. Services are with small Cessna Caravans (14 passengers) and similar aircraft. Flights leave from the domestic terminal of Juan Santamaría international airport, 17km from the center of San José. Demand

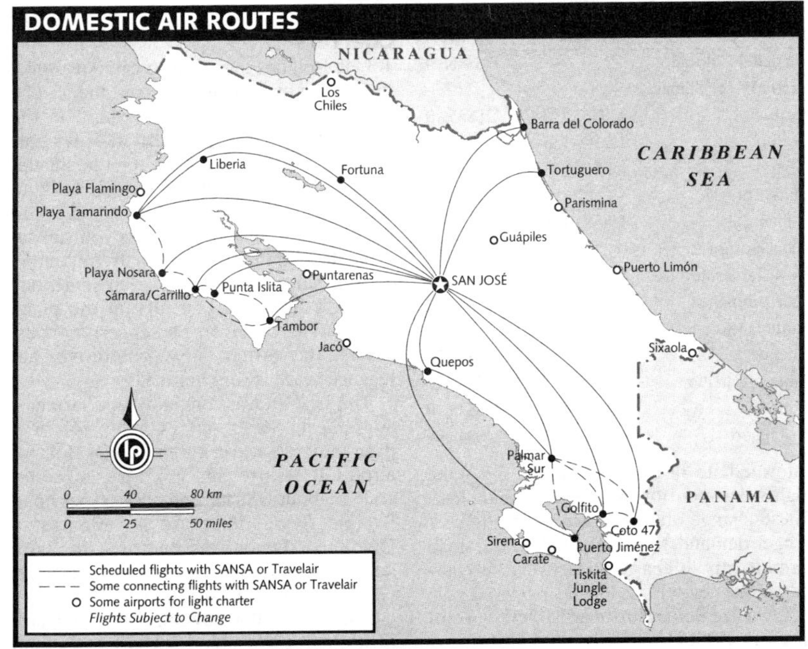

for seats is high, so try to book as far in advance as possible. Because the aircraft are small, baggage allowance is limited to 12kg (about 26lb).

Travelair is the newer domestic airline and is more expensive than SANSA. Travelair tends to provide better on-time service and fewer canceled flights than SANSA. Travelair works with Adobe Rent a Car to provide free pickup and drop-off at any of the destinations listed in the table below.

Travelair flies from the smaller Tobías Bolaños airport in Pavas, about 5km from the center of San José. Service is with nine-passenger Britten Islanders, 15-passenger Britten Trislanders, and similar planes. Again, book as far in advance as possible and remember to limit your luggage to 12kg.

Fares given are for high-season one-way/roundtrip flights from San José and are subject to change. Most flights are daily; some are more frequent. Destinations served can change from season to season. Low-season fares are slightly cheaper.

destination	Travelair	SANSA
Barra del Colorado	–	US$45/90
Carrillo – see Sámara		
Fortuna	US$63/103	US$45/90
Golfito	US$96/155	US$55/110
Liberia	US$100/165	US$55/110
Neily/Coto 47	–	US$55/110
Palmar Sur	US$89/145	US$55/110
Playa Nosara	–	US$55/110
Playa Tamarindo	US$100/165	US$55/110
Puerto Jiménez	US$100/165	US$55/110
Punta Islita	US$93/151	–
Quepos	US$58/93	US$35/70
Sámara/Carrillo	US$89/145	US$55/110
Tambor	US$76/122	US$45/90
Tortuguero	US$58/103	US$45/90

Intermediate fares are available for some flights between towns outside of San José. These change often and are subject to passenger demand, so ask. If all else fails, small aircraft can be chartered between any airports (see below).

Oversize items (surfboards, bicycles) cost an extra US$15.

As a general rule, the most popular destinations are Playa Tamarindo, Quepos, Palmar Sur, and Puerto Jiménez, so you should book as far ahead as possible for those destinations if you want to fly on a particular day. Barra del Colorado and Tortuguero are also fairly popular. Both airlines suggest that you not book a flight to connect with an international flight the same day because, if the domestic flight has to be canceled (which happens a few times each season), you will probably miss your international flight, and nobody wants to be responsible.

The head offices of SANSA and Travelair are in San José, though any travel agent can book your flight. Remember that reservations with SANSA must be prepaid in full before they can be confirmed. Most agents, especially if you are calling from outside Costa Rica, add a booking fee of a few dollars. Details of other offices are given under the appropriate towns in the regional chapters of this book.

Charters

Tobías Bolaños airport also caters to small single- and twin-engined aircraft that can be chartered to just about anywhere in the country where there is an airport. Fares start at about US$300 per hour for the smaller planes, and it takes about an hour to fly to most coastal destinations. You also have to pay for the return flight, unless you can coordinate with the company to fly you out on a day when they are picking up somebody else. If a group of you fills up the plane (three, five, or seven passengers in most cases), the fare is not prohibitive, but luggage space is very limited.

The best-known company for charters is Aero Costa Sol (☎ 441-1444, fax 441-2671, flyacs@sol.racsa.co.cr), at the Tobías Bolaños airport. It has five- and seven-passenger aircraft at about US$360 and US$500 per hour. Sample flying times are 40 minutes to Quepos or Puntarenas, one hour to Barra del Colorado, and 90 minutes to Tamarindo, Golfito, Sixaola, or Los Chiles.

Many towns that have an airport will have light aircraft available for charter; those of particular interest to the traveler are mentioned in the text.

You can arrange flights directly by going to Tobías Bolaños airport, or you can look in the Getting There & Away section of the San José chapter for the telephone numbers of several companies that charter aircraft. Many tour agencies will charter planes for you if you take one of their tours.

BUS

The ICT tourist office in San José (see Tourist Offices in the Facts for the Visitor chapter) has a (usually) up-to-date listing of many bus departure points and the destinations they serve. Other places to find bus timetables are Ecole Travel in San José (see Organized Tours, below) and on the web at www.yellowweb.co.cr/crbuses.html.

San José is the center of the country's bus network, and buses depart from the capital for just about anywhere in the country. See the San José chapter for details.

There are few central bus terminals. In San José, some bus companies leave from what used to be the old Coca-Cola bottling plant in San José – the area is still known as 'La Coca-Cola.' A few blocks north, the Atlántico Norte terminal serves some northern destinations, and the Caribbean area is served by the Caribe terminal, in another location (see the San José chapter).

Other companies leave from their own offices elsewhere in the city. Still others leave from bus stops on the street, and some leave from street corners without even a bus stop to mark their departure point. The addresses or street intersections of bus companies, bus stops, or bus departure points are given under the appropriate city headings in this book. This combination of different bus terminals, offices, and stops is how it is throughout much of the country.

The larger companies with offices and buses serving major destinations sell tickets in advance. The smaller companies with just a bus stop expect you to wait in line for the next bus, but normally there is room for everyone. If you don't have a ticket, buy one when you board; the fares should be clearly posted inside the bus.

The exceptions are the days before and after a major holiday, especially Easter, when buses are ridiculously full. Note that there are *no buses at all* from the Thursday morning to the Saturday afternoon before Easter. Friday-night and Saturday-morning trips out of San José can be very crowded, as can Sunday-afternoon and evening return trips; try to avoid those if possible. I have resorted to hitchhiking in these cases.

If this all seems chaotic, take heart. Costa Ricans are used to the system and know where buses depart – just ask.

Fares are generally cheap, with even the longest and most expensive run out of San José costing under US$7.

Long-distance buses are of two types, *directo* and *normal* (or *corriente*). The direct buses are a little faster and more expensive. Travelers on a budget can save as much as a quarter of the direct bus fare by taking a normal bus, which stops on demand at various intermediate points and usually takes an hour or two longer.

Roads are narrow and winding and sometimes unpaved; normal buses are rather old, so comfort is not one of the things that the bus journeys are known for, particularly those to smaller and more remote destinations served by battered old Bluebird school buses. But they get you there. Trips longer than four hours have a rest stop, and no trips are scheduled to take longer than about nine hours. If you want reasonable comfort, take the more expensive direct buses.

Luggage space is limited, so I suggest breaking your Costa Rican stay into sections and leaving what you don't need for a certain section in San José. A small bag is certainly much easier to travel with and easier to keep your eye on, as you can take it aboard with you. There have been reports of checked luggage on buses getting 'lost,' particularly on the route from San José to Puntarenas.

If your bag is too big to take aboard the bus with you, watch it getting loaded and keep your eyes open during any stops the bus makes to ensure that it isn't 'accidentally' given to the wrong passenger. Another suggestion is to put your backpack in a large burlap sack, thus making it less conspicuous.

TRAIN

The railway lines in Costa Rica were severely damaged in the 1991 earthquake and have been closed since then. They were running at a financial deficit before the closure, so it is unlikely that the system will be repaired or reopened. This is a shame, because the run from San José to the Caribbean coast was a famous and well-loved ride. There is occasional talk of privatizing the system with foreign money, but nothing has come of this yet.

CAR & MOTORCYCLE

Few people drive to Costa Rica in their own vehicle, though it is certainly possible (see the Getting There & Away chapter for details). Renting a car after arrival, on the other hand, is something many travelers do for part of their trip. A few people rent motorcycles, though this is not such a popular option. Motorcycle tours (on Harleys) are offered (see Organized Tours, below).

Road Rules

San José is notorious for its narrow streets, complicated one-way system, heavy traffic, and thefts from cars. I certainly would not recommend driving a rental car or motorcycle around San José, except to get out of the city.

Once out of San José, the roads vary from barely passable to very good. But even the good ones can suffer from landslides and thick fog, so you should always be prepared for the unexpected. Most roads are single-lane, lack hard shoulders, and are very winding, so defensive driving is recommended. Always be prepared for cyclists, pedestrians, a broken-down vehicle, heavily laden, slow-moving trucks, or even an ox cart around the next bend. Potholes of varying sizes and depths are an unfortunately frequent occurrence (and a grim national joke).

After major hurricanes or earthquakes, the Interamericana may be closed for weeks, so always be prepared for delays. During the June to November wet months, sudden heavy storms can cause landslides and flooding, which can close roads or render them passable only to 4WD vehicles. This can happen locally at any time. For information about a particular route, call the National Transit Police (☎ 222-9245, Spanish only) for recent road conditions.

Some roads have a reputation for being especially dangerous. The Cerro de la Muerte area on the Interamericana between Cartago and San Isidro de El General (the highest section of the Interamericana) suffers from frequent landslides and dense fog at any time of day or night. (I have driven this section several times with visibility down to under 10m.) The busy San José-to-Puntarenas road is steep, narrow, and tortuously winding, but local drivers familiar with the road drive it very fast. The section between San Ramón and Esparza is especially notorious: there is one area that suffers from permanent earth subsidence, and the road sometimes goes over a chassis-breaking drop – be careful. The new road from San José to Guápiles goes through Parque Nacional Braulio Carrillo and is subject to landslides and heavy fog, especially later in the day. Similarly, the stretch of the Interamericana from Palmar Norte to Buenos Aires is subject to frequent rockfalls and landslides. The Pacific coastal highways, especially between Quepos and Jacó, are deceivingly well paved and maintained in places, changing suddenly to slick, bumpy, and unguarded one-way bridges with little warning. Don't drive this road too fast, especially at night (which is generally not recommended anyway).

If you are involved in an accident, you should not move the car until the police get there. Injured people should not be taken from the scene until the Red Cross ambulance arrives. Try to make a note or sketch of what happened, and don't make statements except to authorized people.

Because of difficult driving conditions, there are speed limits of 100km/h or less on all primary roads and 60km/h or less on secondary roads. Traffic police use radar, and speed limits are enforced with speeding tickets. You can also get a traffic ticket for not wearing a seat belt. All rental cars have seat belts. It is illegal to enter an intersection unless you can also leave it, and it is illegal to make a right turn on a red light unless a sign indicates that a turn is permitted. At unmarked intersections, yield to the car on your right. Driving in Costa Rica is on the right, and passing is allowed only on the left.

If you are given a ticket, you have to pay the fine at a bank; instructions are given on the ticket. If you are driving a rental car, the rental company may be able to arrange your payment for you – the amount of the fine should be on the ticket.

Fines can be expensive: US$150 for driving 40km/h over the speed limit, US$70 for running a red light, and US$15 for not wearing a seat belt. Police have no right to ask for money under any circumstances. Police have no right to confiscate a car unless the driver cannot produce a license and ownership papers, the car lacks license plates, or the driver is drunk or has been involved in an accident causing serious injury.

If you are driving and see oncoming cars with headlights flashing at you, it often means that there is some kind of road problem or a radar speed-trap ahead. Slow down immediately. Also watch for a branch on the side of the road: this often means that a vehicle is broken down just ahead. Police cars are blue with white doors and have a small red light on the roof – they can be small sedans or pickups. White or red police motorcycles are also in use.

Many foreign drivers complain that the roads are inadequately signed. This is often

Traffic Signs

Traffic signs are in Spanish and don't always have an internationally recognized symbol. Drivers should be aware of the following, to help prevent accidents.

One of the most important signs is found at one-lane bridges (of which there are many). On one side of the bridge there will normally be a *Cede el Paso* sign, which means 'Yield' or 'Give Way.' The driver who has this sign must stop for oncoming traffic – it is not the first car to enter the bridge that has the right of way. Important signs to know are the following:

Adelante	Ahead
Alto	Stop
Cede el Paso	Yield; Give Way
Curva Peligrosa	Dangerous Curve
Derrumbes en la Vía	Landslides or Rockfalls in the Highway
Despacio	Slow
Desvío	Detour; Alternate Route
Hundimiento	Dip
Mantenga Su Derecha	Keep to the Right
No Adelantar	No Passing
No Estacionar	No Parking
No Hay Paso	No Entrance
Peligro	Danger
Puente	Bridge
Trabajos en la Vía	Roadworks
Transito Entrando	Traffic Entering the Highway

Know and take these signs seriously. An *Hundimiento* can be an axle-breaking sinkhole that needs to be negotiated in first gear. A *Puente* might be a one-lane bridge just after a blind curve, with no guardrails. Be prepared!

– Rob Rachowiecki

Police Corruption

The problem of police corruption has diminished dramatically in recent years. Government officials now have a low tolerance for police corruption, instead of turning a blind eye as they did a few years ago. Still, isolated incidents do occur.

In 1999, while I was driving to the Nicaraguan border on the Interamericana, a uniformed police officer pulled me over for speeding. Following some suggestive and heartfelt banter about his desire to help me out, the officer indicated that rather than pay an official ticket of US$80, I could drop US$20 through the open window of his car onto the backseat. After a moment or two of temptation (during which I wondered whether he might take my US$20 and still give me the ticket), I ruefully expressed my preference for the official channels. The official ticket turned out to be only US$25, and we parted ways amicably.

Always remember that an officer does not have the right to take money directly. Tickets are often turned in and paid at a bank. I was able to pay this speeding ticket through the rental company when dropping off the car – simple, cheap, and legal.

– John Thompson

true, though more signs have been placed in the last few years. Still, you should get a decent road map and ask locals when you are not sure of directions. They are nearly always able and willing to give assistance.

Rental

There are plenty of car rental agencies in San José, but few in other cities. Several agencies also have offices at Juan Santamaría international airport.

Car rental is popular because a car can get you to places where you can't go by public transport. It also gives you the freedom to travel when you want and to stop wherever you like. Because buses to remote areas are not very frequent, you can cover more ground in a shorter time with a car.

Realize that car rental is not very cheap. Discounts are available if you rent by the week, but expect to pay about US$300 per week for a subcompact car in the high season. Almost all cars now come with air-conditioning and a cassette/radio, so bring a few of your favorite tapes. The cost includes (mandatory) insurance and unlimited mileage (or *kilometraje*, as they call it). If you plan on driving 500km or more in a week, you should get unlimited kilometers; less than that and you might save by paying a daily base rate plus the per-kilometer charge.

The insurance accounts for about US$12 per day of your cost (up to US$20 for larger vehicles); rental companies won't let you rent a car without it because they say that your policy at home will not be valid in Costa Rica in case of an accident or theft of the car. Even if you use a gold or platinum credit card, which will often provide free insurance in many countries, you'll find that Costa Rican car rental companies won't accept their insurance coverage. Perhaps this is because of the terrible condition of many Costa Rican highways – cars often come back damaged from hitting a pothole at a fast speed. Even with insurance, there is a high deductible (as much as US$1500 in some cases), but you can pay an extra fee (US$8 to US$10 per day) to waive this. Even with the extra fee, you are still held accountable for damage if you are deemed to have been negligent, so don't drive off a bridge!

If you want more than a subcompact car, expect to pay about US$400 for a medium-size car or sports jeep, and about US$500 to US$700 for a van or larger 4WD vehicle. All rates are per week, including free kilometers and insurance. These are high-season rates.

For travel during the rainy season, many rental agencies insist that you rent a 4WD vehicle if you are going to places where you need to drive on dirt roads – the Península de Nicoya, for example. The rainy season is also the low season, and discounted rates may apply, but it's still not cheap.

Many of the major car rental companies, such as Avis, Budget, Dollar, Hertz, and National, have offices worldwide, so you can rent a car in advance from home. Normally, you need to book a car at least 14 days in advance, and the rate when booked at home is often a little cheaper than it is in San José, though you should check that no extra fees will be charged after you arrive. You can also book through the Internet (see Internet Resources in the Facts for the Visitor chapter).

To hire a car you need a valid driver's license, a major credit card, and your passport. If you don't have a major credit card, some companies may allow you to make a cash deposit of about US$1000. Your driver's license from home is acceptable for up to three months if you are a tourist; you don't need an international driving permit.

The minimum age for car rental is 21 years. One reader wrote in to report that the maximum age for car rental in Costa Rica is 70. While this has not been confirmed, senior travelers should plan ahead.

Dozens of other companies are listed in the San José yellow pages. I haven't heard too many complaints about any rental agencies – most are fairly reputable. However, I have received a few reports from readers who told me that the rental company added surcharges for damage after the vehicle was turned in, or provided shoddy vehicles in the first place, or otherwise was unreliable. My advice is to rent a vehicle (if you can) through a reputable hotel or travel agent in San José. They pass a fair volume of travelers on to the car rental companies, and you are more likely to receive the benefit of the doubt in the case of a problem if you go through a hotel or travel agent.

When you rent a car, carefully inspect it for minor dents and scratches, missing radio antennae or hubcaps, and anything else that makes the car look less than brand new. (Minor nicks are acceptable.) These damages must be noted on your rental agreement; otherwise, you may be charged for them when you return the car. The insurance won't cover it, because of the deductible. This can be a problem in Costa Rica, because rental vehicles typically see well over 50,000km of driving before they are sold, unlike, say, in the USA, where rental vehicles are renewed almost every year.

If your car breaks down, call the rental company. Don't attempt to get the car fixed

Driving Accidents

If you are involved in an accident while driving, call the Red Cross to help injured parties. Also call the Instituto Nacional de Seguros (National Insurance Institute; ☎ 800-835-3467) as soon as possible. Then call the transit police or Guardia Civil to make a report for insurance purposes. Note that the following numbers are correct at the time of this writing but are liable to change.

province	all emergencies	Red Cross	Transit Police	Guardia Civil
San José	911	128, 911	222-9245, 222-9330	911
Alajuela	911	441-3939	117	441-6346
Cartago	911	551-0421	117	551-0455, 117
Heredia	911	237-1115	117	237-0044, 117
Guanacaste	n/a	666-0994	117	666-0213, 117
Limón	n/a	758-0125	117	758-0365, 117
Puntarenas	n/a	661-0184	117	661-0640, 117

Note that there are plans to expand the ☎ 911 emergency system nationwide.

– Rob Rachowiecki

yourself, because most companies won't reimburse you for your expenses without prior authorization from them.

Rental cars have special license plates and it is immediately obvious to everyone that you are driving a rental car. There have been many instances of theft from rental cars. You should never leave valuables in sight when you are away from the car, and you should remove luggage from the trunk when checking into a hotel overnight. Many hotels will provide parking areas for cars. It is better to park the car in a guarded parking lot than on the street. This cannot be overemphasized – don't leave valuables in the car.

Small mopeds and dirt bikes can be rented in a few places in San José and along the coast, but aren't much cheaper than compact cars. In San José, try Peisa Corporación (☎ 257-3831). Large touring bikes can be rented from Rent-a-Harley Davidson & Tours (see Organized Tours, below).

The price of gas (petrol) is about US45¢ per liter of regular (about US$1.70 per US gallon or US$2.05 for an imperial gallon), although it has been a little higher and lower in the past. Most stations sell regular and diesel; unleaded and super are available in larger towns. Most rental cars take regular. The price of gas is the same at all stations nationwide, so gas up wherever you want.

TAXI

It may come as a surprise to most people that taxis are considered a form of public transport outside urban areas. Taxis can be hired by the hour, the half day, or the day. Meters are not used on long trips, so arrange the fare with the driver beforehand.

There are various occasions when you may want to consider using a taxi. Visiting some of the national parks by public transport is not possible. Your alternatives are to take a tour, rent a car, hitch a ride, walk, cycle, or catch a taxi.

The roundtrip journey from San José to Volcán Poás, for example, is about 110km. An all-day excursion allowing a couple of hours at the volcano and photo stops along the way costs around US$50 to US$70, depending on the taxi driver and your bargaining ability. That's not a bad deal, and it's cheaper than a tour if you share your cab with other travelers.

When you are out in the country, you may need to take a taxi to a remote destination on a bad road. During the rainy season, 4WD may be required. Many taxis are 4WD jeeps and can get you just about anywhere.

BICYCLE

All the warnings under the Road Rules section, above, apply here – but even more so. There are no bike lanes and traffic can be hazardous on the narrow, steep, winding roads. Cycling is a possibility, however, and long-distance cyclists report that locals tend to be very friendly toward them. It is possible to cycle all the way from the USA, or you can fly your bicycle down as luggage. Check with airlines for regulations – often a bicycle will be carried free of charge if it is properly packed and doesn't exceed luggage size and weight requirements (see Mountain Biking in the Facts for the Visitor chapter).

A few companies rent bikes and/or arrange escorted tours; some are listed in the Organized Tours section, below; some in the Getting There & Away chapter; and others in the San José chapter.

HITCHHIKING

Hitchhiking is never entirely safe in any country, and Lonely Planet doesn't recommend it. Travelers who hitchhike should understand that they are taking a small but potentially serious risk. People who do hitchhike will be safer if they travel in pairs and let someone know where they are planning to go.

On the main roads, the frequency of inexpensive buses makes hitchhiking unusual, except during the holiday periods when buses may be full. If you do get a ride, offer to pay for it when you arrive: '*¿Cuánto le debo?*' ('How much do I owe you?') is the standard way of doing this. Often, your offer will be waved aside; sometimes you'll be asked to help with gas money. If you are driving, picking up hitchhikers in the countryside is normally no problem and often gets you into some interesting conversations.

Tico hitchhikers are more often seen on minor rural roads. If you hitch, imitate the locals. They don't simply stand there with their thumbs out. Vehicles may pass only a few times per hour and ticos try to wave them down in a friendly fashion, then chat with the driver about where they're going and how lousy the bus service is. (This gives you a chance to size up the driver and car occupants; if you don't feel comfortable, don't take the ride.)

BOAT

There are various passenger and car ferries in operation. Three cheap ferries operate out of Puntarenas across the Golfo de Nicoya. One is a huge car ferry that leaves several times a day for Playa Naranjo (a 1½-hour trip). The others are a car ferry and a small passenger ferry that crosses to Paquera two or three times a day, taking about 1½ hours. Buses meet the ferries at Paquera to transport you onward into the Península de Nicoya. Complete details are given in the appropriate town sections in this book.

There is also a car ferry operating across the mouth of the Río Tempisque, which cuts two or three hours off the road trip to the Península de Nicoya – if you can time the ferry crossing just right. The ferry runs every hour from 5 am to 8 pm; see the Northwestern Costa Rica chapter for details.

A daily passenger ferry links Golfito with Puerto Jiménez on the Península de Osa; the trip takes about 1½ hours. This ferry is subject to cancellation. Puerto Jiménez is the nearest town of any size to Parque Nacional Corcovado.

Motorized dugout canoes ply the Río Sarapiquí once a day on a scheduled basis and more frequently on demand. See Puerto Viejo de Sarapiquí in the Northern Lowlands chapter for more details. Daily motorboats also go to Tortuguero (see the Tortuguero Area section in the Caribbean Lowlands chapter).

Other boat trips can be made, but these are tours rather than rides on scheduled ferries. These include canal boats up the inland waterway from Moín (near Puerto Limón) to Parque Nacional Tortuguero and Refugio Nacional de Fauna Silvestre Barra del Colorado.

Boats can be hired at Puerto Viejo de Sarapiquí down the Río Sarapiquí to the Río San Juan, which forms much of the Costa Rica/Nicaragua border. It's possible to travel along the border down the Río San Juan as far as its mouth, and then down into the Refugio Nacional de Fauna Silvestre Barra del Colorado. This is not a regularly scheduled trip, but it can be arranged – see under Puerto Viejo de Sarapiquí or Barra del Colorado for further information.

People staying in the Bahía Drake area usually arrive or leave via an exciting boat trip on the Río Sierpe.

For adventurous types, river running or floats down Ríos Pacuare, Reventazón, Corobicí, Chirripó, and Sarapiquí for one or more days is one option – see Organized Tours later in this chapter for further information. Fishing trips, either on Laguna de Arenal or offshore, are another option.

One-day sailing trips in the Golfo de Nicoya can be booked on various boats, the best known of which is the yacht *Calypso* (see Organized Tours, below); others can be arranged with travel agents in San José.

LOCAL TRANSPORT

Bus

Local buses serve urban and suburban areas, but services and routes can be difficult to figure out. Many towns are small enough that getting around on foot is easy. Some local bus details are provided in the Getting There & Away sections for major towns in this book.

Local people are usually very friendly, and this includes bus drivers, who will often be able to tell you where to wait for a particular bus.

Taxi

In San José, taxis have meters, called *marías*, but these might not be used, particularly for foreigners who can't speak Spanish. (It is illegal not to use the meter.) Outside San José, taxis don't have meters and so fares are agreed upon in advance; bargaining is acceptable. In rural areas, 4WD jeeps are used as taxis.

Within San José, a short ride should cost about US$1. A ride across town will cost around US$2, and it's about US$4 to suburbs. Rates are comparable in other parts of the country. Taxi drivers are not normally tipped. Taxi cabs are red and have a small sticker in the windshield identifying them as a 'TAXI.'

ORGANIZED TOURS

Over 200 tour operators are recognized by the Costa Rican Tourist Board, with the majority in San José.

Many companies specialize in nature tours, with visits to the national parks and wilderness lodges. They can provide entire guided itineraries (with English-speaking guides) and private transport to any part of the country, especially the nature destinations. Many of these nature-tour companies also specialize in adventure tourism, such as river running or mountain biking. Almost all agencies also provide services such as day trips around the Central Valley, San José city tours, hotel reservations, and airport transfers.

Prices vary depending on the services you require. Two people wishing to travel with a private English-speaking guide and a private vehicle will obviously pay a lot more than two people who are prepared to join a group or can understand a Spanish-speaking guide. Note that although these companies are in Costa Rica, most will happily take advance reservations from abroad. For detailed information on operators that arrange tours of Costa Rica from abroad, see the Organized Tours section in the Getting There & Away chapter.

For an overview of things to do on tours, see the Activities section in the Facts for the Visitor chapter. For more on fishing trips, see the coastal chapters.

Tour Companies in Costa Rica

The oldest (since 1978) and biggest nature/adventure-tour company is **Costa Rica Expeditions** (☎ 257-0766, 222-0333, fax 257-1665, www.costaricaexpeditions.com), at Calle Central, Avenida 3. It pioneered adventure and nature tourism in Costa Rica and has received awards for both its work and its environmental awareness, including honorable mentions in the *Condé Nast Traveler* Ecotourism Awards in 1995 and 1996 and the *Travel and Leisure* Critics' Choice Award in 1999. The top guides are well-qualified naturalists or ornithologists – all the staff is very professional and the company is highly recommended. It specializes in natural history tours, particularly to Parque Nacional Tortuguero and Reserva Biológica Monteverde (where it has its own luxurious lodges), and Parque Nacional Corcovado (where it has a tent camp and a rainforest canopy platform). It also does river rafting (it is the oldest rafting company in Costa Rica) and other trips. The standard of services is excellent (their motto is 'legendary service…unforgettable memories'), and the trips are priced accordingly. The mailing address is Dept 235, PO Box 025216, Miami, FL 33102-5216, USA.

Another highly recommended nature-tour company is **Horizontes** (☎ 222-2022, fax 255-4513, www.horizontes.com), Calle 28, Avenidas 1 & 3. It has been arranging nature and adventure tours for 15 years and has built up an excellent reputation. Some of the tours are recommended for families with children over five. Horizontes is Costa Rica Expeditions' biggest competitor, but it speaks well for both companies that they regard themselves as colleagues in the sense of running environmentally and socially responsible operations.

Costa Rica Sun Tours (☎ 255-3418, fax 255-4410, www.crsuntours.com) is at Calle 36, Avenida 4. It does the normal nature tours and fishing trips, and operates the Arenal Observatory Lodge at Volcán Arenal, where fishing trips on Laguna de Arenal can also be undertaken, and Tiskita Jungle Lodge, which is on a private reserve on the far southern Pacific coast. The company is recommended.

Several other companies specialize in nature tours and have also been recommended. **Tikal** (☎ 223-2811, 257-1494, fax 223-1916), Avenida 2, Calles 7 & 9, has a wide variety of tours ranging from day trips to weeklong tours. **Los Caminos de la Selva** (Jungle Trails; ☎ 255-3486, fax 255-2782), Calle 38, Avenidas 5 & 7, specializes in trips to Volcán Barva and, if you can get a group together, will arrange a tree-planting tour where you learn about the ecological value of native trees. You get to plant a tree of your choice. It also visits other parks in the Central Valley.

Green Tropical Tours (☎/fax 292-5003, 380-1536 cellular, information@greentropical.com) specializes in trips to Monumento Nacional Guayabo and to a private cloud forest reserve near Los Juncos. It can arrange trips to many other places and also offers bilingual driver/guides (one person who drives and guides). The office is in San Isidro de Coronado (about 12km north of San José, in the Central Valley) on Calle El Rodeo, 1.5km north of the Catholic church. Owner Juan Carlos Ramos does a great job and often accompanies groups himself.

Several companies specialize in river rafting. Especially recommended is **Ríos Tropicales** (☎ 233-6455, fax 255-4354, www.riostro.com), Calle 32, Avenida 2 (100m south of Pollo Kentucky on Paseo Colón), which has river rafting and kayaking trips and sea kayaking expeditions. It has a lodge on the Río Pacuare for overnight trips. Owned and operated by Costa Rican kayaking champions, this is an excellent organization that does much to improve the sport and protect the rivers in Costa Rica.

Aventuras Naturales (☎ 222-0333, fax 253-6934; in the USA ☎ 800-514-0411, www.toenjoynature.com), on Avenida Central, Calles 33 & 35, also has hiking and cycling tours. You can combine tours and stay overnight at its Río Pacuare Lodge. **Safaris Corobicí** (☎/fax 669-1091, safaris@sol.racsa.co.cr) specializes in Río Corobicí float trips; **Sarapiquí Aguas Bravas** (☎ 292-2072, fax 229-4837, www.aguas-bravas.co.cr) rafts the Río Sarapiquí and offers biking trips; and **Iguana Tours** (☎/fax 777-1262, info@iguanatours.com) does rafting and kayaking from Parque Nacional Manuel Antonio. Also check out Costa Rica Expeditions (see earlier reference in this section).

One of the most famous boat trips is an all-day yacht cruise through the Golfo de Nicoya to Isla Tortuga – excellent food and good swimming opportunities. The longest-running of these cruises is by **Calypso Tours** (☎ 256-2727, fax 256-6767, www.calypsotours.com). The office is in Edificio Las Arcadas, Avenida 2, Calles 1 & 3. It uses a luxurious catamaran, the *Manta Ray*, and does other cruises, too; see the Islands Near Bahía Gigante section in the Península de Nicoya chapter for more details.

There are cruises along the Caribbean canals to Tortuguero, too. These usually involve one or two nights at lodges in either Parque Nacional Tortuguero or Barra del Colorado, and can be combined with bus or airplane returns, wildlife watching, and fishing trips, depending on your time and budget. These companies are listed under the Tortuguero Area section in the Caribbean Lowlands chapter.

The MV *Temptress Voyager* is a 53m vessel with 30 double and three single air-conditioned cabins with private showers and outside windows. The ship is run by **Temptress Adventure Cruises** (☎ 232-6672, fax 220-2103; in the USA ☎ 800-336-8423, www.temptresscruises.com). Seven-day cruises along the Pacific coast visit the following: Manuel Antonio, Corcovado, Bahía Drake, Golfo Dulce, Curú, and Isla Coiba. There are naturalist and biologist guides aboard. Scuba diving is also possible for certified divers with their own gear – the boat has air, tanks, and weights. Cruises leave from Bahía Herradura, though prices are all-inclusive from San José. High-season fares for seven nights are from US$1995 to US$2695 per person in doubles, with most cabins at US$2495 per person. Children get big discounts.

There are many fishing lodges and boats on both coasts. **Americana Fishing Services** (☎ 223-4331, fax 221-0096, fishing@sol.racsa.co.cr), with an office in the lobby of the Hotel del Rey, Avenida 1, Calle 9, San José, can advise you about these and arrange a customized itinerary to fit your needs.

Cosmos Tours (☎ 234-0607, fax 253-4707, cosmos@sol.racsa.co.cr), Avenida 7, Calles 37 & 39, is good for airline reservations and hotel and tour bookings. Other agencies that readers have recommended for general travel and tours include **Central American Tours** (☎ 255-4111, fax 255-4216), with an office in the Cariari Hotel (☎ 239-0281) and a friendly staff. **Camino Travel** (☎ 234-2530) does general bookings and arranges hiking guides for climbing Chirripó.

Ecole Travel (☎ 223-2240, fax 223-4128, ecolecr@sol.racsa.co.cr), Calle 7, Avenidas Central & 1, specializes in budget travel, especially to Tortuguero and Corcovado, but also to other destinations. Budget tours mean that you might stay in rock-bottom-priced hotels, and meals might not be included, but they get you there. Some tours are more costly but include meals or better accommodations.

Canopy Tour (☎/fax 257-5149, 256-7626, www.canopytour.com) has pioneered adventurous rainforest canopy tours that involve a rope ascent or a rope traverse to a platform built in a tall tree, followed by traverses to other platforms. This is not recommended for someone who is afraid of heights! The first platform/rope systems were built near Monteverde and at Iguana Park near Orotina. Others have since been added on Isla Tortuga and near Ciudad Quesada. The Canadian founders' objective is to provide an adventurous ecological experience while helping to preserve the rainforest through direct financial support.

Costa Rica Rainforest Outward Bound (☎/fax 777-1222, 777-0052; in the USA ☎ 800-676-2018, www.crrobs.org) has an 85-day adventure course that visits Costa Rica, Ecuador, and Peru, with academic credit available. The course fee is US$7400 from Costa Rica (including flights to Ecuador and Peru). It also does 10-, 15-, 24-, and 30-day courses within Ecuador; some are suitable for 14-year-olds, and others are for older students.

Rent-a-Harley Davidson & Tours (☎ 289-5552, 228-9072, fax 289-5551, www.arweb.com/harleytours/) offers either rental of Harley-Davidsons or tours ranging from one to 10 days. Rentals cost US$110 to US$195 per day, depending on the bike, and weekly rentals cost the same as six days. Rates include helmets, insurance, rain gear, locks, and unlimited mileage. Renters must be 25 years old, be experienced at riding big bikes, and have a credit card and passport. Contact the company about escorted tours including hotel arrangements, etc, or unescorted tours with hotel arrangements. Passengers can ride with guides.

Other agencies that serve just a local area are mentioned in the appropriate sections of the regional chapters.

San José

For the traveler who arrives at the Costa Rican capital overland from other Central American nations, as I first did in 1980, San José comes as something of a surprise. Compared to other capitals of the region, it is more cosmopolitan, even North Americanized. There are department stores and shopping malls, fast-food chain restaurants, and blue jeans.

It takes a day or two to start getting the real *tico* feeling of the city. Perhaps the first sign of being in Costa Rica is the friendliness of the people. Asking someone the way will often result in a smile and a genuine attempt to help you out – a refreshing change from many other capital cities.

Although the city was founded in 1737, little remains from the colonial era. Indeed, until the Teatro Nacional was built in the 1890s, San José was a small and largely forgotten city. Today, the capital boasts several excellent museums, good restaurants, and a fine climate – the main attractions for visitors. But most visitors have a quick look at the museums, then go on to the national parks, rainforests, and beaches – tasty food and an agreeable climate can be found elsewhere in the country. Because Costa Rica's public transport and road system radiates from San José, the capital is often used as a base from which to visit the many attractions of the country.

Although Costa Rica is known for trying to preserve the environment with one of the best national park systems in Latin America, the environmental effort is less evident in urban areas. In the late '90s, the phasing out of leaded fuel and the introduction of a vehicle emissions program ('Ecomarchamo') were followed by a slight decrease in lead and carbon monoxide levels; however, air pollution, mainly from street traffic, remains a definite problem in the city. Signs posted around the city with the hopeful slogan *Limpio y Verde* – 'Clean and Green' – are part of a recent anti-litter campaign.

The population of the city itself is about a third of a million, but the surrounding suburbs boost the number to about 900,000. The population of the whole province is about 1.2 million, or 40% of the country. Inhabitants of San José are sometimes referred to as *josefinos*.

ORIENTATION

The city stands at an elevation of 1150m and is set in a wide and fertile valley known throughout Costa Rica as the Valle Central (Central Valley).

The city center, where many visitors spend most of their time, is arranged in a grid. All the streets are numbered in a logical fashion, and it is important to learn the system because all street directions and addresses rely on it (see the boxed text 'Costa Rican Street Addresses'). This system is also applied in many other Costa Rican towns.

The center has several districts, or *barrios*. These are rather loosely defined, but they are well known to josefinos. Perhaps the most interesting to downtown visitors is Barrio Amón, northeast of Avenida 5 and Calle 1, which has the best concentration of turn-of-the-century buildings, most of which tend to be residential or small commercial structures rather than major public edifices. East of Amón is Barrio Otoya, a less trendy version of Amón. East of downtown is the semiresidential barrio of Los Yoses, with an increasing number of first-class restaurants and hotels, followed by San Pedro, which is a major suburb in its own right and is where the main university is found, with the accompanying university-area ambience.

West of the center is La Sabana, named after the biggest park in San José. Northwest of La Sabana lies Rohrmoser, which has many elegant addresses, including several ambassadors' residences. In the hills several kilometers south of La Sabana is the suburb of Escazú, with many B&Bs offering fine views of central San José below.

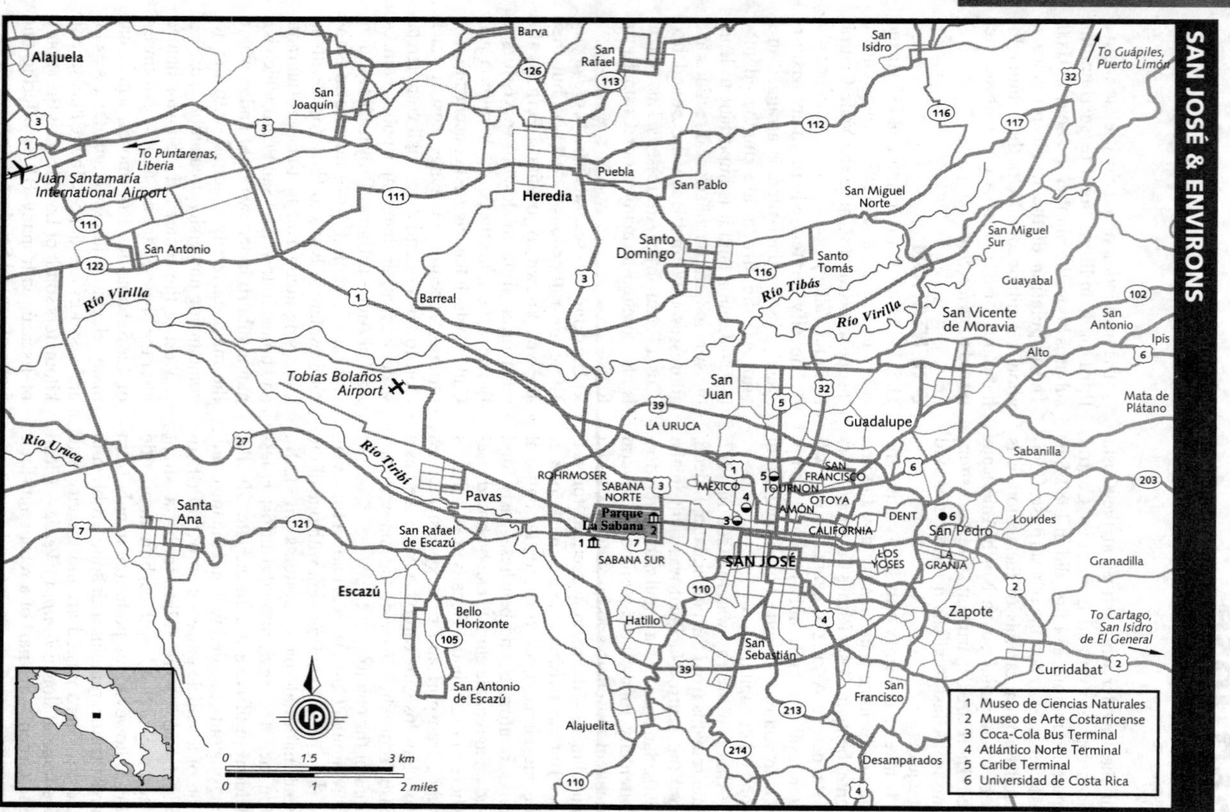
SAN JOSÉ & ENVIRONS
1 Museo de Ciencias Naturales
2 Museo de Arte Costarricense
3 Coca-Cola Bus Terminal
4 Atlántico Norte Terminal
5 Caribe Terminal
6 Universidad de Costa Rica
To Guápiles, Puerto Limón
To Cartago, San Isidro de El General
To Puntarenas, Liberia
Juan Santamaría International Airport
Tobías Bolaños Airport
SAN JOSÉ
Parque La Sabana
SABANA NORTE
SABANA SUR
ROHRMOSER
LA URUCA
MÉXICO
TOURNÓN
AMÓN
OTOYA
SAN FRANCISCO
CALIFORNIA
LOS YOSES
DENT
LA GRANJA
San Pedro
Zapote
Curridabat
Granadilla
Sabanilla
Lourdes
Guadalupe
San Vicente de Moravia
Guayabal
Alto
San Antonio
Ipís
Mata de Plátano
San Miguel Sur
San Miguel Norte
Santo Tomás
San Isidro
Santo Domingo
San Pablo
Puebla
San Juan
Heredia
San Rafael
Barva
Barreal
San Joaquín
San Antonio
Alajuela
Pavas
San Rafael de Escazú
Escazú
Bello Horizonte
San Antonio de Escazú
Santa Ana
Hatillo
Alajuelita
San Sebastián
Desamparados
San Francisco
Río Virilla
Río Tibás
Río Tiribí
Río Uruca
0 1.5 3 km
0 1 2 miles

INFORMATION

The friendliness of the Costa Ricans has already been mentioned – but it really is one of the outstanding features of this country. The local people can often be your best source of information.

Tourist Offices

The main tourist office of the Instituto Costarricense de Turismo (ICT; ☎ 222-1090, 222-1733 ext 277, fax 223-1090, Web: www.tourism-costarica.com) is on the Plaza de la Cultura at Calle 5 & Avenida Central, next to the Museo de Oro, open 9 am to 5 pm weekdays, with a flexible lunch hour. There is also an ICT office at the airport to greet arriving travelers, which is open for longer hours.

Money

Any bank will change foreign currency into *colones*, but US dollars are the most accepted currency. The commissions, when charged, should be small – never more than 1% of the transaction; otherwise, go elsewhere. Banco Nacional de Costa Rica and Banco de Costa Rica are very slow; the non-national banks tend to give the fastest service.

Recommended non-national banks include the following:

Banco Banex
(☎ 257-0522) Calle Central, Avenida 1

Banco de San José
(☎ 256-9911) Calle Central, Avenidas 3 & 5

Banco del Istmo
(☎ 257-9011) Calle 2, Avenidas Central & 1

Banco Mercantil
(☎ 257-6868) Calle 2, Avenida 3

Banco Metropolitano
(☎ 257-3030) Calle Central & Avenida 2

Banco Popular
(☎ 257-5797) Calle 1, Avenidas 2 & 4

Each has many branches, and there are many other banks. Most banks are open 9 am to 3 pm weekdays. A few banks are open longer than normal hours. The Banco Nacional de Costa Rica at Avenida 1, Calle 7, is open 10 am to 5 pm weekdays.

Most of the major banks have, or are planning to have, 24-hour ATMs, accepting a variety of cards. ATMs outside of San José often do not work, so if you are financing yourself through an ATM, do it before you leave the capital. Aside from credit cards, cards that bear the Plus and Cirrus logos are the most commonly accepted. Withdrawal limits can vary significantly, so look around; also, depending on the charges incurred with your card, getting cash from an ATM can be more economical than paying a commission to a teller. A convenient nonbank ATM is at the western entrance of the Omni Center at Calle 3, Avenida 1. Another option is stopping at a Burger King; for some reason, they often have ATMs that accept Visa and MasterCard.

The better hotels have exchange windows for their guests. Rates should be fairly similar to those at banks, but sometimes they aren't, so check before changing large sums. The advantage of changing money at your hotel is speed and convenience.

Another alternative to banks is an exchange house, although there are few of these. Their service is fast and their exchange rates good. Also, they claim to accept foreign currency other than US dollars. The following were operating recently:

Compania Financiera de Londres
(☎ 222-8155, fax 221-2003)
Calle Central, Avenida Central

Especialides Electricas
Avenida Central, Calles 5 & 7

GAB International Money Exchange
In the Edificio Las Arcadas arcade, Avenida 2, Calles 1 & 3; open 8:15 am to 4 pm weekdays

Changing money on the streets gives you almost no advantage over the banks; rip-offs, forged currency, and other scams abound, so changing money on the streets can't be recommended. Still, if you are desperate after hours, moneychangers are a choice – they hang out around Avenida Central & Calle 2. Go with a friend and be very careful. There are also moneychangers at the airport.

Credit cards are widely accepted and you can use them to buy colones in banks (see

Costa Rican Street Addresses

Few addresses in Costa Rica have the street and number system that many visitors are used to. Instead, addresses are given from nearby street intersections or from local landmarks. The system is described here and uses San José for specific examples, but it is similar in other Costa Rican towns.

The streets running east-west are *avenidas,* and the streets running north-south are *calles*. Avenida Central runs east-west through the middle of the city; avenidas north of Avenida Central are odd-numbered, with Avenida 1 running parallel and one block north of Avenida Central, followed by Avenida 3, and so on. The avenidas south of Avenida Central are even-numbered. Similarly, Calle Central runs north-south through the heart of downtown, and calles east of Calle Central are odd-numbered and calles west of Calle Central are even-numbered. If you ask a passerby for directions, you'll probably be told to go seven blocks west and four blocks north *('Siete cuadras al oeste y cuatro cuadras al norte')*. Often, 100m is used to mean a city block, so you may be told, *'Setecientos metros al oeste y cuatrocientos metros al norte.'* This does not literally mean 700m west and 400m north; it refers to city blocks. *Cincuenta metros* (50m) means half a block. Perhaps one reason for this method of giving directions is the lack of street signs, especially away from downtown.

Street addresses in San José are rarely given by the building number (although some numbers do exist). Instead, the nearest street intersection is given. Thus, the address of the Museo Nacional is Calle 17, Avenidas Central & 2. This means it is on Calle 17 between Avenida Central & Avenida 2 (*y* means 'and' in Spanish). This is often abbreviated in telephone directories or other literature to C17, A Ctl/2, or occasionally C17, A 0/2, with 0 replacing the Central. If an address is on or near a corner, just the street intersection is given.

the Money section in the Facts for the Visitor chapter). American Express (☎ 223-0116, 223-0112) in the Banco de San José sells US-dollar traveler's checks to American Express cardholders. If your AmEx credit card or traveler's checks are lost or stolen, call them toll-free at ☎ 800-528-2121 or 800-828-0366.

Post

The Correo Central (Central Post Office) is on Calle 2, Avenidas 1 & 3. Hours are 8 am to 5 pm weekdays. The post office is open for machine stamp sales 24 hours a day. The better hotels have mailboxes and sell stamps. Most people use the post office to mail their letters. (Most ticos also use the post office to receive their mail at a PO box, or apartado, because of the lack of precise street addresses.)

You can receive mail addressed to you c/o Lista de Correos, Correo Central, San José, Costa Rica. They are very strict about whom they give mail to. You must produce identification (usually your passport) before they will even look for your mail. They will not give mail to friends or family members; you must get it in person. There is a US25¢ fee per piece of mail received. Mail is held for a month before being returned to sender. American Express in the Banco de San José (see Money, above) will hold mail for AmEx customers addressed to the cardmember, c/o American Express, Banco de San José, Calle Central, Avenidas 3 & 5, San José.

Receiving packages can be problematic because of customs requirements – try to have only letters sent to you. Mail theft is a perennial problem, so don't have valuables sent to you in the mail if you can avoid it.

Telephone

You can make local calls and international calls from most public telephone booths, which accept five-, 10-, and 20-colón coins or the new CHIP telephone cards – see Post & Communications in the Facts for the Visitor

Costa Rican Street Addresses

Note that San José's Avenida Central becomes Paseo Colón west of Calle 14. The building on the north side of Paseo Colón, Calles 38 & 40, is known as Centro Colón and is a local landmark.

Many ticos use local landmarks to give directions, or even addresses in smaller towns. Thus, an address may be 200m south and 150m east of a church, a radio station, a restaurant, or even a *pulpería* (corner grocery store). Sometimes, the landmark may no longer exist, but because it has been used for so long, its position is known by all the locals.

A good example is La Coca-Cola, which is a bus terminal in San José where a Coca-Cola bottling plant used to be for many years. Everyone knows this, except for the first-time visitor! This can get confusing, but persevere. The friendly ticos will usually help you out. Note that taxi drivers especially like to know the landmark address. Drivers will sometimes say that they don't understand where you want to go until you explain your destination in terms of landmarks. It pays to use them – cab drivers are unlikely to overcharge you if you look like you know where you're going!

Street signs in central San José are plentiful, but there is a dearth of them away from the center and in many towns. Although the city maps in this book show the official names of the streets, beware of the fact that very few streets have their names posted at every corner. Many locals don't know street addresses and will be much more likely to use local landmarks. Many hotels have business cards with landmark addresses rather than street addresses.

To have mail delivered, many places have a post office box *(apartado)*, so if you see an apartado or 'apdo' address, don't look for it on the map.

– Rob Rachowiecki

chapter. An ICE office selling telephone cards and providing quiet public booths for making international calls is located near the Plaza de la Cultura, at Avenida 2, Calle 1. They are open 8 am to 8 pm daily.

You can also make off-street international calls at Radiográfica (☎ 287-0087), Calle 1, Avenida 5. They are open 7 am to 10 pm daily and also provide email, telex, and fax services. They will hold faxes for you for up to a month and charge about US50¢ a page for receiving and holding them. The better hotels will put international calls through from their switchboards, but these calls are more expensive.

Telephone directories are available in hotels and at Radiográfica. There are none in the public telephone booths.

Email & Internet Access

At this writing, the best place to access the Internet in downtown San José is the CyberCafe (☎ 233-3310), on Avenida 2 just west of the Teatro Nacional, downstairs in the Edificio Las Arcadas. Owner Roger Pilon and his right-hand man, the charming Fernando Muñoz, speak Spanish and English and will give you all the help you need with accessing or setting up an email account. Good coffee and sandwiches are available, and the place is as much a café and meeting place as it is an Internet outlet. KitCom Communications (☎ 258-0303), Calle 3, Avenidas 1 & 3, has a few computers in a small office. They provide good information about public transportation and other tourist industry services, including a reliable bus schedule and terminal map. In San Pedro, the Internet Cafe de Costa Rica (☎ 224-7295), 50m east of the Banco Popular, is open 24 hours. Though they include some food in their hourly charge, they will charge you for two hours if you stay online for 61 minutes, and charge you double if a friend sits at the computer with you. Also see the Email & Internet Access section in the Facts for the Visitor chapter.

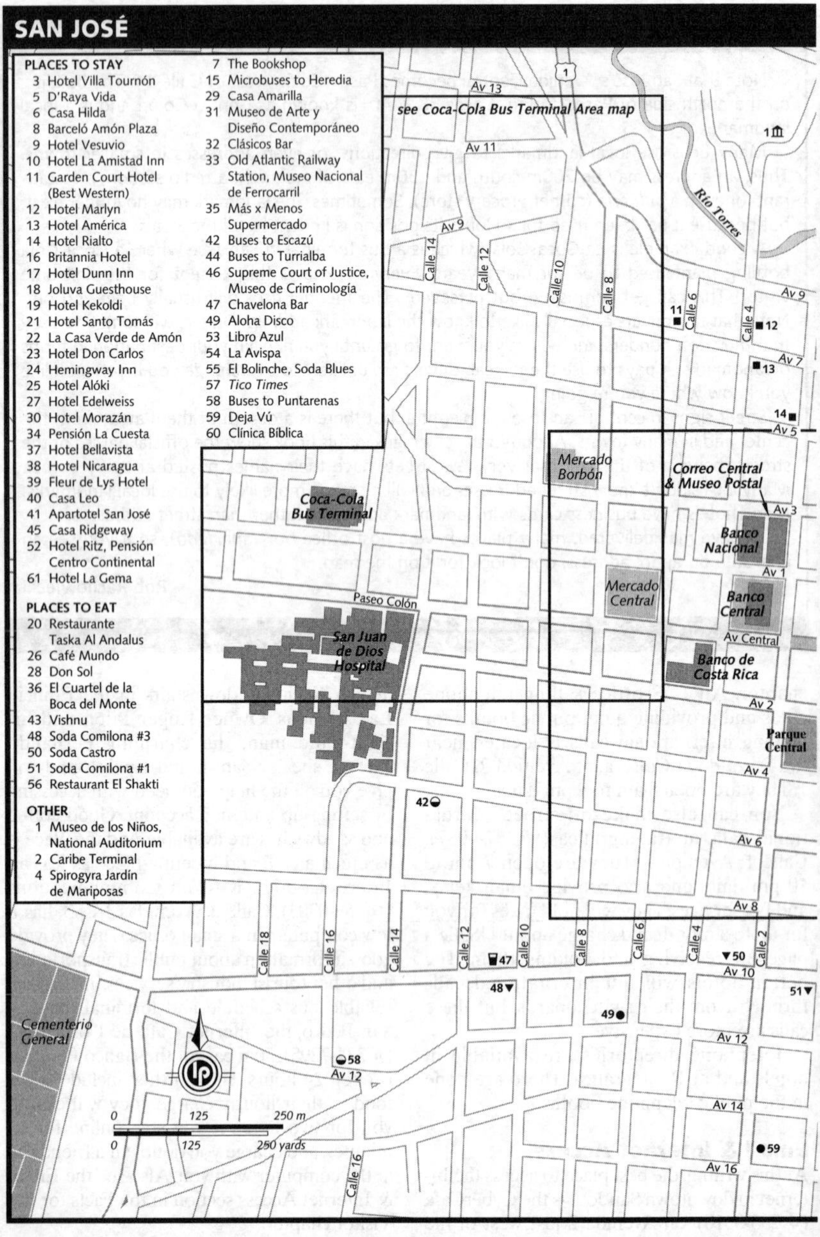

SAN JOSÉ

PLACES TO STAY
3 Hotel Villa Tournón
5 D'Raya Vida
6 Casa Hilda
8 Barceló Amón Plaza
9 Hotel Vesuvio
10 Hotel La Amistad Inn
11 Garden Court Hotel (Best Western)
12 Hotel Marlyn
13 Hotel América
14 Hotel Rialto
16 Britannia Hotel
17 Hotel Dunn Inn
18 Joluva Guesthouse
19 Hotel Kekoldi
21 Hotel Santo Tomás
22 La Casa Verde de Amón
23 Hotel Don Carlos
24 Hemingway Inn
25 Hotel Alóki
27 Hotel Edelweiss
30 Hotel Morazán
34 Pensión La Cuesta
37 Hotel Bellavista
38 Hotel Nicaragua
39 Fleur de Lys Hotel
40 Casa Leo
41 Apartotel San José
45 Casa Ridgeway
52 Hotel Ritz, Pensión Centro Continental
61 Hotel La Gema
PLACES TO EAT
20 Restaurante Taska Al Andalus
26 Café Mundo
28 Don Sol
36 El Cuartel de la Boca del Monte
43 Vishnu
48 Soda Comilona #3
50 Soda Castro
51 Soda Comilona #1
56 Restaurant El Shakti
OTHER
1 Museo de los Niños, National Auditorium
2 Caribe Terminal
4 Spirogyra Jardín de Mariposas
7 The Bookshop
15 Microbuses to Heredia
29 Casa Amarilla
31 Museo de Arte y Diseño Contemporáneo
32 Clásicos Bar
33 Old Atlantic Railway Station, Museo Nacional de Ferrocarril
35 Más x Menos Supermercado
42 Buses to Escazú
44 Buses to Turrialba
46 Supreme Court of Justice, Museo de Criminología
47 Chavelona Bar
49 Aloha Disco
53 Libro Azul
54 La Avispa
55 El Bolinche, Soda Blues
57 Tico Times
58 Buses to Puntarenas
59 Deja Vú
60 Clínica Bíblica
see Coca-Cola Bus Terminal Area map
Av 13
Av 11
Av 9
Av 7
Av 5
Av 3
Av 1
Av Central
Av 2
Av 4
Av 6
Av 8
Av 10
Av 12
Av 14
Av 16
Calle 18
Calle 16
Calle 14
Calle 12
Calle 10
Calle 8
Calle 6
Calle 4
Calle 2
Río Torres
Mercado Borbón
Correo Central & Museo Postal
Coca-Cola Bus Terminal
Banco Nacional
Mercado Central
Banco Central
Paseo Colón
San Juan de Dios Hospital
Banco de Costa Rica
Parque Central
Cementerio General
0 125 250 m
0 125 250 yards

SAN JOSÉ

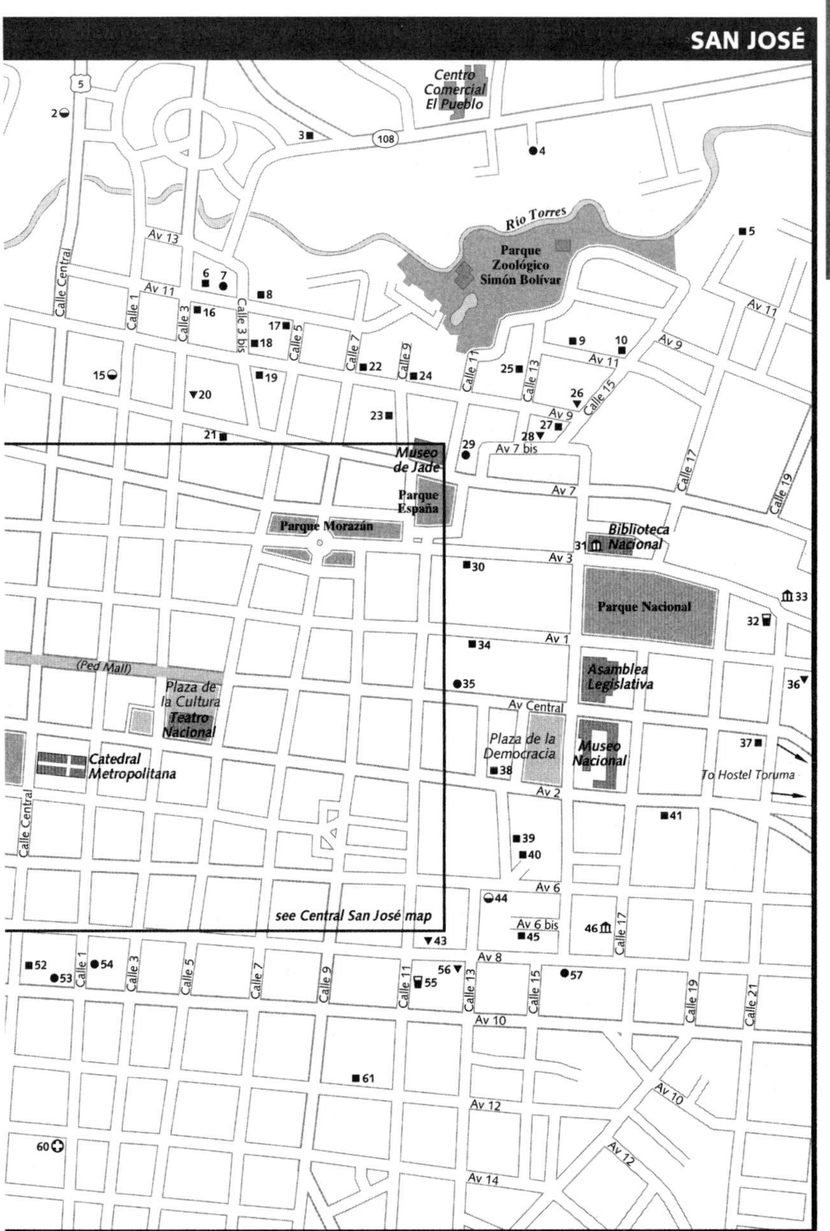
Centro Comercial El Pueblo
Río Torres
Parque Zoológico Simón Bolívar
Museo de Jade
Parque España
Parque Morazán
Biblioteca Nacional
Parque Nacional
Asamblea Legislativa
Plaza de la Cultura
Teatro Nacional
Catedral Metropolitana
Plaza de la Democracia
Museo Nacional
(Ped Mall)
To Hostel Toruma
see Central San José map
Calle Central
Calle 1
Calle 3
Calle 3 bis
Calle 5
Calle 7
Calle 9
Calle 11
Calle 13
Calle 15
Calle 17
Calle 19
Calle 21
Av 13
Av 11
Av 9
Av 7 bis
Av 7
Av 3
Av 1
Av Central
Av 2
Av 6
Av 6 bis
Av 8
Av 10
Av 12
Av 14
5
108

Bookstores

The following bookstores are among the most noteworthy:

7th Street Books
(☎ 256-8251) Calle 7, Avenidas Central & 1. This is an attractive shop with an excellent selection of books in English and other languages, both new and used, as well as wildlife guides and guidebooks. A large selection of magazines and newspapers is also available. The owners are very helpful and speak English. They share space with the budget travel agency Ecole Travel (see the Getting Around chapter) and are planning to expand into a second floor.

Mora Books
(☎/fax 255-4136, 383-8385). This is an atmospheric secondhand bookstore in the same complex as the mall-like Omni Center, run by Darren Mora, who is hands-down the coolest guy in San José. Books are mainly in English; guidebooks and comic books are also a specialty. Darren is a well-traveled tico with flawless English who can give you advice on everything from hiking in indigenous reserves to where to go dancing or get late-night *bocas*. There's usually a friendly mixture of foreigners and ticos hanging out in his store.

Librería Internacional
(☎ 253-9553, fax 280-5473) in Barrio Dent behind the San Pedro Mall, 300m west of Taco Bell. Though less centrally located than 7th Street Books, they offer a similar range of books (new only) – from Latin American authors (in original and translation) and international literature (in English and other languages) to travel and wildlife guides. They also have a selection of children's books. The staff is helpful and speaks English. They have a second location, the Librería Internacional Multiplaza (☎ 288-1138, fax 288-1139), in the Escazú area, in the Multiplaza near the Camino Real hotel.

The Bookshop
Avenida 11, Calle 3 & Calle 3 bis. The longest-running English bookshop in Costa Rica, the Bookshop has relocated to an attractive early-20th-century house (old by local standards). There is a noteworthy gallery of modern local and indigenous art (for sale), a coffee shop with good coffee, pastries, and light snacks, and a helpful staff. At last visit, only a small selection of books (in English and Spanish) was available, but the owners are planning to bring in more. Hours are 10 am to 7 pm Monday to Saturday. They are open during most holidays as well – but don't have a phone.

Lehmann's
(☎ 223-1212) Avenida Central, Calles 1 & 3. This shop has some books, magazines, and newspapers in English and a selection of Costa Rican maps (in the map department upstairs).

Librería Francesa
(☎ 223-7979) Calle 3, Avenidas Central & 1. This store sells French books.

Librería Universal
(☎ 222-2222) Avenida Central, Calles Central & 1. This is one of the biggest bookstores in Costa Rica. It has maps and a few books in English, and tends to be crowded.

Libro Azul
Avenida 10, Calles Central & 1. This is a tiny shop offering secondhand books in Spanish.

English-language magazines, newspapers, and some books are also available in the gift shops of the international airport and several of the top-end hotels.

Laundry

There are few laundries or launderettes in San José (or, indeed, in Costa Rica), though there are plenty of *lavanderías,* most of which only do dry cleaning. To simply wash your own clothes, go to Lava-más (☎ 225-1645), Avenida 8, Calle 45 (next to the Los Yoses Spoon coffee shop). It's about US$4 per load to wash and dry, self-service. Lavandería Lavamex (☎ 258-2303), Calle 8, Avenidas Central & 1 (across from the Mercado Central), will wash and dry your clothes in about two to three hours for US$5.50 per load; they are open 8 am to 6 pm Monday to Saturday.

Burbujas (☎ 224-9822), 50m west and 25m south of the Más x Menos Supermercado in San Pedro, is open 8 am to 6:30 pm weekdays and 8:30 am to 5 pm Saturday. They have coin-operated machines. Nearby is Lava y Seca (☎ 224-5908), 10m north of the Más x Menos, which has drop-off wash and dry or dry-cleaning service.

Downtown, the Sixaola (☎ 221-2111), Avenida 2, Calles 7 & 9, charges US$4 a load (wash and dry) and has same-day service. They claim to have been scrubbing since 1912. Also, there's Sol y Fiesta, Avenida 8, Calles 7 & 9, which charges US$5 a load, including soap.

Most hotels will arrange for your laundry to be washed, but beware that the top-end hotels charge as much for a couple of items as you'd pay to get a whole load washed elsewhere.

Medical Services

The most central (free) hospital is Hospital San Juan de Dios (☎ 257-6282) at Paseo Colón, Calle 14.

If you can afford to pay for medical attention (costs are much cheaper than in the USA or Europe, for example), go to the well-recommended Clínica Bíblica (☎ 257-5252 or, in an emergency, 257-0466) on Avenida 14, Calles Central & 1. They have some English-speaking staff and are open 24 hours for emergencies. They will carry out laboratory tests (stool, urine, blood samples, etc) and recommend specialists if necessary. They also have a full range of other medical services, including a 24-hour pharmacy. There are plenty of other pharmacies in San José.

Your embassy is a good source of references for specialists if you need one. Embassy staff get sick too – and they usually know the best doctors, dentists, etc around.

Emergency

Call ☎ 911 for all emergencies. Call ☎ 128 for a Red Cross ambulance, ☎ 118 for the fire department, and ☎ 222-9330 or ☎ 222-9245 for the Policía de Transito (Traffic Police).

Dangers & Annoyances

There has been a noticeable increase in street crime over the past few years. That doesn't make San José as dangerous as some other Latin American capitals, or parts of many North American and European cities, but you should exercise basic precautions.

Sneak theft is much more likely than getting mugged – the generally peaceful outlook of ticos seems to extend even to street crime. Pickpockets and bag snatchers abound, so carry your money in an inside pocket, and carry bags firmly attached to your body with a strap rather than letting them dangle loosely over your shoulder. Keep day packs in front of you rather than on your back, where they can be unzipped and pilfered in a crowd. Don't wear expensive jewelry, watches, etc downtown – they can be snatched off.

In 1999, most thefts from travelers, including a number of muggings, happened in the area west of the Mercado Central, especially around the Coca-Cola bus terminal, so be careful in this area. The lively, popular area around Avenida 2 and the Parque Central has been the scene of many pick-pocketing attempts, particularly late at night.

Take the precautions you would when traveling to any large city with typical crime problems – don't carry valuables, keep money hidden, and keep your eyes open.

Don't leave cars parked on the streets – find a guarded parking lot. Don't leave any packages inside the car, even in a guarded lot, as they invite window smashing and theft. Men should beware of friendly prostitutes – they may pair up with you on quiet streets and pickpocket you while distracting you. Prostitutes are known for their abilities to take more than their customers bargained for, including lifting wallets during a sexual encounter. Another occasional scam is getting sprayed with ketchup and robbed by the person who steps in to help 'clean up' – yet another is being invited out by a well-dressed stranger for an evening that ends with too many stiff drinks and missing belongings. Women traveling alone have complained of being harassed by cab drivers at night – certainly, you should firmly discourage a macho driver at the first sign of an inappropriate comment, or ask to be dropped off immediately in a central area if you feel uncomfortable. (None of this happens very frequently.)

The best way to prevent problems is to first find out (from your hotel or other travelers) about the area you are going to, and, especially if bar-hopping at night, to go with a friend.

Finally, noise and smog are unavoidable components of the San José experience. Most central hotels have some street noise, and some are very noisy indeed. Even the best hotels are liable to suffer from some street noise, which might not be a problem if you live in a major city and are used to traffic. There is a fair amount of smog, which detracts from the walking experience during the day and may create a problem in some cheaper hotels in the bus station area.

Also, watch out for open gutters and potholes in the sidewalks, some of which are big enough to swallow a dog (a big dog).

THINGS TO SEE

The downtown area is small and congested with heavy traffic. Driving is not recommended, parking is very difficult, and sightseeing is best done on foot. The cluster of parks northeast of the center, and the neighborhoods between them, offer the most pleasant walking – particularly Barrio Amón, northeast of Avenida 5 and Calle 1, which has the best concentration of turn-of-the-century buildings. East of Amón is Barrio Otoya, a less-trendy version of Amón. The Avenida Central, from the Mercado Central through the Plaza de la Cultura to the Plaza de la Democracia, is a pedestrian mall most of its length and makes for a good urban walk. The Plaza de la Democracia is just below the Museo Nacional and the Parque Nacional and offers decent views of the mountains sur-

CENTRAL SAN JOSÉ

PLACES TO STAY
1 Hotel Compostela
2 Nuevo Hotel Central
3 Hotel Capital
5 Hotel Europa
9 Pensión Otoya
10 Aurola Holiday Inn
12 Hotel Astoria
13 Hotel ABC
23 Diana's Inn
27 Hotel del Rey
38 Hotel La Gran Viá
40 Hotel Balmoral
43 Gran Hotel Centroamericano
44 Hotel Diplomat
46 Hotel Plaza
47 Hotel Royal Dutch
49 Hotel Royal Garden
50 Pensión Americana
56 Gran Hotel Costa Rica
62 Tica Linda
63 Hotel Presidente
68 Hotel Avenida 2, Pensión Salamanca
70 Hotel Doral
71 Park Hotel
77 Hotel Fortuna
78 Hotel Príncipe
79 Hotel Boston
80 Casa 429
83 Gran Hotel Doña Inés

PLACES TO EAT
4 Soda Nini
8 Coffee Station
17 Vishnu
18 Naturama Uno
19 Restaurante Omni
20 Soda Central
21 La Vasconia
24 Restaurante Lung Mun
25 Pasta Factory & Pizzeria
27 City Café
42 Balcón de Europa
45 Mönpik
48 Churrería Manolos
51 Soda Palace
56 Café Parisienne
58 Soda B&B
59 Spoon
60 La Hacienda, L'Ile de France
61 Restaurant Fulusu
62 La Esmeralda Bar & Restaurant
64 Chelle's
66 Churrería Manolos
67 Panadería Schmidt, Pops Ice Cream
73 Ristorante Pizza Metro
74 Restaurante El Campesino
84 Restaurantes Tin-jo, Don Wang

OTHER
6 Banco de San José, American Express
7 Radiográfica
11 Galería Namu
14 Costa Rica Expeditions
15 KitCom Communications
16 Salsa 54
19 Omni Center, Mora Books
22 Nashville South Bar
26 Banco Nacional de Costa Rica
28 Serpentario
29 Beatle Bar
30 Casino Club Colonial
31 Banco del Istmo
32 La Casona
33 Companía Financiera de Londres (Money Exchange)
34 Las Risas
35 Librería Universal
36 TAM Travel Agency
37 Lehmann's
39 Ecole Travel & 7th Street Books
41 Lucky's Piano Blanco Bar, El Túnel de Tiempo Disco
52 Teatro Melico Salazar
53 Banco Metropolitano
54 ICE Telephone Office
55 Edificio Las Arcadas (CyberCafe, GAB International Money Exchange, Calypso Tours)
57 ICT Tourism Information Office, Museo de Oro Precolombino
65 Chelle's Taberna
69 Tiny's Tropical Bar & Restaurant
72 Buses to Irazú
75 Lavandería Sixaola, Tikal Tours
76 TICA Bus (International)
81 Sirca (International Buses)
82 Mercado Nacional de Artesanía

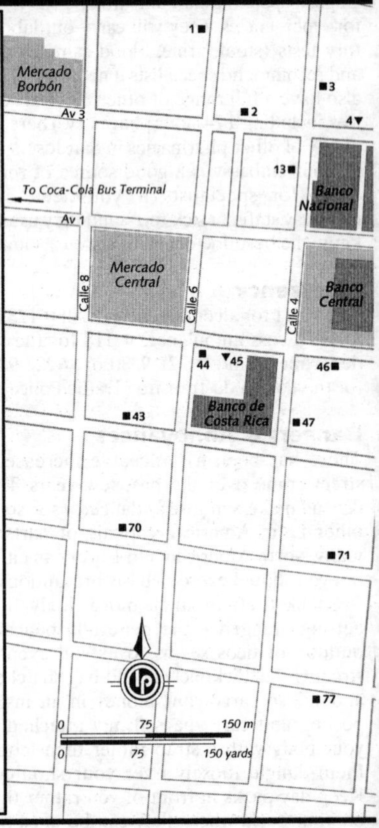

rounding the city. It will be fairly easy for you to find a route to join some of the sites of interest to you that are described below. Author Vernon Bell of Bell's Home Hospitality (see Books in the Facts for the Visitor chapter and Places to Stay, below) has produced a useful booklet describing suggested walks. Avenida 2 carries the main flow of traffic from west to east. Many downtown streets are one way.

Museum Hours & Admission Opening hours sometimes fluctuate, especially at the smaller museums; before making a long trek, call ahead to ensure that the museum will be open when you arrive. Ticos often pay less than foreign visitors; the non-tico admission fees are given in this book.

Museo de Jade

This is perhaps Costa Rica's most famous museum. It houses the world's largest collection of American jade, and hundreds of pieces are on display. Many pieces are mounted with a backlight so that the exquisite translucent quality of this gemstone can be fully appreciated. There are also archaeological exhibits of ceramics, stonework, and gold, arranged by cultural regions.

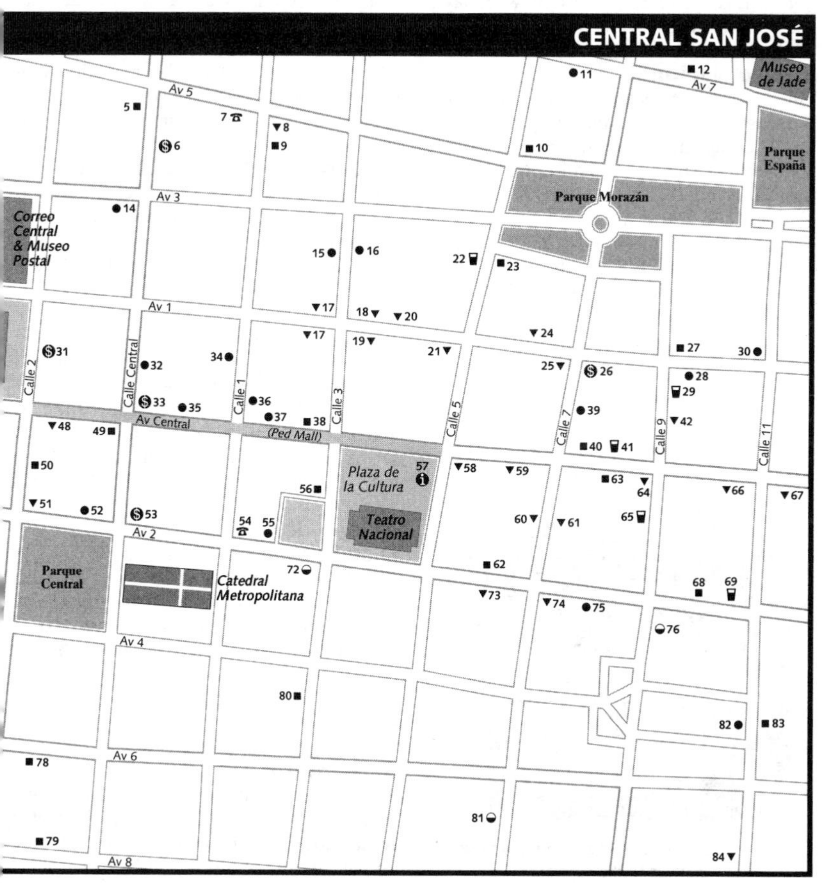

The 11th-floor vantage point offers a good view of the city – bring your camera. There's an interesting metal building to the southwest. It was designed in France and shipped over in prefabricated sections; it is now a school. With the city view and world-class jade collection, this museum is at the top of most visitors' lists of places to see.

Note that 'jade' is written the same as in English but is pronounced 'HA-day' in Spanish.

The museum (☎ 287-6034, 223-5800 ext 2584) is on the 11th floor of the Instituto Nacional de Seguros (INS) at Avenida 7, Calles 9 & 11. It is open 8:30 am to 4 pm weekdays, and admission costs US$2.50.

Museo Nacional

The National Museum is housed in the Bellavista Fortress, the old army headquarters. The small museum displays Costa Rican archaeology, some jade and gold, colonial furniture and costumes, colonial and religious art, and historical exhibits. Some pieces are labeled in English as well as Spanish. There is a small garden with cannons, and some of the walls are pockmarked with bullet holes from the 1948 civil war.

The museum (☎ 257-1433) is on Calle 17, Avenidas Central & 2. Opening hours are 8:30 am to 4:30 pm Tuesday to Saturday and 9 am to 4:30 pm on Sundays and holidays. Admission costs US$2 (students with ID and kids under 10 free). There is also a gift shop here. This is another favorite museum for visitors.

The Museo Nacional is a favorite among visitors to the capital.

Museo de Oro Precolombino

This museum houses a dazzling collection of pre-Columbian gold pieces and is well worth seeing. There is also a small numismatic museum and a display of Costa Rican art.

The museum (☎ 223-0528) is in the basement of the Plaza de la Cultura complex on Calle 5, Avenidas Central & 2, under the tourist information office. The museum, owned by Banco Central, is open 9 am to 4:30 pm Tuesday to Saturday, and admission costs US$6 or US$2.50 for students. Security is tight: you must leave your bags at the door.

Museo de Arte Costarricense

This small museum of Costa Rican art contains a collection of local paintings and sculpture from the 19th and 20th centuries. The sculptures are especially worth a look. There are also changing shows of local artists.

The museum (☎ 222-7155) is in Parque La Sabana, which was San José's airport until 1955. The collection is housed in the old airport terminal just off Calle 42, Paseo Colón & Avenida 2. Hours are 10 am to 4 pm Tuesday to Sunday; admission costs about US$2, free to children and students with ID. Everyone gets in free on Sundays.

Museo de Arte y Diseño Contemporáneo

The Museum of Contemporary Art and Design (☎ 257-7202) houses changing shows by working Costa Rican artists. It is next to the Biblioteca Nacional (National Library) on Avenida 3, Calles 15 & 17. Hours are 10 am to 5 pm Tuesday to Saturday; admission is free.

Serpentario

This is a small but unusual collection of live snakes and other reptiles housed in the center of San José. Anyone interested in reptile or amphibian identification will benefit from a visit to this live display of many of Costa Rica's exotic species.

A bilingual biologist is sometimes available to explain the collection, and there is a small gift shop. The serpentarium (☎ 255-4210) is on Avenida 1, Calles 9 & 11, and is open 9 am to 6 pm weekdays and 10 am to 5 pm weekends; admission costs US$4.

Museo de los Niños

The Children's Museum (☎ 233-2734, 223-7003, 223-7154) is in the old *penitenciario* (penitentiary) at Calle 4, north of Avenida 9. The hands-on displays allow children to learn and experience science, music, geography, and other subjects. Part of the old jail can still be visited. There are exhibits about children in Costa Rica, children's rights, and so on. It's a big place and there's lots to do! Hours are 8 am to 3 pm Tuesday to Friday, 10 am to 4 pm Saturday and Sunday. Adult admission costs US$5, with substantial discounts for children, depending on age.

Museo de Ciencias Naturales

The Natural History Museum is housed in the old Colegio (high school) La Salle near the southwest corner of Parque La Sabana. Basically, it is a large collection of stuffed animals and mounted butterflies, a resource for those wishing to identify some of the species they may see in the wild. There are also exhibits on paleontology and archaeology.

The museum (☎ 232-1306) is open 8 am to 4 pm Monday to Saturday, 9 am to 5 pm Sunday. Admission costs about US$2 (half price for students).

Most cab drivers know the Colegio La Salle and charge less than US$2 to get there. A Sabana-Estadio or Sabana-Cementario city bus from Parque Central will take you there for a few colones – ask the driver to let you know where the museum is.

Museo de Insectos

Also known as the Museo de Entomología, this is a fine collection of insects curated by the Facultad de Agronomía at the Universidad de Costa Rica. It is claimed that this is the only insect museum of any size in Central

Kids' Stuff

The youngest will enjoy swinging and sliding in the playground in the Parque Morazán. Older kids will have fun at the Museo de los Niños. Other museums that are often a hit with children are the Serpentario (my kids certainly like looking at live snakes and lizards) and, for those into nature, the butterflies at the Spirogyra Jardín de Mariposas. The gruesome exhibits at the Museo de Criminología may also be of interest. Teenagers check one another out and meet at the Plaza de la Cultura, near which, on Avenida Central, are several fast-food joints (including the ubiquitous McDonald's, which I realize some kids love but others wouldn't be caught dead in!) and ice-cream bars. (All these places are described in the text of this chapter.)

A few kilometers west of town is the Acua Mania water park – great for the whole family. See the entry in the Alajuela Area section of the Central Valley chapter for details.

The Tico Times (see Newspapers & Magazines in the Facts for the Visitor chapter) has a page specially for children, and it sometimes reviews plays and movies (many in English) that will appeal to children. The Teatro Eugene O'Neill (see the Theater section in Entertainment, later in this chapter) has a Children's Theater group; seeing a performance might be a fun Spanish lesson. Movies screened at cinemas include G-rated ones suitable for the whole family, and in original English (with Spanish subtitles).

Most kids, though, will probably want to get out of San José as fast as possible to experience the adventures of the rainforests, beaches, exploding volcanoes, and national parks.

I encourage families traveling with kids to write me with your 'Kids' Stuff' recommendations for future editions.

– Rob Rachowiecki

America – whether or not that's true, the collection is certainly extensive and many splendid and exotic insects can be seen.

Surprisingly, the museum (☎ 207-5318, 207-5647) is housed in the basement of the Artes Musicales building on campus. It is signposted, or you can ask for directions. Hours are 1 to 5 pm weekdays, and admission costs US$1.50; ring the bell to gain admission. A cab to the university (in San Pedro) costs about US$2 to US$3, or take a San Pedro bus along Avenida 2 from Calle 5.

Parque Zoológico Simón Bolívar

This small national zoo (☎ 233-6701) is in Parque Simón Bolívar; hence its name. You can see many of Costa Rica's animals, along with a small sprinkling of exotics.

Unfortunately, as in many Latin American countries, the cages are too small, although not as bad as in some zoos I've seen. There are also dozens of labeled Costa Rican plants on the grounds, and a brochure describing them is available. The zoo is popular with josefinos on weekends. The gate is at Avenida 11, Calles 7 & 9 (go north on Calle 7 and east on Avenida 11 to get there). Hours are 8 am to 4 pm weekdays and 9 am to 5 pm weekends; admission costs US$2.

Spirogyra Jardín de Mariposas

Not to be confused with the large butterfly farm in La Guacima, this smaller version offers close-up looks at Costa Rican butterflies in a garden setting close to downtown. The garden is 100m east and 150m south of Centro Comercial El Pueblo and can be reached on foot (about a half hour from downtown), by taxi, or by bus to El Pueblo (where there is a sign). Spirogyra (☎ 222-2937) is open 8 am to 4 pm daily. Admission costs US$6.

Museo Postal, Telegráfico y Filatélico de Costa Rica

This postal, telegraphic, and stamp-collecting museum (☎ 223-9766 ext 269) is upstairs in the central post office, Calle 2, Avenidas 1 & 3. Hours are 9 am to 2 pm weekdays; admission is free.

Museo de Criminología

The stated objective of this museum (☎ 223-0666 ext 2378) is the prevention of crime through the presentation of exhibits of criminal acts. It reportedly contains such niceties as limbs that have been separated from their rightful owners by machete-wielding criminals.

The museum is in the Supreme Court of Justice, Calle 17, Avenidas 6 & 8, and is open 7 to 11 am and 1 to 5:30 pm weekdays.

Museo Nacional de Ferrocarril

Railroad buffs may want to take a walk past the National Railroad Museum to see the old locomotive that served the San José-Puerto Limón run.

The museum (☎ 221-0777) is appropriately housed in the old Atlantic railway station at Avenida 3, Calle 21; closed in 1999, it may reopen. The locomotive is outside and visible to passersby; the exhibits – a model railway, old photographs, and railroad paraphernalia – are still inside, and you may be able to find a caretaker who'll let you look around.

Teatro Nacional

The National Theater (☎ 221-1329, 233-6354) is considered San José's most impressive public building. Built in the 1890s (see Arts in the Facts about Costa Rica chapter), the Teatro Nacional is the center of Costa Rican culture and stands on the south side of the Plaza de la Cultura, Calles 3 & 5, Avenidas Central & 2. The outside is elegant, though not particularly impressive, with statues of Beethoven and Calderón de la Barca (a 17th-century Spanish dramatist) flanking the entrance, and a columned façade.

Inside the more interesting interior are paintings of Costa Rica, the most famous of which is a huge canvas showing coffee harvesting and export. It was painted in Italy in the late 19th century and was reproduced on the five-colón note. (This note is now out of circulation, but can sometimes be obtained in banks – or by paying about US$1 to one of the street vendors outside.)

The marble staircases, gilded ceilings, and parquet floors made of local hardwoods are worth seeing. These were all severely damaged in the 1991 earthquake, but most have been restored.

There are regular performances in the theater, and this is the best way to see the splendid public areas inside the building. The private box seats are certainly a treat – bring your opera glasses and a fan. Otherwise, the theater is open 9 am to 5 pm Monday to Saturday; it costs about US$3 to visit. There is a pleasant coffee shop to the left of the lobby with changing shows by local artists, good coffee, and a quiet atmosphere in which to write postcards – though it gets very crowded at lunchtime. Café hours are 9 am to 6 pm Monday to Saturday.

Mercado Central

This market is interesting to visit if you've never been to a Latin American market, although it is a little tame compared to the markets of many other countries. Nevertheless, it is crowded and bustling and has a variety of produce and other goods ranging from live turkeys to leatherwork for sale. Some of the cheapest meals in town are served here.

The Central Market is at Avenidas Central & 1, Calles 6 & 8. A block away at Avenida 3, Calle 8, is the similar Mercado Borbón. Beware of pickpockets in these areas. The streets surrounding the markets are jam-packed with vendors.

Parque Nacional

This pleasant and shady park is between Avenidas 1 & 3, Calles 15 & 19. It has two statues of note. In the center of the park is the Monumento Nacional showing the Central American nations driving out William Walker (see History in the Facts about Costa Rica chapter). At the southwest corner is a statue of national hero Juan Santamaría.

Important buildings surrounding the park include the Asamblea Legislativa (Legislative Assembly or Congress Building) to the south, the Biblioteca Nacional (National Library) to the north, and the Fábrica Nacional de Licores (National Liquor Factory, founded in 1856 and now housing an art gallery) to the northwest.

Parque España

This small park seems to have some of the tallest trees in San José. It is a riot of birdsong just before sunset, and a riot of color on Sunday when there is an outdoor art market. The park is between Avenidas 3 & 7, Calles 9 & 11.

To the north of the park is the INS building, housing the Jade Museum and fronted by a huge statue. To the west is the famous iron building (now a school), which was designed in France, shipped from Belgium in parts, and welded together in Costa Rica during the 1890s; to the east is the old Liquor Factory; and to the northeast is the Casa Amarilla (Yellow House), which is Costa Rica's Ministry of Foreign Affairs.

Parque Morazán

This park intersects at four city blocks at Calle 7 and Avenida 3, and is graced in the center by a dome-roofed structure, the so-called Templo de Música. There are several other statues and monuments, as well as a small Japanese garden in the northeast quarter. Parents with small children should note that there is a playground here.

Plaza de la Cultura

This plaza is not particularly prepossessing in itself, but it is the site of the Teatro Nacional, Museo de Oro Precolombino, and ICT

Kissing Parks

Many ticos live with their families until they get married, which puts a premium on good public locales for romancing. This gives travelers a way of gauging the safety of city parks after dark – if you see more than two couples smooching, chances are it's a safe area.

– John Thompson

office. Young people hang out here and check out what everyone else is doing – it's a good place to people watch.

Street vendors wander around the plaza, especially at its western end by the terrace café at the Gran Hotel – every once in a while the municipal authorities ban them from the plaza, but they seem to drift back again a few weeks later.

Parque Central

This park is between Avenidas 2 & 4, Calles Central & 2. These streets are very busy (especially Avenida 2), and the park is known as the place to catch many of the local city buses. To the east is the fairly modern and not very interesting Catedral Metropolitana. To the north is the well-known Teatro Melico Salazar.

Plaza de la Democracia

Situated below the Museo Nacional, this mostly bare plaza has a few interesting sculptures and, on its western side, an open-air market of arts and crafts – it gets very busy just before Christmas and around other holidays, although there is often plenty of stuff for sale at any time of year. There are decent views of the mountains surrounding San José.

Parque La Sabana

This park, at the western end of the Paseo Colón, is home to both the museum of Costa Rican art and the national stadium, where soccer matches are played. It is a spacious park, with a lagoon, fountain, and a variety of sports facilities (see below). It is a decent place for a daytime stroll or a picnic beneath the trees, and offers something of a respite from the congestion of downtown. Don't wander the grounds after dark.

ACTIVITIES

Parque La Sabana has a variety of sporting facilities. There are tennis courts, volleyball, basketball, and baseball areas, jogging paths, and an Olympic-size swimming pool, but it costs about US$3 to swim, and it is open only between noon and 2 pm. Many ticos prefer the excursion to the Ojo de Agua pool (near Alajuela, frequent buses), where swimming is available all day.

The Cariari Country Club (☎ 239-2455, fax 239-2366) has Costa Rica's only 18-hole championship golf course (6700 yards, par 71), charging US$40 per day plus a US$10 caddie fee; club rental (US$15) and golf carts (US$25) are available. The country club also has 11 tennis courts (most are lighted), a pro shop, an Olympic-size swimming pool, and a gym. The Costa Rica Country Club (☎ 228-9333, 228-0988) in Escazú has a nine-hole course. Tennis is also available at the at the Costa Rica Tennis Club (☎ 232-1266) on the south side of La Sabana. You can join a local gym for about US$20 a month or use the facilities in the best hotels if you happen to be staying in one. Gyms are listed under 'Gimnasios' in the yellow pages telephone directory.

If you're interested in knocking down some pins, near the North American-Costa Rican Cultural Center you'll find the Compañis de Bolinche (☎ 253-5745), Avenida Central, Calle 23, where you can rent bowling shoes for US$1.50 per person and bowl for US$11 per hour.

LANGUAGE COURSES

There are some excellent Spanish-language schools in and near San José, but they are not particularly cheap. Classes are usually intensive, with class sizes varying from two to five pupils per teacher. Individual tutoring is also available. Classes usually last for several hours every weekday. Most students are encouraged to stay with a Costa Rican family to immerse themselves in the language. Family homestays are arranged by the schools, as are the necessary visa extensions. Cheaper classes usually involve larger group sizes and/or fewer hours. Short and long courses are available.

Most schools offer more than just language courses. Lectures, discussions, field trips, and other activities may be available – topics include the environment, women's issues, human rights, social studies, economics, political studies, agriculture, culture, and travel.

Spending a month learning Spanish in Costa Rica is an excellent and recommended way of seeing and learning about the country.

Many language schools advertise in *The Tico Times* every week. If you want to arrange classes in advance, write to or call the schools in the following list (arranged alphabetically) for details. There are dozens of existing schools – noninclusion here does not automatically mean that the school is not good. The schools listed meet one or both of the following criteria: they have been operating for at least five years, or they have received several reader recommendations. Most schools are in San José, but those in nearby suburbs are also included. Also see Language Courses in the Central Valley chapter and the Central Pacific Coast chapter for other options.

Brief descriptions give an idea of price – most schools have longer or shorter programs than those described and will tailor a program to fit your needs. Also, you can arrange more or fewer hours of class time. Note that if you opt for the language course only, rather than staying with a local family, this can easily be arranged at much cheaper rates (though you'll probably end up paying more to stay in a hotel and pay for your own meals).

Academia Costarricense de Lenguaje
(☎ 221-1624, fax 233-8670; in the USA ☎ 800-854-6057, crlang@sol.racsa.co.cr). In the capital's San Pedro suburb, this academy gives students a chance to learn about Costa Rican culture through (optional) lessons in music, cooking, dancing, and customs. From US$10 per hour for lessons, US$100 per week for homestay. Recommended by readers.

Academia Latinoamericano de Español
(☎ 224-9917, fax 225-8125, recajhi@sol.racsa.co.cr). This school at Avenida 8, Calles 31 & 33, offers 20 hours of tuition a week for US$145 plus family homestay for another US$135 a week.

American Institute for Language & Culture
(☎ 225-4313, fax 224-4244, Apartado 2200-1001, San José). This San Pedro suburb school offers homestay and four hours daily of instruction for individuals and small classes. Cultural and community activities are available. Rates start at US$300 per week.

CELL – Centro Linguístico Latinoamericano
(☎ 293-0128, fax 239-1869, cellcr@sol.racsa.co.cr). For those who don't want to stay in San José, this school is in San Antonio de Belén (near Alajuela). Individual instruction with homestay costs US$295 a week. Dance and cooking classes, laundry, and airport pickup are also available – recommended by readers. In the USA, contact Latin American Language Center (☎ 916-442-4883, fax 916-428-9542).

Centro Cultural Costarricense-Norteamericano
(☎ 225-9433, fax 224-1480, acccnort@sol.racsa.co.cr). This school, at Calle 37, Avenidas 1 & 5, Los Yoses, offers all levels of classes at a wide range of costs, with or without homestays. It also teaches English, has a large library of English books, and offers other bicultural programs funded by the US government. This school has been in San José for over 50 years.

Centro Linguístico Conversa
(☎ 221-7649, fax 233-2418, conversa@racsa.co.cr). There are two locations: Paseo Colón, Calles 38 & 40 in San José, and a Santa Ana suburb. Cheap classes without homestays and for short periods are available in San José. Classes in Santa Ana are intensive and include homestays and cultural programs – they start at US$560 per week and go up to US$2300 per month.

Forester Instituto Internacional
(☎ 225-3155, 225-1649, 225-0135, fax 225-9236, forester@sol.racsa.co.cr), about 75m south of the Automercado, Los Yoses. The school charges about US$1360 for four weeks of classes (20 hours a week) with homestays and excursions.

ICADS – Institute for Central American Development Studies
(☎ 225-0508, fax 234-1337, icads@netbox.com), or write to Dept 826, PO Box 025216, Miami, FL 33102-5216. This school, in the suburb of San Pedro, offers intensive 30-day programs (4½ hours daily, three students maximum) for US$1400, including homestay and meals. It offers many extra lectures and activities devoted to environmental, women's, and human rights issues, and will place you in volunteer positions with local grassroots organizations. 'Semester abroad' programs for college credit are also offered.

ICAI – Central American Institute for International Affairs
(☎ 233-8571, fax 221-5238, icai@expreso.co.cr). In a residential area 10 minutes from the heart of San José, this program offers two-week total-immersion courses with homestays, lectures, and field trips for US$815.

ILISA – Instituto Latinoamericano de Idiomas (☎ 225-2495, fax 225-4665; in the USA ☎ 800-454-7248, spanish@ilisa.com), or ILISA, PO Box 3006, Peoria, IL 61612. About 400m south and 50m east of the San Pedro church. It offers small groups (four students maximum), intensive studies (four to six hours a day), family homestays, and a Central American history and culture program. A four-week course including homestays costs from US$1300 (four hours a day).

Instituto Británico
(☎ 234-9054, fax 253-1894, instbrit@sol.racsa.co.cr). About 75m south of the Subaru dealership in Los Yoses. Homestays and cultural activities are emphasized.

Instituto Universal de Idiomas
(☎ 257-0441, fax 223-2980, info@universal-edu.com). It offers classes with a six-student maximum, ranging from three-day crash courses (six hours a day, US$130) to economy packages (four weeks, three hours per day, homestay with meals, textbook, and airport pickup, US$900). Individual instruction is available for US$15 per hour.

Intensa
(☎ 224-6353, fax 253-8912, intensa@sol.racsa.co.cr). At Calle 33, Avenidas 5 & 7, Barrio Escalante, it offers a variety of programs.

ISLS – Institute for Spanish Language Studies (☎ 257-1622; in the USA 800-765-0025, 213-765-0028, www.isls.com), 1011 E Washington Blvd, Los Angeles, CA 90021. This company represents many schools throughout the country.

Universidad Veritas
(☎ 283-4747, Apartado 1380-1000, San José). In the Edificio ITAN, Carretera a Zapote (20-minute walk southeast of San José), this school has a wide range of levels and courses – recommended by several readers.

ORGANIZED TOURS

The following is a list of the most popular tours offered in, around, and out of San José. Approximate prices per person are provided, but be sure to look around for occasional bargains, such as two people for the price of one.

Day tours normally include lunch and pickup and return from your San José hotel; multiday tours normally include overnight accommodations, meals, and transport. Bilingual guides, usually fluent in English, accompany most tours.

For information on tour operators in Costa Rica, see the Organized Tours section in the Getting Around chapter.

Half-day city tour – US$20 to US$25.

Half-day tours to one of the following: Volcán Irazú, Volcán Poás, ox-cart factory at Sarchí, Valle de Orosi, coffee tour, butterfly farm – US$25 to US$55.

Full-day tours combining two of the above – US$65 to US$100.

Full-day tours to one of the following: Rainforest Aerial Tram, Jungle Train with Parque Nacional Braulio Carrillo, Volcán Arenal, Volcán Barva, Reserva Biológica Carara with Playa Jacó, Cerro de la Muerte, Parque Nacional Tapantí, Colonia Virgen del Socorro, Golfo de Nicoya cruise to Isla Tortuga, horseback riding, white-water rafting trip on one of the Ríos Reventazón, Sarapiquí, or Corobicí – US$50 to US$100. (Note: one-day tours from San José to Manuel Antonio, Tortuguero, Caño Negro, or Monteverde are offered from about US$100, but these generally involve too much travel to be comfortable one-day trips. Volcán Arenal is also pushing it a bit in one day.)

Two days/one night river rafting and camping – US$250 to US$320 (four passengers is the minimum).

Three days/two nights at Tortuguero – per person, double occupancy, US$235 and up depending on transport, accommodation, and guides desired.

Three days/two nights at Monteverde – per person, double occupancy, US$360 and up. (Note that cheaper options for the last two may lack good hotels, meals, or naturalist guides.)

PLACES TO STAY

There are about 200 hotels of all types in San José, but accommodations may be tight in some of the better ones during the high season (December to May) and especially in the week before and after Christmas and the week before Easter. If you want to stay in a particular hotel at these times, you should make reservations – as much as three months in advance for Christmas and Easter. Reservations should be prepaid, or they will sometimes be ignored. If you have no reservations, you can still find rooms, but your choices are limited.

Although there is a large choice of hotels, accommodations are generally lackluster, especially downtown. Many hotels, although clean and secure, tend to suffer from musty carpets, street noise, and unappealing decor (though there are exceptions – especially the smaller hotels, which are often in beautifully restored older houses).

For people staying for a while, *apartotels* offer furnished rooms with kitchens at medium hotel rates; you can also look in the newspapers for apartments to rent. Those advertised in the Spanish-language *La Nación* are generally a little cheaper than those advertised in the English-language *The Tico Times*. The most luxurious hotels are good, but not many travelers want to pay well over US$100 for a place to sleep. Budget rooms are usually grim and noisy little boxes, but at least they are fairly cheap. There is also one youth hostel associated with Hostelling International.

Since the early 1990s, a large number of small bed & breakfast hotels have appeared on the scene that offer a reasonably priced alternative to the more traditional top-end hotels. B&Bs offer more than just breakfast with your room – they also tend to provide a family-like atmosphere in a house rather than a more impersonal hotel. There are several outlying suburbs with middle to top-end hotels and B&Bs. People like to stay there to get out of the hustle and bustle of San José, or to be closer to the airport (17km away), or because of the quiet, rural atmosphere. These areas are served by local buses, described in the Getting Around section later in this chapter.

Prices given here (and in the rest of the book) are current high-season rates, including the 16.39% government and tourist tax. Rates are subject to demand and may change substantially (both up and down) over the life of this book. Some of the mid-priced hotels are actually a little cheaper than they were a few years ago, which reflects the increase in the number of hotels in San José, combined with the flattening out of the tourist boom of the early 1990s.

Note that there are many B&Bs and hotels (especially mid- to top-end ones) in Escazú and on the way to the international airport, both west of San José. These are listed under the Escazú and Other Areas sections that follow the Places to Stay – In the City listings.

Making Reservations

Many of the mid-priced and all of the top-end hotels accept reservations from outside Costa Rica by phone, email, or snail-mail. Some have US telephone numbers (occasionally toll free). A reservation deposit is normally required. A good travel agent can help you make reservations from home.

Local phone numbers and street addresses are given below, and, for those hotels that accept reservations from abroad, email and postal addresses (apartados) and/or US phone numbers are also given. Email is fast becoming the most common way to make reservations, and hotels are rushing to get online; if a hotel below doesn't have an email address listed, it is worth a quick call to see if it has added one since this writing. If you are making mail reservations, allow several months – letters can be very slow. Phoning, faxing, emailing, or using a travel agent are the best ways to make reservations.

Budget hotels may not accept reservations, but the phone numbers will at least enable you to find out if they have rooms available.

Homestays

This is an alternative to staying at a hotel or B&B. You stay with a local family (most are ticos, a few are foreign residents) that provides a room (or perhaps two) for one to three guests per room. Thus, you or your small group will be the only guests, and you'll receive a more in-depth look at Costa Rica, often participating in family activities and so on. Host families may or may not speak English, smoke, have children or pets, have private showers for guests – all are unique.

A well-recommended agency is run by Vernon Bell (a Californian who has lived in Costa Rica for over 20 years) and his tica wife, Marcela. They have some 70 homes available, each of which has been personally inspected to maintain their high standards of cleanliness and wholesomeness. All are close to public transportation, and I have received only positive comments about these places. If you like the idea of staying with a local family, this is a good way to go. The Bells will also help with arranging car rental and other reservations.

Rates are US$35/45 single/double, including breakfast, or an extra US$5 with private bath; dinners can be arranged and discounts are available for stays over two weeks. Contact Bell's Home Hospitality *(☎ 225-4752, fax 224-5884, homestay@racsa .co.cr)*.

PLACES TO STAY – IN THE CITY

Budget

Hostels There is one youth hostel that is associated with Hostelling International. This is the clean and attractive ***Hostel Toruma*** *(☎ 234-8186, ☎/fax 224-4085)*, Avenida Central, Calles 29 & 31, a little over a kilometer east of downtown. There are over 100 bunk beds (with railway-compartment-like shutters) in segregated dormitories, and hot water is available at times. The charge is US$9 per person for HI members and US$12 for nonmembers, which is pricey for a dorm bed. Nevertheless, it's popular and often booked up well in advance. Laundry facilities are available in the afternoons, and there is a spacious lounge. There is a message board, and it is a good place to meet other budget travelers.

The hostel is also the headquarters for the network of Costa Rican youth hostels, and information and reservations for the others can be made here. Note that the San José hostel is the cheapest – the others offer private rather than dormitory rooms.

An interesting small hostel is the ***Casa Ridgeway*** *(☎ 221-8299, ☎/fax 233-6168)*, Calle 15, Avenida 6 bis. This hostel was formerly known as the Peace Center and continues to be affiliated with and operated by Quakers. It is a useful place for information on and discussion of peace issues. There is a small library, and the center is staffed mainly by volunteers. Accommodations cost US$8 per person in clean, small rooms with four beds and individual lockers, or US$10/20 for a few singles/doubles. There are basic kitchen and laundry facilities, communal hot showers, and quiet hours from 10 pm to 7 am.

Hotels Many cheap hotels are found west of Calle Central. There have been reports of occasional thefts and muggings in the area around the Coca-Cola bus terminal, Mercado Central, and Parque Central – keep your eyes open and use taxis if arriving at night. Certainly, unless you're a die-hard fan of grunge and bustle, this is one of San José's least pleasant neighborhoods.

Many shoestring travelers head for the basic ***Gran Hotel Imperial*** *(☎ 222-7899)*, Calle 8, Avenidas Central & 1. Fronted by an unprepossessing chained iron door leading into a bare stairwell, this cavernous hotel provides all the basic necessities – security, reasonably clean beds, communal showers with spasmodic hot water, and one of the best-value restaurants in town, with a balcony where you can sip a beer while watching the busy market action below. Rooms cost US$4 per person (though there are few singles) and the place is full of international backpackers. The hotel will hold a room for you until the afternoon if you call ahead.

Another place that is popular with young travelers on the 'gringo trail' is ***Tica Linda*** *(☎ 233-0528, fax 257-2272)*, at Avenida 2, Calles 5 & 7. It's next door to La Esmeralda Bar & Restaurant, where *mariachis* play late into the night. (Mariachis are Mexican street bands whose members dress elegantly in tight-fitting sequined suits and enormous sombreros.) The sign is just a tiny plate on the door – ring the bell to get in. The place is cramped and noisy but friendly and secure. Laundry facilities and hot showers are available, but its main attraction is as a place to meet other budget travelers. The rate is about US$5 per person, but there are few

MICHAEL FOGDEN

Cloud forest hiker, Monteverde

FRANK BALTHIS

Gecko on screen

BUDDY MAYS

Visitors enjoy the Tabacón hot springs near Parque Nacional Volcán Arenal.

ROBERT WINSLOW

Canoeing beneath the rainforest canopy

NIK WHEELER

White-faced capuchin monkey

JAN BUTCHOFSKY-HOUSER

City view and surrounding mountains from the Museo de Jade, San José

ERROL D SEHNKE

Girl at window, San José

DAVID MADISON

Girl with ice cream, Cartago

DAVE G HOUSER

Church and town center, Zarcero

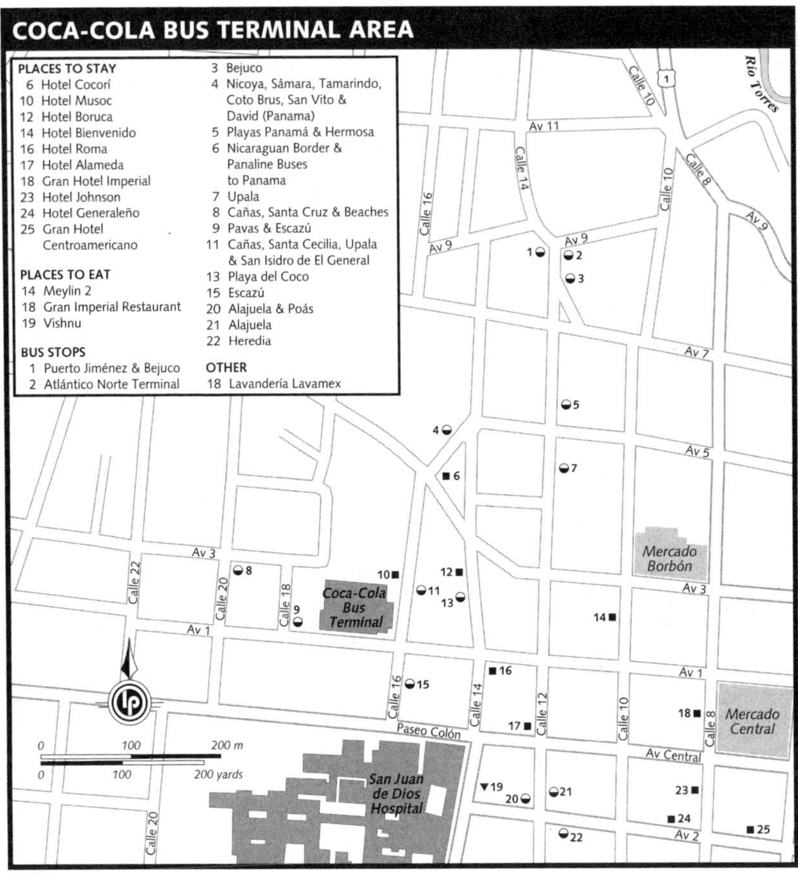

singles. Rooms sleeping four cost about US$16.

Other basic places to try include the ***Hotel Nicaragua*** (*☎ 223-0292*), Avenida 2, Calle 13, which charges US$5/7 single/double. The small, family-run hotel is reasonably clean and secure. There are only cold-water showers, and the hotel is often full of travelers from other Central American countries. Close by is the basic but clean ***Hotel Avenida 2*** (*☎ 222-0260, fax 223-9732*), at Avenida 2, Calles 9 & 11, which has hot communal showers and charges US$7.50/12 single/double. On the same block is the super-basic ***Pensión Salamanca***, at Avenida 2, Calles 9 & 11. The charge is US$3 per person in boxlike rooms, and there are only cold showers. Unfortunately, Avenida 2 is very noisy.

Another reasonable cheapie is the ***Hotel Rialto*** (*☎ 221-7456*), Calle 2, Avenida 5, which is decent, has hot water in the mornings, and charges US$5/9 single/double, or US$11 with a private bath. The ***Hotel América*** (*☎ 221-4116*), Calle 4, Avenida 7, is clean but lacks hot water – rooms cost US$11 a double. Another cheap place is the ***Hotel Marlyn*** (*☎ 233-3212*), Calle 4,

Avenidas 7 & 9, which charges US$6 for a small single with communal showers, or US$12 with private bath and hot water. This is very secure – the entrance is always locked and the owners let you in personally.

The ***Hotel ABC*** *(☎ 221-5007)*, Calle 4, Avenidas 1 & 3, has been recommended by readers. Rooms with fans and private baths cost US$10/16. There is a public lounge area with a TV and phone. The ***Hotel Generaleño*** *(☎ 233-7877)*, Avenida 2, Calles 8 & 10, is stuffy and basic. Spartan rooms with shared cold showers cost US$5/8, and a double with private hot shower costs US$13.

The ***Hotel Boruca*** *(☎ 223-0016, fax 232-0107)*, Calle 14, Avenidas 1 & 3, is convenient for buses, but some rooms are rather noisy because of them and the bar below. It is open 24 hours, but it's family-run, friendly, secure, clean, and has hot water some of the time. Rooms are small and cost US$4.50/7.50. Nearby is the slightly more expensive ***Hotel Roma*** *(☎ 223-2179)*, Calle 14, Avenidas Central & 1. It is adequate, clean, and secure, but spartan and has cold water only.

The ***Hotel Astoria*** *(☎ 221-2174)*, Avenida 7, Calles 7 & 9, has been popular for years and is often full, though it's not especially remarkable. It has a few very basic rooms in the back and some much better ones in the front, so look around. Doubles cost US$8 with shared hot baths or US$10.50 to US$13 with private baths. Laundry service is available, as are discounts for longer stays. The ***Hotel Morazán*** *(☎ 221-9083)*, Avenida 3, Calles 11 & 15, has large, clean, bare rooms, and it is secure. The staff is friendly, and double rooms cost US$10 with a communal cold shower or US$13 with private hot showers. At last visit, it was closed for remodeling, and the hotel may change hands.

The ***Pensión Americana*** *(☎ 221-4171, 221-9799)*, Calle 2, Avenidas Central & 2, charges US$6.50 per person in large clean rooms with electric showers. There is a TV room, and the management is friendly. The ***Hotel Boston*** *(☎ 221-0563, fax 257-5063)*, Avenida 8, Calles Central & 2, has large rooms with private baths and tepid water for US$12.50/16.50 single/double. The management is friendly; some rooms are noisy, but inside rooms are reasonably quiet. A block away, Calle 2 has a seedy red-light district, so solo women travelers may want to avoid this area. Also in this area, the ***Hotel Príncipe*** *(☎ 222-7983, fax 223-1589)*, Avenida 6, Calles Central & 2, is secure and has decent rooms with private warm showers for US$14/18 single/double.

The ***Pensión Otoya*** *(☎ 221-3925)*, Calle 1, Avenidas 3 & 5, is clean, friendly, has long been popular with foreigners, and is often full. Decent single/double rooms cost US$7/10 with shared baths or US$10/13 with private baths and hot water. The secure ***Hotel Compostela*** *(☎ 257-1514)*, Calle 6, Avenidas 3 & 5, charges US$16 for very clean single or double rooms – each room has a private hot bath, but you have to cross the corridor to reach it. There also are double rooms with communal hot showers for US$14 and small rooms with communal cold showers for US$5 per person. A reasonable choice is the ***Nuevo Hotel Central*** *(☎ 222-3509, 221-2767, fax 223-4069)*, at Avenida 3, Calles 4 & 6. It has large clean rooms for US$12/16.50 single/double with private hot baths. Four people can share a room for US$22. The upstairs rooms are the nicest.

The ***Pensión Centro Continental*** *(☎ 222-4103)*, Calle Central, Avenidas 8 & 10, is run by the same folks who run the neighboring mid-priced Hotel Ritz. It is a small, popular hotel with kitchen facilities and tepid electric communal showers. Rooms cost US$8/15 single/double (beware of surprise 'taxes' on the bill).

The ***Hotel Musoc*** *(☎ 222-9437, fax 255-0031)*, Calle 16, Avenidas 1 & 3, is a large building (with some noisy rooms) very close to the Coca-Cola bus terminal. The hotel is clean, has some English-speaking staff, and accepts credit cards. Singles/doubles cost US$8/13 with shared baths and US$10/15 with private hot showers. The ***Hotel Cocorí*** *(☎ 233-0081, 233-2188)*, Calle 16, Avenida 3, charges US$12/18 for adequate singles/doubles with private hot showers. Be careful at night around the nearby bus terminal areas.

The ***Casa Leo*** *(☎ 222-9725)*, Avenida 6 bis, Calles 13 & 15, charges US$10 per person in very clean dormitories, US$12/22 for singles/doubles, and US$15/25 with private baths. Bathrooms have hot showers, and laundry and kitchen privileges are available; the owners are friendly and helpful with tourist information, and the place attracts budget travelers.

The ***Hotel Johnson*** *(☎ 223-7633, 223-7827, fax 222-3683)*, Calle 8, Avenidas Central & 2, accepts credit cards and reservations, has hot water in the private showers, and offers reasonably sized rooms with telephones and use of the fax. This makes it popular with Central Americans in town on business. The hotel has about 60 rooms. The quiet inside rooms are a bit on the dark side, and the beds have seen better days – but you can't expect the Hilton for these prices. There is a mid-priced restaurant and bar on the premises, with music on Friday nights. Rates are US$14.50/16 single/double. Some 'suites' with TVs that can accommodate up to six people cost about US$24.50.

The friendly ***Hotel Capital*** *(☎ 221-8497, fax 221-8583, Apartado 11094-1000, San José)*, Calle 4, Avenidas 3 & 5, charges US$16.50 for simple but clean doubles with hot water, fans, and TVs. The outside rooms are noisy (par for the course throughout the city center), but some interior rooms are quieter, though darker.

The ***Hotel Bellavista*** *(☎ 223-0095; in the USA 800-637-0899)*, Avenida Central, Calles 19 & 21, is friendly and clean and has pleasant rooms with private baths and hot water for US$19/25 single/double; some readers complain that the walls are very thin. Welcome to Central America!

At the ***Gran Hotel Centroamericano*** *(☎ 221-3362, fax 221-3714)*, Avenida 2, Calles 6 & 8, are clean, though rather small, rooms with private electric showers for US$19 a single and about US$5 more for each additional person (up to six people). Its main attraction is its central location; the management is friendly and laundry service is available. The ***Hotel Bienvenido*** *(☎ 233-2161, fax 221-1872)*, at Calle 10, Avenidas 1 & 3, is secure and has helpful staff and good clean rooms with hot water (sometimes). Rates are US$18 for single or double rooms. There is a restaurant, open at 7 am, with good cheap food.

Mid-Range

B&Bs The B&B phenomenon has swept San José, from a couple of places in the 1980s to dozens today. Those places listed here are mid-priced – see under Top End and Escazú for more options.

Pensión La Cuesta *(☎/fax 255-2896, ggmnber@sol.racsa.co.cr)* is on a little hill *(cuesta)* behind the Asamblea Legislativa on Avenida 1, Calles 11 & 15. It is an attractive house with plenty of artwork and a pleasant living room for hanging out. Eight simple but clean and pleasant bedrooms sharing communal baths rent for US$23/33 single/double, with discounts for cash and longer stays. The place has 24-hour security, is safe and friendly, has kitchen and laundry facilities, and has received several readers' recommendations. The ***Hotel Aranjuez*** *(☎ 256-1825, fax 223-3528, info@hotelaranjuez.com)*, Calle 19, Avenidas 11 & 13, has rooms with shared hot showers for US$20/24 and rooms with private hot showers and TVs for US$28/35, all with breakfast included. All rooms have phones with free local calls. The place is run by a friendly Costa Rican family that enjoys international guests. There is plenty of parking.

The gay-friendly ***Joluva Guesthouse*** *(☎/fax 223-7961, joluva@sol.racsa.co.cr)*, Calle 3 bis, Avenidas 9 & 11, is a clean, well-run place in a historical barrio. About eight fairly quiet rooms rent for US$45 a double with private baths and TVs; simpler rooms cost US$20. Also gay-friendly is ***Colors*** *(☎ 296-1880, fax 296-1597; in the USA ☎ 800-934-5622)*, a more expensive and larger place in the quiet Rohrmoser district. Call for directions.

The ***Ara Macao Inn*** *(☎ 233-2742, fax 257-6228, aramacao@hotels.co.cr)*, Calle 27, Avenidas Central & 2, is a nice place in a quiet area about four blocks east of the Museo Nacional (tell cab drivers it's 50m south of the Pizza Hut in Barrio California). Eight rooms all have private bathrooms, fans, clock radios, and TVs; some rooms have kitchenettes. The staff is bilingual and friendly, and there is a pleasant outdoor courtyard for dining. Rates are US$38/48/58 for one/two/three people.

Hotel La Amistad Inn *(☎ 221-1597, fax 221-1409, wolfgang@sol.racsa.co.cr)*, Avenida 11, Calle 15, has 22 rooms in a German-operated villa. Rates range from US$33 to US$38 single and US$46 to US$61 double; 'suites' are available for US$94 for up to four people. All rooms have cable TV, fans, and private hot showers. There are a couple of tiny rooms that are a bit cheaper. It's an OK place, though a little large for its B&B category.

Diana's Inn *(☎/fax 233-6542, dianas@sol.racsa.co.cr)*, Calle 5, Avenida 3, is an attractive clapboard house overlooking the Parque Morazán near the center of town. Pleasant, air-conditioned rooms with private baths, TVs, and phones rent for US$28/38.

The ***Hemingway Inn*** *(☎/fax 221-1804, hemingway@amerisol.com)*, Calle 9, Avenida 9, is in a solid-looking 1930s house in the traditional Barrio Amón. About 16 slightly old-fashioned rooms each bear the name of a (male) 20th-century writer and offer comfortable beds, ceiling fans, TVs, clock radios, and electric hot showers. The only phone for guest use is at the reception desk. The hotel is attractive, though some rooms are very small. There is a hot tub. Rates start at US$38/51 single/double, with a 10% discount for paying in cash or with traveler's checks. Breakfast is served in a plant-filled patio.

Another B&B choice is the ***Casa 429*** *(☎ 222-1708, fax 233-5785, 429 Calle 3)*, Avenidas 4 & 6, in an older San José home close to Plaza de la Cultura in the heart of downtown. Five large and comfortable rooms rent for about US$60 a double with shared bath, or a bit more with private bath. This is a retreat for adults only. Amenities include a lovely breakfast room (full breakfast is served) and a spa. The owners, however, are thinking of closing, so definitely call ahead.

The ***Don Paco Inn*** *(☎ 283-2012, fax 283-2033)*, Avenida 11, Calle 33, is in a more modern home dating from the 1940s. The rooms are light and cheerful, and the hotel is clean, quiet, and recommended. Two smaller downstairs rooms rent for US$52/58 single/double, and eight larger upstairs rooms cost US$68 for one or two people and US$82/93 for three/four people. Breakfast is included.

Hotels The Swiss-run ***Hotel Ritz*** *(☎ 222-4103, fax 222-8849, ecobraun@sol.racsa.co.cr)*, Calle Central, Avenidas 8 & 10, also runs the cheaper Pensión Centro Continental next door. They are friendly and helpful. Rooms cost US$12/24 single/double or US$21/29 with private bathrooms and hot water.

A clean and quiet choice is ***Hotel Fortuna*** *(☎ 223-5344, fax 221-2466)*, Avenida 6, Calles 2 & 4, which has decent rooms with good beds and private hot showers for US$22/28 single/double, though the neighborhood is close to the Calle 2 red-light district.

The ***Petit Hotel*** *(☎ 233-0766, fax 233-4794)*, Calle 24, Paseo Colón & Avenida 2 (25m south of the Mercedes-Benz dealer on Paseo Colón – tell that to the cab driver and get tico treatment), is a friendly but not fancy hotel with a restaurant attached. The rate is US$30 for a double with private hot shower and bathroom.

Casa Hilda *(☎ 221-0037, fax 221-2881, Apartado 8079-1000, San José)*, Avenida 11, Calles 3 & 3 bis, has nice rooms with private bathrooms and hot water for US$20/30. The owners are friendly, and tour services are available nearby.

The ***Hotel Diplomat*** *(☎ 221-8133, 221-8744, fax 233-7474, Apartado 6606, San José)*, Calle 6, Avenidas Central & 2, has a decent restaurant. Standard, slightly musty rooms with TVs and private hot showers cost US$18/28: a fair deal.

At the ***Park Hotel*** *(☎ 221-6944, fax 233-7602)*, Avenida 4, Calles 2 & 4, which charges US$30/34 for a room with hot water, the management turns a blind eye to one-night stands, including those of a professional nature. At least the rooms are clean.

The ***Hotel Royal Garden*** *(☎ 257-0022/23, fax 257-1517)*, Calle Central, Avenidas Central & 2, charges US$35/40 single/double. It has a casino, a bar, a balcony overlooking the avenue, a good restaurant, and quiet, pleasant rooms with air-conditioning, TVs, and telephones.

The ***Hotel Doral*** *(☎ 233-9410, fax 233-4827, Apartado 5530-1000, San José)*, Avenida 4, Calles 6 & 8, has nice rooms with TVs, telephones, and private hot showers for US$28/40/51, including breakfast. There is a bar and restaurant.

The friendly ***Hotel La Gema*** *(☎ 257-2524, fax 222-1074, Apartado 1127-1002, San José)*, Avenida 12, Calles 9 & 11, has pleasant rooms with fans, hot water, TVs, and telephones for US$32/41, and there is a decent restaurant and bar on the premises. Smaller, noisier rooms facing the street start at US$15 single.

The ***Hotel Plaza*** *(☎ 222-5533, 257-1896, fax 222-2641, hotplaza@sol.racsa.co.cr)*, Avenida Central, Calles 2 & 4, charges US$36/43/57 (including breakfast) for nice rooms in the heart of downtown.

An older house converted into a small hotel, the ***Gran Hotel Doña Inés*** *(☎ 222-7443, 222-7553, fax 223-5426, Apartado 1754-1002, San José)*, Calle 11, Avenidas 2 & 6, charges US$35/45 for quaint rooms around a pretty inside courtyard. Breakfast is included, and this is a good deal. Most rooms are off the street (quiet). All come with TVs, radios, phones, and private hot baths, and there is parking and 24-hour security. The staff speaks English, Spanish, and Italian and helps with travel arrangements. The hotel is popular with European and Costa Rican guests.

The ***Hotel La Gran Vía*** *(☎ 222-7737, fax 222-7205, hgranvia@sol.racsa.co.cr)*, Avenida Central, Calles 1 & 3, has some attractive rooms with balconies facing the street, which is a pedestrian zone, so traffic noise is minimized, and even quieter inside rooms, some of which are air-conditioned. The cost is US$40/48 single/double. It has a reasonably priced restaurant.

Another small hotel in a refurbished turn-of-the-century house is the ***Hotel Petit Victoria*** *(☎ 233-1812, 233-1813, fax 233-1938)*, Calle 24, Avenida 2. The original tiled floors are attractive. The 16 fairly simple rooms have large bathrooms and cost US$45/50 single/double including breakfast. Guests have kitchen privileges. Unfortunately, the rooms at the front are very close to the street and somewhat noisy.

The extravagantly colorful ***Hotel Kekoldi*** *(☎ 223-3244, fax 257-5476, kekoldi@sol.racsa.co.cr)*, Avenida 9, Calle 3 bis, is gay-friendly and also popular with younger travelers wanting to stay in the Barrio Amón. The decor is simple, but imaginative, and the airy, colorful rooms cost US$37/52/68 single/double/triple, including a light, healthy breakfast. Luggage storage is available; the owners have opened a similar hotel in the Manuel Antonio area.

The ***Hotel Royal Dutch*** *(☎ 224-1414, fax 233-3927)*, Calle 4, Avenidas Central & 2, has a casino and charges US$40/54 single/double. Rooms are large, air-conditioned, and have TVs and phones.

The ***Garden Court Hotel*** *(☎ 255-4766, fax 255-4613, garden@sol.racsa.co.cr)*, Avenida 7, Calle 6, is a large hotel with a pool, tour information, guarded parking, bar, and restaurant. In late 1996, it was bought by the Best Western chain (in the US ☎ 800-528-1234). Rooms are air-conditioned and have TVs, telephones, and hot water. The price of US$46/58 includes breakfast, free local calls, coffee, and an evening cocktail. This is fair value – but the neighborhood is poor. Take a taxi and then ask the desk to show you the safest walking route.

The ***Hotel Cacts*** *(☎ 233-0486, 221-6546, fax 221-8616, hcacts@sol.racsa.co.cr)* is a little out of the way at Avenida 3 bis, Calles 28 & 30, but is quiet because of that. This is a small but popular hotel. Friendly and helpful management, clean and spacious rooms with TVs and phones, hot water in the private baths, and buffet breakfast are included in the price of US$47/59 single/double, or 22% less in older rooms (which lack TVs and phones and some of which have shared baths). There is also a TV lounge, a roof-top terrace (where breakfast is served), and a travel agency. Discounts for multinight stays can be arranged.

The ***Hotel Dunn Inn*** *(☎ 222-3232, 222-3426, fax 221-4596)*, Calle 5, Avenida 11, is a small hotel in an attractive late-19th-century house. A few rooms face the noisy street; some newer rooms added onto the back are more modern but quiet. There is a nice plant-filled restaurant, courtyard, and bar, and a guarded parking lot. Unpretentious but comfortable and attractive rooms with TVs, radios, fans, and phones begin around US$60 single or double (US$70 for larger rooms with two beds). Breakfast is included.

The family-owned and -managed ***Hotel Vesuvio*** *(☎ 221-8325, ☎/fax 221-7586, Apartado 477-1000, San José)*, Avenida 11, Calles 13 & 15, is on a quiet street. The hotel basically consists of a long corridor with a total of 20 rooms on either side, but, because the corridor angles away from the street, it is one of the quietest hotels near downtown. Smallish, but clean and adequate, carpeted rooms with TVs, telephones, fans, and private showers cost US$46.50/58 including breakfast. Larger rooms with two queen-size beds cost US$87 for four people. There is a terrace and private parking.

The ***Hotel Edelweiss*** *(☎ 221-9702, fax 222-1241, edelweis@sol.racsa.co.cr)*, Calle 15, Avenida 9, has a simple elegance and is located in a quiet area near the Parque Nacional. Rooms cost US$47/58/70 single/double/triple, and the hotel is across the street from the romantic new restaurant Café Mundo. Airport pickup can be arranged.

An excellent downtown choice is the ***Hotel Santo Tomás*** *(☎ 255-0448, fax 222-3950, hotelst@sol.racsa.co.cr)*, Avenida 7, Calles 3 & 5. There are about 20 rooms with tiled or wood floors and high ceilings in a refurbished early-20th-century house. The interesting original ventilation system built into the ceilings is still in use and works well. Antique pieces and Persian rugs add to the elegance of the public areas and rooms. There is a small bar and TV lounge. The hotel is very comfortable and has helpful and friendly staff who go out of their way to arrange hotel reservations, car rentals, and tours for you. Spanish, English, French, German, and Portuguese are spoken. Affable North Carolinian owner Thomas Douglas prides himself on choosing top-notch staff. Rates include continental breakfast and are US$50/60 single/double for the standard rooms (one double bed), US$63/70 for the superior room (queen bed), and US$80 for a deluxe (two queen beds); all have private hot showers, TVs, and phones. Stay a few days and get a discount. The hotel has a locked gate for 24-hour security, and the rooms are set back from the busy street so that traffic noise is minimal.

The modern ***Hotel Ambassador*** *(☎ 221-8155, fax 255-3396, info@hotelambassador.co.cr)*, Paseo Colón, Calles 26 & 28, has over 70 large, comfortable double rooms that cost US$58 (standard), US$70 (deluxe), and about US$105 for top-floor suites with good views. Group discounts are available, and children under 12 years old stay free in the same room as their parents. The staff is friendly and the hotel is popular, but its restaurant is pricey.

The ***Hotel Balmoral*** *(☎ 222-5022, fax 221-1919; in the USA ☎ 800-691-4865, balmoral@sol.racsa.co.cr)*, Avenida Central, Calles 7 & 9, is a centrally located hotel used by tourist groups and businesspeople. The executive business center has computer hookups. The 116 air-conditioned rooms are comfortable enough, with TVs and telephones, though the bathrooms are a bit small and the walls are thin. There is a restaurant, bar, and casino. Rates are about US$50/65.

A popular hotel in this price category is ***Hotel Don Carlos*** *(☎ 221-6707, fax 255-0828, hotel@doncarlos.co.cr; in the USA, Dept 1686, PO Box 025216, Miami, FL 33102-5216)*, at Calle 9, Avenidas 7 & 9. The hotel is in a beautifully remodeled mansion, and each of the approximately 40 rooms is different but comfortable and attractive (some more so than others). However, those on the street side suffer from traffic noise, so make sure you ask for a room away from the street. Their excellent gift shop is one of the best in town, and they have a tour desk and, occasionally, live marimba music. There is an attractive indoor patio and pre-Columbian-themed garden. Rates are US$52 to US$58 single, US$64 to US$70 double, and include continental breakfast and a welcome cocktail.

About 5km west of downtown, just off the freeway to the airport, is the ***Hotel Irazú*** *(☎ 232-4811, fax 232-454; in the USA ☎ 800-528-12349, bestwestern@irazu.co.cr)*. With over 300 rooms, this hotel is the largest in the city. It has been bought and renovated in recent years by the Best Western chain. There is a small shopping mall, tennis court, swimming pool and sauna, casino, discotheque, restaurant, cafeteria, and bar. The hotel is used by charter tour groups escaping the North American winter and, with the facilities available, some guests don't leave the hotel! Too bad – there's nothing especially Costa Rican about the hotel, but some folks like it that way. If you do want to get away, there is a minibus shuttle to downtown and a daily bus to a beach resort in Jacó. Rates start at about US$67 double for rooms with TVs and telephones; some have private balconies. Guests without reservations may be able to arrange a cheaper rate, particularly in the wet season.

The ***Gran Hotel Costa Rica*** *(☎ 221-4000, fax 221-3501; in the USA ☎ 888-401-7337, Gran@centralamerica.com)*, Calle 3, Avenidas Central & 2, dates from the 1930s and has a certain old-world charm. The 105 rooms are modern, however, and all have TVs, telephones, and room service. The pavement café outside the lobby is an attractive and popular place for breakfast as well as meals and drinks throughout the day, and, with its view of the Teatro Nacional, it is downtown's prime people-watching spot. This alone brings guests back time and time again. There is a 24-hour casino and restaurant on the top floor. Rates start at US$58/72/81 single/double/triple for rather small standard rooms; varying suites are also available for US$15 to US$100 more for a double. Discounts aren't hard to get if the hotel isn't full.

The ***Hotel Don Fadrique*** *(☎ 225-8166, 224-7583, fax 224-9746, fadrique@centralamerica.com)*, Calle 37, Avenida 8 in Los Yoses, is a family-run hotel decorated with a fine private collection of contemporary Central American and Costa Rican art, and it features a large plant-filled patio with a fountain. There are 20 rooms with hardwood floors and comfortable furnishings, all with TVs, fans, telephones, and baths. Rates are US$64/76 single/double, including continental breakfast. There is a decent restaurant and bar. They provide transport for guests to or from the airport for US$15.

If a safe neighborhood is your priority, try ***La Casita Inn*** *(☎ 231-6304)*, which is near the Canadian and US embassies in Rohrmoser (west of Parque La Sabana and downtown). Call for the exact address. The hotel has 48 rooms (more are being built) as well as a garden, restaurant, balcony, pool, and entertainment lounge for guest use. Rates are US$60 to US$80 double. If you have a reservation, staff will pick you up at the airport. Parking and laundry facilities are available.

Out in the suburb of San Pedro, a short bus ride away from the center of San José, is the well-recommended ***Hotel Milvia*** *(☎ 225-4543, fax 225-7801, hmilvia@sol.racsa.co.cr)*. This is the best hotel in San Pedro and one of the best values in the greater San José area. It is housed in the 1930 home of Ricardo Fernández Peralta, an artillery colonel who fought in Costa Rica's last war (the 1948 civil war). The home was lovingly restored to its original architecture and interior ambience by the colonel's grandson, Mauricio Jurado Fernández, who named the hotel for his Italian-born wife, Milvia.

Their pride in the hotel's and family's history are evinced by the various old family photographs and artifacts decorating some of the public areas. Hand-painted tiles created by Milvia adorn the bathrooms, and other ceramics (some for sale) grace the shelves. Nine spacious and charmingly appointed guest rooms are named after members of the family, and each comes with TV, phone, mini-bar, fan, and a large bathroom with oodles of hot water in the shower. A small games/reading room (chess, backgammon, maps, novels) opens out onto an upstairs terrace overlooking a garden. The friendly receptionists will help with travel arrangements, or lend you a hair dryer or alarm clock if you need one. Rates are US$64/70 single/double, including continental breakfast served as early (or late) as you need it. Lunch and dinner are available on request from noon to 8 pm, and there is free coffee or tea at any time.

Guarded parking and a free security box are available. Spanish, Italian, and English are spoken. The hotel is 50m north and 200m east of the Supermercado Muñoz y Nanne, a local landmark well known to all cab drivers, on Avenida Central. The street the hotel is on is quiet.

The ***Hotel Europa*** *(☎ 222-1222, fax 221-3976; in the USA ☎ 800-223-6764, europa@sol.racsa.co.cr)*, Calle Central, Avenidas 3 & 5, has a pool, a restaurant, and a car rental and tour agency, and it is central. Spacious, air-conditioned rooms cost US$58/70 single/double. Cheaper rooms overlooking the street are available, but they are pretty noisy.

The ***Hotel del Rey*** *(☎ 257-7800, fax 221-0096, info@hoteldelrey.com)* is a shocking-pink, five-story, 105-room, and renovated neoclassical building at the corner of Avenida 1 and Calle 9. It is popular with anglers and gamblers and has one of San José's liveliest 24-hour bars, known for its flirtatious atmosphere. The casino starts with US$2 roulette bets. There's also a good restaurant and a deli. The reception area has a tour and fishing desk staffed by people who really know Costa Rican waters like the backs of their hands. They also set up car rentals and ecotourism, etc. Rooms are fairly standard for US$64/79/87; all come with TVs, telephones, private showers, carpeting, and either fans or air-conditioning. Some larger and more expensive rooms and suites are available for US$10 more per person. Some interior rooms lack windows but are very quiet.

Apartotels These are a cross between an apartment building and a hotel. Rooms are fully furnished and have TVs and telephones, private bathrooms, and kitchen units with utensils. There is often a separate sitting room and perhaps laundry or maid facilities. Apartotels are designed for people who wish to cater for themselves to some extent. Although singles and doubles are available, rooms are also suitable for families.

Apartotels can be rented by the day, but discounts are available for stays of a week or a month. Some owners prefer long-stay rentals of a week or month. If you do not need to be in the town center and do not need restaurant, casino, or travel agent facilities in the hotel, then these apartotels provide some of the best-value accommodations in San José. You should think ahead, however, as they are often booked up during the high season.

There are two downtown. ***Apartotel San José*** *(☎ 256-2191, 222-0455, fax 221-6684, amstel@sol.racsa.co.cr)*, Calle 17, Avenida 2, charges US$60/72 single/double in one-bedroom apartments and US$77 double in two-bedroom apartments (which sleep five for US$12 for each extra person). It is run by the owners of the Barceló Amón Plaza hotel. ***Apartamentos Sudamer*** *(☎ 221-0247, 381-3183, fax 222-2195, Apartado 2873-1000, San José)*, Calle 7, Avenidas 14 & 16, charges US$650 a month.

The following places are west of the center. The ***Apartotel Ramgo*** *(☎ 232-3823, fax 232-3111, Apartado 1441-1000, San José)* is at Sabana Sur, a block south of Parque La Sabana. Buses to downtown stop nearby. All apartments have two bedrooms. The daily rate is US$52 double, US$63 for four people. The newer and recommended ***Apartotel La Sabana*** *(☎ 220-2422, fax 231-7386, Apartado 11400-1000, San José)* is 50m west and 150m north of the Burger King on the street along the north side of La Sabana. It has a pool, sauna, laundry service, and air-conditioned apartments ranging from US$45 to US$90, depending on their size and the number of occupants. The newest is the recommended ***Apartotel El Sesteo*** *(☎ 296-1805, fax 296-1865, sesteo@sol.racsa.co.cr)*, 150m south of McDonald's on the street that runs along the south side of Parque La Sabana. It has a garden with pool and spa, laundry machines, and a guarded parking lot. Hotel-style rooms with TVs, telephones, fans, and private baths cost US$51 for one or two people (US$1032 a month); one-bedroom apartments with kitchenettes and living areas cost US$64 (US$1148 a month); two-bedroom apartments sleeping up to four with kitchens cost US$99 (US$1717). A 10% weekly discount is available. Continental breakfast is included.

In Los Yoses, east of the center, is ***Apartotel Los Yoses*** *(☎ 225-0033, 225-0044, fax 225-5595, losyoses@sol.racsa.co.cr)*, 150m west of the Fuente de la Hispanidad (a large fountain on Avenida Central between Los Yoses and San Pedro). There is a pool, and a variety of apartments begin at US$52 for one or two people and range from US$87 to US$110 for three or four people.

Apartamentos Scotland *(☎ 223-0833, 257-4374, fax 257-5317, scotland@sol.racsa.co.cr)*, Avenida 1, Calle 27, caters mainly to long-term guests. One-bedroom apartments cost US$650 to US$850 a month.

Top End

B&Bs The ***D'Raya Vida*** *(☎ 223-4168, 223-4157, rayavida@costarica.net; in the USA, PO Box 025216-1638, Miami, FL 33102-5216)* is 100m north of Hospital Calderón Guardia on Calle 17, then 50m west on Avenida 11, where a sign directs you 50m north to the hotel (tell this to your cab driver). This elegant Costa Rican house is described as an 'antebellum estate' (alluding to the years preceding the Costa Rican, not the US, civil war; the architecture is, however, reminiscent of the USA's Deep South). The attractive bedrooms and dining and sitting areas reflect the owner's interests in art, antiques, and decorating. Stained glass, hardwood floors, a patio with fountain, and a fireplace make this a nice place to spend a few days. Owner Michael Long will help with car rental and reservations elsewhere in the country; he knows most of Costa Rica's B&Bs. Guests have kitchen privileges on request. Four bedrooms share three bathrooms and cost US$85 double including full breakfast and airport pickup. Ask for weekly/monthly/low-season discounts.

La Casa Verde de Amón *(☎/fax 223-0969, casaverd@sol.racsa.co.cr; in the USA, Dept 1701, PO Box 25216, Miami, FL 33102-5216)*, Calle 7, Avenida 9, is a distinctive mint-green clapboard house dating from 1910. It received Costa Rica's 1994 Best Restoration Award and is now a National Historic Site in the heart of Barrio Amón. There are eight rooms and suites, all with queen- and king-size beds, TVs, telephones, radios, fans, and private baths. A sitting room with a grand piano and a garden patio are available for guests, and the gracious staff speaks English. Decor is attractively Victorian throughout, and this is one of San José's best-looking small hotels; unfortunately, the beautiful old construction does little to dampen the traffic noise, though a couple of inside rooms are marginally quieter. Rates range from US$75 to US$112 for double rooms and suites (with discounts for single occupancy), and some suites will sleep four for US$123. Buffet breakfast is served on the patio from 7:30 to 9 am, and smoking is allowed outside only.

Hotels An early-20th-century mansion turned into an attractive hotel is the ***Hotel Grano de Oro*** *(☎ 255-3322, fax 221-2782, granoro@sol.racsa.co.cr; in the USA, PO Box 025216-36, Miami, FL 33102-5216)*. This hotel is at Calle 30, Avenidas 2 & 4, and features 35 rooms, categorized as standard (US$82/87), superior (US$105/110), the somewhat larger deluxe (US$118/123), and a family suite for US$150 double (US$5 for extra people). A few suites with a private spa and a miniature garden or panoramic view cost US$169/174 to US$192/197. All rooms are nonsmoking, have TVs and telephones, and are comfortably furnished. The hotel has an attractive courtyard, serves delicious meals in a sunny restaurant (which attracts in-the-know locals as well as hotel guests), and is friendly and recommended. The staff works hard to provide a comfortable stay and makes travel arrangements for guests, many of whom are North American.

Also good is the ***Fleur de Lys Hotel*** *(☎ 233-1206, 257-2621, fax 257-3637, florlys@sol.racsa.co.cr)*, Calle 13, Avenidas 2 & 6. Housed in a beautifully restored 1926 building, the hotel features 20 comfortable and individually decorated rooms, each named after a native flower and all with TVs, telephones, and private baths. The hotel is owned by the local adventure tour company Aventuras Naturales, which has a tour desk at the reception. The hotel restaurant is locally well known and very good, with Costa Ricans coming in for the *plato del día*. Rates are US$75/87 for standard rooms and US$99/110 for larger junior/master suites. Rates include breakfast.

The 18-room ***Hotel Le Bergerac*** *(☎ 234-7850, fax 225-9103, Apartado 1107-1002, San José)*, Calle 35, 50m south of Avenida Central, Los Yoses, is also recommended. Owned by

French Canadians, the hotel has a decidedly French flair in its dining room and artwork, as well as in its name. Rooms are elegant, and all have TVs, telephones, and private baths. Some of the larger rooms also boast private patios or a balcony. A conference room with computer hookup, slide and video screen, and fax machine is available for business meetings. Rates are US$67 to US$90 single and US$79 to US$102 double and include continental breakfast.

The ***Hotel Alóki*** (*☎ 223-1598, 222-6702, fax 221-2533, Apartado 1040-2050, San Pedro, San José*) is a Spanish-style house at Calle 13, Avenidas 9 & 11. It is furnished with antiques and has six rooms and a presidential suite around a central courtyard. Under new, friendly management, it now also has a restaurant/pub. Rooms cost US$81/104 single/double and the suite costs US$128/162, including breakfast.

The ***Hotel Torremolinos*** (*☎ 222-5266, fax 255-3167; in the USA ☎ 800-948-3770, email: torremolinos@centralamerica.com*), Calle 40, Avenida 5 bis, has a pool, spa, sauna, and gym, and is in a quiet neighborhood. Smallish, but very clean, carpeted rooms with TVs, radios, and telephones cost US$81 single or double; larger suites with air-conditioning, minifridges, and terraces cost US$105. There is an Italian restaurant and bar. Across the street is ***Hotel Ejecutivo Napoleon*** (*☎ 222-2278, fax 222-9487, napoleon@sol.racsa.co.cr*). Modern, spacious, air-conditioned rooms with TVs, telephones, and radios cost US$73/85 (US$68/73 without air-conditioning). There is a pool and bar, and a buffet breakfast is included in the price, although there is no restaurant on the premises. Both of these places are quiet, clean, and recommended.

The ***Hotel Presidente*** (*☎ 222-3022, fax 221-1205; in the USA ☎ 800-972-0515, info@hotel-presidente.com*), at Avenida Central, Calles 7 & 9, has large air-conditioned rooms, a casino, a decent restaurant, and a disco. Rates in 'junior suites' are US$81/93 and there are some older rooms for US$70/81.

The small but elegant ***Britannia Hotel*** (*☎ 223-6667, fax 223-6411; in the USA ☎ 800-263-2618, britania@sol.racsa.co.cr*), Calle 3, Avenida 11, is in a renovated 1910 mansion in the heart of Barrio Amón. It is one of the loveliest hotels in the area, with a spacious and gracious lobby that is an inviting place to sit, rest, and relax. There is a good restaurant, bar, and equipped conference room, and the hotel has 24 attractive rooms. The 14 standard rooms are a little on the small side, so you should opt for the better-value deluxe rooms if you can get them. Standard rooms have direct-dial phones, TVs, fans, and good-sized bathrooms, and run US$89/103. Five much larger deluxe rooms have air-conditioning, hair dryers in the bathrooms, and writing desks for US$108/122, and the five junior suites cost US$123/136. All rates include breakfast. Children under 10 stay free.

A large downtown hotel is the ***Barceló Amón Plaza*** (*☎ 257-0191, fax 257-0284; in the USA ☎ 800-575-1253, amonpark@sol.racsa.co.cr*), Avenida 11, Calle 3 bis & 5. This is an attractive, modern, international hotel in the elegant old Barrio Amón. The place is spotless, with a good restaurant, bar, 24-hour café, casino, spa, business center, underground parking, and travel agency. All units are air-conditioned and have TVs and phones, and some have nice views. Street noise is minimal. The 60 spacious standard rooms cost US$133 single or double, the 24 junior suites cost US$168, and a few deluxe suites cost US$244. Continental breakfast is included. Recently, it was bought by the Barceló group, which has been much criticized for the way it has developed its Playa Tambor megahotel (see the Península de Nicoya chapter).

The ***Quality Hotel*** (*☎ 257-2580, fax 257-2582; in the USA ☎ 800-228-5151, quality@centralamerica.com*), Avenida 3, Calles 38 & 40, is a member of the well-known Quality Hotel chain in the USA. The 126 rooms and suites with air-conditioning, TVs, hairdryers, phones, and private baths are at the standards you would expect from this chain (ie, fairly high but rather bland). There is a 24-hour cafeteria and room service, a bar, and a casino. The rate is US$104 single or double, US$10 for additional people.

About 750m north of downtown and across the Río Torres is the modern ***Hotel Villa Tournón*** (☎ *233-6622, fax 222-5211, hvillas@sol.racsa.co.cr*). There is a decent restaurant, pool, spa, and a spacious feel, and the popular Centro Comercial El Pueblo is nearby. Cab drivers know it as 300m east of the *La República* newspaper office. Rooms with air-conditioning, bathtubs, and TVs range from US$82 to US$95 single, US$88 to US$101 double.

Next we get into the modern, luxury-class resort hotels with many facilities, such as restaurants, shops, pools, gyms, saunas, casinos, discotheques, convention facilities, travel agents, etc. These include the ***Hotel Corobicí*** (☎ *232-8122, fax 231-5834; in the USA* ☎ *800-227-4274, corobici@sol.racsa.co.cr*), Calle 42, 200m north of Parque La Sabana. The cavernous architecture is interesting to look at, but the huge lobby area echoes loudly into some bedrooms. On the other hand, the air-conditioned rooms are spacious and comfortable and the restaurants, although very expensive, serve excellent food and provide room service. There are about 200 air-conditioned rooms with TVs, telephones, mini-bars, and large bathrooms. There is an executive floor for business travelers, a casino, a spa, a sauna, a disappointing pool, massage services, and a gym. The rates are US$145 single or double for standard rooms, and about US$170 for executive rooms, US$190 for junior suites (some with a whirlpool bath), and US$200 to US$500 for other suites.

Farther out, along the road to the airport near La Uruca suburb, is the 280-room ***San José Palacio Hotel*** (☎ *220-2034, fax 220-2036, palacio@sol.racsa.co.cr*). This modern hotel is owned by the Barceló group. Rates are US$129/144 and up for luxurious single/double rooms, and the hotel has all the amenities you expect. Still farther out along the road to the airport are other luxury resort hotels (see Places to Stay – Other Areas, later in this chapter).

Right downtown you'll find the ***Aurola Holiday Inn*** (☎ *233-7233, fax 222-2621; in the USA* ☎ *800-465-4329, aurola@sol.racsa.co.cr*), at Calle 5, Avenida 5. This luxurious, 17-story building topped with a fancy restaurant is a San José landmark – ticos and cab drivers know it as Hotel Aurola rather than the Holiday Inn. This is the most convenient large luxury hotel to downtown, and it has all the amenities you might expect, including a pool and parking. Rooms start at US$128 single or double, US$160 on the executive floor, and there are more expensive suites, including the presidential suite, which you can rent for about US$550 per night. Children under 12 years of age stay free in their parents' rooms.

PLACES TO STAY – ESCAZÚ

The Escazú suburb has a variety of accommodations, as well as some elegant residential areas that are popular with foreign residents. San Rafael de Escazú, about 7km west of downtown San José, and San Antonio de Escazú, about 1.5km south of San Rafael, are the central areas (see the Escazú map), but around them are several other districts with delightful rural accommodations with urban amenities.

B&Bs

These have really proliferated in the suburbs of San José over the past few years, especially in the Escazú area. Most are within walking distance of a bus line or are a 15-minute cab ride from San José. Many are owned by North American expats who can't imagine a better place to live than Escazú, and they show a genuine pride in their properties, many of which are very attractive or have great views (or both). Street addresses aren't given here – refer to the map or call the hotel for directions. Most B&Bs will give low-season or long-stay discounts.

Park Place B&B (☎ *228-9200; in the USA, Interlink 358, PO Box 025635, Miami, FL 33102*) is a small but friendly place run by Barry Needman, who can hook you up with reasonably priced tours run by locals. Park Place is an attractive alpine-style house with four guest bedrooms sharing two bathrooms and kitchen privileges. Rates are US$40/45 single/double. To maintain peace and quiet, guests must be over 12 years old. Buses to San José stop just outside several

ESCAZÚ

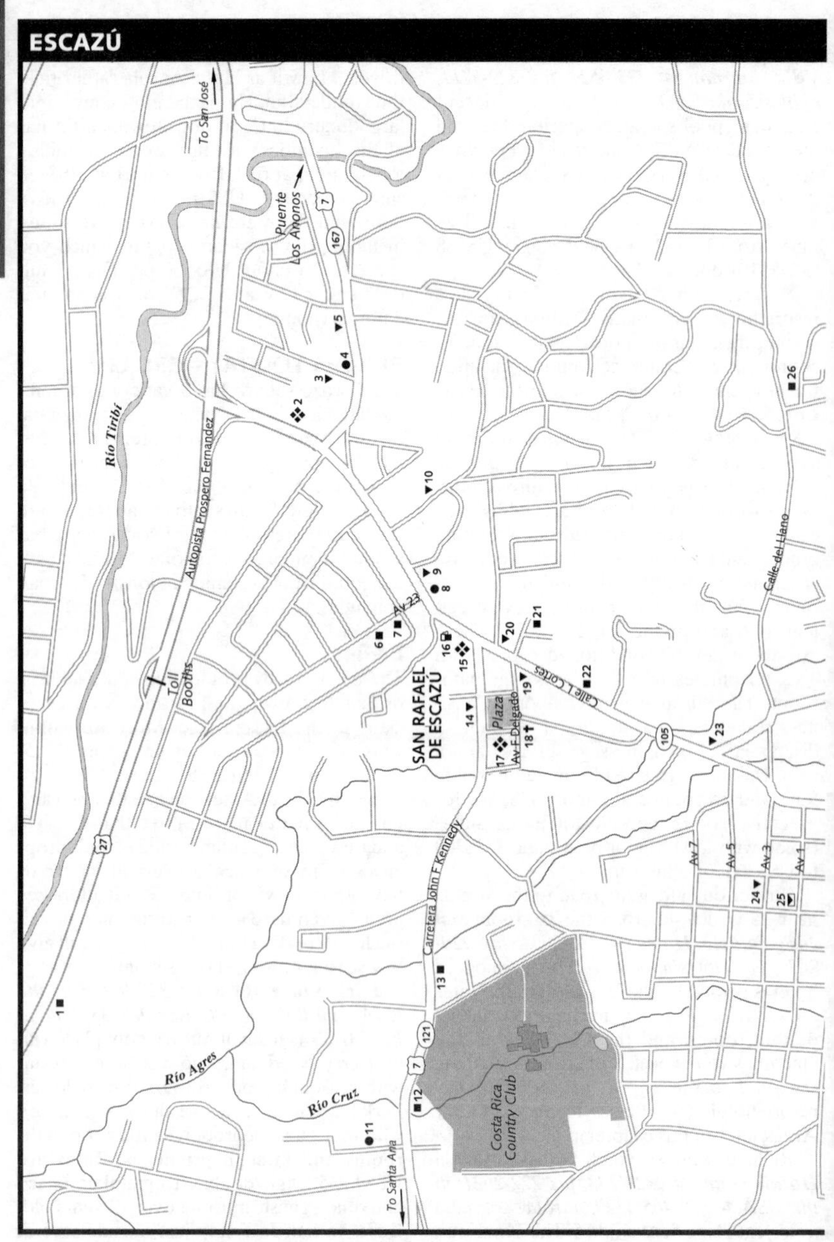

To San José
Puente Los Anonos
7
167
Río Tiribí
Autopista Prospero Fernandez
Toll Booths
27
Av 23
SAN RAFAEL DE ESCAZÚ
Plaza
Av F Delgado
Calle L Cortes
105
Calle del Llano
Av 7
Av 5
Av 3
Av 1
Carretera John F Kennedy
121
Río Agres
Río Cruz
Costa Rica Country Club
To Santa Ana
1
2
3
4
5
6
7
8
9
10
11
12
13
14
15
16
17
18
19
20
21
22
23
24
25
26

ESCAZÚ

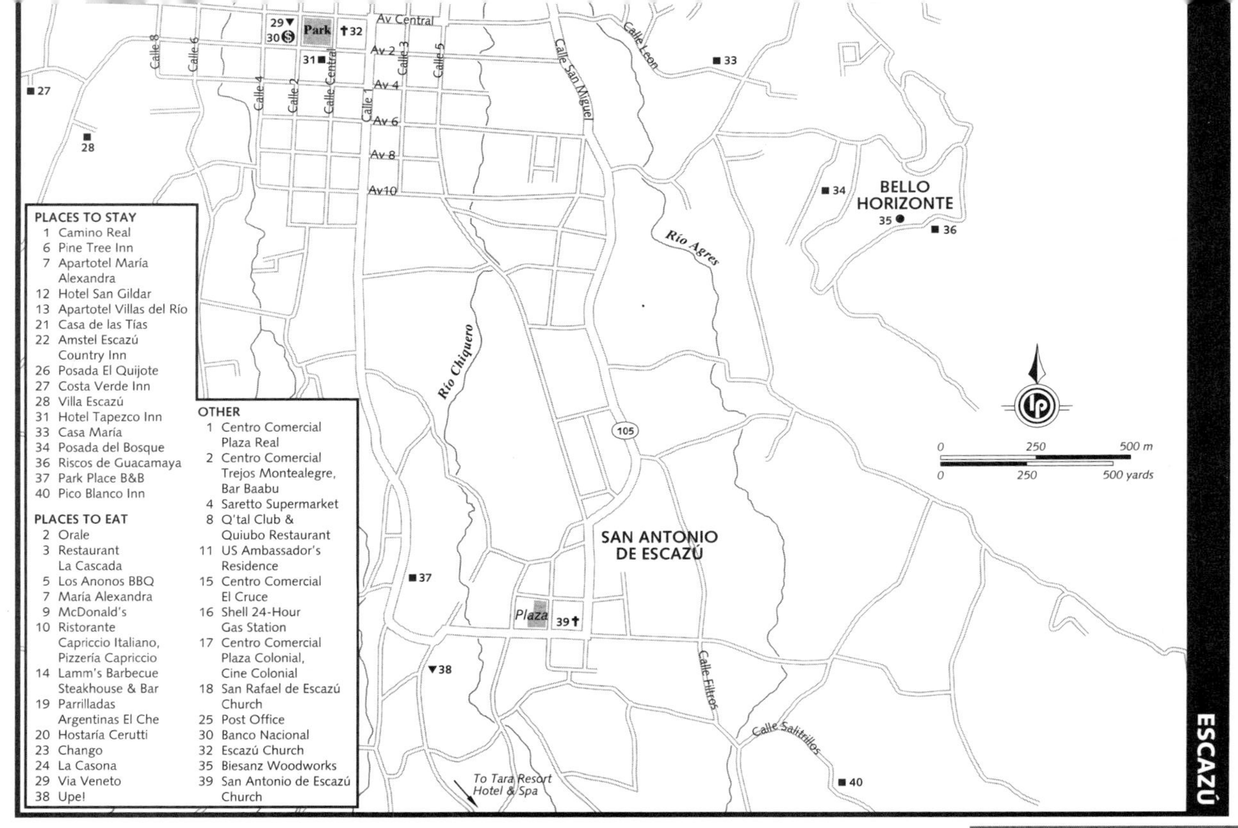
BELLO HORIZONTE
SAN ANTONIO DE ESCAZÚ
Río Agres
Río Chiquero
Calle Leon
Calle San Miguel
Calle Filtros
Calle Salitrillos
To Tara Resort Hotel & Spa
Plaza
Park
105
Av Central
Av 2
Av 4
Av 6
Av 8
Av10
Calle 8
Calle 6
Calle 4
Calle 2
Calle Central
Calle 1
Calle 3
Calle 5
0 250 500 m
0 250 500 yards
PLACES TO STAY
1 Camino Real
6 Pine Tree Inn
7 Apartotel María Alexandra
12 Hotel San Gildar
13 Apartotel Villas del Río
21 Casa de las Tías
22 Amstel Escazú Country Inn
26 Posada El Quijote
27 Costa Verde Inn
28 Villa Escazú
31 Hotel Tapezco Inn
33 Casa María
34 Posada del Bosque
36 Riscos de Guacamaya
37 Park Place B&B
40 Pico Blanco Inn
PLACES TO EAT
2 Orale
3 Restaurant La Cascada
5 Los Anonos BBQ
7 María Alexandra
9 McDonald's
10 Ristorante Capriccio Italiano, Pizzería Capriccio
14 Lamm's Barbecue Steakhouse & Bar
19 Parrilladas Argentinas El Che
20 Hostaría Cerutti
23 Chango
24 La Casona
29 Via Veneto
38 Upe!
OTHER
1 Centro Comercial Plaza Real
2 Centro Comercial Trejos Montealegre, Bar Baabu
4 Saretto Supermarket
8 Q'tal Club & Quiubo Restaurant
11 US Ambassador's Residence
15 Centro Comercial El Cruce
16 Shell 24-Hour Gas Station
17 Centro Comercial Plaza Colonial, Cine Colonial
18 San Rafael de Escazú Church
25 Post Office
30 Banco Nacional
32 Escazú Church
35 Biesanz Woodworks
39 San Antonio de Escazú Church

times an hour. This place is a good value and recommended.

Villa Escazú *(☎/fax 228-9566, villaescazu@yellowweb.co.cr)* is a Swiss chalet-type building surrounded by terraced gardens and fruit trees. A verandah is good for watching birds and eating the full gourmet breakfast that is included in the US$35/60 single/double rent; no smoking allowed inside, and no small children. There are six attractively decorated rooms sharing three bathrooms (two rooms per bathroom, and one room can be closed off on request to create a room with private bathroom at an extra charge). A pleasant sitting room with a fireplace invites you to relax in the evening.

The ***Costa Verde Inn*** *(☎ 228-4080, fax 289-8591, costaverdeinn@hotmail.com)* is an attractive country inn with hot tub, tennis court, small pool, Jacuzzi, sundeck, barbecue area, and fireplace. Rooms with fans, king-size beds, and private hot showers rent for US$52 double. Two apartments with balconies cost US$76 double. All include full breakfast served on an outdoor terrace. Low-season and weekly discounts are available.

Casa María *(☎ 228-0190, fax 228-0015, costarica@costarica.org)* is a small hotel that includes a full breakfast in its rates, which range from US$57/80 to US$80/103 single/double depending on the room. (Some share baths, others don't.) There is a pool, and lunches and dinners are provided on request. The owners are friendly, and maps, books, and travel information are available to help guests plan their trips. Decor includes walls covered with psychedelic murals and traditional art prints that combine to…well, look and decide for yourself.

Casa de las Tías *(☎ 289-5517, fax 289-7353, casatia@costarica.net)* is in a quiet area of San Rafael de Escazú. The tico owners provide typical breakfasts and other meals on request. The house is decorated with art and crafts from all over Latin America. English, French, and Hebrew are spoken. Five rooms share three bathrooms and rent for US$57 single, US$68/80 to US$81/93 double/triple. Smoking is allowed outside only, children are accepted with advance notice, and free airport pickup is available if you have a reservation.

The ***Posada El Quijote*** *(☎ 289-8401, fax 289-8729, quijote@sol.racsa.co.cr; in the USA, PO Box 025216, Miami, FL 33102-5216)* is a splendid B&B on the east side of Escazú, in the Bello Horizonte district. The huge and sumptuously appointed living room has a magnificent view down onto the Central Valley, and the well-chosen modern artwork found in the living room continues throughout the house. Rooms are bright and spacious, with cable TV, telephones, and modern bathrooms with excellent showers. A full breakfast is served in the plant-filled breakfast/bar area. Outside are an attractive garden and terrace with lounge chairs. Three standard and five deluxe rooms rent for US$58 to US$81 single and US$70 to US$83 double, with discounts for weeklong stays or in the low season. Air conditioning is available for US$5. Two bedrooms are designated for nonsmokers. If you like small, elegant B&Bs, this one is hard to match for top quality at a very fair price. Airport pickup and tours can be arranged by the friendly US owners, who also speak French and Spanish.

Riscos de Guacamaya *(☎ 228-9074, fax 289-5776, faberr@sol.racsa.co.cr)* is also in the Bello Horizonte district. Its doubles with private baths cost about US$40; a suite costs US$50, including continental breakfast. Units have cable TV but no telephones. A swimming pool is available. The hotel will provide meals on request. The public areas are nicer than the guest rooms. An apartment with a sitting area and kitchenette may be available.

Posada del Bosque *(☎ 228-1164, fax 228-2006, villela@sol.racsa.co.cr)* is a country inn set in pleasant gardens. The friendly and helpful tico owners will cook for you on request and enjoy chatting in English with their international guests. There are about eight rooms (another is planned), most with private baths and nonsmoking rules. There is a fireplace, laundry service, and a barbecue area. A swimming pool, tennis, and horseback-riding trails are nearby. Children are invited. Rates are US$57.50/63 single/double including full breakfast – several readers have recommended this place. Airport pickup is available.

In the hills south of San Antonio de Escazú is ***Las Golondrinas*** *(☎ 228-6448, fax 228-6381, Apartado 672-1250, Escazú)*. This is one secluded wooden cabin with verandah (good views), flower-filled garden, bathroom, and kitchenette. Lunches and dinners can be provided on request – the owners will tailor services to suit the guests. Rates for a double room are US$53/207/592 per day/week/month.

Hotels & Apartotels

The ***Apartotel María Alexandra*** *(☎ 228-1507, fax 289-5192, matour@sol.racsa.co.cr)*, Calle 3, Avenida 23, San Rafael de Escazú, is clean and quiet and has a pool, sauna, parking, VCR rentals, and laundry facilities. The restaurant (☎ 289-4876) is medium priced and well recommended – people come from the city to eat. This is one of the most comfortable apartotels and is usually booked up several months ahead, especially for the dry season. Apartments with one bedroom and bathroom cost US$81 for two people. Apartments with two bedrooms sleeping four people cost US$99, and apartments with two bedrooms, two bathrooms, and a studio sleeping up to five cost US$116. All apartments have fully equipped kitchenettes, dining areas, air-conditioned bedrooms, TVs, clock radios, and direct telephones. Maid service is included. Discounts of 5% or 10% for a week or month are available.

Just beyond the Apartotel is the ***Pine Tree Inn*** *(☎ 289-7405, fax 228-2180, pinetree@sol.racsa.co.cr)*, with 15 rooms, each with fans, cable TVs, telephones, and private hot baths. There is a swimming pool and snack bar. Rates are US$46/51 including breakfast, US$10 for additional people.

The ***Amstel Escazú Country Inn*** *(☎ 228-1764, fax 228-0620, escazu@sol.racsa.co.cr)* is 300m south of the Centro Comercial El Cruce. It offers parking, a pool, gardens, and a barbecue area. There are 16 air-conditioned rooms with cable TV, phones, and private bathrooms for US$64 single or double, and one suite for US$87, additional people US$10, including continental breakfast.

Near the Escazú church is the ***Hotel Tapezco Inn*** *(☎ 228-1084, fax 289-7026)*, with a Jacuzzi, sauna, and small restaurant/bar looking out over the valley. The management is friendly, and the rooms are nice enough at US$35/45 single/double. It is a short walk from a San José bus stop and the cafés around the town park.

On the northwest side of Escazú is the ***Hotel San Gildar*** *(☎ 289-8843, fax 228-6454, info@hotelsangildar.com)*. A pool set in a pretty garden is surrounded by the modern and attractive hacienda-style building, which houses about 30 very comfortable rooms. The management is friendly and helpful, and the flute of champagne presented to guests upon arrival is a classy welcome. There is a good restaurant and bar that attracts diners from outside the hotel. Spacious, air-conditioned rooms with cable TV and phones in both the bedroom and bathroom run US$114 single or double, US$17 for additional people, including breakfast. Near the San Gildar is the exclusive-looking ***Apartotel Villas del Río*** *(☎ 289-8833, fax 289-8835, info@villasdelrio.com)*, where modern, air-conditioned apartments range from US$145 to US$350 a night, US$2610 to US$4640 monthly. It has a pool, sauna, playground, gym, bar, travel agency, and sundries shop.

About 2km northwest of Escazú, just off Hwy 27/Autopista Prospero Fernandez, is the posh ***Camino Real*** *(☎ 289-7000, fax 289-8930, caminoreal@ticonet.co.cr)*. The five-story building has 260 deluxe air-conditioned rooms with cable TV, mini-bars, direct-dial phones with voice mail, clock radios, and hair dryers. It also houses a pool, spa, gym, casino, two restaurants, two bars, a convention and business center, concierge services including baby-sitting, and a small shopping lobby. The rate is about US$250 for most rooms, and there are a few suites. The country's largest shopping mall, the Multiplaza, is close by.

The ***Pico Blanco Inn*** *(☎ 228-1908, 289-6197, fax 289-5189, Apartado 900-1250, Escazú)* is a 20-room, friendly, and pleasant countryside hotel in the hills about 3km southeast of central Escazú. There are balconies with views of the mountains and of

San José below, a pool, and a restaurant and bar. Rooms are fairly simple, but have queen-size beds and private hot showers, and rent for US$35 to US$46 single and US$45 to US$65 double. Many rooms have great views (which are a good deal) and some have refrigerators. Three cottages (which lack views) sleep up to six and rent for US$65 to US$77. You're pretty high in the hills here, and the driveway leading up to the hotel is quite steep and narrow. You can call for a pickup from the airport, Escazú, or San José.

The ***Tara Resort Hotel & Spa*** *(☎ 228-6992, fax 228-9651; in the US ☎ 800-405-5112, tara@tararesort.com)* is in one of Costa Rica's most elegant buildings, in the hills above Escazú. As the name implies, it is modeled after the plantation mansion in the movie *Gone with the Wind*, and its setting will take your breath away. It has a fine dining room serving continental cuisine. There is a pool, sauna, steam room, gym, and complete spa. Health and beauty packages are offered, ranging from half a day to several days. These include a variety of massages, facials, loofah scrubs, herbal treatments, manicures, pedicures, scalp treatments, personal diet and training sessions, etc. There are 12 rooms and suites ranging from US$151 to US$226 double, a bungalow for US$232, and a stunning penthouse suite for US$290, including continental breakfast and use of spa facilities. All rooms have sitting areas, telephones, and cable TV, and some have balconies or fireplaces. Packages including various tours of the country are available. The spa is open 9 am to 6 pm Tuesday to Sunday (previously closed on Mondays, so call to confirm).

PLACES TO STAY – OTHER AREAS

The suburbs of Santa Ana (several kilometers west of Escazú) and San Antonio de Belén (en route to the international airport in Alajuela) have several good places to stay. Beyond that, look in the Central Valley & Surrounding Highlands chapter.

Camping

There is a full-service campground in San Antonio de Belén, 2km west of the San Antonio-Heredia intersection with the Interamericana, near the Cariari Hotel. In San Antonio, there are signs for the ***Belén Trailer Park*** *(☎ 239-0421, 239-0731, fax 239-1613, Apartado 143, San Antonio de Belén, Heredia)*. There are full hookups for camper vehicles, as well as safe tenting areas for backpackers. Hot showers, laundry facilities, public phone, local information, and nearby public buses to San José are all available. Rates are US$10 per tent or small vehicle, US$13 for a larger motorhome.

Hotels & Apartotels

There are two luxury hotels near the Cariari Country Club, about 9km northwest of San José on the way to the international airport. Both hotels have country club privileges. (For information about golf at the Cariari Country Club, see the Activities section earlier in this chapter.)

The ***Cariari Hotel*** *(☎ 239-0022, 231-6442, fax 239-2803, 220-1914; in the USA ☎ 800-227-4274, cariari@centralamerica.com)* has two pools, sauna, children's play area, casino, shopping mall, restaurants, and bars in addition to guest privileges at the neighboring country club. Over 200 rooms and suites cost US$162 standard to US$545 for the presidential suite. All come with air-conditioning, cable TV, telephones, and mini-bars, and many have a private balcony. There is 24-hour room service.

Not far away is the ***Hotel Herradura*** *(☎ 239-0033, fax 239-2292, hherradu@sol.racsa.co.cr)*. This place also has privileges at the neighboring Cariari Country Club and has full convention facilities managed by Grupo Costa Sol International, which also operates Aero Costa Sol (for airplane charters) and the Isla de Pesca fishing lodge in Barra del Colorado, as well as a fleet of fishing boats and river rafts. A travel desk will make arrangements for these. The hotel features a huge pool with waterfalls and swim-up bar, five Jacuzzis, a 24-hour casino, sauna, and concierge services. There are four restaurants (Japanese, Spanish, a coffee shop, and a 24-hour international restaurant) and two bars. Shuttle service to downtown is available. Over 200 rooms and suites start at US$162.

Still closer to the airport is the ***Marriott Hotel*** *(☎ 298-0000, fax 298-0044, marriott@sol.racsa.co.cr)*, part of the international Marriott chain. The village of San Antonio de Belén is 5km south of the airport. The hotel features a pool, tennis courts, gym, sauna, spa, golf driving and putting areas, and a game room. There are five restaurants and bars, a casino, 254 rooms, and seven suites. Conference and banquet rooms are available. Rates are US$244/267 to US$226/238 single/double; suites cost US$520. Free airport transportation is offered. Several readers have written to say they enjoyed staying here.

In the small rural town of Santa Ana, about 7km west of Escazú and 14km south of the airport, is the Canadian-run ***Apartotel Paraíso Canadiense*** *(☎/fax 282-5870, email: lynandre@sol.racsa.co.cr)*, with four one-bedroom apartments at US$50/225/525 for a night/week/month, and a two-bedroom apartment for US$65/250/650. All apartments have kitchenettes, TVs, and laundry facilities, and share a swimming pool. Parking is available, and there are frequent buses into San José.

PLACES TO EAT

Cosmopolitan San José has a wide variety of restaurants – something to satisfy most tastes and budgets. You'll find Peruvian and Middle Eastern restaurants, as well as the old standbys: Italian, Chinese, and French. American chain restaurants are also popular if you need a fast-food fix. And, of course, there are tico specialties. This section is broken down into restaurants in and around the city, and places in Escazú.

Remember that most restaurants, apart from the very cheapest, add a 13% tax plus a 10% service charge to your bill. Many of the better restaurants can get quite busy, so a telephoned reservation may help you avoid a wait. (Telephone numbers are given here only for the finer restaurants.) Where approximate prices are given as a guide, bear in mind that anything with shellfish (shrimp, lobster, or crab) will be far more expensive.

Some of the popular bars also have good food; see the Entertainment section later in this chapter.

In the City

Budget Restaurants Shoestring travelers trying to economize may find San José a somewhat expensive city in which to eat. Apart from the sodas (see below), here are some suggestions. The ***Mercado Central***, at Avenidas Central & 1, Calles 6 & 8, has a variety of cheap sodas and restaurants inside. It's a great place to eat elbow-to-elbow with local ticos – plenty of atmosphere. There are several other cheap places to eat near the market, especially on the Avenida 1 side. The area around the market is not dangerous, but it is a little rough: women may prefer not to go there alone. There are pickpockets, too. Don't wander around with cameras and cash bursting out of your pockets, and leave that diamond-studded gold tennis bracelet at home.

The ***Restaurant El Campesino***, Calle 7, Avenida 2, is a pleasant place with booth seating and a homey atmosphere, open 10 am to midnight daily. It serves a few Chinese dishes and chicken roasted over a wood fire (not fried) – the latter is about US$2 for a quarter chicken with tortillas or mashed potatoes and a drink. There is take-out as well.

La Vasconia, Avenida 1, Calle 5, is a cheap but decent place with plenty of local atmosphere, a largely tico clientele, and a wide variety of food on the chalkboard menu. A *pinto con huevo* breakfast (rice and beans with an egg) is about US$1, and they have set *casado* (cheap meal of the day) lunches for about US$2. Some nights musicians stroll in and play awhile. Nearby, next to the Omni Cinema, is the clean ***Restaurante Omni***, Avenida 1, Calles 3 & 5, where a good set lunch is served 11:30 am to 1:30 pm for about US$2. It also has Chinese dishes for US$3 or US$4.

Most restaurants offer a casado for lunch at a price well below eating à la carte. These fixed-price meals can cost from about US$1 in the very cheapest places to US$4 or US$5 in the fancier restaurants, where the meal may be called an *almuerzo ejecutivo* (business lunch) but are often be very good value.

The ***Meylin 2***, adjoining the Hotel Bienvenido at Calle 10, Avenidas 1 & 3, and the ***Gran Imperial Restaurant***, in the hotel of that name at Calle 8, Avenidas Central & 1, are both inexpensive and popular.

A reader recommends ***Restaurante y Cafeteria La Criollita*** in Barrio Amón, 50m west of INS. It's open 7 am to 8 pm and serves full American or tico breakfasts, with coffee and juice included, for about US$4, with free refills on coffee and fast, friendly service.

Sodas These luncheonette-type snack bars are usually cheap and are a good choice for the budget traveler, particularly for breakfast or lunch, when you can have a light meal for as little as US$1. Most are rather featureless and certainly not fancy, but are popular with ticos. They cater to students and working people, and hence some tend to close on weekends. There are dozens of sodas in San José, so what follows is just a selection.

An inexpensive and popular one is the ***Soda Central***, Avenida 1, Calles 3 & 5, where the *empanadas* are good and you can have *gallo pinto con huevo* for US$2.50 or a casado for US$3. The ***Soda B&B*** is on the northeast corner of the Plaza de la Cultura and has been discovered by and is popular with tourists – the 23% for tax and service is charged and credit cards are accepted. The menu has a few tico dishes but mainly offers hamburgers (about US$2.50) and hot dogs, shakes, and sandwiches.

The cheap ***Soda Nini***, Avenida 3, Calles 2 & 4, serves large portions of both tico and Chinese food. ***Soda Magaly***, at Avenida Central, Calle 23, has a good variety of cheap meals under US$2 and is close to the Hostel Toruma. There are several other sodas near here. Also close to the hostel is the ***Soda Pulpería La Luz***, at Avenida Central, Calle 33 – this old *pulpería* is a local landmark. The menu is limited to cheap but tasty local snacks and meals.

Another is ***Chelle's***, at Avenida Central, Calle 9, also open 24 hours. It is a bit quieter than the others (musicians don't usually come in here) and has similar prices and a full bar. Some ticos say you haven't really experienced San José until you've had a wee-hours breakfast here after a night of drinking. Other 24-hour options are ***Soda Comilona #1*** and ***Soda Comilona #3***, five blocks away from each other on Avenida 10, at Calle Central and Calle 10 respectively, in an area of town where a taxi is advisable late at night. In fact, a lot of taxi drivers hang out at these places. ***Soda Castro***, at Avenida 10, Calles 2 & 4, serves desserts and fruit salads and is an old-fashioned tico family spot – check out the sign prohibiting public displays of romance.

If you're out by Parque La Sabana, stop by the locally popular ***Soda Tapia***, Calle 42, Avenida 2, which serves sandwiches as well as set meals.

Cafés & Coffee Shops These are very popular among Costa Ricans, who seem to have a sweet tooth for pastries and cakes. They are often good places for travelers to catch up on journal or letter writing. Prices are not necessarily cheap, but you don't have to buy much and can sit for hours.

A favorite people-watching place is the ***Café Parisienne***, the pavement café of the Gran Hotel Costa Rica at Calle 3, Avenida 2, where you get a good view of the comings and goings in the Plaza de la Cultura. Full meals are also served here. In the Plaza de la Cultura itself is the Teatro Nacional, within which you'll find the elegant ***Café Ruiseñor***, which is very popular and always full at lunchtime – come early and people watch. Changing art is displayed on the walls. Hours are 9 am to 6 pm Monday to Saturday (later if there's a show on). It's not cheap, but it serves some of the best coffee in Costa Rica.

The ***City Café***, part of the Hotel del Rey downtown but with a separate entrance, is a

24-hour place that serves excellent huge sandwiches (about US$5) as well as pies and coffee. Often, blues or jazz plays in the background, and an all-night guard makes this a safe place to eat in the wee hours.

Spoon has several locations: Avenida Central, Calles 5 & 7 downtown; Avenida 8, Calle 45 in Los Yoses (a local landmark); and others in the Central Valley. It is known for a great selection of pastries and cakes, as well as light lunch items. Similar, and perhaps slightly upmarket, are ***Ruiseñor***, 100m east of the Automercado in Los Yoses, and ***Choices***, across the street and 150m east of the Los Yoses Automercado. (On a map, you'll find them on Avenida Central near Calle 41.) The new, spacious ***Coffee Station***, at Avenida 5, Calle 1, has done a good job of imitating a certain North American coffee chain and has a well-kept if not exactly local ambience. You can get a bagel sandwich for about US$3, pastries, and all kinds of espresso drinks.

Churrería Manolos, at Avenida Central, Calles Central & 2, and Avenida Central, Calles 9 & 11, is famous for its cream-filled *churros* (hollow doughnut tubes) as well as a variety of other desserts and light meals. The first location is especially popular and has a 2nd floor from which you can watch the people going by on the pedestrian-only street below. It's a popular breakfast spot. Nearby, ***Panadería Schmidt*** also has two locations: on Avenida 2, Calle 4; and Avenida Central, Calle 11. It's locally popular for cakes, pastries, and breads for carry-out (though there are small eat-in areas).

The Bookshop (see Bookstores under Information, earlier in this chapter) has a nice little coffee shop where you can read the book you just bought. Ice-cream eaters should look for ***Pops***, ***Walls***, and ***Mönpik*** for the best ice cream; each chain has several locations in San José and can also be found outside the capital.

Vegetarian Although vegetarianism still isn't very big in Costa Rica, there are several reasonable vegetarian restaurants, most of them fairly inexpensive. There are three ***Vishnu*** restaurants: at Avenida 8, Calles 11 & 13; Calle 14, Avenidas Central & 2; and Avenida 1, Calles 1 & 3. The last, which has expanded to both sides of the avenue, seems the most popular. Try the veggie burger and fruit drink combo. There is a daily set meal for about US$3. Read carefully when ordering their fruit salads, or you may end up with something looking more like an ice-cream sundae than a healthy meal. The attractive ***Restaurant El Shakti***, Avenida 8, Calle 13, is also recommended; the US$3 set lunch is good and filling, and it has a small display of health-food products (vitamins, granola, dietary supplements, and the like) for sale. The newer ***Naturama Uno***, Avenida 1, Calles 3 & 5, has a good three-course vegetarian lunch plus fruit drink for about US$3, as well as a good variety of other plates from US$1.50 and up. It's open 7 am to 7 pm daily except Sunday.

For good-value macrobiotic lunches, try ***Don Sol*** at Avenida 7 bis, Calles 13 & 15, two blocks east of the Museo de Jade. A slightly more upmarket macrobiotic/vegetarian restaurant is the recommended ***La Mazorca***, 100m north and 25m west of the Banco Anglo in San Pedro. It also has a store selling health-food products.

Fast Food US-style fast-food restaurants in Costa Rica serve food similar in taste and price to what you get in the USA (about US$3 for a medium-size meal, less for just a small burger). They are popular among ticos, especially the younger ones.

McDonald's, at Calle 4, Avenida Central & 1, and on the north side of the Plaza de la Cultura at Avenida Central, Calles 3 & 5, and elsewhere, has been recommended for its clean bathrooms. (Note that McDonald's restaurants are found in a few other Costa Rican towns, where they seem to be used as local landmarks because all the locals know where a new one has opened.) Also on the north side of the Plaza de la Cultura is ***Archi's***, a Costa Rican version of US fast food serving both hamburgers and chicken.

For some reason, the ***Kentucky Fried Chicken*** (Pollo Kentucky) restaurants, at Paseo Colón, Calles 32 & 34, and in Los Yoses at Avenida Central, Calle 31, have both become local landmarks. Tell a cab driver that you want to go 125m north of the

Pollo Kentucky on Paseo Colón and you'll be taken there directly and probably charged exactly the same fare as a local! (This is actually the address of the Machu Pichu restaurant, described farther on.)

Other fast-food restaurants include ***Hardee's***, Calle 1, Avenida Central, for hamburgers, and ***Don Taco***, Avenida 1, Calle 2, for instant burritos and tacos. There's also a ***Taco Bell*** at Calle 5, Avenidas Central & 2. More open every year.

Costa Rican As much as anything else, national specialties include steak and seafood, so most of the restaurants in the next section can also be thought of as Costa Rican. There isn't a very strong typical culinary tradition in Costa Rica, but a few restaurants serve what could be considered tico country cooking, and the food is very good.

The best-known one is ***La Cocina de Leña*** *(☎ 223-3704, 255-1360)*, in the Centro Comercial El Pueblo. The restaurant's name literally means 'the wood stove,' and the atmosphere attempts to be country kitchen and homey. The owners had so much success, however, that they moved to bigger premises, which detracts from the homey feel somewhat, and their prices are no longer 'country kitchen.' Still, it's a nice enough place, the food is well prepared, and they continue their charming tradition of printing their menu on a brown paper bag. A selection of typical dishes includes corn soup with pork, black bean soup with eggs, tamales, beef casado, gallo pinto with meat and eggs, stuffed peppers, ox tail served with yucca and plantain, and, of course, steak and fish. Most meals cost US$10 to US$20. They also serve local desserts and alcoholic concoctions, including the tico firewater, *guaro*. They may have a band or dance group on busy nights in the high season.

Also try ***El Cuartel de la Boca del Monte*** *(☎ 233-1477)*, Avenida 1, Calles 21 & 23, which is a coffee house and restaurant during the day, serving some Costa Rican dishes – casually elegant and moderately priced – and a bar at night. It's usually fairly quiet at lunch but gets busier in the evening. The food is as much North American as tico, but the restaurant attracts locals and feels tico to a gringo like me. Eat during the day – at night, it's loud with young people and live bands.

If you come right down to it, the ***Mercado Central*** is as good a place as any for a plate of pinto beans with sour cream or a couple of banana-leaf-wrapped tamales. It'll be your cheapest option.

Out in Santa Ana, 100m north and 250m east of the Santa Ana church, is ***Casa Quitirrisí*** *(☎ 282-5441)*, which is a locally popular weekend spot open from noon till late Thursday to Sunday. It often has marimba music.

Steak & Seafood Some of these restaurants are for dedicated carnivores; side salads are usually available, but otherwise the meals are very meaty. Many have a good selection of both meat and seafood dishes, while others tend to have seafood only.

For mainly meat, ***La Hacienda*** *(☎ 223-5493)*, at Calle 7, Avenidas Central & 2, is quiet and unpretentious and has very good steaks for around US$10 and lunch specials for US$3 or US$4.

Other steakhouses are away from the center. ***Los Ranchos*** *(☎ 232-7757)*, on the north side of the Parque La Sabana, behind the ICE building (most cab drivers know it), is a little pricier than La Hacienda but has good service and is also recommended. ***El Chicote*** *(☎ 232-3777)* is another good steakhouse on the north side of La Sabana, 400m west of the ICE building, and it includes seafood on its menu. You can get to the north side of the Parque La Sabana on the Sabana Estadio bus, which goes out along Paseo Colón.

For barbecued ribs, ***JR House of Ribs*** *(☎ 225-5918)*, Avenida Central, Calles 33 & 35, in Los Yoses, is a reasonably priced choice if you want a big portion. There are other JRs in the northeastern suburb of Guadalupe and the western suburb of Rohrmoser – cab drivers know them.

In the Centro Comercial El Pueblo (which has a variety of restaurants, bars, and nightspots as well as shops), about 1.5km north of downtown, is the elegant ***Rías Bajas*** *(☎ 221-7123, 233-3214)*, which specializes in seafood but also has meat dishes.

Also specializing in seafood is the moderately priced ***La Fuente de Mariscos*** *(☎ 231-0631)*, in the Centro Comercial San José 2000 next to the Hotel Irazú, a few kilometers northwest of downtown. ***Oceanos*** *(☎ 260-7809)*, which is one of the country's most exclusive seafood (and international) restaurants, open for dinner only, has moved to Heredia. Moderately priced, ***La Princesa Marina*** *(☎ 232-0481)* is open 11:30 am to 10:30 pm daily on the west side of La Sabana (150m south of Canal 7 TV station). A fried-fish dinner starts around US$5.

Chinese Chinese restaurants are found all over the Americas from Alaska to Argentina, and San José has its fair share (a *Tico Times* reporter claims there are over 250 in San José and the Central Valley area). Most are good and medium priced. The best downtown is the recommended ***Restaurante Tin-jo*** *(☎ 221-7605)*, Calle 11, Avenidas 6 & 8, which has expanded its seating and added Thai cuisine to its menu. The restaurant is attractive and cozy, and the waitstaff is gracious and friendly. Expect to pay about US$5 to US$10 for a meal.

For inexpensive Chinese, the ***Restaurante Lung Mun***, Avenida 1, Calles 5 & 7, has a lunch menu with big portions for not much over US$2. It's popular with local office workers and budget travelers, and there is sometimes a line to get in when they open at noon.

For dim sum downtown, the restaurant in the ***Hotel Royal Garden*** *(☎ 257-0023)*, Calle Central, Avenida Central, has been recommended. Dim sum and other Chinese dishes are served all week.

Other recommended Chinese restaurants include the downtown ***Restaurant Fulusu*** *(☎ 223-7568)*, Calle 7, Avenidas Central & 2, for spicy Szechuan and Mandarin food, and the locally well-known and popular ***Ave Fénix*** *(☎ 225-3362)*, serving Szechuan meals 200m west of the San Pedro church.

Japanese Some excellent Japanese restaurants are found in the top hotels and tend to be pricey, though the food is good. One of the best is the ***Sakura*** *(☎ 239-0033)* in the Hotel Herradura (see Places to Stay – Other Areas, above, for details). It serves authentic Japanese food and may be closed on Monday. Another recommended Japanese restaurant is the ***Fuji*** in the Hotel Corobicí (see Places to Stay – Top End for details). It is closed on Sunday.

Arirang *(☎ 223-2838)*, at Paseo Colón, Calles 38 & 40, serves more moderately priced Japanese and Korean food but is closed on Sunday.

Mexican ***Los Antojitos*** has several locally popular locations; the best known is in Los Yoses *(☎ 225-9525)* on Avenida Central, 50m west of the fountain. The food is inexpensive, though not as authentic as some might like (they call it Mexican-tico). Hours are 11 am to midnight daily, and there are mariachis on Friday and Saturday nights. Also open daily and with weekend mariachis is ***La Hacienda de Pancho's*** *(☎ 224-8261)*, which is 200m east of the rotunda to Zapote (south of San Pedro) and has more authentic Mexican cuisine. ***El Jorongo*** *(☎ 253-5028)*, almost across from the Muñoz & Nanne supermarket in San Pedro, is a small Mexican-owned place with authentic meals for about US$4 or US$5. South of the center, a great little hole-in-the-wall place is ***Huarachez***, at Avenida 22, Calles 5 & 7, which is run by Don Ernesto, who used to make his living in Mexico as a dolphin trainer. The place is open to 11 pm and gets crowded.

On the way to Escazú, there's ***Andale*** *(☎ 231-5164)*, 400m west of Parque La Sabana on the old road (not the freeway).

Also see the entries under Entertainment, later in this chapter, for other suggestions.

Spanish One of the longest-running Spanish restaurants (though it has moved a couple of times) is ***La Masía de Triquell*** *(☎ 296-3528)*, Edificio Casa España in Sabana Norte. It specializes in Catalan cuisine and is expensive but worth the splurge. The service is excellent, and the surroundings are attractive.

A newer and more moderately priced choice is ***Restaurante Taska Al Andalus*** *(☎ 257-6556)*, at Calle 3, Avenidas 7 & 9. It specializes in Andalusian cuisine but has good international dishes as well.

Out in San Pedro, the ***Marbella*** *(☎ 224-9452)*, in the Centro Comercial Calle Real, 75m east of the Banco Popular, has a Spanish chef who claims to make the best paella in Costa Rica (though Francisco, at La Masía, might well disagree!).

French There are several French restaurants in San José, most of them very expensive (at least by Costa Rican standards), and all recommended by and for lovers of French cuisine. Downtown there's the classy ***L'Ile de France*** *(☎ 222-6525)*. The weekday lunch special costs about US$10, which gives you an idea of the prices – but the food is good. It is closed on Sunday. Out along Paseo Colón is the elegant ***La Bastilla*** *(☎ 255-4994)*, Paseo Colón, Calle 22, with excellent main courses starting around US$12. It is also closed on Sunday.

Le Chandelier *(☎ 225-3980)*, in Los Yoses, is the best French restaurant in town – and is also closed on Sunday. Tell the cab driver to go to the Los Yoses ICE building, then 100m west and 100m south. The restaurant is lovely, with dining in a choice of outdoor patios, indoor areas next to a fireplace, or larger and smaller private rooms. Main courses cost in the US$10 to US$40 range.

Italian Pizzas and pastas vie with Chinese cuisine and American hamburgers for the most widespread foreign cuisine in Costa Rica. One of San José's most popular restaurants is the ***Balcón de Europa*** *(☎ 221-4841)*, Calle 9, Avenidas Central & 1. The restaurant has been in San José (though not always in the same location) since 1909 and claims to be the oldest eatery in Costa Rica. Italian chef Franco Piatti took over the restaurant in 1984, fired all but one of the staff, and retrained the new employees to his own specifications. The restaurant became an enormous success and is usually packed with both ticos and visitors. Sadly, Chef Piatti died in November 1996. The restaurant is now being run by his wife, an able Costa Rican businesswoman. Piatti's trained staff is still here, and the restaurant continues to be a local culinary landmark.

La Piazetta *(☎ 222-7896)*, Paseo Colón near Calle 40, has a mouth-watering menu of creative Italian food served on silver platters – locals call this the most elegant Italian restaurant in San José. Another elegant Italian place vying for the title of 'best Italian' is at the other end of town, in San Pedro. This is ***Il Ponte Vecchio*** *(☎ 283-1810)*, 150m east of La Fuente de Hispanidad (or 200m west of the San Pedro church), and 10m north. The chef survived 18 years of preparing Italian food in New York, and his work is recommended so much that the restaurant was named one of the 100 best restaurants in Central America. Call for opening hours, which vary. Also on the upscale Italian scene is ***Fellini*** *(☎ 222-3520)*, Avenida 4, Calle 36 (or 200m south of the Toyota dealership on Paseo Colón), which has good food and a decor that gives more than a nod to its namesake film director.

The new ***Pasta Factory and Pizzeria*** *(☎ 222-4642)*, Avenida 1, Calle 7, is a pleasant and reasonably priced place; meals start at about US$5. ***San Remo*** *(☎ 253-7880)* serves pizza and other reasonably priced Italian and tico food; it has moved to Guadalupe. The ***Ristorante Pizza Metro*** *(☎ 223-0306)*, Avenida 2, Calles 5 & 7, is locally popular and has pizzas and pastas in the US$5 range. Students like to grab a pizza at the lively ***Pizzería Il Pomodoro*** *(☎ 224-0966)*, 100m north of the San Pedro church and near the Universidad de Costa Rica. Locals claim it's the best pizza in town. There is also a ***Pizza Hut*** chain with two locations: Calle 4, Avenidas Central & 2, and Paseo Colón, Calle 28. It has a salad bar.

Continental Several restaurants serve food with a European flair. ***La Galería*** *(☎ 234-0850)*, 125m west of the ICE building in Los Yoses (behind Apartotel Los Yoses), has long been popular for its well-prepared and reasonably priced food served in a classical setting. The cuisine has a strong German influence, and many main courses are priced under US$10. Hours are noon to

2:30 pm weekdays and 7 to 11 pm Monday to Saturday.

Café Mundo *(☎ 222-6190)*, Avenida 9, Calle 15, is a new restaurant with a romantic ambience and good selection of international dishes starting at about US$5, including some with a Costa Rican flavor. This is also a nice place for a dessert and espresso. Hours are 11 am to 11 pm Monday to Thursday, noon to midnight Friday and Saturday.

A fancy and expensive place for fondues and other Swiss delights is ***Zermatt*** *(☎ 222-0604)*, Avenida 11, Calle 23 (100m north of the Santa Teresita church). The ***Fleur de Lys***, in the hotel of the same name, also has a good Swiss-influenced menu. See Places to Stay – Top End, earlier in this chapter, for details.

Several other hotels offer fine continental dining and are open to the public. Foremost among them is the ***Grano de Oro*** (see Places to Stay – Top End), which has received good reviews both for its attractive dining area and its fine food at moderate prices.

Other Cuisines There is a host of other international restaurants with food from several countries. A favorite is the ***Machu Pichu*** *(☎ 222-7384)*, Calle 32, Avenidas 1 & 3, 125m north of the Pollo Kentucky. It serves authentic Peruvian cuisine, especially seafood, at moderate prices. It also makes *pisco* sours (the Peruvian national cocktail). Hours are 11 am to 3 pm and 6 to 10 pm daily. Nearby is ***El Ceviche del Rey***, Calle 32, Avenida 1, which also serves Peruvian food, though it has a menu in English with prices higher than the Spanish version! Another recommended Peruvian restaurant is ***Café 1900*** *(☎ 225-0819)*, 100m north of La Fatíma church in Los Yoses.

For good Lebanese food, the place to go is ***Lubnán*** *(☎ 257-6071)*, Paseo Colón, Calles 22 & 24. It is closed on Monday.

In the Centro Comercial de la Calle Real in San Pedro, ***Ambrosia*** *(☎ 253-8012)* has an unconventional and indefinable menu, with many adventurous recipes. It is closed on Sunday. Just south of San Pedro, in Barrio La Granja, 300m south of the Más x Menos Supermercado, ***Restaurante Bijahua*** *(☎ 225-0613)* prepares nouvelle tico food. It's pricey but popular.

Escazú

For Costa Rican food, ***Tiquicia*** *(☎ 289-5839, 228-0468)* is upmarket price-wise, with a rustic setting. In a farmhouse up in the hills of Escazú, this restaurant gives diners great views and sometimes has live local music. Hours are erratic – call first and ask for directions. After rain, you might need a 4WD to get there. Also offering views from its terrace, much easier to reach, and a little cheaper is ***Upe!*** *(☎ 228-0183)*, in San Antonio de Escazú, open 5 to 11 pm on Thursday and Friday, 11 am to midnight on Saturday, and 11 am to 10 pm on Sunday. It often has marimba players, and the food is definitely tico.

In the center of Escazú, ***La Casona*** is a small, typical restaurant. On the central plaza, ***Via Veneto*** is a nice bakery/coffee shop.

Out on the road approaching Escazú is the well-known ***Los Anonos BBQ*** *(☎ 228-0180)*, which has served barbecued steaks and other food for three decades. Prices are very reasonable. It is closed on Monday. Nearby is another longtime favorite, ***Restaurant La Cascada*** *(☎ 228-0906, 228-9393)*, with a good selection of seafood as well as grilled steaks. An upscale choice, nicely located on the north side of the church plaza in San Rafael de Escazú, is ***Lamm's Barbecue Steakhouse & Bar*** *(☎ 289-6184)*. If you prefer Argentine-style grills, there's ***Parrilladas Argentinas El Che*** a few minutes' walk away.

Orale *(☎ 228-6437)*, in the Centro Comercial Trejos Montealegre, serves pretty good Mexican food.

Recommended Italian restaurants include ***Hostaría Cerutti*** *(☎ 228-4511)*, with authentic Italian dishes in the US$6 to US$10 range. From the clients to the chef, you'll hear a lot of Italian spoken here. It's closed on Tuesday. Also good is the ***Ristorante Capriccio Italiano*** *(☎ 228-9332)*, which is closed on Wednesday. Adjoining the restaurant is the ***Pizzería Capriccio,*** which serves pastries as well as pizza.

There are several excellent continental restaurants in Escazú. The classiest is the

Atlanta Dining Gallery *(☎ 228-6992)* in the Tara Resort Hotel, where the view is as splendid as the interior elegance, and the continental menu has a Costa Rican twist.

The ***María Alexandra***, in the apartotel of the same name in Escazú, is a small and locally recommended restaurant. The story goes that when John F Kennedy visited Costa Rica in 1963, he was accompanied by his personal chef, Hans Van Endel. The chef liked Costa Rica so much that he gave up his job cooking for the president and stayed in Costa Rica to work in the María Alexandra, where he supervises a Dutch-influenced continental menu. It is closed on Sunday.

Note that many shopping centers in Escazú have several decent restaurants each. A new place in an attractive turn-of-the-century building, ***Chango*** has a good international menu and has been recommended by a few readers.

ENTERTAINMENT

Stop by the ICT information center in the Plaza de la Cultura for leaflets with information on live music and nightclub acts. Of San José's newspapers, *La Nación* has the best listing (in Spanish) of clubs, theaters, cinemas, etc in its 'Viva' section. *The Tico Times* has a 'Weekend' section that tends to cover more theater, music, and cultural events, though it will occasionally profile a local band or nightclub.

Music Scene

Area bands and musicians are locally popular but haven't made much impact outside of Costa Rica. Having said that, there are some good Costa Rican acts that will get you listening or dancing – especially dancing, which ticos love to do. Occasionally, a famous foreign touring band will come through. Street musicians and mariachi bands looking for tips wander in and out of many downtown bars (see Bars & Dance Clubs, below).

Some groups have been together for a decade or more and are institutions on the tico music scene. Marfil, founded in Limón in 1974, is a 10-member band that gets audiences jumping with standard Latin rhythm – salsa, merengue, and Carlos Santana covers. Rock, jazz, and *nueva trova* (modern Latin folk music, often with a political, anti-establishment, human rights, social, etc theme) bands are also popular. A good guru for information on the music scene is Darren Mora of Mora Books (see Bookstores, earlier in this chapter), who helped start a number of radio stations in the country and knows the latest on what's going on.

A number of concerts on the beach (mostly rock and reggae) have been organized in recent years, some with bus caravans leaving from San José; look for signs around town. (Also see the Monteverde & Santa Elena section in the Northwestern Costa Rica chapter and the Puerto Viejo de Talamanca section in the Caribbean Lowlands chapter for information on the Monteverde Music Festival and South Caribbean Music Festival.)

Bars & Dance Clubs

Although there are some bars you go to just to have a drink, and some nightclubs you go to just to dance, ticos delight in mixing the two, and they are also mixed together in this section. Places that have withstood the test of time are emphasized; there are a few new listings, but the scene is a bit more sparse than it was in the mid-'90s. In the late '90s a tough crackdown on after-hours drinking (previously something of a tradition in San José) led to a number of popular places being shut down. New places open and close every year, and the most changeable and happening scene is, predictably, in San Pedro, home to the Universidad de Costa Rica and plenty of student hangouts. Gay and lesbian visitors may also want to see that section below.

El Cuartel de la Boca del Monte *(☎ 233-1477)*, Avenida 1, Calles 21 & 23, is a restaurant by day but is transformed at night into one of the capital's busiest and most popular nightspots for young people. The music is sometimes recorded and sometimes live (Wednesday is a good night for live bands), but always loud, and it's elbow-room only in the back room, where there is a small dance floor. In front, it's rather less frenzied but still crowded. This is a good place to meet young ticos.

Club Cocodrilo, Calle Central about 200m east of the San Pedro church, is a large bar with dance floor and videos, popular with students from the nearby university and with yuppies hanging onto their youth. The Cocodrilo has a reputation for serving up good hamburgers. ***La Villa***, 125m north of the Cocodrilo on Calle 3, is a favored university-area bar housed in a great old house.

The Centro Comercial El Pueblo has a good variety of restaurants and nightspots – most are rather pricey. Wander around on Friday or Saturday night and take your pick; some spots are cheaper than others. The ***Bar Tango Che Molinari*** *(☎ 226-6904)* is an Argentine bar featuring live tango for a small cover charge. Nearby, ***Bar Los Balcones*** *(☎ 223-3704)* is a small bar with folk or acoustic musicians and no cover charge. Other bars in El Pueblo feature jazz or reggae; still others are just quiet places to have a drink without any music. The selection of live music lessens midweek, but there's usually something going on. Several discos here charge as much as US$4 to get in – and then may ask you to buy at least US$4 worth of drinks. The best known is the ***Infinito*** *(☎ 221-9134)*, which has three separate dance areas, one with Caribbean sounds like salsa and reggae, another with rock and pop music, including US and European hits, and a third with romantic music. One cover gets you into all three; this place attracts a wide variety of people, but the person flirting with you may be on the job. Another popular dance club in El Pueblo is ***Coco Loco*** *(☎ 222-8782)*. Opposite El Pueblo is ***La Plaza*** *(☎ 233-5516)*.

Dance clubs downtown include ***El Túnel de Tiempo Disco***, Avenida Central, Calles 7 & 9, with flashing lights and disco music, and the ***Dynasty*** and ***Partenón***, both in the Centro Comercial del Sur, near the old Puntarenas railway station (around Calles Central & 4, Avenidas 20 & 24), with soul, reggae, calypso, and even rap music. All these have cover charges of about US$2 to US$4. A cheaper place is the ***Salsa 54***, Calle 3, Avenidas 1 & 3, with Latin music, especially salsa. The local dancers here are expert *salseros*.

If disco isn't your scene, there are several alternatives. The ***Beatle Bar*** *(☎ 257-7230)*, Calle 9, Avenidas Central & 1, has the cheapest beer and is the busiest of the downtown bars favored by expats and tourists. It's friendly and fun.

A US-style bar that tends to be frequented by travelers from the US and other English-speaking foreigners is ***Lucky's Piano Blanco Bar***, Avenida Central, Calles 7 & 9, featuring videos of North American sports events and an occasional piano player. Street bands wander in on occasion. Similar venues include ***Nashville South Bar*** *(☎ 221-7374)*, Calle 5, Avenidas 1 & 3, which has country music and good hamburgers, chili dogs, and other bar meals. The new owner is a feisty gringa who hasn't let leaving her 50s behind slow down her partying. ***Tiny's Tropical Bar & Restaurant*** *(☎ 233-7325)*, Avenida 2, Calles 9 & 11, was inhabited by

Dance Schools

Speak all the Spanish you need and want to meet some locals? Dance classes are offered not for tourists, but for ticos. Travelers who speak Spanish are welcome. Latin dancing – salsa, cha-cha-cha, merengue, bolero, tango, etc – as well as the latest local dance crazes are taught. Classes are inexpensive – around US$20 a month gives you two hours of group classes per week. Private lessons cost US$7 to US$14 per hour.

Academia de Bailes Latinos
(☎ 233-8938)
Avenida Central, Calles 25 & 27
Bailes Latinos
(☎ 221-1624, 223-4052, fax 233-8670)
Avenida Central, Calles 25 & 27
Danza Viva
(☎ 253-3110) San Pedro
Malecón
(☎/fax 222-3214)
Avenida 2, Calles 17 & 19
Merecumbe
(☎ 224-3531, 234-1548, fax 225-7687)
San Pedro; or (☎ 231-7496) next to the US Embassy in Rohrmoser

– Rob Rachowiecki

middle-aged US tourists on fishing vacations the first time I stopped by, but it has a dart board and attracts local expat English teachers (second visit) as well as surfers (third visit). It serves bar meals and shows US games on the cable TV sports channel.

More popular with ticos is ***Las Risas*** *(☎ 223-2803)*, Calle 1, Avenidas Central & 1, on two floors in an attractive older building. There's a disco upstairs, and rock videos in the bar. ***Soda Blues*** *(☎ 221-8368)*, Calle 11, Avenidas 8 & 10, has occasional live blues or jazz, and blues karaoke! Next door, ***El Bolinche*** *(☎ 221-0500)* is a more upscale drinks bar that is popular among young professional ticos out for a night of fancy clothes and flirting. Also popular is ***Río Bar & Restaurant*** *(☎ 225-8371)*, Avenida Central, Calle 39, in Los Yoses. As it's close to the university, it attracts a younger crowd that spills over onto the outdoor verandah on weekends, when there may be a live band and the place gets really packed. The ***Sand Bar***, on Avenida Central in Los Yoses, in the shopping center just west of the fountain, is the loudest and most popular dancing place for the latest rock and heavy metal. Also here is the new ***All Star Bar & Grill***, a big, friendly sports bar with a large-screen TV and a variety of beers on tap. Occasionally, there is live music and dancing. The crowd here is a mix of ticos, students, and travelers.

JAN BUTCHOFSKY-HOUSER

Wandering minstrel with tools of his trade

Many a visitor to San José checks out the well-known ***La Esmeralda Bar & Restaurant*** *(☎ 221-0530)*, Avenida 2, Calles 5 & 7. It's open 11 am to 5 am and is the center of the city's mariachi tradition. You can get a meal any time (set lunches for US$4, very popular with the business crowd, or à la carte entrées from US$5 to US$9), but the action begins later at night, when there are dozens of strolling musicians around. They'll come to your table and offer to sing. The going rate per song is about US$2 for a soloist to US$8 for a large group, and you can negotiate a cheaper price for several songs. Of course, you can listen to mariachis playing for other people for free.

Out on Avenida 2, Calle 28, is ***The Shakespeare Bar*** *(☎ 257-1288)*, so called because it's next to a couple of small theaters and is the place to go before or after a show. It has a dart board, piano bar, and occasional live jazz. Hours are 3 pm to midnight.

An interesting and somewhat upscale bar with delicious bocas and great mariachi music (some nights) is ***México Bar*** *(☎ 221-8461)*, Avenida 13, Calle 16, next to the Barrio México church. The beer is kind of pricey, but the free bocas that come with it are excellent. A reader recommends the margaritas. The bar itself is good, although the neighborhood leading to it is a poor one; you'd be best off taking a cab.

A seven-days-a-week, 24-hour downtown bar that has been there for decades and has become something of a local landmark is ***Chelle's*** *(☎ 221-1369)*, at Avenida Central, Calle 9. It serves simple, medium-priced meals and snacks, and, of course, beer and other drinks, but its main attraction is that it's always open. You never know who may come wandering into this harshly lit bar. Just around the corner is the newer, more intimate, and less bright ***Chelle's Taberna***, Calle 9, Avenidas Central & 2. ***Clásicos Bar***, near the Parque Nacional, plays music videos and is a standard San José hole-in-the-wall bar.

Where to Get Cheap Beer & What to Avoid

Most of the bars mentioned in this chapter charge about US$1 to US$2 for a beer – over US$2 is considered very expensive indeed for a beer in a bar. These bars are generally OK for women to visit alone. Cheaper beers, at US50¢ to US75¢, can be had in many bars in town, but the cheaper bars may not be suitable for women to enter alone. As you start heading west of Calle 5, toward the market area, you'll find frequent bars catering to workmen. Here you'll find cheap beer and bocas in a spit-and-sawdust, macho atmosphere. Cheaper bars often advertise their beer prices on signs in the window.

Out along Calle 2 near Avenida 8 is a small red-light district with expensive strip joints. It's best avoided.

– Rob Rachowiecki

The ***Chavelona Bar***, Avenida 10, Calles 10 & 12, is a fun place in a mainly deserted neighborhood south of the center; it is open all night (take a taxi). The nearby ***Aloha Disco***, Avenida 12, Calle 6, has Caribbean music and dancing. There are many other bars in San José; this is just a selection to start with.

The ***Q'Tal Club*** *(☎ 228-4091)* is associated with Quiubo Restaurant and has upscale dinner and dance shows with live bands, as well as live jazz evenings. Cover varies depending on who's playing, but isn't cheap. ***Bar Baabu***, in the Centro Comercial Trejos Montealegre, has live music and dancing.

Gay & Lesbian Venues

There are a good number of gay and lesbian nightclubs in San José. These range from slightly dangerous meat markets to raving dance clubs to quiet places for a drink and talk. The main street action is in the blocks south of the Parque Central, but some blocks (though not all) are somewhat dangerous at night, so don't go around alone unless you know how to look after yourself or have good local information. There are also clubs in other areas. Clubs may close on some nights (especially Mondays) and may have women-only or men-only nights, so call before you go.

The following are among the most established gay places: ***La Avispa*** *(☎ 223-5343)*, Calle 1, Avenidas 8 & 10, is in a black-and-yellow building (*avispa* means 'wasp') and is a popular gay and lesbian dance club; Sunday and Tuesday are big nights. There's also a pool table and big-screen TV upstairs. ***Deja Vú*** *(☎ 223-3758)*, Calle 2, Avenidas 14 & 16, is known for spectacular shows and plenty of dancing, especially by men. Although the clientele are elegantly dressed, the area is poor, so take a taxi. ***Los Cucharones*** *(☎ 233-5797)*, Avenida 6, Calles Central & 1, is a loud and racy disco frequented by young, working-class people. All these clubs charge a cover on most nights – about US$2 to US$6, depending on what's happening. ***La Tertulia*** *(☎ 225-0250)* is near the entrance to the Universidad de Costa Rica; go one block north of the San Pedro church, then a block east, and turn left. This is a quiet lesbian-owned bar-restaurant with several intimate little dining areas. It's mostly for lesbians, though gay men come here, too.

Contact Triángulo Rosa (Pink Triangle; ☎ 234-2411 in English, 258-0214 in Spanish, atrirosa@sol.racsa.co.cr), an organization founded to support human rights for all members of the gay and bisexual community, for information on at least another dozen places, some of which may have just opened in the fast-changing world of gay nightlife.

See the Gay & Lesbian Travelers section in the Facts for the Visitor chapter for additional information and resources.

Theater

Theaters advertise in the local newspapers, including *The Tico Times*. Although many performances are in Spanish, prices are so moderate that you'll probably enjoy yourself even if you don't understand Spanish all that well. A few performances are in English.

The most important theater is the ***Teatro Nacional*** *(☎ 221-5341)*, Avenida 2, Calles 3 & 5, which stages plays, dance, opera, symphony, Latin American music, and other cultural events. The season is from March to November, although less-frequent performances occur during other months. Tickets start as low as US$4. The National Symphony Orchestra plays here and is of a high standard. The new ***National Auditorium*** *(☎ 222-7646)* also hosts a variety of performances.

The English-language ***Little Theater Group*** *(☎ 228-9369)* presents several plays a year – the LTG is always on the lookout for actors, so if you plan on being around for a few months and like to act, give them a call.

The restored 1920s ***Teatro Melico Salazar*** *(☎ 222-2653)*, Avenida 2, Calles Central & 2, has a variety of performances, including music and dance, as well as drama. Every Tuesday evening there's a folkloric dance performance aimed at foreign tourists, which people say is well done. ***Teatro de la Aduana*** *(☎ 225-4563)*, Calle 25, Avenidas 3 & 5, is where the National Theater Company performs. ***Teatro La Máscara*** *(☎ 255-4250)*, Calle 13, Avenidas 2 & 6, also has dance performances, as well as alternative theater. The ***Teatro Carpa*** *(☎ 234-2866)*, Avenida 1, Calles 29 & 33, is known for alternative and outdoor theater, as well as performances by the Little Theater Group, which also performs at the ***1887 Theater*** *(☎ 273-3643)*, Avenidas 5 & 7, Calles 11 & 13, and the ***Teatro Laurence Olivier*** *(☎ 223-1960)*, Calle 28, Avenida 2. This last is a small theater, coffee shop, and gallery, where anything from jazz to film to theater may be showcased. ***Teatro Chaplin*** *(☎ 223-2919)*, Avenida 12, Calles 11 & 13, is known for mime; ***Teatro del Angel*** *(☎ 222-8258)*, Avenida Central, Calles 13 & 15, for comedy; ***Teatro Sala Vargas Calvo*** *(☎ 222-1875)*, Avenida 2, Calles 3 & 5, for theater-in-the-round; ***Teatro Arlequin*** *(☎ 222-0792)*, Calle 13, Avenidas Central & 2, for original works; and ***Teatro Eugene O'Neill*** *(☎ 225-9433)*, Calle Los Negritos, Barrio Escalante, for performances sponsored by the North American-Costa Rican Cultural Center.

Most theaters are not very large, performances are popular, and ticket prices are very reasonable. This adds up to sold-out performances, so get tickets as early as possible. Theaters rarely have performances on Mondays.

Other important theaters are ***Teatro de la Comedia*** *(☎ 255-3255)*, Avenida Central, Calles 13 & 15; ***Teatro Sala de la Calle 15*** *(☎ 222-6626)*, Avenida 2, Calles 13 & 15; and ***Teatro Bellas Artes*** *(☎ 207-4327)*, at the east side of the Universidad de Costa Rica campus in San Pedro.

Cinemas

Many cinemas show recent US films with Spanish subtitles and the original English soundtrack. Occasionally, films are dubbed over in Spanish *(hablado en Español)* rather than subtitled; ask before buying a ticket. Most have two screens; the Cine San Pedro has 10 screens. The Rex is the 'grande dame' of the city's theaters, with enormous murals depicting Costa Rican and Hollywood history. The Teatro Sala Garbo offers international films tending toward the avant-garde, rather than box-office, Hollywood-type movies. You'll also find more independent films at Variedades. Movies cost about US$3 per screening. Cinemas advertise in *The Tico Times* and in other local newspapers. Some of the best cinemas are as follows:

Bellavista
(☎ 221-0909) Avenida Central, Calles 17 & 19

Capri 1 & 2
(☎ 223-0264) Avenida Central, Calle 9

Cine San Pedro
(☎ 283-5715) Planet Mall, San Pedro

Colón 1 & 2
(☎ 221-4517) Paseo Colón, Calles 38 & 40

Colonial 1 & 2
(☎ 289-9000) Plaza Colonial, Escazú

Magaly
(☎ 221-9597) Calle 23, Avenidas Central & 1

Omni
(☎ 221-7903) Calle 3, Avenidas Central & 1

Rex
(☎ 221-0041) Calle Central, Avenidas 6 & 8

Teatro Sala Garbo
(☎ 222-1034) Avenida 2, Calle 28

Variedades
(☎ 222-6108) Calle 5, Avenidas Central & 1

Casinos

Gamblers will find casinos in several of the larger and more expensive hotels, including the Aurola Holiday Inn, Balmoral, Barceló Amón Plaza, Camino Real, Cariari, Corobicí, del Rey, Gran Hotel Costa Rica, Herradura, Irazú, Marriott, Presidente, Quality, Royal Dutch, Royal Garden, and San José Palacio (see the Places to Stay sections earlier in this chapter for addresses). These are fairly informal places, and dress codes are often neat but casual, especially in the non-luxury hotels. One of the most popular and casual is in the Hotel del Rey. There are a few other casinos outside hotels; one is the ***Casino Club Colonial*** (☎ *258-2807*), Avenida 1, Calles 9 & 11, just down the street from the del Rey. Minimum bets in most places are 500 colones (about US$2), though you can also play with US cash in some places (US$5 minimum).

Gambling Tico-Style

The most popular game is 21, which is similar to Las Vegas-style blackjack, but with tico rules. You get two cards, and ask for another card *(carta)* or stay put with the two you have *(me quedo)*. As in blackjack, the idea is to get as close to 21 points as possible without going over, with face cards counting as 10 points and aces counting as one or 11. If your first three cards are the same number (eg, three kings) or a straight flush (eg, five, six, seven of the same suit), you have a 'rummy' and you are paid double. And if your three-of-a-kind happen to be three sevens (which equal 21), you get an even higher bonus. If you get 21 with two cards or get five cards without breaking 21, there's no double bonus as you get in many international casinos. Splitting pairs is allowed.

Other games played include roulette, where the numbers are drawn from a lottery tumbler rather than spun on a roulette wheel, and electric slot machines. There are also other, uniquely tico, card games you'll need to learn before you can play!

– Rob Rachowiecki

SPECTATOR SPORTS

The national sport is soccer (see the Facts for the Visitor chapter for more details). International and national games are played in the Estadio Nacional in Parque La Sabana. (See Things to See, earlier in this chapter.)

SHOPPING

This section deals with stores in San José. If you have the time and the inclination you can find wide selections of well-priced items in the suburb of Moravia, about 8km northeast of downtown, or by taking a day trip to the village of Sarchí, where many of Costa Rica's handicraft items are produced. (Both villages are described in the next chapter, Central Valley & Surrounding Highlands.) For buying books, see Bookstores under Information, earlier in this chapter.

A recommended souvenir shop is Annemarie's Boutique (☎ 221-6063) in the Hotel Don Carlos, Calle 9, Avenida 9. This is not the usual hotel gift store with a limited selection of overpriced gift items for guests with little time to shop around; the public is welcome and both the prices and selection are very good. The new Galería Namu (☎ 256-3412), Avenida 7, Calles 5 & 7, is recommended for those interested in indigenous art (see the boxed text). The Bookshop (see Bookstores, earlier in this chapter) has a nice art gallery in an attractive neighborhood; some of the work is for sale.

Other reasonably priced stores with good selections include government-organized crafts cooperatives such as CANAPI (☎ 221-3342), Calle 11, Avenida 1, and Mercado Nacional de Artesanía (☎ 221-5012), Calle 11, Avenida 4 (there are also branches inside the Museo Nacional and in Moravia). Also reasonably priced are Arte Rica, Avenida 2, Calles Central & 2, specializing in folk art; and ANDA (☎ 233-3340), Avenida Central, Calles 5 & 7, specializing in pottery and gourd crafts produced by the few local Indians. Sol Maya (☎ 221-0864), Avenida Central, Calles 16 & 18, sells handicrafts with a Mayan theme, mostly made from Guatemalan textiles.

La Casona, Calle Central, Avenidas Central & 1, is a large complex of many stalls with a wide selection of items, including imports from other Central American countries. Malety, Avenida 1, Calles 1 & 3 (☎ 221-1670) and Calle 1, Avenidas Central & 2 (☎ 223-0070), specializes in leather goods.

Some galleries carry top-quality work that is excellent but expensive (though this doesn't necessarily mean overpriced). If you are looking for top quality and are prepared to pay for it, try the following selection. La Galería (☎ 223-2110), Calle 1, Avenidas Central & 1, is perhaps the most elegant, with good displays of pieces by renowned woodworker Barry Biesanz and other artisans.

Suraksa (☎ 221-0129), Calle 5, Avenida 3, has a good selection of gold work in pre-Columbian style, and fine ceramicware. Atmósfera (☎ 222-4322), Calle 5, Avenidas 1 & 3, has a wide selection of paintings, wall hangings, and Indian work. Both of these also have Biesanz's splendid woodwork.

If you want to see more of his work, call Biesanz Woodworks in Bello Horizonte, Escazú (☎ 228-1811, fax 228-6164, biesanz@sol.racsa.co.cr), to arrange a viewing (by appointment only). His work has been presented to visiting presidents, and some pieces cost nearly US$1000. A good crafts store in Escazú is the Ara Macao (☎ 239-3563) in the Plaza Real Cariari shopping center near the Hotel Herradura.

The Plaza de la Cultura area often doubles as an impromptu arts market, with everything from T-shirts to carvings to paintings to inexpensive jewelry. The stalls that used to be located here have moved to the Plaza de la Democracia. The Mercado Central, Avenidas Central & 1, Calles 6 & 8, has a small selection of handicrafts (leatherwork, sandals, clothing, wooden toys).

Also look for Café Rica, the local liquor that looks and tastes rather like the better-known Kahlua. And, of course, bring home a 500g bag of local coffee beans – the country's most traditional export.

Heading east on Avenida Central beyond San Pedro, look for the huge indoor arts and crafts market on the south side of the road in the suburb of Curridabat. It has the largest collection of crafts and souvenirs for sale in San José.

Indigenous Art

Galería Namu (☎ 256-3412), Avenida 7, Calles 5 & 7, which was selected as an official site for the annual Costa Rican Arts Festival in San José, is a new gallery that has done an admirable job of bringing together artwork and crafts from Costa Rica's small but diverse population of indigenous tribes. If you want a quick education about indigenous culture in the country, this is a good place to come. Owner Aisling French regularly visits artists in remote villages around the country and can provide background information on the various traditions represented. Boruca ceremonial masks, Guaymí dresses and dolls, Bribri dugout canoes, Chorotega čeramics, Huetar carvings and mats, and Guatuso blankets are all among the works that can be found at the gallery.

Some work by contemporary urban artists, including art produced by street children through a city program, is also available.

– John Thompson

GETTING THERE & AWAY

San José is not only the capital and the geographical heart of Costa Rica; it is also the hub of all transport around the country.

Unfortunately, the transport system is rather bewildering to the first-time visitor. Most people get around by bus, but there is no central bus terminal. Instead, there are dozens of bus stops and terminals scattered around the city, all serving different destinations. In recent years, efforts have been made to consolidate bus services, and the new Atlántico Norte and Caribe terminals have made the situation more coherent. There are also two airports.

Fortunately, the tourist office does pretty well keeping up with what goes where and when, so check with them if you get stuck. The inherent friendliness of the Costa Rican people also goes a long way toward easing transport difficulties – if you need directions or advice, ask.

Air

Airports The two airports serving San José are Juan Santamaría international airport (☎ 443-2942) in Alajuela and Tobías Bolaños international airport (☎ 232-2820) in Pavas – the latter is officially called an international airport because you can charter flights out of the country, but there are no scheduled international departures from this small airport.

The Juan Santamaría airport, as of 1999, is undergoing extensive and (some say) long-overdue renovations; a new terminal will be added, as well as more facilities to deal with the expected increase in tourism.

Domestic Airlines SANSA and Travelair are the two domestic airlines with scheduled flights. San José is the hub for both of them. In addition, air taxis provide charter services to a host of airstrips all over the country. For details, see the Getting Around chapter.

SANSA will check you in at its office downtown and provide transportation to Juan Santamaría international airport's domestic terminal, which is a few hundred meters to the right of the international terminal. Remember that reservations with SANSA must be prepaid to SANSA in full before they can be confirmed. You should also reconfirm in advance, preferably several times.

Travelair, the newer domestic airline, flies from Tobías Bolaños airport in Pavas. You can buy Travelair tickets from any travel agent, or from the Travelair desk at the airport. There are no buses to Tobías Bolaños – a taxi costs about US$3 from downtown.

SANSA, Travelair, and a number of air-taxi companies provide reasonably priced charters with small (mainly three- to five-passenger) aircraft to many airstrips in Costa Rica:

Aéro Costa Sol
(☎ 441-1444, 441-0922, fax 441-2671)
Juan Santamaría airport

Aerolíneas Turísticas de America (ATA)
(☎ 232-1125, fax 232-5802)
Tobías Bolaños airport

Aviones Taxi Aéreo SA
(☎ 441-1626, fax 441-2713)
Juan Santamaría airport

Helicópteros del Norte
(☎ 232-7534)
Tobías Bolaños airport

SANSA
(☎ 221-9414, 233-3258, 233-4179, fax 255-2176)
Calle 24, Paseo Colón & Avenida 1
(☎ 441-8035) Juan Santamaría airport

Travelair
(☎ 220-3054, 232-7883, fax 220-0413
Tobías Bolaños airport

Viajes Especial Aéreos SA (VEASA)
(☎ 232-1010, 232-8043, fax 232-7934)
Tobías Bolaños airport

International Airlines International carriers that serve Costa Rica or have offices in San José are listed here, with their country of origin in parentheses (where it isn't obvious). Airlines serving Costa Rica directly are marked with an asterisk; they also have desks at the airport.

Air France
(☎ 222-8811, fax 223-4970)
Avenida 1, Calles 4 & 6

Alitalia (Italy)
(☎ 222-6009, 222-6138, fax 233-7137)
Calle 38, Avenida 3

American Airlines* (USA)
(☎ 257-1266) Avenida 5 bis, Calles 40 & 42

Avianca (Colombia)
(see SAM, below)

Aviateca* (Guatemala)
(☎ 255-4949) Calle 40, Avenida 3

British Airways
(☎ 233-5648, fax 223-4863) Calle 7, Avenida 7

Condor* (Germany)
(☎ 234-9292, fax 234-8442)

Continental Airlines* (USA)
(☎ 296-4911, 296-5554, fax 296-4920)

COPA* (Panama)
(☎ 222-6640, fax 221-6798) Calle 1, Avenida 5

Iberia* (Spain)
(☎ 257-8266, fax 223-1055)
Paseo Colón, Calle 40

Japan Air Lines
(☎ 233-1489) Calle 4, Avenida Central

KLM* (Netherlands)
(☎ 220-4111, fax 220-3092) Sabana Sur

Lacsa* (Costa Rica)
(☎ 221-0111, fax 232-3622) Calle 1, Avenida 5

Ladeco (Chile)
(☎ 233-7290) Calle 11, Avenida 1

Lloyd Aéreo Boliviano
(☎ 255-1530) Avenida 8, Calles 20 & 24

Lufthansa (Germany)
(☎ 221-7444, fax 233-9485)
Calle 5, Avenidas 7 & 9

Mexicana*
(☎ 257-6334, fax 257-6338)
Calle 5, Avenidas 7 & 9

SAM (Avianca)* (Colombia)
(☎ 233-3066) Centro Colón

Singapore Airlines
(☎ 255-3555) Avenida 1, Calles 3 & 5

Taca* (El Salvador)
(☎ 222-1790, 222-1744, fax 223-4238)
Calle 40, Avenida 3

United* (USA)
(☎ 220-4844, fax 220-4855)
Sabana Sur

Varig* (Brazil)
(☎ 290-5222, fax 290-0200)
Avenida 5, Calles 3 & 5

Bus

Read the general information in the Getting Around chapter about Costa Rican bus travel before you begin taking buses around the country. This section lists the addresses, and some phone numbers, for the long-distance bus companies. However, at many bus stops there may be no clear evidence of a particular company – bus stops are more often identified by destination than by company (with the exception of international bus companies). Many companies have no more than a bus stop; some have a tiny office with a window opening onto the street; some operate out of a terminal.

The ICT information office at the Plaza de la Cultura has up-to-date bus information and will provide you with a computerized printout of bus services upon request. Kit-Com Communications also produces a regularly updated schedule and map for intercity buses; it's available at 7th Street Books (see Bookstores, earlier in this chapter) and many other locations around the city. Calling bus companies themselves is usually more frustrating than helpful; the most reliable way to find out about routes and schedules is to go personally to the bus stop and ask for information. Talk to the ticket seller, if there is one, or the bus conductor. Individual departure points (listed by destination) and general terminals are listed on the city maps.

Try to avoid leaving San José on Friday nights and Saturday mornings, when the buses are full of josefinos off for the weekend. If you must travel then, try to book ahead. Buses during Christmas and Easter are very crowded indeed.

In addition to the old Coca-Cola terminal, named after a Coca-Cola bottling plant that used to exist on the site many years ago, San José now has two new general bus terminals. The Coca-Cola terminal is between Calles 16 & 18, north of Avenida 1, and is one of the best-known landmarks in San José. The new Caribe terminal, north of Avenida 13 on Calle Central, serves the Caribbean coast. The new Atlántico Norte terminal, at Avenida 9, Calle 12, serves northern destinations, including Monteverde, the Arenal area, and Puerto Viejo de Sarapiquí.

Several companies serve a number of different towns from the Coca-Cola terminal. There are a few small signs in the terminal, and it seems a little bewildering at first, but just ask someone to show you where your bus is; everyone seems to know where each bus leaves from. Several other companies have buses leaving from within three or four blocks of the Coca-Cola terminal, so this is an area to know. It is not in the best part of town, so watch for pickpockets and use common sense. The area is generally safe during the day, though after dark you might think about taking a taxi rather than walking, particularly if you are a solo woman traveler. Some travelers suggest that you take a cab at any time – many travelers do walk through here in daytime without hassles, but it is also true that in recent years reports of muggings have increased.

The Atlántico Norte terminal is in the same neighborhood, but is better organized and often has a guard on duty.

The Caribe terminal is a longish walk from downtown through a somewhat deserted area that is considered safer than the Coca-Cola area; a taxi is certainly the easiest way to go. The terminal itself is modern and bursting with amenities – restaurants, shops, bathrooms, and phones! For general information about either the Atlántico Norte or Caribe terminals, call ☎ 256-8129.

Bus fares (in US dollar terms) have stayed remarkably stable for internal routes over the past few years, but schedules change more often. Try calling, or go by the bus stop for the latest departure times.

To Nicaragua See the Getting There & Away chapter for details of what to expect when taking international buses. TICA Bus (☎ 221-8954), Calle 9, Avenidas 2 & 4, has buses to Managua daily at 6 am (there may be a second bus, or fewer buses, depending on demand, so check locally). The trip takes 11 hours and costs about US$9 from San José (it varies from year to year depending on exchange rates). These buses continue to San Salvador or Tegucigalpa and Guatemala City (2½ days; passengers sleep in hotels in Managua and San Salvador). Buses to San José leave Managua at 6 am.

A cheaper but less reliable service to Managua is provided by Sirca (☎ 222-5541, 223-1464), Calle 7, Avenidas 6 & 8. Office hours are 8 am to 5 pm weekdays and 8 am to 1 pm on Saturday. You have to wait on the street outside the office for the bus to come by. Departures for Managua are at 5 am on Wednesday, Friday, and Sunday. Sirca recommends that you buy tickets three days in advance. Fares from Managua are rarely the same as from San José because of differences in currency regulations.

To Panama TICA Bus has a daily service to Panama City at 10 pm (US$18, 20 hours). It leaves Panama City at 11 am for the return to San José. Buses have onboard bathrooms and video. Buy tickets in advance. This company will also sell you a ticket to David, the first major town in Panama. Another company with buses to David is Alfaro (☎ 222-2666), Calle 14, Avenidas 3 & 5, with direct buses at 7:30 am daily (US$9, nine hours) and at midday if there is enough demand.

A company with fairly comfortable express bus service to Panama City is Panaline (☎ 255-1205), in the Hotel Cocorí at Calle 16, Avenida 3. The trip costs US$21 and takes 15 hours, with daily departures at 2 pm. Buses to San José leave Panama City at 2 pm as well. Panaline also has a service to Changuinola, Panama (16km east of the border at Sixaola), leaving at 10 am.

Note that fares from Panama City are rarely the same as from San José because of differences in currency regulations.

To Southern Costa Rica TRACOPA (☎ 221-4214, 223-7685), Avenida 18, Calle 4, has six daily buses to Neily and on to the Panamanian border at Paso Canoas. It is about seven hours to Neily, eight hours to the border. Fares are US$5.50/6.50 to Neily/Paso Canoas direct, or a little cheaper on the normal route. TRACOPA also has seven daily buses to Palmar Norte (US$4.50, five hours) and two daily buses to Golfito (US$5.75, eight hours). TRACOPA buses to Coto Brus en route to San Vito, leave four times a day from the TRACOPA/Empresa Alfaro station (☎ 222-2750, 223-8361), Calle 14, Avenidas 3 & 5.

Buses to Puerto Jiménez in the Península de Osa (US$6.75, eight hours) leave at 6 am and noon with Autotransportes Blanco (☎ 771-2550, 257-4121) from the stop at Calle 12, Avenida 9.

Buses to San Isidro de El General are with Transportes Musoc (☎ 222-2422, 771-0414, 223-0686), under the Hotel Musoc, Calle 16, Avenidas 1 & 3, next to the Coca-Cola bus terminal Alternatively, go with TUASUR (☎ 222-9763), across the street. The fare is US$3 for the three-hour trip, with about 15 daily departures

To the Central Valley Buses to Cartago leave several times an hour from the SACSA station (☎ 233-5350) at Calle 5, Avenida 18. The trip takes almost an hour, depending on traffic, and costs about US40¢. Some of these buses continue to Turrialba, but more Turrialba buses leave from the TRANSTUSA station (☎ 556-0073) at Avenida 6, Calle 13. The two-hour ride costs just over US$1.

Microbuses to Heredia leave several times an hour between 5 am and midnight and every half hour between midnight and 4 am from Calle 1, Avenidas 7 & 9; the half-hour trip costs about US40¢. Microbuses to Heredia also leave from the south side of Avenida 2, Calles 10 & 12 (across from the Alajuela bus stop), every 15 minutes between 6 am and 8 pm.

Buses to Alajuela leave every few minutes from the TUASA terminal (☎ 222-5325) at Avenida 2, Calle 12. Most of these buses stop at the international airport.

Buses to Grecia (US40¢, one hour) and continuing on 7km to Sarchí (US50¢) leave hourly from the Coca-Cola terminal. It is often easier to go to Alajuela and change.

Buses to San Ramón, halfway to Puntarenas, leave several times an hour from Calle 16, Avenidas 1 & 3, across the street from the Hotel Musoc.

To the Pacific Coast Buses to Quepos and Manuel Antonio leave from the Coca-Cola terminal with Transportes Morales (☎ 223-5567). Direct buses to Manuel Antonio, with reserved seats, leave at 6 am, noon, and 6 pm, and cost US$5 for the 3½-hour trip. Slower and cheaper buses to Quepos leave five times a day. Other Transportes Morales buses (☎ 232-1829, 223-1109) go to Jacó at 7:30 and 10:30 am and 3:30 pm from the Coca-Cola terminal. The journey costs about US$2.

Buses to Puntarenas leave two or three times an hour during the day (6 am to 7 pm) from a terminal at Calle 16, Avenida 12, with Empresarios Unidos de Puntarenas (☎ 222-0064, 233-2610, 221-5749). The two-hour trip costs about US$2.50.

To the Península de Nicoya Buses to the Península Nicoya and its popular beaches have to negotiate the Golfo de Nicoya, a formidable body of water. Buses either cross the Río Tempisque (at the northwest end of the Golfo de Nicoya) on the ferry linking the mainland and peninsula highways, which leaves about every hour, or take the longer overland route through Liberia. Thus, bus times can vary considerably depending on the route chosen and, if using the ferry, whether you have to spend a long time waiting for it – it leaves about every hour. A bridge is being built north of the current ferry crossing, which, when completed, will make this route quicker. The car ferry from Puntarenas does not normally take buses.

Empresa Alfaro (% 222-2750), Calle 14, Avenidas 3 & 5, has seven daily buses to Nicoya (US$5.25, six hours), also going to Santa Cruz and Filadelfia. More interestingly, they also have daily buses to beaches at Sámara (noon, US$6, six hours) and Tamarindo (3:30 pm, US$6, five hours), as well as a bus to Quebrada Honda, Mansión, and Hojancha (2:30 pm).

On Calle 12, Avenidas 7 & 9, is a small office with buses to Jicaral and the beaches at Bejuco and Islita (US$5.50, five hours).

TRALAPA (☎ 221-7202), at Calle 20 Avenida 3, has daily buses to Playa Flamingo (8 and 10 am, US$8), Junquillal (2 pm, US$8), and Santa Cruz (nine daily, US$5.25).

The Pulmitan station (☎ 222-1650), Calle 14, Avenidas 1 & 3, has two buses to Playa del Coco at 8 am and 2 pm daily (US$4.50).

Buses to Playas Panamá (five hours) and Hermosa leave at 3:20 pm daily from the bus stop in front of Los Rodriguez lumber store on Calle 12, Avenidas 5 & 7.

These schedules are for the dry season, when people go to the beach – during the wet season, services may be curtailed. Beach resorts are very popular among Costa Ricans and buses tend to be booked up ahead of time, especially during dry-season weekends. Reserve a seat if possible.

To Northern & Northwestern Costa Rica Unless otherwise noted, the following buses now leave from the new Atlántico Norte terminal (☎ 222-3854) at Avenida 9, Calle 12. Express buses to Monteverde leave at 6:30 am and 2:30 pm daily for the four-hour trip, which costs about US$5. It is worth getting tickets the day before departure because the buses get booked up quickly; the ticket office is closed from 12:30 to 2 pm. Buses to Tilarán leave at 7:30 and 9:30 am and 12:45, 3:45, and 6:30 pm.

Buses to Ciudad Quesada (US$2, three hours) via Zarcero (one hour) leave at least every hour; a few buses are express to Ciudad Quesada. (Note that Ciudad Quesada is also known as San Carlos.) From Ciudad Quesada you can take buses west to Fortuna, Volcán Arenal, and on to Tilarán, or east toward Puerto Viejo de Sarapiquí and Río Frío. There are also direct buses to Fortuna at 6:15, 8:40, and 11:30 am (US$3.75)

Direct buses to Puerto Viejo de Sarapiquí (not to be confused with Puerto Viejo de Talamanca on the southeastern Caribbean coast) leave eight times a day between 6:30 am and 6 pm and cost about US$3. Most of these buses go via Río Frío and Horquetas (for Rara Avis) and return to San José via Varablanca and Heredia; a few do the route in reverse. If going to Horquetas, make sure you go via the Río Frío route or you will get stuck on the bus for four hours instead of 2½. The Heredia/Varablanca route is much more scenic. Check departures with the bus stop or the ICT – they have changed frequently in the last few years.

Buses to Los Chiles (US$3.75, five hours) leave at 5:30 am and 3:30 pm.

The following buses do not leave from the Atlántico Norte terminal.

Buses to Cañas with Transportes La Cañera (☎ 222-3006) leave six times a day from Calle 16, Avenidas 1 & 3, opposite the Coca-Cola terminal. TRALAPA also operates buses from Calle 20, Avenida 3. The trip takes about 3½ hours and costs about US$2.50. There also is one bus to La Cruz (near the Nicaraguan border), continuing to Santa Cecilia, at 2:45 pm. A bus to Upala leaves at 6:30 am daily (6 am on Saturdays). Buses to Upala also leave from Calle 12, Avenidas 3 & 5, at 3 and 3:45 pm daily.

Buses to the Nicaraguan border at Peñas Blancas, with stops at the entrance to Parque Nacional Santa Rosa and La Cruz, leave from behind the Hotel Cocorí, Calle 14, Avenidas 3 & 5, with Carsol (☎ 224-1968). There are four buses daily, and the cost is about US$4 for the six-hour trip to the border.

Buses to Liberia (US$3, 4½ hours) leave 11 times a day from Pulmitan (☎ 222-1650), Calle 14, Avenidas 1 & 3.

To the Caribbean Coast The following buses all leave from the new Caribe terminal. Buses to Guápiles leave about every half hour between 6 am and 9 pm. Buses to Sixaola that stop at Cahuita and Puerto Viejo de Talamanca leave at 6 and 10 am and 1:30 and 3:30 pm. Tickets cost about US$5; the trip to Cahuita takes about four hours, to Puerto Viejo about 4½ to five hours, and to Sixaola about six hours. Direct buses to Puerto Limón leave hourly from 5 am to 6:30 pm; the trip takes three hours and costs about US$4. From Limón there are frequent buses southeast along the coast.

Train

The railway was severely damaged in the 1991 earthquake, causing all services to be canceled, and it is highly unlikely that the services from San José to Puerto Limón or to Puntarenas will resume. The famous and attractive route to Puerto Limón was known as the 'banana train.' Ask at the ICT in the Plaza de la Cultura about day tours on old trains.

GETTING AROUND

Downtown San José is very busy and relatively small. The narrow streets, heavy traffic, and complicated one-way system often mean that it is quicker to walk than to take the bus. The same applies to driving: if you rent a car, don't drive in downtown – it's a nightmare! If you are in a hurry to get somewhere that is more than a kilometer away, take a taxi.

To/From the Airport

For the main international airport (Juan Santamaría) there is no airport bus as such, but most buses to Alajuela will stop at the international airport. Look for a sign in the bus window, or ask before boarding (*'¿aeropuerto?'*). Alajuela buses leave every few minutes from Avenida 2, Calle 12, and cost about US40¢, irrespective of whether you go to the airport or Alajuela. (From midnight to 5 am, buses go about every hour.)

Heading into San José from the airport, you'll find the bus stop outside the international terminal, behind the car rental agencies. This may change when current airport renovations are finished; ask at the airport. During the rush hour, the Alajuela to San José buses may be full when they come by, and you may have to wait for some time.

Airport taxis are orange, and the fare to or from the airport is a set US$10 – though it has been US$10 for a few years now and may go up. In 1999, many taxis going from San José to the airport were asking US$12. Cab drivers at the airport will try to hustle you, either by trying to charge more than US$10 or by asking you to share the cab with another passenger into San José, and then charging each of you US$10. Don't start a cab journey without establishing the fare first.

There are no direct buses to the local airport at Tobías Bolaños. Your best bet is to take a taxi – about US$3.

Bus

Local buses are very useful to get you into the suburbs and surrounding villages, or to the airport. They have set routes and leave regularly from particular bus stops downtown. Buses run from about 5 am to 10 pm and cost from US5¢ to US50¢.

Buses from Parque La Sabana head into town on Paseo Colón, then go over to Avenida 2 at the San Juan de Dios hospital. They then go three different ways through town before heading back to La Sabana. Buses are marked Sabana-Cementario, Sabana-Estadio, or Cementario-Estadio. These buses are a good bet for a cheap city tour. The Sabana-Cementario bus has been particularly recommended. Buses going east to Los Yoses and San Pedro go back and forth along Avenida 2, going over to Avenida Central at Calle 29 outbound. They start at Avenida 2, Calle 7, near the Restaurante El Campesino.

Buses to the following outlying suburbs and towns begin from bus stops at the indicated blocks (though they pick up passengers at other stops along the way, which you'll figure out by asking or doing the journey once from the beginning):

Escazú
  Avenida 1, Calle 18 *or*
San Rafael de Escazú
  from Calle 16, Avenidas Central & 1 *or*
San Antonio de Escazú
  Avenida 6, Calles 12 & 14
Guadalupe
  Avenida 3, Calles Central & 1 (though some leave from one or two blocks away – ask)
Moravia
  Avenida 3, Calles 3 & 5
Pavas
  Avenida 1, Calle 18
Santa Ana
  Calle 18, Avenidas 1 & 3 (at the back of the Coca-Cola terminal)

If you need buses to other suburbs, inquire at the tourist office.

Electric Trams

Trams were the main form of city transport in the early 1900s but stopped running in 1950. Plans to reopen a section of track have yet to materialize.

Car

There are about 50 car rental agencies in San José, and new ones keep coming – look in the newspaper or the yellow pages under *Alquiler de Automóviles* for a comprehensive listing. *The Tico Times* often carries ads for those companies that are having specials. However, car rental is quite expensive, at least by North American standards. You should review the sections on Car & Motorcycle Rental and Road Rules in the Getting Around chapter before venturing onto the roads. As long as you're careful, you can have fun with a car in Costa Rica.

Car rental rates vary about 10% among companies, so shop around.

Motorcycle

Given the narrow roads and difficult driving conditions, I can't recommend riding a motorcycle here. However, if you are an experienced and careful biker, renting a motorcycle is an option, but don't think about suing me if you die. Rent is about US$40 per day including unlimited mileage, insurance, and one (or two) helmets. Weekly discounts are available. Rental bikes are usually small, in the 185cc to 250cc range.

A few motorcycle rental companies have come and gone over the years. One that has been withstanding the test of time is Heat Renta Moto (☎ 221-6671, 221-3848, fax 221-3786), Avenida 2, Calles 11 & 13. Others advertise occasionally in the newspapers (but may not be in the yellow pages).

Taxi

San José taxis are red, with the exception of airport cabs, which are orange. Downtown, meters *(marías)* are supposed to be used, but some drivers will pretend they are broken and try to charge you more – particularly if you are a tourist who doesn't speak Spanish. Driving with a broken maría is illegal and happens less and less – but there are always a few cab drivers who will try to pull a fast one. Always make sure that the maría is working when you get in – if it isn't, you can get out and hail another taxi or negotiate a fare to avoid being grossly overcharged at your destination.

The official 1999 rates are 165 colones (US60¢) for the first kilometer (which should be the total on the meter when you get in) and 80 colones for each additional kilometer. (Due to currency devaluation, rates in terms of colones will go up, but should still be about US60¢ for the first kilometer.) Short rides downtown should cost around US$1, longer rides around US$2, and a cab to Escazú about US$3 to US$4. There is a 20% surcharge after 10 pm, which may not appear on the maría. Waiting time has to be negotiated – about US$5 an hour is reasonable. San José cab drivers are the toughest in Costa Rica; on the other hand, they are a lot more friendly than cab drivers in many other countries.

You can hire a taxi and driver for half a day or longer if you want to do some touring around the Central Valley. Around US$40 is reasonable for half a day, depending on how far you want to go. Cabs will take three or four passengers. To hire a cab, either ask your hotel to help arrange it or flag one down on the street. Alternatively, talk to drivers at any taxi stand. There are cab stands at the Parque Nacional, Parque Central, near the Teatro Nacional, and in front of several of the better hotels. Taxi drivers are not normally tipped in Costa Rica.

You can have a taxi pick you up if you are going to the airport or have a lot of luggage. The most difficult time to flag down a taxi is when it's raining (especially afternoons in the May to November wet months).

Bicycle

Trek of Costa Rica (☎ 296-3383, fax 289-7013) in San José has good bikes from US$20 a day. Ciclo Profesional (☎ 224-8318), 75m west of Parque Central in the Guadalupe suburb, charges US$15 a day for a mountain bike (plus a hefty cash deposit).

Central Valley & Surrounding Highlands

The 'Central Valley' is the popular English name for the region in the center of Costa Rica around San José. It is not really a valley, and a more appropriate name would be the 'central plateau' or 'central tableland.' This is, in fact, the literal translation of the Costa Rican name for the area, Meseta Central.

This region is both historically and geographically the heart of Costa Rica. To the north and east, the Central Valley is bounded by the mountain range known as the Cordillera Central, which contains several volcanoes, including the famous Volcán Poás and Volcán Irazú.

To the south, the region is bounded by the north end of the Cordillera de Talamanca and a short mountainous projection called the Fila de Bustamente. Between the Cordilleras Central and Talamanca is the beautiful Río Reventazón valley, which gives San José its historical access to the Caribbean. To the west, the plateau falls off into the Pacific lowlands.

This chapter covers the Central Valley (except San José) and, additionally, the upper Río Reventazón valley and the volcanoes of the Cordillera Central. Although not geographically part of the Central Valley, these surrounding highlands are usually visited on day trips from San José.

About two-thirds of Costa Rica's population live in the Central Valley. The region's fertile volcanic soil and pleasant climate attracted the first successful Spanish settlers. Before the arrival of the Spaniards, the region was an important agricultural zone inhabited by thousands of Indian farmers, most of whom were wiped out by diseases brought by the Europeans. The first colonial capital city was at Cartago.

Today, four of Costa Rica's seven provinces have fingers of land within the Central Valley, and all four have their political capitals there. Thus, we see an unusual situation in which three provincial capitals are within a scant 25km of San José, which itself is the capital of San José Province. The others are the cities of Cartago, Alajuela, and Heredia, all capitals of provinces of the same names.

Despite their provincial capital status, the cities of the Central Valley do not have a well-developed hotel infrastructure, although Alajuela, close to the international airport, does have a few good places to stay. Most visitors use San José as a base for day trips to the other cities, as well as many of the other attractions of the Central Valley region. A bus ride from San José out to Central Valley towns for a day trip is as good a way as any of seeing some of rural Costa Rica – and it'll cost you next to nothing. As visitors travel the area, they pass through attractive rolling agricultural countryside full of green shiny-leafed plants bearing the berries that made Costa Rica famous – coffee.

On the way to Volcán Poás, huge areas of hillsides are covered with what appear to be black plastic sheets, rather like a modern environmental sculpture. These are, in fact, *viveros* (plant nurseries). Closer inspection reveals that the black plastic is a protective mesh under which a variety of plants are grown for sale to greenhouses.

The essentially rural nature of Costa Rica is made evident by the roads of the Central Valley. Thin, winding strips of tarmac provide tenuous links among the cities and many villages of the area. There are no freeways, and the road system is difficult to navigate unless you keep a sharp eye out for the few small road signs, which are easy to miss. It's quite confusing unless you've been here for a while.

It is, therefore, hard to arrange the Central Valley into a logical sequence that follows obvious routes and cities. For want of a better solution, this chapter is arranged in a roughly west-to-east sequence around San José.

Alajuela Area

ALAJUELA

The provincial capital of Alajuela lies about 18km (as the crow flies) northwest of San José. The city is on a gently sloping hill that has an altitude of 920m on the southwestern side of town, rising to 970m on the northeastern side. It is about 200m lower than San José and has a slightly warmer climate, thus attracting *josefinos* on summer outings. Alajuela's town center is a slightly scaled-down version of the busy market areas in San José, but it generally enjoys a more unhurried pace of Costa Rican life than the nearby capital. Several nearby villages and other attractions (the Butterfly Farm and Zoo-Ave) are popular places on the tourist circuit, and these are described later in the Alajuela Area section.

The city and its immediate suburbs have a population of about 172,000, making it the second-largest city in the country. It was founded in 1782 (the original name was Villa Hermosa), but no 18th-century architecture survives. The Juan Santamaría international airport, serving San José, is only 2.5km southeast of Alajuela. This makes Alajuela a convenient alternative to more bustling and smoggy San José for those using the nearby airport. There are several good mid-priced hotels in Alajuela to serve this segment of the traveling public.

The map shows the streets and avenues, but, as in most Costa Rican towns, locals prefer landmark addresses, and street addresses are rarely used.

Information

A periodically talked-about tourist office has yet to appear; try the Instituto Costarricense de Turismo (ICT) at the airport (☎ 442-1820). There are half a dozen banks within two blocks of the Parque Central to change money (see the Alajuela map). Internet access is available at SAEC (see map), which is open 7 am to 9 pm weekdays and 7 am to 7 pm Saturday. The Hospital San Rafael (☎ 441-5011) is at Avenida 9, Calles Central & 1, and the 24-hour Norza Clinic (☎ 441-3572) is at Avenida 4, Calles 2 & 4; it has an English-speaking staff.

Museo Juan Santamaría

Alajuela's main claim to fame is being the birthplace of the national hero, Juan Santamaría, after whom the nearby international airport was named.

Santamaría was the drummer boy who volunteered to torch the building defended by filibuster William Walker in the war of 1856 (see History in the Facts about Costa Rica chapter). He died in this action and is now commemorated by the museum and a park in Alajuela.

The Museo Juan Santamaría (☎ 441-4775) is in what used to be a jail on Calle 2, Avenida 3, to the northwest of the Parque Central. The museum, which contains maps, paintings, and historical artifacts related to the war with Walker, is open 10 am to 6 pm Tuesday to Sunday (as always, hours are subject to change); admission is free. There is a small auditorium in the museum where performances are occasionally staged.

Other Attractions

The shady **Parque Central** is full of mango trees and is a pleasant place to relax. It is surrounded by several 19th-century buildings, including the **cathedral**, which suffered severe damage in the 1991 earthquake. Two presidents are buried here. The interior is spacious and elegant rather than ornate. A more baroque-looking church (though it was built in 1941) is the **Iglesia La Agonía**, five blocks east of the Parque Central.

Where Am I?

Note that most of the maps throughout this book give official street names, but the locals rarely use them, preferring the *tico* landmark system instead. Read the boxed text 'Costa Rican Street Addresses' in the San José chapter for a full discussion of this phenomenon.

– **Rob Rachowiecki**

CENTRAL VALLEY & SURROUNDING HIGHLANDS
Florencia
Aguas Zarcas
Venecia
Ciudad Quesada (San Carlos)
Parque Nacional Juan Castro Blanco
Río Toro
San Miguel
Laguna Hule
Cariblanco
Heredia
Rara Avis
Río Sarapiquí
Parque Nacional Volcán Poás
Volcán Poás 2704m
Poasito
Varablanca
Parque Nacional Braulio Carrillo
Volcán Barva 2906m
Bajos del Toro
To Los Angeles Cloud Forest Reserve, La Tigra
Zarcero
Alajuela
Río Barranca
Laguna Fraijanes
Sacramento
Paso Llano
Monte de la Cruz
Túnel Zurquí
San José de la Montaña
El Castillo
San Ramón
Naranjo
Sarchí
Grecia
World of Snakes
Río Poás
San Pedro de Poás
Palmares
Interamericana
To Puntarenas
Santa Bárbara
Barva
San Isidro de Heredia
Alajuela
San Rafael de Heredia
Zoo-Ave
Juan Santamaría International Airport
Heredia
San Isidro de Coronado
Atenas
La Garita
To San Mateo, Jacó
La Guácima
San Antonio
Butterfly Farm
Ojo de Agua
Moravia
Túrrucares
Río Virilla
Río Tárcoles
Ciudad Colón
Escazú
SAN JOSÉ
San Pedro
Reserva Indígena Quitirrisí
Santiago de Puriscal
San José
Tarbaca
San Ignacio de Acostá
San Gabriel
Río Candelaria
Frailes
Reserva Indígena Zapatón

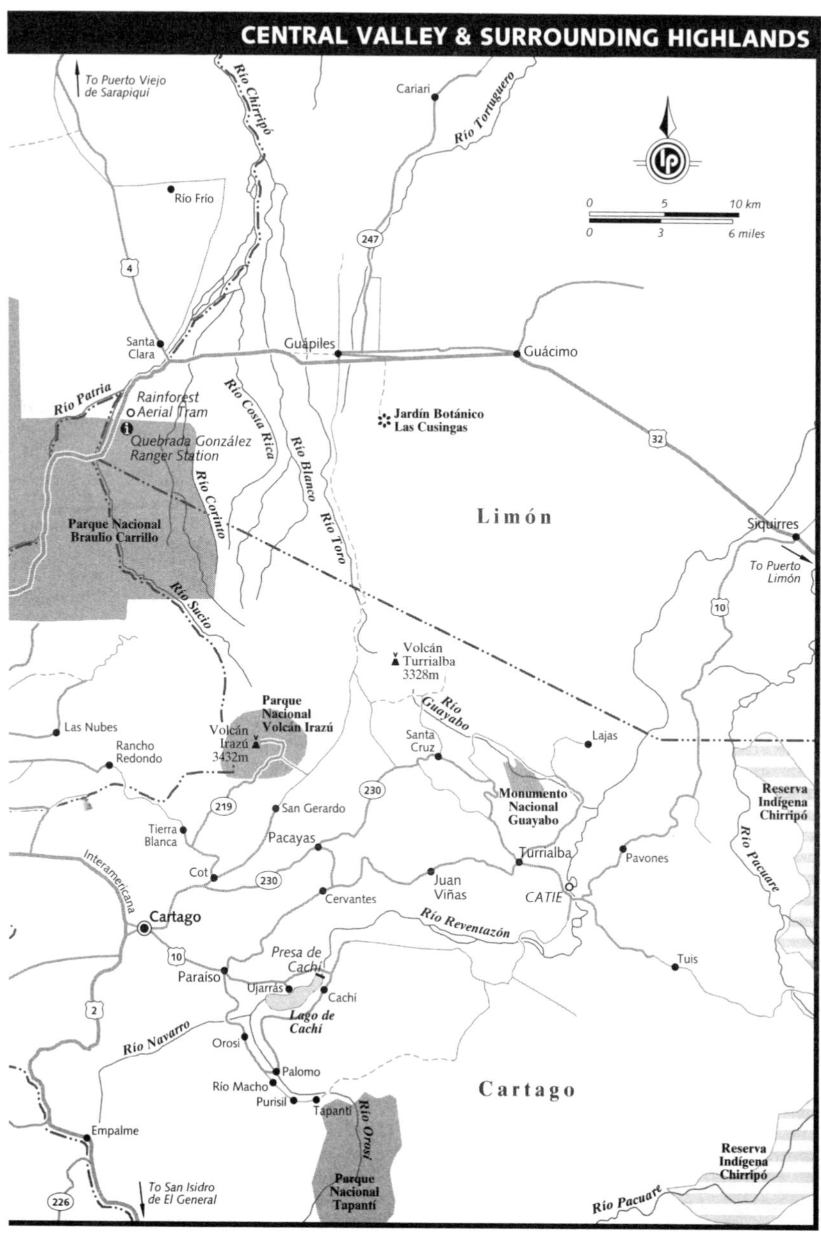
CENTRAL VALLEY & SURROUNDING HIGHLANDS
To Puerto Viejo de Sarapiquí
Río Chirripó
Cariari
Río Tortuguero
Río Frío
0 5 10 km
0 3 6 miles
247
4
Santa Clara
Guápiles
Guácimo
Río Patria
Rainforest Aerial Tram
Quebrada González Ranger Station
Río Costa Rica
Río Blanco
Río Corinto
Río Toro
Jardín Botánico Las Cusingas
32
Limón
Parque Nacional Braulio Carrillo
Siquirres
To Puerto Limón
Río Sucio
10
Volcán Turrialba 3328m
Río Guayabo
Parque Nacional Volcán Irazú
Las Nubes
Volcán Irazú 3432m
Santa Cruz
Lajas
Rancho Redondo
230
Monumento Nacional Guayabo
Reserva Indígena Chirripó
219
San Gerardo
Tierra Blanca
Pacayas
Turrialba
Pavones
Río Pacuare
Interamericana
Cot
230
Juan Viñas
Cervantes
CATIE
Cartago
Río Reventazón
10
Presa de Cachí
Tuis
Paraíso
Ujarrás
Cachí
2
Lago de Cachí
Río Navarro
Orosi
Palomo
Río Macho
Cartago
Purisil
Tapantí
Río Orosi
Empalme
Reserva Indígena Chirripó
To San Isidro de El General
Parque Nacional Tapantí
226
Río Pacuare

Two blocks south of the Parque Central is the rather bare **Parque Juan Santamaría**, where there is a statue of the hero in action, flanked by cannons.

Special Events

The anniversary of the Battle of Rivas, April 11, is particularly celebrated in Alajuela, the hometown of the battle's young hero, Juan Santamaría. There is a parade and civic events.

The Fiesta de Los Mangos is held every July, lasts over a week, and includes an arts & crafts fair, parades, and some mild revelry.

Saturday is market day, and the streets around the market can get very congested.

Places to Stay

Budget There are few really cheap hotels, though you'll do fine if you can spend about US$10 to US$15 a person.

The ***Hotel La Central*** *(☎ 443-8437)*, by the bus terminal (the entrance is off Avenida Central), is under new, pretty friendly management. Basic rooms with shared cold showers cost US$6/10 single/double.

A good budget choice is the ***Villa Real Hostel*** *(☎ 441-4022)*, which is clean and friendly (English is spoken), has one hot shower in the shared bathrooms, a funky sitting area with movies on cable TV, and a porch. The rate is US$11 per person, US$13 with breakfast. Kitchen privileges are available, and the place is popular among budget travelers. The owners are well connected in the local music and nightlife scene (though the hostel itself remains tranquil). The ***Mango Verde Hostel*** *(☎/fax 441-6330)*, Avenida 3, Calles 2 & 4, is also a good choice, with all the amenities – hot water, a sitting/TV room, and kitchen privileges. Its decent rooms cost US$13/20 single/double with shared baths and US$17/30 with private baths.

The ***Pensión Alajuela*** *(☎/fax 441-6251, Apartado 1416-4050, Alajuela)* is four blocks north of the Parque Central. It's a friendly place with a nice little bar for guests and charges US$20 for a double with a shared bathroom or US$24 for a double with a private bath (no single rates).

Charly's Place *(☎/fax 441-0115)*, two blocks north of Alajuela's Parque Central, is popular with gringos (though it's tico-run), but it is up for sale, so it may change. Rooms cost US$20/25 with shared showers, US$30/35 with private bathrooms; hot water, breakfast, kitchen privileges, and parking are available.

Out by the airport is the ***Hotel El Avion*** *(☎ 441-2079, fax 443-3447; in the USA ☎ 800-330-4663)*, which has hot water and double rooms for US$24 but is recommended only for its convenience. The hotel arranges airport pickup, which is sometimes free, depending on, well, you know, however things may be at the moment.

Mid-Range ***Islands B&B*** *(☎ 442-0573, fax 442-2909, eic30732@irazu.una.ac.cr)*, 50m west of Iglesia La Agonía on Avenida 1, Calles 7 & 9, has clean rooms with private hot baths for US$25/35 including breakfast. The friendly English-speaking owner, David Quesada, plays for the San José soccer team and is also very knowledgeable about the Alajuela team and Costa Rican soccer in general, as well as about places to eat and drink in Alajuela.

Around the corner from Charly's Place is the ***Hotel 1915*** *(☎/fax 441-0495)*, which has simple, nice rooms in an elegant house with private hot baths for US$45 double, including breakfast served in a pleasant courtyard. Readers have sent warm recommendations of this hotel.

The Canadian-run ***Tuetal Lodge*** *(☎ 442-1804, tuetal@sol.racsa.co.cr)* is about 4km north of the center (see Getting There & Away, later in this section, for buses; you could also take a taxi). There are six clean and roomy cabins (US$42 double), or cabins with kitchenettes (US$5 more). There is a restaurant that serves vegetables from the lodge's own organic garden and a bar; the lodge is in a nice location fairly close to the airport, and pickup can be arranged.

In the Tuetal area, near the crossroads, is the ***Pura Vida B&B*** *(☎ 441-1157, fax 441-1157)*, which charges about US$40/50 single/double with continental breakfast.

The ***Hotel Alajuela*** *(☎ 441-1241, 441-6595, fax 441-7912, Apartado 110-4050, Alajuela)* is on Calle 2, just south of the Parque Central.

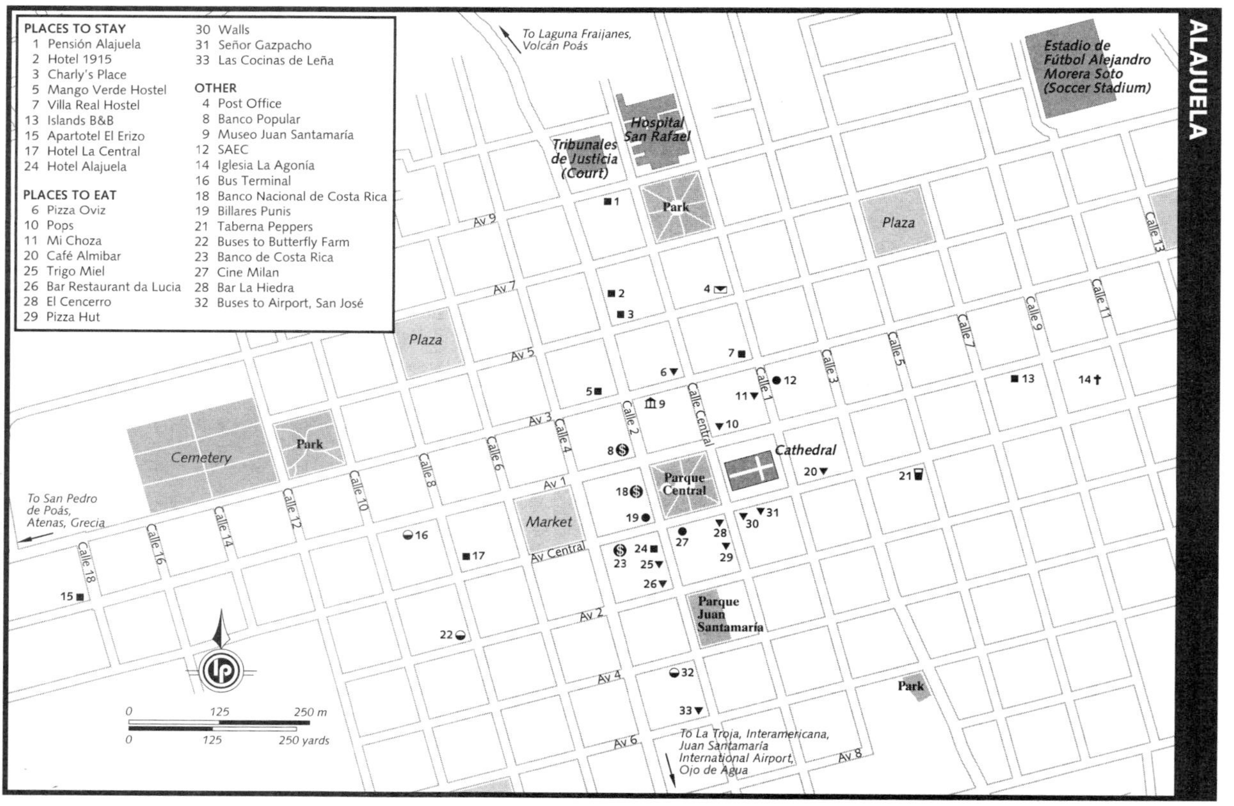
ALAJUELA
PLACES TO STAY
1 Pensión Alajuela
2 Hotel 1915
3 Charly's Place
5 Mango Verde Hostel
7 Villa Real Hostel
13 Islands B&B
15 Apartotel El Erizo
17 Hotel La Central
24 Hotel Alajuela
PLACES TO EAT
6 Pizza Oviz
10 Pops
11 Mi Choza
20 Café Almibar
25 Trigo Miel
26 Bar Restaurant da Lucia
28 El Cencerro
29 Pizza Hut
30 Walls
31 Señor Gazpacho
33 Las Cocinas de Leña
OTHER
4 Post Office
8 Banco Popular
9 Museo Juan Santamaría
12 SAEC
14 Iglesia La Agonía
16 Bus Terminal
18 Banco Nacional de Costa Rica
19 Billares Punis
21 Taberna Peppers
22 Buses to Butterfly Farm
23 Banco de Costa Rica
27 Cine Milan
28 Bar La Hiedra
32 Buses to Airport, San José
Estadio de Fútbol Alejandro Morera Soto (Soccer Stadium)
Hospital San Rafael
Tribunales de Justicia (Court)
Park
Plaza
Cathedral
Parque Central
Parque Juan Santamaría
Market
Cemetery
Calle 13
Calle 11
Calle 9
Calle 7
Calle 5
Calle 3
Calle 1
Calle Central
Calle 2
Calle 4
Calle 6
Calle 8
Calle 10
Calle 12
Calle 14
Calle 16
Calle 18
Av 9
Av 7
Av 5
Av 3
Av 1
Av Central
Av 2
Av 4
Av 6
Av 8
To Laguna Fraijanes, Volcán Poás
To San Pedro de Poás, Atenas, Grecia
To La Troja, Interamericana, Juan Santamaría International Airport, Ojo de Agua
0 125 250 m
0 125 250 yards

This hotel is friendly and well run, but, unfortunately, it is often full during the high season because of its proximity to the international airport. Rates are US$35/40/43 single/double/triple with private hot baths, and an extra US$2 for a TV. There are a few rooms with kitchenettes and a few less expensive rooms with shared baths for US$18/28. Long-stay discounts are available.

On the south side of the airport, about 4km from town, is the ***Posada Aeropuerto B&B*** *(☎/fax 441-7569; in the USA ☎ 800-697-5154)*. It charges US$44 for a double room with private hot bath, including breakfast and airport transfer. The ***Hampton Inn*** *(☎ 443-0043, 0800-426-7866 toll free in Costa Rica, fax 442-9532; in the USA ☎ 800-426-7866, hampton@sol.racsa.co.cr)* is 1.5km east of the airport and is the easiest hotel to reach from there. It is a very clean and modern American-style hotel with a pool, 24-hour coffee, and a staff that works hard to please – the staff guarantees 100% satisfaction! Spacious singles/doubles with cable TVs and free local calls cost US$70/77, including continental breakfast and free airport pickup. The third and fourth occupants of a double room can stay for free. This hotel will ease the cultural shock between the USA and Costa Rica.

The ***Apartotel El Erizo*** *(☎/fax 441-2840, apartotelerizo@sol.racsa.co.cr)* is eight blocks west of the Parque Central and is the fanciest place near the center of town. It has one- and two-bedroom apartments with kitchenettes/dining areas, air-conditioning, and TVs for US$60 and US$80, as well as double rooms without kitchenettes for US$40.

About 5km west of Alajuela on the road to San Pedro de Poás (call for precise directions) is the US-owned ***Orquideas Inn*** *(☎ 433-9346, fax 433-9740, orchid@sol.racsa.co.cr)*, an attractive Spanish-style mansion with a pool and spacious, airy rooms with wood parquet floors. Air-conditioned rooms with private bathrooms cost about US$50 to US$80, depending on the room. There is a restaurant and bar: the first is well recommended for excellent breakfasts, and the second is famous for its Marilyn Monroe paraphernalia (presided over by a cat named Marilyn, of course). No children are allowed in either hotel or bar.

The ***Hotel Buena Vista*** *(☎ 442-8595, fax 442-8701, bvista@sol.racsa.co.cr)*, run by the friendly Ed Pratt, who has 'retired' to Costa Rica from Florida, is 5km north of Alajuela on the road to Poás and has good views of the Central Valley and nearby volcanoes. There is a swimming pool, restaurant, and bar. Rates are US$75 double, US$85 for rooms with balcony views of the volcanoes.

Top End ***Xandari Plantation*** *(☎ 443-2020, fax 442-4847, hotel@xandari.com; in the USA ☎ 800-686-7879, paradise@xandari.com)* is about 6km north of Alajuela. Set in a coffee plantation overlooking the Central Valley, this is a lovely, low-key resort with great views, walking trails, and waterfalls you can either gaze at or dive under. Many comforts are available, including a library, a video room (with nightly classic films), swimming pools, heated Jacuzzi, open-air exercise room, and restaurant. Rates are US$175 to US$250 double (discounts in low season) for spacious, individually decorated villas. Breakfast (on your private terrace) and airport pickup are included.

Places to Eat

Most places worth trying are on or near the Parque Central. ***Señor Gazpacho*** is a cheerful, popular place serving Mexican food. The pleasant ***Bar Restaurant da Lucia*** is upstairs at the corner of Calle 2, Avenida 2, and has pasta and pizza for about US$5 and up. Some of the tables are out on little balconies with views of the Parque Juan Santamaría and the statue.

For good, inexpensive breakfasts, try ***Mi Choza***, Calle 1, Avenidas 1 & 3. Coffee and a variety of yummy desserts are the standbys at the ***Café Almibar***, on Avenida Central, Calles 1 & 3. Another cozy retreat for coffee and pastries is the ***Trigo Miel*** bakery, south of the Parque Central on Calle 2. At the southeast corner of the park is ***Walls***, a favorite for ice cream and snacks; at the northeast corner is ***Pops***, also good for ice cream.

Pizza lovers have the choice of the locally owned ***Pizza Oviz*** or the internationally owned ***Pizza Hut*** (with a salad bar), both on Calle Central.

On the Parque Central, ***El Cencerro*** (☎ *441-2414)* – the name translates to 'the cowbell' – serves steaks as the house specialty, although it serves other food as well. Meals cost in the US$6 to US$12 range. ***Las Cocinas de Leña***, Avenida 2, Calle 6, serves typical steaks and seafood cooked over wood-burning grills or in wood-burning ovens.

Entertainment

There is a movie theater, ***Cine Milan***, on Avenida Central near Parque Central.

Nice places for a drink include ***Bar La Hiedra*** (☎ *441-1366)*, next to El Cencerro (see above), and ***Taberna Peppers***, a friendly little corner bar that has good *bocas*. ***La Troja*** (run by the family that operates the Villa Real Hostel) is a favorite among young people wanting to listen to live music, which it has most nights. It has relocated a short distance south of the center; taxi drivers will know where to drop you off. At the friendly ***Billares Punis***, a small upscale pool hall (air-conditioning!) that overlooks the Parque Central, you can't drink beer, but staff can give you suggestions about other good nightspots farther out from the center. There are five good tables, which rent for US$3.50 per hour, and an unobtrusive cable TV.

The 1996 Costa Rican soccer champions, Alajuela's own La Liga, play at the stadium at the northeast end of town on Sundays during the soccer season. For more information, see the Islands B&B entry under Places to Stay earlier in this section.

Getting There & Away

TUASA buses for Alajuela (US40¢) leave San José from Avenida 2 and Calle 12 every 10 minutes between 5:30 am and 7 pm. From 7 pm till midnight, buses leave at 15- or 20-minute intervals. Late-night buses are also available at less frequent intervals from Calle 2, Avenida 2. The return buses from Alajuela to San José leave from the stop at Avenida 4, Calles 2 & 8.

The Alajuela bus terminal, off Avenida 1, Calles 8 & 10, is the departure point for buses to other towns and to Volcán Poás. To reach the Tuetal Lodge, take a Tuetal Norte bus (leaving every hour) and watch for lodge signs.

To get to the airport, either take a San José bus and get off at the airport (make sure that the bus stops there) or take a bus from Avenida 4, Calles 2 & 4, or take a taxi. Taxis to the airport are available from the Parque Central (west side) at any hour of the day or night. The fare is about US$2 during the day, more at night. A taxi to San José costs about US$12.50.

OJO DE AGUA

About 6km south of Alajuela are the Ojo de Agua springs, a favorite resort for working-class people from both San José and Alajuela. Thousands of liters of water gush out from the spring each minute. This fills swimming pools and an artificial boating lake before being piped down to Puntarenas, for which it is a major water supply.

The recreational complex can be very crowded as picnicking locals flock there on weekends; it is quieter midweek. Entrance to the complex costs about US$1, and there are places to eat, game courts, and a small gym. The end of the dry season is reportedly the least impressive time to visit, because water levels are low, partly due to local deforestation.

Another water park in the Alajuela area is the more upscale **Acua Mania** (☎ 293-2890, 293-2891), which has several pools (including children's pools) with a variety of water slides, as well as underwater caves, a wave machine, an artificial river for float trips, and water volleyball. Lifeguards are on duty. In addition, there is a miniature golf course and a go-cart track (US$3 each), a video arcade, a picnic area, and a restaurant. It is not open to the general public for day visits, but individual and family memberships are available starting at US$55. Call for directions and more information.

Getting There & Away

Buses leave from the terminal in Alajuela. Buses also leave every hour (more frequently on weekends) from Avenida 1, Calle 20, in San José.

Drivers from San José should take the San Antonio de Belén exit off the Interamericana (in front of the Hotel Cariari) and go through San Antonio to Ojo de Agua.

BUTTERFLY FARM

Yes, they farm butterflies in Costa Rica, and it's a fascinating process. The Butterfly Farm (☎ 438-0400, fax 438-0300, info@butterflyfarm.co.cr) opened in 1983 and was the first commercial butterfly farm in Latin America. Informative guided tours take you through tropical gardens filled with hundreds of butterflies of many species. You can see and learn about all the stages of the complex butterfly life cycle as well as find out about the importance of butterflies in nature. Every Monday and on Thursdays from March to August, visitors can watch thousands of pupae being packed for export all over the world. Sunny weather (mornings in the rainy season) is usually the best time to see activity.

There are also traditional ox-cart rides, a bee garden, and tropical birds that abound in the gardens. Bring your camera – there are good photo opportunities.

The Butterfly Farm is open 9 am to 5 pm daily. Guided butterfly tours (in English, Spanish, French, and German) last two hours and run continuously from 9 am to 3 pm for US$15/7 for adults/children (five to 12 years). Kids under five are free; students over 12 with ID get a 25% discount. Once your tour is over, you can stay as long as you want. There is a restaurant serving snacks.

The Butterfly Farm also offers complete tour packages from San José with hotel pickups at 7:20 and 10 am and 2 pm; the cost is US$25/14 for adults/children. In addition, staff can arrange a tour with lunch combined with the Coffeetour at Café Britt Finca (see Around Heredia, later in this chapter) for US$60/45, with hotel pickups beginning at 8 am; this combined tour includes lunch.

Getting There & Away

The farm is in front of El Club Campestre Los Reyes (a country club) in the village of La Guácima, 12km southwest of Alajuela. Buses to La Guácima leave San José at 11 am and 2 pm daily from a stop marked 'San Antonio/Ojo de Agua' at Avenida 1, Calles 20 & 22. The bus returns to San José at 3:15 pm.

There are also buses from Alajuela at 6:30, 9, and 11 am and 1 pm, leaving from Calle 8, Avenida 2; ask locals, as the stop is poorly marked. Make sure your bus goes to La Guácima Abajo. The last bus departs for Alajuela at 5:45 pm.

Drivers from San José should take the San Antonio de Belén exit off the Interamericana by the Hotel Cariari and drive through San Antonio to La Guácima. There are butterfly signs as you get close to the farm. Tours are available from San José travel agencies as well as direct from the farm.

WEST TO ATENAS

West of Alajuela is a road that leads to Atenas, a small village about 25km away. En route to Atenas you pass Zoo-Ave and La Garita. **Zoo-Ave** (☎ 433-8989, fax 433-9140, zooave@sol.racsa.co.cr) is about 10km west of Alajuela and has a collection of tropical birds, including over 60 Costa Rican species, displayed in a pleasant, parklike setting. There is a program to breed endangered native species and reintroduce them into the wild; a current red macaw project, at the Dolphin Quest lodge on the Golfo Dulce, is a nice example of how the twin aims of ecotourism can complement each other (see Playa San Josecito in the Península de Osa & Golfo Dulce chapter). There are also a few mammals (including all four species of Costa Rican monkeys) and reptiles, but the birds are certainly the highlight.

The zoo is open 9 am to 5 pm daily, except Christmas; admission costs US$9 for foreign adults and under US$1 for ticos and all children. If you are driving west from San José or Alajuela on the Interamericana, at the Atenas exit go east for 3km to Zoo-Ave. Buses between Alajuela and La Garita pass by the entrance every half hour.

A few kilometers beyond Zoo-Ave is **La Garita**, with an unusual restaurant that serves every dish you could imagine – as long as it is made from corn *(maize)*. The restaurant, called ***La Fiesta del Maíz*** *(☎ 487-7057)*, is open 8 am to 9 pm Friday to Sunday and on additional days during the high season.

The area is famous for its viveros, where local flora are grown and sold for use within Costa Rica.

Places to Stay

There are a few small hotels in the area. ***Ana's Place*** *(☎/fax 446-5019, Apartado 66 Atenas, Alajuela)* has seven decent rooms, some with private baths, around a quiet backyard populated by a few large, exotic birds. The rate is US$35 double, including breakfast. Ana's Place is near the Atenas bus station and about four blocks southwest of the Atenas Parque Central – call for directions if you can't find it. Just south of Atenas, reachable only by car, is ***Vista Atenas*** *(☎/fax 391-3209)*, a B&B with a few modern, hotel-like rooms, a small pool, and views over the Central Valley. The rate is US$35 double, including breakfast.

About 4km from Atenas is the ***Hotel Colinas del Sol*** *(☎/fax 446-6847, colinas@hotels.co.cr)*, which has modern bungalows scattered around a hilly and tranquil 6-hectare property surrounded by farmland; the airport is only 20 minutes away and pickup can be arranged. Each unit has a kitchenette, terrace, and private hot bath and costs US$45 per day, US$300 per week; there is a large pool, bar, coffee shop, and 24-hour security.

Everyone raves about the friendly and clean ***El Cafetal Inn B&B*** *(☎ 446-5785, fax 446-5140, cafetal@sol.racsa.co.cr)*, about 5km north of Atenas (in Santa Eulalia de Atenas) – there are plenty of signs. There's a large garden and pool, and a dozen attractive rooms with private baths, which cost in the US$55 to US$75 range, including breakfast. On Sundays in the dry season, an all-you-can-eat lunch buffet is served (US$12) that includes complimentary coffee liqueurs and use of the pool; this attracts people from San José.

Getting There & Away

Buses go to Atenas from the San José Coca-Cola terminal several times a day, but they do not pass Zoo-Ave. To get to Zoo-Ave and La Garita, take one of the buses from Alajuela's bus terminal to La Garita, which leave about every half hour. Call Coopetransatenas (☎ 446-5767) for bus information.

NORTHWEST TO ZARCERO

Northwest of Alajuela are the villages of Grecia (22km), Sarchí (29km), Naranjo (35km), and Zarcero (52km). They all have colorful churches typical of the Costa Rican countryside.

All of these small towns can be reached by buses that depart either from the Coca-Cola terminal in San José or the bus terminal in Alajuela. The drive to Zarcero is along a narrow, winding, and hilly road with pretty views of the coffee *fincas* (farms) that cover the Central Valley hillsides.

GRECIA

Grecia is an agricultural center (pineapples, sugarcane) and is known for its red church, a local landmark. There is a small regional museum in the Casa de Cultura (☎ 444-6767), open sporadically, which also features a tiny insect museum.

A new attraction in the Grecia area, located about 2km south of the town center, is the **World of Snakes** (☎/fax 494-3700, snakes@sol.racsa.co.cr), an open-air public exhibit with a commitment to research and to breeding endangered species. Some 150 snakes, representing over 50 species of snakes (as well as some frogs and reptiles, including baby caimans and crocodiles), are on display in cages simulating the species' home environments. The snakes are from all over the world, with an emphasis on Costa Rica. Informative tours in English, German, or Spanish last a minimum of 45 minutes; if there's time, they'll talk to you for as long as you're interested – and make available exciting options like snake-handling. Admission costs US$11 for adults; any bus to or from Grecia can drop you at the entrance.

Otherwise, Grecia's main importance for the traveler is as a place to change buses to continue to Sarchí (although there are also direct buses to Sarchí from the Coca-Cola terminal in Sán José).

The citizens pride themselves on the fact that Grecia was once voted the cleanest little town in Latin America!

Places to Stay

For the cheapest digs near the town center, try ***Pensión Familiar*** *(☎ 444-5097)*, run by the Quíros family. A mid-range option is the ***Hotel Healthy Day Inn*** *(☎/fax 444-5903, healthi@sol.racsa.co.cr)*, 800m northeast of the red church on the main road out of town. A loosely organized variety of health services are available (homeopathic therapies, massage, macrobiotic meals), as well as a tennis court, gym, and Jacuzzi. The rooms are cute and a decent value at US$35 to US$48 double.

The best place for miles around is the critically acclaimed ***Vista del Valle Plantation Inn*** *(formerly known as Posada Las Palomas; ☎ 450-0800, 450-0900, 661-2401, ☎/fax 451-1165, mibrejo@sol.racsa.co.cr)*. It is near the village of Rosario, about 7km southwest of Grecia as the crow flies, and borders the small Zona Protectora Río Grande, a cloud forest reserve at about 800m, as well as coffee fincas and fruit orchards. The Plantation has extensive grounds, much of which form an orchard and a botanical garden. Trails lead into the adjoining reserve past a 90m-high waterfall, and a pool and Jacuzzi are on the hotel grounds. The rooms are lovely and airy with balconies and views; a few are in garden cottages with kitchenettes. Meals, airport pickup (20 minutes away, about US$30 roundtrip, US$20 one way if before 6 am or after 10 pm), and tour information are available from the owners, one of whom was a US Peace Corps volunteer here in the 1960s and knows the country intimately. From different parts of the property it is possible to get views of volcanoes and of San José city lights. Meals can be eaten in a common area or privately. Eight suites of varying sizes with kitchens or kitchenettes cost US$115 to US$130 single or double, US$20 for additional people; two rooms in the main house cost US$85/100 single/double.

SARCHÍ

This small town is Costa Rica's most famous crafts center, and tour buses and locals stop here to buy crafts, particularly woodwork. It is, of course, commercial, but in a charmingly understated Costa Rican way. Some readers complain that it is too touristy, while others write and say that it's wonderful. Although I would qualify it as a tourist trap, there is no pressure to buy anything, and there is the opportunity to see crafts being made. Unfortunately, though, the shopping is mainly in the modern area, away from the older and nicer part of town.

Among the best-known crafts are the *carretas* (see Arts in the Facts about Costa Rica chapter), which are often used nowadays to decorate people's gardens; scaled-down versions are made for use as indoor tables, sideboards, and bars, and miniature models are available for use as indoor sculptures. All sizes come apart and fold down for transport.

You can see them being made in a couple of *fábricas de carretas* (cart factories), where the most interesting part of the process is watching local artisans paint colorful mandala designs onto the carts. The oldest and best-known factory is Fábrica de Carretas Joaquín Chaverri (see below).

The bright paintwork is also used to decorate wooden trays, plates, and other souvenirs. Unpainted woodwork, such as salad bowls, kitchen cutting boards, serving dishes, jewelry boxes, letter openers, statuettes, toy cars and planes, and a variety of other utilitarian knickknacks, are also sold.

There are also furniture factories in Sarchí. While the elegantly carved headboards and bedsteads, tables and chairs, and sitting room furniture are mainly designed for local sale and use, some travelers buy the leather and wood rocking chairs – these come apart and fold down for transport.

Whatever you do, leave a shopping trip to Sarchí until the end of your trip. Thus, you won't be encumbered by presents while you are traveling around the country. And shop around – there are plenty of factories and stores to choose from in Sarchí. Note that almost everything here is also available in San José.

Orientation & Information

Sarchí is divided by the Río Trojas into Sarchí Norte and Sarchí Sur and is rather spread out, straggling for several kilometers along the main road from Grecia to Naranjo.

At the Plaza de la Artesanía in Sarchí Sur is an information booth with sketch maps of Sarchí.

In Sarchí Norte, you'll find the main plaza with the twin-towered typical church, a hotel, and some restaurants. There is also a Banco Nacional (☎ 454-4262), open 8:30 am to 3 pm weekdays; it cashes traveler's checks and dollars.

Crafts

In Sarchí Sur, you will find the Plaza de la Artesanía (☎ 454-4271), a shopping mall with over 30 souvenir stores and restaurants, as well as local musicians playing marimbas. Nearby are several factories specializing in rocking chairs and other furniture, including Los Rodriguez (☎ 454-4097), La Sarchiseña (☎ 454-4062), El Artesano (☎ 454-4304), and others. All these are on the main road.

The oldest and best-known carretas factory is Fábrica de Carretas Joaquín Chaverri (☎ 454-4411, fax 454-4944), in Sarchí Sur.

There are more factories and stores, including Taller Lalo Alfaro, Sarchí's oldest workshop, at the far north end of town, and Artesanía Sarchí (☎ 454-4267), at the south end of Sarchí Norte, specializing in typical Costa Rican clothing. Pidesa Souvenirs (☎ 454-4540), by the main plaza, specializes in hand-painting all local souvenirs, including full-size milk cans. Get a couple for that person in your life who already has everything.

Places to Stay & Eat

Few people stay here, as most visitors come on day trips. A decent budget option is the friendly ***Hotel Daniel Zamora*** *(☎ 454-4596, 382-6684)*, on a quiet street just east of the soccer field; the rate for clean doubles with private baths and cable TV is US$25. If you get stuck, try the decent-looking ***Hotel Cabinas Sarchí***, on the noisy main road.

Restaurante Tipico La Finca, at the north end of Sarchí Norte, overlooks a tranquil garden – a nice break from the hurly-burly of shopping. ***Super Mariscos***, next to the Banco Nacional in Sarchí Norte, specializes in seafood; it is open daily except Tuesday. There are also the restaurants in Plaza de la Artesanía in Sarchí Sur.

Getting There & Away

The quickest way to get to Sarchí from San José is to take one of the frequent buses to Grecia from the Coca-Cola terminal and then connect with an Alajuela-Sarchí bus going through Grecia. There are numerous other possibilities. If you are driving, you can take the unpaved road northeast from Zarcero to Bajos del Toro and on through Colonia del Toro to the northern lowlands at Río Cuarto. The main attraction of this route is the beautiful waterfall north of Bajos del Toro. Look for local signs for the 'Catarata.'

Getting Around

Taxis Sarchí (☎ 454-4028) will shuttle you from Sarchí Norte to Sarchí Sur and drive you to any workshop you wish to visit.

PALMARES

Driving west along the Interamericana between the turnoffs for Naranjo and San Ramón (see below), you'll see a turnoff to Palmares, a village that is a few kilometers south of the highway. Palmares' main claim to fame is the annual fiesta, held for 10 days in the middle of January. This country fair attracts ticos from all over the Central Valley and has events for the whole family, including carnival rides, bullfights (the bull is not killed in Costa Rican fights), food, beer stands, and a variety of unusual sideshows. One year's fair featured robot ponies and snake caves.

SAN RAMÓN

From Sarchí, the road continues west to Naranjo, where it divides. You can then continue 13km south and west to San Ramón or 17km north to Zarcero.

San Ramón is a pleasant small town located about halfway between San José and Puntarenas, just off the Interamericana, which joins the capital with the Pacific coast. The town is known locally as the 'city of presidents and poets,' because several of them were born or lived here. Ex-president Rodrigo Carazo lives a few kilometers to the north and owns a tourist lodge surrounded by the Los Angeles Cloud Forest. A museum in town has further information about famous native sons and daughters of San Ramón. The Saturday farmers' market is a big one with lots of locals and few tourists. There are smaller markets on Wednesday and Sunday.

Museo de San Ramón

This museum, on the south side of the Parque Central, has interesting exhibits on local history and culture. It's open 1 to 5 pm weekdays, but museum hours tend to be a bit erratic. It's well worth a look, and there is no admission fee.

Places to Stay

There are some cheap and basic places in town. Close to the center, try ***Hotel Gran*** *(☎ 445-6363)*, ***Hotel El Viajero*** *(☎ 445-5580)*, ***Hotel Washington*** *(☎ 445-7349)*, or ***Hotel Nuevo Jardín*** *(☎ 445-5620)*.

A Peace Corps volunteer who lived in the area for two years writes that ***La Posada B&B*** *(☎ 445-7359)*, 100m south and 50m east of the hospital, is the first nice, affordable hotel to open in central San Ramón; clean rooms cost US$25/40/52 single/double/triple, including breakfast.

Getting There & Away

Buses to San Ramón leave San José from in front of the Hotel Musoc on Calle 16, Avenidas 1 & 3.

SAN RAMÓN TO LA TIGRA

A paved road links San Ramón with La Tigra and Fortuna (see the Northwestern Costa Rica chapter). This road goes north from San Ramón, across the central highlands, and down to Fortuna, and it could also be placed in the next chapter. The road goes through cloud forest and coffee fincas, but it is steep, narrow, and winding and there are few landmarks and pull-offs for the driver.

Los Angeles Cloud Forest Reserve

This private reserve is about 20km north of San Ramón; look for signs along the highway. The last few kilometers are on an unpaved but good road to the west of the paved highway.

The reserve is centered around a dairy ranch owned by ex-president Rodrigo Carazo and his wife. Some 800 hectares of primary forest have a short boardwalk trail and longer horse and foot trails leading to waterfalls and cloud forest vistas. Bilingual naturalist guides are available to lead hikes, and the birding is good. Horse rentals cost US$10 per hour and guided hikes cost US$22.50 (unguided hikes cost US$14.75). A canopy tour costs US$35. Tours of the reserve are arranged through the Hotel Villablanca (see below). There are relatively few tourists in this cloud forest, which has a good variety of species, some of which, however, are hard to see.

Places to Stay & Eat

The ***Hotel Villablanca*** *(☎ 661-8003, fax 661-1600, information@villablanca-costarica.com)* has a large main lodge and restaurant with about 30 whitewashed, red-tiled, adobe cabins scattered around, all surrounded by the cloud forest described above. The rustic cabins cost US$92/115 single/double.

'Rustic' describes the ambience rather than the amenities – the cabins have refrigerators, hot water, bathtubs, fireplaces, and even electric kettles for hot drinks. Meals (buffet-style country cooking) are served in the main lodge for about US$15 (US$8 breakfast). Call the hotel about day trips from San José including transportation, a guided horseback ride, canopy tour, or hike, lunch at the hotel, and snacks, all for US$77. Ask about programs and discounts for students and groups staying in a building with dormitory-style accommodations.

About halfway between the Hotel Villablanca and the village of La Tigra is the ***Valle Escondido Lodge*** *(☎ 231-0906, fax 232-9591, hotel@valleescondido.com)*, on a working farm that grows ornamental plants and citrus fruits. There are over 100 hectares of preserved forest, and the whole place is good for birding. Horseback rides cost US$8 an hour, or you can hike the trails yourself (US$5 trail fee for nonguests). There is a pool and a locally popular restaurant with Italian specialties. Tours to various parts of the country and special 'green season' packages can be arranged. About two dozen spacious and attractive rooms cost US$64/81/99 single/double/triple. Meals cost about US$15 (US$7 for breakfast, US$6 for a boxed lunch).

ZARCERO

North of Naranjo, the main road climbs for 17km to Zarcero, a town at over 1700m at the western end of the Cordillera Central. The town is famous for its topiary garden in front of the town church. The bushes and shrubs have been cut into a variety of animal and human shapes and the effect is very pretty. (Look to your right if you're traveling northbound by bus from San José.)

The surrounding mountainous countryside is attractive and the climate cool and refreshing. The area is also well known for peach jam and homemade cheese, both of which are for sale in town.

Places to Stay & Eat

Hotel Don Beto *(☎ 463-3137)*, on the north side of the town church, is clean, friendly, and pleasant. It has eight rooms of varying size, some with shared baths and others with private baths, for about US$20 to US$30 double. Breakfast is available. The owner has lots of local information.

There are a number of simple ***restaurants*** around Zarcero's main square.

Getting There & Away

Buses for Ciudad Quesada (San Carlos) via Zarcero leave San José's Atlántico Norte terminal every hour from 5 am to 7:30 pm. There are also buses from Alajuela. From San José to Zarcero, it takes almost two hours, and from Alajuela a little less.

Buses from Zarcero leave from the red bus stands at the northwest corner of the park (the church plaza with the topiary art).

Northbound buses continue over the Cordillera Central and down to Ciudad Quesada, 35km away. Southbound buses go to San José every hour; some of them will drop you in Alajuela. Because Zarcero is on the busy San José to Ciudad Quesada run, buses may be full when they come through, especially on weekends.

PARQUE NACIONAL JUAN CASTRO BLANCO

This 14,285-hectare park was created in 1992 to protect the slopes of Volcán Platanar (2183m) and Volcán Porvenir (2267m) from logging. This is an important watershed area for several rivers that would have been

DAVE G HOUSER

Zarcero is famous for the elaborate topiary garden in front of the town church.

severely damaged by the erosion caused by logging. Now, the premontane rainforest and montane cloud forest shelter a great variety of flora and fauna and safeguard the quality of the watershed.

This national park has almost no infrastructure for visitors. You can enter the edge of it by driving north from Sarchí for about 18km to the village of Bajos del Toro at the edge of the park. Alternately, a shorter road to Bajos del Toro goes east from Zarcero, but is in worse shape. From Bajos del Toro, footpaths and 4WD tracks travel a short way into the park as they follow along the Río Toro, which was dammed in 1995. There are several waterfalls near here, some of which are now dry because of the hydroelectric project. You can also approach the park from the north (see West of San Miguel in the Northern Lowlands chapter).

LAGUNA FRAIJANES AREA

This small lake (☎ 482-2166 information) is surrounded by trails, play areas, and picnic sites, and is a stopping place en route to Volcán Poás. Laguna Fraijanes is 15km north of Alajuela on Route 130 and is open 9 am to 3:30 pm (except Monday).

Places to Stay & Eat

If you don't want to picnic, you'll find several recommended restaurants in the area. ***Chubascos***, a kilometer north of the lake, with a terrace, pine trees, and a spacious garden, serves good typical Costa Rican food. ***Las Fresas*** *(☎ 448-5567)*, west of the lake on the road joining Volcán Poás with San Pedro de Poás, serves steaks and pizzas. Las Fresas is named after the many strawberry fields and blackberry patches in the area – berry drinks and shakes are a specialty of local restaurants – and it offers a few cabins to stay in, with private hot showers, for US$30.

Farther north, several other country-style restaurants are dotted along the road to the volcano.

Getting There & Away

Coopetransasi (☎ 449-5141) has buses from three blocks west of Alajuela's Mercado Central. Weekend departures are hourly from 9 am to 5 pm; from Tuesday to Friday, buses leave at 9 am, noon, and 2, 4:15, and 6:15 pm, returning one hour later. You can also visit the lake by car en route to Volcán Poás.

Drivers should note that although the road is a fairly important route to Poás, it is in poor shape with many potholes, and, on one hairpin bend, there is a one-way bridge with no guardrails. The locals deal with these problems by driving as quickly as possible.

PARQUE NACIONAL VOLCÁN POÁS

This 5599-hectare park lies about 37km north of Alajuela by road and is a popular destination for locals and visitors alike. It is one of the oldest and best-known national parks in Costa Rica.

The centerpiece of the park is, of course, Volcán Poás (2704m), which has been active since well before records started in 1828. There have been three major periods of recorded activity, from 1888 to 1895, 1903 to 1912, and 1952 to 1954.

It appears that the volcano is entering a newly active phase, and the park was briefly closed in 1989 after a minor eruption in May of that year sent volcanic ash over a kilometer into the air. Since then, lesser activity intermittently closed the park in 1995.

At the present time the crater is a bubbling and steaming cauldron, but it doesn't pose an imminent threat, and the park is steadily open. This volcanic activity, though, has resulted in acid rain that has damaged the coffee and berry crops of the area. Rangers don't recommend drinking water in the park; buy bottled water.

The mountain is composed of composite basalt. The huge crater is 1.5km across and 300m deep. Geyser-type eruptions take place periodically, with peaceful interludes lasting minutes or weeks depending on the degree of activity within the volcano. Because of toxic sulfuric acid fumes, visitors are prohibited from descending into the crater, but the view down from the top is very impressive. This park is a 'must' for anyone with an interest in seeing what an active volcano looks like.

Apart from Volcán Poás itself, there is a dwarf cloud forest near the crater, the best example of this kind of habitat in the national park system. Here you can wander around looking at the bromeliads, lichens, and mosses clinging to the curiously shaped and twisted trees growing on the volcanic soil.

Birds abound, especially the magnificent fiery-throated hummingbirds, which are high-altitude specialties of Costa Rica.

Other highland specialties to look for include the sooty robin, as well as the resplendent quetzal, which has been reported here.

A nature trail leads through this cloud forest to another crater nearby (this one extinct), which forms the pretty Laguna Botos. There are other walking trails as well.

Information

Current park hours are 8 am to 3:30 pm daily. Entrance to the park costs US$6 per (non-tico) person. The park is very crowded on Sunday, and the annual number of visitors is around half a million. There is a visitor center with a coffee shop, gift shop, and video shows every hour from 9 am to 3 pm. There is also an insect museum with explanations in both Spanish and English. Admission to the museum costs an extra US50¢ for adults.

The best time to go is in the dry season, especially early in the morning before the clouds roll in and obscure the view. Nevertheless, I have been there in late afternoon and had great views, and readers traveling in the rainy season have reported the same, so it's partly luck. If it's clouded in, don't despair! Winds may blow the clouds away, so walk around the cloud forest and keep checking back on the crater. Overnight temperatures can drop below freezing, and it may be windy and cold during the day, particularly in the morning, so dress accordingly. Poás receives almost 4m of rain a year, so be prepared for it.

There are well-marked trails in the park. It is easy to walk (about 1km) to the active crater lookout for spectacular views; the trails through the cloud forest are somewhat steeper but still not very difficult or long. The route to the crater is a paved road that is shut to cars, but disabled people who are unable to negotiate it can request permission to drive to the rim. This is normally OK early in the day at midweek but difficult on Sundays, when the road is too crowded with pedestrians.

There is a parking lot where rangers on patrol look after your car during your visit. Parking costs vary slightly depending on the size of your vehicle.

A reader reports that there is a new tourist office open in San Pedro de Poás. Ask locally for details.

Organized Tours

Numerous companies advertise tours that depart from San José just about every day. Typically, they cost US$20 to US$70 per person, and you arrive at the volcano by about 10 am or a little later. Some tours spend very little time at the crater, so check carefully before you fork out your hard-earned cash. The cheaper tours are large group affairs providing only transportation, park entrance, and limited time at the crater. The more expensive tours feature smaller group size, bilingual naturalist guides, and lunch. There are now daily buses to the park from San José (see Getting There & Away, below) that offer the cheapest way to visit.

Artavio's Trekking (☎ 448-5122), on the south side of the church in San Pedro de Poás, has daily hiking tours (by advance reservation) for US$39 to US$65, depending on the number of participants. It also operates Snacks Lodge at US$12 per person; ask staff for directions.

Places to Stay & Eat

There are no overnight accommodations within the park, and camping is prohibited.

The coffee shop has a limited menu, so bringing your own food is a good idea. There are picnicking areas, but it is best to bring your own drinking water; you can buy bottles at the café, but it may run out, so it's best to bring your own.

There are several places to stay outside the park. The following are described in the order that you would encounter them after leaving the park. High up on the southwestern flanks of the volcano is ***La Providencia Reserva Ecológica*** *(☎ 232-2498, 387-3757, fax 231-2204)*, which is reached by taking a 2.5km dirt road (normally passable to cars) leaving from the paved highway about 2km after the national park entrance/exit. The 572-hectare property adjoins the national park and is a working dairy ranch with about 200 hectares of primary forest and much secondary forest. There are four small rustic guest cabins with private bathrooms for US$42 double, including breakfast. Electricity and hot showers have been added to some; alcohol is not allowed. Another cabin sleeps four, and the sixth cabin sleeps 10 people; both cost US$17 per person without breakfast. Some cabins are quite isolated. Three-hour horseback tours with a resident biologist guide are sometimes available for US$25, and there are several trails; some are good for birding (quetzals have been seen) and others for views. Reportedly both oceans, Lago de Nicaragua, and San José – plus a wee glimpse of Arenal – can be seen from here if it's clear. The decidedly rustic restaurant (dirt floor, wood stove, wooden stools) is open to the general public and serves breakfast, lunch, and dinner, though it's best to call ahead to arrange meals.

About 3.5km from the park exit, a sign indicates the ***Lagunillas Lodge*** *(☎ 448-5506)*, which is reached by a steep 1km dirt road (you need 4WD to get out). This small lodge (which is recommended by the park rangers) offers five rooms with baths (hot water available on request) for US$20 single and US$5 for up to four extra people. Typical meals cost US$4 to US$7, and horse rental costs US$8 per hour; staff say they'll take you to the Poás crater. Quetzals have been seen on the property from June to October.

Just over 5km from the park entrance is ***Lo Que Tu Quieres Lodge*** (this translates as 'Whatever You Want Lodge'), which has three basic little cabins with private hot showers for about US$20 (sleeping up to three people). There is a small restaurant and sweeping views of the valley; the owners are friendly.

Poás Volcano Lodge *(☎/fax 482-2194, poasvl@sol.racsa.co.cr)* is about 16km east of the volcano near Varablanca, in a dairy farm set at 1900m; it has good mountain views (though none of the rooms have views of the volcano). The attractive stone building blends rural architectural influences from Wales, England, and Costa Rica (the original owners were English farmers), and this is the nicest lodge in the Poás area. Trails surround the lodge, and common areas include a billiard room ('pool' doesn't do it justice) and a sitting area with a gorgeous, sunken fireplace. Six large comfortable rooms (they're called suites) cost US$52/75 single/double; a master suite with a fireplace and French doors that open onto a garden costs US$70/115. A couple of smaller rooms with shared baths cost US$40/65; rates include breakfast. Lunch and dinner cost around US$9 to US$14.

Also close to Varablanca is the slightly cheaper ***Juanbo Cabinas and Restaurant*** *(☎ 482-2099)*, which is also on a dairy farm. A reader reports that the food and views are good; rates are US$50 double, US$40 without breakfast.

Getting There & Away

From San José, a bus leaves from Avenida 2, Calles 12 & 14, at 8:30 am daily, sometimes followed by a second bus if there is passenger demand. Get there early (especially in the high season) to get onto the first bus, and when you get to the volcano, make a beeline for the crater to have the best chance of seeing it before the clouds roll in. The fare is about US$4 (roundtrip), the journey takes almost two hours, and the return bus leaves at 2:30 pm. This bus also stops in Alajuela. A taxi from Alajuela costs about US$35, including a couple hours at the park; it costs twice that from San José.

CATARATA LA PAZ

This waterfall, whose name means 'Peace Waterfall,' is perhaps the most famous waterfall in Costa Rica. This is partly for its impressive size and partly because it is just off the highway, about 8km north of Varablanca. It makes a nice side trip after visiting Volcán Poás. The Río La Paz cascades down the flanks of Volcán Poás' almost 1400m in less than 8km, culminating in a dramatic waterfall visible from the road. A short trail leads behind the falls so that you can stand between the mountainside and the plunging water – haven't you always wanted to do that?

A local guidebook reports that 'according to experts in the subject, the drops of water are charged with negative electricity, a kind of energy that reduces the stress of modern life.' Cool.

Heredia Area

HEREDIA

This small but historic city is the capital of the province of Heredia and lies about 11km north of San José. It has a population about half that of nearby Alajuela and retains more of a small-town colonial air than the neighboring capitals.

The elevation is 1150m above sea level, about the same as San José. The Universidad Nacional is on the east side of town, and there is a sizable student population. Despite this, there is little nightlife, and most people head into San José to party.

Information

There is no tourist office. Several banks in the town center change money. Banco Interfin (☎ 238-3633), Avenida 4, Calles Central & 2, and Banco Popular (☎ 261-0536), Avenida Central, Calles 1 & 3, are usually faster than most. Credomatic (☎ 257-4744), Calle Central, Avenidas 3 & 5, is the Visa/MasterCard office. A good Internet 'café' (no food at last visit) is near the university; it is currently open 10 am to 7 pm weekdays, but hours may expand. The Hospital San Vicente de Paul (☎ 261-0091) is at Calle 14, Avenida 8, or call the Red Cross Ambulance (☎ 237-1115).

Things to See

The city was founded in 1706, and its colonial character is the main reason to visit. The **Parque Central** is the best place to see the older buildings. To the east of the park is the church of **La Inmaculada Concepción**, built in 1797 and still in use. Opposite the church steps, you can watch old men playing checkers at the park tables while weddings and funerals come and go. The church's thick-walled, squat construction is attractive in an ugly sort of way – rather like how Volkswagen Beetles are attractive to many people. The solid shape has withstood the earthquakes that have damaged or destroyed almost all the other buildings in Costa Rica that date from this time.

To the north of the park is a colonial tower simply called **El Fortín** (the small fortress). This area is a national historic site. At the park's northeast corner is the **Casa de la Cultura**, formerly the residence of President Alfredo González Flores (1913-17), now housing art and historical exhibits. The center of the park has a covered bandstand where there are occasional performances.

Uphill and north from the center is a somewhat untended park that offers views across stretches of the valley and the mountains to the south.

A visit to the campus of the Universidad Nacional is of interest. The marine biology department has a **Museo Zoomarino** (☎ 277-3240), open 8 am to 4 pm weekdays; admission is free. Almost 2000 displayed specimens give an overview of Costa Rica's marine diversity.

The countryside surrounding Heredia is almost completely dedicated to growing coffee. Tour companies in San José sometimes arrange visits to these fincas. The countryside is attractive and has several points of interest and good hotels. See the Around Heredia section for details.

Language Courses

The following seem to do a good job. These are good choices if you'd like to stay near San José without actually being in the capital.

Centro Panamericano de Idiomas (☎ 265-6866, ☎/fax 265-6213; in the USA ☎ 800-903-8950, anajarro@sol.racsa.co.cr) Apartado 151-3007, San Joaquín, Heredia. In a suburb about 10 minutes by bus from Heredia, this school offers four weeks of classes for about US$1000, including family homestay, all meals, and field trips. Classes average two or three students (four maximum). This center has been recommended by several students.

Instituto de Lenguaje Pura Vida (☎/fax 237-0387, info@costaricaspanish.com) Avenida 3, Calles 8 & 10; Apartado 890-3000, Heredia. Courses cost US$320 to US$370 a week, all with family homestay, meals, four hours of tuition a day, and extracurricular activities and tours every afternoon; extra tutoring is available for US$16 per hour. Courses without homestay cost US$230 a week. Classes for seven- to 13-year-olds are also available.

Intercultura (in the USA ☎ 309-692-2961, 800-552-2051, fax 309-692-2926, info@langlink.com) PO Box 3006, Peoria, IL 61612. It prefers bookings made in the USA. Rates vary from US$330 to US$580 for a week with homestay, depending on the number of hours and whether you want group or private lessons. Discounts are given for two or more weeks.

Places to Stay

With San José so close, most travelers stay in the capital, though some elect to stay here because it is quieter. There are quite a few hotels in Heredia, however, partly to cater to the student population of the nearby university. Cheap hotels may give monthly discounts to students, but they are also used for short-term rentals – the walls are often thin. (We're talking young lovers rather than prostitutes.)

The basic ***Hotel El Parqueo*** *(☎ 238-2882)*, Calle 4, Avenidas 6 & 8, at US$5 per person, is friendly and clean enough but lacks hot water. The ***Hotel Verano*** *(☎ 237-1616)*, Calle 4, Avenida 6, is similar at US$5 per person. The ***Hotel Colonial*** *(☎ 237-5258)*, Avenida 4, Calles 4 & 6, is clean and family-run and charges US$7.50/12.50 single/double with fans (bargain it down US$2 or so in the low season). There's hot water in the shared baths.

The ***Hotel Heredia*** *(☎/fax 238-0880)*, Calle 6, Avenidas 3 & 5, is clean, will change US dollars, and charges US$11/18 single/double with private baths and hot water. Meals are available. The ***Casa de Huéspedes Ramble*** *(☎ 238-3829)*, Avenida 8, Calles 10 & 12, is pleasant and attractive and charges US$26/30 single/double with private hot baths. Also slightly away from the center, the ***Hotel Las Flores*** *(☎ 261-8147)*, Avenida 12, Calles 12 & 14, is a friendly, family-run place with private parking and rooms with private baths with hot showers for US$11/16.

The ***Hotel America*** *(☎ 260-9292, fax 260-9293, hamerica@sol.racsa.co.cr, Apartado 1740-3000, Heredia)*, Calle Central, Avenidas 2 & 4, has light and reasonably sized rooms with private hot baths for US$35/45 and suites sleeping up to four for US$110. There is a 24-hour restaurant and bar.

On the northwest side of Heredia (head north on Calle 12 about 1km) is ***Apartotel Vargas*** *(☎ 237-8526, Apartado 87-1300, Heredia)*, which has good apartments with kitchenettes, hot-water showers, TVs, and laundry facilities for about US$30/40.

The best hotel is the ***Hotel Valladolid*** *(☎ 260-2905, fax 260-2912, Apartado 93-3000, Heredia)*, Calle 7, Avenida 7. The five-story building features a sauna/spa/solarium on the top floor with good views of the surrounding area. Attractive air-conditioned rooms with kitchenettes, cable TVs, and hot showers rent for US$60/72. A good restaurant and bar are on the premises.

There are a number of mid-range and top-end hotels in the countryside surrounding Heredia; see Around Heredia, later this chapter.

Places to Eat

Near the Parque Central, ***Gran Chaparral*** is a locally popular place serving tico and Chinese meals for about US$3 to US$4. There are some student bars and cafés close to the university; ***El Bulevar*** and ***Restaurant La Choza*** have been recommended. Nearby, ***Restaurant Fresas*** serves good, fairly typical meals in the US$4 to US$7 range and has an outdoor dining area. Just down the street, ***Mango Verde***, a branch of the San José-area Vishnu chain, has good vegetarian food; try the veggie burger and fruit shake combo. Carnivores can try the ***Cowboy Steak House*** a few blocks away. Some students prefer ***Pizza Hut*** or ***McDonald's***, which are also around here (McDonald's has become a local landmark).

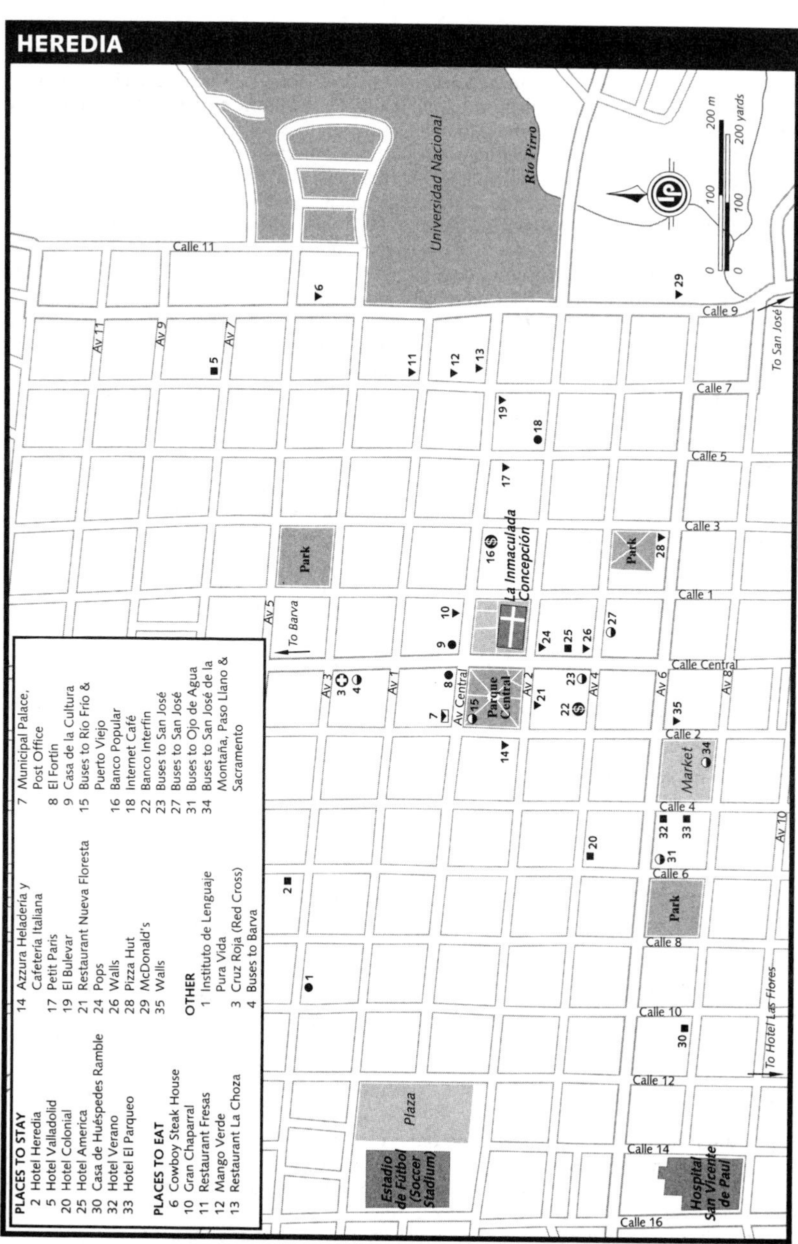

CENTRAL VALLEY

There are clean sodas in the market for inexpensive meals. For something slightly less basic, a good choice is ***Restaurant Nueva Floresta***, overlooking the south side of Parque Central, which serves Chinese food – a serving of decent chop suey with shrimp costs about US$4.

For good ice cream, deluxe coffee, or light snacks, the best places are ***Azzura Heladería y Cafetería Italiana***, on the west side of the Parque Central, or ***Petit Paris***, closer to the university, which also serves good crepes. There are also a couple of ***Walls*** and ***Pops*** ice-cream parlors.

Entertainment

Ask around the university area for currently popular nightspots. Again, many students recommend going into San José for nightlife.

Getting There & Away

Bus Minibuses leave San José for Heredia every 15 minutes from Avenida 2, Calles 10 & 12, from 6 am to 10 pm.

In Heredia, there is no central bus terminal, and buses leave from bus stops near the Parque Central and market areas. Destinations, departure points, and approximate frequency are as follows:

Barva – by the Cruz Roja (Red Cross), Calle Central, Avenidas 1 & 3, every 30 minutes

Ojo de Agua – Avenida 6, Calle 6, several times a day

Paso Llano (Porrosatí) & Sacramento (for Volcán Barva in Parque Nacional Braulio Carrillo) – Avenida 8, Calles 2 & 4, at 6:30 and 11 am and 4 pm

Río Frío & Puerto Viejo de Sarapiquí – west side of Parque Central, at 6:30 am, noon, and 3 pm

San José – Calle Central, Avenida 4, and Avenida 4, Calles Central & 1, every few minutes

San José de la Montaña – Avenida 8, Calles 2 & 4, every hour

Ask around the market for information on other destinations.

Taxi A ride to San José costs about US$5; a ride to the airport costs about US$8.

AROUND HEREDIA

The small colonial town of **Barva**, 2.5km north of Heredia, was founded in 1561 and is a national historic monument. Its church and surrounding houses date from the 1700s. Although there is no particular building to see, the town as a whole has a pleasant old-world ambience and is fun to stroll around in.

A short distance south of Barva is the famous **Café Britt Finca** (☎ 260-2748, fax 238-1848, turismo@cafebritt.com), which does 'coffeetours.' These begin with a visit to the coffee finca and continue with a bilingual (Spanish-English) multimedia presentation using actors to describe the historical importance of coffee to Costa Rica. The tour also shows parts of the production process. The presentation finishes with coffee-tasting sessions led by experienced coffee cuppers (as the tasters are called). It's a real eye-opening experience! Then you can buy as much coffee as you want along with coffee paraphernalia at the Café Britt gift shop.

'Coffeetours' are held at 9 and 11 am year-round and cost US$20 (or US$25 if you go from San José). The Café Britt bus will pick you up from major San José hotels – call for a reservation. If you drive or take the bus, you can't miss the signs between Heredia and Barva.

Other tour choices include combining this tour with the Butterfly Farm (see the Butterfly Farm entry, earlier in this chapter) or with a visit to the Museo de Cultura Popular (☎ 260-1619) in Santa Lucía de Barva, about 1.5km southeast of Barva. The museum is open 9 am to 4 pm daily and is housed in a century-old farmhouse that is restored with period pieces and gives a look at late 19th-century life in rural Costa Rica. Admission costs US$1.50. A combined Café Britt/museum tour runs at 3 pm from December to May and costs US$25 from San José. From mid-November to mid-March, a full-day tour visiting Volcán Poás, an organic coffee farm (where you can pick coffee), and a working coffee mill, and including a typical lunch costs about US$80 from San José. The all-day tours are led by an agronomist guide and go with a minimum of four people.

West and then north of Barva, buses go to **San Pedro de Barva** (where there is a coffee research station) and on to **Santa Bárbara** (where there is an exclusive hotel – see below).

About 1km north of Barva, the road forks. The right fork continues to the village of **San José de la Montaña**, about 5km north of Barva. The village is pleasantly located at about 1550m on the south slopes of Volcán Barva. The higher elevation gives a fresh nip to the air, and you should bring some warm clothes, particularly if you're staying overnight in one of the country inns north of the village. From San José de la Montaña, three buses a day continue toward **Sacramento**, and this is the route to the trails up Volcán Barva, part of Parque Nacional Braulio Carrillo.

Three kilometers northeast of Heredia is San Rafael de Heredia, where a road leads about 8km north to **Monte de la Cruz** and its inexpensive restaurant that serves local food. Here are great views of the mountains, the Central Valley, and San José. There is pleasant hiking in the area.

A couple of kilometers before you get to Monte de la Cruz is the **Club Campestre El Castillo** (☎ 267-7111, 267-7115); you can use its facilities for a few dollars. Among the attractions are a pool, sauna, ice-skating rink (in the tropics!), and go-carts. There is a restaurant, bar, and picnic area, and camping is allowed.

Some 5km east of San Rafael is San Isidro de Heredia, which has a couple of B&B hotels (see below).

In the village of Santo Domingo de Heredia, about halfway between Heredia and San José, is the **Museo Joyas del Trópico Húmedo** (☎ 244-5006, ☎/fax 236-4521), 100m east of the Santo Domingo cemetery. The name of the museum means 'Jewels of the Humid Tropics' – the jewels are some 50,000 insects, spiders, centipedes, and crustaceans that make up the lifetime collection of a North American biologist who now resides in Costa Rica. Museum visits feature education and fun, including interpretive tours and videos, and even sing-alongs! Hours are 9 am to 5 pm daily except Sunday, when hours are 10 am to 6 pm. Admission, including a tour, costs US$5 for adults, US$2.50 for children.

Places to Stay

Santa Bárbara Just before Santa Bárbara is the ***Finca Rosa Blanca*** *(☎ 269-9392, fax 269-9555; in the USA, SJO 1201, PO Box 025216, Miami, FL 33102-5216, rblanca@sol.racsa.co.cr)*, one of the most exclusive small country hotels in Costa Rica. It has only eight suites (two are two-bedroom garden villas), ranging in cost from US$157 to US$250 single and US$174 to US$273 double, including full breakfast. Extra people are charged US$25 each; kids three to 12 pay half-price.

The most expensive room is surreal: a tower with a 360° view reached by a winding staircase made of a single tree trunk. The bathroom is painted like a tropical rainforest and has water flowing out of an artificial waterfall – not your run-of-the-mill hotel bathroom! The other rooms, all different, are also intriguing and feature murals, handmade furniture, and interesting modern architecture. All rooms have a private patio or deck. There is a lovely outdoor pool, a game room, a library, and a restaurant and bar for the guests. A top-notch four- or five-course dinner (about US$25) may be reserved in advance. The owners and staff are gracious and helpful with tour reservations and airport pickups.

San José de la Montaña A few kilometers north of San José de la Montaña (and at a higher elevation) are several comfortable country hotels, all known for their attractive settings. Pleasant walks and birding are the main activities. Although three buses a day (from Heredia to Sacramento) come close to the hotels, they will provide you with courtesy pickup. Alternatively, get a taxi from San José de la Montaña. The hotels are small and sometimes close temporarily midweek if there is no demand. During the weekends, they may well be full with locals, so you should call first to make reservations, get precise directions, or arrange to be picked up.

Las Ardillas Resort *(☎/fax 260-2172, ardillas@sol.racsa.co.cr)* has seven cabins, each with its own fireplace, kitchen area, and accommodations for two to four people, and another seven cabins nearby in its Cabañas Las Milenas annex. There is a spa and a restaurant. A massage with a US-trained physical therapist costs US$30, and mud treatments cost US$20. The per-cabin rate is US$60 double including breakfast; ask about long-stay discounts.

The ***Hotel El Cypresal*** *(☎ 237-4466, fax 237-7232, Apartado 3094-1000, San José)* has two dozen standard rooms with terraces, fireplaces, TVs, and private hot showers. There's a small swimming pool, a sauna, horse rental, and a restaurant. Rates are US$30/40 single/double.

The ***Hotel El Pórtico*** *(☎ 260-6000, 237-6022, fax 260-6002, Apartado 289-3000, Heredia)* has 18 heated rooms, a restaurant, sauna, and pool. Horses can be rented. The room rate is about US$40 double, and it is very popular with ticos.

Monte de la Cruz Between Monte de la Cruz and Club Campestre El Castillo, you'll find a recommended small country hotel, the ***Hotel Chalet Tirol*** *(☎ 267-6228, fax 267-6229, info@chalet-tirol.com)*. It has a variety of comfortable suites set at 1800m in the foothills of the Cordillera Central. There is a good French restaurant and tennis courts. Pleasant trails head into the cloud forest on the grounds and beyond, and horses are available for rent. Trout fishing and birding are other activities. The rate is US$90 double, depending on the suite. The staff will pick you up from San José or the airport for an extra US$15; reservations are recommended. (This hotel also manages the Dundee Ranch Hotel near Carara.)

Santo Domingo de Heredia Another good country hotel is the ***Bougainvillea Santo Domingo*** *(☎ 244-1414, fax 244-1313, bougain@sol.racsa.co.cr)* in Santo Domingo de Heredia, about halfway between Heredia and San José. There are orchards on the extensive grounds, and there is a restaurant, pool, and tennis court. Free shuttle buses run to San José, and tours and car rental can be arranged. The rooms with balconies cost US$75/87 single/double.

Coffee farms blanket the Heredia countryside.

San Isidro de Heredia This village is about 8km northeast of Heredia. ***Debbie King's Country Inn/B&B***, formerly Finca Wa Da Da *(☎/fax 268-8284, 380-8492 cellular; in the USA, SJO 381, PO Box 025216, Miami, FL 33102-5216, debbiek@costarica.net)*, is in a small fruit and coffee farm and has nice views. The owner personally arranges tours and is helpful. Three 2nd-story rooms in the main house all have balconies and views and rent for US$41/57/68 single/double/triple including full breakfast. Two guesthouses with kitchens and private hot baths will sleep six people. The rate is US$68 double plus US$10 for each additional person. Airport pickup costs US$15 for two people. The inn is a couple of kilometers from the center of San Isidro; call for directions.

PARQUE NACIONAL BRAULIO CARRILLO

This national park is a success story for both conservationists and developers. Until the 1970s, San José's links with the Caribbean coast at Puerto Limón were limited to the (now defunct) railway and a slow narrow highway. A fast, paved, modern highway was proposed as an important step in advancing Costa Rica's ability to transport goods, services, and people between the capital and the Caribbean coast.

This development was certainly to Costa Rica's economic advantage, but the most feasible route lay through a low pass between Volcán Barva and Volcán Irazú to the northwest of the Central Valley. In the

1970s, this region was virgin rainforest, and conservationists were deeply concerned that the development would lead to accompanying colonization, logging, and loss of habitat, as well as damage to the watershed that is the single greatest source of water for the San José area.

A compromise was reached by declaring the region a national park and allowing this one single major highway to bisect it. This effectively cuts the region into two smaller preserved areas, but it is considered one national park.

Parque Nacional Braulio Carrillo (named after Costa Rica's third chief of state) was established in 1978. The San José-to-Guápiles highway was completed in 1987, and 45,899 hectares have been protected from further development. The pristine areas to either side of the highway are large enough to support and protect a great and varied number of plant and animal species, and San José has its much-needed modern connection with the Caribbean coast.

The way most people see the park is simply by riding through it on one of the frequent buses traveling the new highway between San José and Guápiles or Limón. The difference between this highway and other roads in the Central Valley is marked; instead of small villages and large coffee plantations, the panorama is one of rolling hillsides clothed with thick montane rainforest. About 75% of Costa Rica was rainforest in the 1940s; now less than a quarter of the country retains its natural vegetative cover, and it is through parks such as Braulio Carrillo that the biodiversity represented by the remaining rainforest is protected.

The buses traveling the new highway may stop on request, but most passengers just gaze out of the window and admire the thick vegetation covered with epiphytes (air plants) such as bromeliads and mosses. On the steepest roadside slopes are stands of the distinctive huge-leafed *Gunnera* plants that quickly colonize steep and newly exposed parts of the montane rainforest. The large leaves can protect a person from a sudden tropical downpour – hence the plant's nickname is 'poor folks' umbrella.' A walk into the forest will give you the chance to see the incredible variety of orchids, ferns, palms, and other plant life, although the lushness of the vegetation makes viewing the many species of tropical animals something of a challenge. You will certainly hear and see plenty of birds, but the mammals are more elusive.

Part of the reason why there is such a huge variety of plant and animal life in Braulio Carrillo is that it encompasses a wide spread of altitudinal zones. Elevations within the park range from the top of Volcán Barva (2906m) to less than 50m in the Caribbean lowlands. Five of the Holdridge Life Zones are represented, and the differences in elevation create many different habitats.

A visit to the park can consist of anything from sightseeing from a bus crossing the park to a difficult and adventurous trip of several days, climbing Volcán Barva and perhaps the nearby Volcán Cacho Negro (2150m) before descending to the lowlands on foot. The observant naturalist may see Costa Rica's most famous bird, the resplendent quetzal, as well as umbrella birds, toucans, trogons, guans, eagles, and a host of other avifauna.

Mammals living in the park include cats such as the jaguar, puma, and ocelot, and also tapirs and sloths, all of which are difficult to see. More likely sightings include peccaries or any one of the three species of monkeys present in the park.

Orientation & Information

There are two main ways to access the park. One is from the new highway; the second is from the road north of San José de la Montaña toward Sacramento (see Getting There & Away, later in this section). On both these routes are ranger stations where you can get further information, though the station on the second route doesn't keep regular hours.

The park entrance on the new highway is about 20km northeast of San José. From the highway toll booth (US$1 for cars), continue on the new highway almost 2km to the Puesto Zurquí ranger station on the right, where there is a short nature trail (but no other facilities). Less than 1km past the station, the road goes through the 600m-long

Túnel Zurquí. About 22km beyond the tunnel is the Quebrada González ranger station on the right – keep your eyes peeled or you'll miss it. It's open 8 am to 3:30 pm Tuesday to Sunday. There is a guarded parking lot, toilets, and two 1.5km-long walking trails. The usual US$6 per person national park fee applies. The gate isn't normally locked, so if you arrive before 8 am, you can open the gate, park, hike, and pay when you return.

Note that there is no fee to simply drive through the park. Also note that, although there are numerous restaurants along the highway out of San José, they peter out by the time you reach the toll booth and there are none afterward for many kilometers. It is possible to get to the park by public bus, but this is not recommended because on the way back you have to walk 2km along the highway to reach a stop at a restaurant; a vulnerable position (see below).

Warning Unfortunately, there have been many reports over the last few years of thefts from cars parked at entrances to other trails, as well as armed men robbing tourists hiking on the trails or walking along the highway. Readers have reported hearing shots fired on the trails, and hitchhikers have reported being told it is a dangerous area. Don't leave your car parked anywhere unless there is a park ranger on duty, such as at Quebrada González.

CENTRAL VALLEY

Rainforest Aerial Tram

The Rainforest Aerial Tram is the brainchild of biologist Don Perry, one of the pioneers of rainforest canopy research. He first started exploring the canopy using rope-climbing techniques in 1974 and began stringing ropes together into a canopy-exploration web in 1979 (see the June 1980 *Smithsonian* magazine). In 1984, he started work on an Automated Web for Canopy Exploration (AWCE) in Rara Avis (see the Northern Lowlands chapter), and in 1992 he began construction of the Rainforest Aerial Tram. It opened in late 1994 and is located just past the northeastern exit from Parque Nacional Braulio Carrillo (on the right coming from San José).

The 2.6km aerial tram has 22 cars, which each take five passengers and a naturalist guide. The ride is designed to go silently through and just over the rainforest canopy and takes 45 minutes each way, thus affording riders a unique view of the rainforest and unusual plant and birding opportunities. Although there are platforms, ropes, and walkways in the rainforest canopy in Costa Rica and other countries, this is the first time (that I know of) that a canopy project on this scale has been accessible to the general public anywhere in the tropics.

Amazingly, the whole project was constructed with almost no impact on the rainforest. A narrow footpath follows the tram and all the 250,000kg of construction material was carried in on foot or by a cable system to avoid erosion, with the exception of the 12 towers supporting the tram that were helicoptered in by the Nicaraguan Air Force (Costa Rica has no armed forces!). The pilot involved in the project called it 'the best work' he had ever done.

There is a 400-hectare reserve around the tram, and visitors often go for a guided introductory hike (about an hour) before embarking on the tram. Three kilometers of the reserve boundary is contiguous with Parque Nacional Braulio Carrillo. Perry emphasizes, and I concur, that this is not a zoo and the numbers of animals seen will not be high, although many have been recorded in the area – about 118 species of reptiles and amphibians, 300 species of birds, 85 species of bats, and about 50 other mammals.

The sheer density of the vegetation makes observing animals difficult. Mammals are spotted only very occasionally, though there are fairly good opportunities to get close to rain-

Unfortunately, the Servicio de Parques Nacionales (SPN) doesn't have the money to patrol most of the park. An alternative is to go with an organized tour, but even these are prone to being robbed if the group is very small. This situation may improve in the near future, but exercise extra caution in the meantime.

Climbing Volcán Barva

Use the park entrance via San José de la Montaña if you plan to climb this volcano. From the road, foot trails go to the summit of Barva, which is climbable in about four or five hours roundtrip at a leisurely pace. A trail goes from Paso Llano (Porrosatí) to the summit of Barva (about 9km) and returns to Sacramento. However, at last check the trail from Paso Llano was reported to be badly overgrown and poorly maintained. Most people go from Sacramento, about 5km beyond Paso Llano. There is a guard post near Sacramento, open at erratic hours. Sometimes the rangers will take you to the top: about 4km one way.

The trail up Barva from Sacramento is fairly obvious, and it's marked by a sign. On the park border, near the guard post, is a small cabin; to arrange accommodations call ☎ 283-5906, and they will contact the rangers by radio at Cordillera 13. If you wish to continue from Barva north into the lowlands, you will find that the trails are not marked and not as obvious. It is possible, however, to

Rainforest Aerial Tram

forest birds. The best time to go is first thing in the morning, though most tours arrive later. When I went at about 9 am, I had the opportunity to glimpse an unusual white bat as well as get a nice close view of a pair of toucans. The most lasting impression, though, is of silently swooping through the different layers of rainforest, sometimes just a meter above the ground and at other times 30m above a chasm clothed in trees. Certainly, riding the tram was a memorable experience and one that I would recommend.

It doesn't come cheaply, however, and several budget travelers have complained to me that it's too expensive. Personally, I think the experience is unique enough to warrant the cost, but you'll have to decide for yourself.

The Rainforest Aerial Tram (in San José ☎ 257-5961, fax 257-6053, doselsa@sol.racsa.co.cr) is open 6 am to 3:30 pm every day of the year. (The tram stays open until dusk.) Note that on Mondays no trams run until 9 am (for maintenance), although you can enter and walk around. There is a guarded parking lot at the entrance, where tickets are sold, but it's worth getting tickets in advance to save time. The San José office is at Avenida 7, Calles 5 & 7, and is open 7 am to 6 pm on weekdays and till 4 pm on weekends, or you can buy tickets through a travel agent. Tickets cost US$49 (half-price for students and five- to 18-year-olds; children under five are not permitted). From the parking lot, a truck takes you about 3km to the tram loading area, where there is a small exhibit/information area (there was a live pit viper there once – on a log, not in a cage!) and a restaurant and gift shop. Here, you can see an orientation video, and there are short hiking trails that you can use for as long as you want. Tram riders should be prepared for rain – although the cars have tarpaulin roofs, the sides are open to the elements.

If you are not driving, you can take a bus to Guápiles (under US$2, every 30 minutes, from the Caribe terminal in San José) and ask the driver to drop you at the entrance. The people at the entrance will help you flag down a return bus. Alternately, for US$65, you can arrange a tour with a bus pickup from major San José hotels to the tram and return. Allow about eight hours for this.

– Rob Rachowiecki

follow northbound 'trails' (overgrown and unmaintained) all the way through the park to La Selva near Puerto Viejo de Sarapiquí. A tico who has done it told me that it took him four days and is a bushwhacking adventure only for those people used to roughing it and able to use a map and compass.

The slopes of Barva are one of the best places in the park to see the quetzal. Near the summit are several lakes; the biggest are Lagos Danta, Barva, and Copey, with diameters of 500, 70, and 40m, respectively. Camping is allowed anywhere you can pitch a tent, but no facilities are provided, so you must be self-sufficient.

There is plenty of water (the park receives between 3 and 6m of rain per year depending on locality), and there are innumerable lakes, streams, and waterfalls. This means that trails are often very muddy and that you should be prepared for rain at any time of year.

The best time to go is supposedly the 'dry' season (from December to April), but it is liable to rain then, too, though less than in the other months. If you're going on a day trip, leave as early as possible, as the mornings tend to be clear and the afternoons cloudy. The night temperatures can drop to several degrees below freezing.

Organized Tours

Only a few companies in San José offer guided day hikes to Volcán Barva, some with bilingual naturalist guides to help with birding – they try to point out quetzals if possible. Try Los Caminos de la Selva (see the Getting Around chapter). The cost is about US$75 per person (four-person minimum), including transportation from San José and lunch. Ask these companies about the current status of trips to Parque Nacional Braulio Carrillo along the main highway.

Getting There & Away

Via the New Highway It is possible to get one of the buses going through the park to Guápiles along the new highway and get off where you want (the Quebrada González ranger station is the suggested place). However, taking a public bus is not recommended, as you will have to flag one down from the highway when you want to leave – this is a problem in part because buses are often full and don't want to stop (especially on weekends), but mainly because it can be dangerous; see the Warning earlier in this section about visiting this area. Hitchhiking is also, for the same reason, not a good idea. Unfortunately for budget travelers, the best options are to go on a tour or hire a car.

Via San José de la Montaña For the entrance via San José de la Montaña, three buses a day (currently at 6:30 and 11 am and 4 pm) leave Heredia for Paso Llano (Porrosatí on some maps) and Sacramento. Ask the driver to set you down at the track leading to Volcán Barva. During the wet season, the bus might not make it up to Sacramento, when 4WD may be necessary. The bus returns at 5 pm. It's about 13km from San José de la Montaña to the park entrance.

MORAVIA

This village is named San Vicente de Moravia or San Vicente on many maps but is known as Moravia by the local inhabitants. It's about 7km northeast of San José and used to be the center for the area's coffee fincas. Today, the village is famous for its handicrafts, especially leather, but also ceramics, jewelry, and the ubiquitous wood.

The best-known store (it's been there for three-quarters of a century) is the Caballo Blanco (☎ 235-6797) on the corner of the spacious and attractive Parque Central. It started as a saddle shop but now sells a good variety of leather and other goods. Other good stores nearby include La Rueda (home to an odd pair of the world's largest birds), Artesanía Bribri (which sells work made by the Bribri Indians of the Caribbean slope), La Tinaja, Ceramicas Buchanan, and many others.

The Mercado de Artesanías Las Garzas (☎ 236-0037) is a mall-like complex with arts & crafts stores, simple restaurants serving tico food, and clean toilet facilities. It's 100m south and 75m east of the *municipio* (town hall). It is open 8:30 am to 6 pm daily except Sunday (9 am to 4 pm). Shoppers who are planning a spree should note that some stores are closed on Sunday, especially in the low season.

There are frequent buses (Nos 40, 40A, and 42) from Avenida 3, Calles 3 & 5, in San José to (San Vicente de) Moravia. A taxi from San José costs about US$2.

CORONADO

This is the general name for several villages centered on San Isidro de Coronado, about 6km east of Moravia. About 1km before San Isidro de Coronado is San Antonio de Coronado, and close to this is Dulce Nombre de Coronado.

San Isidro de Coronado is at 1383m above sea level, 200m higher than San José. It is a popular destination during the dry season for josefinos looking for an escape from the city. There are some simple restaurants but no accommodations. The ***Lone Star*** is a popular steakhouse where the well-respected Costa Rican classical composer Fulvio Villalobos Sandoval occasionally puts on a hilarious country-western performance at the piano, singing in English and Spanish. The village has an annual fiesta on May 15.

Instituto Clodomiro Picado

The main reason to visit Coronado is to see the snake 'farm' at Instituto Clodomiro Picado (☎ 229-0344, 239-3135, fax 292-0485) at Dulce Nombre.

The institute is run by the University of Costa Rica and has a selection of local poisonous snakes on display. At 2 pm on Friday, visitors can see the snakes being 'milked' for their poison, which is then used to make antivenin. On other days of the week, the visitor must be content with the opportunity to view the snakes, learn about the serum-making process, or buy some serum. The institute is open 9 am to noon and 1 to 4 pm weekdays; entrance is free.

Getting There & Away

Take a bus from Avenida 3, Calles 3 & 5, in San José. From San Isidro, it is 1km or so back to the snake institute – ask the bus driver for directions. It is a pleasant downhill walk back to Moravia, about 6km away.

LOS JUNCOS

The road east of San Isidro continues through Las Nubes to Los Juncos, a private cloud forest preserve on the southern edge of Parque Nacional Braulio Carrillo. The preserve, approximately 1350 hectares, is the largest tract of privately owned virgin forest left in the Central Valley. There are excellent birding and wildlife-watching opportunities here. There is also a farmhouse that once belonged to two ex-presidents of Costa Rica.

Los Juncos is owned and managed by Green Tropical Tours (☎ 229-4192, fax 292-5003, information@greentropical.com), which offers one-day tours for US$75 per person (two-person minimum) including transportation from San José, a bilingual naturalist guide, breakfast, and lunch. It will also do overnight trips for US$160 per person (six-person minimum preferred), which includes sleeping at the rustic farmhouse (bunk beds, shared bathrooms) and eating hearty country cooking. This seems like a good way to beat the crowds!

RANCHO REDONDO

This little community is a pleasant 16km drive east of San José. The road climbs slowly to about 2000m, giving picturesque views of agricultural countryside and San José.

Hacienda San Miguel *(☎ 229-5058, ☎/fax 229-1097)* is a beautiful country lodge with spa, sauna, pool (both the swimming and the snookering varieties!), and a relaxing recreation area with a fireplace. Room rates range from US$38 to US$76 double, including breakfast. The hacienda operates horseback tours through rainforest on the 400-hectare property.

Most people drive here, but buses for Rancho Redondo (Route 47) leave San José from Avenida 5, Calles Central & 2.

Cartago Area

CARTAGO

This is the fourth provincial capital of the Central Valley, and the most historic one. The city was founded in 1563 and was the capital of the country until 1823. Unfortunately, major earthquakes in 1841 and 1910 ruined almost all the old buildings, and there is not a great deal of architecture left to see.

Cartago was built at an elevation of 1435m in the valley between the Cordillera Central and Cordillera de Talamanca; Volcán Irazú looms nearby.

The metropolitan area, including the densely settled suburbs, has a population of about 120,000 and is the nation's third-largest urban area. It's 22km southeast of San José, and the two cities are connected by a good road and frequent buses.

Information

There is no tourist office. Several banks in the town center change money; Banco Interfin (☎ 591-1000), Avenida 2, Calle 2, is usually faster than most. The Hospital Max Peralta (☎ 551-0611) is located at Calle 5, Avenidas 1 & 3.

Churches

The most interesting sights in Cartago itself are churches. The church at Avenida 2, Calle 2, was destroyed by an earthquake in 1910. **Las Ruinas** (The Ruins) was never repaired, and the solid walls of the church now house a pretty garden. Las Ruinas is a major landmark of downtown Cartago, and it is a pleasant spot to sit on a park bench and watch people go about their business.

East of the downtown area at Avenida 2, Calle 16, the **Basílica de Nuestra Señora de los Angeles** is the most famous church of the Central Valley, if not of all Costa Rica. The Basilica was destroyed in the 1926 earthquake and rebuilt in Byzantine style.

The story goes that a statue of the Virgin was discovered on the site on August 2, 1635, and miraculously reappeared on the site after being removed. A shrine was built on the spot, and today the statue, known as La

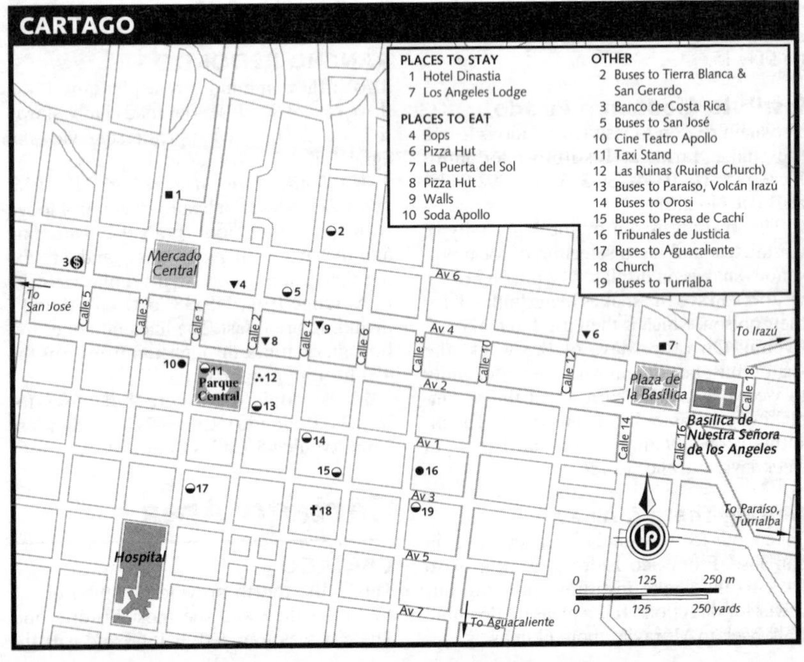

Cartago's Basílica de Nuestra Señora de los Angeles

Negrita, is considered a pilgrimage destination. The Virgin associated with the statue is the patron saint of Costa Rica.

Miraculous healing powers are attributed to La Negrita, and pilgrims from all over Central America come to the Basilica to worship every August 2. There is a procession on foot from San José, 22km away. Inside the Basilica is a chapel dedicated to La Negrita where gifts from cured pilgrims can be seen. The gifts are predominantly metal (including gold) models of parts of the human body that have been miraculously healed.

Other Attractions

A few kilometers out of the city are several interesting sights, the most famous of which is Volcán Irazú (see Parque Nacional Volcán Irazú, later in this chapter). A favorite trip for locals is to the suburb of Aguacaliente, about 5km south of Cartago. Here are natural hot springs that have been dammed to form a swimming pool; it is a popular picnic spot.

Special Events

The annual August 2 pilgrimage to La Negrita at La Basílica de Nuestra Señora de los Angeles is a major Costa Rican event.

Places to Stay & Eat

Most visitors stay in nearby San José. There are only a couple of decent places in Cartago.

Los Angeles Lodge *(☎ 551-0957, 591-4169)*, on the north side of the Plaza de la Basílica, charges US$20/35 for simple singles/doubles with private hot baths and breakfast. The family-run ***Hotel Dinastia*** *(☎ 551-7057)*, 25m north of the market, charges US$8 per person with shared hot bathrooms and US$15/20 with private hot bathrooms; the rooms are nothing special but clean, and laundry service is available. There are some cheap but very basic flophouses near this hotel that are not recommended.

There are no outstanding restaurants, but there are several reasonable places where you can get a meal. Just stroll along the main streets of Avenida 2 and Avenida 4 downtown and take your choice. A few suggestions are marked on the map – ***La Puerta del Sol*** is probably the best for simple tico food. The ***Soda Apollo***, opposite the park, is open 24 hours and has atmosphere. Or, take a picnic lunch to one of the scenic spots in the Cartago area.

Getting There & Away

SACSA (☎ 233-5350) buses leave San José several times an hour from Calle 5,

Avenida 18. Services run from about 5 am to midnight, the journey takes almost an hour depending on the traffic, and the fare is US50¢. There are also hourly night buses.

Buses arriving in Cartago from San José come in on Avenida 2 from the west and head east, stopping every few blocks, until reaching the Basilica, the last stop. Buses from Cartago back to San José (☎ 551-0232) leave from Avenida 4, Calles 2 & 4.

You can also take a *colectivo* (shared) taxi from Avenida Central, Calles 11 & 13, in San José. They charge almost US$2 per person and leave when they have five passengers.

To continue from Cartago to the town of Turrialba, take a TRANSTUSA bus (☎ 556-0073) from Avenida 3, Calles 8 & 10 (in front of the Tribunales de Justicia). There are buses every 30 minutes from 6 to 10:30 am and every hour from 10:30 am to 10:30 pm. It takes about 1½ hours to reach Turrialba and costs less than US$1. Some of these buses originate in San José and come through town on Avenida 3. Space may be limited on these buses.

Local destinations are served by a variety of bus stops; if what you need isn't listed here or if the stop has moved, ask locals for directions. For Paraíso (and the turnoff for Lankester Gardens), the bus leaves from Avenida 1, Calles 2 & 4. For Orosi, the bus leaves from Calle 4 near Avenida 1. For Aguacaliente, the bus leaves from the corner of Calle 1, Avenida 3. For the Presa de Cachí (Cachí Dam), the bus leaves from Calle 6 and Avenida 3. All of these buses are cheap and leave at least every hour.

Buses to Tierra Blanca (a village 18km before Volcán Irazú) leave from Calle 4, Avenidas 6 & 8. Buses leave Cartago at 7 and 9 am for Tierra Blanca, where you can walk or hitch to the volcano. Walkers should remember that the altitude will make the hike a breathlessly difficult one. Buses for San Gerardo (en route to Volcán Turrialba; see later) also leave from this stop, at 6:15 am and 2:30 pm.

There is no daily bus service to Volcán Irazú. You can take a weekend bus from San José, leaving from Avenida 2, Calles 1 & 3 (opposite the Gran Hotel), at 8 am, which also stops in Cartago at 8:30 am outside Las Ruinas and returns from the volcano about 1 pm.

There is a taxi stand on the west side of the plaza and west of the ruined church. You can hire cabs to take you to any of the local destinations. A cab to Irazú costs about US$25 (bargain hard), including a short wait at the crater.

PARQUE NACIONAL VOLCÁN IRAZÚ

The centerpiece of this national park is the highest active volcano in Costa Rica, Volcán Irazú, at 3432m. It is because of eruptions of this and other volcanoes that the soil of the Central Valley is so fertile. Eruptions have been recorded since 1723, when the governor of the (then) Province of Costa Rica, Diego de la Haya Fernández, reported the event. His name is now given to one of the two main craters at the summit.

The last major eruption of Irazú was a memorable one; it occurred on March 19, 1963, the day that US President Kennedy arrived on a state visit. San José, Cartago, and most of the Central Valley were covered with several centimeters of volcanic ash – it piled up to a depth of over half a meter in some places. The agricultural lands northeast of the volcano were rendered temporarily uninhabitable due to the rocks and boulders that were hurled out of the crater. Since that explosive eruption, Volcán Irazú's activity has been limited to gently smoking fumaroles that can be observed by the curious visitor.

The national park was established in 1955 to protect 2309 hectares in a roughly circular shape around the volcano. The summit is a bare landscape of volcanic ash and craters. The Principal Crater is 1050m in diameter and 300m deep, while the Diego de la Haya Crater is 690m in diameter and 100m deep and contains a small lake.

There are two smaller craters, one of which also contains a lake. In addition, there is a pyroclastic cone, formed of fragmented rocks from volcanic activity. A few low plants are slowly beginning to colonize the landscape – if it wasn't for these, you might feel that you were on a different planet. A few high-altitude bird species, such as the volcano junco, hop around. A 1km trail goes from the parking lot to a lookout over the craters. A longer, steeper trail leaves from behind the bathrooms and gets you closer to the craters. Trails are marked by blue and white pedestrian symbols – other 'trails' that are marked by a sign saying *'Paso Restringido'* (Restricted Access) are precarious and should be avoided.

From the summit, it is possible to see both the Pacific and the Caribbean, but it is rarely clear enough for this to be actually possible. The best chances for a clear view are in the very early morning during the dry season (from January to April). It tends to be cold, windy, and cloudy on the summit, with temperatures ranging from -3°C to 17°C and an annual rainfall of 2160mm. Come prepared with warm and rainproof clothes as well as food.

Below the summit is a thicker cloud forest vegetation with oak and *madroño* trees covered with epiphytic plants. The lower you get, the lusher the vegetation. As you emerge from the park boundary, the land is agricultural, with much cattle and dairy farming.

Information

A paved road leads to the summit, where there's a parking lot and a small information center, open 7 am to 5 pm. There is a small café and souvenir shop, but no overnight accommodations or camping facilities. A mobile soda wagon serves simple meals during dry-season weekends. The main gate is open 8 am to 3:30 pm. The entrance fee is US$6 per person.

Organized Tours

Tours from San José will take you to Volcán Irazú for about US$22 to US$40 for a half-day tour, or up to US$60 for a full day combined with visits to Lankester Gardens and the Río Orosi Valley. Many companies will arrange this; see Organized Tours in the Getting Around chapter for recommendations.

Places to Stay & Eat

If you insist on staying on the volcano, there's ***Hotel Gestario Irazú*** *(☎ 253-0827)*, about 11km below the summit. Basic, cold rooms with private heated showers cost in the US$20s, and the restaurant is not always open. The best place to eat is ***Restaurant Linda Vista***, a few kilometers below the summit on your right as you descend, which claims to be the highest restaurant in Costa Rica and is decorated with license plates and business cards from all over the world.

Getting There & Away

Bus Buses Metrópoli (☎ 272-0651, 591-1138) operates a weekend bus to the national park. The bus leaves San José from Avenida 2, Calles 1 & 3, at 8 am on Saturday, Sunday, and holidays (and sometimes on Thursday during the high season). The bus stop is across the street from the front of the Gran Hotel Costa Rica, and the roundtrip fare is US$5. The bus also stops on Avenida 2 in front of the ruined church (Las Ruinas) in Cartago. The return bus leaves the summit parking lot at 1 pm, allowing a little over three hours at the top.

You can also take an early-morning bus from Cartago to Tierra Blanca and walk the remaining 18 or 20km, but it is hard work at this elevation. You could also hitch, but there isn't much traffic midweek.

Car & Taxi In a car, you'll find the road occasionally has signs, but not at every turn. Leave Cartago from the northeast corner of the Basilica on Hwy 8, which goes all the way to the summit. If there is no sign at road forks, either look for the more major-looking road or avoid signs for highways with numbers other than 8 (you will intersect with Hwys 233, 230, 227, and 6 on the way up). It is not difficult to find your way. A taxi from Cartago costs about US$25.

LANKESTER GARDENS

This is an orchid garden run by the University of Costa Rica (☎ 551-9877, 552-3247, fax 552-3151). Originally a private garden run by British orchid enthusiast Charles Lankester, it is now open to the public and is frequently visited by plant lovers. The gardens are about 6km east of Cartago.

You can visit the gardens year-round, but the best time for viewing orchids in bloom is from February to April. With some 800 species of orchid, however, there is always something flowering year-round. Apart from orchids, there are many other plants and an arboretum representing a variety of Costa Rican ecosystems. This trip is recommended to all interested in plants.

Hours are 8:30 am to 3:30 pm daily; admission costs about US$3.50. To get there, catch a Paraíso bus and ask the driver to let you off at the turnoff for Lankester Gardens. From the turnoff, it is 0.75km farther on foot to the entrance; there is a sign.

A taxi costs about US$2 from Cartago, or you can walk the 6km. Tour buses from San José often stop by the gardens on the way to either Irazú or the Río Orosi.

RÍO OROSI VALLEY

This river valley southeast of Cartago is famous for its beautiful views, colonial buildings, hot springs, the lake formed by a hydroelectric damming project, and a national park. Most people visit the valley by taking a tour from San José or by driving their own cars. It is possible to get around by public bus as well.

The first village passed is **Paraíso**, 8km east of Cartago. Here, you can eat at the ***Bar Restaurant Continental*** and other restaurants, which have decent food.

Beyond Paraíso, you have the choice of going east to Ujarrás and the lake formed by the Presa de Cachí (Cachí Dam) or south to Orosi.

From Cartago, buses go to both the village of Orosi and the Presa de Cachí. The two roads are linked by a gravel road. You can drive this road, which is often used by some of the tour groups, in your own car. However, if you are traveling by public bus, you'll have to do one leg of the trip and then backtrack in order to do the other.

East of Paraíso

The Cachí bus will drop you off at the entrance to **Ujarrás**, about 7km east of Paraíso. It's a little over a kilometer to hike in. This village was damaged by the flood of 1833 and abandoned. The waters have since receded and the ruins are a popular tourist sight; the ruined 17th-century church is particularly interesting and is surrounded by a parklike setting. The ruins are open daily from dawn till dusk. Every year, usually the third Sunday in April, there is a procession early in the morning from Paraíso to the ruins, mass is said, and local food and music celebrate the day of La Virgen de Ujarrás (April 16). Information (in Spanish) is available from an office in Paraíso (☎ 574-6656).

A short distance above Ujarrás is a good lookout point for the artificial **Lago de Cachí**. On the north shore of the lake, about a half hour on foot to the east of Ujarrás, is **Charrara**, a government-run tourist complex with a swimming pool, a reasonable restaurant, picnic areas, walking paths, and boats for hire on the lake. It is closed on Monday, which makes this the least-crowded day to visit the area. The hydroelectric dam itself is at the northeastern corner of the lake.

Near the village of Cachí is ***La Casona del Cafetal Restaurant*** *(☎ 533-3280)*, with international food. Main dishes range from US$5 to US$11. It is open 11 am to 6 pm daily, with extended hours till 9 pm on Friday and Saturday and till 10 pm daily in the high season.

This is in an attractive, rural, and not overtoured area.

South of Paraíso

At the beginning of the road to Orosi, a gravel road leads a short way to ***Linda Vista B&B*** *(☎ 747-7632)*, charging US$15 per person with shared hot showers and kitchen privileges. About 2km south of Paraíso are the ***Mirador Sanchirí*** tourist center and cabins *(☎/fax 533-3210, 573-3068, sanchiri@sol.racsa.co.cr)*, with an excellent view of the Río Orosi Valley; there's also a restaurant and picnic area, and a few cabins for rent (US$40 double with private hot baths on high-season weekends, breakfast included).

This area has some of the best views of the entire valley. There are trails, and horses can be rented.

A little farther, the ICT-run ***Mirador Orosi*** also has parking and good views. Adjacent to it is ***Lost in Paradise*** *(☎ 574-6047)*, a café with yummy cookies and coffee as well as light meals. It is closed Monday and Tuesday. Less than a kilometer beyond is ***Hacienda del Río*** *(☎/fax 533-3308)*, with a pool and nice rooms for US$70 double including breakfast.

The bus continues on to the village of Orosi (see below), about 6km farther south. The Orosi bus usually continues about 4km south of Orosi through the villages of **Río Macho** and **Palomo**. Río Macho has a power plant on the river of that name, and there is good fishing here. Near the end of the bus run, just after crossing a large river bridge, look on the left for the ***Hotel Río Palomo*** *(☎ 533-3128, ☎/fax 533-3057, Apartado 220-7050, Cartago)*, which has an adequate restaurant open 7 am to 5 pm daily. The motel has a swimming pool, and cabins with private electric showers cost US$20 single or double (US$10 per additional person). Some cabins with private kitchenettes cost US$30 single or double.

About 5km east of the Río Palomo on the road to Cachí is the **Casa del Soñador** (Dreamer's House), a whimsical house designed and built by the renowned tico carver Macedonio Quesada and now, since his death in 1995, run by his sons. The house, completely built of bamboo and wood, is filled with carvings of local campesinos and religious figures. Many are life-size and carved from the gnarled and twisted roots of the coffee tree, and a selection is available for sale. Entrance is free.

About 4km south of Río Macho, near the village of **Purisil**, is the private **Monte Sky** cloud forest preserve. It is good for birding and has a trail system. The preserve can be entered with a guide for US$8, and you can stay there overnight for US$25, including meals – ask at Montaña Linda in Orosi (see below) for details. There is camping but only cold showers. Also near Purisil are trout ponds where you can fish and pay for what you catch – about US$4.50 per kilo of trout. They'll prepare it for you.

About 2 or 3km beyond Purisil is the friendly ***Kiri Lodge*** *(☎ 284-2024, 533-3040)*, the closest lodging to Parque Nacional Tapantí (see below). Its 50-hectare property has six cabins with hot showers at US$35 double, including breakfast. There's a trout-fishing pond (US$5 per kilo) and a restaurant-bar. You can camp here for US$5. It has access to free trails behind the property leading into the Río Macho Forest Preserve, adjacent to Tapantí, with much of the same wildlife.

OROSI

Orosi was named after a Huetar Indian chief who lived here at the time of the conquest. The town and surrounding district have a population of about 8000 people. The main product here is coffee, and a nearby finca offers tours.

This is one of the few colonial towns to survive Costa Rica's frequent earthquakes. It boasts an attractive church built in the first half of the 18th century – probably the oldest church still in use in Costa Rica. It's on the west side of town. There is a small religious art museum adjacent to the church; it is open 9 am to 5 pm daily except Monday (but call ahead, as hours change), and admission costs US50¢. There are hot springs and swimming pools (US$2, open 7:30 am to 4 pm) on the southwest side of town near the Montaña Linda hostel. There's another set of hot springs, called Los Patios (US$2, open 8 am to 4 pm), about 1km south of town. It's a small place – ask anyone for directions.

Organized Tours

Most travel agencies in San José offer day tours to this area; see Organized Tours in the Getting Around chapter for recommendations. The Montaña Linda hostel (see below) organizes tours throughout the valley and rents bicycles.

Places to Stay & Eat

Montaña Linda *(☎ 533-3640, mtnlinda@sol.racsa.co.cr)* is two blocks south and three blocks west of the bus stop by the soccer field (where you get off from Cartago). It has a fun hostel environment and charges US$5.50 per person, mainly in dormitories, but there are a few doubles for couples at US$8/12. Camping costs US$3.50 per person, US$2.50 if you bring your own tent. There are hot showers and kitchen privileges, and cheap meals are available. Helpful, friendly owners Toine and Sara are a good source of local information and organize tours in the valley. Day trips to Volcán Irazú and Monumento Nacional Guayabo cost US$10 and US$25 per person, respectively, and whitewater rafting costs US$70. Bicycle rental costs US$3 per day. They also run a small, inexpensive language school, which has received recommendations from readers. Maximum class size is three, and teachers live in the village, so even without homestay (which can be arranged), part of the appeal is getting involved with the local community. A basic package of five three-hour classes including breakfast, dinner, and accommodation for six days costs US$120; shorter and longer packages are available, and accommodations at places other than the hostel can be arranged.

Media Libra Cabinas is a new place that reportedly charges about US$30 for doubles with private baths and satellite TVs. The owners of the Pulpería Coto run ***Albergue Montaña Orosi*** *(☎ 533-3032)*, with simple rooms at US$15 single or double. Bathrooms are shared. A new, popular restaurant in the town 'center' is the ***Palacio del Pollo***. There are also some inexpensive but good and friendly sodas.

Getting There & Away

Buses run between Cartago and Orosi about once an hour between 8 am and 10 pm (US30¢ to US45¢, depending on the bus).

PARQUE NACIONAL TAPANTÍ

This 6080-hectare park (a wildlife refuge until 1992) is in wild and wet country on the rainforested northern slopes of the Cordillera de Talamanca. Although not a large park, there are reportedly over 150 rivers within it, which gives an indication of the area's wetness. Waterfalls and trees abound, and the wildlife is prolific, though not easy to reach because the terrain is rugged and the trails are few. Rainfall reportedly is about 2700mm in the lower sections but supposedly reaches over 7000mm in some of the highest parts of the park – maybe you should pack an umbrella. Nevertheless, Tapantí is a popular destination for dedicated birders, and it opens at 6 am to accommodate them.

Quetzals are said to nest on the western slopes of the valley, where the park information center is located. Well over 200 other bird species have been recorded, including eagles and hummingbirds, parrots and toucans, and difficult-to-see forest floor inhabitants such as tinamous and antbirds.

There is a large variety of other animals: amphibians, reptiles, mammals, and butterflies. The rare jaguar, ocelot, jaguarundi, and little-known oncilla (caucel) tiger cat have been recorded here, but more usual sightings include squirrels, monkeys, raccoons, and agoutis. Tapirs are occasionally spotted.

A well-graded dirt road runs through a section of the park and is quite popular with mountain bikers.

Information

The park is open 6 am to 4 pm daily. Admission costs US$6 per person. There is an information center near the park entrance and a couple of trails leading to various attractions, including a picnic area, a swimming hole, and a viewpoint with great views of a waterfall. Fishing is allowed in season (from April to October; permit required), but the dry season (from January to April) is generally considered the best time to visit the refuge, although you should be prepared with rain gear even then. Camping may be allowed with a permit, and you may be able to arrange to sleep in the ranger station or for a ranger to show you around. (See the National Parks & Protected Areas section in the Facts about Costa Rica chapter for general contact information.)

Getting There & Away

If you have your own car, you can take a gravel road (passable year-round) from Orosi through Río Macho and Purisil to the park entrance. Most buses from Cartago to Orosi go as far as Río Palomo, which is a 9km walk from the park (or hire a taxi).

There is a daily early-morning bus from Cartago to Orosi going as far as Purisil, from where it is a 5km walk. A taxi from Orosi costs US$5 to US$10 one way. Several tour companies in San José do day trips. Some of the best are with bilingual naturalist guides from Costa Rica Expeditions or Horizontes, which charge US$99 per person including lunch and entrance fees (four-person minimum). See Organized Tours in the Getting Around chapter for contact information. Cheaper tours are available in Orosi; see above.

Turrialba Area

RÍO REVENTAZÓN

From the northeast end of Laguna Cachí flows one of the more scenic and exciting rivers in Costa Rica, the Río Reventazón. (In fact, the Cachí Dam across the Río Reventazón created this artificial lake.) The river tumbles from the lake at 1000m above sea level and down the eastern slopes of the mountains to the Caribbean lowlands. It is a favorite river for rafters and kayakers; some sections offer Class III and IV white water, while others are relatively flat and placid. Minimum age for rafters is usually nine.

Single- and multiday river trips are offered by several agencies in San José, including Costa Rica Expeditions, which is the oldest and best-known company. Ríos Tropicales, Horizontes, and Aventuras Naturales are also all reputable (see Organized Tours in the Getting Around chapter for contact information). A day trip costs about US$69 to US$85, depending on which section of the river you want to run, and includes the following: roundtrip bus transportation from San José, a breakfast stop in a country restaurant, all river equipment and life jackets, a delicious gourmet picnic lunch on the river, and several hours of guided fun on the thrilling white water. All the guides speak English.

Because of higher and more constant rainfall on the Caribbean side of the country, it is possible to run this river year-round, but June and July are considered the best months.

TURRIALBA

This small town is attractively perched on the Caribbean slope of the Cordillera Central at an elevation of 650m above sea level. It is on the banks of the Río Turrialba, which flows into the Reventazón, 4km to the east.

The town used to be the major stopping point on the old highway from San José to Puerto Limón, but, since the opening of the new highway via Guápiles, Turrialba has been bypassed by travelers heading to the coast and has suffered economically. Nevertheless, it is a pleasant town and makes a good base for several nearby excursions, so tourism, while still very low-key, is increasingly important.

With the surge of interest in river running during the 1980s, the town became somewhat of a center for kayakers and rafters. Turrialba is also an excellent base for visits to the nearby agronomic center (CATIE) and the archaeological site at Guayabo, as well as for climbing Volcán Turrialba – all these are described later in this section.

Turrialba is a minor agricultural center for the coffee fincas in the highlands around the town and the sugarcane and banana plantations in the lowlands to the east. The population of the town and surrounding district is about 70,000.

Information

Change money at the Banco Popular (☎ 556-6098), Banco de Costa Rica (☎ 556-0422), or Banco Nacional (☎ 556-1211). The William Allen Hospital (☎ 556-1133) is at the end of Calle 2. There are also several clinics, pharmacies, and private doctors in the center.

Places to Stay

In Town On the south side of the old railway tracks is the best of the budget places, the clean and friendly ***Hotel Interamericano*** *(☎ 556-0142, hotelint@sol.racsa.co.cr)*. A popular place with river runners, it is run by a mother and daughter who trade time between Turrialba and New York (the global village in

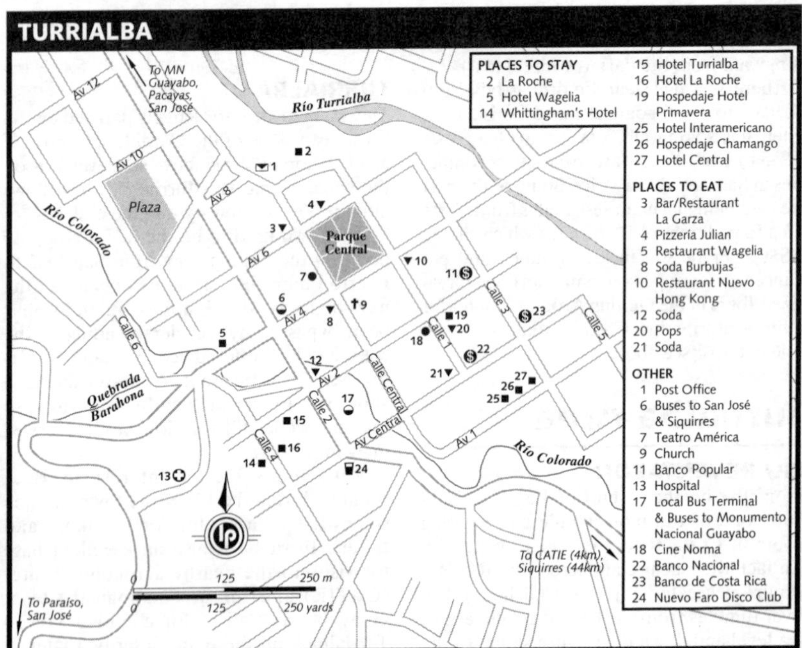

action). They charge US$7 per person for decent rooms with shared baths or US$10 for double rooms with private baths. There is a snack bar and Internet service on the premises. The nearby Hotel Central and Hospedaje Chamango are just a couple of dollars cheaper but are not recommended.

Hotel La Roche *(☎ 556-1624)* is basic but clean, with rates similar to the Interamericano's. Another popular cheapie to try is ***Whittingham's Hotel*** *(☎ 556-8822, 556-6013)*, which has large but rather dark and dismal rooms (though frequent groups of athletic river types brighten the atmosphere). Doubles with private baths and hot water cost about US$12.50. Also, there's the very basic but friendly ***Hospedaje Hotel Primavera*** at about US$4 per person. North of the park on the edge of town (look for signs) is another place called ***La Roche*** *(☎ 556-7915)*, which looks decent and tranquil; rooms with private cold bath cost about US$15 double.

The ***Hotel Turrialba*** *(☎ 556-6654)* has rooms with TVs, fans, and private hot baths for US$13/16. The best hotel in town is the ***Hotel Wagelia*** *(☎ 556-1566, fax 556-1596)*, Avenida 4, Calles 2 & 4, which charges US$30/40 single/double in the 14 standard rooms with private baths, fans, and hot water. Better rooms with air-conditioning, TV, and mini-refrigerator cost US$50 double. However, if you reserve in advance, prices are often US$10 or US$20 higher. Although it's cheaper to just show up, the hotel is often full. The hotel is clean and set in an attractively landscaped garden.

The restaurant on the premises is one of the best in town and has meals in the US$5 to US$10 range. The management will arrange one-day Reventazón river-running excursions and other local trips.

Out of Town There are several small but pleasant country hotels several kilometers east of Turrialba. About 8km away on the road to Siquirres and Limón is the ***Turrialtico*** *(☎ 556-1575, ☎/fax 556-1111, turrialt@sol.racsa.co.cr)*, which is known for the good tico meals served in its restaurant and favored by river runners. Outside, there's a small kids' playground. There are a dozen attractively rustic rooms with private baths and hot water renting for about US$30/36/42 single/double/triple; meals range from US$5 for breakfast to US$8 for dinner. Reservations are recommended. The hotel is set on a little hill and has great views. Management arranges river-running trips and allows camping.

About 11km away from Turrialba, also on the road to Limón, is the ***Pochotel*** *(☎ 556-0111, fax 556-6222)*, a favorite of local river guides. The hotel is above the village of Pavones, and there is a sign for the hotel in the village. There is also a tico-style restaurant here (breakfast costs about US$5, other meals about US$10) and a lookout tower with great views and a small playground for kids. Eight rooms with private baths and hot water cost about US$35 single or double and US$5 for an additional person; again, reservations are recommended.

Both hotels can help arrange nearby excursions or river-running trips. If you call in advance, staff will pick you up in Turrialba, or you can get off the Turrialba-Siquirres bus at the appropriate spot. Both are well recommended.

About 8km southeast of Turrialba is the elegant ***Casa Turire Hotel*** *(☎ 531-1111, fax 531-1075, turire@ticonet.co.cr)*. The three-story building features wide and shady verandahs and is set in well-landscaped grounds with sugarcane, coffee, and macadamia nut plantations nearby. There is a swimming pool, a six hole golf course, and a game room with a pool table. Children under 16 years old are not accepted. Spacious rooms, most with private balconies, hot water, telephones, and cable TVs, cost US$113/130 single/double, and four suites (with refrigerators and king-size beds) go for US$154 to US$237. The most expensive suite has two floors, a balcony that takes up the whole side of the building, and a spa. Breakfast (US$7.50), lunch (US$16), and dinner (US$18.50) are served. Horse and mountain-bike rental and guided walks in the rainforest and plantations are available. This is about as nice as hotels get in Costa Rica.

Other country hotels are found near Monumento Nacional Guayabo and at the Rancho Naturalista, described later in this chapter.

Places to Eat

The hotels ***Wagelia***, ***Turrialtico***, ***Pochotel***, and ***Casa Turire*** all have good restaurants. The ***Restaurant Kingston*** *(☎ 556-1613)*, on the outskirts of town on the road to CATIE and Limón, is the best in Turrialba and has meals from US$3 to US$10 – mostly at the higher end. The locally well-known chef is Jamaican, and this shows in some of the meals.

The following are other restaurants where you can have a decent meal for about US$2 to US$6. ***Pizzería Julian*** is popular with young locals. ***Soda Burbujas***, near the park, is a pleasant place and has good tico meals and fruit shakes. ***Bar/Restaurant La Garza*** has a good variety of seafood, chicken, and meat dishes. The ***Restaurant Nuevo Hong Kong*** serves slightly cheaper Chinese food. An inexpensive (and yet unnamed) locally popular ***soda*** is on the corner of Calle 2 and Avenida 2; another one is at the corner of Calle 1 and Avenida Central opposite the open-air

CENTRAL VALLEY

Breakfast at Cervantes

In Cervantes is a popular country restaurant, ***La Posada de la Luna*** *(☎ 534-4288)*, that serves good local food and is especially popular at breakfast time with river runners on their way to the Reventazón or the Pacuare. The restaurant is cluttered with bits and pieces of Costa Rican history, ranging from old guns and swords to household artifacts to archaeological pieces – an interesting place.

– Rob Rachowiecki

market along the old railroad tracks. For ice cream, there's the ubiquitous ***Pops***.

Entertainment

Turrialba doesn't have much in the way of entertainment. The ***Cine Norma*** looks like it has seen better days. The ***Teatro América*** used to be a movie theater but now is used occasionally for concerts. You can dance at the ***Nuevo Faro Disco Club***.

Getting There & Away

TRANSTUSA (☎ 556-0073) buses from San José to Turrialba leave hourly from Calle 13, Avenidas 6 & 8, and take about two hours. The cost is US$1.25 direct or US$1 with stops. The route runs through Cartago and then either through Pacayas or through Paraíso and Cervantes (see the boxed text 'Breakfast in Cervantes,' above) to Turrialba.

There are two main bus terminals in Turrialba. The main stop on Avenida 4 near Calle 2 serves San José (you can get off at Cartago) with hourly buses. From this stop you can also go to Siquirres (connecting for Puerto Limón), with buses every two hours.

The other terminal is between Avenidas Central & 2 and Calles Central & 2. This terminal has buses serving the local communities such as La Suiza and Tuis every hour, and Santa Cruz three times a day. Buses to Santa Teresita (which travel within 4km of Monumento Nacional Guayabo) leave at 10:30 am and 1:30 pm. Other local communities served include Juan Viñas, Pejibaye, Tucurrique, and Pavones.

Buses to Monumento Nacional Guayabo (☎ 556-0583) also leave from here; at last check the schedule was at 9:30 am on Saturday and Sunday only, returning at 4 pm, allowing several hours at the ruins. On weekdays, the bus leaves at 5 pm and returns at 5:30 am the following day – not convenient for a day trip! Also, a weekday bus at 11 am returns at 12:45 pm – not enough time for a day trip! These may be subject to change, so ask locally.

AROUND TURRIALBA

The Centro Agronómico Tropical de Investigación y Enseñanza, known throughout Costa Rica by its acronym of **CATIE** (which is just as well), is comprised of about 1000 hectares dedicated to tropical agricultural research and education. Agronomists from all over the world recognize CATIE (☎ 556-6431, 556-1149, fax 556-1533) as one of the tropics' most important agricultural stations.

The attractively landscaped grounds of CATIE lie just to the left of the main road to Siquirres, about 4km east of Turrialba. Visitors are allowed to walk around the grounds, and birders will enjoy a visit to the small lake on the site where waterbirds such as the purple gallinule are a specialty. Another good birding area is the short but steep trail descending from behind the administration building to the Río Reventazón.

Those with a serious interest in tropical agriculture are encouraged to visit the facilities at CATIE. These include one of the most extensive libraries of tropical agricultural literature anywhere in the world, a teaching and research facility with student and faculty accommodations, laboratories, greenhouses, a dairy, an herbarium, experimental fruit, vegetable, and forest plots, and a seed bank.

Livestock and seeds suitable for the tropics are available for sale (although these require special permits to be exported). Research interests at CATIE include conservation of crop genetic diversity, high-yield/low-impact farming techniques for small farms, and the development of agricultural strains suitable for tropical environments worldwide.

Although the grounds can be visited without prior arrangement, a tour of the complex should be arranged beforehand, either with one of the tour agencies in San José or direct with CATIE (see numbers above). Tours cost about US$10. Arrangements to obtain seeds or carry out research at the center can be made by writing to CATIE, Turrialba, Costa Rica.

About 10km east of Turrialba, in the village of Pavones (500m east of the cemetery) is **Parque Vibrona**, known for its serpentarium. Here, you can see a variety of Costa Rican snakes, including some unusual albino specimens and several boas, one of which weighs as much as a good-size person. The serpentarium has a rustic visitors' area with educational exhibits. Stop by if you're driving east of Turrialba.

MONUMENTO NACIONAL GUAYABO

Guayabo lies 20km northeast of Turrialba and contains the largest and most important archaeological site in the country. Although interesting, it does not compare with the Mayan and Aztec archaeological sites of Honduras, Belize, Guatemala, and Mexico to the north. Nevertheless, excavations have revealed a number of cobbled roads, stone aqueducts, mounds, retaining walls, and petroglyphs that interested visitors can examine. Some pottery and gold artifacts have been found and are exhibited at the Museo Nacional in San José.

Archaeologists are still unclear about the pre-history and significance of the site. It seems to have been inhabited perhaps as far back as 1000 BC and reached the pinnacle of its development around 800 AD, when some 10,000 people were thought to have lived in the area.

Guayabo is considered an important cultural, religious, and political center, but more precise details remain to be unearthed. The site was abandoned by 1400 AD, and the Spanish conquistadors, explorers, and settlers left us no record of having found the ruins.

The area was rediscovered in the late 19th century by Anastasio Alfaro, a local naturalist and explorer, who began some preliminary excavations and found a few pieces that are now in the Museo Nacional.

In 1968, Carlos Aguilar Piedra, an archaeologist with the University of Costa Rica, began the first systematic excavations. As the importance of the site became evident, it was obviously necessary to protect it, and it became a national monument in 1973, with further protection decreed in 1980. The latest round of excavations began in 1989 and is still underway.

The monument is small, some 218 hectares, and the archaeological site itself is thought to comprise no more than 10% of the total. Most of these ruins are yet to be excavated. The remaining 90% of the monument is premontane rainforest. It is important because it protects some of the last remaining rainforest of this type in the province of Cartago. However, because of its small area, there aren't many animals to be seen. The few that do live in this rainforest, though, are interesting.

Particularly noteworthy among the avifauna are the oropendolas that build colonial sacklike nests in the trees of the monument. Other birds include toucans and brown jays – the latter are unique among jays in that they have a small, inflatable sac in the chest, which causes the popping sound that is heard at the beginning of their loud and raucous calls. Mammals include squirrels, armadillos, and coatis, among others.

Information

The archaeological site is being worked on during the week and sections may be closed to visitors. Opening hours are 8 am to 3 pm; park rangers or trained guides are available to take you around for a nominal fee. This is as much to protect the site as to give you a cheap tour, but it's a good deal anyway!

There is an information center near the monument entrance where you pay the US$6 national park admission fee. There is a small interpretive display, and maps are available. Within the monument are trails, picnic areas, latrines, and running water. Camping is allowed. You can visit the park midweek if you just want to visit the rainforest, bird-watch, picnic, or camp.

Average annual rainfall is about 3500mm, and the best time to go is during the January to April dry season (when it can still rain).

Places to Stay & Eat

Apart from camping in the monument, visitors can stay in the one nearby country hotel, the ***Albergue La Calzada*** *(☎ 556-0465, fax 556-0427)*, less than 1km from the entrance to the monument. It is a small place with a few rooms at about US$16 to US$24, without and with private baths. There is also a fun kids' playground with bicycle-powered swings and boats, as well as a restaurant open to the public.

Calling ahead for reservations is recommended – the friendly and helpful owners will help you with current bus information from Turrialba and pick you up from the bus stop nearest to the hotel.

Getting There & Away

There are buses from Turrialba to Guayabo (the community at the north entrance to the monument), but the schedule should be checked in Turrialba as it changes often.

There are also buses from Turrialba to Santa Teresita (marked as Lajas on just about every map I've seen!) that pass the turnoff to the southern entrance of the monument; it's a 4km walk to the monument from this entrance. You could try hitchhiking or hire a taxi from Turrialba (about US$15 one way). Once you've sussed out the constantly changing bus schedules, your best bet might be to take a taxi in the early morning and return by bus later.

Tours to the monument can be arranged with travel agencies in San José for about US$75 including lunch in Turrialba, and can be combined with visits to Irazú, Cartago, or Lankester Gardens. Green Tropical Tours specializes in this area; see Organized Tours in the Getting Around chapter for details.

VOLCÁN TURRIALBA

This 3329m-high (some sources say 3339m) active volcano is actually part of the Irazú volcanic massif, but it is more remote and difficult to get to than Irazú. The name of the volcano was coined by early Spanish settlers, who named it Torre Alba, or 'white tower,' for the plumes of smoke pouring from its summit in early colonial days. The volcano is only about 15km northwest of Turrialba as the crow flies, but over twice as far by car and continuing on foot.

The last eruption was in 1866. Although the volcano lies dormant today, it is likely that the tranquil farmlands on Turrialba's fertile soils will again be disturbed by earth-shattering explosions sometime in the future.

The summit has three craters, of which the middle one is the largest. This is the only one that still shows signs of activity with fumaroles of steam and sulfur. Below the summit is a montane rain and cloud forest, dripping with moisture and mosses, full of ferns, bromeliads, and even stands of bamboo.

To climb Turrialba, take a bus to Santa Cruz, where a 21km track climbs to the summit. A 4WD vehicle will get you over halfway, then you have to walk. It is reported that horses can be hired from the village of Pacayas (halfway between Turrialba and Cartago), and there are horse trails to the summit. Another approach is to take a bus from Cartago to the village of San Gerardo on the southern slopes of Volcán Irazú. From here, a rough road continues to Volcán Turrialba – it's farther than from Santa Cruz, but San Gerardo, at 2400m, is a higher starting point than Santa Cruz is at 1500m. Either way, hiking the rough roads would be a good trip for backpackers. There are several farms and forests where you can camp. The best time to go is the January to April dry season.

Places to Stay

About 8km northwest of Santa Cruz is the ***Volcán Turrialba Lodge*** *(☎/fax 273-4335, volturri@sol.racsa.co.cr)*, which is accessible by 4WD only (call for directions or they'll pick you up if you have a reservation). Rooms cost about US$57 per person, including all meals. The lodge is high up between the Turrialba and Irazú volcanoes. Visitors report great views and interesting, well-guided tours.

RANCHO NATURALISTA

This 50-hectare ranch is about 20km southeast of Turrialba near the village of Tuis. The ranch has a small 10-room lodge called the ***Albergue de Montaña***, which is popular with birders and naturalists. The North American owners are avid birders who have recorded over 400 species of birds in the area (over 200 species have been recorded from their balcony alone!). Hundreds of species of butterflies can be found on the grounds as well. The ranch lies at 900m above sea level in montane rain and wet forest – there is a trail system. This is a recommended destination for people who would like some quiet days of birding and nature study in a tranquil and undisturbed environment.

Costs here are not cheap, but once you decide to go you'll find almost everything is included. Because the owners wish to maintain a relaxed atmosphere, they ask guests to book for a minimum of three days to enjoy and explore their surroundings at a leisurely pace. Many guests stay for a week. Accommodations cost US$135 per person per day or US$877 per week. Discounts for groups or longer stays are available.

The prices include taxes, roundtrip transportation from San José (if you stay a minimum of three days), three home-cooked meals a day, maid and laundry service, guided birding trips, horseback riding, and (with stays of a week or more) a day trip to another area. About the only things not included are bottled or canned drinks.

Rooms are comfortable and most have private baths and hot water. Three rooms share a bath if the lodge is full. Most rooms have very good or excellent views, one room lacks views, and two have only fair to good views, so check which room you are reserving.

Reservations can be made with the owners, Kathy and John Erb (*☎/fax 267-7138, johnerb@sol.racsa.co.cr*) or with Mark Erb in the USA (*☎ 800-593-3305, fax 870-942-1949, Costa Rica Gateway, 3428 Hwy 46 S, Sheridan, AR 72150*). They'll be happy to send you a description of each room.

RÍO PACUARE

The Río Pacuare is the next major river valley east of the Reventazón (described earlier in this chapter). It is arguably the most scenic rafting river in Costa Rica and one of the world's classic white-water experiences. The river plunges down the Caribbean slope through a series of spectacular canyons clothed in virgin rainforest. The Class IV rapids are exciting and separated by calm stretches that enable you to stare at the near-vertical green walls towering hundreds of meters above the river – a magnificent and unique river trip.

The Pacuare does not lend itself to one-day trips (although they are available) because it is relatively remote and inaccessible – two- or even three-day trips are done more often, with nights spent camping on the riverbanks. During the day, stops are made for swimming and exploring the beautiful tributaries of the main river. Some of these tributaries arrive at the Pacuare in a plunging cascade from the vertical walls of the canyon, and your raft may pass directly beneath the falls.

The usual agencies in San José do this trip. Costa Rica Expeditions provides excellent service. Ríos Tropicales, Horizontes, and Aventuras Naturales are other options. See Organized Tours in the Getting Around chapter for details. The river can be run year-round, though June to October are considered the best months. One-day trips cost US$89, and two-day trips cost about US$250 per person, with seven passengers. Three-day trips cost US$305 per person. Costs are more per person in smaller groups, but you can often join another group to cut costs. Combined tours with other rivers are also available.

Another option is to look for signs in Turrialba; a number of smaller companies advertise around town, offering the possibility of more personalized service and lower prices. One such company recommended by several readers is the tico-owned Ticos River Adventures (☎ 556-1231), which has English-speaking guides and offers day trips for US$70, as well as longer raft trips. Costa Rica Rios Aventuras (☎ 556-9617, reservations@costaricarios.com), also based in Turrialba (look for signs just northeast of the Parque Central), offers kayak trips that have also been recommended by readers. Owner Ray McClain writes a regular column for *The Tico Times* and is a personable and enthusiastic guide. Lessons and trips all around the country can also be arranged.

In 1986, the Pacuare was declared a 'wild and scenic river,' and protected status was conferred upon it by the government – the first river to be so protected in Central America. Despite this, the National Electric

Company began an 'exploratory feasibility study' for a hydroelectric dam.

It is not clear whether the dam would be successful in generating electricity, but it would certainly ruin the Río Pacuare valley by flooding it, thus destroying the most beautiful tropical river valley in Costa Rica, and one of the most beautiful and unique in the world. As of 1999, plans to build a dam are still underway.

In 1994, Ríos Tropicales established the nonprofit Fundación Ríos Tropicales to assist in the preservation, protection, and restoration of Costa Rican rivers. Contact Ríos Tropicales for further information (see Organized Tours in the Getting Around chapter for contact information). In addition, most professional river guides with the other rafting companies are aware of what is happening with river conservation in Costa Rica.

Northwestern Costa Rica

Costa Rica's spectacular central highlands stretch out to the Nicaraguan border. To the northwest of the Cordillera Central lie two more mountain chains, the Cordillera de Tilarán and the Cordillera de Guanacaste.

The Cordillera de Tilarán is characterized by rolling mountains that used to be covered with cloud forest. The famous cloud forest reserve at Monteverde is an important and popular destination for those wishing to see something of this tropical habitat. Separating the Cordillera de Tilarán and Cordillera de Guanacaste are Laguna de Arenal and the nearby Volcán Arenal, currently the most active volcano in Costa Rica and one of the most active volcanoes in the world. It is also the centerpiece of Parque Nacional Volcán Arenal. The spectacular sights and sounds of the eruptions draw visitors to the nearby town of Fortuna.

The Cordillera de Guanacaste is a spectacular string of dormant or gently active volcanoes, five of which are protected in Parque Nacional Rincón de la Vieja, Parque Nacional Guanacaste, and Parque Nacional Volcán Tenorio. To the west of the Cordillera de Guanacaste, shortly before the Nicaraguan border, is the Península Santa Elena, which contains a rare dry tropical forest habitat descending down to remote Pacific beaches. The dry forest and coastline are preserved in the beautiful and historic Parque Nacional Santa Rosa, which is well worth a visit. All in all, this is a very scenic part of Costa Rica and, apart from the Monteverde and Arenal areas, one that is not much visited by foreign tourists.

This next section describes the towns, parks, reserves, and mountains found along the northwestern section of the Carretera Interamericana, while the second section deals with a less frequently traveled route on minor roads around the northeast side of the mountains, past the explosive Volcán Arenal, and connecting eventually with the Interamericana at Cañas. If you have the time, consider taking the rougher back route. Otherwise, the well-paved Interamericana will quickly take you through this spectacular part of Costa Rica.

Interamericana Norte

Overland travelers heading from San José to Managua (Nicaragua) usually take buses along the Interamericana. This highway heads west from San José almost to Puntarenas in the Pacific lowlands and then swings northwest to the Nicaraguan border. The highway from the highlands to the lowlands is steep, winding, and often narrow. Because it is a major highway, however, it is heavily used and is plied by large trucks that hurtle down the steep curves at seemingly breakneck speeds. While the truck drivers probably know the road very well, travelers driving rental cars are advised to keep alert on this road. This advice comes from both the Costa Rican authorities and from me – I've driven it several times and found it a little nerve-racking to take a bend and be confronted by a truck trying to pass another on the narrow road.

The lowlands are reached at the village of Esparza, where there is a popular roadside restaurant and fruit stalls. Tour buses and private cars often stop here for refreshments, but public buses are usually in a hurry to press on. (Esparza is linked with Puntarenas by frequent buses; see the Central Pacific Coast chapter for further information.) Five kilometers beyond Esparza, and 15km before Puntarenas, the Interamericana turns northwest. It continues through the small town of Cañas and the larger city of Liberia before ending up at the Nicaraguan border. Liberia and, to a lesser extent, Cañas are the most important towns in the area and, although not major destinations in themselves, provide transportation and accommodation facilities. The Interamericana Norte provides

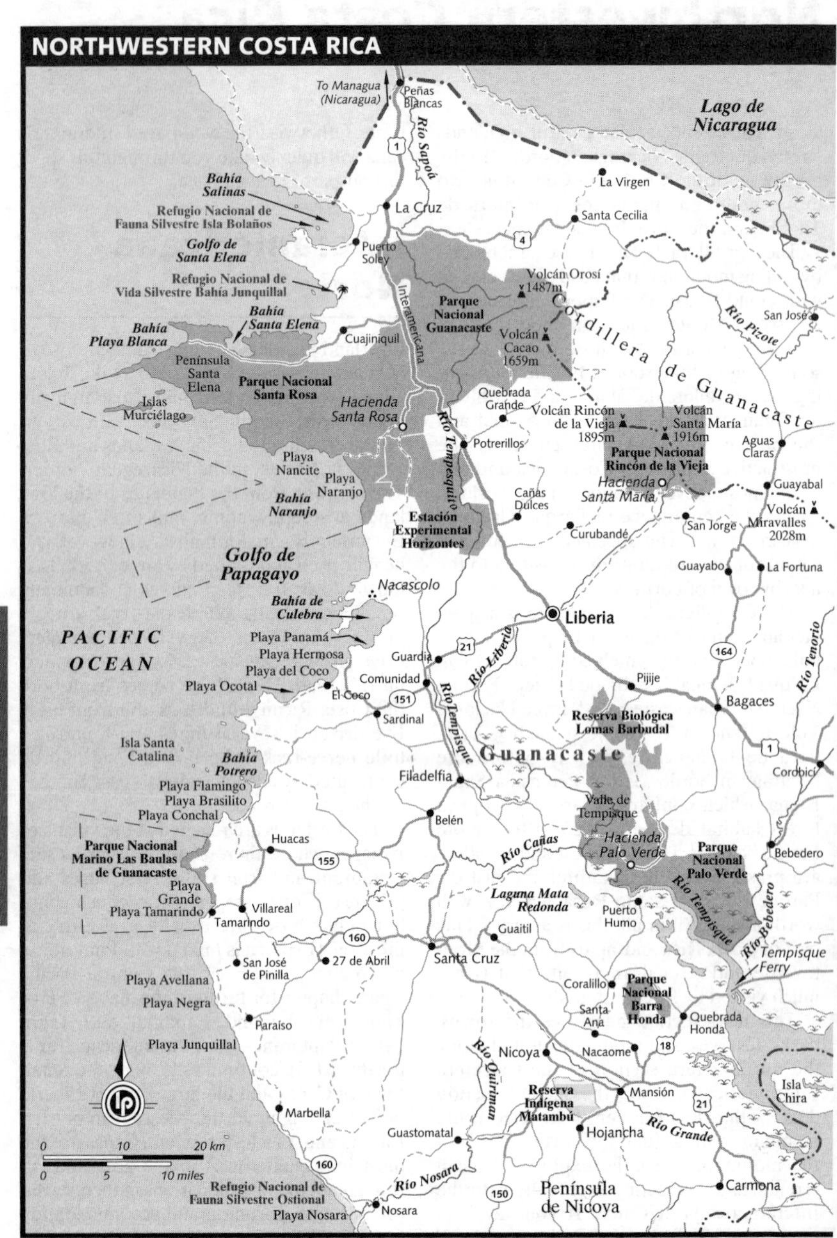

NORTHWESTERN

NORTHWESTERN COSTA RICA
NICARAGUA
Archipiélago Solentiname
San Carlos
Río San Juan
Los Chiles
Río Frío
Llanura de Guatusos
Upala
Caño Negro
Refugio Nacional de Vida Silvestre Caño Negro
Lago Caño Negro
Canalete
Colonia Puntarenas
Río Mónica
Alajuela
Santo Domingo
Bijagua
Llanura de San Carlos
Volcán Tenorio 1916m
San Rafael de Guatuso
Reserva Indígena Guatuso
Parque Nacional Volcán Tenorio
Río Cote
Río San Carlos
Boca Tapada
Lago Coter
Tierras Morenas
Río Tres Amigos
Río Pital
Arenal
Venado
Boca de Arenal
Laguna de Arenal
Unión
Parque Nacional Volcán Arenal
Río Arenal
Río Corobici
Puerto San Luis
Balneario Tabacón
El Tanque de La Fortuna
Muelle de San Carlos
Tilarán
Volcán Arenal 1633m
Fortuna
Pital
Quebrada Grande
Cañas
Chiripa
Parque Nacional Volcán Arenal Ranger Station
Chachagua
Platanar
Reserva Santa Elena
Cordillera de Tilarán
Jabillos
Aguas Zarcas
Ciudad Cutris
Florencia
Venecia
Río Cuarto
La Tigra
Ciudad Quesada (San Carlos)
To Puerto Viejo de Sarapiquí
Interamericana
Santa Elena
Monteverde
Reserva Biológica Bosque Nuboso Monteverde
Río Balsa
Parque Nacional Juan Castro Blanco
Laguna Hule
Juntas
Río Lagarto
Parque Nacional Volcán Poás
Bajos del Toro
Puntarenas
Zarcero
Volcán Poás 2704m
Refugio Nacional de Fauna Silvestre Peñas Blancas
Río Barranca
Rancho Grande
San Ramón
Naranjo
San Pedro de Poás
Miramar
Isla de Los Pájaros
Grecia
Golfo de Nicoya
Reserva Biológica Isla de Los Pájaros
Palmares
Alajuela
To San José
Esparza
Atenas
Ferry
Barranca
Juan Santamaría International Airport
Jicaral
Lepanto
Puntarenas
Robles
To San Mateo
4
6
35
142
141
140
18
1
144
17
3
NORTHWESTERN

the best access to the private cloud forest reserve at Monteverde as well as a host of national parks and reserves.

Views from the highway are spectacular, particularly at the northern end. A seat on the right-hand side of a bus heading north will give you excellent views of the magnificent volcanoes in the Cordillera de Guanacaste.

REFUGIO NACIONAL DE FAUNA SILVESTRE PEÑAS BLANCAS

This 2400-hectare refuge is administered by the Servicio de Parques Nacionales (SPN). Peñas Blancas lies about 6km northeast of the village of Miramar, which itself is 8km northeast of the Interamericana (see the Puntarenas section of the Central Pacific Coast chapter for details on buses to Miramar). The Miramar turnoff is at Cuatro Cruces near the rustic ***Miramar Restaurant***. The Miramar serves tasty and inexpensive food and is a good place to stop after enduring the rigors of the descent from San José.

The road is in fairly good shape as far as Miramar but then deteriorates. You can either hike 6km northeast into the refuge or continue east on a poor road through Sabana Bonita to the tiny community of Peñas Blancas, which is near the refuge and 14km from Miramar. An alternative approach is to head north from the Interamericana at Macacona, which is 3km east of Esparza. A dirt road heads north 20km to Peñas Blancas – 4WD is recommended in the wet months. There are no facilities at Peñas Blancas.

The refuge clings to a steep southern arm of the Cordillera de Tilarán. Elevations in this small area range from less than 600m to over 1400m above sea level. Variation in altitude results in different types of forest, such as tropical dry forest in the lower southwestern sections, semideciduous dry and moist forests in middle elevations, and premontane forest in the higher northern sections. The terrain is very rugged and difficult to traverse – there are two short trails. The refuge was created to protect the plant species in the varied habitats and also to protect an important watershed. Before the refuge's creation, however, parts of the area were logged, which is partly why it is not particularly noted for its animals.

The name Peñas Blancas means 'white cliffs' and refers to the diatomaceous deposits found in the reserve. Diatoms are unicellular algae that have a 'skeleton' made of silica. Millions of years ago, when Central America was under the sea, countless dead diatoms sank to the ocean floor and in places built up thick deposits. Diatomaceous rock is similar to a good-quality chalk. The whitish deposits are found in the steep walls of some of the river canyons in the refuge.

There are no facilities at the refuge. Camping is allowed, but you must be self-sufficient and in good shape to handle the very demanding terrain. There are some hiking trails. The dry season (from January to early April) is the best time to go – it's not likely that you'll see anyone else there.

RESERVA BIOLÓGICA ISLA DE LOS PÁJAROS

This reserve forms part of a small group of islands (Reservas Biológicas Guayabo, Negritos, and Los Pájaros) administered as part of the Area de Conservación Tempisque (ACT), Subregión Cañas (☎/fax 669-0533), from which permission must be obtained to visit. Isla de Los Pájaros (Bird Island) lies less than a kilometer off the coast at Punta Morales, about 15km northwest of Puntarenas. There are no facilities on the 3.8-hectare islet, which has a small colony of nesting seabirds. The predominant vegetation is wild guava.

With help from the ACT authorities, it is possible to charter a boat to visit the island and see the birds, but camping is prohibited and normally landing is limited to researchers working on the birds. Generally speaking, biological reserves were created to protect flora and fauna, and in the more fragile areas part of the protection consists of not encouraging visitors. This is a case in point.

MONTEVERDE & SANTA ELENA

Monteverde is one of the more interesting places in Costa Rica and is one of the most popular destinations for both foreign and local visitors. The name 'Monteverde' refers to a small but spread-out community founded by North American Quakers in 1951 and to the cloud forest reserve that lies adjacent to the community. The entrance point for this area is the village of Santa Elena, a *tico* settlement that, in response to Monteverde's popularity, is developing a tourism infrastructure of its own.

Orientation

Driving from the Interamericana, you will arrive first at Santa Elena. This is where the public bus stop and ticket office (☎ 645-5159) are located, as well as the cheapest *pensiones* and restaurants. The community of Monteverde is spread out along an unpaved road running roughly southeast from Santa Elena. At the end of this road, about 6km from Santa Elena, is the entrance to the Monteverde cloud forest reserve and the visitor center. In between, about 4km from the reserve, is a district locally called Cerro Plano. Hotels of various price levels are strung out along and just off this road.

Five kilometers northeast of Santa Elena is the Reserva Santa Elena. Both this and the Monteverde cloud forest reserve are described following this section. The nearby village of San Luis, south of Monteverde, has an interesting biological station and ecolodge, also described later in this chapter

Various businesses provide detailed maps of the area, many of which were produced

The Quakers of Monteverde

The story of the founding of Monteverde is an unusual one that deserves to be retold. It begins in Alabama with four Quakers (a pacifist religious group also known as the 'Friends') who were jailed in 1949 for refusing to register for the draft in the USA.

After their release from jail, they, along with other Quakers, began to search for a place to settle where they could live peacefully. After searching for land in Canada, Mexico, and Central America, they decided on Costa Rica; its peaceful policies and lack of an army matched their own philosophies. They chose the Monteverde area because of its pleasant climate and fertile land, and because it was far enough away from San José to be (at that time) a relatively cheap place to buy land.

Forty-four original settlers (men, women, and children from 11 families) arrived in Monteverde in 1951. Many flew to San José. They loaded their belongings onto trucks, and a few of the pioneering Quakers drove from Alabama to Monteverde, a journey that took three months. If you think the roads to Monteverde are bad now, imagine what they must have been like five decades ago! The road in 1951 was an ox-cart trail, and it took weeks of work to make it barely passable for larger vehicles.

The Quakers bought about 1500 hectares and began dairy farming and cheese production. Early cheese production was about 10kg per day; today, Monteverde's modern cheese factory produces over 1000kg of cheese daily, which is sold throughout Costa Rica. The cheese factory is now in the middle of the Monteverde community and can be visited by those interested in the process.

There has been talk of paving the really rough road from the Interamericana to Monteverde. Many locals don't want this to happen, though, rightly concerned that a paved road would dramatically change the area for the worse.

Note that due to the Quaker influence and the high level of tourism, much of the local population speaks English and many local places are named in English as well as Spanish. Also remember that there were a few rural Costa Rican families in the area before the Quakers arrived – Geovanny Arguedas (of the Hotel El Sapo Dorado) had grandparents who were among the first tico farmers here.

– Rob Rachowiecki

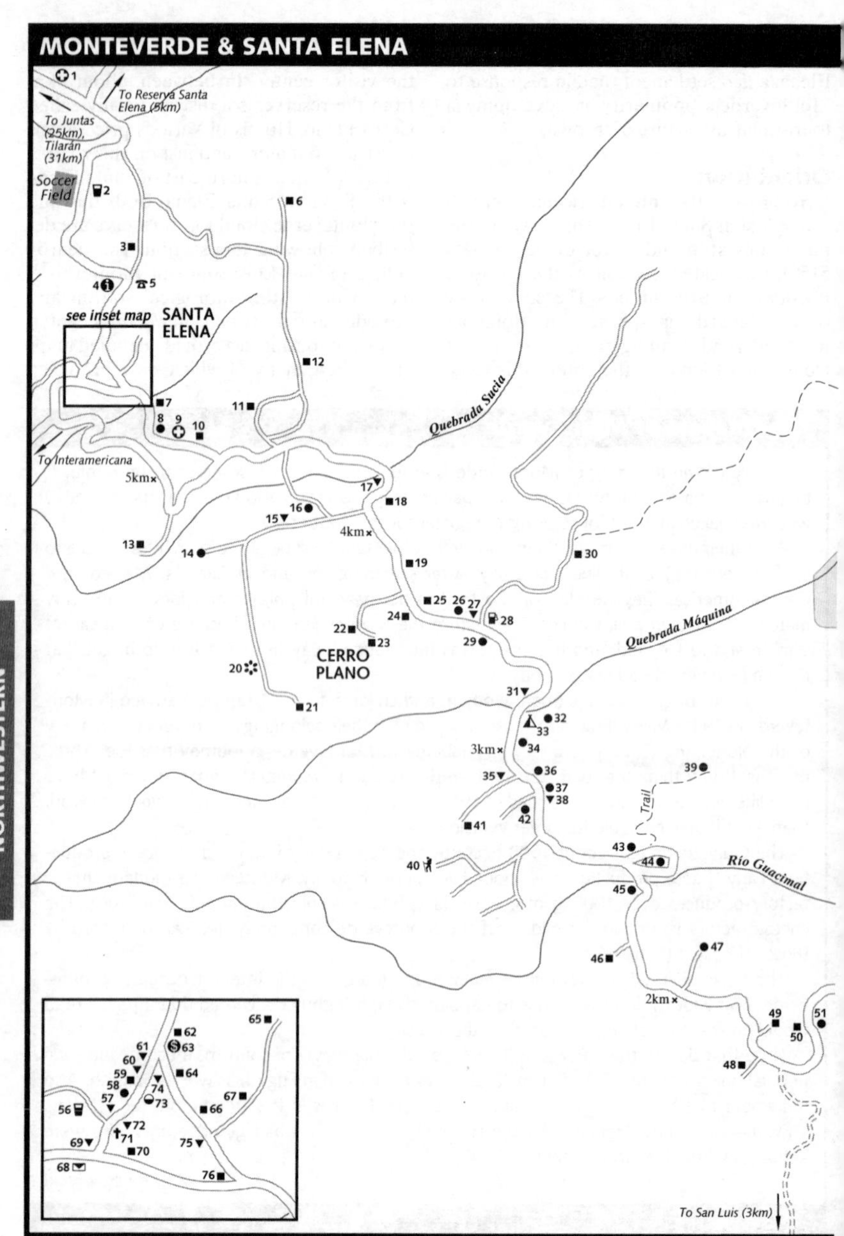
MONTEVERDE & SANTA ELENA
To Reserva Santa Elena (5km)
To Juntas (25km), Tilarán (31km)
Soccer Field
see inset map
SANTA ELENA
To Interamericana
5km
4km
3km
2km
Quebrada Sucia
Quebrada Máquina
Río Guacimal
CERRO PLANO
Trail
To San Luis (3km)
NORTHWESTERN

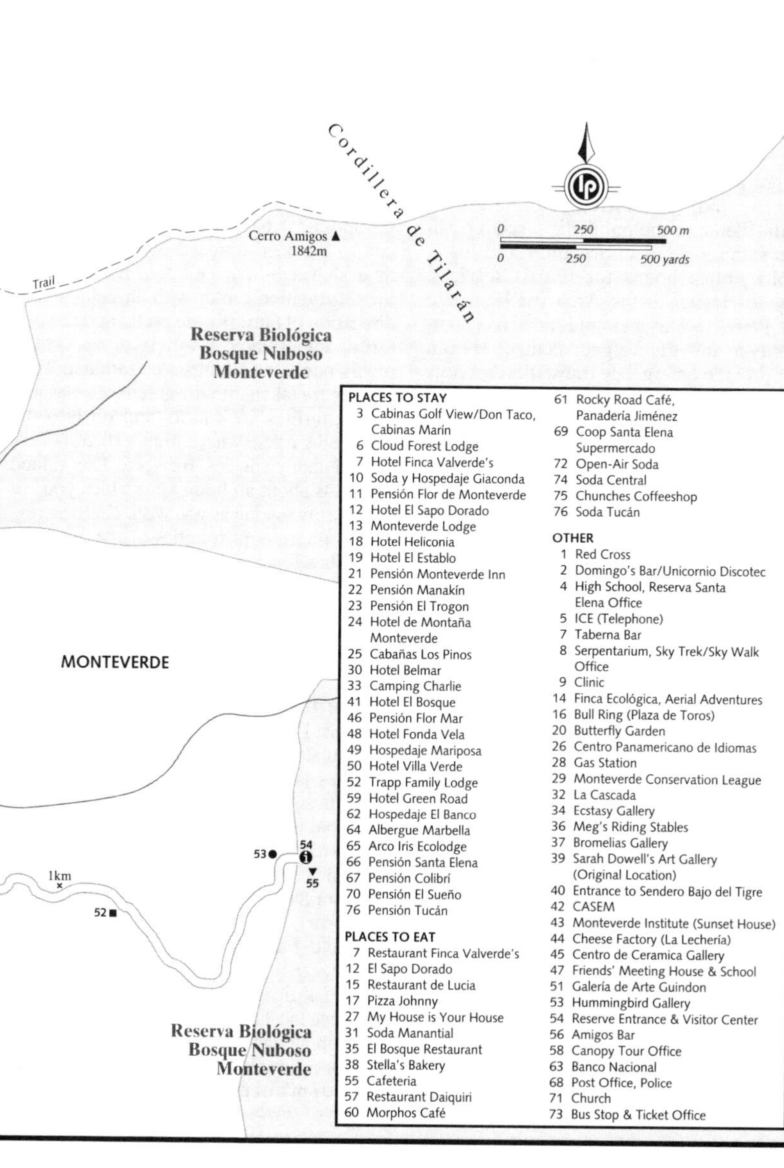
MONTEVERDE & SANTA ELENA
Cordillera de Tilarán
Cerro Amigos ▲ 1842m
Trail
0 250 500 m
0 250 500 yards
Reserva Biológica Bosque Nuboso Monteverde
MONTEVERDE
1km
53
54
55
52
Reserva Biológica Bosque Nuboso Monteverde
PLACES TO STAY
3 Cabinas Golf View/Don Taco, Cabinas Marín
6 Cloud Forest Lodge
7 Hotel Finca Valverde's
10 Soda y Hospedaje Giaconda
11 Pensión Flor de Monteverde
12 Hotel El Sapo Dorado
13 Monteverde Lodge
18 Hotel Heliconia
19 Hotel El Establo
21 Pensión Monteverde Inn
22 Pensión Manakín
23 Pensión El Trogon
24 Hotel de Montaña Monteverde
25 Cabañas Los Pinos
30 Hotel Belmar
33 Camping Charlie
41 Hotel El Bosque
46 Pensión Flor Mar
48 Hotel Fonda Vela
49 Hospedaje Mariposa
50 Hotel Villa Verde
52 Trapp Family Lodge
59 Hotel Green Road
62 Hospedaje El Banco
64 Albergue Marbella
65 Arco Iris Ecolodge
66 Pensión Santa Elena
67 Pensión Colibrí
70 Pensión El Sueño
76 Pensión Tucán
PLACES TO EAT
7 Restaurant Finca Valverde's
12 El Sapo Dorado
15 Restaurant de Lucia
17 Pizza Johnny
27 My House is Your House
31 Soda Manantial
35 El Bosque Restaurant
38 Stella's Bakery
55 Cafeteria
57 Restaurant Daiquiri
60 Morphos Café
61 Rocky Road Café, Panadería Jiménez
69 Coop Santa Elena Supermercado
72 Open-Air Soda
74 Soda Central
75 Chunches Coffeeshop
76 Soda Tucán
OTHER
1 Red Cross
2 Domingo's Bar/Unicornio Discotec
4 High School, Reserva Santa Elena Office
5 ICE (Telephone)
7 Taberna Bar
8 Serpentarium, Sky Trek/Sky Walk Office
9 Clinic
14 Finca Ecológica, Aerial Adventures
16 Bull Ring (Plaza de Toros)
20 Butterfly Garden
26 Centro Panamericano de Idiomas
28 Gas Station
29 Monteverde Conservation League
32 La Cascada
34 Ecstasy Gallery
36 Meg's Riding Stables
37 Bromelias Gallery
39 Sarah Dowell's Art Gallery (Original Location)
40 Entrance to Sendero Bajo del Tigre
42 CASEM
43 Monteverde Institute (Sunset House)
44 Cheese Factory (La Lechería)
45 Centro de Ceramica Gallery
47 Friends' Meeting House & School
51 Galería de Arte Guindon
53 Hummingbird Gallery
54 Reserve Entrance & Visitor Center
56 Amigos Bar
58 Canopy Tour Office
63 Banco Nacional
68 Post Office, Police
71 Church
73 Bus Stop & Ticket Office

by accomplished local cartographer Linda Mather. The map in this book shows only those places that welcome the public. Some maps published for the use of the residents of the zone are not readily available, to protect the privacy of the locals.

Information

There is no general information office; most places advertising tourist information are geared toward steering you into their own hotel or tour. The office of the Reserva Santa Elena, at the public high school, can give some general information and has a public notice board for tourist services. Haymo Heyder at the Arco Iris Ecolodge (see Places to Stay, below) is an active community member and a good contact. He can also provide emergency translation services in English, German, French, Italian, and Dutch for travelers who need assistance with medical or police problems. Please ask for this service only in emergencies.

Chunches Coffeeshop (☎/fax 645-5147), in Santa Elena, is a bookstore/coffee shop with a fine selection of books (many in English), including travel and natural history guides and some US newspapers. It provides public fax services (sending and receiving) and laundry service (US$5 to wash and dry a load). Chunches also serves as a useful meeting place and is a good source of information. It is open 9 am to 6 pm Monday to Saturday.

There is a Banco Nacional (☎ 645-5027) in Santa Elena, open 8:30 am to 3:45 pm weekdays. They will most likely want to see your passport to change US dollars or traveler's checks; they will give cash advances on Visa cards. Most hotels will accept US dollars or change small sums of money. US dollars and traveler's checks in amounts under US$100 can be changed at the upstairs office of the Coop Santa Elena Supermercado (☎ 645-5006) in Santa Elena. Hours are 8 am to noon and 1 to 5 pm on weekdays and 8 am to noon Saturday.

Internet access is available at the Pensión Santa Elena, as well as the Canopy Tour office (see below); ask around for new providers and the best price. Many hotels allow guests to check or send email.

Santa Elena also has a small clinic (☎ 645-5076), which is closed from 3 pm Friday to 7 am Monday. The Red Cross station (☎ 128, 645-6128), just north of Santa Elena, is open 24 hours. The police can be reached at ☎ 117 or 645-5127.

Butterfly Garden

One of the most interesting activities is visiting the Butterfly Garden (El Jardín de las Mariposas; ☎ 645-5512). Admission entitles you to a guided tour led by a naturalist (in Spanish, English, or German) that begins in the information center with an enlightening discussion of butterfly life cycles and the butterfly's importance. A variety of eggs, caterpillars, pupae, and adults are examined. Then visitors are taken into the greenhouses where the butterflies are raised, and on into the screened garden, where hundreds of butterflies of many species are seen. The guided tour lasts about an hour, after which you are free to stay as long as you wish. There are excellent photo opportunities of the gorgeous butterflies. Keep your entrance ticket and you can visit the garden the next day if you wish. There are good volunteer opportunities here.

The garden is open 9:30 am to 4 pm daily; admission is US$7, or US$6 for students.

Serpentarium

Biologist Fernando Valverde has a collection of about 20 snakes and lizards well displayed in cages labeled with informative signs in English and Spanish. Tours and talks are available for groups. The Serpentarium (☎ 645-5238) is open 8 am to 5 pm daily; admission is US$3. It now also serves as the office for Sky Trek and Sky Walk (see below).

Cheese Factory

The cheese factory (also called La Lechería or La Fábrica) has a shop where you can buy fresh local cheese and ice cream. Behind the shop, a huge window allows you to watch the workers making the cheeses. Store hours are 7:30 am to 4 pm daily, except Sunday and holidays.

Art Galleries

A number of art galleries can be visited. They are all more than just souvenir stores for tourists. A local women's arts and crafts cooperative (CASEM; ☎ 645-5190) sells embroidered and hand-painted blouses and handmade clothing as well as other souvenirs and crafts. Profits benefit the local artists and community. Hours are 8 am to noon and 1 to 5 pm Monday to Saturday. In the high season, they are also open 10 am to 4 pm Sunday.

The Hummingbird Gallery (☎ 645-5030), just outside the cloud forest reserve entrance, has feeders that constantly attract several species of hummingbirds, including the violet sabrewing, Costa Rica's largest hummer, and the coppery-headed emerald, one of only three mainland birds endemic to Costa Rica. Great photo opportunities! An identification board shows the nine species that are seen here. Inside, slides and photographs by the renowned British wildlife photographers Michael and Patricia Fogden are on display and for sale. At 4:30 pm, a slide show of their work is narrated by local biologists; it costs US$3. Gallery hours are 9:30 am to 5 pm daily.

Sarah Dowell's Art Gallery is currently in her home up a steep path through pleasant woodlands – her work is bold and distinctive and can be seen in some of the Monteverde hotels as well. Dowell is moving some (and perhaps all) of her work to the new Bromelias Gallery, a two-story gallery near Stella's Bakery planned by the owners of the Hummingbird Gallery. Sarah Dowell and other artists from Costa Rica will be represented here; music, books, medicinal plants, and a garden café will also be available.

Galería de Arte Guindon, on the main road, is open noon to 4 pm most days and showcases another local artist from the locally well-known Guindon family. Farther up the main road, Ecstasy Gallery specializes in woodwork. Centro de Cerámica Gallery, also on the main road, specializes in pottery.

Monteverde Studios of the Arts

Organized by the enterprising Sybil Terres Gilmar, the Studios of the Arts (☎ 645-5434; in the USA ☎ 800-370-3331, mstudios@sol.racsa.co.cr) offer the wonderful new opportunity of taking classes with artists from the Monteverde community. Held in homes and studios, the classes include woodworking, photography, stained glass design, painting and drawing, paper and textile work, cooking, and storytelling. Most classes last a week and cost about US$235, with additional materials fees in some cases; ask about shorter classes. Food and lodging with private bath can be arranged for about US$330/265/200 per person single/double/triple for six nights.

Nature Trails & Hiking

The Monteverde Conservation League (MCL; ☎ 645-5003, fax 645-5104, acmmcl@sol.racsa.co.cr) has an office and welcomes visitors with serious questions (see map). Office hours are 8 am to noon and 1 to 5 pm weekdays. They operate a 3.5km trail system called **Sendero Bajo del Tigre**, which is open 7:30 am to 5:30 pm daily. There is parking. A day-use fee of US$5 benefits the MCL. Children and students with ID pay US$2. The trail offers more open vistas than do those in the cloud forest and hence spotting birds tends to be easier. You can join the MCL for US$25 – this entitles you to a subscription to their quarterly publication, *Tapir Tracks*.

The **Finca Ecológica** (☎ 645-5222) is a private property with four loop trails (the longest takes about 2½ hours at a slow pace) offering hikes of varying lengths through premontane forest, secondary forest, a couple of waterfalls and lookout points, and a small area of coffee and banana plantations. Coatis, agoutis, and sloths are seen on most days, and monkeys, porcupines, and other animals are sometimes seen as well. Birding is good and a bird list is available. Some of these animals are seen at feeders, but they are wild. There is an information booth where you can find out where animals are being seen and get help with identification. The *finca* is open 7 am to 5 pm; admission is US$5, or US$3 for children and students with ID.

Another small private reserve with trails is the **Reserva Sendero Tranquilo** (Quiet Path Reserve), which limits visitation to two groups at any one time, with two to six people per group. Visitation is permitted with a trail guide only, and the average hike lasts three to four hours – you see no one outside your group. Information is available from Hotel El Sapo Dorado (☎ 645-5010). The cost of the guided hike is US$12.50 per person.

The **Hidden Valley Trail** is behind the Pensión Monteverde Inn (see Places to Stay, below). This is free to inn guests and US$5 to others.

The new **Sky Walk** (☎ 645-5238), as a way of getting up among the treetops, is a serene alternative to the zip-wire tours offered by Canopy Tour and Sky Trek (see below). Five suspension bridges, averaging 101m in length, stretch high across valleys along a circular trail winding 3.5km through a 228-hectare private reserve. Swaying gently on the bridges and gazing down through green layers of cloud forest is akin to snorkeling among reefs in deep water. Quetzals have been seen along the trail, as well as monkeys, and it is a treat for birders to see their quarry dart by beneath them. The walk is open 7 am to 4 pm and tickets cost US$8 per person, US$6 with student ID; transportation from the Santa Elena bank costs US$2 per person (US$4 from hotels along the Monteverde road). Dawn and night tours can be reserved in advance but may only be available to groups. The Sky Walk is only 2km from the entrance to the Reserva Santa Elena, so a combined day trip is easy to arrange.

Hiking and nature trails in the Monteverde and Santa Elena reserves are described later in this chapter.

A free hiking option is the track up to **Cerro Amigos** (1842m). This hill has good views of the surrounding rainforest and, on a clear day, of Volcán Arenal, 20km away to the northeast. The track leaves Monteverde from behind the Hotel Belmar and ascends roughly 300m in 3km; from the hotel, take the dirt road going downhill, then the next left. Near the end of the track are a couple of TV/radio antennae, so the route is easy to follow.

Monteverde's Sky Walk is a treat for birders.

Canopy Tour

The Canopy Tour (☎ 645-5243) opened its first site here, in the grounds of the Cloud Forest Lodge. They also have an information office in Santa Elena (see map). Their adventure in the cloud forest canopy has become popular and reservations are needed in the high season. Tours leave four or five times a day.

The tour begins with a short guided hike through the forest to a series of three platforms between 20 and 33m up in the trees. The first platform is reached by a rope ladder that goes up the inside of a giant hollow fig tree; then you whiz across on a pulley harness attached to fixed ropes to the second and third platforms, and finally make a rappel descent to the ground. All participants are harnessed to safety equipment throughout the tour, which lasts about 2½ hours. Costs are US$45 for adults, US$35 for students with ID and US$30 for children. See Organized Tours in the Getting Around chapter for more details.

An alternative to the Canopy Tour (and currently being sued for patent infringement, though some observers say that knock-off tours are inevitable and that there's nothing that original about a zip-line) is the **Sky Trek** (☎ 645-5238), which offers a similar ride through the treetops. Sky Trek also operates the Sky Walk (see above).

Neither of these tours is particularly about wildlife observation; the thrill of the ride (which produces the high-spirited yells that scare off most wildlife) is more the point.

The newer **Aerial Adventures** (☎ 645-5960), located off the road to Finca Ecológica (see map), offers a much more sedate ride through the trees. Essentially a ski-lift, the tour offers a 1.5km journey in electrically propelled gondola chairs along rails attached to towers; heights range from near ground level to 12m up. The ride lasts between one and 1½ hours; you have the option of pausing your car briefly to look around. Lacking in the thrills offered by the zip-line tours, this quieter tour offers similar views and probably a better chance of seeing birds and wildlife. Tickets are US$10, including the loan of tree and bird identification guides, and it is open 6 am to 8 pm daily, making dawn and dusk visits possible.

Horseback Riding

Horseback tours are another option. There are plenty of outfitters in the area, and your hotel can arrange a tour for you. One well-recommended outfitter is Meg's Riding Stables (☎ 645-5052), which charges US$10 per hour (or less for longer rides) and takes you on private trails. Their horses are well looked after. Caballeriza La Estrella (☎ 645-5075) has also been recommended. Other outfitters are available, charging US$7 an hour and up. Apart from forest tours, day treks can be arranged to viewpoints from which Volcán Arenal can be seen (see the boxed text in the Fortuna section, later, about horse trips to Fortuna).

Viewing Volcán Arenal

A rough road goes 8 or 9km north of Santa Elena, past the turnoff to the Reserva Santa Elena, to an area where there are great views (if it's clear) of the volcano exploding away about 15km to the northeast. You could drive, bike, or hike along this road for the views. There are a couple of places to

Responsible Tourism

Monteverde started as a Quaker community founded by peaceful people who wanted to live in a quiet and friendly environment. This has changed drastically in the last fifteen years with the large influx of visitors. There is a limit to the number of visitors Monteverde can handle before losing its special atmosphere, and there is a limit to the number of people who can visit the Monteverde reserve without causing too much damage.

Quakers have traditionally been adept at peaceful resolution of problems, and they have handled their status as a tourist attraction with grace and common sense. The income from tourism is important, but preserving their own lifestyle and surroundings is equally, if not more, important to the inhabitants. Monteverde is a special but fragile place – visitors are very welcome but should remember that they are visiting a peaceful community and/or a cloud forest reserve.

Most visitors are delighted with their stay, but a few complain about how muddy the trails are (you have to expect mud in a cloud forest), how boring the nightlife is (Quakers traditionally don't do much nightclubbing), or how difficult it is to see the quetzal (this is not a zoo). Monteverde is not for everybody – if clouds and Quakers, cheese and quetzals do not sound like your idea of fun, head for a resort more to your liking.

– Rob Rachowiecki

stay out here, described below. The lookout tower at the Reserva Santa Elena (see later in this chapter) and Cerro Amigos (see above in Hiking & Nature Trails) also offer volcano-viewing opportunities.

Organic Farming

There is a fair amount of organic farming in the area for those interested in learning more about how it's done. Information about volunteering on Finca La Bella, which gives locals an opportunity to learn organic coffee farming methods, is available through the Monteverde Institute (see Courses, below). Behind Stella's Bakery, Rigo Alvarado oversees a well-developed organic garden, whose produce goes to Stella's and comes back again as compost. Rigo can be reached through Meg Wallace (Stella's daughter and operator of Meg's Riding Stables; see above in Horseback Riding); he can tell you about other organic farming projects in the area.

Courses

The Monteverde Institute (☎ 645-5053, fax 645-5219, mvipac@sol.racsa.co.cr) is a nonprofit educational institute founded in 1986. The institute offers interdisciplinary courses in tropical biology, agroecology, conservation, sustainable development, local culture, Spanish, and women's studies. There is also a volunteer placement program for people who wish to teach in local schools or work in reforestation programs. Homestay costs US$9 per day and the placement fee is US$50. Teaching positions last a minimum of three months; workstays on Finca La Bella, their organic farm, can last two weeks to two months. Another volunteer opportunity is with Vida Familiar, a program addressing domestic violence and family health; this is open only to those with experience in the field.

The Institute's short courses (10 to 14 days) give high school and college students and adults the opportunity to learn about conservation and land use in the Monteverde area. Costs are US$700 to US$1500, all inclusive from San José. Long courses (eight to 10 weeks) are university-accredited programs for undergraduates and emphasize tropical community ecology. Costs are about US$4000. Graduate students interested in doing thesis research in the area can apply for office space and housing through the institute; the application fee is US$25.

The Centro Panamericano de Idiomas (☎/fax 645-5448, anajarro@sol.racsa.co.cr) has opened a Spanish-language program in Monteverde, with homestays available. (Also see the entry under Heredia in the Central Valley & Surrounding Highlands chapter.)

Monteverde Music Festival

The Monteverde Music Festival is held annually throughout January and February and has gained a well-deserved reputation as one of the top music festivals in Central America. Music is mainly classical, jazz, and Latin with an occasional experimental group to spice things up. Concerts are held daily at the Monteverde Institute. Tickets are US$9. Note that musicians play for about four nights, then a new group begins, so if you're only here for a couple of nights, you probably won't be able to listen to more than one performance.

For those seeking musical entertainment, the smaller South Caribbean Music Festival offers a similar mix of music, with a more Caribbean and folk flavor, on a similar schedule (see Puerto Viejo de Talamanca in the Caribbean Lowlands chapter).

Places to Stay

During Christmas and Easter, most hotels are booked up weeks or even months in advance. During the January-to-April busy season, and also in July, hotels tend to be full often enough that you should telephone before arriving to ensure yourself of a room in the hotel you want. You may have to book well in advance to get the dates and hotel of your choice. If you're flexible, you can almost always find somewhere to stay. The Santa Elena bus stop is one of the few places in Costa Rica where you're likely to be besieged on arrival by people trying to offer you a place to sleep.

Places to Stay – Budget

Camping ***Camping Charlie*** is a small, loosely organized spot in an attractive riverside location. It charges about US$3 per person and is planning to add a shower. Camping is also sometimes permitted on the grounds of a few hotels – the charge is about US$2 per person and allows you to use a shower. Check at Pensión Flor Mar and Cabinas El Bosque (see below) and ask around about other places.

Hotels Many, though not all, of the cheapest hotels are in Santa Elena, about 5 to 6km from the reserve. ***Pensión El Sueño*** *(☎ 645-5021)* is a family-run place with basic quadruple rooms from US$5 per person, and slightly better rooms with private bath for about twice as much. There is hot water, and they will cook for you on request.

Pensión Santa Elena *(☎ 645-5051, fax 645-6060, mundonet@sol.racsa.co.cr)* is clean, friendly, and popular. Lodging in small rooms costs US$5 to US$8 per person, depending on whether you want a private bath with a non-electric hot shower (!); there are electric showers in the communal bathrooms. You can get wine, beer, and Internet access; there is a communal kitchen and an attractive eating area. The proprietors also manage ***Albergue Marbella***, which is next door and is a quieter place to stay. Rates are slightly higher and there are more rooms with private baths. Nearby, the small, clean, and friendly ***Pensión Colibrí*** *(☎ 645-5682)* charges US$5 per person for basic rooms with shared bathroom and hot electric shower. Some rooms have sunny windows, and there is a little balcony; the place as a whole feels perched among the trees. Rooms with private bath cost US$20 double. The people will cook for you on request (US$3.50 for a *casado*), and horse rental is available – a day trip to Reserva Santa Elena is US$20 per person.

Hospedaje El Banco *(☎ 645-5204)*, behind the bank, is basic but friendly and charges about US$7 per person. The shared electric showers are warm and laundry service and meals are available on request. ***Hotel Green Road*** *(☎ 645-5916)* has laundry service, will change small amounts of money, and has clean basic rooms for US$5 per person with shared bath, US$8 with private bath.

About a half kilometer north of Santa Elena, past the school and radio tower, is the quiet ***Cabinas Golf View/Don Taco*** *(☎ 645-5263)*, which has clean rooms with bunk beds, communal bath, and hot showers for US$6 per person. Breakfast costs US$4. Nearby is the similarly priced ***Cabinas Marín*** *(☎ 645-5279)*, which also has a few doubles with private bath for US$15.

The helpful ***Pensión Tucán*** *(☎ 645-5017)* has 14 small but clean double rooms with hot water. Seven rooms have shared bathrooms for US$7 per person, and seven others cost US$10 with private bath. The pensión will rent cabins with kitchenettes from US$125 a month. Meals are available and the owner is a good cook.

A good new budget place, just outside the village to the southwest, is ***Cabinas Tina's Casitas*** *(☎ 645-5641)*. Three little cabins around an outdoor terrace, from which you can see the Golfo de Nicoya on a clear day, offer rooms ranging from US$6 to US$15 per person, depending on size and whether you share a bathroom. From behind the Santa Elena supermarket, it's about a 200m walk down a dirt road and up a small hill; there are signs. The cabins are simple but nicely built.

At the southeast end of Santa Elena, ***Soda y Hospedaje Giaconda*** has four basic little rooms with shared hot showers for US$5/8 single/double. It serves tasty, filling casados, meat and vegetarian, for US$3. Farther out is the small, clean, friendly, family-run, and helpful ***Pensión Flor de Monteverde*** *(☎/fax 645-5236)*. Owner Eduardo Venegas Castro has worked at both the Monteverde and Santa Elena reserves and was director of the latter. He charges US$7 per person, or US$10 with private hot shower, and offers three meals a day for another US$15. Tours and transportation can be arranged, a number of wildlife guides are available to guests, and there is laundry service.

In Cerro Plano, the little ***Pensión El Trogon*** *(☎ 645-5130)* has rooms with bunk beds and shared warm showers for US$6 per person and rooms with private bath for US$10 per person. The phrase 'Antigua El Pino' (Formerly El Pino) on its roadside sign refers to the fact that it was forced to change its name by the nearby and larger Cabañas Los Pinos. Laundry, meals, and horse rental are all available. Almost next door, the 11-room ***Pensión Manakín*** *(☎ 645-5080, fax 645-5517, manakin@sol.racsa.co.cr)* is simple but friendly and has hot water. Rates are US$10 per person in rooms with shared bathrooms. A few rooms with private bath cost US$30 double. Good breakfasts cost US$2 to US$5, depending on what you want to eat. The pensión also provides Internet access, picnic lunches, laundry service, and basic kitchen privileges, and can arrange local tours and transportation. Ask about the simple lodge/campground that the owners operate in a remote area of the foothills of the Caribbean coast. They also organize community music and poetry evenings.

In a remote part of Cerro Plano is the friendly ***Pensión Monteverde Inn*** *(☎ 645-5156)*, from which the Hidden Valley Trail goes into a deep canyon behind the hotel and through an 11-hectare reserve. The owners' daughters, Lisetta and Vanessa, are fun and enjoy guiding folks along the trail. The rooms are spartan but adequate and have private hot showers for US$10/18 single/double; breakfast is available on request for US$5, and the owners can pick you up at the bus stop if you have a reservation. The remote and very quiet location is the main attraction here.

About 3 or 4km northwest of Santa Elena on the road to Tilarán is ***Monte Los Olivos Ecotourist Lodge*** *(☎ 645-5059, fax 645-5131)*, a community project supported by the Arenal Conservation Area, the Canadian World Wildlife Fund, and the Canadian International Development Agency. The project is intended to develop a grass-roots ecotourism that protects forests and directly benefits small communities such as this one. Two similar lodges have opened in northwestern Costa Rica (see the Volcán Tenorio Area, later in this chapter). This one has nine rustic but clean cabins with hot water. Five cabins that have shared bathrooms cost US$10/15 single/double, and four with private bathrooms cost US$17/24/29/35 for one to four people. Breakfasts (US$2) and other meals (US$5) are served. You can arrange guided hikes and horseback rides with the locals.

Places to Stay – Mid-Range

The ***Pensión Flor Mar*** *(☎ 645-5009, ☎/fax 645-5088)* was opened by Marvin Rockwell, one of the original Quakers, who was jailed for refusing to sign up for the draft and then spent three months driving down from Alabama. Recently he sold the pensión, but he still lives next door – the new owner wants Marvin to remain a presiding spirit, and he comes over regularly for meals and conversation. He and his Costa Rican wife, Flory, are very friendly. The little pensión is pleasant, though the rooms are simple and small; the new owner may renovate and prices may change. Rooms with shared bath cost US$10 per person; with private bath, US$15 per person. All three meals are provided for an additional US$17 per person, but no alcohol is served. There are hot electric showers. Horses are available for rent. The hotel is just over 2km from the reserve.

Some 9km north of Santa Elena, near San Gerardo Abajo, is ***El Gran Mirador*** *(☎ 381-7277, ☎/fax 645-5087)*, a rustic lodge that has good views of Arenal. Dormitory-style rooms with shared baths cost US$20 per person; double rooms with private bath cost about US$50. One or two of the doubles are in separate, private little cabins with great volcano views. A restaurant serves home-cooked meals in the US$2 to US$7 range. Guided hiking and horseback tours are available for about US$8 per person per hour – some primary forest and waterfalls are nearby. To get to the lodge, you need 4WD for the last kilometer in the dry season or the last few kilometers in the wet months – this place is not on the beaten track.

The ***Hospedaje Mariposa*** *(☎ 645-5013)* is a small and friendly family-run place with just three simple but clean rooms with a double and single bed and private warm shower. The best feature of this place is that it is only 1.5km from the reserve. Rates are

US$20/25/30 for one to three people, including a Costa Rican breakfast. Other meals can be arranged.

About 1.5km out of Santa Elena toward the Reserva Santa Elena is the ***Sunset Hotel*** (*☎ 645-5048, 645-5228, fax 645-5344*), a small, well-kept place with a quiet location and great views. Seven rooms with private bath and hot water are US$24/36/46 including breakfast. Readers have reported substantial wet-season discounts.

The small ***Arco Iris Ecolodge*** (*☎ 645-5067, fax 645-5022, arcoiris@sol.racsa.co.cr*) is on a little hill overlooking Santa Elena and the surrounding forests. The multilingual owners are active in local tourism issues, have been recognized for running an environmentally sensitive hotel, and are generally helpful. The quiet hotel has a large garden that produces some of the organic vegetables served in its restaurant, which currently only offers breakfast to guests but may reopen to the public for other meals. They have six pleasant rooms, all with private hot shower. Two rooms cost US$25, three cost US$45, and one particularly nice cabin costs US$50 (all double rates). The price differences are because of size and view. All the local tours are organized quickly. Trails and a sunset lookout point are being developed on the mountain behind the lodge.

The ***Hotel El Bosque*** (*☎ 645-5221, ☎/fax 645-5129, elbosque@sol.racsa.co.cr*) is a few hundred meters behind the popular restaurant of the same name. The 22 rooms are simple but clean, bright, and spacious and have private hot showers for US$25/40 – good for the money. Guests get a 10% discount in the restaurant. A small campground is being built here.

Just outside Santa Elena on the road to Juntas is the pleasantly situated ***Swiss Hotel Miramontes*** (*☎ 645-5152, fax 645-5297*), with six rooms of varying size for US$30 to US$50 double, all with private hot bath. Four languages are spoken, and the restaurant offers an international menu.

The ***Hotel El Establo*** (*☎ 645-5033, 645-5110, fax 645-5041, establo@sol.racsa.co.cr; in San José ☎ 225-0569*) is named after the stable next door and is set in a 60-hectare property, half of which is primary forest. Horses are available for rent at about US$10 per hour. The 18 rooms are simple but comfortable, with good beds, hot showers, carpeting, and access to a spacious and relaxing sitting area decorated with early photographs of the region. Rates are US$30/40/50. The restaurant is for guests only and serves breakfast for US$7 and other meals for US$10.

About 7 or 8km north of Monteverde in San Gerardo – a district, not a village – is the new ***Vista Verde Lodge*** (*☎ 380-1517*), with spectacular views of Volcán Arenal 15km to the northeast. This lodge has 10 rooms, some with huge picture windows facing Arenal, all spacious and attractive with hot showers. Rates are US$35/45/55 single/double/triple including breakfast, and there is a nice restaurant and bar with an outdoor viewing deck. Call the lodge to find out what the view is like, then drive up for a meal or beer. The owner will arrange horseback rides and hikes.

In Cerro Plano, ***Cabañas Los Pinos*** (*☎ 645-5252, ☎/fax 645-5005*) has six separate cabins scattered through its forested property, offering 11 rooms in all. All cabins have private hot baths and a kitchenette. Rates are US$45 for a double, US$85 for a unit with two rooms sleeping four to six, and US$95 for a unit with three rooms. Horseback rides from US$7 per person per hour can be arranged.

The ***Hotel Villa Verde*** (*☎ 645-5025, fax 645-5115, estefany@sol.racsa.co.cr*) was until recently the closest hotel to the reserve, a little over a kilometer away. It is an attractive stone and wood building with a good restaurant/bar, a conference room with a free slide show about the area most nights at 8 pm, and laundry service. All local tours are quickly arranged by the helpful owners. Eighteen standard rooms with private hot bath cost US$43/56/69 for one to three people, including breakfast. Five suites with kitchenette and fireplace cost US$89 and sleep up to five people. They advertise low-season, student, and long-stay discounts.

The closest lodge to the reserve is now the ***Trapp Family Lodge*** (*☎ 645-5858,* *fax 645-5990, trappfam@ticoweb.com)*, and, yes, the owners are related to the Trapps of *Sound of Music* fame, though part of the family has local Costa Rican roots. This new lodge (which is slightly less than a kilometer from the reserve entrance) has high wooden ceilings and simple spacious rooms with private hot bath for about US$50 double. The friendly owners can arrange tours and transportation.

Places to Stay – Top End

Outside Santa Elena is ***Hotel Finca Valverde's*** *(☎ 645-5157, fax 645-5216, fincaval@sol.racsa.co.cr)*, a working coffee farm. There are five cabins, each with two clean and spacious (if rather bare) units with private bathtubs and hot water, an upstairs loft, and a balcony. Most have two double beds; two have four singles. Note that three of the cabins are a short (20 to 50m) but very steep hike up from the parking lot. Rates are US$64/87 single/double, US$17 for additional people. Eight standard rooms cost US$52/75. Discounts are available for student groups. A simple but pleasant restaurant serves Costa Rican food, and the attached bar is locally popular. Restaurant hours are 7 am to 9 pm, and it is open to the public.

The ***Cloud Forest Lodge*** *(☎ 645-5058, fax 645-5168, taylor@catours.co.cr; in San José ☎ 297-0343, fax 236-5270)*, now owned and operated by Costa Rica Tours, is in an out-of-the-way location northeast of Santa Elena. It has a private cloud forest that is the home of the Canopy Tour (see earlier). The 28-hectare property has about 6km of hiking trails (free for hotel guests). Nine duplex cabins with porches are on a steep hillside surrounding a central restaurant/bar. Simple but clean and spacious rooms are separated by a stone wall to minimize neighbors' noise, and each has a private bath and hot water. Rates are US$64/70 and US$12 for additional people. Children under 11 sharing a room with two adults stay for free. Meals are mainly typical tico cuisine, with bread baked on the premises, all served family style. Box lunches are available for hikers.

The ***Hotel Heliconia*** *(☎ 645-5109, 223-3869, fax 645-5007, heliconi@sol.racsa.co.cr)* is 4km away from the reserve and is a family-run hotel. The attractive wooden lodge and bungalows behind it offer 25 good-size rooms, each with private bath and hot water. A separate building houses a spa, and there is a nice-looking restaurant and bar. Rates are US$74/77/89 for one to three people. Full breakfasts cost US$8; other meals cost US$12.50.

The ***Hotel Fonda Vela*** *(☎/fax 645-5125, 645-5114, fax 645-5119; in San José ☎ 257-1413, fax 257-1416, fondavel@sol.racsa.co.cr)* is the closest top-end place to the reserve at just over 1.5km away. Trails through the 14-hectare grounds offer good birding possibilities and stables provide horses very quickly. The restaurant is in a beautiful building that was home to the Monteverde Music Festival until the new Institute was built, and the owners' father, Paul Smith, is a well-known local artist whose work, along with others', graces the walls. Other music events are held irregularly throughout the year.

Seven separate structures house a total of 20 spacious, wood-accented standard rooms with large windows, six junior suites, and two master suites. All have private hot showers and two queen-size beds, and some have great views. Many rooms are wheelchair accessible. The suites have a sitting room, refrigerator, bathtub, balcony, and loft. Room rates are US$68/78, junior suites cost US$76/86, and master suites cost US$85/96. Extra people are charged US$11. Set meals are served from 6:15 to 9 am, noon to 2 pm, and 6:30 to 8:30 pm; the restaurant is open to the public. Breakfast costs US$8, lunch costs US$11, and dinner costs US$13 – the food is good. Readers wrote to recommend this place.

Also recommended is ***Hotel Belmar*** *(☎ 645-5201, fax 645-5135, belmar@sol.racsa.co.cr)*, a beautiful wooden hotel on a hill almost 4km from the reserve. Its two Alpine-looking buildings have 34 rooms. The road up to the hotel is steep and slippery for the last 300m, and cars don't always make it in heavy rain. But once you get there, you are rewarded with superb views of the Golfo de Nicoya when the weather is clear. Attractive spacious rooms (most have balconies) cost

US$64/70 to US$81/87 single/double (US$12 to US$15 for each additional person). Breakfast costs about US$9, lunch or dinner costs US$13, and the food is good. Apart from the restaurant, there is a pizza bar with a pool table. For US$10 you can get a ride to the reserve and be picked up again at a prearranged time. Horse rides and the usual tours are arranged.

The ***Hotel de Montaña Monteverde*** *(☎ 645-5046, fax 645-5320; in San José ☎ 224-3050, fax 222-6184, monteverde@ticonet.co.cr)* opened in 1978 as the first top-end hotel in Monteverde. It has over 30 rooms and suites, all with private hot showers and some with balconies and views. Some suites have fireplaces. There is a good restaurant, and the spacious gardens of the 6-hectare property are pleasant to walk around. There is a sauna and Jacuzzi that can be used for US$1 per hour. All the local tours and activities are arranged. A slide show (US$2) is screened most nights at 8 pm. Rates are US$53/81; junior suites cost US$91 double, and the honeymoon suite, with a balcony and private Jacuzzi, costs US$125. Additional occupants are charged US$15. The single rooms are small with cramped bathrooms, and the double rooms have moderately sized bathrooms.

Hotel El Sapo Dorado *(☎ 645-5010, fax 645-5180, elsapo@sol.racsa.co.cr)* is owned by long-time residents Geovanny Arguedas and Hannah Lowther, a tico-Quaker couple who met as children in school at Monteverde. They are active in the community, promoting sustainable tourism and other values. The private forest behind the hotel has trails. Their restaurant/bar serves excellent and healthy meals, with vegetarian main courses always among the choices. They occasionally have live music and a musically accompanied slide show by noted area photographer and naturalist Richard Laval. The restaurant is open to the public 6:30 to 9:30 am, noon to 3 pm, and 6 to 9 pm. The bar is open 7 am to 10 pm and serves snacks. They also have professional massage services for US$29 per hour.

There are 20 spacious rooms in 10 large cabins. All have two queen-size beds, table and chairs, and private hot-water showers. Their 'Mountain Suites' have mountain views, a small balcony, and a fireplace. Rates are US$89/103/118/133 for one to four people. Larger 'Sunset Terrace Suites' have a minibar and fridge, and French doors open to a private terrace with views down to the Golfo de Nicoya. Rates are US$93/111/129/147. Light sleepers should opt for the Sunset Terrace Suites, which have thicker walls than the Mountain Suites.

The ***Monteverde Lodge*** *(☎ 645-5057, fax 645-5126, ecotur@expeditions.co.cr)* is 5km from the reserve and is the most upscale hotel in the Monteverde area. A progressive recycling policy, a solar energy system, and a procedure whereby sheets and towels are changed on guest request (just as at home), rather than every day, are noteworthy environmentally sound aspects of this upscale hotel. The rooms are larger than most and have picture windows with garden or forest views. Apart from a smoking wing, most guest rooms and the restaurant have a nonsmoking policy. The large lobby is graced by a huge fireplace and, adjoining the lobby, a huge solar-powered but nice and hot Jacuzzi allows up to 15 guests to soak away the stresses of hiking steep and muddy trails.

The grounds are attractively landscaped with a variety of native plants, and a short trail leads to a bluff with an observation platform. The bluff is at the height of the forest canopy, with good views of the forest and a river ravine. Rooms cost US$95.50/115/133/149. Children under five years old stay and eat for free; children from ages six to ten stay for free (with their parents) and receive a 50% discount on meals. Meals cost US$13 for breakfast, US$18.50 for lunch, and US$21 for dinner. Transportation to the Monteverde or Santa Elena reserve costs US$8 per person; to San José it's US$40. The staff will arrange guided reserve visits, horseback rides, and all other activities.

Reservations should be made with lodge owner/operator Costa Rica Expeditions (see Organized Tours in the Getting Around chapter). Complete guided tours that include transportation, meals, and accommodations are also available (for example, three days/two nights from San José, including a half day at the Monteverde reserve, costs US$439 per person, double occupancy).

Places to Eat

Many people eat in their hotels, most of which provide meals and will also provide picnic lunches on request. Several hotel restaurants are open to the public. Other possibilities include the following.

El Bosque Restaurant *(☎ 645-5158)* is a very pleasant and popular place serving good lunches and dinners for about US$5 to US$9. It is open noon to 9 pm daily. The restaurant is nearly 3km from the reserve.

Pizza Johnny *(☎ 645-5066)* is popular with both travelers and locals. It serves other good Italian dishes as well as pizza, and is a pleasant place for a meal. On the road to the Butterfly Garden, the Chilean-owned ***Restaurant de Lucia*** *(☎ 645-5337)* is one of Monteverde's best restaurants, though not very expensive at under US$20 for a meal for two people. The ***Soda Manantial***, by the Quebrada Máquina, serves inexpensive tico meals. The cook from the former Muelle 595 has taken his seafood dinners to ***My House is Your House***, near the Centro Panamericano de Idiomas.

There are cheap places to eat in Santa Elena, especially if you stick with basic plates like the casado, which can be had for under US$3. The ***Soda Central*** is popular. Next to the church, a small ***open-air soda*** is open early. ***Chunches Coffeeshop*** (see Information, earlier in this chapter) has espresso coffee and delicious homemade cookies and snacks.

Morphos Café has good sandwiches and vegetarian dishes. The friendly ***Rocky Road Café*** has sandwiches, hamburgers, barbecued chicken, and ice cream. Below is ***Panadería Jiménez*** for baked goods. Other places along the same road include the ***Restaurant Daiquiri***, which stays open longer than most, and those associated with the hotels (see Places to Stay, above).

Stella's Bakery has fresh salads, soups, and sandwiches (many of the ingredients are grown organically behind the bakery), coffee drinks, and a variety of pastries, delicious home-made bread, and rolls – all of which make for good picnic lunches. It is open 6 am to 6 pm. At ***La Lechería*** (the cheese factory), you can pick up some fresh cheese or ice cream. Opposite Stella's, there is a ***grocery store*** next to CASEM. In Santa Elena, stop by the supermarket.

There is a decent ***cafeteria*** just inside the entrance of the Monteverde reserve.

Entertainment

La Cascada is a popular dance club open 9 pm to 1 am Thursday to Sunday. There may be a cover charge. The locals go to ***Domingo's Bar/Unicornio Discotec***, next to the soccer field at the north end of Santa Elena. Popular bars are ***Amigos Bar*** in Santa Elena, which has a pool table, and the ***Taberna Bar*** by the Hotel Finca Valverde's, which has a small dance floor. You can stop by the ***Pensíon Santa Elena*** for a beer or glass of wine in its communal eating area. Several of the better hotels have slide shows and bars for evening entertainment. Also see the Monteverde Music Festival, earlier in this chapter.

Getting There & Away

Bus After stopping in Santa Elena, most buses to the Monteverde area continue on to La Lechería, about 2.5km before the reserve. Ask to be dropped off anywhere before that point, near the hotel of your choice. These buses also begin the return trip from La Lechería, stopping at several points, including the bus office (☎ 645–5159) next to the Soda Central in Santa Elena, before continuing. Departure times from La Lechería for buses that follow this route are 5:30 am for Las Juntas, 5:45 am for Puntarenas, and 6:30 am and 2:30 pm for San José – all these buses pick up passengers at the Santa Elena bus office about 10 minutes later.

Buses to the Monteverde area leave from Las Juntas at 2:30 pm, from Puntarenas at 2:15 pm (about three hours), and at 6:30 am and 2:30 pm from San José (about four to five hours).

The bus to Tilarán leaves at 7 am from the church in Santa Elena; the departure from Tilarán to Santa Elena is at 12:30 pm (about three hours). Try to buy tickets for all buses a day in advance, especially in the high season. Several hotels arrange private transportation to or from San José.

Car Drivers will find all the roads to Monteverde in poor condition, and 4WD may be necessary during the rainy season. Many car rental agencies will refuse to rent you an ordinary car during the wet season if you state that you are going to Monteverde. Ordinary cars are OK in the dry months, but it is a slow and bumpy ride, on which cars occasionally break down or sustain damage to the undercarriage – drive with care.

There are two roads from the Interamericana to Santa Elena and Monteverde. Coming from the south, the first turnoff is at Rancho Grande, 18km northwest of the turnoff for Puntarenas. All there is at Rancho Grande is the Bar Rancho Grande and a sign for 'Sardinal, Guacimal, Monteverde,' both on the right (north) side of the highway. Unfortunately, the sign is placed so that you can't easily see it unless you are coming from the north, so keep your eyes peeled for the bar.

The second turnoff is at the Río Lagarto bridge (just past Km 149, and roughly 15km northwest of Rancho Grande). Here there is another not very obvious sign: 'Guacimal, Santa Elena, Monteverde.' Both routes are steep, winding, and scenic dirt roads with plenty of potholes and rocks to ensure that the driver, at least, is kept from admiring the scenery. (There is good birding en route.)

Which road should you take? Good question. Both are about the same distance (32 or 33km from the Interamericana to Santa Elena). The Rancho Grande road is reached more quickly from San José, and many bus drivers prefer it for that reason, but the Río Lagarto road seems to be favored by local drivers and may be in marginally better condition. Both are poor but driveable. If you're driving, talk to everyone you can about current conditions and weigh the (invariably conflicting) advice received – once you are thoroughly confused, you can begin your journey!

It is possible to drive from Tilarán, but the road is just as bad (some people say it's worse – a point that is debated by road-warriors having an evening drink in the hotel bars). It's driveable in an ordinary car during the dry season, at least – drive carefully.

Jeep & Boat When leaving for Fortuna, it's possible to take a 4WD jeep taxi to Río Chiquito, then a boat across Laguna de Arenal, and be met by a taxi on the other side to continue to Fortuna. This takes about five hours and the whole package costs US$75 for two people or US$115 for four. Both morning and afternoon departures are available. To make a reservation for this service, call ☎ 645-5263.

Horse Horseback rides between Monteverde and Fortuna are offered by a number of people, but are not recommended as this trip is very hard on the horses – there have even been reports of horses dying on the trail. (See the 'To Ride or Not to Ride?' boxed text near the end of this chapter.)

RESERVA BIOLÓGICA BOSQUE NUBOSO MONTEVERDE

When the Quaker settlers first arrived, they decided to preserve about a third of their property in order to protect the watershed above Monteverde. In 1972, with the help of organizations such as the Nature Conservancy and the World Wildlife Fund (WWF), more land was purchased adjoining the already preserved area. This was called the Reserva Biológica Bosque Nuboso Monteverde (Monteverde Cloud Forest Biological Reserve), which the Centro Científico Tropical (Tropical Science Center) of San José bought and operated. Gradually, more land was acquired and added to the reserve.

In 1986, the Monteverde Conservation League (MCL) was formed, and it continues to buy land to expand the reserve. In 1988, the MCL launched the International Children's Rainforest project whereby children and school groups from all over the world raise money to buy and save tropical rainforest adjacent to the reserve. This project does more than ask children to raise money for rainforest preservation – it is an educational program as well. Estimates place the size of the Monteverde reserve at about

17,000 hectares, combined with another 7000 hectares (or more) of the neighboring Children's Rainforest.

The most striking aspect of this project is that it is a private enterprise rather than a national park administered by the government. Governments worldwide must begin to count conservation as a key issue for the continued well-being of their citizens, but it is interesting to see what a positive effect ordinary people can have on preserving their environment. This preservation relies partly on donations from the public. Donations directly to the reserve can be sent to Centro Científico Tropical, Apartado 8-3870-1000, San José. Donations to the Children's Rainforest and to aid educational work and sustainable development in the local community can be sent to Monteverde Conservation League, Apartado 10581-1000, San José. US residents can send tax-deductible contributions to Friends of the Monteverde Cloud Forest, PO Box 6255, Zephyrhills, FL 33540. If you contribute US$25 or more, you receive a newsletter and a membership card that allows free admission to the reserve on your next visit.

Visitors should note that many of the walking trails are generally very muddy, and even during the dry season (from late December to early May) the cloud forest tends to drip. Therefore, rainwear and suitable boots are recommended. (Rubber boots can be rented at the entrance for about US$1 – bring your own footwear for the best fit.) A few of the trails have been stabilized with concrete blocks or wooden boards and are easier to walk. During the wet season, the unpaved trails turn into quagmires, but there are usually fewer visitors. The annual rainfall here is about 3m, though parts of the reserve reportedly get twice as much. It's usually cool (high temperatures around 18°C or 65°F), so wear appropriate clothing. Dry-season visitors who plan to stay on the main trails really don't need rubber boots – I've seen sweaty-footed hikers looking elegant in their personal pink rubber boots with barely a splash of mud on them. Binoculars rent for US$10 per day.

Because of the fragile environment, the reserve will allow a maximum of 120 people in at any given time. During the dry-season months, it can be busy in the mornings, though the 120 limit is not often reached. It is usually less crowded in the afternoons. The least busy months are May, June, September, October, and November. If you are traveling in the dry season, consider going to the less-crowded Reserva Santa Elena, described later in this chapter.

It is important to remember that the cloud forest is often cloudy and the vegetation is thick. This combination cuts down on sounds as well as visibility.

I have received several letters from readers who have been disappointed with the lack of wildlife sightings in the cloud forest, and they have asked me not to raise people's expectations with enthusiastic descriptions of the fauna. Personally, I find the cloud forest exhilarating and mysterious even on those cloudy and stormy days when the forest reveals few of its animal secrets – but I do emphasize that, for many people, the secretive wildlife is a disappointment. If your expectations are not met, I am sorry – but, please, don't blame me for that!

Information

The information office (☎ 645-5112, fax 645-5034, montever@sol.racsa.co.cr) and gift store at the entrance of the reserve, and the reserve itself, are open 7 am to 4 pm daily. Entrance to the reserve costs US$8.50 per day, or US$4.50 for children over 11 and students with ID. Younger children are admitted free.

You can get information and buy trail guides, bird and mammal lists, and maps here. The gift shop also sells T-shirts, beautiful color slides by Richard Laval, postcards, books, posters, and a variety of other souvenirs. A slide show of Laval's work is shown at 11 am daily for US$3 per person; a group of four or more people can arrange for a special showing after 1 pm.

Tours & Guides

Although you can hike around the reserve without a guide, you'll stand a better chance of seeing a quetzal or other wildlife if you hire a guide.

Guided natural history tours are offered by the reserve (☎ 645-5112) every morning at 8 am and, on busy days, at 7:30 and 8:30 am

Who Has Seen the Golden Toad?

One animal you used to be able to see so often that it almost became a Monteverde mascot was the golden toad, *Bufo periglenes.* Monteverde was the only place in the world where this exotic little toad appeared. The gold-colored amphibian used to be frequently seen scrambling along the muddy trails of the cloud forest, adding a bright splash to the surroundings. Unfortunately, no one has seen this once-common toad since 1989, and what happened to it is a mystery.

During an international conference of herpetologists (scientists who study reptiles and amphibians), it was noted that the same puzzling story was occurring with other frog and toad species all over the world. Amphibians once common are now severely depleted or simply not found at all. The scientists were unable to agree upon a reason for the sudden demise of so many amphibian species in so many different habitats.

One of several theories holds that worldwide air quality has degenerated to the extent that amphibians, who breathe both with primitive lungs and through their perpetually moist skin, were more susceptible to airborne toxins because of the gas exchange through their skin. Another theory is that their skin gives little protection against UV light, and increasing UV light levels in recent years have proven deadly to amphibians. Perhaps they are like the canaries miners used in the old days to warn them of toxic air in the mines. When the canary keeled over, it was time for the miners to get out!

Are our dying frogs and toads a symptom of a planet that is becoming too polluted?

– Rob Rachowiecki

NORTHWESTERN

as well. Call the day before to make a reservation. Tours are usually limited to about 10 participants and cost US$15 per person, plus the US$8.50 or US$4.50 cost of entrance to the reserve. Participants meet at the Hummingbird Gallery, where a short 10-minute orientation is given, followed by a 2½- to three-hour walk, followed by a 30-minute slide show (this is the same as the one shown at 4:30 pm at the gallery; the slides are by renowned wildlife photographers Michael and Patricia Fogden). The guides all speak English and are trained naturalists. Once your tour is over, you can return to the reserve on your own as your ticket is valid for the entire day. Proceeds from the tours benefit environmental education programs in 16 local schools.

The reserve also offers tours at 7:30 pm nightly. These are by flashlight (bring your own for the best visibility) and led by guides who know about nocturnal natural history. Reservations are not required; the night tour costs US$13 and lasts 2½ hours.

If a reservation is made the previous day, the reserve will arrange guided birding tours in English. Various options are available. A morning tour begins at Stella's Bakery at 6 am, and usually over 40 species are sighted. This costs about US$28 per person, including reserve admission, with a minimum of three and maximum of six participants. Longer tours go on into the afternoon by request at a higher fee, and usually over 60 species are seen. All-day tours begin at 5:30 am with a hotel pickup and visit both the Monteverde reserve and the San Luis Biological Station (described later in this chapter) and include breakfast, lunch, and transportation. The cost is US$55 per person, four minimum and six maximum, including reserve admission. Normally, over 80 species are seen. Profits from all these tours and entrance fees go directly to the reserve.

Most hotels will be able to arrange for a local to guide you either within the reserve or in some of the nearby surrounding areas.

You can also hire a guide for a private tour. Costs vary depending on the season, the guide, and where you want to go, but average about US$30 to US$65 for a half-day tour. Entrance costs may be extra, especially for the cheaper tours. Full-day tours are also available. The size of the group is up to you – go alone or split the cost with a group of friends.

The following guides all work for the reserve and, as such, are recommended. All of them have good general natural history knowledge. They can be contacted through the reserve or personally. Alex Villegas (☎ 645-5343) is one of the best local young birders. Debra de Rosier (☎ 645-5220) is doing research on the importance of hedgerows as corridors in bird flyways and is a good birder. Mark Wainwright (☎ 645-5598) has been recommended for his enthusiasm. Eric Bello (☎ 645-5291) likes to talk about plants. For generalists, any of the following are good:

Samuel Arguedas	☎ 645-5142
Pedro Bosques	☎ 645-5470
Gary Diller	☎ 645-5045
Ricky Guindon	☎ 645-5085
Adrian Mendez	☎ 645-5282
Victorino Molina	☎ 645-5643
Eduardo Neil	☎ 645-5220
Jorge Quesada	☎ 645-5546

Other guides are available. Because of the historical Quaker influence, many locals and most guides speak English as well as Spanish.

Nature Trails & Hiking

Inside the reserve are various marked and maintained trails. The most popular are found in a roughly triangular area ('El Triángulo') to the east of the reserve entrance – these trails are all suitable for day hikes. There are some seven trails, which vary from 200m to 2km one way. The 1.75km-long Chomogo Trail climbs 150m to reach 1680m above sea level, the highest point in the triangle. A free trail map is provided with your entrance fee.

Longer trails stretch out east across the reserve and down the Peñas Blancas river valley (it's not connected with the Peñas Blancas refuge) to lowlands north of the Cordillera de Tilarán. These longer trails have shelters (see Places to Stay & Eat, below). Ask at the reserve about hiking through to the northern lowlands.

The bird list includes over 400 species that have been recorded in the area, but the one that most visitors want to see is the resplendent quetzal (see the Wildlife Guide at the back of this book). The best time to see the quetzal is when it is nesting in March and April, but you could get lucky any time of year.

There is a host of other things to observe. A walk along the Sendero Bosque Nuboso (Cloud Forest Trail; see the 'A Hike on the Sendero Bosque Nuboso' boxed text) will take you on a 2km (one-way) interpretive walk through the cloud forest to the continental divide. The US$2 trail guide (with numbers matching discrete markers on the trail) describes plants, weather patterns, animal tracks, insects, and ecosystems that you'll see along the way. Ask about a new suspension-bridge trail.

Places to Stay & Eat

Almost all visitors stay in one of the many hotels, pensiones, and lodges in either the Monteverde community or Santa Elena; see details earlier in this chapter.

There is ***dormitory-style accommodation*** near the park entrance, where one of 39 bunks costs US$10. These bunks are often used by researchers and student groups but are sometimes available to tourists – contact the reserve (☎ 645-5112, 645-5564) for information. There are shared bathrooms and full board can be arranged in advance.

Backpackers can stay in one of three basic ***shelters*** on the reserve. Each has at least 10 bunks, drinking water, shower, electricity, stove, and cooking utensils. You need to carry a sleeping bag and food. The shelters are about two, three, and six hours' hike from the entrance along muddy and challenging trails. Each shelter is locked, but you can get a key from the reserve office after

A Hike on the Sendero Bosque Nuboso

When I walked this trail, the clouds were low over the forest and the gnarled old oak trees, festooned with vines and bromeliads, looked mysterious and slightly foreboding. Palm trees and bamboos bent menacingly over the trail, and I felt as if I were walking through a Grimm fairytale – a wicked witch or grinning goblin would not be out of place.

Suddenly the cold, clammy mist was rent by the weirdest metallic BONK!, followed by an eerie high-pitched whistle such as I had never heard before. I stopped dead in my tracks.

For a full minute I listened and heard nothing but the sighing of the faintest of breezes and a lone insect circling my ear. Then again, the strange BONK! and whistle were repeated, louder and high overhead. I craned my neck and searched the treetops with my binoculars.

Finally, after several more extremely loud BONK! sounds and whistles, I spied an odd-looking large brown bird with snow-white head and shoulders just visible on a high snag.

At first, I thought the bird was eating a lizard or small snake – through my binoculars I could clearly see the wormlike objects hanging from the bill. But then the beak gaped wide open and, instead of a seeing a reptile wriggling away, I heard another BONK! and whistle. Finally, I realized that I was watching the aptly named three-wattled bellbird.

The three black, wormy-looking wattles hanging from the bill were fully 6cm long – about a fifth of the length of the entire bird. The metallic BONK! did sound rather bell-like, but it traveled over an incredible distance. It seemed to be flooding the forest with sound, but the bird itself was probably 100m away or more, barely visible in the top of the cloud forest.

– Rob Rachowiecki

making a reservation. Usually, you can leave the day after making a reservation. The cost is US$3.50 per person per night, plus the usual daily entrance fee; the farthest-in shelter costs US$5 per person and has room for 22 people.

There is a small ***cafeteria*** by the park entrance, open till 4:30 pm. It has a small and inexpensive selection of snacks and meals. Otherwise, carry your own lunch on day hikes in the reserve.

Getting There & Away

The entrance to the reserve is uphill from all the hotels; there are two public buses, leaving Santa Elena at 6 am and 1 pm, which can be flagged down anywhere along the road. Ask your hotel what time the buses usually pass its doorstep; return trips leave the reserve at noon and 4 pm, and the one-way fare is about US$1. The better hotels can arrange a vehicle to take you up to the reserve, or you can take your own vehicle to the small parking lot by the entrance. A taxi from Santa Elena will charge about US$5 to US$6.

You can also walk – look for paths that run parallel to the road. There are views all along the way, and many visitors remark that some of the best birding is on the open road leading up to the reserve entrance, especially the final 2km.

RESERVA SANTA ELENA

This reserve was created in 1989 and opened to the public shortly thereafter. It is now managed by the high school board and bears the quite unwieldy official name of Reserva del Bosque Nuboso del Colegio Técnico Profesional de Santa Elena (☎ 645-5390, fax 645-5014, forestse@sol.racsa.co.cr). You can visit their office in the high school.

The reserve provides a welcome alternative to the more visited one in Monteverde. The Reserva Santa Elena is about 6km northeast of the village of Santa Elena. The cloud forest in the reserve is slightly higher than, but otherwise similar to, Monteverde, and you can see quetzals here too – I did. Within an hour or two of hiking from the entrance, you reach lookouts from which you can see Volcán Arenal exploding in the distance – I didn't. I reached the lookouts, but it was too cloudy and the 20m visibility just didn't quite make it. Rule No 407 of cloud forest travel: It's often cloudy.

The Reserva Santa Elena is less visited than Monteverde yet has a good (though not 'concrete blocked') trail system. The Reserva Santa Elena offers a good look at the Costa Rican cloud forest, despite the cachet conferred by the Monteverde name.

Over 12km of trails are currently open, and expansion of the reserve and trail system is planned. Currently, four circular trails offer walks of varying difficulty and length, from 45 minutes to 3½ hours. There is a program of cloud forest study for both local and international students. Projects for volunteers (minimum age 16) are also available, with housing provided, though volunteers must contribute toward food and other expenses. Contact the reserve office in Santa Elena (see above) for information about studying or volunteering. Donations are gladly accepted.

Information

The reserve is open 7 am to 4 pm daily. There is an information center at the entrance where you can see a small exhibit, obtain trail maps and information, and pay the entry fee of US$6 (US$3.50 for students with ID). Rubber boots can be rented here; bring your own for a better fit. Guided tours can be arranged for US$13, and night tours are available by reservation at the Santa Elena office. At the entrance, there's a small gift shop as well as a coffee shop. Dorm beds can be reserved in advance; there are four little cabins with room for 14 people at US$4 per person. You can also get permission to camp in the reserve. All proceeds go toward managing the reserve and to environmental education programs in local schools.

Getting There & Away

The reserve can be reached by car or on foot; head north from Santa Elena and follow the signs. A taxi from Santa Elena costs about US$8 each way; at the reserve entrance they can radio for a return taxi. Sky Trek (see the Canopy Tour section, earlier in this chapter) is nearby; following a tour there, you could walk the remaining 2km to the reserve. Ask at the office about a daily early-morning bus to the reserve.

ECOLODGE SAN LUIS & BIOLOGICAL STATION

Formerly just a tropical biology research station, this facility now integrates research with ecotourism and education. It is directed by on-site tropical biologists and has hosted many researchers and university courses. The addition of comfortable accommodations has made this a station to rival better-known places like La Selva as a great place to stay for travelers interested in learning about the cloud forest environment and experiencing a bit of traditional rural Costa Rica.

The 70-hectare site is on the Río San Luis and adjoins the southern part of the Monteverde reserve. The average elevation of 1100m makes it a tad lower and warmer than Monteverde, and birders find that this is a good place to find species that prefer slightly lower elevations. About 230 species have been recorded in this small protected area, and the list will grow. Many mammals have been sighted as well, and visitors have a good chance of spotting coatis, kinkajous, tayras, sloths, monkeys, and others. There are a number of trails into primary and secondary forest, and there's also a working farm with tropical fruit orchards and a coffee harvest from November to March.

Activities include day and night hikes guided by biologists, horseback rides, excellent birding, farm activities, seminars and slide shows, research and cultural programs, and relaxing activities like swimming in the river or swinging in a hammock.

Places to Stay

There are three types of lodging available. Two dormitory rooms with 12 bunks and shared segregated bathrooms cost US$55 per person. There are a couple of smaller bunk rooms with shared bathrooms. All bathrooms have hot water. Rooms with private hot bath cost US$75 per person. Twelve larger rooms with private hot bath, a double and a single bed, and view porches cost US$90 per person. Children seven to 14 staying with parents pay US$45. Rates include three meals a day (tico home cooking served family-style), guided hikes, slide shows, and participation in seminars, research activities, etc. Horseback riding costs an extra US$9 an hour. Discounts can be arranged for students, researchers, large groups, and long stays. Ask about their week-long rainforest ecology course. Reservations can be made at the ***Ecolodge San Luis*** *(☎/fax 645-5277, 380-3255 cellular; in the USA ☎ 800-699-9685, ☎/fax 615-297-2155, edutropical@nashville.net)*. A minimum of two nights' stay is recommended so that you can enjoy at least one full day at the station.

Getting There & Away

From Santa Elena, you can take a taxi (about US$25) or walk down on the dirt road from Monteverde (see the Monteverde & Santa Elena map) for about 3km. This dirt road may be passable to 4WD vehicles, but most taxis take the driving route that goes south of Santa Elena to an orange kiosk about 12km away. Here, a sign points left to San Luis and the ecolodge, about 8km away. You can also arrange in advance with the ecolodge to ride to/from Santa Elena by horse for about US$20 per person.

If you are driving from the Interamericana, follow the directions to Santa Elena and turn right at the orange kiosk.

JUNTAS

Although marked only as 'Juntas' on some Costa Rican maps, the full name of this town is Las Juntas de Abangares. This small town on the Río Abangares used to be a major gold-mining center in the late 19th and early 20th centuries, attracting fortune seekers and entrepreneurs from all over the world. The gold boom is now over, but a museum opened in 1991 and a small tourist industry is beginning in this sleepy Costa Rican town. It makes an interesting side trip for travelers wishing to get away from the tourist hordes.

Named the **Ecomuseo de las Minas de Abangares**, the small museum is 5km beyond Juntas and has photographs and models depicting the old mining practices of the area. (It is unclear why a mining museum should be called an 'Ecomuseo' – it seems that everyone is trying to jump on the ecological bandwagon.) In the grounds outside the museum are a picnic area and children's play area; trails above the museum lead to mine artifacts, such as bits of railway. I found some good birding along these trails – it's very quiet here and the birds are rarely disturbed. Also, the area is several hundred meters above the coastal lowlands and attracts some different species. Hours are 6 am to 5 pm daily. Admission to the Ecomuseo is by contribution (300 colones suggested – about US$1.50), but there was nobody around to take it when I was there.

Although major mining is over, there are still a few minor mine operations – ask around about visiting or touring these.

Places to Stay & Eat

Cabinas Las Juntas *(☎ 662-0153)* has rooms with air-con and private cold showers for about US$5.50 per person. A double with hot shower, air-con, and TV costs US$18. A reasonable restaurant is attached.

There are several other places to eat – try the ***Soda La Amiga*** by the bus terminal and the restaurant on the Parque Central.

On the way out of town toward the museum, you pass the ramshackle ***El Caballo Blanco*** bar, which is an interesting place full of mining artifacts and colorful characters. Closer to the museum is ***La Sierra Alta Super Bar***, which serves cold drinks.

Getting There & Away

Bus There are buses from Cañas to Juntas at 9:30 am and 2:50 pm. There are also buses from the Puntarenas terminal in San José at 11 am and 5 pm. From Santa Elena, there is a bus at 5 am. There are no buses to the Ecomuseo, though 4WD taxis can be hired to take you there.

Buses leave Juntas for San José at 6 and 11 am, for Cañas at 6:30 am and 12:30 pm, and for Monteverde and Santa Elena at 2:30 pm.

Car The turnoff from the Interamericana is 27km south of Cañas and is reasonably well signed: 'Las Juntas 6km, Ecomuseo 11km.' (There is a place called Irmas at this intersection where you can stay and get information about tours of Juntas mines.) The road is paved as far as Juntas. To get to the Ecomuseo, follow the paved road for 100m past the Parque Central, turn left, cross a bridge and pass the Caballo Blanco on your left, then turn right; you'll see a sign indicating 'Ecomuseo 4km.' Then, the road becomes unpaved and progressively worsens. A couple of kilometers past Juntas, the road forks – a sign indicates a poor road going left to Monteverde (30km), rarely used by tourists but passable with 4WD, and to the right to the Ecomuseo (3km). In the small community of La Sierra, you can stop for a drink – you may have to park your car here and walk the last kilometer or so.

TEMPISQUE FERRY

About 23km south of Cañas on the Interamericana is a turnoff to the Tempisque ferry, 25km to the west. If you are headed to the Península de Nicoya, this will save you about 110km of driving via Liberia. Some buses from San José to Nicoya and the Península de Nicoya beaches come this way – ask about the route in the San José bus offices. Note that bus passengers must get off, buy a passenger ticket, and board the ferry on foot – don't miss the boat, because the bus won't wait.

The ferry runs every hour from 5 am to 8 pm (westbound) and 5:30 am to 8:30 pm (eastbound). The crossing takes 20 minutes and costs US$3 per car and US25¢ for foot passengers. The ferry holds about 10 to 20 vehicles (depending on their size); you might have to wait for the next ferry at peak times, especially Sunday afternoons when you're heading back to the mainland from the Península de Nicoya.

A bridge is being built north of here – it is projected to open sometime in the early years of the new millennium.

CAÑAS

Cañas is a small agricultural center serving about 25,000 people in the surrounding area. If you're coming from the south, this is the first town of any size in Costa Rica's driest and dustiest province, Guanacaste, known for its cattle ranches and folk dances. You'll see an occasional cowboy hat and swagger on the streets of this little town. It's 90m above sea level (hot!) and about 180km from San José along the Interamericana. There is not much to do in Cañas itself, but travelers use it as a base for visits to the nearby Parque Nacional Palo Verde and other reserves, the Ecomuseo in Juntas, and for Corobicí river trips (see later in this chapter). There is a small ACT office (☎/fax 669-0533) here that administers Reserva Biológica Isla de Los Pájaros. Cañas is also the beginning or end point for the Arenal backroads route, described later in this chapter.

Places to Stay

Cañas is a cheaper place to stay than Liberia, which may be why so many long-haul truck drivers spend the night here. Get in by midafternoon for the best choice of rooms.

Two basic but adequate hotels on the southeastern side of the Parque Central are the ***Hotel Guillén*** *(☎ 669-0070)* and ***Hotel***

Parque, which is cleaner and has a balcony; both charge about US$3.50 per person. The ***Gran Hotel***, on the northwestern side of the park, is similarly priced and has basic double rooms with private bath for a few dollars more. At the southeastern end of town, on Avenida 2 near Calle 5, the ***Cabinas Corobicí*** *(☎ 669-0241)* is better, charging about US$7 per person with private bath. None of these hotels has hot showers.

The best place in downtown Cañas is the ***Hotel Cañas*** *(☎ 669-0039, 669-1319)*, Calle 2, Avenida 3. Simple rooms with private cold baths and fan cost about US$15/21 single/double; with air-conditioning, rates are US$28 for a double. This hotel has a good restaurant and is very popular – the air-conditioned rooms go very fast. A block away, their 'annex,' the ***Nuevo Hotel Cañas*** *(☎ 669-0039, 669-1319)*, takes the overflow; it has newer, slightly more expensive rooms and a pool (available to nonguests for a small fee).

The most expensive place is the ***Hotel El Corral*** *(☎ 669-1467)*, which is right on the Interamericana. Its basic air-conditioned rooms with private electric showers rent for US$25/40.

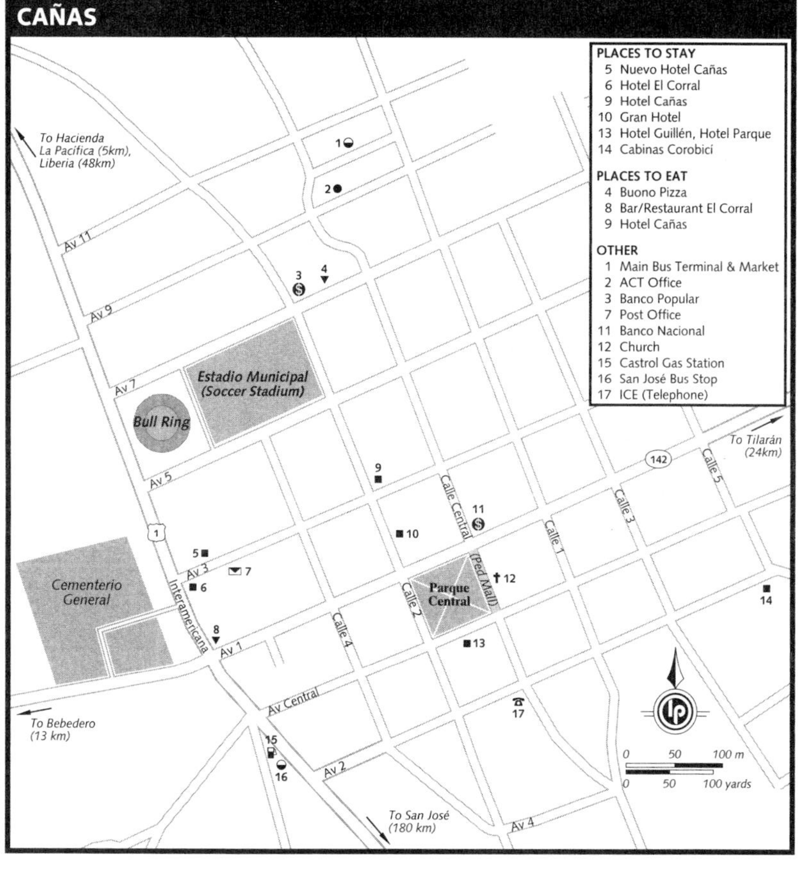

Three kilometers northwest of Cañas on the Interamericana is the tranquil ***Capazuri Bed & Breakfast*** *(☎ 669-0580)*, which charges US$16/27 per person for a room with fans, TV, and private shower, including a good breakfast served at a large family table. The spacious grounds offer many shade trees and hammocks. Camping is about US$3.50 per person; breakfast for campers is an additional US$2 to US$5. Also consider the upscale ***Hacienda La Pacífica***, 5km north of Cañas (see below).

Places to Eat

The ***Hotel Cañas*** restaurant is good – its breakfast attracts some of the town's important people to sit around and plan the day's events. Around and near the park are some typical sodas as well as a few unremarkable Chinese restaurants with adequate meals in the US$2 to US$5 range. There's also ***Buono Pizza***, near the stadium on Avenida 7. Down on the Interamericana is the ***Bar/Restaurant El Corral***, which is run by a lady who speaks English well.

Getting There & Away

Buses for Cañas leave San José six times a day from Calle 16, Avenidas 1 & 3, opposite the Coca-Cola terminal. There are also TRALAPA buses from Calle 20, Avenida 3. The trip takes about 3½ hours and costs about US$2.50.

Cañas has two bus stops. The main bus terminal and produce market is at Calle 1 and Avenida 11 – most buses leave from here. In addition, many San José-bound buses can be flagged down outside the Castrol gas station (see map). By the time you read this, all buses may be leaving from the main terminal. Call Transportes La Cañera (☎ 669-0145) for departure times.

The terminal has about seven daily buses to Liberia, seven to Tilarán, two to Juntas at 9:30 am and 2:50 pm (this may change, so check), six to Bebedero (near Parque Nacional Palo Verde), five to Upala, and seven to Puntarenas. Not all buses originate in Cañas – many just stop here, such as the Liberia-Cañas-Puntarenas bus.

HACIENDA LA PACÍFICA

La Pacífica is a working hacienda just off the Interamericana about 5km north of Cañas. There are cattle, rice paddies, sorghum fields, cashew trees, and other crops, but about 600 of its 2000 hectares have been left covered with forest. The owners, to put it in their own words, have attempted an equilibrium between rational exploitation of the natural resources and conservation.

To a certain extent, this concept has been successful. Many species of birds are attracted to the hacienda, and howler monkeys, armadillos, and anteaters are among the mammals that can be seen in the forest. Observation of the flora and fauna is encouraged and there are trails for hiking and horseback riding. There is a small library of reference books. Bilingual naturalist guides and horses are available free to guests. Bicycle rental is US$3 per hour or US$15 a day.

Ríos Tropicales offers a variety of tours from La Pacífica to the nearby national parks, rivers, and reserves. Contact them through La Pacífica (see number below) or through their San José office (☎ 233-6455, fax 255-4354, www.riostro.com).

Although the hacienda is on the Pacific side of the country, it is not named after the ocean. Its name derives from Doña Pacífica Fernandéz, who designed the Costa Rican flag near the turn of the century and was the wife of President Bernardo Soto. Her *casona* (old ranch house) has been restored and is now a museum of rural turn-of-the-century life. It can be visited on foot or horseback.

The hacienda can be visited on day trips, but most visitors stay in one of 33 comfortable bungalows with private hot baths and fans. Rates are about US$70/80. Three-day/two-night packages are offered. Call the hacienda *(☎ 669-0050, 669-0266, fax 669-0555; in San José ☎ 220-4047, fax 231-4429)* for details and reservations.

There is a swimming pool and a good, tastefully decorated restaurant that is open to the public. Main courses are in the US$7 to US$15 range. If this is too expensive for you, there is also the pleasant and slightly cheaper restaurant ***Rincón Corobicí***, which is just past La Pacífica on the banks of the Río Corobicí – people swim off the rocks behind the outdoor terrace, a nice break from the highway.

RIVER TRIPS

Tour companies in San José arrange one-day rafting trips on the Río Corobicí with roundtrip transportation from San José. Most people use a local outfitter, Safaris Corobicí (☎/fax 669-1091, safaris@sol.racsa.co.cr), which has an office on the Interamericana about 400m southeast of Hacienda La Pacífica. The emphasis of these trips is wildlife observation rather than exciting white water. The river is Class I to II – in other words, pretty flat.

Safaris Corobicí offers daily departures on the Corobicí. A two-hour float costs US$35 per person, a three-hour birding float covering 12km costs US$43 per person, and a half-day 18km float including lunch costs US$60 per person. All prices are based on a two-person minimum; children under 14 accompanying adults receive a 50% discount, and large groups can ask for a better rate, depending on group size.

Safaris Corobicí also has half-day saltwater estuary trips along the Bebedero and Tempisque rivers, bordering Parque Nacional Palo Verde, for US$60 per person (four minimum, lunch included). Birds and other animals seen on some of these float trips (both Corobicí and estuary trips) include motmots, parrots, sungrebes, boat-billed and other herons, trogons, wood storks, spoonbills, coatis, river otters, howler monkeys, and caimans. These are good trips for nature enthusiasts – you can bring a camera and binoculars because the ride is not wild. Bring a swimsuit for a refreshing river dip, and don't forget sun protection.

LAS PUMAS

Las Pumas (☎ 669-0444, 669-0544) is a wild-animal shelter directly behind Safaris Corobicí. It was started in the 1960s by the Swiss former owners of La Pacífica and is said to be the largest shelter of its kind in Latin America. The emphasis, as the name suggests, is on cats – you may get to see pumas, jaguars, ocelots, and margays, plus peccaries and a few birds. The animals were either orphaned or injured, and it has clearly been a labor of love to save and raise them. Although the cages aren't large, the animals are well looked after and are certainly much better off than being left to die. Some animals are reintroduced into the wild.

The shelter is open 8 am to 5 pm daily except Monday. Admission is free, but there is a donation box. Las Pumas is not officially funded and contributions help offset the high costs of maintaining the shelter.

VOLCÁN TENORIO AREA

The 58km paved highway to Upala goes north from the Interamericana about 1.5km northwest of La Pacífica. This road passes in between Volcán Miravalles (2028m) to the west (see below) and Volcán Tenorio (1916m) to the east. Tenorio is an active volcano, though activity is limited to fumaroles, hot springs, and mud pots, with none of the spectacular activity of Volcán Arenal.

Tenorio is part of **Parque Nacional Volcán Tenorio**, one of Costa Rica's newest national parks and part of the Area de Conservación Arenal (ACA). Services at this park are pretty much nonexistent at this writing, although it can be visited via the Bijagua Heliconia Ecotourist Lodge (see below). The park boasts five life zones, and the virgin forests near the volcano's summit are the haunts of tapirs and pumas. At the summit is a small lake surrounded by epiphyte-laden cloud forests. On the northeastern flanks of the volcano, the Río Celeste, named after the blue color caused by many minerals dissolved in its waters, is a scenic attraction. Its thermal headwaters contain springs and boiling mud pots – take great care not to scald yourself when you're exploring the area.

About 33km north of the Interamericana and 25km south of Upala is the community of **Bijagua**. The ***Bijagua Heliconia Ecotourist Lodge***, sponsored by the Canadian WWF and ACA, is 3km east of Bijagua on a bumpy, unpaved road. The lodge is operated by an association of 12 local families, with a friendly, helpful brother-and-sister team (who speak some English) serving as the main managers. A few trails surround the lodge, including a short walk to a canopy platform that gives a bird's-eye view of the rainforest and valley. Guests can visit local farms or go on locally guided hikes and horseback rides to waterfalls, hot springs, and rivers in Parque Nacional Volcán Tenorio. Tours cost US$20 to US$40 per person. The adventurous can get information about where they can hike and camp on the volcano without guides.

The lodge has six simple, comfortable cabins with private hot showers renting for US$15/22/27/33 for one to four people. A restaurant with sweeping views of the valley, Volcán Miravalles, and (on a clear day) Lago de Nicaragua serves breakfast (US$2) and other meals (US$5). For reservations, call ☎ *259-3605, fax 259-9430, cooprena@sol.racsa.co.cr*. If you speak Spanish, you can leave a message at the public phone near the lodge (☎ 470-0622) or ask if the lodge's direct line has been installed. The signed turnoff to the lodge is by Bijagua's Banco Nacional, where you can change money.

Two or three kilometers north of Bijagua, a sign points east to ***La Carolina Lodge***. This lodge is about 8km east of the highway toward the village of Santo Domingo. This is a rustic country farm offering inexpensive accommodations (two double rooms and a dorm with seven beds) with shared showers and family cooking. Horseback and hiking tours onto neighboring Volcán Tenorio are offered, and other tours may also be available. Rates are about US$40 per person including a bed, three meals, and a guided horseback ride. Ask about discounts for longer stays.

VOLCÁN MIRAVALLES AREA

Volcán Miravalles (2028m) is the highest volcano in the Cordillera de Guanacaste. It is afforded a modicum of protection by being within the Zona Protectora Miravalles. Although the main crater is dormant, there is some geothermal activity at Las Hornillas (a few bubbling mud pools and steam vents), at about 700m above sea level on the south slopes of the volcano.

Volcán Miravalles is 27km north-northeast of Bagaces and can be approached by a paved road that leads north of Bagaces through the communities of Salitral, La Ese, Guayabo, and on to Aguas Claras. A parallel paved road to the east avoids La Ese and Guayabo – instead, it goes through Salitral and then the community of La Fortuna before rejoining the first road just north of Guayabo. The road beyond Aguas Claras is a rough one continuing to Upala. North of La Fortuna is the government-run Proyecto Geotérmico Miravalles, a project that generates electrical power from geothermal energy. A few bright steel tubes from the plant snake along the flanks of the volcano, adding an eerie touch to the remote landscape. The project can be visited. There are small signs for both the project and Las Hornillas along the road. There are no guard rails around the vents and mud pools – stay away from their edges, which occasionally collapse. Four kilometers north of the plant is the **Yoko Hot Springs**, a small locally owned resort where you can buy a drink and relax in the thermal waters. Admission is about US$4; call the Miravalles Lodge (see below) to ask about opening hours.

The village of Guayabo is about 30km north of Bagaces in the saddle between Parque Nacional Rincón de la Vieja and Volcán Miravalles. In the village are a couple ***sodas***; if you ask around, you could probably find somewhere to stay in someone's home.

A couple kilometers north of Guayabo is ***Cabinas Las Brisas*** (☎ *673-0333*), run by Armando Rodriguez, a former Cuban who cooks up good, simple Cuban cuisine and offers basic rooms for US$8 per person. About 5km farther north is the ***Miravalles Lodge*** (☎ *673-0823, fax 673-0350, mvolcano@sol.racsa.co.cr*), an attractive lodge with great views of the volcano. There is a spacious restaurant/bar, tours are available, and the owners speak English. A short path leads from the lodge through a neighbor's farm to a small hot spring in a cool brook; there are other trails nearby. High-ceilinged, wood-paneled rooms with private bath cost about US$40 double. Dan Stasiuk, the Canadian foreman of a nearby cattle ranch, can be contacted through the lodge for horse tours; he is a friendly, experienced horseman whose enthusiasm and respect for Guanacaste culture make him an enjoyable guide.

In La Fortuna, near the soccer field, is the basic, friendly ***Cabinas Jesse***, with small rooms for about US$3 per person.

A daily bus goes from Liberia to Aguas Claras, leaving at 1:30 pm; from Bagaces, there are four buses a day for Aguas Claras, which can drop you near any of the places to stay described above. Several buses a day go from Bagaces through La Fortuna and can drop you at the power plant or hot springs.

BAGACES

This small town is about 22km northwest of Cañas on the Interamericana. The main reason to stop here is to visit the national park offices or the Friends of Lomas Barbudal offices (or both).

The headquarters of the Area de Conservación Tempisque (ACT), which administers Parque Nacional Palo Verde, Reserva Biológica Lomas Barbudal, and several smaller and less-known protected areas, is in Bagaces. The ACT office (☎ 671-1062, fax 671-1290) is on the Interamericana opposite the main entry road into Parque Nacional Palo Verde (which is signed). The office is mainly an administrative one, though sometimes rangers are available. The staff is friendly and will try to help – you can ask them to call Palo Verde to get information directly from the rangers. Office hours are 8 am to 4 pm weekdays.

Friends of (Amigos de) Lomas Barbudal (☎ 671-1203, fax 671-1029) is a nonprofit organization begun in 1986 to protect tropical dry forest in general and Reserva Biológica Lomas Barbudal in particular. It is still in existence but currently operates at a much reduced level and is not running any projects. In the past, 'Friends' put a lot of work into community involvement and education and constructed a visitor and community center staffed by locals, which is now closed. You are still welcome to visit the office in Bagaces to ask for information about the reserve – there is no street address, but most *bagaceños* know where it is.

Places to Stay & Eat

There aren't many places to stay in this small town. The best is ***Albergue Bagaces*** *(☎ 671-1267, fax 666-2021)*, on the Interamericana opposite the ACT office. The charge is US$12.50 per person for clean rooms with private bath and fan. The town's best restaurant is also here, open 9 am to 10 pm (though sometimes it shuts down for the day if business is slow). There's a good, cheap roadside ***soda*** by the gas station. There are a couple of cheap and basic ***pensiones*** in town; ask around to see which one is currently the best maintained.

Getting There & Away

The bus terminal here is a block north of the village park; ask for directions from the highway. Most buses going to Liberia or Cañas can drop you off on the Interamericana at the entrance to town. Everything is within a few blocks of the highway. See the Volcán Miravalles Area section (above) for information on buses from Bagaces to that area.

PARQUE NACIONAL PALO VERDE

The 16,804-hectare Parque Nacional Palo Verde lies on the northeastern banks of the mouth of Río Tempisque at the head of the Golfo de Nicoya, some 30km west of Cañas and 30km south of Bagaces. It is a major bird sanctuary for resident and migrating waterfowl as well as forest birds. A large number of different habitats is represented, ranging from swamps, marshes, mangroves, and lagoons to a variety of seasonal grasslands and forests. Some 150 species of trees have been recorded in the park. A number of low limestone hills provide lookout points over the park. The dry season, from December to March, is very marked, and much of the forest dries out. During the wet months, large portions of the area are flooded.

Palo Verde is a magnet for birders, who come to see the large flocks of herons (including the country's largest nesting colony of black-crowned night-herons on Isla de Los Pájaros), storks (including the only Costa Rican nesting site of the locally endangered jabiru stork), spoonbills, egrets, ibis, grebes, and ducks. Inland, birds such as scarlet macaws, great curassows, keel-billed toucans, and parrots may be seen. Approximately 300 bird species have been recorded in the park. Other possible sightings include crocodiles (reportedly up to 5m in length), iguanas, deer, coatis, monkeys, and peccaries.

The recommended time for a visit is September to March because of the huge influx of migratory and endemic birds. This is one of the greatest concentrations of waterfowl and shorebirds in Central America. December to February are the best months. September and October are very wet, and access may be limited. When the dry season begins, the birds tend to congregate in the remaining lakes and marshes. Trees lose their leaves and the massed flocks of birds become easier to observe. In addition, there are far fewer insects in the dry season and the roads and trails are more passable. Mammals are seen around the waterholes. Binoculars or a spotting scope are highly recommended.

Information

Admission to the park is US$6 a day, which you pay at the park entrance station.

The Hacienda Palo Verde research station, 8km from the park entrance station, is run by the Organization of Tropical Studies (OTS).

Several trails lead from the station area into the national park, and there is also an observation tower in the area. A couple of kilometers farther into the park, you'll reach the Palo Verde park headquarters and the ranger station.

The ACT office in Bagaces can be contacted for information about the park (see Bagaces, above), but the best source for information or reservations for day or overnight visits is the OTS (see below).

Places to Stay & Eat

The research station allows travelers to stay for US$38 per day, US$13 for children between the ages of six and 12 (though researchers and those taking OTS courses get preference). Accommodation is in dormitory rooms with shared bathrooms and includes three meals. A few two- and four-bed rooms with shared bathrooms are available. Overnight guests must make all arrangements with the ***OTS*** *(☎ 240-6696, fax 240-6783, reservas@ns.ots.ac.cr, www.ots.ac.cr)*. If you just want a day visit, you can make all reservations via the above OTS contacts. Visits include lunch and either a talk by station personnel or a guided walk. These cost US$15. Both overnight and day visitors must also pay the US$6 park fee, because the station is in the national park.

Camping is permitted near the Palo Verde ranger station, where toilets and shower facilities are available to campers. A camping fee of US$2 per person is charged (in addition to the US$6 park fee). Meals with the park rangers can be arranged in advance by calling ACT in Bagaces *(☎ 671-1062, fax 671-1290)*.

On the Península de Nicoya side of the park is Puerto Humo (see the Península de Nicoya chapter), where there is lodging near the park boundary and boat tours can be arranged.

Getting There & Away

There are several routes into the park, but it is difficult to get there unless you have your own transportation, are on a tour, hire a taxi, or walk. If you call in advance, park rangers may be able to pick you up in Bagaces; try the ACT office in Bagaces (see above).

The most frequently used route begins in Bagaces, where there is a signed turnoff from the Interamericana. From here, follow signs for the national park. At times, the road forks – if in doubt, take the fork that looks more used. If you can't decide which is the main fork, take the road that has a power line running along it. After about 28km, you reach the park entrance station, where admission fees are paid. Another 8km brings you to the limestone hill, Cerro Guayacán, from which there are good views of the park. This is where the OTS research station is found; a couple of kilometers farther are the Palo Verde park headquarters and ranger station.

The road is supposedly passable to ordinary cars all year-round, but get up-to-date information if you are traveling in the rainy season. Note that the road from the Interamericana to Reserva Biológica Lomas Barbudal, which skirts the edge of the reserve, eventually joins the Bagaces-Palo Verde road near the park entrance. Therefore, both these areas can be visited without having to return to the Interamericana.

From Puerto Humo, you can get boats into the park. Safaris Corobicí (☎/fax 669-1091, safaris@sol.racsa.co.cr) has float trips along the Ríos Tempisque and Bebedero, which border the park. Major tour companies in San José also offer tours, but they're not cheap.

RESERVA BIOLÓGICA LOMAS BARBUDAL

The 2279-hectare Lomas Barbudal reserve is separated from the northern edge of Palo Verde by a narrow strip of privately owned land. About 70% of the area is deciduous forest that contains several species of endangered trees, such as mahogany and rosewood, as well as the common and quite spectacular *Tabebuia ochracea* (it's locally called the *corteza amarilla* or yellow cortez). This tree is what biologists call a 'big bang reproducer' – all the yellow cortezes in the forest burst into bloom on the same day and, for about four days, the forest is an incredible mass of yellow-flowered trees. This usually occurs late in the dry season, about four days after an unseasonable rain shower.

During the dry season, many of the trees shed their leaves just as they do in the autumn or fall season in temperate lands. This kind of forest is known as tropical dry forest – once common in many parts of the Pacific slopes of Central America, but very little of it now remains. In addition, there are riparian forests along the Río Cabuyo, which flows through the reserve year-round, as well as small areas of other types of forest.

Lomas Barbudal is also locally famous for its abundance and variety of insects. There are about 250 different species of bees in this fairly small reserve – this represents about a quarter of the world's bee species. Bees here (and in nearby Palo Verde) include the Africanized 'killer' bees – if you suffer from bee allergies, this is one area where you really don't want to forget your bee-sting kit. Wasps, butterflies, and moths are also locally abundant.

There are plenty of birds to be seen. A checklist published by Friends of Lomas Barbudal in the 1990s has 202 species, and more have been added since. Interesting species include the great curassow, a chickenlike bird that is hunted for food and is endangered. Other endangered species found locally are the king vulture, scarlet macaw, and jabiru stork. Mammals you may see include white-tailed deer, peccaries, coatis, and howler and white-faced monkeys. The 'Friends' published an interesting trail guide under the title of *A White-Faced Monkey's Guide to Lomas Barbudal*. The guide is written as if by a white-faced monkey, who gives the reader six pages of interesting details about the forest from its own perspective: 'Contrary to popular belief, we do not throw fruit or intentionally defecate on humans; however, we do have to discard our garbage *somewhere*, and if you happen to be standing beneath us, it will land on you.'

Orientation & Information

At the reserve entrance, there's a small local museum and information center. The actual reserve is on the other side of the Río Cabuyo, behind the museum, but the river is not passable to vehicles, so you have to wade across at this point. Alternatively, you can drive to the right toward San Ramon de Bagaces (2km) and continue along the edge of the reserve by vehicle, making short incursions at various points. It is difficult to drive into the reserve because of the river, but hikes are certainly possible. This road eventually joins up with the road between Bagaces and Palo Verde.

The biological reserve is administered by the SPN and is part of the ACT; information can be obtained from the ACT office in Bagaces. The Friends of Lomas Barbudal also have an office in Bagaces; the bird checklists and trail guides may still be available. (See Bagaces, earlier in this chapter.)

Entrance to the reserve is by donation or free or costs US$1 or US$6, depending on whom you talk to. Camping is allowed. The dry season is from December to April, and it can get very hot then – temperatures of 38°C (100°F) are sometimes reached. During the rainy season, it is a little cooler, but insects are more abundant; bring repellent.

Getting There & Away

The turnoff to Lomas Barbudal from the Interamericana is near the small community of Pijije, 14km southeast of Liberia or 12km northwest of Bagaces. The road to the reserve is signed – it says '6km,' but it's actually just over 7km to the entrance to the reserve. The road is unpaved but open all year – some steep sections may require 4WD during and after heavy rains. Even during the dry season, it is barely passable to cars.

LIBERIA

Liberia is Costa Rica's most northerly town of any importance. It is the capital of the province of Guanacaste but has a population of only 40,000. This is an indication of how rural most of Costa Rica is once you leave the Central Valley.

The city is 140m above sea level and surrounded by ranches, making it a center for the cattle industry. It's also a fairly important transportation center, lying on the Interamericana at the intersection with the road to the west, which is the main entry route into the Península de Nicoya. Liberia is also a good base for visiting Parques Nacionales Santa Rosa, Guanacaste, and Rincón de la Vieja, all to the north, as well as Parque Nacional Palo Verde and Reserva Biológica Lomas Barbudal to the south.

Orientation & Information

Note that though streets are labeled on the map, very few of them are signed, especially once you get away from Parque Central.

There is a tourist information office (☎ 666-1606) in a historic mid-19th-century house at the corner of Avenida 6 and Calle 1. The office may be moving to a new building, but the phone number will stay the same. The staff is helpful with local details about hotels, bus schedules, national parks information, etc, and has a large-scale map for reference. It helps if you speak Spanish. Ask them about Internet access; if a public venue hasn't opened by the time of your visit, often someone will let you into their home to rent time on their computer.

Most of the better hotels will accept US dollars, and there are also the Banco Popular (☎ 666-0158, 666-1932) and the Banco Nacional (☎ 666-0996), among others. The smaller banks usually have the shortest lines.

The ICE telephone office has international phone and fax facilities – you can send an urgent fax overseas in a couple of minutes from here. This office is relocating – ask at the tourist information center for the new address.

The Hospital Dr Enrique Baltodano Briceño (☎ 666-0011, emergencies 666-0318) is behind the stadium on the northeastern outskirts of town.

The town is busy during the dry season and you should make reservations for the hotel of your choice, particularly at Christmas and Easter and on weekends. Conversely, the better hotels give discounts in the wet season. Mosquitoes can be a problem in the rainy months.

Things to See & Do

There are a number of good hotels, restaurants, and bars, and the main activity is relaxing in one of them as you plan your next trip to a beach or volcano.

The tourist information center has a small museum of local ranching artifacts – cattle raising is an historically important occupation of Guanacaste province. A statue of a *sabanero* (see boxed text) can be seen on the main road into town. The blocks around the tourist information center contain several of the town's oldest houses, many dating back about 150 years.

There is a pleasant Parque Central with a modern church, Iglesia Inmaculada Concepción de María. Walking six blocks northeast of the park along Avenida Central brings you to the oldest church in town, popularly called La Agonía (though maps show it as La Iglesia de la Ermita de la Resurección). Strolling out there and in the surrounding blocks makes as good a walk as any in town.

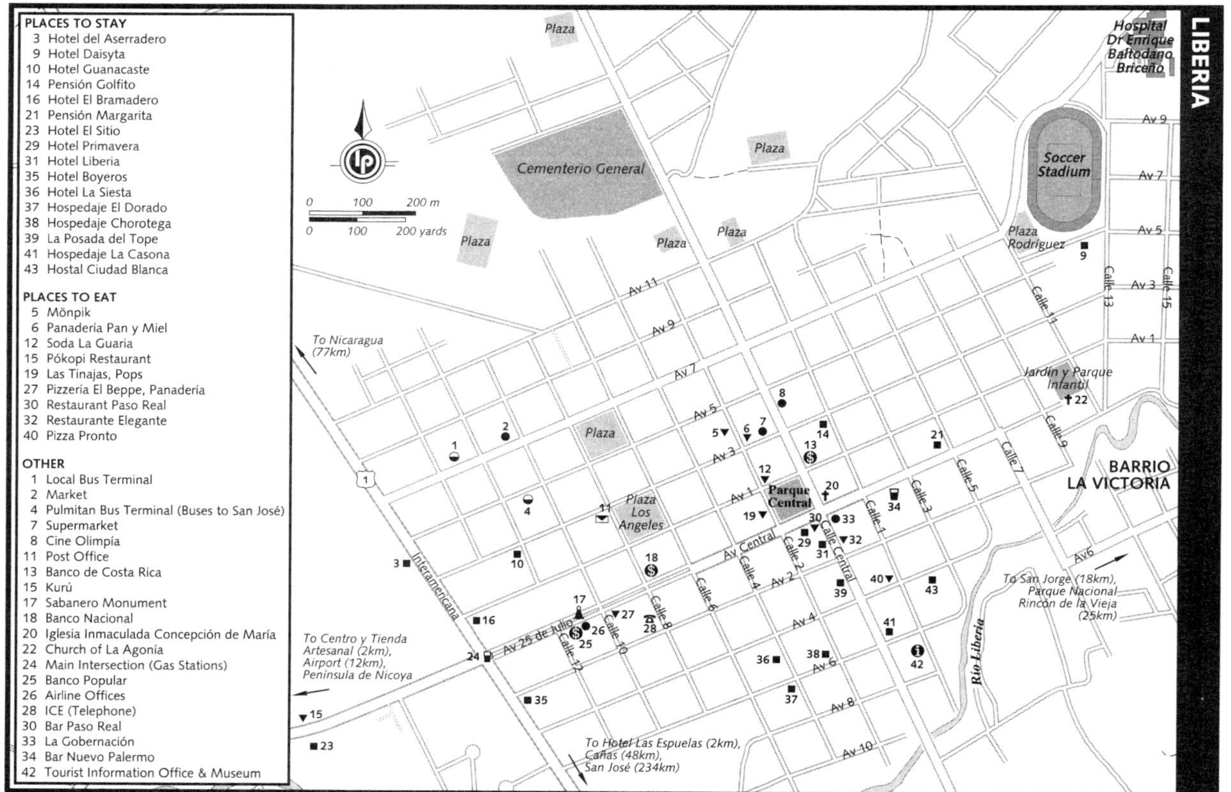

NORTHWESTERN

When I walked by early one morning, I saw a little old *campesino* gravely remove his hat and reverently kiss the locked door of the church, then cross himself three times.

Special Events

Guanacaste Day, July 25, is actively celebrated here in the capital of the province with a *tope* (horse parade), cattle auction, bullfight (the bull is never killed in Costa Rica), music, and rural fair. Ask at the tourist information office about topes and other events in small towns in the area – they happen frequently though irregularly.

Places to Stay

Budget Cheap and basic places to try in the US$3 to US$4 range include the ***Hospedaje Chorotega*** *(☎ 666-0898)*, ***Pensión Golfito*** *(☎ 666-0963)*, and ***Hospedaje El Dorado*** *(☎ 666-2950)*.

The basic but friendly ***Pensión Margarita*** *(☎ 666-0468)* charges US$5 per person. It's in a slightly dilapidated family home with a balcony offering street and sunset views. ***La Posada del Tope*** *(☎ 666-1313, fax 666-2136)* is a mid-19th-century house with an attractive front and lobby. Six basic but clean rooms with fans share one shower. The staff is friendly and allows guests to use the kitchen. Rates are about US$5 per person. ***Hospedaje La Casona*** *(☎/fax 666-2971)* has seven basic rooms with fans, sharing three bathrooms. There is a TV lounge. It is also home of Green Mountain Tours, a local travel office. Rates are US$5 per person.

The ***Hotel Liberia*** *(☎/fax 666-0161)* is in a solid-looking turn-of-the-century house just south of the park. Basic and rather dark little rooms with fans cost US$7.50/12 single/double or US$12/22 with private bath (cold water). Breakfast is included, and there is a café and laundry. The hotel can arrange taxis to Rincón de la Vieja for about US$18 one way for up to five passengers.

The ***Hotel Guanacaste*** *(☎ 666-0085, fax 666-2287, htlguana@sol.racsa.co.cr)* is affiliated with Hostelling International and has a restaurant with outdoor patio attached. It is on Avenida 3, a block off the Interamericana, and is popular with Costa Rican truck drivers and families and is often full. Check in early for the best rooms. Rates are about US$13/19 with a fan or US$24 for a double with air-conditioning. Some rooms have shared bathrooms. Hostelling International members receive a 15% discount. Internet access is available to guests. The hotel has a guarded parking lot, will change US dollars, and has a laundry and a morning and afternoon minibus to Rincón de la Vieja for US$8.50 per person one way. Staff will make local travel arrangements.

Mid-Range The family-run and friendly ***Hotel Daisyta*** *(☎ 666-0197, fax 666-0927)* has about 30 adequate rooms with private bath and fan, a swimming pool and a kids' pool, and a restaurant/bar for guests only. It advertises an underground discotheque, too. It is near the stadium on the northeastern outskirts of town. Rates are US$15 to US$20 per person.

On the other side of town, the ***Hotel El Bramadero*** *(☎ 666-0371, fax 666-0203)*, near the intersection of the Interamericana and the main road into town (Avenida Central), charges about US$20/30 for one of 17 rooms with private bath and air-conditioning, and US$15/22 for one of five rooms with fans. Rooms are plain but clean, and not all of them have hot water. There is an adequate restaurant (open 6 am to 10 pm) and swimming pool.

The ***Hotel Primavera*** *(☎ 666-0464, fax 666-2271)* is on the Parque Central. There are 30 clean and modern rooms with TV, fans, private cold baths, and parking. Rates are US$18/24, slightly more for air-conditioning if the hotel is full.

The ***Hotel La Siesta*** *(☎ 666-0678, fax 666-2532)* is on a quiet street at Calle 4, Avenidas 4 & 6. The rates are US$24/38 for clean singles/doubles with bath (cold shower) and air-conditioning. There is a small restaurant/bar and a tiny swimming pool. This place is nothing fancy, but it does offer a quiet night's sleep and is recommended for that.

The clean ***Hotel del Aserradero*** *(☎ 666-1939, fax 666-0475)* is in a converted old lumber mill on the Interamericana (but set back enough to minimize highway noise). It has 17 nice, fair-sized rooms, each with private hot bath and fan. Rates are US$27/35.

The small ***Hostal Ciudad Blanca*** *(☎/fax 666-2715)* has 12 rooms in a mansion and is one of Liberia's most attractive hotels. Rooms are air-conditioned and have fans, TVs, telephones, nice furnishings, and private (cold) baths. There is a charming little restaurant/bar. High-season rates are about US$22/40.

The ***Hotel Boyeros*** *(☎ 666-0722, fax 666-2529)* is near the intersection of the Interamericana with the main road into Liberia. With about 70 rooms, it's the largest in town. Air-conditioned rooms with private hot showers and TVs cost US$44/50 double/triple. Most rooms have small balconies or patios. There is a restaurant, adults' and kids' swimming pools, and dancing on weekends – get a room away from the music if you are looking for an early night.

Top End Many hotels (especially the more expensive ones) give substantial discounts in the low (rainy) season, except in late July for Guanacaste Day.

The ***Hotel Las Espuelas*** *(☎ 666-0144, fax 666-2441, espuelas@sol.racsa.co.cr)* is on the east side of the Interamericana, about 2km south of the main road into Liberia. It has pleasant grounds, a pool, a restaurant/bar, a casino, and gift shop. Over 40 rooms are US$46/59 single/double with private bath, TV, telephone, and air-conditioning.

The ***Hotel El Sitio*** *(☎ 666-1211, fax 666-2059)*, on the road to Nicoya about 250m west of the Interamericana, has 52 spacious air-conditioned rooms with TVs and private hot baths. The hotel is attractively decorated with original art. Pre-Columbian motifs and sabanero scenes predominate, and there are various *guanacasteco* touches. There is a decent restaurant/bar, a spa, and adults' and kids' pools. The hotel arranges horseback rides, car rental, and tours to beaches and national parks. High-season rates are US$58/75 and US$12 for each additional person.

The Sabanero

The open, dry cattle country of Guanacaste is Costa Rica's equivalent of the USA's West – and the *sabanero* is Guanacaste's cowboy. But in keeping with Costa Rica's mainly peaceful self-image, the sabanero tends to be a figure of steely dignity rather than of fist-fighting rambunctiousness. A sabanero carries himself with an air that will remind you as much of a samurai or knight as of a cowboy. You'll see sabaneros riding along almost any road or even highway in Guanacaste, and will recognize them by their straight-backed posture, casual hand on the reins, holster-slung machetes, and the high-stepping gait of their horses. This distinctive, almost prancing gait is a signature of sabanero culture – it demands endurance and skill from both horse and rider. Every year sabaneros show off their horsemanship at the local *tope*.

A tope is a mix of Western rodeo and country fair. Food stalls, music, and bull-riding – the bulls are not wounded or killed – are all central features. The bull-riding spectacle is where youthful wild oats are sown. A young macho turning pale and crossing himself as the bullring door is thrown open is a sight to remember. For comic relief, there are always a few drunks willing to volunteer as rodeo clowns, dancing around the ring to distract the bull as fallen riders scramble to safety. The horseback riding of the sabaneros is the high point of the day. Almost every little town has a tope; the dates change, so ask locally in any region you're visiting about when the next one will be held.

– John Thompson

Places to Eat

The better hotels have reasonable restaurants. On the southwest side of the Parque Central, ***Las Tinajas*** is a good place to sit outside with a cold drink and watch the unenergetic goings-on in the park. Meals cost US$7 to US$11, and you can get hamburgers and snacks as well. Several Chinese restaurants (the ***Restaurante Elegante*** is as good as any) are near the Parque Central, and several sodas are nearby; the ***Soda La Guaria***, on the northwest side, is cheap and popular with locals.

There are several Italian places. ***Pizza Pronto***, Calle 1 & Avenida 4, is in a 19th-century house and is a nice place, with a wood-burning pizza oven, outdoor patio with a kids' play area, and small art gallery. Another good one is ***Pizzería El Beppe***, on Avenida Central & Calle 10, which also has pastas and other meals for US$5 to US$7.

Restaurant Paso Real, at the southeast corner of the park, is a cheerful, modern place with a balcony; seafood specials cost US$4 to US$8. Inside at the bar is a large TV showing international sports.

For delicious pastries, there are two ***Panaderías Pan y Miel***, one next to Pizzería El Beppe and another a block north of Parque Central. For ice cream, one of your best choices is ***Mönpik***, on Calle 2, a couple of blocks north of the park, or ***Pops***, next to Las Tinajas.

Perhaps the best place in town, judging by its many recommendations, is the ***Pókopi Restaurant***, opposite the Hotel El Sitio. It serves a variety of seafood and meat dishes for US$7 to US$12.

Entertainment

Next door to the Pókopi Restaurant is the ***Kurú*** discotheque for you to dance off your dinner. Near Parque Central, the ***Cine Olimpía*** shows movies in English. Some of the bars in the upscale hotels may have live music at times. ***Las Tinajas*** has traditional music shows at 7 pm on Thursday and Sunday. The ***Bar Nuevo Palermo***, in the center, is a decent place for a beer.

Shopping

About 2km west of the Hotel El Sitio on the main road to the Península de Nicoya, you'll find the Centro y Tienda Artesanal de Liberia, a large complex of art galleries and crafts stores specializing in area crafts. Pottery from the Guaitil area (see the Península de Nicoya chapter) as well as local woodwork and paintings can be purchased, and often you can watch crafts being made.

Getting There & Away

Air The airport is about 12km west of town. Since early 1993, it has served as Costa Rica's second international airport, which allows sun-starved North American tourists trying to escape harsh winters to fly almost directly to Costa Rica's Pacific beach resorts. However, these international flights are definitely in development and subject to changes. In 1999, most international traffic here originated, for some reason, in Canada. There is a modern terminal (with pleasant air-conditioning!), but this is not a busy airport. It opens up when a flight is due – one or two daily domestic flights and occasional international ones. (Yes, there are immigration and customs here if you happen to be coming from abroad.)

SANSA flies San José-Liberia at 7 and 11 am and 2, 5:40, and 8:30 pm, returning at 6 and 8:35 am and 12:10, 3:15, and 7 pm. The fare is US$55 each way. Travelair flies San José-Tamarindo-Liberia daily at 8:20 am, returning from Liberia at 9:55 am directly to San José. The San José-Liberia fare is US$100 one way or US$165 roundtrip. Schedules to Liberia seem to change more often than anywhere else in Costa Rica; there have been flights via Tambor and Nosara in the past. Tickets for both airlines can be bought at the airport – call the San José offices for information: SANSA (☎ 221-9414), Travelair (☎ 220-3054).

A taxi to the airport will cost a few dollars. Or take any of the buses headed to Nicoya or the Playa del Coco region and ask to be let off at the entrance road – note that you'll have to walk about 1.6km from the main road to the airport terminal, so this is only an option for travelers willing to carry their luggage that far.

Bus Most visitors arrive by bus (or car). Pulmitan buses leave San José (US$3, 4½ hours) 11 times daily from Calle 14, Avenidas 1 & 3. From the Liberia Pulmitan terminal (☎ 666-0458), on Avenida 5, buses for San José leave 11 times a day between 4 am and 6 pm (a few of them may originate in Playa del Coco).

The bus terminal on Avenida 7, a block from the Interamericana, has departures for local and provincial destinations. Two companies service Filadelfia, Santa Cruz, and Nicoya (about US$2), with buses leaving roughly every hour from 5 am to 8 pm. Buses for Playa del Coco leave six times a day. Buses for Playa Hermosa and Playa Panamá leave at 7:30 and 11:30 am and 3:30, 5:30, and 7 pm. These three are the closest beach resorts to Liberia (see the Península de Nicoya chapter), but bus services may be curtailed in the rainy season.

Buses for La Cruz and Peñas Blancas (on the Nicaraguan border) leave about every hour during the day – some buses stop en route from San José, but seats are usually available. These are the buses to take if you want to get dropped off at the entrance to Parque Nacional Santa Rosa. Other northbound destinations include Cuajiniquil (north side of Santa Rosa) at 3:30 pm, Santa Cecilia (passing Hacienda Los Inocentes) at 7 pm, Quebrada Grande at 3 pm, and several buses for the nearby towns of Colorado and Cañas Dulces.

Southbound buses go to Bagaces and Cañas at 5:45 am and 1:30 and 4:30 pm, and to Puntarenas at 5, 8:30, 10, and 11:15 am and 3:15 pm. All these schedules are liable to change, but they give you an idea.

Car From Liberia, the Interamericana heads south to Cañas (48km) and San José (234km). Northbound, the highway reaches the Nicaraguan border at Peñas Blancas (77km). A paved highway to the west is the major road into the Península de Nicoya, which is famous for its good beaches and surfing, cattle ranches, terrible roads, and friendly inhabitants. A poor road to the east leads to Parque Nacional Rincón de la Vieja.

Rental cars are available – you should check their condition even more than in San José. However, with more international flights arriving (maybe?!), car rental agencies will be improving their services. Travelair can arrange for Adobe Rent a Car to meet you at the airport. In Liberia, shop around for the best deal. Ada (☎ 666-2998), 2km before the airport; National (☎ 666-1211); Sol (☎ 666-2222, fax 666-2898), by the Hotel El Bramadero; and Toyota Rent a Car (☎ 666-0016) rent cars at prices similar to those in San José.

Taxi There is a taxi stand at the northwest corner of the Parque Central. These cabs will take you to the beaches if you can't wait for a bus. They will also take you to Parque Nacional Santa Rosa (US$15 to US$20 per cab) and up the rough road to Parque Nacional Rincón de la Vieja (US$30 to US$40 per cab). Most cab drivers consider four passengers to be their limit. During the wet season, 4WD taxis are used to get to Rincón de la Vieja.

PARQUE NACIONAL RINCÓN DE LA VIEJA

This 14,084-hectare national park is named after the active Volcán Rincón de la Vieja (1895m), which is the main attraction. There are several other peaks in the same volcanic massif, of which Volcán Santa María is the highest (1916m). The numerous cones, craters, and lagoons in the summit area can be visited on horseback and foot.

Major volcanic activity occurred many times in the late 1960s, but at the moment the volcano is gently active and does not present any danger (ask locally to be sure). There are fumaroles and boiling mud pools, steam vents, and sulfurous springs to explore.

Thirty-two rivers and streams have their sources within the park, and it is therefore an important water catchment area. It was to protect this that the park was created in 1973. Forests protect the rivers from evaporation in the dry season and from flooding in the wet season.

Elevations in the park range from less than 600m to 1916m, and the changes in altitude result in the presence of four life zones. Visitors pass through a variety of different habitats as they ascend the volcanoes. Many species of trees are found in the forests. The area has the country's highest density of Costa Rica's national flower, the purple orchid *Cattleya skinneri*, locally called *guaria morada*.

Because of its relative remoteness, the park is not heavily visited, but several lodges just outside the park provide access, and transportation is easy to arrange from Liberia. Rincón de la Vieja is the most accessible of the volcanoes in the Cordillera de Guanacaste.

Orientation & Information

Admission to the park costs US$6 per day and camping costs US$2 per person. The park is part of the Area de Conservación Guanacaste (ACG), which also includes the parks of Santa Rosa and Guanacaste as well as other protected areas. The ACG has its headquarters in Parque Nacional Santa Rosa (☎ 666-5051, fax 666-5020), where you can get information. They maintain radio contact with the park.

There are two entrances to the park, with a park ranger station and camping area at each. Las Pailas, with trails past various volcanic features and waterfalls and up to the summit, is the most visited. At the Santa María ranger station is the Casona Santa María, a 19th-century ranch house with a small public exhibit, which was reputedly once owned by US President Lyndon Johnson. This station is the closest to the hot springs (which are 6km from Las Pailas) and also has an observation tower and a nearby waterfall.

Wildlife Watching

The wildlife of the park is extremely varied. Almost 300 species of birds have been recorded here, including curassows, quetzals, bellbirds, parrots, toucans, hummingbirds, owls, woodpeckers, tanagers, motmots, doves, and eagles – to name just a few.

Insects range from beautiful butterflies to annoying ticks. Be especially prepared for ticks in grassy areas such as the meadow in front of the ranger station – long trousers tucked into boots and long-sleeved shirts offer some protection. A particularly interesting insect is a highland cicada that burrows into the ground and croaks like a frog, to the bewilderment of naturalists.

Mammals are equally varied: deer, armadillos, peccaries, skunks, squirrels, coatis, and three species of monkeys are frequently seen. Tapir tracks are often found around the lagoons near the summit, and you may be lucky enough to catch a glimpse of this large but elusive mammal as it crashes away like a tank through the undergrowth.

Several of the wild cat species have been recorded here, including the jaguar, puma, ocelot, and margay, but you'll need a large amount of patience and good fortune to observe one of these.

Trails & Hiking

Trails to the summit and the most interesting volcanic features begin at Las Pailas. Sign in at the ranger station when you arrive and they will give you maps.

A circular trail east of the ranger station (about 8km in total) takes you past the boiling mud pools (Las Pailas), sulfurous fumaroles, and a miniature volcano (which may subside at any time).

North, trails lead 8km (one way) to the summit area. Below the summit is the Laguna de Jilgueros, which is reportedly where you may see tapirs – or more likely their footprints, if you are observant. About 800m west of the ranger station is a swimming hole. Farther away are several waterfalls – the largest, 5km west, is a classic, dropping straight from a cliff into a small lagoon where you can swim. This trail winds through forest, then comes out onto open grassland on the volcano's flanks, where you can get views as far as the Golfo de Nicoya. The slightly smaller 'hidden waterfalls' are about 4km west on a different trail; there are cliff views and swimming.

From the Santa María ranger station, a trail leads 3km west through a forest (nicknamed the 'enchanted forest') and past a waterfall to sulfurous hot springs with supposed therapeutic properties. You shouldn't soak in them for more than about half an hour (some people suggest much less) without taking a dip in one of the nearby cold springs to cool off. The observation tower is 450m east of the station. Though the hikes here are shorter than at Las Pailas, you should still check in with the rangers to let them know where you're going.

Places to Stay

Inside the Park At either ranger station, you can camp (US$2 per person), or a basic and inexpensive room and board can be arranged with the park in advance – bring a sleeping bag. The campground has water, pit toilets, showers, tables, and grills. Mosquito nets or insect repellent are needed in the wet season. Meals can also be arranged for about US$3 each, and horses can be hired.

Camping is allowed in most places within the park, but you should be self-sufficient and prepared for cold and foggy weather in the highlands – a compass would be very useful. Beware of ticks in the grassy areas. The wet season is very wet, and there are plenty of mosquitoes then. Dry-season camping is much better, and February to April are the best months.

Outside the Park Just outside the Santa María sector of the park, near the village of San Jorge, is the very rustic but friendly ***Rinconcito Lodge***. This is the cheapest of the lodges near the park. Rates are US$9 per person in cabins sharing a couple of cold-water bathrooms. Rural tico breakfasts cost US$3; other meals cost US$5. Guides and horses can be hired for US$15, and both the Rincón de la Vieja and Miravalles volcanoes can be visited on tours. Make reservations and get directions from the owners, Gerardo and María Inés Badilla, who have an office and house in Liberia (*☎ 666-4527, or 224-2400 to leave a message in English for 'Rinconcito'*). They offer transport to the lodge for about US$35 roundtrip and will take up to six people for that price.

Also in this area is the equally rustic ***Miravieja Lodge*** (*☎ 666-4945*), run by Geovanny Murillo, which has similar prices, accommodations, and tours; call for details. Reportedly, some budget rooms are available in the village of San Jorge itself.

There are several lodges near the Las Pailas sector at the southwest corner of the park, reached by the gravel road described in Getting There & Away, below.

The first lodge reached on the road to Las Pailas, about 4km from the Interamericana, is the new ***Posada El Encuentro Inn*** (*☎/fax 382-0815, encuentro@arweb.com*), which has attractive rooms, cliffside views, a billiards table, a star-gazing telescope, and a small pool. Rates are US$55/70 for standard rooms with private hot bath and US$80/95/110 for larger junior suites, including breakfast. The friendly staff speaks some English.

Closer to the park is the ***Hacienda Lodge Guachipelín*** (*☎ 442-2818, fax 442-1910, hacienda@intnet.co.cr*), on the site of a 19th-century ranch, parts of which are incorporated into the current building. The hacienda has some 1200 hectares, part primary forest, part secondary forest, and part a working cattle ranch. Accommodations are in simple duplex cabins (US$40 double). There is an even simpler bunkhouse (water during certain hours only) where you can stay for US$10 per person. Inside the ranch house is a dormitory with beds for US$16 per person and private rooms for US$45 for a double. Showers are cold and electricity can be erratic. Buffet-style meals are served for US$7 (breakfast or lunch) and US$10 (dinner). The food quality and quantity have been criticized, so you may wish to bring your own.

Horses are available for US$14 a half day or US$20 a full day, and guides can also be hired to take you up into the national park. The lodge can provide transportation from Liberia for about US$20 roundtrip per person (larger groups get discounts).

Five more kilometers bring you to the ***Rincón de la Vieja Mountain Lodge*** (*☎/fax 695-5553; in San José ☎ 256-8206, fax 256-7290, rincon@sol.racsa.co.cr*). This lodge is the closest to the park and is therefore more popular and crowded than the Hacienda Lodge Guachipelín. It is about 2km from the mud pools and 5km from the fumaroles described earlier. There are 27 rooms, some with private bath and hot showers, others with cold showers or with dorm-style bunks. There is 24-hour electricity and the rooms are screened – insects are abundant in the wettest months, and the screens help. There is a small swimming pool and a reference library. Rooms cost US$44/56/75 for one to three people and US$16 for extra people. Dorm beds cost about US$20 per person.

Meals at the lodge are available for US$9 (breakfast) or US$11 (lunch or dinner).

Various tours are offered, including a canopy tour arranged by Top Tree Trails (not associated with the Canopy Tour). They have 16 platforms joined by steel cables and charge US$45 for a four-hour tour. Guides (US$30), horses (US$45 all day), and transportation from Liberia are all available, as are multiday packages – call the lodge for details.

These are growing tourism developments, and you can expect changes during the life of this book. The latter two lodges offer discounts for Hostelling International members.

On a different road via Cañas Dulces is the ***Buenavista Lodge*** *(☎/fax 695-5147)*, on an 1800-hectare farm. It offers horseback and hiking tours into Rincón de la Vieja, birding, an entomology tour for butterfly lovers, and a spa, sauna, and private mud and steam pools. You can rent dormitory-style rooms for about US$15 per person and private bungalow rooms for US$50 a double. There is a bar and restaurant.

Getting There & Away

To Las Pailas Almost 5km north of Liberia on the Interamericana is a signed turnoff to the northeast onto a gravel road; from here, it is just over 20km from the Interamericana to the station at Las Pailas. Most hotels (or the tourist office) in Liberia can arrange transport for about US$17 roundtrip. (Frequent public buses from Liberia to Colorado or Cañas Dulces can drop you at this turnoff, if you want to walk up. Reportedly, there are three buses a week from Liberia to Curubandé, 10km from the park, at 2:30 pm on Monday, Wednesday, and Friday.)

The road passes through the grounds of the Hacienda Lodge Guachipelín (there are signs for the lodge along the way). There is a guarded gate (open during daylight hours) and a US$2.50 vehicle fee for use of what is now a private road. This is reimbursed if you stay at the Hacienda Lodge Guachipelín, but if you continue to the Rincón de la Vieja Mountain Lodge, there is no refund. The Hacienda Lodge Guachipelín is 3km beyond the gate, and the Mountain Lodge is 5km farther still.

Alternatively, you can walk about 8km from the Santa María ranger station to Las Pailas or the Rincón de la Vieja Mountain Lodge.

To Santa María The park is 25km northeast of Liberia by a poor road that often requires 4WD in the rainy season but is passable in ordinary cars in the dry. To get to the Santa María ranger station, drive, walk, or take a taxi (US$30 to US$40) on the road that heads northeast out of Liberia through the Barrio La Victoria suburb. After about 18km, the road passes the village of San Jorge and then continues as far as Santa María. Sometimes a ride from Liberia can be arranged when a park service vehicle is in town. Most people drive or arrange a ride with the lodge where they are staying. If you want, you can simply walk the 25km along the road – there's not much traffic, and the walk is no problem if your body is up to it.

To Buenavista Lodge This is reached from the Interamericana by driving 12km north from Liberia and turning right on the signed road. The 5km drive from this point to Cañas Dulces is on paved road (there are buses to Cañas Dulces from Liberia); the additional 13km drive to the Buenavista Lodge is on unpaved and rough road.

PARQUE NACIONAL SANTA ROSA

This national park is one of the oldest (established 1971) and biggest (37,117 hectares) in Costa Rica and has one of the best-developed (though still simple) camping facilities of the nation's parks.

Santa Rosa covers most of the Península Santa Elena, which juts out into the Pacific at the far northwestern corner of the country. The park is named after the Hacienda Santa Rosa, where a historic battle was fought on March 20, 1856, between a hastily assembled amateur army of Costa Ricans and the invading forces of the North American filibuster William Walker. In fact, it was mainly historical and patriotic reasons that brought about the establishment of this national park in the first place. It is almost a coincidence that the park has also become extremely important to biologists.

Santa Rosa protects the largest remaining stand of tropical dry forest in Central America, and it also protects some of the most important nesting sites of several species of sea turtles, including endangered ones. Wildlife is often seen, especially during the dry season, when animals congregate around the remaining water and the trees lose their leaves. So for historians and biologists, campers and hikers, beach and wilderness lovers, this park is a great attraction.

One of the most innovative features of Parque Nacional Santa Rosa is that local people have been involved in preserving and expanding the park. Through a campaign of both education and employment, locals have learned the importance of conservation and have been able to put it to their own use by working as research assistants, park rangers, or other staff, and also by using conservation techniques to improve their own land use on the surrounding farms and ranches. This attitude of cultural involvement has made the relationship between the national park authorities and the local people one that benefits everybody. It stands as a model for the future integration of preservation and local people's interests in other parts of Costa Rica and in other countries.

The best season is the dry season, when there are fewer biting insects, the roads are more passable, and the animals tend to congregate around waterholes, making them easier to see. But this is also the 'busy' season when, particularly on weekends, the park is popular with Costa Ricans wanting to see some of their history. It is less busy midweek, but it's always fairly quiet compared to parks like Volcán Poás or Manuel Antonio. In the wet months, you can observe the sea turtles nesting and often have the rest of the park virtually to yourself. The best months for sea turtles are September and October, though you are likely to see some from July to December as well. An increase in large tour groups wanting to see the turtles nesting prompted a closure of Playa Nancite (the best-known turtle-nesting beach) to large groups, though individuals and small groups can sometimes obtain a permit to see the nesting. Visitation during turtle season is limited to 25 people per night, and you should make a reservation with the park headquarters (☎ 666-5051, fax 666-5020).

Orientation

The entrance to Parque Nacional Santa Rosa is on the west side of the Interamericana, 35km north of Liberia and 45km south of the Nicaraguan border. From the entrance, a 7km paved road leads to the main center of the park. Here, there are administrative offices, scientists' quarters, an information center, campground, museum, and nature trail.

From this complex, a 4WD trail leads down to the coast, 12km away. It's impassable and closed from May to November (wet season). Horses and walkers can use the road all year. About a third of the way down this trail are two lookout points with views of the ocean. There are several beaches, with a camping area at the southern end of Playa Naranjo, though you need permits from the park rangers to camp on the beach and camping may be prohibited during turtle nesting months. There are also other jeep, foot, and horse trails that leave the main visitor complex and head out into the tropical dry forest and other habitats.

The park's Sector Murciélago encompasses the wild northern coastline of the Península Santa Elena. There is a ranger station and camping area here. The story is that this area was once owned by the Nicaraguan dictator Anastasio Somoza – after he was deposed, the area became part of the national park. You can't get there from the main body of the park (except perhaps by bushwhacking). To reach the Sector Murciélago, you need to return to the Interamericana and travel farther north, as described in Getting There & Away, below.

The Interamericana forms the eastern border of Santa Rosa and also the western border of Parque Nacional Guanacaste – the two parks are contiguous.

Information

The park entrance station (just off the Interamericana) is open 7:30 am to 4:30 pm daily. At the entrance booth you pay the US$6 park admission and, if you plan on camping, an extra US$2 per person. Maps of the park are sometimes available for sale.

It is another 7km to the park headquarters (☎ 666-5051, fax 666-5020) and campground. There are no buses, so you must walk or hitch if you don't have a car. Rangers may allow travelers to accompany them on their rounds of the park. Note that the park headquarters also administers the Area de Conservación Guanacaste (ACG) and has information about (and maintains radio contact with) Parque Nacional Rincón de la Vieja, Parque Nacional Guanacaste, and other protected areas.

Several of the park rangers have been trained as naturalist guides and will accompany you on tours of Santa Rosa and other areas within the ACG.

La Casona

The historic La Casona (the main building of the old Hacienda Santa Rosa) houses a visitor center and small museum, open 7:30 am to 4:30 pm; admission is free. The battle of 1856 was fought around this building, and the military action is described in documents, paintings, maps, and diagrams. Other battles were fought in this area in 1919 and 1955. You can view antique firearms and other weapons, as well as a collection of period antique furniture and tools, and a typical country kitchen that is set up as it would have been in a hacienda over 100 years ago. A display interpreting the ecological significance and wildlife of the park is also here. Some of the old rooms of La Casona are favorite bat roosts. Don't be surprised should you disturb several dozen bats upon entering one of the side rooms, and don't worry, the bats are completely harmless.

Behind La Casona, a short trail leads up to the Monumento a Los Héroes and a lookout platform.

Wildlife Watching

Outside La Casona is a fine example of the national tree of Costa Rica, the guanacaste *(Enterolobium cyclocarpum)*. The province is named after this very large tree species, which is found along the Pacific coastal lowlands. Nearby is a short nature trail with signs interpreting the ecological relationships among the plants, animals, and weather patterns of Santa Rosa. The trail is named El Sendero Indio Desnudo after the common tree whose peeling orange-red bark can photosynthesize during the dry season, when the tree's leaves are lost. The reddish bark is supposed to represent a naked Indian, though local guides suggest that 'sunburnt tourist' might be a better name. The tree is also called gumbo limbo. Although the Indio Desnudo nature trail is short (a little over 1km roundtrip), you will certainly see a variety of plants and birds and probably, if you move slowly and keep your eyes and ears open, monkeys, snakes, iguanas, and other animals. Markers along the trail explain what you see – also look out for the petroglyphs (probably pre-Columbian) etched into some of the rocks on the trail.

The wildlife is certainly both varied and prolific. Over 250 species of birds have been recorded. One highly visible bird, common in Santa Rosa and frequently seen and heard around the park campground, is the white-throated magpie jay. This raucous blue-and-white jay is unmistakable with its long crest of maniacally curled feathers. The forests contain parrots and parakeets, trogons and tanagers, and as you head down to the coast, you will be rewarded by sightings of a variety of coastal birds.

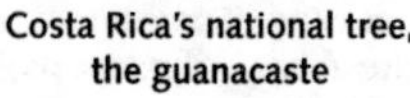

Costa Rica's national tree, the guanacaste

Research at Santa Rosa

Santa Rosa is a mecca for scientists, particularly tropical ecologists. Near the park headquarters are simple accommodations for researchers and students, many of whom spend a great deal of time both studying the ecology of the area and devising better means to protect the remaining tropical forests of Costa Rica.

Tropical ecologist Dr Daniel H Janzen has spent much of his research time in Santa Rosa and has been a prime mover in the conservation of not just this national park, but also in the creation of the conservation area system that is making protection of all the national parks more effective. He has been very vocal about how the needs of local people must be addressed in order for conservation to become truly effective on a long-term basis. Most recently, Janzen has been involved in the INBio project to catalogue as many species as possible and to screen them for potential pharmaceutical value.

Janzen has also done much solid research on the tropics and is noted for a plethora of scientific papers. The titles of these range from the whimsical ('How to Be a Fig' in *Annual Review of Ecology & Systematics*, vol 10, 1979) to the matter-of-fact ('Why Fruits Rot, Seeds Mold, and Meat Spoils' in *American Naturalist*, vol 111, 1977) to the downright bewildering ('Allelopathy by Myrmecophytes: The Ant *Azteca* as an Allelopathic Agent of *Cecropia*' in *Ecology*, vol 50, 1969). But perhaps Janzen's strangest claim to fame, among students of ecology at least, is his experiment on tropical seeds. He studied how seed germination is affected by the seeds being eaten and passed through the digestive systems of a variety of animals. Facing a lack of suitable animal volunteers, Janzen systematically ate the seeds himself, then recovered the seeds and tried to germinate them. Tropical ecology can be a messy business!

– Rob Rachowiecki

At dusk, the flying animals you see probably won't be birds. Bats *(murciélagos)* are very common: about 50 or 60 different species have been identified in Santa Rosa. Other mammals you have a reasonable chance of seeing include deer, coatis, peccaries, armadillos, coyotes, raccoons, three kinds of monkeys, and a variety of other species – about 115 in all. There are many thousands of insect species, including about 4000 moths and butterflies.

There are also many reptiles – lizards, iguanas, snakes, crocodiles, and four species of sea turtles. The olive ridley sea turtle is the most numerous, and during the July to December nesting season, tens of thousands of turtles make their nests on Santa Rosa's beaches. The most popular beach is Playa Nancite, where, during September and October especially, it is possible to see as many as 8000 of these 40kg turtles on the beach at the same time! The turtles are disturbed by light, so flash photography and flashlights are not permitted. Avoid the nights around a full moon as those are too bright. After nesting has been completed, the olive ridleys range all over the tropical eastern Pacific, from the waters of Mexico to Peru. Playa Nancite is strictly protected and restricted, but permission can be obtained from the park headquarters (☎ 666-5051, fax 666-5020) to see this spectacle.

The variety of wildlife reflects the variety of habitats protected within the boundaries of the park. Apart from the largest remaining stand of tropical dry forest in Central America, habitats include savanna woodland, oak forest, deciduous forest, evergreen forest, riparian forest, mangrove swamps, and coastal woodlands.

Surfing

Playa Naranjo, the next major beach south of Playa Nancite, is near the southern end of the national park's coastline. The surfing here is reportedly good, especially near Witches Rock. This is a popular place to camp and surf, but you'll need to pack everything in – surfboards, tents, food, and drinking water (though brackish water is available for washing off after a day in the waves). The hike in takes several hours. Surfing and boat tours to Witches Rock are offered from Playa del Coco (see the Península de Nicoya chapter).

Places to Stay & Eat

There is a ***campground*** at the park headquarters. Facilities are not fancy but do include drinking water, picnic benches, grills, flushing toilets, cold-water showers, and garbage cans. Large fig trees provide shade. The campsites on the coast (when open) have pit toilets but no showers. Ask the rangers whether drinking water is available; you may need to pack in your own. Camping fees are US$2 per person. At Playa Naranjo is another campground with more basic facilities and limited drinking water – ask at the ranger station about current supplies, but be prepared to pack in your own.

The ***research station*** at the park headquarters has eight rooms, each sleeping up to eight people. Showers are shared. Researchers and students stay here, but there is often room for travelers. The cost is about US$20 a night, not including meals, which cost about US$3 to US$4 each. Make arrangements for accommodations and meals in advance with the ranger station (☎ 666-5051, fax 666-5020).

A ***snack bar*** sells soft drinks and a few snacks. Occasionally, simple meals may be available (when rangers or guests haven't eaten all the food!) and they may rustle up lunch with a couple of hours' notice.

Getting There & Away

To get to the main park entrance by public transport, take any bus between Liberia and the Nicaraguan border and ask the driver to set you down at the park entrance. When you are ready to leave, you can ask the ranger on duty for a timetable of passing buses. There are about 12 buses a day heading to the border and about six each to Liberia and San José. If you are driving from the south, watch for the kilometer posts on the side of the road – the park entrance is about 300m south of Km 270.

To get to the northern Sector Murciélago of the park, go 10km farther north along the Interamericana, then turn left to the village of Cuajiniquil, 8km away by paved road. There are passport controls both at the turnoff and in Cuajiniquil itself, so don't have your passport buried. Buses go here once or twice a day from La Cruz, and buses from the main park entrance go here at 4 and 5:30 pm (subject to change), or you could hitch or walk the 8km if you don't have a car. At Cuajiniquil there is a basic soda/*pulpería* but no accommodations. (The paved road continues beyond Cuajiniquil and dead-ends at a marine port, 4km away – this isn't the way to the Sector Murciélago, but goes toward Refugio Nacional de Vida Silvestre Bahía Junquillal.) Park rangers say it is about 8km beyond Cuajiniquil to the Murciélago ranger station by poor road – 4WD is advised in the wet season, though you might make it in a high-clearance ordinary vehicle if you drive carefully. At the Murciélago ranger station, you can camp and, if you advise the Santa Rosa headquarters in advance, eat meals. The dirt road continues beyond the ranger station for about 10 or 12km, reaching the remote bays and beaches of Bahía Santa Elena and Bahía Playa Blanca. This road may be impassable in the wet season.

REFUGIO NACIONAL DE VIDA SILVESTRE BAHÍA JUNQUILLAL

This 505-hectare wildlife refuge is part of the Area de Conservación Guanacaste, administered from the park headquarters at Santa Rosa. The quiet bay and protected beach provide gentle swimming, boating, and snorkeling opportunities, and there is some tropical dry forest and mangrove swamp. Short trails take the visitor to a lookout for marine birding and to the mangroves. Pelicans and

NORTHWESTERN

frigatebirds are seen, and turtles nest here in the appropriate seasons. Volcán Orosí can be seen in the distance.

Information

There is a ranger station in radio contact with Santa Rosa. Entrance here costs less than at the national parks (about US$1), and camping is allowed for US$2 per person. During the dry season especially, water is at a premium and is turned on for only one hour a day. There are pit latrines.

Getting There & Away

From Cuajiniquil (see Parque Nacional Santa Rosa, above), continue for 2km along the paved road and then turn right onto a signed dirt road (the sign may say 'Playa Cuajiniquil,' but it's the correct turn). Continuing 4km along the dirt road (passable to ordinary cars) brings you to the entrance to Bahía Junquillal. From here, a poorer 700m dirt road leads to the beach, ranger station, and camping area.

PARQUE NACIONAL GUANACASTE

This newest part of the ACG was created on July 25, 1989, Guanacaste Day. The park is adjacent to Parque Nacional Santa Rosa, separated from it by the Interamericana, and is only about 5km northwest of Parque Nacional Rincón de la Vieja.

The 32,512 hectares of Parque Nacional Guanacaste are much more than a continuation of the dry tropical forest and other lowland habitats found in Santa Rosa. In its lower western reaches, it is an extension of Santa Rosa's habitats, but the terrain soon begins to climb toward two volcanoes, Volcán Orosí (1487m) and Volcán Cacao (1659m). Thus it enables animals to range from the coast to the highlands, just as many of them have always done.

Scientists have come to realize that many animal species need a variety of different habitats at different times of year, or at different stages of their life cycles, and if habitats are preserved singly, the animals within them may not thrive. If a series of adjoining habitats is preserved, however, the survival of many species can be improved. This is one of the main reasons for the formation of conservation areas such as the ACG.

Not all the preserved areas are natural forest. Indeed, large portions of the ACG are ranchlands. But researchers have found that if the pasture is carefully managed (and much of this management involves just letting nature take its course), the natural forest will reinstate itself in its old territory. Thus, crucial habitats are not just preserved, but in some cases they are also expanded.

For information on this park, contact the ACG headquarters in Parque Nacional Santa Rosa (☎ 666-5051, fax 666-5020).

Research Stations

Research is an important aspect of Guanacaste, and there are no less than three biological stations within its borders. They are all in good areas for wildlife observation or hiking.

Maritza Biological Station This is the newest station and has a modern laboratory. To get there, turn east off the Interamericana opposite the turnoff for Cuajiniquil (see Parque Nacional Santa Rosa, earlier). The station is about 17km east of the highway along a dirt road that may require a 4WD vehicle, especially in the wet season. The main problem with driving the road is entering it from the Interamericana – there is a very steep curb – but once you've negotiated that, the going gets better.

From the station, at 600m above sea level, rough trails run to the summits of Volcán Orosí and Volcán Cacao (about five to six hours). There is also a better trail to a site where Indian petroglyphs have been found, about an hour away.

Cacao Biological Station This station is high on the slopes of Volcán Cacao at an elevation of about 1060m above sea level. The station is reached from the southern side of the park. At Potrerillos, about 9km south of the Santa Rosa park entrance on the Interamericana, head east for about 7km on a paved road to the small community of Quebrada Grande (marked as Garcia Flamenco on many maps). A daily bus leaves Liberia at 3 pm for Quebrada Grande. From the village square, a 4WD road heads left (north) toward the station, about 10km away. Contact the ACG headquarters in Parque Nacional Santa Rosa (☎ 666-5051, fax 666-5020) to find out if the road is passable. From the station, there are rough trails to the summit of Volcán Cacao and to the Maritza Biological Station.

Pitilla Biological Station This station is a surprise – it lies on the northeast side of Volcán Orosí in forest more like that found on the Caribbean slopes than on the Pacific, although the Pacific is only 30km to the west while the Caribbean is 180km to the east. Because the station is on the eastern side of the continental divide, the rivers flow into the Caribbean and the climate and vegetation are influenced by the Caribbean.

To get to the station, turn east off the Interamericana about 12km north of the Cuajiniquil turnoff, or 3km before reaching the small town of La Cruz. Follow the paved eastbound road for about 28km to the community of Santa Cecilia. From there, ask about the poor dirt road heading 10 or 12km south to the station – you'll probably need 4WD. (Don't continue on the unpaved road heading farther east – that goes over 50km farther to the small town of Upala.)

NORTHWESTERN

Places to Stay & Eat

Inside the Park Since the creation of the national park in Guanacaste, the biological research stations are sometimes available for tourist accommodations. ***Maritza*** or ***Cacao*** are where you are most likely to be allowed to stay – Pitilla is the province of research biologists or students. The stations are all quite rustic, with dormitory-style accommodations for 30 to 40 people and shared cold-water bathrooms. A bed and three meals cost about US$20 a day. Permission to camp near the stations can also be obtained; the fee is about US$2 per night. You should make arrangements to stay in the stations with the Santa Rosa headquarters (☎ 666-5051, fax 666-5020). Research personnel and students always get preference. Park personnel in Santa Rosa may be able to arrange transport from that park's headquarters to the biological stations for about US$10 to US$20, depending on where you go.

Outside the Park There are two lodges within a few kilometers of the park boundaries, one on the south side and one on the north. Either can be used as a base to explore the national park.

The ***Santa Clara Lodge*** *(☎ 391-8766, 257-8585 beeper; in Liberia ☎ 666-4054, fax 666-4047)* is on the south side of the park. This is a small, rustic, friendly, family-run lodge in a working dairy farm on the banks of the Río Los Ahogados (River of the Drowned) – a not-very-reassuring name! A cold-water mineral spring near the lodge is channeled into a dip pool; the locals claim the water is good for the skin. Rooms are clean but very small and simple. Electricity is available from 6 to 10 pm; otherwise, candles are provided. Showers are cold. The owners are completely up-front about this – they even tell you that there may be noise in the early mornings because of the farm animals!

Rooms in the lodge cost about US$9 per person; rooms in individual cabins cost about US$30 double (some have shared baths). Ask about low-season and youth hostel discounts. Meals cost US$3 to US$5 for breakfast and US$5.50 for lunch and dinner.

The lodge is about 7km due south of Parque Nacional Guanacaste and 9km west of Parque Nacional Rincón de la Vieja. Horseback and taxi tours are available around the ranch and to local waterfalls and thermal springs; to Santa Rosa, Rincón de la Vieja, and Junquillal; and, on weekends only, to **Sutton Ostrich Farm** (unique in Costa Rica as of this writing), which is on the western outskirts of the nearby village of Quebrada Grande. Tours cost US$20 to US$65 and usually require a minimum of three participants. Ask about visiting other places.

The lodge is reached by heading 4km south of Quebrada Grande on a dirt road (see Cacao Biological Station, above, for information about reaching Quebrada Grande).

The ***Hacienda Los Inocentes*** *(☎/fax 679-9190; in Heredia ☎ 265-5484, fax 265-4385; in the USA ☎ 888-613-2532, orosina@sol.racsa.co.cr)* is a ranch on the north side of Parque Nacional Guanacaste. The owners are interested in wildlife and conservation as well as ranching; they promote recycling and solar energy and host scientists engaged in environmental research. The hacienda building itself is a very attractive century-old wooden house converted into a comfortable country lodge owned and operated by the Viquez family, who have been here for generations. Current owner Jaime Viquez embodies the graciousness and confidence of traditional Guanacaste. The setting below Volcán Orosí is quite spectacular. About two-thirds of the 1000-hectare ranch are forested (mainly with secondary forest), and bird- and animal-watching opportunities abound. Howler monkeys are seen frequently on foot trails by the nearby Río Sábalo, as well as a variety of parrots in the forest and king vultures overhead.

Trips into Parque Nacional Guanacaste can be arranged, and Volcán Orosí, looming high on the horizon about 7km to the south, can be climbed. Naturally, horses are available (by this stage in the chapter, you probably realize that horses are an important way of getting around rural Costa Rica). The lodge building has about a dozen spacious wooden bedrooms upstairs – each room has a private bathroom with electric shower on the ground floor, so though you never have to share a bathroom, you do have to walk downstairs to reach it. The upper floor is surrounded by the beautiful shaded wooden verandah with hammocks and volcano views – a good spot for sunset and moonrise. A few cabins with private bath are near the main lodge. Accommodations cost US$35 per person or US$71 with meals – the food is good. You can wander around at will, but guided tours are extra, though very reasonably priced.

Reach the hacienda by driving 15km east from the Interamericana on the paved road to Santa Cecilia. It is just over half a kilometer from the entrance gate to the lodge itself. Buses from San José to Santa Cecilia pass the lodge entrance at about 7:30 pm, and buses from Santa Cecilia returning to San José pass the lodge around 5:15 am. More frequent buses join La Cruz with Santa Cecilia and can drop you at the hacienda entrance. Taxis from La Cruz charge about US$10 for the 20km ride.

In **Santa Cecilia** itself, you'll find a ***soda, pulpería,*** and several basic ***pensiones*** where you can find lodging for about US$4 per person; two of them are right next to where the bus stops. Ask around for others; it's a remote but friendly little place. About 3km out of Santa Cecilia, on a poor dirt road that passes by orange groves on the way to the village of La Virgen, you can get views of the islands in Lago de Nicaragua.

Getting There & Away

See the descriptions of the three biological research stations and two nearby lodges, earlier in this section, for details on how to get to the park. Note that access to the research stations can be difficult in the wet months. Also see the section on Parque Nacional Santa Rosa, which adjoins the park.

REFUGIO NACIONAL DE FAUNA SILVESTRE ISLA BOLAÑOS

This 25-hectare island is a national wildlife refuge because brown pelicans, magnificent frigatebirds, American oystercatchers, and other seabirds nest here. There are several hundred pelicans in a nesting colony on the north end of the island, and hundreds of frigatebirds nest on the southern cliffs. The rocky and largely barren island is 81m at its highest point. The refuge is part of the ACG, administered in Parque Nacional Santa Rosa (☎ 666-5051, fax 666-5020).

The island is in Bahía Salinas on the Nicaraguan-Costa Rican border. The nearest point on the mainland is Punta Zacate, 1.5km away, but there is no road here. The nearest habitation is at Puerto Soley, about 6km southwest of La Cruz by road. In Puerto Soley, you can hire a boat to take you the 4km across the bay to the refuge.

There are no facilities on the island, and you should contact the Santa Rosa headquarters for permission if you need to land on the island. No permit is necessary for birding from a boat.

LA CRUZ

This is the first and last settlement of any size you'll encounter before reaching the Nicaraguan border at Peñas Blancas, 20km farther north on the Interamericana. It's a small town, and everything is within two or three blocks of the Parque Central, with its bright-blue concrete benches. The town is on a small hill overlooking Bahía Salinas in the distance – there is a good lookout point with sweeping views of the coast.

Information

The Banco Nacional (☎/fax 679-9110) is at the junction of the Interamericana and the short road into the center. Changing money is slow. There is a small clinic (☎ 679-9116) and police station (☎ 679-9197).

Places to Stay

A good budget choice is the cheap and clean ***Cabinas Maryfel*** *(☎ 679-9096)*, opposite the bus station. A more basic choice is the ***Hotel El Faro***, on the road leading into town from the Interamericana. Double rooms in both cost US$10 or less. A couple of blocks south of the Parque Central is ***Cabinas Santa Rita*** *(☎ 679-9062)*, which has clean rooms with shared cold showers for US$8 double or US$15 with private shower. Rooms with air-conditioning and private bath cost US$18/25 single/double. It is popular and often full, especially in the dry season.

The ***Hostal de Julia*** *(☎/fax 679-9084)*, north of the gas station on the road into town from the Interamericana, has a dozen clean rooms around a whitewashed courtyard with fans and private hot bath for about US$18/25 single/double.

Amalia's Inn *(☎/fax 669-9181)* is a seven-room family inn with a small pool. It's on a coastal bluff with good sea views and is the nicest place to stay. Amalia, the knowledgeable tica owner, can tell you about the area and arrange horse and boat trips. The house is filled with paintings and drawings by her North American husband, who passed away recently. Rates are about US$35, US$5 more with breakfast. Next door is the simple and small ***Iguana Lodge*** *(☎ 679-9015)*, which charges about US$20 a double.

About 12km north of La Cruz is the ***Hotel Colinas del Norte*** *(☎/fax 679-9132)*, an attractive ranch that arranges local tours and has rooms with private hot baths for about US$40 per person. Children are welcome, and there is a small miniature golf course on the back lawn. You can rent a horse for US$15 per hour, and discounts are given for longer stays.

Places to Eat

The ***Restaurante Ehecatl*** *(☎ 679-9104)*, locally called *el mirador* or 'the lookout point,' is on the bluff overlooking Bahía Salinas, a few blocks uphill from the park. There are spectacular views, and lunches and dinners are pretty good. It is open 10 am to 10 pm, and its mid-priced menu is varied, though seafood is an obvious main feature.

Cheaper places include the ***Bar y Restaurante Thelma*** *(☎ 679-9150)*, with decent meals in a friendly atmosphere. ***Restaurante Dariri***, a couple of blocks before the park, is a small, friendly *típico* place open 7 am to 9 pm. Just past the park is the hole-in-the-wall ***Soda Santa Marta***, which serves cheap local breakfasts and meals. Just south of the park, a ***coffee shop*** was under construction at last visit.

Getting There & Away

Bus Buses connect La Cruz with San José, Liberia, and the Nicaraguan border. Buses come through on the way to San José five times a day, to Liberia five times a day, and to the border nine times a day.

In La Cruz, the bus station is next to a pulpería (☎ 679-9108) that sells tickets and has bus schedules. Many of the southbound buses begin at the border, and locals complain that it's sometimes difficult to board by the time the bus comes through La Cruz. If this is the case, you could try backtracking 20km to the border and catching a bus there – though many of the buses to the border originate in Liberia or San José and may also be full as they come through La Cruz. Catch-22.

Local buses leave La Cruz for Santa Cecilia (passing Hacienda Los Inocentes)

NORTHWESTERN

about six times a day. In Santa Cecilia, there are basic pensiones and connections with buses on to Upala in the northern lowlands. Call the Santa Cecilia public telephone (☎ 679-9105) for further information. There are also local buses from La Cruz to Puerto Soley at 5 am and 1 pm and to Cuajiniquil at 12:30 pm. (See the Parque Nacional Guanacaste section, earlier, for more information on Santa Cecilia.)

Taxi A taxi to the border charges about US$6.

BAHÍA SALINAS

A dirt road (normally passable to ordinary cars) leads down from the lookout point in La Cruz past the small coastal fishing community of Puerto Soley and out along the curve of the bay to where there are a couple of newer resorts. Boats can be rented here to visit Isla Bolaños and other places; horse rental is also available. The bay is becoming something of a windsurfing spot, and there is a windsurfing school where you can rent boards and get lessons (see below).

One map shows a small archaeological site named 'Las Pilas' in the area – ask locally for information if you're interested.

Windsurfing

Next to the Hotel Three Corners (see below) is the Tommy Friedl Windsurfing School (costarica@procenterfriedl.com). Board rental begins at US$20 per hour and US$55 per day, with weekly rates available. A three-day beginner course (comprising six two-hour lessons) costs US$165, including equipment; a three-hour introductory course costs US$55, not including equipment. Call Three Corners for information.

Places to Stay & Eat

On Playa Morro, off the road to Puerto Soley, is a ***campground*** *(☎ 289-6474, ask in Spanish for Rodolfo Gonzales)* with shade trees, showers, drinking water, fire pits, and views of Isla Bolaños in the distance. At the entrance to the campground is a bar/restaurant; the campground itself is 300m off the road and rates are US$5 per person.

At Puerto Soley is a rustic ***beachfront restaurant*** where you can have good, cheap fresh fish and cold beer, and ask about renting a boat to visit the Isla Bolaños refuge. Expect to pay about US$20 per hour for a boat that will hold eight or 10 passengers.

Following the road beyond Puerto Soley along the coast, you come to the new ***Hotel Three Corners Bolaños Bay Resort*** *(☎/fax 679-9444, 3cornco@sol.racsa.co.cr)*, set on an attractive, windy point overlooking the bay. There are adult and children's pools, a spacious bar/restaurant, and a variety of activities, tours, and rentals. Pleasant bungalows on well-kept grounds are about US$60 double. Also in this area, the ***Hotel Ecoplaya*** *(☎ 679-9380, fax 289-4536, ecoplaya@sol.racsa.co.cr)* has similarly attractive accommodations and prices.

Getting There & Away

There are two buses a day from La Cruz that can drop you at any of the places described above; current departure times are 10:30 am and 1:30 pm, but check with the La Cruz bus station (☎ 679-9108). A taxi to one of the resorts charges about US$8.

PEÑAS BLANCAS

This is on the border with Nicaragua – it is a border post, not a town. There isn't anywhere to stay, although meals and money-changing are available.

See the Getting There & Away chapter for full details of crossing the border here in either direction.

Arenal Route

The route described here goes from San José in a northwesterly direction through Ciudad Quesada (San Carlos), Fortuna, Arenal, and Tilarán, connecting with the Interamericana at Cañas. From Cañas, you could head north toward Liberia and Nicaragua, or turn south along the Interamericana and thus make a loop trip back to San José. Fortuna makes a good base for visiting the active Volcán Arenal, and there are adequate bus connections. Drivers can do the complete circuit on paved roads, with the exception of a 10km stretch on the north shores of Laguna de Arenal, which is passable to cars. It is also possible to connect with Monteverde, although the roads are not in such good shape, and with the northern lowlands of Costa Rica.

CIUDAD QUESADA (SAN CARLOS)

The official name of this small city is Ciudad Quesada (sometimes abbreviated to Quesada), but all the locals know it as San Carlos, and local buses often have San Carlos as the destination. The town lies at 650m above sea level on the northwestern slopes of the Cordillera Central, overlooking the plains of Llanura de San Carlos stretching off to Nicaragua. The population, including outlying suburbs, is about 33,000.

Roads north and east of the city take the traveler into the northern lowlands. Roads to the northwest lead to Fortuna and the spectacular Volcán Arenal, and over the mountains to the Interamericana.

Ciudad Quesada makes a convenient place to spend the night if you like to travel slowly and want to see one of Costa Rica's smaller cities. It's an important agricultural and ranching center and the Feria del Ganado, or cattle fair and auction, held every April, is the biggest in the country. This is accompanied by the usual carnival rides and a *tope* (horse parade). If you're interested in horses, check out the *talabarterías* or saddleshops found near the town center. They make and sell some of the most intricately crafted leather saddles in Costa Rica; a top-quality saddle can cost US$1000. Just walking into a talabartería and smelling all the leatherwork is a memorable olfactory experience.

The town's focal point is the large Parque Central, with shade trees and benches. Almost everything of importance is either on this square or within a few blocks of it.

Information

Tourist information offices have been open intermittently.

There are several banks, including the Banco del Comercio (☎ 460-2233), a block south of the west side of the Parque Central, and the Banco Popular (☎ 460-0534), a block north of the park.

Emergency medical attention is available at the Hospital de San Carlos (☎ 460-1176) and Clinica Monte Sinai (☎ 460-1080).

Places to Stay

Budget The cheapest place is the ***Hotel Terminal*** *(☎ 460-2158)*, which is in the bus terminal, half a block from the plaza. This hotel is very basic and noisy and not particularly recommended. A much better place is the clean ***Hotel del Norte*** *(☎ 460-1959, 460-1758)*, which is three blocks north of the bus terminal and charges US$3.75 per person with hot shared showers and has a few rooms with private showers for US$7.50/11 single/double. On the same block is the ***Hotel San Carlos*** *(☎ 460-6394)*, with rooms with private baths at US$11 double.

Budget travelers could stroll along the first two blocks of Calle 2, north of the northwest corner of Parque Central. There is a produce market along here and also several budget hotels, on or just off this street, including the ***Hotel Cristal*** *(☎ 460-0541)*, ***Hotel Ugalde*** *(☎ 460-0260)*, ***Hotel Diana*** *(☎ 460-3319)*, ***Hotel del Valle*** *(☎ 460-0718)*, and ***Hotel Axel Alberto*** *(☎ 460-1423)*. Some of these have hot water and rooms with both shared and private bathrooms for US$3 to US$6 per person. I didn't inspect any of the rooms, but shoestring travelers will have a good choice here.

Mid-Range The ***Hotel El Retiro*** *(☎ 460-0463)* is on the Parque Central and charges about US$10/15 single/double. Rooms are basic but clean and have private baths with electric showers. There is a parking lot.

The ***Hotel Conquistador*** *(☎/fax 460-0546, 460-1877)* is 600m south of the park on Calle Central and has 46 clean and adequate rooms that have private hot showers for US$10/18. There is a restaurant for early breakfast, and a parking lot.

A block south of the Parque Central, the ***Hotel Don Goyo*** *(☎ 460-1780, ☎/fax 460-6383)* has 20 small but very clean and pleasant rooms with fans and private hot showers. There is a guarded parking area and a restaurant. Rates are about US$15/20.

The ***Hotel La Central*** *(☎ 460-0301, 460-0766, fax 460-0391)*, on the park, has 50 small and clean but older rooms with fans, private baths, and hot water for around US$15/26. There is a restaurant, public fax services, and a tiny casino. The hotel is popular with local businesspeople.

On the northwestern outskirts of town is the ***Balneario San Carlos*** *(☎ 460-6857, fax 460-2145)*, which has 10 cabins with private baths renting for about US$20 a double. There is a swimming pool, restaurant and bar, and dancing on weekends.

Top End The ***El Tucano Resort & Thermal Spa*** *(☎ 460-6000, fax 460-1692, Tucano@centralamerica.com)* is 8km northeast of Ciudad Quesada on the left-hand side of the road leading to Aguas Zarcas – look for the large white gate. Facilities include a recommended Italian restaurant, swimming pool, Jacuzzi and sauna, and various sports facilities ranging from tennis courts to miniature golf. Nearby thermal springs are tapped into three small hot pools where you can soak away your ills. The thermal waters are said to have medicinal and therapeutic properties. Horse, boat, and vehicle excursions can be arranged to anywhere in the region. The whole complex is well run and popular, and the 182-hectare resort offers 90 rooms.

Full high-season rates include breakfast and dinner and are US$99/162/209 for standard singles/doubles/triples. Rates for junior suites are US$186 double, the suites cost US$209, and master suites cost US$278. Day visitors are charged about US$3 Monday to Thursday and US$9 on weekends to use the pools and facilities.

Outside the hotel is a public park and recreation area named Aguas Termales de la Marina – popularly known as 'El Tucanito' by the locals – through which flows the same hot river used in the hotel. You can bathe directly in the hot springs for US$2. A short walk away is La Marina (☎ 460-0946, 460-3663), a small private zoo that cares for orphaned or injured Costa Rican wildlife. Hours are 8 am to 4 pm daily; admission is US$2.

Both the hotel and hot springs can be reached from Quesada by taxi or by a variety of buses to Puerto Viejo, Pital, Venecia, Río Frío, etc.

Several other good hotels are found to the north in or near Muelle de San Carlos, as described in the Northern Lowlands chapter.

Places to Eat

Apart from the hotel restaurants, there are several places to eat within a couple of blocks of the park, and there is a good selection on the park itself. This is cattle country and the best steakhouse, ***Restaurant Coca Loca*** *(☎ 460-3208)*, is on the east side. Also on this side is ***Pollos Jeffry*** *(☎ 460-3351)* for chicken and ***Pops*** for ice cream. The ***Restaurante Tonjibe*** *(☎ 460-1585)*, on the south side, has a good and varied selection of meat and seafood dishes. The ***Restaurante La Jarra*** *(☎ 460-0985)*, by the southeast corner, is also one of the town's better places.

Getting There & Away

Buses to Ciudad Quesada leave San José from the Atlántico Norte terminal about every hour from 5 am to 7:30 pm. The journey costs about US$2 and is an attractive ride over the western flanks of the Cordillera Central, reaching 1850m at Laguna, just beyond Zarcero. Then begins the long and pretty descent to Quesada at 650m. The bus makes many stops and takes three hours unless you get a direct one all the way to Quesada (2¹/4 hours).

The bus terminal in Quesada (☎ 460-0638) is half a block south of the Parque Central's southeast corner. Buses return to San José about every hour from 5 am to 6:15 pm. Buses to Fortuna take just over an hour, leaving at 6 and 10:30 am and 1, 3:30, 5:15, and 6 pm; there are several routes, so ask at the station. Buses to Tilarán take four or five hours and leave at 6 am and 3:30 pm, stopping in Fortuna. At other times, buses from other towns to Fortuna come through here; seats may be available.

Eastbound buses leave for Río Frío (via Venecia, Puerto Viejo de Sarapiquí, and other intermediate communities) three times a day. Two more buses go as far as Puerto Viejo and terminate there, and there are other buses for small local villages to the east. Buses north to Los Chiles leave numerous times a day; and northwest to San Rafael de Guatuso, buses leave five times a day. Ask at the bus terminal for other local destinations.

FORTUNA

Officially called La Fortuna de San Carlos, this small town (population about 7000) is the nearest to the spectacular Volcán Arenal. Fortuna is 250m above sea level and has excellent views of the 1633m volcano only 6km to the west. The volcano attracts many travelers, and Fortuna's tourist industry has expanded greatly in recent years, which means you'll see many other travelers here. It's a friendly town, and various attractions are found nearby – a lovely waterfall, hot springs, a lake, and tours to caves and the nearby Caño Negro wildlife refuge (described in the Northern Lowlands chapter).

Orientation & Information

The map shows no street names because there are no street signs in Fortuna. Local landmarks are used instead.

There's no impartial tourist office, though tour offices give tourist information (see

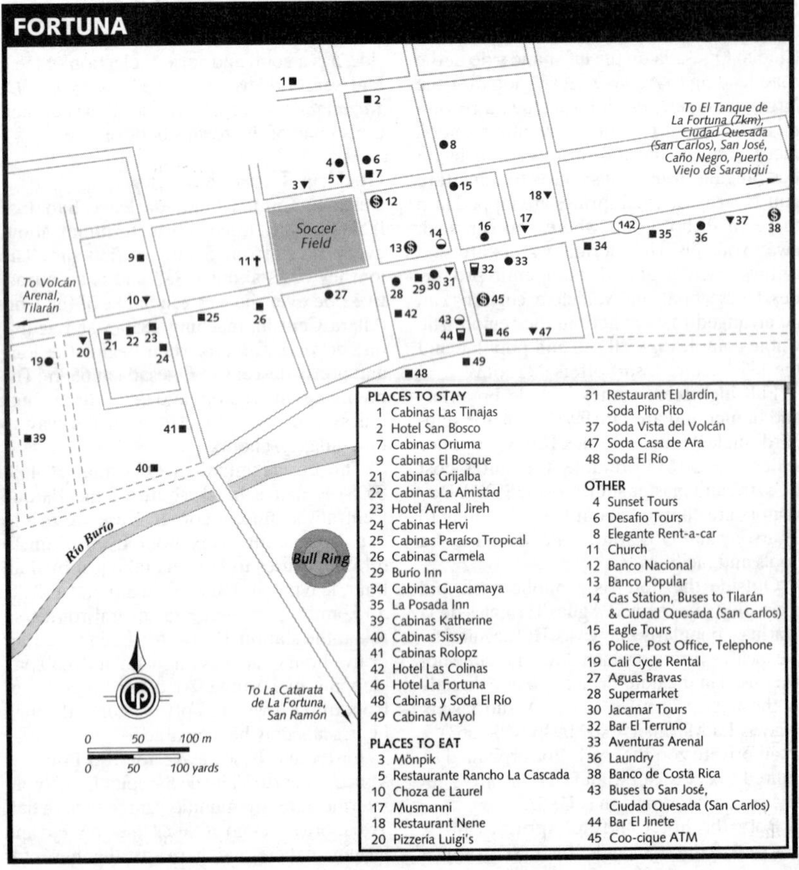

Organized Tours, below). Most of the hotels provide tourist information, too.

The Banco Popular, Banco de Costa Rica, and Banco Nacional change money, with the first giving the fastest service. Both the Banco Popular and Coo-cique have ATMs.

Internet access is available at Desafio Tours (see below) and some hotels, but it isn't cheap. Plan on quickly checking your email, not surfing.

La Catarata de La Fortuna

A visit to this long and narrow waterfall is one of the area's most popular excursions, after the obligatory visits to the Arenal volcano and lake. It is easy to visit the falls from town – you don't need a guide unless you want one.

A signed road runs from the south side of the church (the sign claims it is 5.5km to the falls). After almost 1km, the paved road becomes dirt and makes several twists and turns; each one of these is marked, though the signs are sometimes hard to see. It makes a pleasant walk through agricultural countryside. Alternately, ride a horse (these short trips don't wear out horses as does the slog described in the boxed text) or drive, though you'll need 4WD in the rainy months. Early risers will find good birding along this road.

At the overlook to the falls, you must park. From here there's a good view of the long, ribbonlike falls cascading down the far side of a very steep forested canyon. There's plenty of water, even in the dry season. There is a US$1.75 fee to continue down an extremely steep trail to the base of the falls. People swim there, though it can get pretty wild after heavy rains, so take care and don't swim under the falls themselves, which is very dangerous. Remember that the hike out afterward is steep uphill! The admission fee has been used to stabilize the trail and build steps in the steepest sections. Allow several hours roundtrip if you are walking, and bring a picnic lunch.

Organized Tours

A number of tour operators have sprung up in the last few years. Many operate out of hotels. Prices and quality of tours can vary substantially, so shop around and try to talk to someone who has just been on a tour to see what's good.

The most popular tour is, of course, a visit to Volcán Arenal. You can go by day or night, though an increasingly popular option is a midafternoon departure to take a short hike in daylight, watch the sunset, and observe nocturnal volcanic activity. If the weather is clear, red-hot lava rolling down the slopes and being ejected from the crater can be seen at night. If it is cloudy in late afternoon, it is unlikely that you will see the lava, and there is no refund if you don't see anything (though some operators offer a cut-price second trip the following day). You will hear the explosions in the distance. Many tours allow time for a soak in the Tabacón hot springs, which becomes a sort of second prize on cloudy nights, but this is at extra cost. (Both the volcano and Balneario Tabacón are described in detail later in this chapter.) Night tours leave every day and cost US$10 to US$30 per person – shop around. Discounts are sometimes available if you buy the tour through the hotel where you are staying. The cheapest tours are more crowded and may offer a dip in some free hot springs. The pricier tours include national park entrance and better guides and vehicles. Always check to see which hot springs might be part of the tour and whether the entry fee is included or extra.

Tours are also available to La Catarata de La Fortuna waterfall (see above) by horseback (half day, US$15 per person), Caño Negro by bus and boat (US$45 for a full day), the caves at Venado, fishing on Laguna de Arenal (US$135/250 for half/full day per boat, which takes two anglers), and other local places on request. The Caño Negro tour is one of the most popular, and Fortuna is as good a base as any to do this trip. Note that these prices vary; the cheaper tours aren't necessarily better value.

Other tours include white-water rafting on the Ríos Toro and Peñas Blancas. Tours range from 1½ to 3½ hours of river time, with Class III and IV rapids. The trips vary depending on local conditions and cost US$40 to US$70 per person.

Of the several tour operators, Sunset Tours (☎ 479-9415, ☎/fax 479-9099, mcastro@sol.racsa.co.cr) is one of the best established and most helpful. Apart from tours, the staff will help with flight reconfirmation, international phone and fax messages, and local information. Desafio Tours (☎ 479-9464, fax 479-9463, desafio@sol.racsa.co.cr) has been recommended by readers for adventure tours and specializes in local river rafting. Aventuras Arenal (☎ 479-9133, 479-9656, fax 479-9295) is another well-established option and offers bicycle rental.

To Ride or Not to Ride?

The Arenal area is fascinating: an active volcano and cloud forests attract ecotourists from all over the world. The only towns with a tourism infrastructure here are Fortuna and Monteverde and, although they are only a few kilometers apart, this region's rugged terrain requires a day of hard driving over rough roads to get from one to the other.

Local entrepreneurs have discovered that ecotourists are interested in visiting both Fortuna and Monteverde and have provided a horseback-riding tour that joins the towns. The catchphrase is 'The shortest and most convenient connection,' which has proved successful and popular, and many 'outfitters' have jumped on the horseback tour bandwagon. Tourists often think that riding a horse from Fortuna to Monteverde or vice versa is a good way to cover the route and see some of the countryside. Demand for horseback rides has risen and competition is fierce to earn the tourists' dollars.

The result is cut-throat competition and severe price-cutting in order to attract tourists, who often look for the best prices. Unfortunately, this has led to unethical practices such as buying cheap old horses for a few hundred dollars and literally working them to death. The trails between Fortuna and Monteverde are steep, slippery, and often very muddy, and the horses are sometimes forced to work without adequate rest breaks or days off. There have been a few cases of horses dying on the trail; more often they are worked until they can't carry a rider and then sold to a butcher.

Many travelers have written to let me know that they were saddened and, in some cases, outraged to see their tour horses treated so poorly. I have received repeated reports of animals that are old, thin, worn-out, plagued by sores, underfed, and beaten by the guides to make them move faster. Because some owners buy the horses as a short-term investment, the animals do not receive the necessary veterinary care and blood tests. In 1999, an outbreak of a deadly disease locally called 'equine anemia' caused the destruction of dozens of horses; this was attributed to uncared-for hacks purchased to service ecotourists and spreading the disease from one area to another.

I have spoken with several local outfitters about this. The reply is usually, 'Oh, no, we always look after our animals. It's the other companies.' Unfortunately, I haven't been able to find a company that really does provide healthy, strong, well-cared-for animals. If you do find one, let me know. And you should expect to pay a lot more than the other companies charge; it's worth it.

Clearly, horses provide pleasurable transportation for tourists. Equally clearly, the tourists who may never have ridden before and don't know any better are being exploited along with the horses on the Fortuna-Monteverde tours. I do not recommend these tours. There are plenty of shorter, gentler rides available in Costa Rica where the animals are not treated as expendable sources of short-term profits.

– Rob Rachowiecki

Aguas Bravas (☎ 229-4837) has river trips and bicycle rentals (from US$15 a day). Eagle Tours (☎/fax 479-9091, 479-9485) and Jacamar Tours (☎/fax 479-9456, jacamar@sol.racsa.co.cr) also appear to be reputable. Cali Cycle Rental (see map) has basic bicycles for US$1 an hour or US$7 a day.

Places to Stay – In Town

Fortuna is popular with both ticos and foreign travelers interested in seeing the famous exploding volcano. On weekends, especially in holiday periods, the cheaper hotels can be full, so try to arrive early or make a reservation if possible. Prices tend to be a little higher during holiday weekends and lower when the town isn't full. I give approximate busy weekend rates.

A number of small, family-run places, each with just a few simple rooms with private bath and electric showers or shared showers, provide cheapish lodging. Some aren't well signed, and you may hear about them through word of mouth. These places will help arrange local tours and are a good way to help locals cash in on the tourism boom. Hotel touts meet the buses and are a little more aggressive with their wares than in most of Costa Rica.

Note that hotels beyond the town center are listed separately here (see the additional Places to Stay sections below).

Budget ***Cabinas Sissy*** *(☎ 479-9256, 479-9356)* charges US$2 per person to camp; bathroom and kitchen are available. (For another camping option, see Jungla & Senderos Los Lagos, under Places to Stay – West of Town, below.) Cabinas Sissy also has 12 basic but clean rooms with fans and electric showers for US$7/12 single/double. There are kitchen privileges.

La Posada Inn *(☎/fax 479-9793)* is a basic but clean and friendly place, popular with young backpackers. Rates are US$5 per person; showers are shared. ***Cabinas Rolopz*** *(☎ 479-9058, ☎/fax 479-9576)* has four rooms with fans and electric showers from US$7 single to US$20 for four people. Its soda (next door) is open 6 am to 9 pm and houses a small tour agency. The ***Burío Inn*** *(☎ 479-9076)* charges US$8 per person including breakfast. Rooms have hot showers.

Cabinas Katherine *(☎ 479-9542)* has rooms with shared and private showers for US$6 to US$8 per person.

Several small places charge about US$10 per person for a room with hot bath; they prefer to rent doubles but will rent the same rooms as singles if they're not busy. All seem clean and adequate. They include the ***Cabinas Grijalba*** *(☎/fax 479-9129)*, ***Cabinas La Amistad*** *(☎ 479-9364, fax 479-9342)*, and ***Cabinas El Bosque***.

The decent ***Hotel La Fortuna*** *(☎ 479-9197)* has 13 rooms with hot showers for US$12/20. They have a soda. The clean ***Cabinas Carmela*** *(☎ 479-9010)* has fairly large rooms with private hot-water bath and fan for US$15/20. ***Cabinas Mayol*** *(☎ 479-9110)* has eight clean double rooms with fans and hot bath for US$12/20/25/30 for one to four people. It has a pool and restaurant. The reader-recommended ***Cabinas Hervi*** *(☎ 479-9430, 479-9100)* has four good-size rooms with bath and fan for US$19 double, and four rooms sharing two baths and a kitchen for US$5.50 per person.

Mid-Range The ***Cabinas y Soda El Río*** has a popular little restaurant and rooms for about US$24 double with bath. ***Cabinas Las Tinajas*** *(☎ 479-9308, fax 479-9099)* has just four clean and spacious rooms with fans and hot water at US$25 double. It is on a quiet street.

Hotel Las Colinas *(☎ 479-9305, ☎/fax 479-9107, hcolinas@sol.racsa.co.cr)* is clean and good with friendly and helpful management. Internet access is available. Nineteen rooms with both hot water and fans cost US$15/30/35/40 for one to four people. ***Cabinas Oriuma*** *(☎/fax 479-9111)* is a family-run place (the office is in the hardware store downstairs) with six rooms, most with a queen and two single beds and private hot shower. They advertise US$10 per person, but this is usually for three or four people. Singles and doubles have to be negotiated according to demand.

Cabinas Guacamaya *(☎ 479-9393, ☎/fax 479-9087, info@cabinasguacamaya.com)* has nine good-size, air-conditioned rooms with refrigerator and hot water for US$35/40. They have a patio with volcano views, a parking area, and a small gift shop, and are planning to add a swimming pool and breakfast room.

Cabinas Paraíso Tropical *(☎ 479-9222, fax 479-9722)* has 10 pleasant rooms. Five standard rooms have fans and private baths for US$35 a double. Five air-conditioned rooms with TV cost US$50 a double. A swimming pool is planned for 2000. ***Hotel Arenal Jireh*** *(☎ 479-9236, ☎/fax 479-9004, jirehcr@sol.racsa.co.cr)* has a pool and six air-conditioned rooms with TV. Rates are in the US$30s and US$40s.

The ***Hotel San Bosco*** *(☎ 479-9050, fax 479-9109, fortuna@sol.racsa.co.cr)* has balcony views of Arenal, a pool, a Jacuzzi, and a guarded parking lot, and it can arrange tours. Fourteen pleasant rooms with fans and private hot shower cost US$35/40/45 single/double/triple and 19 air-conditioned and more spacious rooms cost US$45/50/55, but few single rooms are available. Some rooms sleep four or five. Two furnished houses with kitchens and fans cost US$80 (six beds, one bathroom, maximum eight people) and US$100 (10 beds, two bathrooms, maximum 14 people).

Places to Stay – East of Town

Almost 1km east of town is ***Cabinas Villa Fortuna*** *(☎/fax 479-9139)*, set in pleasant gardens that have chili-pepper plants and uncaged pet toucans. There are clean rooms with a fridge and private hot showers for US$35 to US$40 a double, some with air-conditioning and most with views of the volcano. Almost 1.5km east of Fortuna is ***Las Cabañitas Resort*** *(☎/fax 479-9400, 479-9408, cabanita@sol.racsa.co.cr)*, which has a pool, tour desk, restaurant and bar, and 30 spacious individual cabins, all with ceiling fans and porches and many with great volcano views; no TVs or telephones in the rooms. Rates are US$80 single and US$12 per additional person.

In the village of El Tanque de La Fortuna, which is 7km east of Fortuna, is the clean, comfortable, and helpful ***Hotel Rancho Corcovado*** *(☎ 479-9300, ☎/fax 479-9090)*, which has a swimming pool and restaurant and arranges local tours and horse rental. Rooms cost US$55/65.

Beyond El Tanque, the road continues to Muelle de San Carlos, which is described in the Northern Lowlands chapter.

Places to Stay – South of Town

The paved road to San Ramón passes ***Arenal Country Inn*** *(☎ 479-9670, 479-9669, fax 479-9433, arenal@costaricainn.com)*, about 1km south of town. Here, 20 spacious, modern, air-conditioned rooms, all with two queen-size beds and private patio, rent for US$70 single and US$12 for each additional person, including full breakfast. The restaurant/bar is an interesting open-air affair, housed in a restored cattle corral. Spacious grounds include an adults' and children's pool, volcano views, and a river running through the property.

By the entrance to La Catarata de La Fortuna is the new (parts were still under construction in 1999) ***Americas' Paradise Hotel*** *(☎ 479-9327, 392-2342, fax 479-9311; in the USA ☎ 800-648-2141, trimed@soflo.net)*, owned by a Costa Rican doctor who practices in Miami and is involved in various health-care projects, including accommodating medical groups. The hotel is set in 160 hectares, and hiking trails, a swimming pool, tennis and volleyball courts, horseback riding, and tours are planned. This is a no-smoking facility and alcohol is limited to wine with dinner. Thirty rooms are planned – 10 were open when I visited and appeared spacious, attractive, and comfortable; one was wheelchair accessible. Rates range from the US$50s to US$80s depending on the room but will increase when the hotel is finished.

Chachagua Rainforest Lodge *(☎ 231-0356, fax 290-6506, chachagua@novanet.co.cr)* is about 12km south of Fortuna, 2km off the main highway to San Ramón. The rough final stretch into the lodge may require 4WD after rains. It is a working cattle and horse ranch adjacent to a private rainforest reserve; horse rides are available and the wildlife watching is reportedly excellent. Rates for one of two dozen comfortable wooden bungalows with spacious baths are US$84/98, and there is an open-air restaurant from which you can watch birds and horses.

Places to Stay – West of Town

Several hotels are nearby on the road that heads west toward the volcano. Two kilometers west of town, ***Hotel Arenal Rossi*** *(☎ 479-9023, fax 479-9414, cabrossi@sol.racsa.co.cr)* offers 25 rooms with private hot bath, TV, and minifridge. Fifteen rooms with fans cost US$30/35 single/double, and 10 larger, air-conditioned rooms cost US$50 double, all including breakfast. There is a gift shop, swimming pool, and small kids' playground. Close by, friendly ***Cabinas Las Flores*** *(☎ 479-9307)* has clean rooms with private hot bath for US$10/15 single/double, though the helpful owner often gives discounts if things are slow.

La Catarata Ecotourist Lodge *(☎ 479-9612, 479-9522, fax 479-9168, ccoprena@sol.racsa.co.cr)* is on a side road south of the above *cabinas*. It is another of the ecotourism projects run by local communities and funded by the Canadian WWF, ACA, and other agencies (see the Volcán Tenorio Area and Monteverde & Santa Elena sections, earlier in this chapter, for similar projects). As such, it is well worth supporting. Of course, great volcano views and tours led by locals are highlights. There are nine cabins with private hot showers for US$30/48/66 for one to three people, including full breakfast. A simple restaurant serves casados (US$6) for the other meals. A butterfly garden, orchid house, and paca breeding house can be visited (US$1 for nonguests).

Continuing west out of Fortuna, you come to the new ***Baldi Thermae*** *(☎ 479-9651, fax 479-9652)*. It has four soaking and swimming pools of various temperatures, from 62°C down to 37°C. Hours are 10 am to 10 pm; admission is US$7 and there is a bar and restaurant. A hotel is planned with private thermal Jacuzzis in the rooms. There are good volcano views.

About 6km west of Fortuna is ***Jungla & Senderos Los Lagos*** *(☎ 479-8000, 479-9126, fax 479-8009)*, which bus drivers and locals also know as El Mirador. This is a resort spread out over a large area of the northern flanks of the volcano. Near the entrance is a rock garden with pools full of caiman and crocodiles. An aquarium and other pools have fish from the area, and one pool is stocked for fishing (loaner rods available). There are two swimming pools – both with unheated water. One has a rather scary-looking stone waterslide that I would hesitate to use (OK, so I'm a wimp). Nearby are a restaurant, gift shop, and about 20 pleasant air-conditioned rooms with cable TV, phone, minifridge and private hot showers for US$42/57/72/87 for one to four people. From the entrance area, a dirt road with scenic views climbs steeply to two lakes in the foothills of the volcano, about 3km away from the entrance. Here, there are eight camping cabins with beds (you provide bedding or a sleeping bag), electricity, and cold-water showers; rates are US$18/21.50/25/28.50. There is a campground by the lakes with drinking water, toilets, showers, grills, and picnic benches. Camping (your tent) costs US$6 per person for one night and US$3 for additional nights. Nearby is the mirador (lookout) with fine views of the volcano. Rowboats can be hired for US$2 per half hour minimum. There are hiking trails and good birding opportunities. Day use of the area costs US$3.50 (free if you are staying here). Horses are available for rent. This is an uncrowded place with simple but adequate facilities, recommended for camping. Tico families like to drive up here on weekends.

Eight kilometers west of Fortuna, on the north side of the volcano, the ***Hotel Arenal Paraiso*** *(☎ 460-5333, fax 460-5343, arenalpa@sol.racsa.co.cr)* has 12 clean standard cabins with fans, refrigerators, private baths, and patios with volcano views for US$53 double, and eight larger air-conditioned cabins with cable TV for US$72 double. There is a restaurant and a Jacuzzi; a pool is planned. Short walking trails behind the hotel go to a private waterfall.

Nine kilometers to the west of town, the ***Montaña del Fuego Inn*** *(☎ 460-1220, 479-9579, 460-6720, fax 460-1455)* has two dozen wooden duplex cabins, each with a patio and picture windows facing the volcano. On clear nights, views are spectacular. All rooms sleep up to four and have views, fans, and hot showers, and some have air-conditioning. There is a restaurant. Rates are US$60 double and extra people are US$11. Junior suites cost US$80 double, and horseback riding and other local excursions can be arranged.

Farther west are more places to stay beyond the volcano and around Laguna de Arenal, described later in this chapter.

Places to Eat

The ***Soda El Río*** serves good, reasonably priced food in a simple setting. The ***Soda Casa de Ara*** is locally recommended for cheap food. The ***Soda Vista del Volcán*** is another decent budget choice. The ***Restaurant El Jardín*** is overpriced and mediocre but popular with tourists because of its central location. Locals eat at the outside window counter, called ***Soda Pito Pito***, where prices are reasonable though selection is limited. ***Musmanni*** is a bakery with the best selection of breads, etc for a picnic.

If you want more than the basic casado, the attractive, thatch-roofed ***Restaurante Rancho La Cascada*** *(☎ 479-9145)*, at the corner of the soccer field, has average food, with both Italian and tico specialties. One of the nicest places (though very reasonably priced) is the recommended ***Restaurant Nene*** *(☎ 479-9192)*, where a big steak costs about US$7 and there are plenty of cheaper options. At the west end of town, the rustic ***Choza de Laurel*** has good meals in the US$3 to US$7 range. It is open 6 am to 10 pm and serves espresso and cappuccino. Nearby is the reasonably priced ***Pizzería Luigi's***. There's also a ***Mönpik*** for ice-cream lovers.

Just under 2km west of town on the road to the volcano is the recommended ***La Vaca Muca*** *(☎ 479-9186)*, an attractive tico-style country restaurant with good food. Meals are in the US$6 to US$12 range. It is closed on Monday.

Entertainment

You can dance in the nightclub over the ***Restaurante Rancho La Cascada***, which is usually empty except on weekends. Otherwise, there's not much in the way of entertainment in Fortuna apart from hanging out with other travelers or locals over a beer. A couple of popular basic local bars are ***Bar El Jinete***, which also does cheap food, and ***Bar El Terruño***, which serves *bocas*.

About 5km west of town is ***Volcán Look***, supposedly the biggest discotheque in Costa Rica outside of San José. It's usually dead except on weekends and holidays.

Getting There & Away

Air Travelair flies to from San José to Fortuna for US$63/103 one way/roundtrip at 12:05 pm daily, returning at 1 pm. SANSA flies from San José at 10 am for US$45/90, continuing to Tamarindo (US$50/100), and returning to San José in the early afternoon. These are new schedules, subject to changes and civil aviation approval. Local travel agencies sell tickets.

Bus Direct buses from San José to Fortuna leave the Atlántico Norte terminal at 6:15, 8:40, and 11:30 am. Alternatively, take one of the frequent buses to Ciudad Quesada and connect there with an afternoon bus. There are also buses from Tilarán.

In Fortuna, there are two bus stops. The one in front of the gas station is for buses to Tilarán; the one a block to the south is for San José buses. Buses for Ciudad Quesada leave from both bus stops. Buses for San José (US$2.50, 4½ hours) leave at 12:45 and 2:45 pm. Buses for Ciudad Quesada leave at 5 and 8 am and 12:15 and 3:30 pm. Some of these connect in Ciudad Quesada with a San José bus. Other buses may be available passing through Fortuna from somewhere else; ask. Transportes Jocar (☎ 479-9633), opposite the Restaurant El Jardín, has daily shuttles to San José for US$15 that are faster and more comfortable.

Buses for Tilarán leave at 8 am and 5:30 pm. For most other northern destinations, ask locally; you'll usually be told to go to Ciudad Quesada and change buses.

BALNEARIO TABACÓN

The Tabacón hot springs, 12km west of Fortuna, is a good spot from which to view Volcán Arenal, and many tours to the volcano include a visit and a soak in the natural hot pools. The most well-known place is the upscale ***Tabacón Resort*** (*☎ 256-7373, fax 256-8412, sales@tabacon.com*), which features hot tubs, water slide, swim-up bar, waterfalls, and 12 cold and hot swimming and soaking pools. Temperatures vary from 22°C to 41°C. The area is open 9 am to 10 pm daily, and there is a US$15 admission fee (US$8 for children). The spa offers a multitude of treatments such as volcanic mud masks, massages, manicures, and aromatherapy, ranging from US$20 to US$60 and lasting 20 to 75 minutes. Packages of treatments cost US$45 to US$110 and last one to three hours. Admission is free to just visit their bar, café, and restaurant, from which you can watch either the bathers bathing or Arenal exploding, depending on where you sit. The views are good, especially on a clear night when your dinner is enhanced with periodic volcanic fireworks to liven up what could be called a hot date.

A short walk from the spa is the lodge, with 42 modern, large, air-conditioned rooms with cable TV and volcano views. Rates are US$122/140 single/double including breakfast and admission to the spa. Local tours are offered.

Across the street from the resort is another facility, with a soda and several swimming pools; you can bathe in the same thermal water for US$6 from 10 am to 9:30 pm. Take your choice.

There are places where you can bathe for free. Continue on the road toward the lake past the resorts for a few hundred meters and look for trails leading off into the bushes. There are no signs, but undeveloped pools of hot mineral water can certainly be found.

PARQUE NACIONAL VOLCÁN ARENAL

This park was created in 1995. Along with Tenorio, Miravalles, the Monteverde cloud forest reserve, and other areas, it is part of the Area de Conservación Arenal, which protects most of the Cordillera de Tilarán. This area is rugged and varied and the biodiversity is high. It contains roughly half the species of land-dwelling vertebrates (birds, mammals, reptiles, and amphibians) known in Costa Rica.

Obviously, the centerpiece of this park is the volcano. Arenal was temporarily dormant from about 1500 AD until July 29, 1968, when huge explosions triggered lava flows that destroyed two villages and killed about 80 people and 45,000 head of cattle. Despite this massive eruption, the volcano retained its almost perfect conical shape, which, combined with its continuing activity, makes Arenal everyone's image of a typical volcano. Occasionally, the activity quiets down for a few weeks, but generally Arenal has been producing huge ash columns, massive explosions, and glowing red lava flows almost daily since 1968.

Every once in a while, perhaps lulled into a sense of false security by a temporary pause in the activity, someone tries to climb to the crater and peer within it. This is very dangerous – climbers have been killed or maimed by explosions. The problem is not so much getting killed (that's a risk the foolhardy insist is their own decision) but rather risking the lives of Costa Rican rescuers. I must admit that I was young, uninformed, and impetuous enough to climb the volcano in 1981 and came close to terminating my climbing career just below the summit. I strongly discourage anyone from attempting the climb.

The best nighttime views of the volcano are usually from the west and north sides of the volcano, although spectacular activity can sometimes be seen from any direction, including Fortuna. Still, most visitors drive or take a tour around to the west side in the hopes of seeing the most impressive views. The degree of activity varies from week to week; sometimes it can be a spectacular display of flowing red-hot lava and incandescent rocks flying through the air; at other times the volcano subsides to a gentle glow. During the day, the glowing lava isn't easy to see, but you can still view the great clouds of ash thrown up several times a day by massive explosions.

Be aware that clouds can cover the volcano at any time, and tours don't guarantee a view (though often you can hear the explosions).

Orientation & Information

The ranger station/information center is on the west side of the volcano and is reached by driving west of Fortuna for 15km, then turning left at a 'Parque Nacional' sign and taking a 2km dirt road to the entrance, open 7 am to 10 pm. Here you pay the US$6 park fee. There is a restroom and visitor information here. A road continues 1.4km toward the volcano, where there is a parking lot. From here, a 2km trail continues toward the volcano. Rangers will tell you how far you are allowed to go.

It should be noted that this route gets you close to the volcano but, because the view is foreshortened, many visitors prefer more distant views from some of the lodges west of the volcano or from Laguna de Arenal. However, the explosions do sound loud!

Places to Stay

Inside the Park No camping is allowed inside the park, though people have camped (no facilities) off some of the unpaved roads west of the volcano by the shores of the lake. Rangers told me that a park camping facility is planned by the lake.

There are plenty of places to stay in Fortuna (see earlier) and outside of the park around Laguna de Arenal (see below), but there is only one lodge within the park itself. This is the ***Arenal Observatory Lodge***, operated by Costa Rica Sun Tours (see contact information under Organized Tours in the Getting Around chapter). It was originally a private observatory established in 1987 on a macadamia nut farm on the south side of Volcán Arenal. Volcanologists from all over the world have come to study the active volcano, including researchers from the Smithsonian Institute in Washington, DC. A seismograph operates around the clock.

The lodge has 24 rooms and is a good base for exploring the nearby countryside. It is set on a ridge just over 2km away from the volcano, and views and sounds of eruptions are excellent. Laguna de Arenal is visible in the other direction. Hikes can be made to a nearby waterfall (short hike), to see recent lava flows (2½ hours), to see old lava flows (three hours), or to climb Arenal's dormant partner, Volcán Chato, which is 1100m high and only 3km southeast of Volcán Arenal (four hours). There is a lake in Chato's summit crater, and canoes and paddles are provided for those who can't resist the chance to boat out on a volcano. Maps or local English-speaking guides are available for these hikes.

You can wander around the macadamia nut farm or through the primary forest that makes up about half of the 347-hectare site. Guided walks cost US$30 for one to four people up Volcán Chato. (There are trails up Chato, and a guide is not essential.) A guided hike to the waterfall and to a lava flow is included in the cost of an overnight stay. The US$6 per-person park fee is extra. Horse rental costs US$7 per hour. There is good birding as well as good volcano views. Full-day Caño Negro tours cost US$70 per person, and Venado caves tours cost US$55.

There are three main areas of the lodge. The Observatory Block is where the observatory was built and now houses the office, restaurant/bar, and about half the rooms. These are nine standard rooms without volcano views for US$62/74/85/95 for one to four people. They are cramped, older rooms; some are noisy because of people watching the volcano from the patio outside. Four newer rooms with volcano views cost US$97/114 single/double. About 200m away is the Smithsonian block, reached on foot by a suspension bridge over a forested ravine – quite dramatic. The 10 newer, spacious rooms here have picture windows with volcano views and rent for US$87/105/112 for one to three people. There is a viewing deck, conference room, and seismograph here. All the rooms have private hot showers. Finally, La Casona is about a half kilometer away in the original farmhouse. It now houses five double rooms sharing two hot showers; there are volcano views from the house porch. Rates here are US$41/49/61/80. Children get discounts. Day use of the grounds and trails costs US$3.50 for nonguests.

Various multiday packages are available that include transport from San José or Fortuna. Otherwise, take a bus to Fortuna and hire a taxi to the lodge. Drivers from Fortuna should turn left on the road toward Parque Nacional Arenal and drive about 9km to the lodge. There's only one major fork (after about 5.5km) where you go left – there are several signs.

Outside the Park If you follow the road past the ranger station to the fork described above and turn right (instead of left to the Arenal Observatory Lodge), you'll come to two other hotels. Just over 3km beyond the fork, after you have forded two rivers (high clearance needed in the wet months, though bridges are planned), you reach the ***Linda Vista del Norte*** *(☎ 380-0847, fax 479-9443, lindav@costaricabureau.com)*, which has 10 simple but clean rooms with fans and private hot showers. Set up on a ridge, the rooms have good forest and lake views, but only two have volcano views. However, the restaurant/bar has a huge picture window and outdoor terrace that have super volcano views. Rates are US$47/65/75 for one to three people including breakfast. They offer all the usual local tours at competitive prices.

About 2.5km farther, after you've forded yet another river and gone through the tiny communities of El Castillo and Pueblo Nuevo, you come to the attractive ***Arenal Vista Lodge*** *(☎ 221-0965, 221-2389, fax 221-6230, arenalvi@sol.racsa.co.cr)*, which has 25 spacious rooms, all with fan, private hot shower, balcony, and volcano views. Rates are US$70 single and US$12 for additional people (up to four). There's a restaurant (meals cost US$7 to US$12.50), a conference room, and a volcano-viewing room. Horseback rides to a waterfall and lava flow (US$20) and other places are offered, and fishing and other excursions can be arranged.

LAGUNA DE ARENAL AREA

It's about an 18km drive west from Fortuna, past Tabacón and the national park road, to the dam that marks the beginning of the lake. The dam is crossed by a 0.75km-long causeway, and the road continues around the north and west shores of the lake past the village of Arenal to the small town of Tilarán. Along the way are frequent splendid lake and volcano views. Many small hotels and other establishments have been built along this road, and they are described here in the order that they are passed as you drive west around the lake. Distances given are from the dam. Mostly, these are mid-range to top-end places, except in the village of Arenal.

The lake is an artificial body of water formed when the dam was built in 1973, flooding small towns such as Arenal and Tronadora. Laguna de Arenal is Costa Rica's largest lake and now supplies water for Guanacaste and hydroelectricity for the region. Winds are usually strong and steady, especially at the western end during the dry season, and the lake is recommended for sailing and windsurfing. (See the Activities section of Facts for the Visitor and the 'World-Class Windsurfing' boxed text later in this chapter).

Rainbow bass (locally called *guapote*) weighing up to 4kg are reported by anglers, who consider this a premier fishing spot. Boats and guides can be hired for fishing expeditions – ask at any of the major hotels in the area.

While most of the road is supposedly paved, repairs have been infrequent, and there are some huge potholes. Some of the unpaved road is passable to cars only with care. Don't expect to drive this stretch quickly.

Arenal

This small village, sometimes called Nuevo Arenal, replaced the earlier Arenal that was flooded by the lake formed in 1973. It is

29km west of the dam and is the only town between Fortuna and Tilarán.

Arenal has a gas station, a bank, a few simple places to stay and eat, and a bus stop near the park. It also offers a disco and live Costa Rican music and dancing on weekends.

Arenal Botanical Gardens

These gardens (☎ 694-4273) are 25km beyond the dam and 4km southeast of Arenal village. They were founded in 1991 as a reserve and living library of tropical and subtropical plants. Well-laid-out trails lead past 1200 varieties of tropical plants from Costa Rica and all over the world, and guide booklets in English, German, and Spanish describe what you see. Plenty of birds and butterflies are attracted to the gardens, and there is a butterfly farm and trails through primary forest. Michael LeMay is the helpful and knowledgeable English-speaking owner. Hours are 9 am to 4 pm daily; admission is US$4.

Places to Stay & Eat

The following listings start from the dam and work west. About 400m west of the dam, a paved but incredibly steep road rises 2.5km to the right to ***Arenal Lodge*** *(☎/fax 383-3957, arenal@sol.racsa.co.cr)*. There are exceptionally fine volcano views as well as forests surrounding the attractive grounds, which give wildlife-watching opportunities. The lodge has a Jacuzzi with a volcano view, a billiards room, a pricey restaurant, and a variety of first-class accommodations. Six economy rooms that sleep two and lack volcano views cost US$79/87 single/double. Twelve spacious junior suites with a good-size bathroom (hot water) and a balcony with volcano views cost US$149/156. Four junior suites that have kitchenettes cost US$161/167. The suites sleep three. Ten chalets sleep four and have kitchenettes and good views for US$168/176. Two larger suites sleeping up to five are available. Extra people are charged US$23. Look for big low-season discounts here. Breakfast is included, as is use of mountain bikes, a horseback ride around the property, and transfers to Tabacón hot springs. The staff arranges all tours and has experienced fishing guides on hand.

Just over 14km west of the dam is the ***Hotel Los Heroes*** *(☎/fax 284-6315, fax 441-4193, heroes@sol.racsa.co.cr)*, an unmistakable and slightly incongruous Alpine-style building with wooden balconies and window shutters. The volcano is visible from some parts of the grounds. Facilities include a Jacuzzi, swimming pool, chapel, and good European-style restaurant with a heavy Swiss influence; it's popular with European tourists. Meals seem a fair value in the US$4 to US$11 range. There's a nice bar with a cozy fireplace. Thirteen large and comfortable rooms with private hot bath cost US$55 double (US$65 with a balcony) including breakfast. Three apartments with huge bathrooms and balconies sleep up to six and rent for US$115. Credit cards are *not* accepted. They also run a two-deck Swiss-style tour bus from San José, leaving from the Gran Hotel Costa Rica at 8 am on Tuesday, Thursday, and Saturday. Rates are US$87 per person, double occupancy for the roundtrip, including lunch and dinner with wine, cocktail, overnight accommodations, breakfast, and an Arenal volcano visit. Make reservations at their Escazú office (☎/fax 228-1472, 284-6315). This seems like a good deal if you don't mind traveling with a group of mainly European travelers.

A little over 2km farther west in the tiny community of Unión is the charming ***Toad Hall*** *(fax 479-9178)*, which is a great place to stop for a coffee and a homemade snack or meal. The restaurant overlooks the forest and is open 8 am to 5 pm, serving a short but interesting and tasty menu for breakfast and lunch. While there, you can browse the art gallery, which has a small but very high-quality collection of local and indigenous art and jewelry, as well as a bookstore (travel and wildlife guides in English) and a pulpería-type general store where local farmers stop for sundries.

Just beyond Toad Hall, a dirt road to the right goes to **Venado** and on into the northern lowlands. Near Venado are caves that can be explored with guides (see San Rafael de Guatuso in the Northern Lowlands chapter).

Immediately past the Venado turnoff is the ***Marina Club Hotel & Resort*** *(☎/fax 284-6573)*, which is close to the lake and has a dock just over a kilometer away from the hotel. Rowing boats, windsurfers, and kayaks are available for guest use at no charge. There also is free horseback riding for guests, as well as attractive grounds with a swimming pool and a good restaurant and bar. Twelve huge split-level rooms, each with private terrace, hot bath, and a CD player, cost US$70/87 single/double, including breakfast (long stay discounts offered). Two spacious suites with kitchens cost US$140. You can rent three CDs for US$1. Fishing trips on the lake cost US$65 per half day, and other excursions are arranged.

Two kilometers farther west is the small ***Complejo Turístico La Alondra*** *(☎ 284-5575)*, with 10 standard rooms with private bath for US$30 a double. Rooms have a small terrace and lake view. There is a restaurant (open 7 am to 10 pm), and hiking trails are behind the property. A kilometer beyond is ***Restaurante Sabor Italiano***, which is a tiny place in the owner's house. Pizzas and pastas cost about US$5.

Continuing almost 4km farther brings you to ***La Ceiba Tree Lodge*** *(☎/fax 385-1540, 694-4297, ceibalodge@hotmail.com)*, which has five spacious, cross-ventilated rooms and one apartment, all with private hot baths and attractive decor. Rates are US$35/49, including breakfast. Sailors can rent Hobie 16s and Hobie 21s, and tours can be arranged. Mountain bikes are available and a Jacuzzi is planned. Lake views from the huge ceiba tree by the house are pretty, and the grounds have a collection of 70 local orchids and good birding possibilities. The friendly owners will cook dinner for you by advance request.

Continuing west, you pass the Botanical Gardens described above and, 3km beyond La Ceiba, arrive at the recommended ***Villa Decary B&B*** *(☎ 383-3012 cellular, fax 694-4330, email: villadecary@costarica.net, info@villadecary.com)*. This place is an all-around winner with bright, spacious, well-furnished rooms, a Jacuzzi, delicious full breakfasts, and super hosts. Five rooms each have private hot showers, a queen and a double bed, and balconies with excellent views of woodland immediately below (good birding from your room!) and the lake just beyond. Rates are US$69/80 single/double, US$12 per extra person, including breakfast. There is also a separate *casita* with a kitchenette that costs US$92 double. Credit cards are not accepted. Paths into the woods behind the house give good opportunities for watching wildlife, including howler monkeys. Guests can borrow binoculars and a bird guide to identify what they see. Jeff, one of the US owners, has gotten the bird bug and can help out with identification. His partner, Bill, is a botanist and specializes in palms (Decary was a French botanist who discovered a new palm). They are very enthusiastic about the area and enjoy accompanying guests into nearby Arenal on weekends to listen to tico music and introduce you to the locals. They know all the best places to eat and visit.

Arenal village is just a few kilometers beyond the Villa Decary B&B, on the left side of the highway from this direction. On the shoreline, ***Aurora Inn*** *(☎ 694-4245, 694-4071, fax 694-4262, AuroraInn@hotmail.com)* has a swimming pool and can arrange fishing trips on the lake. It has a restaurant, bar, and 10 rooms at US$41/54 single/double including breakfast.

The friendly ***Cabinas Rodriguez*** is the cheapest place in the village. Rooms with shared bath cost US$5 per person, with private bath US$10 per person. Nearby, ***Pipas Restaurant*** is a good choice for budget travelers. About 100m west of the gas station, the simple but clean and well-priced ***Restaurante Lajas*** *(☎ 694-4169)* has also been recommended. The ***Bar Restaurant El Toro Bravo*** *(☎ 694-4112)* is a lively place next to the soccer field. The restaurant is open from 11 am daily and has a good-value menu of steaks, burgers, and barbecue in the US$3 to US$8 range.

Also in Arenal, I recommend ***Pizzeria e Ristorante Tramonti*** *(☎ 694-4282)*, which is a classy Italian-run place with a wood-burning pizza oven, attractive outdoor patio, and good-value Italian meals in the US$5 to US$7 range. Hours are 11:30 am to 3 pm and 5 to 10 pm, but it may close on Monday.

On the other side of the main highway, a dirt road leads about 2km to the Canadian-run ***Joya Sureña*** *(☎ 694-4131, 694-4058, fax 694-4059, joysur@sol.racsa.co.cr)*. This classy hotel set on spacious grounds has a pool, sauna, and exercise room. The deck restaurant (room service is available) and bar have pretty views. All the usual local tours can be arranged and mountain bikes can be rented. Large and airy rooms with TV, telephone, writing desk, and ceiling fan cost US$64 single and US$12 for extra people (up to four). Breakfast is included.

Two kilometers west of Arenal is ***Willy's Caballo Negro*** *(☎/fax 694-4074)*, serving vegetarian and European fare; locals recommend the food. The restaurant has forest and lake views, and a canoe can be rented for rides on the lake, which is stocked with fish. Also look for iguanas, turtles, and birds while you are dining. Monica, one of the owners, is a professional massage therapist and can be hired for a relaxing Swedish massage.

Two or three kilometers northwest of Arenal is the attractive little ***Chalet Nicholas*** *(☎/fax 694-4041, chaletnicholas@costarica.net)*. Owners Catherine and John Nicholas are helpful and knowledgeable hosts; co-owners are four Great Danes, so don't be alarmed when they come bounding out to greet you. Two downstairs rooms have a private bath; the upstairs loft has two linked bedrooms sharing a downstairs bathroom. On clear days, all rooms have views of the volcano at the end of the lake, 25km away as the parrot flaps. The owners enjoy natural history and have a living collection of dozens of orchids. Birding is good too – one guest reported seeing 80 species of birds in four days on the reforested property alone; trails behind the lodge lead into the forest. Rates are US$45/69 including breakfast. Smoking is not allowed and credit cards aren't accepted. This place has many repeat guests.

Less than a kilometer west of Chalet Nicholas is the **Stable Arenal**, owned by a friendly guy nicknamed Gordo. He has horses for both beginners and experienced riders. Many local hotels use his services, or you can stop by yourself for a guided ride.

Four or five kilometers west of Arenal is a sign for the ***Lago Coter Ecolodge*** *(☎ 694-4470, fax 694-4460, in San José ☎ 257-5075, fax 257-7065, ecolodge@sol.racsa.co.cr, www.Eco-Lodge.com)*. A 3km unpaved but OK road leads to the lodge, which is near Lago Coter. The emphasis is on natural history and adventure – amenities include naturalist guides for hiking and birding, canoes (US$20/day), kayaks (US$25/day), and horses (US$30/day). There are trails through the nearby cloud forest, and birding is promising – the lodge brochure claims that over 350 species of birds have been recorded in the area. Guided hikes (US$20), canopy tours (US$35), and fishing (US$75/day) are offered, and a variety of nearby excursions are available. There is a fireplace and relaxation area – billiards, TV, and a small library. Food is buffet-style and plentiful and costs about US$6 for breakfast and US$12.50 for lunch or dinner. Twenty-three small but comfortable standard rooms cost US$48/56/66 single/double/triple and 14 larger cabins cost US$56/77/87. Many visitors come on complete packages that include rental equipment and activities led by naturalist guides and all meals and lodging. Prices start between US$148 and US$163 for two nights/three days per person (double occupancy) and go up to US$506 to US$586 for eight days/seven nights. Tours away from the lodge cost extra.

Back on the main road to Tilarán, a short distance past the Lago Coter turnoff, is ***La Rana de Arenal*** *(☎/fax 694-4031)*, with seven rooms at US$25/40 including breakfast, and an apartment at US$60. It offers a German-influenced restaurant and three cars for rent with advance notice. Six or seven kilometers west of Arenal is the ***Hotel Alturas del Arenal*** *(☎/fax 694-4039)*, which has 12 rooms for US$20/25/30 single/double/triple. Meals are available and all local tours can be arranged.

NORTHWESTERN

Just over 3km farther west is the American-run ***Cabinas Los Lagos*** *(☎ 694-4271; in the USA fax 847-574-0611, loslagos@sol.racsa.co.cr)*, which has a locally popular restaurant and 11 simple rooms with private bath for US$15/25 single/double. They run a backpackers' special for US$10 per person and give long-stay discounts. Camping costs US$5 per person, including use of hot showers. There are good views from here. The place has a slightly hippyish feel. Internet access is available for US$1.75 for five minutes and tours can be arranged. One reader reported a theft from a wallet left in the storage deposit. A kilometer beyond is the ***Villas Alpino*** *(☎/fax 695-5387, 284-3841 cellular)*, which has four nice bungalows with kitchenettes and balconies with lake/volcano views. Rates are US$35 per bungalow (they sleep up to four people).

Next is the ***Rock River Lodge*** *(☎/fax 695-5644, rokriver@sol.racsa.co.cr)*, which has six rooms in a long, rustic-looking wooden building with a porch and lake/volcano views. Eight separate bungalows have larger rooms and private terraces. Rates are US$52 double in the rooms and US$76 in the bungalows; extra people are charged US$12. The staff specializes in arranging mountain biking (rental US$20 a day) and windsurfing (rental US$35 a day), with discounts to lodge guests, and can arrange other excursions. They tend to close down the windsurfing outside of the December-to-April high wind season. There is a good restaurant open to the public; breakfasts cost US$7.50 and dinners cost US$15 (no lunch). A few hundred meters beyond is the ***Hotel Vista Lago Inn*** *(☎/fax 661-1363)*, with four simple rooms with private bath for US$29/35/45/55 for one to four people and nice views from the porch. At this point you are 12km west of Arenal and about 19km away from Tilarán.

Four kilometers beyond Vista Lago are the ***Equus Bar/Restaurant*** and ***Xiloe Lodge*** *(☎ 259-9806, fax 259-9882)*, both popular with ticos. The Equus specializes in barbecued meats, and the lodge next door has rustic wooden cabins, some with kitchenettes and all with private baths and balconies. Rates are US$40 to US$50; some units sleep four people.

A few hundred meters west, at the northwest end of the lake, a signed dirt road goes to Tierras Morenas, 7km away. (It continues – 4WD recommended – to Bijagua, 36km away on the flanks of Volcán Tenorio.) Four hundred meters farther up this road is the ***Mystica Resort*** *(☎ 382-1499, fax 695-5387, Barbara_Moglia@nacion.co.cr)*, with great views of the 30km length of Laguna de Arenal and the volcano puffing away just beyond the end of it. The friendly Italian owners run a good pizzeria (open noon to 9 pm) with a wood-burning oven on the premises, and the bar/restaurant is cozy and has a fireplace. Each of the six comfortable, good-size rooms with hot showers has a double and a bunk bed, so families can use them. Rates are US$35/50 single/double including breakfast (served 7:30 to 9:30 am). All the usual sporting and touring options can be arranged.

Almost 6km beyond the Tierras Morenas turnoff and 9km north of Tilarán, a sign points to the ***Hotel Tilawa*** *(☎ 695-5050, fax 695-5766; in the USA ☎ 800-851-8929, tilawa@sol.racsa.co.cr)*, which is the most upscale lodge in the Tilarán area, with frescoes, columns, and architecture reminiscent of the Palace of Knossos in Crete. It is 400m off the main road and has good lake and volcano views from its hillside location.

The Tilawa has a windsurfing school (see boxed text) and a 12m yacht that will take 20 passengers. Two-hour sailing tours cost about US$25. Excursions in faster boats to Arenal Dam are also offered, as are numerous other local tours. The hotel has a swimming pool, tennis court, horse and mountain bike rental, day tours, a restaurant, and a very lively bar, with a pool table, videos, and dance music some nights. The bar is backed up by the only microbrewery that I know of in Costa Rica, serving amber, pale, and stout ales. I tried the sampler (three small glasses), and found them better than the local bottled beers. Professional massage is available on the premises. Simply put, you won't be bored, and active guests have really enjoyed this place. Two dozen spacious rooms with

World-Class Windsurfing

The Hotel Tilawa (see Places to Stay & Eat) runs a windsurfing school that has the largest and best selection of sailboards in Costa Rica; the boards are all top quality and rent for US$55/day (US$45 for hotel guests). This area is considered one of the three best windsurfing spots in the world, and Hotel Tilawa is the best place from which to windsurf. Lessons are available; complete beginners pay US$45 for a sailboard and instruction during the first day, much of which begins on land with stationary boards so you can learn what to do before going out on the water.

Some folks think that the high winds, waves, and world-class conditions are too much for a beginner to handle. The folks at Tilawa disagree, and say that if you don't enjoy your first day of lessons and can't get at least a short ride by the end of the day, they'll refund your money. After the first day, lessons become more expensive and cater to all skill levels – once you have learned the basics, self-motivated practice, with short instructional periods, is the best way to learn.

– Rob Rachowiecki

two queen-size beds cost US$59/77/100/118 for one to four people; four junior suites cost US$147 (one to four guests). Contact them about the many packages (with or without windsurfing and tours) that are available.

Four kilometers beyond the Tilawa turnoff, the road forks. South, the road leads 5km to Tilarán (see below); east, the road leads along the lake past the communities of Puerto San Luis and Tronadora. Two kilometers down this road, the ***Hotel Bahia Azul*** *(☎/fax 695-5750)* is on the shores of Laguna de Arenal. Rooms have private hot showers, two queen-size beds, refrigerators, cable TV, and fans for about US$25/35 including breakfast. There is a restaurant. Ask about boat rental; a kayak and a rowboat are available and other rentals can be arranged.

Getting There & Away

Bus Puerto San Luis can be reached from Tilarán on the Tronadora bus that leaves Tilarán at 11:30 am and 4 pm. (Tronadora is a village a couple of kilometers beyond Puerto San Luis).

The rest of Laguna de Arenal can be reached by buses between Tilarán and Fortuna or Ciudad Quesada. Also, there are buses from Tilarán to Arenal village (1¼ hours) at 6 and 10 am and 12:30 and 4 pm, returning at 7:30 am, noon, and 6 pm. These schedules change more often than most.

There is an afternoon bus from Arenal to San Rafael de Guatuso – the bus is simply marked 'Guatuso' and goes to several other small villages in the northern lowlands.

Car Most of the road is narrow and winding, and there is an unpaved section of about 8km on the east side of Arenal, which will slow you down further. This section is improved regularly, and there are plans to pave it. The paved sections are often badly potholed. Although it is only

60km from Tilarán around the lake to the dam at the eastern end, allow about two hours to drive.

TILARÁN

This is a small, quiet market town 550m above sea level near the northern end of the Cordillera de Tilarán. For most foreign visitors, Laguna de Arenal (5km away) is the principal attraction. Cattle farming is important in the area, and there is a rodeo and fiesta (Días Cívicas) on the last weekend in April that is very popular with tico visitors, and hotels are often full at that time. There is another fiesta on June 13.

The pleasant climate, rural atmosphere, annual rodeo, and proximity of Laguna de Arenal have brought about the development of a small tourist industry. A local leaflet proclaims Tilarán as 'the city of broad streets, fertile rains, and healthful winds, in which friendship and progress is cultivated.' I have no quibbles with that.

Places to Stay

The friendly, remodeled ***Hotel y Restaurant Mary*** *(☎ 695-5479, 695-5758)*, on the south side of the park, is good, clean, and pleasant, and has a reasonably priced restaurant attached. About 18 rooms with private bathrooms (hot water) and fans cost about US$20 double or a little more with TVs. Good value.

The ***Hotel Central*** *(☎ 695-5363)* is near the southeast corner of the town church, 50m from the park and 350m south of the principal road into town. Basic but clean rooms (some with shared baths) cost about US$5 per person; cabins with private baths cost about US$20 and will sleep up to four people. There are a couple of other basic budget places in the center with unlisted phone numbers.

The friendly and recommended ***Cabinas El Sueño*** *(☎ 695-5347, fax 695-6072)*, a block from either the bus terminal or the Parque Central, is clean and has a restaurant. Twelve rooms with private baths, warm water, and ceiling fans surround a courtyard and cost about US$12/18 single/double with TVs, a little less without. The owners are helpful. Also at about this price, the newer ***Hotel Guadalupe*** *(☎ 695-5943, fax 695-5387)*, a block south and a block east of the cathedral, has nine pleasant rooms with private baths, hot water, and TVs.

The ***Hotel Naralit*** *(☎ 695-5393, fax 695-6767)*, opposite the church, has two dozen clean rooms with private baths and hot water, some with cable TVs and minifridges, from about US$18/24 single/double. A restaurant and bar are attached. The Naralit ('Tilarán,' reversed!) is currently the most comfortable central hotel.

Places to Eat

The restaurant under the ***Hotel y Restaurant Mary***, open 6 am to 10 pm, is fairly inexpensive and well recommended. ***El Parque*** restaurant, under the Cabinas El Sueño, is also good, though slightly pricier. Both serve tico food.

The US-operated ***La Carreta*** *(☎ 695-6654)*, behind the church, has a pleasant garden terrace (dine in or out) and specializes in Italian and North American cooking that has received good reviews. It also has homemade bread and tico casados. Hours are 7 am to 9 pm daily except Sunday, when it opens at noon.

Getting There & Away

Bus Autotransportes Tilarán buses from the Atlántico Norte terminal in San José cost about US$2.50 and take 3½ hours. They leave at 7:30 and 9:30 am and 12:45, 3:45, and 6:30 pm from Calle 12, Avenida 9. Buses from Puntarenas leave at 11:30 am and 4:30 pm. Buses from Ciudad Quesada (San Carlos) via Fortuna leave at 6:30 am and 3 pm. There are several buses a day from Cañas.

Buses leave Tilarán from the bus terminal, half a block from the Parque Central as you head away from the cathedral. Buses to San José on Sunday afternoon may be sold out by Saturday. Buses between Tilarán and San José go via Cañas and the Interamericana, not via the Arenal-Fortuna-Ciudad Quesada route.

As of this writing, the timetable for departures from Tilarán is as follows:

Arenal – 6, 10 am, 12:30, 4 pm; 1¼ hours
Cañas – 5, 7:30, 10 am, 12:30, 3:30 pm; 45 minutes
Ciudad Quesada (via Fortuna) – 7 am, 12:30 pm; 4 hours
Puntarenas – 6 am, 1 pm; 2 hours
San José – 5, 7, 7:45 am, 2, 4:45 pm; 3½ hours
Santa Elena – 12:30 pm; 2½ hours
Tronadora – 11:30 am, 4 pm; use for Puerto San Luis

The travel times given in the preceding table are minimum advertised times, but buses often take longer. A few other local villages are also served by bus from Tilarán; inquire at the terminal for details.

Car Tilarán is 24km by paved road from the Interamericana at Cañas. The route to Santa Elena and Monteverde is unpaved and rough, though ordinary cars can get through with care.

Península de Nicoya

This peninsula juts south from the northwestern corner of Costa Rica and, at over 100km in length, it is by far the largest in the country. Despite its size, it has few paved roads, and most people get around on gravel or dirt roads. Some of Costa Rica's major beach resorts – sometimes remote and difficult to get to – are here, offering beaches and sun rather than villages, culture, or wildlife. Most visitors come for the beaches, and if all you want to do is swim, sunbathe, and relax, you'll probably enjoy a few days on part of the beautiful shoreline of the peninsula. Otherwise, you could become bored very quickly. An adventurous traveler, however, may still discover remote beaches and villages where a friendly conversation with a smiling local could be more memorable than a hammock on the beach.

There are several small wildlife reserves and a national park in the peninsula that are worth visiting if you are in the area. In 1940, about half of the peninsula was covered with rainforest; this was mostly cut down by the 1960s. Much of the peninsula has been turned over to cattle raising, which, along with tourism, is the main industry.

The main highway through the peninsula begins at Liberia (see the Northwestern Costa Rica chapter) and follows the center of the peninsula through the small towns of Filadelfia and Santa Cruz to Nicoya, which is the largest town in the area. (Nevertheless, it is a small town.) From Nicoya, the main road heads east to the Río Tempisque ferry or southeast to Playa Naranjo, from where the ferry to Puntarenas leaves several times a day. These roads are good, and, for the most part, paved. Many drivers arrive from the main part of Costa Rica by taking the car ferry from Puntarenas (to Playa Naranjo or Paquera) or the car ferry across the Río Tempisque. In this chapter, however, I describe the peninsula from north to south.

From this main central highway, side roads branch out to a long series of beaches stretching along the Pacific coastline of the peninsula. Many of these roads are gravel or dirt and may be in poor condition. Once you get to the beach area of your choice, you are usually stuck there and cannot continue north or south along the coast for any long distance because there is no paved coastal road. If you have a 4WD vehicle, it is possible to more or less follow the coast on the poor dirt roads. If you are traveling by bus or in an ordinary car to the next set of beaches, you often need to backtrack to the main central highway and then come back again on another road. Some beaches have a hotel but no village, and bus service may be nonexistent. If there is a small village, the bus service is often limited to one per day. Many visitors come by car rather than relying on the bus services, though there is no problem with using buses if you have plenty of time and patience. Note that bus services may be curtailed during the wet season, when few *ticos* go to the beach.

The beaches at Tamarindo, Nosara, Sámara, and Tambor have regularly scheduled flights from San José with SANSA or Travelair. This avoids the difficulties of road travel but limits your visit to just one beach. Some people rent a car (4WD is useful in the dry season and recommended in the wet – many car rental companies won't allow you to rent an ordinary car to go to the Península de Nicoya in the wet season), but this is an expensive option if you are going to park your car by the beach for a few days. If you decide to hire a car, be prepared for a frustrating lack of road signs and gas stations. Fill up whenever you can and ask frequently for directions.

Budget travelers using public buses should allow plenty of time to get around. Hitchhiking is a definite possibility – given the paucity of public transport, the locals hitchhike around the peninsula more than in other parts of Costa Rica. If you want to cook for yourself, bring food from inland.

Stores are few and far between on the coast, and the selection is limited and expensive.

What this all means is that most of the Península de Nicoya beaches are more suitable for a leisurely visit of several days. If you are looking for a quick overnight getaway from San José, the beaches at Jacó, Manuel Antonio, Puerto Viejo, or Cahuita are generally easier to get to and have more of a tourist infrastructure. Playas del Coco, Hermosa, Panamá, and Ocotal, all of which are detailed below, are among the most popular on the peninsula as they are linked to Liberia by a paved road and have good bus service. The airport near Liberia is beginning to receive more international flights, mainly servicing visitors to 'all-inclusive' beach resorts in the northern part of the peninsula and surfers heading straight for the more renowned beaches.

As with beach areas throughout the country, reservations are a good idea, especially during dry-season weekends and Easter week. Prices in this chapter are the high- and dry-season prices (from December to Easter). Substantial rainy-season discounts are usually given.

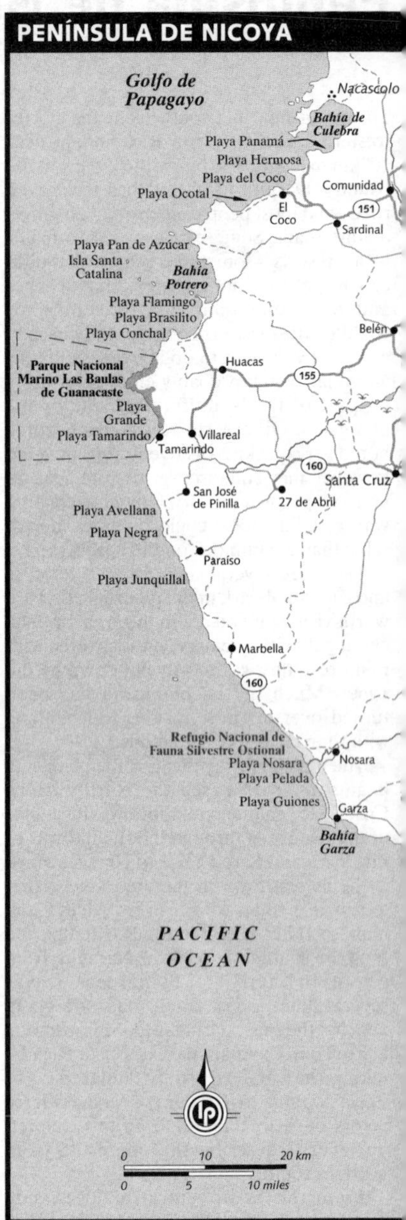

PLAYA DEL COCO

This beach is only 35km west of Liberia and, of the Península de Nicoya beaches, it's the most easily accessible by road from San José. It is attractively set between two rocky headlands and is a growing scuba diving center (see Activities, below). There are a number of hotels to choose from, a small village, good bus connections from San José and Liberia, and more nightlife than most beaches on the peninsula. It's a popular resort for young ticos, and on weekends the town has a cheerful boardwalk beach atmosphere (think young Bruce Springsteen). In recent years, the town had garbage bins installed near the beach and organized a litter campaign that has minimized the impact of partying visitors. Many buildings around town have for-sale signs up; this is not because the town is fading, but because longtime owners are hoping to strike it rich by selling to a big developer. However, it

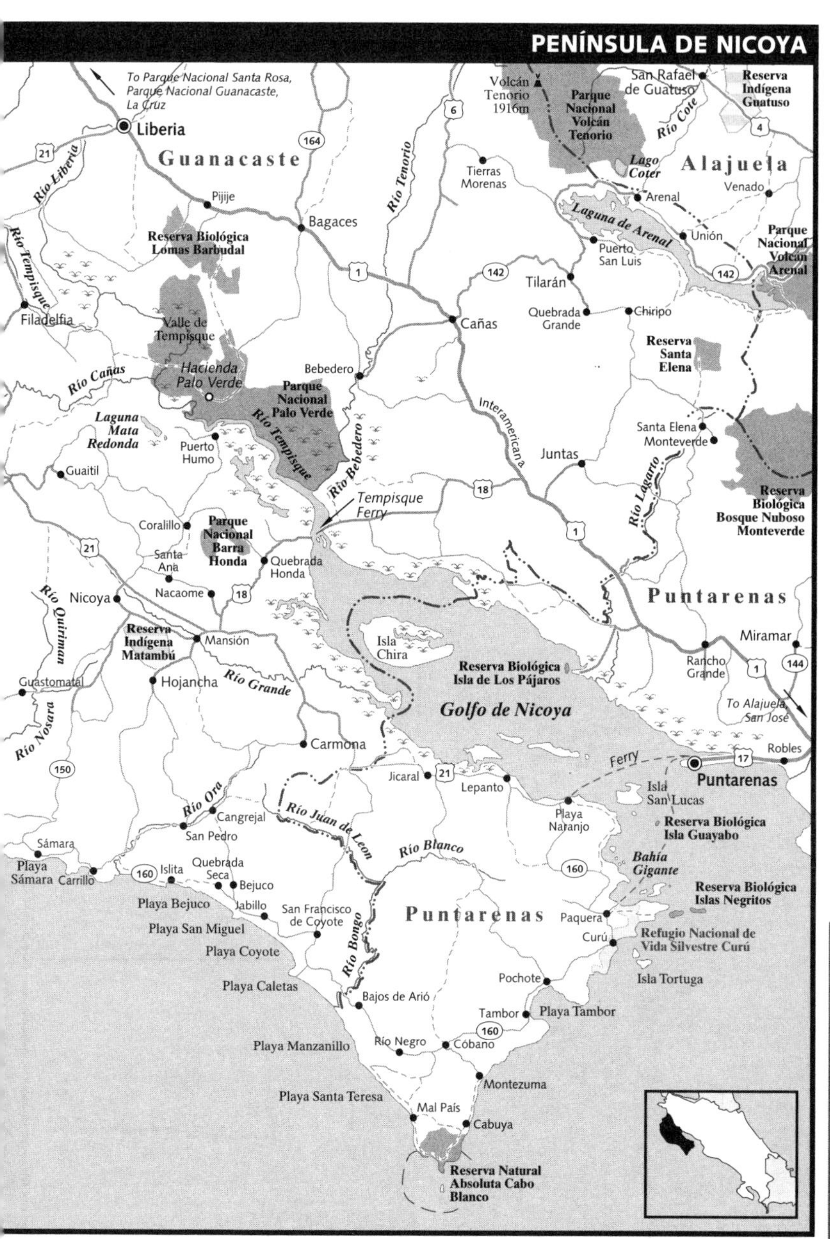

PENÍNSULA DE NICOYA

remains one of the less expensive beach towns in the peninsula.

Information

The police station and post office are both on the southeast side of the plaza by the beach. The few people arriving at Playa del Coco by boat will find the immigration service in the police post. The Banco Nacional will change cash US dollars and traveler's checks. There's a laundry near the south corner of the plaza. Note that some maps combine this beach with a neighboring one and call them Playas del Coco.

Activities

Playa del Coco and the surrounding beaches have several dive shops, most of which have opened in the last few years. They offer offshore scuba diving, and most can arrange snorkeling, sailing, sportfishing, and other trips. Scuba diving is the main attraction, and this is the best place for it in the country. There is no good beach diving in this area, so dives are around volcanic rock pinnacles near the coast, or farther off at Isla Catalina (about 20km to the southwest) or Islas Murciélago (40km to the northwest near the tip of Península Santa Elena), from a boat.

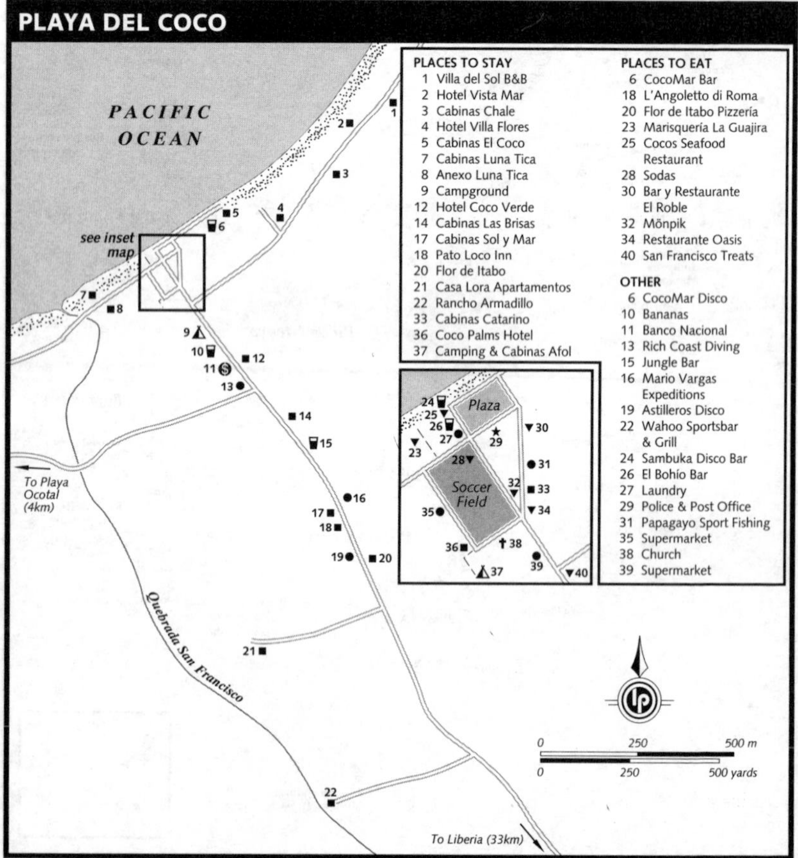

The diving is mediocre from a visibility standpoint (6 to 24m visibility, though it's usually well under 20m) but pretty good in other aspects. The water is warm – around 26°C at the surface, with a thermocline at around 20m below the surface, where it drops to 23°C. This means you can skin dive (no wet suit) if you want to. The best feature is the abundant marine life, with possibilities of sighting manta rays with 4 to 6m fin spans, other rays, sharks, huge schools of fish, and plenty of coral reef life. Most of the dive sites are less than 25m deep, allowing three dives a day. This is a relatively little-known area, still being explored by divers.

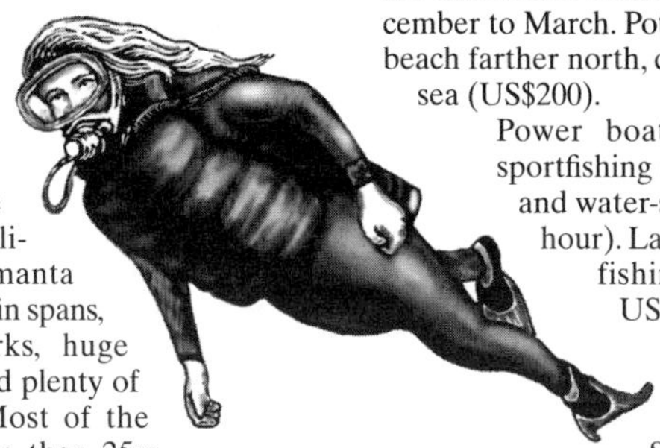

Most of the dive shops are competitively priced. Typical rates are US$70 for two dives including all gear and US$45 if you have your own gear. Trips out to the Islas Murciélago (also called Bat Islands) are more expensive and for experienced divers. Rates are US$130/170 for two/three dives including equipment, US$20 less if you bring your own. Trips to Isla Catalina cost US$105/135 for two/three dives with equipment. Nondivers can go on snorkeling trips from the boat for US$25 with gear. Boats should have divemasters or instructors aboard. Instruction is offered, ranging from certification for beginners to advanced courses teaching night diving and other specialties. A complete certification course costs about US$300. People who have never dived can take an introductory lesson for about US$75, which includes a guided dive to see if they like it before they shell out for complete certification. Hotel and dive packages are also available. Always ask for low-season or multiday or group discounts.

Sailing is also offered. A five-hour sunset cruise with open bar costs about US$50, for example, and a full day of sailing costs about US$85 with lunch. Other cruises can be arranged.

Surfers can hire a boat for about US$175 to take up to six people to Witches Rock, which is within Parque Nacional Santa Rosa and difficult to reach by land. This has one of the best beach breaks in the area from December to March. Potrero Grande, a surfing beach farther north, can be reached only by sea (US$200).

Power boats are available for sportfishing (from US$35 an hour) and water-skiing (from US$45 an hour). Larger boats for offshore fishing may range up to US$700 a day.

Sea kayaks can be hired for US$8 or for US$10 a day. Jet Skis have recently been added to the list of activities. But, when all is said and done, scuba diving is the main attraction here. The following is a list of outfitters in Playa del Coco and nearby Playa Hermosa:

Aqua Sport
(☎ 670-0353) Playa Hermosa. This general store/water-sports office near the middle of the Playa Hermosa beach rents kayaks, surfboards, snorkeling gear, etc. It can also arrange boat excursions for anglers, divers, water-skiers, parasailers, and sightseers.

Bill Beard's Diving Safaris
(☎/fax 670-0012; in the USA ☎ 800-779-0055, fax 612-931-0209, diving@sol.racsa.co.cr) in the Sol Playa Hermosa Resort, Playa Hermosa. These folks have been scuba diving and snorkeling here for over 20 years and are very experienced. They also do Nitrox courses and dives and can arrange extended adventure tours.

El Ocotal Resort
(☎ 670-0323, fax 670-0083, elocotal@sol.racsa.co.cr). This resort overlooking Playa Ocotal has a dive shop that can handle large groups of up to 40 divers, does fishing charters (it has six boats), and offers kayak rentals. Complete resort packages are offered.

El Velero
(☎ 672-0036, ☎/fax 672-0016, elvelero@costarica.net) Hotel El Velero, Playa Hermosa. *El velero* means 'the sailboat' in Spanish, and the hotel owns a yacht and offers daily cruises. It also rents Jet Skis and kayaks.

Mario Vargas Expeditions
(☎/fax 670-0351) Apartado 194, Playa del Coco, Guanacaste; on the main street of Playa del Coco. Tico Mario Vargas is the country's best-known divemaster and has taken President Figueres diving, which speaks for itself. Spanish, English, French, and Italian are spoken.

Papagayo Sport Fishing
(☎ 670-0374, fax 670-0446) on the main road of Playa del Coco, near the beach. This operator offers boat trips to the surfing areas as well as sportfishing.

Rich Coast Diving
(☎/fax 670-0176; in the USA ☎ 800-434-8464, richcoas@sol.racsa.co.cr) on the main street of Playa del Coco, just past the Playa Ocotal turnoff. This young and enthusiastic company has been well reviewed by readers. It prides itself on small groups (maximum of three divers per staff member) and customer service. It also has a trimaran for sailing and overnight diving trips and pangas for fishing, water-skiing, and surfing trips.

Places to Stay

Budget There's a ***campground*** just off the main road and ***Camping & Cabinas Afol*** just southwest of the soccer field (look for signs). Both have several basic bathrooms and showers. The rate for camping is about US$3 per person per night. Afol also has a few basic cabinas with fans and kitchens for about US$7 per person.

Cabinas Catarino *(☎ 670-0156)* is friendly and clean but has only six rooms (for three, four, or five people) at US$6 per person. It is on the main road fairly close to the beach. Otherwise, bottom-end hotels are pricier than in most areas of Costa Rica.

Cabinas El Coco *(☎ 670-0110, 670-0276, fax 670-0167)* is to the right as you arrive on the beach and is one of the cheaper hotels. There are about 80 rooms, and the place is fairly popular, though not because the rooms are anything special. There is a decent mid-priced restaurant on the premises and a disco next door. Rates are US$12 per person in rooms with fans and US$23/28 for air-conditioned singles/doubles. All have private showers.

Cabinas Luna Tica *(☎ 670-0127)* has rather stuffy rooms with private baths, fans, and double beds for US$21 double, as well as some larger air-conditioned rooms for US$26 double. There is a decent restaurant, and breakfast is included in the low season. Across the street, the ***Anexo Luna Tica*** *(☎ 670-0279)* is similarly priced, but the rooms seem breezier and better.

Cabinas Las Brisas *(☎ 670-0155)* has basic rooms with showers and fans for about US$22 double. The ***Cabinas Chale*** *(☎ 670-0036)* is 100m from the beach and a 600m walk from town, to the right as you arrive (there are signs). There are 25 clean but unexciting air-conditioned rooms with private baths for about US$25 double. There is a big pool on the premises, and the staff is friendly. On the road into town, ***Cabinas Sol y Mar*** *(☎ 670-0808, fax 670-1111)* is a new, motel-like establishment with air-conditioned doubles for US$29 (US$4 less for fan) and a small, unshaded pool. Rooms sleeping four people cost US$54.50.

Mid-Range The ***Pato Loco Inn*** *(☎/fax 670-0145, patoloco@sol.racsa.co.cr)* is a small, European-style hotel. Why 'European-style'? Well, the owners are a Dutch/Italian couple who also speak English, French, and Spanish, and they say their place is Eurostyle, so why disagree? They run a small and friendly inn with three triple rooms and one double, each with a desk, fan, cross ventilation, and hot-water bathroom. All local activities can be arranged for you. Their L'Angoletto di Roma restaurant (see Places to Eat, below) is attached. Rates are US$24/35/47 single/double/triple.

The ***Coco Palms Hotel*** *(☎ 670-0367, fax 670-0117, pfleme@sol.racsa.co.cr)* has a good restaurant. Clean, spacious rooms with fans and private baths with hot water cost US$22/38/47 single/double/triple, including breakfast. A larger room that sleeps six costs US$73.

Some good little B&B hotels have recently opened. The French-Canadian-run ***Villa del Sol B&B*** *(☎/fax 670-0085, villasol@sol.racsa.co.cr)*, quietly located about a kilometer north of the main road, offers five large and very clean rooms with private baths and two more with semiprivate baths, all with hot water. It is about 100m from the beach, which is little visited at this end. The villa has a pool and a balcony with ocean view, and may serve meals if requested in advance. All local activities can be arranged. Room rates are US$41 to US$53 double with breakfast, and at least US$12 less in the green season.

The Italian-run ***Hotel Villa Flores*** *(☎/fax 670-0269)* is about 300m from the main road, and quiet because of that. There is an open-air restaurant and a TV lounge, and the owner is a scuba diver who loves to arrange dives for his guests (and go along with them when he can). He has eight simple but clean rooms, each with fans and a private bath, for US$42 double with breakfast.

The ***Casa Lora Apartamentos*** *(☎/fax 670-0642, 385-1300)* has a few breezy, two-story houses set in a lovely garden, with a small pool, for US$52. The houses sleep up to seven people and have balconies and small kitchens. The showers are solar-heated – the owners, a friendly German couple, did most of the building themselves and are planning a few smaller cabinas. The ***Cabinas Costa Alegre*** *(☎ 670-0218)* is 5km before you reach the beach on the road from Liberia. It has cabins with kitchenettes, fans, and private baths; they sleep up to five people for US$50. There is a pool and restaurant.

The secluded ***Hotel Vista Mar*** *(☎ 670-0753, jplamar@sol.racsa.co.cr)* is on a shady, grassy beachfront lot north of town. The rooms range from a double with a private bath and air-conditioning for US$60 to a double with shared bath and fan for US$35 (US$10 more for air-conditioning). Breakfast is included, and discounts are available for longer stays.

The ***Hotel Coco Verde*** *(☎ 670-0494, 670-0544, fax 670-0555, cocoverd@sol.racsa.co.cr)* has 33 big air-conditioned rooms with private hot baths. There is a pool, and the attractive restaurant/bar is open 6 am to 10 pm daily. Rates are US$64/75 single/double, 15% to 20% less in low season.

Near the entrance of town, Texan-owned ***Rancho Armadillo*** *(☎ 670-0108, fax 670-0441)* is a large ranch-style building with a variety of rooms, some air-conditioned, for US$42 to US$71 double, including breakfast. Extra occupants are charged US$12. The hotel is quietly located on a hillside about 400m off the main road. The owners are helpful with arranging fishing and surfing trips. There is a swimming pool, and plenty of armadillos. Above the ranch is the Wahoo Sportsbar & Grill (see Entertainment, below), which has a view over the bay.

The most upscale hotel is the low-key, friendly ***Flor de Itabo*** *(☎ 670-0011, fax 670-0003, Apartado 32, Playa del Coco, Guanacaste)*, which is 1.5km before the beach, on the right-hand side as you arrive. There is a good restaurant and both children's and adults' pools. The spacious air-conditioned rooms with hot water cost US$60 double, and cabins and smaller rooms with fans cost US$15 less. Cabins with kitchenettes and refrigerators cost about US$70. The cabins each have one double and two single beds. The owners will help arrange fishing and diving excursions, and there are horses for rent. The bar has a reputation for attracting anglers.

Places to Eat

Italian food is big in Playa del Coco; most Italian restaurants are linked with hotels. The ***Flor de Itabo Pizzería*** is good and has a good number of Italian specialties other than just pizza, but it is a bit more expensive than the rest. ***L'Angoletto di Roma***, associated with the Pato Loco Inn, is Italian-run and specializes in spaghetti and other pasta dishes at reasonable prices.

About 200m before the beach, the US-operated ***San Francisco Treats*** will cater to any homesick expat, with fabulous homemade cakes and cookies and a variety of California-style cuisine ranging from huge sandwiches to vegetarian lasagna. A ***Mönpik*** ice-cream shop has opened nearby.

Closer still to the beach, there are a bunch of inexpensive ***sodas*** at the northeast corner of the soccer field. Almost opposite, ***Bar y Restaurante El Roble*** and ***Restaurante Oasis*** serve tico food. Around the small plaza, you can eat seafood at ***Cocos Seafood Restaurant*** (which serves pizza as well). Just off the plaza, ***Marisquería La Guajira*** is a local seafood place and ***CocoMar Bar*** is popular with ticos on vacation. It serves a variety of food, and most tables are far enough away from the adjacent disco that you can hear yourself speak. All these places are almost on top of one another, so walk around and choose what's best for you.

Entertainment

If you're into dancing, the loud ***CocoMar Disco*** is right in the middle of the beachfront scene, adjacent to the CocoMar Bar restaurant. Farther inland on the main road, ***Bananas*** also has dancing and is popular with visiting foreigners; you can also play pool here, or catch a breeze on the balcony bar. The restaurants around the plaza double as bars, and ***El Bohío Bar*** is something of a favorite. The former ***Sambuka Disco Bar***, on the west corner of the plaza, is currently in transition – beach party life doesn't tend to be about lasting commitments, and hip spots come and go. A quick walk around will let you know what's currently in vogue.

Out on the main road is the newly popular French-owned ***Jungle Bar***. The once famous ***Astilleros Disco***, farther out on the main road, now only operates a few times a year but reportedly draws in the crowds when it opens (usually around holidays; inquire locally for opening times).

At the entrance to town, the ***Wahoo Sportsbar & Grill***, above the Rancho Armadillo, has a view over the bay, ice-cold beer, bar food, and a satellite dish bringing in US sporting events. The ***Flor de Itabo*** hotel has a small casino and is popular with anglers.

Getting There & Away

The main bus stop in Playa del Coco is on the plaza in front of the police station. There is another stop in front of the Hotel Coco Verde.

Pulmitan (☎ 222-1650) has a bus leaving San José from Calle 14, Avenidas 1 & 3, at 8 am and 2 pm daily (US$4.50). The return bus leaves Playa del Coco at the same hours.

Buses leave Liberia for Playa del Coco at 5:30 am and 12:30, 2, and 4:30 pm, returning from Playa del Coco at 7 and 9:15 am and 2 pm. These hours are subject to change, and there are fewer departures in the wet season.

A taxi from Liberia costs US$12 to US$15.

PLAYA HERMOSA

This gently curving and relatively safe beach is about 7km (by road) north of Coco, and it is quieter and less crowded, although the ongoing development of the so-called Papagayo Project beginning at the next beach (see Playa Panamá, later) may change this dramatically. See Activities under Playa del Coco, above, for a list of activities in the area and outfitters in Playa Hermosa.

Places to Stay & Eat

Many ticos camp on the beach, which is free; there are some good, shady spots. Out on the main road, by the southern entrance to the beach, ***Cabinas Roberta*** looks about to fade into the undergrowth, but it might be a place to crash. Down near the south end of the beach, ***Cabinas Playa Hermosa*** *(☎ 672-0046)* is a quiet hotel. Clean beachfront rooms with fans, private baths, and electric showers cost US$25/40 single/double. There is an Italian restaurant on the premises. Several cheaper oceanfront restaurants serve fresh fish on this part of the beach. Cheaper rooms (and groceries) are available nearby at ***Cabinas y MiniSuper El Cenizaro*** *(☎ 672-0186)*, from US$10 per person with fans and showers.

The friendly ***Cabinas La Casona*** *(☎ 672-0025)*, opposite the Hotel El Velero (see below), has basic beach cabins starting at US$24 double, US$28 with a kitchenette; ask for a room with cross breezes. A room sleeping five costs US$31. Set 100m back along the north entrance to the beach is the ***Iguana Inn*** *(☎ 672-0065)*, a friendly eco-surfer kind of place with a pool, a pizza restaurant, and a bar with satellite TV. About a dozen simple but clean rooms with semiprivate baths start at around US$25 double.

Nearer the northern end of the beach is the tico-owned ***Playa Hermosa Inn*** *(☎/fax 672-0113)*, which has received enthusiastic recommendations from our readers. The grounds are very pleasant, and a pool and restaurant round out the comforts at this low-key establishment. Spacious, clean rooms with fans and private hot-water bathrooms go for US$30/50 single/double, including breakfast; add US$10 for air-conditioning or extra people.

The well-maintained ***Villa Huetares*** *(☎ 672-0081, fax 672-0051)* has about 16 small apartments with air-conditioning, kitchenettes, dining areas, and private baths. Some rooms sleep up to six people. Rates are US$60 to US$80, depending on the number of people, with some discounts for longer stays. There is a pool and a TV lounge.

The French-Canadian-owned ***Villas del Sueño*** *(☎/fax 670-0027)* is a couple of hundred meters back from the south end of the beach, has a pool and pretty garden, and offers 15 pleasant rooms with high ceilings and private baths. In an area subject to more and more large-scale development, the owners have committed themselves to creating unobtrusive, upscale comfort. Their restaurant has a limited but excellent home-cooked menu and attracts people from the area; the owners are also musicians and perform here several times a week. Most dinners cost US$10 to US$12; lunches start at US$4. Standard rooms (smaller spaces intended for people who want a nice place to sleep but plan to be mainly out by the pool or beach) cost US$63 double; larger rooms cost US$91 double. Extra guests are charged US$10 each; rooms without air-conditioning cost US$10 less. Ask them about the ***Monkey Bar***, a fun new nightspot along the main road.

The ***Hotel El Velero*** *(☎ 672-0036, ☎/fax 672-0016, elvelero@costarica.net)* is also run by French-Canadians. The place seems a bit faded and overpriced but has all the facilities of a big hotel and a good location. It has 14 beachfront rooms with private baths and air-conditioning for about US$100 double (high season). There's a pool and restaurant. The hotel yacht provides guests and others with a variety of cruises (roughly US$55 per person including meals) for snorkeling or just enjoying the sunset with an open bar.

The ***Sol Playa Hermosa Resort*** *(☎ 672-0001, fax 672-0212; in San José ☎ 257-0607, fax 223-3036)* is proud to offer the quiet and insulation of a gated community. This condominium complex has over 100 units (and is still growing) renting for US$118 double. Each has a kitchenette, hot water, and air-conditioning. There are tennis courts, a pool, discotheque, restaurant, and bar on the grounds, and diving, snorkeling, fishing, kayaking, boating, and horseback riding can be arranged.

The previously mentioned ***Aqua Sport*** (see Activities under Playa del Coco) has a good seafood restaurant with international dishes; it has received several recommendations.

Getting There & Away

Empresa Esquivel (☎ 666-1249) buses leave Liberia for Playa Hermosa at 7:30 and 11:30 am and 3:30, 5:30, and 7 pm, returning at 5, 6, and 10 am and 4 and 5 pm. Some of these may not go all the way to Playa Panamá – ask locally. An express bus leaves San José from Calle 12, Avenidas 5 & 7, at 3:20 pm and takes about five hours, stopping first at Playa Hermosa and then Playa Panamá. It returns from Playa Panamá at 5 am. A taxi from Liberia costs about US$12 to US$15, and a taxi from Coco costs about US$4.

If you are driving from Liberia, take the signed turnoff to Playa Nosara about 3 or 4km before reaching Playa del Coco.

PLAYA PANAMÁ & THE PAPAGAYO PROJECT

This protected dark-sand beach is one of the best swimming beaches in the area. About 3km north of Playa Hermosa, this friendly rural beach, scattered with campers and toddlers splashing in the shallows, used to be the end of the road. It is now faced across the bay by the beginnings of a massive condo colonization – the huge and controversial Papagayo Project, which aims to put a large number of luxury hotels, condominiums, and villas in the hitherto almost deserted area surrounding Bahía Culebra, the most protected large bay on the peninsula. As many as 15,000 rooms as well as golf courses are planned in this development, which has drawn attacks from those who feel that this project is a blatant misuse of the area. The tropical dry forest (see Parque Nacional Santa Rosa in the Northwestern Costa Rica chapter) that surrounds the bay is being bulldozed, and the few mangrove swamps have been destroyed, to provide what the Mexican developer claims is an ecologically sensitive tourism project. No environmental impact studies were done. Go figure!

In 1995, several lawsuits were pressed charging, among other things, embezzlement and corruption among top-level government tourism officials, including the former Minister of Tourism. The project is rolling on despite the legal wrangling.

Tourists visiting Papagayo Project Hotels will be selling themselves short in the sense that they will not really be seeing Costa Rica, but just a big, self-contained mega-resort plunked down on top of (not within) an area of tropical forest. You could be almost anywhere. The parallels with soulless Cancún have been frequently drawn. Curious locals hanging around outside gates manned by officious guards, through which busloads of foreigners on package trips occasionally pass, give the whole thing a somewhat feudal air. The intimacy and friendliness that characterize most interactions between tourists and ticos are lost here.

Places to Stay & Eat

Two large and luxurious resort hotels are already operating here. ***Costa Smeralda*** has about 70 huge air-conditioned rooms and suites for about US$150 and US$250. Two restaurants, bar, casino, pool, tennis courts, ocean view, and activities are offered. Newer still, the ***Blue Bay*** is even more expensive and offers about 100 villas with more of the same, plus a gym, sauna, and spa. More hotels are under construction. Further information is easily obtainable from travel agencies.

NACASCOLO

This is a pre-Columbian Indian ruin north of Playa Panamá. There isn't a great deal to see, but you can get here by boat across Bahía Culebra from Playa Panamá or one of the other nearby beaches. Ask around for someone to take you over. It is possible to camp at Nacascolo, but there are no facilities or drinking water.

PLAYA OCOTAL

This attractive but small beach is 3 or 4km southwest of Coco by unpaved road. It is the cleanest, quietest beach in the area, offering good swimming and snorkeling. Scuba diving is available, and nearby Isla Catalina is a recommended diving spot; it is the best place to see huge schools of rays, including the giant manta ray. Accommodations are good but not cheap. Camping is possible but not that common; be discreet and you'll have a better time. The south end of the beach is recommended for snorkeling.

Places to Stay

El Ocotal Resort (*☎ 670-0321, 670-0323, fax 670-0083, elocotal@sol.racsa.co.cr*) is on an oceanside cliff with spectacular views. Rooms cost US$86/97/103 single/double/triple with hot water, air-conditioning, and refrigerators. Rates are higher around Christmas, New Year, and Easter, lower in the wet season. Roomier bungalows cost about US$125 double, and oceanview suites cost about US$173 double. Most of the rooms were crisply remodeled in the late '90s, and some new suites (some with Jacuzzis) are on the way. A new restaurant showcasing the cliff views was built, and there is a pool, tennis court, dive shop, and boating facilities. Complete dive packages for four to seven nights are available, including two or three daily boat dives (you don't have to dive every day), overnight accommodations, and breakfast only or all meals. Equipment and transportation from San José can be included. Prices vary tremendously depending on services required – contact them for rates. If you don't want to go as part of a package, you can rent all the gear, get instruction, and do day dives. Sportfishing is also available, both as all-inclusive packages and for daily rates if boats are not booked for packages. Sea kayaks can be rented.

Down closer to the beach, ***Los Almendros*** *(☎ 670-0442, 257-0815)* is a well-maintained, easygoing villa development (ie, no feudal fortress-size walls or helicopter pads) popular with vacationing tico families. Fully furnished three-bedroom houses, all with kitchens, carports, telephones, and satellite TV, rent for US$130 per night in high season, US$80 per night in low season. Each house has two floors, with a living room, two bathrooms, a double bed in each bedroom, and big closets. Ask about monthly rates. Communal services include an oceanview swimming pool, a playground, cleaning service in the houses, and 24-hour security.

The ***Hotel Bahía Pez Vela*** *(☎ 670-0797)* closed down in the late 1990s so the site could be devoted to the current villa boom. Once villa construction is done, the hotel may reopen; the owners are aiming for 2002.

Between Playa del Coco and Playa Ocotal is the attractive ***Villa Casa Blanca*** *(☎/fax 670-0448, vcblanca@sol.racsa.co.cr)*, in a pleasant hilltop location a few minutes' walk from the beach. This is a small, friendly B&B with about 10 pleasant rooms, some with romantic canopy beds, each with private bath, fan or air-conditioning, and porch hammocks, renting for US$68/80, including a huge and varied breakfast. Free transport to the restaurant at El Ocotal is available. There is a pool with a garden bridge, bar, and views that make for delightful lounging. In the lobby is a souvenir shop with some English books. Receptionist Fulvie Marie Forero is a charming host.

Places to Eat

Apart from the hotels (where the food is pricey), there's the ***Father Rooster Restaurant***, an adjunct to El Ocotal Resort located down near the beach. The 'Rooster' is an inexpensive and fun place serving snacks and burgers as well as seafood dinners. It makes a good margarita.

ACCESSING BEACHES SOUTH OF PLAYA OCOTAL

To visit beaches farther south than Ocotal, you have to return to the main peninsula highway at Comunidad. Then head south for 12km through the little town of Filadelfia, the community of Belén (18km), and the small town of Santa Cruz (35km south of Comunidad).

A paved road heads 25km west from Belén to the small community of Huacas, where shorter paved roads radiate to a number of popular beach areas. From Santa Cruz, a 16km paved road heads west to the tiny community of 27 de Abril, where unpaved roads also radiate to a number of beaches. It is possible to drive from 27 de Abril to Huacas, thus making all the beaches described in this section accessible from Santa Cruz.

Filadelfia and the beaches near Huacas are described first, then Santa Cruz and the beaches reached via 27 de Abril.

FILADELFIA

Filadelfia is about 32km from Liberia. The population of Filadelfia and the surrounding district is about 6600.

There is an inexpensive hotel here, the ***Cabinas Amelia*** *(☎ 688-8087, ☎/fax 688-9172)*, which is three blocks from the central park. Also try the basic ***Cabinas Tita*** *(☎ 688-8073)* nearby. There are a couple of local places to eat around or near the park.

The bus terminal, half a block from the park, has several buses a day to San José and hourly buses passing through en route to Nicoya or Liberia.

PLAYA BRASILITO

The road from Huacas hits the ocean at the village of Brasilito, which has a few small stores and restaurants and the cheapest accommodations in the area. There is a beach, but the other beaches nearby are better. On weekends, buses from the capital roll in, the beach fills up, and accommodations prices rise.

Activities & Organized Tours

Brasilito Excursiones (☎ 654-4237) operates out of the Hotel Brasilito and offers horseback riding, sailing, and scuba diving. An hour-long beach ride costs US$25, guide included; a two-hour guided ride to Playa Grande costs US$35. A two-hour sailing trip to Isla Catalina costs US$45, or US$75 with diving included. Tourpro (☎ 654-4585, fax 654-4130, tour@crinfo.com), a branch of the San José company Costa Rica Temptations, has an office on the main road that can arrange tours and car rental. It also runs a beach shuttle between Playas Tamarindo and Flamingo.

Places to Stay & Eat

Just off the beach, near ***La Casita del Pescado***, a tiny soda serving fresh fish, is a shady area for ***camping*** *(☎ 654-4452)*. Showers are available, as well as some basic cabins; putting up a tent costs US$2 per person. Away from the beach, opposite the village plaza on the main road, is the unsigned ***Cabinas Olga*** *(☎ 654-4013)*, which charges US$7 per person for basic rooms. A couple hundred meters south along the main road is the somewhat ramshackle ***Cabinas Ojos Azules*** *(☎ 654-4346)*, which has big, comfy beds complete with mirrored headboards for about US$22 double, US$3.50 more for hot water. There is a supermarket nearby and a communal kitchen. A nicer cheapie a bit farther is the ***Rancho El Caracol*** *(☎ 654-4073, 654-4085)*, which has clean, roomy doubles for US$26. Its restaurant is open daily.

On the beach side of the plaza in Brasilito is the ***Hotel Brasilito*** *(☎ 654-4237)*, which has simple rooms with private baths and fans for US$25/30 single/double, US$5 more for a seaview room. A restaurant is attached. There are a couple of other simple places to eat near the plaza.

About half a kilometer before reaching Brasilito is the ***Hotel Conchal*** *(☎ 654-4257)*, with clean, spacious rooms with fans and private baths for US$30 double, US$40 for a room sleeping four, and US$50 for six – less during the week and low season. It can arrange bicycle and horse rentals as well as boating and fishing excursions.

About half a kilometer north of Brasilito and set back from the beach somewhat is ***Villas Pacifica*** *(☎ 654-4137, 654-4139, fax 654-4138)*, which has air-conditioned condo units with kitchens and satellite TV for about US$100 and up. The premises have a pool, restaurant, bar, and ocean views, and staff can arrange fishing.

The best place to eat is reputedly the large beachfront ***Restaurante y Bar Camarón Dorado*** *(☎ 654-4028)*, a couple of blocks north of the school.

Getting There & Away

See Playa Flamingo, below, for details.

PLAYA CONCHAL

Playa Conchal, so called for the many shells *(conchas)* that pile up on the beach, is the most common name given to a pretty sweep of bay beginning about 2km south of Brasilito. The beach is most easily reached from Brasilito by car, beach shuttle, or foot. The clear water makes for nice snorkeling. A large, though unobtrusive, hotel has been built on the northern stretch of the beach, which means there is no shortage of equipment and horse rentals on this mainly quiet beach.

Places to Stay & Eat

At the far south end of the beach, accessible from the main road, is the ***Condor Club Hotel*** *(☎ 667-4050, fax 667-4044; in San José fax 220-0670)*, which has functional rooms with air-conditioning, fans, TVs, private hot baths and king-size beds for about US$80. There is a restaurant, bar, pool, and disco, all with good views.

Next door is the little ***Hotelito La Paz*** *(☎ 654-4259)*, with various-sized rooms from about US$30 to US$60. Some rooms have hot showers and air-conditioning, and there is a pool. The ***Pizzería La Paz*** here is one of the cheaper places to eat in the area. Overlooking the beach below the Condor Club, ***Restaurant Encanto*** *(☎ 654-4345)* has big seafood lunches for about US$8. If it's not too windy, staff will give you a free boat ride to and from the Brasilito end of the beach.

The ***Hotel Melia Playa Conchal*** *(☎ 654-4123, fax 654-4181, melia.playa.conchal@solmelia.es)* is an enormous new resort development that extends its walls up to the edge of the beach but is, nonetheless, relatively unobtrusive. All the usual amenities are available, including a golf course. Rates start at US$215 double.

Getting There & Away

See Playa Flamingo, below, for details.

PLAYA FLAMINGO

Three or 4km north of Brasilito, the road comes to Flamingo, a beautiful white-sand beach. It has been developed for sportfishing and boating and is one of the better-known beaches in Costa Rica. Many maps mark the beach with its original name, Playa Blanca, but it is now known as Playa Flamingo after the famous Flamingo Beach Hotel. (There are no flamingoes in Costa Rica.) It is the original upscale beach resort in the country and has one of the largest fleets of sportfishing boats. An upscale marina being built at Playa Herradura (see the Central Pacific Coast chapter) may begin to draw boats away, but there's plenty of resort life to be found here.

There are many luxurious private houses and villas (many owned by well-heeled North Americans), but there is no village as such here, so if you are looking for life beyond the hotels, forget it unless you want to go to Brasilito or Potrero. But if you want luxury with comfortable hotels, a pretty beach, and first-class boating facilities – and have enough money to pay for them – this is a popular destination.

Activities & Organized Tours

If you want to enjoy the beach and bay or get a glimpse of resort lifestyle without paying for an expensive room, The Edge Adventure Company (☎/fax 654-4578) offers a full range of rentals and tours. Snorkels and bikes rent for US$5 per hour, body boards for US$2; boat trips for diving or snorkeling and sunset sails start at about US$40 per person. It is across from the Flamingo Marina. The new beach bus shuttle between Flamingo and Tamarindo stops at the marina, making day trips from Tamarindo or Brasilito possible.

Places to Stay & Eat

There are no cheap places here. Some possibilities include the ***Flamingo Tower B&B*** *(☎ 654-4109, fax 654-4275),* which has five unique rooms for about US$70 double, including breakfast. Within the same price range is the ***Mariner Inn*** *(☎ 654-4081, fax 654-4024)*, which has a dozen clean and spacious air-conditioned rooms with hot water and TVs, starting at about US$70. There is a restaurant and bar, and all the local water activities are easily arranged.

Somewhat more expensive is the ***Hotel Club Villas Pacífica*** *(☎ 654-4137, fax 654-4138)*, with the area's most elegant and expensive restaurant as well as sportfishing packages. The ***Villas Flamingo*** *(☎/fax 654-4215)* has villas with kitchens and maid service.

Other more luxurious accommodations include ***Hotel Flamingo Marina Resort*** *(☎ 654-4141, fax 654-4035; in San José ☎ 290-1858, fax 231-1858, hotflam@sol.racsa.co.cr)*, which offers a variety of rooms starting at US$90 single or double. There are two pools, a Jacuzzi, tennis court, restaurant, tour agency, and a nearby marina with all the sportfishing you could possibly want.

At the far end of the road, the famous ***Flamingo Beach Hotel*** *(☎ 654-4011, 654-4010, fax 654-4060; in San José ☎ 233-7233, auroven@sol.racsa.co.cr)* was bought by the Holiday Inn chain and thoroughly remodeled in 1995, and it is now also known as the Aurola Playa Flamingo. It has everything you might want for a beach resort vacation. There is a huge pool with a swim-up bar, a children's pool, restaurants, bars, and casino; it also has snorkeling, boating, diving, and fishing facilities. Car rental is also available. Rates for rooms are in the US$100s, and suites with kitchenettes cost in the US$200s.

Apart from the hotel restaurants, there are a few other places to eat. ***Marie's*** *(☎ 654-4136)*, with a variety of snacks and meals, is open 7 am to 9 pm and is one of the longest-established ones. There's also the ***Sunset Pizzería*** (nice views); ***Amberes***, which is a classy dinner place with a casino and disco; and ***Tío's Bar & Restaurant***, on the road leading into Playa Flamingo, which is the most down-home.

Getting There & Away

Air The Flamingo Beach Hotel has a private airstrip, and plane charters are possible there. Alternatively, you can fly to Tamarindo, which is the nearest airstrip with scheduled flights. The airstrip is about 20km from Flamingo and, if you have hotel reservations, you can arrange to be picked up.

Bus TRALAPA in Santa Cruz has buses for Playas Conchal, Brasilito, Flamingo, and Potrero at 6:30 am and 3 pm, returning from Potrero at 9 am and 5 pm; the schedule changes often. TRALAPA (☎ 221-7202, 223-5859) has express buses to Flamingo at 8 and 10 am from Calle 20, Avenida 3 in San José. Return expresses leave at 9 am and 2 pm. The fare is about US$8 for the five- or six-hour ride.

BAHÍA POTRERO

This stretch of bay is 6 or 7km north of Brasilito and is separated from Flamingo by a rocky headland. There is a small community at Potrero, just beyond the north end of the beach. This is the end of the bus line, and the beaches here don't get the weekend rush found at Brasilito. Though upscale Playa Flamingo is visible across the bay, this is still an area where monkeys can be heard in the trees and oxen come down to the shore to lick salt out of the water.

There are several beaches strung along the bay. The black-sand beach is Playa Prieta, the white-sand beach is Playa Penca, and Playa Potrero, the biggest, is somewhere in between – these names, it should be noted, are used loosely. Hotels on the beaches rent water-sports equipment. The rocky islet 10km due west of Playa Pan de Azúcar is **Isla Catalina**. It is one of the few places in Costa Rica where the bridled tern is known to nest, which occurs from late March to September. Birders could rent a boat from any of the nearby resorts to go and see this bird in season. The waters around the island are popular diving spots (see Playa del Coco).

Places to Stay

Budget You can camp on the beach. At the far south end of the beach, the friendly ***Mayra's*** *(☎ 654-4213, 654-4472)* has a shady camping area for US$2.50 per person, with beach showers and a mini-soda available. A few rooms with baths and fans cost in the US$20s. Mayra's companion, Alvaro Chinchilla, is a retired newspaperman and is well stocked with stories. Close to the village, ***Cabinas La Penca*** *(☎ 654-4107)* has clean, high-ceilinged rooms sleeping four for US$36, set in a two-story pink building in the backyard of Bar La Penca. Set back from the north end of the beach is ***Cabinas Isolina Beach*** *(☎ 654-4333)*, which has nice, simple rooms surrounded by hibiscus for US$25 double. Cheaper rooms can sometimes be found in the village center; ask around.

Mid-Range ***Cabinas Cristina*** *(☎ 654-4006, fax 654-4128)* is about 700m away from the sea near the north end. There is a small pool, the management is friendly, and local tours and boat rentals can be arranged. Clean cabins with kitchenettes, refrigerators, fans, and private baths cost US$40 double and US$65 for five people. In the same price range is ***Windsong Cabinas*** *(☎/fax 654-4291)*, which has clean, spacious rooms with kitchens and air-conditioning, behind a little supermarket on the way into the village.

About 50m east of the village center, ***Bahia Esmeralda*** *(☎ 654-4480, fax 654-4479)* is a new place with clean, comfortable rooms with heated water and fans for US$30/44 double/triple. A four-person villa with a kitchen rents for US$73 per day. An Italian restaurant is on the premises.

Casa Sunset House *(☎ 654-4265)* has seven nice cabins on a lush hillside north of the village, with views over the bay. Monkeys and birds are often seen on the grounds, and a nearby estuary provides good birding in the wet season. Owner Martha Herbst is a friendly and knowledgeable host. Each cabin has fans and a private bath; a shared open-air kitchen with fridge and ice machine is available. The price is US$50 double (additional people US$10 each), with discounts for longer stays.

Hotel El Sitio Cielomar *(☎ 654-4194, fax 666-2059)* is set in attractive, grassy grounds next to Playa Penca. Bicycles, horses, snorkeling equipment, and kayaks are available for rent. Plain doubles with air-conditioning and hot water cost US$45/57 single/double including breakfast; extra people are charged US$15 each.

Top End The ***Bahía Potrero Resort*** *(☎ 654-4183, fax 654-4093)* is the best-known resort in Potrero and offers sportfishing, scuba, other water sports, horseback riding, and tours. There is a pool, a children's pool, and a good, reasonably priced restaurant. Large rooms with refrigerators, air-conditioning, and hot water cost US$70 double, US$10 more for beachfront rooms, US$12 more for additional people. Full-service condos are being built, which will rent for US$122. Nonguests can rent kayaks for US$10 per hour, US$50 per day, or boogie boards for US$2 per hour.

New large resort hotels planned for the area seem to have stalled for the time being.

Places to Eat

Aside from the hotel restaurants mentioned above, there are several options. ***Hardens Gardens***, 50m inland from the Bahía Potrero Resort, serves pizzas and pastries. Another 200m inland, ***La Perla*** does barbecue and burgers. ***Bar La Penca***, by the hotel of the same name, is locally recommended for food and has a Wurlitzer jukebox. At the far end of the bay past the village, ***Las Brisas Bar*** claims to be the oldest bar in Guanacaste. Bill Enell, formerly of Texas, came to the area some 20 years ago and serves up big Texas-style *bocas* and tall tales. The pool table is popular with ticos from the village, and the open-air bar is a great place to watch the sunset while lights come on in yachts moored across the bay.

Getting There & Away

See Playa Flamingo for details.

PLAYA PAN DE AZÚCAR

This small white-sand beach is 2 or 3km north of Potrero and is the last beach reachable by road. The waters are protected by rocky headlands at either end of the beach and offer good snorkeling.

The ***Hotel Sugar Beach*** *(☎ 654-4242, fax 654-4239; in North America ☎ 800-458-4735)* is a small, lovely hotel attractively located in rambling grounds above Playa Pan de Azúcar. A long-established hotel with excellent service, it remains the only accommodations here. About 30 good rooms, each with an individually carved wooden door, have air-conditioning, private baths, and hot water, and cost in the low US$100s double. Three suites or apartments cost US$200 to US$350 each. The restaurant is good and has a great view. There is some forest in the area, and you can watch monkeys and birds near the hotel. Boat charters are available for fishing, diving, and snorkeling, and horse and sailboard rental are also offered.

The nearest bus goes to Playa Potrero, from where you'll have to walk or drive on a rough road.

PLAYA TAMARINDO

Instead of turning north from Huacas to Brasilito and Flamingo, you can head south to Tamarindo. The road is paved most of the way to the village, with more pavement on the way, and is in decent shape. The village of Tamarindo is spread along the last 1.5km. Both commercial fishing and tourism are of economic importance here, though you'll see far more surfers than fishermen wandering around the village.

Both surfing and windsurfing are good, and there is a wildlife refuge and marine national park nearby. The beach is attractive and large enough that nonsurfers can still find quiet stretches. Parts of the beach have rip currents or barely submerged rocks, so make local inquiries before swimming. This beach has better access by public transport than most of the beaches in the area and is bustling with small-scale development.

Tamarindo's combination of attractions is well served with accommodations, restaurants, and equipment rentals, all of interest to nonsurfers here to enjoy village beach life or the nearby refuges. However, Tamarindo is definitely a surfer town. Except for the global village flavor of the tattoos and the smaller, sharper boards, you might think you'd walked into California in the '50s. There are good waves at the river estuary north of town and at Playa Grande across

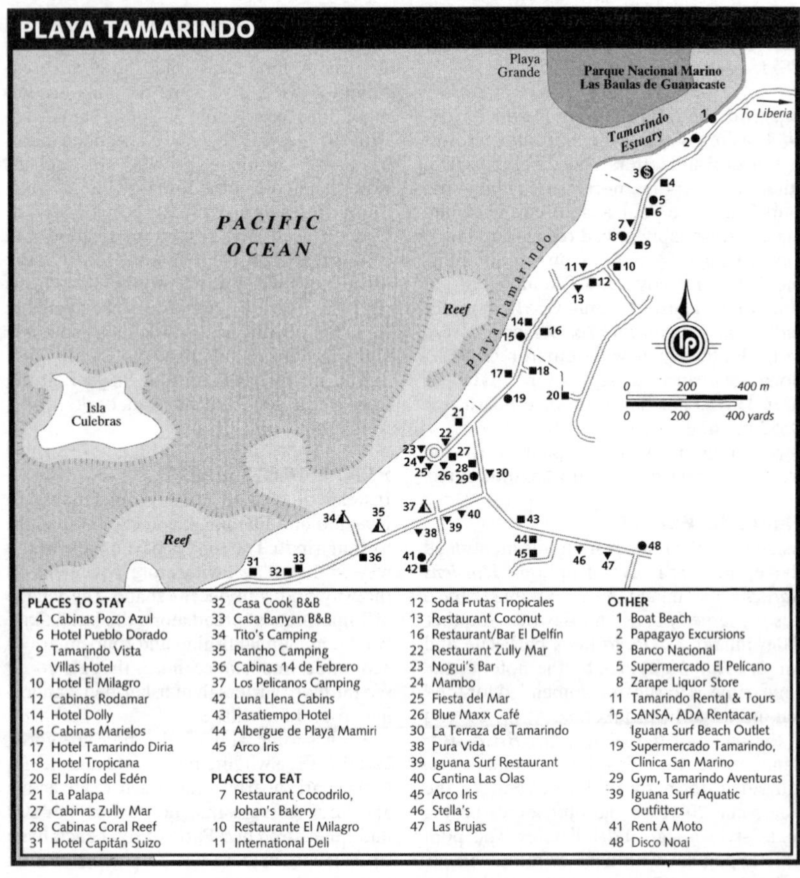

the estuary. There is some surfing right off Playa Tamarindo, but the rocks make for limited space. Playa Langosta, a couple of kilometers south of Tamarindo, is a favorite and uninhabited surfing beach. About 6 or 7km farther south is Playa Avellana, described later in this section. Sea kayaking is also good.

Information

Tourist information is available from any of the equipment outfitters (see below); this is also an easy town in which to ask around. The Blue Maxx Café is a popular meeting place and also offers Internet access, as does Iguana Surf. There are a number of public CHIP phones (see Post & Communications in the Facts for the Visitor chapter for information) on the road circle at the south end of town. The Banco Nacional changes US cash and traveler's checks. The small Clínica San Marino offers medical attention a few hours a day on weekdays. Hotels can help get you a doctor in case of emergency.

Activities & Organized Tours

Many new outfitters have opened up shop in the past few years, which attests to Tamarindo's popularity. A passport or credit card may be necessary for some rentals. Also look for flyers at hotels and cafés for people offering services like group transport to surf beaches.

The friendly, well-run Iguana Surf Aquatic Outfitters (☎/fax 653-0148) is the largest equipment rental shop and has opened another small outlet near the beach. It has reasonably priced bike, kayak, surfboard, body board, snorkeling, Hobie Cat, and other rentals, including some camping equipment, and sells many other beach needs. It also offers local tours and surfing or kayaking lessons. Typical rental rates for a full day are US$25 for a surfboard, US$12.50 for snorkeling gear, a bike, or a body board, and US$45 for an ocean kayak, with hourly rates available. Surf taxi service is also available – US$10 to Playas Avellana and Grande, or US$20 to Playa Negra, minimum two passengers. 'Quad' tours, the newest and noisiest thing to do (like bungee jumping, popular but hard to recommend), are also available.

Papagayo Excursions (☎ 653-0254, fax 653-0227), near the entrance of town, is one of the longest-running outfitters and arranges excursions such as boat tours, scuba diving, snorkeling, sportfishing, horse rentals, and visits to turtle nesting areas on Playa Grande in Parque Nacional Marino Las Baulas de Guanacaste.

Also on the way into town, Tamarindo Rental & Tours (☎ 653-0078) rents surfboards, kayaks, snorkels, bikes, and other beach gear. It arranges all kinds of tours and has a souvenir shop with international newspapers and paperbacks.

Tamarindo Aventuras (☎/fax 653-0640) rents scooters for US$32 per day, as well as water-sports equipment. It also offers quad tours. Rent A Moto (☎ 653-0082) specializes in scooter rental, from US$20 for four hours to US$200 for a week, insurance included.

The *Samonique III* is a 52-foot ketch available for sunset cruises, day cruises, or overnight charters (it sleeps up to six guests). The owners, Sam and Moni, have completed a 13-year circumnavigation and now own the Finca Monte Fresco (see Places to Stay, below). Rates range from US$45 per person for a sunset cruise with drinks and snacks to US$775 for a seven-day/six-night cruise including all meals. These cruises have been recommended by readers.

Sportfishing charters are offered by Tamarindo Sportfishing (☎/fax 653-0090), which has Captain Randy Wilson's 38-foot Topaz *Talking Fish* and a 22-foot Boston Whaler. Osprey Sportfishing (☎/fax 653-0162) has Captain Brock Menking's 31-foot *Rampage*. Capullo Sportfishing (☎ 653-0048) has a 36-foot Topaz and 22-foot Boston Whalers. Both inshore and offshore fishing are available for half-day (US$250 to US$500) and full-day (US$350 to US$800) trips. Papagayo Excursions and Tamarindo Rental & Tours, above, can give you more details.

Agua Rica Diving Center has moved several times but can be contacted through Papagayo Excursions, above, or Tamarindo Rental & Tours. A four-day PADI certification course for beginners costs US$300; two-tank dives from a boat cost US$65.

Places to Stay

Budget There is much more of a price selection here than in most of the towns on this coast, but it's almost impossible to get cheap single rooms during the high season, so budget travelers need to find a buddy.

There are three campsites near the beach at the south end of town, all offering basic facilities for about US$2 per person. ***Tito's Camping*** has the best beachfront location and has a couple of tents that rent for US$3 per person. Meals can be bought here. ***Rancho Camping*** offers more room and better shade. ***Los Pelicanos Camping*** is run by old-style Guanacaste señora Doña Paula, who serves up inexpensive local food from her beachfront home.

Cabinas Rodamar *(☎ 653-0109)* has basic, airy room with private showers for US$11 double. There is an open-air kitchen, and you can camp in the backyard for US$2 per person. ***Cabinas Coral Reef*** *(☎ 653-0291)* has small doubles for US$14.50. The place is a bit disheveled, but the owner is cheery.

The ***Hotel Dolly*** offers small rooms with fans and private baths that get snapped up quickly at about US$24 double. Opposite, the pleasant ***Cabinas Marielos*** *(☎ 653-0141)* provides slightly larger rooms with fans and baths for about US$27 double.

The ***Cabinas Pozo Azul*** *(☎ 653-0280; in Santa Cruz 680-0147)* is rather spartan-looking, with basic rooms in bare grounds. All have private baths and shaded patios, with a choice of fans or air-conditioning. Most rooms have a kitchenette and refrigerator, and there is a pool. Rates start in the US$20s with fan and in the US$30s with air-conditioning.

At the end of the road is a reasonably priced favorite – the ***Cabinas Zully Mar*** *(☎ 653-0140)*. Basic rooms with private baths and fans cost in the US$20s; better rooms with refrigerators cost a couple of dollars more; the best rooms (in the US$40s) are air-conditioned and have refrigerators and electric warm showers.

Cabinas 14 de Febrero *(☎ 653-0238)* has roomy doubles and triples with private showers for US$25/30. The slightly faded though charming ***Albergue de Playa Mamiri*** *(☎ 653-0079)* has rooms with private baths for about US$30.

Mid-Range The Italian-owned ***Arco Iris*** has a cluster of pretty hillside cabinas, each individually and imaginatively decorated. Some are quite romantic; doubles with private hot baths cost US$45 (open to negotiation if times are slow). An open-air kitchen is available, as are shiatsu massage (US$15 per hour), a karate dojo, herbal therapies, and impressive tattoos. The vegetarian restaurant is excellent. The ***Hotel Tropicana*** *(☎/fax 653-0261)* is a large white building with about 40 clean and pleasant rooms, all with private hot baths. Some rooms are air-conditioned. The rate is about US$65 for a double. There is a pool, a restaurant, and a tower that gives a view of the sea.

The ***Pasatiempo Hotel*** *(☎ 653-0096, fax 653-0275, passtime@sol.racsa.co.cr)* is a small hotel with a great reputation. The 10 rooms are not fancy, but they are good-sized and clean and have comfortable beds, hot baths, and fans or air-conditioning. Each has a little patio with a hammock. There is a pool, and the bar has satellite TV and live music jams once or twice a week. High-season rates are US$58 double, or US$70 with air-conditioning, adding another US$12 per extra person.

The ***Hotel El Milagro*** *(☎ 653-0042, fax 653-0050, flokiro@sol.racsa.co.cr)* is under European management, and the staff speaks some Spanish, English, Dutch, French, and German. There is a small pool, the recommended Restaurante El Milagro, and a bar. It is popular with youngish Europeans. Local tours of all kinds are arranged. The rooms are a bit close together, but the grounds are nice, and each room has its own little patio and private bath with hot water for US$57 double. Add US$10 for air-conditioning and extra people (up to four). Breakfast is included. Rooms cost about 30% less in the low season.

La Palapa *(☎ 653-0362)* is a new beachfront hotel in the center of town. Reception is in a photo shop of the same name; French owner Denis is friendly. Simple, pretty beachview cabinas cost US$40 double, US$50 with hot water and fridge, US$60 with air-conditioning and kitchen. Extra people are charged US$10.

The ***Hotel Pueblo Dorado*** *(☎/fax 653-0008, Apartado 1711-1002, San José)* is very clean and has a pre-Columbian motif throughout. There is a small pool and restaurant. Sportfishing and touring can be arranged. Pleasantly bright air-conditioned rooms with hot showers cost US$70/80 single/double.

The ***Casa Cook B&B*** *(☎ 653-0125, casacook@sol.racsa.co.cr; in the USA ☎ 925-846-0784, fax 925-426-1141, wsmith3019@aol.com)* is a very pretty and well-kept little inn in a private house. There is a pool and garden. The 2nd floor of the house (the 'villa') offers two large bedrooms with private baths, a kitchen, outdoor deck, and dining and living rooms; there are sofabeds, and up to eight people can sleep comfortably here. On the beach are two one-bedroom cabinas, also with kitchens, sleeping up to four. Hammocks hang in the trees by the beach and body boards are available to guests. The rate for the villa is US$260 per night for four people; the cabina rate is

US$130 double. Extra people and air-conditioning cost US$10 per night. Almost next door is the similar ***Casa Banyan B&B***, administered by the same owner. For information about other similar villas in Tamarindo, call Donna at ☎ 653-0044.

Luna Llena Cabins *(☎ 653-0082)* has undergone a complete remodeling and now offers round two-story towers with treehouselike sleeping lofts for US$80 double, including breakfast. Slighter cheaper hotel accommodations are being built by the Italian owner. There is a pool and a bar.

There are a few other places on the road leading into town. The ***Finca Monte Fresco*** *(☎ 653-0241, fax 653-0243, samoniqe@sol.racsa.co.cr)* is high up on the right about 3km before the beginning of town. This 6-hectare property has great views of the surrounding forest down to the ocean. The owners have the *Samonique III* ketch (see Activities & Organized Tours, earlier). There are five clean, mid-size apartments, each complete with a full kitchen and bathroom. There is a pool and covered Ping-Pong area. Horses, bikes, and surfboards are available for rent, and all tours can be arranged. Rates are US$46/70/93 single/double/triple, and full (US$7) or continental (US$3) breakfast is served, though you hardly need it with your own full kitchen.

Top End On a hill overlooking Tamarindo is the elegant, luxurious, and recommended ***El Jardín del Edén*** *(☎ 653-0137, ☎/fax 653-0111, hotel@jardin-eden.com)*. This friendly Italian/French-run hotel has beautiful rooms, each with a private patio or balcony (and some of Tamarindo's best views) and a sitting area. All rooms have fans and air-conditioning, refrigerators, and private baths with hot water. There is a lovely big pool with a swim-up bar, a Jacuzzi, and a restaurant. All the usual local tours can be arranged, and a professional masseuse/acupuncturist is available. Although not right on the beach, the hotel has the advantages of being high on a hill: good views and ocean breezes. The pool and grounds of the hotel are very inviting, and it takes only a few minutes to walk to the beach. Rooms vary in size, and prices start at

Massage & Yoga

A distinctive thing about tourist services in Costa Rica is that many entrepreneurs have founded their businesses around a holistic mission of one kind or another. One side benefit of this is that you can find massage and yoga classes offered almost anywhere there are hotels – ecotourism at the level of the body.

– John Thompson

US$100 single for the smaller rooms, going up to US$122/145 single/double for the largest. There are two apartments with kitchenettes for US$170. Extra adults pay US$23; extra children five to 12 years pay US$18; kids under five stay free. These prices include breakfast. The recommended restaurant specializes in French and Italian dishes, which vary from night to night. The hotel can arrange a private bus to and from San José (US$25 per person, four minimum).

In town next to the beach is the large ***Hotel Tamarindo Diria*** *(☎ 653-0033, fax 653-0032; in San José ☎ 290-4340, fax 290-4367, tnodiria@sol.racsa.co.cr)*, which is popular with German-speaking tourists (Spanish and English are also spoken). This is Tamarindo's first luxury hotel and has a faithful older clientele. A recent facelift has kept it in pretty good shape. It has two pools set in plant-filled tropical gardens and a good restaurant and bar; staff also make all tour arrangements. There are 70 air-conditioned rooms with fans, cable TV, phones, and hot-water bathrooms at about US$130 double. One reader writes that, during the wet season, the management brings mosquito repellent around to the diners at its outdoor restaurant! (Indoor seating is available as well.)

A recommended hotel right on the beach at the far south end is the ***Hotel Capitán Suizo*** *(☎/fax 653-0292, 683-0075, capitansuizo@ticonet.co.cr)*. This expertly Swiss-run hotel features beautiful spacious rooms with bigger bathrooms than anywhere else. The large free-form pool is right next to the beach, so you can choose a freshwater float or a salty swim. There is a good restaurant and bar, kayaks and horses are available for rent, and all the other tours can be arranged. It's a bit far away from the center of things, but if you prefer peace and quiet, you'll be delighted with this. There are 22 rooms on two levels; the lower 11 are air-conditioned, and the upper 11 have fans and are designed with cross-breezes in mind. All have a mini-fridge, a sitting area with a futon, and a terrace or balcony. There are also eight bungalows, which are larger still, with huge sunken bathtubs and fans but no air-conditioning. High-season rates are US$110 for a room, US$133 for an air-conditioned room, and US$162 for a bungalow, all for two people. Rates go up US$10 to US$20 during Christmas, New Year, and Easter, and drop US$15 to US$40 in the low season. Additional people pay US$15 each.

Near the Hotel Capitán Suizo, ***Casa Sueca*** *(☎/fax 653-0021, vikings@sol.racsa.co.cr)*, a B&B run by Ann and Kjell, a young Swedish couple, offers suites for about US$75 double and has been warmly recommended by readers. South of the hotel, the road continues about a kilometer to Playa Langosta. Here there's the fine ***Sueño del Mar B&B*** *(☎/fax 653-0284, suenodem@sol.racsa.co.cr)*. There are three rooms in the beautifully and eclectically decorated house, a small cottage with kitchen and loft alongside, and a new honeymoon suite. The rooms have open-air (but private) showers, which is a nice touch. All the usual activities can be arranged, including (they say) horseback rides along the beach at dawn. High-season rates are US$133 for double rooms with breakfast, US$174 for four people in the cottage with breakfast or for the honeymoon suite.

Another choice is to rent an apartment or a house. Top of the line for apartments is ***Tamarindo Vista Villas Hotel*** *(☎ 653-0114, fax 653-0115, tamvv@sol.racsa.co.cr)*. It has modern air-conditioned apartments with one bedroom each and modern bathrooms, ocean views, well-equipped kitchens with dining areas, patios or balconies, and living rooms with two fold-out futons. Up to four people can be accommodated. It also has larger two-bedroom units with two bathrooms; with the futons in the sitting room, these can sleep up to eight people. High-season rates range from US$115 for one-bedroom to US$185 for two-bedroom apartments; there is one larger suite for US$230 and discounts for longer stays and in low season. Maid service is provided. The owners are helpful with local information.

Tamarindo Sunset House *(☎/fax 653-0098, pacific@sol.racsa.co.cr)* is an attractive beach house with tiled floors and murals by local artists, on the north side of the Banco Nacional. The two-story home has a carport, two bedrooms with two double beds each, and a third bedroom with a queen-size bed, two hot-water bathrooms with towels, fully equipped kitchen, outdoor beach shower, lawn furniture, hammock, and barbecue. There are body boards, a cassette player, and daily maid and laundry service. Monkeys, iguanas, birds, and other animals frequent the tropical trees in the garden. The nightly rate is about US$200 for two people, US$25 per additional person, up to nine. Next to the house, a one-bedroom apartment with a kitchenette is available for US$100 nightly.

Other houses can be rented. Tamarindo Rental & Tours (see Activities & Organized Tours) may know of some; otherwise, look for signs around the village.

Places to Eat

There is a good selection of restaurants in Tamarindo, and more seem to open every year. One that has been around the north end of town for years is ***Johan's Bakery***, which opens soon after dawn and is a favorite breakfast place with great croissants and coffee, a variety of pastries and breads, and pizza for lunch and early dinner. Right next door is ***Restaurant Cocodrilo***, a popular bar that serves tasty bar food, seafood, snacks, and bocas.

Continuing into town from the north, there are a couple of good and not too pricey (by local standards) snack bars. ***Soda Frutas Tropicales*** is a tourist-friendly soda with good fruit drinks. Opposite is the ***International Deli***, a new place serving up US-style sandwiches. Just beyond is ***Restaurant Coconut***, which advertises French cuisine but is rather more international in flavor and is one of Tamarindo's better restaurants. It opens at 3 pm, and dining is upstairs in a tropical bamboo setting – rather romantic. Most dinner entrées cost over US$10. A little farther is the ***Restaurant/Bar El Delfín***, an inexpensive local place.

There are several places to eat at the road circle at the southwest end of the road into town. ***Mambo*** makes real cappuccinos and has good sandwiches and salads starting at US$2.50. There is a small pool table in back. The more-or-less open-air ***Restaurant Zully Mar*** is open from 7 am to 10 pm, has meals in the US$5 to US$10 range, has good sea views, and is a reliable local favorite. Also right on the beach, ***Nogui's Bar*** is a popular little place for beer, sandwiches, and seafood. The most upscale in this area is the large, high-roofed, and attractive ***Fiesta del Mar***, which serves good steaks, seafood, and tropical cocktails. Most entrées cost around US$10.

The ***Blue Maxx Café*** opens early and is a popular meeting spot. Fabulous North American breakfasts, big sandwiches, espresso drinks, and Internet access can all be found here. Canadian owner Phil Baker is a helpful source of information.

La Terraza de Tamarindo has a good view from the upstairs dining room, where excellent pizza and Italian food are served. Farther up the road are a couple of Italian restaurants, the small ***Las Brujas*** and the more elegant and popular ***Stella's***. The ***Arco Iris*** serves an excellent and international array of vegetarian dishes. ***Pura Vida*** is open 8 pm to 1 am Monday to Saturday and is the place for a late-night meal. The ***Iguana Surf Restaurant***, an addition to the outfitter, serves a variety of snacks and exotic entrées. Nearby, ***Cantina Las Olas*** is a Mexican-food restaurant and bar. Another good place for Mexican food is ***Ranch Mexico***, about three-quarters of a kilometer north of town on the main road.

Don't forget the recommended restaurants in the more upscale hotels.

Entertainment

There's usually live or recorded dance music happening at one or more of the road-circle restaurants on weekends. The ***Pasatiempo Hotel*** has live music jams once or twice a week. The new ***Disco Noai*** has live music some nights.

Getting There & Away

Air The Tamarindo airstrip is about 2.5km from the north end of the village; a hotel bus is usually on hand to pick up arriving passengers. SANSA (☎ 653-0001) has an office on the main road, and the Hotel Pueblo Dorado is the Travelair agent. Both airlines have daily flights to and from San José; the trip takes about an hour, and return flights leave Tamarindo immediately following arrival. In the high season, SANSA has departures from San José at 5:15, 8:30, and 11:35 am and 1:30 pm. In the high season, Travelair offers a daily flight from San José via Liberia at 8:20 am and two direct flights at 1 and 3:30 pm. In the past, some flights continued on to Nosara or Sámara, but this was not the case recently. Check locally for the ever-changing schedules. One-way/roundtrip fares from San José are US$55/110 with SANSA and US$100/165 with Travelair.

Bus Empresa Alfaro (☎ 222-2750), at Calle 14, Avenidas 3 & 5, San José, has a daily bus at 3:30 pm. Its bus returns from Tamarindo direct to San José at 6 am, with an extra bus at 1 pm on Sunday. A bus leaves Santa Cruz at 8:30 pm daily for Tamarindo, returning at 6:45 am the next day.

Car & Taxi If you are driving, the better road is from Belén to Huacas and south. It is also possible to drive from Santa Cruz 17km to 27 de Abril on a paved road and then northwest on a dirt road for 19km to Tamarindo; this route is rougher, though still passable to ordinary cars. A taxi from Santa Cruz should cost about US$12 to US$15. Allow twice that from Liberia.

Getting Around

Many people arrive in rental cars. If you arrive by air or bus, you can rent bicycles and motorbikes from Tienda Tamarindo or cars from ADA Rentacar next to the Neomundo Travel Agency. Travelair passengers can arrange for a rental car to be waiting for them at the airport. However, there seems to be a different car rental agent in town almost every year, so things will probably have changed by the time you arrive. There is no gas station, though you can buy gas from drums in a shack near the entrance of town. Fill up in Santa Cruz.

PARQUE NACIONAL MARINO LAS BAULAS DE GUANACASTE

Formerly a national wildlife refuge, this national marine park was created in 1991 and covers about 420 hectares on the north side of the Río Matapalo estuary, just north of Tamarindo village. In addition, 22,000 hectares of ocean are also protected. Most of the land portion is mangrove swamp containing all six of the mangrove species found in Costa Rica – two species of black mangrove as well as tea, white, red, and buttonwood. This creates a great habitat for caimans and crocodiles, as well as numerous bird species, including the beautiful roseate spoonbill.

But the main attraction and *raison d'être* of the park is undoubtedly **Playa Grande**, which is the country's important nesting site for the leatherback turtle *(baula)*, briefly described in the Wildlife Guide. Its nesting season is from October to March (especially from November to January), and more than 100 reptiles may be seen laying their eggs on Playa Grande during the course of a night (dark nights are best); about 2500 nests are made each season. Other species are occasionally seen in other months.

Mangrove swamps are home to many species.

Playa Grande is also a favored surfing beach, its break touted as the most consistent in Costa Rica. So far, surfers and turtles have co-existed within the national park with few problems. The park was created more to control unregulated tourism and to protect the nests from poaching.

Until the formation of the park, tourists arrived by the boatload and harassed the animals by using flash photography, touching the animals, and generally acting like yahoos. Now turtle-watchers pay a US$6 entry fee to the park and must watch the activities from specified viewing areas. You must be accompanied by a guide or ranger, and no flash photography or lights are allowed as they disturb the laying process.

Other things to look for when visiting this reserve are howler monkeys, raccoons, coatis, otters, and a goodly variety of crabs.

The park office (☎/fax 653-0470) is by the northern entrance and is open 9 am to 6 pm. Maps and brochures about park wildlife are available. The US$6 entrance fee is generally only charged for the nighttime turtle-watching tours.

Turtle-Watching

Tamarindo hotels and agencies will organize turtle-watching tours in season. Some of these are by boat. Tours cost about US$16 and up, depending on the size of the group, where you start from, the quality of the guide, etc. A limited number of visitors are allowed in the park at any one time, and seeing a turtle is never guaranteed; don't pressure your guide to break the rules!

A recommended way to begin your tour is with a visit to **El Mundo de la Tortuga** (☎/fax 653-0471), an excellent exhibit about leatherback turtles that opened recently near the north end of the park. The exhibit is a self-guided introduction to the life of a leatherback turtle, narrated over headphones in English, French, German, or Spanish and accompanied by beautiful photographs. A visit here will make your turtle-watching tour much more rewarding. Most of the tours offered from the exhibit itself are guided by reformed poachers who know the turtles well. The museum is open from 4 pm until dawn, with tours running all night. Show up early to put your name on the tour list; when turtles arrive, small groups are led out to the beach in the order that they signed up. A full tour costs US$18, including entrance to the exhibit (US$5 for the exhibit alone); transport to and from Tamarindo can be arranged for an additional US$7.

Places to Stay & Eat

Most people stay in Tamarindo, just south of the park. At the north end of Playa Grande (at the north end of the park) are a few small hotels.

Hotel Las Tortugas *(☎/fax 653-0458, nela@cool.co.cr)* has spacious air-conditioned rooms with private baths for US$85 double and suites sleeping up to four for US$125. It gives a 40% low-season discount. There is a pool, Jacuzzi, and restaurant, and tours to the national park and elsewhere can be arranged. The owners, Marianela Pastor and Louis Wilson, were instrumental in organizing protection for the turtles and have designed their hotel so that the lights, which are quite dim, shine away from the beach area, even though the hotel is right on the beach. Surfboards, body boards, sea kayaks, snorkels, and horse rentals are offered. You can get a massage here from an experienced chiropractor for US$40 per hour.

At the southern end of the park, just across the estuary from Tamarindo, is ***Villa Baula*** *(☎ 653-0493, fax 653-0459, hotelvb@sol.racsa.co.cr)*, a pleasantly rustic beachfront complex with family cabins (two adults and two children) with hot water and ceiling fans for US$69. Cabins sleeping five with kitchenettes cost US$116. There is a pool, and surfboards, body boards, kayaks, and bikes are available. Ask about exploring the estuary, where birds, monkeys, and caimans can be seen. Also in this area and price range is the ***Hotel Cantarana*** *(☎ 653-0486, fax 653-0491)*, which has a good restaurant near the estuary and offers massage.

Several hundred meters inland from the north end of the beach, the ***Rancho Diablo Surf Camp*** *(☎ 653-0490)* is overseen by friendly Bob. Simple, nice doubles cost US$45 with fans and private showers. Good barbecue and beer can be had here, as well as Ping-Pong, VCR movies, and use of a swimming pool. The latter is attached to the former Hotel Parque de Agua, next door to Bob's and now an annex to the surf camp. Air-conditioned doubles go for US$60. Try bargaining.

A few hundred meters back from the beach on the main road is the ***Centro Vacacional Playa Grande*** *(☎/fax 653-0467)*, which is popular with vacationing tico families and surfers. The owner, Kike, is friendly, and this is the cheapest place in the area. Rooms with private baths and fans, some with kitchenettes, cost about US$20 double, and some cheaper basic rooms are available. There is a restaurant and pool.

You can also contact the Hotel Las Tortugas (see above) about several modern, spacious, fully equipped and furnished ***beachfront houses*** that are available for rent. These have porches right onto the beach and come with maid service. Most are air-conditioned. Sample rates for a two-bedroom house are US$150/800/2500 for a night/week/month; for a three-bedroom house, US$250/1500/4000; for a four-bedroom house, US$350/2000/5000.

They also have air-conditioned apartments about 400m back from the beach. These have one or 1½ bedrooms, kitchenettes, maid service, and shared pool. Rates are US$75 to US$125 a night, US$300 to US$600 a week, and US$1000 to US$2000 a month.

Other new places are being developed, including a huge resort project with a golf course.

Getting There & Away

There are no buses to Playa Grande. You can drive to Huacas and then take the dirt road through Matapalo to Playa Grande. This is a dirt road that may be hard to negotiate in a regular car during the wet months of May to November. If you are staying at one of the hotels on Playa Grande, ask them to pick you up from the Matapalo turnoff (where the bus from San José can drop you off). It is also possible to take day tours to the reserve from Tamarindo, or get a local boatman to take you across the estuary from Tamarindo to the southern end of Playa Grande (see Playa Tamarindo).

PLAYAS NEGRA & AVELLANA

These popular surfing beaches offer both left and right breaks. Avellana is a long stretch of white sand about 15km south of Tamarindo by road (unpaved south of Villareal), but closer to 10km if you walk in along the beaches. Negra, a few kilometers farther south, is a darker beach broken up by rocky outcrops that offer exciting surfing. If you're not coming from Tamarindo, head west on the paved highway from Santa Cruz, through 27 de Abril to Paraíso, then follow signs or ask locals. The last section is unpaved. Either way, the road is rough and may require 4WD in the wet season, so get local updates. The relatively difficult access means that these beaches are frequented by those who appreciate them, mainly surfers. Some of the places to stay are nice enough in themselves to be a destination for those looking for a remote beach experience.

Places to Stay & Eat

These are listed from north to south. ***Cabinas Las Olas*** *(☎ 682-4366)*, set in spacious grounds, has 10 airy individual cabins with porches and hammocks for US$45/55 single/double. Boardwalk trails lead through mangrove down to Playa Avellana; there are very few surfers at this end of the beach. The attractive ***Lagartillo Beach Hotel*** *(☎ 257-1420, fax 221-5717)* has rooms with private baths and fans for US$40/50 single/double. There is a pool and restaurant, and there is forest around the grounds.

The ***Avellanes Surf Ranch*** has cabins, camping, and a soda. It doesn't seem very well organized, which may be a plus for some people. ***Cabinas Gregorios*** has three basic cabins with private baths for US$9 per person; try bargaining. You can camp on the beach, and there are a couple of sodas/bars nearby.

More or less between Playas Avellana and Negra, the ***Mono Congo Lodge*** *(☎/fax 382-6926)* is a large open-air ranch building surrounded by monkey-filled trees. This place is one of those inspiring examples of a dream well realized. When the owners arrived 10 years ago, this was scrub farmland; the beautiful wooden building, trees, and gardens are all their doing. Their vegetarian restaurant is excellent too. There is a comfortable common living room and a star-watching deck. Simple, well-designed rooms cost US$35 double. Bunkhouse beds are available for US$10 per person.

A bit closer to Playa Negra is a variety of surfer-oriented places. The side-by-side ***Aloha Amigos*** and ***Juanitos Ranchitos*** share a phone *(☎ 680-0280)* and charge about US$10 per person. Kitchen, laundry, bikes, and transport to Paraíso are available. On the beach, ***Hotel Playa Negra*** *(☎ 382-1301, fax 382-1302, info@playanegra.com)* offers spacious, circular bungalows for US$50/60 single/double, US$10 for extra people. Tours and rentals are available. ***Pablo's Picasso*** *(☎ 382-0411)*, 400m from the beach, is another classic surfers' hangout, with hamburgers 'as big as your head,' huge surfing murals, laundry, TV, and cabins and dorms for about US$10 per person. Some have kitchens and air-conditioning.

PLAYA JUNQUILLAL

This is a wide and wild beach, with high surf, strong rip currents, and few people. The beach is 2km long and has tide pools and pleasant walking. The local people go surf fishing here.

Junquillal is about midway between Las Baulas de Guanacaste and Ostional. Ridley sea turtles nest here in December and January, but in smaller numbers than at the refuges. There is no village as such (the nearest is **Paraíso**, about 4km inland), but there are several nice places to stay near the coast. Because of the length of the beach and the lack of a village, the beach is uncrowded, and there is a pleasant away-from-it-all feel to the place. Some hotels don't even have phones, and those that do suffer from occasional cuts in service. Hotels lower their rates by 20% to 40% outside the mid-December to mid-April high season.

Places to Stay & Eat

As you arrive, the first place you pass is the entrance to the recommended Canadian-run ***Hotel Iguanazul*** *(☎ 653-0124, ☎/fax 653-0123; in the USA or Canada ☎ 800-948-3770, iguanazul@ticonet.co.cr)*. It's about a kilometer from the entrance to the hotel itself, which is elegant and secluded, but friendly and fun. There is a pool, game room with pool table, darts, and table tennis, volleyball, a small souvenir shop with a well-chosen selection of gifts, and a recommended restaurant and bar with a good view of the beach. The beach is a short walk away by trail. Snorkeling gear (US$5 a half day) and horse rental (US$15 for the first hour, US$10 for each additional hour) are available. Sportfishing, diving, and local tours can be arranged. High-season rates for the 24 airy and attractive rooms with fans and private hot showers are US$65/80/92 single/double/triple. There are four rooms with air-conditioning, two of them poolside, for US$92 to US$105 double.

There is an excellent ***campground*** near the hotel, on a shady hillside overlooking the ocean; look for signs. Campers are sometimes allowed to use the hotel facilities.

The Iguanazul also has information about renting a two-room ***beach apartment*** with a hot-water bathroom, fans, a kitchen, dining area, and balcony. One room has a double bed; the second room has two double beds. High-season rates are about US$100 for the whole apartment and US$70 for the apartment without the second room. You can use all the hotel facilities.

On a hilltop about half a kilometer beyond the Iguanazul entrance is the small, seven-room, German/tica-owned ***Hotel El Castillo***, which looks like a little white castle. It has a panoramic view from the rooftop bar – a breezy place to laze in a hammock and watch the sunset – and rooms cost around US$35/50 in the low/high season. The tower bedroom faces the ocean. This is a place only a dreamer could build, and the owners are enthusiastic hosts. Good meals are available, and it's well under a kilometer from the beach itself. A short way beyond is the six-bungalow, Swiss-run ***Guacamaya Lodge***, which charges US$35/50 for low/high-season doubles with fans and private hot-water baths. There is a pool and restaurant/bar, and it's a quiet and pleasant little place. Another half kilometer brings you past the ***Tatanka Resort*** *(☎ 653-0426)*, which is a row of motel-like rooms; readers write that the Italian management is friendly and that the restaurant is good. Triples cost US$40. Just beyond is the ***Hospedaje El Malinche*** *(☎ 653-0433)*, run by a somewhat confusing and quarrelsome family. A few low-budget rooms and camping may be available.

The ***Hotel Playa Junquillal*** *(☎ 653-0432)* is US-owned but run by friendly locals Bernardo and Senjia Sánchez, who speak some English. Basic but pleasant beach cabins with fans and private hot showers cost about US$36 double, half that in low season. Hammocks and body boards are available. The cabins are often full in the dry season – you can try calling Coco in Santa Cruz *(☎/fax 680-0053)* for a reservation. There is a restaurant/bar that is popular with locals and serves good tico meals. You could ask to camp here, or you could probably camp almost anywhere along the beach if you have your own food and water. Almost opposite is the tico/French-run ***Hotel Hibiscus*** *(☎ 653-0437)*, which has five pleasant rooms with fans and private hot showers for about US$40/46, including breakfast. It serves French-inspired cuisine and has a flower-filled garden.

About half a kilometer beyond the Hibiscus, the ***Hotel Villa Serena*** *(☎ 653-0430, serenaho@sol.racsa.co.cr)* has modern bungalows spread around a small pool where open-air musical aerobics classes are held. Instructor Xinia Amador also performs typical dances on occasion. Palm trees abound, and there is a sauna, tennis court, and horses for rent. Spacious doubles with fans, private hot-water bathrooms, and (in some cases) patios facing the beach rent for US$65. The restaurant has a good ocean view.

The ***Hotel Antumalal*** *(☎/fax 653-0425, antumal@sol.racsa.co.cr)* is almost a kilometer beyond at the end of the road, on spacious grounds frequently visited by wild monkeys. There are two dozen attractive cabins with private hot baths, fans, and terraces, and nine larger furnished villas. There is a pool and a kids' pool, discotheque (sometimes), tennis court, good restaurant, and two bars. Horses are available for rent (cheap rates, and nonguests are welcome), boats are available for fishing and diving, and PADI certification courses can be arranged from the hotel's dive shop. The room rates are about US$69/78/90 single/double/triple, and the villas cost about US$100. About half of the clients are German, and the owners speak German, English, and Spanish. This place has received several reader recommendations.

Apart from the hotels, there is nowhere to eat unless you return 4km to the village of Paraíso, where there are a few simple local restaurants, sodas, and bars. These include the ***Restaurant Las Vegas***, with a menu that ranges from cheeseburgers to lobster, and the ***Tamarindo Surf Restaurant***, which is a bar serving sandwiches and burgers. The public telephone in the village is ☎ 680-0846.

Getting There & Away

Bus TRALAPA (☎ 221-7202), Calle 20, Avenida 3 in San José, has a daily bus to Junquillal at 2 pm, taking about five hours. The return bus leaves Junquillal at 5 am. There is also a daily TRALAPA bus from Santa Cruz at 6:30 pm, returning at 5 am. The bus may go only as far as Paraíso, which is 4km by foot or taxi from the beach.

Car & Taxi If you are driving, it is about 16km by paved road from Santa Cruz to 27 de Abril, and about a further 17km by unpaved road via Paraíso to Junquillal.

From Junquillal you can head south by taking a turnoff about 3km east of Paraíso. This road is marked 'Reserva Ostional' and is passable in ordinary cars, at least during the dry season. Most people visiting the beaches south of Junquillal reach them from Nicoya. Expect to have to ford some rivers (especially if it has been raining), and carry spare everything. There are no gas stations on this coastal dirt road, and it carries little traffic.

A taxi from San José costs about US$125 to US$150; from Santa Cruz, it's about US$20.

SANTA CRUZ

This small town is on the main peninsula highway 25km south of Filadelfia, 57km south of Liberia, and 23km north of Nicoya. A paved road leads 16km west to 27 de Abril, from where dirt roads continue to Playa Tamarindo, Playa Junquillal, and other beaches. Santa Cruz is a possible overnight stop when you're visiting the peninsula – it gives the visitor a chance to experience Costa Rican life in a small country town. It also has some of the cheapest places to stay in the peninsula.

About three city blocks in the center of town were burned to the ground in a devastating fire in 1993. A major town landmark, the Plaza de Los Mangos, a large grassy square named after the four mango trees growing on the north side, is now not much more than a vacant lot. However, many town addresses are still given from that plaza. The attractive and shady Parque Bernabela Ramos, a new park with folklore-themed statues, has opened 400m south of here. Across from a ruined clock tower and a modern church with interesting stained glass windows, the new park is a nice place to soak in Santa Cruz life.

There is an annual rodeo and fiesta during the second week in January, with plenty of Guanacasteco dancing, marimba music, and traditional food. Another fiesta is held in late July. Santa Cruz is considered the folklore center of the region, if not the entire country, although not much seems to happen here outside of fiesta time. Nearby villages (see the boxed text 'Guaitil') are famous as Chorotega pottery centers. The population of Santa Cruz and the surrounding district is over 15,000.

You can change money at the Banco Anglo Costarricense, by the Palacio Municipal at the northwest corner of Parque Ramos.

Places to Stay

Budget The ***Pensión Isabel*** *(☎ 680-0173)* is 400m south and 50m east of the Plaza de Los Mangos and has basic but OK rooms for about US$5 per person. Basic wooden boxes are available for US$3 at the ***Hotel Anatolia*** *(☎ 680-0333)*, a boardinghouse-like place with a restaurant, 100m west and 200m south of the Plaza de Los Mangos. Another cheapie is the ***Hospedaje Amadita***, 250m north of the same Plaza. Also try (350m south and 100m west) the family-run ***Hospedaje y Restaurante Avellanas*** *(☎ 680-0808)*, which charges about US$3.50 per person for simple rooms with baths. A block away is the slightly cheaper ***Posada Tu Casa***, with basic but clean rooms and friendly people. Also try the friendly ***Cabinas Tauro*** *(☎ 680-0289)*, a row of decent rooms in a family garden, 100m north and 100m west of the Plaza de Los Mangos. A room for two or three costs US$9.

Mid-Range The ***Hotel La Estancia*** *(☎ 680-0476, 680-1033, fax 680-0348)* is 100m west of the Plaza de Los Mangos. There are 16 clean rooms with fans, TVs, and private baths for US$13/25/29 single/double/triple. On the west side of the Plaza de Los Mangos is the ***Hotel Plazza*** *(☎ 680-0169)*, which has 13 clean, simple rooms with fans and private showers. It charges US$13 per person. The ***Hotel La Pampa*** *(☎ 680-0586)* is 50m west of the Plaza de Los Mangos and has 20 simple but clean modern rooms with private baths. Rooms with air-conditioning cost US$28/42, and rooms with fans cost US$18/23.

On the northern outskirts of town, at the intersection with the main peninsula highway and about 500m north of the Plaza de Los

Guaitil

An interesting excursion from Santa Cruz is the 12km drive by paved road to the small pottery-making community of Guaitil. Get there by taking the main highway toward Nicoya and then taking the signed Guaitil road to the left, about 1.5km out of Santa Cruz. This road is lined by trees and is very attractive in April when all the trees are in bloom. The road used to be the main highway to Nicoya and passes the small town of Santa Bárbara before reaching Guaitil, where you can see people making pots outside their houses.

NIK WHEELER

The attractive pots are made from local clays, using natural colors in the pre-Columbian Chorotega Indian style. They come in a variety of shapes and sizes – many of the huge pots seen decorating houses and hotels in Guanacaste come from here. Ceramics are for sale outside the potters' houses in Guaitil and also in San Vicente, 2km beyond Guaitil by unpaved road. If you ask, you can watch part of the potting process. One of the artisans told me that approximately 100 families are engaged in this industry. Many of them are descendants of the Chorotega Indians who once inhabited the area but who have now been largely assimilated into Costa Rican culture.

There are local buses from Santa Cruz.

– Rob Rachowiecki

Mangos, is the best hotel in town – the ***Hotel Diria*** *(☎ 680-0080, 680-0402, fax 680-0442, Apartado 58, Santa Cruz, Guanacaste)*. It has a pool and restaurant, and 50 air-conditioned rooms with private baths, TVs, and telephones cost US$32/47 single/double. Occasionally, the hotel may host entertainment on weekends – live marimba music or recorded dance music are both possibilities. (Marimbas are wooden xylophone-like instruments of African origin, although some musicologists claim that the Central American version is of Guatemalan Indian origin.)

Places to Eat

Check out ***Coopetortillas***, also known as La Fabrica de Tortillas, on a side street 700m south of the Plaza de Los Mangos (250m south of Parque Ramos). It's a huge corrugated-metal barn that looks like a factory. Inside are plain wooden tables, and you eat whatever is available – always homemade typical Costa Rican food cooked right in front of you in the wood-stove kitchen. It's interesting, and the food is tasty and inexpensive. Hours are 5 am to 6:30 pm.

A popular place is ***Geroca #1***, 100m south and 25m east of the plaza, where you can get a *casado*, hamburger, or super taco and pint-glass-size fruit drinks. ***Geroca #2***, 200m north of the plaza, is a quieter version serving the same menu in a breezy shaded patio. Just west of Hotel La Estancia, past an auto shop, ***El Portoncito*** is a cute local soda. ***Bar Restaurant Barbará***, 50m south of the plaza, has a Guanacaste cowboy ambience. There are a few Chinese restaurants; ***Restaurant Jardín de Luna***, at the northeast corner of Parque Ramos, looks like a nice place.

Getting There & Away

There are two bus terminals and some other bus stops. Check all departure points carefully. Unscheduled services to the beaches west of here crop up frequently; ask around. Folklorico, a little company in a wooden building 100m south and 25m west of the plaza, is worth checking. Transportes La Pampa buses (☎ 680-0111) leave the terminal on the north side of the Plaza de Los Mangos for Nicoya 17 times a day from 6 am to 9:30 pm, and for Liberia 16 times a day from 5:30 am to 7:30 pm.

The main terminal is 400m east of the center. TRALAPA (in San José ☎ 221-7202; in Santa Cruz 680-0392) has buses leaving Calle 20, Avenida 3, in San José nine times a day for Santa Cruz (five hours, US$5.25). Buses to San José leave Santa Cruz at 3, 4:30, 6:30, 8:30, and 11:30 am and 1 pm. Expect one or two buses fewer in the wet season. Alfaro buses between San José and Nicoya also go through Santa Cruz. Buses to Puntarenas leave at 6:20 am and 3:20 pm. Various local villages are also served, including Guaitil about six times a day.

Buses for the beach also leave from the main terminal. There are buses for Playas Conchal, Brasilito, Flamingo, and Potrero four times a day during the dry season – fewer in the wet. Some TRALAPA beach buses also go via Santa Cruz. A bus leaves for Junquillal at 6:30 am and for Tamarindo at 6:45 am and 8:30 pm.

> **The Earthquake**
>
> Nicoya has a history of being hit by an earthquake about every 50 years, and starting in 1999, residents of the area have begun waiting for the next one. No one knows for sure if it will happen, but people certainly have opinions about the subject! For more information on earthquakes in Costa Rica and safety tips, see the Facts for the Visitor chapter.
>
> **– John Thompson**

ACCESSING BEACHES SOUTH OF PLAYA JUNQUILLAL

To visit any of the beaches south of Junquillal, many people return to the main peninsula highway and go through Nicoya, 23km south of Santa Cruz. Dirt roads to the southwest reach the attractive beaches at Playas Nosara, Garza, Sámara, and Carrillo, and the wildlife refuge at Ostional. There are airstrips with scheduled flights at Nosara and Sámara/Carrillo. Paved roads east of Nicoya pass the national park at Barra Honda en route to the Tempisque car ferry to the main part of Costa Rica. Paved and unpaved roads to the southeast lead to Playa Naranjo and the Puntarenas car ferry. Travelers using public buses will find it difficult to continue farther south to the popular beach at Montezuma and other areas – you'll need to return to Puntarenas and take the passenger ferry back to Paquera.

NICOYA

Nicoya is the most important town on the peninsula and has a population of about 25,000 (including the surrounding district). The town is named after the Chorotega Indian chief Nicoya, who welcomed the Spanish conquistador Gil González Dávila in 1523. The Indians presented the Spaniard with rich gifts, which is part of the reason why the country became known as Costa Rica. The Chorotegas were the dominant Indian group in the area at the time of the conquest, and many of the local inhabitants can claim to be at least partly of Indian descent.

A major landmark is the attractive white colonial Church of San Blas in the Parque Central, which dates back to the mid-1600s. The church, whose mosaic tiles are crumbling, is slowly undergoing restoration but can be visited. There is a small collection of colonial religious artifacts; more are on display at the Banco Nacional de Costa Rica. The park is an inviting spot to stroll and people-watch, and the wooden-beamed church is appealingly peaceful.

Nicoya is now the commercial center of the cattle industry as well as the political capital and transportation hub of the peninsula. US dollars can be exchanged at any of the several banks in town. The main hospital on the peninsula is the Hospital La Anexión (☎ 685-5066), north of town. The Area de Conservación Tempisque Oficina de Nicoya (☎/fax 685-5667) has some information about wildlife in the region and can make reservations for camping, accommodations, or cave exploration at Parque Nacional Barra Honda (see below).

Places to Stay

Budget The cheapest place is the ***Hotel Ali*** *(☎ 685-5148)*, on the southwest corner of the park. Basic rooms cost US$3.50 per person. On the north side of the park, the ***Hotel Venecia*** *(☎ 685-5325)* charges US$3.50/6.50 single/double for basic but clean rooms with shared cold showers and US$12 double with private showers. Next door, the ***Hotel Elegancia*** *(☎ 685-5159)* is in the same price range. The best cheap hotel, which is often full, is the clean ***Hotel Chorotega*** *(☎ 685-5245)*, two blocks south of the park. It has basic rooms with fans for US$4 per person and fairly decent rooms with private showers and fans for US$5 per person.

Mid-Range The ***Hotel Las Tinajas*** *(☎ 685-5081, 685-5777, fax 685-5096)* is clean and has 28 decent rooms. Reception is open 24 hours. It is 200m west and 100m north of the park. Rooms with private baths and fans cost US$10.50/14.50/20.50 single/double/triple. It also has some larger rooms with private baths sleeping up to seven people for US$40. The ***Hotel Jenny*** *(☎ 685-5050)*, 100m south of the park, is clean and helpful, so it is popular and often full. Air-conditioned rooms with private baths and TVs cost US$14/18.50 single/double. ***Cabinas Nicoya*** *(☎ 686-6331)*, 500m east of the Banco Nacional de Costa Rica, is a small new place with parking, a tiny pool, and clean rooms with TVs for US$13 per person.

The best place is the ***Hotel Curime*** *(☎ 685-5238, fax 685-5530)*, a rustic resort complex about half a kilometer south of town on the road to Playa Sámara. There is a pool and restaurant, tennis and volleyball courts, and horses. Rooms have TVs, refrigerators, and private hot showers. Rates are US$22/29 single/double for rooms with fans and US$29/42 with air-conditioning.

Places to Eat & Drink

There are three or four Chinese restaurants in the town center, and they are among the best places to eat. Two good ones are the ***Restaurant Teyet***, which has three tables in a little outdoor patio (as well as more tables inside), and the ***Restaurant Cam Mun***, on the park.

Café Daniela, a block east of the park, serves breakfasts, casados, burgers, pizzas, and snacks and is a local favorite. Next door, the Chinese-run ***Bar/Restaurant Nicoya*** is good for standard meals. A new place is the ***Jardín Cervecero***, under construction at last visit, which hopes to be an upscale dining and drinking spot. Opposite is an unlikely looking ***piano bar***, which seems worth checking out.

Cheap snacks are available from several stands and sodas around the park. The ***Soda Colonial*** has cheap local food, and ice cream is served at ***Mönpik*** and ***Baloons***. Next door to Baloons is the discotheque ***El Cuartel Latino***.

Getting There & Away

The bus terminal at the south end of Calle 5 is where most buses depart. An antique bus on display here was the first bus to make the San José to Nicoya run, on December 11, 1958.

Alfaro (in Nicoya ☎ 685-5032; in San José 222-2750), at Calle 14, Avenidas 3 & 5, San José, has seven buses a day to Nicoya (US$5.25, six hours). Most of these go through Liberia, Filadelfia, and Santa Cruz – a few cross on the Río Tempisque ferry. Buses

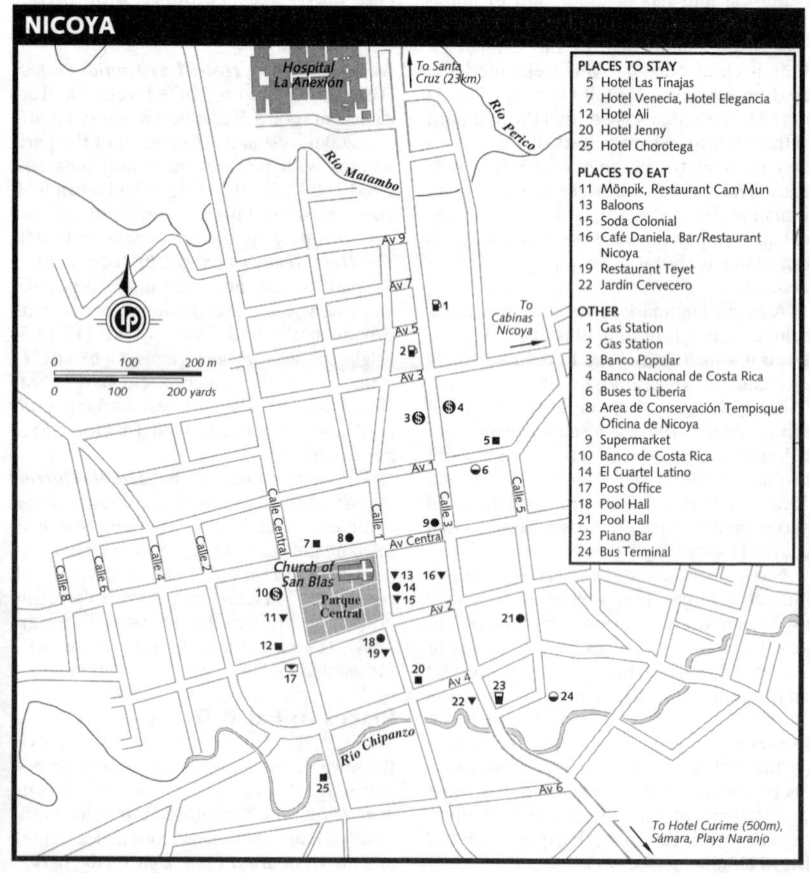

from Nicoya to San José leave six to eight times a day between 4 am and 4 pm. Buses to Playa Naranjo leave at 5:15 am and 1 pm, connecting with the ferry from Naranjo to Puntarenas. There is a 1 pm bus to Playa Nosara, four daily buses to Playa Sámara (fewer in the wet season), buses at 10 am and 3 pm to Quebrada Honda, and one or two a day to a variety of other nearby villages.

Departures for Liberia (US$1.25) leave 18 times a day between 5 am and 7 pm from Transportes La Pampa (☎ 685-5313) at Avenida 1 and Calle 5. These buses go through Santa Cruz and Filadelfia.

PARQUE NACIONAL BARRA HONDA

This 2295-hectare national park is unique in that it was created to protect an area of great geological and speleological interest rather than to conserve a particular habitat.

The park lies roughly midway between Nicoya and the mouth of the Río Tempisque in a limestone area that has been uplifted into coastal hills over 400m in height. A combination of rainfall and erosion has created a series of deep caves, some in excess of 200m in depth. There are reportedly 42 caves. Only 19 of them have been explored, so Barra Honda is of special interest to speleologists looking for something new.

The caves come complete with stalagmites, stalactites, and a host of beautiful and (to the nonspeleologist) lesser-known formations with intriguing names such as fried eggs, organs, soda straws, popcorn, curtains, columns, pearls, flowers, and shark's teeth. Cave creatures, including bats, sightless salamanders, fish in the streams running through the caves, and a variety of invertebrates, live in the underground system. Pre-Columbian human skeletons have also been discovered, although who these people were and how they got into the caves remain a mystery.

A few of the caves have access to the public. The 62m-deep Terciopelo Cave is one of the most beautiful and frequently visited (though don't worry, there are no terciopelos here). Visitors may be required to get permits from the Servicio de Parques Nacionales to enter some of the other caves. These include Santa Ana, the deepest, at 249m; the Trampa ('trap'), 110m deep with a vertical 52m drop; the Nicoya, where human remains were found; and the Pozo Hediondo ('stinkpot'), which has a large bat colony. In all cases, a guide is required (see Proyecto Nacaome, below).

Above the ground, the Barra Honda hills have trails and are covered with the deciduous vegetation of a tropical dry forest. The top of Cerro Barra Honda boasts a lookout with a view that takes in the Río Tempisque and Golfo de Nicoya. There are waterfalls (adorned with calcium formations) in the rainy season and animals year-round. Howler and white-faced monkeys, armadillos, and coatimundis are sometimes seen and certainly heard. Striped hog-nosed skunks are supposedly frequently sighted.

Information

The dry season is considered to be the best time for caving because entering the caves is dangerous and discouraged during the rainy months. However, you can come any time to climb the hills, admire the views, and observe the wildlife. If you come in the dry season, however, be sure to carry several liters of water and let someone know where you are going. Two German hikers died at Barra Honda in 1993; they planned a short hike of about 90 minutes and didn't want to hire a local guide. They got lost, had no water, and died of dehydration.

There is a ranger station in the southwest corner of the park where maps and information may be obtained. Park entry is US$6 per day. Near the station is an area with bathrooms and showers where camping is permitted for about US$2 per day. Trails from the ranger station lead to the top of Cerro Barra Honda – allow about half a day for the roundtrip. These trails can be hiked using only a map, but, again, take lots of water and tell the rangers where you are going.

The park is part of the Area de Conservación Tempisque, with administrative headquarters in Nicoya (☎/fax 685-5667, Spanish only). You should obtain permits from this office if you wish to explore the cave system. You can also reserve guides as well.

Proyecto Nacaome

Formerly Proyecto Las Delicias, this locally run project is now administered through the park and provides a basic tourist infrastructure as well as work for local people. At the park entrance it has food, accommodations, and information. Guides from the area come by here daily looking for clients. It has proven to be an excellent way to involve the local population in conserving the area. A visit here is ecotourism at its best grass-roots level.

Three small cabins, each with a shower and six beds, are available for US$5.50 per person. Camping costs US$2 per person. A simple restaurant serves typical local meals for about US$3 each; it's best to arrange meals in advance. A guide service is available for hiking the trails within the park and also for descending into the most popular caves. A descent costs about US$40 for a group of up to eight cavers. This covers the costs of guide and equipment – ladders and ropes are used, and you should be reasonably fit.

To make reservations for accommodations or guide service, call the park office in Nicoya (☎ 685-5667, leave a message in Spanish). Guides are also available from Barra Honda, El Flor, and Corralillo. Only Spanish is spoken by the guides, though a few of the rangers at the park itself speak English and can help with arrangements.

Getting There & Away

Getting to the park is somewhat confusing, because a map shows two ways to enter the park. Barra Honda is shaped like an inverted U; at the east end is the village of Quebrada Honda, with a dirt road leading north from it into the park. This is not the best way to enter the park.

The west arm of the inverted U is the way to the ranger station. If you are driving from the Tempisque ferry, you will see a sign on the right-hand side for 'Barra Honda' about 16km after leaving the ferry and 1.5km before you reach the main peninsula highway between Nicoya and Carmona. If you are driving from the peninsula highway, take the turnoff for the Tempisque ferry and look for the Barra Honda road to your left after 1.5km – there is no sign if you are coming this way. From the turnoff, the road goes 4km to the small community of Nacaome, where a signed dirt road goes a further 6km into the park. The community of Santa Ana is passed en route. This road has some steep and rough stretches, and may require 4WD in the rainy season.

No buses go to the park, but you can get a bus from Nicoya to Santa Ana and walk the last kilometer. Two buses a day leave Nicoya for Santa Ana, at 12:15 pm and 4 pm. The ride costs less than US$1 and takes about 45 minutes, with the return buses leaving Santa Ana at around 1 pm and 6:15 pm. A taxi from Nicoya to the park entrance costs about US$10.

PUERTO HUMO

This little riverside settlement is about 28km northeast of Nicoya, due north of Barra Honda on the Río Tempisque and across the river from Parque Nacional Palo Verde. A dock here is a possible entry point to the park (see Northwestern Costa Rica). This is a remote area that is definitely off the beaten track. Aside from birding and wildlife-spotting opportunities on the river, the road here passes through pretty stretches of rural Guanacaste.

Places to Stay & Eat

There are a couple of options for camping or staying in people's homes. ***Aventuras Arenal*** *(in Fortuna ☎ 479-9133)* has an 'office' here; it will let you camp in a grassy lot near the river dock for about US$2 per person.

Sulma Fonseca lives in a little blue house near the dock and can make meals or find you an inexpensive room in a family home if you call ahead. Leave a message (in Spanish) with her mother, who operates the public phone at the Bar San Gerardo *(☎ 669-0594)*. Sulma's husband, Israel, arranges river tours: US$50 for up to three people, US$11 per person for more than three. Leave a message (in Spanish) for him or Alexander Piñar at ☎ 233-3333. They also sell fresh fish and shrimp. Camping along the river is also a possibility; there are two ***pulperías*** in the village where you can buy groceries.

A few kilometers outside of Puerto Humo is the 1000-hectare, tico-owned ***Rancho Humo*** *(☎ 255-2463, fax 255-3573, ecologic@sol.racsa.co.cr)*. Modern rooms with air-conditioning, private hot-water bathrooms (with bathtubs!), and balconies overlooking Parque Nacional Palo Verde cost US$93 double. The large, circular restaurant offers panoramic views of the river and park; meals cost US$6 to US$10. Horses and bikes and a variety of local tours are available. River tours start at US$35 per person, with discounts increasing with group size; a tour of the park and islands costs US$65 per person. Elderhostel groups make regular visits here, and guests may get to sit in on nature talks. Transport from San José costs US$150 per person by land, US$400 per person by air.

Getting There & Away

If you're driving, the dirt road is in good condition, and there are signs at all the turns (keep your eyes peeled, though); near the river, a couple of spots may require 4WD in the rainy season. There are two daily buses from Nicoya to Puerto Humo, leaving at 10:30 am and 2:45 pm and returning at 6 am and 12:30 pm.

TEMPISQUE FERRY

The car and passenger ferry crossing is 17.5km from the main peninsula road. See the description of the Tempisque ferry in the Northwestern Costa Rica chapter for more details. A bridge is being built near here and will be ready sometime in the early years of the new millennium.

PLAYA NOSARA

This attractive white-sand beach is backed by a pocket of luxuriant vegetation that attracts birds and wildlife. The area has seen little logging, partly because of the nearby wildlife refuge and partly because of real-estate development – an unlikely-sounding combination.

There are many houses and condominiums, some of which are lived in year-round, and others that can be rented by the week or month. The permanent occupants are mainly foreign (especially North American) retirees. The expatriate community is interested in protecting some of the forest, which makes Nosara an attractive area to live in, and you can see parrots, toucans, armadillos, and monkeys just a few meters away from the beach. So far, there has been a reasonable balance between developing the area and preserving enough habitat to support wildlife. The residents' association has been winning legal battles to keep out large-scale development. The hotels and other places to stay are spread out along the coast and a little inland, set unobtrusively into the forest and mixed in with private houses, condos, and a cosmopolitan selection of restaurants.

Note that the village and airport of Nosara are 5km inland from the beach. Basic food supplies and gas are available in the village. There are three distinct beaches. The southernmost is Playa Guiones, a long stretch of white sand with corals and the best snorkeling opportunities; Playa Pelada, in the middle, is a small crescent with shady trees and a simple restaurant near which you can camp; Playa Nosara, north of the river and hardest to access, has surf. Thus the Nosara area (three beaches, airport, and village) is very spread out and lacks a real center. There are many unidentified little roads. This makes it hard to get around if you don't know the place – look for signs and ask for local help.

Activities & Organized Tours

Most hotels and cabinas offer tours and rentals. The presence of the nearby Nosara Retreat (see the boxed text) means that yoga and massage are available at many. By the soccer field in the village, the Dutch-run Tuanis (☎ 682-0249) offers the usual rentals and tours, as well as conversation groups for those interested in practicing Spanish and meeting locals, and local crafts.

Places to Stay & Eat

The cheapest accommodations are in the village, inland, or you can camp on the beach. The basic but clean ***Cabinas Chorotega*** *(☎ 680-0836)* has a pleasant courtyard balcony and rooms with fans for about US$5 per person, US$7 with private shower. The owners are friendly. A bit closer to the village

The Nosara Retreat

Unique in Costa Rica, the ***Nosara Retreat*** is a health and yoga center housed in a sparkling white hilltop villa overlooking the ocean. Spiritual and physical rejuvenation are the goals of the retreat directors, who have many years of experience in holistic health. Dr Don Stapleton is a director of the renowned Kripalu Center in Massachusetts, where he has developed many of the programs. His wife, Amba Camp, has taught at Kripalu for years and has also developed an exclusive clientele in Hollywood. Together, they opened the Nosara Retreat a couple of years ago and offer personalized and professionally supervised programs in a vibrant and friendly setting. Their young son lives at the retreat, and families are welcome.

Activities at the retreat include Hatha yoga classes from beginner to advanced levels, breathing and meditation classes, massage (including their trademarked Yogassage therapy, which combines yoga, acupressure, and massage), reflexology, communication skills training, fasting and detoxification programs, and nutritional counseling. Guests are also encouraged to swim, watch wildlife, surf, and enjoy the beach on foot or horseback.

The villa houses 10 guests in five comfortable double rooms, all with private baths, fans, and view balconies. There is a swimming pool and a VCR room that is stocked with videos (Hollywood as well as yoga programs). The daily rate is US$250 per person in a shared room and US$350 in a private room; a two-night minimum is required. Reservations are needed. All meals are included and are healthy, nutritious, and tasty. Daily yoga instruction and use of beach equipment is included in the base rate, and various other activities are added according to individual wishes. Six-day/five-night Wellness Adventure Plans are offered and can be customized. The Nosara Retreat was a recommended outfitter in the 1995 *Condé Nast Traveler* Ecotourism Award.

If you are driving, follow the blue frog symbols to the retreat. If you are flying, they will pick you up from the Nosara airport. Further information is available from the Nosara Retreat *(☎/fax 682-0071, fax 682-0072; in the USA ☎ 888-803-0580, yogacr@sol.racsa.co.cr).*

– Rob Rachowiecki

center is the roomier but less cared-for ***Cabinas Agnel***, at US$4.50 per person. ***Sodita Vannessa***, on the main road by the public phone, is locally popular. There are other sodas and restaurants around the soccer field.

A five-minute walk from Playa Guiones, ***Olas Grandes*** *(☎ 682-0080)* is a surf lodge with spacious, clean octagonal bungalows. Each is split into two cabins sharing a hot-water bathroom, for US$15/25/30 single/double/triple. Mountain bikes, body boards, and snorkels rent for US$8 per day, kayaks for US$16. ***Josy's*** is the restaurant here, open for breakfast and lunch. Josy makes great omelettes and fruit crepes. In the same price range are ***Alan's Surf House*** and ***Rancho Conga***, just off the main road between Playas Guiones and Pelada. Between the beaches and the village, ***Casa Rio*** *(☎ 682-0117, fax 682-0182, casarionosara@nosara.com)*, run by Tony and Beatrice Kast, has rustic, pleasant bungalows by the river for about US$15 per person. The Kasts are friendly hosts and organize all kinds of tours, on water and horseback. Readers have written to recommend them. Breakfast is available.

High on a hill overlooking Playa Pelada, ***Almost Paradise*** *(☎ 682-0172, fax 682-0173, almost@nosara.com)* has six pleasant rooms with private baths. A balcony gives fine ocean views, and there is a good restaurant. Rates are US$25/30 single/double, US$5 for breakfast.

A few minutes' walk from Playa Pelada is the reasonably priced and recommended

Rancho Suizo Lodge *(☎/fax 682-0057, fax 682-0055, Apartado 14, Bocas de Nosara, Guanacaste 5233)*. Run by René and Ruth, a friendly Swiss couple, the lodge provides 11 pleasant bungalows with private baths and fans for US$35/45 single/double and three larger, newer units for US$57 double. There is a small pool, whirlpool, and restaurant (make advance reservations for dinner), and horse rental and tours (eg, turtle-watching in season or as far afield as Volcán Arenal) can be arranged on request. A 'Pirate Bar' has been installed near the beach where you can barbecue, and they also have a camping area.

The Italian/Swiss-run ***Estancia Nosara*** *(☎/fax 682-0178, Apartado 37, Nosara, Guanacaste)* is about 1km away from the beach at the south end of the Nosara area. Rooms with refrigerators, kitchenettes, private electric showers, and fans cost in the US$50s double and in the US$60s quadruple. There is a pool and plenty of trees; rentals and tours are available. In the same price range, the ***Lagarta Lodge*** *(☎ 682-0035, fax 682-0135, lagarta@sol.racsa.co.cr)* is high on a steep hill above the private Reserva Biológica Nosara and offers stunning views over the estuary, reserve, and beach. Trails lead directly from the lodge through the reserve down to the river; guided tours of the reserve cost US$5. Birding is good here. The Swiss manager, Rene, and his Costa Rican wife, Nieves, are friendly, knowledgeable hosts, and their hilltop bar and restaurant is worth a sunset visit.

Air-conditioned rooms in the US$50 to US$80 range are offered at the ***Hotel Villas Taype*** *(☎ 682-0188, fax 682-0187)*, with a large pool and plenty of activities available.

The ***Hotel Playas Nosara*** *(☎ 682-0121, fax 682-0122, Apartado 4, Nosara, Guanacaste)*, with its incomplete minaret-like tower, is the most unusual and most visible of Nosara's hotels. On an attractive hilltop between Playas Pelada and Guiones, this hotel has been here for 20 years and has a *1001 Nights* feel – fanciful and apparently eternally under construction. The balconied rooms offer beautiful beach views. There is a restaurant and pool. The North American owners speak many languages and will help with organizing local tours. Rooms have private baths with hot water and fans and cost in the US$50s double, US$10 less for unheated showers.

The ***Condominio Los Flores*** *(☎ 680-0696)* is perched on a hill overlooking the beach and rents two-bedroom apartments with kitchens and hot water. Expect to pay about US$500 per week. Owners Terry and Ed Kornbluh are longtime members of the residents' alliance.

Down beside Playa Guiones, ***Casa Romantica*** *(☎/fax 682-0019, casaroma@sol.racsa.co.cr)* is a private home converted into a small hotel. Swiss owners Rolf Sommer and Angela Schmidt run the place with professionalism and grace. Their restaurant is popular with local residents, and the poolside garden and bar are a nice respite from the beach, which is a short walk away. Spacious modern rooms cost about US$56/67/87 single/double/triple. Nearby, the ***Casa Tucan*** *(☎/fax 682-0113, casatucan@nosara.com)* has four theme-decorated studio apartments (from 'jungle' to 'Victorian') with kitchenettes and living rooms for US$40/60 single/double. Owners Richard and Nancy Moffat are Californians who vacationed here for years before realizing their dream of settling. They organize sportfishing trips, and their popular restaurant (open daily, except Monday, for all meals) often serves the catch of the day. Farther south, back out on the main road, the ***Café de Paris*** *(☎ 682-0087, fax 682-0089, cafedeparis@nosara.com)* is a hotel, restaurant, and bakery. You can have a good meal followed by an espresso or drink at the bar, and they'll let you take a dip in the pool. New bungalow-style rooms with ceiling fans and private hot showers start at US$29/39 single/double.

The ***Gilded Iguana Bar & Restaurant*** *(☎ 682-0259)* has been recommended for its famous Black Panther cocktail and good sandwiches and snacks; from the main road, follow the signs to Olas Grandes. It has rooms with kitchenettes for rent in the US$50s. ***La Dolce Vita*** is an upscale Italian restaurant open for dinner only, Tuesday to Sunday. Down on Playa Pelada, grab a casado for just US$3 at the popular tico-owned ***Olga's Bar & Restaurant***, or get a fish dinner for about US$6. Olga passed away recently, but the restaurant is still run by her family.

Getting There & Away

Air SANSA has flights from San José to Nosara daily except Sunday. Flights leave at 7:30 am and continue to Sámara before returning to San José. One-way/roundtrip fares are US$55/110. Schedules and fares change often, and advance reservations are recommended.

Bus There is a daily bus from Nicoya's main bus terminal at 1 pm, returning to Nicoya at 6 am. The journey lasts about 2-½ hours, but it can take much longer depending on road conditions. There is a daily bus (about six hours) from San José with Empresa Alfaro (☎ 222-2750, 222-2666), Calle 14, Avenidas 3 & 5, at 6 am, returning from Nosara at 12:45 pm.

Car The 35km dirt road from Nosara to Nicoya (via Guastomatal) is a poor one – locals say it is passable only to 4WD vehicles, and there are no signs. Most people take the longer paved road from Nicoya toward Playa Sámara. You turn off about 5km before Sámara (there's a sign). The last 27km to Nosara has many sudden dips and washboarded areas, and there may be rivers to ford, especially in the wet season – but this is the way the bus comes. You may have some difficulty getting through in an ordinary car during the rainy season. It is also possible to continue north, past Ostional, to Paraíso and Junquillal, though you will have to ford some small rivers and will need 4WD in the rainy season.

REFUGIO NACIONAL DE FAUNA SILVESTRE OSTIONAL

This coastal refuge includes the beaches of Playa Nosara and Playa Ostional, the mouth of the Río Nosara, and the beachside village of Ostional.

The reserve is a narrow strip about 8km long but only a few hundred meters wide. The protected land area is 162 hectares; 587 hectares of adjoining sea are also protected.

The main attraction and reason for the creation of the refuge is the annual nesting of the olive ridley sea turtle on Playa Ostional. This beach and Playa Nancite in Parque Nacional Santa Rosa are the most important nesting grounds for the olive ridley in Costa Rica (see Parque Nacional Santa Rosa in the Northwestern Costa Rica chapter for more information). The nesting season lasts from July to November, and August to October are peak months.

The turtles tend to arrive in large groups of hundreds or even thousands – these mass arrivals, or *arribadas*, occur every three or four weeks and last for about a week, usually on the dark nights preceding a new moon.

However, you can see turtles in lesser numbers almost any night you go during the nesting season. Villagers will guide you to the best places.

Coastal residents used to harvest both eggs and turtles indiscriminately, and this made the creation of a protected area essential for the continued well-being of the turtles. An imaginative conservation plan has allowed the inhabitants of Ostional to continue to harvest the eggs from early layings. Most turtles return to the beach several times to lay new clutches, and earlier eggs may be trampled or damaged by later layings. Thus, it seems reasonable to allow the locals to harvest the first batches and sell them – they are popular snacks in bars throughout the country.

The leatherback and Pacific green turtle also nest here in smaller numbers. Apart from the turtles, there are iguanas, crabs, howler monkeys, coatis, and many birds. Some of the best birding is at the southeast end of the refuge, near the mouth of the Río Nosara, where there is a small mangrove swamp.

The rocky Punta India at the northwest end of the refuge has many tide pools abounding with marine creatures such as sea anemones, sea urchins, starfish, shellfish, and fish-fish. Along the beach are thousands of almost transparent ghost crabs, bright red Sally Lightfoot crabs, and a variety of lizards. The vegetation behind the beach is sparse and consists mainly of deciduous trees such as frangipani and stands of cacti.

The rainy season lasts from May to December, and the annual rainfall is about

2000mm. The best time to see the turtles is the rainy season, so be prepared. The average daytime temperature is 28°C. There is a Universidad de Costa Rica research station, and the villagers of Ostional are helpful with information and will guide you to the best areas. There have been some clashes between the villagers and the research station in recent years, but tensions may be resolved by the time you visit.

Ostional has a small pulpería where you can get basic food supplies. Beware of very strong currents off the beach – it is not suitable for swimming.

Places to Stay

Camping is permitted, but there are no camping facilities. The ***Hospedaje Guacamaya***, next to the Ostional pulpería, advertises a few rooms with air-conditioning for about US$4 per person with bath. It is usually full during the best turtle-nesting nights. The nearby ***Cabinas Ostional*** has clean, basic rooms in a pleasant family backyard for US$4 per person. Neither has a phone, but you can try calling the public phone at the pulpería (☎ 682-0267) and leaving a message.

Getting There & Away

The refuge begins at Playa Nosara, and Ostional village is about 8km northwest of Nosara village. This unpaved road is passable, but some minor rivers need to be forded, and 4WD is necessary in the wet season. From the road joining Nosara beach and village, turn north just before the Supermercado La Paloma. After 0.4km, take the right fork and continue another 0.4km, across a new bridge over the Río Nosara. After the bridge, there is a T-junction; take the right fork and continue another 1.2km to a T-junction where you take the left fork. From here, continue on the main road north to Ostional, about 5.5km away. The road from Santa Cruz to just before Paraíso and south along the coast to Ostional is in similar condition – passable to an ordinary car in the dry season, but with some small rivers to ford; in the rainy season 4WD is necessary. The rivers have firm bottoms; walk across to find the shallowest route, then roar through in low gear.

During the dry months, there are two daily buses from Santa Cruz – these may or may not run during the wet season, depending on road conditions. Hitchhiking from Nosara is reportedly easy. Many of the better hotels in the region offer tours to Ostional during egg-laying periods.

BAHÍA GARZA

This small bay is about 10km south of Nosara along a dirt road. A beach is picturesquely set in a rocky cove with an island at the mouth of the bay.

There is one good hotel, the ***Villagio La Guaria Morada*** (*☎ 680-0784, 233-2476, fax 222-4073, Apartado 860-1007, Centro Colón, San José*). There are 30 pleasant cottages, each with private bath, renting for US$130 double including breakfast and dinner. There is a good restaurant, pool, and disco, and horseback riding, fishing, and snorkeling can be arranged. A reader writes that recent renovations have damaged watercourses leading to the ocean.

PLAYA SÁMARA

This beach is 16km southeast of Bahía Garza and about 35km southwest of Nicoya. Sámara has a beautiful, gentle, white-sand beach that has been called one of the safest and prettiest in Costa Rica. It has gained much popularity in recent years. Former president Oscar Arias has a vacation house near here, as do many other wealthy ticos. It is also a favorite beach for tourists and has good bus and air service. One drawback is the relative lack of forest, which means there is less wildlife and shade than at other Nicoya beaches.

The village has a few stores and discos and several hotels, restaurants, and bars. Things are a little spread out – ask for directions to places away from the center. Local inhabitants (other than retirees) do a little farming and fishing.

Playa Sámara is still a fairly tranquil place, but development has picked up since the paved road arrived in early 1996. There is a fair amount of construction going on in the

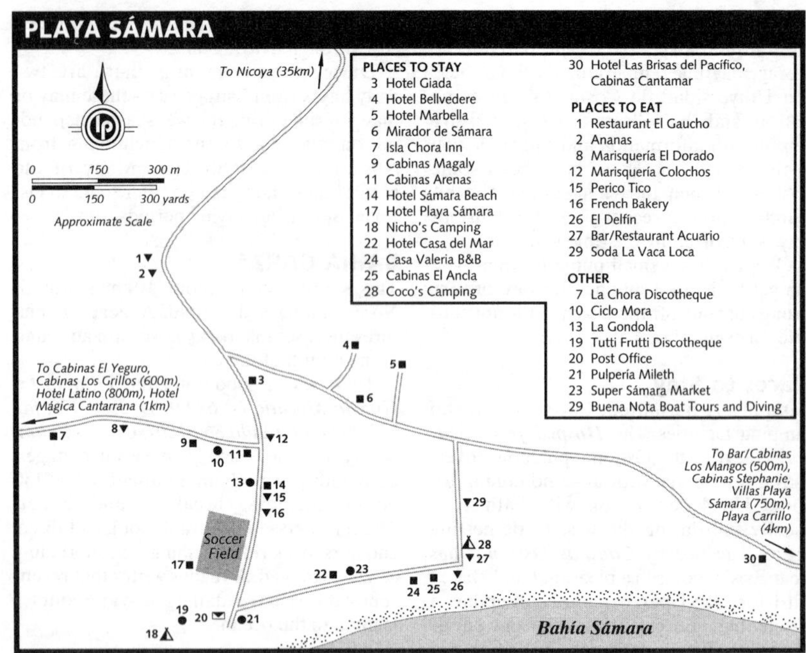

village center, and new places will continue to open.

Activities & Organized Tours

Captain Rick Ruhlow, a well-known local skipper, has a boat for sportfishing here. Ask at any hotel to get in touch with him. Captain Rob Gordon (☎ 656-0170) offers his boat, the *Kitty Cat*, for sportfishing. Buena Nota Boat Tours and Diving (☎ 656-0265) also offers diving trips and scuba instruction. Ciclo Mora, about 100m west of Cabinas Arenas, rents bicycles. Horse rentals can be arranged through several of the hotels, as mentioned below. Popos (☎ 656-0086, fax 656-0092), based in Playa Carrillo and run by the friendly Tad Cantrell, offers a variety of exciting, well-orchestrated, and reasonably priced kayak tours, including a few designed especially for families. The Flying Crocodile (☎ 656-0483), several kilometers west along the road to Nosara, offers ultra-light flights.

Places to Stay

Budget Just behind the sign for ***Coco's Camping*** are several places to camp at about US$3 per person; ask around for the best price. ***Nicho's Camping***, behind the Tutti Frutti Discotheque on the beach, is another option.

A popular, cheap, and basic place to stay is the ***Hotel Playa Sámara*** *(☎ 656-0190)*, which charges about US$5.50 per person. It's usually full with tico beachgoers on weekends. This hotel isn't very well maintained, so check to see if the water is working (if you care). There is a cheap but decent soda attached, and the Tutti Frutti Discotheque is nearby. Other cheap and basic places to try are the ***Cabinas Magaly***, which has rooms with shared baths; ***Cabinas Stephanie*** *(☎ 656-0308)*, about 1km southeast of town, which has fridges and kitchens; and ***Bar/Cabinas Los Mangos*** *(☎ 656-0356)*. The latter two are casually managed and don't have firm prices in mind – bargain.

Entrepreneurial surfer types occasionally rent a house and put up a sign offering cheap rooms. New places are opening, so definitely ask around – ***Cabinas El Yeguro*** *(☎ 656-0196)* and ***Cabinas Los Grillos***, about 600m west of the village center, look like they'll be worth a try. ***Cabinas El Ancla*** *(☎ 656-0254)* has simple, clean rooms by the beach for US$7.50 per person. There is a restaurant and cheerful bar.

Mid-Range ***Cabinas Arenas*** has 12 basic but adequate rooms with private baths and fans for about US$30 double – they'll give you the room for US$15 single if there is space.

In a quiet, shady spot at the eastern end of the beach, ***Cabinas Cantamar*** *(☎ 656-0284)* has three simple wooden cabins of varying size that sleep two for US$25 to US$35. Each room is decorated with owner Jamie Koss' vivid, peaceful paintings. In the village, the ***Casa Valeria B&B*** *(☎ 656-0511, fax 656-0317)* has a grove of trees and hammocks by the beach. Clean rooms with private hot showers cost US$15/25 single/double, and a communal kitchen is available.

One of the nicest places in this price range, on the main road down to the beach, is the friendly, Italian-owned ***Hotel Giada*** *(☎ 656-0132, fax 656-0131)*, with plants and bamboo giving it a tropical feel. It has 13 large and pleasant rooms, all with balconies or patios, private hot baths, and fans. Rates are US$35/53/61/73 for one/two/three/four people, including breakfast. A pool and Jacuzzi have been added. The hotel can arrange horse rental and all local tours and has bar and laundry service and tourist information. The SANSA agent has an office in the lobby.

The ***Hotel Casa del Mar*** *(☎ 656-0264, fax 656-0129)* is next to the Super Sámara grocery store close to the beach and has spacious, very clean, pleasant rooms with fans. Some have private bathrooms; others share. Rates are in the US$30 to US$60 range.

The ***Hotel Bellvedere*** *(☎/fax 656-0213)* is in a breezy garden with nice views. Three rooms, all with private hot baths, fans, and access to a small terrace, go for US$20/30 single/double, including breakfast. One room is rather bigger than the others. Nearby, the Czech-run ***Hotel Marbella*** *(☎/fax 656-0122)* offers simple rooms with private hot showers and fans for US$25 single or double. There is a pool, restaurant, and bar, and tours and horse rental can be arranged. Also near here is the ***Mirador de Sámara*** *(☎ 656-0044, fax 656-0046, mdsamara@sol.racsa.co.cr)*, built on a hill and with a tall white-and-blue tower that is a prominent landmark. It's a great place to eat breakfast or hang out with a beer in the afternoon and watch for monkeys. There are six good-size apartments with airy high ceilings, private hot showers, fans, and equipped kitchens. They sleep up to five people, and high-season rates are about US$70 double, US$93 for four to five people. The owner, Max Gerd Mahlich, who speaks German and English, will take guests on car tours anywhere they want to go.

The ***Hotel Sámara Beach*** *(☎ 656-0218)* has air-conditioned rooms with private baths, hot water, and balconies for about US$60 double, US$10 less with fan; a breakfast is included. It has a small pool, nice grounds, and a restaurant.

A couple of new hotels, nice in themselves, have opened along the dusty (in dry season) rural road west of the center. The ***Hotel Latino*** *(☎/fax 656-0043)* is 300m from the beach and has spacious rooms with two double beds, fans, and private hot showers for US$30/40 single/double, US$10 for each additional person. Breakfast is included. The Swiss-run ***Hotel Mágica Cantarrana*** *(☎ 656-0071, fax 656-0260, magica@sol.racsa.co.cr)* is a small, modern complex built around a pool. Rooms with private baths cost US$25/52 single/double; apartments of varying sizes are also available. There is a restaurant.

Top End At the west end of town is the attractive ***Isla Chora Inn*** *(☎ 656-0174, fax 656-0173, hechombo@sol.racsa.co.cr)*, which is the best hotel in town. It has spacious and light rooms in five two-story buildings around a large central pool, and four apartments. The rooms each have private balconies or patios, large modern bathrooms with hot water, fans, two queen-size beds, and free safety deposit boxes. Eight rooms have air-conditioning. High-season rates are US$85 single or double, US$10 each for additional people up to four. The apartments have fans and air-conditioning, kitchenettes, large balconies with breakfast areas, bedrooms with queen-size beds, and sitting rooms with two futons opening into queen-size beds. Rates are US$150 for up to four people, US$160/170 for five/six people. There is a good Italian restaurant that has a three-meals-a-day plan for US$25, or you can eat à la carte. Also, there's a genuine Italian ice-cream parlor (they imported the ice-cream maker and make their own – it's delicious). During high-season weekends, there is a discotheque and occasional live bands, and pool aerobics and Latin American dance lessons may be offered. All year long, the usual local activities and tours are quickly arranged.

The ***Hotel Las Brisas del Pacífico*** *(☎ 656-0250, fax 656-0076, labrisa@sol.racsa.co.cr)* has a pool, spa, and good restaurant with a German chef. The hotel has a gift shop and horses, boats, surfboards, and diving gear are available for rent. Comfortable and spacious rooms, all with private hot showers, cost US$70 to US$110 double, depending on whether you want air-conditioning and how big the room is. A third person can be added for US$17, but single rates are difficult to get during the dry season.

A little over a kilometer southeast of the village center is the ***Villas Playa Sámara*** *(htlvilla@sol.racsa.co.cr)*, which has a guard at the gate and aerobics by the pool. Its 73 rooms and villas are spread out in a huge resort complex that offers many amenities but doesn't seem in keeping with the small-hotel feel of this beach. The units are large and attractive but lack air-conditioning – this supposedly attracts European rather than North American visitors. The rate for a bedroom is US$113 double, and villas for two/four/six people cost US$148/219/284.

Places to Eat

Budget travelers can find reasonably cheap meals at the ***Soda La Vaca Loca***. Campers can stock up on supplies at the ***Pulpería Mileth*** or ***Super Sámara*** market. There are also cheap eateries on the beach.

El Delfín is a new beachfront restaurant that is quite romantic at night. It specializes in gourmet pizzas, but all its food is good. ***Perico Tico*** is a creperie and restaurant that serves French and Costa Rican meals and is open late.

For seafood, the ***Marisquería Colochos*** is a long-time and reasonably priced favorite. It's getting a run for its money from ***Marisquería El Dorado***. Both are good. On the coast, ***Bar/Restaurant Acuario*** has cheap seafood and a lively collection of cassettes to keep you entertained. Up on the hill as you enter town is ***Restaurant El Gaucho***, with more meaty dishes. Next door, ***Ananas***, for a dessert or antidote, offers fruit shakes.

Some hotels also have good restaurants, especially the one at ***Isla Chora Inn***, which serves Italian food.

Entertainment

La Gondola is a fun nightspot, with pool, darts, Ping-Pong, and an unlikely mural of Venice. The ***Tutti Frutti Discotheque*** operates most weekends of the year. ***La Chora Discotheque***, in the Isla Chora Inn, operates during high-season weekends and is classier.

Getting There & Away

Air The airport is between Playa Sámara and Playa Carrillo (actually a bit closer to the latter) and serves both communities. Sometimes the airport is referred to as Carrillo. The SANSA agent is at the Hotel Giada.

SANSA has flights from San José via Nosara daily, except Sunday. Travelair has daily flights, also stopping at Punta Islita. The one-way/roundtrip fare is US$55/110 with SANSA and US$89/145 with Travelair.

Bus Empresa Alfaro (☎ 656-0269; in San José 222-2750, 222-2666) has a daily bus to Sámara at noon (six hours), continuing on to Playa Carrillo and costing US$6. The bus returns to San José (starting from Carrillo) at 4:30 am, 1 pm on Sunday.

Buses from Nicoya leave at 10 am and 12:30, 3, and 5 pm, take about two hours, and cost US$1.25. The returns are at 5:30, 6:30, and 11:30 am and 1:30 pm. On weekends, buses leave at 4 pm, and during the wet season there may be only one bus a day. The 3 pm bus from Nicoya continues to Playa Carrillo; this service may expand, so ask. In Playa Sámara, get bus information and tickets at Pulpería Mileth.

PLAYA CARRILLO

This beach begins 3 or 4km southeast of Sámara and is a smaller, quieter version of it. With its curving boulevard of palm trees, clean sand, and rocky headlands, Carrillo is a postcard-perfect tropical beach. Over holiday periods like New Year and Easter, the beach has traditionally been popular with ticos. A recent prohibition on camping has cut down on the number of visitors and is a source of some controversy – some complain that big developers are trying to restrict the beach to the well-off. The signs are still up but are sometimes ignored. The two beaches are separated by the narrow Punta Indio and thus are almost, but not quite, contiguous.

Places to Stay & Eat

Just off the beach, ***Victorio's*** offers basic camping facilities. At the southern end of the beach, cheap rooms are sometimes available at the ***Bar Restaurant Chala***, which has a hilltop view of the bay. Nearby, ***Casa Pericos*** *(☎/fax 656-0061)* has double rooms with ocean views, private baths, and fans for US$24. Dormitory beds cost US$9 per person; there is a large, pleasant verandah, living room, and communal kitchen. You can also camp here. The owners are friendly, speak German and English, and offer scuba courses. There are a couple of other unsigned places in this area that sometimes offer cheap cabins – ask around. Farther up the hill, off the main road, ***Cabinas El Tucan*** *(☎ 656-0305)* has clean, bamboo-bedecked rooms sleeping up to four people for US$22, including breakfast. It has a ***pizzeria***, and the staff will drive you down to the beach or airport.

The ***Hotel Sunset*** calls itself 'an ecological beach resort' and is up a hill inland from the beach. There are nice views, a pool, and a few air-conditioned rooms for about US$80 in the high season (half that in the low).

The most famous place is the 41-room, Japanese-run ***Guanamar*** *(☎ 656-0054, fax 656-0001; in San José ☎ 239-2000, fax 239-2405, hherradu@sol.racsa.co.cr)*. It is attractively located at the south end of the beach on a cliff with good views and ocean breezes. There is a pool, casino, and restaurant. Air-conditioned rooms with balconies and ocean view, TVs, telephones, carpeting, and private baths cost US$109 double; without ocean views, US$98. Suites cost US$170. Horses, mountain bikes, snorkeling gear, body boards, and sea kayaks are available for rent. Water-skiing is also available. Sportfishing, however, is the big and most expensive attraction.

Downhill from the hotel are a couple of restaurants. ***El Mirador*** is an OK place with good views of the bay; ***Restaurant El Yate*** serves good, inexpensive seafood – seabass in garlic costs US$4. A reader reports that ***Manolo*** serves good paella.

About a kilometer southeast of Playa Carrillo, ***El Suño Tropical*** *(☎ 656-0151, fax 656-0152, suetrop@sol.racsa.co.cr)* has pleasant bungalows with private baths and patios for US$44/50 single/double, US$10 more for air-conditioning. There are two pools and an Italian restaurant.

Getting There & Away

See under Playa Sámara, above.

ISLITA & BEYOND

It is possible to continue southeast beyond Playa Carrillo, more or less paralleling the coast, to reach the southern tip of the peninsula. Although Punta Islita is less than 10km by road southeast of Playa Carrillo, the road is so bad that when a small luxury resort opened near there in the mid-1990s, Travelair began stopping at the small Punta Islita airstrip en route to Sámara and Nosara. The coast southeast of Playa Carrillo remains the most isolated stretch in the peninsula. There are various small communities and deserted beaches along this stretch of coast, but accommodations and public transport are minimal.

Places to Stay & Eat

You can camp in many places (usually without facilities) if you have a vehicle and are self-sufficient. Otherwise, the few hotels are described heading southeast from Playa Carrillo.

The hilltop ***Hotel Punta Islita*** *(☎ 231-6122, 296-5787, fax 296-0715; in the USA ☎ 800-525-4800, ptaisl@sol.racsa.co.cr)* offers about two dozen rooms and suites overlooking Playa Islita. One guidebook sticks its neck out and suggests this is Guanacaste's best hotel – without going that far, it's clearly not too shabby. It has a fine restaurant, beautiful rooms, and a lovely pool and spa. You can rent equipment for snorkeling, mountain biking, tennis, boating, fishing, etc. Rates start at about US$150 for rooms and go up to about US$500 for suites.

Playa San Miguel has an unnamed ***beach hotel*** where very basic cabins rent for about US$4 per person. A bar/restaurant is attached. This is typical along the coast. A more attractive option by this beach is the ***Blue Pelican*** *(☎ 233-6421)*, run by multilingual Frank Teixeira. Romantic doubles (canopy beds) cost US$25, with fans and private baths. Simpler rooms sleeping up to five cost US$25. Frank cooks delicious local and international food and boasts the coldest beer in this remote area. A pool is on the way; kayaks and horses rent for US$5 per hour.

Inland from the beach is the ***Hotel Arca de Nue*** *(☎/fax 656-0065, arcanoe@sol.racsa.co.cr)*, a pleasant complex with a pool and bar. Attractive doubles cost US$45. Horses and kayaks can be rented.

In San Francisco de Coyote (☎ 671-1236 public phone), a small village 4km inland from Playa Coyote, are a couple of sodas and pulperías. The friendly folk at ***Soda Familiar*** offer clean cabinas sleeping up to four people for US$11 and horse rental for US$3 per hour. The family-run ***Rancho Loma Clara*** is similarly priced. Both places prepare simple country meals. The ***Centro Social Los Amigos*** offers beer and pool.

About 300m from Playa Coyote is the ***Bar/Cabinas Veranera***, which offers cheap accommodations.

Getting There & Away

Air Travelair flies to Punta Islita from San José daily. The one-way/roundtrip fare is US$93/151.

Bus Arsa (☎ 257-1835) has a daily bus that crosses the Golfo de Nicoya on the Puntarenas ferry and continues through the villages of Jicaral, San Francisco de Coyote, and on to Playa San Miguel and Bejuco. The bus leaves San José at 6 am and 3 pm, passing through San Francisco de Coyote at 11:30 am and 10 pm and arriving at Playa San Miguel at noon and 10:30 pm. The return bus leaves Bejuco at 2 am and 12:30 pm, passing through Playa San Miguel at 2:30 am and 1 pm, San Francisco de Coyote at 3 am and 2 pm. This service may not run in the rainy season.

There don't seem to be buses from Nicoya, or any other bus services going south along this coast between Playa Coyote and Mal País. Mal País can be reached via Cóbano (see Mal País, later).

Car It is about 70km by very rough road from Playa Carrillo to the town of Cóbano – allow about four hours for the trip if you have a 4WD vehicle and encounter no delays. Several rivers have to be forded, including the Río Ora about 5km east of Carrillo. This river can be impassable at high tide, even to 4WDs, so check the tides and water levels. If you time it right and are ready for adventurous driving, you can make it in an ordinary car in dry season.

A slightly easier route, if you are driving, is to head inland from Playa Carrillo through the communities of San Pedro, Soledad (also known as Cangrejal), and Bejuco and down to the coast at either Islita (to the northwest) or Jabilla (to the southeast). This loop takes about 18km and is very steep in places – a regular car can just make it in the dry season, but you'll probably need 4WD in the wet.

Adventurous drivers with 4WD (or maybe a regular car in the dry season) can continue on past Playa Coyote, Playa Caletas, Playa Arío, and Playa Manzanillo (camp at any of these places if you are self-sufficient) before heading inland via Río Negro to get to Cóbano, Mal País, Montezuma, and Cabo Blanco. There are several rivers to be crossed in this stretch as well. Be prepared to get lost and to ask directions frequently. These last three places are usually reached by the road that connects with the Puntarenas-to-Playa Naranjo ferry and follows the southeastern part of the peninsula; they are described below.

SOUTHEAST CORNER

From Nicoya, buses go southeast through Jicaral and Lepanto to the car ferry terminal of Playa Naranjo, about a 72km drive. From Jicaral, you can get buses to Playas Coyote and San Miguel (see above). Otherwise, to travel beyond Playa Naranjo into the southern part of the peninsula, you need your own transportation – all buses either end at the car ferry or cross over to Puntarenas. In fact, Playa Naranjo and the southern end of the peninsula are part of the province of Puntarenas, even though it looks as if this area should belong to the province of Guanacaste, as does the north and central part of the peninsula described thus far in the chapter. If you want to go farther south from Playa Naranjo and don't have your own car, cross the Golfo de Nicoya on the car ferry to Puntarenas and then recross the gulf on the Puntarenas-Paquera passenger ferry. Buses go from Paquera farther south.

Jicaral and **Lepanto** are two villages of note on the Nicoya-Playa Naranjo run. There are a couple of cheap and basic places to stay in Jicaral. There are 4WD taxis available to take you anywhere you want to go.

Near Lepanto, salt pans are visible from the road. This is a good place to stop and look for waders – you may see roseate spoonbills here, among others.

PLAYA NARANJO

This tiny village is the terminal for the Puntarenas car ferry. The beach is not very exciting. Most ferry passengers continue on to Nicoya by bus or drive farther south into the Península de Nicoya. Several hotels offer lodging for those waiting for a ferry, though they also offer plenty of activities if you just feel like spending a few days.

Places to Stay & Eat

The ***Hotel Del Paso*** *(formerly the Hotel Deyekų; ☎ 661-2610, fax 223-0140)* has clean rooms with air-conditioning and TVs for US$38 double. There is a pool, plenty of hammocks, and a good restaurant serving fresh seafood. Boat and horse excursions are arranged.

The ***Hotel Oasis del Pacífico*** *(☎/fax 661-1555, Apartado 200-5400, Puntarenas)* has adults' and children's pools, pleasant grounds, volleyball, tennis, and horses and boats for rent. Sportfishing is available. The owner, a Floridian named Lucky, is a sailor who has an Unlimited Masters License and welcomes yachting visitors, who can call him on the radio at VHF channel 22A. He has mooring in front of the hotel for US$5 a day, giving access to all the hotel facilities, including showers. The restaurant is good and not too expensive. Food and decor have an Asian touch from Lucky's wife, Aggie, who is from Singapore. The 36 rooms with fans and private baths have hammocks in their patios and rent for about US$50/60 single/double in the high season. Lucky has put the hotel up for sale, so things may change by the time you visit.

Reportedly, there are a couple of other smaller places in the area. There are several simple restaurants and sodas near the ferry boat dock.

Getting There & Away

All transport is geared to the arrival and departure of the ferry. The hotels pick up ferry passengers if they know you are coming – although you could walk, as it's not far.

Buses meet the ferry and take passengers to Nicoya, three to four hours away. There are no other public transport options except for 4WD taxis, which can take you to Paquera for about US$25.

The ferry (☎ 661-1069 for information) leaves Playa Naranjo daily at 5:10 and 8:50 am and 12:50, 5, and 9 pm, and the crossing to Puntarenas takes 90 minutes. (These times have changed often and some crossings may be canceled in the rainy season, so plan accordingly.) Fares are about US$10 for car and driver, US$1.50 for adults, US75¢ for children, and US$2.50 for bicycles and motorbikes. Note that on most buses using the ferry, passengers have to get off the bus to buy a separate ticket – don't dally in the nearby sodas, as the bus may leave without you! If you are driving, you may need to show up a couple of hours early during holiday periods.

The road from Playa Naranjo to Paquera is in very poor shape (4WD may be essential in the rainy season), but it improves beyond Paquera.

BAHÍA GIGANTE

This bay is about 9km southeast of Playa Naranjo.

The good ***Rancho Bahía Gigante*** *(☎/fax 661-2442)* has pleasant views of the bay and large forested grounds where you can hike and watch wildlife. Monkeys and other mammals can be seen, and there are plenty of birds and butterflies. There's a marina, and sportfishing, sea kayaking, and other boat trips to the nearby islands are available. Diving can be arranged. Tours by horseback to a nearby waterfall are also offered. There is a restaurant and pool. Ten spacious rooms with fans and private baths cost about US$50 double; there are also a few more expensive condo apartments. Staff will pick you up at Playa Naranjo.

The ***Bahía Luminosa Resort*** *(☎ 381-2296, 288-2292, bahia-luminosa@getawaynow.com)* is on a little hill overlooking the beach. The French owners offer a variety of sailing and boating excursions, including diving, fishing, and multinight charters. They have anchorage for visiting yachters, who can radio them on VHF channel 16. Water-skiing, windsurfing, and snorkeling are other activities here. There's a large pool, restaurant, and bar, and the 14 rooms have private hot baths and a choice of fans or air-conditioning. The rate is US$35 per person. There is also a two-bedroom house with a kitchenette for about US$150.

You can also stay at Isla Gitana (see below).

ISLANDS NEAR BAHÍA GIGANTE

The waters in and around Bahía Gigante are studded with islands, 10 large enough to be mapped on the 1:200,000 map, and many smaller little rocks and islets. In fact, this area packs in more islands than anywhere on Costa Rica's coasts, and they attract a variety of sightseers and boat traffic.

The biggest of these islands is the 600-hectare **Isla San Lucas**, which is about 4km northeast of Bahía Gigante and 5km west of Puntarenas. The island used to be a prison and had a reputation of being the roughest jail in Costa Rica. The prison was closed in 1992, and now tourists can visit the island (see Organized Tours, below) and see the largely overgrown remains of the prison cells, some of which are over 100 years old.

A few hundred meters off the coast, **Isla Gitana** (shown on most maps as Isla Muertos because of the Indian burials found here) is smack in the middle of Bahía Gigante. The almost 10-hectare island is a sort of rustic resort, with trails through the forest, a nice beach, and a saltwater pool. There is a small ***lodge*** *(☎/fax 661-2994)* here with a couple of simple cabins for about US$50 per person including meals, or less if you cook for yourself. Cabins are cooled by sea breezes and sleep up to six – no luxuries. The ramshackle ***restaurant/bar*** on the beach attracts the occasional boater, and the owners have various boats and kayaks, snorkeling gear, and windsurfers available for guests. This is an unusual place where you can get away from it all. Remember to bring lots of spare batteries for your flashlight. Call for information and reservations and to arrange pickup from Puntarenas (US$50), Paquera (US$15), or Bahía Gigante. If you can't get through, call the Rancho Bahía Gigante (see above), which can pass on a message via radio.

Isla Guayabo and **Islas Negritos** are well-known seabird sanctuaries but, for the protection of the birds, no land visitors are allowed except researchers with permission from the Servicio de Parques Nacional. The reserves can be visited by boat, however, and you can observe many of the seabirds from the boats. The Paquera ferry is the cheapest way to get fairly close, and the Isla Tortuga trips and chartered boats are another way to go.

Isla Guayabo is a 6.8-hectare cliff-bound rocky islet about 3km east of Punta Gigante (at the north end of Bahía Gigante). There is very little vegetation. Costa Rica's largest nesting colony of brown pelicans (200 to 300 birds) is found here, and the peregrine falcon overwinters on the island. The Islas Negritos are two islands 10km southeast of Bahía Gigante and just a few hundred meters east of the easternmost point of the peninsula. They have a combined size of 80 hectares and are covered with more vegetation than Guayabo. Frangipani, gumbo limbo, and spiny cedar have been reported as the dominant trees. Both Guayabo and the Negritos have colonies of magnificent frigatebirds and brown boobies.

The best-known island in the area is **Isla Tortuga**, which is actually two uninhabited islands about 5km southwest of Islas Negritos. There are beautiful beaches for snorkeling and swimming. The islands can be reached by daily boat tours from Puntarenas (see below).

Organized Tours

The most well-known tour goes to Isla Tortuga. This was pioneered in 1975 by the yacht *Calypso* (see Calypso Tours under Organized Tours in the Getting Around chapter), which has built up a reputation for excellence in food and service and has many repeat customers. Calypso Tours has added the luxurious 70-foot motor catamaran *Manta Ray* to its fleet. This air-conditioned boat is built for fun and speed – there are even a couple of outdoor Jacuzzis, as well as an underwater viewing window. Onboard freshwater showers are available as well.

The *Manta Ray* does tours to Isla Tortuga from San José. They cost US$99 per person (US$94 from Puntarenas) and include a dawn departure from San José, a private bus to Puntarenas with a continental breakfast, boat trip to the islands, delicious (with no exaggeration) four-course picnic lunch and cocktails on the beach, plenty of time for swimming, snorkeling, and sunbathing, and transport back to San José, returning around 8 pm. The two island biological reserves of Guayabo and Negritos are passed en route, with opportunities to see the bird colonies from the boat.

This is undoubtedly a classy trip, and several other companies also do the trip (though none have a boat as sophisticated as the *Manta Ray*), which has led to some complaints that Isla Tortuga is getting a little more crowded than it was in earlier years. Other options include various local hotels and tour operators (see Montezuma, later in this chapter) in the southern Península de Nicoya. Better hotels in Puntarenas and San José and travel agents in San José can make reservations on this cruise for you. Go midweek to avoid the crowds. Canopy Tours (see Organized Tours in the Getting Around chapter) has opened one of its adventurous canopy platform and ropes tours on Isla Tortuga.

Partly in response to the competition, *Calypso* now does a tour that stops at the prison island of San Lucas, cruises by the various wildlife islands, and lands at Punta Coral, a private beach at the easternmost point in the peninsula. Guided nature walks, swimming, snorkeling, and sea kayaking are offered, along with the usual superb lunch. This full-day tour departs San José on Wednesdays and Sundays. Also, it offers a night cruise through these islands aboard the *Manta Ray* every Friday, accompanied by a professional astronomer. A landfall is made for a barbecue dinner, and a telescope is set up for stargazing.

PAQUERA

It is about 25km by road from Playa Naranjo to the village of Paquera, which is 4km from the Paquera ferry terminal. Most travelers pass straight through on their way to or from Montezuma – perhaps that is a good reason to stop here for a night and meet some locals for a change. There is a Banco de Costa Rica.

Places to Stay & Eat

There are a couple of cheap hotels in the village of Paquera. The ***Cabinas and Restaurant Ginana*** (*☎ 641-0119*) is considered the best, with rooms with private showers and fans renting for about US$7/11 and a decent restaurant. The ***Cabinas Jardín*** (*☎ 641-0003*) has rooms with private baths and fans for US$20 double, US$10 more for air-conditioning.

Getting There & Away

Boat The passenger ferries (☎ 661-2830) leave Puntarenas for Paquera at 6 and 11 am and 3:15 pm and return from Paquera to Puntarenas at 7:30 am and 12:30 and 5 pm daily. The fare is US$1.50 for adults, US$1.20 for motorbikes, and US90¢ for bicycles and children. Crossing time is about 90 minutes.

Naviera Tambor (☎ 661-2084) has car ferries from Puntarenas at 5 am and 12:30 and 5 pm. They return at 8 am and 2:30 and 8:30 pm. The fare is about US$10.50 for car and driver and US$1 for extra adults. There is a 1st-class lounge that costs about US$2 per person extra. Children under 12 pay half fare. Another car ferry, charging the same fares, leaves from the same dock in Puntarenas at 8:45 am and 2 and 8:15 pm, returning at 6 and 11:15 am and 6 pm.

Bus, Car & Taxi A very crowded truck takes passengers into Paquera village. Most travelers take the bus from the ferry terminal to Montezuma (two hours, US$2.25). Some ferries may not be met by buses; ask at the terminal. The bus can be crowded; try to get off the ferry early to get a seat.

Parts of the road from Paquera to Montezuma have been paved, though much remains unpaved. Work has been slowly progressing on this road. During the wet season, this bus may stop in Cóbano, 6km short of Montezuma, and you can continue by 4WD (about US$5). This road is being improved, however, and this might not be a problem by the time you get there. A 4WD taxi from Paquera to Montezuma costs about US$30; taxis usually meet the ferry.

There are no northbound buses. A 4WD taxi to Playa Naranjo costs about US$25.

REFUGIO NACIONAL DE VIDA SILVESTRE CURÚ

This small 84-hectare refuge is at the eastern end of the Península de Nicoya, about 5km south of Paquera village. Despite its small size, a great variety of habitats exists here. There are deciduous and semi-deciduous forests with large forest trees, mangrove swamps with five different mangrove species, sand beaches fringed by palm trees, and rocky headlands. The forested areas are the haunts of deer, monkeys, agoutis, and pacas, and three species of cats have been recorded. Iguanas, crabs, lobsters, chitons, shellfish, sea turtles, and other marine creatures are found on the beaches and in the tide pools. The snorkeling and swimming are good. Birders have recorded about 200 species of birds, but there are probably more. For such a small place, it has a lot of wildlife.

An intriguing feature of this national wildlife refuge is that it is privately owned. The owners, Señora Julieta Schutz and children (☎ 661-2392), can provide tours, very rustic accommodations, and simple home-cooked meals when arranged in advance. However, the Schutzs also run a working ranch and are often busy. Most of the better hotels in the area will arrange guided day tours to Curú. The reserve is not signed and is down a dirt road (as is everything in this area). Call in advance if you want to visit without a guide to get directions, and to make sure the gate is open.

PLAYAS POCHOTE & TAMBOR

These two long beaches are protected by Bahía Ballena (Whale Bay), the largest bay on the southern peninsula coastline. The beaches begin 14km south of Paquera at the tiny community of Pochote in the north, and stretch for about 8km to the village of Tambor – they are divided by the narrow and wadable estuary of the Río Pánica. The calm beaches are safe for swimming, and whales are sometimes sighted in the bay.

There are a few fairly cheap places to stay, mainly in the village of Tambor or at Playa Pochote. There are also three luxury hotels, and more are planned.

Places to Stay

Budget At the south end of the bay, in the village of Tambor, is the ***Hotel Dos Lagartos*** *(☎/fax 683-0236)*. It is clean and friendly and has beach views and a restaurant. A few rooms with private baths and fans cost in the US$20s double; most rooms have shared bathrooms and cost about US$10 less. Tours can be arranged to nearby areas. The ***Cabinas Tambor Beach*** *(☎ 683-0057)* has cabins sleeping up to four people for US$30. There is a campsite halfway between Tambor and the Bahía Ballena Yacht Club (see

PENÍNSULA DE NICOYA

Places to Eat), which has basic cold showers and charges about US$2.50 per person.

At Playa Pochote, ***Zorba's Place*** has rooms on the beach at US$18 double or US$28 double with private bath. There are fans, breakfast is included, and there is a restaurant with meals for about US$5 to US$10. There's not much else in the immediate vicinity – the owner says that Erich von Daniken has stayed here for weeks while writing his books.

Top End Right in the middle of the Bahía Ballena shoreline is the ***Hotel Playa Tambor*** (☎ *683-0303, fax 683-0304, tambor@sol.racsa.co.cr*), which, with over 400 guest rooms, is by far the largest hotel in the country. It is like a Club Med, with all activities (and there are many) and food covered in one price of about US$200 double. It is also the most controversial hotel in the history of tourism in Costa Rica; see the related boxed text, 'Clamor in Tambor.'

Tango Mar Resort (☎ *683-0002, fax 683-0003; in San José* ☎ *289-9328, reservations@tangomar.com; in North America* ☎ *800-648-1136*) is 3km south of Tambor village. This is an attractive, romantic, and secluded beachfront resort and country club with a pool, 10-hole golf course, lighted tennis courts, and first-class restaurant where guests are offered a complimentary after-dinner cigar. The club is built on 50 hectares of property and has some primary forest left. Tours are available, and you can rent 4WDs, horses, boats, and fishing and diving gear. It has spacious oceanfront rooms with two queen-size beds, air-conditioning, fans, satellite TVs, mini-bars, large hot-water showers, and picture-window balconies with access to the beach. Two honeymoon suites are similar but have king-size beds and whirlpool bathtubs. Cliffside king suites are bigger and have Jacuzzis. There's also a Presidential Villa with a kitchen, family room, private pool, and four bedroom suites, each with private terrace and sound system. This is a luxury resort and prices are commensurate – approximately US$200 double in the high season. Nonguests can play golf for US$35.

Clamor in Tambor

Grupo Barceló, the Spanish owners of Hotel Playa Tambor, were sued in 1992 for a long series of environmental violations during construction. The claims in these suits included illegally filling in a swamp, taking massive amounts of sand off beaches and gravel from rivers (causing serious erosion), improperly treating sewage, and harassing passersby on the beach. (By law, the first 50m of all Costa Rican beaches are public property and available to everyone.) Some workers have complained of inadequate health care and safety rules – two employees have died in accidents in questionable circumstances.

The Costa Rican Supreme Court ordered the project halted in April 1992, and, in September 1992, the Minister of Tourism ordered Grupo Barceló to stop building within the 50m zone because, they said, necessary permits for the project had not all been obtained. Despite these restraining orders and alleged violations, the project proceeded as planned and opened in November 1992. This led to criticism of the (then) government for their perceived inability to enforce the law and also led to boycotts of the hotel by tourism operators who felt that the highly touted 'environmentally sensitive ecotourism' image of Costa Rica was being destroyed. Some European groups even called for a boycott of all tourism in Costa Rica until the environmental and social impact of the hotel has been studied and the problems addressed.

As of 1999, most of these issues remain unresolved. Grupo Barceló has been fined (US$9000 – a tiny sum in proportion to the amounts spent on and earned by the hotel) for the unambiguously illegal act of destroying a mangrove swamp. However, the 1992 suit is still in the courts and the hotel is still in operation.

– Rob Rachowiecki

The newest resort is ***Tambor Tropical*** *(☎ 683-0011, fax 683-0013; in the USA ☎ 503-365-2872, fax 503-371-2471, info@tambor .tropical.com)*, which has 10 spacious rooms in five split-level cabins on the beach. Each room has a queen-size bed, a fully equipped kitchen, fans, a verandah, and a large hot-water bathroom. There is a pool, Jacuzzi, restaurant, and open-air bar. Guided horseback riding, snorkeling, parasailing, water-skiing and Jet Skiing, windsurfing, boating, diving, and fishing trips are available at extra cost. The swimming off the beach in front of the cabins is safe. Year-round rates are US$148 double in lower rooms and US$177 in upper rooms, including breakfast. Children under 16 are not allowed.

Places to Eat

Nearby are several places to eat, of which ***Scruffy's*** is considered the best (and priciest), serving international food. ***Salsa*** is a coffee shop that is good for breakfast, and you can also eat at the reasonably priced ***Cristinas Restaurant*** or ***Carlos's Restaurant***. You can get supplies at ***Pulpería de Los Gitanos***; next door is ***Los Gitanos Bar/Restaurant***. There are also some beachfront sodas. About 1km south is the ***Bahía Ballena Yacht Club***, which has a restaurant and bar and provides mooring facilities, boat rentals, water-taxi services, and scuba diving. See also ***Zorba's Place*** in Places to Stay.

Getting There & Away

The airport is just north of the entrance to Hotel Playa Tambor. SANSA has daily flights from and to San José; the fare is US$45 each way. Travelair has daily flights from San José for US$76/122. There may be fewer departures in the low season.

The Paquera-Montezuma buses pass through here. A taxi to Montezuma reportedly is more expensive from here than from Paquera.

CÓBANO

This small inland town is the most important community in the far south of the Península de Nicoya, though most people go on to Montezuma. There is a Banco Nacional (☎ 642-0210), gas/service station (☎ 642-0072), clinic (☎ 642-0208), shops, and other services.

There are a few cheap sodas and basic pensiones, including ***Cabinas Grelmar*** and ***Hotel Caoba***. Both have restaurants. ***Cabinas Villa Grace***, on the way out of the village toward Montezuma, looks a bit nicer than these two.

The Paquera-Montezuma bus comes through here. A 4WD taxi to Montezuma costs US$5.

MONTEZUMA

This little village near the tip of the Península de Nicoya has beautiful beaches, friendly residents, and plenty of hotels. It wasn't always like this, though.

Once a very remote fishing village, Montezuma gained popularity in the 1980s and early 1990s with younger gringo travelers who enjoyed both the beautiful surroundings and the laid-back atmosphere. Accommodations were very cheap, and it became a party beach on the Costa Rican part of the gringo trail. In fact, there now seem to be more gringos than locals in town (which one reader described as 'Gringolandia'). Some of the more remote beaches to the north attract nude sunbathers, a custom that is not much appreciated by most of the local people, except, perhaps, some of the young machos who enjoy a leer.

Montezuma's popularity inevitably led to an increase in room rates, and there are many more mid-priced options than before, though there are no very expensive resorts. Also, reports began to surface of undesirable characters, drug abuse, and litter spoiling the area.

The locals were aware of the problems and began working to resolve them. Most of the hotels banded together to form a chamber of commerce called CATUMA (Cámara de Turismo en Montezuma). CATUMA organizes weekly beach clean-ups, has placed litter barrels in appropriate places, improved the water supply and other services, planted trees, discouraged undesirable elements, and educated Montezumeños about the importance of preserving their surroundings. They are making every effort to avoid the overdevelopment so much criticized in the Manuel Antonio and Tambor areas, and it appears that they are succeeding.

Montezuma remains one of the most popular destinations on the coast, and many people like to stay for at least several days (which is a good way to get beyond the hippie-frat-party aspect of the place) to enjoy not only the beaches and village, but also the nearby nature reserves and various activities. Readers fall into two groups: those who absolutely love the place, and those who claim that there are too many tourists. If you want a remote little coastal village to get away from other travelers, this is not the place for you.

Information

Monte Aventuras (☎/fax 642-0025) provides international faxing, phone, and email. It can arrange some tours. The most comprehensive tour agency in town is Rodel Tours/Nicoya Expeditions (☎/fax 642-0467). El Sano Banano (see Places to Eat, below) is a good source of local information and contacts.

There are no banks, but you can change your US cash or traveler's checks at Monte Aventuras. You might also be able to change

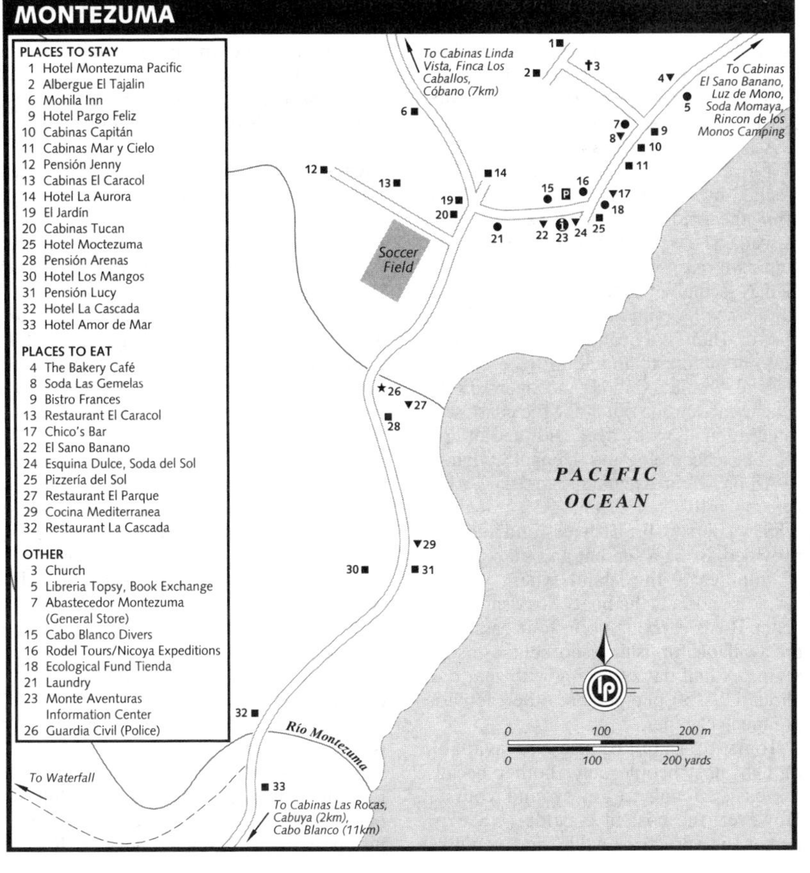

US cash at either Chico's or El Sano Banano restaurants – if they have enough colones available. There is a laundry and book exchange (see the Montezuma map for location details).

It's a small town, and parking can be a problem. There is a parking lot in the center that charges US$2.50 per day.

Activities & Organized Tours

Ask at the tour agencies listed above or your hotel about the following. Bicycle rentals cost US$15, motorbikes go for around US$40, and a 4WD Suzuki jeep costs about US$75, all per day. A half-day horseback ride runs about US$25. Several readers have recommended Roger Rojas for local guided horseback rides. Snorkeling gear and body boards cost about US$5 per day, and a variety of tours with snorkeling opportunities are offered, starting at US$35.

A 20-minute stroll to the south takes you to a lovely waterfall with a swimming hole, reached by taking the trail to the right just after the bridge past the Restaurant La Cascada. The waterfall can be climbed, but at your own risk – visitors have fallen here and died. A second set of falls, which some visitors consider to be even prettier, is found farther upriver. There is a beautiful nature reserve a few kilometers to the south (see Reserva Natural Absoluta Cabo Blanco, later). Lovely beaches are strung out along the coast, separated by small rocky headlands and offering great beachcombing and tidepool studying.

All-day boat excursions to Isla Tortuga (see Islands Near Bahía Gigante) cost US$35 a person. Fruit, snacks, and juices are provided. Bring a sun hat and sunblock. It's 90 minutes to the island, where you can swim or snorkel (the boats carry snorkeling gear). Boats carrying up to four passengers are available for fishing, snorkeling, or sightseeing. A half day of fishing with gear costs about US$150 per person; other activities are much cheaper.

Tours to Cabo Blanco are available, though most people don't bother because it's easy enough to get around yourself. However, the cost of a guide (US$5 per person) is very reasonable, and you'll see more. Tours to other destinations may be offered if there is enough demand – lunch is often not included, so bring your own and plenty of drinking water as well.

Places to Stay – Montezuma

The high season (from December to April) occasionally gets crowded, and reservations aren't a bad idea on weekends, though you'll certainly find something even if you just show up. If you arrive on a Friday afternoon, though, don't expect much choice! Take whatever you can get. If you arrive midweek, first thing in the morning, you may need to wait a couple of hours for people to leave to catch the afternoon ferry for rooms to become available. As usual, low-season discounts are common, especially in the higher-priced places – high-season prices follow. Note that most hotels are small: most have about a dozen rooms or fewer.

Budget Single travelers might have a hard time finding a cheap room during the high season, as most places want to charge for a double or even triple. The cheapest places have had some thefts reported, so keep your stuff locked up.

Camping in town itself is locally discouraged. A short walk north along the beach is ***Rincon de los Monos Camping*** (next to the hip Soda Momaya; see Places to Eat, below), which has showers, lockers, laundry, darts, and Ping-Pong. It charges about US$3.

Pensión Jenny is in a quiet location on a hill above the soccer field and has a view of the sea from the common porch. Rooms are basic but clean, and a fair deal for US$5.50 per person in dormitory rooms (four bunk beds) or US$11 for double rooms. All bathrooms are shared. Nearby, ***Cabinas El Caracol*** *(☎ 642-0194)* has bare but large rooms with communal baths for US$6 per person; rooms with private baths cost US$16 double. A cheap restaurant is attached, though one reader reports being grossly overcharged here.

The ***Mohila Inn*** *(☎ 642-0030)*, run by the friendly Gonzalo, is on a quiet, lush hillside on the way into the village. Look for a path just past the ICE telephone sign. Rooms cost about US$10 per person with shared bathroom and communal kitchen.

The ***Pensión Lucy*** *(☎ 642-0273)* charges only US$6/11 for airy rooms with shared showers. The hotel has verandahs overlooking the ocean, and the upper rooms get cooling sea breezes. ***Cabinas Tucan*** *(☎ 642-0284)* has decent little rooms for US$8/13 single/double with communal cold showers. ***Pensión Arenas*** *(☎ 642-0306)* is similarly priced but has rooms with private showers and is in a good location right on the beach. A family-run restaurant is attached.

The ***Hotel Moctezuma*** *(☎ 642-0258, fax 642-0058)* is right in the center and has a restaurant and popular bar with music. Light sleepers should bring earplugs if they plan on an early night. With over two dozen rooms, this is a good place for budget travelers with no reservations to try. Clean, large rooms with fans and private bathrooms cost US$12/18 single/double, or US$8/11 in a few rooms with shared baths. Single rates are hard to get in the high season. Some triples and quads are available.

Cabinas Capitán *(☎ 642-0069)* has basic but clean rooms with fans for US$10 single (shared showers) or US$15 double with private cold showers. The ***Cabinas Mar y Cielo*** *(☎ 642-0036, 642-0261)* is also clean, and charges about US$25 to US$30 for two to six people in rooms with private baths and fans. The upstairs rooms are breezy with nice views.

The ***Hotel Pargo Feliz*** *(☎ 642-0065)* is next to a recommended restaurant and also has well-kept rooms with fans and private baths for about US$25 double.

Mid-Range The recommended ***Hotel La Aurora*** *(☎ 642-0051, fax 642-0025)* is a pleasant-looking vine-covered mansion up on the hill as you come into town. About eight clean but simple rooms with fans and mosquito nets cost US$25 to US$30 double, some with private cold baths. There are homey touches like a kitchen, free coffee and tea, a library, and nice areas to hang out in. This is one of Montezuma's first hotels and has been here for about 20 years under the same management (though different names). They have a good local reputation for recycling and being involved in environmental issues.

One of the newest places is ***Albergue El Tajalin*** *(☎ 642-0061, fax 642-0527)*, which has nice clean rooms with fans and private hot baths for US$18/31, and rooms with air-conditioning and TVs for US$30/45. The owners speak English, Spanish, and Italian. Almost next door, the quiet ***Hotel Montezuma Pacific*** *(☎ 642-0204)* has decent air-conditioned rooms with private hot-water bathrooms for US$30/40 single/double, or less with fans. Some rooms have balconies, and breakfast is included. Near the entrance of town, ***El Jardín*** *(☎ 642-0074)* has six cabins with private baths and fans for about US$40 double, or US$50 with hot water. There are nice ocean views.

Hotel La Cascada *(☎ 642-0057)* recently opened next to the restaurant of the same name. Clean rooms with fans, private cold baths, and ocean views cost US$36 double, though the owner will lower rates substantially (he said by over half!) in the low season. It's in a nice location by the river en route to the waterfalls.

The ***Hotel Los Mangos*** *(☎/fax 642-0076)* is a lovely place with a good restaurant and Montezuma's first (and, as of this writing, only) swimming pool. The hotel has rooms in the main building and bungalows in the spacious grounds, which are filled with – you guessed it – mango trees. Fairly big hotel rooms with fans cost US$30 double with shared showers, or US$48 with private bath and cold water. The wooden bungalows are cozy, with a thatched roof, verandah with hammocks, chairs, ocean views, and private hot showers. Rates are US$72 double.

At the south end of town is the quiet ***Hotel Amor de Mar*** *(☎/fax 642-0262, shoebox@sol.racsa.co.cr)*, which has pleasant grounds and a beautiful shorefront with a tidepool big enough to swim in. A 2nd-floor balcony area overlooks the sea. There is a restaurant that serves breakfast and, in the high season, lunch. Good rooms with fans and shared cold bath cost US$30 double, US$55 for rooms with private hot baths sleeping up to three people.

The folks who run ***El Sano Banano*** restaurant *(☎/fax 642-0068, elbanano@sol.racsa.co.cr)* have pleasant and quiet bungalows next to a pretty beach about 15 minutes' walk north of town (you can't drive there). The buildings are intriguingly shaped polygons or geodesic domes, all with private baths, fans, coffeemakers, fridges, porches, and sea views. Some have kitchen facilities. Three rooms cost US$53 double, seven larger bungalows cost US$71 double, and an apartment costs US$90 double. Four of the bungalows have kitchenettes, and the apartment has a full kitchen. Some of the rooms and bungalows sleep up to four people, and the apartment sleeps up to eight. Extra adults pay US$5 per person, and children stay free.

Places to Stay – Around Montezuma

A budget option is the ***Cabinas Linda Vista*** *(☎ 642-0274)*, about 1.5km out of town toward Cóbano. It is clean and basic with, yes, good views.

About 3km north of town, just off the road to Cóbano, is ***Finca Los Caballos*** *(☎/fax 642-0047)*. Caballos is Spanish for 'horses,' and the Canadian owner prides herself on having the best-looked-after horses in the area. Apart from horse rentals, they do bike rentals, arrange tours, and have a swimming pool. Eight pleasant rooms with private baths and patios cost about US$40 double, and a nice restaurant is on the premises.

About 2.5km south on the road to Cabuya is ***Cabinas Las Rocas*** *(☎ 642-0393)*, in a tranquil spot near rocky tidepools. Rooms with shared bath cost US$15/20 single/double. One-bedroom apartments with private baths and kitchens cost US$45. Discounts are made for longer stays. The mellow Swiss owner will pick you up in Montezuma if you call ahead.

Places to Eat

Chico's Bar is the traditional place to go for a beer and a simple meal. These days it's also a popular place for a beer, with loud music till about 11 pm (a town rule to allow folks to sleep!). A number of other places have opened in recent years – they cater to tourists and may charge 23% tax on top of the bill: if you are on a budget, ask. Some places close down or have limited hours during the rainy months.

Cheap places that recently didn't add tax include the typical ***Soda La Gemelas*** and ***Restaurant El Parque***. You can get a fish casado at these places for about US$3.50, perhaps a little less with chicken, or around US$5 for a fish dinner. They don't sell alcohol, but you can bring your own. These places offer the best budget values and are very popular with young travelers – you should go by about 6 pm for the best choice of food and tables. ***Restaurant El Caracol***, situated in the cabins of the same name, is similarly priced. ***Soda del Sol*** serves North American as well as typical Costa Rican meals and is reasonably priced. Next door, ***Esquina Dulce*** is a good place for dessert. ***Soda Momaya***, north along the beach, is popular among travelers and has good cheap food; on Thursday night there's Indian cuisine.

Other places that serve decent meals but are a little more expensive include the ***Bistro Frances***, which serves large portions of good French food; ***Restaurant La Cascada***, which is a quiet and pleasant place next to a stream; and the popular restaurant/bar in the ***Hotel Moctezuma***. Next door to the Moctezuma is the inexpensive ***Pizzería del Sol***, which serves pizzas whole or by the slice.

The well-known and popular ***El Sano Banano*** *(☎/fax 642-0068)* serves yogurt, juices, fruit salads, and sane bananas (*sano* actually means healthy, but 'sane' seems like a better translation!) as well as full vegetarian and seafood meals and pizzas. It shows movies every night (US$2.50 minimum consumption). It will also prepare picnic lunches for day tours. The owners are actively involved in community and environmental affairs and are a good source of information on the area.

The Bakery Café has a nice little verandah and good coffee and pastries. Farther along the same road is one of the newest places, with an elegant outdoor ambience: ***Luz de Mono*** offers a 'calendar of flavors' – theme cooking from Italian to Thai nights. There is live music some nights. ***Cocina Mediterranea***

offers excellent northern Italian and seafood dinners for around US$7.

Entertainment

Soda Momaya, north along the beach, has music and is the current hip spot to hang out. There may be live music at ***Luz de Mono***, and there is talk of a new disco opening; ask around. Otherwise, take in a 7:30 pm movie at ***El Sano Banano*** and go on to ***Chico's Bar*** for a beer.

Shopping

The Ecological Fund Tienda sells miscellaneous items ranging from condoms to postage stamps, and 5% of the proceeds go toward keeping the beaches clean. Nearby are several souvenir shops and street stands.

To make your own picnic lunches, buy supplies at the Abastecedor Montezuma. Some gringos report getting overcharged in the Montezuma stores; this may not be true, but it never hurts to stay alert and use your Spanish.

Getting There & Away

The ferries from Puntarenas connect with the Paquera-Montezuma bus. Buses leave Montezuma for Paquera at 8:15 am, noon, and 4 pm to connect with the ferries to Puntarenas. This schedule may change; be sure to ask locally. The fare is US$2.50 (US50¢ as far as Cóbano). During the rainy season, the section to Cóbano may be impassable to 2WD vehicles. A jeep taxi between Cóbano and Montezuma costs US$5.

A 4WD taxi from Montezuma to Paquera costs about US$30, to Cabo Blanco about US$14.50, and to Mal País about US$20, though there aren't many taxis around.

MAL PAÍS

This small village is on the west coast of the peninsula, about 4km north of Cabo Blanco, in an area that is more and more popular with surfers. Two or 3km north, next to the attractive Playa Santa Teresa, is a tiny community nicknamed Santa Teresita. The road from Cóbano reaches the beach road between the two communities, with Mal País to the south (left). The Mal País end of the beach is rockier, emptier, and good for tidepool exploration; the Santa Teresa end is sandier and better for surfing. Horses can be rented for the 4km down to Cabo Blanco.

Places to Stay & Eat

Frank's Place *(☎ 640-0096)* is at the intersection of the Cóbano road and the beach road and is a central landmark. Frank is a friendly local tico who has become a pillar of the surfing community. There is a popular restaurant here and an information booth with helpful maps of the area and 24-hour photo developing. A small store (cold beer!) will sometimes change US cash and traveler's checks. Nice cabinas cost US$8 per person with shared bath, US$10 with private. If you walk straight to the beach from Frank's, you'll find many surfers camping and the ***Mambo Café***, which serves veggie burgers and smoothies (when there's ice). It has a shady verandah and a bamboo rack where surfboards are stacked like horses tied up at a saloon. A flyer board advertises the many temporary services a surfer community generates – massage, grocery delivery, photos of you surfing...

The following are all along the beach road south of Frank's, toward Mal País. The ***Mal País Surf Camp & Resort*** *(☎/fax 640-0061)* has accommodations for a variety of budgets on 20 lush acres. This is a friendly, well-built place; its restaurant/bar is good and, with its pool and Ping-Pong table, is a popular hangout. It has bungalow rooms starting at US$25/35 for two/four people and a campground. Surfboard repairs and rentals, horseback riding, satellite TV, and surf videos are all available. The beachfront ***Cabinas Atardecer*** is a good budget option and allows camping. Near here is a ***shoreside soda*** that serves good local and North American breakfasts (strong coffee!). ***Cabinas Bosque Mar*** *(☎ 640-0074)* has big rooms with private hot showers for US$25/28 and some rooms with kitchenettes for a few dollars more. There's a good Italian restaurant here. The friendly, tico-owned ***Cabinas Mar Azul*** *(☎ 640-0075)* overlooks a picturesque rocky headland and has a restaurant and bar. Decent cabins cost US$15/20/25 single/double/triple. Just before the road to Cabuya, ***Mary's*** is a locally owned café serving good pizza. In the village itself are a few sodas; ask around about camping.

The ***Star Mountain Eco Resort*** *(☎/fax 642-0024, info@starmountaineco.com)* is off the rough road between Mal País and Cabuya, about a kilometer from the beach road, alongside the Cabo Blanco reserve boundary. This small resort was built without cutting down trees, on areas that had been previously logged, and the forest around is full of birds and monkeys. With its pool, Jacuzzi, and verandah restaurant, this is a tranquil retreat from the beach. A pretty row of four hillside rooms cost US$45/65 single/double, and a less expensive family room with bunk beds is available.

The following are north of Frank's, toward Playa Santa Teresa. ***Tropico Latino Lodge*** *(☎/fax 642-0062, tropico@centralamerica.com)*, run by a friendly surfer who can still remember life in England, has a large pool and Jacuzzi next to the beach. Thatched bungalows have king-size beds, fans, private hot-water bathrooms, and patios with hammocks. Tours can be arranged. The rate is US$60 double. ***Rancho Itáuna*** *(☎ 640-0095)* has four rooms in two octagonal towers, each with a double bed, bunk bed, private heated shower, and fridge for US$50. The restaurant serves Brazilian food and prides itself on its music selection. ***Cabinas and Restaurant Santa Teresa*** *(☎ 640-0137)* has a sherbet-colored row of clean cabins sleeping four for US$18. ***Cecilia's B&B*** *(☎ 640-0115)*, run by French-Canadians, has a few simple, clean doubles near the beach for US$45. ***Milarepa*** *(☎ 640-0023, milarepa@mail.ticonet.co.cr)* is an upscale beachfront development with spacious bungalows in a simple, safari-elegance style for US$90 double.

A reader reports the existence at Punta Cuevas of the ***Sunset Reef Marine Lodge*** *(☎ 640-0012, sunreef@sol.racsa.co.cr)*, with doubles for about US$90.

Getting There & Away

From Cóbano, there are buses at 10:30 am and 2:30 pm Monday to Saturday and 11 am on Sunday. From Mal País, there are buses to Cóbano at 7 am and noon Monday to Saturday and 8 am on Sunday. The fare is US$1.50. A taxi from Cóbano costs US$15.

CABUYA

This tiny village is about 9km south of Montezuma and 2km north of Cabo Blanco. An interesting feature is the local cemetery, which is on Isla Cabuya, just to the southeast. The cemetery can be reached only at low tides because the (otherwise uninhabited) island is cut off from the mainland at high tide.

The ***Ancla de Oro*** *(☎/fax 642-0369)* restaurant and cabinas is one of the original places to stay here. There are simple thatched-roof huts in a pleasant garden and rooms in the house. You can stay here for US$10 or less per person, depending on the room. A cabin equipped with a kitchen costs US$30 double. The restaurant serves decent seafood, and the owners arrange local boat, horse, and vehicle tours to various local sites of interest. You can rent a horse for about US$20 a day.

There are three cabins with baths and fans at ***Cabinas Yugo*** *(☎/fax 642-0303)*. The rate is about US$20 double. Cheaper rooms are available at the rustic ***Cabinas Cabo Blanco*** *(☎/fax 642-0025)*, which has a restaurant. Nearby, the ***Hotel Cabo Blanco*** *(☎ 642-0332)* has spacious rooms with private hot baths and TVs for US$25, US$35 with air-conditioning. The ***Hotel Celaje*** *(☎ 642-0374)* has nice air-conditioned rooms, a pool, and a restaurant for US$30/40/50 single/double/triple. More places may open as this village begins to take some of the overflow from Montezuma and to cater to travelers who want to stay closer to the Cabo Blanco reserve.

RESERVA NATURAL ABSOLUTA CABO BLANCO

This beautiful reserve encompasses 1172 hectares of land and 1790 hectares of surrounding ocean and includes the entire southern tip of the Península de Nicoya. The reserve was established in 1963 by the late Karen Morgenson and Olof Wessberg, who donated it to the Costa Rican nation several years before a park system had even been created. Thus, it is the oldest protected area in Costa Rica.

Until the late 1980s, Cabo Blanco was called an 'absolute' nature reserve, because no visitors were permitted. Now there are trails and visits are allowed, but the recent upsurge in the popularity of the Montezuma area has led to greater visitation than expected. Accordingly, park directors have closed the reserve on Mondays and Tuesdays to minimize tourist impact.

Information

Just inside the park, south of Cabuya, is a ranger station (☎/fax 642-0093) where you pay a US$6 entrance fee and can obtain a trail map. The reserve is open 8 am to 4 pm Wednesday through Sunday.

The average annual temperature is about 27°C, and annual rainfall is some 2300mm at the tip of the park. The easiest months for visits are from December to April – the dry season.

Camping is not permitted. No food is available, so bring snacks and plenty of drinking water.

Wildlife Watching

The reserve preserves an evergreen forest, a couple of attractive beaches, and a host of birds and animals. There are several kilometers of trails, which are excellent for wildlife observation. Monkeys, squirrels, sloths, deer, agoutis, and raccoons are among the more common sightings – ocelots and margays have also been recorded, but you'd have to be very lucky to see one of these elusive wild cats. Armadillos, coatis, peccaries, and anteaters are also present.

The coastal area is known as an important nesting site of the brown booby. Some nest on the mainland, but most are found on Isla Cabo Blanco, 1.6km south of the mainland. The island supposedly gains its name ('white cape') from the bird droppings *(guano)* encrusting the rocks. Other seabirds in the area include brown pelicans and magnificent frigatebirds. The beaches at the tip of the peninsula abound with the usual marine life – starfish, sea anemones, sea urchins, conchs, lobsters, crabs, and tropical fish are a few of the things to look for.

Trails & Hiking

A trail (about 4.5km) leads from the ranger station south of Cabuya to the beaches at the tip of the peninsula. The hike takes a couple of hours and passes through lush forest before emerging at the coast – a great opportunity to see many different kinds of birds, ranging from parrots and trogons in the forest to pelicans and boobies on the coast. You can visit two beaches at the peninsula tip and then return by a different trail. The high point of the reserve is 375m, and parts of the trail are steep and strenuous.

Check with the park rangers about trails and tides. The trail joining the two beaches at the tip of the reserve may be impassable at high tide.

Getting There & Away

The reserve is about 11km south of Montezuma by a decent dirt road – though 4WD is needed for the last section in the rainy season. Taxis with 4WD charge US$15 from Montezuma and will carry several passengers; it's normally not a problem to get a group together to share the fare. Nicoya Expeditions (see the entry under Information at the beginning of the Montezuma section) also arranges daily transportation. A bus service from Montezuma may be starting; ask at El Sano Banano (see the entry under Places to Eat, above). Some stalwarts walk or rent a mountain bike from Montezuma. Hitching is reportedly not bad.

Northern Lowlands

The traveler heading north from San José, over the volcanic ridges of the Cordillera Central, soon arrives in the flat tropical lowlands stretching from just 40km north of the capital to the Nicaraguan border and beyond. The northern halves of the provinces of Alajuela and Heredia both contain large tropical plains, called *llanuras*. It is the northern slopes of the central mountains (Cordillera Central) and the two llanuras beyond that are described in this chapter.

The original vegetation of much of the northern lowlands is mixed tropical forest that becomes increasingly evergreen as one heads east to the Caribbean. The climate is generally wet and hot. The dry season is more pronounced in the western part of the northern lowlands, near the slopes of the Cordillera de Guanacaste, but as one moves east toward the Caribbean, the dry season tends to be shorter and not entirely dry. Much of the original vegetation has been destroyed and replaced by pasture for raising cattle, which is the main industry in most of the northern lowlands.

In much of the more remote areas near the Nicaraguan border, especially in the Llanura de los Guatusos and the Llanura de San Carlos, the pastureland floods extensively during the wet season, creating vast swamps and lakes. One such area has been protected in Refugio Nacional de Vida Silvestre Caño Negro – one of the more remote of Costa Rica's national wildlife refuges and parks. Other swamp areas have been utilized for rice cultivation.

The northern lowlands generally have a very low population density, with only a few small towns, mainly rough roads, poor public transport, and relatively little in the way of tourist facilities. A major exception to this is in the northeastern lowlands around the small town of Puerto Viejo de Sarapiquí, which is well served by public buses. Here there are many hotels, and nearby are several tourist lodges and a biological station. The Puerto Viejo area is the destination of most visitors wanting to see some of the northern lowlands.

The Caño Negro area has seen an increase in visitation. Visitors traveling in between Puerto Viejo and popular Volcán Arenal (see the entry in the Northwestern Costa Rica chapter) are starting to discover this area, which now has several hotels, the national wildlife refuge with excellent birding, and a number of small towns that have not yet been much visited by gringos. Los Chiles, which provides the easiest access to the refuge, is often busy midday with tour buses making day trips from the Arenal area, but for the most part the Caño Negro area retains a remote and unvisited feel.

Caño Negro Area

From Muelle de San Carlos, two paved roads head out across the northern lowlands. These are the road northwest to San Rafael and Upala and the road north to Los Chiles. The Caño Negro area is between these two roads.

MUELLE DE SAN CARLOS

This small crossroads village is locally called Muelle, which means 'dock.' It is one of the first places from which the Río San Carlos is navigable. There is a 24-hour gas station at the main highway intersection. Unless you are staying at the comfortable Tilajari Resort Hotel, there's nothing to do here apart from deciding whether you want to go north, south, east, or west. The resort offers a variety of tours; see the entry in Places to Stay & Eat, below, for details.

Places to Stay & Eat

The cheap-looking ***Cabinas Violetas*** is near the middle of the village (almost 2km north of the main road intersection), but most overnight visitors stay at the modern ***Tilajari Resort Hotel*** *(☎ 469-9091, fax 469-9095, info@tilajar.com)*, which is the most

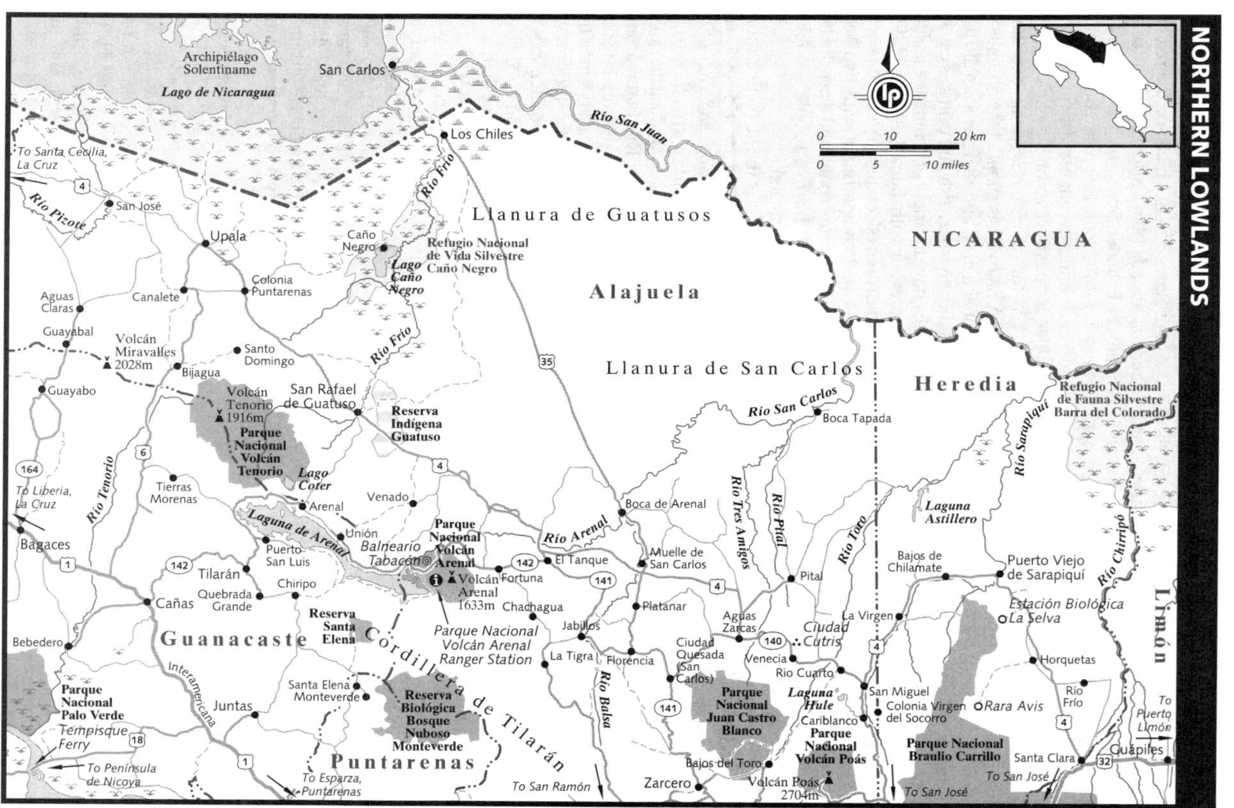
NORTHERN LOWLANDS
NICARAGUA
Heredia
Alajuela
Limón
Guanacaste
Puntarenas
Llanura de Guatusos
Llanura de San Carlos
Cordillera de Tilarán
Lago de Nicaragua
Archipiélago Solentiname
San Carlos
Los Chiles
Río San Juan
Río Frío
Río Pizote
Río Tenorio
Río Arenal
Río Balsa
Río San Carlos
Río Tres Amigos
Río Pital
Río Toro
Río Sarapiquí
Río Chirripó
Refugio Nacional de Vida Silvestre Caño Negro
Refugio Nacional de Fauna Silvestre Barra del Colorado
Lago Caño Negro
Caño Negro
Reserva Indígena Guatuso
Upala
Colonia Puntarenas
Canalete
San José
Aguas Claras
Guayabal
Guayabo
Volcán Miravalles 2028m
Bijagua
Santo Domingo
San Rafael de Guatuso
Volcán Tenorio 1916m
Parque Nacional Volcán Tenorio
Lago Coter
Tierras Morenas
Venado
Arenal
Unión
Laguna de Arenal
Balneario Tabacón
Parque Nacional Volcán Arenal
Volcán Arenal 1633m
Parque Nacional Volcán Arenal Ranger Station
Fortuna
Chachagua
El Tanque
Puerto San Luis
Chiripo
Tilarán
Quebrada Grande
Cañas
Bagaces
Bebedero
Juntas
Interamericana
Reserva Santa Elena
Santa Elena
Monteverde
Reserva Biológica Bosque Nuboso Monteverde
Parque Nacional Palo Verde
Tempisque Ferry
To Península de Nicoya
To Esparza, Puntarenas
To Liberia, La Cruz
To Santa Cecilia, La Cruz
To San Ramón
Boca de Arenal
Muelle de San Carlos
Platanar
Florencia
Jabillos
La Tigra
Ciudad Quesada (San Carlos)
Aguas Zarcas
Zarcero
Bajos del Toro
Parque Nacional Juan Castro Blanco
Venecia
Río Cuarto
Ciudad Cutris
Pital
Boca Tapada
La Virgen
Laguna Hule
Cariblanco
Parque Nacional Volcán Poás
Volcán Poás 2704m
San Miguel
Colonia Virgen del Socorro
Bajos de Chilamate
Laguna Astillero
Puerto Viejo de Sarapiquí
Estación Biológica La Selva
Rara Avis
Parque Nacional Braulio Carrillo
Horquetas
Río Frío
Santa Clara
Guápiles
To Puerto Limón
To San José
0 10 20 km
0 5 10 miles

luxurious hotel in the area and a good base for exploring the surrounding attractions (see below for tour options). One of the owner/managers is Jaime Hamilton, who came to the area with the Peace Corps and has lived in Costa Rica since the 1960s – but still remembers how to speak English! His business partner, Don Ricardo, is Costa Rican. The hotel used to be a country club, but it also offers 60 spacious, air-conditioned rooms and suites. All come with private hot showers, ceiling fans, telephones, private patios or balconies, and two double beds; the suites have living rooms, TVs, refrigerators, and larger terraces. Two suites have a loft with three single beds, recommended for families with children. Rates are US$86/98 single/double and US$123 for the suites; children under 12 years old stay free (one child per adult). Additional people are charged US$10. An attractive, open-sided restaurant serves excellent meals, with continental breakfasts for US$8.75 and lunches and dinners for US$17.

There are two pools, a sauna, a spa, four lighted tennis courts, two racquetball courts, a game room, and a small gift shop. The hotel is set in pleasantly landscaped grounds with good views of the Río San Carlos. There is an enclosed Butterfly Garden (US$3) on the grounds, with good opportunities to photograph butterflies. The grounds are surrounded by a 240-hectare working cattle ranch adjacent to a 400-hectare private rainforest preserve with several trails. The preserve is unusual in this area where most of the land has been deforested for cattle. It is about a 20-minute hike from the hotel to the preserve. Horseback riding is available.

Tours offered by the hotel are expensive unless you can join a group – with so many people staying at the hotel, this is reasonably feasible. The following prices are for day tours per person for groups of one, two, and three or more: to Volcán Arenal and the Tabacón Hot Springs (US$90/45/35), La Catarata de La Fortuna and jungle lakes (US$70/35/25), and the Venado Caves (US$90/45/30). Guided boat trips at Caño Negro, including transportation from the hotel and box lunch, cost US$48 per person (two-person minimum). Boat and fishing tours are available from US$60 per person.

About 5km south of Muelle on the road to Ciudad Quesada (San Carlos) is the tiny community of Platanar, near which is ***La Quinta Inn*** *(☎/fax 475-5260)*. This rustic B&B, with a pool and sauna available, is run by the Ugaldes, a friendly *tico* couple who taught in the USA for years and speak excellent English. A macaw has adopted the grounds as its personal aviary, and there is a small river behind the inn where fish and caimans can be seen. They have a variety of rooms available: a 10-person cabin with bunk beds for US$10 per person, rooms sleeping up to three people for US$33, and an apartment with two bedrooms, kitchen, sitting room, and a private hot shower for US$60 for five people – weekly discounts can be arranged.

Also near Platanar is the attractive, more upscale ***Hotel La Garza*** *(☎ 475-5222, fax 475-5015; in the USA fax 888-782-4293, information@hotel-lagarza-arenal.com)*, a 600-hectare working dairy and cattle ranch with relaxing views of the Río Platanar and far-off Volcán Arenal – the parking lot is on the bank of the river, and visitors enter the ranch via a graceful suspension footbridge. It has large, clean, polished wooden cabins with big porches, ceiling fans, and good-sized private bathrooms. Tennis, basketball, and volleyball courts are available, as well as a swimming pool and Jacuzzi. The rate is about US$100 double, and meals are served in the adjoining farmhouse (US$7 for breakfast, US$13 for lunch and dinner). Manager Minor Castro is a capable and gracious host; a number of tours are available, and horseback rides through the extensive grounds (US$25 to US$40 for two to four hours) are quickly arranged.

Some 9km north of Muelle is the small ***Hotel Río San Carlos*** *(☎ 460-0766, 460-0301, 469-9194, fax 460-0391, 469-9179, Apartado 345-4400, Ciudad Quesada, San Carlos)*, in the village of Boca de Arenal. Reservations can be made at the Hotel Central in Ciudad Quesada (San Carlos). There are five pleasant rooms with fans, air-conditioning, and private electric showers – two rooms have views of the Río San Carlos.

The hotel is set in pleasant gardens with a pool. The rate is US$60 double including breakfast. The inexpensive ***Restaurant La Galería***, less than 1km away, serves dinner.

Getting There & Away

Bus Buses to and from San Rafael de Guatuso and Los Chiles pass through Muelle and can drop you off. (See the entries for those towns, below, for details.)

Car Drivers will find paved roads north to Los Chiles (74km; lots of potholes); east to Aguas Zarcas (22km; under repair in '99) and Puerto Viejo (55km); south to Ciudad Quesada (San Carlos) (21km) and on to San José (124km); west to Fortuna (28km) and Volcán Arenal; and northwest to San Rafael de Guatuso (58km). This is certainly a crossroads town.

SAN RAFAEL DE GUATUSO AREA

Although marked on most maps as San Rafael, this small community is locally known as Guatuso. About 6000 people inhabit the town and the surrounding district. San Rafael is on the Río Frío, 19km northeast of Boca de Arenal by poor dirt road or 40km northwest of Fortuna (de San Carlos) by paved road. This latter road gives good views of Volcán Arenal to the south.

About 10km before San Rafael, a dirt road heads south for about 10km to Venado (which means 'deer'), where there are basic *cabinas* and a public telephone (☎ 460-4118, 460-4145).

Things to See & Do

Four kilometers south of Venado are caves that can be explored; an entry fee of about US$3 is charged, and you should be prepared with several sources of light and clothes that you don't mind getting wet and dirty. There are local guides in Venado, or you can take a tour from any of the larger hotels in the Caño Negro and Fortuna areas. There is an afternoon bus from Ciudad Quesada.

Just before reaching San Rafael, the road passes through the Reserva Indígena Guatuso, although there is nothing that obviously demarcates the reserve.

A few kilometers north of Guatuso is the Ujuminica Caiman Farm, where the animals are raised for release into the wild. Tours can be arranged with hotels in Guatuso.

From San Rafael, you may be able to hire a boat in the wet season to take you up the Río Frío to Refugio Nacional de Vida Silvestre Caño Negro.

Places to Stay & Eat

The most tranquil budget option in Guatuso is the ***Cabinas Milagro*** *(☎ 464-0037)*, a quiet, family-run place on the edge of town; from the center, go past the church toward the Río Frío bridge and turn right just past the soccer field. Rooms with private baths cost about US$4 per person. In the center is the former Albergue Tío Henry (still known by this name by many locals), now ***Albergue Segana*** *(☎ 464-0344)*, with a small locked parking area and about 10 rooms, some with fans and shared baths and others with private baths, air-conditioning, and cable TVs. Rates are US$10 to US$20 double. Tío Henry still arranges local tours. There are a few other cheaper and more basic places to stay – the 'best' of them appears to be ***Hotel Las Brisas***. The ***Cabinas El Bosque*** *(☎ 464-0235)*, just north of town, which advertises air-conditioning and a parking lot, seems worth checking out; at last visit, the bridge was out.

There are a handful of inexpensive eateries on the main street. The ***Restaurant El Turista*** has good *casados* for US$2; ***Soda La Macha*** has a homey atmosphere and woodfire cooking; across the way, ***Río Celeste*** is a popular place with a modern diner counter and a TV.

Getting There & Away

Buses leave about every two hours for either Tilarán or Ciudad Quesada (some continue to San José). Ciudad Quesada is the most frequent destination.

A paved road leads 40km northwest to Upala.

UPALA

This small town is 9km south of the Nicaraguan border, in the far northwestern corner of the northern lowlands. About 10,000 people live in Upala and the surrounding district. Dirt roads lead up to and across the border, but these are not official entry points into either Costa Rica or Nicaragua. There is sometimes a passport check by the bridge at the south end of town (coming from San Rafael de Guatuso) and another near Canalete (coming from the Carretera Interamericana on the paved road from Cañas).

Upala is the center for the cattle and rice industries of the area. A few remaining Guatuso Indians live in the region. It has become increasingly important – the paved secondary road from the Interamericana opened in the 1980s, so there are good bus connections with San José. Few travelers go to Upala, however, and those who do are mostly heading to or from the infrequently visited west side of Caño Negro. The trip to Upala and its surroundings is an interesting off-the-beaten-track experience.

Places to Stay & Eat

Although few travelers come through, Upala is visited by a relatively large number of ticos, especially businesspeople at midweek, when the hotels may be full. Call ahead and get there early in the week for the best choice of rooms.

A popular place is the ***Cabinas Buenavista*** *(☎ 470-0186)*, near the Super San Martín (the sign for the cabinas is under a large advertisement for 'Glidden' paint). The rooms, with fans, private cold showers, and parking, cost about US$6 per person; they are a bit stuffy, but the courtyard is nice and the owners friendly – it's often full, especially midweek.

Another good place, just off the open plaza behind the bus station, is the ***Cabinas Maleku*** *(☎ 470-0142)*, with rooms for US$5 to US$8 per person; some rooms are nicer and have TVs. A ***soda*** is attached. Also off the plaza is the ***Hotel Restaurante Upala*** *(☎ 470-0169)*, with basic, clean rooms with private cold showers for US$5/10 single/double. The owner is nice and reception is open 24 hours.

The ***Restaurante Buena Vista*** is still open but has been sold to new owners; it is in a pleasant, breezy location overlooking the river, just to the right after you cross the bridge entering town from the south.

Across from the bridge is the ***Hotel Rosita*** *(☎ 470-0198)*, another clean, cheap place to stay. The ***Cabinas del Norte*** *(☎ 470-0061)* is right next to the bus station and market – convenient but noisy. Both charge about US$4 per person.

Getting There & Away

There are two or three buses a day from San José and an afternoon bus from Ciudad Quesada (San Carlos). The most frequent bus service is from Cañas, with at least five departures a day.

From the Upala bus station, there are buses to San José two to four times a day (US$4, five to six hours). There is a morning bus to Ciudad Quesada, five or six daily buses to Cañas, and buses to a variety of small local destinations, including Santa Cecilia, three times a day. There is a bus to Caño Negro two times a day, if the road is OK. Call Auto Transportes Upala (☎ 470-0061) in the Cabinas del Norte for schedule updates.

If you are driving to Upala, have documents accessible for passport controls on the outskirts.

REFUGIO NACIONAL DE VIDA SILVESTRE CAÑO NEGRO

This 9969-hectare refuge is of interest especially to birders, who come to see a variety of waterfowl including anhingas, roseate spoonbills, storks, ducks, herons, and the

Dogs

You'll see many dogs running loose in Costa Rica; generally, they are not a cause for alarm. If dogs are a good barometer of local attitudes toward strangers, then the friendliness of strays in this country – dogs are rarely kept at home as pets – reflects the friendly, cosmopolitan attitude of most ticos. If you stop to ask for directions in a remote area, it's as unusual to get hassled by a dog as it is to get an unfriendly response from a person.

– John Thompson

largest Costa Rican colony of the olivaceous cormorant. The refuge is the only place in Costa Rica where the Nicaraguan grackle regularly nests. In addition, pumas, jaguars, and tapirs have been recorded here more often than in many of the other refuges. It certainly is in a remote and sparsely populated area that is conducive to these rare large mammals. Many smaller mammals have also been reported.

The Río Frío flows through the refuge and offers good birding and some wildlife spotting. During the wet season, the river breaks its banks and forms an 800-hectare lake. During the dry months of January to April, the lake shrinks and is no longer accessible by boating down the river; by April it has almost completely disappeared – until the rains in May begin. During the dry season, the lake is accessible from the Caño Negro village, where you can rent boats, and there are also some foot and horse trails, but the only way to go for most of the year is by boat. January to March is the best time for seeing large flocks of birds, though smaller flocks can be seen year-round.

Orientation & Information

In the tiny community of Caño Negro, you'll find a ranger station. Aside from administering the park, the rangers are contact points for a few community projects, including a butterfly garden put together by a local women's association (ASOMUCAN) and a turtle nursery. Park entrance officially costs US$6; camping runs US$2.50, or you can stay in the rangers' house for US$6 if it is arranged in advance. There are cold showers, and meals can be arranged. There are few visitors here.

The Caño Negro public phone (☎ 661-8464) is one way to leave messages (in Spanish) to arrange for local guides and boat transport or to contact the ranger station. Arrangements can also be made by asking the San José office (☎ 283-8004) to radio ahead. Boats can be hired for about US$12 per hour (including driver) to take you on fishing and birding trips. There are about five local boat pilots; Carlos Sequera and Napoleon Sequera both speak English. Fishing is not allowed from April to June, but during the rest of the rainy season you can catch a variety of fish if you have a license, which you can buy at the station for US$30. Two local guides who have been recommended are Elgar Ulate and Vicente Mesa. Horse rental can also be arranged.

Most visitors come on guided tours either from one of the area's better hotels or, more cheaply, by arranging them in the town of Los Chiles. A few visitors arrange tours from the San Rafael de Guatuso or Upala areas.

Organized Tours

Several hotels in this area arrange tours to Caño Negro (see Muelle de San Carlos earlier in this chapter and Fortuna in the Northwestern Costa Rica chapter), and there are a couple tour operators in Los Chiles (see the entry below). Travel agencies in Fortuna and San José also arrange tours. Horizontes, in San José, has some of the best tours, but not the cheapest (see the entry under Organized Tours in the Getting Around chapter).

Places to Stay & Eat

Aside from the ranger station, accommodations in Caño Negro are few; this is definitely still an off-the-beaten-track place, although the recently built bridge between Caño Negro and Los Chiles may change things. The ***Cabinas Arguedas*** *(☎ 224-2400 to leave a beeper message in Spanish)*, at the eastern edge of the community, just off the main road, has a few basic rooms on spacious grounds for about US$4 per person. The rooms have fans, mosquito nets, and cold showers. Camping is available for US$3 per person. Don Alvaro Arguedas has set up an information booth about the area at the cabinas' entrance, and he rents boats and arranges trips on the river. The ***Cabinas and Restaurante Machon*** *(☎ 233-3333 to leave a beeper message with Carlos Sequera)*, near the center of the community (look for signs), is friendly and can feed you. Small, bamboo-paneled cabins with screened windows and cold showers cost US$4 per person. There is a small ***soda*** in the middle of the community near the public phone and the bus stop, where you can get snacks and some meals. Other local people may provide meals or a place to stay; ask around.

Getting There & Away

The reserve can be reached by road from Upala and Los Chiles or by boat from Los Chiles or San Rafael de Guatuso. Buses to and from Caño Negro usually stop at the center of the community, near the public phone and the small soda. However, if you are leaving the area, ask locals about the best place to meet the bus.

From Upala There is a daily bus between Upala and Caño Negro, but it might not run when the road is bad. Call Auto Transportes Upala for updates (☎ 470-0061). Pickup trucks drive along this road a couple of times a day and will pick up people. If you're driving, take the road southeast toward San Rafael de Guatuso. After 11km, at the community of Colonia Puntarenas, there is a signed turnoff for Caño Negro. It is 26km away by very rough road, though the first half is in better shape. A normal car can just barely get through in the dry season (let's hope the car rental companies aren't reading this!), but you'll definitely need 4WD in the wet season.

From Los Chiles Access from Los Chiles is easier. There are fewer buses (the bus to Upala, leaving around 1 pm on Monday, Wednesday, and Friday, passes through Caño Negro), but there are many boats going down the Río Frío. These are day trips, described under the Los Chiles entry. During the wet season, boats coming down the river can reach the lake in the center of the park, and these could leave you near the Caño Negro village and ranger station.

A good bridge has been built over the Río Frío, so the road from Los Chiles to Caño Negro is now open. Beyond the bridge, the dirt road is in good shape and may be passable all year in a normal car. However, Hurricane Mitch raised water levels and badly damaged the stretch between Los Chiles and the river; ask locally how repairs are going.

LOS CHILES

Los Chiles is about 70km north of Muelle by paved road, though many stretches of the road are riddled with potholes that slow driving down to around 30km per hour. The drive offers long green vistas underscored by the red soil typical of the northern regions. The small town is on the Río Frío, 3km before the Nicaraguan border. About 8000 people inhabit the Los Chiles district. Although the town is midway between the Pacific and Caribbean coasts, the elevation is only 43m above sea level – it's not for nothing that this region is called the northern lowlands.

Los Chiles was originally built to service river traffic on the nearby Río San Juan; the south bank forms the Nicaragua-Costa Rica border for much of the river's length. A landing strip connects Los Chiles with the rest of the country. Since the construction of a road, there is no scheduled air service, although aerotaxis can be hired from San José (see information on air charters in the Getting Around chapter), and Travelair has talked of scheduling flights here.

This is a small town, and you can ask almost anybody for directions to places mentioned below. Information is available from Servitur and Ecodirecta (see Organized Tours, below).

In the 1980s, Los Chiles was on an important supply route for the Contras, which explains why the authorities were touchy about the border crossing here. In fact, until Violeta Chamorro became the Nicaraguan president in 1990, this crossing was closed except to ticos and Nicaraguans *(nicas)*. This crossing is now open to all travelers with proper documents. Some nationals need a visa; many don't. (See the Getting There & Away chapter for additional information.)

Organized Tours

From the main highway, you have to drive west through town to reach the Río Frío. Caño Negro tours are recommended if you enjoy watching wildlife; there are plenty of monkeys, caimans, sloths, turtles, lizards, butterflies, and toucans, parrots, and other birds. Wildlife sightings are comparable to the

Sí a Paz

An interesting side effect of the Contra-Sandinista hostilities was that many of the local inhabitants living on or near the Río San Juan left for a safer area. Because fighting in the area was relatively low-key compared to, for example, Vietnam, where defoliants and herbicides destroyed much of the countryside, most of the rainforest in the Río San Juan area has been protected from colonization and preserved in its virgin state. While forests were being cut for pasture in northern Costa Rica, the San Juan area remained free of farmers.

Since the cessation of hostilities in 1990, the colonists are drifting back, though the discovery of unexploded mines in the area has somewhat stemmed the tide of resettlement.

Meanwhile, environmentally aware Costa Rican authorities have been working with their Nicaraguan counterparts in an attempt to establish an 'international' park – a national park that spans the border. The proposed name of the park is Si a Paz (literally, 'yes to peace'). It is hoped that it will stretch north from the Caño Negro refuge to Lago de Nicaragua and east through a large tract of primary rainforest in southeastern Nicaragua and along the Río San Juan to the Caribbean coast, joining up there with the existing Barra del Colorado refuge. This park is part of the proposed Paseo Pantera, an innovative project to preserve biological diversity and enhance wildlife management throughout the Caribbean side of Central America. Paseo Pantera is the brainchild of the Carr brothers, sons of Archie Carr Jr, who founded the Caribbean Conservation Corporation and is considered the father of turtle conservation in Central America.

The project is still in the planning stages, even though several international organizations have put financial support into the park. Environmentally, this is a perfect region to preserve because it has been so little disturbed, but political, social, and economic factors have a way of making such projects difficult to realize.

– Rob Rachowiecki

more frequently visited Tortuguero (some readers say they saw more here than they did in Tortuguero). Tours are available year-round; guides almost always increase your chances of seeing wildlife.

Individual travelers looking to join a group and save money may find it easier to hook up with the tours that are offered in Fortuna, where there are many other travelers (see the Fortuna entry in the Northwestern Costa Rica chapter). Los Chiles is a lot quieter – however, people who stay overnight here and take a locally organized morning tour (before day visitors from Fortuna hit the river) usually see more wildlife. There are currently two tour operators in Los Chiles, and visits to the river are increasing.

Servitur (☎ 471-1055), run by the friendly Manfred Vargas Rojas, now operates out of Cabinas Jabirú. The name may change, but the company has been in the area awhile and, in addition to the well-known Caño Negro trips, it runs tours to the nearby private reserve of Medio Queso (with horse-back riding, the opportunity to observe traditional farming techniques, and a typical farm lunch – a chance to see some of rural Costa Rica not yet discovered by tourists), as well as tours and guided camping trips to the islands in Lago de Nicaragua (about US$65 per person, including food). A half-day tour to Caño Negro, including lunch, costs US$70 for two people and US$20 per person for groups over two.

Ecodirecta (☎/fax 471-1197), with an office near the docks, is a Dutch-run reforestation company that has a tourism wing offering tours along the river and simple accommodations in town (see Places to Stay, below). Three-hour Caño Negro trips, not including lunch, cost US$60 for two people and US$20 per person for groups. Oscar Rojas is the helpful tico manager of the tours; the Dutch owners can provide details about how tourists can involve themselves with the reforestation investment project.

At the boat dock, you can also hire individual boatmen to take you up the Río Frío during the dry season and all the way into Lago Caño Negro during the rainy season. Boat rental costs about US$45 to US$80 for a trip lasting at least three or four hours, depending on the size and type of boat (a canopied boat is usually more expensive; it protects you somewhat from direct sun and rain, but cuts down a little on your field of view).

Going upriver to San Carlos in Nicaragua is also easy to arrange; ask either a tour operator or at the public dock (sometimes there is a passenger boat making regular trips).

Places to Stay

The rock-bottom options in town are the ***Hotel Onassis***, on the corner of the 'parque' (actually, a soccer field), and the ***Hotel Río Frío***, near the immigration office, which have rooms with shared cold baths for about US$3 per person; neither are particularly welcoming to travelers (this is a border town in a mainly agricultural region). A better cheapie near the center is the ***Hotel Los Chiles*** *(☎ 471-1262)*, which has basic rooms, some with skylights, and shared showers for US$3.50/5.50 single/double. Opposite the 'park,' the ***Hotel Central*** has basic rooms with shared showers for about US$7 double.

The ***Cabinas Jabirú*** *(☎ 471-1055)* is the nicest budget option in town; the Servitur office is currently located here. There are 12 simple but good-sized and attractive units around a backyard garden, each with a double and two single beds (separate little bedrooms), a private bath with hot shower, fans, and a small sitting room. There is a parking area. The rate is about US$8 per person.

On the west side of the main road, about 1km south of town, is the ***Hotel Restaurante Cuajipal*** *(☎ 471-1197)*, operated by Ecodirecta, which also has nice rooms by its tour office in town. Clean, plain rooms with private baths and fans, some with air-conditioning, cost US$15/24 single/double.

Places to Eat

Restaurant El Parque *(☎ 471-1032, 471-1090)* serves pretty good tico food, has a nice self-service coffee bar, and is open 6 am to 9 pm. It's the standard recommendation – tour-bus groups eat lunch here, but breakfast and dinner are a more private affair. Another place to try is the ***Soda El Tucan***, near Cabinas Jabirú, which is a tiny soda with a limited but cheap menu and a couple of Nicaraguan dishes. Nearby, the ***Heladeria Fantasía*** serves ice cream, juices, and snacks and is locally popular (the owner also runs Servitur). ***Los Petates*** and, close to the police post on the main highway, the ***Soda Sonia*** are both good for simple local food.

Getting There & Away

About 10 buses a day run between Ciudad Quesada (San Carlos) and Los Chiles. Direct buses from San José leave for Los Chiles at 5:30 am and 3 pm from the Atlántico Norte station and return at 5 am and 3 pm. A bus to Upala, leaving around 1 pm on Monday, Wednesday, and Friday, passes through Caño Negro.

LA LAGUNA DEL LAGARTO LODGE

This lodge *(☎ 289-8163, ☎/fax 289-5295, 231-3816, laguna-del-lagarto@adventure-costarica.com)* is one of the most isolated places in the country, which is why it gets its own heading. Also, it is one of the few places where the increasingly rare great green macaw can be seen frequently. This macaw nests near the lodge, which has been the base for researchers studying the bird. Many other birds have been recorded – almost 300 species at the last count. Monkeys, poison-arrow frogs, and caimans are routinely seen.

The lodge is set in a 500-hectare area, most of which is rainforest. Some of it is swampy and there is a lagoon, but canoes are available to explore these parts. There are about 10km of foot trails, and horseback trips (US$15 for two hours) are offered. You can also take a boat tour down the Río San

Carlos to the Río San Juan on the Nicaraguan border (US$25, three hours). The lodge will lend you a poncho if it's raining – though you really should bring your own, along with insect repellent.

The lodge has 18 screened rooms with private baths, fans, and large verandahs for US$52/68/79 single/double/triple. Two more rooms share a bath for US$40/57/67. Meals cost US$5.50 for breakfast, US$7.50 lunch, US$11 dinner.

To get there, drive on the paved road to Pital (north of Aguas Zarcas) and continue on a graveled road 29km to the tiny community of Boca Tapada, from where it is a further 6 or 7km to the lodge (there are signs). 4WD is recommended, though not absolutely essential (call ahead to find out how the road is). Buses from Ciudad Quesada go to Pital several times a day. From Pital, there are two buses a day to Boca Tapada. There are also two buses from the Coca-Cola bus terminal in San José at 5:30 am and 12:30 pm daily that go to Pital and connect with a Pital-Boca Tapada bus. If you have a reservation, lodge staff will pick you up from Boca Tapada. A jeep taxi from Pital to the lodge costs about US$25. The lodge will provide roundtrip transportation from San José for US$150 per person (two-person minimum).

Alternatively, the lodge offers complete three-day/two-night package tours including transportation from San José, meals, a guided jungle hike, a four-hour boat tour, a two-hour horseback ride, and unlimited canoeing and trail use. These cost US$220 for each person (four minimum).

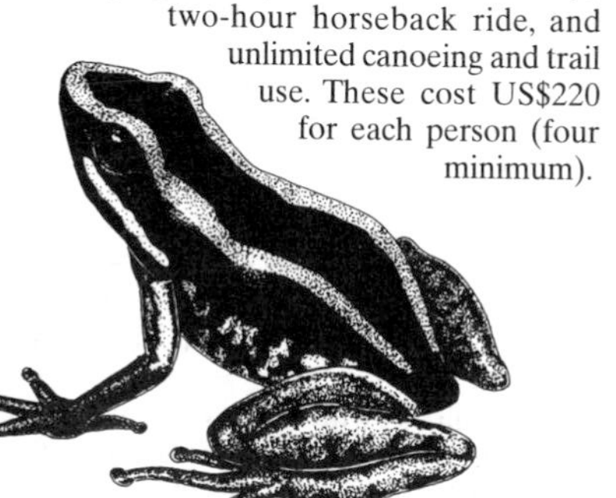

Poison-arrow frog

San José to Puerto Viejo de Sarapiquí

Puerto Viejo de Sarapiquí can be approached from San José from either the west or the east, so a roundtrip can be done without backtracking. The western route goes via Heredia, Varablanca, Catarata La Paz, San Miguel, La Virgen, and Chilamate. The eastern route goes via the new highway through Parque Nacional Braulio Carrillo and on from the turnoff (about 13km before Guápiles) to Horquetas and Puerto Viejo. Both routes are paved.

WESTERN ROUTE

San José to San Miguel

The western road is spectacular and a favorite of tour companies. The road leaves San José via Heredia and Barva and continues over a pass in the Cordillera Central between Volcán Poás to the west and Volcán Barva to the east (see the Central Valley & Surrounding Highlands chapter). The steep and winding mountain road climbs to over 2000m just before the tiny community of Varablanca.

A couple of kilometers past the highest point is a turnoff to Poasito and Volcán Poás; then a dizzying descent with beautiful views begins. People on tours or with their own vehicles can stop for photographs or for high and middle-elevation birding. Travelers on public buses must be content with the excellent window gazing.

About 8km north of Varablanca, the Río La Paz is crossed by a bridge on a hairpin bend. On the left side of the bridge is an excellent view of the spectacular Catarata La Paz (described in the Central Valley & Surrounding Highlands chapter). Several other waterfalls may be seen, particularly on the right-hand side (heading north) in the La Paz river valley, which soon joins with the Sarapiquí river valley.

About 6 or 7km beyond Catarata La Paz is a turnoff to the right on a dirt road leading to **Colonia Virgen del Socorro**, a small community several kilometers away across the river. This road (which may require 4WD) is famous among birders, who will often spend several hours looking for unusual species along the quiet road, with a forest, a river, clearings, and elevational changes contributing to species diversity in this one spot.

On one of my birding trips to this area, a friend who had been birding in Costa Rica for over a decade saw his first solitary eagle, a large and uncommon bird that likes remote forested mountainous terrain and is therefore difficult to see. This was a big find. My observations were less unusual but more colorful. I saw the sunbittern (a water bird with a striking sunburst pattern on its spread wings) and the psychedelically colored red-headed barbet. The area is certainly a birder's delight. Costa Rica Expeditions (see the entry under Organized Tours in the Getting Around chapter) organizes day trips to the area accompanied by an expert bird guide.

Barely a kilometer north of the turnoff for Virgen del Socorro, just past the community of Cariblanco (which has one of the only gas stations on this road), is a turnoff to the left that leads along a poor dirt road to the attractive **Laguna Hule**. The 9km road is just passable to ordinary cars in the dry season, but 4WD is advised in the wet season. The lagoon is the remnant of a volcanic crater and is set amid luxuriant rainforest – though away from the lake, most of the forest is gone. The lake is reputedly good for fishing.

About 7km north of the Virgen del Socorro turnoff, the road forks at the community of San Miguel. The westbound fork goes to Ciudad Quesada, about 35km away by paved road, while the north fork heads for Puerto Viejo de Sarapiquí to the northeast.

West of San Miguel

The westbound road hugs the northern limits of the Cordillera Central, and there are occasional views of the northern lowlands. About 14km west of San Miguel along this road is the village of **Venecia**, where there is a basic pensión. Halfway between San Miguel and Venecia is the hamlet of Río Cuarto, from which an unpaved road heads southeast past the beautiful waterfall near Bajos del Toro, through Parque Nacional Juan Castro Blanco, and on to Zarcero (see the Central Valley & Surrounding Highlands chapter).

A few kilometers north of Venecia is the pre-Columbian archaeological site called **Ciudad Cutris**, which can be reached by 4WD vehicle or on foot. The site has not been properly excavated, has no tourist facilities, and is on private land. Inquire locally about permission to see it.

About 8km west of Venecia is the small town of **Aguas Zarcas**, which is the largest settlement between the Puerto Viejo and Caño Negro areas, with a couple of cheap and basic places to stay.

San Miguel to Puerto Viejo de Sarapiquí

The road north from San Miguel drops for 12km to the village of **La Virgen** (not Colonia Virgen del Socorro, mentioned previously), which is truly in the northern lowlands. The now-flat road goes through mainly agricultural country an additional 13km to **Bajos de Chilamate**, and then 6km on to Puerto Viejo de Sarapiquí. Lodges along this route include Rancho Leona near La Virgen and Islas del Río and Selva Verde, both near Chilamate. These lodges are described later in this chapter, as are several others in the Puerto Viejo area. There is also a nice budget option near the river in La Virgen.

Río Sarapiquí Trips Parts of the Sarapiquí are good for river running from May to November. The put-in point is usually around Virgen del Socorro, where Class II and III rapids are encountered. Alternatively, you can put in at Chilamate, where it is a more gentle float with mainly Class I and maybe a few Class II rapids. Check to ensure you are signing up for the level you want. Tours run most days with one company or another and cost about US$70 per person. Costa Rica Expeditions, Horizontes, and Ríos Tropicales all run day trips that involve 3½ hours of driving from San José, four hours on the river, and 3½ hours back to San José. Lunch and bilingual river guides are provided; see

Organized Tours in the Getting Around chapter for contact information. Next to Islas del Río Lodge near Chilamate is Sarapiquí Aguas Bravas (☎ 292-2072), which also offers river rafting here, as does the Sarapiquí Outdoor Center (☎/fax 761-1123, 297-1010 beeper) in La Virgen, run by the friendly David Duarte Soto.

Another option is a kayak tour operated by Rancho Leona in La Virgen (see the Rancho Leona entry, later in this section).

EASTERN ROUTE

After visiting the interesting Puerto Viejo de Sarapiquí area, you can return to San José via the eastern road. (You can also arrive in Puerto Viejo by the eastern road; buses go in both directions.)

About 4km southeast of Puerto Viejo, the road passes the entrance to La Selva Biological Station (described later in this chapter). About 15km farther is the village of **Horquetas**, from where it is 15km to the rainforest preservation project and lodge at Rara Avis (also described later in this chapter).

From Horquetas, the paved road continues about 17km through banana plantations to the main San José-Puerto Limón highway near the village of Santa Clara. Turn east for Guápiles and the Caribbean; turn west for San José. This route to San José takes you through the middle of Parque Nacional Braulio Carrillo.

About 2km south of Horquetas, an unpaved road goes east for 9km to the village of **Río Frío**, which is an important banana center. This used to be on the main road between Santa Clara and Horquetas, and some buses still go through here, even though it is about 9km farther and the road is not paved. Río Frío has an airstrip, and flights can be chartered to and from Tortuguero. There is a basic hotel, and buses between San José and Puerto Viejo often stop here for a meal break. You can catch buses several times a day from here to Puerto Viejo, San José, or Guápiles.

Bananas

Everywhere you look in this region, you'll see banana plants. Bunches of bananas are often covered with large blue plastic sacks while the fruit is still on the tree. The plastic keeps the plants warm (as in a miniature greenhouse) and also concentrates ethylene gas, which is produced by ripening fruit.

Strange-looking little tractor-trains pull wagons loaded with fruit to processing centers. In some plantations, bunches of bananas are hung on wire contraptions, which are pushed by workers into the processing area. The bananas are washed and sprayed to prevent molding and then shipped off in crates and boxes to the coast and the world.

The banana companies have been criticized for a multitude of ills over the decades. Rainforests have been replaced by plantations, blue plastic bags litter and clog the streams and rivers, and the insecticide and fungicide sprays used have caused health problems, including sterility, in thousands of workers.

These problems have been largely ignored, mainly because the plantations give workers minimum housing and a livelihood, and bananas have been, along with coffee, the main source of foreign income for Costa Rica.

Slowly, however, the health and environmental problems are being addressed. Though the damage already done cannot be easily reversed, some attempt is being made to minimize further pollution, degradation, and sickness. Most of this is 'too little, too late,' but it is better than nothing at all.

– Rob Rachowiecki

PUERTO VIEJO DE SARAPIQUÍ

The locals simply refer to the town as Puerto Viejo, but its full name distinguishes it from another popular destination, Puerto Viejo de Talamanca on the Caribbean coast.

The town is at the confluence of the Río Puerto Viejo and the Río Sarapiquí. About 6000 people live in the Puerto Viejo district, which, despite its ramshackle appearance, has an interesting history. It used to be an important port on the trade route to the Caribbean before the days of roads and railways. Boats plied the Sarapiquí as far as the Nicaraguan border and then turned east on the Río San Juan to the sea. Despite its distance from Nicaragua, it has something of the feel of a jungle border town – there is an immigration post near the small wooden dock, and (especially since Hurricane Mitch) emigrating Nicaraguans sometimes share the river with local fishermen and visiting birders. With the advent of roads and railways, Puerto Viejo lost its importance as a river port, but adventurous travelers can still travel down the Sarapiquí in motorized dugout canoes.

Today, the region is known for its nearby undisturbed premontane tropical wet forest that extends from the northern arm of Parque Nacional Braulio Carrillo. A biological research station and several forest lodges nearby have made this undisturbed habitat accessible to scientists and travelers. A new addition is an ambitious rainforest reserve, museum, and lodge called Centro Neotropico Sarapiquí (see the entry below).

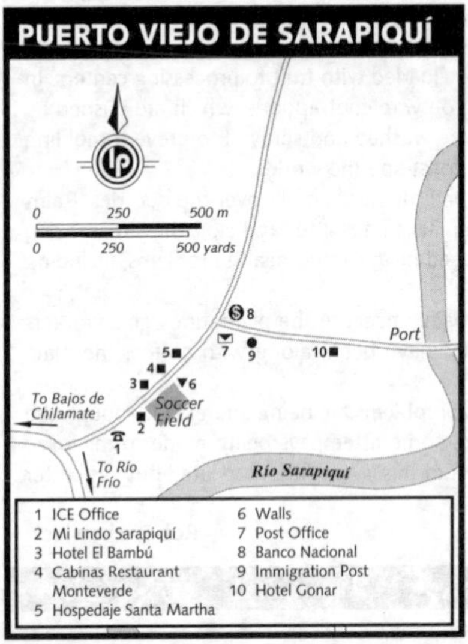

Grassroots environmental activity is also strong in this area – a good contact for those interested in finding out about or contributing to local activity is local guide Alex Martínez (owner of the Posada Andrea Cristina B&B; see the entry below under Places to Stay & Eat). He is co-founder of the Asociación para el Bienestar Ambiental de Sarapiquí (ABAS), which promotes environmental education in local schools and communities, is experimenting with models for organic banana agriculture, and has established conservation programs for local endangered species – its most successful program has been with the green macaw. Contact Alex through his B&B or call ABAS (☎/fax 766-6732, 235-5394).

A few kilometers southeast of Puerto Viejo (just off the main road and signed, or ask anybody) is a women's herb cooperative called MUSA. It is a small farm that produces herbs for medicinal, culinary, cosmetic, and incense purposes. But more importantly, it provides local support and advice for women. Products made from the herbs are for sale and visits are encouraged.

There is no dry season in this area, but late January to early May is the less wet season. A weather station at La Selva, just outside Puerto Viejo, records about 170mm of rain in February (the driest month) and close to 500mm in December, the wettest month. The drier season means fewer insects and less muddy trails, but it's never really dry.

Places to Stay & Eat

Budget Although most foreign visitors stay in one of the more expensive lodges in the Puerto Viejo area, budget travelers will find a few cheap and basic hotels in Puerto Viejo itself. Most are along the one main street, so you won't have any difficulty finding them. The problem is that the best cheap rooms

PUERTO VIEJO DE SARAPIQUÍ

1 ICE Office
2 Mi Lindo Sarapiquí
3 Hotel El Bambú
4 Cabinas Restaurant Monteverde
5 Hospedaje Santa Martha
6 Walls
7 Post Office
8 Banco Nacional
9 Immigration Post
10 Hotel Gonar

are often full of local workers who use them on a long-term basis, so the choice of rooms may be limited. There are several inexpensive restaurants, bars, and sodas.

The ***Cabinas Restaurant Monteverde*** *(☎ 766-6236)* charges US$6/8 for six fairly basic singles/doubles with private cold showers and table fans. The restaurant here is popular and reasonably priced. Just opposite is a ***Walls*** ice-cream shop. The ***Hotel Gonar*** is above a hardware shop, Almacén y Ferretería Gonar *(☎ 766-6196)*, and has 18 bare rooms with beds and fans, sharing one basic cold shower. Call the store to see if it has a room available. The rate is about US$3 per person, plus a $6 deposit for the key. A last-resort cheapie is ***Hospedaje Santa Martha***, for about US$3 per person; rooms all share baths, the place looks pretty run-down, and the owner won't let you see a room before you pay.

The nicest budget rooms are in ***Mi Lindo Sarapiquí*** *(☎ 766-6074)*, on the south side of the soccer field. It has only six rooms, all simply decorated but clean with private hot showers and fans. The rate is US$7.50 per person. Below the hotel is a decent, locally recommended restaurant open 9 am to 10 pm.

If all these are full, budget travelers can try the basic ***Cabinas Yacaré***, in the small village of Guaria, almost 3km west of Puerto Viejo on the main road to Chilamate. Six rooms with shared baths cost US$5 per person, and four more rooms with private cold showers cost US$7.50/12.50.

About 5km west of Puerto Viejo is the new ***Hotel Tucan Lodge*** *(☎ 766-6281)*, built by the tico owners of Mi Lindo Sarapiquí, described above. Below the nice cabins are a fish pond, stream, and horses, and the cabins are available for US$9/16 single/double.

Mid-Range ***Posada Andrea Cristina B&B*** *(☎/fax 766-6265)* is about 1km west of the center, on the road to Chilamate. This is a clean, family-run place with six quiet little cabins set in a plant-filled garden. Each cabin has a fan and a private hot bath. The rate is US$20 per person, including a big home-cooked breakfast with some of Costa Rica's best coffee. The owner, Alex Martínez, is an excellent and charming guide and a passionate front-line conservationist. He arrived here 30 years ago as a tough young hunter exploring what was virgin forest, saw firsthand the rapid destruction of the forest, changed his philosophy, and is now a volunteer game warden – who will abandon a Saturday night soccer match to chase down poachers on the river. He helped found ABAS, a local environmental protection and education agency (see above). Alex speaks perfect English and can tell you as much as you want to know about environmental issues of the area as well as help with transport and tour arrangements.

The ***Hotel El Bambú*** *(☎ 766-6005, fax 766-6132)*, on the west side of the soccer field, has 12 roomy, standard rooms, all with fans, TVs, and hot water, for US$25/50 single/double including breakfast. Children under 12 years old stay free if they are with their parents, and substantial discounts are offered in the wet season. The large and modern dining room is open 7 am to 10 pm and has meals in the US$4 to US$8 range.

Getting There & Away

Bus Express buses from San José via Braulio Carrillo leave from the Atlántico Norte terminal about eight times a day between 6:30 am and 6 pm (about 1½ hours). Three buses a day, at 6:30 am, noon, and 3 pm, take the scenic route via Heredia and Varablanca (four hours). There are also buses from Ciudad Quesada (San Carlos) and Guápiles. Note that arriving buses will continue down to the port (a five-minute walk) if you ask the driver.

Buses leave Puerto Viejo for San José on a similar schedule, from a bus stop on the main street – ask anyone. A nearby stop has buses for Ciudad Quesada and other destinations. About eight buses a day stop in Guápiles between 5:30 am and 6 pm.

Boat The port is small and not very busy. A few motorized dugouts are available for hire. A daily boat leaves around noon for Oro Verde and Trinidad on the Río San Juan, returning the next morning at 4:30 am – the fare is US$3 to Trinidad (see North of Puerto Viejo de Sarapiquí, later in this chapter).

Sailing to Nicaragua

Sailing down the Río Sarapiquí to the Río San Juan is a memorable trip. If the water is low, dozens of crocodiles can be seen sunning on the banks. If the water is high, river turtles climb out of the river to sun themselves on logs. Birds are everywhere. North of Puerto Viejo, much of the land is cattle pasture with few trees, but as you approach the Nicaraguan border, more stands of forest are seen. In trees on the banks, you may see monkeys, iguanas, or maybe a snake draped over a branch.

On my trip, the boatman suddenly cut the engine, so I turned around to see what was the matter. He grinned and yelled, in his none-too-good English, 'Slow! Slow!' It was obvious that we were going slow, and it took me a while to realize that he was trying to say, 'Sloth!' It was not until the dugout had gently nosed into the bank beneath the tree, and the sloth raised a languid head to see what was going on, that I finally realized what we were stopping for. How he managed to make out the greenish-brown blob on a branch (the color is caused by the algae that grows in the fur of this lethargic animal) as a sloth is one of the mysteries of traveling with a sharp-eyed *campesino*.

We continued on down to the confluence of the Sarapiquí with the San Juan, where we stopped to visit an old Miskito Indian fisherman named Leandro. He claimed to be 80 years old, but his wizened frame had the vitality of a man half his age. From the bulging woven grass bag in the bottom of his fragile dugout, Leandro sold us fresh river lobster to accompany that evening's supper.

The official border between Nicaragua and Costa Rica is the south bank of the San Juan, not the middle of the river, so you are technically traveling in Nicaragua when on the San Juan. This river system is an historically important gateway from the Caribbean into the heart of Central America. Today, it remains off the beaten tourist track and is a worthwhile trip to see a combination of rainforest and ranches, wildlife and old war zones, and deforested areas and protected areas.

– Rob Rachowiecki

Local lodges can arrange transportation almost anywhere. Three local boatmen to try are William Rojas (☎ 766-6260), Jorge Enriques (☎ 766-6658), and Juan Guzman Mena (☎ 224-2400), for whom you can leave messages in Spanish. They will take you anywhere; short trips along the river cost about US$6 per hour for a group of four, US$20 per hour for a single person. Trips to Tortugero and back cost about US$50 per person, with a minimum of four people. Check with lodges for their current prices to use as a starting point in negotiating a price down at the dock.

Taxi There is a taxi sign on the main street of Puerto Viejo. If a taxi isn't there, wait by the stand and one will eventually cruise by. (Conveniently, a bar behind the taxi stand has a serving window to the street, so you can have a beer while you're waiting, or Walls ice cream is just a few meters away.) Taxis will take you to the nearby lodges and biological station for US$3 to US$5.

WEST OF PUERTO VIEJO DE SARAPIQUÍ

Selva Verde

Selva Verde *(☎ 766-6800, fax 766-6011; in the USA ☎ 800-451-7111, email: travel@holbrooktravel.com)* is in Chilamate, about 7km west of Puerto Viejo. It is a private *finca* that has been turned into a tourist facility. Well over half of its approximately 200 hectares are forested; the rest contain the lodge buildings in attractively landscaped grounds.

The main lodge (called the River Lodge) has 45 double rooms in a series of modules surrounding a large conference hall. This facility is often used by Elderhostel groups, and slide shows, lectures, and discussions on a variety of topics are presented on nights when Elderhostel groups are staying there and at irregular intervals at other times. If you happen to be staying at the lodge when an Elderhostel group is there, discreetly sitting in on their slide shows is usually not a problem – the Elderhostel folks are generally a nice bunch. The dining area is in a large thatched building linked to the bedrooms by a long covered walkway. Meals are served buffet-style at set times. There is a small reference library for guests.

Rooms are rustic but comfortable, with private hot showers and large communal verandahs with hammocks and forest views. Rates are US$85/136/174/192 single/double/triple/quad including three meals. Children under 12 sharing with adults stay free; children over 12 sharing with adults pay US$32 each. Green-season discounts (US$12 less per person) apply April 16 to December 14.

The lodge is owned and operated by Holbrook Travel of the USA (see Organized Tours in the Getting There & Away chapter). Because of the travel agency connection, the lodge is popular with tour groups from the USA and other countries.

Things to See & Do There are several kilometers of walking trails through the grounds and into the forest (premontane tropical wet forest); trail maps are available, or you can hire a bilingual guide from the lodge. There are plenty of birds and butterflies, and observant visitors may see mammals, frogs, and reptiles. Bilingual guides charge US$15 for a three-hour hike or US$25 for a six-hour hike on the trails. Costs are per person, and it is customary to tip the guide.

On one visit, I saw a pair of nesting sunbitterns on the banks of the Río Sarapiquí. Stiles and Skutch write in their authoritative *A Guide to the Birds of Costa Rica* that 'the sunbittern's nest has rarely been found, and the best available account of its breeding is that of a pair that nested in the gardens of the Zoological Society of London more than a century ago.' Seeing a pair of sunbitterns in a nest in the wild is not a bad way to start a day of birding.

There is also a garden of medicinal plants, as well as a butterfly garden planted with flowers, shrubs, and trees designed to attract a variety of butterfly species. Explanatory tours are offered. Guests at the lodge can visit for free; others pay US$5 admission.

Various boat tours on the Río Sarapiquí are also available. You can rent a small boat, raft, or canoe with a guide for four or five hours for US$45 per person. Three-hour motorized boat trips on the Sarapiquí cost US$25 per person from the lodge. These trips give you a good chance of seeing a sloth in the trees, but only if you have a local guide – most tourists just can't spot them. Mountain bikes can be rented for US$25 a half day, and locally guided horseback rides (US$20 for two to three hours) can also be arranged.

Getting There & Away Buses en route to or from Puerto Viejo will drop you off at the entrance – all the drivers know where it is. Taxis from Puerto Viejo to the lodge cost about US$4. If you make arrangements with Selva Verde, above, it can arrange private transportation from San José.

Islas del Río

Almost 2km west of Selva Verde, at the community of Bajos de Chilamate, is the Islas del Río Lodge (*☎ 766-6574*), which was bought in 1996 by its tico owner returning home after years in California. There are about 3km of trails that can be visited on foot or horseback – some trails may involve stream crossings. The lodge is called Islas del Río (Islands of the River) because tributaries of the Sarapiquí have divided the grounds into small islands. Longer foot or horseback tours beyond the lodge area into the rainforest are also available.

There are about 30 rooms, half of which have private baths with electric hot showers (or, in some cases, bathtubs). The other rooms have shared bathrooms. All rooms have fans. A large open dining room serves good tico fare. A few rooms will sleep up to six people. The rate is about US$20 per person, including a continental breakfast.

Sarapiquí Aguas Bravas offers river running here. A 2½-hour run on Class III rapids costs US$40 per person, including lunch. Inner-tubing, motorboating, horseback riding, and mountain bike rental are all offered – most adventures run about US$25 for two to four hours.

Reservations for these activities can be made at Islas del Río. See the Selva Verde entry, above, for transport details.

La Quinta de Sarapiquí Lodge

About 5km north of the village of La Virgen, a 1km-long gravel road to the west leads to La Quinta de Sarapiquí Lodge (*☎/fax 761-1052, laquinta@costarica.net*), a pleasant little family- run lodge on the banks of the Río Sardinal. Friendly tico owner Beatriz Gámez is very active in local environmental issues and is a good source of information on the area.

Activities at the lodge include swimming in the river (there is a good swimming hole near the lodge), a butterfly garden, a 'frog land' trail where poison-dart frogs are commonly seen, horseback riding, fishing, boat trips, mountain biking, and birding. Fishing and horseback rides are free to lodge guests. There are 15 rooms in bungalows set in a garden, all with terraces, ceiling fans, and private hot showers. Rates are US$52 for one or two people, US$70 for three. There is an air-conditioned dining room where meals cost US$7 for breakfast, US$8 for lunch, and US$9 for dinner. There's also a game room with Ping-Pong, a small swimming-hole-like pool overlooking the river, and an informal bar.

Beatriz helps administer the Camara de Turismo de Sarapiquí (CANTUSA), which works to promote a balance between conservation and tourism. La Quinta was host to the brainstorming sessions for the new Centro Neotropico Sarapiquí (see below) and is organizing discussions about a dam planned for the Río Sarapiquí. Its informal bamboo conference center is available to visiting groups.

Centro Neotropico Sarapiquí

This new project, which was declared by presidential decree a 'Project of National Interest' at its inception in 1997, is 2km east of the village of La Virgen. The Centro Neotropico Sarapiquí (*☎/fax 761-1004, magistra@sol.racsa.co.cr*) lodge, museum, and botanical garden are the gateway to a 350-hectare rainforest reserve. The aim of the museum and lodge is to heighten visitors' awareness of both the cultural and natural history of the rainforest before they enter the reserve itself. This is done through a mixture of ambience and education. Cars are left near the highway and visitors walk through orange groves and gardens to the lodge, which is modeled after a 15th-century pre-Columbian village. Four conical Palenque-style buildings with palm-thatch roofs house comfortable rooms decorated with pre-Columbian motifs. The restaurant serves meals incorporating spices and edible flowers used in pre-Columbian indigenous cuisine, as well as fresh fruits and vegetables from the surrounding gardens. The museum chronicles the history of the rainforest (and human interactions with it) through a mixture of displays, audio presentations, and animation. The tour is interactive and is 'led' by the 19th-century Costa Rican naturalist/explorers Anastasio Alfaro and José Cástulo Zeledon. Following the museum tour, visitors enter the reserve via a 250m suspension bridge.

At last visit, parts of the project were still under construction. If any of the passion and vision of designer/architect Jean Pierre Knockaert (who was on hand for a personal tour) are realized, the center should be well worth a visit. Knockaert is the president of Landscape Foundation Belgium, the project's nonprofit developer.

The lodge and reserve were operational in late 1999, and the museum is due to open in January 2000. A four- to six-hour visit to the museum, botanical gardens, rainforest reserve, and canopy skywalk costs US$25 (US$12.50 for children under 12), including a naturalist guide. The overnight rate for the 24 lodge rooms is US$99 single or double; all have private baths and Internet connections (!), some have views of the valley and reserve, and others look out on the orchards and gardens. Meals cost US$6 for breakfast, US$12 for lunch and dinner buffets of vegetarian and Costa Rican food. A research center is available to students, scientists, and visitors.

Rancho Leona

Rancho Leona *(☎/fax 761-1019, rleona@sol.racsa.co.cr)* is a rustic lodge 19km west of Puerto Viejo in the village of La Virgen. The US/tica owners, Ken and Leona, are artisans and musicians who provide a laid-back family atmosphere. Musicians are welcome to stop by and jam with Ken on the piano. The focus of their artwork is Tiffany-style stained glass using a copper foil technique. Their studio/workshop is a dazzling display of windows, glass hangings and, especially, lampshades, all of which are custom-designed; they have done work for customers all over the world, working out sketches via fax, and many of the pieces hanging in the studio are also for sale. This artistic technique is a painstaking and time-consuming process and the results are exquisitely lovely, but they don't come cheap. They also sell T-shirts and tropical jewelry made from local seeds and beads that will meet the needs and pocketbooks of casual souvenir shoppers.

Rancho Leona has a restaurant serving Italian food, salads, and sandwiches, all freshly made and moderately priced (US$3 to US$7). Stop by for lunch and, while you wait for your order to be prepared, take a tour of the studio.

Kayaking trips are another focus of the lodge. They offer a trip that gives you two nights at the lodge with a day of kayaking. The price is US$75 per person and includes kayak and equipment, river guide, transportation to/from put-in and take-out points, and a picnic lunch. The one-day kayaking trip is designed for all levels; a brief introductory lesson is provided for those with no experience. Extra days of instruction can also be arranged. Experienced kayakers can arrange adventurous trips on rivers with Class III and IV rapids. Group trips can also be arranged.

Guests are welcome to hang out at the lodge, swim in the nearby river, or hike to riversides and a waterfall (about an hour's walk along roads and then through pasture and forest). Guides are available, and all the people who work here speak English. Accommodations at the lodge are in bunks. Solar-heated showers, a sweat lodge, a hot tub, a restaurant and bar, and a games/reading area are all available (another recent interest of Ken's is the computer strategy games Star Craft and War Craft).

They also have a geodesic dome deep in the rainforest, with a screened-in loft with 360° view. The dome is next to the Río Peje on the border of Braulio Carrillo, about 10km east of the lodge. It has basic cooking facilities, and a composting outhouse; bathing is in the river. Costs are about US$80 per person per night, including food supplies and a guide to take you there. Longer stays and group rates are negotiable.

Buses out of San José and Ciudad Quesada can drop you off in front of the lodge on their way to Puerto Viejo. All the drivers know Rancho Leona in La Virgen. Buses from Puerto Viejo to San José or Ciudad Quesada can drop you here too.

La Virgen

This is the largest village on the road between Puerto Viejo and San Miguel (although it is just a tiny community), and it has one of the best budget options in the area, the friendly ***Sarapiquí Outdoor Center*** *(☎/fax 761-1123, ☎ 297-1010 beeper)*, run by David Duarte Soto, who also runs river trips. The rooms are simple and a fair value at $8 per person – the draw is that behind the cabinas are lovely views of the river and landscaped grounds. You can camp here for US$3 per person; there is a communal kitchen and a covered terrace in case of rain. Breakfast, in a small for-guests-only café overlooking the river, costs US$4; lunch and dinner cost US$5. A white-water rafting day trip costs US$40, other boat trips cost US$28, and horseback trips can be arranged for US$25.

Other clean and friendly budget accommodations in La Virgen are the ***Hotel Claribel*** *(☎ 761-1190)*, offering rooms with TVs and private showers for US$8 single, and the slightly cheaper and simpler ***Cabinas Tia Rosita*** *(☎ 761-1032)*, which gets a lot of truckers. The ***Restaurante Nuevo Cevi*** has a nice porch and a cook with a good local reputation; Ken at Rancho Leona recommends the fish soup. The friendly ***Restaurant and Bar Sansi*** *(☎ 761-1163)* has seafood specialties; it is open until 2 am on weekends, when it may have dancing. It's a locally popular place.

The Green Tortoise overland bus tour company has one of its stop-over activity centers close to La Virgen; call ☎ 761-1035 for information. About 1km southwest of Rancho Leona, a signed turn to the left advertises Bijagual Butterfly Sanctuary in San Ramón, 6km away.

NORTH OF PUERTO VIEJO DE SARAPIQUÍ

El Gavilán

El Gavilán is a private 100-hectare preserve about 4km northeast of Puerto Viejo. Reservations can be made in San José with El Gavilán partners Peace Rainbow Travel Agency *(☎ 234-9507, fax 253-6556, gavilan@sol.racsa.co.cr)*. There is no phone at the lodge, which used to be a cattle hacienda and is surrounded by attractive gardens with large trees that are great for birding. One of the receptionists, Eric Castro, is an avid birder and can guide you. There is also a variety of tropical fruit harvested for meals. Horses are available for hire, and guides will take you into the rainforest, or you can wander around at will on 5km of trails. There is a nice outdoor Jacuzzi for relaxation.

A variety of boat trips are available, ranging from short jaunts down the Río Sarapiquí for a couple of hours to multiday trips down the Sarapiquí to the San Juan and then on to the coast and down to Barra del Colorado or Tortuguero.

The lodge has 12 good-sized rooms and cabins, each with a private large bathroom, hot shower, and fan. Three more rooms share two bathrooms. Rates are US$45/60 single/double including breakfast, though several readers have arranged a discount just by dropping in. Tico-style lunches or dinners are available for US$9. Note that the restaurant serves no alcohol – bring your own if you wish. Guided hiking or horseback tours cost US$15 per person (three hours), Sarapiquí river rides cost US$20 per person (two hours), day tours to the Río San Juan cost US$60 per person (two minimum, lunch included), and on to Tortuguero costs US$300 one way (several people can go for this price). Rafting and tours to Volcán Arenal are also offered.

To get here, take any Puerto Viejo de Sarapiquí bus, then a taxi for about US$2 or US$3. Boatmen from the Puerto Viejo dock (if you can find one readily available) will take you across the river to the lodge for about the same price. El Gavilán will arrange transportation from San José for US$25 per person one way (four-person minimum). It also offers day trips from San José, including a ride on the Río Sarapiquí and lunch, for US$70 per person. Overnight packages, including transportation from San José, accommodations, meals, and tours, start at US$380 double for two days and one night and go to US$760 double for five days and four nights. If you are driving, there is a sign to the right about 2km before Puerto Viejo coming from Horquetas; from the main road, it's about 1km to the lodge.

The prices given for accommodations at El Gavilán are the officially advertised prices; if you just show up and there's space, you can often get a discount. Several readers have written in praise of this place.

Oro Verde

Oro Verde is a private preserve on the Sarapiquí near the Nicaraguan border, two to three hours by motorized dugout from Puerto Viejo. There are about 2500 hectares, of which 80% is forested. In '99 it was put up for sale, and plans for it are uncertain.

LINDSEY P MARTIN

LINDSEY P MARTIN

Sky Walk and shadows on cloud forest canopy, Monteverde

CAROL HUGHES

Playa Nancite, Parque Nacional Santa Rosa

FRANK BALTHIS

Expect muddy trails in the cloud forest of Monteverde.

BUDDY MAYS

Malachite butterfly, Monteverde

FRANK BALTHIS
Nesting olive ridley turtle and observers at Playa Grande, PN Marino Las Baulas de Guanacaste

DAVID MADISON
Estación Biológica La Selva

BUDDY MAYS
Fishing boat on quiet beach, Península de Nicoya

NIK WHEELER
Local bar in Puerto Humo, Península de Nicoya

Contact former owner Wolf Bissinger for information (wolfbiss@sol.racsa.co.cr).

Trinidad Lodge

This budget travelers' lodge, also rather grandiloquently called Cabinas Paraíso de las Fronteras, is in the village of Trinidad at the confluence of Río Sarapiquí and Río San Juan, across from the Nicaraguan border post. It is a working ranch, and there are about six clean and spacious cabins with three beds and private baths; rates are variously reported as US$7.50 and US$10 per person. Reasonably priced and tasty home-cooked meals are available. Birding is good, and horse rentals and boat tours can be arranged. Trinidad is served by a daily boat from Puerto Viejo at 11 am, returning around 2 pm. There is no phone at the lodge, but information is available from English-speaking Cesar *(☎ 259-1679)* in San José.

SOUTH OF PUERTO VIEJO DE SARAPIQUÍ

Estación Biológica La Selva

La Selva (☎ 766-6565, fax 766-6335, nathist@sloth.ots.ac.cr), not to be confused with Selva Verde in Chilamate, is a biological station, not a lodge, though you can stay here if you have an advance reservation. The biological station is the real thing, teeming with research scientists and graduate students using the well-equipped laboratories, experimental plots, herbarium, and library to investigate the ecological processes of the rainforest.

La Selva is run by the Organization for Tropical Studies (OTS; ☎ 240-6696, fax 240-6783, reservas@ots.ac.cr), which is a consortium founded in 1963 for the purpose of providing leadership in the education, research, and wise use of tropical natural resources. Member organizations from the USA, Puerto Rico, and Costa Rica include 46 universities and two museums.

Many well-known tropical ecologists have received training at La Selva. Twice a year, OTS offers an eight-week course open mainly to graduate students of ecology. The students visit several of the other OTS sites, but La Selva is the biggest and most frequently used one. Course work is grueling, with classes, discussions, seminars, and field work running from dawn till dusk and into the evening. Various other courses and field trips are also offered. There are many long-term and ongoing experiments underway at La Selva, and many researchers come here year after year.

The area protected by La Selva is almost 1600 hectares of premontane wet tropical rainforest. Most of the land has not been disturbed. It is bordered to the south by the almost 46,000 hectares of Parque Nacional Braulio Carrillo, thus affording a large enough area to enable a great diversity of species to live here. Over 400 species of birds have been recorded at La Selva, as well as 120 species of mammals, 1900 species of vascular plants (especially from the orchid, philodendron, coffee, and legume families), and thousands of species of insects. The list goes on, and increases every year.

Information You can visit La Selva all year round, but with almost 200mm of rain falling in each of the months of February and March (the driest months), you should be prepared with rainwear or an umbrella.

Insect repellent, a water bottle, clothes that you don't mind getting covered in mud, and footwear suitable for muddy trails are also essential. The total annual rainfall is 4100mm, and temperatures average 24°C but are often higher. The elevation is about 35m at the research station and goes up to about 150m by the time Braulio Carrillo is reached.

There is a small exhibit room and a gift shop selling books, maps, posters, and T-shirts.

Nature Trails & Hiking Birding in particular is excellent because of the very well-developed trail system at La Selva. A few of the trails have a boardwalk to enable relatively easy access even during the wet season (though watch your footing – those wet boards can get very slick). The total length of trails is about 60km, many of which are rough jungle paths. Guided hikes are offered daily, but unguided hiking is no longer allowed. This happened because of the rising popularity of the research station with visitors, which led to a conflict with research interests. Now, guided 3½-hour hikes are offered at 8 am and 1:30 pm daily. These cost US$20 per person, or US$30 for both hikes. Children aged five to 12 accompanied by an adult pay half-price. The hikes are mainly on cement or boardwalk trails, suitable for all abilities – some trails are wheelchair or walker accessible. You come here to learn, not to have a remote wilderness experience. Profits from these walks help to fund the research station. Mandatory reservations for guided hikes can be made directly with La Selva; see above contact information.

Places to Stay & Eat You can come on a day trip or stay overnight. There are simple but comfortable bungalows with four bunks per room, and a limited number of singles and doubles. Bathrooms are communal, but there are plenty of them. There is a dining room that serves meals, although researchers and students always have priority. If room is available, tour groups (especially birding ones) and individual travelers can use the facilities, but reservations must be made in advance. There is usually space available if reservations are made a few weeks in advance, though during the popular dry season the place may be fully booked for two or three months ahead. Reservations for overnight stays should be made with OTS; see above contact information.

The overnight foreign tourist rates are US$75/120 single/double, US$45 for extra adults, and US$25 for children (five to 12 years) sharing with adults; ticos, researchers, and students stay for heavily discounted rates. This is, after all, a research station. Prices include three meals a day and one guided hike each day. Beer is available if ordered in advance; other alcohol is not available. Laundry machines are available in the afternoons only.

Getting There & Away The public bus to Puerto Viejo via the Río Frío and Horquetas route can drop you off at the entrance road to La Selva, about 3km before Puerto Viejo. From here it is almost 2km on a dirt road to the research station. Taxis from Puerto Viejo will take you there for about US$3.

OTS runs buses from San José (8 am) to La Selva and back (3 pm) on Monday, Wednesday, and Friday. The fare is US$10 one way, and reservations should be made when you arrange your visit. Researchers and students have priority.

OTS also runs a van service into Puerto Viejo and back several times a day (except Sunday, when there is only one trip).

Sarapiquí Ecolodge

Just outside of La Selva is the Sarapiquí Ecolodge *(☎ 766-6122 mornings or afternoons)*, on an 80-hectare dairy ranch run by the Murillo family. Rustic accommodations in bunks in the family ranch house are available for US$10 per person; country-style meals cost US$5 to US$6. There are a total of 18 beds in four rooms upstairs, and they share four bathrooms with hot showers downstairs. Behind the lodge, the Río Puerto Viejo (a tributary of the Sarapiquí) provides swimming and boating. Horses can be rented and boat tours are available. Get there by using the same entrance road as for La Selva (above) and then following a dirt road another kilometer to the left just before the La Selva gate.

Rara Avis

Rara Avis (☎ 764-3131, fax 764-4187, raraavis@sol.racsa.co.cr) is a remote private preserve of 1335 hectares of tropical rainforest between 600 and 700m in elevation on the northeastern slopes of the Cordillera Central. The land borders the eastern edge of Parque Nacional Braulio Carrillo. The rainforest preserve was founded by Amos Bien, an American who came to Costa Rica as a biology student in 1977. As has happened to many biologists who have worked in the tropics, he became fascinated by the incredible complexity of the rainforest ecosystems. Instead of becoming a research biologist bent on discovering more about the rainforest, Amos wanted to help conserve it. The result is the Rara Avis preserve, which was created with the goal of demonstrating that an intact and preserved rainforest could be just as profitable, if not more so, than one that is logged and turned into cattle pasture, which has been the fate of much of Costa Rica's tropical rainforests.

Bio-Projects at Rara Avis

Biologists at Rara Avis have rediscovered the stained glass window palm, *Geonoma epetiolata*, which had been considered extinct in Costa Rica for about half a century. It is an attractive palm that grows only in deep shade, with potential as an ornamental house plant. Silvana Marten has been doing research on this plant, and it is now being cultivated commercially in the rainforest understory for sale to nurseries. The third crop of several hundred seedlings was being grown in 1996. Growing other rainforest plants such as canopy orchids in situ (in their natural habitat) is also being considered.

Some philodendron species produce aerial roots that are harvested and treated by local artisans to produce wicker. This product can then be woven into baskets, furniture, mats, and other utilitarian items. A local craftsman, Federico Vargas, has been actively producing wicker furniture from philodendron roots for some years. He has appeared on CNN television and was featured in a documentary made by Cultural Survival (the international human rights group for indigenous people and ethnic minorities). The philodendron is a rainforest plant, and workers at Rara Avis have studied the ecology of the plant to determine what a sustainable harvest size would be and whether it would be an economically practical crop.

Another enterprise is butterfly farming. At Rara Avis, Isidro Chacón, former curator of entomology at the Museo Nacional in San José, began sustainable butterfly farming in a project funded by the Worldwide Fund for Nature. The farm raises certain species of moths and butterflies for sale to tropical hothouses in Europe and North America, where it is difficult to raise butterflies economically. Butterflies are important in the hothouses both as an attraction in themselves and as natural pollinators. Another purpose of the project is to learn more about these insects and provide education. The butterfly farm was so successful that five similar family-run projects are now flourishing in the area.

Straightforward biological research is also a goal at Rara Avis, but with an innovative twist. It is here that biologist Donald Perry built his Automated Web for Canopy Exploration (AWCE). This radio-controlled ski-lift-style machine traveled up, down, and across about 4 hectares of forest canopy, enabling researchers to get a close look at the many epiphytic plants, mosses, beetles, ants and other insects, frogs, reptiles, fungi, parasites, and other creatures that spend their entire life cycles in the rainforest treetops. Many of these were unknown to scientists until exploration of the canopy began.

The story of the AWCE can be read in Perry's book *Life Above the Jungle Floor*. Although the original AWCE is no longer functioning, Don Perry has since gone on to develop the Rainforest Aerial Tram (see the Central Valley & Surrounding Highlands chapter for details). At Rara Avis, he built a cabin platform 30m up in a *Vantanea* tree. It is reachable by climbing a rope using mechanical ascenders if you're accompanied by a guide. Don is hoping to install more canopy platforms at Rara Avis.

– Rob Rachowiecki

Visitors can use the trail system at Rara Avis, either alone or accompanied by guides. The birding is excellent, with a list of over 350 species. Birds seen here but not very often elsewhere include the blue-and-gold tanager, the black-and-yellow tanager, and the snowcap hummingbird (all of which I saw near the lodge), as well as many others.

Very common mammals include white-faced, spider, and howler monkeys, coatis, anteaters, and pacas. Peccaries, jaguars, tapirs, and sloths are also present in reasonable numbers but are hard to see.

Insects are, of course, abundant, and the plants and trees are as varied as anywhere in the tropics – over 500 species of trees are known on the property, which is more than the tree species in all of Europe. Reference books are available at the lodge.

Rara Avis can be visited year-round. The dry season is from January to December inside the lodge. Outside, it rains over 5000mm every year, and there are no dry months, although from February to April is slightly less wet. This is definitely rainforest.

A short trail from the lodge leads to La Catarata – a 55m-high waterfall that cuts an impressive swath through the forest. With care, it is possible to take a gloriously refreshing swim at the base of the falls, though you have to beware of flash floods, so ask the lodge staff for advice.

Places to Stay & Eat Contact Amos Bien *(☎ 764-3131, fax 764-4187, raraavis@sol.racsa.co.cr)* to make the required reservations at any of the accommodations listed below.

El Plastico is at the edge of the preserve, 12km from Horquetas by a very bad road through farmland. (Horquetas itself is about 18km south of Puerto Viejo and 10km west of Río Frío.) It is a ramshackle building built in 1964 by prisoners from a now defunct jungle penal colony. The prisoners were given pieces of plastic to sleep under – hence the name. The building was abandoned in 1965 and renovated for Rara Avis in 1986. It is available mainly for use by biologists, students, and groups. Accommodations are quite basic – 30 bunk beds in about seven rooms. There are communal showers with hot water on demand and an open-air dining area with simple but plentiful and tasty food. Accommodations cost US$45 per person per day, including meals, with a minimum of eight people. Discounts are available for large student and research groups.

A further 3km of an equally bad (if not worse) road through the rainforest brings you to the ***Waterfall Lodge***, named after the falls nearby. This is a rustic but comfortable and attractive jungle lodge. Ten rooms have private showers and hot water, with balconies overlooking the rainforest. Even when it's pouring outside, you can watch birds from your private balcony. Because access is time-consuming and difficult, a two-day minimum stay is recommended. Prices include meals, guided walks, and transport from Horquetas. There is no electricity, but kerosene lanterns are provided. The open-air dining room serves good and plentiful meals. The rates are US$90 per person per day in single rooms, US$80 per person in doubles, and US$70 per person in triples or quads. Children four to 16 years old sharing rooms with their parents are charged half-price.

Also, there is the two-room ***Riverside Cabin***, with similar facilities to those at the Waterfall Lodge but set in the rainforest about a half kilometer away from the dining room.

The cabin platform (see the boxed text 'Bio-Projects at Rara Avis,' above) is also available for overnighting. There is room for two people, and bathroom facilities consist of water (which has to be hauled up in a can) and a portable toilet. The platform is operated separately by Donald Perry Adventures; contact Amos Bien at Rara Avis for details (see above).

Getting There & Away First get a bus to Horquetas – you are given a schedule when you make your reservation. In Horquetas, you will be met and transported to Rara Avis. The road climbs from Horquetas at 75m to the lodge at 710m above sea level.

En route, two rivers must be forded (there are footbridges).

The road is so bad that a tractor is used to pull a wagon with padded bench seats; Rara Avis asks guests to pack lightly, and it has a storage facility in Horquetas for extra luggage. The tractor leaves Horquetas every morning at 9 am and returns from Rara Avis at 2 pm. The 15km trip takes three to five hours. You can arrange to have a 4WD jeep take you the first 12km (up to El Plastico), taking under an hour, but then you must walk for the last 3km. Horses are available if you want to ride.

Caribbean Lowlands

The Caribbean and Pacific coasts of Costa Rica are very different. The Pacific coast is indented, resulting in a very long and irregular coastline, while the Caribbean is a smooth, relatively short sweep of beaches, mangroves, and coastal swamp forest. The tidal variation on this smooth coastline is very small. The Pacific has a dry season; the Caribbean can be wet year-round (though from February to March and September to October are less rainy). About half of the Caribbean coastline is protected by two national parks and two national wildlife refuges, while less than 10% of the Pacific coastline is protected.

The entire Caribbean coast is part of Limón province, which covers 18% of Costa Rica but has only 7.5% of the population, making it the least-populated and second most sparsely inhabited province in the country (after Guanacaste). One-third of the province's 250,000 inhabitants are blacks of mostly Jamaican descent. Most of them live on or near the coast and many still speak English, albeit a dialect that sounds old-fashioned to most nonlocal ears. They add a cultural diversity missing in the rest of Costa Rica. Also, in the southern part of the province, several thousand indigenous Bribri and Cabecar people inhabit the region.

Partly because of the low population of the region and partly because, until the development of the 1949 constitution, blacks were legally discriminated against, the Caribbean lowlands have been developed at a much slower rate than the Pacific. There are proportionately fewer roads and more areas that can be reached only by boat or light aircraft. Limón province has less than 10% of the country's hotel rooms, while the Pacific coastal provinces of Guanacaste and Puntarenas have a combined total of over 40%. Traditionally, Costa Ricans from the populous Central Valley have vacationed on the Pacific, and even today, the Caribbean is not a primary destination for most nationals. This slowly began to change with the 1987 opening of the San José-Puerto Limón highway, which cut driving time to the coast in half, but traditions die hard.

Foreign travelers, on the other hand, are more attracted to the Caribbean, partly for the romance associated with the word 'Caribbean' and partly for the cultural diversity found there. The main road from San José to the Caribbean ends at the provincial capital of Puerto Limón. From here there is just a single road heading south along the coast to the Panamanian border. Northbound travelers must rely on boats to take them up the Intercoastal Waterway (a series of canals locally known as *los canales*), through wilderness areas, past remote fishing villages, and on to Nicaragua. Limited access to the region has helped maintain a sense of traditional values in its inhabitants, making a Caribbean visit more culturally interesting than a trip to the Pacific beaches, though not as luxurious.

There are exceptions, of course. The Tortuguero and Barra del Colorado areas both have first-class lodges and fishing resorts in wilderness environments, and the hotel quality is improving in the south. But most of the Caribbean coast has a gentle, laid-back, unhurried feel to it.

The devastating earthquake that struck Costa Rica on April 22, 1991, was centered south of Puerto Limón, which was the city most seriously affected by the disaster. Roads to the coast were closed (at least 17 bridges were impassable), the railway was destroyed, thousands of buildings suffered damage, and parts of the coastline rose by more than a meter, in some cases exposing coral reefs. This was one of the worst earthquakes to hit the country, but there are frequent minor ones. The highways from San José to Puerto Limón have been repaired but still show signs of earthquake and other damage. Highway motorists tend to speed once they get to the flatlands on the way to Puerto Limón – beware of very severe dips, potholes, or bumps in the road. Some of these could certainly damage your car if you hit them at 80km/h. The highway is also prone to closure because of mudslides during the wettest season – closures normally last from a few hours to a day or two. The southbound road from Puerto Limón has suffered severe cracking and potholes – average speeds of 20km/h are normal for long stretches.

San José to Puerto Limón

GUÁPILES & ENVIRONS

This town is the transport center for the Río Frío banana-growing region. It is in the northern foothills of the Cordillera Central, 62km northeast of San José, and is the first town of any size on the San José-Puerto Limón highway. The region is home to several small B&B-style hotels, which offer an excellent base for visiting the Rainforest Aerial Tram (only 20km west of Guápiles, described in the Central Valley & Surrounding Highlands chapter), some small local reserves (see Places to Stay & Eat, below), and the banana-growing region to the north. Most travelers speed through on Hwy 32, which connects most of the places described in this section, but increasing numbers are finding a stop in the region worthwhile. There is a lively agricultural market on Saturdays, but for the most part, there is little of interest in Guápiles itself.

Jardín Botánico Las Cusingas

This is not your typical botanical garden. The *tico* owners (Jane Segleau and Ulyses Blanco) emphasize education about a variety of subjects including medicinal plants, rural Costa Rican life, conservation, the ethical use of plants for profit, and information on a variety of other nature-related subjects. The owners give interesting tours (in English or Spanish) of the grounds for US$5; tours last about two hours. The grounds have 80 species of medicinal plants, 80 species of orchids, 30 species of bromeliads, and over 100 species of birds recorded. The grounds cover 20 hectares and the owners work with neighbors to protect surrounding areas. Two trails go into the forest: the longer one is 1.5km and leads to a river, while a shorter loop is carefully graded to allow access to people of any age and fitness level (though not to those in wheelchairs). Various courses, research projects, and a library are all available to visitors and locals.

Banana Trains

Bananas, Costa Rica's most important export, used to be loaded onto steam trains and hauled to the Caribbean coast. Today, trucks have superseded trains for transporting bananas, though small sections of track remain for hauling banana cargo in the Caribbean lowlands.

– **Rob Rachowiecki**

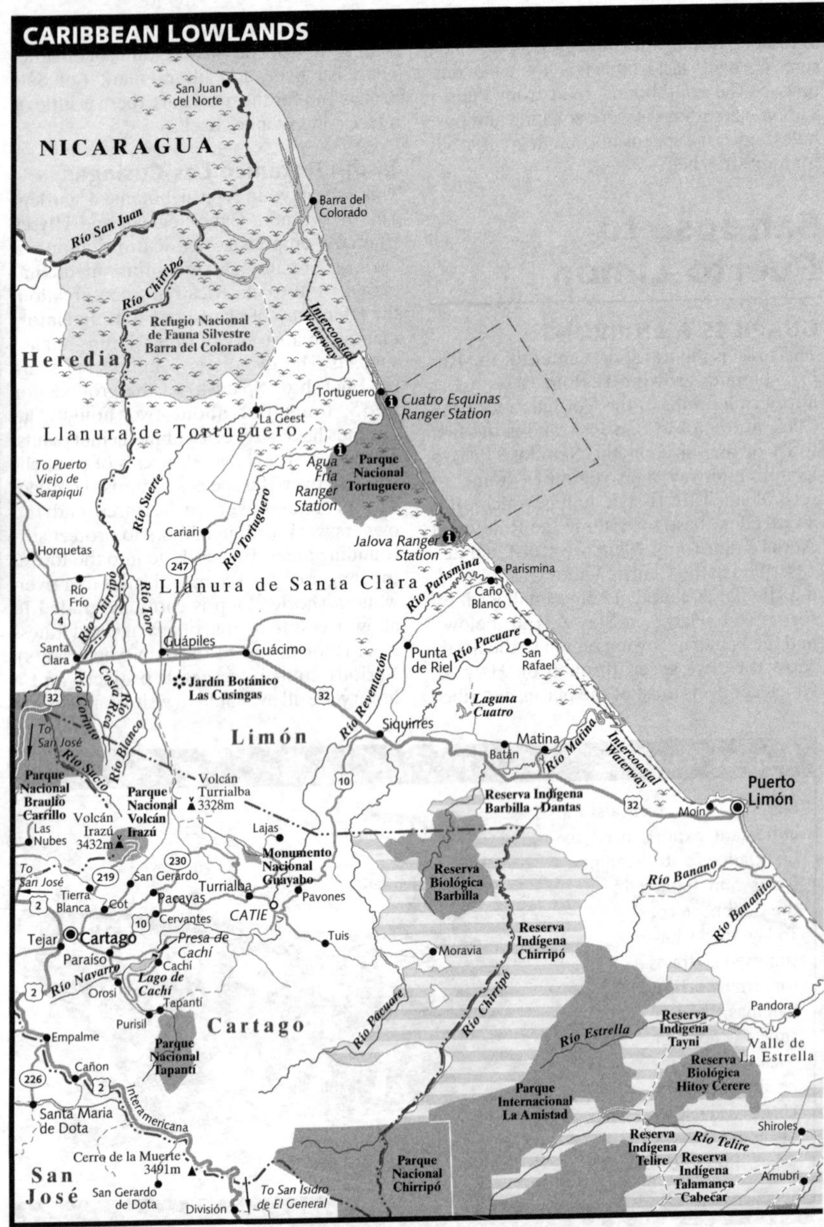
CARIBBEAN LOWLANDS
NICARAGUA
San Juan del Norte
Barra del Colorado
Río San Juan
Río Chirripó
Refugio Nacional de Fauna Silvestre Barra del Colorado
Intercoastal Waterway
Heredia
Tortuguero
Cuatro Esquinas Ranger Station
La Geest
Llanura de Tortuguero
Agua Fría Ranger Station
Parque Nacional Tortuguero
To Puerto Viejo de Sarapiquí
Río Suerte
Río Tortuguero
Cariari
Jalova Ranger Station
Horquetas
Parismina
Río Parismina
Caño Blanco
Río Frío
Río Toro
Llanura de Santa Clara
Guápiles
Guácimo
Santa Clara
Punta de Riel
Río Pacuare
San Rafael
Río Reventazón
Jardín Botánico Las Cusingas
Río Costa Rica
Río Corinto
To San José
Río Blanco
Laguna Cuatro
Limón
Siquirres
Matina
Batán
Río Matina
Río Sucio
Parque Nacional Braulio Carrillo
Volcán Turrialba 3328m
Parque Nacional Volcán Irazú
Reserva Indígena Barbilla - Dantas
Puerto Limón
Moín
Volcán Irazú 3432m
Las Nubes
Lajas
Monumento Nacional Guayabo
Reserva Biológica Barbilla
To San José
San Gerardo
Tierra Blanca
Cot
Pacayas
Turrialba
Pavones
Cervantes
CATIE
Río Banano
Río Bananito
Tejar
Cartago
Presa de Cachí
Tuis
Moravia
Reserva Indígena Chirripó
Paraíso
Cachí
Río Navarro
Lago de Cachí
Orosi
Tapantí
Purisil
Parque Nacional Tapantí
Cartago
Río Pacuare
Río Chirripó
Río Estrella
Reserva Indígena Tayni
Pandora
Valle de La Estrella
Empalme
Reserva Biológica Hitoy Cerere
Cañon
Interamericana
Parque Internacional La Amistad
Santa Maria de Dota
Reserva Indígena Telire
Río Telire
Shiroles
Cerro de la Muerte 3491m
Parque Nacional Chirripó
Reserva Indígena Talamança Cabecar
Amubri
San José
San Gerardo de Dota
División
To San Isidro de El General
32
247
4
10
230
219
2
226

Jane is a 2nd-degree practitioner of Reiki (a hands-on natural healing technique).

There is a rustic cabin with two rooms sleeping up to four people, a sitting room, and wood-burning stove with kitchen equipment (no microwave!), or you can eat with the owners' family with advance notice. Hot showers are available. The cabin rents for about US$30 (one to four people). This place is recommended for people who want to spend a few days studying natural history in a rustic setting. Reservations should be made for both the cabin and for guided tours (☎ 382-5805, leave a message).

Get to the garden by going 4km south by unpaved road from the main highway (Hwy 32) at the Soda Buenos Aires/Servicentro Santa Clara (gas station), on the eastern outskirts of Guápiles.

Places to Stay & Eat

In Town There are no street signs, so you have to ask for these places. The ***Keng Wa***, near the center of town, is probably the best of the basic places at US$4 per person for rooms with fans and shared cold showers; two rooms, at US$8 double, have private baths and fans. There are a few other poorer-looking cheap hotels.

The family-run ***Restaurant y Cabinas Madrigal*** *(☎ 710-0520)*, 50m east of the Almacén Ugalde, has eight clean (though windowless) rooms for US$7/11 single/double. The ***Cabinas Irdama*** *(☎ 710-7034, ☎/fax 710-7177)* has 21 decent and brighter rooms for about US$10/13 single/double. There's also a little restaurant. (Ask the owners about the three apartments with two double beds, kitchenettes, and warm showers that go for US$17, or about US$300 per month.) ***Cabinas Car*** *(☎ 710-0035)*, 50m west of the Catholic church, has 10 rooms for US$10 per person. All three hotels are clean, well run, and have TVs, fans, and private cold showers in the rooms.

The best in town is the ***Hotel Suerre*** *(☎ 710-7551, fax 710-6376)*, with 26 spacious, tiled, air-conditioned but bland rooms with cable TVs, telephones, and private hot showers for US$70/87 in the high season. There is a restaurant, Olympic-sized pool, tennis court, and sauna and spa for guests. Four suites with a sitting room cost about US$120 to US$150. The hotel is 1.8km north of the Servicentro Santa Clara on the main highway, east of town.

West of Town Note that the phones don't work well in this area, so when calling the following establishments be patient or try a fax.

Casa Río Blanco *(☎ 382-0957, 710-2652 to leave a message, fax 710-6161, rioblanco@compusource.net)* is a small B&B and reserve recently bought by Dee Bocock, a very friendly North American. The place is very environmentally conscious, and local tours can be arranged. Three cabins are set overlooking the Río Blanco (20m below), with great rainforest canopy views and excellent birding and other wildlife-watching. Volunteer positions in the reserve can be arranged. Two rooms inside the main house have garden views. All are fully screened, with private baths and hot water. Kerosene lanterns are used for lighting and there is solar electricity in the bathrooms. Rates are US$52/69/87 single/double/triple including breakfast and a guided nature hike on private trails. Rubber boots for hiking and inner tubes for river floating are available.

The entrance road to the Casa Río Blanco is 5km west of Guápiles on the west side of the Río Blanco bridge. From here it's about 1.5km south. If you're not driving, ask the bus driver to stop by the ***Restaurant La Ponderosa*** *(☎ 710-7144)*, which is 300m west of the entrance road. Call from here and you can arrange to get picked up. The Ponderosa, which is complete with a photograph of Ben Cartwright and the boys from the TV show *Bonanza*, serves delicious *bocas* (US50¢ each or free with a beer) as well as sandwiches and steaks. Another good place to eat is the ***Río Blanco Restaurant and B&B*** *(☎ 710-7857)*, just east of the Río Blanco bridge. There are a few motel rooms behind the restaurant that cost about US$15/20 single/double, each with fan, TV, and private hot bath. The rates include breakfast.

Continuing up the road from the main highway past the Casa Río Blanco for another 2km brings you to the ***Happy Rana Lodge*** *(☎ 385-1167 cellular; in the USA ☎ 520-743-8254; Apartado 348, Guápiles, Limón)*. Large rustic cabins with one queen and two single beds, hot private showers, and a spacious verandah cost US$40 single and US$10 for each additional person, including breakfast. Other meals are available on request. Electricity is available in the evenings. Owned by a young US-tico couple, the lodge has nearby hiking trails into the rainforest and horse rental (free for guests spending a few days). The best time to call is early afternoon.

For another lodging option outside of Guápiles, see the Jardín Botánico Las Cusingas section, above.

Getting There & Away

Buses to San José (under US$2) or Puerto Limón leave about every hour. Buses to Río Frío leave three or four times a day. There are also buses to Cariari, from where one or two buses a day go to Puerto Lindo on the Río Colorado in the Refugio Nacional de Fauna Silvestre Barra del Colorado. The road is paved as far as Cariari.

GUÁCIMO

This small town is 12km east of Guápiles and is the home of **EARTH** (Escuela de Agricultura de la Región Tropical Húmeda; ☎ 255-2000, fax 255-2726). This school has a college-level program designed to teach students from all over Latin America about sustainable agriculture in the tropics. A banana plantation, a 400-hectare forest reserve, nature trails, and horse rental attract visitors. Overnight visitors (by prior arrangement) are accommodated in rooms with fans and private hot showers. Rates are about US$27/40 single/double.

Also of interest is **Costa Flores** (☎/fax 717-5457; in San José ☎ 220-1311, Apartado 4769, San José), north of Guácimo on signed roads. This 120-hectare tropical flower farm claims to be the largest in the world. Six hundred varieties of tropical plants are grown here for export. Visitors and shoppers are welcome – call for information.

The ***Hotel Restaurant Río Palmas*** *(☎ 760-0305, fax 760-0296, Apartado 6944-*

1000, San José) is 600m east of EARTH and is the best motel directly on the highway to Puerto Limón. The rooms are good-sized, clean, and pleasantly decorated, and the glass windows are more effective than screens in keeping bugs out, though they keep the heat in. Large fans alleviate the heat and there is a TV and hot shower in each room. The hotel has a good restaurant and an attractive swimming pool, and trails behind the property allow hiking and horseback riding in a 200-hectare reserve (about US$4 per hour; horses must be reserved in advance). High-season rates are about US$45/50. The 24-hour gas station on the main highway at the entrance to Guácimo is a popular stopping place for truckers and tico families – the food is inexpensive and quite good. Aficionados of truck-stop menus may want to give the tico version a try.

SIQUIRRES

This town, 25km southeast of Guácimo, was a railway junction until recently. It remains significant as the road junction of the old San José-Turrialba-Puerto Limón route (Hwy 10) with the new highway to the coast (Hwy 32). The old route is slower but very scenic, for those with a little time on their hands. Siquirres is the last major town on the main highway before Puerto Limón, 58km farther east. Note that if you want to drive to Turrialba from here (on Hwy 10), you have to take a poorly signed overpass over the main highway. Most travelers go straight through or maybe stop at the ***Caribbean West Restaurant***, on the main highway just west of town. There are a few interesting-looking buildings (see the round church), and the center is small but bustling. There are a few cheap and basic hotels.

PUERTO LIMÓN

This port is the capital of Limón province and ticos refer to the city as Limón. The mainly black population of Limón and the surrounding district is about 76,000, so some 30% of the province's inhabitants live in and around the provincial capital. Limón is quite lively and busy, as ports tend to be, but is not considered a tourist town, although there are good hotels and something of a beach resort at Playa Bonita, 4km northwest of the town center. The recent addition of direct bus service from San José to the coastal villages south of Limón has decreased casual tourist traffic here, which means that despite the port town atmosphere, you may actually get less negative attention here than in the smaller, more visited villages.

Orientation

Streets are poorly marked and most do not have signs. Calles and avenidas go up one number at a time (Calle 1, Calle 2, etc) instead of going up in two's, as they do in most other towns. Locals get around by city landmarks such as the market, Radio Casino, and the *municipalidad* (town hall) on Parque Vargas. If you ask where the intersection of Calle 5 and Avenida 2 is, most people will have no idea where it's located. (It's 500m west of the municipalidad, or 100m west of the southwest corner of the market.)

Avenida 2 is considered one of the main streets – Parque Vargas, the municipalidad, the market, a couple of banks, the museum, and the San José bus terminal are all on or just off this street.

Limón is on the rocky Punta Piuta; the point shelters the main port at Moín, about 6 or 7km west of Limón.

Information

There is no tourist office. For information on tours, ask at some of the better hotels; for local information, the Internet places are a pretty good bet (see below). Jugos Viagra, a juice stand by the central market, has a sign advertising tourist information (which means they'll give you friendly street directions).

Immigration The Migración office is on Avenida 1, Calle 5. Visa extensions are normally given in San José.

Money Banco de Costa Rica (☎ 758-3166) and other banks will change money. The ATM at the Banco de San José accepts the widest variety of cards. The better hotels all

CARIBBEAN LOWLANDS

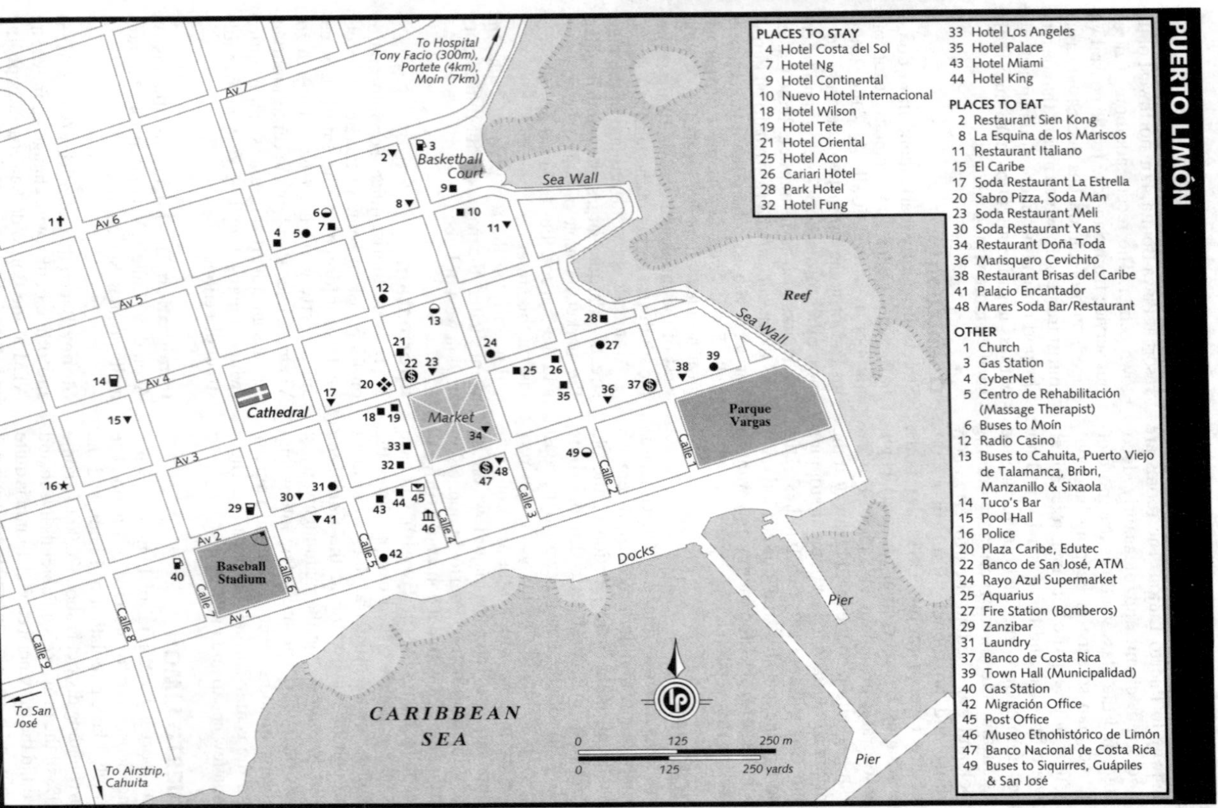
PUERTO LIMÓN
PLACES TO STAY
4 Hotel Costa del Sol
7 Hotel Ng
9 Hotel Continental
10 Nuevo Hotel Internacional
18 Hotel Wilson
19 Hotel Tete
21 Hotel Oriental
25 Hotel Acon
26 Cariari Hotel
28 Park Hotel
32 Hotel Fung
33 Hotel Los Angeles
35 Hotel Palace
43 Hotel Miami
44 Hotel King
PLACES TO EAT
2 Restaurant Sien Kong
8 La Esquina de los Mariscos
11 Restaurant Italiano
15 El Caribe
17 Soda Restaurant La Estrella
20 Sabro Pizza, Soda Man
23 Soda Restaurant Meli
30 Soda Restaurant Yans
34 Restaurant Doña Toda
36 Marisquero Cevichito
38 Restaurant Brisas del Caribe
41 Palacio Encantador
48 Mares Soda Bar/Restaurant
OTHER
1 Church
3 Gas Station
4 CyberNet
5 Centro de Rehabilitación (Massage Therapist)
6 Buses to Moín
12 Radio Casino
13 Buses to Cahuita, Puerto Viejo de Talamanca, Bribri, Manzanillo & Sixaola
14 Tuco's Bar
15 Pool Hall
16 Police
20 Plaza Caribe, Edutec
22 Banco de San José, ATM
24 Rayo Azul Supermarket
25 Aquarius
27 Fire Station (Bomberos)
29 Zanzibar
31 Laundry
37 Banco de Costa Rica
39 Town Hall (Municipalidad)
40 Gas Station
42 Migración Office
45 Post Office
46 Museo Etnohistórico de Limón
47 Banco Nacional de Costa Rica
49 Buses to Siquirres, Guápiles & San José
To Hospital Tony Facio (300m), Portete (4km), Moín (7km)
Basketball Court
Sea Wall
Reef
Cathedral
Market
Parque Vargas
Baseball Stadium
Docks
Pier
CARIBBEAN SEA
To San José
To Airstrip, Cahuita
Av 1
Av 2
Av 3
Av 4
Av 5
Av 6
Av 7
Calle 1
Calle 2
Calle 3
Calle 4
Calle 5
Calle 6
Calle 7
Calle 8
Calle 9
0 125 250 m
0 125 250 yards

take credit cards and some will exchange dollars. Exchange facilities are poor elsewhere along the coast (though the better lodges and hotels accept cash US dollars or even traveler's checks).

Email & Internet Access Edutec (☎ 798-5717), upstairs at the Plaza Caribe, is open 8 am to 10 pm daily. Also try CyberNet, next to the Hotel Costa del Sol.

Medical Services The Hospital Tony Facio (☎ 758-2222), on the *malecón* at the north end of town, serves the entire province. The tiny Centro de Rehabilitación (☎ 798-5073) offers a half-hour upper-back massage for US$7.50; a full-hour therapeutic rub costs US$13.

Dangers & Annoyances People have been mugged in Limón, so stick to the main well-lit streets at night. Also watch for pickpockets during the day. These are fairly normal precautions for many port cities – Limón is not especially dangerous.

Don't park anywhere after dark except in a guarded parking lot. Break-ins are common.

Things to See & Do

The main attraction is **Parque Vargas** by the waterfront. The park has tall attractive palms and other tropical trees and flowers, and birds and sloths hang out (literally) in the trees. It's not easy to see the sloths, but locals will help you spot one.

From the park it's a pleasant walk north along the **sea wall** of Puerto Limón with views of the rocky headland upon which the city is built.

There are no beaches clean enough for swimming in Limón. At **Playa Bonita**, 4km northwest of town, there is a sandy beach with decent waves that is OK for swimming. There are places to eat and picnic areas, and the backdrop of tropical vegetation is attractive.

On his fourth and last transatlantic voyage, Columbus landed at **Isla Uvita**, which can be seen about 1km east of Limón. It is possible to hire boats to visit the island,

CARIBBEAN LOWLANDS

DAVE G HOUSER

Municipal building in the neocolonial style, Puerto Limón

and the better hotels can arrange tours there. Organized tours to Tortuguero, Cahuita, and other destinations of interest can also be arranged from all the better hotels (as well as in San José).

Another focal point of the town is the colorful **central market**, which has a variety of cheap places to eat and plenty of bustling activity.

The small **Museo Etnohistórico de Limón** (☎ 758-2130, 758-3903) has exhibits about local culture and history but is open only erratically (supposedly 9 am to 5 pm Tuesday to Friday).

Special Events

Columbus Day (October 12), locally known as El Día de la Raza, is celebrated with more than the usual enthusiasm because of Columbus' historic landing on Isla Uvita. Tens of thousands of visitors, mainly ticos, stream into town for a *carnaval* of street parades and dancing, music, singing, drinking, and general carrying-on that goes on for four or five days. Hotels are booked well in advance of this event.

Labor Day is also especially colorful around Puerto Limón; people come up from the beach villages and there are dances and cricket matches.

Places to Stay

Hotels all along the Caribbean coast are in demand on weekends during the San José holiday seasons (Christmas, Easter, and the months of January and February) and especially during the Columbus Day celebrations, when prices rise. Reserve ahead if possible during those periods.

Some hotels reportedly operate on two price structures: one for locals and a higher one for visitors.

Budget The cheapest hotels are dirty and a poor value. Prostitutes and their clients use them. While not salubrious, these places don't seem particularly dangerous, though solo women travelers should avoid them. Basically, they are places to crash for a night; the ones listed here are on the more wholesome end of the spectrum. This is a town where it's worth spending a little more for a better room.

The ***Cariari Hotel*** *(☎ 758-1395)* has an atmospheric balcony-sitting area and small, basic rooms with fans for US$5.50/7.50 single/double. The ***Hotel Oriental*** *(☎ 758-0117)* has rooms for US$7 double with shared cold showers and is a decent, basic place. The ***Hotel Ng*** *(☎ 758-2134)* is filled with workers during the week but is less busy on weekends. The place seems friendly, though rooms are very basic for US$6/10 single/double or US$7.50/11.50 with private cold shower. The ***Hotel Wilson*** *(☎ 758-5028)* also seems friendly and takes boarders who often fill up the single rooms, though the clacking of domino games and TV create some noise. Double rooms with private baths and fans cost US$9.

A good choice in this price range is the clean ***Hotel King*** *(☎ 758-1033)*, which is well-run and cheerful. The rate is US$4 per person for rooms with communal bath; doubles with private cold showers cost US$12. Most rooms have fans. The ***Hotel Fung*** *(☎ 758-3309)* is fair and rooms cost US$4/8 with communal cold showers or US$6.50/10.50 with private cold showers; most rooms have fans and some have sunny windows. The new ***Hotel Costa del Sol*** *(☎ 798-0707, fax 758-4748)* has parking, is open 24 hours, takes credit cards, and has clean, decent rooms with private baths for US$9/12 single/double. The hotel was being expanded at time of writing.

The ***Hotel Palace*** *(☎ 758-0419)* charges US$5/9.50 for basic, dark rooms with communal baths, or US$13 to US$16 for better doubles with private baths and a fan. The hotel is housed in an interesting-looking old building around a courtyard with flowers. Despite the 24-hour sign, this is not a place used for prostitution – the owner allows visitors only in the sitting area. The ***Hotel Los Angeles*** *(☎ 758-2068)*, where rooms cost US$11 for a double with a fan or US$14 with air-conditioning, is clean but noisy.

The ***Nuevo Hotel Internacional*** *(☎ 798-0545, Apartado 288, Puerto Limón)* has good, clean rooms with private baths and hot water in the morning. Rooms cost

US$7/11 with fans and US$10/19 with air-conditioning, and are a fair value for Limón. Across the street is the similar ***Hotel Continental***, owned by the same individual. The Continental has a parking lot.

Mid-Range The clean ***Hotel Miami*** *(☎/fax 758-0490, Apartado 266, Puerto Limón)* charges US$12.50/17.50 for single/double rooms with private cold showers and fans; the air-conditioned rooms with TVs cost US$15/20. There is a café and parking.

The ***Hotel Tete*** *(☎ 758-1122, fax 758-0707, Apartado 401-7300, Puerto Limón)* has a nicer interior than exterior and is a good deal; rooms with private hot showers and fans cost US$10/18, or US$18/20 with air-conditioning. The ***Hotel Acon*** *(☎ 758-1010, fax 758-2924, Apartado 528, Puerto Limón)* charges US$18/25 for decent rooms with private hot showers, air-conditioning, TVs, and phones. It has a reasonable restaurant and a popular dance club on the 2nd floor (see Entertainment, below). Major credit cards are accepted at both these hotels.

The ***Park Hotel*** *(☎ 798-0555, 758-3476, fax 758-4364)* has doubles with TVs, air-conditioning, and private baths with hot water for US$40. A few nicer rooms with sea views and little balconies cost US$5 more. Ask if cheaper single and double rooms with fans are still available. There is a parking lot and a simple but adequate restaurant. This is downtown Limón's best hotel.

There are also better hotels to be found northwest of Limón (see the following Around Puerto Limón section).

Places to Eat

There are many snack bars and sodas around the market – one of the best is ***Restaurant Doña Toda***, where snacks and simple meals cost around US$2. Rather more upscale, popular, and clean is the ***Mares Soda Bar/Restaurant*** on the south side of the market. It offers a variety of snacks and meals for US$3 to US$7 and is a good spot for people-watching. ***El Caribe*** is a friendly little local eatery with a Creole flavor; there are two or three different dishes a day, good prices, and cold beer. ***Soda Restaurant Meli***, on the north side of the market, is also cheap and popular with locals.

At the Plaza Caribe, ***Sabro Pizza*** and ***Soda Man*** have off-street courtyards and are relatively relaxing places for a meal, or to have a coffee and write postcards. A block west, the ***Soda Restaurant La Estrella*** is one of the cleaner cheap places you'll find in town. The ***Restaurant Brisas del Caribe***, on the north side of Parque Vargas, is mid-priced, pleasant, and airy.

Near the north end of the seawall is a cute Italian place called ***Restaurant Italiano***. House specialties here start at US$5; the restaurant is open until 2 am daily. Farther from the center, the best Chinese restaurant is the ***Restaurant Sien Kong*** *(☎ 758-0254)*, with meals from US$5 to US$10. A couple of blocks west of the market is the clean ***Palacio Encantador***, offering decent Chinese food. Within a block are a couple of sodas that have small menus but are very popular among locals – one is ***Soda Restaurant Yans***. A rather upscale seafood restaurant with good meals in the US$13 to US$15 range is ***La Esquina de los Mariscos***. The restaurant is in the process of relocating; ask around. Another seafood place to try is the ***Marisquero Cevichito*** on the pleasant pedestrian mall; dishes start at US$5.

The better hotels (see above) have decent restaurants that are open to the public.

Entertainment

Various bars by Parque Vargas and a few blocks west are popular hangouts for a variety of coastal characters: sailors, ladies of the night, entrepreneurs, boozers, losers, and the casually curious. These aren't places for a quiet drink and certainly not for solo women travelers. Go at your own risk!

The ***Zanzibar***, Avenida 3 & Calle 6, is a slightly more sedate bar popular with locals. ***Tuco's Bar*** is a fairly cozy place for a drink and has good bocas that come with the cheap beer. (This is the best place for serious drinking, according to the Hano Crew – an intrepid trio who spent a couple weeks here while trying to ship a vehicle home, and so ought to know.) Nearby is a friendly ***pool***

hall, which has also received the Hano Crew seal of approval.

For dancing check out ***Aquarius***, the disco in the Hotel Acon (see Places to Stay, above). It's lively on weekends, with Latin music and a small cover charge. See the Around Puerto Limón section for more bars.

Getting There & Away

Limón is the transportation hub of the Caribbean coast, though this role has declined with the introduction of direct bus service between San José and the southern coast.

Air The airstrip is about 4km south of town, near the coast. Chartered flights are available, and Travelair and SANSA (☎ 666-0306) have daily flights for US$100/165 and US$55/110 one way/roundtrip. A taxi from the airstrip into town costs about US$3.

Bus Express buses from San José to Limón leave the new Caribe terminal hourly from 5 am to 6:30 pm, returning to San José from the bus terminal on Calle 2, a block east of the market. The fare is US$4 for the three-hour ride. From the same terminal there are buses to Siquirres and Guápiles many times a day.

Buses heading south leave from a block north of the market. Currently, buses from Limón to Cahuita (US80¢) leave six times a day from 5 am to 6 pm. Buses normally continue to Puerto Viejo de Talamanca (US$1.20). Some then go on to Bribri (US$1.40) and Sixaola (US$2, three hours). The 6 am and 2:30 and 6 pm buses go on to Manzanillo instead. The buses are crowded, so try to get a ticket in advance and show up early. Advance tickets are sold next to the soda by the *parada* (bus stop). Note that buses from the south to San José don't go into central Limón.

Buses also leave from here to Penshurst and Pandora (Valle de La Estrella) several times a day. From Pandora you can go to the Reserva Biológica Hitoy Cerere.

Car If you are driving, take note that south of Limón, there is only one gas station on the coast, at the crossroads just north of Cahuita. There is also one inland at Pandora in the Valle de La Estrella. Last-ditch options are the roadside stands near some of the villages, which sell fairly dirty gasoline out of drums.

Boat Limón is the country's major Caribbean port, and cruise ships occasionally dock at Moín, about 7km northwest of Limón, for a short visit. Boats to Tortuguero and points farther north leave from Moín.

Taxi A taxi to Cahuita costs about US$20 (though foreigners may get charged twice that – bargain hard). If you make this trip at night, be sure you have a hotel reservation in Cahuita on weekends. Taxis to the good hotels around Portete, about 4km northwest of Limón, cost around US$3.

AROUND PUERTO LIMÓN

Portete & Playa Bonita

Portete and Playa Bonita both offer decent little beaches and a handful of pleasant accommodations; if you are staying in the area, these places make a nice break from downtown Puerto Limón. If you are driving toward Limón from the west, take the Moín turnoff to the left, about 6km before reaching Limón, to avoid downtown. If you go this way, 3km after turning off the main highway, just before the Moín dock, take a right for Portete and Playa Bonita, and follow the coast road east past the coastal hotels. This route eventually leads back to Limón itself. If you are not driving, take the Moín bus from downtown Limón, though this bus is often very crowded; a taxi would be a better way to go.

Places to Stay & Eat About 4km out of Limón, or 2.5km from the Moín dock, is ***Hotel Cocori*** *(☎ 758-2930, ☎/fax 798-1670),* which is on the small beach at Playa Bonita. The hotel offers cabins with kitchenettes, air-conditioning, and refrigerators for US$30 double. There is an open-air restaurant with an ocean view. This is a good budget option outside of town. Across the street from the Hotel Cocori is the ***Hotel Matama*** *(☎ 758-1123, fax 758-4499, matama@sol.racsa.co.cr).* It is about 300 to 400m to the beach at Playa

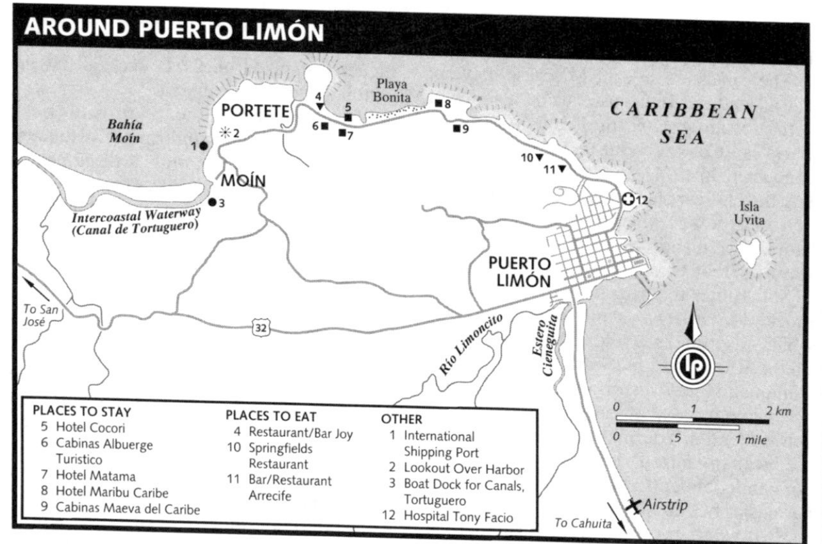

Bonita. The Matama has a swimming pool, bar, and restaurant. The air-conditioned rooms are in a variety of bungalows and cabins – there are eight double rooms, four rooms sleeping four, and four rooms sleeping six. The buildings are set in hilly gardens with jungle vegetation; inside some of the bathrooms are miniature jungle gardens, which I rather liked. It made a nice change from the thousands of hotel bathrooms it's been my good fortune to gaze at. Rates are US$58/64 single/double including breakfast in the high season, much less in the low season.

Between these two hotels and Portete is the small, friendly ***Cabinas Albuerge Turistico*** *(☎ 798-3090)*, a new place with plans for expansion. Clean doubles with private baths cost US$20. The ***Hotel Maribu Caribe*** *(☎ 758-4010, 758-4543, fax 758-3541, Apartado 623-7300, Puerto Limón)* is just over a kilometer east of the Matama, or about 3km northwest of Puerto Limón. It is on a small hill that catches ocean breezes and offers a good view, especially from the restaurant. There are two pools in addition to the restaurant and bar. Accommodations are in private, air-conditioned, thatched bungalows and cost US$85 single or double (US$50 in the low season). Most of these top-end hotels will arrange local tours.

About 200m east of the Maribu Caribe is ***Cabinas Maeva del Caribe*** *(☎ 758-2024)*, which has pleasant and quiet cabins for US$12.50/21 and a restaurant on the premises. There is some talk locally of new hotels being built in the area; ask around town for newer options.

The ***Bar/Restaurant Arrecife*** *(☎ 758-4030)*, about 500m northwest of downtown Limón on the road to Portete, serves good seafood. A few hundred meters farther is ***Springfields Restaurant*** *(☎ 758-1203)*, which serves Caribbean food and is locally popular in the evenings.

Apart from the hotel restaurants, there are several places to eat in Playa Bonita. One of the best is the ***Restaurant/Bar Joy***, which serves good seafood in the US$6 to US$10 range and is known locally as 'Johnny's,' after the friendly owner.

Moín

This port is about 7km west of Puerto Limón. The main reason to come here is to take a boat up the canals to Parque Nacional

Tortuguero and on to Refugio Nacional de Fauna Silvestre Barra del Colorado.

The canals are so called because they are not all natural. There used to be a series of natural waterways north of Limón as far as Barra del Colorado, but they were not fully connected. In 1974, canals were completed to link the entire system, thus avoiding the need to go out to sea when traveling north from Moín. This inland waterway is a much safer way to go than traveling up the coast offshore.

Sometimes the canals north of Moín are blocked by water hyacinths or log jams, in which case the riverside village of Matina, on the Río Matina halfway between Puerto Limón and Siquirres, or other ports that are accessible by road are used until the blockage is cleared. You may go this way if you are on an organized tour, but if you are traveling independently, go via Moín because it has easier bus connections.

Near where boats leave for Tortuguero is the **Bamboo Mission**, a Chinese mission where locals are taught how to make bamboo furniture and other bamboo handicrafts, all for sale to visitors.

Getting There & Away

Bus Buses to Moín depart from Limón several times an hour starting at 6 am. The bus stop is 100m north of Radio Casino at Calle 4, Avenida 5, in central Limón.

Boat Most travelers get to the national parks on organized tours with prearranged boat or plane transport. These tours are usually good but not very cheap, although it is possible to pay for just the travel portion and then stay in cheaper accommodations in the Tortuguero area. There are also some new, cheaper ways of getting to Tortuguero (see Boat under Getting There & Away in the Tortuguero Area section, later in this chapter).

To arrange transportation independently, go down to the Moín dock early and start asking around. The boat dock for Tortuguero is about 300m to the left of the main port, through a guarded gate. There are passenger and cargo boats leaving most days, but it takes a little bit of asking around about schedules. Cargo boats are cheaper but are officially for cargo only, though you might persuade the captain to allow you aboard. The trip to Tortuguero can take from 2½ hours to all day, depending on the type of boat.

Most travelers take a private boat; boatmen offer the roundtrip to Tortuguero for US$50 per person with a three-person minimum, or less with large groups. There are often boatmen hanging around the dock area in the early morning and boats normally leave between 7 and 8 am. The trip takes about five hours to Tortuguero (allowing for photography and wildlife viewing). After lunch and a brief visit to Tortuguero, the return trip is done in 2½ hours. Overnights and returns on the following day can be arranged. There is a locked and guarded parking area for those driving to the dock area (but don't leave valuables in the car).

You can make arrangements for the trip in advance in San José (or in Cahuita), or with boatmen and agencies in Limón. Laura's Tours (☎ 758-2410) has been recommended; roundtrip transport to Tortuguero costs US$65, with up to two nights' stay between journeys. Alfred Brown Robinson of Tortuguero Odysseys Tours (☎ 758-0824) offers US$75 overnight tours including a cheap hotel and meals, or a day tour for US$50. Ask about discounted trips, especially for groups. Other boatmen who have been recommended include Willis Rankin (☎ 798-1556), Modesto Watson (in San José ☎ 226-0986, fvwatson@sol.racsa.co.cr), and Mario Rivas.

Northern Caribbean

PARISMINA

This village is at the mouth of the Río Parismina, about 50km northwest of Limón. It boasts some of the better fishing lodges on the Costa Rican Caribbean. Record-breaking Atlantic tarpon and snook are the fish to go for. Offshore reef fishing is also good. Traditionally, the tarpon season is from January to mid-May and the season for big snook is from September to November.

However, all the locals will tell you that the fishing is good during any month of the year, because these fish don't migrate. Parismina's proximity to the south end of Parque Nacional Tortuguero means that nature tours can also be enjoyed (see listings under Places to Stay & Eat, below).

Places to Stay & Eat

The ***Río Parismina Lodge*** (☎ *229-7597, fax 292-1207; in the USA* ☎ *800-338-5688, 210-824-4442)* is a comfortable fishing lodge that also provides local nature tours on request. The lodge has a pool, Jacuzzi, and nature trails on its 20-hectare property and is the best place to fish in Parismina. Absolutely everything is provided (except tips for fishing guides and lodge staff) in the lodge's all-inclusive fishing packages, which include a night in a 1st-class San José hotel at either end of your lodge stay, plus air or land transfers from San José. Rates range from US$1800/3400 single/double for three days of fishing to US$2800/5200 for seven days of fishing. Extra days of fishing cost US$550 per person. Reduced rates are offered for nonfishers.

Other places to try for fishing packages are ***Campo de Pesca y Albergue Naturalista Río Parismina*** (☎ *236-7480, fax 236-7480)* and the ***Parismina Tarpon Rancho*** (☎ *771-2583, fax 222-1763)*. The rooms all have fans, screens, and private hot showers.

If you just want budget accommodations, there are a couple of cheap and pretty basic *cabinas* charging about US$20 for a double with shared cold shower or a bit more with private hot shower. The ***Parismina Lodge*** (☎ *768-8636)* charges about US$90 per person per day, including meals and transport. The lodge will arrange relatively cheap fishing packages.

Getting There & Away

You pass Parismina on the canal boats to Tortuguero from points farther south; the dock at Caño Blanco, which is reached by bus, is only a few minutes by boat from the fishing lodges. Some visitors fly in to the local airstrip (charter flights only).

Pacuare Nature Reserve

This 800-hectare private reserve is near the mouth of the Río Pacuare, about 30km northwest of Puerto Limón. It is owned by the Endangered Wildlife Trust, which works to protect the area in partnership with the British charity Rainforest Concern. The highlight is a 6km-long beach that is used for nesting by giant leatherback turtles from March to June, and by green turtles from June to August.

Volunteers work at the reserve, patrolling the beaches, moving nests to safer areas, tagging turtles and monitoring hatchlings from mid-March through July of each year. Rustic but comfortable accommodations and food are provided and volunteers are requested to stay for at least one week and pay US$100 per week toward living expenses. In 1998, 133 volunteers from 17 countries worked on the reserve. If you're interested, contact Rainforest Concern (☎ 020-7229-2093, fax 020-7221-4094, rainforest@gn.apc.org), 27 Lansdowne Crescent, London W11 2NS, England. In Costa Rica, contact La Reserva Pacuare (☎ 233-0451, fax 221-2820, fdezlaw@sol.racsa.co.cr), Avenidas 8 & 10, Calle 19, No 837, San José.

The reserve has a lodge with three double rooms and a kitchen available for rent; a cook is provided on request. Also, two cottages sleep larger groups (maximum 20). Contact the reserve about availability and rates. Minimum stays of one week are the norm. Trails from the lodge lead along the beach and into the forest, where a rich variety of birdlife and various mammals can be observed.

– Rob Rachowiecki

PARQUE NACIONAL TORTUGUERO

This 19,211-hectare coastal park (plus about 52,000 hectares of marine area) is the most important breeding ground for the green sea turtle in all of the Caribbean. There are eight species of marine turtles in the world; six nest in Costa Rica and of those, four are in Tortuguero (see the Wildlife Guide at the back of this book). The many turtles give the national park its name. The Tortuguero nesting population of the green turtle, *Chelonia mydas*, has been continuously monitored since 1955, and is the most studied. Comparatively little is known about other marine turtles.

Parque Nacional Tortuguero is under extreme pressure. With only a handful of personnel to work in the three ranger stations, the protected area is being encroached upon by loggers, banana and oil palm plantations, ranches, colonists, and some tourist developments. Arriving by air is frightening. If you fly in, you'll see nothing but plantations and cattle ranches until you reach the Caribbean. At the last possible moment, there is a narrow swath of coastal land that looks relatively undisturbed. Visitors arriving by boat are treated to rainforest views along the canal banks, but a few minutes' walk into the forest will reveal that these views are cosmetic in many cases. The western parts of the national park are being eroded and it is difficult to stop this effectively.

Nevertheless, locals are becoming increasingly aware of the problems of forest loss and you can still see more wildlife here than in many parts of Central America. Devastatingly, the inhabitants of inland Caribbean-slope villages such as Cariari and towns such as Guápiles are illegally trying to push a road through the national park to Tortuguero village. The completion of such a road would change the tranquil nature of the village and encourage illegal logging and colonization, and the abundant wildlife would soon be forced away. I encourage you to discuss conservation issues with local boatmen, tour operators, and whomever else you come across on your journey.

Green turtle

Orientation & Information

Humid is the driest word I can think of to describe Tortuguero. With rainfall of up to 6000mm in the northern part of the park, it is one of the wettest areas in the country. Rainwear is a must year-round: an umbrella is a good idea. There is no dry season, although it does rain less in February and March and again in September. The average temperature is 26°C, but it is often hotter during the middle of the day. Bring insect repellent – you'll use it.

There are two ranger stations visited by travelers. The Jalova station is on the canal at the south entrance to the national park. Here, there is a short nature trail, a bathroom, and drinking water.

Most visitors go to the Cuatro Esquinas station (and park headquarters), which is at the north end of the park along the canal. (The village of Tortuguero is a few minutes' walk away, just beyond the park boundary.) Information is available here. From the headquarters there is a 2km-long loop nature trail (returning along the beach), which is maintained but is often flooded or otherwise impassable during rainy months.

Although the beaches are extensive, they are not suitable for swimming. The surf is very rough, the currents strong, and, if that's not enough to faze you, sharks regularly patrol the waters.

Fees The entrance fee to the park is US$6 per day – most visitors pay the fee at the headquarters. In 1998, nocturnal boat visits into the park were prohibited because the bright lights, engine exhaust, and noise were impacting the wildlife. In 1999, a nine-month experimental program was initiated to allow a limited number of night tours, but only in boats with a maximum of 17 passengers and accompanied by a guide and park ranger, using quiet electric motors and one light of 200,000 candlepower or less. Park fees for two-hour night tours are US$5 and several local lodges operate the tours (if there is a demand) at costs as high as US$30 per person. Local guides charge US$10 and are knowledgeable. Also in 1999, a US$10 ticket valid for four days to visit both Tortuguero and the Barra del Colorado refuge was available on an experimental basis.

For detailed information on organized tours of Parque Nacional Tortuguero, see the Tortuguero Area section, later in this chapter.

Turtle-Watching

Travelers are allowed to visit the nesting beaches at night and watch the turtles lay their eggs or observe the eggs hatching. However, camera flashes, VCRs, and flashlights are prohibited by law as they disturb the egg-laying process or attract predators to the hatchlings. The best seasons to visit the beaches are from April 1 to May 31 (when leatherbacks lay in small numbers) and July 1 to October 15 (when green turtles lay in large numbers). Officially designated by the park, these dates may occasionally be extended by a week or two, depending on whether or not nesting is occurring; the highest numbers nest from late July to late August. Guides (available by asking anyone in the area) must accompany visitors to the viewing areas. Some of the nesting beaches are outside the park.

Several years ago, scientists wrote that anywhere from several hundred to over 3000 female green turtles came to the Tortuguero nesting beach during any given season, compared to tens of thousands in earlier decades. However, in the mid-1990s, 15,000 to 20,000 were estimated to have nested here because of conservation efforts.

The story of the decline and return of the green turtle and the setting up of turtle conservation projects in the Caribbean is told in two popular books by Archie Carr, a herpetologist who did much work with turtles and played an important role in getting Tortuguero protected. The books are *The Windward Road: Adventures of a Naturalist on Remote Caribbean Shores* and *The Sea Turtle: So Excellent a Fishe.*

If you are unable to visit during the green turtle breeding season, leatherback turtles nest in small numbers from February to July, with a peak from mid-April to mid-May. Hawksbill turtles nest sporadically from March to October and loggerhead turtles are also sometimes seen. Stragglers have been observed during every month of the year. Only the green turtle nests in large numbers; the other species tend to arrive singly.

Watching Other Wildlife

Turtles are by no means the only attraction at Tortuguero. The national park offers great wildlife viewing and birding opportunities, both from the few trails within the park and on guided or paddle-yourself boat trips. All three of the local species of monkeys (howler, spider, and white-faced capuchin) are often seen. Sloths, anteaters, and kinkajous are also sighted. Manatees are protected but not often seen. Peccaries, tapirs, and various members of the cat family have also been recorded, but you have to be exceptionally lucky to see them.

The area's reptiles and amphibians are also of great interest. Apart from the sea turtles, there are seven species of freshwater turtles. Look for them lined up on a log by the river bank, sunning themselves. It seems that as soon as you see them, they see you, and one by one they plop off the log and into the protective river. Lizards, caimans, crocodiles, and snakes are also seen; a friend of mine saw a 2m-long fer-de-lance. A variety of colorful little frogs and toads hop around in the rainforest, including tiny poison-arrow frogs and large marine toads. About 60 species of amphibians have been recorded in the park.

There are over 400 species of birds recorded in the Tortuguero area. These include oceanic species such as the magnificent frigatebird and royal tern; shore birds such as plovers and sandpipers; river birds such as kingfishers, jacanas, and anhingas; and inland forest species such as hummingbirds and manakins.

Many migrant birds from North America pass through on their way south from the North American winter or going north for the North American summer.

The variety of habitats within the park contributes to the diversity of birds. On just one boat ride near Tortuguero I saw six species of herons, including the chestnut-bellied heron, which Stiles' and Skutch's *A Guide to the Birds of Costa Rica* describes as an uncommon to rare resident of the humid lowland forests of the Caribbean slopes.

Over 400 species of trees and at least 2200 species of other plants have been recorded, but there are undoubtedly more to be identified.

Places to Stay

There's a camping area at the park headquarters where you can stay for US$2 per person – just make sure your tent is waterproof. Drinking water, showers, and toilets are provided. However, in wet months (most of them) the camping area is subject to flooding and is not recommended.

Just outside the northern boundary of the park in the village of Tortuguero (see the following section), you can find basic, inexpensive accommodations, food, boats, and guides. Between 1 and 4km north of the village are several comfortable and more expensive jungle lodges.

TORTUGUERO AREA

The 600 inhabitants of the sleepy little village of Tortuguero, just north of the national park, make most of their living from turtles and tourism. They work in the hotels and tour lodges, or as park rangers or researchers, or as guides and boatmen, and a few do a little farming and fishing. Generally speaking, a good balance has been struck between the interests of the local people, visitors, and the turtles. This is mainly because access is limited to boats and planes – if there was a road here it would undoubtedly be a different story. Unfortunately, outside interests are trying to push a road through to the village; if this ever happens, I would strongly discourage travelers from using it.

Instead of harvesting the turtles, the people exploit them and the accompanying park in nondestructive yet economically satisfactory ways. The community appears to take some pride in 'its' turtles and national park.

Information

In the center of the village is an informative kiosk explaining the natural history, cultural history, geography, and climate of the region.

Apart from the kiosk, several places offer local information. The Tortuguero Information Center, in front of the Catholic church (ask anyone), can recommend local guides and businesses catering to independent travelers. Local guides use dugout canoes or skiffs with electric motors to avoid disturbing the wildlife, while allowing tourists to get good views. Canadian biologist Daryl Loth, who has lived in the area for years, leads inexpensive local tours and knows the best local guides. He can be contacted at the Information Center or by email at canals@sol.racs.co.cr (put 'Daryl' in the subject line). You can try phoning (☎ 392-3201), but the reliability of the phone service is erratic, so keep trying.

Also ask in the Jungle Shop, which has handicrafts and souvenirs, and the Paraíso Tropical Store (☎ 710-0323), which has a wide selection of souvenirs and sundries, a public phone, and sells Travelair tickets. A tiny park outside this store has towering bird statues and benches. The Super Morpho Pulpería, in the center of the village, has another public phone and the best food selection (though no alcohol). Booze is sold across the street in the rough La Culebra Bar.

There is a small police post and a medical center – the latter has a doctor one day a week (currently Wednesdays), so plan your illnesses with care.

Caribbean Conservation Corporation

The Caribbean Conservation Corporation (CCC; ☎ 710-0547; in the USA 800-678-7853, ccc@cccturtle.org, www.cccturtle.org) operates a research station about 1km north of Tortuguero village. The station has a small but well-run visitor center and museum explaining the turtle conservation and research work, and an 18-minute video (in English or Spanish) about the history of local turtle conservation is shown on request. Hours are 10 am to 12:30 pm and 2 to 5:30 pm daily except Sunday (2 to 5 pm); admission costs US$1. The research station teaches courses in various biological fields – contact the CCC for information. Visitors with a background or interest in biology may be able to stay in the CCC's dorms (four to six beds each) if they're not full.

During July and August, there are volunteer programs for people interested in assisting scientists with turtle tagging and research. Volunteers pay US$1890 for 15 days, including flights from Miami, one night's lodging in San José at the beginning and end of the trip, and room and board in the research station. (Cheaper rates can be arranged for those making their own way to San José). These are popular projects, and advance reservations are needed through the US office of the CCC.

Canoeing & Kayaking

Several places in Tortuguero just north of the entrance to the park have signs announcing boats for hire. You can paddle yourself in a dugout canoe for about US$2 per person per hour, or go with a guide for a little more. Miss Junie's and the Manati Lodge (see Places to Stay & Eat, below) have plastic kayaks for rent, as do other places – ask around.

Hiking

Apart from visiting the waterways and beaches of the park, hikers can climb the 119m-high **Cerro Tortuguero**, about 6km north of the village. You need to hire a boat and guide to get there. Cerro Tortuguero is the highest point right on the coast anywhere north of Puerto Limón – it actually lies just within the southern border of Refugio Nacional de Fauna Silvestre Barra del Colorado. The path is very steep and usually muddy, but it offers good views of the forest, canals, sea, birds, and other wildlife. I saw several howler monkeys hanging out in the trees below the trail.

Organized Tours

Many travel agencies in San José and elsewhere offer tours of the Tortuguero area, but they normally end up subcontracting (at the same price) with the companies associated with the lodges listed under Places to Stay & Eat (see below). Usually, you get what you pay for – the cheaper options are not as well-organized and may have mediocre guides.

COTERC

The acronym stands for Canadian Organization for Tropical Education and Rainforest Conservation, a nonprofit organization with many local education, research, and conservation activities. COTERC operates the Estación Biológica Caño Palma in the Caño La Palma area just north of Cerro Tortuguero and about 7km north of Tortuguero village. Although the biological station is actually within the southern boundary of Refugio Nacional de Fauna Silvestre Barra del Colorado, access is easiest from Tortuguero.

The station accommodates researchers, student groups, and volunteers who pay a nominal fee for food and board and help with the upkeep of the station and assist ongoing research projects. Other guests (nature tourists) are accepted when space is available. The buildings are 200m from the Caribbean, but separated from it by a river. Rivers, streams, and lagoons can be explored and there is a trail system into the rainforest. Researchers, volunteers, and visitors stay in simple dormitories with bunks and bedding, and outdoor showers and bathrooms. The capacity is 14 people, though there are plans to add more sleeping space in 2000. There is also a covered area with four hammocks, a study area, and a kitchen and dining area. The rate is US$40 per person per day including three meals and the use of the trails. Guided boat excursions can be arranged.

The station can be reached by hiring a boat from Tortuguero. If you make prior arrangements, the staff will pick you up either at Tortuguero airport or village for US$10.

COTERC relies on members and donors to run its programs. Members receive the quarterly newsletter *Raphia*. For further information and reservations, contact Marilyn Cole, COTERC (in Canada ☎ 905-831-8809, fax 905-831-4203, coterc@interhop.net, PO Box 335, Pickering, ON L1V 2R6, Canada). Drop-in visitors can usually find space.

– Rob Rachowiecki

Tours from San José include one-day and overnight options. For those with limited time, a rushed one-day tour is offered by Caño Blanco Marina (☎ 259-8216, 256-9444, 284-2017 cellular, fax 259-8229, tucanti@sol.racsa.co.cr). This includes a dawn flight from San José to Tortuguero, a park tour with bilingual guide, breakfast and lunch in Tortuguero, a visit to the CCC museum (at the visitor center), a return along the canals by speedboat to Caño Blanco, continuing to San José by bus and arriving at 5:45 pm. This costs US$89, plus US$6 park and US$1 museum fees.

Overnight options of one, two, or three nights are available, with the three-day/two-night option being the most popular and providing a reasonably good look at the area.

The cheaper three-day/two-night tours start with a drive from San José to Moín (or another dock closer to Tortuguero), where you board a boat for a two- to five-hour journey (depending on departure point and power of the boat) through the canals to Tortuguero. The journey itself is part of the adventure – the boat slows down for photographs, and a bilingual guide identifies what you see. On the second day, guided walking and boat tours of the area are provided (these may or may not be included in the price). A night visit to the beach is added during the turtle nesting season, or a night canoe tour might be offered for an extra charge. You return by boat and bus on the third day. More expensive tours will utilize more comfortable lodges, offer better guides, and cut down on travel time by flying one way (all those described in the following sections can be upgraded with a one-way flight). During the low season, 'green season' discounts are offered – shop around in San José.

Fran and Modesto Watson (☎/fax 226-0986, fvwatson@sol.racsa.co.cr), who own and operate the riverboat *Francesca*, offer guided overnight tours that include transport from San José to Moín by van, boat ride to Tortuguero, lodging at the Laguna Lodge, a two-hour boat tour of the park, entry fees, and meals for US$185 per person, inclusive. They can customize tours.

Budget or independent travelers can stay in Tortuguero village and hire local guides. See also the Moín section, earlier in this chapter, for tours from Puerto Limón.

Places to Stay & Eat

Tortuguero Village Budget travelers normally stay in the village. You might be able to bargain the following prices down by US$1 to US$2 per person per day if you're staying for a few days. The friendly and family-run ***Cabinas Mariscar*** *(reservations in San José ☎ 290-2804, 296-2626 messages)* has small, basic but clean rooms with fans and shared baths for US$6 per person. They also have a couple of more expensive rooms with private baths.

The basic but clean ***Cabinas Sabina*** is the biggest place, with 31 rooms near the ocean at US$10/15 double/triple, but the owner is unfriendly (locals told me that 'fighting is what keeps her alive'). The ***Tropical Lodge***, just north of the park entrance, has a few basic cabins at US$5 per person. The ***Cabinas Tortuguero*** is clean and good; the rate is US$10 per person.

Rooms with baths are found at ***Cabinas Pancana*** and the slightly better ***Cabinas Aracari*** *(☎ 798-3059)*, both with only a few rooms; the rate is about US$10 per person or less. At the north end of the village is ***Miss Junie's*** *(☎ 710-0523)*, with 12 clean rooms (more are planned) with fans and private baths for US$25/35 single/double. Miss Junie is Tortuguero's best-known cook and she (and now her daughter) does good Caribbean-style meals (such as fish in coconut sauce) for about US$5, but you need to order a meal several hours in advance or the day before.

Restaurants charge about US$3 per meal, and it is fairly basic food. One of the best places is ***La Caribeña***, across from the Super Morpho Pulpería, and there are a few others.

North of the Village About 1km north of Tortuguero, the ***Mawamba Lodge*** *(☎/fax 710-7282)* caters mainly to prearranged tours but will rent you a room if it is not full. There are 54 pleasant and spacious rooms with fans and private hot showers. Verandahs with hammocks and rocking chairs allow for relaxation. The lodge has a good restaurant and a second dining-bar area next to an attractive swimming pool, complete with a waterfall and a bridge to swim under. The food and tropical drinks are definitely tasty. There is a souvenir shop and the beach is 100m away (not suitable for swimming here or anywhere in the Tortuguero area). An air-conditioned conference room enables local guides to give natural history presentations. This is the best lodge within fairly close walking distance of the village, and it has received several recommendations from our readers. Tours here are provided by the Mawamba Group (☎ 223-2421, 223-7490, fax 222-5463, mawamba@sol.racsa.co.cr). Its three-day/two-night package includes a breakfast stop at the company's Río Danta Restaurant, within Parque Nacional Braulio Carrillo, and begins the canal portion from a private dock at Matina. Rates are US$252 per person, double occupancy, or US$201 for a two-day/one-night package.

The ***Laguna Lodge*** *(☎ 710-0355)* is about 2km north of the village. About 30 rooms with fans, hardwood floors, and tiled private bathrooms with hot water look attractive. The lodge's rustic restaurant serves good tico food, family style, and there's an attractive free-form pool. Laguna Lodge Tours (☎ 225-3740, fax 283-8031) offers three-day/two-night packages for US$234 per person, double occupancy, or US$187 for one night. Guides speak decent English. Walk-in clients are accepted on a space-available basis.

Other Areas The remaining lodgings all require a boat ride to get to and from Tortuguero village, which means you pretty much are stuck in the lodge for meals and other activities, though transportation to the village can be arranged (at extra cost) if you want.

The friendly and *tranquilo* ***Manati Lodge*** *(☎/fax 383-0330)* has eight simple rooms (four doubles, three triples, and a quintuple), each with a warm private shower and fan.

The rate is US$35 double (US$25 single if available) including breakfast, or US$15 per person in rooms with three or more people. Lunches and dinners cost US$7 each. Trails lead to the canals on either side of the lodge. Kayaks are available for US$5 for two hours. The grounds are attractive and good tico home cooking is featured. This lodge is used as a base for research on the endangered manatee, and is recommended for folks interested in conservation and local issues.

The ***Ilan Ilan Lodge*** has 24 medium-sized, plain but clean rooms with fans and cold private showers. The hotel is placed in about 8 hectares of nicely landscaped grounds. Packages with mainly Spanish-speaking guides are arranged in advance with Mitur Tours (☎ 255-2031, 255-2262, fax 255-1946, mitour@sol.racsa.co.cr), on Paseo Colón, Calles 20 & 22, in San José. The rate is US$224 per person, double occupancy, for three days/two nights. Walk-ins can be accommodated on a space-available basis.

The ***Jungle Lodge*** *(☎/fax 256-6942)* has 50 nicer rooms with hot showers and fans. The grounds have a small swimming pool, and several dozen trees are numbered so that you can identify the species using a list (which was unavailable when I stopped by). Across the Laguna Penitencia, the lodge has opened a butterfly garden that is available for guest visits (it may be open to visitors from other lodges in the future). A restaurant serves buffet-style meals, and a separate bar features a small dance floor and free dance lessons (so the bartender tells me). As with others described above, this lodge accepts walk-ins, but relies on tour groups booked through Cotur (☎ 233-0155, 233-6579, fax 233-0778, cotour@sol.racsa.co.cr), Calle 36, Paseo Colón and Avenida 1 (50m north of the Toyota dealership), in San José. Cotur offers three-day/two-night tours for US$240 per person, double occupancy. Two-day/one-night trips cost about US$50 less. This company often services large groups.

The ***Pachira Lodge*** *(☎ 256-7080, fax 223-1119, paccira@sol.racsa.co.cr)* has some of the prettier rooms in the Tortuguero area, with pleasant pastels offering a break from the interminable wood. It has 44 airy rooms with good ventilation and hot water, and a spacious restaurant-bar area with good food. In addition, there are six simpler cabins with baths and hot water next to a basic above-ground swimming pool on the other side of Laguna Penitencia, in an area locally called 'Hollywood.' Walk-ins are often accommodated there. Rates for a three-day/two-night package from San José, including the usual services, are US$239 per person, double occupancy, and US$313 single.

The ***Caribbean Magic Eco-Lodge*** *(in San José ☎/fax 240-3318, bayislan@sol.racsa.co.cr)* has 16 fairly simple rooms with fans and hot showers, an attractive thatched restaurant, and a small swimming pool. The base rate is US$60 double including breakfast. It will arrange a complete three-day/two-night package from San José for about US$224 per person, double occupancy, or US$249 single.

Just south of here is the rustic ***Tortuguero Caribe Lodge*** *(☎ 385-4676, in San José ☎ 259-0820, 259-1811)*, with seven very simple cabins with shared baths for US$14 per person. Good home-cooked meals cost US$10 each (this includes a wide spread; you can eat more cheaply if you ask for a simple dish). Two basic rooms with private baths cost US$17 per person. Ecole Travel (☎ 223-2240, 255-4172, ☎/fax 223-4128, ecolecr@sol.racsa.co.cr), Calle 7, Avenidas Central & 1, arranges overnight tours here for US$89/125 for one/two nights per person, double occupancy. This starts and ends at the dock at Moín (Ecole gives you up-to-date instructions on how to get there by public transport) and does not include lunch or dinner, but does include breakfast and some local tours. Ecole Travel also does the same trip using the Caribbean Magic Eco-Lodge (if you want a more comfortable room) for US$105/150 per person for one/two nights.

The ***Tortuga Lodge & Gardens*** *(☎ 710-6861)* was the first comfortable lodge built in the area and remains the most comfortable place to stay, with superior rooms (spacious, screened, cross-ventilated, large bathrooms with hot showers, and fans), rocking chairs and hammocks in covered walkways outside all the rooms, an airy bar-restaurant built on the riverside, with verandah dining next to the water, and an adjoining swimming pool (being built in 1999). A solar energy system is used here, which is one of the reasons that the lodge has been recognized with ecotourism awards from *Travel & Leisure* and *Condé Nast Traveler*. Other reasons include the fact that the lodge supports the local community through sustainable development, hires locals, and supports local conservation projects. The food is plentiful, served family style, includes plenty of vegetables and local specialties, and is very well-prepared. The staff and guides are helpful and well-trained, and many speak English.

The lodge is on 20 hectares of attractively landscaped gardens with ornamental tropical trees, palms, shrubs, orchids, and other flowers that attract birds, lizards, and butterflies. The tropical rainforest begins beyond the gardens, and a troop of howler monkeys is usually heard near the lodge (they were visible from some guest rooms when I visited recently). Red and black poison-arrow frogs are found in the forest behind the lodge.

Tortuga's current high-season prices are US$95/115/133 single/double/triple. Large and delicious all-you-can-eat meals cost US$13 for breakfast, US$18 for lunch, and US$21 for dinner.

Many guests come on packages with tours included. Tours that might be extra include climbing Cerro Tortuguero (US$11 per person), night turtle walks in season (US$20 per person), and night tours (US$30 per person). Tortuga Lodge also provides fishing boats and guides, who often go up to the Barra del Colorado area (less than an hour away) if that's where the best fishing is. See Barra del Colorado Area, later in this chapter, for more fishing information. Boat rental for fishing (including guide and tackle) is US$45 per hour (minimum two hours and up to five people) for local fishing; US$180 per person (two minimum) for a full day of inshore fishing; and US$297 per person (two minimum) for deep-sea fishing with highly experienced guides. Fishing depends on weather and other local conditions.

Costa Rica Expeditions (see Organized Tours in the Getting Around chapter) owns the Tortuga Lodge, has the best-trained guides, and is well recommended. A complete two-day/one-night package, including roundtrip flights from San José, hotel transfers, two guided boat tours, meals, and park fee, costs US$487 for one person down to US$379 per person in a group of four. Extra days cost US$110.

Boat rentals for natural history tours (with motor and driver/guide) cost US$40 per hour and accommodate up to five people. Night tours of the canals, with a superpowerful searchlight to seek out crocodiles, sleeping animals, and night animals on the prowl, cost US$30 per person (two-person minimum) and last about three hours. Speedboats from Moín to the lodge cost US$50 per person (three minimum, five maximum, 2½ hours). Slower boats taking four hours cost US$350 for up to 12 passengers.

Getting There & Away

Air The small airstrip is 4km north of Tortuguero village, across the canal from the Tortuguero Lodge. Travelair has daily flights from San José at 6 am for US$49/89 one way/roundtrip (fares have been 50% higher in the past, but the airline is currently competing with SANSA). The designated ticket-sales agent for Travelair in Tortuguero is the Paraíso Tropical Store (☎ 710-0323). SANSA also has daily flights at 6 am for US$45 each way; ask in Tortuguero about who is the current SANSA agent. Planes can be chartered into this airport.

Boat See Organized Tours, above, or the Moín section for details on transport by passenger boat, especially if you come on a tour.

The cheapest way to arrive and leave from Tortuguero at time of writing is to take a bus from San José's Atlántico Norte bus terminal to Cariari (about US$2.50, two hours) first thing in the morning, then take a bus from Cariari to La Geest (about US$1.50, 90 minutes). La Geest is a dock in a banana plantation on the Río Suerte (locally called Caño Suerte). Here, you will be met by Bananero, who runs a daily boat at 1 pm to Tortuguero (about US$10, one hour). Bananero will take you back in the morning in time to catch the bus from La Geest to Cariari and San José. His dock/office is just north of the national park at the south end of Tortuguero village – ask anyone.

Also see the entry on Caño Blanco Marina (under Organized Tours, above). The staff will sell you a spot on their boat-bus connection back to San José on a space-available basis – the folks at the Paraíso Tropical Store in Tortuguero can help you get in contact with them. Ecole Tours also provides roundtrip transportation from Moín for US$55 if arranged in advance.

BARRA DEL COLORADO AREA

At 92,000 hectares, Refugio Nacional de Fauna Silvestre Barra del Colorado (locally called Barra, which also refers to the neighboring village of Barra del Colorado) is the biggest national wildlife refuge in Costa Rica. It is virtually an extension of Parque Nacional Tortuguero, and the two are combined to form a regional conservation unit.

There are several differences between Tortuguero and Barra del Colorado. Barra is more remote, more difficult to visit cheaply, and is not as famous for its marine turtles. (Although they are found in the reserve, they don't nest in large numbers.)

Despite being a national wildlife refuge, Barra has traditionally attracted visitors for the sportfishing rather than for natural history tours. But this is beginning to change: Barra receives as much rainfall as Tortuguero, and has much of the same variety of wildlife, best seen from a boat. Locals say that because it covers more land area and is more remote than Tortuguero, Barra is still undiscovered as a superb natural history destination. During a recent visit, I found that the birding was excellent, and I had good looks at monkeys, sloths, and a whole family of baby caimans that had recently hatched and were sitting together on a log, each one about the length of my hand. The rainforest and river scenery was lovely. Although fishing is still the bread and butter of most of the area's lodges, wildlife tours are attracting increasing numbers of visitors and are less likely to encounter other tour groups than in Tortuguero. If you want to do a wildlife tour, let the lodge staff know in advance, as most guides are more oriented toward fishing (though I've found that many of the locals are very adept at spotting wildlife).

The northern border of the refuge is the Río San Juan (also the border with Nicaragua). This area was politically sensitive during the 1980s, which contributed somewhat to the isolation of the reserve. Since the relaxing of Sandinista-Contra hostilities in 1990, it has become easier to journey north along the Río Sarapiquí and east along the San Juan to the reserve. This is an interesting trip and is described below.

The western part of the refuge is less accessible, but that doesn't mean that no one goes there. Infrared satellite photography is showing large amounts of unauthorized logging and road construction at the western boundary of the refuge. Undoubtedly, illegal logging activity is going on within Barra del Colorado, but there are not enough reserve wardens to police the area properly. The western part of the refuge is now accessible to vehicles and there is a daily bus (road and weather conditions allowing) to Puerto Lindo, on the Río Colorado, in the heart of the reserve. This road brings in loggers, ranchers, farmers, and colonists and does not bode well for the western part of Barra del Colorado, but the eastern sections (where the lodges are) are very swampy and not conducive to easy logging; that area, at least, may be less vulnerable to change.

Surprisingly, there are over 2000 inhabitants in the area, and they want the rough road to Puerto Lindo to be improved and have petitioned the government to make the road all-weather. However, this is not on the cards in the near future; in fact, after Hurricane Mitch in 1998 the road was badly damaged and Barra remains one of the most remote parts of Costa Rica.

Orientation & Information

The village of Barra del Colorado lies near the mouth of the Río Colorado and is divided by the river into Barra del Norte and Barra del Sur. There are no roads. The airstrip is on the south side of the river, but

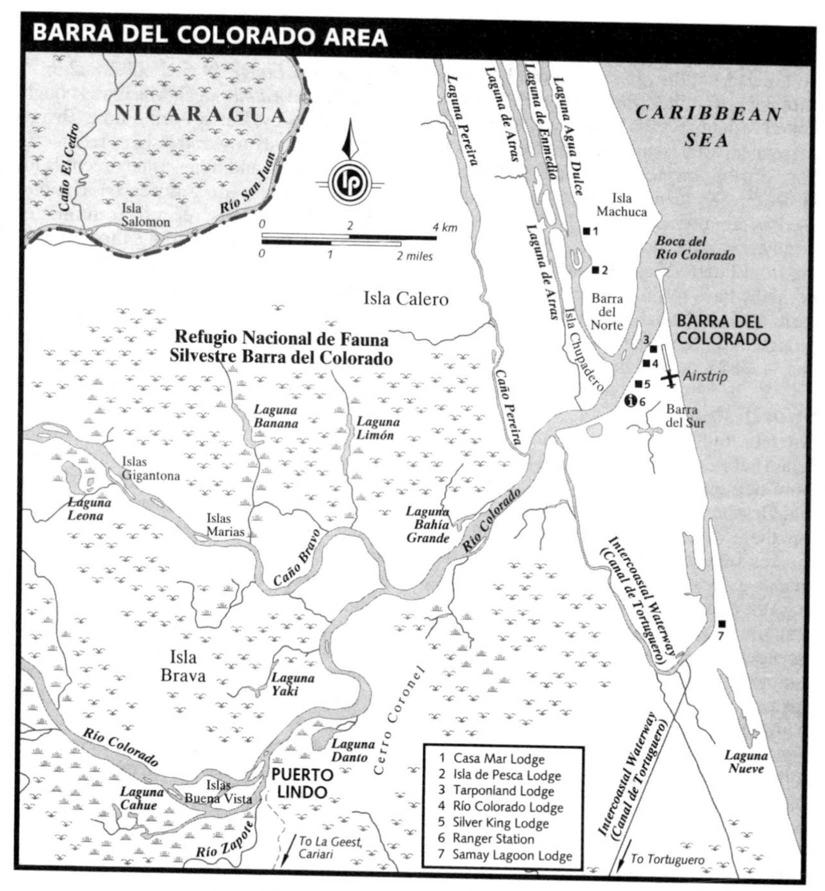

more locals live on the north side. The area outside the village is very swampy and travel is almost exclusively by boat, though some walking is possible around some of the lodges scattered in the area.

The Servicio de Parques Nacionales (SPN) maintains a small ranger station on the south side of the Río Colorado near the village. However, there are no facilities here. Officially, US$6 is charged to enter the refuge, but this was not being enforced at time of writing.

From the airport, only the Tarponland and the Río Colorado Lodges (see Places to Stay & Eat, below) are accessible on foot. All other lodges require a boat ride (a boatman will be waiting for you at the airport if you have a reservation).

C&D Souvenirs (☎ 710-6592), near to the airport, has a public phone and fax and offers tourist information. There's a small grocery store about 100m away.

Entering Nicaragua Day trips along the Río San Juan and some offshore fishing trips enter Nicaraguan territory, but no special visa is required (though you should carry your passport for checkpoints along the San Juan).

The Nicaraguan village at the mouth of the Río San Juan is San Juan del Norte. There are no hotels here, though lodging can be found with local families. San Juan del Norte is linked with the rest of Nicaragua by irregular passenger boats sailing up the San Juan to San Carlos, on the Lago de Nicaragua. However, San Juan del Norte is not normally used as an entry point into Nicaragua – ask locally about the possibilities. People traveling from Puerto Viejo de Sarapiquí to Barra normally have to show their passports at the various Nicaraguan border checkpoints, even though they are not actually entering Nicaragua. A US$5 fee may be charged.

Sportfishing

Anglers find that tarpon from January to June (February to May are best) and snook from September to December (September and October are best) are the fish of choice, but there is decent fishing year-round and the seasons seem to vary somewhat from year to year. Other fish include barracuda, mackerel, and jack crevalle, all inshore; or bluegill, rainbow bass *(or guapote)*, and *machaca* in the rivers. There is also deep-sea fishing for marlin, sailfish, and other fish, but this option is better on the Pacific (though available here in some lodges for those whose time is limited). Dozens of fish can be hooked on a good day, so 'catch and release' is an important conservation policy of all the lodges.

Places to Stay & Eat

Budget & Mid-Range Most visitors stay in one of several lodges in the area, which cater primarily to anglers but also to naturalists. Most of these are beyond the pocketbook of shoestring travelers, although there are a few moderately priced places.

Visitors to Barra del Colorado are allowed to camp in the refuge, but there are no facilities. The rangers at the station told me that visitors can set up a tent in front of the ranger station if they want. It is also possible to find somewhere inexpensive (about US$8 per person) to stay with a family in Barra del Colorado village if you ask around – try C&D Souvenirs near the airport for information.

In the village of Barra del Colorado, the cheapest hotel is next to the airport. This is the ***Tarponland Lodge*** *(☎ 383-6097, 382-3350, 710-6592, leave a message)*, which was bought in late 1996 by Barra-born Eddie Brown Silva, who holds a world fishing record for cubera snapper, and other fishing records for Costa Rica. There are a dozen basic rooms with baths and fans recently renting for US$45 per person including three meals. Fishing, boat tours, and transportation can all be arranged; I've heard that the Tarponland only rents to anglers fishing with Eddie.

The German-run ***Samay Lagoon Lodge*** *(in San José ☎ 284-7047, fax 383-6370, samaycr@sol.racsa.co.cr)* is an excellent mid-range option for those who wish to visit the area without an emphasis on sportfishing. Located about 8km south of Barra del Colorado airport, the lodge has 22 standard rooms with tiled bathrooms and hot showers, fans, and a restaurant-bar. The beach is a couple of minutes' walk away (but heavy surf, strong currents, and sharks preclude swimming). Most visitors come on a three-day/two-night package that begins at San José with a bus ride through Braulio Carrillo to Puerto Viejo de Sarapiquí, continuing with a 3½-hour boat ride down the Ríos Sarapiquí, San Juan, and Colorado to the lodge. The second day includes a guided canoe trip-hike into the rainforest and the third day return takes you back the way you came. The tour costs US$278 per person, double occupancy, from San José (plus a US$5 Nicaraguan border fee) and includes meals, two nights' lodging, transportation, and a tour. Extra days cost US$50 per day including meals and canoe use. Guided horseback riding, fishing, and other tours can be arranged.

Top End The ***Isla de Pesca Lodge*** *(☎ 710-6776)* is run by the Japanese-owned Grupo Costa Sol International, which owns the upscale Hotel Herradura in San José (see that chapter for further contact information). The lodge is 2 or 3km north of Barra village and has cabins with fans and private hot showers; the lodge also offers full fishing packages. In 1999, the lodge was closed for renovation and it's not clear when/if it will reopen.

The ***Casa Mar*** *(☎ 381-1380, fax 433-9287; in the USA ☎ 800-543-0282, 714-578-1881, fax 800-367-2299; 2634 W Orangethorpe No 6, Fullerton, CA 92833)* is about 1km north of Isla Pesca. It's a small sportfishing lodge with six duplex cabins set in a pleasant 2.8-hectare garden that attracts lots of birds; ecotourists stay here for that reason. Rooms all have fans and tiled hot showers; all-you-can-eat home-cooked meals are included in the rates. Casa Mar is open year-round. Its seven-day charters cost US$2695/4390 single/double and include transfers from the Barra del Colorado airport, all fishing, accommodations, meals, and an open bar. Three-day trips cost US$1275/2100 and trips of other lengths can be arranged. The lodge staff will make San José hotel reservations and SANSA or private air charter arrangements (at additional cost) upon request.

The longest-established lodge (built in 1971) on the Caribbean coast is the well-known ***Río Colorado Lodge*** *(☎/fax 710-6879; in San José ☎ 232-8610, 232-4063, fax 231-5987, tarpon@sol.racsa.co.cr; in the USA ☎ 800-243-9777, tarpon4@cyberspy.com)*. The lodge also has an office in the Hotel Corobicí in San José. The rambling tropical-style lodge buildings are constructed on stilts near the mouth of the Río Colorado, and the carpenter who erected the original buildings was still working on lodge upkeep in 1999 – a nice touch. Cages around the covered walkways house tropical birds and some small monkeys, and a tapir named Baby wanders around. All 18 rooms have fans and hot showers, and are breezy and pleasant. Six of the rooms also have air-conditioning (including a 'honeymoon suite' with wicked ceiling mirrors!) and two rooms have wheelchair access. The food has been recommended and is all-you-can-eat, served family style. For relaxation after a day of fishing, the lodge features a happy hour with free rum drinks, a lounging area with a pool table and other games, a breezy outdoor deck, and a video room with satellite TV.

This is the only upscale lodge from which you can walk to the airport and, as its brochure states, villagers often drop by with their guitars in the evening and it doesn't take much to get a party started. The Río Colorado has a reputation for being a 'party lodge' and is run by Mississippian Dan Wise, a colorful character who meets guests with a killer Belgian Malinois that responds only to commands in German.

Most guests are anglers, but nonfishing visitors can stay here for US$90 per day including meals. For those interested in natural history, the staff can arrange local rainforest tours or transportation by boat from Puerto Viejo de Sarapiquí to the lodge, returning to San José via Tortuguero. The lodge is open year-round and offers boats, bilingual guide, all meals, and accommodations at a daily rate of US$360 per person. Air-conditioned rooms cost about US$10 per day extra. Complete packages from San José, including hotels in the capital if desired, can also be arranged. The lodge locally advertises discounted super summer saver specials from June 15 to August 15. They'll take you fishing in Nicaragua on request for an extra charge.

The best sportfishing lodge on this coast is the ***Silver King Lodge*** *(☎/fax 381-1403, 381-0849; in the USA ☎ 800-847-3474, slvrkng@sol.racsa.co.cr, www.silverkinglodge.com; Aerocasillas, Dept 1597, PO Box 025216, Miami, FL 33102)*. This place, about 1.5km southwest of the Barra del Colorado airport, has the largest rooms of any lodge, in 10 duplexes; each room has a big tiled bathroom with hot water and a coffeemaker (complimentary coffee). There is a large indoor Jacuzzi, a small but attractive outdoor pool with waterfall surrounded by loungers and hammocks, a dining room with excellent and varied all-you-can-eat meals (served family style with complimentary wine), and a screened 24-hour bar with river views and a TV/VCR with videos. Soft drinks and local beer and rum are free, and all boats come with a well-stocked ice chest of soft drinks and beer. Covered walkways link all the areas. An especially nice feature is the free daily laundry service. A recreation room with exercise machines is planned. The lodge's fax/phone and email are available for client use.

Boats used for fishing include 19-foot unsinkable, self-bailing skiffs with 65hp engines, suitable for two anglers and a guide, and

13 new 23-foot, deep-v-hull boats with 150hp engines. An offshore boat with two 150hp engines, downriggers, outriggers, radio, and sonar is also available. All guides are English-speaking local fishers. Rods and reels are provided for regular fishing and a wide selection of lures is sold in the lodge's tackle shop. Loaner rods and reels are free, unless you lose or break them, in which case you are charged. Fly-fishing gear is also available for anglers wishing to try for a tarpon on a fly rod!

To see the wildlife, you can use one of the Silver King's 17-foot aluminum canoes, either on your own or with a guide. They'll give you a lift to a recommended area and then leave you to explore if you want, picking you up at a prearranged time. Multi-day canoeing tours are available for those more interested in land-based wildlife such as monkeys, birds, and caimans than in snook and tarpon.

The lodge has developed a reputation as the best in the area. Managed and owned by genial Ray Barry, who has a fund of wild stories to entertain you with, and smiling Shawn Feliciano-Barry, one of the few women anglers on the coast, the lodge guarantees complete satisfaction. If you aren't happy with the services, they'll transport you to another Barra lodge of your choice for the remainder of your trip. Their staff and service are exceptional. The lodge is usually full during the busiest months (mid-January to mid-May); you should book several months in advance to get the dates you want. This lodge closes in July and December.

Sample rates are US$1995/3290 single/double for three full days of fishing, all lodge

Sleeping in a Houseboat

The *Rain Goddess* is a 65-foot-long, 18-foot-wide air-conditioned houseboat that plies the waters of Tortuguero and Barra del Colorado, allowing guests to see the area in comfort. There are six spacious cabins, four with a queen-size and single bed, and two with a double bed (no bunks here!). Each cabin has its own sink, and there are three shared bathrooms, each with hot shower. There is an elegant dining salon and bar, and the chef does a first-class job. The owner, Dr Alfredo Lopez, is an affable medical doctor who sometimes cruises along with the guests and offers free medical services to locals in the remote settlements visited, which means that the houseboat is a welcome sight to local residents.

Both sportfishing and natural history cruises are offered, with a minimum of six and maximum of 12 passengers for the fishing trips and a minimum of eight for the natural history tours. The latter are accompanied by bilingual naturalist guides. If you arrange your own minimum-sized group, you can rent the whole boat; otherwise, you can share with other travelers. Small boats are towed both for fishing and jungle exploration.

Three nights with three full days of fishing, plus a night in a San José hotel and flights to/from Barra, cost US$1750 per angler (US$850 for nonanglers), including all airport transfers, meals, and an open bar. Basic fishing tackle is provided. The same tour for five nights and five days of fishing costs US$2250/1070 per angler/nonangler. Extra days cost US$350/110. Three-day/two-night natural history tours leave San José by bus to Puerto Viejo de Sarapiquí, where an express boat connects guests with the *Rain Goddess* on the Río Colorado in early afternoon. On the second and third days, the boat cruises through the Barra area and back to Puerto Viejo, where passengers board an afternoon bus to San José. The cost is US$475 per person, all inclusive.

Fur further information and reservations, contact Blue Wing International (☎ 231-4299, fax 231-3816; in the USA ☎ 877-258-9464, www.bluwing.com).

– Rob Rachowiecki

Epiphyte-laden tree

NORMAN OWEN TOMALIN

Exploring the canals near Parque Nacional Tortuguero

JANIS BURGER

Immature green turtle *(Chelonia mydas)*, Caribbean coast

ERWIN & PEGGY BAUER

Near the summit of Cerro Chirripó, Costa Rica's highest peak

ROB RACHOWIECKI

Water lily at Genesis II

BUDDY MAYS

FRANK BALTHIS

FRANK BALTHIS

Fisherman and his catch near Marenco, Península de Osa

DAVE G HOUSER

Black-sand beach, Puntarenas

DAVID MADISON

DAVID MADISON

Almendro tree and a quiet place to rest at Marenco Beach & Rainforest Lodge facilities for three nights, roundtrip air from San José, and luxury hotels in San José at either end if needed. For five full days, it's US$2876/4576; extra days cost US$441/762. Nonfishing stays cost US$117 per day, including all lodge facilities but not air transportation. The only extra fees are US$38 for a fishing license, plus gratuities, the cost of lures, imported liquors, and phone calls.

Canoeing tours cost about US$50 per day with a guide, depending on the number of clients.

Getting There & Away

Air Most visitors arrive by air from San José. You can charter a light plane or take a regularly scheduled flight with SANSA (see the Getting Around chapter for details).

Boat A few of the boats from Moín to Tortuguero continue to Barra, but there is no regular service. Boats can be hired in Tortuguero to take you up to Barra for about US$50 (two hours); they'll take three to five passengers. If you don't have a group and have time on your hands, you could probably do it more cheaply by asking the locals and going with them.

Occasional and irregular passenger boats go from Barra to Puerto Viejo de Sarapiquí via the Ríos San Juan and Sarapiquí, or boats can be hired to make this trip anytime. Several lodges (especially the Samay Lagoon Lodge; see above) arrange parts of their tours to include a boat ride from Puerto Viejo.

One can also hire a boat from Barra to the small riverside community of Puerto Lindo, less than an hour by motorboat up the Río Colorado. From Puerto Lindo, vehicles go to the town of Cariari, from where there are buses to Guápiles. The road is often closed after heavy rains, but provides the cheapest link with San José for local inhabitants who share transportation. There used to be a bus service between Puerto Lindo and Cariari, but Hurricane Mitch damaged the road in 1998 and a taxi with 4WD must now be hired. Ask in Barra or Cariari about possibilities. This road is the subject of much contention between developers and conservationists.

Southern Caribbean

The road southeast of Puerto Limón approximately parallels the coast, first offering views of freighters scattered outside the port – near Isla Uvita, where Columbus made a landing – and then miles of palm trees, waves, and empty beaches.

The inhabitants of this district are predominantly blacks of Jamaican descent who settled on the Costa Rican coast in the middle of the 19th century; many speak a Creole form of English. This can be confusing at first, because some words and phrases do not have the meanings that other speakers of English are accustomed to. For example, 'All right!' means 'Hello!' and 'Okay!' means 'Goodbye!'

These settlers have traditionally lived by small-time agriculture and fishing, although catering to tourists is now becoming an industry of its own. The influx of tourist cash helps improve the standard of living, but at a cultural cost. Traditional ways slowly become eroded and, inevitably, local people have some difficulties in adjusting to the new – and sometimes demanding or obnoxious – tourist presence. Some of the younger locals have become demanding or obnoxious as well. Nevertheless, much of the Creole and indigenous culture remains for those who look for it, particularly in cooking, music, and local knowledge of medicinal plants.

The mixture of black and indigenous culture on this stretch of coast is very interesting: you can buy Bribri handicrafts and listen to reggae or calypso music, take horseback rides into local indigenous reserves, go fishing with the locals, go surfing, snorkeling, and swimming, or just hang out with the old-timers and talk. There's plenty to do, but everything is very relaxed. Take your time and you'll discover a beautiful way of life – rush through and you'll end up feeling frustrated. The villages are places to hang out for a few days, not to spend a quick day visiting or passing through.

The wet and dry season are not as clearly distinguished in this region as in other parts of the country; the relative warmth of the Caribbean Sea, combined with the proximity of the Cordillera de Talamanca and the cooler air pushing over from the Pacific side, means that rain is a possibility any time of year. In the wettest season, it can rain hard for days on end. However, sun is a year-round possibility as well – even during the rainiest months, cloud patterns often adopt a regular rhythm that will give you several predictable hours of sun a day. Come prepared for rain, but hope that the best of this microclimate will smile your way.

Until the 1970s, this area was quite isolated from the rest of Costa Rica. A ride in an old bus on a dirt road, a river-crossing by wobbly canoe, and a train ride were required just to get from Cahuita to Puerto Limón – this journey could take half a day. The 1987 opening of the highway from Limón to San José means that the coast is now about three hours from the capital – and the paved road leading southeast from Limón has cut the journey to Cahuita to a 45-minute drive (under good conditions), with Puerto Viejo de Talamanca only another 20 minutes farther south. Since the '91 earthquake, which pushed some reefs in the area a foot or two out of the water, this stretch of road is still fairly tumultuous; potholes will slow down those drivers interested in safety. Recently, direct bus service from San José to the coastal villages has eliminated the need for a bus change in Limón.

Despite the increasing ease of access, the area retains much of its remote, provincial, and unhurried flavor. Most Costa Ricans still head to the Pacific coast for their beach vacations, and there are few luxury hotel developments on the Caribbean.

In addition to the reserves described below, a number of organic farm communities have sprung up in the area in recent years, many of them founded by immigrants from the USA and Europe interested in creating sustainable agriculture and in tapping into local knowledge of flora, fauna, and farming methods. Some of these communities can be contacted through tour agencies in the villages.

Just northeast of Puerto Viejo, the main road turns inland toward Bribri, then turns southeast again before reaching Sixaola, on the Panamanian border. This border is commonly used as a gateway to the Bocas del Toro islands in Panama.

CONSELVATUR

This tour company owns a private 850-hectare reserve, one-third of which is a family farm; the remainder is rainforest preserved for tourism. Conselvatur arranges various tours in the area (and throughout the country). The farm is reached by driving almost 20km south of Limón, then turning west at the Río Bananito and heading up the Río Bananito valley for about 15km. You'll need a 4WD for the last few kilometers, though staff can pick you up if requested. Contact the lodge for information on combining the use of public transportation with getting picked up. What bus the staff instruct you to take (ie, where they pick you up) depends on what they're up to at the time.

On the farm is the seven-cabin ***Selva Bananito Lodge*** *(☎ 284-4278, ☎/fax 253-8118, fax 224-2640, costari@netins.net)*. Each cabin has a solar-heated tiled shower, two beds, a large deck with hammock and rainforest views, but no electricity (portable bedside lamps are available). Complete packages with three meals cost US$100/160/201/244 for one to four people per cabin (there are discounts for kids under 12), including one or two tours for those staying two or three nights. Tour options include hiking to waterfalls, birding, and mountain biking. Bicycle rental costs US$12 per day.

AVIARIOS DEL CARIBE

This small wildlife sanctuary and B&B (☎/fax 382-1335, aviarios@costarica.net) is 31km south of Limón, or about 1km north from where the coastal highway crosses the Río Estrella. The sanctuary is an 88-hectare island in the delta of the Río Estrella, where the owners (Luis and Judy Arroyo) have recorded 314 species of birds – and are still counting. A variety of local nature-oriented excursions are offered. The most popular is the US$30 kayak tour that lasts about three hours. A guide paddles you quietly through the Estrella delta, getting close to a variety of birds and animals. Sloths, monkeys, caiman, and river otters are seen – in fact, there is an orphaned sloth named Buttercup on the grounds. Buttercup's mother was killed by a car and the owners raised the youngster, who was about five weeks old when they found it. They also have all sorts of other interesting animals, as well as an ant house and a poison-arrow frog hatchery! Visits and tours are available to nonguests as well.

The small B&B is an attractive place to stay. Art by Mindy Lighthipe graces the walls – her paintings of butterflies are stunning. A balcony provides a view of the garden and forest, and there is a library and a game room. Rooms are spacious with fans, comfortable beds, restful decor, and well-designed bathrooms with hot water. High-season rates, including full breakfast, are about US$65 double. If calling for reservations, keep trying; it can sometimes be hard to get through on the phone.

Any bus to Cahuita will drop you off at the entrance to Aviarios del Caribe.

VALLE DE LA ESTRELLA

The Río Estrella valley is a long-established banana- and cacao-growing region. There are plantations producing several other types of tropical fruit as well. Traveling south from Limón, the valley is reached by turning right (west) on the signed road just south of the bridge over the Río Estrella. This is the route to Reserva Biológica Hitoy Cerere. Buses from San José leave from the Caribe terminal at 3 pm, returning at 6 am the next day.

RESERVA BIOLÓGICA HITOY CERERE

This 9154-hectare reserve is 60km south of Limón by road, but only half that distance as the vulture glides. Although not far from civilization, it is one of the most rugged and rarely visited reserves in the country. There is a ranger station but otherwise there are no facilities – no campsites, nature trails, or information booths. The reserve lies at between about 150 and 1000m in elevation on rugged terrain on the south side of the Río Estrella valley.

Few people come to Hitoy Cerere, but that is no reason to ignore it. The reserve sounds like a fascinating place and, being so rarely visited, offers a great wilderness experience in an area that has been little explored. It has been called the wettest reserve in the parks system – expect almost 4m of rain each year in these dense evergreen forests.

Hiking is permitted, but the steep and slippery terrain and dense vegetation make it a possibility only for the most fit and determined hikers. Heavy rainfall and broken terrain combine to produce many beautiful streams, rivers, and waterfalls. These often take several hours of difficult hiking to reach. Hiking along a stream bed is the best way of getting through the dense vegetation. Reportedly, there is one more-or-less maintained trail leading south from the ranger station. The reserve is home to many different plants, birds, mammals, and other creatures, many of which have not yet been recorded because of the remoteness of the site.

Information

Visitors should call ahead (see National Parks & Protected Areas in the Facts about Costa Rica chapter) to see if somebody will be at the ranger station when they arrive. Sleeping at the ranger station is possible for a small fee.

Getting There & Away

Take a bus to Valle de la Estrella from Limón. From the end of the bus line it is an additional 10 to 15km to the reserve along a dirt road. There are 4WD taxis available to drive you there for US$10 or so one way. The drivers are reliable, and will come back to pick you up at a prearranged time. From Cahuita (about 30km away), 4WD taxis will take you to the reserve for about US$30. (Ordinary cars can get there during the drier months.)

CAHUITA

This small village lies about 43km southeast of Puerto Limón by road. It is known for the attractive beaches nearby (more suitable for snorkeling and swimming than for surfing), some of which are in Parque

Nacional Cahuita, which adjoins the village to the south.

After a mid-1990s slump, Cahuita is beginning to revive as a tourist destination, with the construction of a few hotels and new restaurants and locally run tour companies opening for business. But the main street is still made of sand – more suited to horses and clunky wheeled bicycles than to the cars and 4WDs with which tourists send up clouds of choking dust. One local woman said that the tourists' vehicles were the biggest problem that tourism has caused. She couldn't even hang her laundry out to dry in front of her house because of the dust – one example of the clash between 20th-century tourism and a 19th-century way of life. As always, travelers are urged to enjoy their experience without imposing their own values upon the areas they are visiting.

Information

Tourist information is available from the places listed in the following Activities & Organized Tours section.

Money Cash US dollars are readily exchanged. Some hotels will change traveler's checks if they have enough *colones*, as will some of the tour operators; rates may vary significantly from place to place.

Email & Internet Access Internet access is now available at some businesses and hotels, but in the village center businesses tend to overcharge; ask around for the best deal. At time of writing, Cahuita Tours & Rentals charged US$3.50 per 15 minutes while Cabinas Palmer charged US$3.50 per hour; definitely look around for new options.

Dangers & Annoyances The following warnings are applicable, to a certain extent, in all the beach towns. They are placed here because Cahuita has received, generally unfairly, a bad rap for theft and drugs. This reputation peaked about four years ago, when several violent holdups (one resulting in a death) occurred along the road to Puerto Limón, even though the holdups weren't very near town. As a result, tourism dropped off substantially in 1995 and 1996 while it increased somewhat farther south, around Puerto Viejo de Talamanca, which reputedly was safer.

Although in terms of safety there's really not much difference between Cahuita and Puerto Viejo, the temporary decrease in tourism means that Cahuita is currently the least developed of the two. Most travelers find that the area's relaxed pace, generally friendly people, lack of a highly developed tourist infrastructure, cultural diversity, and attractive environment all contribute to an enjoyable visit.

As for the drug situation, not too many of the locals are into smoking ganja or snorting coke, but those who are usually hang around the few bars in town and they can be rather insistent with their approaches. These individuals don't reflect the nature of the population as a whole: most residents are not particularly happy with young travelers coming in search of drugs. There are plenty of Rasta wannabes hanging around. Remember that buying drugs is illegal as well as dangerous (dealers may be crooked or collaborating with the police). Though policing has improved in the area, travelers should still be alert to prevent rip-offs. Keep your hotel room locked and the windows closed; there have been several reports of theft from rooms, including some employing the 'fishing' technique, which involves slicing open the netting over a window and using a long, hooked stick to fish out whatever valuables are 'caught.' Never leave gear unattended on beaches when swimming, don't walk the beaches alone at night, and be prudent if entering some of the local bars. Don't give money for a service in advance as you might not see the person again, and always count your change.

Some solo women travelers have complained that local men can be too demanding in their advances. Female travelers may feel that traveling with a friend is safer than traveling alone. Some women do travel alone and have a good time, but not everyone is adept at avoiding unpleasant situations. Some local men have a reputation for picking up female travelers (especially

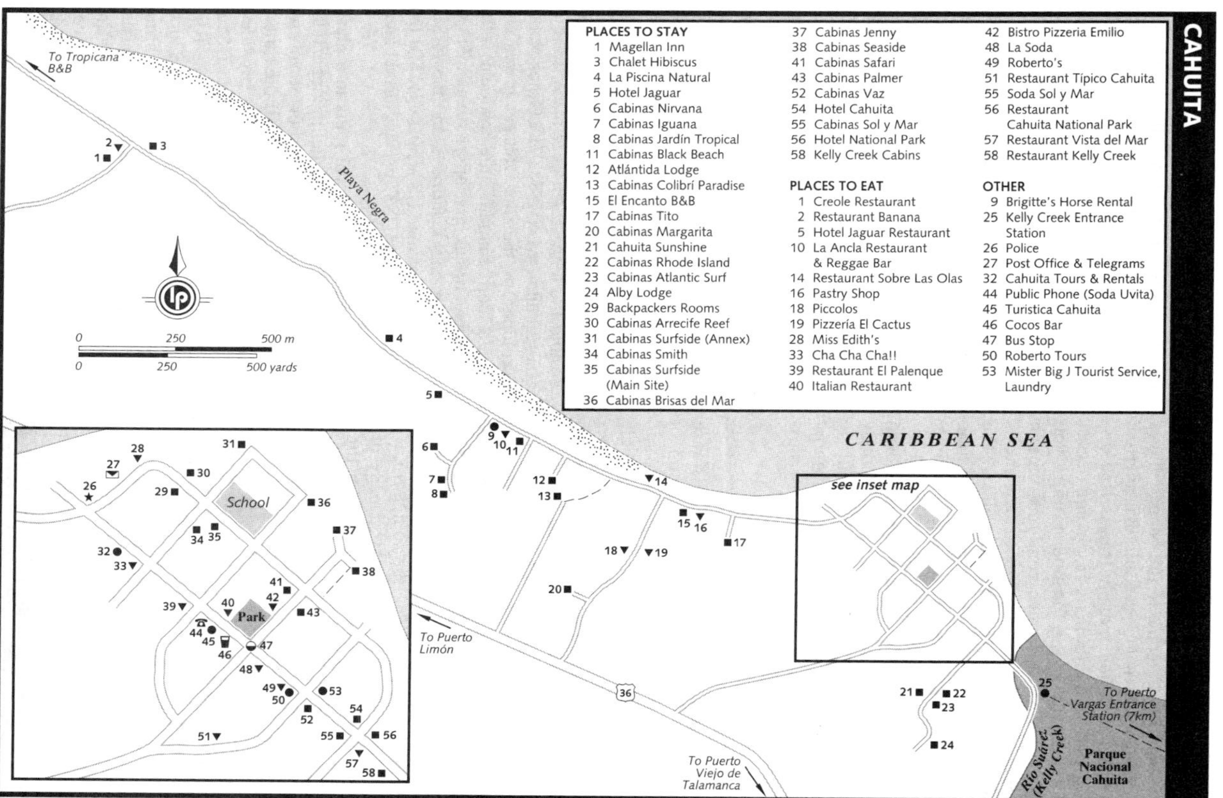
CAHUITA
PLACES TO STAY
1 Magellan Inn
3 Chalet Hibiscus
4 La Piscina Natural
5 Hotel Jaguar
6 Cabinas Nirvana
7 Cabinas Iguana
8 Cabinas Jardín Tropical
11 Cabinas Black Beach
12 Atlántida Lodge
13 Cabinas Colibrí Paradise
15 El Encanto B&B
17 Cabinas Tito
20 Cabinas Margarita
21 Cahuita Sunshine
22 Cabinas Rhode Island
23 Cabinas Atlantic Surf
24 Alby Lodge
29 Backpackers Rooms
30 Cabinas Arrecife Reef
31 Cabinas Surfside (Annex)
34 Cabinas Smith
35 Cabinas Surfside (Main Site)
36 Cabinas Brisas del Mar
37 Cabinas Jenny
38 Cabinas Seaside
41 Cabinas Safari
43 Cabinas Palmer
52 Cabinas Vaz
54 Hotel Cahuita
55 Cabinas Sol y Mar
56 Hotel National Park
58 Kelly Creek Cabins
PLACES TO EAT
1 Creole Restaurant
2 Restaurant Banana
5 Hotel Jaguar Restaurant
10 La Ancla Restaurant & Reggae Bar
14 Restaurant Sobre Las Olas
16 Pastry Shop
18 Piccolos
19 Pizzería El Cactus
28 Miss Edith's
33 Cha Cha Cha!!
39 Restaurant El Palenque
40 Italian Restaurant
42 Bistro Pizzeria Emilio
48 La Soda
49 Roberto's
51 Restaurant Típico Cahuita
55 Soda Sol y Mar
56 Restaurant Cahuita National Park
57 Restaurant Vista del Mar
58 Restaurant Kelly Creek
OTHER
9 Brigitte's Horse Rental
25 Kelly Creek Entrance Station
26 Police
27 Post Office & Telegrams
32 Cahuita Tours & Rentals
44 Public Phone (Soda Uvita)
45 Turistica Cahuita
46 Cocos Bar
47 Bus Stop
50 Roberto Tours
53 Mister Big J Tourist Service, Laundry
To Tropicana B&B
Playa Negra
CARIBBEAN SEA
see inset map
To Puerto Limón
To Puerto Viejo de Talamanca
36
To Puerto Vargas Entrance Station (7km)
Río Suárez (Kelly Creek)
Parque Nacional Cahuita
School
Park
0 250 500 m
0 250 500 yards

blonde ones) and expecting the woman to pay for both their expenses during the affair.

Some people come to the beach villages looking for sexual flings. Caution is advised; AIDS and other sexually transmitted diseases are certainly here. If you can't resist the temptations the Caribbean offers, you should bring your own condoms, though persuading a local *macho* to use one is another matter. Better still, talk to the locals about AIDS – sharing information about this subject is never a waste of time.

Please note that, despite the casual atmosphere both here and in other coastal areas, nude or topless bathing is definitely not accepted. Also, wearing skimpy bathing clothes in the villages is frowned upon. Wearing at least a T-shirt and shorts is expected and appreciated.

Beaches

Three beaches are within walking distance of the village. At the northwest end of Cahuita is Playa Negra, a long black-sand beach with good swimming. Some people think that the black-sand beach has better swimming than the white-sand beach at the eastern end of town, though ask about currents at both. This latter beach is in the

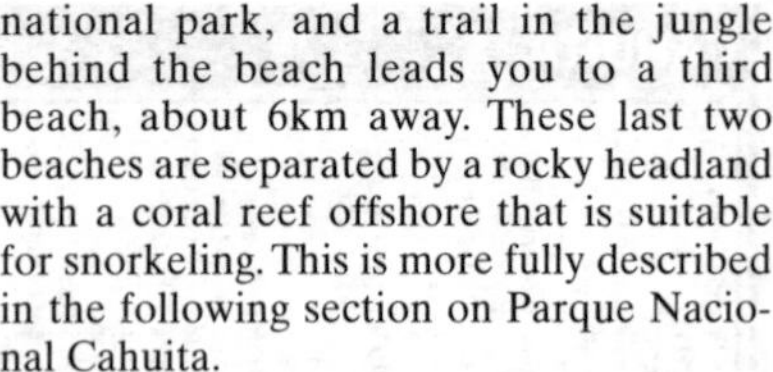

national park, and a trail in the jungle behind the beach leads you to a third beach, about 6km away. These last two beaches are separated by a rocky headland with a coral reef offshore that is suitable for snorkeling. This is more fully described in the following section on Parque Nacional Cahuita.

Activities & Organized Tours

A number of places rent equipment and arrange tours. Brigitte (☎ 755-0053), a Swiss woman who has lived by Playa Negra for years, offers half-day guided horseback tours for US$25 to US$35 and horse rental (for unguided exploration) at US$10 per hour. Mister Big J Tourist Service (☎ 755-0328) and Roberto Tours (☎/fax 755-0117) are both recent additions, presided over by personable locals who cover all the standards and have individual specialties. Mister Big J has been leading horse tours in the area for over 10 years; Roberto will take you fishing and then cook your catch at his restaurant (see Places to Eat, below), or organize a visit to a nearby organic farm. Cahuita Tours & Rentals (☎ 755-0232, fax 755-0082) has been around the longest. Another place is Turistica Cahuita (☎/fax 755-0071). Other places may open by the time you get there. You should shop around for the best deals – the following prices are approximate. These places rent masks, snorkels, and fins (US$7 per day), bicycles (US$7.50 to US$10 per day), surfboards (US$7 per day), and binoculars (US$7 per day).

Boat trips to the local reefs in a glass-bottomed boat, with snorkeling opportunities, cost US$15 to US$20 per person for three or four hours (about half the time is spent on the water). Drinks are provided. Day trips to Tortuguero cost about US$65 to US$75. River-running trips on the Ríos Reventazón and Pacuare cost US$70 to US$90. (Trips include two or three hours of actual rafting; the rest of the day is spent getting there and back and eating meals, which are included in the price). Guided horseback and hiking trips into the local national park areas are available, as are a variety of taxi services and visits to

Organic Farms

A number of organic farm communities have sprung up along the southern Caribbean coast in recent years, many of them founded by immigrants from the USA and Europe interested in creating sustainable agriculture and in tapping into local knowledge of flora, fauna, and farming methods. Roberto Tours in Cahuita and Earth Connect in Punta Mona, south of Manzanillo, are good contact points for people interested in visiting these communities.

Monteverde (see the Northwestern Costa Rica chapter) is another good place to find organic farmers.

– **John Thompson**

places like Hitoy Cerere and the indigenous reserves.

Often, the best prices are available directly from the guides. The Asociación Talamanqueña de Ecoturismo y Conservación (ATEC), based in Puerto Viejo de Talamanca (see that section for more information), has local guides who will take you on half- to full-day hiking tours through old cacao plantations and into the rainforest around Cahuita – the emphasis of these tours is the Afro-Caribbean lifestyle plus natural history. ATEC also offers visits to Parque Nacional Cahuita and birding walks. Some local guides who have been recommended are Walter Cunningham, who specializes in birding, Carlos Mairena, and José McCloud. Ask for these men at your hotel; all of them are well known in Cahuita (you don't need to go through ATEC).

Places to Stay

There are two possible areas in which to stay. In town, hotels are generally cheaper and noisier, but close to restaurants and the national park. Northwest of town, along Playa Negra, you'll find more expensive hotels and a few cabinas, which offer more privacy and quiet but a more limited choice of restaurants unless you travel 1 or 2km into town. A few of these hotels are overpriced – you're paying for the location. None are deluxe.

In the early 1990s, reservations were recommended for holidays and high-season weekends, but a small increase in hotel building combined with a drop in tourism meant that in the late '90s, rooms were usually available at any time. Room rates have remained level or even dropped since the last edition of this guide and bargains can be found, especially midweek. This situation will be changing again as Cahuita's reputation revives, and prices may rise. Rates below are for busy weekends; they may be lower at other times or for longer stays.

Budget Solo budget travelers may have difficulty finding cheap rooms because many are intended for rental to two to four people. For camping options, see the following Parque Nacional Cahuita section.

A sporadically open cheapie is simply signed ***Backpackers Rooms*** and offers four basic but reasonably clean rooms with foam mattresses on the beds for US$5 per person.

The ***Cabinas Surfside*** *(☎ 755-0246)* has modern, concrete-block rooms; they are plain but clean and have fans and private baths. There is a night guard on duty at the gate and you can park here. The rate is US$12 double, and there are a couple of better cabins a block away, right near the rocky shoreline, for US$18. Nearby, the clean ***Cabinas Smith*** *(☎ 755-0068)* is run by a friendly local woman and has good rooms with electric showers and fans for US$15.

Cabinas Vaz *(☎ 755-0283)* offers clean concrete-block rooms with baths and fans for US$9/13 single/double, which is a decent value, though it can get noisy. The similarly priced ***Cabinas Rhode Island*** *(☎ 755-0264)* has clean rooms with baths and fans. Across the street, the slightly more expensive ***Cahuita Sunshine*** *(☎ 755-0368)* offers clean, modern rooms with bathtubs, beanbag chairs, and kitchen facilities. Almost next door, the pretty ***Cabinas Atlantic Surf*** *(☎ 755-0086)* has pleasant wooden rooms, offering a nice change from the mainly concrete-block construction of Cahuita's hotels. Rates here are US$7.50/12.50/14.50 for rooms with fans, cold showers, and porches.

Cabinas Brisas del Mar *(☎ 755-0011)* charges US$15 to US$20 for clean double rooms with cold showers and good beds. The ***Cabinas Sol y Mar*** *(☎ 755-0237)* has decent rooms with fans and hot showers for US$13/15 single/double.

Cabinas Jenny *(☎ 755-0256, jenny@racsa.co.cr)* is right on the shore and charges US$15 double for the cheapest rooms, which are fairly basic; US$20 gets you a better upstairs room with a private bath, or a spacious downstairs cabin that also has a porch and hammock – both offering more privacy and sea views. Next door is the equally pleasant ***Cabinas Seaside*** *(☎ 755-0210)*, run by the easygoing Nan, which has a number of hammocks strung beneath the coconut palms – a good place to relax and chat or just watch the waves roll in. The rate is US$12 double for basic, clean rooms with two double beds and private cold showers, US$5 each additional person. Tour information is available.

The decrepit and charming ***Hotel Cahuita*** had just shut down at time of writing, with no clear plans for the future – fixer-upper, anyone? The ***Cabinas Palmer*** *(☎ 755-0243, kpalmer@sol.racsa.co.cr)* is owned by some friendly locals and offers Internet access for US$3.50 per hour. Most of the plain but clean rooms have hot showers and go for US$15/20 single/double. Rooms vary; ask to have a look. Across the street, the rooms at ***Cabinas Safari*** *(☎ 755-0078, fax 755-0020)* are consistently nicer and come with hot showers for US$15/20. Parking and money-exchange services are available.

Out toward Playa Negra, ***Cabinas Nirvana*** is a good budget choice with a variety of options from US$8 to US$12 per person. Built by a friendly Italian, all the cabins are nice; some have porches and hammocks. Though tucked down a side road several hundred meters from the beach, coral juts up from their grassy lawn area. Farther out from town is ***La Piscina Natural*** (meaning 'the natural pool'), named after a small inlet on the beach. Simple but adequate cabins with hot showers cost about US$18 double.

Almost at the entrance to Parque Nacional Cahuita, the ***Hotel National Park*** *(☎/fax 755-0244)* has decent clean rooms with hot showers for US$10/20 single/double, or US$15/25 with views. A popular restaurant is attached (see Places to Eat, below).

Cabinas Margarita *(☎ 755-0205)* has clean rooms with electric showers for US$15/20. ***Cabinas Arrecife Reef*** *(☎ 755-0081)* has plain rooms with hot showers for US$15/20, but the breezy, shaded porch has good sea views. ***Cabinas Black Beach*** *(☎ 755-0251)* has four pleasant rooms with balconies and private baths for US$25 double (each has a double bed and a bunk bed).

Mid-Range Conveniently attached to a soda, ***Cabinas Jardín Tropical*** *(☎ 755-0033)* has two nice cabins for rent with hot water, fans, refrigerators, and porch hammocks for US$30; there's a larger house that rents for US$50. ***Cabinas Iguana*** *(☎ 755-0005, fax 755-0054)* has three nice rooms with shared cold showers for US$15 double (often full of long-term guests) and a couple of even nicer cabins with refrigerators and hot plates; these sleep two to four people and rent for US$36 to US$48. The staff will pick you up at the bus stop if you have reservations. There is a swimming pool and book exchange. Both of these cabinas are quiet and out of the way.

The friendly ***Cabinas Tito*** *(☎ 755-0286)* has six pleasant rooms with cold showers and fans, some of them with kitchenettes, for US$25/30. The ***Cabinas Colibrí Paradise*** *(☎ 755-0055)* is also very attractive, in a quiet location behind the soccer field. It's easy enough to walk there on a footpath from the beachside road, but if you have a car you need to drive in from the main Puerto Limón-Sixaola road (Hwy 36). The handful of cabins (about US$30) come with fans, kitchenettes, refrigerators, and hot showers. There are many trees on the premises and the multilingual owner is friendly.

Right by the entrance to Parque Nacional Cahuita is the ***Kelly Creek Cabins*** *(☎ 755-0007)*, with very attractive and spacious wooden cabins with hot showers renting for US$35 and up. There's a restaurant here, too (see Places to Eat, below). Nearby, the German-run ***Alby Lodge*** *(☎/fax 755-0031)* has pleasant grounds with attractive thatched wooden cabins renting for US$30 to US$50. All have hot showers, fans, mosquito nets, and a porch with a hammock. The high-roofed and stilted architecture helps keep the rooms cool. At the other edge of town is the friendly ***El Encanto B&B*** *(☎/fax 755-0113)*, run by US expats Karen and Michael Russell. They have three comfortable and attractive wooden bungalows for US$42/50, including breakfast. All have hot water, ceiling fans, comfortable beds, and private patios.

The ***Chalet Hibiscus*** *(☎ 755-0021, fax 755-0015)* is set in attractive beachside gardens with many flowering bushes and plants. It's almost 2.5km northwest of the main bus stop in 'downtown' Cahuita – a good location if you're looking for peace and quiet. Pleasant, rustic-looking wooden rooms with private hot showers, table fans, and mosquito screens cost around US$40 to US$50 double (depending on size), and there are two houses that go for US$80 and US$100. There is a pool, and low-season discounts are offered. In an equally quiet area farther along the beach road, ***Tropicana B&B*** *(☎/fax 755-0059, borgato@sol.racsa.co.cr)* has doubles/triples for US$35/45 in a simple lodge-style building set amidst spacious, shady grounds. There's a wrap-around wooden verandah upstairs and a kitchen downstairs. Continental breakfast is included and the owners speak Italian, Spanish, and English.

The ***Hotel Jaguar*** *(☎ 755-0238; in San José 226-3775, fax 226-4693, jaguar@sol.racsa.co.cr)* is almost 2km from downtown. The hotel has a pool and trails where sloths and other animals have been sighted. The owners have opened a botanical garden and there is a guidebook available describing the plants (a small fee is charged to nonguests). The spacious rooms are built so that cross-breezes and natural ventilation keep them airy and comfortable without fans. Most rooms have large bathrooms with hot showers. Rates are US$30/55 single/double for standard rooms, including breakfast, and US$40/70 for larger, better-furnished superior rooms. There are also a few cold-water budget rooms with one bed for US$28 single or double without breakfast (these are aimed at students and budget travelers). There's also a poolside restaurant.

The ***Atlántida Lodge*** *(☎ 755-0115, fax 755-0213, atlantis@sol.racsa.co.cr)* is a nice place with about 30 rooms set in very pleasant gardens. Rooms with fans and hot showers go for about US$53/66 single/double including full breakfast. There's a swimming pool and an attractive thatched restaurant-bar, and the owners and staff are friendly and helpful. The lodge is about 1km northwest of the central bus stop – if you have a reservation, the staff will pick you up. The hotel also arranges a private bus from San José several times a week – call for times. The fare is US$25 one way per person direct to the lodge.

The ***Magellan Inn*** *(☎/fax 755-0035)* is almost 3km northwest of Cahuita at the north end of Playa Negra, and far enough removed from the village to be a destination in itself. The inn looks attractive with Asian rugs on the wooden floors and there is a small pool set in a pretty sunken garden. The inn has six carpeted rooms with fans, good hot showers, comfortable queen-size beds, and private patios looking out onto the grounds. The rate is about US$65 double including breakfast. Other meals are available in the fine restaurant (see below).

Places to Eat

An eatery that has attracted the attention of travelers over the years is ***Miss Edith's***. (As the local people get older, they traditionally earn a place of respect in the community. This is reflected by their form of address; they are called Miss or Mister, followed by their first name – hence, Miss Edith. You wouldn't refer to a young person in this way.) Guidebooks have rhapsodized about Miss Edith 'cooking up a storm' of Caribbean food, and she has been so successful that the restaurant is no longer just a little local place on someone's front porch but also a popular tourist hangout. The food is still good, however, and meals cost around US$4 to US$6, or US$10 and up for shrimp and lobster dishes. Alcohol isn't served. Service can be extremely slow and several readers have complained about this. It seems that the more in a hurry you are, the slower the staff works! Be friendly and willing to try whatever's on hand – this is a good place to reap the rewards of behaving like a guest in someone else's home. Miss Edith herself usually doesn't cook anymore; that's done by sisters and daughters.

As tourism begins to rebound here, a few new and well-liked restaurants have opened, taking over the premises of eateries that faded away in the latter '90s. ***Restaurant El Palenque*** serves tasty vegetarian as well as fish and meat dishes. ***Cha Cha Cha!!*** offers *cuisine del mundo*. ***Roberto's***, next to the tour company run by the same genial owner, is a relaxed place serving good, simple,

Caribbean-inflected meals. The mission statement on the wall reads, 'Let's go fishing and later we'll cook the fish for you.' Near the park, an as yet unnamed ***Italian restaurant*** has a good Italian chef, some wines, and a cheerful menu detailing the ingredients and spices in each dish. On the other side of the park is the little ***Bistro Pizzeria Emilio***, which looks charming.

On a side road northwest of downtown is the ***Pizzería El Cactus***, with pizzas and pastas in the US$3 to US$6 range. It's open for dinner only. At the northwest end of town is the popular beachfront ***Pastry Shop***, which offers delicious fresh-baked bread, cakes, and pies, and has picnic tables by the shore – a good place for a snack while being cooled by ocean breezes. Nearby is the ***Restaurant Sobre Las Olas***, rumored to be closing but traditionally a good place for a beachfront meal or a beer, though the location means slightly higher prices. ***La Ancla Restaurant & Reggae Bar*** is another choice; it has a limited menu but is a popular place for a beer with the Rastas. The relatively new ***Piccolos*** is a small, Caribbean-style pizza and burgers place, with a good pool table and cable TV. Farther out is the poolside ***Hotel Jaguar Restaurant***. For people staying out at the far end of Playa Negra, the ***Restaurant Banana*** sells good local food and the ***Creole Restaurant*** at the Magellan Inn is reportedly excellent (Creole and French cooking), but you should call the hotel to see if reservations are required.

Back in the heart of town, the ***Restaurant Cahuita National Park*** is by the entrance to Parque Nacional Cahuita and is a little pricey, but popular because of its location. The restaurant serves breakfast, lunch, and dinner. The food is decent and the place tends to be frequented by tourists who eat and drink at the outside tables. The newer ***Restaurant Vista del Mar***, across the street, is also open all day long and serves seafood dishes starting at US$3. Right by the park entrance, the ***Restaurant Kelly Creek*** specializes in paella and other Spanish cuisine and offers a standard menu for US$8 as well as other pricier but well-prepared options. Between these two restaurants is a little snack hut that is open erratically, selling delicious homemade *empanadas* (stuffed turnovers; US50¢) and other snacks until they're gone. Local women sometimes set up shop and sell their homemade meals (US$2.50) and snacks direct from the cooking pot.

For breakfasts and other meals, nearby are the ***Soda Sol y Mar*** (attached to the cabinas of the same name) and the somewhat self-consciously named ***La Soda***, which advertises natural food and real-estate deals. The nearby ***Restaurant Típico Cahuita*** has a variety of pricey but decent fish dishes – budget travelers should order the *casado* (bargain special) for US$3.

Entertainment

This can be summed up in one word: bars. The 'safest' bet is any one of the restaurants mentioned above, many of them out of the center. ***Cocos Bar***, in the middle of town, has taken over the location of the venerable Salon Vaz, and dominoes seems to be on the wane, though you can still hear games clacking out at older sodas around town. At night, the Cocos back room pounds to the sounds of Caribbean disco and there are occasional salsa nights. Local 'Calypso King' and storyteller Walter Gavitt Ferguson (his music sounds a bit like a Caribbean talking-blues) no longer plays publicly, but sometimes hangs out in the park across from Cocos. A tape of his original and traditional songs is available at Roberto Tours (see Activities & Organized Tours, earlier in the Cahuita section).

Getting There & Away

Express buses leave from the Caribe terminal in San José at 6 and 10 am, 1:30 and 3:30 pm. The fare is US$5 and the trip takes about four hours. Return buses leave from the central crossroads in Cahuita at 7:30, 9:30, and 11 am and 4 pm. Alternately, take a bus from San José to Puerto Limón and change there for service to Cahuita; there are six buses daily between Limón and Cahuita. These buses go on to Puerto Viejo de Talamanca, three of them also continuing to Manzanillo. About four buses go to Bribri and Sixaola daily. You may have to catch these buses out on the highway, southwest of the bus crossroads in town; ask locally. For the Puerto Vargas entrance to Parque Nacional Cahuita, take any bus to Puerto Viejo de Talamanca, Manzanillo, or Sixaola.

Schedules are liable to change, and given the potholed condition of the roads, don't be surprised if buses are late!

PARQUE NACIONAL CAHUITA

This small park of 1067 hectares is one of the more frequently visited national parks in Costa Rica. The reasons are simple: easy access and nearby hotels combined with attractive beaches, a coral reef and coastal rainforest with many easily observed tropical species. All of these combine to make this a popular park. Fortunately, Cahuita is still relatively little-visited compared to Manuel Antonio on the Pacific coast.

The park is most often entered from the southeast end of Cahuita village, through the 'donate what you want' Kelly Creek entrance station. A steep increase of national park fees to US$15 a few years ago (since reduced to US$6) had the locals up in arms because they thought that travelers would refuse to fork out US$15 to go sit on the beach, and feared that visitors would go elsewhere instead. Accordingly, villagers closed down the park entrance booth and encouraged visitors to use the beach for free. This resulted in the Minister of National Resources, René Castro, blaming the situation upon drug-taking budget travelers!

Currently, the village entrance station is open on a well-run 'donation only' basis. (Although locally known as Kelly Creek, some maps show the river at the entrance as Río Suárez.) Almost immediately upon entering the park, the visitor sees a 2km-long white-sand beach stretching along a gently curving bay to the east. About the first 500m of beach have signs warning about unsafe swimming, but beyond that, waves are gentle and swimming is safe. (It is unwise to leave clothing unattended when you swim; take a friend. Mister Big J Tourist Service, near the entrance, stores valuables in individual security boxes for US$1 per day.)

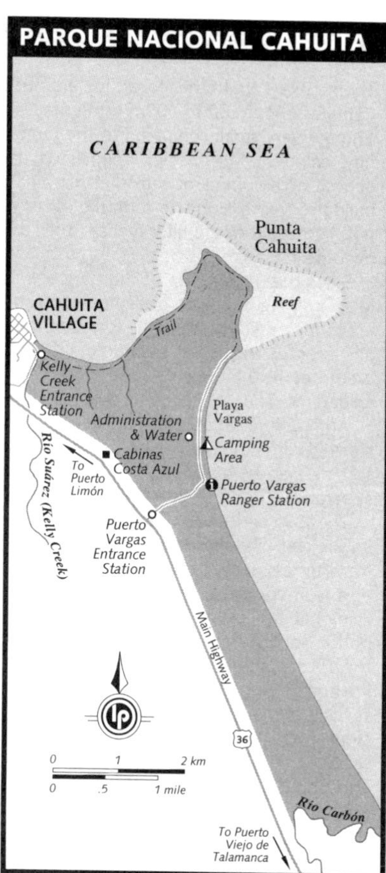

A rocky headland known as Punta Cahuita separates this beach from the next one, Playa Vargas. At the end of Playa Vargas is the Puerto Vargas ranger station, which is about 7km from Kelly Creek. The two stations are linked by a trail that goes through the coastal jungle behind the beaches and Punta Cahuita. The trail ends at the southern tip of the reef, where it meets up with a paved road leading to the ranger

Coral Reefs

The monkeys and other forest life are not the only wildlife attractions of Parque Nacional Cahuita. About 200 to 500m off Punta Cahuita is the largest living coral reef in Costa Rica (though very small compared to the huge Barrier Reef off Belize, for example). Corals are tiny, colonial, filter-feeding animals (cnidarians, or, more commonly, coelenterates) that deposit a calcium carbonate skeleton as a substrate for the living colony. These skeletons build up over millennia to form the corals we see. The outside layers of the corals are alive, but, because they are filter feeders, they rely on the circulation of clean water and nutrients over their surface.

Since the opening up of the Caribbean coastal regions in the last couple of decades, a lot of logging has taken place, and the consequent lack of trees on mountainous slopes has led to increased erosion. The loosened soil is washed into gullies, then streams and rivers, and eventually the sea. By the time the coral reef comes into the picture, the eroded soils are no more than minute mud particles – just the right size to clog up the filter-feeding cnidarians. The clogged animals die, and the living reef along with them.

After deforestation, the next step is often plantations of bananas or other fruit. These are sprayed with pesticides which, in turn, are washed out to sea and can cause damage to filter-feeding animals that need to pass relatively large quantities of water through their filtering apparatus in order to extract the nutrients they need.

The 1991 earthquake that was centered near the Caribbean coast also had a damaging effect on the reef. The shoreline was raised by over a meter, exposing and killing parts of the coral. Nevertheless, some of the reef has survived and remains the most important in Costa Rica.

It is important to note that the coral reef is not just a bunch of colorful rocks. It is a living habitat, just as a stream, lake, forest, or swamp is a living habitat. Coral reefs provide both a solid surface for animals such as sponges and anemones to grow on and a shelter for a vast community of fish and other organisms – octopi, crabs, algae, bryozoans, and a host of others. Some 35 species of coral have been identified in this reef, along with 140 species of molluscs (snails, chitons, shellfish, and octopi), 44 species of crustaceans (lobsters, crabs, shrimps, barnacles, and a variety of fleas, lice, and others), 128 species of seaweed, and 123 species of fish. Many of these seemingly insignificant species represent important links in various food chains. Thus logging has the potential to cause much greater and unforeseen damage than simply destroying the rainforest.

On a more mundane level, the drier months in the highlands (from February to April), when less runoff occurs in the rivers and less silting occurs in the sea, are considered the best months for snorkeling and seeing the reef. Conditions are often cloudy at other times.

Visitors can reach the reef by swimming from Punta Cahuita, but this is not recommended. Several readers have reported cutting their feet on the coral (which also damages the living reef) and getting into difficulties. It is best to hire a boat in Cahuita and snorkel from the boat.

– Rob Rachowiecki

station. At times, the trail follows the beach; at other times hikers are 100m or so away from the sand. A river must be waded through near the end of the first beach and the water can be thigh-deep at high tide. Various animals and birds are frequently seen, including coatis and raccoons, and ibises and kingfishers.

From the Puerto Vargas ranger station, a 1km road takes you out to the main coastal highway, where there is another park entrance station.

Information

The park entrance stations are open daily from 8 am to 4 pm, and while park entry fees are officially US$6, at the Kelly Creek entrance station only a voluntary donation is requested (see above for a bit of history on this). At the Puerto Vargas entrance you'll pay US$6. No one stops you from entering the park on foot before or after these opening hours at Kelly Creek. However, if you are driving to the Puerto Vargas area (where you can camp), you'll find a locked gate prevents entry to vehicles outside of opening hours.

There is not much shade on the beaches, so remember to use sunscreen and a sun hat to avoid painful sunburn. Don't forget your sensitive untanned feet after you take your shoes off on the beach. Also, carry plenty of drinking water and insect repellent.

Places to Stay

Camping is permitted at Playa Vargas, less than 1km from the Puerto Vargas ranger station. There are outdoor showers and pit latrines at the administration center near the middle of the camping area. There is drinking water, and some sites have picnic tables. The area is rarely crowded; in fact it is often mostly empty and many people opt to camp close to the administration center for greater security. This is safe enough if you don't leave your gear unattended (this is important). Easter week and weekends tend to be more crowded, but the campsite is rarely completely full. The daily camping fee is about US$2 per person. With a vehicle it's possible to drive as far as the campsite via the Puerto Vargas ranger station.

About 1km northwest of the Puerto Vargas entrance station is the recently built ***Cabinas Costa Azul*** (*☎ 755-0431*), which has basic, clean cabins with private baths for about US$10 per person.

Getting There & Away

It's very easy to enter the park by just walking in from central Cahuita village via the Kelly Creek entrance station. You could hike as described above and then bus back, or go as far as you want and return the way you came. Both are straightforward day trips for anyone in reasonably good shape. Alternatively, take a 6 am Puerto Viejo de Talamanca bus (catch it at the central bus stop in Cahuita village) and ask to be put down at the Puerto Vargas park entrance road. A 1km walk takes you to the coast, and then you can walk the further 7km back to

An Eerie Hike

I have a special memory of the trail behind the beaches of Parque Nacional Cahuita. I was hiking along it early one morning when I began to notice a distant moaning sound. It seemed as if the wind in the trees was becoming more forceful and I wondered whether a tropical storm was brewing. I decided to continue, and as I did, the noise became louder and eerier. This was definitely unlike any wind I had heard – it sounded more like a baby in pain.

I am not normally afraid of sounds, but the cries began sounding so eerie that I had to reason with myself that there was nothing to be apprehensive about. Finally, after much hesitant walking and frequent examinations of the forest through my binoculars, I found the culprit: a male howler monkey – the first I had ever seen. At the time, I knew only that the name of the monkey related to its vocalizations; I had no idea how weird and unsettling these cries could be. For more information on the howler monkeys, see the Wildlife Guide at the back of this book.

– Rob Rachowiecki

Cahuita. However, you will have to pay the full US$6 entrance fee.

PUERTO VIEJO DE TALAMANCA

This small village is known locally as Puerto Viejo – don't confuse it with Puerto Viejo de Sarapiquí. There is more influence here of the local Bribri indigenous culture than in Cahuita. Lately, there has also been much more development, though mainly of an individual, low-key variety. The cabinas, bars, and craft stalls strung along the shoreline nicely sum up the feel of the village. As a whole, Puerto Viejo is more exposed to the sea than Cahuita, which encourages shoreside strolling (and partying). Also, the Puerto Viejo area has the best surfing on this coast, if not the whole country. If you're looking for peace and quiet rather than a lively beach village, head south toward Manzanillo; there are many places to stay near stretches of empty shore.

Poor surfing conditions in September and October mean that these are the quietest months of the year (though snorkeling improves at this time).

Information

Tourist Offices The acronym ATEC stands for Asociación Talamanqueña de Ecoturismo y Conservación, an organization with headquarters in Puerto Viejo. The office (☎/fax 750-0191, 750-0398, atecmail@sol.racsa.co.cr, www.greencoast.com/atec.htm) is open 7 am to noon and 1 to 9 pm daily (with slight variations depending on staff scheduling). If you are interested in the local culture and environment, this is the place to come for information; the office also has a large flyer board posting general tourist information and the staff can field most questions. Internet access is available by the minute, with a 10-minute minimum, at US$6 per hour.

ATEC is a nonprofit grassroots organization that began in the 1980s. Its purpose is to promote environmentally sensitive local tourism in a way that supports and enhances local people and communities while providing a meaningful and enjoyable experience for the traveler wishing to learn something about the region.

ATEC can provide you with information ranging from the problems caused by banana plantations to how to arrange a visit to a nearby indigenous reserve. ATEC is not a tour agency, but will arrange visits to local areas with local guides and, as such, is recommended. Homestay opportunities with local people are currently rare, but possible. Trips can be slanted toward the visitor's interests and include emphases on natural history, birding, indigenous and Afro-Caribbean cultures, environmental issues, adventure treks, snorkeling, and fishing. (There are over 350 birds recorded in the area; one group reported 120 species sighted on a two-day trip.) ATEC trains local guides to provide you with as much information as possible and they do a good job – if all your questions aren't satisfactorily answered, follow up at the ATEC office. Most trips involve hiking – ask about necessary levels of endurance. Fairly easy to difficult hikes are available. For the very adventurous, information is available about a hiking route across the Continental Divide to Buenos Aires.

Although these trips aren't dirt cheap, they are a fair value. The idea is to charge the traveler less than the big tour companies, but to pay the guides more than they might make working for the big tour companies. This avoids the middle person, giving more profits to local guides while saving the traveler some money.

A percentage of fees goes toward supporting community activities and prices start at about US$15 per person for half-day trips, early morning birding hikes, and nightwalks. All-day trips cost about US$25 and a variety of overnight trips are available, priced depending on your food and lodging needs. Group sizes are limited to six for outdoor activities.

ATEC can arrange talks about a variety of local issues for around US$45 per group. Staff can arrange meals in local homes for various prices, depending on the meal required.

Money The acceptance of credit cards and payment in US dollars is spreading to more hotels and cabinas, but the nearest bank is in

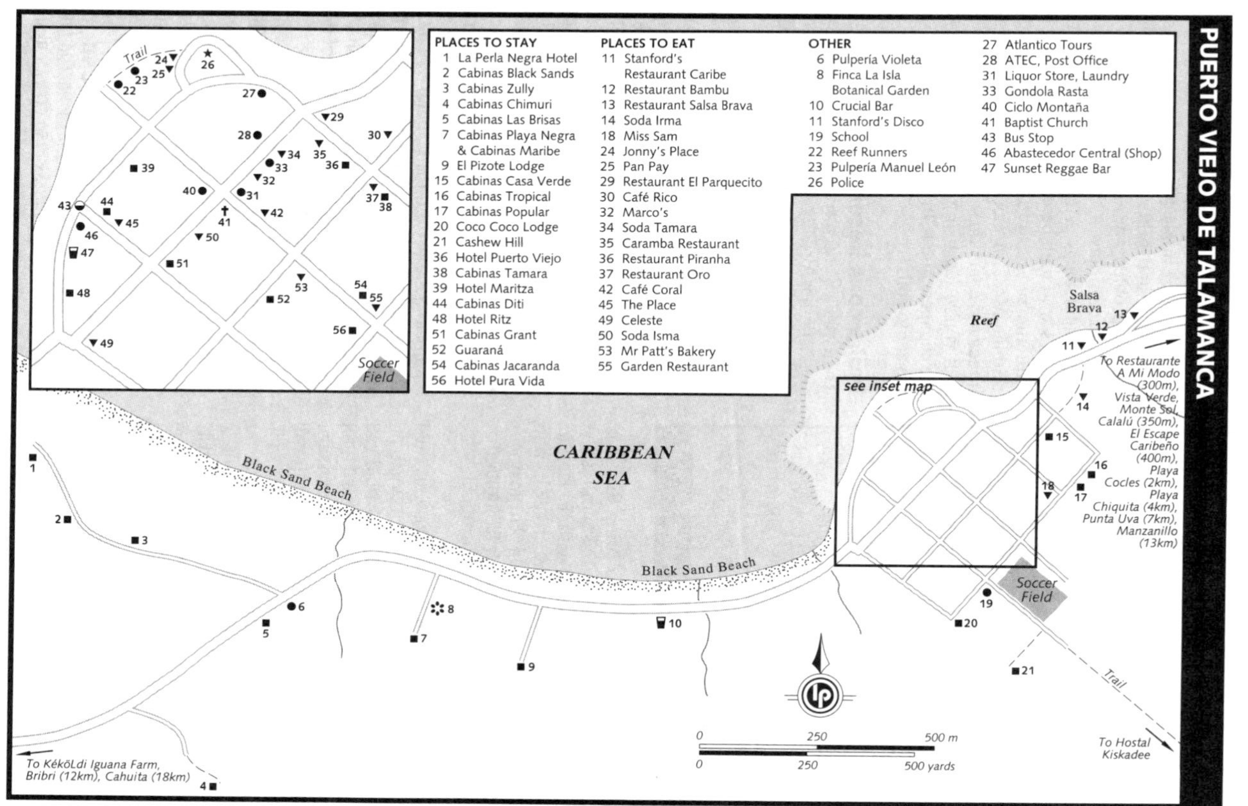

CARIBBEAN LOWLANDS

Books on Local Culture

Some of the older black and indigenous inhabitants of the area told their life stories to Paula Palmer, who collected this wealth of oral history, culture, and social anthropology in books that are sometimes available in San José or at ATEC in Puerto Viejo (see Books in the Facts for the Visitor chapter for specific titles).

The titles of these books include the phrases 'What happen' or 'Wa'apin man,' which are common forms of greeting among Costa Rican coastal blacks. Some foreign visitors may find this greeting somewhat mystifying; 'All right' is probably as good a response as any. The books are well worth reading. ATEC also has some interesting pamphlets about the area's history.

– Rob Rachowiecki

Bribri (see below); try to bring as many colones as you'll need. At this writing, the best place to change is still with 'El Chino,' the owner of Pulpería Manuel León, who now charges 1% commission. He may not change large amounts of cash US dollars or traveler's checks; then again, he might.

Telephone & Email Until 1996, you could literally count the phones in Puerto Viejo on the fingers of one hand. Visitors would call the local Pulpería Manuel León, the Hotel Maritza, or ATEC and leave a message asking for the hotel of their choice to call them back. This system worked quite well, considering the circumstances. Now over 200 lines have been installed, but the new phone book listings have been notoriously inaccurate. The numbers listed in this section are those given out directly by businesses; at time of writing, ATEC was compiling a list of verified numbers for the area.

The only public email and Internet access service at this time is at ATEC. Also inquire wherever you're staying.

Dangers & Annoyances See the corresponding section under Cahuita for general warnings that apply here as well, and ask hotel staff and other travelers about any current problems or areas to avoid. Use the usual precautions – don't flash valuables, avoid unlit areas at night, beware of drug dealers who may be crooked or in cahoots with the police, and don't wear skimpy clothing. Most travelers don't have problems if they use common sense.

If you're sensitive to bugs and staying in the cheapest hotels, bring insect repellent or mosquito coils.

Indigenous Reserves

There are several reserves in the Caribbean slopes of the Cordillera de Talamanca, including the Reserva Indígena Cocles/KéköLdi, which comes down to the coast just east of Puerto Viejo. Together with the nearby national parks and wildlife reserves they are part of the Amistad-Talamanca Regional Conservation Unit or 'megapark.' These reserves protect the land against commercial development in a variety of ways. Hunting is prohibited except among Indians hunting for food. Entrance to the reserves is limited to those visitors who receive the necessary permits from the Reserve Associations – these are difficult to obtain for the Talamanca reserves. ATEC is the most comprehensive source for those interested in going to the reserves. Mauricio Salazar from the Cabinas Chimuri (see Places to Stay, below) can guide you on day tours to the small KéköLdi reserve (twice a week, US$25 per person including lunch, two minimum, six maximum), and 10% of the tour cost goes directly to the reserve.

The Talamanca Cabecar reserve is the most remote and difficult to visit. The Cabecar indigenous group is the most traditional and the least tolerant of visits from outsiders. The Bribri people are more acculturated. Access to the reserves is generally on foot or on horseback.

Finca La Isla Botanical Garden

To the west of town is the Finca La Isla Botanical Garden (☎/fax 750-0046, email:

jarbot@sol.racsa.co.cr), a working tropical farm where the owners have been growing local spices, tropical fruits, and ornamental plants for over a decade. Part of the farm is set aside as a botanical garden, which is also good for birding and wildlife observation (look for sloths and poison-arrow frogs). There is a picnic area. The garden is open 10 am to 4 pm daily and admission costs about US$8, including an informative guided tour (in English).

KéköLdi Iguana Farm

Recently opened to tourists, this KéköLdi-run farm raises iguanas for release to the wild and for food; some indigenous crafts are also available for sale. The farm is out on the road to Cahuita and is accessible by bus; inquire about visiting at ATEC. Admission costs about US$1.

Samasati Retreat Center

Set on a lush hillside north of Puerto Viejo, the Samasati Retreat Center (☎ 224-1870, fax 224-5032, samasati@samasati.com) is a well-built, attractive complex with sweeping views of the coast – the village is just visible far below. Daily programs of different meditation techniques are offered in its large open-air meditation/group room. There is a calendar of special events and instruction in, among other things, yoga, bodywork, herbalism, and nutrition. Tasty vegetarian meals are served buffet-style on a wooden terrace with ocean views. Rates for ten private bungalows are US$79 double or US$46 double in a guesthouse with shared bathrooms, all with hot showers; continental breakfast is included. Full meals cost US$5 for breakfast, US$7 for lunch, and US$12 for dinner. A yoga class costs US$8, a meditation session US$2, a massage US$45, and an astrology session US$50. Packages and long-stay discounts are available and tours of the area can be arranged. There is a sign for the retreat center about 1km north of the fork on the main highway where the road splits southeast to Puerto Viejo and west to Bribri; you can drive to the entrance or have a bus drop you off on the highway. From the entrance, which is about 1km off the highway, a 4WD jeep will take you the rest of the way up the hill. If you just show up, someone may be around to take you up but it's best to arrange transport when you make reservations.

Water Sports

In the village, the owner of the Hotel Puerto Viejo is a local surfing expert and many surfers stay here (see Places to Stay, below). Dan Garcia is a respected local board maker who works out of his home; ask for him anywhere in town or at ATEC.

Surfers say that the best surfing is at the famous 'Salsa Brava,' outside the reef in front of Stanford's (see Places to Eat, below). The reef here is very shallow and sharp so if you lose it, you're liable to smash yourself and your board on the reef; this wave is for experienced surfers only. If this doesn't appeal to you, try Playa Cocles, about 2km east of town (an area commonly referred to as 'Beach Break' after the restaurant there), where you'll find good and less-damaging breaks as well as some cabinas popular with surfers. Pay attention to the posted warning signs about currents. Ask around for other places and up-to-date conditions.

The waves are generally best from December to March, and there is another miniseason for surfing in June and July. From late March to May, and in September and October, the sea is at its calmest.

Generally, underwater visibility is best when the sea is calm; ie, when surfing is bad, snorkeling is good. The best snorkeling reefs are at Cahuita, Punta Uva, and by Manzanillo, which has the greatest variety of coral and fauna. Researchers have recently realized something locals have known for years: that there is a small barrier reef off Manzanillo. For diving companies, see the next page.

The safest swimming around town is along Black Sand Beach, or in the natural sea-pools in front of Pulpería Manuel León and Stanford's. Be cautious of currents at all beaches, particularly if the waves are high.

Reef Runners (☎/fax 750-0480, 750-0099, reefrun@sol.racsa.co.cr) offers all levels of diving. Introductory courses start at US$50 for three hours, and half-tank boat dives start at US$40. Aquamor (see under Manzanillo, below), which has helped coordinate reef research as well as compile data on nearby dolphin communities, also offers diving trips and courses, sea kayaking, and snorkeling.

Other Activities & Organized Tours

Two cheery, somewhat raffish tour operators have recently set up shop in the village. Ed Oliver runs Atlantico Tours (☎ 750-0004, fax 750-0188), which offers tours up and down the coast. Day trips to Refugio Nacional de Vida Silvestre Gandoca-Manzanillo and Parque Nacional Cahuita cost US$35, including lunch and guide; a two-day/one-night trip to Tortuguero costs US$55, not including accommodations. Rafting and surfing trips are also available and you can rent snorkels, bikes, and surfboards for about US$8 per day. Captain Marlon and Magnificent Marco at Gondola Rasta (☎ 750-0273, 750-0186) rent snorkeling and fishing equipment and can also take you out by boat. Other options include onboard reggae music, beach tours, and dolphin watches, with tour rates starting at US$30 per person. Look around for other small rental places.

Places renting bicycles tend to come and go, but there are usually several in operation. Look for signs and shop around for bike quality and price – rust works fast on the coast. Good possibilities at time of writing were Ciclo Montaña and Cabinas Diti. For horse rental, ask at ATEC.

South Caribbean Music Festival

The South Caribbean Music Festival was first held in 1999, from the beginning of February to the end of March, with different performers appearing on every weekend evening and featuring music ranging from Caribbean and folk to classical and jazz. The festival brought foreign and local performers together in an intimate setting near the beach and was a great success. Organizer Wanda Paterson (who is originally from Cahuita and lived in Paris and New York before settling again on the Caribbean) consulted with one of the original organizers of the long-standing Monteverde Music Festival. In the future she plans to have the schedules of the two overlap, making it possible to attend both the mountain and the coastal festivals within the same week or month. Proceeds go to music programs for children on the southern Caribbean coast; tickets cost US$4 and transport from Puerto Viejo to the festival site is made available for a small fee. The first festival was held at the Playa Chiquita Lodge; see East of Puerto Viejo de Talamanca, below. For more information contact Taller de Musica (☎/fax 750-0062, wolfbiss@sol.racsa.co.cr).

Places to Stay

Puerto Viejo has developed much more rapidly than Cahuita in recent years, and there are many new places in town, as well as along the road to Manzanillo (described later in this chapter). Keep your eye out for new places and competition-induced bargains. Places may fill up during weekends in the surfing season, and, of course, during the Christmas and Easter holidays. Most of the rates below are for a one-night stay during the high season. Bargain for long-term and low-season discounts.

Ask around about camping on hotel grounds, which is sometimes a possibility.

Budget Cold water is the norm in budget places, but the tropical weather makes this a minor inconvenience, perhaps even a blessing. Water pressure can be an occasional problem in the cheaper places. The majority of hotels will provide either mosquito netting or fans (a breeze fanning the bed will help keep mosquitoes away). Check the facilities before getting a room. Solo travelers are often charged as much or almost as much as two, so find a partner to economize.

Note that apart from the places listed below, local people may hang out a 'Rooms for Rent' sign and provide inexpensive accommodations. ATEC staff often know which local families are offering rooms.

Two recommended budget places are the friendly and tranquil ***Hostal Kiskadee***

(☎ *750-0075)*, which is a six- or seven-minute walk southeast of the soccer field and, closer to the soccer field, ***Cashew Hill*** *(☎ 750-0256)*. Both are on secluded hills that offer good birding and monkey sightings. The path to the former is steep and is slippery after rain, so you should carry a flashlight if arriving after dark; simple dormitory-style accommodations are provided for US$5 per person. At Cashew Hill, two simple cabins, each with a double and single bed, cost US$10/15 single/double including kitchen privileges and a warm shared shower. A larger room with private bath costs US$15/20. The owners, Mike and Amy, settled here in the early 1990s and are warm, knowledgeable hosts. You can check the surf down at Salsa Brava from their hilltop hammock area.

The ***Hotel Puerto Viejo*** has over 30 double rooms and is the biggest place in town. It is popular with surfers and budget travelers. The bare, basic but reasonably clean upstairs rooms cost US$5 per person; a few downstairs rooms are not as good. Doubles with private cold showers cost about US$16.

An OK cheapie is the ***Hotel Ritz***, which charges US$10 for a single cubicle with shared baths or US$15/18 for a single/double room with private cold baths; it's reasonably clean. ***Cabinas Jacaranda*** *(☎ 750-0069)* has pleasant rooms with shared cold showers and provides fans and mosquito nets – not bad for US$13/16 single/double (a good value at the double rate). It also has a few doubles with private hot baths for US$22. There's a restaurant on-site.

Cabinas Diti *(☎ 750-0311)* is OK and has rooms with private baths for US$9/13 single/double; a bike rental/souvenir-clothing store is attached. The attractive and clean ***Hotel Pura Vida*** *(☎/fax 750-0002)* charges US$13/17 in decent rooms with fans and sinks – shared hot showers are down the hall. Two rooms with private baths cost US$10 more. ***Cabinas Grant*** *(☎ 758-2845)* has decent rooms with private cold baths and fans for US$15/20 and offers a locked parking area. The owners are helpful with local advice and operate a restaurant. The pleasant, Italian-owned ***Guaraná*** *(☎ 750-0244)* has hot water, fans, some balconies, and kitchen use for US$25 single or double. ***Cabinas Tamara*** *(☎ 750-0157)* offers good doubles with private baths and fans for US$16. ***Cabinas Popular*** *(☎ 750-0087)* has doubles with private cold showers for about US$20.

Cabinas Las Brisas (over 1km west of town) is locally known as 'Mister O'Conner's,' after the owner. He has four basic but decent rooms for about US$12 double and a couple of larger ones for US$24. Nearby is ***Cabinas Zully***, run by the friendly Miss Julie. She charges US$8/10 for one simple room with cold water, but it also has a stove. Farther west is the friendly ***Cabinas Black Sands*** *(☎ 750-0124, bsands@sol.racsa.co.cr)*, an attractive thatched cabin in the local Bribri style set in a pleasant garden near the black-sand beach. There are three simple rooms, each with two beds and mosquito nets, and communal kitchen and bathroom facilities. This is a nice place to stay for peace and quiet near the beach, though restaurants are not very close. The rate is US$10 per person and you get a US$10 discount if you book all three rooms (six beds total).

The ***Cabinas Playa Negra*** *(☎ 750-0063)*, on a quiet road just west of town, manages several houses for people looking for cheap group lodgings. The houses have two or three rooms, kitchens, bathrooms (cold water), and TVs, and rent for US$33 for up to six people. The cabinas, with doubles costing US$14, are basic and have bathing-suit-beauty beer posters on the walls. Nearby is ***Cabinas Maribe*** *(☎ 750-0182)*, offering decent rooms with cold baths and fans for about US$15 double.

Just east of the village are three newer good budget choices, clustered at the end of a short side road that begins 250m east of Stanford's. ***Vista Verde***, run by a kindly German named Michael, has five rooms of varying sizes at US$10 per person, including shared baths (an outdoor shower is also an option) and access to a communal kitchen – a nice place to meet people. ***Monte Sol*** *(☎/fax 750-0182)* has simple, attractive rooms for US$20 double, some with imaginatively tiled bathrooms. The youthful German owners are building a bar and restaurant, and one of them, Birgit, also runs a hair salon here. The French-owned ***Calalú*** *(☎ 750-0042)* has well-built bungalows with hammock porches for US$20 double, or US$25 for a bungalow with a private kitchen; there's US$5 charge per each additional person. There is a communal Ping-Pong table on-site.

Mid-Range The ***Hotel Maritza*** *(☎ 750-0003, fax 750-0313)* charges US$22 double in nice cabins with fans, private baths, and electric showers. There are also a few basic rooms with shared cold bath over the attached restaurant. These cost US$13 double. This helpful hotel accepts credit cards and has a parking area.

The friendly, multilingual ***Cabinas Casa Verde*** *(☎ 750-0015, fax 750-0047, atecmail@sol.racsa.co.cr)* is centrally located and has four pleasant rooms with warm water in the communal bathroom and a poisonous-frog garden. Rates are US$15/20 for clean singles/doubles; six more rooms have private bathrooms for US$25/30. The prices may be lowered midweek. The ***Cabinas Tropical***, at the southeast end of town, has nice clean rooms with private cold showers for US$25/30. The new ***Coco Loco Lodge*** *(☎/fax 750-0281, atecmail@sol.racsa.co.cr)*, on the quiet edge of town, has bungalows with private baths and hot water for US$25/30 single/double set in spacious, pleasant grounds.

In the hills west of town is ***Cabinas Chimuri*** *(☎ 750-0119)*, owned by Mauricio Salazar (and his European wife, Colocha), who knows as much about the Bribri culture as anyone in Puerto Viejo. There are a few small, simple, attractively thatched A-frame cabins in the Bribri style on stilts renting for US$17/25 single/double and one quadruple cabin for US$35. Students get big discounts. There is a communal kitchen and simple cold bathroom facilities. The cabins are set in a 20-hectare private preserve with trails and good birding possibilities. (The cabinas are a 10-minute hike uphill from the end of the road.) This is the place to go for trips to the local indigenous reserves (see the Indigenous Reserves section, above, for details and rates) and to learn more about the Talamanca region. You are paying for the wild location and the owners' knowledge rather than for the comfort of the rooms.

About half a kilometer east of town is ***El Escape Caribeño*** *(☎/fax 750-0103, escapec@sol.racsa.co.cr)*, which has pleasant bungalows with fans, private hot baths, refrigerators, and porches for US$40 double, or US$50 for larger cabins closer to the ocean; there's a US$10 charge for each additional person. Kitchen privileges are available.

At the far west end of the beachfront road is ***La Perla Negra Hotel*** *(☎ 750-0111, fax 750-0114)*, which has pleasant rooms with hot private baths for US$45 double, though they'll rent for US$25 in the low season. There is a restaurant and a pool on-site.

About 1km west of town on a quiet backroad is the relatively comfortable ***El Pizote Lodge*** *(☎ 750-0088, fax 750-0226; in San José ☎ 221-0986, fax 255-1527, pizotelg@sol.racsa.co.cr)*. The rooms are large and clean but don't have private baths. That is not a real problem, however, as there are four shared bathrooms for eight rooms. There are also pleasant wooden bungalows with private baths that are more expensive. The lodge is set in a garden, and there are bicycles, horses, and snorkeling gear for rent to clients; boat and snorkeling tours are also available. Good meals are served in the rather pricey restaurant. Rooms with shared bathrooms cost US$34/50 single/double and bungalows with private baths cost US$75 double. Ask about big discounts in the low season. The owner also has some larger houses for rent.

La Danta Selvaje is a rustic lodge near a waterfall in a private rainforest reserve on the Caribbean slope, reached from Puerto Viejo by a 4WD road followed by a three-hour hike. The owners, David and Dalia Vaughan, live in Puerto Viejo and can be contacted through ATEC or via email *(ladanta@sol.racsa.co.cr, ladanta@yahoo.com)*. They arrange guided four-day visits to their lodge; costs are around US$200 per person.

Places to Eat

Several small locally owned places serve meals and snacks typical of the region – ask at

ATEC for recommendations if you'd like to eat with a family or at a small local place. Some of these include the reasonably priced ***Miss Sam***, ***Soda Isma***, and ***Soda Irma***, all run by women who are long-term residents of the area and will cook a good local meal for about US$3 or US$4. Doña Juanita cooks out of her house, which is shortly before the Cabinas Las Brisas as you enter Puerto Viejo. Doña Guillerma does the same a couple hundred meters away – ask locally for directions.

The ***Café Coral*** serves breakfast daily (except Monday) from 7 am to noon. It serves a variety of healthful items such as yogurt and granola, homemade whole wheat bread, and, of course, the tico specialty – *gallo pinto*. Eggs and pancakes are also served. Down the street is ***Mr Patt's Bakery*** for a variety of yummy cakes and pastries. Also popular for breakfasts and meals throughout the day is the friendly ***Soda Tamara*** (☎ *750-0148*) – it has coconut bread, cakes, and casados. ***Pan Pay*** has strong coffee, croissants, and fresh pastries.

Restaurant El Parquecito is decent and offers meals for around US$4. The ***Restaurant Piranha***, in the Hotel Puerto Viejo, serves Mexican-style snacks and meals at reasonable prices, and the ***Caramba Restaurant*** serves Italian food. More expensive but better Italian food and wine are served at the ***Restaurante A Mi Modo***, which features relaxing jazz as background music.

The Place is a recent recommended addition, with meals ranging from healthy breakfasts and veggie burger lunches to kebab dinners, all reasonably priced; look for the chalkboard specials. ***Stanford's Restaurant Caribe*** is good for seafood, which ranges from US$3 to US$20 depending on how exotic a meal you order (most cost US$5 to US$8). There's a lively disco here on weekends. ***Café Rico*** has cheap but good breakfasts. The ***Restaurant Bambu*** serves fruit shakes and sandwiches within sight of the wave action at Salsa Brava and becomes a popular bar in the evenings. ***Restaurant Salsa Brava*** has candlelit seafood and steak dinners for US$6 to US$12. The variously spelled ***Jonny's Place*** has satisfying and cheap Chinese-style meals (although the restaurant may be closing) and dancing on weekends. ***Restaurant Oro*** has good local food and, with its little open-air terrace, is closer to a small restaurant than just a soda.

A popular recent addition is ***Marco's***, which serves good pizza and a variety of dinner entrées. ***Celeste*** serves French cuisine.

One of the best places in town is the warmly recommended ***Garden Restaurant***, whose Trinidadian chef, Vera, is a local legend. Caribbean, Asian, and vegetarian food is served. Try the Jamaican jerk chicken, chicken curry, or well-prepared red snapper. Desserts are also good. Vegetarian main courses begin at about US$5.50; others start at US$6.50 and go up from there – red snapper is US$8, for example. Service and preparation are a step or three above what you might expect in such a small, out-of-the-way town. The restaurant is closed on Wednesday.

Entertainment

The ***Sunset Reggae Bar*** is a good and locally popular establishment that plays both Caribbean and rock music and has live entertainment on occasion; Wednesday nights there is an open jam session. ***Jonny's Place*** is the most happening dance club on weekends – some nights the sand and rocks around the shoreside tables are liberally decorated with lit candles, a lovely complement (or contrast) to the flashing lights in the disco. There's also weekend dancing at the quieter ***Stanford's Disco***; its shoreside attraction is the occasional bonfire and circle of chairs. The ***Restaurant Bambu*** has a popular bar and has good reggae nights (with DJ) on Monday and Friday. Out along Black Sand Beach is the new, currently hip ***Crucial Bar***.

Getting There & Away

From San José, express buses leave at 6 and 10 am and 1:30 and 3:30 pm and cost about US$5 for a five-hour trip (the first morning bus may leave you at a crossroads 5km out of town; ask). Alternatively, go from Puerto Limón, where buses leave from a block north of the market six times a day – again, check that they will go all the way into Puerto Viejo.

Buses from Puerto Viejo leave from the bus stop shown on the map. Buses usually start from somewhere else and are liable to be late going through Puerto Viejo. The following is a recent schedule of departures from Puerto Viejo. Check with ATEC (see Information, above) for the latest schedule.

San José – US$5; 7, 9, 11 am, 4 pm
Bribri/Sixaola – US50¢/US$2.50; 6:20, 9:30 am, 5:30, 7:30 pm
Bribri only – US50¢; 11:30 am
Cahuita/Limón – US50¢/US$1.20; 5:45, 6 am, 1, 4, 5 pm
Manzanillo – US$1.20; 7:15 am, 4, 7:30 pm

EAST OF PUERTO VIEJO DE TALAMANCA

A 13km dirt road heads east from Puerto Viejo along the coast, past sandy, driftwood-strewn beaches and rocky points, through the small communities of Punta Uva and Manzanillo, through sections of the Reserva Indígena Cocles/KéköLdi, and ending up in the Refugio Nacional de Vida Silvestre Gandoca-Manzanillo.

The locals use horses and bicycles along this narrow and sandy road, though vehicles get through easily. Drive slowly and carefully; not only are there horses, bicycles, and small children to watch out for, but there are slick little one-lane bridges offering the unwary driver an intimate visit to the creek below.

This road more or less follows the shoreline, and a variety of places to stay and eat can be found along the road. Most have opened in the last decade; this area is experiencing a minor boom in tourism, and aside from what is listed here there are (and will be) other places along the way – among them there are certain to be some hidden treasures.

A number of people are buying land in this area, among them members of wealthy, influential Costa Rican families; not all of them are developing their property responsibly. The local people realize that the tourist industry is a double-edged sword and are trying to control its development to ensure that *talamanqueños* benefit fairly, and also that the environment is not irreparably damaged. They are hampered by a bureaucratic jungle within which such apparently straightforward things as the borders of the KéköLdi reserve and the Gandoca-Manzanillo refuge are poorly defined. Some of these problems are addressed briefly below; interested Spanish-speaking visitors should read *La Loca de Gandoca* (see Books in the Facts for the Visitor chapter for a brief review).

Places to Stay & Eat

Playa Cocles Beginning 2km to the east of town, Playa Cocles has very good surfing and is benefiting from the organization of a lifeguard system (a praiseworthy effort). The first place you come to after leaving Puerto Viejo is ***El Tesoro*** *(☎ 750-0128, 284-7493)*, a nice little place with several cabinas ranging from US$7 to US$10 per person; cabinas have private hot showers. The owners are energetic promoters of the area and offer free morning coffee, free email and phone service, and a communal kitchen; discounts and free taxis to town are available for longer stays. Next is ***La Isla Inn***, which has a few spacious and clean doubles with hot water, fans, and sea views for about US$40; it was up for sale at time of writing. Slightly farther along is the ***Beach Break Restaurant***; opposite is one of the more popular surfing beaches. Many surfers stay at the nearby ***Cabinas & Soda Garibaldi***, which charges US$12 for fairly basic double rooms with private baths and sea views, and at the ***Surf Point***, which is also popular with surfers and has nicer rooms for about US$25.

Just before the Garibaldi is ***Cariblue*** *(☎ 750-0057, cariblue@sol.racsa.co.cr)*, built by a friendly young Italian surfer couple; this is one of the nicest recent additions to the area. Spacious hardwood bungalows with bathrooms (each with a different tile mosaic) set in lovely grounds cost US$45 to US$65 double, breakfast included. A little farther down the road is another attractive bungalow-style place on nice grounds, ***La Costa de Papito*** *(☎/fax 750-0080, atecmail@sol.racsa.co.cr)*, offering a mellow philosophy on life and doubles for US$50. The ***Río Cocles Cabinas*** *(☎/fax 750-0142)*, the next down the road, has nice doubles with private baths and hot showers for US$30. This is a growing area and there are several other places available, as well as houses where rooms are rented.

Between Playa Cocles and Playa Chiquita is the bright and fanciful ***Yaré Hotel & Restaurant*** *(☎ 750-0086; in San José 284-5921, fax 231-7280)*, with clean and pleasant rooms for about US$40 to US$60 double; family cabins sleeping four people cost about US$90 to US$100. All rooms and cabins have private hot showers and fans, and covered walkways lead to a decent restaurant. The owner is both helpful and friendly. Travelers write that the surrounding jungle has great frog noises at night.

It isn't exactly clear where Playa Cocles ends and Playa Chiquita begins; the names are used fairly loosely.

Playa Chiquita There are several places to stay along Playa Chiquita, a series of beaches about 4 to 7km east of Puerto Viejo. New places are opening up along this stretch of waterfront.

The most luxurious place on this beach is ***Villas del Caribe*** *(☎ 750-0202; in San José 233-2200, fax 221-2801, info@villascaribe.net)*, which has nice beachfront apartments with sea views, hot showers, and fans, and can sleep up to five people. Rooms rent for about US$80 double. They give discounts to drop-in guests if they are not full. In 1992, it emerged that part of the hotel had been built illegally within the limits of the KéköLdi indigenous reserve and the Gandoca-Manzanillo wildlife refuge. Part of the problem was that surveying errors had been made and boundaries of the reserve and refuge were unclear. The managers are working to make this hotel as low-impact as possible, and the controversy has died down. It should be noted that several of the other smaller places mentioned here have also been in violation of reserve or refuge boundaries, but their impact has been minimal. ***Hotel La Caracola*** *(☎ 750-0248, fax 750-0135)* has simple, cheerfully painted rooms near the beach, US$50 double, US$10 more for doubles with a kitchen. ***Aguas Claras*** has several pretty houses for rent near here; get their number through ATEC (see Information, above).

About 5km from Puerto Viejo is the entrance, on the right, to the ***Hotel Punta Cocles*** *(☎ 750-0117, 750-0338; in San José fax 234-8033, gandoca@sol.racsa.co.cr)*, a modern hotel development that is gaining popularity with tico families. The Punta Cocles has several dozen comfortable rooms, some with air-conditioning, some with kitchenettes, and all with private hot showers and private patios. There is a swimming pool, spa, playground for kids, restaurant, bar, and local trails into the forest, though the grounds around the buildings themselves are bare. Guides and rental items (snorkels, surfboards, binoculars, horses, and bicycles) are available. Rooms cost US$60 double; larger bungalows that sleep four and have kitchenettes cost about US$90.

Also in the area is the clean little ***Ranchita Blanca***, with a few rooms with private baths for US$30 double and bicycles for rent. ***Kashá*** *(☎ 750-0205, fax 283-7896)* charges US$32 double for pleasant bungalows with private hot showers and satellite TVs; there is a restaurant and bar on the premises.

A bit farther east is the ***Miraflores Lodge*** *(☎ 750-0038, mirapam@sol.racsa.co.cr)*. This small B&B-style lodge has a private trail leading 500m to the beach and offers about eight rooms in an attractive private home, as well as a variety of more basic budget options tucked away on the beautiful grounds. These range in price from US$40 for a double with a balcony shower shared between two rooms (US$5 more for private shower) to US$10 per person for lodging in a bunk room. Owner Pamela Carter has been living in the area since 1988 and has gradually financed the construction of the lodge by growing and selling exotic flowers. She is very knowledgeable about local botany and wildlife, has long-term relationships with members of some of the indigenous tribes, and can organize trips to visit Bribri farming families or practicing medicine men. A number of interesting healing and local culture workshops are available. Breakfast includes fruits grown on the grounds (in season); local people often stop by the restaurant for a morning snack and chat. The place is small and popular, so reservations are recommended.

There are half a dozen small restaurants within a few hundred meters, as well as a few small cabinas and houses advertising rooms for rent. ***Elena Brown's Soda & Restaurant*** is no longer run by Elena (she rents it out) but is still a locally popular place to eat and drink; a TV has been added. The ***Soda Acuarius*** offers homemade bread and has a couple of basic rooms for rent.

On lush grounds almost 6km from Puerto Viejo is the attractively thatched ***Playa Chiquita Lodge*** *(☎ 750-0408, ☎/fax 750-0062, wolfbiss@sol.racsa.co.cr)*, which is 200m from the beach – you can't see the ocean from the lodge because the owner, Wolf Bissinger, wanted to leave the intervening forest standing. Instead, a short but scenic jungle hike leads to the beach. His partner, Wanda Paterson, is actively involved in local community issues and is the organizer of the South Caribbean Music Festival (see under Puerto Viejo de Talamanca, earlier in this chapter), which was first held at the lodge. Rooms with overhead fans and private baths are simple but spacious and nicely designed. There is a good restaurant on the premises, open to the public. Full breakfasts cost US$6, lunches and dinners cost about US$8 to US$12. Local guided tours by boat or van can be arranged; massage is available for US$20 per hour and a steam room is planned. High-season room rates are US$30/40/50/60 for one to four people; discounts are available for groups, students, and low-season visitors. A fully equipped four-room house is available nearby for US$60 per night or US$275 per week.

Across the road, the upscale ***Shawanda Lodge*** *(☎ 750-0018, fax 750-0037)* has a variety of large, airy bungalows – all with the fabulous bathroom mosaics that seem to be a minor cultural movement on this stretch of coast – for about US$80 double including breakfast. The restaurant is a bit pricey but elegant. The ***Rinconcito Peruano*** is a locally recommended Peruvian restaurant.

Punta Uva About 7km east of Puerto Viejo is the Punta Uva area, which offers several places to stay and eat. The protected curve on the western side of this lovely point offers tranquil swimming. A sign advertises *'Caminata Guiada al Bosque'* ('Guided Forest Hikes') and there is a trail leading up into the forest along the Quebrada Ernesto (*quebrada* means 'gorge' or 'stream'). Ask at the house near the sign for guides and horses.

Near the beach is the long-standing ***Selvin's Cabins***, with several basic rooms with shared bath for about US$16 double; there's another room with private bath sleeping four people for US$30. Selvin is a member of the extensive Brown family, noted for their charm and unusual eyes (Selvin is from the one blue/one brown branch), which have attracted them both romantic and scientific attention. There is a locally popular restaurant-bar on-site, which is closed on Monday and Tuesday. A small dirt lane leads past Selvin's to the beach, where you'll find the awkwardly named ***Come A Lot*** *(☎ 750-0431, 255-4087, jstewart@costarica.net)*, with two secluded beachfront cabinas for US$25 for a double with a shared kitchen. Back on the main road, 200m farther along is the reasonably cheap and popular ***Walaba Cabinas***, offering both basic rooms and dormitories starting at about US$10 per person. The staff arrange house rentals, as do the people at the nearby ***La Casa del Sol*** *(☎ 272-0004)*. Look for other house rentals in this area as well. Down near the point is ***Ranchito***, a beachfront restaurant, which so far has been restrained enough in its development to not spoil the beauty of this spot. Kayaks and snorkeling equipment can be rented.

Just beyond Punta Uva, about 9km east of Puerto Viejo, is ***Las Palmas Beach Resort*** *(☎ 750-0049, fax 750-0079, hpalmas@sol.racsa.co.cr)*. This 80-room resort offers rooms with ocean views, private hot showers, and air-conditioning for about US$70 double. There is a pool, a somewhat dilapidated tennis court, and a bar and restaurant; tours are available.

Unfortunately, this resort was built within the boundaries of the Gandoca-Manzanillo wildlife refuge and has violated a number of environmental laws. This caused the Ministry of Natural Resources to order that the hotel be torn down, a decision that was revoked by the Supreme Court. Meanwhile, owner Jan Kalina, born in Czechoslovakia but a Canadian resident, was ordered deported because he was in Costa Rica on an expired tourist visa.

In the drawn-out legal battle, local conservation organizations reported the many infringements early on, but government bureaucracy, ineptitude, and confusion led to a chaotic situation not only with this development, but with the tourism boom on the entire coast. Kalina won the suit against him on the grounds that he had, in fact, received government permission for his activities here, thus releasing him from responsibility for any infractions committed. He has since sold a chunk of this property, on which the ***Hotel Suerre*** *(☎ 750-0181, fax 750-0196)* now stands. The 1999 brochure promoting this hotel states that it is 'surrounded by coarse and impressive places,' and it offers facilities similar to those at Las Palmas for US$60 double. Readers have written to complain about poor service at both hotels – a bad situation all around.

The next few kilometers of coastal road are within the wildlife refuge and have few tourist developments, although the village of Manzanillo offers some facilities within the refuge.

Getting There & Away

For information on accessing the beach areas east of Puerto Viejo de Talamanca, see the Manzanillo entry, below.

MANZANILLO

The school of Manzanillo, which marks the beginning of the village, is 12.5km from Puerto Viejo de Talamanca (Manzanillo village already existed when the Gandoca-Manzanillo wildlife refuge was established in 1985). The road continues for about one more kilometer and then peters out. From the end of the road, footpaths continue around the coast through the Gandoca-Manzanillo refuge. Costa Rica's Ministry of Natural Resources has an office here (in a lime green wooden building a few hundred meters past the school), where information on the refuge is sometimes available.

Water Sports

Aquamor Talamanca Adventures in Manzanillo (☎ 391-3417 cellular, 225-4049 beeper, aquamor@sol.racsa.co.cr) offers scuba diving at prices ranging from US$30 for a one-tank beach dive to US$55 for a two-tank boat dive; rates include equipment and guide. PADI open-water certification courses cost US$300. Kayak rentals for sea and river trips cost US$5 per hour, snorkeling gear is US$12 per day, and various discounts are offered for all-day or overnight kayaking, diving, camping, and snorkeling adventures. The guides speak Spanish and English and are concerned about the environment, particularly the fragile coral reefs. Dolphin-watching tours by boat or kayak are available for US$25 to US$55; note that the owners of Aquamor helped found the Talamanca Dolphin Foundation (see the boxed text).

Places to Stay & Eat

Near the bus stop in Manzanillo, you'll find the basic, seaside ***Maxi's Cabinas***, where rooms cost about US$15. There is a restaurant and a bar here, and even a disco on the weekends. Eating seafood here is a local tradition; craft stalls and picnickers gather on the beach outside of Maxi's. On the way into the village, by the *pulpería*, is ***Cabinas Las Veraneras*** *(☎ 754-2298)*, with clean rooms for about US$15 per person.

The Italian-owned ***Pangea B&B*** has two pleasant rooms for about US$20 per person; leave messages with Aquamor (see Water Sports, above).

Almonds and Corals Lodge Tent Camp *(in San José ☎ 272-2024, 272-4175, fax 272-2220, almonds@sol.racsa.co.cr)* is on the outskirts of Manzanillo. The spacious, comfortable tents are on raised wooden platforms and contain single beds, mosquito nets, fans, lights, tables, and hammocks. A central lodge provides family-style dining, and there are hot showers, toilet facilities, and a swimming pool. Guided hikes, snorkeling, bicycle rental, birding, and horseback riding are offered. The surrounding area is undeveloped and full of wildlife – insects and frogs call all night and howler monkeys wake you at dawn. Rates are about US$65/80 single/double and meals cost about US$7 each.

Several local women will prepare traditional Caribbean meals in their homes for travelers – ask around for details. For breakfast (and other meals), there is a little ***soda*** just inland past the Aquamor office. At the entrance to the village, ***Bar Restaurant La Selva*** is slightly more upscale in ambience.

Getting There & Away

Buses leave Limón for Manzanillo at 6 am and 2:30 and 6 pm, passing through Cahuita and Puerto Viejo and arriving in Manzanillo about 2½ hours later. Return buses leave Manzanillo at 5 and 8:30 am and 5 pm.

For any of the destinations described above between Puerto Viejo and Manzanillo, simply ask the bus driver to let you off.

EARTH CONNECT

Earth Connect is a camp that is being developed upon Punta Mona by Costa Rican Adventures (☎ 391-2116 cellular, leave a message; in the USA ☎ 800-551-7887, info@costaricanadventures.com), a small travel company that brings high school and college students to Costa Rica for a week of fun and environmental education. In 1997, Costa Rican Adventures bought 30 acres of

Talamanca Dolphin Foundation

The new millennium stretches ahead, the blunt truths of evolution and two world wars are behind us, and everybody wants to know why the dolphins look so happy. These days, getting a glimpse of these graceful, social, and apparently communicative sea mammals is high on the list of many travelers. Tours have been springing up rapidly to meet this desire, with the predictable result that dolphins find themselves getting chased down by tour operators with high-powered motors and boatloads of expectant customers. A central aim of the Talamanca Dolphin Foundation is to promote respectful interactions with wild dolphins, who, when not harassed, often seem just as interested in us as we are in them. The foundation, which has formed a countrywide alliance with other dolphin tour operators, has published sensible guidelines for approaching dolphins – a step reminiscent of the early days of ecotourism in the rainforests. A related aim has been to include local communities in the profits earned from tours; local fishermen often have intimate knowledge of the habits of dolphins in the area and make good captains for tours. The foundation also combines the tours with scientific research, using them as opportunities to collect observational data. It has also been instrumental in banning the capture of dolphins in Costa Rica.

A good local contact point for the foundation is Aquamor (see Water Sports under Manzanillo), whose owners are founding members. Steve Larkin of Aquamor is a fount of information on dolphins and other marine life and can steer those who want more than a day trip toward ongoing research projects – student internships and volunteer positions for data collection can be arranged. The Talamanca Dolphin Foundation can be contacted through the Internet or through the Adventures travel company (☎ 750-0093; in the USA ☎ 800-231-7422, info@dolphinlink.org, www.dolphinlink.org). Other dolphin tours operating on the foundation's principles are Planet Dolphin in Quepos and Dolphin Quest in Golfo Dulce.

– John Thompson

land on Punta Mona (which is a few kilometers south of Manzanillo, accessible by boat or on foot) and started an organic farm. Currently, as part of their week-long trip, students spend two days at the farm learning about sustainable agriculture – the camp will eventually offer longer programs. Cabins are planned for independent travelers interested in visiting the property, and camping can be arranged with advance notice. Volunteer positions are also available for those who would like to work on the farm or with visiting students.

The camp organizers are dedicated to integrating the local community into their efforts; one of their aims is to revive indigenous and other traditional methods of sustainable farming and teach them to young ticos in the area. The original owner of the camp property, who was born on Punta Mona in the 1930s, still lives and works there; farmers from nearby reserves and organic farms also provide advice and help. The camp and travel education company are run by the energetic and idealistic Stephen and Lisa Brooks, a brother and sister team from the USA; it will be interesting to see how the project develops. For further information, contact Costa Rican Adventures directly.

REFUGIO NACIONAL DE VIDA SILVESTRE GANDOCA-MANZANILLO

This refuge lies on the coast around Manzanillo and extends southeast as far as the Panamanian border. It encompasses 5013 hectares of land plus 4436 hectares of sea. This is the only place in the country apart from Cahuita where there is a living coral reef. It lies about 200m offshore and snorkeling is one of the refuge's attractions.

The land section has several different habitats, not least of which is farmland. The little village of Manzanillo is actually within the boundaries of the refuge, which also contains an area of rainforest and some of the most beautiful beaches on the Caribbean, unspoiled and separated by rocky headlands. Coconut palms form an attractive tropical backdrop. There is a coastal trail leading 5.5km from Manzanillo to Punta Mona. South of this trail is an unusual 400-hectare swamp containing holillo palms and sajo trees. One map shows a trail that leaves from just west of Manzanillo and skirts the southern edges of this swamp and continues to the small community of Gandoca, roughly 8 to 10km away. Experienced hikers could follow the Punta Mona trail, but a guide may be necessary for the trail to Gandoca; ask locally.

Beyond Punta Mona is the only red mangrove swamp in Caribbean Costa Rica, protecting a natural oyster bank. In the nearby Río Gandoca estuary there is a spawning ground for Atlantic tarpon, and caimans and manatees have been sighted. The endangered Baird's tapir is also found in this wet and densely vegetated terrain.

Marine turtles have nested upon the beaches at the southeast end of the refuge, especially leatherbacks, which nest from March to July with a peak in April and May. Local conservation efforts are underway to protect these nesting grounds – the growth in the human population of the area has led to increased theft of turtle eggs to the point that the species is declining locally. The people taking turtle eggs may be doing it out of economic necessity, but destroying this resource will not solve anyone's problems.

Currently, there is a grassroots organization called the Asociación Nacional de Asuntos Indígenas (ANAI; National Association of Indigenous Affairs) that is working with locals to protect the sea turtles – the staff are definitely looking for volunteers if you are interested in sea turtle conservation. Volunteers collect nesting and size data, patrol beaches, and move eggs that are in danger of being destroyed by high tides or predation. Volunteering involves long hours, no pay, hot and humid conditions, and a chance to help sea turtle conservation while seeing a remote part of Costa Rica. If this appeals to you, contact ANAI in San José (☎ 224-6090, 224-3570, fax 253-7524, anaicr@sol.racsa.co.cr) or write the organization for information at 1176 Bryson City Rd, Franklin, NC 28734, USA. If you can't volunteer, contributions are welcome – donations are tax-deductible in the USA for US taxpayers. Steve Cansell of the UK, who volunteered for ANAI in 1996, writes that 'studying these beautiful giant turtles is something that will stay in my memory for a long time.' ANAI is supported by The Nature Conservancy and US AID. Accommodations for the volunteers range from camping to housing with local families; a minimum stay of seven days is required and volunteers must contribute to the cost of meals and housing (from US$5 to US$25 per day, depending on how much comfort you want).

The variety of vegetation and the remote location of the refuge attract many tropical birds; the very rare harpy eagle has been recorded here. Other birds to look for include the red-lored parrot, the red-capped manakin, and the chestnut-mandibled toucan, among hundreds of others. The birding here is considered to be very good. I saw a flock of several hundred small parakeets come screaming overhead at dusk – quite a sight and quite a sound!

Information

Ask for Florentino Grenald, who lives in Manzanillo and used to serve as the reserve's administrator. He has a local bird list and can recommend guides. A local boatman, Willie Burton, will take you boating and snorkeling from Manzanillo. His house is the last one on the road through Manzanillo before you reach the trails leading to Punta Mona. If you have a car, you can leave it by his house while you go hiking. Horses and guides can also be hired locally. ATEC in Puerto Viejo de Talamanca (see Information in that section, earlier in this chapter) offers a variety of tours into the refuge, including day and overnight trips on foot, horseback, or by boat.

Places to Stay

Camping is permitted, but there are no organized facilities unless you are volunteering with ANAI (see above). Reportedly, camping on the beach is best, as there are fewer insects and more breezes. See also the entry for Earth Connect, above. Most visitors take day hikes and stay in the Puerto Viejo area.

Getting There & Away

The Gandoca-Manzanillo reserve is accessible from Manzanillo by trail or by boat.

BRIBRI

This small village is passed en route from Cahuita to Sixaola, on the Panamanian border, at the end of the paved (and badly potholed) coastal road. From Bribri, a 34km gravel road takes the traveler to the border.

Bribri is the center for the local indigenous communities in the Talamanca mountains, although there is not much to see here. Ask locally about a large waterfall near Volio, about 3km from Bribri.

The Ministry of Health operates a clinic in Bribri that serves both Puerto Viejo and the surrounding Indian communities. There is a Banco Nacional de Costa Rica here, also serving Puerto Viejo (about 12km away) and surrounding communities. There are a few public phones (☎ 754-2273, 754-2171, 754-2253, 754-2287).

Places to Stay & Eat

There are a couple of basic lodging options and some restaurants in Bribri. Accommodations tend to fill up on market days (Monday and Tuesday). ***Cabinas El Piculino*** has rooms with private cold showers for US$6/9 single/double and has a soda attached. Slightly better rooms can be found at the ***Bar Restaurant Los Mangos*** *(☎ 754-2253)*, where doubles cost US$9. It is a few hundred meters out of town toward Puerto Viejo. Buses sometimes stop for a meal or snack at the ***Soda Restaurant Bribri***.

Getting There & Away

Bribri is a regular stop for all buses to/from Sixaola. Buses leave from Bribri and travel via the communities of Chase and Bratsi (☎ 754-2175, public phone) to the village of Shiroles (☎ 754-2064, public phone), 17km away. ANAI has built a vocational training center located in Shiroles. Nearby, Don David and Doña Patricia Sharp are US missionaries conducting leadership training courses for local Indian church leaders.

They welcome visitors and are known in the community.

From Shiroles, horse and foot traffic continues on into the indigenous reserves. One village that can be reached is Amubri (☎ 754-2215, public phone), which reportedly has a mission with a place to stay.

Buses for other coastal towns stop outside the Soda Restaurant Bribri. If going to Puerto Viejo, ask if the bus is going into town or just as far as the *cruce* (crossroads).

SIXAOLA

This is the end of the road as far as the Costa Rican Caribbean is concerned. Sixaola is the border town with Panama, but few foreign travelers cross the border here – most overlanders go via Paso Canoas on the Carretera Interamericana.

Sixaola is an unattractive little town, with nothing to recommend except the border crossing itself, which is fairly relaxed. Most of the town is strung along the main street. The public phones are ☎ 754-2152, 754-2002, 754-2004, and 754-2127. Remember, Panama's time is one hour ahead of Costa Rica's.

For details on crossing the border at this point, see the Getting There & Away chapter.

Places to Stay & Eat

There are several basic restaurants and a few places to stay; ask around. Accommodations are generally unappealing, though OK for the unfastidious looking for something different. It's best to get here as early as possible if going to or coming from Panama to avoid getting stuck here. There are better accommodations on the Panamanian side.

The ***Cabinas Sanchez*** *(☎ 754-2105)* has seven fairly clean rooms with cold baths for US$9 double. There's no sign, so ask. The ***Pizza Yuli*** and ***Soda Los Almendros*** are decent enough places to eat. The ***Restaurant Hong Wing*** is friendly and has a few basic rooms upstairs. There are several other places to eat – on one visit, every restaurant had a bunch of argumentative drunks in it at about 10 am. Maybe it was the day after payday for workers on the local cacao *fincas*.

Getting There & Away

Direct buses from San José leave from the Caribe terminal at 6 and 10 am and 1:30 and 3:30 pm, returning to San José at 5, 7:30, and 9:30 am and 2:30 pm (US$5.75, six hours). There are also a few buses a day to/from Puerto Limón via Cahuita and Puerto Viejo. A new service from San José to Changuinola, Panama (16km east of Sixaola), leaves the Hotel Cocorí near the Coca-Cola terminal at 10 am.

Taxis with 4WD are available to visit local villages. You can reach Gandoca (within the Refugio Nacional de Vida Silvestre Gandoca-Manzanillo) from here. Taxis can also be hired for the journey to Almirante, Panama, for about US$20.

Southern Costa Rica

The southbound Carretera Interamericana leaves San José to the east and skirts Cartago before truly heading south. The highway begins to climb steadily, reaching its highest point at over 3300m near the somberly named peak of Cerro de la Muerte (Death Mountain; 3491m). This area is about 100km south of San José and is often shrouded in mist. The next 30km stretch is a particularly dangerous section of highway. From the high point, the road drops steeply to San Isidro de El General at 702m. San Isidro is the first important town south of Cartago and is the main entry point for nearby Parque Nacional Chirripó, which contains Costa Rica's highest mountain, Cerro Chirripó (3820m), and others almost as high.

From San Isidro, the Interamericana continues southeast through mainly agricultural lowlands to the Panamanian border, a little over 200km away. There are no more big towns on this route, but several smaller ones are likely to be of interest to visitors wanting to see parts of Costa Rica that are not on the usual 'gringo trail.' From these towns, roads lead out to some of the more remote protected areas in the country, including the rarely visited and difficult-to-get-to Parque Internacional La Amistad and the Wilson Botanical Garden, arguably the best in the country.

Note that the little yellow-topped, numbered posts along the Carretera Interamericana south of San José are kilometer markers and are referred to in the chapter text.

The magnificent wilderness of Parque Nacional Corcovado and the popular nearby Bahía Drake area in the Península de Osa are accessed from southern Costa Rica, but are covered in the separate Península de Osa & Golfo Dulce chapter. Some of Costa Rica's best surfing beaches are found at Pavones in the far south, which is also covered in that chapter. Dominical, another popular surfing beach often accessed through San Isidro, is covered in the Central Pacific Coast chapter.

RUTA DE LOS SANTOS

The so-called Route of the Saints is a scenic backroads drive that leads from the Interamericana south of Cartago and winds back north to San José. It is named for the villages it passes through: San Pablo de León Cortés, San Marcos de Tarrazú, Santa María de Dota, San Cristóbal Sur, and several others named after saints. The towns themselves are not especially exciting, but the drive takes you through typical hilly farm country – coffee, cattle, and clouds. Narrow, steep roads twist through a splendid landscape – green and inviting or dark and forbidding, depending on the weather.

Places to Stay & Eat

Most visitors tend to just drive through on a day trip, but some of the towns have inexpensive country hotels for those in need of lodging.

In Santa María de Dota, the ***Hotel Bar Restaurante Dota*** *(☎ 541-1026)* has rooms with private baths for US$7 per person.

In San Marcos de Tarrazú, ***Hotel Zacatecas*** *(☎ 546-6073)* has doubles with private hot baths for US$10 and larger rooms for US$22; the ***Hotel Bar y Restaurante Continental*** *(☎/fax 546-6225)* charges US$13 double, and ***Hotel Tarrazú*** *(☎ 546-7711)* charges US$18.

Two kilometers north of the Empalme junction on the Interamericana is ***Albergue Turístico Cerro Alto*** *(☎ 382-2771, ☎/fax 710-6852)*. It has nine rustic but comfortable cabins of various sizes, all of which sleep up to four people and have private hot showers, fireplaces, and kitchenettes. The rate is US$36 for the cabin; rates for fewer people depend on whether the place is full. It is often empty midweek but may fill up on weekends, when prices may rise accordingly. The restaurant is open weekends. (Another simple ***restaurant*** is less than a kilometer away, and there are places to eat on the Interamericana at the turnoff to Santa María de Dota as well.) If you are returning to San

José by road from southern Costa Rica, Cerro Alto is probably the last lodging option before Cartago.

Getting There & Away

Most visitors drive south on the Interamericana to Empalme, a small gas station and *soda* stop almost 30km south of Cartago. Shortly beyond there, a paved road turns west toward Santa María de Dota (about 10km away), San Marcos (7km farther), and San Pablo (4km farther). From there, a choice of paved roads takes you back to the Interamericana via San Cristóbal or winding north through San Gabriel and other villages to San José. A regular car can travel these roads, but available maps and road signs are poor – ask locals for directions.

Autotransportes Los Santos (☎ 223-1002) buses bound for Santa María de Dota leave from Avenida 16, Calles 19 & 21, in San José, several times a day. Some of these buses go via San Marcos de Tarrazú.

GENESIS II

At about 2360m above sea level, this private nature reserve is possibly the highest in the country. Situated in the Cordillera de Talamanca, the reserve covers 38 hectares, almost all of which are virgin cloud forest (or, technically, tropical montane rainforest). This consists of evergreen and oak forest with epiphytic bromeliads, ferns, orchids, lichens, mosses, and other plants covering every available surface. A species of tree fern generally thought to be extinct also grows here.

For those interested in looking for highland species of birds, plants, and butterflies, this is the place to stay. Some of the more spectacular birds include the resplendent quetzal, collared trogon, and emerald toucanet. About 200 birds are estimated to inhabit this highland region, and identifying and classifying them is an ongoing project. Tropical red squirrels are often seen.

There are about 20km of trails within the reserve, of which 3.5km are well maintained; the rest are much wilder. The 'dry' season is from January to May, but it can rain at any time, so rain gear is essential. Mornings are usually clear – even during the rainy season. Average annual rainfall is 2300mm. The altitude makes for colder weather – bring warm clothes.

Admission to the reserve for day visitors costs US$10.

Volunteer Programs

The reserve runs a program for motivated volunteers over age 21 to help with trail construction and maintenance (the primary job) or on other jobs including repairing fences, producing brochures/maps, counting birds, reforestation, housework, gardening, and landscaping. Volunteers pay US$600 for four weeks of food and lodging (two work periods of 10 six-hour days followed by four days off). Details and applications are available from the owners (see below).

Places to Stay & Eat

There are five simple, small guest bedrooms (one with a double bed and four with two singles) in the main house, and two separate, very basic cabins sleeping up to four people (usually student volunteers). All guests share the two hot-water showers and toilets in the main house. Electricity is available, but there is no TV. Tasty family-style meals are served using fresh garden and local produce. The large balcony affords forest views.

The English-speaking owners suggest a minimum stay of three days and recommend a week. The rate is US$85 per night including all meals and guide service. Students can stay for US$45. Guests staying four or more nights get complimentary laundry service and a free guided half-day trip to an alternate habitat. The weekly rate is US$450 and includes a full-day trip to an alternate habitat.

Get further information and reservations from the on-site owners, Steve and Paula Friedman *(☎ 381-0739, genesis@yellowweb.co.cr, www.yellowweb.co.cr/genesis)*.

Getting There & Away

The turnoff for Genesis II is at the Cañon church, just south of Km 58 on the Interamericana. Turn east and follow the rough road 4km to the refuge. You'll need 4WD. If traveling by bus, get off at the Cañon church and the owners will pick you up if you make arrangements with them, or you can walk. Roundtrip transportation from San José can also be arranged.

FINCA DEL EDDIE SERRANO

Near Km 70 on the Interamericana is a sign for Finca del Eddie Serrano (☎ 381-8456), also called Mirador de Quetzales, which is about 1km off the highway to the right (heading south). Quetzals are seen very often from November to early April, and sometimes during other months. This farm doubles as a friendly budget lodging option with seven simple rooms, each with four bunk beds, and there are two shared hot showers. The rate is US$34 per person per day, including three meals and a guided hike (one to two hours) to view quetzals. To protect the birds, hiking without a guide is not allowed. Day visitors can take a guided hike for US$5 each. The *finca* has good views of valleys and volcanoes when it's clear.

SAN GERARDO DE DOTA

This small and spread-out little farming community on the western slopes of Cerro de la Muerte is famous for excellent highland birding. Quetzals have been reported here regularly every April and May (during breeding season) but are often seen during the rest of the year as well. In fact, many people feel this is one of the best places in the country to see quetzals. The trout fishing in the Río Savegre is also very good: the seasons are May and June for fly-fishing and from December to March for lure-fishing.

Places to Stay & Eat

Almost 7km from the Interamericana, you pass the turnoff for ***Trogon Lodge*** *(☎ 223-2421, 771-1266)*, which is part of the Mawamba Group (see the Mawamba Lodge entry under Tortuguero Area in the Caribbean Lowlands chapter). This hotel has nicely landscaped grounds, a stocked trout fishing pond (not much of a challenge to catch your own trout for dinner), and 10 rooms in attractive wooden cabins. Horse rental (US$10 per hour) is available. Rates are US$40/58 single/double with hot baths and heaters. Full breakfast (US$7), lunch, and dinner (US$9) are offered.

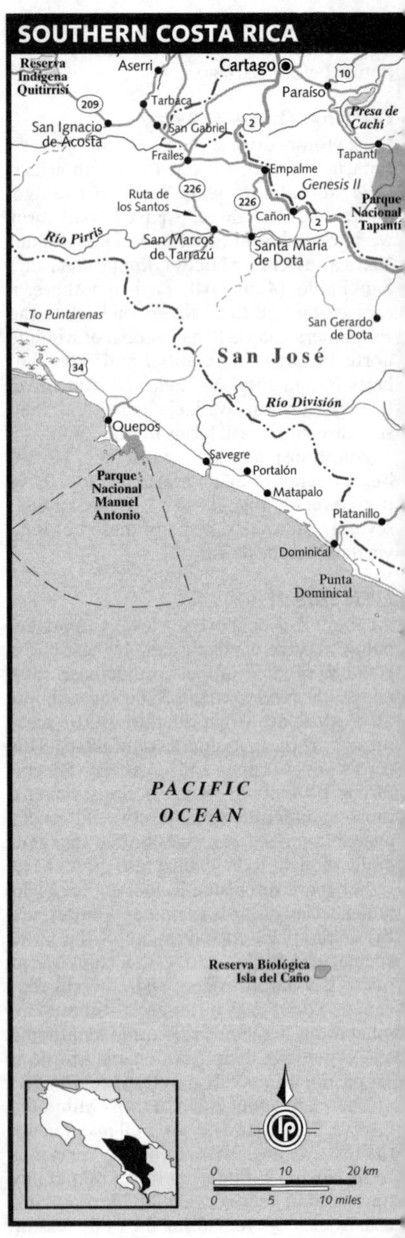

SOUTHERN COSTA RICA
CARIBBEAN SEA
Cartago
Limón
Puntarenas
PANAMA
PANAMA
Tuis
Moravia
To Puerto Limón
Pandora
Cahuita
Parque Nacional Cahuita
Puerto Viejo de Talamanca
Bribri
Reserva Indígena Cocles/KéköLdi
Río Sixaola
Shiroles
Bratsi
Amubri
Río Urén
Reserva Indígena Talamanca Bribri
Reserva Indígena Talamanca Cabecar
Reserva Indígena Telire
Río Telire
Reserva Biológica Hitoy Cerere
Reserva Indígena Tayni
Río Estrella
Reserva Indígena Chirripó
Río Chirripó
Río Pacuare
Cerro de la Muerte
▲3491m
Parque Nacional Chirripó
Cerro Chirripó
▲3820m
Parque Internacional La Amistad
Cordillera de Talamanca
División
Avalon Reserva Privada
Herradura
San Gerardo de Rivas
Canaán
Rivas
San Isidro de El General
Río Chirripó
243
2
Río Convento
▲Cerro Durika 3280m
Reserva Indígena Ujarrás
Ujarrás
Reserva Indígena Salitre
Río Cuabrí
Río Ceibo
Buenos Aires
Reserva Indígena Cabagra
Río Teribé
Parque Internacional La Amistad
Uvita
34
Piñuela
Tortuga Abajo
Parque Nacional Marino Ballena
Isla Ballena
Río General
Valle del General
Reserva Indígena Térraba
Río Cabagra
Potrero Grande
Finca Colorado
Río Cedro
Zona Protectora Las Tablas
Reserva Indígena Boruca
Boruca
Paso Real
Curré
Río Cotón
Bahía de Coronado
Ciudad Cortés
Palmar Norte
Palmar Sur
Río Grande de Térraba
Reserva Indígena Curré
Valle de Coto Brus
Santa Elena
Río Jaba
Progresso
Las Mellizas
Humedal Nacional Térraba-Sierpe
Valle de Diquis
2
237
Sierpe
Río Sierpe
Río Sierpe
Isla Violín
Reserva Indígena Guaymí de Coto Brus
San Vito
Wilson Botanical Garden
Sabalito
Río Sereno
Río Chiriquí Viejo
Chacarita
Fila Costeña
Agua Buena
Cañas Gordas
Laguna Sierpe
Río Chocuaco
Rancho Quemado
Interamericana
Bahía Drake
Agujitas
Rincón
Parque Nacional Corcovado (Piedras Blancas Sector)
Gamba
Río Claro
Reserva Indígena Guaymí de Osa
La Palma
Refugio Nacional de Fauna Silvestre Golfito
Neily
Golfito
Golfo Dulce
14
Reserva Indígena Guaymí de Abrojos Montezuma
Ferry
Laguna Corcovado
Dos Brazos
Puerto Jiménez
Playa Zancudo
Río Coto Colorado
Paso Canoas
Parque Nacional Corcovado
Península de Osa
Carate
Reserva Indígena Guaymí de Conte Burica
SOUTHERN COSTA RICA

The resplendent quetzal

A cheaper option is ***Cabinas El Quetzal*** *(☎ 771-2077)*, about 1km after the Trogon Lodge turnoff. Four rooms sleeping three or four people with fireplaces and hot showers cost US$29 per person including meals, but no guides or tours are offered. The staff here say that because they are lower in elevation than the Albergue de Montaña Savegre (see below), quetzals are seen nearby from December to February.

Opposite Cabinas El Quetzal is ***Restaurant/Bar Los Lagos***, a nice little local place.

Two kilometers beyond is the longest-established, best-known, and recommended ***Albergue de Montaña Savegre*** *(☎/fax 771-1732, 284-1444, Apartado 482, Cartago)*, formerly Cabinas Chacón. The hotel is on the Chacón farm, which was carved out of the wilderness by Don Efraín Chacón in 1957 – an interesting story in its own right – and is still in the same family. The 400-hectare farm is now part orchard, part dairy ranch, and 250 hectares remain as virgin forest. The elevation here is about 2000m.

The owners are enthusiastic about their birds; they have a bird list and usually know where the quetzals are hanging out. Often, they'll set up telescopes on their property so that guests can get a close look at the nest. The owners helped set up the Quetzal Education & Research Center in cooperation with US scientists. There are trails of 4 and 8km and a hiking trail that leads to a waterfall. More trails are planned. Horseback rides with a bilingual guide cost US$10 per hour, and trout fishing is available near the hotel (in both the river and a stocked pond). The 27 remodeled rooms have porches and hot showers. The rate is US$60 per person including home-cooked meals. The restaurant-bar is popular with *ticos* on weekends.

Getting There & Away

Buses to San Isidro de El General can drop you off at 'La Entrada a San Gerardo' (near Km 80), from where the Chacóns at the Albergue will pick you up for US$12 if you have a reservation. Or you can walk – it's downhill. It's just over 9km to the Albergue and less to the other places.

You can drive down there, but the road is very steep, though just passable to an ordinary car in good condition.

CERRO DE LA MUERTE

The mountain overlooking the highest point on the Carretera Interamericana got its name before the road was built – but the steep, fog-shrouded highway in the area is known as one of the most dangerous for accidents in Costa Rica. Take care if driving. During the rainy season, landslides may partially or completely block the road. On a dark and misty night, visibility can drop to a car length – frightening! The local wisdom is never to drive this section at night; if you do, take it slow.

This area is the northernmost extent of the *páramo* habitat – a highland shrub and tussock grass habitat more common in the Andes of Colombia, Ecuador, and Peru than in Costa Rica. Nevertheless, here it is – and you can drive through it. Birders look for highland bird species here, such as the sooty robin, volcano junco, and two species of silky flycatchers. Costa Rica Expeditions and Horizontes both arrange guided day and overnight birding excursions to this highland region, but all departures are on request only (see the Getting Around chapter for contact information).

When the weather is clear, the views can be very good, but drivers should concentrate on the very winding, steep, and narrow road.

About 5km beyond the highest point on the Interamericana is the friendly ***Hotel Georgina*** *(☎ 771-1299)*, where buses often stop for a meal and a break. Basic rooms cost about US$5 per person (less for groups or families). Simple meals are served, and there is good high-altitude birding nearby. Hot showers and electric blankets are offered – it's cold up here. Rooms with private baths cost about US$10 per person.

Another place to stay along the highway, closer to San José and just north of Km 62 on the Interamericana, is the ***Albergue de Montaña Tapantí*** *(☎ 231-3332, ☎/fax 232-0436)*. The 10 rooms have sitting areas or terraces or both; private bathrooms have hot water, and room heaters are available. Rates are about US$50/60/70 double/triple/quad including breakfast.

Time & Space

One of the treats offered by Costa Rica's astonishingly diverse landscape is the opportunity to change the season by changing your location. In the space of a few hours, you can travel from the dusty heat of Guanacaste to the cool 'eternal spring' of San José – or from the summery humidity of a coastal mangrove swamp to the crisp autumnal air of a highland forest. At high points on the Interamericana, it's cold enough to see your breath, and if you hike to the top of Chirripó, your water bottle can freeze – while far below, you might see the sunny beaches of the Caribbean and the Pacific.

– John Thompson

AVALON RESERVA PRIVADA

This 150-hectare reserve is about 3.5km west of the Interamericana by way of the tiny community of División, just past Km 107. The unpaved road is passable to cars. Avalon (☎ 380-2107 cellular, ☎/fax 770-1341, glenmom@racsa.co.cr) is a cloud forest reserve with high-altitude birds including quetzals, bellbirds, trogons, and toucanets. There are hiking trails and good views of the mountains of southern Costa Rica. A local birding guide is available with advance notice (US$60 per day – you decide on how big a group you want to get together). Horse rental (US$9 per hour, US$40 per day) is also available.

A wide range of lower-end budgets is accommodated, weekly and low-season discounts are offered, and work-stay is an option. Day use costs US$3 and camping costs US$6 per person. A dormitory room with shared bath costs US$10 per person and a private double room with shared bath costs US$25 to US$30. There are also two cabins with private baths that cost US$50 double. All bathrooms have hot water. There is a restaurant with home cooking for US$3 to US$8 per meal. The hot tub is heated by a wood-burning stove and takes a while to heat up, but it is a great place to take in the clear air and stars. Yoga classes and massage are sometimes available.

Travelers arriving by bus should get off at División and walk or ask for a taxi at the *pulpería* (grocery store).

SAN ISIDRO DE EL GENERAL

Some 136km from San José, San Isidro de El General (commonly known as simply San Isidro) is the most important town on the southern Interamericana. The town and its surrounding district are home to a population of about 40,000.

The Valle del General is important for agriculture, as you can see when descending from the bleak páramos of the Cerro de la Muerte through the increasingly lush farming country of the valley. San Isidro is the commercial center of the coffee fincas, cattle ranches, and plant nurseries that dot the mountain slopes. The town is also an important transport hub.

San Isidro is a bustling, pleasant, and fairly modern town. With the exception of a small museum, there really isn't much to see or do here, though its position as a gateway to other places makes it of interest to the traveler. San José, to the north, and Panama, to the southeast, are the most obvious destinations. A road to the northeast leads to the village of San Gerardo de Rivas (covered later in this chapter), where there's the ranger station for Parque Nacional Chirripó. To the southwest, another road leads to the Pacific coast and the beaches at Dominical; this road allows a roundtrip to be made from San José to Dominical and Parque Nacional Manuel Antonio without retracing your route. Other minor roads lead into quiet farming country. River-running trips on the nearby Ríos Chirripó and General can be

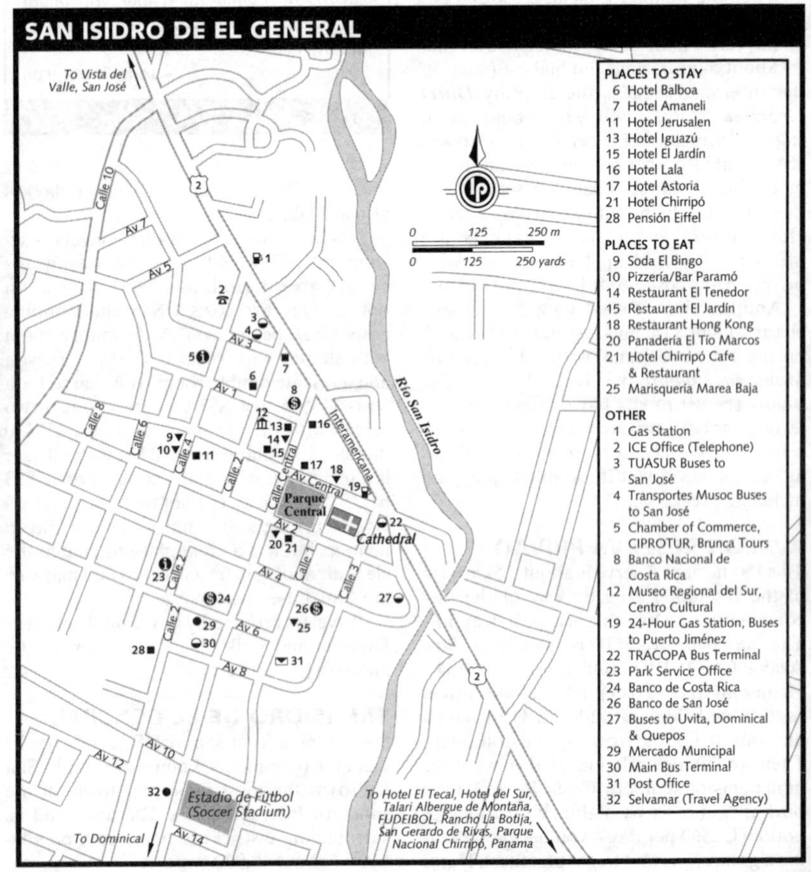

arranged in San José, with overnight stops in San Isidro (see River Running, below).

Orientation & Information

Note that streets, though labeled on the map, are poorly signed and the locals don't tend to know street names or use them much. Hotel business cards, for example, list a telephone number and either no address at all or something like '100m northeast of the park.' Fortunately, the town center is compact, and it's fairly easy to find your way around.

The Cámara de Comercio (Chamber of Commerce), on Calle 4, Avenidas 1 & 3, houses CIPROTUR (☎ 771-6096, fax 771-2003), a well-organized and helpful tourist information center. In the same building, Brunca Tours (☎ 771-3100, fax 771-2003) arranges local excursions.

Selvamar (☎ 771-4582, 771-4579, ☎/fax 771-1903, selvamar@sol.racsa.co.cr) is on Calle Central four blocks south of the park, opposite the soccer stadium. This is a helpful reservation service for over a dozen hotels in the San Isidro and Dominical areas (see the Central Pacific Coast chapter for the latter) and can arrange tours and airline tickets as well. The agency also offers international phone, fax, and email services.

Several banks in town (see map) change cash US dollars and traveler's checks, but shop around for the best rate. The Banco de San José gives cash advances on credit cards. The post office is two blocks south of the park. There is a row of CHIP phones in the Parque Central.

There is a park service office (☎ 771-3155, fax 771-4836) where you can make reservations for Parque Nacional Chirripó on Calle 2, Avenidas 4 & 6; it's open 8 am to noon and 1 to 4 pm weekdays. Information is also available here regarding Parque Internacional La Amistad, which, combined with Chirripó and a host of other protected areas, forms the UNESCO Reserva de La Biosfera La Amistad.

Museo Regional del Sur

This small regional museum at Calle 2, Avenida 1, has a small display of items of local cultural, social, historical, and archaeological interest. Hours are erratic; inquire locally.

In the same complex is a cultural center with a theater, art gallery, and lecture hall.

FUDEIBOL

Seven kilometers northeast of San Isidro, FUDEIBOL (roughly an acronym for the Fundación para el Desarrollo del Centro Biológico Las Quebradas; ☎/fax 771-4131) is a community-run reserve along the Río Quebradas (a source of drinking water for the region). There are nature trails, views, and a butterfly garden; local and foreign volunteers work together on a variety of conservation projects. Admission costs US$6 per person, and camping is possible for about US$3 per person. Call for directions.

Rancho La Botija

This coffee finca and recreation area (☎ 771-2253, 771-1401) is 8km from San Isidro, in the community of Rivas on the left side of the road to San Gerardo de Rivas. The grounds afford views of the valley, and trails lead to an archaeological site with petroglyphs. A small museum features 19th-century implements and antiques, a working *trapiche* (sugar mill), a swimming pool, small restaurant, and horse rental. Locals use this as a place to relax on weekends. Hours are 9 am to 5 pm weekends and holidays, 2 to 5 pm weekdays; admission costs US$2.50/1.50 for adults/children.

River Running

Costa Rica Expeditions and Ríos Tropicales have three- and four-day river-running trips on the Río Chirripó from mid-June to mid-December (see Organized Tours in the Getting Around chapter for contact information). This is mainly a Class IV river.

Trips include roundtrip transportation from San José, all boating gear including life vests, tents for camping by the side of the river, expert bilingual river guides, and all meals. Costs depend on the number of people; ask about joining other groups if your party has fewer than eight people.

Running the Río General is also possible, although none of the major river-running outfitters currently offer trips here on a regular basis. Ask around if you have a group and want to go – most likely something can be arranged.

Special Events

The annual fair is held during the first week in February (occasionally it's held beginning at the end of January) and features agricultural, horticultural, and industrial shows and competitions.

San Isidro is the patron saint of farmers, who bring their stock into town to be blessed on the saint's feast day, May 15.

Places to Stay

San Isidro There are plenty of cheap hotels in town; the fancier ones are on the outskirts.

The cheapest place in town is the rather poor ***Hotel Lala*** *(☎ 771-0291)*, which charges US$2.50 per person in basic rooms, or US$6.50 (one or two people) for a room with a double bed and private cold-water shower. The ***Hotel El Jardín*** *(☎ 771-0349)* has clean, basic rooms for US$3.75 per person and a cheap restaurant (see Places to Eat, below). The family-run ***Pensión Eiffel*** *(☎ 771-0230)*, near the bus terminal, has rooms for about US$4.50 per person but is often full. The ***Hotel Balboa*** has basic singles/doubles for US$4/6 and doubles with baths for US$7; the management is friendly. ***Hotel Jerusalen*** is another cheap place to try.

The ***Hotel Astoria*** *(☎ 771-0914)* has dozens of very basic, tiny rooms for US$5/9 single/double and slightly better boxes for US$6/10 with private cold showers. Half a dozen nicer rooms cost US$15 double but are often full. There's a parking lot too. The 40-room ***Hotel Chirripó*** *(☎ 771-0529)* is modern and a good value at US$5.50/9.50 or US$9/15 for simple rooms with private electric showers. There's a decent restaurant and café on the premises (see Places to Eat).

The best budget option is the ***Hotel Amaneli*** *(☎ 771-0352)*, which charges US$9 per person. The 30 very clean rooms with private hot showers and fans sleep up to five people; try to avoid rooms facing the highway. The café opens at 5 am.

The best standard hotel in town is the clean and secure ***Hotel Iguazú*** *(☎ 771-2571)*. There are 21 rooms with private hot showers, TVs, and fans for US$14/21 per single/double.

Around San Isidro The best standard hotel is a few hundred meters farther along the Interamericana, on the other side of the highway. This is the ***Hotel del Sur*** *(☎ 771-3033, fax 771-0527)*, which has a swimming pool, a tennis court, a sauna, and a pleasant restaurant and bar. Horse and mountain bike rentals are offered. Rooms of varying sizes have private baths, hot water, carpeting, and telephones for US$30 to US$52 double. More expensive rooms also have air-conditioning. Ten cabins with fans, refrigerators, and hot water, sleeping up to five people, are available for US$58.

Overlooking San Isidro, 15km to the north on the Interamericana, ***Vista del Valle*** *(☎/fax 284-4685)* has a pleasant balcony restaurant with great views and hummingbird feeders. It has a few *cabinas* costing US$50 double, including breakfast and dinner.

Seven kilometers northeast of San Isidro, en route to San Gerardo de Rivas and Parque Nacional Chirripó (just before the village of Rivas), is the recommended ***Talari Albergue de Montaña*** *(☎/fax 771-0341, leave a message; talaripz@sol.racsa.co.cr)*. Pilar and Jan, the friendly, multilingual tica-Dutch couple who own this place, will help organize hikes up Cerro Chirripó, arrange horseback tours, and provide local information. They also have a bird list; this is a good center for high-altitude birding. The 8-hectare property has a river running through it, a swimming pool, and a small restaurant and piano bar. (Jan is an accomplished pianist.) Four rooms with two single beds or one queen-size bed and private hot showers cost about US$30/40 single/double, including breakfast. Four larger rooms, each with a single and a queen-size bed, fridge, and hot shower, cost about US$40/50 with breakfast. Other meals are available on request. Low-season discounts are also available.

Places to Eat

There are many inexpensive sodas downtown and in the market/bus terminal area – this is the place for travelers watching their *colones*. However, none of the restaurants in town are expensive.

The ***Restaurant El Jardín***, in the hotel of the same name, is cheap and good. The ***Hotel Chirripó Cafe*** opens at 6:30 am for breakfast; it is inexpensive and popular. The ***Hotel Chirripó Restaurant*** has pleasant plaza views and is a good value – a *casado* costs US$2.50. The ***Panadería El Tío Marcos***, on the same block, has good pastries and other baked goods. ***Restaurant El Tenedor***, next to Hotel Iguazú, has a balcony overlooking a busy street and serves meals that cost from US$1 (hamburgers) to US$5; pizzas are a specialty. Hours are 9 am to 11 pm Tuesday to Sunday. Another place for pizza is the ***Pizzería/Bar Paramo***. Nearby, the ***Soda El Bingo*** serves decent local casados for under US$2. The ***Restaurant Hong Kong***, on the park, has been recommended for – predictably – Chinese food. For seafood, try the ***Marisquería Marea Baja***.

About 2.5km from the town center on the road to Dominical is ***Non Plus Ultra Bar/Restaurant***, which is locally recommended for steaks.

Getting There & Away

Operated by two companies facing each other across the street, buses bound for San Isidro leave San José from Calle 16, Avenidas 1 & 3 (under the Hotel Musoc or from across the street), more or less hourly from 5:30 am to 5 pm. The fare for both is about US$3; the ride takes three hours.

The bus terminal/market complex in San Isidro opened in 1993, but most long-distance buses still leave from a variety of terminals and bus stops scattered throughout town (see the San Isidro map). This may change in the future, but meanwhile the main bus terminal deals mostly with buses to nearby villages.

Buses to San José with Transportes Musoc (☎ 771-0414) or TUASUR (☎ 771-0419) leave from Calle 2 and the Interamericana 13 times a day from 5:30 am to 4:30 pm.

Buses to San Gerardo de Rivas (for Parque Nacional Chirripó) leave at 5 am and 2 pm and take two hours. The morning bus leaves from the Parque Central, and the afternoon bus leaves from the south side of the bus terminal.

Buses leave for Quepos (on the Pacific coast) via Dominical at 7 am and 1:30 pm, and for Uvita via Dominical at 9 am and 4 pm. Departure points are shown on the San Isidro map. The fare to Quepos is US$2.50; tickets to the other places cost less.

Buses to Puerto Jiménez leave from the fruit stand by the 24-hour gas station on the Interamericana. These buses leave San José at 6 am and noon and pass through San Isidro at about 9 am and 3 pm; tickets are sold on a space-available basis. The five- to six-hour ride costs about US$4.

TRACOPA (☎ 771-0468), at Calle 3 and the Interamericana, has southbound routes. The ticket office is open 7 am to 12:30 pm and 1:30 to 4 pm Monday to Saturday; at other times, buy tickets on the bus. Buses originating in San Isidro for Buenos Aires, Palmar Norte, Río Claro, and Neily (US$3, four hours) leave at 4:45 and 7:30 am and 12:30 and 3 pm. Buses to Buenos Aires, Paso Real, San Vito (US$2.75, 3½ hours), Sabalito, and Agua Buena leave at 5:30 am and 2 pm. These services may be changing, so check.

Alfaro buses from San José pass through San Isidro at approximately the following times for the following destinations – tickets are sold on a space-available basis:

David (Panama) – 10 am, 3 pm

Golfito – 10 am, 6 pm

Palmar Norte – seven times a day between 8 am and 9 pm

Paso Canoas – 8, 10:30 am, 2, 4, 7:30, 9 pm

San Vito – 9, 11:30 am, 2:45, 5:30 pm

If the above buses are full, take one of the buses originating in San Isidro and go to Palmar Norte for better connections to Sierpe and Ciudad Cortés, to Río Claro for connections to Golfito, and to Neily for Paso Canoas.

You can hire a 4WD taxi to San Gerardo de Rivas for US$16. A taxi to the Hotel del Sur costs about US$3.

SAN GERARDO DE RIVAS

About 22km northeast of San Isidro, this small village is the entry point to Parque Nacional Chirripó. The elevation here is about 1350m; the climate is pleasant, and there are hiking and birding opportunities both around the village and in the park.

Everyone comes to climb the mountain, of course! However, when you return, check out the **thermal hot springs**. Walk about 1km north of the ranger station on the road toward Herradura and you'll see a sign pointing right. Follow this trail about another 1km to a house where the owner will charge you about US$1 to hang out in the hot springs as long as you want; if you want to stay overnight, they have a couple of cheap rooms and a small soda. Ease those aching muscles and enjoy the mountains for another day.

Foreigners are beginning to buy land here. As more visitors come simply to enjoy the tranquillity and high-altitude beauty around the village, its character may begin to change. So far, foreign development has been private and discreet.

Orientation & Information

The Chirripó ranger station is about 1km below the village on the road from San Isidro (see the Parque Nacional Chirripó section for hours of operation). Just above the ranger station, the road forks; take the right fork to San Gerardo (the left fork will take you almost 3km to the village of Herradura).

The village pulpería (☎ 771-1866), next to the Hotel y Restaurant Roca Dura Café (see below), has a public phone and local operator. If you speak Spanish, you can call this number and leave a message for one of the hotels – either they'll call you back or you can tell them when you'll call again and they can stand by. Slowly, more telephones are being hooked up, and the same operator can tell you if a particular establishment has a phone yet.

Places to Stay & Eat

Just below the ranger station is the simple and basic ***Cabinas La Marín***, with a couple of rooms at US$4 per person and a small restaurant. Across from the ranger station, ***Cabinas El Bosque*** *(☎ 771-4129 in San Isidro)* has decent rooms for US$4 per person and a restaurant-bar. There is some camping equipment for rent, and nonguests can store luggage for US$2 per day.

As you head up to the village from the ranger station, you pass a few more simple hotels. Owned by the friendly and helpful Francisco Elizondo family, the ***Cabinas & Soda El Descanso*** is a good choice. They charge about US$4 per person for small but clean rooms. There is a shared electric shower, and decent meals are available on request.

Farther up is ***Cabinas Elimar***, which has simple but spacious rooms with private electric showers. Each room has one double and one single bed and rents for about US$15. The restaurant opens on request, and there is a trout pond.

In the center of San Gerardo is the ***Hotel y Restaurant Roca Dura Café*** *(☎ 771-1866)*. Seven small, basic, but clean rooms with two to four beds and shared hot showers cost about US$3 per person, and two rooms with double beds and private hot showers cost US$7. These two rooms are a very good value; they're built into the mountain below the hotel, with one wall made of genuine *roca dura* (hard rock). The hotel has a simple restaurant-bar and rents mountain equipment (a sleeping bag costs US$2 per night), and the village pulpería sells supplies next door. A few steps away is the Río Chirripó. This is one of the most popular options for budget travelers and hikers. There are even discounts for groups and students (hard to believe at these prices)! Owner Luis Elizondo is building a camping area and a few cabinas down by the river.

About 200m below the ranger station is the ***Albergue de Montaña El Pelicano*** *(☎ 382-3000, 771-6096 to make reservations through CIPROTUR in San Isidro)*, owned by Rafael Elizondo, a late-blooming but prolific artist who grew up in the area and gradually began sculpting the shapes he saw suggested in the wood and stone around him. His carvings and rock arrangements dot the grounds, and his studio is always open for viewing – make sure you see his tree stump busts and detailed all-wood motorcycle. None of it is for sale, but it's all worth seeing; this is a kind of anonymous, spirited creativity that makes you pleased to be human. Attractive, simple rooms with a shared balcony overlooking the river valley cost US$11 per person including breakfast. Ten rooms share four bathrooms with heated showers.

About 1.5km below the ranger station, in the community of Canaán, is the most upscale lodge in the area (as of this writing). This is the ***Albergue de Montaña Río Chirripó*** *(☎ 771-6096, fax 771-2003)*, with eight pleasant rustic cabins. The cabins have balconies with river views and private bathrooms with hot water; rates are US$22/34 single/double, US$10 per additional person. There's also an attractive-looking restaurant and bar.

Also in Canaán is the ***Chirripó Lodge***, which has basic rooms with four beds for about US$3 per person. The lodge rents hiking gear.

Getting There & Away

Buses leave San Isidro at 5 am and 2 pm and take almost two hours to get to San Gerardo de Rivas (there is another San Gerardo, so ask for San Gerardo de Rivas by its full name). Return buses leave at 7 am and 4 pm. The final stopping point and the departure points for return buses may vary depending on rain and road conditions; ask locally.

If you're driving, head south of San Isidro on the Interamericana, crossing the Río San Isidro at the south end of town. About 500m farther, cross the Río Jilguero and look for a steep turn up to the left, about 300m beyond the Jilguero. A small wooden sign with yellow lettering indicates the turnoff for the park; more visible above it is a large, red sign for the Universidad Nacional. If you are coming from the south, note that there are two entrances to this road, both most easily identified by the red university signs; if you cross the Río Jilguero, you've gone too far.

The ranger station is about 18km up this road, which is paved as far as Rivas. Beyond that it is steep and graveled, but still passable to ordinary cars.

PARQUE NACIONAL CHIRRIPÓ

This is Costa Rica's principal mountain park and, at 50,150 hectares, one of Costa Rica's largest protected areas. There are three peaks of over 3800m, including Cerro Chirripó itself, which is the highest mountain in the country at 3820m. In fact, of all the Central American countries, only Guatemala has higher mountains. Most of the park lies at over 2000m above sea level. There are hiking trails and, for people wishing to spend a few days trekking at high altitude, a mountaintop hostel. When I first visited Chirripó in 1981, I had spent almost a year traveling around tropical Central America and was delighted to find a park where I could get away from the heat for a while!

The park entrance at San Gerardo de Rivas is at 1350m, so the elevation gain to the top of Chirripó is about 2.5km straight up! That is a lot of climbing. Fortunately, there is an easy-to-follow trail all the way to the top, and no technical climbing is required. Almost all visitors use this trail to get to the top, though alternatives are discussed below. Walking at the lower elevations is also rewarding, with excellent views and opportunities for good birding and butterfly observation.

The climb is a fascinating one because it takes you through constantly changing scenery, vegetation, and wildlife as you ascend. After passing through the pasturelands outside the park, the trail leads through tropical lower montane and then montane rainforests. These are essentially evergreen forests with heavy epiphytic growths in the trees, and thick fern and bamboo understories. Emerging above the main canopy (25 to 30m) are oak trees reaching 40 or even 50m in height.

These highland forests are home to such birds as the flame-throated warbler and buffy tufted-cheek, to name but two. Blue and green frogs and lime-colored caterpillars thickly covered with stinging hairs make their way across the trail, and Baird's tapirs lurk in the thick vegetation (though you are much more likely to see squirrels than tapirs). Eventually, the trail climbs out of the rainforests and into the bare and windswept páramo of the mountaintops.

The Chirripó massif is part of the Cordillera de Talamanca, which continues to the northwest and southeast.

The national park's eastern boundary coincides with the western boundary of the huge and largely inaccessible Parque Internacional La Amistad, thus most of the mountains of the Talamanca range are protected. Chirripó and La Amistad, together with a number of biological and Indian reserves, make up the Reserva de La Biosfera La Amistad (covered later in this chapter under Parque Internacional La Amistad).

Orientation & Information

The dry season (from late December to April) is the most popular time to visit the park. During weekends, and especially at Easter, the park is relatively crowded with Costa Rican hiking groups, and at these times the mountain hostel may well be full. Camping is not allowed anywhere, to protect the delicate páramo ecosystem. February and March are the driest months, though it may still rain at times.

During the wet season, you are likely to have the park to yourself. I once spent almost two weeks hiking in the park during the wet season and found that it rarely rained before 1 pm, and that I didn't see anybody – a great wilderness experience. But it is worth remembering that as much as 7000mm of annual rainfall has been recorded in some areas of the park.

The ranger station outside of San Gerardo de Rivas is a good place to ask about weather conditions and get an idea of how many people are in the park. Officially, you need to make a reservation with the central park office in San José (☎ 233-4160) or the office in San Isidro de El General (☎ 771-3155, fax 771-4836) to stay in the hostel near the summit (see below). In reality, there are a lot of no-shows. It's best to just go to the ranger station near San Gerardo de Rivas and ask for a permit – it helps if you speak Spanish and check in immediately after arriving. Occasionally, travelers may find that the hostel is indeed full – but even then, if you can wait a day or two in the village, space will usually become available. The week before Easter and the Easter weekend are usually reserved well in advance, but there are rarely problems at other times.

You can contact the Chirripó ranger station in advance of your visit through the park service office in San Isidro (☎ 771-3155, fax 771-4836). Ranger station hours are 5 am to 5 pm daily.

At the ranger station, you'll pay the US$6 daily park entrance fee plus US$6 per night for lodging in the hostel. Drivers can leave vehicles near the ranger station and excess luggage can be locked up for US75¢.

Mule hire can be arranged through a local association of guides – ask at hotels in the area or at the ranger station, or make reservations through the regional park office in San Isidro. You can ride a mule or just have one to carry your gear. The locals will not normally rent the animals without a local guide to accompany you. Expect to pay about US$25 per day for a guide and a pack animal. In the rainy season, the mules stay home but the guides will carry up to 15kg for you for about US$20.

See Places to Stay, below, for information on equipment rental.

Maps The maps available at the ranger station are fine for the main trails. Good topographical maps from the Instituto Geográfico Nacional de Costa Rica (IGN) are available in San José (see Planning in the Facts for the Visitor chapter for contact information; note that the hostel, shelters, and trails are not marked on these maps). Chirripó lies frustratingly on the corner of four 1:50,000 scale maps, so you need maps 3444 II San Isidro and 3544 III Durika to cover the area from the ranger station to the summit of Chirripó itself, and maps 3544 IV Fila Norte and 3444 I Cuerici to cover other peaks in the summit massif. (Topographical maps are nice to have but not essential.)

Climbing Chirripó

From the ranger station it is a 16km climb to the Chirripó summit area. Allow seven to 16 hours to reach the hostel, depending on how fit and motivated you are. Anybody can show you the beginning of the trail, which is signed at approximately 2km intervals and easy to follow once you are on it.

There used to be three huts spaced out along the last hour of the trail; currently only the hostel El Paramo is open to the public (see Places to Stay, below). It can freeze at night, so warm clothes and a good sleeping bag are necessary (the latter can be rented at El Paramo). There is a cave (sleeping about six people) about halfway along the trail if you don't want to go from the ranger station to El Paramo in one day. The open-sided, insect-ridden hut at Llano Bonito, about halfway up, can also provide shelter. However, the cave and hut are intended for emergency use. Rangers recommend that hikers on day trips don't ascend beyond these emergency shelters. Carry water on the trail, particularly during the dry season, when the only place to get water before reaching the hostel is at Llano Bonito.

From the hostel it is another 4km or so to the summit – allow at least two hours if you are fit. A minimum of two days is needed to climb from the ranger station to the summit and back again; this gives you little time for resting or visiting the summit. Three days would be a better bet. If you don't return to San Gerardo by 4 pm, you'll miss the last bus out.

Almost every visitor to the park climbs the main trail to Chirripó and returns the same way. Other nearby mountains can also be climbed via fairly obvious trails leading from the hostel. These include Cerro Ventisqueros, at 3812m the second-highest peak in the country, and several other peaks over 3700m. Some maps show a couple of rarely used, non-maintained wilderness trails leading north and south out of the park; however, these are extremely difficult to find and are not recommended.

An alternative, rarely used route to Chirripó is to head north of the ranger station to the community of Herradura, 3km away. Guides can be hired here (about US$20 per day) to take you up a new trail entering the mountains from the west side. Call the public phone at the pulpería in Herradura (☎ 771-1199) and ask for José Mora, who is an active member of the guide association and speaks some English. An overnight camp is necessary below Cerro Urán – the rangers will permit you to camp on this rarely used route. Also ask locally about other rarely used routes through the forest up to the mountain.

Apparently, there are a couple of places to stay beyond Herradura – ask locally. In Herradura, a lady named Mirna rents rooms near the river and Rodolfo Elizondo, who speaks English, can arrange accommodation, fishing, and horse rental. Both of them can be contacted through the public phone.

Places to Stay

Centro Ambientalista El Paramo is the new mountain hostel, a thoughtfully designed stone building that looks something like a monastery and sleeps up to 60 people (US$6 per person). A solar panel provides electric light until 7 pm and some heat for the showers (don't count on it); sleeping bags and cooking equipment are available for rent (about US$4 per item; prices were still being determined at time of writing). See Orientation & Information, above, for reservation information.

BUENOS AIRES

This small village is 64km southeast of San Isidro and 3km north of the Interamericana. It has a nice tree-filled plaza, a couple of banks, a gas station, a disco, and other services.

The village is in the center of an important pineapple-producing region. It is also an entry point for the rarely visited Parque Internacional La Amistad, several Indian reserves to the north, and Reserva Indígena Boruca to the south. A road east of Buenos Aires goes through remote country and Indian reserves and eventually joins with the San Vito road at Jabillo. You probably won't see any other tourists in this area.

The best place to stay is ***Cabinas Violeta***, behind the Banco de Costa Rica in the center of town. A dozen simple but clean rooms rent for US$6.50/7.25 single/double. Other cheap and basic places that charge about US$6 per person include ***Cabinas Kanajaka*** *(☎ 730-0207)*, on the way into town from the highway, and ***Cabinas La Torre*** *(☎ 730-0764)*, closer to the center.

To get here, take buses from San Isidro, or any southbound bus on the Interamericana, and ask to be let off at the turnoff for Buenos Aires. Buses to San Isidro leave about every hour from 5:30 am to 5 pm. There are also a few local buses to nearby towns. The TRACOPA agency (☎ 730-0205) in the center has a few buses a day to and from San José; these originate elsewhere and may be full when they come through.

RESERVA BIOLÓGICA DURIKA

This 700-hectare private biological reserve is 17km north of Buenos Aires on the flanks of Cerro Durika in the Cordillera de Talamanca, and is within the Reserva de La Biosfera La Amistad. Within the Durika reserve is the **Finca Anael**, where a couple dozen people live in a more or less independent and sustainable manner. Community members are committed to local conservation. Most are ticos, but there are a few foreigners and English and French are spoken.

The reserve opened to tourism in 1992, and visitors are welcome. Birding and hiking are the main activities – there is a resident birding guide. Day hikes and overnight tours and camping trips are offered to nearby waterfalls, the Cabecar Indian village of Ujarrás (where crafts such as string bags are sold), local farms, and to climb Cerro Durika (at 3280m) in Parque Internacional La Amistad. You can ride a horse if you prefer. Classes are offered in yoga, vegetarian cooking, and meditation, among other things.

There are five cabins of various sizes sleeping two to eight people. All have private bathrooms and porches with mountain views. Rates are US$40/70 single/double and include vegetarian meals, guided walks, and (for those staying more than one night) transportation from Buenos Aires. There are discounts for groups, students, and long stays. If you have a sleeping bag, there is a basic hut where you can sleep for US$10 (student rate) including meals. Reservations and information are available from Asociación Durika (☎ 730-0657, fax 730-0003, durika@sol.racsa.co.cr). There is no phone at the Finca Anael, so you have to make phone reservations a week in advance by contacting the association. This is for adventurous travelers.

PASO REAL

This tiny community is at the junction of the Interamericana with the paved road (Hwy 237) that goes through the Valle de Coto Brus to San Vito. Immediately east of the village, the road crosses the Río Grande de

Térraba via a bridge that opened in 1994. A car ferry operated here at one time, but this is no longer the case.

RESERVA INDÍGENA BORUCA

This indigenous reserve is centered around the village of Boruca, about 20km south of Buenos Aires. It is one of the few Indian reserves where visitors are welcome, perhaps because Boruca is only some 8km west of the Carretera Interamericana.

The Borucas are known for their carvings, including balsa wood masks and decorated gourds. The women use pre-Columbian back-strap looms to weave cotton cloth and belts; these can sometimes be purchased from the locals. The people live a simple agricultural life in the surrounding hills.

If you are simply driving through the area on the Interamericana, you can stop at the community of Curré, where a small crafts cooperative store sells Boruca handicrafts.

Special Events

The three-day Fiesta de los Diablitos (*diablitos* means 'little devils') is held in Boruca during the month of February (dates vary). About 50 men wearing carved wooden devil masks and burlap costumes represent the Indians in their fight against the Spanish conquerors. The Spaniards, represented by a man in a bull costume, lose the battle. As of 1997, the Borucas charge visitors a photography fee and photographers are required to wear a pass indicating they have paid. A similar fiesta is held in Curré (also in February); check locally for festival dates.

Places to Stay

The village pulpería in Boruca has a few basic rooms for rent, but they aren't really set up for tourism. This is for culturally sensitive travelers who can respect and appreciate the local lifestyle. Some of the local families may provide sleeping space for you in their houses.

Getting There & Away

Buses (US$1.25, 1½ hours) leave the central market in Buenos Aires at 11:30 am and 3:30 pm daily via a very poor dirt road. Drivers will find a better road that leaves the Interamericana about 3km south of Curré – look for the sign. The road is about 8km to Boruca; you'll probably need 4WD during the wet season.

In San José, university anthropologist Mildred Pereira (☎ 253-9935, 253-3127) visits this region (and Ujarrás as well) several times a year and allows travelers to accompany her on a space-available basis. You'll overnight in Buenos Aires.

PALMAR NORTE & PALMAR SUR

These two places are basically the same town on different sides of the Río Grande de Térraba, which the Interamericana has been following for the last 40km (for those traveling southbound). Palmar is about 125km south of San Isidro and 95km northwest of the Panamanian border.

The town is the center of the banana-growing region of the Valle de Diquis, and is also a transportation hub. You might find yourself staying here en route to Sierpe, Bahía Drake, and the Parque Nacional Corcovado region (see the Península de Osa & Golfo Dulce chapter).

The area is interesting to archaeologists because of the discovery of almost-perfect stone spheres up to 1.5m in diameter. The spheres were made by pre-Columbian Indians, but exactly who made them and how remains a mystery. Similar objects have been found on Isla del Caño (now a biological reserve). Ask in town if you want to see the spheres *(esferas de piedra)* – they are found in a variety of places, including backyards and banana plantations.

Palmar Norte has hotels, bus service, and a gas station, and Palmar Sur has the airport. The Banco Nacional (☎ 786-6263) is on the Interamericana in Palmar Norte. Also on the Interamericana is Osa Tours (☎ 786-6534, fax 786-6335), which arranges local tours into the Península de Osa. To get from Palmar Norte to Palmar Sur, take the Interamericana southbound over the Río Grande de Térraba bridge, then take the first right beyond the bridge.

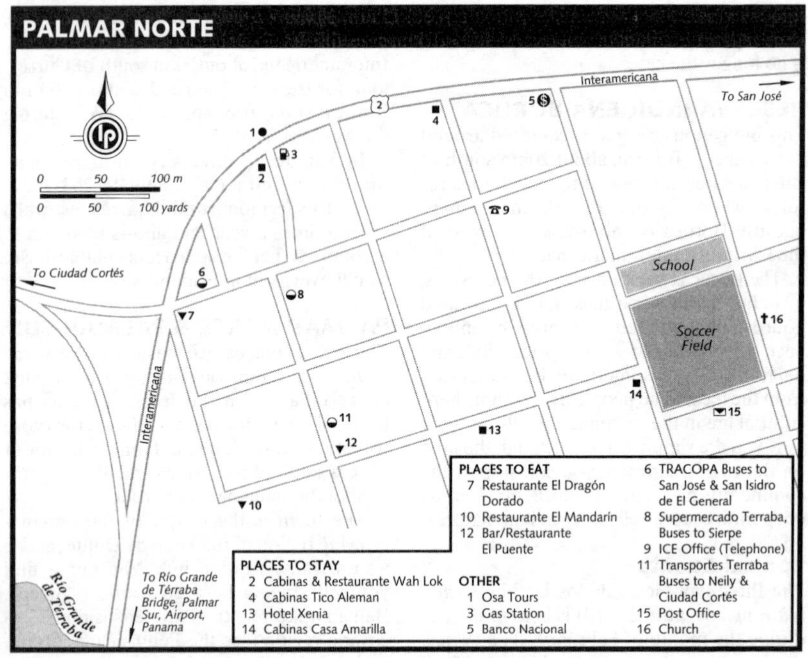

SOUTHERN COSTA RICA

Places to Stay & Eat

One cheap option to try is the ***Hotel Xenia*** *(☎ 786-6129)*, with rooms for US$3 per person. Just off the Interamericana is the ***Cabinas Tico Aleman*** *(☎ 786-6232, 786-6235)*, which has clean, airy rooms with private baths and fans for US$9 per person; there are a few air-conditioned doubles for US$27. Nearby, ***Cabinas & Restaurante Wah Lok*** *(☎ 786-6777)* is a Chinese restaurant with a few adjoining rooms for rent with fans and showers at US$7/11 single/double.

Cabinas Casa Amarilla *(☎ 786-6251)* has a private parking lot and clean, secure rooms with private baths and fans for US$17 single or double, and a few very basic rooms for about US$4 per person.

There are several inexpensive and simple Chinese restaurants, including the ***Restaurante El Dragón Dorado*** and ***Restaurante El Mandarín***. Other options include ***Bar/Restaurante El Puente***, which serves tico food and is popular with locals.

Getting There & Away

Air SANSA (☎ 786-6353) has daily flights from San José (fare US$55/110 one way/roundtrip) and from Quepos. Travelair has daily flights from San José for US$89/145.

These air schedules are very prone to change. Currently, there are scheduled flights to Golfito with both airlines and to Neily/Coto 47 with SANSA.

The airport is in Palmar Sur. Taxis usually meet incoming flights and charge US$3 to Palmar Norte or US$13 to go to Sierpe. The Palmar Norte-Sierpe bus passes through Palmar Sur – you can board it on a space-available basis.

Bus TRACOPA (☎ 786-6511) has buses to San José (US$4.50, five hours) at 5:25, 6:15, 8:15, and 10 am and 1, 2:30, and 4:45 pm Monday to Saturday. On Sunday, buses depart at 6:15, 8:15, and 10 am and 12:15, 1, and 3 pm. Buses to San Isidro leave daily at 8:30 and 11:30 am and 2:30 and 4:30 pm.

Southbound buses sell tickets on a space-available basis only.

Transportes Terraba has six buses daily to Neily between 6 am and 4:50 pm, and hourly buses to Ciudad Cortés.

Buses travel 14km to Sierpe from in front of the Supermercado Terraba at 5:45 and 9 am, noon, and 4:45 pm (US50¢); a taxi will cost you about US$12.50.

PALMAR NORTE TO NEILY

About 40km southeast of Palmar Norte, the Interamericana goes past the junction at Chacarita. The only road into the Península de Osa leaves the Interamericana at this point heading southwest (see the Península de Osa & Golfo Dulce chapter).

Fifteen kilometers beyond Chacarita, a signed road to the right of the Interamericana goes to the Esquinas Rainforest Lodge (see below). Driving an additional 14km brings you to **Río Claro**, which is the junction for the road to Golfito on the Golfo Dulce. Río Claro has a gas station, several restaurants, and a couple of places to stay. The best is ***Hotel y Restaurant Papili*** *(☎ 789-9038)*, which has six small but very clean rooms with private hot baths and fans for US$10 double. This is a better value than anywhere in Neily, which is 16km away. It also has a good restaurant and pizzeria.

Esquinas Rainforest Lodge

This lodge *(☎ 382-5798 cellular)* is in the village of Gamba, less than 6km south of the Interamericana, and above the Piedras Blancas sector of Parque Nacional Corcovado. This Austrian-funded project is ecotourism in the truest sense. Most of the employees are from Gamba and profits from the lodge go into community projects. The lodge is surrounded by 120 hectares of rainforest with trails. Of course, bus, boat, horse, and foot tours are available into the nearby national park as well as other areas.

There are 10 comfortable cabins with private hot showers, fans, and porches. Facilities include a swimming pool and a restaurant with staff trained by one of Austria's foremost chefs. Rates are US$95/150 single/double including three meals. Multiday packages, including tours, are available. For reservations and information, call ☎ 293-0780, fax 293-2632, or email gasguis@sol.racsa.co.cr.

The road from the Interamericana to the lodge is passable to ordinary cars year-round. From the lodge, a rough unpaved road continues to Golfito; this route usually requires 4WD.

NEILY

This town, 17km northwest of the Panamanian border by road, is nicknamed 'Villa' by the locals. It is also sometimes referred to as Ciudad Neily. The town is the main center for the banana and African oil-palm plantations in the Coto Colorado valley to the south of town. At just 50m above sea level, it is a hot and humid place, but pleasant and friendly.

A road winds into the mountains that rise up north of Neily, leading about 30km to the attractive little town of San Vito, which rests at a cooler elevation of 1000m.

Neily's main importance to the traveler is its role as a transport hub for southern Costa Rica – with roads and buses to Panama, San Vito, and Golfito – as well as to a host of small local agricultural settlements. Among these, however, the nearby towns of Golfito and San Vito are the most interesting.

Orientation & Information

Visitors should be aware that this is a town in which the residents don't generally use street names when giving directions; be prepared to rely on local landmarks instead.

There are a number of banks where you can change money; Banco Popular (☎ 783-3076) is usually the fastest. There is a hospital about 2km south of town on the Interamericana.

Places to Stay

There are a number of hotels, all of which are fairly inexpensive. One of the cheapest is the basic but friendly ***Pensión Elvira*** *(☎ 783-3057)*, which charges about US$3 per person, or US$4 for a room with a fan. There is a locked parking lot. Other equally cheap and basic places include the poorer though cheerfully painted ***Hotel El Viajero*** *(☎ 783-5120)*, the somewhat noisy ***Hotel Villa***

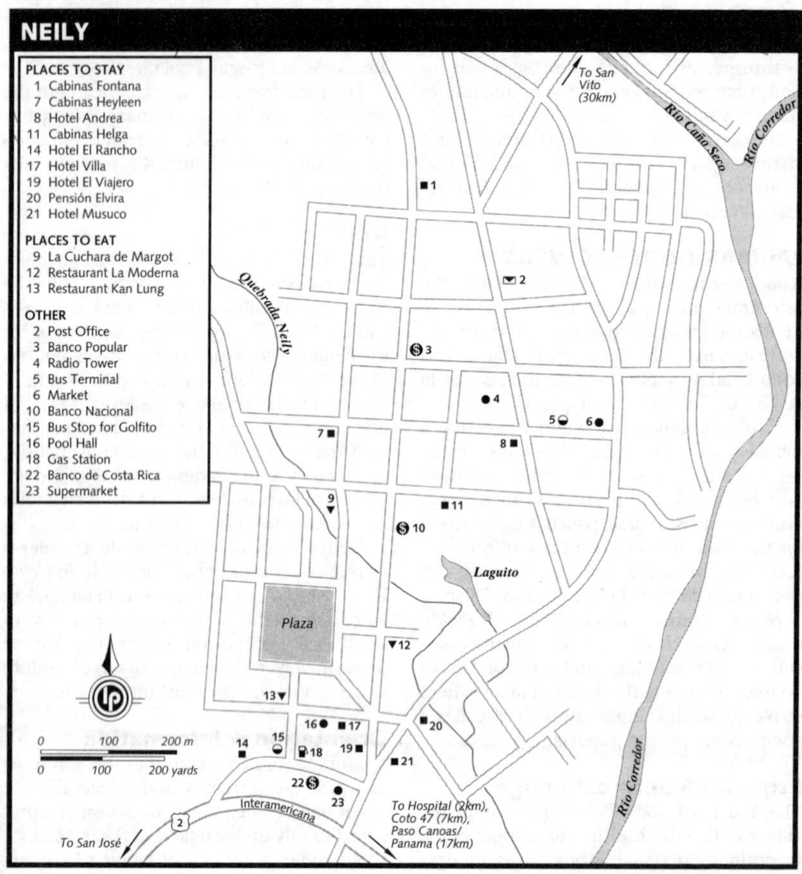

(☎ *783-5120*), and, as a last resort, ***Cabinas Fontana***.

The clean and secure ***Hotel Musuco*** (☎ *783-3048*) offers small basic rooms and shared showers for US$4.50 per person, or US$5.50 for rooms with baths and fans. Other good possibilities for about US$7 per person are the ***Cabinas Helga*** (☎ *783-3146*) and the plant-filled ***Cabinas Heyleen*** (☎ *783-3080*), which is often full.

The ***Hotel El Rancho*** (☎ *783-3060*) is locally popular and has a spartan holiday-camp feel; decent, spacious rooms cost US$7/13 single/double with private cold baths and fans, US$14.50/22 for rooms with TV and air-conditioning. There is a guarded parking lot.

Hotel Andrea (☎/*fax 783-3784*) has 14 rooms and looks like the nicest place in town at this writing. It charges US$12.50/14.50 for decent rooms with cold showers and fans, and US$16.50/22 for slightly larger singles/doubles with TVs and air-conditioning.

Places to Eat & Drink

The ***Hotel El Rancho*** has a decent restaurant attached. The best place in town is the pleasant ***Restaurant La Moderna*** (☎ *783-3097*), which has a variety of meals ranging from hamburgers and pizza to chicken and fish. Prices are in the US$2 to US$6 range. ***La Cuchara de Margot*** serves ice cream, pizza, and snacks and has a couple of outside tables. Of several Chinese restaurants, the ***Restaurant Kan Lung*** is as good as any.

The ***pool hall*** near the Hotel Villa is friendly.

Getting There & Away

Air Coto 47 is about 7km southwest of Neily, and is the closest airport to Panama. Some of the local buses pass near the airport.

SANSA (☎ 783-3275) offers daily flights from San José to Coto 47 for US$55/110 one way/roundtrip. In the past, these flights were routed via Palmar Sur, though as of this writing this is no longer the case. Ask about the frequent schedule and routing changes.

Bus TRACOPA buses from San José leave six times a day from Avenida 18, Calle 4. Most of these buses continue on to Paso Canoas, at the Panamanian border, after stopping at Neily.

In Neily, the bus terminal is next to the market. TRACOPA buses (☎ 783-3227) leave there for the following destinations (with the exception of the frequent buses to Golfito, which leave from the stop opposite the gas station):

Ciudad Cortés (near Palmar Norte) – 5 and 9 am, noon, 2:30 and 4:30 pm

Golfito – (US55¢, 1½ hours) 18 times daily between 6 am and 6:30 pm

Puerto Jiménez – (5 to 6 hours) 7 am and 2 pm

San Isidro – 7 and 10 am, 1 and 3 pm

San José – (US$5.50, 7 hours) 4:30 *(directo)*, 5, 8:30, and 11:30 am, 1:45 and 3:30 pm

San Vito – (US$1.50, 2½ hours) 6 am, 1 and 2 pm via Agua Buena; 11 am and 3 pm via Cañas Gordas

Many local communities are served, including Pueblo Nuevo and Playa Zancudo; these services may depend on rain and road conditions.

Taxi Taxis with 4WD are available to take you almost anywhere. The fare from Neily to Paso Canoas is about US$6; to Coto 47, the fare is about US$2.50. Taxis between Coto 47 and Paso Canoas will cost you about US$8.

PASO CANOAS

This small town is on the Interamericana at the Panamanian border, and is therefore the primary land point of entry between Costa Rica and Panama. A charmless border-crossing town, it is a popular destination for ticos who come on shopping trips to buy goods that are cheaper than in San José. Therefore, hotels are often full of bargain hunters during weekends and holidays, at which time you might seek lodging in Neily, some 17km away. Most of the shops and hotels are on the Costa Rican side. Paso Canoas is only worth a visit on your way across the border to/from Panama; there's nothing else of interest here, and the hotels are poor. Neily is close by and much more pleasant.

See the Getting There & Away chapter for details on crossing the border to/from Panama.

Information

There is a small tourist information office in the same building as the customs post. Paso Canoas has a gas station. Banks are open 8 am to 5 pm weekdays. Money changers hang out around the border and give better rates than banks for exchanging cash US dollars to colones. You can also convert excess colones to dollars, but this exchange is not as good. Try to get rid of as much Costa Rican currency as possible before crossing into Panama. Colones are accepted at the border, but are difficult to get rid of farther into Panama. Other currencies are harder to deal with. Traveler's checks can be negotiated with persistence, but are not as readily accepted as cash. The Panamanian currency is the *balboa*, which is on par with and interchangeable with cash US dollars.

Places to Stay & Eat

None of the hotels in Paso Canoas are particularly good; there's really no reason to stay here unless you have to.

A decent place in the town center is the ***Cabinas Interamericano***, offering clean rooms with private baths and fans for about US$12 double. One of the better restaurants in town is attached. ***Cabinas Hilda*** is also clean and slightly cheaper.

The most secure-looking place in town is the ***Hotel Real Victoria***, which has basic air-conditioned rooms for US$20 double.

Away from the noisy center, ***Cabinas Karla*** *(☎ 732-2234)* is clean and friendly, and has air-conditioned rooms for US$7 per person. Next door, ***Cabinas Los Arcos*** is somewhat overpriced at US$9 per person for rooms with private baths and fans.

A few other cheapies in the US$3 to US$6 range are on the Paso Canoas map. The tourist office can make other recommendations if you're stuck.

Dining options include a number of cheap sodas. Also try the ***Brunca Steak House***, which is popular with international truck drivers, and the relatively pleasant ***Bar/Restaurant Rancho Verde***, which has an outside eating area and is locally popular.

Getting There & Away

Air The airport closest to the border is at Coto 47, near Neily (see the Neily section, earlier in this chapter). There is a SANSA agent (☎ 732-2041) at the Cabinas Interamericano.

Bus Buses from the TRACOPA terminal in San José leave several times a day. Make reservations if you're traveling on Friday night, because the bus is usually full of weekend shoppers. The same applies to buses leaving Paso Canoas on Sundays. Direct buses leave Paso Canoas' TRACOPA terminal (☎ 732-2119) for San José at 4 and 9 am and 1 pm – the fare is US$6.50 for the eight-hour trip. Slightly slower buses leave at 7 am and 3 pm (US$5.40).

Buses to Neily leave at least every hour in daylight hours, from a bus stop less than 100m from the border. Neily has more bus connections than Paso Canoas. If you just miss one and don't want to wait for the next, a taxi will take you the 17km to Neily for US$6.

Taxi For taxi fares between Paso Canoas and nearby Neily and Coto 47, see the Getting There & Away section under Neily, above.

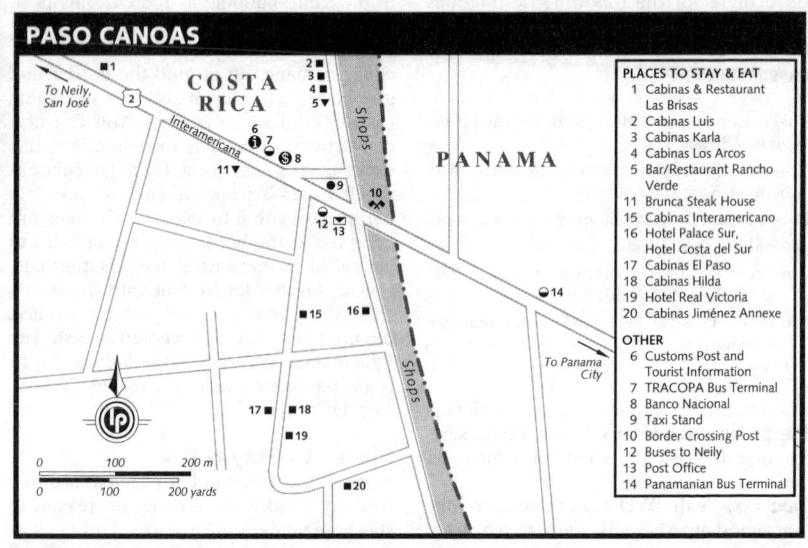

SOUTHERN COSTA RICA

SAN VITO

With a population of about 10,000, this pleasant town at 980m above sea level offers a respite from the heat of the nearby lowlands. The drive up from Neily is a very scenic one, with superb views of the lowlands dropping away as you climb the steep and winding road up the coastal mountain range called Fila Costeña. Drivers should note that the road is ear-poppingly steep, very narrow, and full of hairpin turns; you'll be using 2nd gear much of the way.

Some buses from Neily go via Cañas Gordas, which is on the Panamanian border but is not an official crossing point (though you can see Panama from here). There is reportedly a *pensión* here. The bus continues through Sabalito, a town where there is a gas station and a basic hotel, before reaching San Vito.

Other buses take the more direct route via Agua Buena, passing the Wilson Botanical Garden about 6km before reaching San Vito. This is the route that most drivers take, because it is paved all the way.

You can also get to San Vito from San José via the Valle de Coto Brus – this is an incredibly scenic route with great views of the Cordillera de Talamanca to the north and the lower Fila Costeña range to the south. The narrow, swooping road is paved all the way and there are few tourists.

San Vito was founded by Italian immigrants in the early 1950s. Today you can still hear Italian spoken in the streets, and the most exciting thing to do in San Vito itself is to eat in one of the Italian restaurants. Guaymí Indians, who are known to move undisturbed back and forth across the border with Panama, sometimes come into town, barefoot and in traditional dress. San Vito is also a good base for visits to the splendid Wilson Botanical Garden and to Parque Internacional La Amistad.

Information

There are two banks that will change money. The Centro Cultural Dante Alighieri has some information for tourists and historical displays on Italian immigration. Inquire about Internet access at the ICE telephone office; some employees have computers in their homes and may allow you to check email.

There is a hospital 1km south of the town center.

Places to Stay

The ***Hotel Tropical*** is friendly and secure, but a disco downstairs may keep you awake weekend nights, and buses getting gas at the station across the street may wake you up in the morning. Basic rooms cost about US$3 per person. The ***Hotel Colono*** *(☎ 773-4543)*, another cheap and basic choice, is cleaner and quieter.

The ***Albergue Firenze*** *(☎ 773-3741)* has OK rooms with private electric showers for US$4.25 per person; the office is around back in a house.

For US$5 per person, you can stay at the ***Cabinas Las Mirlas*** *(☎ 773-3054)*, which is clean, quiet, and pleasant and has private electric showers. Windows open onto an orchard. Go down the drive about 150m to the house on the right to ask about the cabins.

The ***Hotel Collina*** *(☎ 773-3173)* charges US$6/10 for basic and dark single/double rooms with private cold showers. The attached bar is locally popular. The ***Centro Turístico Las Huacas*** *(☎ 773-3115)* has decent rooms in the parking lot of a recreation center for US$6.25/10.50 with private electric showers (TVs cost US$2 more).

The small ***Hotel Cabinas Rino*** *(☎ 773-3071, 773-4030 for late-night calls)* has five clean rooms with private hot showers and TVs for US$8.50/13. Reception is available 24 hours, and there is a locked parking lot.

The ***Hotel El Ceibo*** *(☎/fax 773-3025)* is the best in town. It has been renovated; some of the 40 rooms boast little balconies with forest views but others look out on the parking lot. Rooms vary in size and decor but all have private baths with hot water. There is a decent restaurant and bar. Rates are about US$15/24; cable TVs cost US$3 extra.

About 3km south of town, en route to the Wilson Botanical Garden, is ***Cántaros*** *(☎ 773-3760, fax 773-3130)*, owned by the enthusiastic Gail Hewson de Gómez. She rents an apartment in a charming little wooden building on attractive grounds for

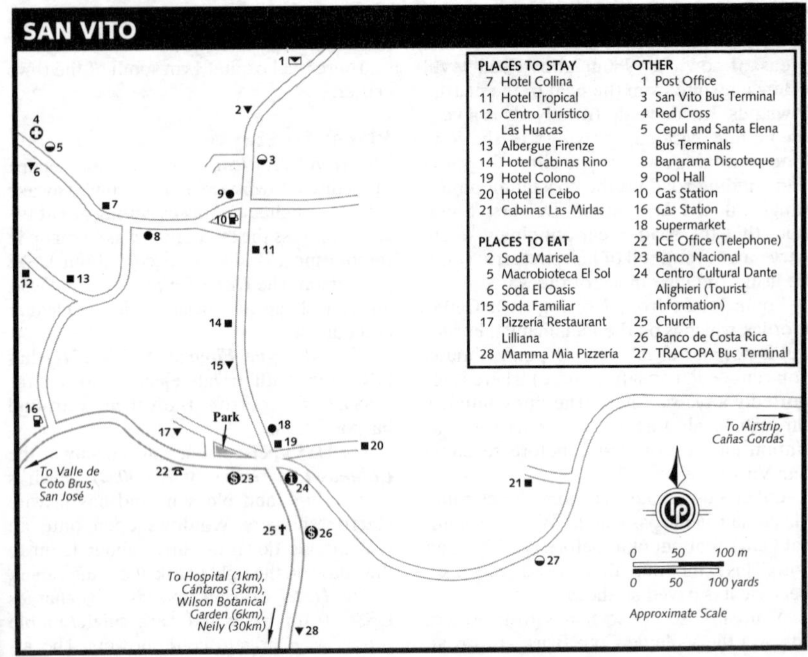

US$30 double. There's a sitting room, a separate bedroom, a TV, hot shower, and a kitchen (the last of these is shared with the library next door).

Wilson Botanical Garden (see below) is the best place to stay in the San Vito area.

Places to Eat

Italian restaurants include the ***Pizzería Restaurant Lilliana***, which has pizza along with Italian and local food for US$3 to US$4; ***Mamma Mia Pizzería***, which has been through several chefs recently but is another good choice; and the restaurant at the ***Hotel El Ceibo***, which also has good Italian and other food.

The ***Soda Familiar*** has cheap meals and is locally popular. ***Soda Marisela*** is one of several other cheap local places. ***Soda El Oasis*** is bright, cheerful, has a special seating section for children, and makes good fruit drinks. Across the street in the Cepul bus terminal, ***Macrobioteca El Sol*** is a macrobiotic health-food store.

Entertainment

After dinner, check out the ***Banarama Discoteque***. Down the street from the Hotel Tropical is a lively ***pool hall***; there's a quieter one in the Hotel Collina.

Shopping

Cántaros (see Places to Stay) is the best gift shop in southern Costa Rica, with a small but carefully chosen selection of local and national crafts – no junk! It's open 8 am to 4 pm Tuesday to Sunday, and it's housed in a great cabin built by early pioneers to the region and now restored. Next to the gift shop are a guest apartment and a children's library (mostly Spanish with some English books) and education area (puzzles, games, crayons). This is a great local resource and is funded by the gift shop.

Getting There & Away

Air You can charter light aircraft at the San Vito airstrip. Otherwise, the nearest airports with scheduled services are at Coto 47 (near Neily) and Golfito (in the Península de Osa).

Bus There are four bus terminals in San Vito. The Cepul and Santa Elena terminals share a location near the Red Cross building. The San Vito terminal is on the main street. The TRACOPA terminal is out on the road to Cañas Gordas.

TRACOPA (☎ 773-3410) has a direct bus to San José at 5 am and slower buses at 7:30 and 10 am and 3 pm (US$6.50, about five to 6½ hours). There are also buses to San Isidro at 6:45 am and 1:30 pm. TRACOPA has buses from San José to San Vito at 5:45, 8:15, and 11:30 am and 2:15 pm, and from San Isidro to San Vito at 5:30 am and 2 pm.

The Cepul terminal (☎ 773-3848) has buses to many local destinations. Buses to Neily (US$1.50, 2½ hours) leave at 5:30, 9, and 11 am and 2 pm. For those wishing to reach Parque Internacional La Amistad, there are buses to Las Mellizas (US$1) at 9:30 am and 2 pm. Other nearby destinations served include Río Sereno and Cañas Gordas on the Panamanian border, Los Reyes, Cotón, and Los Planes.

The San Vito terminal (☎ 773-3028) has local buses to various destinations, including Las Mellizas at 5 pm. The Santa Elena terminal (☎ 773-3460) has buses to Santa Elena five times a day.

WILSON BOTANICAL GARDEN

Despite its small size, Wilson Botanical Garden is truly world-class. About 6km south of San Vito, the garden is very well laid out and many of the plants are labeled. Wandering around the grounds is fun, and the labels turn the walk into a learning adventure. There are many short trails, each named for the plants found alongside it. Trails include the Bromeliad Walk, Heliconia Loop Trail, Tree Fern Hill Trail, Orchid Walk (with over 50 species), Fern Gully, and Bamboo Walk. The most celebrated collection, however, contains 700+ species of palms, one of the largest collections of its kind in the world.

The botanical garden was established by Robert and Catherine Wilson in 1963 and thereafter became internationally known for its collection. The gardens themselves cover 10 hectares and are surrounded by 145 hectares of natural forest. In 1973, the area came under the auspices of the Organization for Tropical Studies (OTS), and in 1983 was incorporated into UNESCO's Reserva de La Biosfera La Amistad.

Today, the well-maintained collection includes over 1000 genera of plants in about 200 families. This attracts both birds and human visitors. As part of the OTS, the gardens play a scientific role as a research center. Species threatened with extinction are preserved here for possible reforestation in the future. Study of conservation, sustainable development, horticulture, and agroecology are primary research aims, and scientific training and public education are also important aspects of the facilities. Students and researchers stay here and use the greenhouse and laboratory facilities. Members of the public can also be accommodated in comfortable cabins that were designed specifically for ecotourists.

The dry season is from January to March; during this time it is easier to get around the gardens. Nevertheless, the vegetation in the wet months is exuberant with many epiphytic bromeliads, ferns, and orchids being sustained by the moisture in the air. Annual rainfall is about 4000mm and average high temperatures are about 26°C. October and November are the wettest months.

A disastrous fire in November 1994 destroyed most of the buildings; as a result, a huge amount of research material was lost. The OTS immediately started picking up the pieces and the new accommodations and facilities for visitors are better than ever. The majority of the grounds were not seriously affected by the fire.

Information

The gardens (☎/fax 773-3278, lcruces@ns.ots.ac.cr) are open 7 am to 5 pm daily (though birders can arrange to enter at dawn) but are closed on December 24 and 25.

Foreign visitors are charged US$8 for a full day (US$3 for children five to 12); lunch costs an additional US$8. Half-day rates drop to US$5 for adults. The staff speaks English and Spanish.

Guided nature walks (in English) lasting 2½ hours cost US$20 for groups of four or less; ask about rates for larger groups. Reservations for guided hikes and visits with lunch must be made with the OTS in San José (☎ 240-6696, fax 240-6783, reservas@ns.ots.ac.cr). For self-guided visits without lunch, no reservation is necessary – just show up. Fees go toward maintaining the gardens and research facilities.

For self-guided walking, a trail map is provided and various booklets are available at low cost so visitors can learn about the collection. The most useful include *Selected Palms of Wilson Botanical Garden*, which identifies palms along a walk that takes about 1½ hours, and a recently compiled checklist of birds. The grounds have about 50 species of trees, some of which are seen on a two-hour walk described in *Selected Trees of Wilson Botanical Garden*. A general overview is given in *The Self-Guided Tour of the Natural History Trail*. Smaller brochures and leaflets describe orchids, hummingbirds, and medicinal plants, and there is also a bird list of 330 species. New publications are developed every year.

For visitors spending the night, the library is available for reference. Talks and slide shows are given on an erratic basis every few days for and by researchers and students; guests are welcome to attend. A one-night visit is not really enough to see what the gardens have to offer. Visitors with a serious interest in natural history are encouraged to spend three nights.

Places to Stay & Eat

Overnight guests can be accommodated if reservations are made in advance with the OTS in San José (see Information, above). Make reservations as far in advance as possible; otherwise, consider staying in San Vito.

The 12 comfortable double cabins have telephones with modem hookups (obviously with the scientist and researcher in mind), private hot showers, and balconies with great views. Rates are US$80/130 single/double including meals and entry to the gardens. There is a 20% discount from August to mid-December. Children under 12 sharing with adults receive substantial discounts. Students with ID can stay in a dorm on a space-available basis for US$32, including meals. There are also four older cabins, two of which have two bedrooms each. These are mainly used by researchers, but may be available to travelers if everything else is full. Meals are a tasty affair, shared family style with interesting scientists, graduate students, and other researchers working here.

Getting There & Away

Buses between San Vito and Neily (and other destinations) pass the entrance to the gardens several times a day. Ask at the bus terminal about the right bus, because some buses to Neily take a different route. A taxi from San Vito to the gardens costs US$2 to US$3. It is a 6km walk from San Vito, mainly uphill, to the gardens. A sign near the center of town claims it's 4km, but it's definitely 6km.

PARQUE INTERNACIONAL LA AMISTAD

This huge park is by far the largest single protected area in Costa Rica. It is known as an international park because it continues across the border into Panama, where it is managed separately.

Combined with Parque Nacional Chirripó and a host of indigenous and biological reserves, La Amistad forms the Amistad-Talamanca Regional Conservation Unit. Because of its remoteness and size, the RCU protects a great variety of tropical habitats ranging from rainforest to páramo, and has thus attracted the attention of biologists, ecologists, and conservationists worldwide. In 1982, the area was declared the Reserva de La Biosfera La Amistad by UNESCO, and in 1983 it was designated a World Heritage Site. Approximately 250,000 hectares form a strictly protected core area that will remain untouched. An additional 340,000 hectares comprise buffer zones with controlled management and development. These areas are joined by some 440,000 hectares of land on the Panamanian side.

Conservation International and other agencies are working with Costa Rican authorities to implement a suitable management plan. This plan must preserve wildlife and habitat and develop resources, such as hydroelectricity, without disturbing the ecosystem or the traditional way of life of the Indian groups dwelling within the reserve.

Reserva de La Biosfera La Amistad has the nation's largest populations of Baird's tapirs, as well as giant anteaters, all six species of neotropical cats – jaguar, puma (or mountain lion), margay, ocelot, oncilla (tiger cat), and jaguarundi – and many other, more common mammals. Over 500 bird species have been sighted (more than half of the total in Costa Rica); 49 of these species exist only within the biosphere reserve. In addition, 115 species of fish and 215 species of reptiles and amphibians have been listed (an unconfirmed report puts this up at 263 species), and more are being added regularly. There are innumerable insect species. Nine of the nation's 12 Holdridge Life Zones are represented in the reserve.

The backbone of the reserve is the Cordillera de Talamanca, which, apart from having the peaks of the Chirripó massif, also has many mountains over 3000m in elevation. The thickly forested northern Caribbean slopes and southern Pacific slopes of the Talamancas are also protected in the park, but it is only on the Pacific side that ranger stations are found. These are on access roads outside of the actual park boundaries.

Within the park itself, development is almost nonexistent, which means backpackers are pretty much limited to their own resources. Hiking through steep, thick, and wet rainforest is difficult and lacks the instant gratification that comes from sighting, say, grizzly bears and North American bison in Yellowstone National Park, or lions and leopards in Kenya's national parks. It is because of the lack of human interference that the shy tropical mammals of Costa Rica are present in relative abundance at La Amistad – but expect to work hard for a glimpse of them. Birding, on the other hand, is likely to yield more successful results.

Orientation & Information

Obtaining information from the parks office in San José (☎ 233-4160) is difficult – this is such a remote area that nobody knows much about it. You are better off trying at the park service office in San Isidro (☎ 771-3155, fax 771-4836), though there isn't much information there either. Officially, as with other parks, admission costs US$6 per day and camping costs about US$2, but often there is nobody around to collect the fees; visitation is so low that it would cost more to collect fees than the income derived from the fees themselves.

Park headquarters is at **Estación Altamira**, near the Zona Protectora Las Tablas. This is the best-developed area of the park; there is a ranger station, a small exhibit room covering the flora and fauna of the park, a camping area, showers and drinking water, electric light (!), and a lookout tower. Several trails offer walks of three to six hours, some passing through primary forest and others offering panoramic views or visits to tiny communities along the border of the park. The longest trail leads to a camping area several kilometers away from the ranger station.

There are also reportedly stations in development at La Escuadra, almost 20km north of Santa Elena, and in the Finca Colorado area, to the northwest of San Vito. Once open, these may not always have rangers on duty.

Very few travelers visit the park, and those who do usually stay at one of two lodges described below.

Places to Stay & Eat

La Amistad Lodge *(☎ 773-3193)* was the first lodge in the area to open to tourists, in the early 1990s. It's about 3km by poor road with signs from the village of Las Mellizas. You'll probably need 4WD for the last section, or you can walk. This is a family-run place, and there are many kilometers of trails into the park as well as opportunities to see a pioneering ranch in action. The owners strive to maintain a balance between organic agriculture and the natural environment, and they appear to have been successful so far. The birding is excellent, and readers recommend this remote place.

There are 10 double rooms, some with shared facilities and others with private hot showers. They are rarely full, unless a group has reserved in advance. More rooms are planned for the near future. Family-style meals are served, and electricity is available for most hours of the day (though you should bring a flashlight). The nightly rate is about US$65 per person including meals and guide service. For reservations and information, contact Tropical Rainbow Tours (☎ 290-3030, fax 232-1913). Major tour operators in San José, including Costa Rica Expeditions and Horizontes, can arrange complete tours here with transportation and guides.

The other facility near the park is the ***Monte Amuo Lodge*** *(☎ 265-6149)*, set on 50 hectares of land bordering La Amistad. This is reached by driving northwest from San Vito on the very scenic Valle de Coto Brus road. About 44km out of San Vito (and only 4km before the bridge over the Río Grande de Térraba at Paso Real), a signed road leads north to the community of Potrero Grande (5km) and continues on into La Amistad. Monte Amuo Lodge is about 10km beyond Potrero Grande on signed but unpaved roads. You'll probably need 4WD beyond Potrero Grande. The rate at the lodge is about US$75 per person in rustic cabins with private hot showers; the rate includes meals and guided hikes into the park. A conference room with panoramic views of the valley and mountains is available for groups. Electricity is available for part of the night (bring a flashlight).

A family in the Las Tablas area provides food and accommodations on their ranch – ask around. Also see the section on Reserva Biológica Durika, earlier in this chapter, for information about visits into La Amistad.

Getting There & Away

Park rangers report that you can get a local bus to the Altamira station from either Buenos Aires or Las Tablas; Las Tablas is accessible by bus from San Vito. For access to La Escuadra station, presently in development, take a bus to Santa Elena.

Taxis with 4WD can usually be hired from the nearest towns to get you to the park stations, but be prepared to do a bit of asking around before finding someone who knows the way. You could also try exploring the area in a rented 4WD vehicle. This is a trip only for those adventurers with plenty of time.

Península de Osa & Golfo Dulce

The large Península de Osa, second only to the Península de Nicoya in size, has the best remaining stands of Central America's Pacific coastal rainforest, preserved in Parque Nacional Corcovado. For many visitors, this is the main reason to come to this region. Budget travelers backpack through the park, while travelers with more upscale budgets stay at a host of comfortable lodges and camps in various parts of the peninsula, using them as a base for guided natural history walks into the park.

Other noteworthy activities in this region include surfing in the Pavones area, where the waves are some of the best in the country, taking a snorkeling or dive trip to the very warm and clear waters of Reserva Biológica Isla del Caño (about 20km west of the peninsula), and going offshore fishing.

There are several ways to get into the peninsula. One route is to take a boat from Sierpe to Bahía Drake, an area where there are several fine lodges. From here, you can walk or boat into Corcovado. It's also possible to charter flights into Bahía Drake or into the national park. Another option is to go to the peninsula's biggest town, Puerto Jiménez, which is reached by air, bus, car, or boat from Golfito. From Puerto Jiménez, a rough road continues around the end of the peninsula to the southeast entrance of the national park. All these options are discussed in this chapter.

To Corcovado via Bahía Drake

SIERPE

This small village is on the Río Sierpe, almost 30km from the Pacific Ocean. Boats to Bahía Drake can be hired here, and most of the lodges around Bahía Drake will arrange boat pickup in Sierpe for guests who plan to use their accommodations.

Sonia Rojas at the Pulpería Fenix (☎ 786-7311) knows boat operators and local hotels. Ask for advice here if you get stuck.

Places to Stay & Eat

Sierpe ***Hotel Margarita*** *(☎ 786-7574)* has five simple but very clean small rooms with private baths for US$11 double. There are also 13 rooms with shared baths for US$3 per person, and the hotel will provide you with a towel. It is on the corner of a grassy square about three blocks from the dock.

A block from the dock, the ***Hotel Pargo*** *(☎ 786-7580)* has 10 rooms with private hot showers for US$20/25 single/double with fans or US$25/30 with air-conditioning. The hotel also has a simple restaurant.

The ***Cabinas Estero Azul*** *(☎ 786-7322)* is on the road about 2km before you get to Sierpe. It has cabins sleeping up to three with fans, private baths, and refrigerators for US$60 per person including meals, though it seemed closed when I visited. Nearby is the ***Eco Manglares Sierpe Lodge*** *(☎ 786-7414, fax 786-7441, ciprotur@sol.racsa.co.cr)*, which has five spacious, rustic cabins with private baths and hot water for US$40 per person including breakfast, or US$52 including three meals. The lodge is across the river and is reached by the narrowest of suspension bridges, which can accommodate a large car but not a bus. This lodge also has playground equipment. Both these places offer fishing, diving, and sightseeing tours.

The most popular restaurant is ***Las Vegas Bar/Restaurant***, right next to the boat dock. There are also a few other cheap *sodas*.

Río Sierpe Area A 30-minute boat ride from Sierpe in an isolated part of the Valle de Diquis is the Italian-run ***Mapache Lodge*** *(☎ 786-6565, fax 786-6458, www.oropesa.net/cr/mapache)*. The 45-hectare property has two developed hectares; the rest is natural rainforest and mangrove. The lodge sponsors the Arborea Project, a conservation initiative dedicated to buying rainforest for

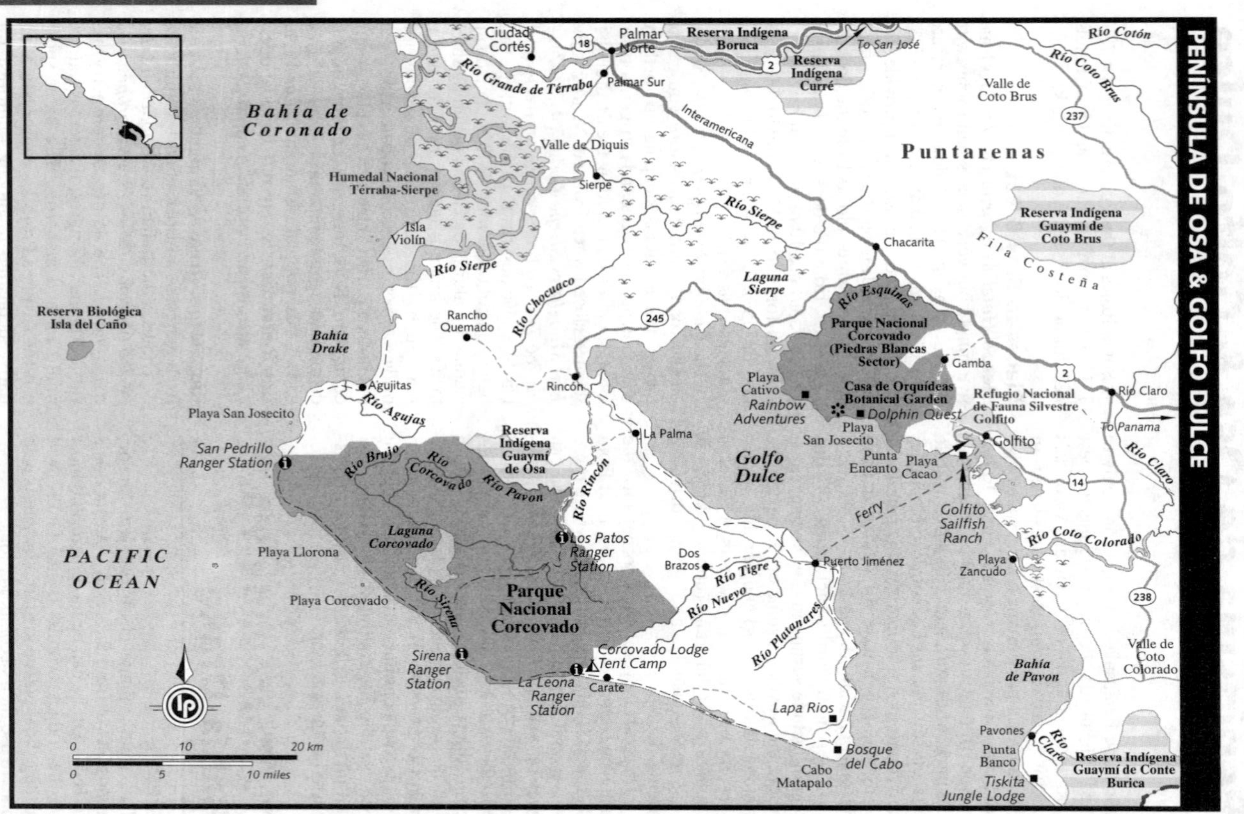

PENÍNSULA DE OSA

protection and agricultural lands for reforestation. Adventurous local tours are offered, including kayaking, horseback riding, and hiking. Tours to Corcovado and other areas are available, as are fishing trips.

The lodge is nonsmoking and features a pool, exercise equipment, and an observation tower. Walking trails on the property offer good birding and wildlife watching. Accommodation is in large, walk-in tents (US$58/104 single/double), rustic cabins with shared baths (US$70/128), and rooms with private baths in the owners' house (US$104/174). Rates include transportation from Sierpe and meals. Contact them about all-inclusive tours ranging from three to 10 days, with various activities available. Italian, English, French, and Spanish are spoken.

The ***Sábalo Lodge*** *(☎ 226-0355, 771-4582, fax 286-2839, 771-1903, sabalo@sol.racsa.co.cr)* is a small, rustic, solar-powered, family-run ecolodge that can accommodate up to eight people in private screened rooms with clean shared bathrooms. A swimming hole and river are nearby, and the lodge has been recommended for wildlife observation and hiking. The friendly owners are certified Spanish teachers and can give personal language classes. Rates are US$55 per person, including three home-cooked meals, and US$48 for roundtrip boat transport from Sierpe (which can be shared). Various local tours can be arranged. Popular packages from San José include three nights at Sábalo Lodge, two nights at a lodge in San Josecito, all meals, roundtrip (land) transportation from San José, one guided tour in Corcovado, and horseback riding, for US$474. Other packages are available.

Within 4km of the ocean and south of Isla Violín, the ***Río Sierpe Lodge*** *(☎ 384-9555, fax 786-6291; in San José ☎ 283-6673, fax 283-7655, vsftrip@sol.racsa.co.cr)* is rustic but comfortable and well run. Nature and birding tours, diving, and sportfishing are featured. There are 17 rooms with private solar-heated showers and six two-story rooms with sleeping lofts. The rooms are spacious; student discounts are available. Food is good and varied, and there is a recreation area with a large library of paperback books. Several trails around the lodge are suitable for birding and wildlife watching. The staff is helpful and friendly.

Room rates include meals, taxes, soft drinks, and road/river transfer from Palmar to the lodge. Independent travelers are charged US$80/130 single/double. Optional full-day excursions (two-person minimum) include Parque Nacional Corcovado or Isla del Caño (US$55 per person), tidal basin angling (US$80), and Pacific Ocean angling (US$225). Half-day trips to Isla Violín (good birding) cost US$25 and mangrove excursions (more birds) cost US$35. The lodge also does two-day overnight camping treks into the rainforest and through remote villages for US$65 per person or US$125 on horseback. These can be combined into excursion packages for naturalists or anglers – they go from three days/two nights to six days/five nights, and internal flights are included. There are substantial discounts for naturalist or student groups of eight or more – call the lodge for details.

Dive packages include boats, all gear, and a PADI- or NAUI-certified divemaster. You just need your swimwear, a mask, and a diver certification card. Prices (including lodging, meals, and flights/transfers from San José) range from US$400 per person for three days/two nights to US$820 for six days/five nights with a six-person minimum; add about 50% if there are just two of you.

Fishing packages, also including everything from San José, cost about US$500 to US$1000 for three days/two nights to six days/five nights of tidal basin fishing or US$600 to US$1200 for the same period of deep-sea fishing.

Getting There & Away

Air Both scheduled flights and charters fly into Palmar Sur, 14km north of Sierpe (see the Southern Costa Rica chapter).

Bus & Taxi Buses depart Sierpe for Palmar Norte at 5:45 and 8:30 am and 3 pm. A taxi charges about US$12.50.

Boat If you have not prearranged a boat pickup with a Bahía Drake or Río Sierpe lodge, ask around at the dock next to Las Vegas Bar or ask at the Pulpería Fenix. The going rate to Bahía Drake is about US$15 per person (four minimum). The trip takes about 90 minutes or more, depending on the size of the boat engine and the tides.

The trip to Bahía Drake is scenic and interesting: first along the river through rainforest, then through the mangrove estuary, and on through the tidal currents and surf of the river mouth into the ocean. Keep your eyes open for monkeys, sloths, herons, macaws, parrots, kingfishers, ibises, and spoonbills along the river and dolphins, boobies, frigatebirds, and pelicans along the coast. The river mouth has a reputation for being dangerous, and in a small dugout it is. The larger boats with strong engines used by experienced operators going to the lodges don't have any problems, though it's pretty exciting riding the swells and avoiding the splashes.

BAHÍA DRAKE (DRAKE BAY)

Simply called Drake locally (pronounced 'DRA-cay' in Spanish), this area is rich in both 16th-century history and natural history. Sir Francis Drake himself supposedly visited the bay in March of 1579 during his global circumnavigation in the *Golden Hind*, and there is a monument at Punta Agujitas to this effect. The bay is only a few kilometers north of Parque Nacional Corcovado, which can be visited from here, as can Reserva Biológica Isla del Caño. (Both Corcovado and Isla del Caño are described later in this chapter.)

Agujitas is a small village on the bay with a *pulpería*, a public phone, a clinic, a school, and a couple of cheapish *cabinas*. You can visit Agujitas and pick up a cola or beer, watch the local kids coming home from school, and chat with the locals. Most people who visit tend to stay in their lodges, but the locals enjoy talking with travelers, so stop by. A dance hall plays music on Saturday nights.

Activities & Organized Tours

The variety of activities offered in this area will keep visitors busy for days, and therefore a stay of at least three nights is recommended by the lodges in the area. Most of them offer the same tours and usually will set you up with another lodge if, for some reason, they can't provide you with your choice. Tours are generally priced fairly competitively among the more expensive lodges, with cheaper tours offered by some of the budget accommodations. The latter will give discounts if you are part of a group, though the better lodges often have the best guides.

Probably the most popular is the day tour to Parque Nacional Corcovado. It includes a boat ride (almost one hour) to the north end of the park, a beach landing (remove your shoes to keep them dry), and a hike. This can be short and easy or long and hard – let the lodge know what you want. The tour costs about US$50 to US$75 plus a US$6 park fee, and includes lunch. The main activities are birding, natural history interpretation, and swimming in rivers and at beaches. It's also possible to go as far as the Sirena ranger station for about US$100.

Reserva Biológica Isla del Caño has great snorkeling and can be visited for US$55 to US$80. Scuba diving is offered for beginners and experts. With advance reservation, beginners can take a PADI certification course (four days required). Certified divers can do two boat dives near Isla del Caño and other sites for approximately US$100 (gear is supplied). Advanced courses are also offered. The best lodges for dive trips are La Paloma Lodge, Jinetes de Osa, Drake Bay Wilderness Resort, and Aguila de Osa Inn (see Places to Stay & Eat, below).

Areas outside the national park and reserve can be visited with guided tours that are a little cheaper, and the birding is still good. You can hike up the Río Claro, visit waterfalls, or take a boat to Isla Violín or mangroves on the Río Sierpe – the latter two are especially good for birding. Horses can be rented for about US$50 per day with a guide, less for shorter rides. You can hike up the Río Claro without a guide if you have wilderness skills – trails aren't signed. You can also hike around the lodge areas and along the beaches yourself.

Although the weather is hot, if you plan on riding a horse, bring a pair of long pants

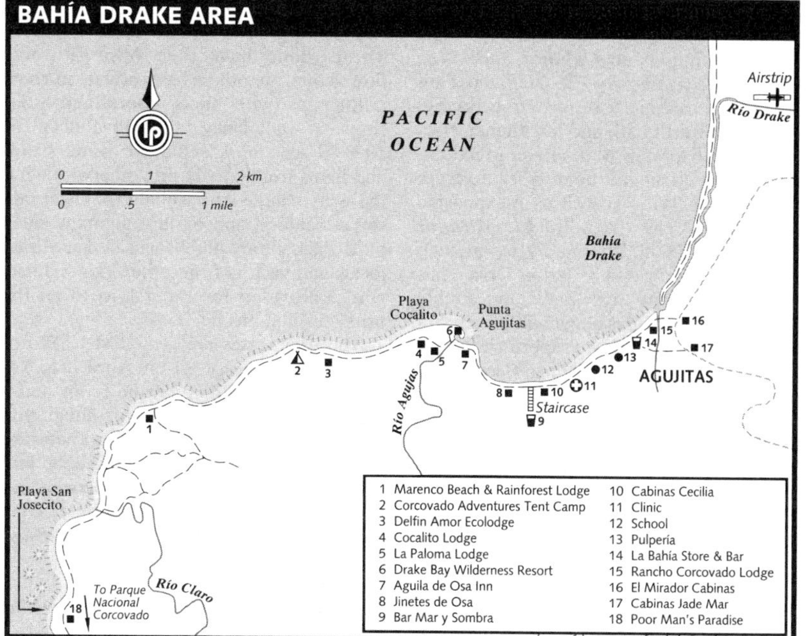

to protect your legs. Long pants are also a good idea for some hikes.

Sportfishing is available, starting at US$35 an hour in small boats and rising to about US$800 a day in a fully equipped 31-foot boat with a professional fishing guide. Up to four anglers can be accommodated in a boat. The best lodge for dedicated offshore anglers is Aguila de Osa, though all the lodges can easily arrange fishing.

Canoes for play on the river and sea kayaks for more serious trips can be borrowed or rented. Drake Bay Wilderness Resort has the best sea-kayaking tours.

The Divine Dolphin (☎ 775-1481; in the USA ☎ 305-443-0222, info@divinedolphin.com, www.divinedolphin.com) opened the tiny Delfin Amor Ecolodge in 1999 (see From Bahía Drake to Corcovado, later in this chapter). Swimming-with-dolphin tours are offered for people who want to interact directly with these animals and who are comfortable with swimming in the ocean several kilometers offshore. Guests of other lodges can take these tours. An all-day tour costs US$85 per person.

And, of course, you can just hang out in a hammock and relax, surrounded by tropical scenery.

Places to Stay & Eat

Reservations are recommended in the high season (mid-November to the end of April), especially in the top-end lodges. Discounts are offered in the low season. High-season prices are given below. (Also see accommodations described in the next section, From Bahía Drake to Corcovado).

Budget & Mid-Range The cheapest places charge about US$35 per person per day, including three meals. Most are in or near the village. You can get a bed for about US$15 or US$20 if you cook for yourself. (There aren't any real restaurants outside the hotels.) A few places allow you to camp. If you can't get through on the phone, call the pulpería (☎ 771-2336) and leave a message.

At the family-run ***Cabinas Jade Mar*** *(☎ 284-6681 cellular, fax 786-6358)*, up a hill behind La Bahía store, are five double rooms, each with bath and fan; there's electricity from 6 to 9 pm. Marta Pérez Mendoza, the owner, arranges boat rides to/from Sierpe for US$15, as well as inexpensive local tours. The friendly ***El Mirador Cabinas*** *(☎ 387-9138 cellular)*, up a steep path at the north end of Bahía Drake, has three rustic rooms with baths and double beds. A fourth cabin is being built on the hill above. All the rooms have superb views, and solar power is used. ***Cabinas Cecilia*** has rooms with private and shared baths on the beach and can also arrange cheap tours. Cecilia is Marleny's sister (see Drake Bay Wilderness Resort, below) and you can leave a message there for Cecilia.

Rancho Corcovado Lodge *(in San José ☎ 240-4085)* has seven rooms with private baths sleeping from two to four people. Rates are US$40 to US$45 including meals. Campers can set up a tent for US$6, which allows use of bathrooms.

Jinetes de Osa *(☎/fax 385-9541, messages ☎ 233-3333; in the USA 800-317-0333, 303-838-0969, crventur@costaricadiving.com)* is a PADI dive facility that offers a certification course for about US$300 as well as two-tank dives at Isla del Caño for US$85. Beginners who don't want to be certified can try a 'resort course' for US$140, which includes two dives. All equipment is provided. The hotel has nine rooms with fans, tiled baths (ocean themes), and solar-heated showers for US$60 double, or US$110 double including meals. More rooms are planned, and other tours can be arranged for about US$50 or less.

Away from the village, over the hill dominated by La Paloma Lodge (see below), a path leads to Playa Cocalito, a small beach. Most of the shoreline in the nearby area is rocky, and this little beach is the best bet for an ocean swim, though not at high tide. Right behind Playa Cocalito is the small and rustic Canadian-run ***Cocalito Lodge*** *(☎ 284-6369; in Canada ☎ 519-782-3978, BerryBend@aol.com)*. There are nine basic rooms sleeping from two to four people. Three rooms have their own bathroom downstairs; the others have private in-room bathrooms with tiled floors and solar showers – not fancy, but renovated in the 1998-99 season. A generator powers fans and lights from 6 to 11 pm; otherwise lighting is by candle or flashlight. A restaurant serves seafood and pasta dinners. A small paperback library and beachside bar attract locals and visitors from other lodges. Local guides are used for excursions to all the usual destinations.

The room rates are a modest US$20 or US$30 per person (less from April 15 to November 15) depending on the room, and a meal plan costs US$35 a day, though you can eat à la carte if you prefer. There are three tents with foam pads, sheets, and towels available for US$10 per person. You can camp here in your own tent for US$7 if you are backpacking through; this allows use of showers, bathrooms, and restaurant.

Top End The ***Drake Bay Wilderness Resort*** *(☎/fax 770-8012; San José reservations ☎ 256-7394; US reservations 561-371-3437, email: emichaud@drakebay.com, Web: www.drakebay.com)* is run by a US-*tica* couple, Herb and Marleny, and is the longest established and most laid-back of the Bahía Drake lodges. The camp is on a low headland, so you can explore the tide pools or swim in the ocean (although the swimming is rocky and depends on the tide). You can borrow a canoe to go up the Río Agujas at high tide to explore the forest and look for birds and monkeys – or you can hang out in a hammock and wait for the monkeys to come to you. A small troop lives around the lodge and can often be seen swinging around the property. All the local tours are offered (see Activities & Organized Tours, above). In addition, mountain bikes are available, there is a trail to a small iguana and butterfly 'farm,' and tours are offered to Isla Violín, a remote and rarely visited area.

Most of the accommodations are in comfortable cabins with fans and private solar-heated tiled showers, and most have patios with ocean views. A few slightly cheaper large walk-in tents with electricity and beds are available only in the January-to-April drier months. Access to bathrooms (for the tents) is nearby, and free one-day laundry service is offered. A generator provides electricity and a radiotelephone provides phone and fax links with the outside world. Tasty and ample home-cooked meals are provided in the screened dining room just a few meters away from the Pacific Ocean. A nice bar by the beach offers complimentary snacks in the evening.

Visitors normally come on one of several tour packages that include flights from San José into the lodge's private airstrip, which is a short boat ride from the lodge (see Getting There & Away). The standard four-day/three-night package, including all meals and two guided tours (normally to Corcovado and to Isla del Caño, though others are available), costs US$695/1240 single/double. Four-day/three-night specialized packages offer kayaking (US$615 per person), fishing (US$740 per person), and scuba diving (US$700 per person, two-person minimum). The lodge has a complete dive facility with a fully certified and experienced dive master. For a bit of everything, try their seven-night/six-day 'Week of Paradise' package with daily tours for US$940 per person (two minimum). Discounts are offered during low season, or with full advance payment, or for families with children. This lodge is especially popular with family groups.

A five-minute walk up a hill above Bahía Drake brings you to the recommended ***La Paloma Lodge*** *(☎ 239-2801, ☎/fax 239-0954, lapaloma@lapalomalodge.com)*. La Paloma's hilltop location gives splendid views of the ocean and forest and catches whatever sea breezes may waft by. There are plenty of birds around; local species often nest on the grounds. English-speaking guides with biology training are on hand to help guests identify what they see.

The lodge has a compressor and diveshop with all equipment. They are justly proud of their 36-foot pontoon boat that makes fast time to Isla del Caño and is currently the most spacious and comfortable dive boat at Drake. In addition, the lodge has a small swimming pool with great ocean views – perfect for a cooling dip after a sweaty rainforest hike. One end is about 9 feet deep and is used for beginner's scuba-diving lessons (or just to practice if you haven't dived for a while).

Scuba diving costs US$110 per person for a two-tank dive, but is discounted to just US$50 if purchased with a package. All the usual tours are available, ranging from US$55 to US$80 per person. Kayaks are available at no charge.

All the lodge buildings are elevated on stilts to take maximum advantage of breeze and views. There are four standard rooms and five deluxe ranchos. The four spacious standard rooms, each with a queen and single bed (another bed can be added on request), have plenty of closet space and great ventilation. The private bathrooms have hot water and are designed with a shoulder-high wall so you can enjoy rainforest views while showering. Each room has a large private balcony with a hammock and rainforest and ocean views. The high-season rate is US$244 double including meals (see below for packages.)

Five secluded, spacious, thatched-roof ranchos, each surrounded by exuberant vegetation and with a wide, wrap-around balcony, can sleep two to five people on two levels – great for families. Each rancho has a private hot-water bathroom. Spending a night listening to the rain beating down on the thatch is very romantic, and these ranchos are my favorite rooms in Drake. Rates are US$291 double or US$122 per person (three to five people).

Single occupancy is possible if there's room. Electric power is available at night. Excellent meals are served in a beautiful dining room/clubhouse with a high thatched roof. Roundtrip boat transfer from Sierpe costs an additional US$35, or US$65 with taxi from the airport in Palmar.

Because of the lodge's smaller size, Mike and Sue Kalmbach, its US owners, try to give personalized service to their guests and hire friendly staff. Complete packages are available. A three-night package, including air travel from San José to Palmar Sur, land and boat travel to the lodge, two tours of your choice, park fees, taxes, and all meals, costs US$735/1350 single/double in standard rooms and US$845/1570 in the ranchos. Four- and five-night packages are offered and children 14 and under get a 15% discount. The Kalmbachs' son, Colby (age 14 in 2000), spends all his vacation time here.

On the east side of the Río Agujas is the ***Aguila de Osa Inn*** *(☎ 232-7722, fax 296-2190, info@aguiladeosa.com)*. This is considered the most upscale lodge in the area, specializing in sportfishing and scuba packages. There are 11 very nice rooms and two suites, all with attractive views, 24-hour electricity, fans, large tiled baths with hot water, and beautifully carved wooden doors on each room. High-season room rates are US$186/291 single/double including tax and all three meals, served with elegant settings in an open-air restaurant. (The food is recommended.) The junior suite costs US$314 and the master suite costs US$349, both double occupancy. The rate for deep-sea fishing is US$800 per day per boat, which will take four anglers. Inshore fishing is cheaper. Scuba diving costs US$110 for a two-tank dive. All the other usual local tours are available. This lodge tends to attract adults rather than families, and the bar stays open later (most other lodges wind down by about 9 or 10 pm, unless they have a partying group). Rooms are far enough away from the bar that its late hours don't preclude sleep.

Entertainment

The ***Aguila de Osa Inn*** stays open later than most lodge bars and has music.

Up some steep stairs at the south end of Bahiá Drake is ***Bar Mar y Sombra***, a small, rustic hilltop bar with great views of the bay. Stop by for a beer, snack, and a game of pool. ***La Bahía*** is a general store and bar at the south end of Agujitas village. There is a pool table. One or the other of these bars has a dance on weekends.

Getting There & Away

Most people arrive by boat from Sierpe (see the Sierpe Getting There & Away section) after either flying to Palmar Sur or traveling by road. If you have a lodge reservation, the boat ride can be arranged for you. An airstrip near Bahía Drake and north of Agujitas can be reached by chartered flights from San José – this is owned by Drake Bay Wilderness Resort, though other lodges can sometimes use it on request. From the airstrip, depending on water levels and sea conditions, you are transported by boat to Bahía Drake (prepare to get your feet wet) or driven in a jeep. It is a couple of hours faster than taking the scheduled SANSA or Travelair flights to Palmar Sur and continuing by taxi and boat.

A terrible road, accessible only by 4WD in the dry season, links Agujitas with Rancho Quemado (a tiny community to the east). This explains the few trucks and 4WDs seen in the village. Rancho Quemado can be reached on foot or by horseback; ask in Agujitas for the latest possibilities. From Rancho Quemado, a daily bus goes to Rincón, on the road to Puerto Jiménez.

Backpackers can hike to or from Parque Nacional Corcovado (see the following section). If you have a reservation at one of the lodges, they'll arrange to pick you up or drop you off in San Pedrillo, the closest ranger station to Bahía Drake. If you have backpacked in, ask around in the Bahía Drake area for a boat on to Sierpe.

FROM BAHÍA DRAKE TO CORCOVADO

It's not difficult to hike from Bahía Drake to Corcovado along the coast. It takes four to seven hours to reach the San Pedrillo ranger station, and trails continue through the park from there. Dropping tides are always the best for coastal walks – high tides may cut you off or delay you. Ask locally about tide tables and conditions.

The route is usually easy to follow. Walk along the beach or, where a headland cuts you off, look inland for a trail over or around the headland, paralleling the coast. This route is hiked often, so if the trail appears to be overgrown, you're probably on the wrong one. Walk back a bit and try again.

Places to Stay & Eat

Places to stay and eat along this section of coast can all be reached by boat from Sierpe or Bahía Drake, or on foot. I describe them here in the order they are passed when hiking west and then south from Bahía Drake. Camping is possible, though there are no organized campgrounds.

About 30 minutes' walk west is ***Delfin Amor Ecolodge*** *(☎ 394-2632, fax 786-7642, sierra@divinedolphin.com)*, which provides dolphin-interaction trips (see Activities & Organized Tours, earlier in this chapter). This is a small lodge in a lovely setting. Rooms are spacious tent-cabins with two double beds, ocean views, and shared bathrooms; cabins with private bathrooms are planned. Rates are US$50/90/105 single/double/triple including three meals (featuring local fish, fruit, and vegetables). You can also camp for US$10 per person and buy meals for US$20 a day. All the usual Drake tours are available. A nine-day/eight-night package that includes being met at San José International Airport, the first night in San José, air/boat roundtrip transportation to the lodge, three days of dolphin tours, a Corcovado park tour, an Isla del Caño tour, and a free day for another tour, costs US$1200. Extensions are available.

Less than an hour's walk from Drake brings you to ***Corcovado Adventures Tent Camp*** *(☎ 284-1679; in San José 289-3595, info@corcovado.com)*. There are nine large tents, each set up on a wooden platform with a double and single bed, nightstand, and thatched roof to guarantee that it won't leak. There are five bathrooms and a dining room/bar. The rate is US$55 per person including meals (though special discounts at US$40 were recently available). All the usual activities and tour options are available (at extra cost) and the staff can arrange US$15 boat transfers from Sierpe.

Marenco Beach & Rainforest Lodge *(☎ 258-1919, fax 255-1346; in the US ☎ 800-278-6223, info@marencolodge.com)* is about 4 or 5km west of Bahía Drake and 5 or 6km north of Corcovado. Once a biological station, it is now a private Costa Rican-run tropical forest reserve set up to protect part of the rainforest. As such, the 500-hectare reserve plays an important role as a buffer zone around Parque Nacional Corcovado. The reserve is set on a bluff overlooking the Pacific and is a good place for trips to Corcovado, Isla del Caño, or simply into the forest surrounding the station. There are 4km of trails around Marenco, and many of the plant, bird, and other animal species seen in Corcovado can be found in the Marenco area. The Río Claro flows through the south part of the reserve. All the usual excursions can be arranged here, though natural history is emphasized. If you want to scuba dive or fish, they can set you up with one of the Bahía Drake lodges. Whales are sometimes seen off the coast from June to September.

Accommodations are in rustic cabins and bungalows that are elevated enough to catch the breeze. Each room has a private bathroom and a verandah overlooking the Pacific Ocean. There are four bunks in some rooms, but double occupancy is the rule except for student or discounted groups. A generator runs for a few hours in the evening. Meals are served family style in the dining room, where a few reference books are available. There are eight small cabins and 17 more spacious bungalows, and reservations are suggested during the 'dry' busy months of December to April. The wettest months are September and October, when the lodge may well be almost empty.

Most people come on a package deal that includes local tours and meals. During the high season, three days/two nights with one tour cost US$712 double; four days/three nights with two tours cost US$1006 double; and five days/four nights with three tours cost US$1212 double. (Single-supplement charges are moderate and low-season discounts are offered.) Transportation costs extra and the hotel will help you arrange bus, plane, or boat travel. Note that there is no dock at Marenco. Arriving guests transfer from launches to small boats that are anchored offshore – you will almost certainly get your feet wet.

Two or three kilometers to the south of Marenco, you reach Playa San Josecito, one of the larger beach areas along this stretch of coast. Here you'll find ***Poor Man's Paradise*** *(nbon@nnex.net)*, owned by Pincho Amaya, a well-known local sportfisherman, and his American wife, Jenny. Pincho's father homesteaded 160 hectares here in the 1960s and the whole family is now involved in running the tourism operation. It is open from November 15 to May 15, when the owners can be reached in Costa Rica *(☎ 383-4209 cellular, fax 786-6358)*. The rest of the year, Jenny and Pincho are in the US *(☎ 715-588-3950, ☎/fax 877-588-9435, 12430 Nixon Rd, Minocqua, WI 54548)*. They are right on the beach, and it's about a 20-minute walk to a snorkeling area and about two hours to the Parque Nacional Corcovado border. Six cabin tents (shared bath) cost US$39 per person, five cabins with private baths cost US$55 per person, and two cabins with shared baths cost US$45 per person, all including home-cooked meals (fish, shrimp, and chicken are featured). This is a chance to hang out with a tico family. Backpackers can camp here for US$7 and use the bathroom facilities. Meals cost US$7 (breakfast or lunch) and US$10 (dinner), though cheaper meals can be arranged if you stay for a few days. There is electricity from dusk till 9 pm. All the local tours can be arranged, and Pincho can take guests sportfishing at moderate rates (by sportfishing standards).

Also near Playa San Josecito is ***Jungle Al's*** *(☎ 768-7323, 786-6534, fax 786-6635, 786-6335)*. Note that these numbers are in Palmar and you may have to leave a message. Jungle Al's has one cabin with a double and single bed, private bath, and ocean view that rents for US$60/80/100 single/double/triple, including meals cooked over a wood fire, and a few rustic bungalows with shared showers rent for US$50/70/90. The staff can arrange an 11-day/10-night package that includes three days of hiking and camping in the rainforest, as well as the more usual excursions, for US$2249 per person (two minimum, four maximum) including air transport from San José.

Finally, a couple of kilometers south of Playa San Josecito, right on the national park boundary, is the comfortable and recommended ***Casa Corcovado Jungle Lodge*** *(☎ 256-3181, fax 256-7409; in the USA ☎ 888-896-6097, corcovado@sol.racsa.co.cr)*. This lodge is a steep 10-minute climb up from the beach (a tractor hauls up luggage and visitors), and trails from the property directly enter the national park (San Pedrillo ranger station is a 45-minute walk away). The lodge has 24-hour electricity from a hydroelectric and solar-power system, and it recycles. There are 10 bungalows, each screened all the way around for cross breezes and good views, and each has ceiling fans and spacious tiled bathrooms with hot showers. Bungalows have one or two beds. The rate is US$100 per person with meals. The restaurant/bar has good forest views (bring binoculars to spot the many birds) and tasty fresh meals. Halfway between the lodge and the beach is the Margarita Sunset Bar, with great sunset views. The staff was friendly and informed when I stopped by, and they offer all the usual tours, excursions, and package deals. For example, three nights cost US$725 per person, roundtrip from San José, including meals, tours to Corcovado and Isla del Caño, and park fees.

RESERVA BIOLÓGICA ISLA DEL CAÑO

This 300-hectare island is roughly 20km west of Bahía Drake. The reserve is of interest to snorkelers, divers, biologists, and archaeologists. About 5800 hectares of ocean are designated as part of the reserve.

Snorkelers will find incredibly warm water (almost body temperature!) and a good variety of marine life ranging from fish to sea cucumbers. The water is much clearer here than along the mainland coast. Scuba diving trips are arranged by the Bahía Drake area lodges – there are four dive sites with coral reefs, underwater rock formations, and abundant sea life. A tropical beach with an attractive rainforest backdrop provides sunbathing opportunities, and a trail leads inland, through an evergreen rainforest, to a ridge at about 110m above sea level.

Near the top, look for some of the rock spheres that were made by pre-Columbian Indian people. Although these spheres have been found in several places in southern

LEE FOSTER

Mysterious pre-Columbian spheres found on Isla del Caño

Costa Rica, archaeologists are still puzzling over their functions. Trees include milk trees (also called cow trees after the drinkable white latex they exude), rubber trees, figs, and a variety of other tropical species. Birds include coastal and oceanic species as well as rainforest inhabitants, but wildlife is not as varied or prolific as on the mainland.

Camping is prohibited, and there are no facilities except a ranger station by the landing beach. The reserve is administered by Parque Nacional Corcovado. Admission costs US$6 per person for land visits and US$3.50 per person per day for scuba diving, which is mainly for divers with some experience. Most visitors arrive with tours arranged with any of the nearby lodges.

PARQUE NACIONAL CORCOVADO

This park has great biological diversity and has long attracted the attention of tropical ecologists who wish to study the intricate workings of the rainforest. The 54,539-hectare park has two sections. Most of it is in

Visiting the Wilderness

Parque Nacional Corcovado is some of the wildest yet most accessible rainforest in Costa Rica. This attracts all kinds of visitors, ranging from young backpackers going it alone for days to retired folks taking a guided day tour.

Corcovado may be accessible and may entice many visitors, but it is definitely a wilderness area, and travel there should not be taken lightly. Recently, a small guided group left Bahía Drake on a day trip to Corcovado. The guide became lost and what was supposed to be a day trip became a nightmare for the tourists, who envisioned spending a night without food or shelter in the rainforest. Fortunately, two group members were able to find their way to the coast (the guide stayed with the rest of the group) and alerted the park rangers, who rapidly raised a search party.

Late that night, the rangers found the group, scratched, shaken, and insect-bitten, but with no major injuries, and helped them back to the coast. Here, a boat took them back to their lodge and safety. The travelers were upset, and understandably so. The park rangers, who work for a pittance and who receive no extra salary for carrying out nighttime rescues, are to be commended for their hard work.

I spoke to several Bahía Drake-area lodge managers and owners following this event. 'What happened?' I asked. The general feeling was that there is no way to have a genuine wilderness experience without some possibility of discomfort, and it is impossible to guarantee that nothing will go wrong. 'There, but for the grace of God, go I,' said one lodge owner. This was an isolated incident.

The bottom line is that this is not Disney's Jungle World. This is the jungle. Even on a guided tour, you are taking a small risk. Live with it and enjoy.

– Rob Rachowiecki

Biological Investigation

A biological station at Sirena houses scientists and students carrying out rainforest research. They get preference over travelers for accommodations. Ongoing research programs mean that some areas close to the station may be off-limits or that trees and sites might be marked with flags, tags, or other markers or equipment. Please avoid disturbing these sites if you come across them.

– Rob Rachowiecki

the southwestern corner of the Península de Osa and protects at least eight distinct types of habitat. This assemblage is considered to be both unique and the best remaining Pacific coastal rainforest in Central America. Later, 12,751 hectares were added on the northeastern side of the Golfo Dulce.

Because of its remoteness, this rainforest remained undisturbed until the 1960s, when logging began in the area. The park was established in 1975, but a few years later gold miners moved into the park with detrimental effects. The miners were evicted in 1986, but some loggers and miners continue to work clandestinely.

Information

Park admission costs US$6 per person per visit. Rangers told me that if you stay for several days, the admission is valid until you leave (in the past you had to pay per day). Puerto Jiménez (see later in this chapter) has the headquarters of the Area de Conservación Osa (Osa Conservation Area, which includes Corcovado; ☎ 735-5036, 735-5580, 735-5282, fax 735-5276). There are several ranger stations; the headquarters is at Sirena, near the coast in the middle of the park. There is also an airstrip at Sirena. Trails link Sirena with three other ranger stations that all permit camping, which costs less than US$2 per person per night. With arrangements made a week in advance, the rangers provide simple but filling meals for about US$7 (less for breakfasts). Food and cooking fuel have to be packed in, and if you just show up, don't expect meals to be available. Camping facilities consist of tent space, water, and latrines.

Sirena provides the main travelers' shelter in the park – a breezy attic area. You still need a sleeping bag and insect netting (or use your tent). There is also a bunkhouse for which you should make reservations in advance. Sleeping fees here are about US$5. The other ranger stations may have sleeping space available, but this is limited and you can't rely on it without reservation. Both La Leona and Los Patos can accommodate up to 12 people.

Reservations for meals at any ranger station or to sleep in the ranger stations can be made through the park's office in Puerto Jiménez (see above). Ask for Carlos Quintero and allow a few days for arrangements to be made. Self-sufficient backpackers can just show up and pay their daily camping fees as they go. Camping is not officially permitted in areas other than at the ranger stations.

Because Corcovado has the best trail system of any rainforest park, it attracts a fair number of backpackers – sometimes as many as two dozen people may be camped at Sirena during the dry season, though there are fewer people at the other stations. During the wettest months (July to November), parts of the trail system or park may be closed; call the park office for current conditions.

Wildlife Watching

The wildlife within the park is varied and prolific. Corcovado is home to Costa Rica's largest population of the beautiful scarlet macaw. Many of the other important or endangered rainforest species are protected here: tapirs, five species of cats, crocodiles, peccaries, giant anteaters, monkeys, and sloths. The rare harpy eagle, which is almost extinct in Costa Rica, may still breed in remote parts of Corcovado. Almost 400 species of birds have been seen here, as well as about 140 mammals and over 500 species of trees. However, it is only fair to say that most of these animals are very hard to see, national park or not, and staying in most of the lodges in the area will yield as good an opportunity for wildlife watching as you'll find in the park.

Trails & Hiking

One of the most exciting aspects of Corcovado for visitors is that there are long-distance trails through the park leading to several ranger stations. At Corcovado, unlike many of Costa Rica's other lowland rainforest parks, backpackers can hike through the park. The trails are primitive, and the hiking is hot, humid, and insect-ridden, but it can be done. For the traveler wanting to spend a few days hiking through a lowland tropical rainforest, Corcovado is the best choice in Costa Rica.

It is safest to go in a small group. One reader claims that he hiked through the park alone and suffered several misadventures. First, he was treed by a herd of 50 to 100 white-lipped peccaries that milled around underneath his tree clicking their teeth in a menacing fashion. Then he was robbed by a gang of youths who apparently were Panamanian poachers capturing scarlet macaws and endangered squirrel monkeys for illegal sale to zoos, collectors, and pet shops. After he had lost, among other things, his insect repellent, his trip ended uncomfortably with hundreds of itchy bug bites.

If, after reading his story, you still want to go, you'll have an easier time of it in the dry season (from January to April) rather than slogging around in calf-deep mud during the wet season. There are fewer bugs in the dry season, too. The largest herds of peccaries are on the Sirena to Los Patos trails, and if you climb about 5 feet off the ground, you'll avoid being bitten if you run into a herd.

You can hike in from the north, south, or east side of the park (see the Península de Osa & Golfo Dulce map) and exit a different way; thus you won't have to retrace your steps.

San Pedrillo to Sirena From the north, walk in along the coast from Bahía Drake and arrive at the San Pedrillo ranger station about a kilometer after entering the park. Allow a day to hike from Drake to San Pedrillo, or hire a boat. Most visitors to this area are on day trips from Bahía Drake lodges. From San Pedrillo, it is an eight- to 10-hour hike to Sirena – check the tide tables or ask at the station. Most of the first few hours' hiking are through coastal rainforest; then the trail follows the beach. En route you'll pass the beautiful waterfall plunging onto the wild beach of Playa Llorona. A few hundred meters south of the waterfall, a small trail leads inland to a cascading river and a refreshing swimming hole. At this point, the Río Llorona must be forded and, at Playa Corcovado two or three hours later, the Río Corcovado must also be crossed. About a kilometer before reaching Sirena, you must ford the Río Sirena, which

A Great Day at Corcovado

One day I was hiking a trail south of Sirena with some friends when we stopped to look at one of the more common rainforest mammals, an agouti. With binoculars, we were all getting excellent looks at this reddish-brown rodent, which looks like an oversize rabbit with a squirrel-like face and an almost nonexistent tail. Suddenly, I saw a slight movement in the bushes behind the agouti and, through binoculars, I found myself staring at a small ocelot. I almost jumped out of my boots in excitement – a jungle cat in the wild! It took a long steady look at me and then melted into the undergrowth. No one else in my group saw it.

That same afternoon I saw all four species of Costa Rican monkeys, a white-nosed coati, and a good number of tropical birds, including trogons, scarlet macaws, a nesting common black hawk, a spectacled owl, and many others. The secret to seeing so much wildlife on one hike is to go in a small group, to hike on a trail that has few visitors, to keep your eyes peeled, and, above all, to have a reasonable amount of good luck. Good luck to you!

– Rob Rachowiecki

Parque Nacional Isla del Coco

This park occupies the entire Isla del Coco (Cocos Island), which is over 500km southwest of Costa Rica in the eastern Pacific. Despite its isolation, Cocos has been known since the early 16th century and was noted on a map drawn by Nicholas Dechiens as far back as 1541. It is extremely wet, with between 6000 and 7000mm of annual rainfall, and thus attracted the attention of early sailors, pirates, and whalers, who frequently stopped for fresh water and, of course, fresh coconuts. Legend has it that some of the early visitors buried a huge treasure here, but, despite hundreds of treasure-hunting expeditions, it has never been found. The heavy rainfall has enabled the island to support thick rainforest that soon covers all signs of digging.

Because of its isolation, Isla del Coco has evolved a unique ecosystem, which is why it is protected with national park status. Over 70 species of animals (mainly insects) and 70 species of plants are reportedly endemic (occurring nowhere else in the world), and more remain to be discovered. Birders come to the island to see the colonies of seabirds, many of which nest on Cocos. Among the approximately 80 birds listed for the park are two species of frigatebirds, three species of boobies, four species of gulls, and six species of storm petrels; more are being added to the list. At least three of the birds are endemic: the Cocos Island cuckoo, Cocos Island finch, and Cocos Island flycatcher. (The Cocos Island finch is part of the group of endemic finches studied in the Galápagos Islands by Darwin; however, the Cocos species was not discovered until almost 60 years after Darwin's visit to the Galápagos.) There are two endemic lizard species. The marine life is also varied, with sea turtles, coral reefs, and tropical fish in abundance. Snorkeling and diving are excellent and are the main activities for visitors.

No people permanently live on the island, although unsuccessful attempts were made to colonize Cocos in the late 19th and early 20th centuries. After the departure of these people,

can be chest-deep in the rainy season and is the largest river on the hike. Note that sharks and crocodiles have been reported near the mouth of this river, so cross as far up from the coast as you can – see where the local rangers and researchers go. The entire distance from San Pedrillo to Sirena is about 23km. This northern trail is the least frequently used one (though there are people hiking it most days during the high season).

La Leona to Sirena From the south, take air or land transportation to Carate, from where it is over an hour's hike to the ranger station at La Leona. From there, it is a six- to seven-hour hike to Sirena, but check that the tides are low – it is a beach hike with several rocky headlands to cross and high tides can cut you off. If you look carefully, you can usually find trails going inland around the headlands. Often, these inland trails offer the best chances to see mammals, though jaguars have been seen loping along the beach. Keep your eyes open for paw prints. The entire distance from Carate to Sirena is about 16km, but parts of the hike are along the beach, where the heat and the loose, sandy footing make it heavy going, especially if you are carrying a big pack. Look for shaded sections in the forest behind the beach.

Los Patos to Sirena From the east, take a bus to La Palma, from where it is about four hours along a rough road to Los Patos ranger station. The road is passable to 4WD vehicles; you can hire a jeep-taxi, or you may be able to hitch a ride in the dry season – but don't count on it, as vehicles are few. This trail/road crosses the river about 20 times in the last 6km before Los Patos. A right turn shortly before the ranger station is easily missed, but there are locals around who can advise you.

Parque Nacional Isla del Coco

feral populations of domestic animals began to create a problem, and today feral pigs are the greatest threat to the unique species native to the island. The pigs uproot vegetation, causing soil erosion that in turn contributes to sedimentation around the island's coasts and damage to the coral reefs surrounding the island. Feral rats, cats, and goats also contribute to the destruction of the natural habitat. Unregulated fishing and hunting pose further threats.

The Servicio de Parques Nacionales is aware of the problem, but lack of funding has made doing anything about it difficult. The island is rugged and heavily forested, with the highest point at Cerro Yglesias (634m). As a practical matter, how *can* you remove a large population of feral pigs from a thickly vegetated and hilly island that is 7.5km long and 4km wide?

Information & Organized Tours

There is a park station, and permission is needed from the park service to visit it. (The dive operator that you choose to use will arrange for the necessary permission.) There are some trails, but camping is not allowed. The few visitors who come stay on their boats; a US$6 per-person park fee is charged.

In Costa Rica, Cocos Travel (☎/fax 290-6737, www.divecocos.com) is the only outfitter specializing in dive trips to Cocos. It operates the 115-foot *Sea Hunter*, sleeping up to 18 passengers in eight cabins, all with private baths, and the slightly smaller *Undersea Hunter*, sleeping up to 14 passengers in six cabins, some with shared bath. The typical cost of a 10-day tour (including seven days of diving with three or four dives a day) is US$3000 from San José.

The US-owned *Okeanos Aggressor* also does 11-day dive cruises. (See Organized Tours in the Getting There & Away chapter.) Note that this trip is for advanced, certified divers; beginners' lessons and certification are not offered.

– Rob Rachowiecki

Try to stick to the 4WD road and you'll find Los Patos more easily; there are other footpaths that have been made by gold miners trying to avoid the ranger station! The birding along this road is reportedly good.

From Los Patos, a 6km trail leads to a small hill with a lookout point from which you can see Laguna Corcovado and a good portion of the park. This makes a good day hike if you want to spend two nights at Los Patos. Backpackers going in through Los Patos continue southwest to Sirena (about six hours). The trail undulates steeply through the hilly forest for two or three hours before finally flattening out near the swampy Laguna Corcovado.

If you hike out of the park through Los Patos, the rangers can help you call a jeep-taxi in the dry months to take you out.

Note that I give fairly conservative times. Fit hikers with light packs can probably move faster, though if you spend a lot of time birding or taking photos, you'll end up taking longer.

Getting There & Away

You can arrange with a Bahía Drake lodge to give you a boat ride to San Pedrillo or Playa Llorona in the northern part of the park; otherwise you'll have to walk.

Several buses a day depart from Puerto Jiménez to La Palma, for entrance via Los Patos.

From Puerto Jiménez it is about 40 or 45km around the southern end of the Península de Osa as far as Carate (see Carate, later in this chapter). A truck or 4WD vehicle leaves Puerto Jiménez at 6 am daily except Sunday for US$6 per person. At other times you can hire a vehicle for US$60. The return to Puerto Jiménez from Carate departs around 8:30 am.

Finally, you can also arrange to fly into either Sirena or Carate with chartered aircraft from San José, Golfito, or Puerto Jiménez. (Allow about US$75 per person for a Puerto Jiménez to Sirena flight.) The Servicio de Parques Nacionales sometimes has planes going in. They may take passengers if space is available, but this is more likely to work for researchers and students, not tourists.

To Corcovado via Puerto Jiménez

FROM THE INTERAMERICANA TO PUERTO JIMÉNEZ

A 78km road joins the Interamericana at Chacarita with Puerto Jiménez. The road is paved but badly potholed for 45km, as far as the small town of **Rincón**, followed by 33km of gravel road to Puerto Jiménez. From Rincón, a very poor road goes to the coast at Bahía Drake. There is a daily bus from Rincón to Rancho Quemado, a community halfway between Rincón and Drake, and unmarked on most maps. Beyond Rancho Quemado, the road is passable to high-clearance 4WD vehicles only in the dry season.

About 9km southeast of Rincón is the village of **La Palma,** from where a rough road goes to Los Patos ranger station. The women of La Palma run a tourist office of sorts, with homemade souvenirs and coffee available. There are restaurants, pulperías, and three inexpensive hotels here, all clustered around a right-angle turn in the main road.

About 21km beyond La Palma and 4km before Puerto Jiménez, a turn to the right leads 8km to **Dos Brazos**, a gold-mining and farming village. A couple of kilometers beyond the village lies the ***Bosque del Río Tigre*** *(fax 735-5045; in the USA ☎/fax 904-532-6775, info@osaadventures.com)*, which is a small private sanctuary and lodge. Run by naturalists Elizabeth Jones and Abraham Gallo, the rustic lodge has four rooms with forest views and shared clean bathrooms and one cabin with a private bath. Solar-powered fans are in the rooms. Rates are US$45 to US$55 per person, including three meals and coffee, tea, and fruit beverages. You can arrange moderately priced horseback rides or hikes to the national park, take gold-panning excursions, or go kayaking. An all-day guided hike across the peninsula ends at Carate, where there are lodges (and where reservations can be made and luggage transported by car). Birding is excellent, and this is a recommended place for a rustic retreat. A *colectivo* taxi (driven by Antonio Garbanzo) leaves from the Super 96 store in Puerto Jiménez at 11 am and 4 pm daily; it leaves Dos Brazos at 7 am and 1:30 pm. If you are driving, 4WD is recommended, as a river must be crossed just before the lodge.

PUERTO JIMÉNEZ

With a growing population of about 7000, Puerto Jiménez is the only town of any size on the Península de Osa. Until the 1960s, the Península de Osa was one of the most remote parts of Costa Rica, with exuberant rainforests and a great variety of plants and animals. Then logging began, and later gold was discovered, creating a minor gold rush and increased settlement. In the face of this, Parque Nacional Corcovado was created in 1975. Logging and gold mining go on around the park, but within the park a valuable and unique group of rainforest habitats is preserved.

The gold rush and logging industry, along with the accompanying colonization, made Puerto Jiménez a fairly important little town and, because access is now relatively straightforward, there is a burgeoning tourist industry. Ticos like to come to Puerto Jiménez partly for its slightly frontier atmosphere and also partly for the pleasant beaches nearby. Foreigners tend to come because this is the entry town to the famous Parque Nacional Corcovado, which has an administration/information office here. It is a pleasant and friendly town and still remote enough that you can see parrots and macaws flying around.

Information

Doña Isabel, the Travelair agent (☎ 735-5062, fax 735-5043, osatropi@sol.racsa.co.cr)

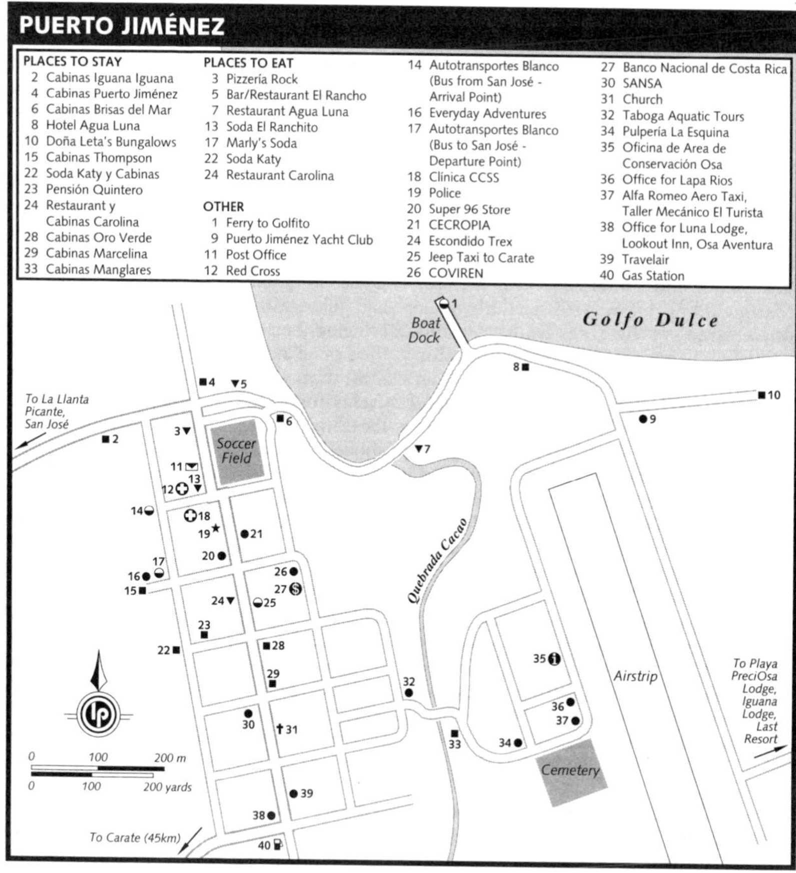

is a good source of local travel information and handles hotel and transportation arrangements of all kinds. She has a radio to call lodges in both the peninsula and Golfito areas. The folks listed under Organized Tours, below, are also an excellent source of local information.

The Oficina de Area de Conservación Osa (☎ 735-5036, 735-5282, 735-5580, fax 735-5276) has information about Corcovado, Isla del Caño, Parque Nacional Marino Ballena (see the Central Pacific Coast chapter), and Golfito parks and reserves. Hours are 8 am to noon and 1 to 4 pm weekdays, though phones are sometimes answered on weekends. They have up-to-date information on Corcovado. Two organizations that work on local environmental issues are CECROPIA (☎ 735-5532) and COVIREN; their information offices are shown on the Puerto Jiménez map.

The Banco Nacional de Costa Rica (☎ 735-5020) changes cash dollars. International phone calls can be made from an office opposite the Restaurant Carolina. Emergency medical treatment can be obtained at the Clínica CCSS, or call the Red Cross (☎ 735-5109).

Organized Tours

Escondido Trex (☎/fax 735-5210, osatrex@sol.racsa.co.cr), which is run by Tom Boylan, has an office in the Restaurant Carolina. They do various tours from half a day to 10 days, involving primarily kayaking for all levels of experience, but also other trips. They can make lodge and hotel reservations. Personable naturalist Andy Pruter runs Everyday Adventures (☎/fax 735-5138, everyday@sol.racsa.co.cr), specializing in sea kayaking and rainforest treks in the Osa area, including hikes with a climb up a hollow strangler fig tree. Both day and overnight adventures are available. Ask for him at the Restaurant Carolina or Travelair office, or check his house, shown on the map. (There's a sign.) Both have been recommended by readers. Rates are negotiable depending on group size, etc, but figure on about US$30 a half day or US$125 a day for multiday trips, including accommodations and meals.

Tours can also be arranged with Osa Aventura (☎/fax 735-5431, osaventura@bananaadventuretours.com), across from the gas station. Run by tropical biologists Mike and Olivier, this company specializes in adventure treks of up to 10 days in the Península de Osa. Juan Blanco S (☎ 735-5440, 735-5310, fax 735-5045) is a local naturalist guide. Taboga Aquatic Tours (☎ 735-5265, fax 735-5121, Marine Radio Channel 12) is run by local fisherman Marco Loaiciga, who has been recommended for fishing and snorkeling trips as well as boat sightseeing. George (☎ 735-5051), down by the Puerto Jiménez Yacht Club, also arranges a variety of boat trips.

About 6km from town, off the road to San José, is the well-recommended and delightfully named La Llanta Picante (☎/fax 735-5414, spicytire@aol.com). Spanish for 'The Spicy Tire,' La Llanta Picante specializes in customized mountain-bike excursions using high-quality Trek and Kona bikes, and they also have bike trailers for pulling small children (or gear) and even a tandem. This is a family-oriented operation run by a small group of American and Costa Rican cyclists and outdoors-people; they also have kayaks available and arrange fishing, hiking, and wildlife-watching excursions. Sample rates are US$65 for a full day of biking, including bike and guide, with discounts for groups, people bringing their own bike, or those staying at their small lodge (see Places to Stay).

In town, Pizzería Rock has a few basic bicycles for rent. Some hotels can arrange local tours, often with the folks mentioned above.

Places to Stay

Budget During Easter week, many hotels are full. On dry-season weekends, hotel choices can be limited. Call ahead to make reservations, or arrive in midweek. Rates below are for the dry high season; the usual discounts apply for wet low season.

You can camp inexpensively on the grass at the so-called ***Puerto Jiménez Yacht Club***, which has a basic bathroom but no lockers.

The ***Pensión Quintero*** *(☎ 735-5087)* has clean rooms, some without windows or fans, though table fans are provided on request. Shared bathroom facilities are rustic, and rates here start at US$4 per person.

The friendly ***Cabinas Marcelina*** *(☎ 735-5007, fax 735-5045, osanatur@sol.racsa.co.cr)* offers six clean rooms with fans and basic private cold showers for US$7/12/17 single/double/triple. The ***Restaurant y Cabinas Carolina*** *(☎ 735-5185)* has five clean rooms with baths that cost US$5.50 per person. Also try the similarly priced ***Soda Katy y Cabinas*** and ***Cabinas Thompson*** *(☎ 735-5140)*.

Cabinas Brisas del Mar *(☎ 735-5012)* rents 14 clean rooms with fans and private showers for US$6.50 per person. ***Cabinas Puerto Jiménez*** *(☎ 735-5090)* rents rooms that are clean, friendly, and good value for about US$7.50 per person with baths and fans. (Both of these are close to El Rancho bar, which can be loud on weekends.) The ***Cabinas Oro Verde*** *(☎ 735-5241)* has good clean rooms with private baths and fans for US$7.50 per person. ***Cabinas Iguana Iguana*** *(☎ 735-5158)* is also in this price range and has a small restaurant and swimming pool (which was closed for repairs when I visited).

Mid-Range The ***Cabinas Manglares*** *(☎ 735-5002, fax 735-5121)* is away from the town center. A small café and a little mangrove area are behind the hotel, where you can look for frogs, etc. Rooms with fans and private baths cost US$15/25.

Near the boat dock, the ***Hotel Agua Luna*** *(☎/fax 735-5393, 735-5108)* has the only air-conditioned rooms in town. Its six air-conditioned rooms with two beds, a large bathroom, TV, and minifridge cost US$40 double. Four smaller rooms without a fridge cost US$35, and four rooms with private baths, TV, and fans cost US$12.50 per person.

Doña Leta's Bungalows *(☎/fax 735-5180, letabell@sol.racsa.co.cr)* has seven separate cabins close to the beach. Cabins are spacious and have screens, with attractively carved wooden doors. All have a kitchenette with minifridge, fans, and warm-water baths. The cabins surround an open-air restaurant/bar that serves beer and seafood. A volleyball net, horseshoe pits, and kayaks are available for guests. Behind the cabins are mangroves where, the owners told me, there is a huge egret rookery with most of the nesting activity in May and June. Published rates are US$45 per person including breakfast, but you can get much better rates by calling locally. Some cabins will sleep up to six people.

La Llanta Picante *(☎/fax 735-5414, spicytire@aol.com)* is 6km from town; to get there, take the San José road and look for a road to the right just beyond the Dos Brazos turnoff. This lodge minimizes ecological impact by using local building techniques, composting toilets (they really do work), and solar energy. Mountain-bike tours are their specialty (see Organized Tours, above). The lodge has four large, screened rooms with porches and shared bathrooms. Three rooms sleep from two to four and a bunkroom can sleep up to 12 people. Rates are US$55/100 single/double including three plentiful and varied meals a day, plus US$10 per child or US$30 per person over 13. Note that the lodge's phone service is limited; it's best to fax them between 8 am and 8 pm, Monday to Thursday, Costa Rican time, or telephone between 2 and 3 pm Monday and Wednesday.

Several lodges have opened on Playa Preciosa/Playa Platanares, about 5km east of the airstrip. The ***Playa PreciOsa Lodge*** *(☎ 735-5062, fax 735-5043)* is popular with German-speaking tourists. Four simple circular thatched bungalows, each with a loft, private bathroom, fan, and patio with hammocks, cost US$65 double, with simple meals available at extra cost. A reader writes that he negotiated rates including meals, but was charged extra for them at the end of his stay. Negotiate carefully to avoid misunderstandings.

Nearby is the small but attractive ***Iguana Lodge*** *(☎ 735-5205, fax 735-5436, info@iguanalodge.com)*, with two cabins, each with a private tiled bath downstairs and a master bedroom upstairs to catch the cooling breezes, and with both ocean and forest views. Rates are US$65/110 single/double, including three good meals in the tall lodge building, which has a Ping-Pong and pool table and is an ideal place to relax. The Tuesday-night spaghetti dinners are locally popular, and the lodge has an information office next to the police station in Puerto Jiménez. Also near here is the beach-side ***Last Resort*** *(☎/fax 735-5474, in Canada ☎ 250-344-7431)*, with six simple rooms with private bath at US$60 double. Meals are available.

Also see South of Puerto Jiménez, below.

Places to Eat & Drink

The reasonably priced and centrally located ***Restaurant Carolina*** is perhaps the town's best-known and most popular restaurant and meeting spot. Other inexpensive little places nearby include ***Soda Katy***, ***Soda El Ranchito*** and ***Marly's Soda***, by the main bus stop; all are OK. The ***Restaurant Agua Luna*** has reasonable seafood and a sea view. The ***Pizzería Rock*** serves pizzas and rents bicycles.

The ***Bar/Restaurant El Rancho*** serves meals, has happy hour from 5 to 6 pm, plays danceable music (with dances on weekends), and occasionally gets mildly wild. This is also a good place to meet people. There are several other locally popular bars on the main street near Restaurant Carolina.

Shopping

If you're stocking up on picnic items, one of the best general stores is Pulpería La Esquina, near the airstrip. The Super 96 Store, on the main drag, also has supplies.

Getting There & Away

Air SANSA (☎ 735-5017) has daily flights from San José for US$55/110 while Travelair charges US$100/165. The Travelair agent (see Information, above) is also helpful with other transportation arrangements.

Alfa Romeo Aero Taxi (☎ 735-5178, fax 735-5112) has charter flights to local destinations like Carate, Sirena, Golfito, and other places. Three-seater aircraft can be chartered into Corcovado for about US$180; five-seaters cost US$220. A five-seater charter to San José costs about US$480.

Bus Autotransportes Blanco has buses at 5 and 11 am daily via San Isidro (US$4.50) to San José (nine hours, US$7), although the 5 am bus might not run in the rainy season. There are separate bus stops for arrivals and departures shown on the map. Next to the departure point, Marly's Soda sells tickets 7 to 11 am daily and 1 to 5 pm Monday to Saturday. Buy tickets in advance, especially for the 5 am departure. In San José, buses leave at 6 am and noon from Calle 12, Avenida 9.

There are also buses at 5:30 am and 2 pm daily for Neily (four to six hours, US$3). The San José and Neily buses take you the 23km to La Palma, the eastern exit/entry point for Parque Nacional Corcovado.

Buses may run to Golfito if the ferry is not running. Ask around town for other destinations.

Truck To go to Carate, south of Puerto Jiménez at the southern end of Corcovado, take a jeep/truck that leaves at 6 am daily except Sunday. There may be more departures in the dry season; some departures may be canceled in the wet. The fare is US$6 per person. At other times, you can hire a truck or 4WD taxi for about US$50 or US$60. Ask at the Travelair office for Cyrilo Espinosa.

Car Drivers will find Taller Mecánico El Turista (☎ 735-5060, 735-5161) next to the Alfa Romeo Aero Taxi office. This is the best mechanic in the area.

Boat The passenger ferry to Golfito leaves at 6 am daily, takes 1½ hours, and costs US$3.

SOUTH OF PUERTO JIMÉNEZ

It is 45km by dirt road around the tip of the Península de Osa to the end of the road at Carate near Parque Nacional Corcovado. The road is driveable in a 2WD vehicle all the way during the dry season, though there are some pretty rough stretches where you'll need to drive very carefully unless you have high clearance. In the wet season, 4WD is needed. All places in this section can be reached by taxi from Puerto Jiménez, or the scheduled jeep/truck to Carate can drop you off at the entrance roads.

About 16km from Puerto Jiménez is the ***Buena Esperanza Bar***, where you can get a cold drink or snack. A kilometer beyond, on the left and slightly set back from the road, is a white cement gate (locally called El Portón Blanco) that leads into a hilly area above the coast, with dirt roads accessing several small lodges and houses for rent; ask in Puerto Jimenéz about others that may be available beyond those I've listed below.

El Portón Blanco Area

Casa Bambu *(in the USA ☎ 512-263-1650, fax 512-263-7553, casabambu@earthlink.net)* is a rustic two-story wooden house set back 100m from the beach. Each of its three bedrooms has a double bed, indoor bathroom and open-air shower, kitchen, dining room, covered porch, and solar-powered fans. Rates are US$90 for two people, US$35 for additional people, three-night minimum, with discounts for larger groups and children. Meals are available at lodges within walking distance, and maid service is offered. ***Encanta La Vida*** *(☎ 735-5062, fax 735-5043; in the USA ☎ 805-969-4270, fax 805-969-0238)* is a 2½-story house (the top story is a lookout tower) with four bedrooms (two with private baths) and nearby beach access; kayaks are available. Rates, including meals and services, are US$70 per person; two-day minimum.

Hacienda Bahía Esmeralda *(☎ 381-8521 cellular, fax 735-5045, pandulce@sol.racsa .co.cr)* has two large rooms in the main lodge and three comfortably appointed cabins, all with private bath and fans. High-season rates are US$100 per person including three excellent meals and beverages; discounts for weeklong stays are offered. The owner, Brett Harter, is a musician, and spontaneous parties have been known to occur!

Lapa Rios

A few hundred meters beyond El Portón Blanco, on the right side of the road, is Lapa Rios, a fabulous wilderness resort in a 400-hectare private nature reserve, 80% of which is virgin forest. Lapa Rios has a commitment to conserve and protect the surrounding rainforest; it created a program for training locals to work at the lodge and built a new school for their children. The excellent local guides include an indigenous shaman who knows medicinal plants and talks about the ancient spiritual value of the rainforest, and natural history guides who can educate guests about their surroundings. The resort won the British Airways 1995 Tourism for Tomorrow Award for the Americas, an award given to encourage environmentally responsible tourism.

The main activities are hiking the extensive trail system and nature observation. Most of the trails are steep and not recommended for people with walking limitations, though a 3km path on the property gives easy access to the rainforest.

A medium-difficulty trail system near the lodge offers scenic looks at a waterfall and huge strangler fig as well as good birding. Longer, more difficult trails require guides (US$20 to US$30 depending on length) and include a hike to the border of the Corcovado park, a wild and difficult trek to a 30m waterfall, a night walk (by flashlight), and other options.

A beach about 500m from the lodge offers tide pools, surfing, swimming, and snorkeling opportunities. Boogie boards can be rented. Horse rental starts at US$30 per half day (two people minimum). A guided boat tour to Casa de Orquídeas botanical garden (US$40 per person) or a guided natural history cruise up the Río Esquinas estuary and mangroves (US$60 per person) can be arranged, as can excursions to Corcovado or fishing trips (about US$500 per day, five or six people). A massage therapist is also available.

The impressive lodge has a pool, restaurant, bar, reading room, and wonderful views. Particularly memorable is the soaring thatched roof of the restaurant, which towers, cathedral-like, over diners. A long spiral staircase climbs three stories to an observation deck near the rooftop. Fourteen spacious and attractive wooden bungalows are scattered over the site, and some of them are a long climb up or down a steep path (with stairs) that would be difficult to access if you have a mobility problem. Each has a large bathroom (two sinks!) and hot water, electricity, fan, two queen-size beds with mosquito nets (more for a romantic display than necessity), large screened view windows, and an ample deck, and rent for US$270/364 single/double, including three meals. A transfer from Puerto Jiménez costs US$20 roundtrip. If you are driving, it's 19km from Puerto Jiménez airport.

Make reservations in Puerto Jiménez *(☎ 735-5130, fax 735-5179, info@laparios .com)*. Lapa Rios has an office near the Puerto Jiménez airport.

Bosque del Cabo

South of Lapa Rios, the road continues through the Cabo Matapalo area, the southernmost cape on the peninsula. There are stands of virgin forest interspersed with cattle ranches and great ocean views.

Two kilometers beyond Lapa Rios, a signed turn to the left leads two more kilometers to Bosque del Cabo, a recommended wilderness lodge set in about 140 hectares, half of it virgin forest. There are eight rustic but attractive thatched-roof bungalows set on a bluff with ocean views (whales pass by from December to March), comfortable beds, and sun-warmed showers. The showers are outside each bungalow and, while completely private, give the impression of bathing in the forest. (The flush toilet is inside.) The bungalows are spaced apart for privacy, and two of them have fantastic ocean views from private patios. Four deluxe units are slightly larger and have solar power and decks or porches; four standard cabins are romantically lit by candles. There is electricity in the main lodge, where good food is served family-style. A swimming pool is naturally filled by a spring and emptied for cleaning every 10 days. It's a 15-minute hike down to the beach.

Birding in the area is excellent and hikes can be taken (alone or with a naturalist guide) through the forest, to the ocean, to nearby rivers, and to a waterfall. Large flocks of scarlet macaws are commonly seen. Horseback riding (US$35 per person), tide pool exploration, and swimming are all options.

Rates are US$134/206 single/double, including three big meals (US$149/238 for the deluxe units). There is also a house with two bedrooms, each with private hot bath, full kitchen, and hydroelectric energy that powers the fridge, blender, and microwave. This is a particularly good place for long-stay visitors who want to prepare their own meals (though they can also buy meals at the restaurant), with rates at US$1050 per week for up to four people.

Make reservations in Puerto Jiménez (*☎ 735-5443, fax 735-5206, boscabo@sol.racsa.co.cr*) or contact the lodge (*☎ 381-4847 cellular, phil@bosquedelcabo.com*).

CARATE

This is the beginning of the road if you are departing from Corcovado, or the end of the road if you are arriving at the park from Puerto Jiménez. There is an airstrip (chartered flights only) and a pulpería. If you are driving, you can leave your car here (US$3 a night) and hike to the tent camp (less than an hour) or La Leona ranger station (under two hours).

Places to Stay & Eat

Apart from the airstrip and pulpería, there is no village as such, but there are small lodges nearby. Note that communication is often through Puerto Jiménez; a fax, telephone message, or email may not be picked up for several days, so be patient.

A couple of kilometers before the airstrip (coming from Puerto Jiménez) is the friendly and rustic ***Playa Carate Jungle Camp*** (*☎ 735-5049, 735-5211, fax 735-5207, leegott@aol.com*). Six large, screened, but simple cabins with shared showers cost US$50 per person, including three meals. There is electricity till 9 pm. Camping costs US$5 per tent (or US$10 in their tent) and meals cost US$5 each.

A little closer to the airstrip, the ***Lookout Inn*** (*☎/fax 735-5431, wendy@lookout-inn.com*) has three lovely rooms with hand-carved wooden doors and private hot showers. The small lodge has an observation deck with pretty coastal and rainforest views (the beach is a short walk away) and a swimming pool. It also has a walk-in wine cellar and homemade tropical fruit wines, which owners Terry and Wendy will be proud to serve you. Guided and on-your-own hikes are available, and kayaking, fishing, and horseback riding can be arranged. Rates are US$99/178 single/double including meals.

Just beyond the airstrip and behind the pulpería, the Río Carate comes steeply out of the rainforested coastal hills. A steep road (4WD needed) goes about 2km up the river valley to the new ***Luna Lodge*** (*☎/fax 735-5431, information@lunalodge.com*), opening at the end of 1999. The hillside location gives superb views, and the high-roofed, open-sided restaurant takes full advantage of them. Five cabins were under construction when I visited; they look like they will be both spacious and comfortable, with private baths and a design that blends into the surrounding rainforest. Lodge owner and operator Lana Wedmore has 20 years of experience in Costa Rican tourism and is sure to do a great job of realizing her dream of a small, special lodge in the rainforest. Rates for 2000 (which will probably rise once the lodge becomes more established) are US$100/175 single/double including meals with plenty of organically grown food from the lodge garden. The usual tours are offered, and you can take a guided hike from here to the Bosque del Río Tigre in Dos Brazos.

CORCOVADO LODGE TENT CAMP

This comfortable tent camp is just 500m from the southern border of Parque Nacional Corcovado, and 1.7km west of Carate along the beach. Owned and operated by Costa Rica Expeditions (see Organized Tours in the Getting Around chapter), it makes an excellent base from which to explore Corcovado in reasonable comfort as well as being a restful place to stay for those who have hiked through the national park. A great feature here is an exciting canopy platform that can be accessed for day and overnight trips.

A sandy beach fronts the camp. A steep trail leads to the rainforest 100m away, where a 160-hectare private preserve is available for hiking and wildlife observation. The lodge is low impact, with 20 walk-in tents, two bath houses (with eight individual showers, toilets, and wash basins), a dining room, and a bar/lounge area. A small generator provides electricity to the dining room and bath houses only – a flashlight is needed in the tents. Each tent is 3m square, high enough to stand up in, is pitched on a platform, and contains a canopied deck and two beds with linens. All sides are screened to allow maximum ventilation. Food is served family-style and is excellent and plentiful.

This is a chance to camp in the wilderness in relative comfort. 'Relative' means that you should think of the possibility of high humidity and temperatures reaching the upper 30°s C, as well as biting insects during the day.

Rates are US$57/96 single/double including breakfast and dinner (the meals are all-you-can-eat, so this is certainly a good budget option if you bring some lunch snacks), or US$75/133 with three meals. Coffee and purified water are available all day, and a bar serves soft and alcoholic drinks. Meals cost US$13 for breakfast, US$18 for lunch, and US$21 for dinner. A tent with no meals costs US$30 per person. While reservations are encouraged, if you just show up, you can eat or sleep if space is available. The staff is friendly and helpful.

A variety of tours and activities are offered. You can take the 3km hike through the rainforest behind the lodge – good views and lots of birds and monkeys – or you can hike along the beach into the park. These hikes are self-guided and free. Guided hikes to more remote areas in the park cost US$25 to US$40 per person, depending on the length and difficulty of the hike. Horses can be rented. Sunset horse rides (3½ hours) cost US$35.

The canopy platform is halfway up a 60m-tall guapinol *Hymenaea courbaril* tree (although the platform is moved every few years). It is within the private reserve, about a 30-minute hike up from the lodge. Access to the platform is by a rope and pulley system. Basically, you sit in a seat that is winched up to the platform by hand, a slow ride that gives you plenty of time to enjoy the changing views of the different levels of the forest. All visitors wear a hard hat and a body harness attached to a separate belay as a safety back-up. The operators of both winch and belay are fully trained and safety is assured. Once you arrive, you are secured to a rope that allows free movement around the platform in safety.

Visitors normally take a half-day tour to the canopy that lasts about four to five hours and allows at least two hours on the platform. Guides are not only trained in platform safety but are well versed in ecology and wildlife spotting and identification. Visitors need to be patient; animals can take an hour or two to appear. The cost is US$69 per person (two minimum, six maximum). Overnight canopy stays for US$125 per person (two maximum) offer the chance to sleep on foam pads in a tent pitched on the platform, accompanied by a guide.

Most guests arrive on a package trip that includes roundtrip flights from San José to Carate, luggage transfer by horse cart from Carate to the lodge (you hike in), meals, tours, and a local canopy guide. One of the most popular packages is for three days and two nights, with a canopy platform tour and preserve hiking. These cost US$569 per person (three minimum) and have fixed departures several times a week. Note that the third day is a travel day, returning to San José about lunchtime. Additional nights can be added at US$67 per person, including meals. Too expensive? Take a bus to Puerto Jiménez, a shared taxi to Carate, and make reservations for the nights you want to stay.

Many other options are available from Costa Rica Expeditions in San José, which is in radio communication with the tent camp. You can also choose to be accompanied by a trained bilingual naturalist guide throughout your trip; this is considerably more expensive but worth it for an in-depth learning experience.

Northern Golfo Dulce Area

GOLFITO

Golfito is named after a tiny gulf that emerges into the much larger Golfo Dulce, a large Pacific Ocean gulf just west of Panama. It is the most important port in the far southern part of Costa Rica, although its maritime importance has declined greatly in recent years. From 1938 to 1985 Golfito was the center of a major banana-growing region, and for many years it was the headquarters of the United Fruit Company. However, a combination of declining foreign markets, rising Costa Rican export taxes, worker unrest, and banana diseases led to the closing of the United Fruit complex in 1985. Some of the plantations have since been turned to African palm-oil production, but this didn't alleviate the high unemployment and economic loss caused by United Fruit's departure.

In the late 1980s a small tourism industry began in the area, and it has since blossomed. The town is pleasantly situated, and visitors often stop by for a day or two en route to somewhere else. There are good surfing and swimming beaches nearby (though none in Golfito itself – Playa Cacao, across the little gulf, is the closest). The town is surrounded by the steep hills of the Refugio Nacional de Fauna Silvestre Golfito, which create a splendid rainforest backdrop and have good birding opportunities. There are a couple of good fishing/boating marinas. Boats and light planes cross the Golfo Dulce to the Península de Osa, where Parque Nacional Corcovado is found. A growing number and good variety of hotels as well as a number of interesting jungle lodges have been pioneered by adventurous expats. The Golfito area has a distinct sense of community, and businesses are often referred to by their owners' names.

In an attempt to boost the economy of the region, Costa Rica built a duty-free facility in the northern part of Golfito. 'Duty-free' is a misnomer, because items for sale here are still heavily taxed and do not offer significant savings for foreign tourists. Nevertheless, the taxes here are substantially lower than elsewhere in Costa Rica, which lures ticos from all over the country into visiting Golfito on shopping sprees for microwave ovens and TV sets. In order to do so, however, they must spend at least 24 hours in Golfito, which can put hotel rooms at a premium on weekends, especially near holidays.

Golfito is still, superficially, two towns strung out along a coastal road with a backdrop of steep, thickly forested hills. The southern part of town is where you find most of the bars and businesses – this sector feels pleasantly decrepit in the way tropical seaports tend to be, but without the usual hustle and danger. Warner Brothers chose this site to film *Chico Mendes*, the true story of a Brazilian rubber tapper's efforts to preserve the rainforest.

The northern part of town was the old United Fruit Company headquarters, and it retains a languid, tropical air with its large, well-ventilated homes with verandahs and attractively landscaped surroundings. Several of these houses now offer inexpensive accommodations. The airport and duty-free zone are also at this end.

The port is a well-protected one, and a few foreign yachts on oceanic or coastal cruises are usually anchored here, as well the occasional freighter looming above the local taxi boats and fishing launches.

Information

Land Sea Tours (☎/fax 775-1614, landsea@sol.racsa.co.cr), located on the shoreline at Km 2, is a good place to get local information – as well as connect to the Internet, get a good sandwich and cup of coffee, book plane tickets and tours, or do your laundry. They also have the best book-exchange selection in town. Katie Duncan, who keeps all these services in motion, is a knowledgeable and enthusiastic advocate of the Golfito area; if she can't connect you with what you're looking for, she'll know who can.

Arriving sailors will find the port captain (☎/fax 775-0487) and immigration authorities (☎ 775-0423) opposite the Muelle de Golfito, also known as the Muelle Bananero (old Banana Company Dock). Hours are 7:30 to 11 am and 12:30 to 4 pm weekdays.

Many places around Golfito communicate with one another by VHF radio. If you need to reach someone by VHF from Golfito, ask at Land Sea Tours, El Balcon Restaurant, Las Gaviotas Hotel, or one of the marinas to borrow their VHF. Alternatively, call Doña Isabel, the Travelair agent in Puerto Jiménez (☎ 735-5062, fax 735-5043), who can put you in radio contact with anywhere in the area. (You should remember that she doesn't work on Sunday.)

Another good and amiable source of information is Dave Corella at Café Coconuts, where there is a public bulletin board. Terry Moore at El Balcon Restaurant is another longtime resident, and Odette López at the Travelair office is friendly and helpful. There are plenty of other local 'experts.'

A couple of banks will change US dollars and traveler's checks. The gas station (locally called La Bomba) changes cash US dollars as well. Mail from abroad can take weeks to reach Golfito, but the post office does have a public fax facility. Laundry service is available next to the Hotel Delfina in the southern part of town. Emergency medical attention can be obtained at the Hospital de Golfito (☎ 775-0011).

Sportfishing & Boating

Sportfishing is a highlight of the Golfo Dulce area, with popular operators leaving both from here and from the more southern Playa Zancudo (see Playa Zancudo, later in this chapter). You can fish year-round, but the best season for the sought-after Pacific sailfish in the Golfito area is November to May.

Banana Bay Marina (☎ 775-0838, VHF 16/11, bbmarina@hotmail.com), run by Bruce Blevins, has a floating dock marina with a full range of services accommodating foreign yachts up to 155 feet for US75¢ per foot per day, or US$12 per foot per month, plus electricity. This is also the base for *Perfect Hooker*, a small luxury sportfisher with an air-conditioned cabin that carries up to six anglers and offers big-game fly fishing Jens Klaus (☎ 775-0225), the boat's owner, speaks English, German, and Spanish. Other charters can be arranged; a full day of fishing on 21- to 25-foot boats, all-inclusive, costs US$450 to US$525. Flights can be booked through the Banana Bay Marina, and a few Jet Skis, bicycles, and kayaks are also available for rent.

The upscale Golfito Sailfish Ranch (☎ 381-4701, fax 775-0750; in the USA ☎ 800-450-9908, advmktl@juno.com) has reopened and

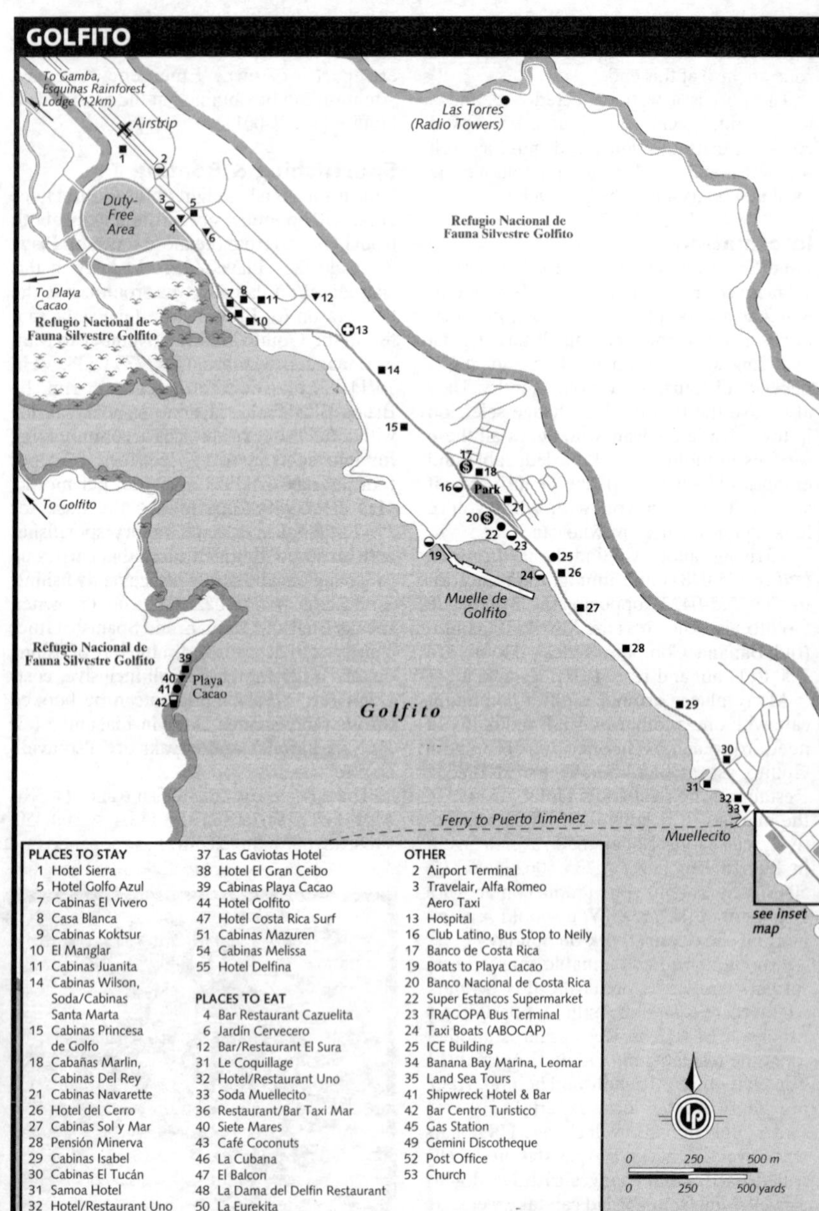
GOLFITO
To Gamba, Esquinas Rainforest Lodge (12km)
Airstrip
Las Torres (Radio Towers)
Duty-Free Area
Refugio Nacional de Fauna Silvestre Golfito
To Playa Cacao
Refugio Nacional de Fauna Silvestre Golfito
To Golfito
Park
Muelle de Golfito
Refugio Nacional de Fauna Silvestre Golfito
Playa Cacao
Golfito
Ferry to Puerto Jiménez
Muellecito
see inset map
0 250 500 m
0 250 500 yards
PLACES TO STAY
1 Hotel Sierra
5 Hotel Golfo Azul
7 Cabinas El Vivero
8 Casa Blanca
9 Cabinas Koktsur
10 El Manglar
11 Cabinas Juanita
14 Cabinas Wilson, Soda/Cabinas Santa Marta
15 Cabinas Princesa de Golfo
18 Cabañas Marlin, Cabinas Del Rey
21 Cabinas Navarette
26 Hotel del Cerro
27 Cabinas Sol y Mar
28 Pensión Minerva
29 Cabinas Isabel
30 Cabinas El Tucán
31 Samoa Hotel
32 Hotel/Restaurant Uno
37 Las Gaviotas Hotel
38 Hotel El Gran Ceibo
39 Cabinas Playa Cacao
44 Hotel Golfito
47 Hotel Costa Rica Surf
51 Cabinas Mazuren
54 Cabinas Melissa
55 Hotel Delfina
PLACES TO EAT
4 Bar Restaurant Cazuelita
6 Jardín Cervecero
12 Bar/Restaurant El Sura
31 Le Coquillage
32 Hotel/Restaurant Uno
33 Soda Muellecito
36 Restaurant/Bar Taxi Mar
40 Siete Mares
43 Café Coconuts
46 La Cubana
47 El Balcon
48 La Dama del Delfin Restaurant
50 La Eurekita
OTHER
2 Airport Terminal
3 Travelair, Alfa Romeo Aero Taxi
13 Hospital
16 Club Latino, Bus Stop to Neily
17 Banco de Costa Rica
19 Boats to Playa Cacao
20 Banco Nacional de Costa Rica
22 Super Estancos Supermarket
23 TRACOPA Bus Terminal
24 Taxi Boats (ABOCAP)
25 ICE Building
34 Banana Bay Marina, Leomar
35 Land Sea Tours
41 Shipwreck Hotel & Bar
42 Bar Centro Turistico
45 Gas Station
49 Gemini Discotheque
52 Post Office
53 Church

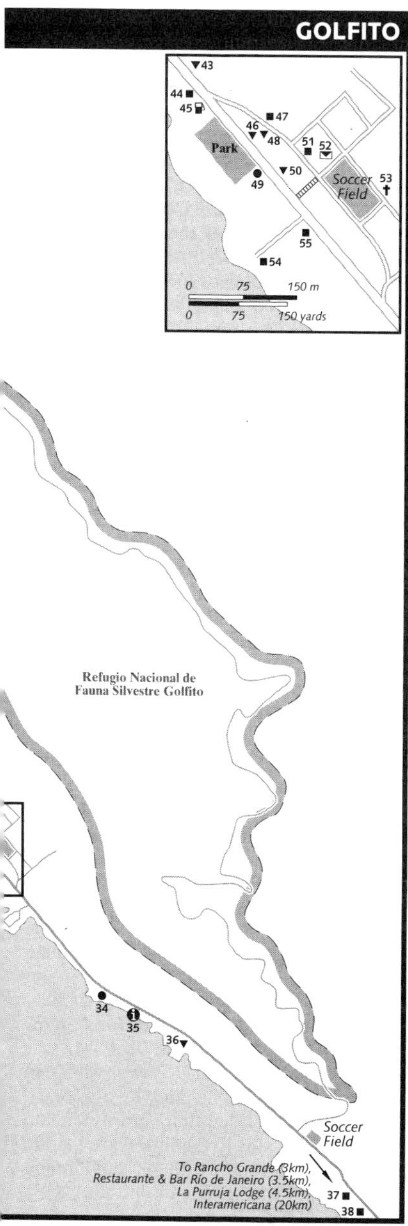

offers three- to seven-day all-inclusive packages for single, double, and triple occupancy, from US$1350 to US$3405 per person; the price includes pickup and overnight hotel in San José, air transport to and from Golfito, boat transport to the lodge, a fishing license, gear, and all meals, lodging, and drinks while at the lodge. Children under 12 are not allowed at the lodge and nonfishers are not permitted on the boats, which are 27-foot, 300hp, 1999 Ocean Masters equipped with all the latest electronics.

Another possibility is Leomar (☎ 775-0230, fax 775-0373), which has a 6.7m boat out of the Banana Bay Marina for US$450 per day and can take you fishing or diving.

For sea kayaking, contact Land Sea Tours (see Information earlier in this section); several of the lodges around the bay also offer kayaks.

Well-known local Joseph Rousseau has for years offered recommended natural history and photography boat trips up the Río Esquinas. He charges about US$40 per person (two minimum) for a four-hour trip. His son, Arjuna Rousseau, and Arjuna's half-brother, Steve Mika, are in the process of inheriting Joseph's knowledge of the river and the tours; snorkeling is now available as well. Steve can be reached on Channel 68, or through Ron MacAllister at Casa de Orquídeas (see that section, later in this chapter).

Places to Stay

Although the number of hotel rooms has grown significantly in the last few years, weekends bring tico shoppers to the duty-free area, and cheaper hotels may well be full then. Come midweek for the best choice of accommodations.

Budget One of the cheapest places is the ***Hotel/Restaurant Uno*** *(☎ 775-0061)*, which has plenty of basic boxes without fans for about US$2 per person. Most rooms lack a window. A better budget choice is the small but friendly ***Cabinas Mazuren*** *(☎ 775-0058)*, which has two rooms with shared bath for US$4 per person and three rooms with private baths and fans for US$5 per person.

Cabinas Sol y Mar *(☎ 775-0418)* rents basic rooms with private baths and parking space for about US$4 per person. The ***Hotel Delfina*** *(☎ 775-0043)* has basic rooms without fans, and many without windows, for US$5 per person. They also have better rooms with private baths and fans for US$15 single or double. ***Cabinas Isabel*** *(☎ 775-1774)* has decent rooms in an attractive old house for about US$6 per person; the staff says they can make tour arrangements. Behind the Delfina, ***Cabinas Melissa*** *(☎ 775-0443)* overlooks the water and offers clean, quiet doubles for US$11/16/20 for two/three/four people.

Another choice on the waterfront is ***Hotel Golfito*** *(☎ 775-0047)*, which rents rooms with private baths and fans for US$12 single or double. The similarly priced ***Cabinas El Tucán*** is basic but friendly and clean. The ***Hotel Costa Rica Surf*** *(☎/fax 775-0034, Apartado 7, Golfito)* has rooms with fans and shared baths for about US$12. Rooms with fans and private baths go for US$18. Many of the rooms either lack windows or have only skylights. There are a few air-conditioned rooms with hot showers, but these are usually booked. The hotel is popular with North Americans and hosts American Legion meetings on the first Tuesday of the month.

In the quieter north end are several families that take guests in their homes. The friendly and interesting Beatham family runs ***Cabinas El Vivero*** *(☎ 775-0217)* and also grows and sells ornamental plants; hence the name. They charge US$4.50 per person for airy rooms with fans and shared baths. Across the street, the family-run ***Casa Blanca*** *(☎ 775-0124)* has rooms with fans and private baths for US$9 single or double. The nearby ***El Manglar*** *(☎ 775-0510)*, ***Cabinas Juanita*** *(☎ 775-0402)*, and ***Cabinas Koktsur*** *(☎ 775-0327)* are also in this price range.

To the south, the ***Cabinas Wilson*** *(☎ 775-0795)* charges in the US$9 range for singles or doubles with fans and private baths. The ***Soda/Cabinas Santa Marta*** *(☎ 775-0508)* costs US$3 to US$5 per person. Across the road and a bit farther south, the ***Cabinas Princesa de Golfo*** *(☎ 775-0422)* has rooms with fans and private baths for US$8/12 single/double.

There are several houses in the area around the park, about 1km south of the north end. These include the ***Cabañas Marlin*** *(☎ 775-0191)*, ***Cabinas Navarette***, ***Cabinas Del Rey***, and others – ask around. They charge in the range of US$3 to US$5 per person. If you're stuck, try the run-down-looking ***Pensión Minerva*** for cheap digs.

The friendly ***Hotel del Cerro*** *(☎ 775-0006, fax 775-0551)*, south of the park, has great views of the bay. The hotel offers a large variety of clean rooms, ranging from dormitories with shared bath (there are plenty of bathrooms) for about US$5 per person ('backpacker rates,' less if several share a room), to rooms with fans and private baths for US$10/15 single/double, to air-conditioned rooms with phones and hot water for US$25 double.

Mid-Range At the entrance to Golfito, about 3 or 4km southeast of town, is ***Hotel El Gran Ceibo*** *(☎ 775-0403)*, which has decent modern rooms with fans and private bath for US$16 double, a few air-conditioned cabins for US$25, and a small swimming pool. The local Golfito bus terminates outside.

The Swiss-run ***La Purruja Lodge*** *(☎/fax 775-1054)* is 7km southeast of the town center on Golfito's main road. It has nice cabins with fans and private bath for about US$20 double. Meals, transportation into Golfito, and tours of the Península de Osa are available, and the owners allow camping on their attractive property.

Right in the north end is the recently refurbished ***Hotel Golfo Azul*** *(☎ 775-0871, fax 775-1849)*, which offers four very clean rooms with fans and hot showers for US$22 (single or double) and 20 rooms with air-conditioning for US$30. A nice restaurant and bar are on the premises, and a parking area is available.

In the far north of town, the ***Hotel Sierra*** *(☎ 775-0666, 775-0275, fax 775-0506)* was formerly the best hotel in town, with two restaurants, two pools, and 72 air-conditioned rooms. It closed (temporarily) in late 1996, but it is slowly coming back to life; decent modern rooms with air-conditioning and TV cost US$32 single or double, US$36 triple. There is a pool.

Almost opposite the Hotel El Gran Ceibo, right on the coast, is the well-known and recommended ***Las Gaviotas Hotel*** *(☎ 775-0062, fax 775-0544, gaviotas@sol.racsa.co.cr)*. It is set in a tropical garden and has an excellent restaurant with good prices, a café, a bar, two pools, and a boat dock from which you can watch the *gaviotas* (gulls). The 18 spacious rooms with fans or air-conditioning and hot water cost US$36 double (fans) or US$42 (air-con), and three larger bungalows with kitchenettes overlooking the ocean cost US$84.

The ***Samoa Hotel*** *(☎ 775-0233, fax 775-0573)* is a large, thatched building north of the center – you can't miss it. Formerly a restaurant, it now has both hotel and restaurant facilities and is a good place working hard to provide services to both locals and visitors. There are 14 clean and spacious rooms, each with two queen-size beds, fan, TV, telephone, and hot water. Rates are US$46, and you can sleep one to four people in each room. Also, its RV campground is a well-known stop for RV vehicles from North America. The charge is US$7 per vehicle and includes the use of showers and the restaurant. There is 24-hour guarded parking. The staff will arrange any local tour you want. Apart from their restaurant, they have a bar with a pool table, darts, and foosball that are in much better condition than most games in Costa Rica. They have a darts club on Monday and Wednesday nights, when you can try beating some of the local champions. They're very good!

Places to Eat

Budget travelers will find several restaurants where the meals start at US$2 to US$3. ***Hotel/Restaurant Uno*** has been around for decades and serves decent Chinese food. ***Café Coconuts***, owned by the friendly Dave Corella, is very popular with local gringos and ticos and is a good place for swapping information and meeting people. A good *casado* costs US$3, the fruit drinks are large and fresh, and a delicious avocado sandwich costs US$2.50. The ***Soda Muellecito*** is popular for early breakfasts by the Muellecito (little dock).

The US-run ***El Balcon***, above the Hotel Costa Rica Surf, has a variety of meals ranging from US$2 to US$7. Breakfast is also served. It has VHF radio communication with many of the local lodges, etc, and the bar is a popular gathering place and information center. There is a dart board, a paperback book exchange, and a pleasant view of the gulf. On Friday afternoons – the day that people around the bay come into town for supplies and a bit of town life – Ron MacAllister and Shane Acton lead an informal jam session. Across the street is ***La Dama del Delfín Restaurant***, which offers pancakes and eggs for breakfast and cheeseburgers or peanut butter-and-jelly for lunch. A gift shop is attached, and a book exchange and games are available.

The nearby ***La Eurekita*** *(☎ 775-1616)* is a breezy open-air restaurant selling good fruit juices and slightly pricey but good tico dishes. Almost next door, ***La Cubana*** is the latest and most long lasting incarnation of a restaurant that has gone through several name changes.

Heading north, you pass ***Le Coquillage***, in the Samoa Hotel (see Places to Stay). Continental cuisine (with a French-Italian emphasis) includes US$2 sandwiches, US$5 fish dishes, US$8 steaks, and US$11 large pizzas. There's good food and good ambience here.

In the northern zone, ***Bar Restaurant Cazuelita*** *(☎ 775-0921)* has decent Chinese meals. Nearby, the ***Jardín Cervecero*** *(☎ 775-0126)*, in a typical two-story house in the Alamedas barrio, claims to have the coldest beer in town and serves good seafood and steaks in a family environment. It opens around 8 am. Also in the northern zone, the ***Bar/Restaurant El Sura*** claims to have the longest bar in the Golfo Dulce region and serves local food. Also in the northern zone are a number of cheap sodas near the duty-free area, across from the school, and near the TRACOPA bus office.

The ***Restaurante/Bar Taxi Mar*** *(☎ 775-0106)*, on the southern route out of town, serves seafood in a nice bay-view setting. ***Las Gaviotas Hotel*** restaurant is open 6 am to 10 pm and serves a variety of pricier food – it is locally popular. Almost 3km farther out of town, the rustic, thatched-roofed ***Rancho Grande*** serves country-style tico food cooked over a wood stove. Margarita, the friendly tica owner, is one of Golfito's many established characters. Prices are US$4 to US$8 for most plates – it's worth the trip out here. Hours are 7 am to 10 pm. Almost a kilometer farther out of town is ***Restaurante & Bar Río de Janeiro*** *(☎ 775-0509)*, a nice roadside bar with a dart board. It has a small but changing menu that ranges from US$2 cheeseburgers to US$12 steaks. You have to ask them what they have – there's no written menu.

Entertainment

In an old port town like Golfito, beer, conversation, and darts have a flavor hard to find anywhere else. Try any of the popular bar/restaurants mentioned above. Right in the center of town, there's also the ***Gemini Discotheque***, which has dancing, especially on weekends.

Shopping

Assuming you're not in town to load up on booze or microwaves at the duty-free area, some of the small restaurants – in particular Café Coconuts and La Dama del Delfín – offer a reasonable selection of crafts and T-shirts.

Getting There & Away

Air SANSA (☎ 775-0303) flies from San José two or three times a day in the high season (less in the low season) for US$55 each way. Travelair (☎ 775-0210) flies from San José every morning for US$96/155 one way/roundtrip. Some flights may stop at Palmar Sur or Puerto Jiménez. Odette López, the Travelair agent, is very helpful and knowledgeable. Alfa Romeo Aero Taxi (☎ 775-1515) has light aircraft (three and five passengers) for charters to Puerto Jiménez, Parque Nacional Corcovado, and other areas.

The airport is almost 4km north of the town center. The terminal consists of four stone benches under the shade of two trees.

Bus TRACOPA (☎ 775-0365) has buses at 7 am and 3 pm daily from San José to Golfito (eight hours). The buses leave from Avenida 18, Calle 4. Return buses from Golfito leave at 5 am (express) and 1:30 pm daily. Fares are US$6 to San José and US$5 to San Isidro. TRACOPA's office hours in Golfito are 7:30 to 11:30 am and 2 to 4:30 pm Monday to Saturday, and 7:30 to 11:30 am on Sunday and holidays.

Buses for Neily leave every hour from the bus stop outside the Club Latino, near the park at the north end of town. Buses will pick up passengers in town as they pass through for the one-hour trip to Neily. Buses for the surfing area of Pavones and for the beach at Playa Zancudo leave from the Muellecito. Departures depend on the weather, the condition of the road, and the condition of the bus – ask locally. Services may be interrupted during the rainy season – it's a poor road. During the dry season, the bus leaves at 10 am and 3 pm for Pavones (three hours) and at 2 pm for Zancudo (three hours), with a transfer at the Río Coto Colorado. The bus might not run after heavy rains.

Boat There are two main boat docks for passenger services (apart from the various marinas). The Muellecito is the main dock in the southern part of town, and boat drivers here will bargain. An association of taxi boats operates from the dock opposite the ICE building near the north end of Golfito; the taxis here have set prices (see below).

The daily passenger ferry (☎ 735-5017) to Puerto Jiménez leaves at 11 am from the Muellecito. It takes 1½ hours and costs US$3. One report claims that there are not enough life jackets aboard for all the passengers. A passenger boat from the Muellecito to Playa Zancudo leaves at around 4:30 am and noon most days and costs about US$2 per person; it returns at 6 am and 1 pm. The boat is captained by Miguel Esquivel (☎ 775-1116); call if you want to catch the morning boat out, as he may leave from home without stopping at the dock. Local boat operators may profess ignorance of this service, because they would prefer to take you themselves!

The Asociación de Boteros (ABOCAP; ☎ 775-0357) has boat taxis from the dock opposite the ICE building that can take eight or more passengers. They have services to Playa Zancudo at various prices, depending on the size and speed of the boat and whom you talk to (average cost is about US$25 per boat). Other destinations (Pavones, Puerto Jiménez, Punta Encanto, Rainbow Adventures, Casa de Orquídeas, and others) can also be reached but cost more; these journeys are more exposed to weather, and conditions may affect prices. Most of the lodges can arrange to have you picked up.

Boats to nearby Playa Cacao are slightly cheaper from a point on the other side of the Muelle de Golfito, because it's the closest point to that beach (described below), but the ride from the Muellecito is a cheap way to get a look across the bay. The fare is US$3 minimum or US$1 per person.

Getting Around

City buses go up and down the main road of Golfito for about US15¢ per ride.

Colectivo taxis go up and down the main road from the airport down to Las Gaviotas Hotel. Just flag one down if it has a seat. The set fare is US75¢.

A private taxi from downtown to the airport costs about US$2.

PLAYA CACAO

This beach is opposite Golfito, and the view of the bay, port, and surrounding rainforest is worth the short boat ride out here. As for swimming, although it's cleaner than the polluted waters just off the town, the water isn't pristine. This is not the Golfo Dulce proper, and though efforts have been made to clean up trash, you're still near a dock visited by freighters.

Places to Stay & Eat

Cabinas Playa Cacao *(☎ 382-1593, fax 256-4850, isabel@sol.racsa.co.cr)* has six spacious cabins with high thatched roofs and tiled floors for US$40 double. Each cabin has a private bath, fan, microwave, and fridge; some have kitchenettes. It is next to the beach, and 'no frills' fishing trips are available for US$20 per hour (discounts for day trips); paddle boats and kayaks are free to guests. Owner Isabel Arias is a friendly host, and with Golfito across the water, this is a tranquil spot from which to enjoy the old port.

The once well-known ***Shipwreck Hotel & Bar***, which used to be a popular and rowdy tavern stop for freighter crews, is currently closed but still worth a look. The owner, Captain Tom, a local fixture for about 40 years, died recently and is buried beneath a small monument behind the dilapidated ship. Rumors that the bar is permanently closed are, some say, greatly exaggerated.

There are reportedly places to camp, some beach houses for rent, and a couple of basic cabinas. Try the ***Bar Centro Turistico*** *(☎ 391-8236; ask, in Spanish, for Juan)*, where you might get a double for US$9, and at any rate you can certainly down a few beers in the shoreside bar. The pulpería is a good source of information.

Siete Mares restaurant is open 7 am to 9 pm for inexpensive breakfasts, lunches, and dinners. It specializes in local dishes and seafood.

Getting There & Away

The five-minute boat ride from Golfito costs about US$1 per person, with a minimum fare of US$3. You can also get there by walking or driving along a dirt road west and then south from the airport – about 10km total from downtown Golfito. (This road is drivable most of the time.)

REFUGIO NACIONAL DE FAUNA SILVESTRE GOLFITO

This small (1309-hectare) refuge was originally created to protect the Golfito watershed. It encompasses most of the steep hills surrounding the town, and while the refuge has succeeded in keeping Golfito's water clean and flowing, it has also had the side effect of conserving a number of rare and interesting plant species. These include a species of *Caryodaphnopsis*, which is an

Asian genus otherwise unknown in Central America, and *Zamia*, which are cycads. Cycads are called 'living fossils' and are among the most primitive of plants. They were abundant before the time of the dinosaurs, but relatively few species are now extant. *Zamia* are known for the huge, cone-like inflorescences that emerge from the center of the plant, which looks rather like a dwarf palm.

Other species of interest include many heliconias, orchids, tree ferns, and tropical trees including copal, the kapok tree, the butternut tree, and the cow tree.

The vegetation attracts a variety of birds such as parrots, toucans, tanagers, trogons, and hummingbirds. Although the scarlet macaw has been recorded here, poaching in this area has made it rare. Peccaries, pacas, raccoons, coatimundis, and monkeys are among the mammals that have been sighted here.

Information

The refuge administration is in the Oficina de Area de Conservación Osa in Puerto Jiménez (see that section, earlier). Camping is permitted in the refuge, but there are no facilities – most people stay in Golfito.

Rainfall is very high: October, the wettest month, receives over 700mm. January to mid-April is normally a dry time.

Getting There & Away

About 2km south of the center of Golfito, before you come to Las Gaviotas Hotel, a gravel road heads inland, past a soccer field, and winds its way up to some radio towers (Las Torres), 7km away and 486m above sea level. This is a good access road to the refuge (most of the road actually goes through the middle of the preserve). You could take a taxi up first thing in the morning and hike down, birding as you go. A few trails lead from the road down to the town, but there is so little traffic on the road itself that you'll probably see more from the cleared road than from the overgrown trails.

Another possibility is to continue on the road heading northwest from the Hotel Sierra, past the end of the airstrip. The pavement soon ends and a dirt road continues about 3km to a sign for 'Senderos Naturales' (Nature Trails). Here, two somewhat overgrown trails plus the abandoned road provide good birding. Crested guan, slaty-tailed trogon, rufous-tailed jacamar, and orange-billed sparrow are among the species reported by birders.

A third way is to take the poor dirt road to Gamba and the Esquinas Rainforest Lodge (see the Southern Costa Rica chapter). This road leaves from a couple of kilometers northwest of the duty-free area and crosses through part of the refuge. You'll probably need 4WD. A local bus goes to the beginning of this dirt road – ask for the bus that goes to the road for Gamba or Esquinas. From where the bus leaves you, it's about 10km to Gamba, so you could walk and bird.

Finally, a very steep hiking trail leaves from almost opposite the Samoa Hotel. A somewhat strenuous hike (allow about two hours) will bring you out on the road to the radio towers, described previously. The trail is in fairly good shape, but easier to find in Golfito than at the top. Once you reach the radio tower road, return the way you came or, for a less knee-straining descent, head down along the road.

NORTH ALONG THE GOLFO DULCE

Boat taxis can take you out of Golfito and up along the northeast coast of the Golfo Dulce, past remote beaches and headlands interspersed with several jungle lodges. The backdrop to the coastline is mainly virgin rainforest; indeed, Parque Nacional Corcovado acquired an extension along this coast. This is called the Piedras Blancas sector and can be visited from the coastal lodges, although this section of the park has no facilities and only limited trails.

Note that some of the following places are difficult to contact directly; you may have to call a local agent and ask for a radio link, or leave a message.

Punta Encanto

About 10km west of Golfito as the crow flies, or about 25 minutes by boat taxi, brings you to the former Punta Encanto Lodge, which was set on a 7.5-hectare property with nature trails and waterfalls. The lodge closed down in the late 1990s; ask in Golfito for news of redevelopment.

Playa San Josecito

A few kilometers north of Punta Encanto, secluded Playa San Josecito has a couple of places to stay.

The Swiss-owned ***Golfo Dulce Lodge*** *(☎ 222-2900 for reservations, 383-4839 cellular, fax 222-5173, aratur@sol.racsa.co.cr)* is set back 250m from the rocky beach on the edge of a 275-hectare property, much of which is rainforest. The owners are informative about local flora and fauna and support a nearby wildcat rehabilitation project. They have five individual wooden cabins, each with a large verandah, and three adjoining rooms with smaller verandahs. All have private bathrooms with warm (solar-heated) water during the day. There is a small, chlorine-free pool. Rates are US$130/210/255 per night for one to three people, minimum two-night stay, including meals and roundtrip boat transfers from either Golfito or Puerto Jiménez.

A large number of excursions at various prices are available, including boat excursions to several destinations for wildlife observation or surfing, and hikes along the beach to Casa de Orquídeas or into the rainforest. Other activities (horseback riding, kayaking, fishing) can be arranged. Packages are available, such as the three-day/two-night package, including boat transfer from Golfito or Puerto Jiménez, meals, a boat excursion, and a guided hike for US$630 double.

Nearby, ***Dolphin Quest*** *(☎ 775-1742, fax 775-0373, dolphinquest@email.com)* is a jungle lodge with a relaxed family atmosphere. It offers access to an interesting community and as much privacy as a mile of beach and 700 acres of mountainous rainforest can offer. Owner Ray first bought property on the beach over 12 years ago and has been slowly developing since then; both of his sons were born here. Three round, thatched-roof cabins sleeping two and a larger house sleeping up to seven are spread out around 5 acres of landscaped grounds. Bunkhouse accommodations and camping are also options. Meals are served communally in an open-air pavilion near the shore, and the food is good; many ingredients are grown organically on the property. A variety of activities are available: horseback rides (US$10 per hour), kayaking (free for the first hour, and then US$5 per hour for a one-person kayak), motorboat excursions (US$25 per hour for a group), snorkeling, scuba diving, dolphin tours, and plenty of hiking. Access to the trails is free after an introductory tour outlining the beauties and dangers of the forest, which costs US$10. A red macaw release program run by Zoo-Ave (see the Central Valley & Surrounding Highlands chapter) is hosted here, and Casa de Orquídeas (see below) is a short walk down the beach.

Other options include massage, acupuncture, a volunteer work program for skilled people who want to stay a while (with housing in the bunkroom), a small library, and local pickup soccer games. Rates, including three meals per day, are US$25/45 single/double for campers (tents are available for US$7 per day), or US$40/70 in the bunkhouse, US$50/80 in the cabins, and US$60/100 in the house. A large private pavilion is available for group retreats, and group rates are available for meals. A birthing raft is also available for those with their own attendants and supplies; one of Ray's sons was born underwater using this raft.

Casa de Orquídeas

This private botanical garden is a veritable Eden. Surrounded by primary rainforest, the garden has been lovingly collected and tended by Ron and Trudy MacAllister, who have homesteaded in this remote region since the 1970s. They first planted fruit trees simply to survive and soon became interested in plants. Self-taught botanists, they have amassed a wonderful collection of tropical fruit trees, bromeliads, cycads, palms, heliconias, ornamental plants, and over 100 varieties of orchids, after which their garden is named.

The gardens are open for guided tours at 8:30 am Saturday to Thursday (the early hours avoid the wilting heat of the midday sun). Guided tours last about two hours and cost US$5 per person. The tours are fascinating and fun – touching, smelling, feeling, and tasting is encouraged. One highlight is chewing on the pulp surrounding a 'magic seed' whose effect is to make lemons taste sweet instead of sour; another is the smell of vanilla. You might also see bats hanging out in a 'tent' made from a huge leaf, insects trapped in bromeliad pools, or torch ginger in glorious flower – available treats vary according to season. The MacAllisters host natural history courses for students. They encourage interested schools to write to them at Apartado 69, Golfito, or contact them by radio from Golfito or Puerto Jiménez on Channel 68.

Casa de Orquídeas is at the west end of Playa San Josecito and can be reached from the lodges on that beach by foot. Otherwise, it is accessible only by boat, and transport and tours can be arranged with all the area's lodges or through Zancudo Boat Tours (☎/fax 776-0012) and Land Sea Tours (☎/fax 775-1614, landsea@sol.racsa.co.cr).

One rustic cabin is available for rental periods of a week or more. The screened two-room cabin can sleep up to four, has a private bath, refrigerator, and kitchenette, and runs on 12V electricity. Linens and kitchenware are furnished, but you need to bring your own food. Fruit can be picked if it's in season. Rates are US$150 a week or US$500 a month, including roundtrip transportation from Golfito.

Rainbow Adventures

This private 400-hectare preserve is bordered by the Piedras Blancas sector of Parque Nacional Corcovado, at the far northeast corner of Golfo Dulce. It is reached by a scenic 45-minute boat ride from Golfito to Playa Cativo. One of the attractions of the trip is 'shooting the rock,' where the boat hurtles through a narrow gap between a rocky islet and the coast. At the preserve, you can walk, swim, or snorkel along the 1.5km-long Playa Cativo or wander into the nearby forest. Howler monkeys and olingos (see the Raccoon Family in the Wildlife Guide at the back of the book) can be seen just a few meters away from the lodge.

The owner has a collection of 8000 natural history publications (in English), which, he says, is the largest private natural history library in Latin America. It can be used by guests staying at one of two luxurious lodges on Playa Cativo, both part of Rainbow Adventures.

The ***Rainbow Adventures Lodge*** is a unique three-story building. The all-wood, wide-balconied, rustic appearance of the lodge belies the elegance within – handmade furniture, silk rugs, turn-of-the-century antiques, and fresh flowers make this a special place in the wilderness. The first level is the dining room, lounge, and relaxation area, and the remaining two levels hold guest rooms. These are not for the average tourist who merely seeks four walls and a bed. Instead, the private rooms are partially open to the outside to allow guests beautiful and unimpeded views of the rainforest, the beach, and the gulf. Each bed is equipped with a fine-meshed mosquito net that can be raised or lowered as desired. It's almost like camping in the jungle, but with all comforts, including a private hot shower, comfortable beds, and balconies. The three rooms on the second level cost US$225/310 single/double, and the 3rd-floor 'penthouse' room costs US$240/330. A hydroelectric system on the property provides power, and there are electric hair dryers in the bathrooms, and a laundry. The lodge also houses the research library.

There are also two attractive and spacious wooden cabins, each with a large bedroom, private bathroom, and spacious verandah – on one visit, a pair of variable finches were nesting immediately outside. The bedroom can be partitioned off into two minibedrooms suitable for parents with children, though they're tight for adult couples. Cabin rates are US$260/350 single/double plus US$65 for extra people (US$50 for four- to 10-year-olds). Outside is a swimming pool.

Almost 1km away along the beach is the equally comfortable ***Buena Vista Jungle & Beach Lodge***. Guests can use the library and pool at the Rainbow Adventures Lodge. Buena Vista has eight rooms in two two-story houses, each with features similar to Rainbow. There is an open-sided dining room and lounge. Depending on the room, rates are US$125 to US$140 single and US$190 to US$230 double, US$55 for extra people, and US$40 for children.

All prices in both lodges include meals (buffet style – vegetarian, dairy free, etc available on request; beer/wine with meals), nonalcoholic drinks, snacks, transportation from and to Golfito airport, a short tour of nearby jungle, and use of snorkeling gear and jungle boots (although it's always wise to bring your own to ensure the best fit).

Boats are available for US$40 per hour per boat (up to four passengers) for fishing or tours. Kayak rental costs US$10 for three hours, US$15 for a double-seater. Guided jungle tours cost US$4 per hour per person.

Information and reservations are available in the US from Michael Medill (*☎ 800-565-0722, 503-690-7750, fax 503-690-7735, info@rainbowcostarica.com, info@buenavista-costarica.com, 5875 NW Kaiser Rd, Portland, OR 97229*). Note that there is no phone at the lodge.

Cabinas Caña Blanca

A couple of kilometers north of Playa Cativo and Rainbow Adventures brings you to a small beach with two well-designed and comfortable cabins. Each has a spacious verandah and private outdoor showers with forest views. Guests have access to rainforest trails and a beach – this is for people who want to do their own thing in a remote area. However, meals can be cooked for you by advance request. Rates are about US$60 double and include transportation from Golfito if you stay for three nights. Boat and fishing excursions cost US$35 an hour. For reservations, call ☎ *735-5062* and leave a message.

Southern Golfo Dulce Area

PLAYA ZANCUDO

This beach, on the south side of the mouth of the Río Coto Colorado, about 15km south of Golfito, is a popular destination for locals, who claim that this 6km-long, dark-sand beach has the best swimming in the area. The surf is gentle and at night the quiet water sometimes sparkles with bioluminescence, tiny phosphorescent marine plants and plankton that light up if you sweep a hand through the water – the effect is like underwater fireflies, which is especially fabulous on a starry night. At the far south end, the waves get big enough for surfing; views all along the beach and out across the bay are beautiful. The beach gets mildly busy during the dry season but is quiet at other times. Many visitors end up hanging out here for a week or more.

There are mangroves in the area around the river mouth that offer wildlife-watching possibilities, even on the boat-taxi ride from Golfito. Look for crocodiles, otter, monkeys, and birds. If you arrive via the estuary, don't be deflated when you first come ashore – the dock and sandy road leading from it are a bit scruffy, but they don't match the rest of the beach.

Activities

The best sportfishing is from December to May, though you can catch something most any month. Sportfishing can be arranged at Roy's Zancudo Lodge (see Places to Stay & Eat, below). Big Al, another longtime local operator, now works out of Roy's place. Captain Jerry Cooper's Golfito Sportfishing (☎ 776-0007, ☎/fax 382-2716, cooper@sol.racsa.co.cr) is based in Playa Zancudo; he offers 24-foot boats for two people for US$375 and for three to four people for US$425 for a day of fishing. Multiday offshore fishing packages for three/five/seven days cost US$890/1450/1850 per person with flights from San José, overnights in Playa Zancudo cabins with hot water, and everything included.

Zancudo Boat Tours (☎/fax 776-0012), run by the friendly and knowledgeable Susan and Andrew of Cabinas Los Cocos, has three- to four-hour boat tours for about US$35 per person. One goes up the river estuary and mangroves behind Zancudo for wildlife watching and some local history. Another goes to Casa de Orquídeas. They have kayaks for rent. A popular kayaking tour is to go by boat up the river and then float back with the tide – about four hours, US$100 for two people. Horse rental is available at Cabinas Sol y Mar and some other places – ask around.

Places to Stay & Eat

Cabins, restaurants, and other businesses are strung out along 5km of beach. There are few single rooms, and on a busy weekend single travelers may get stuck paying triple rate for a room with three beds. At quieter times you should bargain for a single rate.

Most hotels have a restaurant attached. One of the cheapest places is the friendly and recommended ***Bar/Cabinas Suzy*** *(☎ 776-0107)*, which rents basic rooms with shared bath for about US$6 per person and some slightly more expensive rooms with private bath. The friendly Spanish cook, Manolo, is an inconsistent but good chef, and the locally popular bar has a pool table.

The similarly priced ***Restaurant & Cabinas Tranquilo*** (also known as Maria's Place) is a decent budget place popular with European budget travelers. There is a simple and inexpensive restaurant – one traveler reports that Maria is the best cook in town. Other places in this price range include the friendly and popular ***Cabinas Petier*** (also known as Froylan's Place), which has an attached restaurant. Also try the cheaper ***El Coquito***, with basic and rather stuffy cabins with private bath for US$4 and a restaurant serving good inexpensive meals, or ***Río Mar*** *(☎ 776-0056)*, at the north end of the beach (also known as Franklin's Place, though Franklin has passed away and the cabins are up for sale), which has cabins with fans, private baths, and fridges for US$18/22 for three or four people, and a larger cabin with a full kitchen sleeping six for US$55.

Near the path to the public dock is a locally popular place for breakfast, ***Soda Mar y Sol***. A couple minutes' walk south of the dock, on the inland side of the road, ***Cabinas La Palmera de Oro*** *(☎ 776-0121, fax 776-0134)* has simple, modern cabins with air-conditioning, TV, and telephones for US$38 double, US$5 each additional person up to six. There is a small pool, bar, and restaurant.

The beachfront ***Cabinas Los Cocos*** *(☎/fax 776-0012, loscocos@sol.racsa.co.cr)*, about a kilometer south of the public dock, is also the home of the boat taxi/tour service Zancudo Boat Tours, owned by helpful Susan and Andrew. The two of them are artists and Andrew's sculptures, some of which showcase his wry sense of humor, decorate the grounds. Two cabins, which used to be banana company homes, sleep three and rent for US$40 or US$240 a week, and two larger thatched-roof cabins sleeping four cost US$45 or US$260 a week. All are attractively designed, have private baths, hot water, kitchenettes, fridges, fans, boogie boards, and porches with hammocks. There are also two large rustic houses that rent for US$200 a week or US$450 a month.

Just south of Los Cocos, ***Cabinas Sol y Mar*** *(☎ 776-0014, fax 776-0015, solymar@zancudo.com)* is a quiet, friendly place, and owners Rick and Lori are a good source of information on the area. They have four nice cabins with private bath, hot water, and fans for US$25/30. Next door is their recommended restaurant, which serves good food for reasonable prices in a relaxed atmosphere. Prices are about US$3 for breakfast or lunch and under US$6 for dinner. They also have a nice bar. Horse rental is available, and they can arrange fishing and boating excursions.

About another kilometer south is the newer ***Zancudo Beach Club*** *(☎ 776-0087, zbc@costarica.net)*, run by Gary and Debbie, former New Englanders realizing a dream of beach life. It has attractive, spacious cabinas for US$50 double; some smaller rooms for US$30 double are being built. The surf is bigger at this end of the beach, so ask about currents before going swimming. The restaurant is pricier than most on this beach, but excellent; so are the mixed drinks.

Roy's Zancudo Lodge *(☎ 776-0008, fax 776-0011; in the USA ☎ 800-515-7697, fax 813-889-9189)* is one of the oldest places to stay at Zancudo and has a faithful clientele, especially of anglers. The lodge has well over 35 world records for fishing. It can accommodate up to 20 people in various rooms, all with private hot baths and fans, some with kitchenettes or air-conditioning. Most guests come on a fishing package that starts at US$1415 per person double occupancy, and includes airfare from San José, three days of fishing, all meals – including alcohol – and a night in San José. Longer packages are available. Nonfishing guests pay US$75 a day including meals. Owner Roy Ventura has a good reputation.

Estero Mar (also known as Mauricio's) serves decent tico food at reasonable prices and is a popular bar. ***Macondo*** is a good Italian restaurant with a pleasant balcony overlooking a garden.

Getting There & Away

Boat or bus from Golfito is the usual way to get here. It is also possible to drive to Golfito by taking the road south of Paso Canoas to Laurel, and then heading roughly west and north. Signs are infrequent, but stick to the most used-looking dirt roads and ask locals, and you'll get there.

Bus Buses leave Golfito for Zancudo at 2 pm; it is also possible to get buses from Neily and Paso Canoas at 2 pm. From Zancudo, the bus for Golfito leaves El Coquito at 5 am and takes about three hours, with a ferry transfer at the Río Coto Colorado. Service may be suspended in the wet season.

Boat Public boats leave for Golfito at 6 am and 1 pm for about US$2 per person. The boat dock is near the north end of the beach on the inland, estuary side. It can be a kilometer or more from where you're staying.

Zancudo Boat Tours (☎/fax 776-0012) charges US$10 per person to Golfito (two-passenger minimum). The boat can pick you up in Golfito by advance arrangement and can drop you close to where you're staying.

PAVONES

About 10km south of Zancudo is the Bahía de Pavón, which is supposed to have some of the best surfing on the Pacific side of Central America. The name Pavones is used locally to refer to the area comprising both Playa Río Claro de Pavones and, 5km southeast, Punta Banco. There is relatively little infrastructure here and little to do except hang out and surf, which doesn't seem to pose any kind of problem for visitors.

The beach at Pavones is rockier and rougher than at Punta Banco, which is sandier and has less surfers. The best season is from April to October, when the waves are at their biggest and the famous long left can reportedly give a three-minute ride. Legend has it that the wave passes so close to the Esquina del Mar Cantina that you could toss beers to surfers as they come by on their boards. (Camera, anyone?) This is definitely not the beach to bring your small children to for a gentle paddle. Note that the best season coincides with the rainy months.

Places to Stay & Eat

There are several basic places to stay and eat stretched out along a few kilometers of beach. A nice one is the small ***Cabinas La Ponderosa*** *(☎ 384-7430, leave a message; in the USA ☎ 954-771-9166, fax 954-772-8362 for reservations)*, near the south end. Four clean rooms have huge screened windows, electricity, air-conditioning, fans, and private baths. Rates are about US$17 per person or US$40 with three meals. The owners, surfing brothers Marshall and Brian, are friendly and helpful. They surf every day but will also arrange a horseback ride or a spot of fishing for a change of pace. There is a simple dining room and lounge with Ping-Pong and TV/VCR with videos to watch. Surfers hang out here for weeks and get discounted long-stay rates.

Nearby is the ***Impact Surf Lodge***, which also provides decent rooms and all meals. It's not very expensive.

Farther north on the beach is the popular ***Esquina del Mar Cantina***, which has basic and breezy upstairs rooms for about US$5 per person. You are lulled to sleep by the sounds of the surf – and the bar below. The bar owner has other cabins nearby, described as hot and airless. Some new cabins are being built behind the pulpería.

Ask around for other cheap places to stay – new ones will keep opening as both surfers and non-surfers continue to discover this remote area.

Cabinas Mira Olas, set on an 11-acre farm full of wildlife and fruit trees by the Río Claro, is a good choice for those more interested in nature than surfing. Two high-ceilinged cabins with kitchens, private baths, and porch hammocks cost US$35 double (US$165 per week), US$8 for each additional person. A smaller, more rustic cabin costs US$25 double, US$125 per week.

A budget option near the soccer field in Pavones is ***Cabinas Muchas Olas***, which has decent rooms for US$15/20. On a hill above Pavones is ***Casa Siempre Domingo*** *(☎ 775-0631, info@casa-domingo.com)*, a luxurious private home. Rooms cost US$90/120 single/double including meals.

South again, near the Punta Banco soccer field, is ***Marea Alta Cabinas*** *(☎ 775-0131)*, run by Alvaro Baltodano and family, which has nice two-story cabins with private baths for US$10 per person. Fresh fish and other meals are available.

Near the end of the road in Punta Banco is ***Rancho Burica***, a friendly Dutch-run place with a variety of simple, pleasant rooms for US$4 to US$12 per person. Some have decks with ocean views; none have private bath. An attractive bathing option is the nearby waterfall. Snorkeling, surfing, and horse rides are equally regarded options here.

Camping on the beach is possible, but watch your stuff. Thefts from tents have been reported. Don't leave your campsite unattended.

Getting There & Away

The daily bus leaves for Golfito at 5 am and 12:30 pm from the Esquina del Mar Cantina. It returns from Golfito at 10 am and 3 pm. A 4WD taxi will charge about US$40 from Golfito. You can also drive here from Paso Canoas (see above under Playa Zancudo).

Walter Jiménez is a local boatman who can take you to Zancudo, Golfito, and other destinations.

TISKITA JUNGLE LODGE

This is a private biological reserve and experimental fruit farm on 160 hectares of land at Punta Banco, about 30km due south of Golfito and 10km from the Panamanian border. About 100 hectares are virgin rainforest. Tiskita also has a coastline with tide pools and beaches suitable for swimming.

The lodge is run by Peter Aspinall, who is Costa Rican and was educated in North America. His passion is homesteading, and he has an orchard with over 100 varieties of tropical fruits from all over the world. He plans to ship the most suitable of these fruits to San José and abroad. Meanwhile, guests are able to sample dozens of exotic fruits and fruit drinks during their visit to the lodge.

There are trails in the surrounding rainforest, which contains waterfalls and rivers suitable for swimming. The tide pools have a variety of marine life such as chitons, nudibranchs, bristle and feather worms, starfish, sea urchins, anemones, tunicates, crabs, and many shells. Ask for booklets describing the rainforest trail, the tide pools, and the land crabs, and for a butterfly list.

Birders will find that the combination of rainforest, fruit farm, and coastline produces a long list of birds. About 300 species have been recorded here, depending on who's counting. The fruit farm is particularly attractive to frugivorous (fruit-eating) birds such as parrots and toucans, which can be more easily observed in the orchard than the rainforest. Nature trails into the forest help the birder see the more reticent species, and a local checklist is available. This includes such exotic-sounding birds as yellow-billed cotingas, fiery-billed aracaris, green honeycreepers, and lattice-tailed trogons, to name a few. Monkeys, sloths, agoutis, coatis, and other mammals are often seen. Of course, insects and plants abound.

The lodge runs Fundación Tiskita, a non-profit organization involved with arranging medical care in the nearby community of

Punta Banco. It also financially supports local research and conservation efforts to protect marine turtles.

Accommodations are in 16 rustic cabins with private baths and Pacific Ocean views. The private baths are on the outside of the cabins, allowing rainforest views as you shower – a splendid and invigorating way to start the day. A lodge with a small library serves as an informal relaxation area, and a dining room serves home-cooked food. A pool with ocean views has more recently been added.

Reservations are essential, because the lodge is sometimes full of birding groups and the like. Make reservations with Costa Rica Sun Tours (operated by the Aspinalls; see Organized Tours in the Getting Around chapter) or any other major tour operator.

Daily rates are US$145/240/315 single/double/triple (US$60 for children under 12) and include accommodations, meals, and guided walks with a naturalist. Many people come on a package tour that also includes flights from either Golfito or Puerto Jiménez to Tiskita's private airstrip. (A roundtrip flight from San José can also be arranged; on its own, this flight costs US$140.) These packages cost from US$710 for two people for two days/two nights to US$1290 for two people for seven days/seven nights (about 25% less for children under 12).

Various other tours are available. An interesting one is flying from the private Tiskita airstrip to Sirena in Parque Nacional Corcovado, spending about four hours hiking with a local guide, and returning by air. This costs US$150 per person, two minimum. Boogie boards, snorkeling gear, and horse rental are also available.

Getting There & Away

It is possible to drive to the lodge with a 4WD vehicle, but many people opt to fly to the nearby private airstrip that is a five-minute walk from the lodge. Getting there yourself is rather difficult but can be done by public transport or your own vehicle. Ask the Aspinalls for directions.

Central Pacific Coast

Costa Rica's major Pacific coastal town is Puntarenas, about 110km west of San José by paved highway. This has traditionally been the town that highlanders descend to when they want to spend a few days by the ocean, but there are now many other popular vacation spots on the Pacific coast south of Puntarenas.

These include swimming and surfing beach resorts, sportfishing towns, well-developed and almost undeveloped beaches, a biological reserve, a national marine park, and the famous coastal national park at Manuel Antonio.

Generally, the Pacific coast is better developed for tourism than the Caribbean coast, and if you are looking for some luxury, it is easy to find here. You can also find deserted beaches, wildlife, and small coastal villages.

There are marked wet and dry seasons along the Pacific coast. The rains begin in April, and you can expect a lot of precipitation from May to November. This eases in December, and the dry season continues for the next four months.

The dry months coincide with Costa Rican school vacations in January and February and the biggest holiday of the year, Easter. So the dry season is the high season; wherever you travel on the Pacific coast, expect a lot of visitors, and make sure you have hotel reservations on weekends for the better hotels.

Most beach hotels are booked weeks or months in advance for Easter week. If you travel during the low (wet) season, you'll see fewer visitors and have little difficulty booking into hotels.

Low-season discounts (ranging from 10% to 40% or even 50%) are worth asking about. (Prices given throughout this chapter are high-season rates.)

Average temperatures on the coast, year-round, are about 22°C minimum and about 32°C maximum. The dry season is generally a little hotter than the wet.

PUNTARENAS

This city of about 100,000 inhabitants is the capital of the province of Puntarenas, which stretches along the Pacific coast from Golfo de Nicoya to the Panamanian border.

During the 19th century, in the days before easy access to the Caribbean coast, Puntarenas was Costa Rica's major port. Goods such as coffee were hauled by ox cart from the highlands down the Pacific slope to Puntarenas, and then they were shipped around the Horn to Europe – a long trip!

After the railway to Puerto Limón was built, Puntarenas became less significant but remained the most important port on the Pacific side of the country. This was changed in 1981 when a new port was opened at Caldera, about 18km southeast of Puntarenas by road. This facility has become the major Pacific port.

Despite the loss of shipping, Puntarenas remains a bustling town during the dry season, when tourists arrive. During the wet months, however, the city is much quieter.

There are plenty of sandy beaches, but, unfortunately, the water is polluted. Puntarenas has cleaned up its act somewhat, and reportedly the last kilometer of the south side of the point is now OK for swimming. The beaches themselves are regularly cleaned and the views across the Gulf of Nicoya are nice. You can walk along the beach or the aptly named Paseo de los Turistas beach road, stretching along the southern coast of town. Cruise ships make day visits to the eastern end of this beach road, and a variety of souvenir stalls and beach sodas is there to greet passengers – as well as a new indoor complex of shops and restaurants.

Although the town remains somewhat popular with Costa Rican holidaymakers, foreigners tend to look for a destination where they can swim without worrying about pollution. There are plenty of possibilities in the towns and beaches south of Puntarenas, and many people go there and avoid Puntarenas completely.

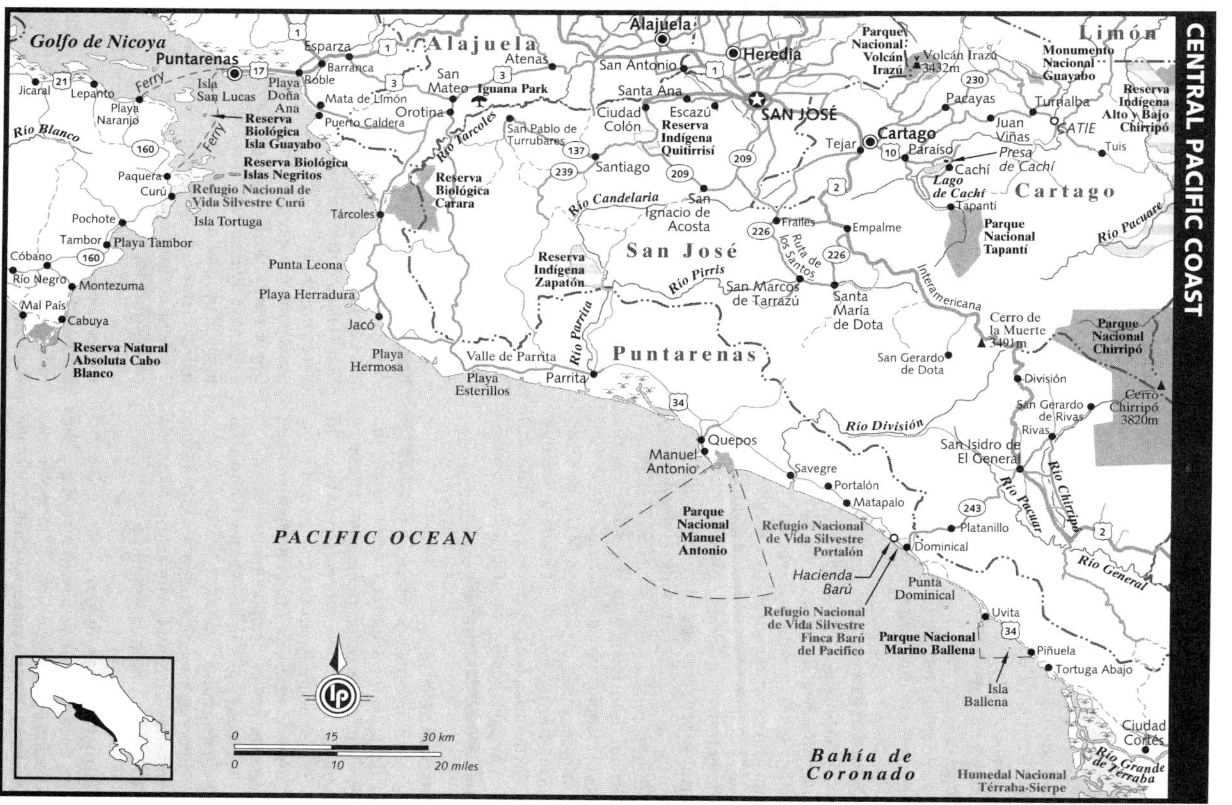
CENTRAL PACIFIC COAST
Golfo de Nicoya
Puntarenas
Alajuela
Heredia
SAN JOSÉ
Cartago
Limón
San José
Puntarenas
Cartago
PACIFIC OCEAN
Bahía de Coronado
Parque Nacional Volcán Irazú
Volcán Irazú 3432m
Monumento Nacional Guayabo
Reserva Indígena Alto y Bajo Chirripó
Parque Nacional Chirripó
Cerro Chirripó 3820m
Cerro de la Muerte 3491m
Parque Nacional Tapantí
Reserva Indígena Quitirrisí
Reserva Indígena Zapatón
Reserva Biológica Carara
Iguana Park
Reserva Biológica Isla Guayabo
Reserva Biológica Islas Negritos
Refugio Nacional de Vida Silvestre Curú
Reserva Natural Absoluta Cabo Blanco
Parque Nacional Manuel Antonio
Refugio Nacional de Vida Silvestre Portalón
Hacienda Barú
Refugio Nacional de Vida Silvestre Finca Barú del Pacífico
Parque Nacional Marino Ballena
Humedal Nacional Térraba-Sierpe
Isla Ballena
Isla San Lucas
Isla Tortuga
Ferry
Río Blanco
Río Tárcoles
Río Candelaria
Río Pirrís
Río Parrita
Río Pacuare
Río División
Río Chirripó
Río Pacuar
Río General
Río Grande de Térraba
Presa de Cachí
Lago de Cachí
Interamericana
Ruta de los Santos
Jicaral
Lepanto
Playa Naranjo
Paquera
Curú
Pochote
Tambor
Playa Tambor
Montezuma
Cóbano
Río Negro
Mal País
Cabuya
Playa Doña Ana
Roble
Esparza
Barranca
Mata de Limón
Puerto Caldera
Orotina
San Mateo
Atenas
San Antonio
Santa Ana
Escazú
Ciudad Colón
Santiago
San Pablo de Turrubares
San Ignacio de Acosta
Frailes
San Marcos de Tarrazú
Santa María de Dota
Empalme
Tejar
Paraíso
Cachí
Tapantí
Pacayas
Juan Viñas
Turrialba
CATIE
Tuis
San Gerardo de Dota
División
San Gerardo de Rivas
Rivas
San Isidro de El General
Platanillo
Tárcoles
Punta Leona
Playa Herradura
Jacó
Playa Hermosa
Playa Esterillos
Valle de Parrita
Parrita
Quepos
Manuel Antonio
Savegre
Portalón
Matapalo
Dominical
Punta Dominical
Uvita
Piñuela
Tortuga Abajo
Ciudad Cortés
0 15 30 km
0 10 20 miles

The locals have a reputation for friendliness. Hang out on the beachfront with the *tico* tourists, and check out the busy comings and goings during the season. Walk by the church – perhaps the most attractive building in Puntarenas. Some people even like to come during the wet season, when it is quiet and fresh with daily rain showers. It is the closest coastal town to San José for a quick getaway, although there are plenty of better beaches elsewhere. The main reason most people spend time here, however, is to wait for a ferry to the Península de Nicoya.

Orientation

The geographical setting of the town is an intriguing one. Puntarenas literally means a 'sandy point' or sand spit. The city is on the end of a sandy peninsula that is almost 8km long, but only 600m wide at its widest point (downtown) and less than 100m wide in many other parts. The city has 60 *calles* from north to south but only five *avenidas* running west to east at its widest point. Driving into town with the waters of the Pacific lapping up on either side of the road is a memorable experience. Make sure you leave or arrive in daylight hours to see this.

With such a long, narrow street configuration, you are never more than a few minutes' walk away from the coast.

Information

A tourist information office (☎ 661-1985) is in the Casa de Cultura (☎ 661-1394); the tourist information office may move to a new complex near the beach, currently home to ICE (see map). Apart from maps and information, travelers can use international and domestic fax and telephone services.

Various banks in the center (shown on the map) change money.

Emergency medical attention is available from the Hospital Monseñor Sanabria (☎ 663-0033), 8km east of town.

Things to See & Do

The **Casa de Cultura** has an art gallery and occasional cultural events. Behind it is the **Museo Histórico Marino**, which describes the history of Puntarenas through audiovisual presentations, old photos, and artifacts – at last visit it was closed, but it may reopen. A block away, the city church is one of the most attractive buildings. A walk along the Paseo de los Turistas is pleasant, and you can swim in **La Punta Municipal Pool** at the very tip of the point. It's open 9 am to 4:30 pm Tuesday to Sunday, and admission costs US$2, or US$1 for two- to 10-year-olds.

Although most cruise ships dock at Caldera for servicing and to unload passengers for land tours, cruise ships do make day visits to a dock at the east end of the Paseo de los Turistas. Near the beach, a large modern building (which houses the new ICE office – see map) will be home to an indoor shopping and dining area. The existing souvenir stalls and beach *sodas* have a festive air, but the new air-conditioned complex will likely provide a more upscale retreat from the heat.

Activities & Organized Tours

Several boat tour companies can take you to visit local beaches and the islands described under Islands Near Bahía Gigante in the Península de Nicoya chapter. Most of these tours are booked in San José. Fred Wagner at Casa Alberta (☎/fax 663-0107) in Roble (10km east of town) offers fishing trips for about US$200 per day, as well as cheaper local sightseeing cruises.

Special Events

Apart from the usual tico holidays, Puntarenas celebrates the Fiesta de La Virgen del Mar (Fiesta of the Virgin of the Sea) on the Saturday closest to July 16. There is the usual parade, except that the gaily decorated floats really do float – fishing boats and elegant yachts are beautifully bedecked with lights, flags, and all manner of fanciful embellishments as they sail around the harbor. There are also boat races, a carnival, and plenty of food, drink, and dancing.

Places to Stay

Budget Make sure your room has a decent fan; otherwise you'll be very hot and, during the wet months, likely to be bitten by mosquitoes.

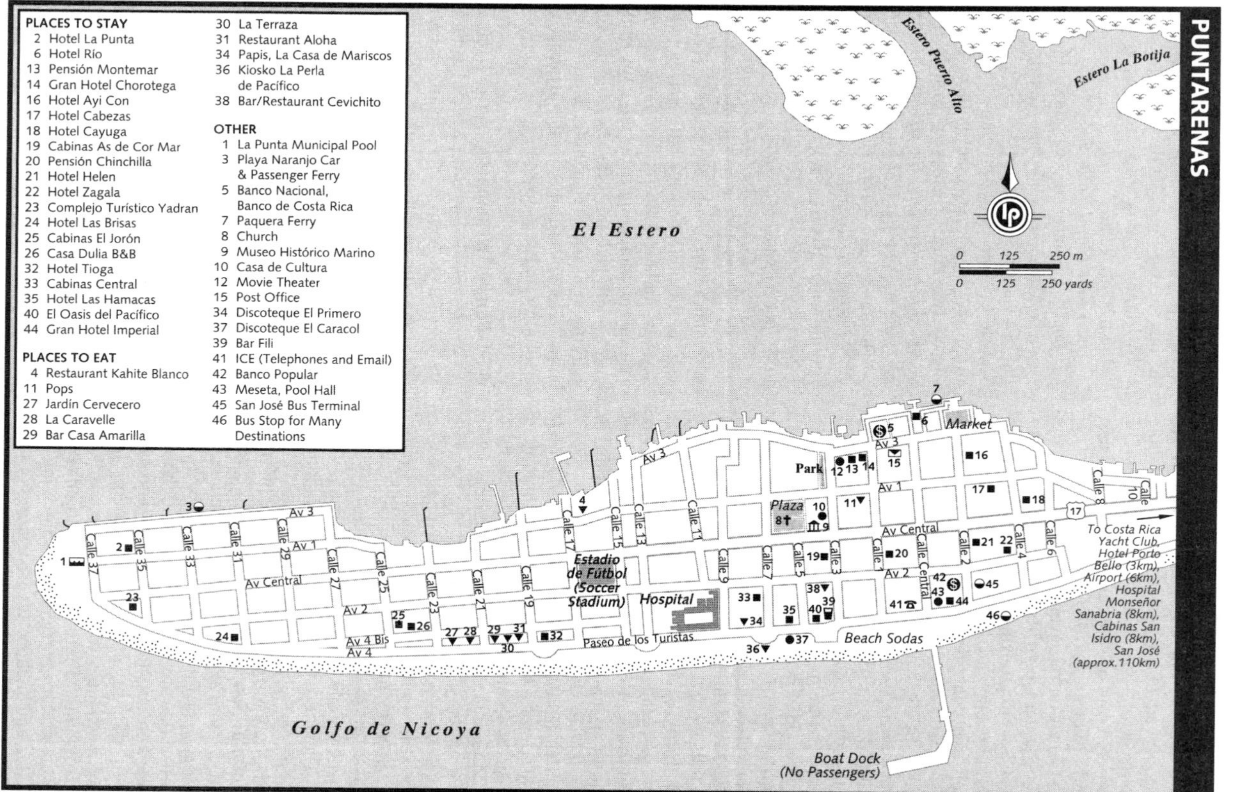
PUNTARENAS
PLACES TO STAY
2 Hotel La Punta
6 Hotel Río
13 Pensión Montemar
14 Gran Hotel Chorotega
16 Hotel Ayi Con
17 Hotel Cabezas
18 Hotel Cayuga
19 Cabinas As de Cor Mar
20 Pensión Chinchilla
21 Hotel Helen
22 Hotel Zagala
23 Complejo Turístico Yadran
24 Hotel Las Brisas
25 Cabinas El Jorón
26 Casa Dulia B&B
32 Hotel Tioga
33 Cabinas Central
35 Hotel Las Hamacas
40 El Oasis del Pacífico
44 Gran Hotel Imperial
PLACES TO EAT
4 Restaurant Kahite Blanco
11 Pops
27 Jardín Cervecero
28 La Caravelle
29 Bar Casa Amarilla
30 La Terraza
31 Restaurant Aloha
34 Papis, La Casa de Mariscos
36 Kiosko La Perla de Pacífico
38 Bar/Restaurant Cevichito
OTHER
1 La Punta Municipal Pool
3 Playa Naranjo Car & Passenger Ferry
5 Banco Nacional, Banco de Costa Rica
7 Paquera Ferry
8 Church
9 Museo Histórico Marino
10 Casa de Cultura
12 Movie Theater
15 Post Office
34 Discoteque El Primero
37 Discoteque El Caracol
39 Bar Fili
41 ICE (Telephones and Email)
42 Banco Popular
43 Meseta, Pool Hall
45 San José Bus Terminal
46 Bus Stop for Many Destinations
Estero Puerto Alto
Estero La Botija
El Estero
0 125 250 m
0 125 250 yards
Market
Park
Plaza
Estadio de Fútbol (Soccer Stadium)
Hospital
Paseo de los Turistas
Beach Sodas
Golfo de Nicoya
Boat Dock (No Passengers)
To Costa Rica Yacht Club, Hotel Porto Bello (3km), Airport (6km), Hospital Monseñor Sanabria (8km), Cabinas San Isidro (8km), San José (approx. 110km)
Av 3
Av 1
Av Central
Av 2
Av 4 Bis
Av 4
Calle 37
Calle 35
Calle 33
Calle 31
Calle 29
Calle 27
Calle 25
Calle 23
Calle 21
Calle 19
Calle 17
Calle 15
Calle 13
Calle 11
Calle 9
Calle 7
Calle 5
Calle 3
Calle 1
Calle Central
Calle 2
Calle 4
Calle 6
Calle 8
Calle 10
17

The ***Hotel Helen*** *(☎ 661-2159)*, on Calle 2, Avenidas Central & 2, is basic but clean and a good budget choice at US$8 for a double room with shared bath (no singles) or US$8/13 with private cold shower. The basic and rather noisy ***Hotel Río*** *(☎ 661-0331)* is on Calle Central, Avenida 3, just next to the old Paquera boat dock. The dock/market area is a little rough, but the hotel is safe and the management is friendly. Rooms with fans and communal bathrooms cost US$4 per person, and rooms with private showers cost US$7 per person. On the east side of the market, the Pacífico (not to be confused with El Oasis del Pacífico) is a flophouse inhabited by drunks and prostitutes – it's not recommended.

For US$4 per person, the ***Pensión Chinchilla*** *(☎ 661-0638)*, on Calle 1, Avenidas Central & 2, is clean and secure, as is the ***Pensión Montemar*** *(☎ 661-2771)*, on Avenida 3, Calles 1 & 3. For US$5.50 per person, stay in the basic but friendly ***Hotel Cabezas*** *(☎ 661-1045)*, on Avenida 1, Calles 2 & 4. The rooms are small but clean and have fans – this is a good choice in this price range. Parking in a locked lot costs US$3.

The ***Hotel Ayi Con*** *(☎ 661-0164, 661-1477)*, on Calle 2, Avenidas 1 & 3, has rather basic and dark but clean rooms. Rates are US$6 per person in rooms with fans, US$8 per person in rooms with fans and private cold showers, and US$10 per person with showers and air-conditioning. The ***Hotel Zagala*** *(☎ 661-1319)*, on Avenida 2, Calle 4, has nicer rooms with fans for US$8/13 single/double, but showers are shared.

The Youth Hostel Association in San José *(☎/fax 224-4085)* can make reservations (strongly suggested) for members at the ***Cabinas San Isidro*** *(☎ 221-1225, 663-0031, fax 221-6822)* for US$10 per person. San Isidro is a Puntarenas suburb about 8km east of downtown Puntarenas, and there are buses to and from town. The *cabinas* are near a beach, and there are cooking facilities, a restaurant, swimming pools, and a playground. The complex is popular with ticos. Cabins vary; air-conditioning, hot water, and kitchenettes are features of some, but not all. Most sleep up to six people, and a few are bigger still. The cabin rate is about US$50 (though hostelers don't get this). Ask the bus to drop you off at the Hospital Monseñor Sanabria bus stop; from there it's about a 300m walk.

The ***Gran Hotel Imperial*** *(☎ 661-0579, 661-0600)* is a large old wooden hotel on Paseo de los Turistas and Calle Central, near the bus stations. The place has atmosphere. The rickety upstairs rooms have balconies, some with ocean views, but bathrooms are shared. The rate is US$10 per person. Darker downstairs rooms have private bathrooms and fans and rent for US$14 per person.

The motel-like ***Gran Hotel Chorotega*** *(☎ 661-0998)*, at Avenida 3, Calle 1, has clean rooms with private baths and fans for US$13/25; rooms with communal baths cost US$9 per person.

The ***Hotel Cayuga*** *(☎ 661-0344)*, on Calle 4, Avenidas Central & 1, has very efficient air-conditioning, which is a relief in the hot temperatures. The rooms have private cold showers and are uninspiring but clean. The restaurant attached to the hotel is quite good – although not very cheap. A locked parking lot is behind the hotel. Room rates are US$13/19 – not a bad deal if you need to park a car and cool down.

Mid-Range The family-operated ***Cabinas Central*** *(☎ 661-1484)*, on Calle 7, Paseo de los Turistas & Avenida 2, is safe and friendly and has a parking area, though the rooms are very small and stuffy, which makes them a poor value. Rates with shared baths are US$10/15, with private baths US$20/25.

The ***Cabinas El Jorón*** *(☎ 661-0467)*, on Avenida 4 bis, Calle 25, has both small, rather dark rooms and roomier cabins. The rooms have private baths, air-conditioning, and refrigerators (locally called a 'refri') and go for US$35 double; the more spacious cabins are more expensive.

The ***Hotel Las Hamacas*** *(☎ 661-0398)*, on the Paseo de los Turistas, Calles 5 & 7, is popular with younger ticos. There is a pool, kiddie pool, restaurant, disco, and bar, but it's noisy if your room is close to the revelries. Basic rooms with private cold baths and fans cost US$23/30, with free dance music all night.

El Oasis del Pacífico *(☎ 661-0209)*, on Paseo de los Turistas, Calles 3 & 5, has a pool, disco, restaurant, bar, and parking and is popular with tico families on vacation. Simple rooms with private hot showers cost US$24/30 and with air-conditioning US$39 double.

The ***Casa Dulia B&B*** *(☎ 661-1292)*, on Avenida 4 bis, Calles 23 & 25, is a pleasant and helpful place, with the rate for most rooms with fans and shared baths at US$30, and one room with private bath for US$36 double with breakfast. It is up for sale, so this may change.

The ***Hotel La Punta*** *(☎ 661-1900, ☎/fax 661-0696)*, on Avenida 1 & Calle 35, at the far western point of town near the car ferry terminal, is a decent little hotel. English is spoken; there is a pleasant bar, small pool, and restaurant; and the rooms have hot water, fans, and balconies. Rooms cost US$22/31 with fans, US$36/41 with air-conditioning.

The ***Hotel Las Brisas*** *(☎ 661-4040, fax 661-2120, hbrisas@sol.racsa.co.cr)*, on Paseo de los Turistas, Calle 31, near the west end of Puntarenas, is a quiet, clean, pleasant hotel with a good restaurant and small pool. Rates are US$40/45. All rooms have air-conditioning, TVs, private baths, and hot water.

The ***Hotel Tioga*** *(☎ 661-0271, fax 661-0127, tiogacr@sol.racsa.co.cr)*, Paseo de los Turistas, Calles 17 & 19, was opened in 1959 and is the 'grand dame' of the downtown hotels. There are 46 rooms, but as it's often full, call ahead. All rooms have air-conditioning and private baths, most with hot water. The more expensive rooms have balconies with a sea view; cheaper ones are inside around the pool. The beach is right outside and guests can borrow a beach umbrella. Rates range from US$39 to US$58 single and US$46 to US$69 double. This includes breakfast in the upstairs dining room with ocean view.

Near the north end of Calle 74 in the suburb of Cocal, at the narrowest portion of the peninsula some 3km east of downtown, is the ***Costa Rica Yacht Club*** *(☎ 661-0784, fax 661-2518, cryacht@sol.racsa.co.cr)*, which caters to members of both local and foreign yacht clubs as well as the public. There is a decent restaurant-bar and a pool, and rooms are spartan but spotless. Standard rooms with fans cost US$26/38 single/double and superior rooms with air-conditioning cost US$32/45, but it's sometimes hard to get in – the place is often full of yachties.

Near the Yacht Club is the ***Hotel Porto Bello*** *(☎ 661-1322, fax 661-0036)*, which is set in pleasant grounds (though the entrance from the road is run down) and has rooms with air-conditioning, TVs, and patios for US$35/50. The restaurant overlooks the estuary.

Top End At the end of town near the point of the sand spit, at Paseo de los Turistas & Calle 35, is the ***Complejo Turístico Yadran*** *(☎ 661-2662, fax 661-1944, yadran@ticonet.co.cr)*, which has two restaurants, a bar, casino, disco, children's and adults' pools, and comfortable rooms with all the usual facilities plus TVs. Rooms cost US$70 and suites cost US$85 double. Bicycles are available for rent at US$12 per day, and tours and fishing can be arranged.

The most luxurious hotel in the area is the ***Hotel Fiesta***, 11km east of downtown near Playa Doña Ana (see Playa Doña Ana, later, for details).

Places to Eat

Eating in Puntarenas (at least in the cheaper places) tends to be a little more expensive than in other parts of Costa Rica. Many restaurants are along the Paseo de los Turistas and tend to be tourist-oriented and a little pricey – but not outrageously so. The cheapest food for the impecunious is in the sodas around the market area, by the Paquera boat dock. This area is also inhabited by sailors, drunks, and prostitutes, but it seems raffish rather than dangerous – during the day, at least. There are also several inexpensive Chinese restaurants within a block or two of the intersection of Calle Central and Avenida Central.

There is a row of fairly cheap ***sodas*** on the beach by the Paseo de los Turistas, Calles Central & 3. They provide good outdoor people watching and serve snacks and nonalcoholic drinks; one specializes in enormous fruit salads (you'll see people eating them). Nearby is ***Meseta***, an air-conditioned coffee shop (ahh!). Four and a half blocks to the west are two reasonably priced restaurants, the popular and friendly ***La Casa de Mariscos***, where most seafood entrées cost US$5 (though jumbo shrimp costs US$10), and ***Papis***, a gangster-themed pizza place. Other good places where a fish meal costs under US$5 are ***Kiosko La Perla de Pacífico*** and ***Bar/Restaurant Cevichito***. There's also a ***Pops***, with ice cream to cool you off.

Just west of the Hotel Tioga are several international restaurants to choose from. They have meals in the US$5 to US$10 range – more for shrimp and lobster, less for a snack. The ***Restaurant Aloha*** *(☎ 661-0773)* is one of the better ones in town. Halfway down the next block is the popular and often crowded ***La Caravelle***, a French restaurant with entrées around US$8 to US$10; it is closed on Monday. Just beyond is a German-style bar and restaurant, the ***Jardín Cervecero***. Apart from beer, it has a variety of snacks and light meals. ***Bar Casa Amarilla*** is also good for snacks by the beach. ***La Terraza***, an Italian restaurant on this block, gets glowing recommendations.

On the north side of town, at Avenida 1 and Calles 15 & 17, is the ***Restaurant Kahite Blanco*** *(☎ 661-2093)*, which is a rambling restaurant popular with the locals. It serves good seafood in the US$4 to US$9 range (more for jumbo shrimp and lobster) and generous *bocas* (appetizers). There is music and dancing on weekends.

Most of the better hotels have decent restaurants. Ones that have been recommended are at the hotels ***Porto Bello*** and ***Las Brisas***.

Entertainment

Look for plays and concerts being presented at the ***Casa de Cultura*** in the high season (from December to late March/early April).

There are several dancing spots. On Paseo de los Turistas near Calle 7 are the ***Discoteque El Caracol*** and the ***Discoteque El Primero***. Several of the hotels may have dancing some nights.

Getting There & Away

Note that passenger train services to San José were discontinued in 1991.

Air There are no regularly scheduled flights here, but you can charter a plane to the Chacarita airstrip, about 8km east of downtown Puntarenas.

Bus The drive from San José takes less than two hours and costs about US$2.50. Buses leave frequently from Calle 16, Avenidas 10 & 12 – there may be a wait during holiday weekends. From Puntarenas, buses for San José leave frequently from the terminal on Calle 2, just north of the Paseo de los Turistas. The first bus leaves at 5:30 am and the last about 7 pm.

Across the Paseo from the San José bus terminal is a covered bus stop right by the ocean, from where buses leave to many nearby destinations. There are 12 buses daily to Miramar (near the Refugio Silvestre de Peñas Blancas) and buses inland to Esparza every hour or so. Buses to Liberia leave at 5:30, 7, 9, and 11 am and 1 and 3 pm.

Other buses include the 11:30 am and 4:30 pm departures for Tilarán, a bus to Guácimal at 1 pm, and a bus to Santa Elena (near Monteverde) at 2:15 pm. Buses to Quepos (which could drop you at Jacó) leave at 5 and 11 am and 2:30 pm. (The 11 am bus may be canceled in the wet season.)

Buses serving the communities on the coast north of Puntarenas include a 1 pm bus to Pitahaya, a 12:15 pm bus to Chomes, and buses to Costa de Pajaro at 5:50 and 10:45 am and 1:15 and 4:30 pm.

Buses for the port of Caldera (also going past Playa Doña Ana and Mata de Limón) leave from the market about every hour and head out of town along Avenida Central.

Boat There are two ferry terminals, one for cars and passengers, one just for foot and bike passengers. The Contranamar terminal (☎ 661-1069, fax 661-2197), at the northwest end of town, has two car/passenger ferries. One makes the 1½-hour trip to Playa Naranjo, on the Península de Nicoya west of

Puntarenas. There are departures at 3:15, 7, and 10:50 am and 2:50 and 7 pm daily in the high season – some crossings may be canceled during the low season, and times change quite often. The fare is US$1.25 for adults, half-fare for children, US$10.50 for car plus driver, and US$2.50 for bicycles and motorcycles. There is rarely any problem with getting a passenger ticket, but cars may be turned away, so try to get in line a couple of hours early. (Note that if you want to continue from Playa Naranjo without a car, the only buses meeting the ferry go to Nicoya.)

Car/passenger ferries also leave the Contranamar terminal for the village of Paquera, a 1½-hour ride away to the southwest across the Golfo de Nicoya. En route, the ferry passes near the Reserva Biológica de Isla Guayabo, which is known for its seabird colonies. Departure times are 8:45 am and 2 and 8:15 pm; rates are the same as for the Playa Naranjo ferry. Another car/passenger ferry to Paquera, operated by Naviera Tambor (☎ 661-2084), leaves this dock at 5 am and 12:30 and 5 pm. Rates are the same, with the added option of sitting in an air-conditioned 1st-class cabin for about US$2.

The old Paquera ferry (☎ 661-2830) departs from the old terminal at the dock behind the market. This ferry is for foot and bike passengers only. Daily departures are at 6 and 11 am and 3:15 pm for Paquera. The fare is US$1.50 for adults, US$1.20 for motorcycles, and US90¢ for bicycles and children under age 11. Buses heading farther south into the Península de Nicoya meet this ferry in Paquera (the Naviera Tambor ferry is not met by a bus, because most passengers drive).

You can charter boats to the above destinations and others throughout the Golfo de Nicoya. Small boats holding up to six passengers are available from Taximar (☎ 661-1143, 661-0331) for US$20 to US$40 per hour, depending on the size and type of boat.

Taxi Bus lines can be very long during dry-season weekends. A taxi back to San José costs about US$80. You can also get taxis to take you south to other beach destinations.

Getting Around

Buses marked 'Ferry' run up Avenida Central and go to the Contranamar (Playa Naranjo) terminal, 1.5km from downtown. The taxi fare from the San José bus terminal in Puntarenas to the ferry terminal is about US$2.

ESPARZA

This small town is about 20km inland from Puntarenas, and the two are linked by hourly buses. It is a clean and pleasant town, with a few inexpensive hotels that can provide an alternative to Puntarenas. These include the ***Hotel Cordoba*** *(☎ 635-5014)* and ***Pensión Fanny*** *(☎ 635-5158)*, which charge about US$4 or US$5 per person, and the ***Hotel Castañuelas*** *(☎ 635-5105, fax 635-5769)*, which has simple rooms with private baths and fans for US$12 double, or US$16 with air-conditioning.

SAN MATEO

There's not much in this village except for the ***Rancho Oropendola*** *(☎/fax 428-8600)*, with half a dozen cabins set in pleasant tropical gardens next to a swimming pool. Local tours can be arranged, and this is a good base for visiting nearby Iguana Park and Reserva Biológica Carara (see below). All cabins have private hot baths, some are air-conditioned, and rates are US$50 to US$70 double, including breakfast.

IGUANA PARK

This is a nonprofit project of the Fundación Pro Iguana Verde (☎ 240-6712, fax 235-2007, iguverde@sol.racsa.co.cr), which protects the endangered green iguana through breeding and release programs. One reason the green iguana is endangered is that it is good to eat and has been severely overhunted. The foundation has developed breeding programs that not only have returned an estimated 100,000 individuals into the wild, but also provide income for breeders who 'farm' the iguana for food.

The foundation also has projects to monitor and protect tropical birds, including the scarlet macaw. Habitat protection and local education are key features. There is a training center where students and biologists from all over Latin America can learn more about both resident and migratory birds. The park has a visitor center where you can see exhibits and videos to learn more about the project, and a restaurant where you can sample iguana meat (tastes like chicken!). A souvenir store sells iguana-leather products. It seems odd that to protect the iguana, it has to be farmed for food and leather, but this is the best way to stop poaching and overhunting.

The 400-hectare park is set in a tropical forest a few kilometers east of **Orotina**. There are 4km of trails in an area of transitional forest between the dry tropical forest of the northern lowlands and the tropical rainforest of the south. In primary forest on the property, the Canopy Tour (see Organized Tours in the Getting Around chapter) has set up canopy platforms that are accessed by cables. Visitors are guided from tree to tree using the cables, traversing high above the forest floor.

Iguana Park is open 8 am to 4 pm daily, and admission costs US$10/6 for adults/children and students with ID. Entrance fees go toward supporting the foundation. The Canopy Tour costs US$45/35/25 for adults/students/children and takes about four hours, including hiking to the access point. Two daily tours are offered. The Canopy Tour organizes a complete package from San José for US$85, including the guided tour, park admission, lunch, and roundtrip transportation from San José. If you want to drive to the park yourself and take a canopy tour, a reservation is recommended; the guides may take the day off if there are no reservations.

Getting there is a little tricky, as there don't seem to be any public buses (other than the Canopy Tour). From just south of Orotina, look for a road to the east signed 'Coopebaro, Puriscal.' This road goes over a wooden suspension bridge to the park, and there are signs, though not many. It's about 9km, and half the road is paved. Call the Fundación or the Canopy Tour for up-to-date directions.

PLAYA DOÑA ANA

This is the first clean beach south of Puntarenas, and it's about 13km away from downtown. There are actually two beaches a few hundred meters from each other: Boca Barranca and Doña Ana. Surfing is reportedly good at both beaches, especially Boca Barranca. The Doña Ana beach has been developed for tourism – there is a sign on the Costanera Sur (coastal highway) south of Puntarenas that reads 'Paradero Turistico Doña Ana.' At the beach entrance is a parking lot (US60¢). Daily-use fees for the beach are US$1 for adults, half that for children, and the beach is open 8 am to 5 pm. There are snack bars, picnic shelters, and changing areas, and the swimming is good.

Places to Stay & Eat

On the east side of the Costanera Sur, a half kilometer north of Playa Doña Ana, is the friendly ***Hotel Río Mar*** *(☎ 663-0158)*, which has rooms with private baths and fans for US$11/18 sisngle/double, US$18/24 with air-conditioning. There is a restaurant and bar.

On the west side of the Costanera Sur, 1.3km north of Doña Ana, is the biggest resort hotel in the area. The ***Hotel Fiesta*** *(☎ 663-0808, fax 663-1176, firehu@mail.powernet.co.cr)* has 191 standard rooms, 34 luxury rooms with ocean views, 18 time-share condos with kitchenettes, 12 junior suites, four master suites, and a presidential suite. There are several restaurants and bars, pools, Jacuzzis, tennis and volleyball courts, a casino, gym, and disco, bicycle and car rental, and full tourist agency. Exciting sailboat and catamaran cruises can also be arranged. There is a beach nearby, and you can walk to Doña Ana. Although tours to local national parks, volcanoes, and reserves are available, most guests treat the place as a destination in itself. A standard room costs US$105 per person, everything included.

Getting There & Away

You can get to this area from Puntarenas on buses heading for Caldera. Hotel Fiesta guests can take a daily bus from San José at 2 pm, returning from the hotel at 9:30 am. The fare is US$15.

MATA DE LIMÓN

This is an old beach resort that has long been popular with locals from Puntarenas, as well as with highlanders. It is near the port of Caldera, and the buses from Puntarenas to Caldera will get you to Mata de Limón. The turnoff is 5.5km south of Playa Doña Ana.

The village is situated around a mangrove lagoon that is good for birding (especially at low tide), though not very good for swimming. It is divided in two by a river, with the lagoon and most facilities on the south side. Aside from the occasional jet-skier buzzing by, this is a sleepy little place.

Cabinas Puerto Nuevo, at the entrance to town, looks nice; the ***Marina Resort***, near the lagoon, has air-conditioning. Other options are the inexpensive ***Hotel Viña del Mar*** and ***Cabinas Cecilia***. There are several restaurants; the ***Costa del Sol***, which has outdoor seating overlooking the water, is the most recommended.

SOUTHEAST OF MATA DE LIMÓN

The major port on the Pacific coast is **Puerto Caldera**, which you pass soon after leaving Mata de Limón. There is nothing to do here apart from looking at the ships – there is no town. Just over 9km southeast of the Mata de Limón turnoff on the Costanera is the turnoff for the ***Dundee Ranch Hotel*** (*☎ 428-8776, 267-6222, fax 267-6229, email: info@dundee-ranch.com, Apartado 7812-1000, San José*), which is only 2km off the highway. Unfortunately, its sign on the highway seems to have fallen down, so it is hard to find the turnoff. The hotel is only 60km from San José's Juan Santamaría international airport via Orotina and Atenas. It is a working ranch on the dry Pacific slopes and has comfortable air-conditioned rooms, a pool, restaurant, and bar, and tours are available to the surrounding sights of interest. You can ride horses and see wildlife on the premises. I haven't stayed here but have received good reports about it. The rate is US$87 single or double occupancy, including breakfast.

Shortly beyond the Dundee Ranch, just outside the village of Cascajal, is the ***Hacienda Doña Marta*** (*☎ 234-0853, fax 234-0958, Apartado 463-1000, San José*). This working ranch, in a renovated hacienda, allows visitors to ride horses, watch the farm activities, go birding, or relax by the pool. There are six rustic but distinctive rooms for about US$70 double. Country-style meals are available.

You can join up with the main coastal highway 18km southeast of Mata de Limón; the rest of this chapter follows this highway (the Costanera Sur) southeast along the coast.

RESERVA BIOLÓGICA CARARA

This 4700-hectare reserve is at the mouth of the Río Tárcoles, around 50km southeast of Puntarenas by road, or about 90km west of San José via the Orotina highway. The reserve is surrounded by pasture and agricultural land and forms an oasis for wildlife from a large surrounding area. It is the northern most tropical wet forest on the Pacific coast, in the transition zone to the tropical dry forests farther north, and five Holdridge Life Zones occur within the park. (See Ecology & Environment in the Facts about Costa Rica chapter for an explanation of life zones.) There are also archaeological remains that you can see only with a guide – but they are not very exciting ruins.

If you're driving from Puntarenas or San José, pull over to the left immediately after crossing the Río Tárcoles bridge, also known as the **Crocodile Bridge**. Basking crocodiles are often seen along the muddy banks below the bridge. Binoculars help a great deal. A variety of water birds may also be seen – herons, spoonbills, storks, and anhingas.

A warning: Armed robbery has been reported in this area. Sometimes a park ranger or policeman is on duty. Otherwise, use caution. Robbers sometimes dress like affluent locals, complete with binoculars – and a gun!

Some 0.6km farther south on the left-hand side is a locked gate leading to the Laguna Meandrica trail. Another 2.5km brings you to the Carara administration building/ranger station, which is open 7 am to 5 pm. There are bathrooms, picnic tables, and a short nature trail. You can get information here and pay the US$6 fee to enter the reserve. Trail maps are available for US$1.

Visitors are advised that cars parked at the Laguna Meandrica trail have been broken into. Recently, there have been guards on duty from 8 am to 4 pm in the high season – but this doesn't help for a crack-of-dawn bird walk. Early risers are advised to park their cars in the much safer parking lot at the Carara ranger station and walk north along the Costanera Sur for 2.5km. Go in a group and don't carry unnecessary valuables. Alternately, park by Restaurante Ecologico Los Cocodrilos (see below).

A variety of forest birds inhabit the reserve but can be difficult to see without an experienced guide. The most exciting bird for many visitors to see, especially in June or July, is the brilliantly patterned scarlet macaw. Other birds to watch for include guans, trogons, toucans, motmots, and many other forest species. Monkeys, squirrels, sloths, and agoutis are among the more common mammals present.

The dry season from December to April is the easiest time to go – though the animals are still there in the wet months! March and April are the driest months. Rainfall is almost 3000mm annually, which is less than in the rainforests farther south. It is fairly hot, with average temperatures of 25°C to 28°C – but it is cooler within the rainforest. Make sure you have insect repellent. An umbrella is important in the wet season and occasionally needed in the dry months.

Slothful Habits

Sloths live in trees for most of their lives. They are fastidious with their toilet habits, always climbing down from their trees to deposit their weekly bowel movement on the ground. Biologists don't know why they do this; one hypothesis is that by defecating at the base of a particular tree, the sloth provides a fertilizer that increases the quality of the leaves of that tree, thus improving the sloth's diet.

– Rob Rachowiecki

BUDDY MAYS

Organized Tours

If you are not experienced at watching for wildlife in the rainforest, you will have difficulty seeing much. Going on a tour with a guide is expensive but worthwhile if you want to see a reasonable number of species. Guides who visit several times a week will know where the wildlife is. Most tour companies have day tours to Carara from San José for about US$75 per person. (For further information, see Organized Tours in the Getting Around chapter.) It takes about 2½ hours to drive down from San José.

Places to Stay & Eat

Camping is not allowed, and there is nowhere to stay in the reserve, so most people come on day trips. The nearest place to stay and eat is the ***Restaurante Ecologico Los Cocodrilos*** (*☎ 428-8005, 428-9009*), on the north side of the Río Tárcoles bridge. It offers basic, clean roadside cabins for US$13 double. Otherwise, the nearest hotels and restaurants are at Tárcoles, 2 or 3km south of the reserve, or at Jacó, 22km south. Several readers have recommended staying in Tárcoles and walking up to the reserve early in the morning before tours begin to arrive.

Getting There & Away

There are no buses to Carara, but you can get off any bus bound for Jacó, Quepos, or Parque Nacional Manuel Antonio. This may be a bit problematic on weekends, when buses are full, so go midweek if you are relying on a bus ride. This budget option has pleased some travelers, though others complain that they 'didn't see anything' in the reserve, which is why it can be worth going on a guided trip.

Many of the more remote parts of the Pacific coast are best visited by car.

TÁRCOLES AREA

Two kilometers south of the Carara ranger station is the Tárcoles turnoff to the right (west) and the Hotel Villa Lapas turnoff to the left. To get to Tárcoles, turn right and drive for a kilometer, then go right at the T-junction to the village, with cabins and a beach. To reach the mudflats of the Río Tárcoles, continue past the village for 2 or 3km; this is a prime area for birders looking for shorebirds, particularly at low tide.

Waterfall

A 5km dirt road past the Hotel Villa Lapas (see below) leads to a waterfall, variously called La Catarata (Waterfall) or El Manatial de Agua Viva (Spring of Living Water). It's about 200m high, and to see it in its full glory, you need to clamber down a steep trail (45 minutes) and then climb back out (90 minutes). It'll probably take you longer if you examine the black-and-green poison-arrow frogs on the trail, watch the many birds above, and stop at various lookout points. The trail and falls are in virgin rainforest. At the bottom of the falls, the river continues through a series of natural swimming holes. A camping area and outhouse are available at the bottom.

The waterfall is on private property owned by Daniel Bedard (☎ 637-0346, fax 236-1506), who cut the trail (reportedly in seven months, working 60-hour weeks with five other men) a few years ago. The trail is open, officially, 8 am to 3 pm December 15 to April 15. It is open in the wet season (when the fall is at its fullest) when conditions and weather permit. Call for information in wet months. Admission to the trail/waterfall costs US$8.

Several kilometers up the road beyond Bedard's trailhead, the Complejo Ecologico Catarata has reportedly bulldozed a trail that gives you a view of the top of the falls.

Crocodile Man Tour

The 'Crocodile Man,' Victor Pineda, takes groups by boat on the Río Tárcoles for birding and crocodile-watching. The 'highlight' is when crazy Pineda gets out of the boat to hand-feed the crocodiles (2.5m to 6m long), while you watch from a safe distance.

The Crocodile Man Tour (☎/fax 637-0426, crocodilemancr@hotmail.com) has an office on the main road in Tárcoles – follow the signs. Tours cost US$25 for two hours and usually are given several times a day. Victor has had troubles since starting this tour, though not the ones you would expect. His first setback was that his boat was destroyed by vandals; then a company with the money to put up large billboards opened a similar tour just down the road. However, Victor has been as scrappy as you would expect someone in this line of work to be, and he is back in business with a new boat and an assistant. *National Geographic* apparently featured his exploits in one of their TV specials. His competitor, the Jungle Crocodile Safari (☎ 383-4612), charges similar prices and its tour seems well run, but Pineda remains the original Crocodile Man.

Places to Stay & Eat

This place can be almost deserted midweek in the wet season. Finding a restaurant can be problematic at that time. In the village is the ***Cabinas Carara*** *(☎ 637-0178)*, which has decent rooms with showers ranging from US$22 to US$30 double, depending on whether you want fans, views, or air-conditioning. It has a small pool. Another possibility is the small, simple, family-run ***Cabinas Mar y Luna***.

Half a kilometer inland from the Tárcoles turnoff is the ***Hotel Villa Lapas*** *(☎ 284-1418, 663-0811, fiesta@sol.racsa.co.cr)*. The hotel has a small pool; its pleasant gardens are surrounded by hillside and forest with good birding along trails that wind up the Río Tarcolitos in a private reserve. There's a butterfly garden (US$3), a pool table, and a mini-golf course. The restaurant opens at 7 am and is open to the public all day. The 47 rooms are clean, spacious, and airy, with fans and private hot showers. Rooms cost about US$90.

The ***Tarcol Lodge*** *(☎/fax 267-7138; in the USA ☎ 800-593-3305, Dept 1425, Box 025216, Miami, FL 33102-5216, johnerb@sol.racsa.co.cr)* is on the south bank of the Río Tárcoles, at the northwest end of the village. At low tide, a huge expanse of mudflats attracts thousands of shorebirds during migration, and hundreds at other times. At high tide, the mudflats disappear, and the river comes up close to the lodge on three sides. Definitely bring binoculars.

The lodge is run by the Erb family, the same folks who have the Rancho Naturalista near Turrialba (see the Central Valley chapter). The focus is similar, with birding and nature tours, rustic but comfortable lodging, and good food. The birding is special – a three-day visit will usually yield at least 150 species, and over 400 are recorded on the lodge list. The owners are friendly, fun, and good birders. This place is highly recommended for birders.

The lodge is small – four double rooms sharing two bathrooms (larger groups can be accommodated in a nearby house). All rooms have fans, and the bathrooms have hot water. The rate is US$99 per person including meals and a free guided tour if you stay three nights or more. Resident naturalists assist with birding around the lodge during your visit. Longer stays cost US$643 per person per week, including two guided tours, meals, and lodging. Bottled drinks cost extra. Tours are led by naturalist guides and visit either two different trails in Carara or the estuary at high tide (by boat), either at night or during the day. Weeks can also be split between the Tarcol Lodge and Rancho Naturalista. Transportation from San José can be arranged for an extra US$60 each way.

Just over 3km south of the Tárcoles turnoff is the ***Chalets Paradise*** *(☎ 637-0168)*, which offers decent double rooms, some with kitchenettes, for about US$30 – its Swiss-style tin roofs (built by the original Swiss owner, who left long ago) have a certain oddball charm. There is a pool.

PUNTA LEONA AREA

This tiny headland is about halfway between Tárcoles and Jacó. There are a couple of upscale places to stay with super views.

Activities

The US-based JD's Watersports (☎ 669-0511 ext 34, fax 661-1414; in San José ☎ 257-3857, fax 256-6391, jdwater@sol.racsa.co.cr; see Organized Tours in the Getting There & Away chapter for US contacts) operates a complete water-sports center here and offers sportfishing (US$165 per person per day, four to six anglers), scuba diving (two-tank boat dives for US$72, or a beginners' resort course for US$94), very popular half-day jungle river cruises (US$55), sunset cruises (US$33), and rentals of ocean kayaks or windsurfers (US$11 per hour), Sunfish sailboats (US$22 per hour), Jet Skis (US$20 per 20 minutes), body boards or snorkeling gear (US$16.50 per day), and scuba gear (US$33 per day). Boat charters to various destinations are available. JD's Watersports arranges complete packages with all meals and your choice of accommodations.

Places to Stay & Eat

About 6km south of Tárcoles and 11km north of Jacó, a guarded gate lets guests onto the 4km dirt road to the ***Hotel Punta Leona*** *(☎ 661-2414, fax 661-1414; in San José ☎ 231-3131, fax 232-0791, puntaleo@sol.racsa.co.cr)*, surrounded by the rainforest. This is a 300-hectare cliff-top resort with beach access and 108 rooms and 73 apartments, all with TVs and air-conditioning. There are three pools, three restaurants, tennis, horseback riding, and children's activities. Rates are about US$90 to US$105 for double rooms (various kinds and sizes) or about US$160 for apartments, which have kitchens and two bedrooms sleeping up to six. Also on this property is the ***Leona Mar Condominium Hotel***, with completely furnished air-conditioned units with kitchens, dishwashers, cable TVs, etc, renting for roughly US$200. The usual weekly and low-season discounts apply.

The luxurious ***Hotel Villa Caletas*** *(☎ 257-3653, fax 222-2059, caletas@ticonet.co.cr)* is 3km south of the Punta Leona entry and 8km north of the Jacó turnoff from the Costanera. A steep 1km paved road leads to the beautiful hotel, decorated with art and antiques. There are stunning views, one of those marvelous pools that appear to drop off at the horizon, and a French-influenced restaurant. The hotel sometimes hosts classical music recitals in a small open-air amphitheater, from which you can watch the sun go down behind the Península de Nicoya. It is about 1km down a steep trail to the beach. Eight spacious rooms in the main hotel and about 20 villas and suites dotted around the steep and forested property all have private view balconies and range from about US$130 to US$250. À la carte meals cost about US$24 for lunch or dinner, US$11 for breakfast. Although tours and activities can be arranged, many guests just do nothing more strenuous than relax, with an occasional dip in the pool. There are no TVs or telephones in the rooms – bring a good book.

PLAYA HERRADURA

The Herradura turnoff is on the Costanera Sur 3.5km north of the turnoff to Jacó. A paved road leads 3km west to Playa Herradura – a quiet, sheltered, palm-fringed, black-sand beach. Until recently this was a rural beach, popular mainly with campers. Now it is home to a marina, hotel, and condominium complex that is one of the largest new tourism developments in the country.

A few hundred meters before the beach on the main road is a ***campground*** with showers and basic facilities, charging about US$3 per person. Facing the beach is ***Cabinas Herradura*** *(☎ 643-3181)*, which charges US$18/32 single/double, US$5 more per additional person, up to six, for simple, spacious cabins with air-conditioning and kitchens; rates may go up on dry-season weekends. About half a kilometer before you reach the beach is the German-owned ***Cabinas del Río*** *(☎ 643-3275)*. Cabins of varying comfort and size are spread out around a tiny creek. Rates are US$11/18 single/double, US$4 more for additional people, slightly more for the two cabins with kitchens. Farther inland, the motel-like ***Cabinas La Turrialbeña*** *(☎ 643-1236)* has a pool and charges US$50 for air-conditioned doubles.

The big change to this beach is the ***Los Sueños Marriott Beach and Golf Resort*** *(☎ 630-9000, fax 630-9090; in the US ☎ 800-228-9290, information@los-suenos.com)*, a US$40 million hotel and condominium project at the north end of the bay that features a 250-slip marina, golf course, tennis courts, 1-acre swimming pool, shopping center, casino, sportfishing, and all the activities and amenities a resort can offer. Hills above the bay have been bulldozed to make way for million-dollar homes. On the plus side, most of the land that the resort is being built on was a cattle ranch, not rainforest, and the builders seem to be obeying the environmental laws that do exist – a refreshing change from the situation at Tambor in Nicoya. Although a resort that advertises 'eco-golf' is kidding itself somewhat, careful steps are being taken to keep pollution produced by the complex within legal limits. The marina will have a customs office for international yachties, and they expect cruise ships to make stops here. At the time of writing, Marriott predicts that rates will start at about US$300 double.

On the beach are a couple of simple restaurants.

JACÓ AREA

Jacó is the first developed beach town on the Pacific coast as you head south. It is a large, pretty beach, and its proximity to San José makes it popular and, by Costa Rican standards, crowded – though it will seem relatively quiet to many visitors who may be used to shoulder-to-shoulder sunbathing on their own crowded beaches. Jacó has something of a reputation as a 'party beach' – especially during the dry season – but it is pretty sedate compared to some North American party beaches, like Daytona Beach in Florida.

Nevertheless, it is popular with young people and vacation-package visitors. Swimming is possible, though you should be careful of rip currents (people drown each year; see Swimming Safety in the Facts for the Visitor chapter) and avoid the areas nearest the estuaries, which are polluted.

The turnoff from the Costanera Sur for Jacó is just 3.5km beyond Herradura. Playa Jacó is about 2km off the Costanera. The beach itself is about 3km long, and hotels and restaurants line the road running behind it. Development has been fast in Jacó – perhaps too fast. The crowded center of Jacó can get somewhat trashed at the end of a busy weekend, although the fringes are quieter and cleaner. However, local hoteliers and tourist industry personnel are making successful efforts to keep the beach clean. Though there are many quieter and less crowded places elsewhere, Jacó continues to grow and draw tourists who want to hang out in a busy beach town.

Information

There is no unbiased tourist information office. Two banks change money. The ICE office has international telephone and fax.

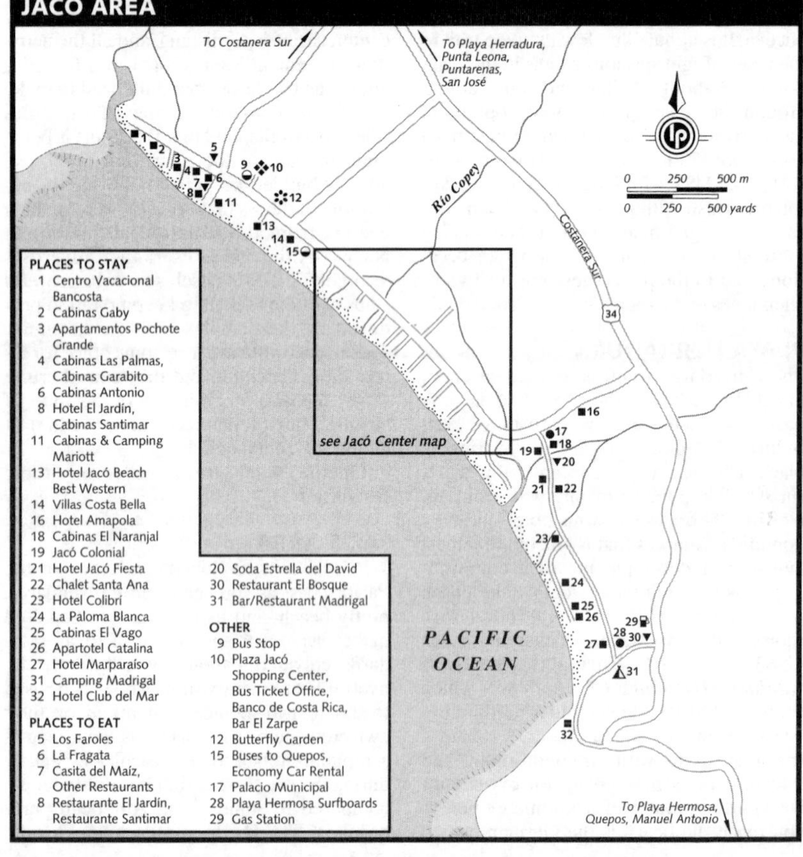

Costa Rica Connection, next to Rad Rentals (see the Jacó Center map), offers Internet access, as does Information Jacó 2000, by the Banco Nacional – also look for signs around town. The Red Cross (☎ 643-3090) can help with medical emergencies, but sick travelers should ask their hotel to call a local doctor, or go to a city hospital in Puntarenas or San José.

Surfing

Jacó is called the surfing capital of Costa Rica – not so much because it has the best waves, but for several other reasons. The waves in the Jacó area tend to be a little more consistent than elsewhere. Although the rainy season is considered the best for Pacific coast surfing, this area has some decent possibilities even in the dry months. Jacó is quickly and easily reached from the capital and provides a huge infrastructure of hotels, restaurants, and surf shops, and it is a central place to get information about surfing conditions anywhere in the country.

Surfers will find a number of places in the center of town competing to rent boards and provide information. At the north end, Chuck's has been around a while. At the south end, Playa Hermosa Surfboards makes custom boards.

The beach at **Playa Hermosa** begins about 5km south of Jacó and has its own small cluster of hotels and restaurants. This beach stretches for about 10km and is for expert surfers; there is an annual contest here in August.

Other Activities & Organized Tours

Several places advertise bike rentals. These usually cost about US$2 an hour or US$6.50 a day. Mopeds and small scooters cost US$25 to US$35 a day (many places ask for a cash or credit card deposit of about US$200); look for signs in the center. One place is Rad Rentals (☎ 643-1310), which also rents boogie and surf boards (US$2 per hour, US$7 per day). There are several car rental agencies, and though rates are a little higher than in San José, they are convenient. The main tour company is Fantasy Tours in the Hotel Jacó Beach lobby. The Jacó Beach

Equestrian Center (☎ 643-1569) offers horseback tours starting at US$25.

Language Courses

The City-Playa Language Institute (☎/fax 643-2122) offers inexpensive courses in Spanish. Ask about group rates.

Places to Stay – Jacó Area

Reservations are recommended during the December to April dry season and definitely required during Easter week and on most weekends. There are plenty of places to stay – but travelers on a shoestring budget will not find many good deals, especially if they're looking for single rooms. Camping is an option, as is staying in cabins that sleep six.

Low-season discounts are available in most hotels, as are surfers' discounts – the latter probably because surfers tend to stay for days or even weeks. If you plan on a lengthy stay (surfer or not), ask for a discount. The rates given here are full high-season rates, but discounts could be as great as 40% to 50% if you're staying for several nights in the low season, especially in the mid- and higher-priced places where good deals can be made. Although single/double rates are given here, many hotels have larger rooms where budget travelers can economize as a group.

Playa Jacó is a growing resort, and new places will have opened since the last edition of this book. Also, many places are expanding, so hotels often have rooms of varying ages and quality. If you are planning on spending a few days, it definitely pays to shop around.

During the rainy season, there are reports of water problems in hotels, because heavy rains can cause landslides and damage water pipes.

Camping In the center, ***Camping El Hicaco*** *(☎ 643-3004)* charges US$2.50 per person and is friendly. It has picnic tables, bathrooms, and a lock-up for your gear. Don't leave valuables in your tent. The campsites are sandy rather than grassy, which may reduce the number of insects you'll encounter. South of the center, for US$2 per person, is the grassier ***Camping Madrigal*** *(☎ 643-3230)*, with a bar/restaurant next door. North of the center, also grassy and US$2 per person, is ***Camping and Cabinas Mariott*** *(☎ 643-3585)*, which despite its name and nice billboard offers pretty basic facilities. It's a nice site, though, at an uncrowded end of the beach, with some good sodas across the road.

Budget At the south end of downtown, the ***Cabinas Calypso*** *(☎ 643-3208, fax 643-3728)* charges US$15 for basic double rooms with fans and shared cold baths, and has some better cabins with private baths for about US$25 triple. Next door, the ***Cabinas Marea Alta*** *(☎ 643-3554)* has fairly basic cabins with private cold showers and refrigerators for US$23 double.

Closer to the center, the ***Cabinas Bohío*** *(☎ 643-3017)* has basic old cabins for US$22 that sleep three or four people. The similarly priced but better-quality ***Cabinas Emily*** *(☎ 643-3513)* is popular with shoestringers and has a good local restaurant next door. Nearby, ***Chuck's Cabinas*** *(☎/fax 643-3328, chucks@sol.racsa.co.cr)* has a few simple rooms with high-powered fans and shared showers for US$7.50 per person, and a larger room with private bathroom for US$25/30/35 double/triple/quad. Chuck also runs a surf shop, has lived in the area for years, and is bursting with information about surfing in Costa Rica; ask about his Bro Deal and Ultra Bro Deal.

At the north end, ***Cabinas Garabito*** *(☎ 643-3321)* has singles for US$10 with shared baths and doubles for US$18 with private baths and cold water. Near the beach, the pleasant ***Cabinas Santimar*** *(☎ 643-3605)* has four basic but clean rooms with shared cold baths at US$15 double.

The basic but friendly ***Cabinas El Recreo*** *(☎ 643-3012)* has doubles with fans and cold showers for US$25. The cabinas have a seafood restaurant next door. The ***Cabinas Mar de Plata*** *(☎ 643-3580)*, in the center, charges US$12 for basic doubles with private cold baths. The friendly, French-Canadian-run ***Cabinas La Cometa*** *(☎ 643-3615)* is popular with international travelers. Four clean rooms with fans and shared cold showers cost about US$22 double, and three rooms with private hot showers cost about US$32 double.

The ***Cabinas Roble*** *(☎ 643-3558)* is clean and a decent value at US$15/20 single/double for rooms with showers. Next door, the friendly ***Cabinas Calu*** *(☎ 643-1107)* has been well recommended by several readers for good-size, clean rooms with private showers and fans for US$20 double. ***Cabinas Marilyn*** *(☎ 643-3215)*, across from the Hotel Cocal, offers large, bare rooms with private baths for US$18 double, US$25.50 with fridges. At the north end of town, the similarly priced ***Cabinas Antonio*** *(☎ 643-3043)* is also OK, with private hot showers and a restaurant next door.

Farther north, the ***Centro Vacacional Bancosta*** *(☎ 643-3016; in San José 223-3326, fax 221-5525)* has basic cabins with cold showers and refrigerators for US$20, which is a good deal for four people. Cabins sleeping six cost US$29, and larger cabins with kitchens cost US$48 (these only sleep five). There is a pool, bar, and restaurant.

The ***Chalet Santa Ana*** *(☎ 643-3233)* is in a quiet area at the far south end of town. The rooms are OK and rent for US$23 double with bath (tepid water) and fans or US$38 with a kitchenette. Some rooms sleep up to five.

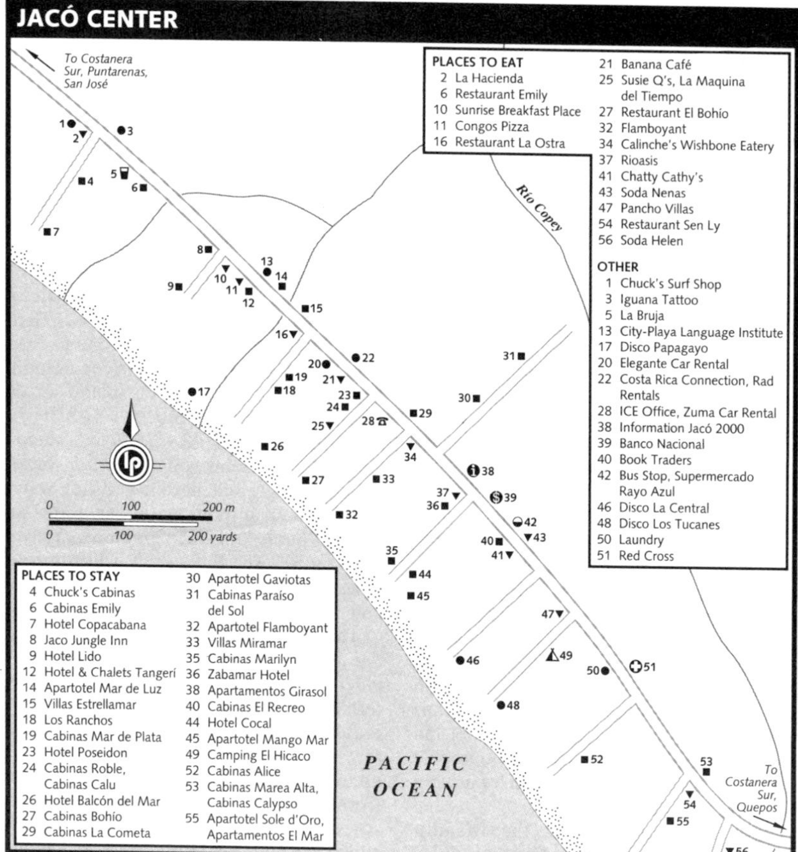

The *Hotel Lido* (☎ *643-3171)* has a pool and charges US$20 per person in rooms with kitchenettes, fans, and cold water.

Mid-Range The *Cabinas Alice* (☎ *643-3061)* has decent clean rooms with private cold baths and fans for US$35 double. The restaurant has been recommended, the beach is just steps away, and there is a pool. At the south end, the *Cabinas El Naranjal* (☎ *643-3006)* has a good restaurant and spacious, clean but bare rooms with hot showers and fans for US$30 double, or US$50 for larger units with kitchens. Also nearby, the *Jacó Colonial* (☎ *643-3727)* is an old mock-Spanish-colonial-style hotel with about a dozen decent rooms with fans and hot water for about US$28 double.

Los Ranchos (☎*/fax 643-3070, Apartado 22, Playa Jacó)* is very popular with English-speaking visitors and has many repeat clients. There is a pool, pleasant garden, small paperback library, and friendly staff offering local tour and surfing information. Rooms are quiet and have fans and private baths with hot water. Some have kitchenettes. The rate is US$30 double in the smaller upstairs rooms. The larger downstairs rooms with kitchens go for US$40 double, and bungalows sleeping up to five rent for about US$65.

The recommended ***Apartotel Mar de Luz*** *(☎/fax 643-3259, mardeluz@ticonet.co.cr)* has attractive, air-conditioned rooms with patios, kitchens, and hot water for US$43 double, and larger rooms for US$55 for four. There is a pool. The management speaks Spanish, English, German, and Dutch and is friendly, knowledgeable, and informative.

The ***Cabinas Bohío*** *(☎ 643-3017)* has a decent restaurant on the premises and, apart from its budget rooms, some newer cabins with two double beds, bathrooms, kitchenettes, refrigerators, and fans for US$42 (two to four people). The ***Apartamentos El Mar*** *(☎ 643-3165, fax 272-2280)* has clean, good-size apartments with hot water, kitchenettes, and fans for US$55 for five people – a good deal. It has a few doubles for US$33, and a small pool. The ***Zabamar Hotel*** *(☎/fax 643-3174)* has a pool and a small, reasonably priced breakfast/snack bar. Clean, pleasant rooms with hot water cost US$30/35 with fans, or US$40/45 with air-conditioning.

At the far north end of town, the ***Cabinas Gaby*** *(☎ 643-3080, fax 441-5922, Apartado 20-4050, Alajuela)* has pleasant rooms with kitchenettes, hot water, and a choice of fans or air-conditioning. There is a small pool and a shady garden. Rooms cost US$40 double with air-conditioning, and US$55 for a cabin with fans that sleeps five.

Also at the north end, the friendly, Belgian-owned ***Hotel El Jardín*** *(☎ 643-3050)* is known for its French restaurant. Rooms are simple but clean and have hot water and fans for US$25/40. There is a pool. Nearby, the ***Cabinas Las Palmas*** *(☎ 643-3005, fax 643-3512)* has a variety of rooms set in pleasant gardens. Older rooms with cold water and fans cost US$23/27. Newer units with hot water, fans, and kitchenettes cost US$40 double, or US$60 with air-conditioning.

The friendly ***Jacó Jungle Inn*** *(☎ 643-1631, conect@sol.racsa.co.cr)* has plain, clean rooms with private baths for US$33 double. The inn has a pool, Jacuzzi, and Tarzan/Jane bathrooms by its small poolside bar. The ***Apartotel Sole d'Oro*** *(☎ 643-3247, 643-3441, fax 643-3172)* has clean, modern, spacious rooms with kitchenettes, cold water, and fans for US$45 double, or US$60 with air-conditioning. Rooms sleep three or four, and there is a pool and Jacuzzi.

The ***Apartotel Gaviotas*** *(☎ 643-3092, fax 643-3054)* has 12 spacious and modern apartments with kitchenettes, refrigerators, sitting areas, fans, and hot water. There is a fine pool, a bar, and a TV room. It's a few hundred meters' walk to the beach – if you can put up with that, you'll find this to be a great deal in the rainy season, when rates as low as US$20 have been reported. High-season rates are US$20/30 for one to three people and US$45 in rooms sleeping up to five. About 100m farther inland is the ***Cabinas Paraíso del Sol*** *(☎ 643-3250, fax 643-3137, Apartado 92-4023, Jacó, Puntarenas)*. Its nice rooms come with fans or air-conditioning, kitchenettes, and hot water. There is a small pool and a bar. Rates are US$37 double and US$62 for a room sleeping up to six. The Italian-run ***Apartamentos Girasol*** *(☎ 643-1119)* has similar facilities and prices.

The ***Hotel Marparaíso*** *(☎ 643-3277; in San José 220-4358)* is a somewhat rundown older hotel that offers a 7% discount for International Youth Hostel members. There are two pools, a game room, and a restaurant. The rate is US$72 for rooms sleeping up to six; some have air-conditioning. ***Villas Costa Bella*** *(☎ 643-3465)* has a pool, beach access, and decent double rooms with fans and hot water for US$42. It also has five condominiums with kitchens for US$76.

The beachfront ***Hotel Balcón del Mar*** *(☎/fax 643-3251, balcon@sol.racsa.co.cr)* has a pool and rooms with private balconies and ocean views for about US$50 double. Some rooms are air-conditioned, and all have hot water and refrigerators. Also on the beach is the good ***Apartotel Mango Mar*** *(☎/fax 643-3670)*, with a dozen nice air-conditioned rooms with kitchenettes, hot water, and balconies overlooking the pool and Jacuzzi. The rate is US$60 double. It also has two larger apartments.

At the quiet south end of town on the beach is the ***Hotel Colibrí*** *(☎ 643-3419,*

643-3770, fax 643-3730). There is a pool, Italian restaurant, and bar. A dozen pleasant rooms with fans and warm showers cost about US$45 double, including breakfast. Nearby, facing the beach, ***La Paloma Blanca*** *(☎ 643-1893, fax 643-1892, iwann@mailcity.com)* is a nice new B&B in a former duplex home. An upstairs room with private bath costs US$45 double, the ground floor suite has a full kitchen and patio for US$60 double, and an upstairs room with a canopy bed and ocean-view verandah costs US$75 double. There is a pool, and discounts are available for longer stays; the house can be rented as a whole for US$120 per night, US$500 per month. The owners are from the USA.

Facing the same stretch of beach, ***Apartotel Catalina*** *(☎ 643-3217, fax 643-3544)* has 20 housekeeping units, all with kitchenettes, hot water, and fans, for US$40 triple. Each unit has a small balcony or patio, and there is a pool. This is a great deal. Between these two hotels is ***Cabinas El Vago*** *(☎ 643-3507)*, with 10 simple but comfortable rooms with fans and hot water for US$40 double – not a bad deal considering the location. (Its 'tropical fish' business card is the most attractive in my vast collection!)

Apartotel Flamboyant *(☎ 643-3146, 643-1068)* has eight clean and pleasant studio rooms just steps from the beach, and there is also a pool. Rooms have fans, kitchenettes, hot showers, and little patios – a good value for US$50/55. The adjoining restaurant is one of the best in Jacó.

The ***Villas Miramar*** *(☎ 643-3003, fax 643-3617)* is a good place with large rooms, kitchenettes, refrigerators, hot water, fans, and a pool. It is set in a pleasant and quiet garden with picnic/barbecue areas. The rate is US$60 double. Similar facilities are found at the pleasant and friendly ***Apartamentos Pochote Grande*** *(☎ 643-3236, fax 220-4979, pochote@sol.racsa.co.cr)*, which charges US$64 double.

Villas Estrellamar *(☎ 643-3102, fax 643-3453)* has a nice pool and pleasant gardens. About 20 good rooms with cable TVs, hot water, and kitchens rent for US$54 double with a fan, US$65 with air-conditioning, dropping to a bargain half-price in the low season. The new ***Hotel Poseidon*** *(☎ 643-1642, fax 643-3558, poseidon@sol.racsa.co.cr)* has simple, attractive rooms with air-conditioning and hot water for US$55 double (slightly less with fans), and an elegant open-air restaurant. There is a pool, wet bar, and private parking; French, Spanish, English, and German are spoken.

The recommended ***Hotel Club del Mar*** *(☎/fax 643-3194, Apartado 107-4023, Jacó)* is the opposite of the brash resorts. It is set in quiet and attractive gardens at the south end of Jacó, with a nice beach nearby. There is a pool and a very good restaurant. The helpful owners speak English, Swahili (!), and Spanish and arrange horseback and other tours. There are 18 varied but attractively furnished rooms with kitchens, fans, air-conditioning, balconies, and sitting areas available in some. All have private hot baths. Rates range from US$55 to US$90 double.

Top End The ***Hotel Cocal*** *(☎ 643-3067, fax 643-3082; in the USA ☎ 800-732-9266, cocalcr@sol.racsa.co.cr)* has 44 pleasant air-conditioned rooms with hot water for US$100 double, including breakfast. There are two pools, a small casino, a good restaurant with ocean views, and a bar. The hotel brochures point out that the two town discos are close by, which is an advantage or disadvantage depending on your point of view. Local tours are arranged.

The ***Hotel & Chalets Tangerí*** *(☎ 643-3001, fax 643-3636)* has air-conditioned double rooms with TVs and fridges for US$71 double. It also has some spacious chalets with three bedrooms and kitchens that are not much more expensive. There is a pool, and the grounds behind the hotel stretch down to the beach.

The ***Hotel Copacabana*** *(☎/fax 643-3131, hotcopa@sol.racsa.co.cr)* is a Canadian-run hotel near the beach. The owners will help arrange car rentals and tours to nearby national parks. There is a pool, restaurant, and sports bar with satellite TV. Standard rooms with fans and hot showers cost about US$70 double, and air-conditioned suites with kitchenettes and private balconies cost US$90 for up to four people.

The ***Hotel Jacó Beach*** *(☎ 220-1725, fax 232-3159; in the USA or Canada ☎ 800-528-1234, htljaco@bestwestern.co.cr)* is the biggest hotel in Jacó, featuring well over 100 rooms, and is now owned by the Best Western hotel chain. Many Canadian charter groups stay here. This is a full-service beach resort, with bicycle, surfboard, kayak, boat, and car rentals. There is a restaurant, disco, casino, swimming pools, and sunbathing areas. Rooms are air-conditioned and have hot water. Rates are US$103 (one to three people) and US$125 for a villa sleeping up to five. The other big resort hotel in town is the ***Hotel Jacó Fiesta*** *(☎ 643-3147, fax 643-3148, Apartado 38, Jacó)*, which is slightly smaller but has four pools, a casino, disco, tennis court, and various tours and rentals. Somewhat faded air-conditioned rooms with refrigerators cost US$85 double or US$100 for four – again, these are often full of charter groups.

The ***Hotel Amapola*** *(☎/fax 643-3668, 643-3337, amapola@sol.racsa.co.cr)* is set back about 700m from the beach. It has 44 tastefully decorated rooms, plus six suites and three villas, all with air-conditioning, hot water, cable TVs, telephones, and refrigerators. There is a large free-form pool, two Jacuzzis, a disco, a casino, and an excellent and reasonably priced Italian restaurant. Local tours can be arranged. This place has much newer and nicer rooms than the older resort hotels mentioned above. Rates are US$95 for a double room, US$148 for the suites, and US$165 for the villas.

Places to Stay – Playa Hermosa

About 4km south of the Restaurant El Bosque on the Costanera (see the Jacó Area map) are a few hotels offering good access to the surfing at Playa Hermosa. ***Restaurante y Cabinas Las Arenas*** is a good deal, with cabins with kitchenettes, cold showers, and four beds for about US$28. ***Cabinas Vista Hermosa*** *(☎ 643-3422)* has beachfront cabins with kitchens starting at about US$25 double, or about US$10 per person in units sleeping up to eight. There is a restaurant, bar, and pool. ***Cabinas Las Olas*** *(☎/fax 643-3687, lasolas@sol.racsa.co.cr)* has nice bungalows with kitchens, fans, and hot water for US$45 double. Rooms sleeping up to seven cost US$10 per person. It has a pool and restaurant and staff will give advice and arrange transportation to the best local surfing and snorkeling spots.

Next door, ***Safari Surf*** has rooms for US$33 double and offers movies and laundry service. Nearby, ***Cabinas Rancho Grande*** *(☎ 643-3529)*, run by a friendly couple from Florida, has cane-paneled rooms with private baths for US$10 per person, including a cute A-frame room on the top floor. Some rooms sleep up to seven and share a communal kitchen.

Just north of the cabins are several more upscale options. The ***Terraza del Pacífico*** *(☎ 643-3222, fax 643-3424, terraza@sol.racsa.co.cr)* has modern, spacious rooms with ocean views, air-conditioning, TVs, and hot water. The hotel has children's and adults' pools, a bar, and a good Italian restaurant. The rate is about US$85 for up to three people. The smaller ***Villa Hermosa Hotel*** *(☎ 643-3373, fax 643-3506, taycole@sol.racsa.co.cr)* offers rooms with air-conditioning and kitchenettes for US$35/45/55 for two/three/up to five people. There is a garden-shaded pool. Nearby, the ***Hotel Fuego del Sol*** *(☎ 643-3737, fax 643-3736, fuegos@costarica.net)* is a small resortlike complex with a pool, bar, and gym. Eighteen rooms with air-conditioning, hot water, coffeemakers, and telephones cost US$50/60/70 for one/two/up to four people. Tours, beach parties, and transportation to surf spots can be arranged.

Places to Eat

Shoestring travelers will find that the set menus at the sodas and restaurants frequented by locals are the best deals for budget meals. *Casados* (bargain meals) are in the US$3 to US$4 range in the following places. (Though slightly cheaper possibilities exist, they won't remain cheaper if I publicize them.) At the north end, the ***Casita del Maíz*** charges US$3.50 for a casado, and there are several other cheapish local places near here, including ***Restaurante Santimar*** *(☎ 643-3605)*, which has a nice beachside patio and good food and fruit drinks. In the center, ***Soda Nenas*** has good casados. Also try ***Soda Helen*** *(☎ 643-3110)*, which is open 7 am to 10 pm in the high season, and ***Soda Estrella del David*** *(☎ 643-3081)*, at the south end.

Plenty of restaurants busily cater to the crowds in the dry season but may falter a bit in the rainy months. New ones open (and close) every year. A stroll through Jacó in the high season can result in an assault of billboards advertising the 'best' places to eat.

There are a number of options for pizza, most with wood-burning ovens. ***Calinche's Wishbone Eatery***, overseen by the charming Calinche, is a good one and has a spacious, shady patio. Mexican and grilled food are also specialties. ***Rioasis*** (the former Killer Munchies) is a fun-looking place with a poster of Salvador Dalí over the door. ***Congos Pizza*** is another pizza-dedicated place, with a jungle theme. There are several other Italian restaurants.

Flamboyant, adjoining the Apartotel of the same name, is known locally as one of the best restaurants in Jacó.

Pancho Villas *(☎ 643-3571)* has Mexican food, but I think the steaks and international food are better (I live an hour's drive from Mexico, so I'm picky about Mexican food). Entrées average US$8. ***Restaurant Sen Ly*** *(☎ 643-3297)* serves satisfactory Chinese food. ***Banana Café*** is good for 'natural' breakfasts. ***Susie Q's*** is open 6 to 9 pm for pretty decent ribs, steaks, and barbecue dinners in the range of US$5 to US$10. Nearby, ***La Maquina del Tiempo*** (The Time Machine) serves more health-oriented food. ***La Hacienda*** *(☎ 643-3191)* has steaks and seafood beginning at US$5. The ***Restaurant El Jardín*** *(☎ 643-3050)* serves French food and is pricey but good.

Several restaurants serve international/tico food. The ***Restaurant El Bohío*** is quite good and has a sea view. It is open for breakfast and serves dinners in the US$4 to US$8 range (except for shrimp or lobster at US$18). The ***Restaurant La Ostra*** is a good low- to mid-priced seafood place. ***Los Faroles*** *(☎ 643-3167)* and ***La Fragata*** *(☎ 643-3043)* are also currently popular for seafood and meat dinners.

Out on the Costanera, the ***Restaurant El Bosque*** *(☎ 643-3007)* is an old standby that has been recommended for breakfast. Check to see if it's actually open for breakfast. It's open throughout the day to cater to highway traffic and serves a good variety of reasonably priced food. Two good breakfast spots in town are the ***Sunrise Breakfast Place***, which serves big North American-style breakfasts, and the Canadian-run (and reader-recommended) ***Chatty Cathy's***, which is a good deal for both breakfast and lunch.

Restaurant Emily, next to the cheap Cabinas Emily, has great local food at reasonable prices and is open all day. The best hotels have decent restaurants open to the public.

Entertainment

There are several dance clubs. Note that the ones in the center are very loud on Friday and Saturday nights and are not places to go if you want to talk. Any hotel within two or three blocks is within reach of the booming music, so if this is a problem for you, find a hotel farther away.

The ***Disco La Central*** *(☎ 643-3076)* is the hip place for foreign travelers and is in the middle of town. ***Disco Papagayo*** is also central and tends to attract a more local crowd. ***Disco Los Tucanes*** is another nearby spot. ***Bar El Zarpe*** *(☎ 643-3473)*, in the Plaza Jacó, is an air-conditioned bar with a mix of travelers and locals. There's a dart board, sports bar with satellite TV, and Californian and Mexican food. ***La Bruja***, closer to the center, is quieter. If you're still going after 2 am, ***Pancho Villas*** restaurant is a popular place to meet and eat. In this fast-changing town, it's definitely worth asking and walking around to find the latest hot spots. Several hotels have a disco and/or a casino.

Shopping

Next to Rad Rental (see the Jacó Center map) is a small paperback-book store that sells and trades books in English. The Plaza Jacó, at the north end, is a shopping center.

Getting There & Away

Bus Direct buses from the Coca-Cola terminal in San José leave at 7:30 and 10:30 am and 3:30 pm daily. The journey takes about three hours and costs about US$3. Buses between either San José or Puntarenas and Quepos could drop you off at the entrance to Jacó. Buses tend to be full on weekends, when extra buses may run, but get to the terminal early if possible.

Buses leave Jacó for San José at 5 and 11 am and 3 pm daily. Departures for Puntarenas are at 6:45 am, noon, and 4:30 pm; and for Quepos at 6 am, noon, and 4 pm. It's best to inquire locally, especially for Puntarenas and Quepos departures, which are the most subject to change. The bus stop is just north of the supermarket in Jacó, and there is another stop near the crossroads toward the north end of town. You can phone for bus information in Jacó (☎ 643-3135, 643-3074). Most hotels know the current timetable.

Taxi Taxi 30-30 (☎ 643-3030) will get you anywhere – for a price.

JACÓ TO QUEPOS

The paved Costanera continues southeast from Jacó to Quepos, 65km away. The road parallels the Pacific coastline but comes down to it only a few times. The route has a few good beaches (some with good surf), which are rather off the beaten track and most easily visited by car, though you could get off buses to Quepos or Manuel Antonio and walk down to the beach.

Esterillos Oeste, **Esterillos Centro**, and **Esterillos Este** are about 22km, 25km, and 30km southeast of Jacó, respectively; all are a couple of kilometers off the Costanera. Between them, the Esterillo beach stretches for several deserted kilometers, and there are several surfing areas. Esterillos Oeste has a few cheap and basic cabinas and camping areas that are used by surfers. At Esterillos Centro is ***La Felicidad Country Inn*** *(☎/fax 779-9003)*, an aging but pleasant beachfront establishment with spacious, homey cabins with private hot baths for US$32 double, US$40 with kitchens. There is a pool, a restaurant-bar, and hammocks.

Esterillos Este also has a few cheap places, as well as some better hotels on the beach that offer off-the-beaten-path relaxation. The French-Canadian-run ***Auberge du Pélican*** *(☎/fax 779-9108)* has been recommended by readers. There are six simple, attractive rooms sharing two baths and four more with private baths, two of which are handicapped-accessible. All have fans and are very clean. There is hot water, a pool, and a restaurant, and boat tours can be arranged. Double rates are US$30 with shared baths, US$40 with private baths. There is a small runway near the hotel, and air transport from San José is available for US$200 in a plane seating five. Another nice little place, also French Canadian, is ***Fleur de Lys*** *(☎ 779-9117, ☎/fax 779-9141, business@sol.racsa.co.cr)*, which has 10 cabins of various sizes, all with hot showers and fans. The rate is about US$60 double, and there is a restaurant.

Infrequently visited beaches beyond Esterillos include Playa Bejuco (good surfing) and Playa Palma, both reached by short side roads from the Costanera. At Playa Bejuco is the ***Hotel El Delfín*** *(☎ 779-9246)*, a sleepy little hotel that has rooms with private baths (hot water) and balconies with sea views for about US$40. Some rooms are air-conditioned, and there is a beachfront restaurant and pool.

Parrita, a bustling little banana town on the river of the same name, 40km from Jacó, has a couple of basic hotels. There are two gas stations and a bank. At the east end of Parrita, you'll see a sign for ***Beso del Viento B&B*** *(☎ 779-9674, fax 779-9675, bdviento@sol.racsa.co.cr)*, which has been recommended by at least one reader and offers rooms with private baths and fans for US$40/45 single/double, US$45/50 with sea views. Also in this area is the larger ***Hotel La Isla*** *(☎ 779-3158, 222-6561)*.

The coastal road is now well inland and continues so until Quepos. The road has been paved all the way, although some sections have bad potholes, and there are several rickety one-way bridges to watch out for. New hotels are beginning to spring up along the coast in the Parrita area. African

Rainmaker

This is an exciting and unique project that enables visitors to walk through the rainforest canopy on a series of suspension bridges attached to the largest trees in the forest. Fabulous! There are aerial walkways like this in the Peruvian Amazon and in Asia, but this was the first in Central America.

Reaching the suspension bridges is almost as interesting as going up into the canopy. From the parking lot/orientation area, visitors walk up a magical rainforest canyon with a pristine stream tumbling down the rocks. To avoid damaging the delicately beautiful canyon bottom, a wooden boardwalk and series of bridges were built along the canyon floor, crossing the stream a number of times and giving lovely views of cascades and waterfalls. After about half a kilometer, the base of the walkway is reached, and visitors climb up several hundred steps to a tree platform, from which the first suspension bridge spans the treetops to another platform. Six linked suspension bridges are planned in all. The longest span is about 90m, and the total walkway is about 250m long. At the highest point, you are some 25 stories above the forest floor.

In addition to the canyon boardwalk and aerial walkway, there are short interpretive trails that enable the visitor to identify some of the local plants, and some long and strenuous trails into the heart of the 2000-hectare preserve that Rainmaker encompasses.

Currently, visits with professional naturalist guides leave hotels in Manuel Antonio and Quepos in the morning and at midday; reservations can be made at most hotels or by calling ☎ 777-1250 ext 207. Tours including a light tropical breakfast cost US$42 per person.

Visitors should come with realistic expectations. This is not a zoo, and you are unlikely to spot large numbers of mammals, though you'll see plenty of birds, plants, and insects. Binoculars are invaluable for watching the birds. Bring sun protection and water.

Rainmaker is reached by turning inland at the large water tower on the Costanera at the north end of the village of Pocares (10km east of Parrita or 15km west of Quepos). From the turnoff, it is 6 or 7km to the parking area. It is not yet open to the general public without reservations, but this may change.

– Rob Rachowiecki

oil-palm plantations stretch for several kilometers before Quepos is reached, and little identical-looking plantation villages are regularly passed. Ten kilometers east of the easternmost gas station in Parrita is the village of Pocares (not marked on any maps), where a side road turns inland to the Rainmaker project (see the boxed text). Fifteen more kilometers bring you to the bridge at the northern entrance of Quepos.

QUEPOS

This town gets its name from the Quepoa Indian tribe, a subgroup of the Borucas, who inhabited the area at the time of the conquest. The Quepoa people's numbers declined because of diseases brought by the Europeans, internecine warfare with other Indian groups, and because they were sold as slaves. By the end of the 19th century, no pure-blooded Quepoa were left, and the area began to be colonized by farmers from the highlands.

Quepos first came to prominence as a banana-exporting port. Its importance has declined appreciably in recent decades because of disease that has severely reduced banana crops. African oil-palms (which stretch away in dizzying rows in the fields around Quepos) have replaced bananas as the major local crop. Processed into oils used in cosmetics, machine oils, and cooking

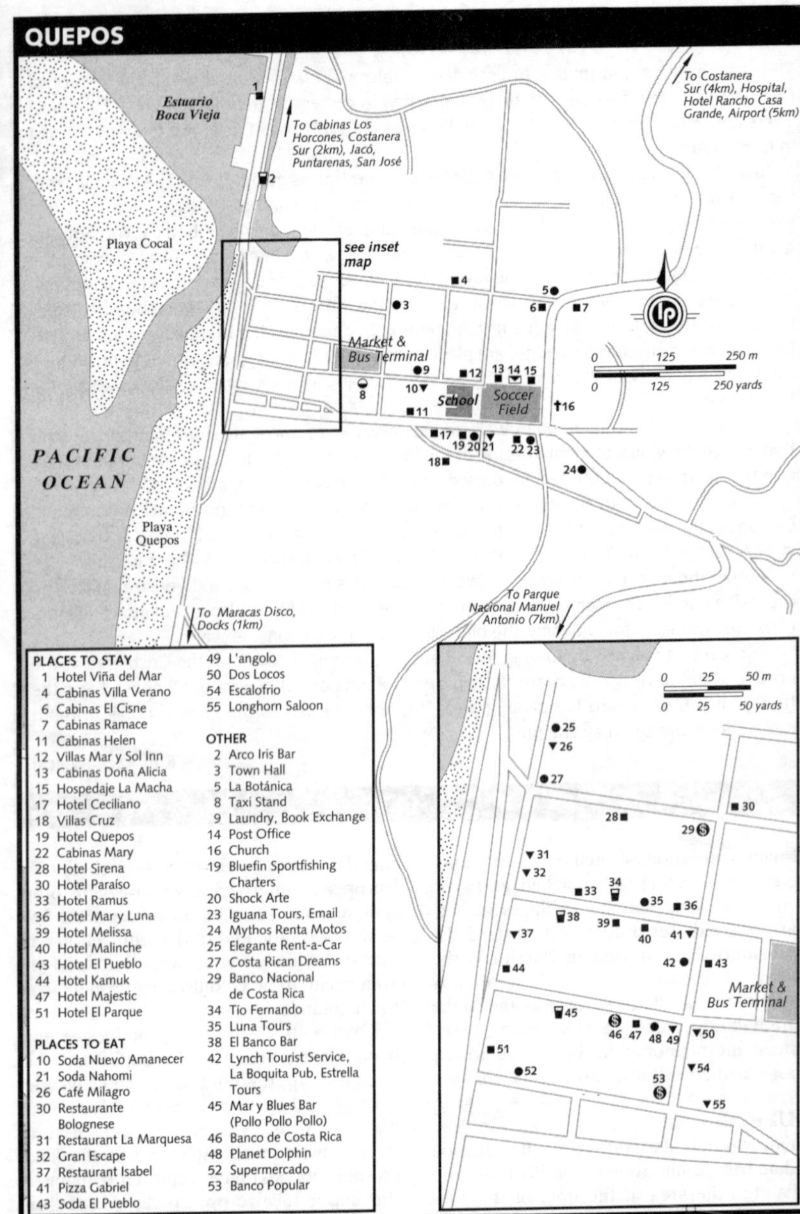
QUEPOS
Estuario Boca Vieja
To Cabinas Los Horcones, Costanera Sur (2km), Jacó, Puntarenas, San José
To Costanera Sur (4km), Hospital, Hotel Rancho Casa Grande, Airport (5km)
Playa Cocal
see inset map
Market & Bus Terminal
School
Soccer Field
0 125 250 m
0 125 250 yards
PACIFIC OCEAN
Playa Quepos
To Maracas Disco, Docks (1km)
To Parque Nacional Manuel Antonio (7km)
0 25 50 m
0 25 50 yards
Market & Bus Terminal
PLACES TO STAY
1 Hotel Viña del Mar
4 Cabinas Villa Verano
6 Cabinas El Cisne
7 Cabinas Ramace
11 Cabinas Helen
12 Villas Mar y Sol Inn
13 Cabinas Doña Alicia
15 Hospedaje La Macha
17 Hotel Ceciliano
18 Villas Cruz
19 Hotel Quepos
22 Cabinas Mary
28 Hotel Sirena
30 Hotel Paraíso
33 Hotel Ramus
36 Hotel Mar y Luna
39 Hotel Melissa
40 Hotel Malinche
43 Hotel El Pueblo
44 Hotel Kamuk
47 Hotel Majestic
51 Hotel El Parque
PLACES TO EAT
10 Soda Nuevo Amanecer
21 Soda Nahomi
26 Café Milagro
30 Restaurante Bolognese
31 Restaurant La Marquesa
32 Gran Escape
37 Restaurant Isabel
41 Pizza Gabriel
43 Soda El Pueblo
49 L'angolo
50 Dos Locos
54 Escalofrio
55 Longhorn Saloon
OTHER
2 Arco Iris Bar
3 Town Hall
5 La Botánica
8 Taxi Stand
9 Laundry, Book Exchange
14 Post Office
16 Church
19 Bluefin Sportfishing Charters
20 Shock Arte
23 Iguana Tours, Email
24 Mythos Renta Motos
25 Elegante Rent-a-Car
27 Costa Rican Dreams
29 Banco Nacional de Costa Rica
34 Tío Fernando
35 Luna Tours
38 El Banco Bar
42 Lynch Tourist Service, La Boquita Pub, Estrella Tours
45 Mar y Blues Bar (Pollo Pollo Pollo)
46 Banco de Costa Rica
48 Planet Dolphin
52 Supermercado
53 Banco Popular

fat, the finished product is much less bulky than bananas. Consequently, Quepos has not been able to recover as a major shipping port. Instead, it has become important as a sportfishing center and as the nearest town to Parque Nacional Manuel Antonio, which is only 7km away and one of the most-visited national parks in Costa Rica. There are regularly scheduled flights and buses from San José, and Quepos has gradually developed a new economic niche for itself as a year-round tourism destination, with outdoor tour companies, bars, and cafés rounding out the attractions of the fishing and nearby park.

Orientation & Information

The town of Quepos is the gateway to Parque Nacional Manuel Antonio – you have to go through the town to reach the park, 7km beyond. There are plenty of hotels and services both in Quepos (described here) and all the way along the road to the park (described in the next section).

Banco Nacional de Costa Rica (☎ 777-0113) changes US dollars and traveler's checks and is extremely air-conditioned – a cool wait. Banco Popular (☎ 777-0344) allows cash withdrawals on Visa cards; it has chairs to wait in and a TV often showing cartoons. Banco de Costa Rica has opened a branch here; its TV favors sports.

Lynch Tourist Service (☎ 777-0161, 777-1170, fax 777-1571, lyntur@sol.racsa.co.cr) will change cash US dollars and specializes in making all local arrangements you might need, as well as reserving places elsewhere in the country and selling international air tickets. Michael Lynch, though he has sold the travel agency to a partner, can still be found at the Costa Rican Dreams sportfishing agency and is a friendly and useful source of information about the Quepos/Manuel Antonio area. The old information center at La Buena Nota has moved to the Manuel Antonio road (see Information in the Manuel Antonio section, later in this chapter).

Internet access is available at a place called Email (☎ 777-0241), run by the helpful Alexis Cubero.

The Hospital Dr Max Teran V (☎ 777-1398, 777-0020) provides emergency medical care for the Quepos/Manuel Antonio area. It is on the Costanera Sur en route to the airport.

Dangers & Annoyances The town's large number of tourists has attracted thieves. In response, the Costa Rican authorities have greatly increased police presence in the area, but travelers should be careful to always lock hotel rooms and never leave cars unattended, except in guarded parking areas. Local kids will volunteer to watch your car for you in many places for a small fee. The area is far from dangerous, but the laid-back tropical beach atmosphere should not lull you into a false sense of security.

Note that the beaches in Quepos are not recommended for swimming because of pollution. Go over the hill to Manuel Antonio instead.

Sportfishing

Sportfishing is big in the Quepos area. Offshore fishing is best from December to April, and sailfish are the big thing to go for, though marlin, dorado, wahoo, amberjack, and yellowfin tuna are also caught. You can fish inshore year-round; mackerel, jack, and roosterfish are the main attractions. Places chartering sportfishing boats may take you out sightseeing, snorkeling, or diving if they don't have any anglers.

A boat for a full day of fishing can cost from US$450 to US$1100, depending on the size and speed of the boat, the experience of the skipper, and whether lunch, drinks, fishing gear, and bait are included. Most boats can take three anglers, and a few can take six. In the December to April season, many boats are reserved well in advance. Individuals looking to join up with a group of anglers can, if they call around, find a spot on a boat for about US$150.

A good place to find out what's going on is the Gran Escape bar and restaurant, which is locally regarded as an anglers' hangout. Because fishing is so expensive, this is a good place to come if you are looking to split costs with a fishing partner. Michael Lynch, at Costa Rican Dreams, is a friendly source of information, though he no longer runs Lynch Tourist Service, an independent sportfishing agent that can book you onto all the local boats (see Orientation & Information, above). If you prefer to talk directly with the charters, call the following:

Baletti Sportfishing (☎/fax 777-0221)
Bluefin Sportfishing Charters (☎ 777-1676)
Boutique El Pescador, Isabel Guillén (☎/fax 777-1596)
Costa Rican Dreams, Richard and Nancy Bebo (☎/fax 777-0593)
Luna Tours (☎/fax 777-0725)

Organized Tours

Outward Bound (☎/fax 777-1222, crrobs@sol.racsa.co.cr) arranges one-day rafting trips (US$60 per person) and a variety of two-, three-, and four-day rainforest expeditions for about US$100 a day (four participants). It also runs longer adventures of 10 to 85 days. Activities include rainforest trekking and staying in remote indigenous villages, canopy climbing, rainforest conservation, mountain trekking and rappelling, and various others.

Iguana Tours (☎/fax 777-1262, email: info@iguanatours.com) arranges park tours and one-day river-rafting, sea-kayaking, and dolphin-watching trips. It also books Ríos Tropicales river trips (see Organized Tours in the Getting Around chapter). Estrella Tours (☎/fax 777-1286) specializes in bike tours and rentals but arranges a variety of other tours as well. Steve Wofford of Planet Dolphin (☎ 777-1647, dolphncr@sol.racsa.co.cr) is a good contact for dolphin-watching tours, which start at US$45 for three hours, including snacks and snorkeling. Look around for other little tour and rental companies – they're there.

Special Events

The Fiesta del Mar (Sea Festival) takes place near the end of January, with processions, street dancing, and general revelry. However, it doesn't occur every year.

Places to Stay

Hotels tend to be full during weekends in the dry season. They are cheaper here than closer to Manuel Antonio. You can get substantial wet-season discounts; rates listed are high-season weekend rates. More and more hotels accept credit cards, but those that do often add a 7% surcharge.

Budget There is an inexpensive ***campsite*** on the road from Quepos to Manuel Antonio (see Places to Stay under Quepos to Manuel Antonio, later in this chapter).

The ***Hotel Majestic*** has basic boxes with fans for about US$4 per person – the cheapest in town. Several shoestring travelers have told me it's OK. The ***Hospedaje La Macha*** *(☎ 777-0216)* is simple and clean, and the rooms have fans. Rates are US$5.50 per person with shared baths, US$11 for doubles with private baths.

Cabinas Doña Alicia *(☎ 777-0419)* has clean rooms with private baths and two double beds for US$16 for up to four people; US$8 for a double with shared baths. ***Cabinas Mary*** *(☎ 777-0128)* charges US$7 per person for clean, acceptable rooms with private baths; so do ***Hotel El Parque*** *(☎ 777-0063)* and ***Hotel Quepos*** *(☎ 777-0274)*. The ***Hotel Ramus*** *(☎ 777-0245)*, also known as Hector's place, charges US$6.50 per person and is a bit dark but is central and has character. Nearby, the friendly ***Hotel Mar y Luna*** *(☎ 777-0394)* is festooned with plants and charges slightly less than Hotel Ramus; the mid-range ***Hotel Malinche*** has a few inexpensive rooms (see below); and ***Hotel Melissa*** *(☎ 777-0025)* has a balcony to read on and clean rooms for US$8 per person. ***Cabinas Villa Verano*** *(☎ 777-1495)* has a few good, clean rooms with private baths for US$11/15 single/double. ***Cabinas Los Horcones*** *(☎ 777-0090)*, north of town, also has good, clean rooms for US$9 per person.

Hotel El Pueblo *(☎ 777-1003)* is right next to the bus station, a minor convenience in a town this small. The 24-hour bar-restaurant downstairs is fun and noisy and brings a lot of traffic through the hotel (ie, lock your doors and windows). Rooms with fans and private baths cost US$8 per person; two rooms with air-con and TVs cost US$32 double. On the road to the Costanera Sur, ***Cabinas El Cisne*** *(☎ 777-0719)* and ***Cabinas***

Ramace (☎ *777-0590*) both offer parking and rooms with private hot baths and fridges for about US$20 double.

The friendly ***Cabinas Helen*** (☎ *777-0504*) has decent rooms sleeping up to three people with private baths and refrigerators for US$18. It has fans and hot water.

Mid-Range The ***Hotel Ceciliano*** (☎/*fax 777-0192*) charges US$30 for clean double rooms with private baths and has a few rooms with communal baths for US$15. It has fans and hot water.

A good choice for various budgets is the ***Hotel Malinche*** (☎ *777-0093*). It has older rooms for US$8/12 with private cold showers and fans. Newer and nicer rooms, with private hot showers and fans, cost US$12 per person or US$20 per person if you want air-conditioning. Several readers have reported much lower prices outside the high season.

Villas Cruz (☎ *777-0271, fax 777-1081*) has nice rooms with private baths, fans, and refrigerators for US$25 – the upstairs rooms are slightly nicer. It also has a two-bedroom villa with a TV and nice views for US$40. These are a good value and a real low-season bargain when rates are about half.

The ***Hotel Paraíso*** (☎/*fax 777-0650*) is part of the Ristorante Bolognese and has a few apartments with kitchenettes, refrigerators, air-conditioning, and private cold or hot showers. The rate is about US$40, depending on the size of the unit. The ***Hotel Viña del Mar*** (☎/*fax 777-0070*) has rooms with hot showers and air-conditioning for US$25/45 and cheaper rooms with fans only.

The ***Villas Mar y Sol Inn*** (☎ *777-0307, fax 777-0562*), run by grumpy French people, has nice, air-conditioned rooms with refrigerators and hot showers for US$30 to US$50. They have a secure parking area, offer massage and laundry service, and arrange sportfishing.

Top End The ***Hotel Sirena*** (☎ *777-0528, fax 777-0165*) has modern air-conditioned rooms, private hot showers, a restaurant, and pool. The hotel arranges horse tours and sportfishing. The rate is about US$55 double, including breakfast.

The most upscale hotel in downtown Quepos is the ***Hotel Kamuk*** (☎ *777-0379, fax 777-0258, info@kamuk.co.cr*). All rooms have air-conditioning, hot water, and phones, and there is a bar, 3rd-floor restaurant with good sunset views, coffee shop, pool, and casino. Standard rooms cost US$65 for one or two people. Better rooms, with balcony and ocean view, cost US$75 to US$95, depending on the size of the room. Rates include breakfast.

Out by the airport, the ***Hotel Rancho Casa Grande*** (☎ *777-1646, 777-0330, fax 777-1575*) has one- and two-bedroom bungalows for about US$80 and US$110. They all have satellite TVs, phones, and spacious hot-water bathrooms, and there is a choice of fans or air-conditioning. There is a restaurant/bar, pool, and Jacuzzi. An 80-hectare private rainforest preserve borders the property, and guided tours on foot or horseback are available. The owners operate Eco-Fan Tours (same telephone number) and offer every kind of local tour and activity.

Places to Eat

Cheap snacks are available at the ***Soda Nahomi***, at the east end of town on the way out to Manuel Antonio beach. ***Soda El Pueblo***, under the hotel of that name, is open 24 hours.

In the center of town are several reasonable places, of which the popular ***Restaurant La Marquesa*** is one of the cheapest for set casados (just over US$2) and breakfasts (US$1 and up). It's a good value. The ***Restaurante Isabel*** is less cheap but also good. There are several inexpensive eateries in the market and near the bus station; a good one is the pleasant little ***Soda Nuevo Amanecer***. Just east of the market is ***Pizza Gabriel***, with good individual pizzas for US$3 to US$5.

Café Milagro (☎/*fax 777-1707*), which recently opened another café on the Manuel Antonio road, serves great cappuccino, espresso, and baked treats and is a nice place to relax and read. Newspapers and magazines in English are available. Say hi to Mike Lynch at Costa Rican Dreams on your way there. ***Escalofrio*** is said to have the best ice cream in the area; it offers 20 flavors and a spacious seating area.

Gran Escape *(☎/fax 777-0395)* is popular with sportfishing visitors ('You hook 'em, we cook 'em,' says the sign) and other tourists and is one of the more lively bars. It serves tasty and varied mid-priced food and is a good value. Hours are 6 am to 11 pm daily except Tuesday. The ***Longhorn Saloon*** (formerly the well-known George's American Bar & Grill) serves steaks, burgers, and seafood. ***Dos Locos*** *(☎ 777-1526)* is a very popular and recommended Mexican-food place open 8 am to 11 pm daily except Sunday, when it opens at 3 pm.

The ***Ristorante Bolognese*** *(☎/fax 777-0650)* serves authentic and recommended Italian food in the US$4 to US$10 range. It is open 10 am to 1 am daily, though it closes for a couple of hours' siesta in the afternoon. Another excellent and similarly priced Italian menu is presented in the tiny but equally recommendable ***L'angolo***. Three indoor tables are air-conditioned, and a couple outdoor tables are usually available. The deli offers sandwiches and other treats – a good choice for picnic lunches.

Entertainment

The ***Arco Iris Bar*** *(☎ 777-0449)* has dancing on weekends. A 20-minute walk south of town, the ***Maracas Disco***, on the road to the docks, has live bands and dancing on weekends, sometimes until dawn. It has a pool and a pool table. These are fun places, but don't walk home alone late at night. Popular places for a beer include ***Mar y Blues Bar*** (also known as Pollo Pollo Pollo) for good music, ***El Banco Bar*** *(☎/fax 777-0478)* for good music and satellite sports TV, ***Gran Escape Bar*** for swapping fishing stories, ***Tío Fernando*** for a quiet drink, ***La Boquita Pub*** for lurid murals and good music, and the ***Longhorn Saloon***. The ***Hotel Kamuk*** has a casino.

Shopping

Café Milagro sells roasted coffee to go, as well as fine cigars and other souvenirs. La Botánica sells organically cultivated herbs, spices, and teas, which make good gifts. Shock Arte is good for local indigenous crafts and other stuff. The street west of here is replete with souvenir and clothing shops.

Getting There & Away

Air Lynch Tourist Service (☎ 777-0161, 777-1170, fax 777-1571, lyntur@sol.racsa.co.cr) is the Travelair agent and sells all airline tickets. The SANSA agent (☎ 777-0683) is below the Hotel Quepos. The San José-Quepos flight takes 20 minutes, and schedules change often. Recently, SANSA had five flights a day (US$35/70 one way/roundtrip). Travelair had four flights a day (US$58/93), with one flight continuing to Palmar Sur.

Make reservations and pay for your ticket well in advance to ensure a confirmed space. Reconfirm your flight as often as you can. Flights are often full, with a waiting list.

It is also possible to charter light planes to Quepos through Lynch Tourist Service, which will also arrange airport transfers for US$3 from anywhere in the Quepos-Manuel Antonio area. The airport is 5km from Quepos.

Bus Buses leave San José several times a day from the Coca-Cola terminal. Direct express buses leave for Manuel Antonio (US$5, 3½ hours) at 6 am, noon, and 6 pm, and regular services to Quepos (five hours) leave at 7 and 10 am and 2 and 4 pm. You can also get here from Puntarenas, Jacó, San Isidro, and Dominical.

The ticket office in the Quepos bus terminal is open 6 to 11 am and 1 to 5 pm daily except Sunday, when it closes at 2 pm. There are regular services to San José at 5 and 8 am and 2 and 4 pm daily (US$3). Direct buses leave three times a day (US$5) from Manuel Antonio (see below) and pick up passengers in Quepos before continuing directly to San José. In the high season, bus tickets to San José are bought days in advance – buy a ticket as early as you can.

Buses to Puntarenas (US$2.75, 3½ hours) via Jacó (US$1.50, two hours) leave at 5 and 11 am and 2:30 pm. There are eight daily buses to Parrita and six to Jacó. Buses leave for San Isidro (via Dominical) at 5 am and 1:30 pm. Buses go to Dominical and on to Uvita at 9:30 am and 4 pm – these services will probably change soon – and to various local communities in the agricultural country surrounding Quepos.

Buses for Manuel Antonio leave about 15 times a day between about 5 am and 9:30 pm, returning from Manuel Antonio as soon as they arrive. There are many more buses in the dry season than in the wet season. The 20-minute trip costs less than US50¢.

Boat Planet Dolphin (☎ 777-1647) operates water-taxi services to anywhere you need to go on the coast. It also advertises dolphin-watching and snorkeling cruises. The boats depart from the Quepos dock.

Taxi Quepos Taxi (☎ 777-0425, 777-1837) will take you to Manuel Antonio for about US$5.

Getting Around

Elegante Rent-a-Car (☎ 777-0115) has an office in Quepos – it's best to arrange car rentals in advance in San José to guarantee getting a car. Elegante will deliver your car to the airport by advance arrangement.

Mythos Renta Motos (☎/fax 777-0006) rents scooters (US$11/26 per hour/day) and motorcycles (US$18/33).

QUEPOS TO MANUEL ANTONIO

From the port of Quepos, the road swings inland for 7km before reaching the beaches of Manuel Antonio village and the national park. The road goes over a series of hills with picturesque views of the ocean. Along this road, every hilltop vista has been commandeered by a hotel that lists 'ocean views' as a major attraction. Certainly, these views are often magnificent. Most people staying in these pricey hotels expect, and get, good services. These hotels are generally so pleasant and comfortable that spending the whole day there is an attractive alternative to visiting the national park.

The Manuel Antonio area has been discovered, and it is no longer the beautiful, unspoiled gem that it was as recently as the 1980s. The proliferation of hotels in an area where the sewage system is primitive at best has led to serious threats of pollution to the once-pristine beaches. The famous national park is overwhelmed by visitors. Hotel prices tend to average much higher here than in the rest of the country. This is perhaps the most publicized stretch of coast in Costa Rica.

Note that the road is steep, winding, and very narrow. There are almost no places to pull over in the event of an emergency. Drive and walk with extreme care.

Information

Costa Rica Adventure Travel (☎/fax 777-0850, 777-1262, iguana@sol.racsa.co.cr), in the Centro Comercial Si Como No about 4km south of Quepos, arranges all local adventure tours and is very helpful. Also see La Buena Nota (in Manuel Antonio village, described later).

At this writing, there are two Internet cafés along the road – the Cantina Internet Café, opposite the Costa Verde hotel, and Net Café, in the Centro Comercial Si Como No.

Jardín Gaia

This is a wildlife breeding center (☎/fax 777-0535) about 2km south of Quepos. The goal is to take care of and rehabilitate animals that have been confiscated from poachers, to breed them, and to reintroduce them into the wild. Teaching locals and tourists about the animals and the problems of habitat destruction is also part of this project. Admission costs about US$1.50; call for hours. The center sometimes takes volunteers.

Language Courses

Escuela de Idiomas D'Amore (☎/fax 777-1143, 777-0233; in the USA ☎ 213-912-0600, damore@sol.racsa.co.cr), which has received enthusiastic reader recommendations, offers Spanish immersion courses at all levels. Classes are small, and local homestays can be arranged. Rates are comparable to those at schools in San José. The school is about 3.5km south of Quepos. The new Escuela del Pacífico (☎/fax 777-0805, info@escueladelpacifico.com) advertises personalized Spanish tutorials; the proprietors are personable and the school seems well run. They offer a variety of housing options and make it easy to arrive and settle in.

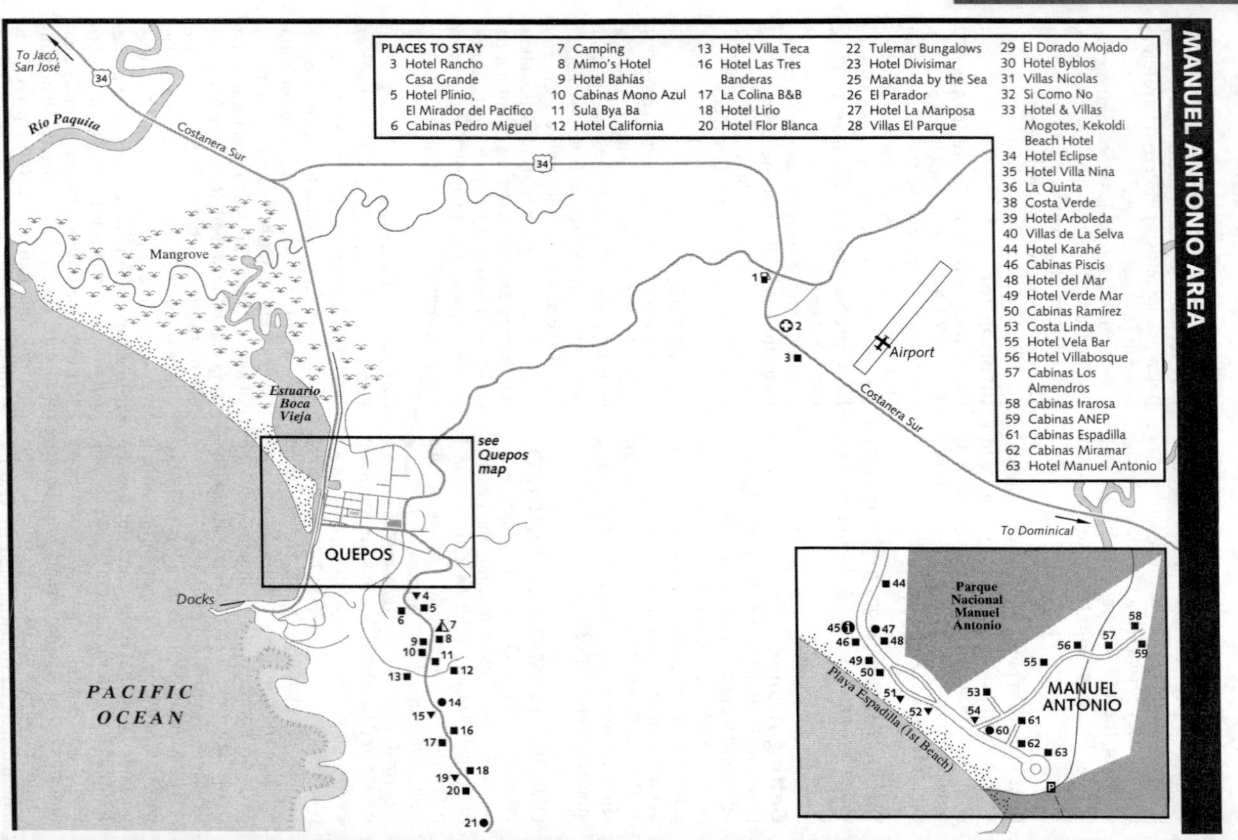
MANUEL ANTONIO AREA
PLACES TO STAY
3 Hotel Rancho Casa Grande
5 Hotel Plinio, El Mirador del Pacífico
6 Cabinas Pedro Miguel
7 Camping
8 Mimo's Hotel
9 Hotel Bahías
10 Cabinas Mono Azul
11 Sula Bya Ba
12 Hotel California
13 Hotel Villa Teca
16 Hotel Las Tres Banderas
17 La Colina B&B
18 Hotel Lirio
20 Hotel Flor Blanca
22 Tulemar Bungalows
23 Hotel Divisimar
25 Makanda by the Sea
26 El Parador
27 Hotel La Mariposa
28 Villas El Parque
29 El Dorado Mojado
30 Hotel Byblos
31 Villas Nicolas
32 Si Como No
33 Hotel & Villas Mogotes, Kekoldi Beach Hotel
34 Hotel Eclipse
35 Hotel Villa Nina
36 La Quinta
38 Costa Verde
39 Hotel Arboleda
40 Villas de La Selva
44 Hotel Karahé
46 Cabinas Piscis
48 Hotel del Mar
49 Hotel Verde Mar
50 Cabinas Ramírez
53 Costa Linda
55 Hotel Vela Bar
56 Hotel Villabosque
57 Cabinas Los Almendros
58 Cabinas Irarosa
59 Cabinas ANEP
61 Cabinas Espadilla
62 Cabinas Miramar
63 Hotel Manuel Antonio
To Jacó, San José
Río Paquita
Costanera Sur
34
Mangrove
Estuario Boca Vieja
QUEPOS
see Quepos map
Docks
PACIFIC OCEAN
Airport
To Dominical
Parque Nacional Manuel Antonio
MANUEL ANTONIO
Playa Espadilla (1st Beach)

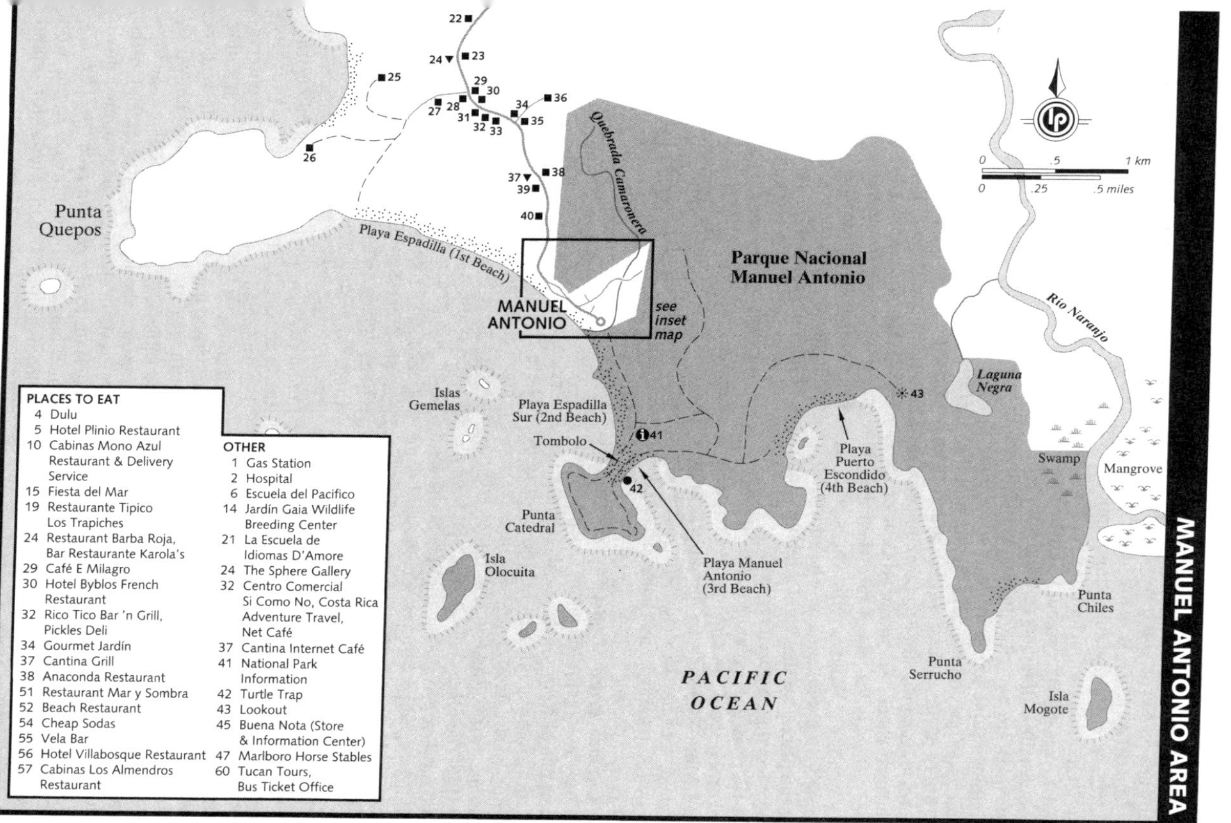
MANUEL ANTONIO AREA
0 .5 1 km
0 .25 .5 miles
Rio Naranjo
Mangrove
Swamp
Laguna Negra
Punta Chiles
Isla Mogote
Punta Serrucho
Parque Nacional Manuel Antonio
Playa Puerto Escondido (4th Beach)
Playa Manuel Antonio (3rd Beach)
PACIFIC OCEAN
Quebrada Camaronera
see inset map
MANUEL ANTONIO
Playa Espadilla Sur (2nd Beach)
Tombolo
Punta Catedral
Isla Olocuita
Islas Gemelas
Playa Espadilla (1st Beach)
Punta Quepos
PLACES TO EAT
4 Dulu
5 Hotel Plinio Restaurant
10 Cabinas Mono Azul Restaurant & Delivery Service
15 Fiesta del Mar
19 Restaurante Tipico Los Trapiches
24 Restaurant Barba Roja, Bar Restaurante Karola's
29 Café E Milagro
30 Hotel Byblos French Restaurant
32 Rico Tico Bar 'n Grill, Pickles Deli
34 Gourmet Jardín
37 Cantina Grill
38 Anaconda Restaurant
51 Restaurant Mar y Sombra
52 Beach Restaurant
54 Cheap Sodas
55 Vela Bar
56 Hotel Villabosque Restaurant
57 Cabinas Los Almendros Restaurant
OTHER
1 Gas Station
2 Hospital
6 Escuela del Pacifico
14 Jardín Gaia Wildlife Breeding Center
21 La Escuela de Idiomas D'Amore
24 The Sphere Gallery
32 Centro Comercial Si Como No, Costa Rica Adventure Travel, Net Café
37 Cantina Internet Café
41 National Park Information
42 Turtle Trap
43 Lookout
45 Buena Nota (Store & Information Center)
47 Marlboro Horse Stables
60 Tucan Tours, Bus Ticket Office

Places to Stay

The hotels below are listed in the order that they are passed as you travel from Quepos to Manuel Antonio. Most are top-end hotels, but there are a few mid-range options as well. Quoted rates include tax for the high and dry season (December to Easter).

Substantial discounts (around 40% is not unusual) are available in the wet season. Getting reservations is a must for weekends and sometimes midweek in the dry months.

Many of these hotels (even the most expensive ones) will not accept credit cards or personal checks, so you need cash or traveler's checks. Ask about this when making reservations. When credit cards are accepted, a 7% surcharge may be added. Most of the places are small and intimate – many have less than a dozen rooms.

There is one option for ***camping*** along this road, between Cabinas Pedro Miguel and Mimo's Hotel; this unnamed, though signed, spot has 15 shady sites, bathrooms, showers, hammocks, and a barbecue spot for US$3 per person.

Cabinas Pedro Miguel (*☎ 777-0035, fax 777-0279*) is up the hill out of Quepos, about 1km out of town on the right. It has fairly basic rooms at US$25 for doubles with baths, plus cabins that sleep three to five people, with kitchenettes, for US$35 to US$55. The place is family-run and friendly, and meals are available. It offers barbecued dinners at which you choose and grill your own cut to your own specifications. This is a big hit with guests and nonguests alike (it's open to the public in the high season), and the hotel is nearly always full.

Hotel Plinio (*☎ 777-0055, fax 777-0558, plinio@sol.racsa.co.cr*) has rooms with fans starting at US$50 (US$60 with air-conditioning) and a variety of air-conditioned suites, some on two levels, starting at US$90 double. There is hot water, the rooms are attractive, and there are plenty of nooks for hammocks and relaxing. Breakfast is included, and both the restaurant and hotel are recommended. The grounds boast two pools and several kilometers of trails into the forest. There is a 17m-high lookout tower along the trails. The restaurant and tower are open to the public, and the staff is friendly.

Just beyond is ***El Mirador del Pacífico*** (*☎/fax 777-0119, email: billdeb@costarica.net*), which has air-conditioned rooms with fans and private hot showers – the rooms lead to a verandah with attractive views. Rates average US$65 double, depending on the room. It has live music on Friday and Saturday – jazz, blues, and southern rock. ***Mimo's Hotel*** (*☎/fax 777-0054*) has spacious rooms with air-conditioning or fans, kitchenettes, hot water, and a pool. Rates are US$45 to US$75 double including breakfast. Also in this price range, ***Hotel Bahías*** (*☎ 777-0350*) has pleasant air-conditioned rooms with hot water; more expensive rooms have Jacuzzis.

Cabinas Mono Azul (*☎ 777-1548, ☎/fax 777-1954, monoazul@sol.racsa.co.cr*) is small and friendly. Eight rooms with hot water and fans cost US$35/40/45 for one/two/three people. Two rooms are air-conditioned. Continental breakfast is included, and the restaurant (closed Monday) has been recommended. Barbecued chicken, pizzas, seafood, homemade bread, and pastries are served, and there is take-out and delivery service to anywhere in Manuel Antonio. There is a pool, and a different movie is shown each night for entertainment. Several readers have been very impressed.

The oddly named ***Sula Bya Ba*** (*☎ 777-0547, fax 777-0279*) is French-owned and offers double rooms with fans and hot water for about US$60. By this point, you are about 1.5km out of Quepos. Look for a driveway to the left for ***Hotel California*** (*☎ 777-1234, ☎/fax 777-1062, hotelcal@sol.racsa.co.cr*), which has 10km of hiking trails into rainforest surrounding the property. The trails lead to waterfalls and an observation tower. Rooms are painted with nature murals and have kitchenettes, coffeemakers, balconies with ocean views, fans, hot water, and cable TVs. There is a pool and Jacuzzi. Rates are about US$65 to US$90. On the other side of the main road, another driveway leads to ***Hotel Villa Teca*** (*☎ 777-1117*), which has 40 air-conditioned rooms with balconies and ocean views for about US$100, including breakfast.

About 2.5km south of Quepos is the recommended ***Hotel Las Tres Banderas*** *(☎ 777-1284, 777-1521, fax 777-1478, TresBanderas@centralamerica.com)*, owned by a couple of super-friendly Polish guys and their tica and US wives – hence 'Tres Banderas,' or three flags. There is an attractive pool with a waterfall and a huge Jacuzzi. Alongside is a nice wooden bar named Pod Papugami after a popular Polish song (that translates to 'Beneath the Parrots'). Eleven spotless rooms and three suites have air-conditioning, large bathrooms, hot water, elegant furnishings including a writing desk (something that I've noticed is missing in many Costa Rican hotels), and private balconies. The suites also have bathtubs and cable TVs with VCR. There is a private dining room and a chicken rotisserie where meals can be prepared on request. Rates are US$64/70 single/double, and the suites cost US$110 for up to four people. If you have a reservation, the owners will pick you up at the bus station or airport.

Just down the road is ***La Colina B&B*** *(☎ 777-0231, lacolina@sol.racsa.co.cr)*, a friendly place built by a young couple from Colorado; some of their rooms offer fabulous views. They have a small public restaurant, swim-up bar, and live music on weekends. Small but clean and attractive rooms with hot water and fans cost about US$40 double; larger rooms with air-conditioning cost about US$50 double. The rooms with the best views are a suite with a wraparound balcony but no air-conditioning (for US$60 double) and another with a smaller balcony, air-conditioning, and TV (US$70 double). The included breakfasts are big and good. The Canadian-run ***Hotel Lirio*** *(☎ 777-0403, fax 777-1182, elirio@sol.racsa.co.cr)* has spacious rooms with hot water and fans, and there is a small pool. Rates are US$35 double, US$45 for a cabin sleeping four people. The hotel is up for sale and may change. ***Hotel Flor Blanca*** *(☎ 777-1620, ☎/fax 777-1633)* has simple, clean rooms with fridges and fans for US$38 double, US$48 with air-conditioning.

The luxurious ***Tulemar Bungalows*** *(☎ 777-1325, fax 777-1579, tulemar@sol.racsa.co.cr)* has 14 modern, air-conditioned octagonal bungalows that sleep up to four people for about US$220 including breakfast. Each has huge picture windows with great views of forest and ocean, and the bungalows are well separated for privacy. They all have bedrooms with two queen-size beds, sitting rooms with two fold-out queen-size beds, well-equipped kitchenettes, telephones, TVs, VCRs, and hair dryers. There is a splendid pool with a snack bar, or you can hike a 15-minute private trail through forest to the beach, where kayaks and snorkeling gear are available free to guests.

Hotel Divisimar *(☎ 777-0371, fax 777-0525, divisamr@sol.racsa.co.cr)* has a pool, whirlpool, and restaurant set in a pleasant garden. A dozen standard rooms cost US$65 double, another 12 superior rooms cost about US$85 double, and a master suite costs US$100; additional people are charged US$15 each in all rooms. All units are air-conditioned, with plenty of hot water. The hotel is popular with affluent ticos as well as with foreign tourists. Horseback, sea kayak, and fishing tours are available, as well as a casino and liquor store.

Just beyond the Divisimar, a side road heads to three of the region's most exclusive hotels. The internationally acclaimed ***Hotel La Mariposa*** *(☎ 777-0355, 777-0456, fax 777-0050; in the USA ☎ 800-223-6510; in Canada ☎ 800-268-0424, mariposa@sol.racsa.co.cr)* has 10 luxurious private villas, each with splendid views. Murals, flowers, hammocks, and balconies are here for the enjoyment of the guests, and there is a pool and expensive restaurant. Children under 15 years are not allowed. Staff will arrange all the usual activities. This was the area's first luxury hotel; rates range from US$90/120 to US$135/180 single/double including continental breakfast and dinner. The restaurant is open to the public, but a few letters report that the food was not outstanding, considering the high price.

About 1km down a very steep gravel road is ***Makanda by the Sea*** *(☎ 777-0442, fax 777-1032, makanda@sol.racsa.co.cr)*, which vies with the Mariposa for peaceful luxury and attentive, helpful staff. There are seven contemporary rooms and villas in a rainforest setting, with good chances of seeing monkeys during your stay. There is a beautiful infinity pool and Jacuzzi with a superb view. Villa 1 (the largest) has a vista that may take your breath away – the entire wall is open to the rainforest and the ocean. The unit has a full kitchen, dining area, king-size bed, balcony, hammock, and large bathroom with hot shower. This rents for about US$200 for one or two people, and US$18 for each additional person.

Three smaller rooms below can all be interconnected to create personalized accommodations. Each one has a king-size bed, kitchenette, and bathroom. Two have a balcony and small Japanese garden; the third has a terrace and air-conditioning, and all rent for about US$150 double. There are also three more large individual villas similar in amenities and price to Villa 1, one with two bedrooms, another with a large Japanese garden, and a third in the forest near the pool. Children under 16 years are not allowed and prepaid reservations are required (credit cards accepted). All rates include continental breakfast delivered to your room, and poolside lunch and dinner are available at extra cost in the high season (and possibly in other months).

About a kilometer down the steep unpaved road is the exclusive ***El Parador*** *(☎ 777-1411, fax 777-1437; in the USA ☎ 800-648-1136, parador@sol.racsa.co.cr)*, one of Manuel Antonio's newest, and certainly most opulent, hotels. It resembles a Spanish fortress on a hill overlooking the ocean, and may put you in mind of a James Bond movie. The formerly forested hilltop was dynamited away to build the 60-room hotel complete with private helicopter landing pad, two swimming pools, tennis court, and miniature golf course. Inside are large conference rooms, a wine cellar and tasting room, dining rooms, a small fitness center, and a library.

This is a place for security-conscious VIPs; the armed guards at the gatehouse wouldn't let me in without an escort. Inside the hotel, the lavish elegance is somewhat overpowering. A wall of photographs shows hotel owners and staff with the presidents and leaders of dozens of countries, including the USA. A priceless collection of 17th- and 18th-century European art, suits of Spanish armor, rare antique model boats, castle doors and gates from England, Italy and Spain — it's all a bit much!

Some guidebooks have gushed about how wonderful this place is. It may be right for some high-powered folks, but others may not feel comfortable. All rooms have a private terrace or balcony, cable TVs, telephones, air-conditioning, hot water, and minibars. Standard rooms cost US$140, but deluxe rooms with larger bathrooms and tubs cost US$190. Nine suites with whirlpool baths, sitting rooms, and coffeemakers cost US$290, and there is also a three-room presidential suite. Rates are double occupancy and include breakfast.

Back on the main Quepos-to-Manuel Antonio road, ***El Dorado Mojado*** *(☎ 777-0368, fax 777-1248, dorplaya@sol.racsa.co.cr)* has four pleasant and spacious rooms with air-conditioning and hot water for US$59/70 single/double, and villas with kitchens for US$106/118 double/triple, including breakfast. Free airport/bus terminal transfers are given for people staying more than one night. Just beyond is ***Villas El Parque*** *(☎ 777-0096, fax 777-0538, vparque@sol.racsa.co.cr)*, with a variety of differently sized and appointed suites, some with kitchens, ranging from about US$70 to US$160.

In the same area is ***Hotel Byblos*** *(☎ 777-0411, 777-0217, fax 777-0009, byblosflof@aol.com)*. Spacious and comfortable bungalows and junior suites are set in the rainforest – there are distant ocean views from the restaurant. Rooms have either air-conditioning or fans, hot water, refrigerators, and TVs, and can accommodate up to four people. There is a pool (open to the public for a small fee) and a French restaurant with a good reputation. The hotel offers sportfishing, kayaking, diving, and yacht cruises (about US$40 for five hours in the morning, US$30 for a three-hour sunset cruise.) Double rates are US$119 for a bungalow with fan, US$127 with air-conditioning, and

US$135 for a junior suite, US$148 with a balcony. Children under 12 stay free.

Villas Nicolas *(☎ 777-0481, fax 777-0451, nicolas@sol.racsa.co.cr)* has a variety of rooms, suites, and villas available for rent most of the year. Some of them are gorgeous, and all are nicely decorated and have hot water, fans, and a balcony. There is a pool and Jacuzzi; the restaurant is open in the high season. The cheapest rooms start at US$68 double and lack ocean views. Bigger rooms with hammocks and views cost US$86; with kitchen US$98 to US$105; suites with two bedrooms, two bathrooms, two balconies with hammocks, and a kitchen cost US$161 to US$178 for four people. Discounts are given for week-long stays and to walk-ins on a space-available basis.

Just beyond is the fabulous ***Si Como No*** *(☎ 777-0777, fax 777-1093; in the USA ☎ 800-237-8201, reservations@sicomono.com)*. This architecturally arresting hotel has been gently eased into the environment with minimal disturbance. The cathedral-like atrium lobby was built around existing trees, and only one full-grown tree was cut during the construction of this 38-room hotel. If you can get past the stained-glass windows, viewing deck, and soothing atmosphere of the atrium, you'll find a lovely pool with a toboggan slide and swim-up bar, a solar-heated Jacuzzi, and the delightful Rico Tico outdoor bar and grill with a varied US-style bar menu. There are trees everywhere, and birds and monkeys treat the property as if it were theirs, which, owner Jim Damalas insists, it is. He built the hotel to incorporate the rainforest, and the result is the best place to stay in the area. In 1996, Si Como No won the grand prize out of a field of 60 contestants in Costa Rica's Biennial of Architecture competition, organized by the College of Architecture every two years.

Other features include a Laser Theater with a state-of-the-art sound system where nature videos and Hollywood films are shown (and which can be used for conferences and presentations). This is free to guests and people dining in one of the restaurants. Rooms are insulated for comfort and conservation and use energy-efficient air-conditioners and fans, water is recycled into the landscaping system, and solar-heating panels are used. Everything has been done right! There is no sacrifice in comfort, however. Each room has a private balcony (a few have picture windows) with unobstructed views of forest below and ocean beyond, as well as queen- or king-size beds and spacious hot-water bathrooms. The double rate, including breakfast, for spacious standard rooms is US$180. Superior suites with wet bars or kitchens cost US$203; larger deluxe suites cost US$226. Extra people are charged US$25 each, and children under 12 stay free. A honeymoon villa has a Jacuzzi.

Hotel & Villas Mogotes *(☎/fax 777-1043)* has great views, a pool, Jacuzzi, and restaurant. Music buffs delight in recounting that this was the summer home of North American singer Jim Croce (1942-73) – this coast must have been incredibly peaceful in those days. There are good views in all but the cheapest units. Double rooms with air-conditioning start at US$70, and larger villas with kitchenettes go for US$100 and up.

Kekoldi Beach Hotel *(☎ 777-1349; in San José 223-3244, fax 257-5476, kekoldi@sol.racsa.co.cr)*, opened by the owners of the Kekoldi Hotel in San José, has five simple and attractive cabins sleeping up to four people, with kitchenettes and fans, for US$70. Some have balconies and views of the islands.

La Quinta *(☎/fax 777-0434)* has four spacious cabins set in pleasant and quiet gardens. Cabins have balconies, patios, views, fans, and kitchenettes. There is a small pool. The rate is US$70 double.

The ***Hotel Eclipse*** *(☎/fax 777-0408, 777-1738, eclipsehcr@sol.racsa.co.cr)* is an unmistakable pure white building with a good restaurant, three swimming pools, and nine attractive split-level houses on the property. The bottom floor of each air-conditioned house is a spacious junior suite with queen-size and single beds, bathroom with hot water, living room, kitchen, and patio. These rent for US$135/160 double/triple. The upper floor is a standard room with queen-size bed, bathroom, and terrace. These have a separate entrance and cost US$95 single or double. A staircase (with lockable door) combines the two and, voilà (the owners *are* French), you have a house sleeping up to five for US$225. If you're adding up, you'll see there's a discount for renting both units. There are also seven more unconnected rooms and suites at the same prices. Breakfast costs about US$6.50, and set dinners cost about US$15 in the hotel's Gourmet Jardín restaurant, with French cooking.

Friendly ***Hotel Villa Nina*** *(☎ 777-1682, fax 777-1497, vilanina@sol.racsa.co.cr)* has nine rooms with balconies, mini-fridges, coffeemakers, and hot showers. Some rooms are air-conditioned, and they come in various sizes. There is a pool. Rates are US$50 to US$70 double.

Costa Verde *(☎ 777-0584, 777-0187, fax 777-0560, costaver@sol.racsa.co.cr)* is the sister hotel of the Escazú Costa Verde. It has a pool with ocean views, a bar, and restaurant, and the helpful staff will arrange local tours and activities. Attractive rooms all have kitchenettes, fans, private hot showers, and balconies with forest or ocean views. Small 'efficiency rooms' cost about US$80, and larger 'studio apartments' US$110. Some of these have whirlpool baths and air-conditioning. It has recently opened the locally recommended Anaconda Restaurant, and, across the road from the hotel, the Cantina Grill, which has an outdoor grill and live music some nights.

Hotel Arboleda *(☎ 777-1056, ☎/fax 777-0092)* has about three dozen stone cabins, some near the beach and others scattered down a forested hillside. The hotel has a pool and restaurant. Some cabins have fans, others have air-conditioning. Rates are about US$60/70 single/double (with fans) or US$80/90 (air-conditioned). The hotel was doing some unspecified building at last visit.

Villas de la Selva *(☎ 777-1137; in San José ☎/fax 253-4890)* has a house and a variety of apartments spread out around a pool. This is a low-key, quiet place (no children) with good views and private access to the beach, a short downhill walk away. Apartments have patios and hammocks, kitchenettes, and hot-water bathrooms for US$55 to US$65 double, depending on the kitchen. The house has two bedrooms, full kitchen, terrace, and barbecue grill and costs US$80 double, US$10 more for each additional person (up to eight).

On the final hill before you reach Manuel Antonio is ***Hotel Karahé*** *(☎ 777-0170, 777-0152, fax 777-1075, karahe@ns.goldnet.co.cr)*. You could easily walk to the national park from here in about 20 leisurely minutes. There is a pool, spa, restaurant, and three levels of rooms. The oldest cabins have superb views and are reached by climbing a flight of steep stairs. All have hot water and fans; some have refrigerators, kitchenettes, and air-conditioning. Rates are about US$70 to US$100 double including breakfast.

Beyond the Karahé, the new ***Hotel Verde Mar*** *(☎ 777-1805, fax 777-1311, verdemar@sol.racsa.co.cr)* now has the honor of being the last upscale hotel on the road from Quepos to Manuel Antonio. Nestled among lush trees, it is also close to the beach. Simple, beautifully decorated rooms cost US$75 double, US$88 with kitchenettes, and US$99 for a suite with kitchenette and two queen-size beds.

A couple of minutes' walk farther, the beach level is reached; there are more accommodations along here and in Manuel Antonio village (all of them cheaper).

Guesthouses If you want to stay for at least a week or more, it is possible to rent a fully equipped house and cater for yourself. The owner of La Buena Nota (see Manuel Antonio, below) has two houses and two two-bedroom apartments near the Hotel La Mariposa, and knows about others. Houses are generally comfortable and come fully equipped, and you can expect to pay between US$350 and US$650 a week.

Places to Eat

Many hotels mentioned above have good restaurants open to the public; the following are particularly recommended, though most hotel restaurants here are good. If you aren't staying in these, call ahead to make a reservation in the high season.

The very popular ***Hotel Plinio*** serves excellent and reasonably priced Italian and German food. The very expensive ***Hotel Byblos*** and the more affordable ***Gourmet JardínIB,*** in the Hotel Eclipse, specialize in French food. ***Villas Nicolas*** has an elegant Uruguayan steakhouse, and the 'grill your own' steakhouse in ***Cabinas Pedro Miguel*** is fun in the high season. The poolside ***Rico Tico Bar 'n Grill***, in Si Como No, is low-key and atmospheric. ***Cabinas Mono Azul*** has take-out and delivery service to anywhere in Manuel Antonio if you want to eat in your room.

There are several good nonhotel restaurants, referred to in the order that they are passed as you head south of Quepos. Some may have reduced hours in the rainy season or may open on their 'off' days in the height of the dry.

Dulu is an interesting-looking restaurant (formerly La Arcada Italian Restaurant) 1km south of Quepos. ***Fiesta del Mar*** *(☎ 777-1127)* is a new seafood place.

Restaurant Barba Roja *(☎ 777-0331)* has well-prepared North American food (hamburgers, sandwiches, Mexican, steak, and seafood), and there is a great view. Fish dinners cost around US$8, hamburgers start at US$3, and its 'margarita sunsets' are good while the sun goes down. There is both inside and outside dining. Breakfast, lunch, and dinner are served Tuesday to Sunday, with dinner on Monday in high season – a good value and recommended. Also check out the Barba Roja's new attraction, The Sphere Gallery.

Bar Restaurante Karola's *(☎ 777-1557)* is right next to Barba Roja and is also recommended. It serves Mexican plates, steaks, and seafood in an attractive garden setting. Entrées cost in the US$5 to US$15 range (more for jumbo shrimp). The macadamia nut pie has been recommended. It opens at 7 am for breakfast and is closed Wednesday. ***Restaurant Tipico Los Trapiches*** will be open by the time you read this, offering tico and international cuisine.

Café Milagro has the same great cappuccino, espresso, baked treats, and tranquil atmosphere you can find in the Quepos outlet. Walking here from the beach for an afternoon coffee, then hopping on the bus back to Quepos, makes a nice outing for budget travelers looking for a way to enjoy the luxuries of the hill.

Pickles Deli *(☎ 777-0048)*, in the little Centro Comercial Si Como No, serves US-style sandwiches (submarines) and other goodies at US prices. It is closed Tuesday.

In the Costa Verde hotel is the new and recommended ***Anaconda Restaurant***; opposite is its outdoor grill spot, the ***Cantina Grill***, built around an old railroad car. There is live music here some nights and views of the ocean every day.

Also see below in Manuel Antonio village and above in Quepos for other suggestions.

Getting There & Away

Many visitors get here by private or rented car, which enables them to drive the few kilometers to Manuel Antonio. Drive carefully on this narrow, steep, and winding road. Others rely on the Quepos taxi service or the frequent Quepos-Manuel Antonio bus service (for more on these options, see the Quepos section, earlier), or walk or hitchhike down to the park.

MANUEL ANTONIO

The small village at the entrance to the national park has a number of less-expensive hotels and restaurants and is popular with younger international travelers. The usual advice regarding hotel reservations during the high season applies here – the village is packed during Easter week, and few rooms are available on weekends. The usual comments about poorly regulated development and subsequent pollution and litter also apply – the government periodically tries to control development, but this has not been very effective. In an effort to protect the nation's coasts, a law was passed in the late 1970s making all of Costa Rica's beaches national and public property and closed to any kind of construction within 50m of the high-tide mark. It remains unclear what to do with those hotels and restaurants that are in violation of the law but were built before it was passed.

There is a good beach (Playa Espadilla), but swimmers are warned to beware of rip currents. Reportedly, there is a nude bathing beach frequented by gay men just beyond the far west end of Playa Espadilla. The town is generally safe, but swimmers should never leave belongings unattended on the beach here, or on the national park beaches. Make sure your hotel room is securely locked when you are out, even briefly.

Information

La Buena Nota (☎ 777-1002, fax 777-1946) has for years functioned as an informal information center in Quepos. Still under Anita Myketuk's management, it is in a spacious building just north of the Cabinas Piscis, at the north end of Manuel Antonio village. It provides assistance and information to travelers (in English) and also sells maps, guidebooks (including this one), new and used books in English, US newspapers, beach supplies, surfboard wax, sundries, and souvenirs galore, including T-shirts hand-painted by local artists and Costa Rican jewelry.

Tucan Tours, in the village near Playa Espadilla, offers Internet access.

Activities & Organized Tours

Marlboro Horse Stables (☎ 777-1108), opposite the Cabinas Piscis, rents horses for US$30 for two or three hours. Body boards are rented at La Buena Nota (see above). Surf and body boards and kayaks are rented all along the beach at Playa Espadilla. The Restaurant Mar y Sombra also rents chairs and umbrellas.

Tucan Tours offers some tours and equipment rentals.

Also see Information in the Quepos to Manuel Antonio section, earlier in this chapter.

Places to Stay

Budget The cheapest place is ***Costa Linda*** *(☎ 777-0304)*, affiliated with the Ticalinda budget travelers' hotel in San José. It is reasonably clean and charges US$7 per person in small, basic, stuffy rooms with shared cold showers. Even cheaper is ***Cabinas ANEP*** *(☎ 777-0565)*, but it may be hard to get into – ANEP is the Asociación Nacional de Empleados Públicos and so the cabinas may be full of tico workers taking a beach vacation. Another cheapie, ***Cabinas Miramar*** *(☎ 777-1253)*, is across from the beach and charges US$7 per person in three basic rooms, one sleeping two and the others sleeping four.

Cabinas Irarosa has simple but clean rooms with fans and private cold baths for US$14/20. ***Hotel Manuel Antonio*** *(☎ 777-1237)* is undergoing renovation; rooms currently have private cold showers and fans, though the hotel is talking about air-conditioning and maybe even hot water. Certainly, it is close to the beach. Rooms cost about US$20 double; they are usually full of young international travelers and are a fun place to stay. The hotel told me it doesn't take reservations. People camp next to the hotel for US$2.50 per person – watch your possessions at *all* times.

Cabinas Ramírez *(☎ 777-0003)* has about 18 rooms with private cold baths and fans for about US$25/30 double/triple. There is direct access to the beach. Rooms on the ocean side are OK, but the ones on the street side are dark and dank. In high season, it may be difficult to get cheaper single rates, but in low season it charges US$7.50 per person. The nearby disco may preclude sleep.

Cabinas Piscis *(☎ 777-0046)* has 12 fairly basic but clean double rooms sharing six baths at US$25 double and six nicer rooms with private baths for US$35/45 double/quadruple. All rooms have fans.

Mid-Range The ***Hotel Vela Bar*** *(☎ 777-0413, fax 777-1071, velabar@maqbeach.com)* has 10 pleasant rooms with private baths and fans for US$28 to US$45 double, depending on the size. Air-conditioning costs an additional US$8 to US$12. It also has a bungalow with a kitchen for US$65. The owners are pleasant and run a popular restaurant. ***Hotel del Mar*** *(☎/fax 777-0543)* has OK spacious rooms on nice grounds with fans and private cold showers for US$45, US$55 with air-conditioning.

Cabinas Los Almendros *(☎/fax 777-0225)* has large, quiet, pleasant rooms with hot water for US$45 double or triple with fans, US$55 with air-conditioning. There is a pool, and a decent restaurant is attached. ***Cabinas Espadilla*** *(☎/fax 777-0416)* has helpful owners and spacious clean rooms with private cold baths and fans. Rooms sleeping up to four, with kitchenettes, cost US$50; some cheaper rooms without kitchenettes are also available. The annex across the street has larger air-conditioned rooms with hot water, sleeping up to four for US$75 on high-season weekends (less midweek). The hotel will give cheaper single and double rates unless it is very busy.

The attractive ***Hotel Villabosque*** *(☎/fax 777-0401)* has nice rooms with fans, balconies, and hot water for US$80 double or US$90 with air-conditioning. There are 16 rooms; 13 are air-conditioned. It has a pool and offers guided tours into the national park.

There is a fair amount of construction in the village; look for new places.

Places to Eat

Vela Bar is the best and priciest restaurant in Manuel Antonio. It serves a variety of meals, including a few vegetarian plates, from US$6 to US$12. The restaurants at ***Hotel Villabosque*** and ***Cabinas Los Almendros*** are also good and slightly cheaper.

Restaurant Mar y Sombra is also popular and serves seafood. It has casados and chicken and pasta plates for about US$3 and fish dinners for twice that. Nearby is a quieter ***beach restaurant*** with inexpensive seafood meals and a pleasant terrace. There are good sunset views at both places. A number of other cheap sodas and roadside stands can be found in the beach area.

Entertainment

The disco at the ***Restaurant Mar y Sombra*** gets down on weekends and, in the busy season, on midweek nights as well.

Getting There & Away

All flights to Manuel Antonio go to Quepos.

Direct buses from San José leave the Coca-Cola terminal at 6 am, noon, and 6 pm daily in the dry season; one of these departures may not run in the wet season. Return buses leave at 6 am, noon, and 5 pm daily, plus 3 pm on Sunday. They will pick you up in front of your hotel if you are on the road to flag them down, or from the Quepos bus terminal, after which there are no stops. The fare is US$5, though shoestring travelers can save by taking a slower bus from Quepos. Buy tickets in advance if possible, particularly on weekends, when they sell out days ahead. Try calling ☎ 777-0263 for bus reservations in Manuel Antonio.

Buses for destinations other than San José leave from Quepos. Buses from Manuel Antonio to Quepos leave about 16 times a day from about 6 am to 9:50 pm – more often on dry-season weekends and less often in the wet season.

PARQUE NACIONAL MANUEL ANTONIO

At 683 hectares, Manuel Antonio is by far the smallest park in the national park system, but it is also one of the most popular. This is because of its beautiful forest-backed tropical beaches, dramatic rocky headlands with ocean and island views, prolific wildlife, and maintained trail network.

Fortunately, Manuel Antonio was declared a national park back in 1972, thus preserving it from hotel development. The many hotels in the area north of the park, however, have made this gem the focus of much visitation. Clearly, large numbers of people in such a small area tend to detract from the experience of visiting the park. Idyllic and romantic beaches have to be shared with others, wildlife is either driven away or – worse still – taught to scavenge for tourist handouts, and there are inevitable litter and traffic problems.

Several steps have been taken to minimize pressure on the park. Camping is no longer allowed. Vehicular traffic is prohibited within the park (and arriving on foot can be a minor adventure in itself). Signs have been installed explaining the dangers of feeding animals – dangerous both to the animals and the people attempting to feed them – and reminding visitors to carry out their garbage. Still, the heavy visitor pressure has led to closure of the park on

Mondays, and the number of visitors is limited to 600 during the week and 800 on weekends and holidays.

If you want to avoid the crowds, go early in the morning, midweek in the rainy season.

Orientation & Information

A visitor information center (☎ 777-0644, fax 777-0654) is just before Playa Manuel Antonio. Drinking water is available at the information center, and toilets are nearby. There are now more toilets farther into the park, as well as beach showers and a refreshment stand. The park is officially open 7 am to 4 pm Tuesday to Sunday, and guards come around in the evening to make sure that nobody is camping. It was once possible to camp, but heavy user pressure caused the closure of the campsite, and visitors have to stay outside the park.

A wildlife guide costs US$15 per person. The only guides allowed in the park are members of AGUILA (a local association governed by the park service) who have official ID badges, and recognized guides from tour agencies or hotels. This is to prevent visitors from getting ripped off and to ensure a good-quality guide – AGUILA guides are trained by the park service and most are bilingual. (French-, German-, or English-speaking guides can be requested from the information center.)

The beaches are often numbered – most people call Playa Espadilla (outside the park) 'first beach,' Playa Espadilla Sur 'second beach,' Playa Manuel Antonio 'third beach,' Playa Puerto Escondido 'fourth beach,' and Playita 'fifth beach.' Some people begin counting at Espadilla Sur, which is the first beach actually in the park, so it can be a bit confusing trying to figure out which beach people may be talking about. The refreshments stand is at third beach.

The average daily temperature is 27°; average annual rainfall is 3800mm. The dry season is not entirely dry, merely less wet, so you should be prepared for rain (although it can also be dry for days on end). Make sure you carry plenty of drinking water and sun protection when visiting the park. Insect repellent is also an excellent idea. Pack a picnic lunch if you're spending the day.

Entrance into the park costs US$6 per person per day.

Trails & Hiking

Visitors must leave their vehicles in the parking lot at the south end of the road in Manuel Antonio village. The Quebrada Camaronera estuary divides the southern end of the village from the park, and there is no bridge, so the estuary must be waded to gain access. The water may be ankle-deep at low tide and thigh-deep at high tide (spring tides in rainy season have been known to be chest-high), so prepare yourself to get at least a little wet.

Once across the estuary, follow an obvious trail through forest to an isthmus separating Espadilla Sur and Manuel Antonio beaches. This isthmus is called a *tombolo* and was formed by the accumulation of sedimentary material between the mainland and the peninsula beyond, which was once an island. If you walk along Playa Espadilla Sur, you will find a small mangrove area. The isthmus widens into a rocky peninsula, with forest in the center. A trail leads around the peninsula to Punta Catedral, from which there are good views of the Pacific Ocean and various rocky islets that are bird reserves and form part of the national park. Brown boobies and pelicans are among the seabirds that nest on these islands.

You can continue around the peninsula to Playa Manuel Antonio, or you can avoid the peninsula altogether and hike across the isthmus to this beach. At the western end of the beach, during the low tide, you can see a semicircle of rocks that archaeologists believe were arranged by pre-Columbian Indians to function as a turtle trap. The beach itself is an attractive one of white sand and is popular for bathing. It is protected and safer than the Espadilla beaches.

Beyond Playa Manuel Antonio, the trail divides. The lower trail is steep and slippery during the wet months and leads to the quiet and aptly named Playa Puerto Escondido (Hidden Port Beach). This beach can be more or less completely covered by high tides, so don't get cut off. The upper trail climbs to a view point on a bluff overlooking Puerto Escondido and Punta Serrucho beyond – a nice vista. Reportedly, rangers limit the number of hikers on this trail to 45 people.

Wildlife Watching

Monkeys abound in the park, and it is difficult to spend a day walking around without seeing some. White-faced monkeys are the most commonly seen, but the rarer squirrel monkeys are also present and howler monkeys may be seen. Sloths, agoutis, peccaries, armadillos, coatis, and raccoons are also seen quite regularly. Over 350 species of birds are reported in the park and surrounding area, and a variety of lizards, snakes, iguanas, and other animals may be observed. All the trails within the park are good for animal-watching – ask the rangers where the most interesting recent sightings have occurred. Some trails may limit the number of hikers to minimize disturbance of the animals. There is a small coral reef off Manuel Antonio beach, but the water is rather cloudy and the visibility limited. Despite this, snorkelers can see a variety of fish, as well as marine creatures like crabs, corals, sponges, sea snails, and many others.

Immediately inland from the beaches is an evergreen littoral forest. This contains many different species of trees, bushes, and other plants. A common one to watch out for is the manzanillo (little apple) tree, *Hippomane mancinella*; this tree has poisonous fruits that look like little crab apples. The sap exuded by the bark and leaves is also toxic, and it causes the skin to itch and burn, so give the manzanillo a wide berth. Warning signs are prominently displayed by examples of this tree near the park entrance.

MANUEL ANTONIO TO DOMINICAL

To continue farther south along the coast from Manuel Antonio, you have to backtrack to Quepos and from there head 4km inland to the Costanera Sur. It is 44km from Quepos to the next village of any size, Dominical. The road is bone-shaking gravel and easily passable in the dry season but requires care to negotiate with an ordinary car in the wet. Residents of this area have long complained to the government that the Costanera Sur should be paved and, in June 1993, coordinated a massive protest by blockading Quepos and effectively shutting down that town and Manuel Antonio. Many travelers were stranded. The government promised to pave and improve this road some time ago, though it has yet to happen. Maybe it'll be paved by the time you get there, though don't bet your last colón on it.

The drive is through kilometer after kilometer of African oil-palm plantations, with identical-looking settlements along the way. These are minor centers for the palm-oil extracting process. Each settlement has a grassy village square, institutional-looking housing, a store, church, bar and, to round out the picture, an Alcoholics Anonymous chapter.

Matapalo offers a mainly unvisited stretch of beach with long vistas and safe swimming (ie, not a surfing beach). In the tiny village, the sign for the ***Express Deli del Pacífico*** announces that Matapalo is 'Center of the World but the World Doesn't Know It!' Near the beach you'll find ***El Oasis Americano Cabinas***, which has a bar, restaurant, English-speaking owners, and basic cabins for US$8 per person. The Swiss-owned ***El Coquito del Pacífico*** (*☎ 222-4103 for reservations only, fax 222-8849, ecobraun@sol.racsa.co.cr*) has six bungalows sleeping up to four people in a pretty, shady spot right next to the beach. It has a pool, restaurant, and bar and can arrange horseback rides. Rates are US$29 single, US$8 for each additional person. Camping on the beach is a possibility and there are probably other cabins in the area, which is still isolated and spread out; this is an area that is sure to see more development. Buses between Quepos and Dominical can drop you in the village, from which it is a couple of kilometers to the beach.

A couple of kilometers northwest of Matapalo is the private ***Reserva Forestal Ecológica Portalón***, where a woman named Sylvia has nice cabins. Also in this area, look for a small wooden sign for ***La Laja***, a bar-restaurant advertising waterfalls, swimming, birds, and butterflies 1km inland off the main road. Sounds nice. Farther to the northwest, 6km inland from Savegre, is the ***Albuerge Agroecoturistico El Silencio***, a local cooperative offering lodging, a restaurant, trails, and horseback riding – it sounds interesting and feedback is welcomed.

South of Matapalo, about a kilometer before reaching the Río Barú, is the private nature reserve at Hacienda Barú. A bridge crosses the Río Barú, and immediately beyond is the village of Dominical on the southeast side of the river mouth. From the west side of the bridge, a steep but paved road climbs 34km inland to San Isidro de El General. Therefore, if you can negotiate the somewhat rough Quepos-to-Dominical road, a roundtrip from San José to Quepos, Dominical, San Isidro de El General, and back to San José is quite possible and, indeed, makes a good excursion.

The road south of Dominical continues through Uvita and reconnects with the Interamericana just southeast of Ciudad Cortés (see below).

HACIENDA BARÚ

This private nature reserve covers only about 330 hectares but manages to pack a large number of species into its small size. This is because its location on the steep coastal hills encompasses a variety of habitats, including 3km of beach, 16 hectares of mangroves, 1km of the Río Barú, pasture and plantations, and lowland and hilly rainforest up to 320m above sea level. About 80 hectares are undisturbed primary rainforest, 50 hectares are rainforest that was selectively logged almost two decades ago and then left, and 25 hectares are secondary forest growing on abandoned pastures. There are tree-growing areas, fruit orchards, cocoa plantations, open pasture, and brushy areas. In addition, the reserve contains several pre-Columbian cemetery sites and petroglyphs.

The Hacienda Barú bird list is well over 300 species and growing; the mammal list is 56 species (including 23 bats); the amphibian and reptile list is 35 species, and there are many frogs, toads, and snakes that are yet to be identified; and the plant list is far from complete with over 100 trees and 75 orchid species. An impressive list!

The owners, Jack and Diane Ewing, have lived and raised their family here since 1970. They are a delightful couple with a fund of stories to tell and information to dispense. They have always been active in pushing for environmentally responsible legislation in Costa Rica and are currently focusing their energy on the creation of biological corridors – stretches of undisturbed land connecting different habitats within Costa Rica and throughout Central America. Buying land is a key part of these projects and if you're interested in contributing you should definitely contact Jack – his fascination with the rainforest is infectious and his dedication to preserving it inspiring.

When they first arrived in the area, transportation was mostly by horseback – now the road goes by and tourism is increasing. Nevertheless, Barú still has a remote feel to it. The Ewings have worked hard at preserving the area and are active in encouraging and helping their neighbors to do likewise; they want to be ready to properly handle the inevitable growth in tourism, which has already begun.

In 1992, they were joined by Steve Stroud, who has worked hard to make the reserve a great place to visit. He has been instrumental in developing ecologically sensitive tours and building a superb rainforest canopy platform, which for many people is the highlight of their visit.

Information

Obtain information and make reservations for tours or accommodations with the Hacienda Barú (☎ 787-0003, fax 787-0004, sstroud@racsa.co.cr) or through Selva Mar (see the Dominical section, below).

The Ewings' El Ceibo gas station, 1.7km north of the hacienda, is the only one for a good way in any direction. A variety of groceries, fishing gear, tide tables, and other useful sundries is available, and there are clean toilets.

Activities & Organized Tours

Three interpretive trails and a new wooden birding tower are open to the public. Trail fees are US$3 per person (60% goes to the government, the rest is for trail maintenance) and, for an extra US$3 per group, you can hire a local schoolkid who knows the trails and has been taught to spot the birds and animals of interest to hikers. An interpretive booklet is also available for US$3. If you want to go in at (or before!) dawn, you can either pay the night before or as you leave.

In addition, there are several guided tours offered at Hacienda Barú. These include a 2½-hour lowland birding walk (US$20); a 5½-hour rainforest hike, including lunch (US$35); a combination of the preceding two hikes (US$40); and an overnight stay in the rainforest with meals and comfortable camping (US$60). These prices are for one person, and there is a two-person minimum. A maximum of eight people are allowed in the rainforest so that you don't meet other hikers. Horseback rides (US$25 for two hours, US$5 each additional hour) are also available. A kayak tour through the mangrove estuary costs US$35. These tour prices include knowledgeable native guides. Jim Zook, a very knowledgeable English-speaking naturalist and ornithologist, Jack Ewing, or another of the English-speaking naturalists will accompany any tour for an additional US$50 per day. One day's advance notice is usually needed.

The most exciting activity is a rope ascent into the canopy. There is a canopy platform about 32m above the ground, built in a tree that is reached after a 15-minute hike through the forest. Each participant is given a safety helmet, attached to a climbing harness, and winched up by rope to the platform. About 45 minutes is spent on the platform, accompanied by a guide who will point out things of interest. The ocean is visible in the distance, but the chance of wildlife observation is more exciting than seeing the ocean. I saw a sloth and a pair of toucans mating on a branch just below the platform, totally oblivious of my presence. Great! On the way down, you can control the pace of descent and spend about 10 minutes hanging, suspended like a spider spinning on a cord, in the middle layers of the canopy. The tour costs US$35 per person with a maximum of three allowed on the platform at a time. No climbing experience is needed – everything is done for you.

If you feel like even more adventure, you can climb into the canopy by a rope hanging from a tree. No platforms, just rope climbing about 35m up into the canopy, accompanied by an experienced climber and naturalist guide. No experience is needed, but this is more strenuous than being winched to a platform, so you need to be in good shape. Two trees are usually climbed, and the cost is US$45 per person.

These tours and activities are open to the public; you don't have to stay here.

Volunteering is a possibility in August and September, to gather olive ridley turtle eggs for a turtle nursery project. You may not get to see the turtles laying, but the chance to be of use in a fascinating and beautiful environment makes this a worthwhile experience.

Places to Stay & Eat

Six simple but spacious two- and three-bedroom ***cabins*** each have a kitchenette, refrigerator, fans in every room, hot shower, sitting room, and insect screens. High-season rates are US$50 double, US$10 for each additional person. Continental breakfast is included, and lunch and dinner are available in the restaurant.

Getting There & Away

The Quepos-Dominical-San Isidro bus stops outside the hacienda entrance. The San Isidro-Dominical-Uvita bus will drop you at the Río Barú bridge, just over a kilometer from the hacienda.

DOMINICAL

This little coastal village is 1.2km south of Hacienda Barú. The Dominical beach is a long one and has a reputation for strong rip currents – exercise extra caution. Despite this, the surfing is good, so a number of surfers hang out here. A small but popular language school in the village means that visitors making extended stays are not all surfers. A small ecotourism industry is developing, and local operators, led by the owners of the Hacienda Barú, are banding together in an effort to promote the area without spoiling it. Apart from surfing, attractions include rainforest hiking and camping, wildlife observation, horseback riding, fishing, and visits to the nearby Parque Nacional Marino Ballena. Slowly, Dominical is being discovered, and the little town can get full on weekends, both with tico and foreign visitors. New hotels can be expected to open over the next few years.

Orientation & Information

The main Costanera highway bypasses Dominical. The entrance to the village is immediately past the Río Barú bridge. There is a main road through the village, where many of the services mentioned are found, and a parallel road along the beach.

Selva Mar (☎ 771-4582, fax 771-1903; in the USA c/o AAA Express Mail, 1641 NW 79th Ave, Miami, FL 33126, selvamar@sol.racsa.co.cr) is a booking agent and tour operator with offices in San Isidro. It works almost exclusively in the Dominical-Uvita area and communicates with over a dozen remote lodges and businesses by radio-telephone. The staff can arrange car rental, horseback rides, boat trips, diving, and fishing.

Surfer Cool

Surfing – which demands strength, skill, and daring, and has the side benefits of a great tan and ocean-buffed physique – is undeniably cool. Unfortunately, this leads some surfers to treat nonsurfers at the beach like caddies that have crashed the country club bar. If you're a surfer, try not to be so stodgy! If you're a nonsurfer, it can help to think of surfers as dolphins – graceful, inexplicable creatures known on occasion to be friendly to mere humans.

– **John Thompson**

There is an ICE office on the main road by Thrusters bar. Internet service is available here. The telephone system reached town in 1996 and is expanding. Selva Mar will pass on radio messages for some local businesses beyond the telephone lines.

Centro Turístico Cataratas Nauyaca

About 10km away on the road to San Isidro, just before the village of Platanillo, an entrance to the right leads into this tourism center (☎ 771-3187, fax 771-2003, ciprotur@sol.racsa.co.cr). There is no vehicle access to the area – you can hire horses for a guided ride to two waterfalls, 20 and 45m high, that plunge into a deep swimming hole. With a day's notice, a tour can be arranged, including guided horseback rides, swimming in the pool under the falls, and country meals with a local family. Tours leave about 8 or 9 am and take six to seven hours. The cost is about US$40 per person. A campground with dressing rooms and toilets is available.

Activities

Although known for surfing, the area is also good for horseback rides to waterfalls in the hills above the coast. The Hacienda Barú and several hotels can arrange horseback rides, or just ask around – Dominical is a very small place.

Language Courses

La Escuelita de Dominical (☎ 787-0090, fax 787-0103, domini@sol.racsa.co.cr) is right on the shore and offers a chance to combine studying Spanish with life in a beach village. Homestays can be arranged; for meals, students are given vouchers that can be used in local restaurants. Rates range from US$350 to US$525 per week, depending on time in the classroom and whether you want jungle tours included, and go down for longer stays. It has a sister school in the Bocas del Toro region of Panama, and another opening in Turrialba in the Central Valley; some packages include stays at both schools.

Places to Stay

Budget Even the cheap places are not very cheap – free camping on the beach is an option. The basic but clean ***Cabinas Coco*** *(☎ 771-2555)* is on the main street and charges US$6.50 per person. Note that the accompanying bar and disco may preclude sleep on weekend nights. Nearby, there are slightly less noisy rooms at this price at ***Sundancer Cabinas*** *(☎ 787-0125)*, which offers basic rooms in a pleasant family home for US$22 double.

On the beach at the north end, the low-key ***La Escuelita de Dominical*** (see Language Courses, above) charges about US$9 per person for a bed if space is available. The head of the school, the brilliantly zany Dr Vern Leicht, is friendly and will let campers use the school's shower and kitchen facilities for about US$3 if things are slow.

Mid-Range On the main road, the shaded ***Albergue Willdale*** *(☎ 787-0023)* has four clean, spacious rooms with private hot showers and fans for US$20/25/30 single/double/triple. Nearby, ***Cabinas Villa Dominical*** *(☎ 787-0030, 771-0621)* has 10 simple, bare rooms with hot water and fans for US$25/30 single/double. Also on the main street, the quiet, friendly ***Posada del Sol*** *(☎/fax 787-0085)* has clean rooms with fans and hot water for US$20/25.

Closer to the beach, ***Cabinas Nayarit*** *(☎ 787-0033)* charges US$30 for rooms with private baths and fans, US$40 with air-conditioning. On a road to the beach, the ***DiuWak*** *(☎ 787-0087, fax 787-0089, diuwak@sol.racsa.co.cr)* has eight clean, spacious rooms with fans and hot water for US$30 double, and four nice air-conditioned units with kitchenettes and refrigerators for US$40 double. It has a restaurant and Jacuzzi. The attractive ***Cabinas San Clemente*** *(☎ 787-0026)*, associated with the bar and restaurant, also has some air-conditioned rooms in this price range on the beach. Also on the beach, the larger ***Tortilla Flats*** *(☎ 787-0033)* has rooms sleeping up to three, US$30 for fans, US$40 for air-conditioning. This place may be up for sale and could change before your visit.

The ***Hotel Río Lindo*** *(☎/fax 787-0028)* is near the entrance to Dominical. It has five clean, attractive, spacious rooms with private baths for US$30 double (US$5 each additional person), and five more with air-conditioning for US$40 double (US$10 each additional person). There is hot water in the evenings, and it has a pool and Jacuzzi, featuring Paco's Maui Pool Bar, and a nearby restaurant.

Just beyond the entrance into Dominical, a sign points under the bridge to ***Hotel Villas Río Mar*** *(☎ 787-0052; reservations in San José ☎ 283-5013, ☎/fax 224-2053)* – about 800 from the village. It has thatched bungalows with 40 spacious rooms, each with fan, wet bar, mini-fridge, private hot shower, and private patio for about US$70/80. There is a pool, Jacuzzi, tennis court, restaurant, and bar. The hotel can arrange local tours and has mountain bikes for rent.

Overlooking a smaller beach about 1km south of the village, the ***Hotel y Restaurante Roca Verde*** *(☎ 787-0036, fax 787-0013, doshnos@sol.racsa.co.cr)* has undergone a big renovation, with new hotel rooms, a spacious restaurant/bar, pool, and Jacuzzi. On Saturdays there is dancing and on Sundays a poolside barbecue complete with a mariachi band; both are popular local events. Nice doubles with air-conditioning cost US$65.

About 2km south of Dominical is the attractive, tranquil, and comfortable ***Costa Paraiso Lodge*** *(☎/fax 787-0025)*. Two fully equipped apartments with fans, living-rooms, and porches overlooking the ocean cost about US$70 double, US$10 per extra person. Spacious rooms with kitchenettes and fans cost about US$55 double, US$10 per extra person.

Places to Eat

There are several inexpensive sodas in Dominical, of which the best are the ***Soda Laura*** and friendly ***Soda Nanyoa***. They open by about 6:30 am for breakfast and serve casados for about US$2. ***Gringo Mike's*** is a new bakery and NYC-style deli with snacks and sandwiches. The popular ***San Clemente Bar & Grill*** has good, big breakfasts and US-style bar food the rest of the day (Tex-Mex and pizza are among the favorites). Its satellite TV shows sports programs and surfing videos. All these are on the main village road. Just off the main road toward the beach (by the ICE office and a surf shop), ***Thrusters Bar*** makes pizzas.

Near the entrance to town, ***La Capanna*** is a new spot manned by two fabulous young Italian chefs; they may be moving to a new restaurant – just ask where they've gone, people will know. Watching them cook is as much of a treat as eating their meals. About 1km south of town, the ***Restaurante Roca Verde*** in the hotel of that name is fun and popular.

On the main Costanera highway, there is a small shopping plaza with a deli. Also see Southeast of Dominical, below, for more suggestions.

Entertainment

The two village hotspots are the ***San Clemente*** and the larger ***Thrusters***; both have pool tables and loud music. The ***Hotel y Restaurante Roca Verde*** has music on weekends.

Getting There & Away

The bus stop in Dominical is by the Soda Nanyoa. It has schedules as well as ticket information.

Buses for Quepos leave at 5:45 and 8:15 am and 3 pm; for San Isidro at 7 and 8 am and3 and 3:30 pm; and for Uvita at 7 am and4:30 and 7 pm.

In addition, buses from San José to Uvita pass through Dominical at about 10:30 am and 9 pm. Buses from Uvita to Quepos and San José pass through Dominical at about 6 am and 2 pm. It is well worth asking locally about all these schedules; some will certainly change as road conditions improve.

SOUTHEAST OF DOMINICAL

The road continues southeast of Dominical about 18km to Uvita. This road has been greatly improved in recent years – bits of it are even paved, though keep your eyes peeled for unexpected and unmarked obstacles created by the ongoing construction. There are occasional glimpses of the ocean but, for the most part, the road is a little ways inland. It is passable to ordinary cars for most of the year. The improvement of the road has heated up real estate business in the area, though most new buyers are private owners rather than entrepreneurs or hotel chains. The beaches are too rough to draw big resort developers, and home owners tend to hide their buildings inside acres of forested land. The most visible difference brought by the improving road will likely be the occasional cluster of shops.

There are several interesting places to stay south of Dominical, off the road to Uvita. You can contact most of them via the Selva Mar (see Orientation & Information in the Dominical section, above).

Places to Stay & Eat

Just over 2km south of the Hotel y Restaurante Roca Verde in Dominical, along the gravel road to Uvita, a sign points to a road to the left for ***Cabinas Bellavista***. Owned by long-time resident Woody Dyer, who has a wealth of stories about his many years in the area, this remote lodge is in a revamped farmhouse 500m above sea level. A balcony gives superb ocean views, and there is rainforest and a waterfall nearby. Accommodations are rustic but clean; solar-heated water is available. Four rooms in the main building cost US$34/45 single/double; bathrooms are communal. Tasty home-cooked meals cost about US$15 per day. A guest house for up to eight people has a private bathroom and a kitchen. This costs US$57 double, plus US$6 each additional person. Rainforest/waterfall hiking or horseback tours with lunch and local guide cost US$40 per person. Bring extra batteries for your flashlight.

This place is difficult to get to. You need 4WD to get up their road, which is locally called the Escaleras (Staircase). If you don't have 4WD, Woody will pick you up in Dominical for US$10. (You might struggle up there with a car in the dry season.) However, it is only about 7 or 8km from Dominical, so the hardy could hike up.

About another kilometer up the Escaleras road is the ***Villas Escaleras Inn*** *(☎/fax 787-0031, crinfo@sol.racsa.co.cr)*, which offers three luxurious villas with gorgeous views. The two larger villas both have a pool and full kitchen; the three-bedroom costs US$325 per night and the two-bedroom costs US$255. A one-bedroom with a splash pool, nearby creeks, and kitchen has a private entrance and rents for US$185 nightly. All have balconies, coffee supplies, and maid service, and surf and body boards can be borrowed; local tours are also arranged and there are discounts for longer stays. The owners have worked in the B&B industry in Los Angeles and pride themselves on their personal touch and the attractiveness of the villas.

Also on the Escaleras road is the ***Finca Brian y Milena***. This is a small, isolated, working farm surrounded by rainforest. It has a screened cabin sleeping up to six with a bathroom. The rate is US$50 per person, including all meals and a short hiking tour. There is a heated rock pool to soak in. There is also the aptly named Birdhouse Cabin, which sleeps two and shares the bathroom with the main house; the rate is US$36 per person. Discounts are given for longer stays, and the staff can also arrange a variety of hiking trips to visit rainforest waterfalls and eat with local campesino families. If you don't have 4WD, you can either hike from the main highway (1½ hours) or ride a horse (about US$10 to US$14 in Dominical) to get to their place.

Eventually, the Escaleras road drops back down to the Costanera but, before it does, you pass the friendly ***Pacific Edge***. It's actually easier to get here by avoiding the first Escaleras entrance to Bellavista and taking the second entrance, where a sign indicates Pacific Edge one steep kilometer up from the Costanera. Four cabins are perched on a knife-thin ridge about 200m above sea level. The rainforest drops off all around and the views are stunning. The cabins are spacious and take advantage of their location with view balconies on the edge of the ridge (don't fall off!). Each has a solar-heated shower and kitchenette, and there is also a restaurant/bar. Rates are US$41/47/53 for one/two/three people, and US$5 extra for use of the kitchenettes. Long-term rentals are cheaper. Meals cost US$5 for breakfast and lunch. Dinner, on request, costs US$10 to US$15.

Cabinas Punta Dominical *(☎/fax 787-0016)* is 3.5km south of Dominical and then to the right on a dirt road to the beach. Built high on a rocky headland named, appropriately enough, Punta Dominical, the cabins are isolated and attractive, yet retain a modicum of comfort. Four pleasant cabins with fans, private baths with electric showers, and porches to hang a hammock rent for US$50 double and US$12 per extra person, up to six people. Reservations are recommended, especially on weekends. The cabins overlook a rocky beach; there is a sandy beach nearby, and boat trips can be arranged. The restaurant on the premises is widely regarded as one of the best in the area and is open to the public. Hours are 8 am to 8 pm daily. Sample prices are US$3.50 for a casado, US$5 for fried fish, and US$15 for a shrimp or lobster dinner.

Seven kilometers south of Dominical is ***Cabañas Escondidas*** *(☎/fax 282-9816, escondi@sol.racsa.co.cr)*, set in attractive gardens surrounded by rainforest. This is a tranquil alternative to other accommodations. The family running the place offers classes in tai chi and chi kung, gives therapeutic massage, and provides international vegetarian meals (meats are available on request), as well as arranges the usual guided rainforest hikes, snorkeling trips, and horseback rides. You can walk to the beach in about 10 minutes. Nine charming and secluded individual cabins all have hot showers and fans. Rates are US$35 to US$65 double, depending on the size of the room and how close it is to the beach (some of are on the inland side of the highway).

Near here is the ***Swiss Tucan*** (fax 771-3060), with six rooms with private baths, and more planned, and a restaurant, bar, and pool. The Swiss owners speak German, French, Spanish, and English and charge about US$40 double, including breakfast.

A couple of kilometers farther is ***Las Casitas de Puertocito*** (*☎/fax 787-0048*), with eight bi-level rustic thatched cabins with private hot showers, fans, patios, and upstairs sleeping decks. There is a small bar and Italian restaurant and nearby beach access. The surroundings are lushly forested and there are ocean views. The rate is US$50 double, including breakfast. You can rent horses and arrange a variety of adventurous two to three day horseback tours, as well as snorkeling day trips.

UVITA

This tiny village is 17km south of Dominical and is the nearest community to Parque Nacional Marino Ballena. There is no real center as such – it is just a loose straggle of farms and houses on both sides of the highway, with a couple of stores, sodas, and places to stay. There are several entrances from the highway and the beaches are locally referred to as Playa Uvita and, to the south, Playa Bahía Uvita. Both are popular with ticos looking for a place to swim – this is not a surfing area. At low tide you can walk out along Punta Uvita. People are friendly and will show you where to go. Most places to stay in this area can also be contacted through Selva Mar (see Orientation & Information in Dominical, above).

Reserva Biológica Oro Verde

This private reserve is on the farm of the friendly Duarte family, who have homesteaded the area for over three decades. About two-thirds of their 150-hectare property is rainforest. They operate tours to see the forest, waterfalls, and wildlife and give you a look at traditional Costa Rican life. Horse rental starts at US$5 per hour, and hikes with a Spanish-speaking local guide cost US$15 per person for three to four hours. They have a simple cabin that will sleep seven people (one room with a double bed and another with five bunk beds) for about US$10 per person. There is a kitchen, shower, and patio. They'll also provide home-cooked meals in their house, about 400m away, for another US$10 per day. This is a recommended local sustainable tourism venture. It is about 3 or 4km inland from Uvita along a signed rough road.

Rancho La Merced

Opposite the turnoff to Oro Verde is Rancho La Merced, a working cattle ranch, over half of which has been left as protected forest. Horseback tours are offered, including 'Cowboy for a Day,' where you ride with the local cowboys and help on the ranch. They'll show you what to do if this is your first time, dude. A three- to five-hour tour costs US$20 (three people minimum) or US$30 (one person). They also offer a variety of other tours on horseback and on foot, with the chance to spot wildlife in various habitats. In 1996, they opened the Profelis Center for feline conservation. It can be visited for free if you are a ranch guest, US$10 for other visitors. Lodging in their Cabina El Kurukuzungo costs US$45/55 double/triple. There are two bedrooms sharing one bathroom, a living room, and a kitchen, for a maximum of six occupants. Meals can be provided for US$7, or US$4 for breakfast.

Places to Stay & Eat

You can ***camp*** on the beach; at the base of Punta Uvita is a soda that will guard your goods for a small fee. Apart from the tourism projects above, Uvita has a few other low-key options; some can be contacted through Selva Mar. These are listed roughly north to south.

The main entrance to Uvita leads inland, east of the highway, where you'll find ***Cabinas Los Laureles***, which has three cabins with bathrooms for US$12/20/25 for one/two/three people. It can arrange horseback tours. You'll find the cabins a few hundred meters to the left of the ***abastecedor*** (general store); there is a sign. Farther up the same road is ***Cabinas El Cocotico***, with six simple but clean rooms with private baths and ceiling fans for US$8/12 single/

double. The staff can tell you how to find a nearby waterfall. A soda is attached.

Near Playa Bahía Uvita is the friendly ***Cabinas Hegalva*** *(☎ 382-5780)*, run by Doña Cecilia who cooks great food and charges US$10 per person for rooms with shared baths, including breakfast. They are building tiny, cute one-person bungalows (imagine a stone tent with a thatched roof) for which they'll charge US$5 per person. You can also camp here for US$3 per person; breakfast costs about US$2. Also in this area are ***Cabinas Betty***, by a soda of the same name, and ***Cabinas Maria Jesus***, both basic rural places charging about US$5 per person.

Villas Bejuco *(☎ 771-0965)* is 2km south of the bridge over the Río Uvita, just inland off the Costanera and only a few hundred meters from the ocean. It has six large, clean cabins with huge screened windows for cross ventilation, private hot baths, and patios. The rate is US$27 double.

Near Villas Bejuco you'll see a big sign for ***Hotel El Chaman*** *(fax 771-7771)*, which is on the beach and has about a dozen simple cabins. Some have private hot showers, and some smaller ones share showers. The rate is about US$30 double. There is a restaurant and a pool. The friendly German owner arranges adventurous horse tours – four days and three nights cost US$148 per person.

On the road leading from the Costanera to El Chaman is ***La Colonia***, which has a few spacious cabins with private baths for US$14.50/18 double/triple.

Getting There & Away

When the road opened to ordinary traffic in 1996, the frequency of buses increased, and the situation is changing all the time. Now there are a couple of buses daily to and from San José, leaving the capital at 5 am and 3 pm and returning at 5 am and 1 pm. Buses to San Isidro de El General, which pass through Dominical, leave at 6 am and 2 pm, returning to Uvita at 9 am and 4 pm. Three buses a day travel the road to Ciudad Cortés; ask locally for times, and whether departures are from the village or the highway.

PARQUE NACIONAL MARINO BALLENA

This national marine park was created in 1990 to protect coral and rock reefs in 4500 hectares of ocean around Isla Ballena, south of Uvita. The island has nesting colonies of magnificent frigatebirds, blue-footed boobies, and other seabirds, as well as many green iguanas and basilisk lizards. Humpback whales migrate through the area and may be sighted from December to March. The Spanish word for whale is *ballena* – this gives the name to the vaguely whale-shaped island as well as the park. Both common and bottle-nosed dolphins are found here year-round, and there is a good variety of other marine life.

From Punta Uvita heading southeast, the park includes 13km of sandy and rocky beaches, mangrove swamps, river mouths, and rocky headlands. By Costa Rican law, the first 50m of coast above the high-tide mark are protected from development and are accessible to everyone – not just here, but throughout the country. The sandy beaches are the nesting sites of olive ridley and hawksbill turtles during the rainy months of May to November, with peak laying occurring in September and October. All six kinds of Costa Rica's mangroves occur within the park: two species of black mangrove, red, tea, white, and (the rarest) buttonwood.

The ranger station is in the community of Bahía, the seaside extension of Uvita. The rangers told me that you can hire boats from Bahía to Isla Ballena for about US$15 to US$20 per hour; landing on the island and snorkeling are permitted. From the ranger station you can walk out onto Punta Uvita and snorkel. This is best on a dropping/low tide (especially when the tides are not extreme). High and extreme tides make the water turbid.

Although there is a ranger station, the park remains undeveloped. There was no park entrance fee at last visit, and there are no campgrounds, though there is a house or two near the station where you might find a place to stay. There are signs to the ranger station from the Costanera. Now that the road southeast of Uvita is passable, this park may develop further by the time you read this.

SOUTHEAST OF UVITA

Beyond Uvita, an improved, though not yet paved, road follows the coast as far as Ciudad Cortés, about 36km away. This road, previously a major challenge even with high-clearance 4WD, was passable to ordinary vehicles for the first time in 1996. There are several remote beaches along here that are becoming discovered as hotels begin opening their doors to visitors who are traveling the Costanera all the way through. This route, which provides an alternative to the Interamericana and had been planned for years, is now a reality. Drivers now have the choice of traveling south along unpaved coastal roads or inland through the mountains along the paved, though sometimes potholed, Interamericana. The three daily buses currently traveling this stretch of road can drop you near any of the places described below.

About 7km south of Uvita is **Playa Bahía Ballena**, which is within the marine boundaries of the park. There is no village here but there are a number of small places to stay along the road, all of them near the beach. ***Cabinas Punta Uvita*** *(☎ 771-2311)* has pleasant grounds and a few rooms with shared baths for US$4.50 per person, US$13 for a double with private bath. You can camp here and horse rental is available. ***Cabinas Flamingo*** *(☎ 771-8078)* has a restaurant/bar and a couple cabins sleeping up to five for US$20. ***Villa Leonor*** *(☎ 225-8151, 280-6284 for reservations)* has an attractive garden and is near a particularly lovely part of the beach, and apparently there's a cavern and waterfall nearby. A few rustic cabins sleeping up to four, with solar-heated water, cost US$17. Meals are available. Reportedly, ***Cabinas Ana*** *(☎ 786-6358)* is somewhere near here; it sounds nice but was harder to find than the others.

About 10km beyond Uvita is **Playa Piñuela**, at the far southeastern corner of the Ballena national park. The ***Cabinas Piñuelas*** was closed at last visit but may reopen.

A few kilometers farther is **Playa Tortuga**, where several hotels have recently opened. It appears to be a French-Canadian enclave – who knows why. In Tortuga Abajo, off the highway, ***Papagayos*** *(☎/fax 788-8210, fax 786-6358; in Canada fax 819-566-5616, 905-548-8527)* has a pool, restaurant, tennis court, horse rental, and a boat for fishing. There are 14 spotless rooms in the US$55 to US$70 range for a double, all with private baths.

Paraíso del Pacífico *(☎/fax 788-8351, fax 786-6358; in Canada ☎ 514-662-7555, fax 514-662-7552)* is on a hill overlooking Playa Tortuga. It has 12 pleasant rooms with hot showers, fans, and private balconies for about US$55 double. There is a restaurant and pool. A new place along the road is the Dutch-run ***Hotel Villas Gaia*** *(☎/fax 256-9996, hvgaia@sol.racsa.co.cr)*. Set in tranquil forested grounds are twelve wooden cabins decorated with tropical colors; each has a private terrace, solar hot water, and ceiling fans. A brief walk leads to a spacious restaurant and hilltop pool. Tours of all kinds (including ultra-light flights) can be arranged. The rate is US$55 double.

Just south and inland is the charming, hilltop ***El Perezoso*** *(fax 786-6358)*, which has great views, a small pool, and pleasant rooms in a small vine-covered villa. Owner John Sevigny (one of the local French-Canadians) is a good cook. Rates are US$30/38 single/double, US$45 for a double with balcony. All the French-Canadian places in this area share a Saturday shuttle service from San José. If you're driving from the south, the sign for El Perezoso isn't visible – look for a turnoff by the Ventana del Pacífico realty office. Just past this office, you'll also see signs for ***Rancho Soluna*** *(fax 788-8351)*, a low-key place in attractive grounds. It has a small bar/restaurant and a pool table on an open-air patio with a thatched roof and mosquito netting. A few simple rooms with private baths cost US$20/25 single/double. You can camp and use the facilities for US$5 per person, or sleep in another net-protected patio for US$7 per person.

Look around for other places to eat, drink, and camp.

The biggest town on the coast south of Quepos is **Ciudad Cortés,** which has a bank and stores, and no doubt will have a hotel soon. The ***Soda Oasis***, near the central park, may have rooms available if you get stuck. From here, a paved 7km road connects with the Interamericana at Palmar Norte. Buses arrive and depart from the park. There are three buses a day to Uvita and seven for Neily, passing through Palmar Norte and Río Claro. From these towns you can make connections to Golfito and the Península de Osa. See the Southern Costa Rica chapter for details and descriptions of these places.

Language

The Spanish Alphabet

Although the Spanish alphabet looks like the English one, it is in fact different. 'Ch' is considered a separate letter, for example, so *champú* (which simply means 'shampoo') will be listed in many dictionaries after all the words beginning with just 'c.' Similarly, 'll' is a separate letter, so *llave* (key) is listed after all the words beginning with a single 'l.' The letter 'ñ' is listed after the ordinary 'n.' Vowels with an accent are accented for stress and are not considered separate letters.

However, the Academia Real de la Lengua Española (in Spain) has decided to eliminate 'ch' and 'll' as separate letters, which means that new Spanish dictionaries will list champú and llave in the same word order that English speakers are accustomed to (although most dictionaries have yet to make this change). Whether this will spread to all Latin American Spanish remains to be seen. The latest Costa Rican telephone directories list names beginning with 'ch' and 'll' in the English way.

Pronunciation

Pronunciation in Spanish is generally more straightforward than it is in English, and if you say a word the way it looks like it should be said, chances are that it will be close enough to be understood. You will get better with practice, of course. A few notable exceptions are 'll,' which is always pronounced 'y' as in 'yacht'; the 'j,' which is pronounced 'h' as in 'happy'; and the 'h,' which isn't pronounced at all. Thus, the phrase '*hojas en la calle*' (leaves in the street) would be pronounced 'o-has en la ka-yea.' Finally, the letter 'ñ' is pronounced as the 'ny' sound in 'canyon.'

Grammar

Articles, adjectives and demonstrative pronouns must agree with the noun in both gender and number. Nouns ending in 'a' are generally feminine and the corresponding articles are *la* (singular) and *las* (plural). Those ending in 'o' are usually masculine and require the articles *el* (singular) and *los* (plural).

There are, however, hundreds of exceptions to these guidelines, which can only be memorized or deduced by the meaning of the word. Plurals are formed by adding 's' to words ending in a vowel and 'es' to those ending in a consonant.

In addition to all the familiar English tenses, Spanish uses the imperfect tense and two subjunctive tenses (past and present). Tenses are formed either by adding a myriad of endings to the root verb, or by preceding the participle form with some variation of the auxiliary verb *haber* (to have, as in 'to have done something').

There are verb endings for first, second and third person singular and plural. Second person singular and plural are divided into formal and familiar modes. If that's not enough, there are three types of verbs – those ending in *ar*, *er*, and *ir* – each of which is conjugated differently. There is also a whole collection of stem-changing rules and irregularities that must be memorized. This sounds a lot more complicated than it really is – you'll be surprised by how quickly you'll pick it up!

Costa Rican Terms

The following colloquialisms and slang *(tiquismos)* are frequently heard and are for the most part used only in Costa Rica.

¡Adios! — Hi! (used when passing a friend in the street, or anyone in remote rural areas; also means 'farewell,' but only when leaving for a long time)

bomba — gas station

buena nota — OK, excellent (literally 'good note')

chapulines — a gang, usually of young thieves

chunche — thing (can refer to almost anything)

cien metros	one city block
¿Hay campo?	Is there space? (on a bus)
machita	blonde woman (slang)
mae	buddy (pronounced 'ma' as in 'mat' followed with a quick 'eh'; mainly used by boys and young men)
mi amor	my love (used as a familiar form of address by both men and women)
pulpería	corner grocery store
pura vida	super (literally 'pure life,' also an expression of approval or even a greeting)
sabanero	cowboy, especially one from Guanacaste Province
salado	too bad, tough luck
soda	café or lunch counter
tuanis	cool!
¡Upe!	Is anybody home? (used mainly in rural areas at people's houses, instead of knocking)
vos	you (informal, same as *tú*)

Greetings & Civilities

Good morning/Good day.	*Buenos días.*
Good afternoon.	*Buenas tardes.*
Good evening/Good night.	*Buenas noches.*
Yes.	*Sí.*
No.	*No.*
Hello.	*Hola.*
See you later.	*Hasta luego.*
How are you? (familiar)	*¿Cómo estás?*
How are you? (formal)	*¿Cómo está?*
Please.	*Por favor.*
Thank you.	*Gracias.*
It's a pleasure.	*Con mucho gusto.*
Excuse me. (when passing by someone)	*Con permiso.*
Sorry!	*¡Perdón!*

Small Talk

Do you speak Spanish/English?
  ¿Habla usted castellano/inglés?
Where (which country) do you come from?
  ¿De dónde (de qué país) es usted?
Where are you staying?
  ¿Dónde está alojado?
What is your profession?
  ¿Cuál es su profesión?
What's the weather like?
  ¿Qué tiempo hace?
It's hot/cold.
  Hace calor/frío.

rain	*lluvia*
wind	*viento*
friend	*amigo/a*
husband/wife	*marido/esposa*
mother/father	*madre/padre*
people	*gente*

Language Basics/Difficulties

When?	*¿Cuándo?*
How?	*¿Cómo?*
Where?	*¿Dónde?*
Why?	*¿Por qué?*
How's that again?	*¿Cómo?*
Do you understand?	*¿Me entiende?*
I don't understand.	*No entiendo.*
More or less	*Más o menos*

Food & Drink

Spanish equivalents for food and drink are given in the Facts for the Visitor chapter.

Directions

Usually, streets running east-west are called *avenidas* and streets running north-south are called *calles*. Often, 100m is used to indicate a city block, and so you may be told '*Setecientos metros al oeste y cuatrocientos metros al norte.*' This does not literally mean 700m west and 400m north; it refers to city blocks.

If you ask a passerby for directions, you'll probably be told to go seven blocks west and four blocks north *('Siete cuadras al oeste y cuatro cuadras al norte'). Cincuenta metros* (50m) means half a block.

north	*norte*
south	*sur*
east	*este*
west	*oeste*
address	*dirección*
ahead	*adelante*
block	*cuadra, cien metros*
meters	*metros*
to the right	*a la derecha*
to the left	*a la izquierda*
go straight ahead	*siga derecho*

downhill *por abajo*
uphill *por arriba*
here *aquí*
there *allí, allá*
around there *por allá*
around here *por aquí*

Getting Around

Where is the...? *¿Dónde está el/la...?*
airport *aeropuerto*
bus station/stop *terminal/parada de autobuses*

What time does the next plane/bus/train leave for...?
¿A qué hora sale el próximo avión/auto bús/tren para...?
where from? *¿de dónde?*
city *ciudad*

Around Town

Where is the...? *¿Dónde está el/la...?*
bank *banco*
cathedral/church *catedral/iglesia*
market *mercado*
police *policía*
post office *correo*
town square *plaza, parque*

Traffic Signs

For traffic signs and related terms in Spanish, refer to the boxed text 'Traffic Signs' in the Getting Around chapter.

Shopping

How much is this?
¿A cómo? ¿Cuánto cuesta esto? ¿Cuánto vale esto?

too expensive *muy caro*
cheaper *más barato*
I'll take it. *Lo llevo.*
The bill, please. *La cuenta, por favor.*

Don't you have smaller change?
¿No tiene sencillo?
Do you accept credit cards?
¿Aceptan tarjetas de crédito?
Where can I change money/traveler's checks?
¿Dónde se cambia dinero/cheques de viajero?

Accommodations

room *cuarto, habitación*
single/double *sencilla/doble*
bed *cama*
double bed *cama matrimonial*
fan *ventilador*
air-conditioned *con aire acondicionado*
bathroom, toilet *baño*
private/shared *privado/compartido*
shower *ducha*

Time & Dates

What time is it? *¿Qué hora es?* or *¿Qué horas son?*
It is one o'clock. *Es la una.*
It is two/three/etc o'clock. *Son las dos/tres/etc.*
midnight *medianoche*
noon *mediodía*
in the afternoon *de la tarde*
in the morning *de la mañana*
at night *de la noche*
half past two *dos y media*
quarter past two *dos y cuarto*
two twenty-five *dos con veinticinco minutos*
twenty to two *veinte para las dos*
spring *primavera*

summer (December to April dry season) *verano*
winter (May to December wet season) *invierno*

today *hoy*
tomorrow *mañana*
yesterday *ayer*
this morning *esta mañana*
this afternoon *esta tarde*
tonight *esta noche*
week/month/year *semana/mes/año*

Days of the Week

Monday *lunes*
Tuesday *martes*
Wednesday *miércoles*
Thursday *jueves*
Friday *viernes*
Saturday *sábado*
Sunday *domingo*

Numbers

0	*cero*
1	*uno/una*
2	*dos*
3	*tres*
4	*cuatro*
5	*cinco*
6	*seis*
7	*siete*
8	*ocho*
9	*nueve*
10	*diez*
11	*once*
12	*doce*
13	*trece*
14	*catorce*
15	*quince*
16	*dieciséis*
17	*diecisiete*
18	*dieciocho*
19	*diecinueve*
20	*veinte*
21	*veintiuno*
30	*treinta*
40	*cuarenta*
50	*cincuenta*
60	*sesenta*
70	*setenta*
80	*ochenta*
90	*noventa*
100	*cien(to)*
101	*ciento uno*
200	*doscientos*
201	*doscientos uno*
300	*trescientos*
400	*cuatrocientos*
500	*quinientos*
600	*seiscientos*
700	*setecientos*
800	*ochocientos*
900	*novecientos*
1000	*mil*
100,000	*cien mil*
one million	*un millón*
one billion	*un billón*

Costa Rica Wildlife Guide

Costa Rica's wildlife is incredibly diverse. This guide is a reasonably comprehensive overview of the most interesting animals and those that are most often seen by observant visitors. For detailed information, see the books listed in the Facts for the Visitor chapter. Also refer to Flora & Fauna in the Facts about Costa Rica chapter for an overview of the country's wildlife and habitats.

The mammals and birds are described in the taxonomic order found in wildlife guidebooks, based on evolutionary history: the most ancient come first and the most recently evolved come last. Spanish names (which vary region to region) and scientific names (which change occasionally with new research) are included.

MAMMALS

Opossums

Opossums are the American representatives of the marsupials, which have one of the strangest methods of mammalian reproduction. Newborns, which look like tiny embryos, crawl from the birth canal through the mother's fur into a pouch containing the teats. Here, the young latch onto a nipple and complete most of their development.

The first marsupial seen in Europe was an opossum, brought home by the Spanish explorer Pinzón in the 16th century. Male opossums have a forked penis, and early naturalists thought that the animals copulated through the nose and the mother then blew the embryo into the pouch! Gestation is 12 days, followed by two months in the pouch.

Nine of approximately 70 opossum species are found in Costa Rica. The most frequently seen is the **common opossum** (zorro pelón; *Didelphis marsupialis*). Resembling overgrown, long-legged rats, they reach almost a meter in length, of which the tail is almost half. Adults weigh 0.6 to 1.8kg, although there have been reports of some reaching 5kg! Males are larger than females. The back and legs are blackish brown or gray and the head and underparts light brown or yellowish, with much variation in color due to the coarse, two-layered fur.

Common opossum

They are mainly nocturnal, often seen foraging for anything edible along watercourses and in garbage dumps. Distribution is nationwide, but normally below 1500m. They are both terrestrial and arboreal and, when cornered, will hiss and attempt to bite, rather than pretending to lie dead, as North American opossums do.

A smaller species seen quite often is the **gray four-eyed opossum** *(Philander opossum)*, found in rainforest regions and recognized by a black face mask with large white spots over the eyes, and a grayer, smoother appearance than the previous species. The **water opossum** *(Chironectes minimus)* is locally common on some rivers and has a light/dark-gray-striped pattern on its back.

Anteaters

Anteaters, members of the New World order Edentata (Latin for 'untoothed'), are unique among land mammals in that they lack teeth and use a long, sticky tongue to slurp up ants and termites. Their eyesight is poor, but strong, heavily clawed forelegs rip open ant nests and a well-developed sense of smell detects their prey.

RICHARD LAVAL

Lesser anteater

All four species are restricted to Central and South America and three are recorded in Costa Rica. The largest is the locally rare **giant anteater** *(Myrmecophaga tridactyla)*, which reaches a length of almost 2m and has a tongue that protrudes an astonishing 60cm up to 150 times a minute!

Much more common is the **lesser anteater** (or northern tamandua; oso mielero; *Tamandua mexicana*), with a distinctive golden-tan and black pattern. Its length is 0.93 to 1.45m and it weighs 4 to 8kg. It too has a prodigious tongue, up to 40cm long, covered with microscopic backward-pointing spines to direct food into its mouth. Graced with a prehensile tail, it is a good tree climber and forages both on and above the ground. The tamandua is nocturnal and diurnal, and is seen, with luck, in most forests below 2000m. Though relatively common, it is, unfortunately, seen more often as roadkill than in the wild. If disturbed, it rears up on its hind legs and slashes wildly with strong front claws – an intimidating and potentially severe defense.

The last Costa Rican species is the 40cm-long **silky anteater** (tapacara; *Cyclopes didactylus*). Nocturnal and arboreal, it eats about 6000 ants per night. By day, it curls up in a tight ball and is hard to see.

Sloths

Sloths are related to anteaters, though they are not true edentates because they have a few rudimentary teeth. They also share skeletal characteristics such as extra joint surfaces between the vertebrae (hence a new sub-order, the Xenarthra, from the Greek 'strange joint'). All five species are found only in the Neotropics; the two Costa Rican species are the **brown-throated three-toed sloth** (perezoso de tres dedos; *Bradypus variegatus*) and the **Hoffman's two-toed sloth** (perezoso de dos dedos; *Choloepus hoffmanni*).

ROB RACHOWIECKI

Three-toed sloth

The diurnal three-toed sloth is often sighted, whereas the nocturnal two-toed sloth is less often seen. Both are 50 to 75cm in length with stumpy tails. The three-toed is grayish brown with a distinctive gray-and-white mask on the face; the two-toed is generally a tan color. Sloths often hang motionless from branches or slowly progress upside down along a branch toward leaves, which are their primary food. Digestion of the tough food takes several days and sloths defecate about once a week (see the 'Slothful Habits' boxed text in the Central Pacific Coast chapter).

They are infrequently sighted on the ground, where their gait is clearly uncomfortable. They are sexually mature at three years and females then have a baby most years. The baby is carried on the mother's chest for 5½ months, feeding on milk for a few weeks but soon being taught to eat leaves. The relationship between mother and offspring is close but not deep during this period – the youngster stays on or perishes. A baby that falls off its mother is ignored.

Some favorite leaves are from the *Cecropia* tree (although others are also eaten). These are common trees on riverbanks in the rainforest; this is the best place to spot sloths in the wild.

Armadillos

Armadillos, armored with bony plates, look very different from their relatives, the anteaters and sloths. Few animal orders have such unlikely looking related members as the edentates.

The armadillos are the only edentates that have migrated as far north as the southern USA. Of about 20 species, two are seen in Costa Rica. The best known is the **nine-banded armadillo** (cusuco; *Dasypus novemcinctus*), which lives in the USA and Central and South America. Despite the name, there can be seven to 10 plates (bands). They are 65cm to 1m in length, of which about one-third is the tail, and weight is 3 to 7kg. Babies are identical quadruplets arising from a single egg.

Mainly nocturnal, they are noisy foragers, blindly crashing around well-drained rainforest slopes. Their eyesight is poor and they have been known to walk into stationary observers! They have few vocalizations, but their snuffling and crashing are sometimes heard in the forest at night. With their primitive teeth, they are limited to a diet of mainly insects, and occasionally fruit, fungi, carrion, and other material. Their burrows dug into the ground are often seen on rainforest hikes.

Nine-banded armadillo

Bats

Of the more than 200 Costa Rican mammal species, 50% are bats. Many lowland open areas have small bats swooping around at dusk, catching insects. Larger bats eat fish, fruit, or small animals, and others drink flower nectar or animal blood.

During the day bats roost in hollow trees (local naturalist guides know where to look) or under wooden roofs. I saw several **white-lined sac-winged bats** (murciélago de saco; *Saccopteryx bilineata*) in buildings in Parque Nacional Santa Rosa. These small social bats roost in colonies of five to 50 individuals and have dark fur with two long wavy white lines on the back.

One of the largest bats is the **fishing bulldog bat** (murciélago pescador; *Noctilio leporinus*), which has a 60cm wingspan. Most of this is skin and bones, so adults weigh under 90g – big as bats go. They fish in both salt and fresh water, and the Tortuguero canals are ideal for watching them grab large insects and small fish with their sharply clawed enlarged feet. You can tell them apart from other bats that are drinking by watching their feet dip into the water.

Another large bat, the **Jamaican fruit bat** (murciélago frutero; *Artibeus jamaicensis*), feeds on fruits of large trees, especially figs, which they grab on the wing and take to a feeding roost for consumption. They have 40cm wingspans and weigh 50g; there are several smaller species of fruit bat. These bats won't feed during the brightest full-moon nights for fear of owls.

Fishing bulldog bat

All three species of **vampire bats** (vampiros) are restricted to the Neotropics (not Transylvania!) and are found in Costa Rica, where the most common is *Desmodus rotundus*. Unusual among bats, vampires are agile on the ground and can hop, run, and crawl toward their prey, which consists of birds and mammals, though cattle are preferred. Razor-sharp incisors make a small cut on the prey, and the flowing blood is licked up, not sucked. Anticoagulants in the bats' saliva ensure the blood flows freely during the meal. The process doesn't cause much harm to cattle, but there is potential danger of bat-borne diseases, especially rabies, which kill the prey (but not the bat).

Because of local misconceptions that all bats are vampires, they may be indiscriminately killed. However, their usefulness in controlling insects and pollinating flowers far outweighs their potential damage.

Most people think of bats as being black, but a variety of browns, grays, yellows, and reds also exists. Two uncommon Costa Rican species are white: the tiny **Honduran white bat** *(Ectophylla alba)* of the Caribbean slopes, and the larger **ghost bat** *(Diclidirus virgo)*, seen in the Península de Osa.

Monkeys

Costa Rica has four monkey species, all members of the family Cebidae. These are the tropical mammals most likely to be seen and enjoyed by travelers. I once saw all four in one day in Parque Nacional Corcovado.

Central American Squirrel Monkey (mono tití; *Saimiri oerstedii*). Weighing under 1kg, these are the smallest, rarest, and most endangered Costa Rican monkeys. Over half of their 63 to 68cm length is a non-prehensile tail. The back and legs are a golden brown, the tail is olive brown with a black tuft at the tip, the chest is light colored, the neck, ears, and areas around the eyes are white, and the cap and muzzle are black. They travel in small to medium-size groups during the day, squealing or chirping noisily and leaping and crashing through vegetation in search of insects and fruit in the middle and lower levels of lowland forests. They exist only in isolated areas of the south Pacific coastal rainforests. Manuel Antonio and Corcovado national parks (especially around Sirena) are good places to see them.

Central American squirrel monkey

White-Faced Capuchin Monkey (mono cara blanca; *Cebus capucinus*). These small and inquisitive monkeys are the easiest to observe in the wild. Like the squirrel monkeys, capuchins travel through the forest in groups searching for fruit and insects and are sometimes seen with squirrel monkeys. Unlike squirrel monkeys, however, they have prehensile tails and forage at all forest levels, occasionally descending to the ground where crops such as corn and even oysters are part of their diet. Their thorough foraging, carefully searching through leaves and litter, peeling off bark, and generally prying into everything, makes them enjoyable to watch.

ROB RACHOWIECKI

White-faced capuchin monkey

These capuchins are black, with a whitish face, throat, and chest. The tail is typically carried with the tip coiled, a feature seen when viewed in silhouette. Ranging in length from 70cm to 1m, of which just over half is tail, they weigh between 1.5 and 3.9kg, with males larger than females. They are widespread in both wet and tropical dry forests on both sides of the country. The dry forests of Parque Nacional Santa Rosa and Reserva Cabo Blanco are two excellent places to view them during the dry season, when few leaves obscure the view. They are seen in most national parks with lowland and mid-elevation forests.

KEVIN SCHAFER

Central American spider monkey

Central American Spider Monkey (mono colorado; *Ateles geoffroyi*). The spider monkeys are named for their long and thin legs, arms, and tail, which enable them to pursue an arboreal existence. They brachiate (swing from arm to arm) through the canopy and can hang supported just by their prehensile tail while using their long limbs to pick fruit. They rarely descend to the ground, and require large tracts of unbroken forest. Logging, hunting (their flesh is eaten), and other disturbances have made them endangered. Recovery is slow because reproductive rates are low, with a 7½-month pregnancy resulting in a single infant about every three years.

The baby rides on the mother's chest for its first two months and then moves onto the mother's back, where it stays for another month before venturing off on brief trips, though returning frequently to the mother to ride or nurse until almost a year old.

Spider monkeys are 1 to 1.5m long, with the tail accounting for 60% of that. They weigh 7 to 9kg. Their color varies from dark brown through reddish brown to gray. They often forage during the day in varisized groups high in the canopy and are also seen resting quietly on high branches. Vocalizations include screams, grunts, barks, and whinnies. When they spot people, a characteristic response is to scream or growl and jump up and down while rattling branches and even hurling vegetation down on the viewers. They favor large tracts of wet forest, as found in some of the larger parks, especially Tortuguero.

KEVIN SCHAFER

Mantled howler monkey

Mantled Howler Monkey (mono congo; *Alouatta palliata*). These large monkeys are often heard before being seen. The loud vocalizations of male howlers can carry for over 1km even in dense rainforest. They howl (or roar or grunt), especially at dawn and dusk, and at other times in response to intruders. Air is passed through a specialized, hollow, and much enlarged hyoid bone in the throat, producing the strange and resonant call. The hyoid bone contributes to the typically thick-necked appearance of the males.

Howlers live in small groups of about a dozen individuals, and the male calls keep the groups spaced out so they don't compete for food, consisting mainly of leaves, supplemented by fruit and flowers. Howlers travel less than other monkeys, preferring instead to maintain separated home ranges of about 10 hectares per group. Therefore howlers have survived better than other species in the face of fragmentation of the forest.

Howlers are stocky, with wide shoulders, large heads and necks (especially in the males), and relatively small hindparts. Their prehensile tail is often carried coiled. They are black, with the exception of their sides and back, where long hairs can give them a golden brown or buff-colored mantle. They weigh 5 to 8kg and are 1 to 1.25m in length, of which just over half is tail. They browse and rest in the canopy, making it hard to spot them from the ground. Good places to see them are hilly forests where you look out over the treetops.

Dog Family

Costa Rica has two canine species, the **coyote** *(Canis latrans)* and the **gray fox** (zorro gris; *Urocyon cinereoargenteus*). The brownish gray coyote (also found in North America) is omnivorous. In Costa Rica it prefers the drier forests and open areas of Guanacaste, although it is found in other regions. Active at any time, it is seen in parks such as Santa Rosa, where its trademark nighttime howling and yapping are heard. It is also common in Monteverde. The gray fox is grayer, much smaller, and more nocturnal. Both species avoid the rainforest.

Raccoon Family

This family, the Procyonidae, has six members in Costa Rica, most of which are quite common. Along with dogs, weasels, and cats, they are classified as carnivores, though many procyonids eat fruit. The classification is based on dental characteristics, not diet.

The **northern raccoon** (mapache; *Procyon loctor*) is the species found in North America. In Costa Rica, they favor water and are commonly found along both coasts as well as near lowland rivers and marshes, where they are often seen at night. When disturbed, they may climb trees. Their most distinctive feature is a white face with a black mask giving a bandit-like appearance. The rest of the body is gray and the tail is gray with black rings. Costa Rican raccoons are smaller than their northern counterparts, measuring under 1m in length, of which one-third is tail, and weighing about 5kg.

Northern raccoon

The similar-looking **crab-eating raccoon** *(Procyon cancrivorous)* is also nocturnal but limited to the Pacific coast. This raccoon has blackish (not gray) fur on the front of its legs and the fur on top of its neck grows forward, toward the head, rather than smoothly away as in most animals.

KEVIN SCHAFER

White-nosed coati

The **white-nosed coati** (pizote; *Nasua narica*) is the most diurnal and frequently seen procyonid. They are brownish and longer, but slimmer and lighter, than raccoons. Their most distinctive features are a long, mobile, upturned whitish snout with which they snuffle around on the forest floor looking for insects, fruit, and small animals, and a long, faintly ringed tail held straight up in the air when foraging. Although they feed on the ground, they are agile climbers and sleep and copulate in trees. They are found countrywide in all types of forest up to 3000m.

The **kinkajou** (martilla; *Potus flavus*) is a cuddly procyonid that lacks the facial markings and ringed tail of its cousins. It is an attractive reddish brown color and is hunted both for food and the pet trade. Nocturnal and mainly arboreal, it jumps from tree to tree searching for fruits (especially figs), which comprise most of its diet.

An animal heard jumping around trees at night is most probably a kinkajou, almost a meter in length, or it might be the smaller and rarer **olingo** *(Bassaricyon gabbi),* which has similar habits. Both have sneezing calls and a two-toned yelp and travel singly or in small groups. The kinkajou has a prehensile tail, which it often curls lightly around tree branches as it travels. The olingo is more gray and has a bushier, faintly ringed tail. Both prefer primary humid forests, but only the kinkajou is found also in secondary forests, tropical dry forests, and even gardens and orchards.

Kinkajou

Similar to the previous two species is the **cacomistle** (cacomistle or olingo; *Bassariscus sumichrasti*); locals don't necessarily differentiate among them. The cacomistle is similar to the ring-tailed cat of North America, having a very bushy white tail with black rings and white spectacles around the eyes. Its ears are more pointed than those of the olingo and it is slimmer and lighter, but otherwise it has a similar body shape and habits. It is more common in highland than lowland forests.

Weasel Family

These tough little carnivores are known for their bite, which is very strong for their size, and their smell – skunks are in the weasel family. Seven members of this family (the Mustelidae) are found in Costa Rica, and some are quite common.

Skunks are perhaps the most obvious. They are widespread but nocturnal, and smelled as often as seen. Their disgusting odor is known to most people in the Americas, and visitors from other continents will be surprised at how badly a skunk can smell! The 'scent' is produced by anal glands and is sprayed at predators (unsurprisingly, skunks tend to get left alone). There are three species in Costa Rica: the **striped hog-nosed skunk** (zorro hediondo; *Conepatus semistriatus*), the **spotted skunk** *(Spilogale putorius)*, and the **hooded skunk** *(Mephitis macroura)*. Despite their smell, they look attractive. The hog-nosed is black with a broad white stripe along its back and a bushy white tail. It is 50 to 75cm in length and widespread throughout the country. The smaller and less common spotted skunk is black with white blotches. The hooded skunk is the least common. All are terrestrial.

Tayra

The **southern river otter** (perro de agua; *Lutra longicaudis*) is the only Costa Rican otter. It lives in and by fast-moving lowland rivers, but is infrequently seen. It is a rich brown color with whitish undersides and has the streamlined shape of an aquatic weasel. The **tayra** (tolumuco; *Eira barbara*) is similarly shaped but is blackish brown, with a tan head, and is terrestrial and arboreal. It can reach over a meter in length (the tail is about 40cm) and is found in forests up to 2000m. If you see what looks like an otter running around the forest, it's probably a tayra.

Grison

The **grison** (grisón; *Galictis vittata*) is a large weasel with distinctive coloration. The body, tail, and crown of the head are light gray and the legs, chest, and lower face are black. A white band across the forehead, ears, and sides of the neck gives the head a black/white/gray tricolor. The tail is shorter than that of most weasels. It is found in the lowland rainforests but is uncommon. The smallest Costa Rican weasel is the **long-tailed weasel** (comadreja; *Mustela frenata*), a nervous brown animal with a pale belly that is reportedly common but rarely seen.

Cat Family

It is every wildlife watcher's dream to see a **jaguar** (tigre, jaguar; *Felis onca*) in the wild. However, they are rare, often silent, and well camouflaged, so the chance of seeing one is remote. This big cat (males occasionally reach over 150kg) is the largest Central American carnivore. They have large territories and you may see their prints or droppings in large lowland parks with extensive forest like Corcovado. Occasionally you may hear them roaring – a sound more like a series of deep coughs. There's no mistaking this 2m-long yellow cat with black spots in rosettes and a whitish belly. Good luck seeing one.

KEVIN SCHAFER

Jaguar

There are five other Costa Rican felids. The **ocelot** (manigordo; *Felis pardalis*) is also yellow but the spotting is variable, often merging into lines. It is a little over a meter in length and the tail is shorter than the hind leg. The most common of the Costa Rican cats, it is shy and rarely seen. It adapts well to a variety of terrain, wet and dry, forested and open, and has been recorded in most of the larger national parks. Smaller still, the yellow **margay** (tigrillo or caucel; *Felis wiedii*) has more distinctive spots and a tail longer than the hind leg, which distinguishes it from the ocelot. The margay, the size of a large house cat, is rare and endangered (as are all the Central American cats). It lives in forests, particularly near rivers, and has been recorded as high as 3000m. Even smaller and rarer is the similar-looking **oncilla** *(Felis tigrina),* which has been recorded in various habitats up to over 3000m. It is hard to differentiate the smaller spotted cats in the field, as you only get a brief glimpse of them, if you are lucky.

KEVIN SCHAFER

Margays

Two cats are unspotted. The **puma** (or mountain lion; león; *Felis concolor*) is almost as large as the jaguar but is a uniform brown (the shade varies from area to area and among individuals), with paler underparts, a white throat and muzzle, and a dark tip to the tail. Like all the cats, they are active both day and night, are fairly widespread but rarely seen, and are endangered. The smaller **jaguarundi** (león breñero; *Felis yagouaroundi*) is darker brown (much variation), with an elongated slim body, long tail, and rather short legs.

KEVIN SCHAFER

Jaguarundi

Peccaries

Known as javelinas in the USA, these animals are related to and look like pigs. The most widespread is the **collared peccary** (saíno; *Tayassu tajacu*), which ranges from the southwestern USA to Argentina in a wide variety of habitats. It is about 80cm long, weighs around 20kg, and has coarse gray hair with a light collar from its shoulders forward to the lower jaw. The larger **white-lipped peccary** (chancho de monte; *Tayassu pecari*) is darker and lacks the collar but has a whitish area on the lower chin.

KEVIN SCHAFER

Collared peccary

Both species move around in varisized groups; numbers of over 300 are reported for the white-lipped, but considerably fewer for the collared peccary. The latter is the more commonly seen but is quieter and shyer. White-lipped peccaries are noisy and rather aggressive with their audible tooth gnashing and clicking – rather frightening if you hear 300 animals performing this way! Corcovado rangers warn visitors to be prepared to climb a tree if they are charged, though this rarely happens. Peccaries leave pungent, churned-up mud wallows, which can be seen (and smelled) in Corcovado.

Deer

The **white-tailed deer** (venado; *Odocoileus virginianus*) is well known to North Americans. The Costa Rican variety is smaller. They are gray to red with a straight back, white belly, and white markings on the throat, eyes, ears, and muzzle. When running, the tail is lifted, revealing the conspicuous white underside. The males have branched antlers, except for the yearlings, which have single prongs.

KEVIN SCHAFER

Red brocket deer

The smaller, shyer, and less common **red brocket deer** (cabro de monte; *Mazama americana*) is reddish (including the belly), with a slightly humped back and no facial markings. The tail is white below and is also raised in alarm. The male antlers are single prongs at all ages. These deer are more likely to be seen in rainforests, while white-tailed deer are fairly common in drier areas such as Guanacaste.

Tapirs

The only Central American tapir is **Baird's tapir** (danta; *Tapirus bairdii*), endangered because of hunting and logging. Weighing 150 to 300kg, it is the region's largest land mammal. Tapirs are among the world's most ancient large mammals; 20-million-year-old fossils have been found. Their closest relatives are horses and rhinos.

They are stocky, rather short-legged, stumpy-tailed animals that are more agile than they appear. They can run as fast as a person and are adept at climbing steep riverbanks. The skin is grayish and covered with sparse, coarse, blackish hairs. Young tapirs are reddish with white spots or stripes. The upper lip is elongated into a mobile snout like a small trunk, which is used in feeding.

KEVIN SCHAFER

Baird's tapir

Their favored habitat is waterside forests and they have been most frequently reported on riverbanks in Corcovado, usually singly and occasionally in small groups. Their eyesight is poor but their senses of smell and hearing are excellent. They will run off when they detect people, probably the result of associating humans with hunting. Kayakers silently gliding up coastal rivers in Corcovado have been able to get good looks at these animals, but hikers have had less luck.

Rodents

Some large rodents are among the most commonly seen rainforest mammals, including the **Central American agouti** (guatusa; *Dasyprocta punctata*) and the **paca** (tepezcuintle; *Agouti paca*), which are relatives of the guinea pig.

The agouti is diurnal and terrestrial and found in forests from the coast up to 2000m. It looks like an oversize cross between a rabbit and a squirrel, with a barely visible tail and short ears. The color is a variable brownish gray. A chunky, brownish, apparently tailless mammal of about 4kg and 50 to 60cm in length running on the forest floor is probably an agouti.

The closely related paca looks similar, except it has white stripy marks on its sides and is twice the size of an agouti. It is common but seen less often because it is nocturnal. It has been much hunted for food and suggestions have been made that pacas might be 'farmed.' They can remain underwater for some minutes, a behavior that has helped them survive hunting. They have been reported in suburban gardens in Costa Rican cities.

There are five squirrel species. The **red-tailed squirrel** (ardilla roja; *Sciurus granatensis*) is grayish with a red belly and red tail, and is quite common. More abundant is the **variegated squirrel** (chiza; *Sciurus variegatoides*), which has various forms. The most frequently seen are mainly whitish with a black back or reddish with a black back and a black-and-white tail with red markings below. The other squirrels are less likely to be seen and are usually smaller and live at high altitudes.

Biologists can't agree what to call the Costa Rican **porcupine** (puerco espín; *Coendou*

KEVIN SCHAFER

Agouti

mexicanus), so various names refer to one species, easily identified by its spiny coat. Generally blackish with a lighter head and belly, it is roughly 40cm long plus a 25cm tail. It is arboreal and mainly nocturnal. During the day it may rest on a branch or den inside a hollow tree; local guides may know about favored sleeping places. A Monteverde guide reports seeing one about every fourth night when leading flashlight nightwalks in the preserve.

Some 40 species of rats, mice, spiny rats, pocket mice, and pocket gophers are of interest to ecologists, agriculturists, and other specialists.

Rabbits

Three species of rabbits are found in Costa Rica. The **eastern cottontail** (conejo cola blanca; *Sylvilagus floridensis*) is familiar to North American visitors. It is a small (about 40cm) brown rabbit with a little brown-and-white tail like a ball of cotton wool. It is widespread at most elevations except inside rainforests, where it is replaced by the **forest rabbit** (conejo de bosque; *Sylvilagus brasiliensis*), which looks similar, except the tail is brown and even tinier. Cottontails are found on the rainforest edge, but not inside it. A third species, *Sylvilagus dicei*, is reported in some highland areas.

Marine Mammals

There aren't many of these. In a few rivers, estuaries, and coastal areas (especially around Tortuguero) you may glimpse the endangered **West Indian manatee** (manati; *Trichechus manatus*), a large marine mammal (up to 4m and 600kg, though usually smaller) that feeds on aquatic vegetation. There are no seals or sea lions, so a manatee is easy to recognize.

Out at sea, dolphins and whales might briefly be seen as they break the water's surface. Off the coast of the Península de Osa and Parque Nacional Marino Ballena, migrating whales, especially the **humpback whale** (ballena; *Megaptera novaeanglia*), may be seen from December to March. The **common dolphin** (delfín; *Delphinus delphis*) and **bottle-nosed dolphin** *(Tursiops truncatus)* live in these waters year-round.

BIRDS

From a newly hatched chick to an adult, a bird goes through several plumage changes or molts, sometimes over a period of years in the cases of larger birds. Juveniles often look nothing like their parents. Descriptions below are for adult birds, unless specified.

Tinamous

There are five Costa Rican tinamous, chunky, almost tailless birds considered the most primitive (or ancient) of the nation's avifauna, which is why they are at the beginning of bird guidebooks. They feed on the forest floor, and fly with alarmingly loud wing beats only when disturbed. Their beautiful songs, a series of tremulous and often deep whistles, are often heard in the forest.

Seabirds

Among the most spectacular seabirds is the **magnificent frigatebird** (rabihorcado magno; *Fregata magnificens*), a large, elegant, streamlined black seabird with a long forked tail that gives it the nickname *tijereta* or 'scissor tail.' They make an acrobatic living by aerial piracy, often harassing small birds into dropping or regurgitating their catch and then swooping to catch their stolen meal in mid-air. This occurs partly because frigatebirds do not have waterproof feathers and so cannot enter the water to catch prey. They are, however, able to catch fish on the surface by snatching them up with their hooked beaks. With a wingspan of over 2m and a weight of only 1.5kg, the birds have the largest wingspan to weight ratio of any bird and are magnificent fliers.

Frigatebirds are found along both coasts but are more common on the Pacific. The males have red throat pouches, which normally look like little skin flaps but are inflated to balloon size when courting and nesting. Unfortunately, nesting in Costa Rica is limited to a few islands off the Pacific coast, so you are unlikely to see this.

The **brown pelican** (pelícano; *Pelecanus occidentalis*) is unmistakable with its large size and huge pouched bill. They have wide fingered wings and are good gliders. They are often seen flying in a squadron-like formation, flapping and gliding in unison to create an elegant aerial ballet.

A pelican feeds by shallow plunge-diving and scooping up as much as 10 liters of water in its distensible pouch. The water rapidly drains out through the bill and the

KEVIN SCHAFER

Magnificent frigatebird

trapped fish are swallowed. It sounds straightforward, but it isn't. Although parents raise broods of two or three chicks, many of the fledged young are unable to learn the scoop-fishing technique quickly enough and starve to death.

Pelicans are found along both coasts but are more common on the Pacific, especially in the Golfo de Nicoya, where they breed on some islands.

Other seabirds are more likely to be seen farther offshore, perhaps on a trip to Isla del Caño biological reserve. These include shearwaters, petrels, storm-petrels, boobies, phalaropes, and jaegers.

Cormorant & Anhinga

The **olivaceous cormorant** (cormorán; *Palacrocorax olivaceus*) and its relative, the **anhinga** (pato aguja; *Anhinga anhinga*), are large blackish waterbirds with long necks and short tails. Both are common in the Tortuguero, Palo Verde, and Caño Negro areas but can be found in other lowland regions. Like frigatebirds, to which they are related, these birds do not have waterproof feathers, yet they are both good swimmers and divers and catch fish underwater. When their plumage becomes waterlogged, they climb onto perches and stand with their wings stretched wide to dry in the sun – this is when they are commonly seen.

ROB RACHOWIECKI

Anhinga

Anhingas have longer necks and tails than cormorants, and silvery streaks on their backs and wings. Female anhingas have a buff-colored head and neck. Cormorants are generally black, though juveniles are a light gray below. Anhingas are able to sink almost below the water's surface, leaving just the lengthy neck, slim head, and long, sharp bill above the water, giving them the descriptive nickname of 'snake bird.'

Herons & Relatives

Herons, wading birds with long legs and necks, are in the same family as egrets and bitterns. Along with storks and ibises, they are in the order Ciconiiformes, which has about 25 representatives in Costa Rica. The best places to see many of these are the Palo Verde and Caño Negro areas and northwestern Costa Rica.

The most commonly seen is the **cattle egret** (garcilla bueyera; *Bubulcus ibis*), which was first recorded in Costa Rica in 1954. Since then, the population of this white heron has exploded dramatically and it is seen countrywide up to about 2000m. It is distinguished from other white herons by its stockier appearance and terrestrial feeding habits (often in pastures), whereas most herons feed in water. In the breeding season, buff-colored head plumes, chest, and back are distinctive.

During non-breeding, you can tell the white herons apart by the colors of their legs and bills. The cattle egret has blackish legs and a yellow bill. The larger **snowy egret**

KEVIN SCHAFER

Great egret

(garceta nivosa; *Egretta thula*) has black legs with bright yellow feet ('golden slippers') and a black bill with yellow facial skin. The immature **little blue heron** (garceta azul; *Egretta caerula*) is white with yellowish legs, a gray bill with a black tip, and gray wing tips. (The adult little blue heron is bluish gray with a purplish head and neck.) The **great egret** (garceta grande; *Casmeroidus albus*) is by far the largest white heron, standing over a meter tall, with a very long neck, black legs, and yellow bill. All these are quite common.

Of the non-white herons, the most abundant is the **green-backed heron** (garcilla verde; *Butorides striatus*), which, at an average length of 43cm, is the smallest heron. A greenish back, maroon neck, white stripe down the front of its throat and chest, black cap, and bright yellow eyes and legs make this quite a colorful bird when seen in sunlight, which is not often. They prefer to forage stealthily, singly or in pairs, in the dense vegetation at the side of most bodies of water and are often seen on boat trips. When disturbed, they squawk and fly to another bush, where they typically pump their tail.

Larger species include the **boat-billed heron** (pico cuchara; *Cochlearius cochlearius*), a stocky, mainly gray heron with a black cap and crest and distinctively large and wide bill. The **yellow-crowned night-heron** (martinete cabecipinto; *Nyctanassa violacea*) is common in coastal areas and has an unmistakable black-and-white head with a yellow crown. Despite its name, it's mainly active by day.

Tiger-herons are large brownish herons with fine horizontal barring on most of their plumage and bright yellow legs. The most common of three Costa Rican species is the **bare-throated tiger-heron** (garza-tigre cuellinuda; *Tigrisoma mexicanum*), with a bare yellow throat.

The descriptively named **roseate spoonbill** (espátula rosada; *Ajaia ajaja*) is the only large pink bird in Costa Rica and is most often seen in the Palo Verde and Caño Negro areas. It has a white head and a distinctive spoon-shaped bill. Unlike most birds, which feed by sight, spoonbills, ibises, and many storks feed by touch. The spoonbill swings its open bill back and forth, submerged underwater, stirring up the bottom with its feet, until it feels a small fish, frog, or crustacean and then snaps the bill shut.

Three ibis species, related to spoonbills, have long and down-curved bills, which probe the bottoms of swamps, streams, and ponds. The **white ibis** (ibis blanco; *Eudocimus*

KEVIN SCHAFER

Green-backed heron

KEVIN SCHAFER

Jabiru stork

albus) is the most often seen, especially in the northwest and Nicoya areas. It is white with black wing tips (seen in flight) and has a bright red bill and legs, which separate it from the **green ibis** (ibis verde; *Mesembrinibis cayennensis*), which is blackish green and more common on the Caribbean coast.

The **wood stork** (cigueñón; *Mycteria americana*) is a large white bird, over a meter tall, with a very heavy bill and bare, blackish head. The flight feathers are black, which gives it a distinctive white-and-black pattern in flight. The rarer **jabiru** *(Jabiru mycteria)* is a much larger white stork with a black head, bill, and neck and a red band at the base of the neck.

Ducks

Of the 15 ducks recorded in Costa Rica, most are uncommon to rare, or are winter migrants from North America. As in other Neotropical countries, ducks and geese are an under-represented bird family.

The most common is the **black-bellied whistling-duck** (pijije común; *Dendrocygna autumnalis*), which favors the Pacific lowlands. It stands rather than swims and has a rusty-brown body with a black belly, whitish wing stripe, reddish feet and bill, and gray-brown face. Also seen fairly often is the **Muscovy duck** (pato real; *Cairina moschata*), which is a large Neotropical duck with a glossy greenish-black body and white wing patches. The most common winter migrant is the **blue-winged teal** (cerceta aliazul; *Anas discors*).

Vultures

These large black birds are often seen hovering ominously in the sky, searching for carrion, which is their main source of food. In common with most vultures, their heads are bare, and the color of the skin on their heads is the best way to identify them.

ROB RACHOWIECKI

Black vulture

The **turkey vulture** (zopilote cabecirrojo; *Cathartes aura*) and the **black vulture** (zopilote negro; *Coragyps atratus*) are both common countrywide below 2000m and occasionally higher. The turkey vulture soars with V-shaped wings and has gray primary feathers, giving the wings a two-toned appearance from below, and has a red head. The black vulture has flatter, broader wings with a whitish patch at the base of the primaries, and a black head. (Young turkey vultures also have blackish heads.) Turkey vultures soar fairly low and can detect carrion by scent, while black vultures soar higher and look for carcasses visually, which is why the latter are more common over open areas and near towns, while the turkey vultures are seen over forests. The black vultures watch for other vultures descending to food, and when both species are present at a carcass, the stockier, heavier black vultures will force the turkey vultures away unless there is an excess of meat.

The **lesser yellow-headed vulture** (zopilote cabecigualdo; *Cathartes burrovianus*) looks like a small turkey vulture with a yellow head but is much less common. The **king vulture** (zopilote rey; *Sarcoramphus papa*) is the largest vulture and is easily identified by its off-white body and legs, black primary wing feathers and tail, and a wattled head colored black with various shades of orange-yellow. It is most often seen in Corcovado, though it lives almost countrywide in small numbers.

Birds of Prey

These include hawks, eagles, kites, falcons, caracaras, and the osprey, all of which hunt for food and are collectively called raptors. About 50 species have been recorded in Costa Rica, and many are hard to tell apart because of similar plumage and flight. Being hunters, they rely on stealth and speed, which makes them hard to observe closely; identification is difficult without binoculars. Raptors are, however, common throughout the country. Among the most frequently seen and easily identified are the following.

The **osprey** (águila pescadora; *Pandion haliaetus*) is one of the few birds found on every inhabited continent. Its prey is unusual for raptors: the Spanish name 'fishing eagle' describes it perfectly. The osprey fishes by plunging into salt or fresh water, feet first, and grabbing the slippery fish. The feet are adapted for the purpose with long, sharp claws and horny spines beneath the toes. The plumage is distinctive – almost completely white below and brown above, with a white head striped black through the eyes. The white underside camouflages it against the sky (so fish can't see it easily) and the dark upperside camouflages it against the water (so predators can't see it). It is found in lowlands along both coasts and in the Caño Negro area.

A long, deeply forked, black tail distinguishes the **American swallow-tailed kite** (elanio tijereta; *Elanoides forficatus*) from other raptors. It has a white head and underparts, black back, and black-and-white wings. It feeds on the wing, plucking insects out of the air or grabbing small lizards from branches, and is normally seen flying gracefully in areas with some humid forests (but not in the drier northwest). The **black-shouldered kite** (elanio coliblanco; *Elanus caerulus*) is a small, almost completely white hawk with black shoulders and a light gray back and primary feathers. The feet are yellow and the yellow bill is tipped black. This bird was first reported in Costa Rica in 1958 but has now become common in open agricultural areas and grasslands.

The **black-chested hawk** (gavilán pechinegro; *Leucopternis princeps*) is a hawk with very broad wings found in mid-elevation humid forests, from 400m (usually higher) to 2500m. Its plumage is mainly black with a white band in its tail, and fine black barring in the white belly and under-wings, giving it a light gray appearance from a distance. The distinct contrast between the black chest and light belly is a good field mark. It is an acrobatic flier and hunts mainly inside the forest. In the lowlands on both coasts, the **common black hawk** (gavilán cangrejero; *Buteogallus anthracinus*) is often seen near water, where it feeds on crabs and other coastal animals. It is quite large and all black except for a white band in the tail, yellow feet, and a yellow base of the bill.

The **white hawk** (gavilán blanco; *Leucopternis albicollis*) is almost all white except for a black band in the tail and black markings at the ends of the wings. Hawks have very broad wings and short, wide tails, while kites have long, slim tails and slim wings that are bent back. This distinguishes the white hawk from the fairly similarly colored black-shouldered kite.

KEVIN SCHAFER

Roadside hawk

The most common resident hawk is the **roadside hawk** (gavilán chapulinero; *Buteo magnirostris*), which perches on trees and posts in open areas waiting for small mammals, reptiles, or large insects to pass below. Because perches in open areas tend to follow roads or tracks, the bird is well named. It is a small hawk with a grayish head and chest merging into a brown-gray back and a pale belly barred with rusty brown. The tail is widely banded in light and dark gray. The throat is whitish and the feet, eyes, and base of bill are yellow. It prefers the lowlands and is more common on Pacific slopes. The most frequently seen hawk from late September to May is the migrant **broad-winged hawk** (gavilán aludo; *Buteo platypterus*),

KEVIN SCHAFER
Crested caracara

which also likes to pounce on its prey from a low perch, often at the forest edge. It looks rather like a browner, larger version of the roadside hawk, with a more distinctly white throat.

Apart from hunting small rodents, reptiles, and amphibians, the **crested caracara** (caracara cargahuesos; *Polyborus plancus*) also eats carrion and is often seen feeding on roadkill, rather like a vulture. Its plumage, however, quickly separates it from the vultures. It has a black body and wings, with a white face and neck merging to a black-and-white barred chest and upper back. The tail is also barred and tipped with black. The front of its face is red, the cap is black, and the legs are yellow. The distinctive **yellow-headed caracara** (caracara cabecigualdo; *Milvago chimachima*) has a buff body and head with a dark brown back. In flight, the underside of the wings is buff with black primaries and a large, pale 'window' at the end of the wings. Although not recorded in Costa Rica until 1973, it is now quite common on the Pacific slope, especially the Corcovado area.

The **laughing falcon** (guaco; *Herpetotheres cachinnans*) looks like a large, slightly paler, yellow-headed caracara with a broad black stripe through the eye and a striped black and pale-buff tail. It is fairly common in the lowlands. Its calls are loud and varied, with the most frequently heard being a hollow 'wah-co' (the pronunciation of its Spanish name) repeated many times, especially at dusk, when it sounds rather eerie. It perches high and searches for snakes.

The **harpy eagle** (águila arpía; *Harpia harpyja*), a spectacular meter-long eagle, was, until recently, widespread in Costa Rica's primary forests but has become almost extinct because of deforestation. It flies strongly and acrobatically through the forest canopy, snatching sloths and monkeys while on the wing! A few reportedly survive in the Corcovado area.

Game Birds

Costa Rica has 13 species of the order Galliformes, descriptively called chickenlike birds, which look and taste a bit like domestic fowl. They are hunted, which makes them rare in populated areas, though they are seen in remote areas and in some national parks. They include guans, chacalacas, curassows, and various members of the pheasant family.

One of the more common game birds is the **black guan** (pava negra; *Chamaepetes unicolor*), a 65cm-long glossy black bird with a long tail. It has bare blue facial skin and red legs. Look for it walking along branches in forests above 1000m, such as in Monteverde, where it isn't much hunted and is seen fairly often.

Rails & Relatives

These birds, members of the order Gruiformes, are represented by 18 species in Costa Rica. Most live on or near water, swamps, or marshes. They are poor fliers and prefer swimming or running. Many rails and crakes are furtive inhabitants of waterside grasses or rushes and, in most cases, are difficult to see even if they are present. Exceptions include the **gray-necked wood-rail** (rascón cuelligrís; *Aramides cajanea*), a large rail (38cm tall) with an olive back and tail; gray head, neck, and upper breast; chestnut lower breast; black belly and thighs; red legs and eyes; and yellow bill – quite a palette! It forages with its short tail pumping, walking over muddy vegetated ground, probing the mud and leaf layer in search of frogs and fruits. It can be found near water below 1400m throughout the country.

In the water, you may see the **purple gallinule** (gallareta morada; *Porphyrula martinica*), a colorful and more common version of the **common gallinule** or **moorhen** (gallareta frentirroja; *Gallinula chloropus*), which is familiar in North America, Eurasia, and Africa. The purple gallinule is violet-purple on the front, neck, and head, bronzy green on the back, and white under the tail. It has bright yellow legs, a red bill with a yellow tip, and a light blue frontal shield on its forehead. It is seen on many ponds below 1500m and is more frequent in Costa Rica than the common gallinule. The **American coot** (focha Americana; *Fulica americana*) is a dark gray to black waterbird with a white bill and frontal shield and white marks under the tail. This migrant is common from October to April.

Purple gallinule

The male **sungrebe** (pato cantil; *Heliornis fulica*) has the remarkable ability to carry its young suspended in a fold of skin under its wings. With a chick under each wing it can swim or even fly. This secretive and shy bird can be seen in several slowly flowing lowland rivers, including the canals of Tortuguero, which is one of the best places to look. It is a mainly brown waterbird with a wide tail tipped in white but has bold and distinctive black-and-white striping on the neck and head, and a red bill, which make identification easy.

The **sunbittern** (garza del sol; *Eurypyga helias*) is a long-legged waterbird with a long bill and slim neck. The head is black with white stripes, the neck and breast brown with fine black lines, the back brown with wider black lines, the belly and throat creamy, the tail gray with two black-brown bands, the bill and legs orange, and the wings gray with large white spots. Its most distinctive feature is the sunburst pattern in a combination of browns, white, and black on its upper wings when it flies. It is an unusual bird, placed in its own family, the Eurypygidae, and high on the 'must see' list of many birders. It lives by rivers in forests in the foothills of the Caribbean and south Pacific slopes but is diminishing in numbers because of deforestation.

Shorebirds & Gulls

Costa Rica has about 70 species of shorebirds and gulls, in the diverse order Charadriiformes. Almost all are known to North American visitors. Some, such as the familiar

herring gull (gaviota argéntea; *Larus argentatus*) are Holarctic (found in all northern continents). Many are winter migrants to Costa Rica and few are seen in summer.

The most common gull is the **laughing gull** (gaviota reidora; *Larus atricilla*), which is a widespread and abundant migrant (September to November and April to mid-May) but is also present in large numbers year-round, especially on the Pacific coast.

The most widespread shorebird is the **spotted sandpiper** (andarríos maculado; *Actitis macularia*), found along inland lakes and rivers up to 1850m as well as on both coasts. It is often seen from August to May but rarely in the summer. It is small, brown above and white below, with a faint white eye stripe and yellowish legs. Its most distinctive feature is its teetering back and forth while walking and foraging. It is usually seen singly. The most abundant shorebird is the **western sandpiper** (correlimos occidental; *Calidris mauri*), which is grayish-brown above with fine streaks and white below. This bird is seen in flocks of hundreds along both coasts, but especially the Pacific, from August to April. Also common is the **sanderling** (playero arenero; *Calidris alba*), especially from mid-August to October and mid-March to early May. Fewer birds are seen in winter and almost none in summer. This shorebird is found in small flocks on both coasts and is paler than other similar shorebirds. It runs up and down the surf line with a distinctive gait like a clockwork toy.

A favorite of many visitors is the **northern jacana** (jacana centroamericana; *Jacana spinosa*), which has extremely long, thin toes that enable it to walk on top of aquatic plants, earning it the nickname 'lily-trotter.' They are common on many lowland lakes and waterways. At first glance, their brown bodies, black necks and heads, and yellow bill and frontal shield seem rather nondescript, but when disturbed the birds stretch their wings to reveal startling yellow flight feathers. This may serve to momentarily confuse would-be predators and makes them easy for us to identify. The female is polyandrous, mating with up to four males within her territory. The males do most of the nest building and incubation – whether the female manages to lay the right eggs in each father's nest remains in doubt.

Northern jacana

Pigeons & Doves

These birds, in the order Columbiformes, are represented by 25 species in Costa Rica. Some are familiar to North Americans, while others are specialties of the tropics. They are unusual among birds because the parents secrete 'pigeon milk' in the crop (part of the esophagus), and this is the chicks' only food during their first days. The milk is similar in constitution to mammalian milk but is thicker and also is produced by both sexes. The milk is regurgitated from the crop and the young eat it from the parent's mouth. After a few days, solid food is also regurgitated and mixed with the milk in increasing amounts. By the time the chicks fledge (about two weeks in small birds and over a month in large ones), milk is only a small portion of the regurgitated mixture.

The largest species is the 35cm-long **band-tailed pigeon** (paloma collareja; *Columba fasciata*), so called because of the dark gray band in its pale gray tail, but better identified by a white crescent on the back of its neck and a yellow bill. It is frequently seen in flocks in the mountains above 900m.

There are several small ground-doves, of which the most common is the **ruddy ground-dove** (tortolita colorada; *Columbina talpacoti*). The male is reddish, distinguishing it from other ground-doves. It has a pale gray head and almost white throat. It prefers open habitat and is often seen in agricultural country and along roads below 1400m on both slopes. As the name implies, these birds spend much of the time on the ground, foraging for seeds, berries, and possibly insects and other small invertebrates.

Band-tailed pigeon

Pigeons and doves generally have cooing calls. One of the most distinctive is that of the **short-billed pigeon** (paloma piquicorta; *Columba nigrirostris*), which sounds like 'cu-COO cu-COO,' accented on the second and fourth notes, and is frequently heard from the middle and upper layers of humid forests up to about 1400m.

Parrots

These are truly tropical birds, found throughout the tropics anywhere there are trees and extending into the subtropics. Of about 330 species in the world, 16 are recorded from Costa Rica. All have a short but very powerful bill with a pronounced hook that is used to open buds and flowers in search of nuts and seeds, which are their main food.

The most spectacular Costa Rican parrot is the **scarlet macaw** (lapa roja; *Ara macao*), unmistakable with its large size (84cm long), bright red body, blue-and-yellow wings, long red tail, and white face. Macaws mate for life (as is generally true of all parrots) and are often seen flying overhead, in pairs or small flocks, calling raucously to one another. Recorded as common in 1900, they have suffered devastating reductions in numbers because of deforestation and poaching for the pet trade. Now, it is rare to see these birds outside of Carara and Corcovado.

Costa Rica's other macaw is the **great green macaw** (lapa verde; *Ara ambigua*), which is similar in size and shape to the scarlet macaw but is mainly green and blue, with some red on top of its tail. This macaw is found on the Caribbean side.

KEVIN SCHAFER

Scarlet macaw

The remaining parrots are much smaller and mainly green. The largest of them (38cm) is the

KEVIN SCHAFER

Scarlet macaw

mealy parrot (loro verde; *Amazona farinosa*). In common with other Amazona parrots, it has a stumpy tail and flies with quick flaps of its short, broad wings, usually in raucously calling flocks. Parakeets, of which there are six species, are also small and green but have long tails. Telling the individual parrots and parakeets apart is not easy because they all are green and usually glimpsed flying. Look for small orange, red, blue, white, and yellow markings on the head and wings, which are best observed when the bird is at rest. For example, the **orange-fronted parakeet** (perico frentinaranja; *Aratinga canicularis*) has an orange forehead, bluish crown, and yellowish white eye ring, is yellowish green below, and has some blue flight feathers – but in flight, it seems generally green.

ROB RACHOWIECKI

Orange-fronted parakeet

Cuckoos

European cuckoos lay their eggs in the nest of another species and then let another bird raise their young, a behavior known as brood parasitism. Only two of Costa Rica's 11 species of cuckoos practice this. Most of the cuckoos are slim, long-tailed birds, skulking stealthily through vegetation rather than flying.

The most common is the **squirrel cuckoo** (cuco ardilla; *Piaya cayana*), which is 46cm long, with the boldly black-and-white-striped tail taking up about half that length. The rest of the body is mainly rufous brown, with a gray belly and yellow bill and eye ring. It is hard to mistake this combination for any other bird. It is found creeping along branches and jumping rather than flying to the next branch – hence the descriptor 'squirrel' in its name. It inhabits woodlands and forest countrywide up to 2400m.

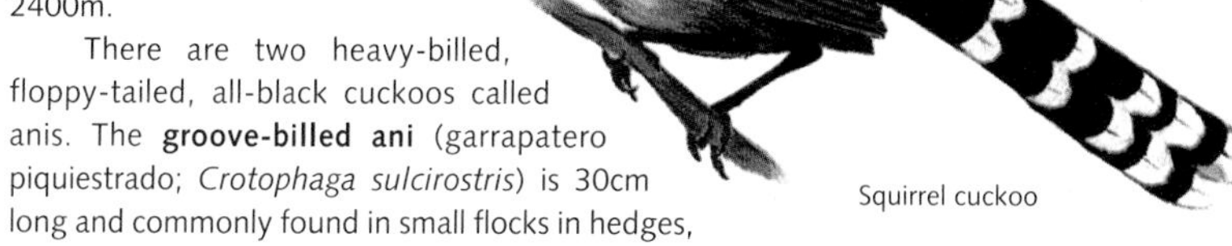

Squirrel cuckoo

There are two heavy-billed, floppy-tailed, all-black cuckoos called anis. The **groove-billed ani** (garrapatero piquiestrado; *Crotophaga sulcirostris*) is 30cm long and commonly found in small flocks in hedges, fields, grasslands, marshes, and watersides throughout the country up to about 2300m, except in the south Pacific region. Their flight is weak and wobbly and they call 'tee-ho' frequently, giving them their local nickname, *tijo*. In the south Pacific, they are replaced by the slightly larger but otherwise similar-looking **smooth-billed ani** (garrapatero piquisilo; *Crotophaga ani*).

Owls

Costa Rica has 17 owl species. As elsewhere, they are nocturnal hunters and are more often heard than seen. They have various hooting, drumming, screeching, and other slightly eerie calls, mainly heard at night or at dawn and dusk.

One species of owl that will occasionally hunt during the day is the widely distributed **spectacled owl** (buho de anteojos; *Pulsatrix perspicillata*). It's one of the larger owls, 48cm in length with conspicuous white markings around the eyes, forming spectacles. Others are generally smaller, but all have the typical owl appearance.

KEVIN SCHAFER

Spectacled owl

Nightjars & Relatives

About a dozen of these mainly nocturnal birds are found in Costa Rica. At dusk they may be mistaken for bats; look for white bars at the ends of the wings to distinguish them. The most abundant is the **common pauraque** (cuyeo; *Nyctidromus albicollis*). You might catch sight of one by car headlights at night. During the day, they roost quietly on branches and flat areas. (I once saw a nightjar sitting in the middle of a hiking trail and it refused to budge even when I stood next to it.) They are camouflaged with a mottled brown, black, and gray, often with a white throat and usually with long bristles around the beak to help them catch insects at night.

KEVIN SCHAFER
Common potoo

Potoos are nightjars found only in the Neotropics. They have a unique camouflage during the day: instead of sitting horizontally, as most birds do, they adopt a vertical posture and often perch on an exposed tree stump, looking very much like an elongation of it. Your guide gets an extra tip for spotting one. At night, their calls are among the eeriest in the forest. The two Costa Rican species are the **great potoo** (nictibio grande; *Nyctibius grandis*) and the **common potoo** (nictibio común; *Nyctibius griseus*).

Swifts

These birds are among the best fliers in the avian world. Their streamlined bodies and long, thin, swept-back wings enable them to spend most waking hours in the air, with their small but wide bills agape to catch insects. They can briefly sleep and even copulate on the wing. Their short legs are poorly developed and they never land on the ground because they would have difficulty taking off. Instead, they have strong feet, and perch and nest on vertical cliffs and buildings from which they can easily glide off.

Costa Rica has 11 species, all mainly dark gray or black, some with white or brown markings. The largest and most common countrywide is the **white-collared swift** (vencejón collarejo; *Streptoprocne zonaris*), which is 22cm long and has a slim white collar and a square or slightly notched tail. The 13cm-long **lesser swallow-tailed swift** (macua; *Panyptila cayennensis*) also has a white collar, which extends over the chin and upper breast. It has a deeply forked tail and is found below 800m on the Caribbean and up to 1000m on the south Pacific slope.

Hummingbirds

All of the world's 330 species of hummingbirds live exclusively in the Americas, predominantly in the tropics. Over 50 species have been recorded in Costa Rica, and their beauty is matched by extravagant names. For many visitors these birds are the most delightful to observe.

Hummingbirds can beat their wings up to 80 times a second, thus producing the typical hum for which they are named. This exceptionally rapid beat, combined with the ability to rotate the whole wing, enables them to hover in place when feeding on nectar (their preferred food), or even to fly backward – unique traits in birds. The energy needed to keep these tiny birds flying is high, and species living in the mountains have evolved an amazing strategy to survive a cold night: they go into a state of torpor, like a nightly hibernation, by lowering their body temperature between 17°C and 28°C depending on the species, thus lowering their metabolism drastically.

Apart from nectar, hummingbirds eat small insects for protein. They are generally quite pugnacious, and many will defend individual feeding territories, driving off any other bird that tries to feed. The males of some species gather together in a lek, a communal displaying area, where they attract females. After mating, however, males play little or no part in nesting or chick rearing.

The often dazzling iridescent colors of hummingbirds are caused by microscopic structures on the end of the feathers. These appear black in certain angles of light but, at other angles, refraction and interference cause the plumage to flash brilliantly. A shining green is the normal color of most hummingbirds, further decorated by brief fiery splashes of red, yellow, purple, or blue, usually in the head and upper breast area. Some have specially modified gorgets, or feathers sticking out from the throat. Normally, the males are the brightest.

KEVIN SCHAFER

Long-tailed hermit

Their small size (many under 10cm), speedy flight, tendency to be metallic green (or black in some lights), and lack of conspicuous coloration in the females make it difficult to tell the hummingbirds apart. With a little practice, however, some species become quickly recognizable. The **long-tailed hermit** (ermitaño colilargo; *Phaethornis superciliosus*) is common in forests of the Caribbean and south Pacific slopes below 1000m. Hikers often notice a sudden 'Zzzip!' as a 15cm-long hummer comes very close and inspects them before zipping off again. This inquisitive bird is probably the long-tailed hermit, identified by its brownish plumage, very long white central tail feathers extending about 3cm beyond the rest of the tail, and a long down-curved bill. If the bird is smaller (9cm) and has short white central tail feathers, it's the **little hermit** (ermitaño enano; *Phaethornis longuemares*). In mid-elevation forests, 600 to 2000m on both slopes, the long-tailed hermit is replaced by the similar-sized **green hermit** (ermitaño verde; *Phaethornis guy*), which is mainly green but has the distinctive elongated white central tail feathers of the hermits.

Other commonly seen lowland hummers include the **white-necked jacobin** (jacobino nuquiblanco; *Florisuga mellivora*), which breeds in the Caribbean and south Pacific lowlands from January to June. From September to December they are rarely seen, but nobody is sure where they disappear to! Their range is Mexico to the Amazon. The male has a blue head and throat with a white collar on the back of its neck and a white belly and outer tail feathers. The females sometimes look like the males but are quite variable; some lose their blue head and white collar and have instead a scaled blue breast. Females, when discovered on the nest, will often flutter off gently like moths, in an attempt to hoodwink predators.

The **violet sabrewing** (ala de sable violáceo; *Campylopterus hemileucurus*) is the largest Costa Rican hummingbird (15cm long) and has a striking violet body and head, with dark green wings and back and white feathers on the outside of the tail. It is found in mid-elevations and is commonly seen at Monteverde. In fact, Monteverde is the single best place in the country to see hummingbirds, though many are attracted to feeders. Also abundant here is the **green violet-ear** (colibrí orejivioláceo verde; *Colibri thalassinus*), a 10cm-long, almost all-green hummer with a violet eye patch and a blackish band near the end of the tail. A highland species found only in the cloud forests of Costa Rica (including Monteverde) and into northern Panama is the **fiery-throated hummingbird** (colibrí garganta de fuego; *Panterpe insignis*). This very pugnacious shimmering green hummer with a blue tail has an amazingly brilliant blue cap and orange-and-yellow throat when viewed in good light.

Trogons

These are 40 species of very colorful, medium-size, upright-perching, long-tailed birds that inhabit the tropics worldwide. Ten species are found in Costa Rica, and the most famous is undoubtedly the **resplendent quetzal** (quetzal; *Pharomachrus mocinno*), perhaps one of the most dazzling and culturally important birds of Central America. It had great ceremonial significance to the Aztecs and the Mayas and is now the national bird and symbol of Guatemala. It is extremely difficult to keep in captivity, where it usually dies quickly, which is perhaps why it became a symbol of liberty to Central Americans during the colonial period.

The male lives up to its name with glittering green plumage set off by a crimson belly, and white tail feathers contrasting with bright green tail coverts stream over 60cm beyond the bird's body. The head feathers stick out in a spiky green helmet through which the yellow bill peeks coyly. The male tries to impress the duller-colored female by almost vertical display flights during which the long tail coverts flutter sensuously. A glimpse of this bird is the highlight of many birders' trips. The quetzal (pronounced 'ket-SAL') is fairly common from 1300 to 3000m in forested or partially forested areas. Locals usually know where to find one; good places to look are Monteverde and various areas in southern Costa Rica. The March to June breeding season is the easiest time to see the birds. At other times, they are less active and quite wary, in common with all the trogons.

KEVIN SCHAFER

Resplendent quetzal

The other nine species of Costa Rican trogons are boldly colored – green and red, blue and red, blue and yellow, and green and yellow are typical combinations for the body, usually with a black-and-white or gray tail. Although they are not uncommon, they sit quietly, motionless on mid-level branches in the forest and, despite their bright colors, are hard to spot. Their calls, which vary from gruff barks to clear whistled notes, are the best way to locate them. This is when a good local bird guide can be invaluable.

Kingfishers

Of the world's 90 species of kingfishers, only six live in the Americas. All six are found in Costa Rica. They are often seen by travelers along rivers. The most common are the ringed and the green kingfishers. The **ringed kingfisher** (martín pescador collarejo; *Ceryle torquata*) is 41cm long and one of the largest kingfishers in the world. The name derives from the white ring around the collar. The rest of the bird is a slaty blue-gray with rufous breast and belly. The less common **belted kingfisher** (martín pescador norteño; *Ceryle alcyon*) is similar but much smaller and has white underparts. Smaller still, the 18cm-long **green kingfisher** (martín pescador verde; *Chloroceryle americana*) is dark green above and white below. The male has a rufous breast band and both sexes have a white collar and white spots on the tail and wings. The similar **Amazon kingfisher** (martín pescador Amazónico; *Chloroceryle amazonica*) is 29cm long and has less spotting on the wings and tail. The other kingfishers are uncommon.

Green kingfisher

Motmots

These birds, related to the kingfishers, are found only in the Neotropics, and Costa Rica has six of the nine known species. They are colorful birds characterized by an unmistakable long racquet-tail (with barbs missing along part of the feather shaft, leaving a tennis-racquet appearance). The most frequently seen are the **blue-crowned motmot** (momoto común; *Momotus momata*) and the **turquoise-browed motmot** (momoto cejileste; *Eumomota superciliosa*). The first has a bright blue crown with black at the very top and a black face, and is otherwise mainly green with brownish underparts. The other has broad turquoise eyebrows, rufous back and belly, a black face, and a large black spot on its chest, and is otherwise green. It has the longest bare area in the 'handles' of its racquets.

KEVIN SCHAFER

Blue-crowned motmot

KEVIN SCHAFER

Keel-billed toucan

Toucans

The 42 species of toucans are Neotropical birds, and six of them are found in Costa Rica. Their best-known feature is their huge bills, which are very light because they are almost hollow, supported internally by thin cross struts. The purpose of these greatly oversized beaks is unknown. Toucans prefer to stay at treetop level and nest in holes in trees. With a little luck, you can see all six species.

The largest is the 56cm-long **chestnut-mandibled toucan** (dios tedé; *Ramphastos swainsonii*), often heard loudly calling with a shrill 'DiOS teDAY teDAY' as it perches high in Caribbean and south Pacific wet forests to about 1800m. It is mainly black with a yellow face and chest and red under the tail, and has a bicolored bill, yellow above and chestnut below. The slightly smaller **keel-billed toucan** (tucan pico iris; *Ramphastos sulfuratus*) is similarly plumaged, but the bill is multicolored. It inhabits the Caribbean slope and the Guanacaste area but not the south Pacific.

Smaller and slimmer are the **collared aracari** (tucancillo collarejo; *Pteroglossus torquatus*) and the **fiery-billed aracari** (tucancillo piquianaranjado; *Pteroglossus frantzii*), about 42cm long. Both have dark olive-green back, wings and tail, black head and chest, and a bright yellow belly with a red-and-black band. The collared's bill is pale yellowish above and black below, while the fiery-billed's is bright orange above. The easiest way to separate the aracaris is by range – the collared is found on the Caribbean side and in the Guanacaste area, while the fiery-billed is found in the south Pacific.

The smaller **yellow-eared toucanet** (tucancillo orejiamarillo; *Selenidera spectabilis*) is the only local toucan with an all-black belly. It is found mainly in the Caribbean lowlands. The smallest is the **emerald toucanet** (tucancillo verde; *Aulacorhynchus prasinus*), which has a green body and lives in the highlands from 800 to 3000m.

Woodpeckers & Relatives

Woodpeckers and their relatives, along with the toucans, are members of the order Piciformes. They share the characteristics of nesting in tree holes and having the first and fourth toe pointing backward and the second and third pointing forward (a zygodactyl foot).

The 16 Costa Rican woodpeckers vary in size, from the 9cm-long **olivaceous piculet** (carpenterito oliváceo; *Picumnus olivaceus*) to the 37cm-long **pale-billed woodpecker** (carpintero picoplata; *Campephilus guatemalensis*). They are often heard drumming on resonant branches before they are seen. The drumming is sometimes done for communication, and at other times to excavate a hole for nesting or to dislodge insects, which are the main food.

Relatives include jacamars, barbets, puffbirds, and nunbirds. The male **red-headed barbet** (barbudo cabecirrojo; *Eubucco bourcierii*) is striking with its bright red head and chest, yellow bill, green back, and yellow belly. It forages in trees at mid-elevations. The **white-fronted nunbird** (monja frentiblanca; *Monasa morphoes*) is an upright-perching black bird of the Caribbean lowlands. It is immediately identified by its bright red bill with white feathers at the base.

Passerines

This order, the Passeriformes, is also called 'perching birds' because all members have a foot with three toes pointed forward and one long toe pointing backward, making a claw suitable for perching on twigs. The passerines also share other anatomical features as well as a unique type of sperm. This is the largest, most recently evolved, and most taxonomically confusing order of birds, and ornithologists are constantly changing the names and relationships of the species, sometimes splitting one species into two or more, sometimes lumping two to make one, and sometimes moving them into a different family.

About half of Costa Rica's birds are passerines, including, among others, the families of flycatchers (78 species), antbirds (30 species), wrens (22 species), ovenbirds (18 species), woodcreepers (16 species), and the huge catchall Emberizidae family, which includes the warblers (52 species, including many North American migrants), tanagers (50 species), blackbirds (20 species), and a confusing array of over 50 sparrows, finches, and grosbeaks. Some, like the woodcreepers, are so similar to one another that ornithologists cannot reliably identify them unless they catch the birds. Others, like some tanagers and cotingas, are so extravagantly and uniquely plumaged that identification is very easy. It is some of the latter that I discuss here.

Tanagers are fairly small but often very colorful birds that mainly live in the Neotropics. The most abundant, and one of the country's most common birds, is the **blue-gray tanager** (tangara azuleja; *Thraupis episcopus*). Its head and body are a pale blue gray, becoming brighter blue on the wings and tail. It prefers open, humid areas and is seen up to 2300m everywhere except the dry northwest and deep inside the forest. The male **scarlet-rumped tanager** (tangara lomiescarlata; *Ramphocelus passerinii*) is jet black with a bright scarlet rump and lower back, a flashy and unmistakable combination. This bird is

KEVIN SCHAFER
White-throated magpie jay

common in the Caribbean and southern Pacific slopes. The females, which travel with the males, are a varied mixture of olive, orange, and gray and look like a different species. Both, however, have a silvery bill.

Costa Rican cotingas flaunt their colors. Two are shining white and two others are a brilliant blue and purple. The white ones are the **snowy cotinga** (cotinga nivosa; *Carpodectes nitidus*), found on the Caribbean slope, and the **yellow-billed cotinga** (cotinga piquiamarillo; *Carpodectes antoniae*), found on the south Pacific slope. In both cases, the female is a pale gray. The blue ones, both with a purple throat and belly, are uncommon though unmistakable if seen. The **lovely cotinga** *(Cotinga amablis)* is found on the Caribbean and the **turquoise cotinga** *(Cotinga ridgwayi)* is in the south Pacific lowlands. One of the strangest cotingas is the **three-wattled bellbird** (pájaro campano; *Procnias tricarunculata*); see the boxed text 'A Hike on the Sendero Bosque Nuboso' in the Northwestern Costa Rica chapter.

The 46cm-long **white-throated magpie jay** (urraca; *Calocitta formosa*) is blue above and white below and on the face, with a very long tail and a crest of forward-curling, black-tipped feathers. It is often seen in the drier northwest slopes and the Península de Nicoya. The slightly smaller **brown jay** (piapia; *Cyanocorax morio*) is mainly brown with creamy outer tail feathers and belly. It is found in deforested areas. Jays are noisy birds with harsh calls.

The colonial **Montezuma oropendola** (oropéndola de Moctezuma; *Psarocolius Montezuma*) weaves a large sacklike nest, sometimes over a meter in length. Colonies of these nests are often seen hanging from branches of tall trees in open areas of the Caribbean lowlands. The bird has a chestnut-colored body, black head and neck, and golden-yellow outer tail feathers that are conspicuous in flight. The dark bill is orange-tipped and there is a bluish patch on the face. The less-common **chestnut-headed oropendola** *(Psarocolius wagleri)* builds similar nests and has yellow tail feathers, but is black with a chestnut head and pale yellow bill. Both are found mainly on the Caribbean slope and occasionally elsewhere. Their calls are varied, loud, gurgling, and at times mechanical sounding.

Montezuma oropendola

CHRIS SALCEDO
Green iguana

REPTILES

Over half of the 200-plus species of reptiles found in Costa Rica are **snakes**. Though much talked about, they are seldom seen. Most are well camouflaged or slither away into the undergrowth when people approach, and few travelers catch sight of one.

More frequently seen reptiles include the common *Ameiva* **lizards**, which have a white stripe running down their backs. Also common, the bright green **basilisk lizard** *(Basiliscus basiliscus)* is seen on or near water. The males are noted for the huge crests running the length of their head, body, and tail, which give them the appearance of small dinosaurs almost a meter in length. Nicknamed Jesus Christ lizards, they can literally run across water when disturbed. They do this on their greatly elongated and webbed hind feet, and the behavior is more common in young, light individuals.

The **green iguana** *(Iguana iguana)* and blackish **ctenosaur** (garrobo; *Ctenosaura*

ROB RACHOWIECKI
Young basilisk lizard

ROB RACHOWIECKI
Spectacled caiman

similis) are large iguanid lizards that are often seen, despite being hunted for food. Ctenosaurs are found in the dry lands of the northwest, while iguanas are also found in wetter regions.

Larger reptiles in coastal national parks such as Tortuguero on the Caribbean or Santa Rosa and Las Baulas on the Pacific include turtles, crocodiles, and caimans. There are 14 species of turtles, some marine and others freshwater or terrestrial. The freshwater ones are often seen sunning in a row on top of a log; as a boat approaches, they quietly slip off, one by one.

KEVIN SCHAFER

Leatherback turtle hatchling

Marine turtles climb up sandy beaches to lay their eggs – a spectacular sight. The largest is the **leatherback turtle** (baula; *Dermochelys coriacea*), which has a carapace (shell) up to 1.6m long and an average weight of 360kg, though 500kg individuals have been recorded. Watching this giant come lumbering out of the sea is a memorable experience (see the Parque Nacional Marino Las Baulas de Guanacaste section). The **olive ridley** (Lora; *Lepidochelys olivacea*) is much smaller (average 40kg) but practices synchronous nesting when tens of thousands of females may emerge from the sea on a single night – another unforgettable sight (see Santa Rosa and Ostional). The most studied is the **green turtle** (tortuga; *Chelonia mydas*), found on the Caribbean coast (see the Parque Nacional Tortuguero section in the Caribbean Lowlands chapter).

The **spectacled caiman** *(Caiman crocodilus)* and the **American crocodile** *(Crocodylus acutus)* are both confusingly called 'lagarto' by locals. Caimans average about 1m in length and are the most commonly seen, especially in the Tortuguero and Caño Negro areas. The much larger crocodile is often seen near the Carara reserve on the Pacific.

AMPHIBIANS

The approximately 150 species of amphibians include the tiny and colorful **poison-arrow frogs**, in the family Dendrobatidae. Some are bright red with black legs, others red with blue legs, and still others are bright green with black markings. Several species have skin glands exuding toxins that can cause paralysis and death in many animals, including humans. Dendrobatids have been used by Latin American forest Indians to provide a poison in which to dip the tips of their hunting arrows. The toxins are effective when introduced into the bloodstream (as with arrows) but don't have much effect when a frog is casually touched.

The so-called **marine toad** (sapo grande; *Bufo marinus*) is actually found both on the coast and inland up to a height of 2000m. Frequently seen in the evenings around human habitations in rural areas, its size makes it unmistakable. It is the largest Neotropical lowland toad and specimens reaching 20cm long and weighing up to 1.2kg have been recorded – one big toad!

KEVIN SCHAFER
Poison-arrow frog

KEVIN SCHAFER
Poison-arrow frog

INSECTS

Over 35,000 species of insects have been recorded in Costa Rica, and many thousands remain undiscovered. Butterflies are abundant. One source claims that Costa Rica has 10% of all the world's butterfly species, and another reports that over 3000 species of butterflies and moths are recorded from Parque Nacional Santa Rosa alone.

The most dazzling butterfly is the **morpho** *(Morpho peleides)*. With a 15cm wingspan and electric-blue upper wings, it lazily flaps and glides along tropical rivers and through openings in the rainforest in a shimmering display. When it lands, however, the wings close and only the brown underwings are visible, an instantaneous change from outrageous display to modest camouflage.

Camouflage plays an important part in the lives of many insects. Some resting butterflies look exactly like green or brown leaves, while others look like the scaly bark of the tree on which they are resting. Caterpillars are often masters of disguise. One species is capable of constricting certain muscles to make itself look like the head of a viper, other species mimic twigs, and yet another species looks so much like a bird dropping that it rarely gets attacked by predators.

KEVIN SCHAFER
Morpho butterfly

ROB RACHOWIECKI

Leaf-cutter ants

There are many hundreds of ant species in tropical forests. **Leaf-cutter ants** *(Atta spp)* are often seen marching in columns along the forest floor, carrying pieces of leaves like little parasols above their heads. The leaf segments are taken into an underground colony and there allowed to decay into mulch. The ants tend their mulch gardens carefully, allowing a certain species of fungus to grow there. Parts of the fungus are then used to feed the colony, which can be several million ants.

Other insects are so tiny as to be barely visible, yet their lifestyles are no less esoteric. The **hummingbird flower mite** *(Rhinoseius colwelli)* is barely half a millimeter in length and lives in flowers. When the flowers are visited by hummingbirds, the mites scuttle up into the birds' nostrils and use this novel form of air transport to disperse themselves to other plants. Smaller still are mites that live on the proboscis of the morpho butterflies. From the tiniest mite to the largest butterfly, insects form an incredibly diverse part of the country's wildlife.

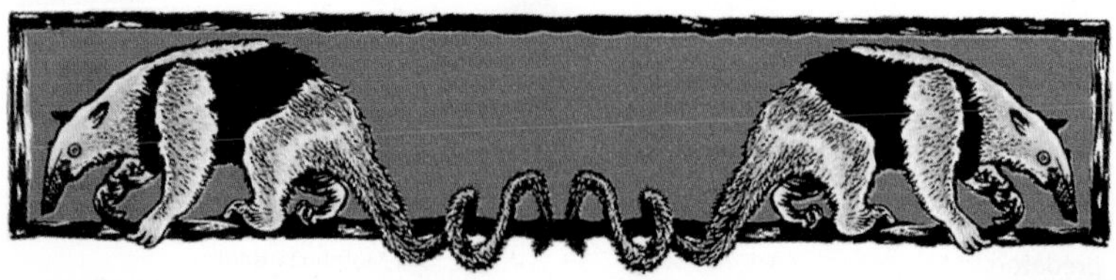

Glossary

For traffic signs and related terms in Spanish, refer to the boxed text 'Traffic Signs' in the Getting Around chapter. Spanish equivalents for common food and drink terms are provided in the Facts for the Visitor chapter.

almuerzo ejecutivo – inexpensive set lunch menu; special of the day (literally 'business lunch')
alquiler de automóviles – car rental
apartado – PO Box

boca – appetizer, often served with drinks in a bar

campesino – peasant; person who works in agriculture
carretas – colorfully painted wooden ox carts, now a form of folk art
casado – a set bargain meal
catedral – cathedral
colectivos – buses, minivans, or cars operating as shared taxis
colón (plural: **colones**) – Costa Rican unit of currency
cordillera – mountain range
corriente – long-distance bus with many stops
costarricense – Costa Rican (see also *tico*)

directo – long-distance bus with few stops

fauna silvestre – wildlife
finca – farm or plantation
frontera – border
fútbol – soccer

guapote – large fish caught for sport, equivalent to rainbow bass

Holdridge Life Zones – A classification system developed in the 1960s by US botanist LR Holdridge, whereby climate, latitude and altitude are used to define 116 distinct natural environmental zones, each with a particular type of vegetation

ICE – Instituto Costarricense de Electricidad; Costa Rican utilities (phone and electricity) company
ICT – Instituto Costarricense de Turismo; Costa Rican tourist authority
iglesia – church
invierno – winter; the wet season in Costa Rica

josefino – resident of San José

kilometraje – distance in kilometers; 'mileage'

lavandería – laundry facility, usually offering dry-cleaning services
llanuras – tropical plains

maize – corn
malecón – pier, sea wall, or waterfront promenade
marías – local name for taxi meters
mercado – market
meseta central – central plateau; central valley
mestizo – person of mixed descent, usually Spanish and Indian
migración (Oficina de Migración) – immigration (Immigration Office)
muelle – dock
museo – museum

normal – long-distance bus with many stops

OTS – Organization for Tropical Studies

parada – bus stop
páramo – habitat characterized by highland shrub and tussock grass; common to the Andes of Colombia, Ecuador, and Peru, as well as parts of Costa Rica
parque – park
playa – beach
PLN – Partido de Liberación Nacional; National Liberation Party
puerto – port
pulpería – corner grocery store

PUSC – Partido Unidad Social Cristiana; Social Christian Unity Party

sendero natural – nature trail
soda – lunch counter; inexpensive place to eat

tico/tica – what Costa Ricans call themselves

UNESCO – United Nations Educational, Scientific, and Cultural Organization
USGS – US Geological Survey

verano – summer; the dry season in Costa Rica
vivero – plant nursery

Acknowledgments

Thanks

Thanks to the following travelers, who read the previous edition of this book and wrote to us about their experiences in Costa Rica (apologies if we misspelled your name):

AJ & ES Bensemann, Achim Queisser, Adrian Bolli, Adrian Farmer, Adrian Hoskins, Adrian Nordenborg, Alaisdair Raynham, Alan Bradley, Aland Hodson, Alessandra Roversi, Algy Sharman, Alison Wiseman, Allan Wallach, Allan Weisbard, Amanda Dunham, Amanda Sumpter, Amir & Simone Zimmermann, Ana Lombardo, Ander Smith, Andrea Schaefer, Andrew Mitchell, Andrew Redfern, Andrew Rymes, Andy Hurst, Angel Sebastian, Angelo Zaragovia, Anke Kohn, Ann Bugeda, Anna Genet, Anne Bowyer, Anne Hamburger, Anne Masorti, Anne Vial, Annette Spates, Anthony Verebes, Anton Medved, Antonio Cuco, Arianna Silvestri, Arleen Sierra & Stuart Kanchuger, Assaf Metuki, BJ Skane, Babette Sohnrey, Barbara MacGregor, Barry Misenheimer, Bauke Van Der Veen, Belle Davis, Bente Sig Nielsen, Beryl Jackson, Beverly Kennedy, Beverly Meyer, Bill Athineos, Bill Schaap, Bjorn Karlsson & Malmoe Sweden, Bob Kurkijian, Bob Morris, Brent & Kathy Evjen, Brian Eggleston, Brian Wolff, Brooke Charles, Bryce Coulter, C & D Timms, Calvin Hill, Caragh Curran, Carol Gigy & Luis Colina, Carole G Jean & Christopher Silke, Carolyn Burnett, Casey Halloran, Catherine Munier, Chad Thompson, Charlotte Targett, Chris Mead, Chris P Robinson, Chris Souilivaert, Christer Garbis & Christina Eriksson, Christian Jacklein, Christian Loncle, Christian Ulrich, Christopher J Cross, Clair Graves, Claire L'Hoer, Claudia Rizzo, Colin Way, Collin McKenny, Craig L Abrams, Curly Carswell, Daan De Cominck, Damon Lenski, Dan Fowler, Daniel De Ugarte, Daniel Fey, Daniel Munday, Daniel van Grootheest, David & Gail James, David & Justine Horton, David Elmore, David Fairweather, David Hunter, David Meagher, David Miller, David Parbery & Lyle Demery, David Townsend, Dawn M Adams, Dean Simonsen, Deborah Pencharz, Deborah Todd, Delia Fasiolo, Dennis Mogerman, Derek Bissell, Derek Hughey, Diana Cafazzo, Diane Eisold, Dirk Kapteyn den Boumeester, Donald Patterson, Donna Roemling, Dorsey Holoppa, Andrea Eggenstein, Irmgard Ehlers, E Pling, E Rabone, Ed & Lorrie Scanlan, Ed Styffe, Eddy Veraghtert & Angeline van Hout, Edward Berkovich, Edward Hill, Edwarda Gutkowski, Eiichi Kawabata, Eliza G Bonner, Elizabeth Leon, Elizabeth Pollard, Ellen Garber, Elly & Oliver Strauss, Elly Kommer, Emanuela Appetiti, Emil Sernbo, Emilie Nolet, Emilio Mayorga, Emily Jones, Erin Longley, Erin Pass & Adrian Miller, Ernest P Dubois, Eshed Doni, Eva Cermak, F Phillips, Felette Dittmer, Florence J Licata, Fran & Frank Conn, Frank Crawford, Frank Van Kampen, Freddie Heitman, Fredrik Gustafsson, Fredrik Naumann, Gabriella Malnati, Gaelen Gates, Gary Bartolacci, Gary W Paukert, Gary W Scott, Geoffrey Tickell, George Anelay, George Bement, Georgia McCall, Gerald Keating, Geraldine Hopper, Gerbert Jansen & Jose Groothuis, Gerry Clift, Gerry Thompson, Gilbert Gimm, Giorgio Carletto, Giuseppe Anzalone, Gladys Fernandez, Graham Whitehead, Grant Stafford, Greg Cornell, Greg Gordon, Gregory Borferding, Guillermo Kimenez Chacon, Gwen & Wilbert Lee, H Walravens, Heidi & Byrne McKenna, Heidi Klose, Heidi Wampfler, Helen Kay, Helle Bjerre, Herman Von Harten, Herold Boertjens, Howard Jamieson, I Vlies, Ian Marsh, Ian Ramsay, Ilse Duijvestein, Impetus Holowillums, Ine van Ham, Ingeborg Chandler, Ingrid Sorg, Inid Schiller, Irene Atting, Irene E Gashu, J Estevez, Jackie Carver, Jackie Robson, Jacob Thyssen, Jacqueline Merlini, Jacques Bertrand, James Brown, James Gobert, James McE Brown, James Shiffer & Kirsten Delegard, Jamie Monk, Jana Durech, Jonathan Katz, Janet Lutz, Janette Denison, Jason M Moll, Jay Connerley, Jaymie Boyum & Dennis Rabun, JD Reed, Jeannie Choi, Jean-Paul Connock, Jeff Caldwell, Jeffrey van Fleet, Jennifer Hopkin, Jennifer Kitson, Jennifer Lange, Jennifer Tassie, Jennifer Widom & Alex Aiken, Jennifer Wilkinson, Jenny Jaffe, Jenny Visser, Jeper & Tina Jensen, Jeremy Bachmann, Jeri Solomon, Jerven Jongkind & Annemarie Breeve, Jesse Kalisher, Jessica Murray, Jill Mathis, Jim McNamara, Jim Satterly, Joanna Dyrr, Joanna Sullivan, Joanne Haase, Jochen & Stefan Bätz, Jochen Starke, Jody & James Bavis, Joe & Helene Tuwai, Joe Davis, Joel & Maria Teresa Prades, Joel Bleskacek, Johannes Schwartlander, John & Eleanore Woollard, John & Elisabeth Cox, John B Frost, John Clark, John Donkin, Joke Schrijvershof, Jolee Martin, Joleen Stran, Jonas Tegenfeldt, Jonathan Wickens, Jorge Artavia, Josh Jones, Judi Wolford, Judy Netherwood, Julia Crislip, Julia Ditrich, Julie Louttit, Julien Stern, June Best, Jurgen Busink, Justin Saunders, Karel Brevet, Karin Jacobsson, Karin Steinkamp & Michael Marquardt, Karl W Werther, Karyn Steer, Katerina Komselis, Katharine Dillon, Kathleen O'Hara, Keri Krupp, Kerry Suson, Ketta Morris, Kevin McGarry, Kim Hauge, Kim Pearson, Kim Van Dyke, Kirsten Hartshorne, Kirsty Morris, KJ Troy, Klaas Nijs, Kristin Wendorf, L Pereira, Langdon W Harris, Laura Galloway, Laura Lee Hartshorn, Lauren Wendle, Leah Archer, Leah Fisher, Lesley James, Leslie Leung, Liam Loftus, Linda Manoll, Linda Nawava, Lisa & John Merrill, Lisa & Ray King, Lisa Nowacki, Lisa Ross, Lisotte Ottingen, Lois & Sherwood Thompson, Louise Curtis, Luc Deschacht, Luis Pereira & Ivonne v/o Vlies, Lyle Webb, Lynn Tomita, Lynn Vogt, Lynne Mitchell, M & N Nakamura, M Fernandez Perez, M Peis, M Ward, M Amsler, Maarten Fischer, Maggie Jamieson, Maggie Sennish, Malene Melgaaard, Manfred & Astrid van Kalkeren-Scheeve, Manfred Melchinger, Marc Anthony Meyer, Marc Dyer & Karen Cooper, Marc Gandelli, Marc Iffenecker, Marc Julien, Marc Sokol, Marc Tebrugge, Marco Akermann, Marcus von Appen & Christine Hillenbrand, Margarita Mooney, Margot Ros, Mari Toyohara, Mariluz Fernández Pérez, Marjo de Kraker, Martin Carter & Diane Scully, Martin Kyllo, Martin Schweinberger, Martin Suter, Martin Vince, Mary Haller, Mary Winston, Matthew Braham, Matthew Salganik, Matthew Smith, Maury Englander, Max Friedman, Max Prokopy, Mayra E August, Megan Smith, Meghan Connolly, Meghan Wheaton, Melanie & Geoff Whitehead, Melanie Knox, Melanie Winskie, Melissa Hewitt, Meredith Witucki, Michael & Karen Russell, Michael Day, Michael Minozzi & Amy Motti, Michael Pfeiffer, Michael Schnitzler, Michele Sanna, Mick Pirie, Mickie Flores, Mike Benveniste, Mike Cotterill, Mike Crimmins, Mike Cunningham, Mike Fee, Mike Rudolph, Mirta Del Frari, Molly & John Bailey, Moos Dohem, Mor Parnass, Moti Bahadur Tailor, N Southern, Nadine Beard, Nancy Matson, Navah Levine, Nerolie & Geoff Stodart, Nick Buckle, Nick Manesis, Nicola Schaab, Nicole Kinson, Nik Katsourides, Nikolaus Baer, Nurit Weiner, Ole Kruse Nielsen & Janne Brunt Henriksen, Oren Postrel, Pat Hoyman, Patricia & Marvin Rosen, Patrick William-Powlett, Paul Bosch, Paul Francis, Paul Robinson & Deidre Gill, Paul Wotherspoon, Paula Bennett, Paula Blanski & James Pospychala, Pauline Smith, Penny Vine, Per Samuelsson, Perer Timmermans, Pete Curtice, Peter Beer, Peter Braat, Peter Mumby, Peter van der Lee, Petra Reck, Petra Schmitz, Philip Bennett, Phillip Boorman, Phillip Owen, Phillip Reineck, Phyllis Hicks, Pia & Michael Dowling, R Roth, Rachel Lynch, Rafa Artavia, Rafael Artavia, Rafael R Martinez, Raffaele Tola, Ralf Kettner, Ramie Blatt, RCB Butler, Regina Phelps, Renata & Peter Deixelberger, Renate Henkel, René Spinnler, RH Payne, Richard Laing, Richard P Rubinstein, Richard Thompson, Rick Scull, Rob Brindamour, Rob Pitts, Robert & Maria Staeheli, Robert Chatenever, Robert Levy, Robert McCorkindale, Robert Meidinger, Robert Perez de la Sala, Robert Saunders, Robert Scott, Robin Irwin, Robyn Christie & Mark Dellar, Rodger Young, Roger Nash, Roger Thiedeman, Roman Kucbel, Ron Alldridge, Ron Cook, Rose Rothe, Rosemary Yeldham, Roslyn Ellison, Rudolf M Ahr, Ruth Masterson, S Shea, Sabina de Serrano, Sage Radachowsky, Sally Laird, Sandra van der Pas, Sandy Johnson, Sanne Reijs & Rokus Groeneveld, Sara Vazquez, Sarah Brodie, Sarah Fullerton, Sarah McKinnon, Scot Stennis, Scott Johnson, Shai Hod, Shannon Nally, Sheila Walker, Silvian Nees, Silvie M, Simon Anderson, Simon Swift, Skadi Heckmueller, Solveig Maisan, Stan Needle, Stef Krook, Stefanie & Bill Raitt, Steve Booth, Steve Cansell, Steve Lidgey, Steve Machemer, Steve Pete, Steve Preston, Steven Hemsley, Steven Jon Gonzales, Steven M Link, Stuart Chambers, Stuart Graham & Beryl Jackson, Stuart Norton, Sue & Nick Howes, Sue Davis, Sue Hill, Susan Doten, Susanna Schlette & Dirk Bremecke, Susanne Hartung, T Burdine, Tania Kemenos, Ted R Feldpausch, Terence Mills, Terry Gardner, Terry Lively, Tevita & Carolyn Fotofili, Therese M Macintyre, Thomas Woltmann, Tim Drummond, Tim Eastling, Tim Hurley, Tim Zijderveld, Tom Croom, Tom Fletcher, Tom Ho, Tom Janet Colleen Liam Hilliard, Tracey McGregor, Travis Lloyd, Trina Tomita, Trish Rohrer, Tristan Baird, Tristram Winfield, Ulla Bunz, Vanessa Van Eeden, Vera Sauviller, Veronique Leblanc, Vicki Cederquist, Volker Seigel, WC & F Leiding, W Shane Turner, Walker Daves, Waltraud Duerst, Warren Leonard, Warren Nunn, Wayne Lewis, Wayne Olson, Wayne Smits, Wendy McClellan, Wes & Jill Barrett, Willem-Henri den Hartog, William E Macauley, Wim Braakhuis, Xenia Marotto, Yoar Aren, Yvo & Hetty Leijnse

Phrasebooks

Lonely Planet phrasebooks are packed with essential words and phrases to help travellers communicate with the locals. With colour tabs for quick reference, an extensive vocabulary and use of script, these handy pocket-sized language guides cover day-to-day travel situations.

- handy pocket-sized books
- easy to understand Pronunciation chapter
- clear & comprehensive Grammar chapter
- romanisation alongside script to allow ease of pronunciation
- script throughout so users can point to phrases for every situation
- full of cultural information and tips for the traveller

'... vital for a real DIY spirit and attitude in language learning'
– Backpacker

'the phrasebooks have good cultural backgrounders and offer solid advice for challenging situations in remote locations'
– San Francisco Examiner

Arabic (Egyptian) • Arabic (Moroccan) • Australian *(Australian English, Aboriginal and Torres Strait languages)* • Baltic States *(Estonian, Latvian, Lithuanian)* • Bengali • Brazilian • British • Burmese • Cantonese • Central Asia (Uyghur, Uzbek, Kyrghiz, Kazak, Pashto, Tadjik • Central Europe *(Czech, French, German, Hungarian, Italian, Slovak)* • Eastern Europe *(Bulgarian, Czech, Hungarian, Polish, Romanian, Slovak)* • Ethiopian (Amharic) • Farsi (Persian) • Fijian • French • German • Greek • Hebrew • Hill Tribes • Hindi & Urdu • Indonesian • Italian • Japanese • Korean • Lao • Latin American Spanish • Malay • Mandarin • Mediterranean Europe *(Albanian, Croatian, Greek, Italian, Macedonian, Maltese, Serbian, Slovene)* • Mongolian • Nepali • Pidgin • Pilipino (Tagalog) • Portugese • Quechua • Russian • Scandinavian Europe *(Danish, Finnish, Icelandic, Norwegian, Swedish)* • South-East Asia *(Burmese, Indonesian, Khmer, Lao, Malay, Tagalog Pilipino, Thai, Vietnamese)* • South Pacific Languages • Spanish (Castilian) *(also includes Catalan, Galician and Basque)* • Sri Lanka • Swahili • Thai • Tibetan • Turkish • Ukrainian • USA *(US English, Vernacular, Native American languages, Hawaiian)* • Vietnamese • Western Europe *(Basque, Catalan, Dutch, French, German, Greek, Irish, Italian, Portuguese, Scottish Gaelic, Spanish (Castilian), Welsh)*

Guides by Region

Lonely Planet is known worldwide for publishing practical, reliable and no-nonsense travel information in our guides and on our Web site. The Lonely Planet list covers just about every accessible part of the world. Currently there are 16 series: Travel guides, Shoestring guides, Condensed guides, Phrasebooks, Read This First, Healthy Travel, Walking guides, Cycling guides, Watching Wildlife guides, Pisces Diving & Snorkeling guides, City Maps, Road Atlases, Out to Eat, World Food, Journeys travel literature and Pictorials.

AFRICA Africa on a shoestring • Cairo • Cairo City Map • Cape Town • Cape Town City Map • East Africa • Egypt • Egyptian Arabic phrasebook • Ethiopia, Eritrea & Djibouti • Ethiopian (Amharic) phrasebook • The Gambia & Senegal • Healthy Travel Africa • Kenya • Malawi • Morocco • Moroccan Arabic phrasebook • Mozambique • Read This First: Africa • South Africa, Lesotho & Swaziland • Southern Africa • Southern Africa Road Atlas • Swahili phrasebook • Tanzania, Zanzibar & Pemba • Trekking in East Africa • Tunisia • Watching Wildlife East Africa • Watching Wildlife Southern Africa • West Africa • World Food Morocco • Zimbabwe, Botswana & Namibia
Travel Literature: Mali Blues: Traveling to an African Beat • The Rainbird: A Central African Journey • Songs to an African Sunset: A Zimbabwean Story

AUSTRALIA & THE PACIFIC Auckland • Australia • Australian phrasebook • Australia Road Atlas • Bushwalking in Australia • Cycling Australia • Cycling New Zealand • Fiji • Fijian phrasebook • Healthy Travel Australia, NZ and the Pacific • Islands of Australia's Great Barrier Reef • Melbourne • Melbourne City Map • Micronesia • New Caledonia • New South Wales & the ACT • New Zealand • Northern Territory • Outback Australia • Out to Eat – Melbourne • Out to Eat – Sydney • Papua New Guinea • Pidgin phrasebook • Queensland • Rarotonga & the Cook Islands • Samoa • Solomon Islands • South Australia • South Pacific • South Pacific phrasebook • Sydney • Sydney City Map • Sydney Condensed • Tahiti & French Polynesia • Tasmania • Tonga • Tramping in New Zealand • Vanuatu • Victoria • Walking in Australia • Watching Wildlife Australia • Western Australia
Travel Literature: Islands in the Clouds: Travels in the Highlands of New Guinea • Kiwi Tracks: A New Zealand Journey • Sean & David's Long Drive

CENTRAL AMERICA & THE CARIBBEAN Bahamas, Turks & Caicos • Baja California • Bermuda • Central America on a shoestring • Costa Rica • Costa Rica Spanish phrasebook • Cuba • Dominican Republic & Haiti • Eastern Caribbean • Guatemala • Guatemala, Belize & Yucatán: La Ruta Maya • Havana • Healthy Travel Central & South America • Jamaica • Mexico • Mexico City • Panama • Puerto Rico • Read This First: Central & South America • World Food Mexico • Yucatán
Travel Literature: Green Dreams: Travels in Central America

EUROPE Amsterdam • Amsterdam City Map • Amsterdam Condensed • Andalucía • Austria • Baltic States phrasebook • Barcelona • Barcelona City Map • Belgium & Luxembourg • Berlin • Berlin City Map • Britain • British phrasebook • Brussels, Bruges & Antwerp • Brussels City Map • Budapest • Budapest City Map • Canary Islands • Central Europe • Central Europe phrasebook • Corfu & the Ionians • Corsica • Crete • Crete Condensed • Croatia • Cycling Britain • Cycling France • Cyprus • Czech & Slovak Republics • Denmark • Dublin • Dublin City Map • Eastern Europe • Eastern Europe phrasebook • Edinburgh • Estonia, Latvia & Lithuania • Europe on a shoestring • Finland • Florence • France • Frankfurt Condensed • French phrasebook • Georgia, Armenia & Azerbaijan • Germany • German phrasebook • Greece • Greek Islands • Greek phrasebook • Hungary • Iceland, Greenland & the Faroe Islands • Ireland • Istanbul • Italian phrasebook • Italy • Krakow • Lisbon • The Loire • London • London City Map • London Condensed • Madrid • Malta • Mediterranean Europe • Mediterranean Europe phrasebook • Moscow • Mozambique • Munich • the Netherlands • Norway • Out to Eat – London • Paris • Paris City Map • Paris Condensed • Poland • Portugal • Portuguese phrasebook • Prague • Prague City Map • Provence & the Côte d'Azur • Read This First: Europe • Romania & Moldova • Rome • Rome City Map • Russia, Ukraine & Belarus • Russian phrasebook • Scandinavian & Baltic Europe • Scandinavian Europe phrasebook • Scotland • Sicily • Slovenia • South-West France • Spain • Spanish phrasebook • St Petersburg • St Petersburg City Map • Sweden • Switzerland • Trekking in Spain • Tuscany • Ukrainian phrasebook • Venice • Vienna • Walking in Britain • Walking in France • Walking in Ireland • Walking in Italy • Walking in Spain • Walking in Switzerland • Western Europe • Western Europe phrasebook • World Food France • World Food Ireland • World Food Italy • World Food Spain
Travel Literature: A Small Place in Italy • After Yugoslavia • Love and War in the Apennines • On the Shores of the Mediterranean The Olive Grove: Travels in Greece • Round Ireland in Low Gear

Mail Order

Lonely Planet products are distributed worldwide. They are also available by mail order from Lonely Planet, so if you have difficulty finding a title please write to us. North and South American residents should write to 150 Linden St, Oakland, CA 94607, USA; European and African residents should write to 10a Spring Place, London NW5 3BH, UK; and residents of other countries to Locked Bag 1, Footscray, Victoria 3011, Australia.

ISLANDS OF THE INDIAN OCEAN Madagascar & Comoros • Maldives • Mauritius, Réunion & Seychelles

MIDDLE EAST & CENTRAL ASIA Arab Gulf States • Central Asia • Central Asia phrasebook • Hebrew phrasebook • Iran • Israel & the Palestinian Territories • Israel & the Palestinian Territories travel atlas • Istanbul • Istanbul city map • Istanbul to Cairo • Jerusalem • Jerusalem city map • Jordan & Syria • Jordan, Syria & Lebanon travel atlas • Lebanon • Middle East on a shoestring • Syria • Turkey • Turkish phrasebook • Turkey travel atlas • Yemen
Travel Literature: The Gates of Damascus • Kingdom of the Film Stars: Journey into Jordan

NORTH AMERICA Alaska • Backpacking in Alaska • Baja California • California & Nevada • Canada • Chicago • Chicago city map • Deep South • Florida • Hawaii • Las Vegas • Los Angeles • Miami • New England • New Orleans • New York City • New York city map • New York, New Jersey & Pennsylvania • Oahu • Pacific Northwest USA • Puerto Rico • Rocky Mountain States • San Francisco • San Francisco city map • Seattle • Southwest USA • Texas • USA • USA phrasebook • Vancouver • Washington, DC & the Capital Region • Washington, DC city map
Travel Literature: Drive Thru America

NORTH-EAST ASIA Beijing • Cantonese phrasebook • China • Hong Kong • Hong Kong city map • Hong Kong, Macau & Guangzhou • Japan • Japanese phrasebook • Japanese audio pack • Korea • Korean phrasebook • Kyoto • Mandarin phrasebook • Mongolia • Mongolian phrasebook • North-East Asia on a shoestring • Seoul • South-West China • Taiwan • Tibet • Tibetan phrasebook • Tokyo
Travel Literature: Lost Japan

SOUTH AMERICA Argentina, Uruguay & Paraguay • Bolivia • Brazil • Brazilian phrasebook • Buenos Aires • Chile & Easter Island • Chile & Easter Island travel atlas • Colombia • Ecuador & the Galapagos Islands • Latin American Spanish phrasebook • Peru • Quechua phrasebook • Rio de Janeiro • Rio de Janeiro city map • South America on a shoestring • Trekking in the Patagonian Andes • Venezuela
Travel Literature: Full Circle: A South American Journey

SOUTH-EAST ASIA Bali & Lombok • Bangkok • Bangkok city map • Burmese phrasebook • Cambodia • Hanoi • Healthy Travel Asia & India • Hill Tribes phrasebook • Ho Chi Minh City • Indonesia • Indonesia's Eastern Islands • Indonesian phrasebook • Indonesian audio pack • Jakarta • Java • Laos • Lao phrasebook • Laos travel atlas • Malay phrasebook • Malaysia, Singapore & Brunei • Myanmar (Burma) • Philippines • Pilipino (Tagalog) phrasebook • Singapore • South-East Asia on a shoestring • South-East Asia phrasebook • Thailand • Thailand's Islands & Beaches • Thailand travel atlas • Thai phrasebook • Thai audio pack • Vietnam • Vietnamese phrasebook • Vietnam travel atlas

ALSO AVAILABLE: Antarctica • The Arctic • Brief Encounters: Stories of Love, Sex & Travel • Chasing Rickshaws • Lonely Planet Unpacked • Not the Only Planet: Travel Stories from Science Fiction • Sacred India • Travel with Children • Traveller's Tales

Lonely Planet Journeys

JOURNEYS is a unique collection of travel writing – published by the company that understands travel better than anyone else. It is a series for anyone who has ever experienced – or dreamed of – the magical moment when they encountered a strange culture or saw a place for the first time. They are tales to read while you're planning a trip, while you're on the road or while you're in an armchair in front of a fire.

These outstanding titles explore our planet through the eyes of a diverse group of international writers. JOURNEYS books catch the spirit of a place, illuminate a culture, recount a crazy adventure or introduce a fascinating way of life. They always entertain, and always enrich the experience of travel.

FULL CIRCLE
A South American Journey
Luis Sepúlveda (translated by Chris Andrews)

'A journey without a fixed itinerary' with Chilean writer Luis Sepúlveda. Extravagant characters and extraordinary situations are memorably evoked: gauchos organising a tournament of lies, a scheming heiress on the lookout for a husband, a pilot with a corpse on board his plane ... *Full Circle* brings us the distinctive voice of one of South America's most compelling writers.

WINNER 1996 Astrolabe – Etonnants Voyageurs award for the best work of travel literature published in France.

GREEN DREAMS
Travels in Central America
Stephen Benz

On the Amazon, in Costa Rica, Honduras and on the Mayan trail from Guatemala to Mexico, Stephen Benz describes his encounters with water, mud, insects and other wildlife – and not least with the ecotourists themselves. With witty insights into modern travel, *Green Dreams* discusses the paradox of cultural and 'green' tourism.

DRIVE THRU AMERICA
Sean Condon

If you've ever wanted to drive across the USA but couldn't find the time (or afford the gas), *Drive Thru America* is perfect for you. In his search for American myths and realities – along with comfort, cable TV and good, reasonably priced coffee – Sean Condon paints a hilarious road-portrait of the USA.

'entertaining and laugh-out-loud funny'– *Alex Wilber, Travel editor, Amazon.com*

SEAN & DAVID'S LONG DRIVE
Sean Condon

Sean and David are young townies who have rarely strayed beyond city limits. One day, for no good reason, they set out to discover their homeland, and what follows is a wildly entertaining adventure that covers half of Australia.

'a hilariously detailed log of two burned out friends' – *Rolling Stone*

Index

Abbreviations
Nic – Nicaragua
Pan – Panama
PN – Parque Nacional
PNM – Parque Nacional Marino
RB – Reserva Biológica
RI – Reserva Indígena
RNFS – Refugio Nacional de Fauna Silvestre
RNVS – Refugio Nacional de Vida Silvestre

Text

A

B

Bold indicates maps.

C

Bold indicates maps.

Bold indicates maps.

Bold indicates maps.